The Routledge Handbook of Audiovisual Translation

The Routledge Handbook of Audiovisual Translation provides an accessible, authoritative and comprehensive overview of the key modalities of audiovisual translation and the main theoretical frameworks, research methods and themes that are driving research in this rapidly developing field.

Divided into four parts, this reference work consists of 32 state-of-the-art chapters from leading international scholars. The first part focuses on established and emerging audiovisual translation modalities, explores the changing contexts in which they have been and continue to be used, and examines how cultural and technological changes are directing their future trajectories. The second part delves into the interface between audiovisual translation and a range of theoretical models that have proved particularly productive in steering research in audiovisual translation studies. The third part surveys a selection of methodological approaches supporting traditional and innovative ways of interrogating audiovisual translation data. The final part addresses an array of themes pertaining to the place of audiovisual translation in society.

This *Handbook* gives audiovisual translation studies the platform it needs to raise its profile within the Humanities research landscape and is key reading for all those engaged in the study and research of Audiovisual Translation within Translation studies.

Luis Pérez-González is Professor of Translation Studies and Co-director of the Centre for Translation and Intercultural Studies at the University of Manchester, UK. He is the author of *Audiovisual Translation: Theories, Methods and Issues* (Routledge, 2014) and co-editor of the Critical Perspectives on Citizen Media series.

Routledge Handbooks in Translation and Interpreting Studies

Routledge Handbooks in Translation and Interpreting Studies provide comprehensive overviews of the key topics in translation and interpreting studies. All entries for the handbooks are specially commissioned and written by leading scholars in the field. Clear, accessible and carefully edited, *Routledge Handbooks in Translation and Interpreting Studies* are the ideal resource for both advanced undergraduates and postgraduate students.

For a full list of titles in this series, please visit https://www.routledge.com/Routledge-Handbooks-in-Translation-and-Interpreting-Studies/book-series/RHTI.

The Routledge Handbook of Audiovisual Translation
Edited by Luis Pérez-González

The Routledge Handbook of Translation and Philosophy
Edited by Piers Rawling and Philip Wilson

The Routledge Handbook of Literary Translation
Edited by Kelly Washbourne and Ben Van Wyke

The Routledge Handbook of Translation and Politics
Edited by Fruela Fernández and Jonathan Evans

The Routledge Handbook of Translation and Culture
Edited by Sue-Ann Harding and Ovidi Carbonell Cortés

The Routledge Handbook of Translation Studies and Linguistics
Edited by Kirsten Malmkjaer

The Routledge Handbook of Audiovisual Translation

Edited by Luis Pérez-González

LONDON AND NEW YORK

First published 2019 by Routledge
2 Park Square, Milton Park, Abingdon, Oxon OX14 4RN
605 Third Avenue, New York, NY 10017

First issued in paperback 2021

Routledge is an imprint of the Taylor & Francis Group, an informa business

© 2019 selection and editorial matter, Luis Pérez-González; individual chapters, the contributors

The right of the editor to be identified as the author of the editorial material, and of the authors for their individual chapters, has been asserted in accordance with sections 77 and 78 of the Copyright, Designs and Patents Act 1988.

All rights reserved. No part of this book may be reprinted or reproduced or utilised in any form or by any electronic, mechanical, or other means, now known or hereafter invented, including photocopying and recording, or in any information storage or retrieval system, without permission in writing from the publishers.

Trademark notice: Product or corporate names may be trademarks or registered trademarks, and are used only for identification and explanation without intent to infringe.

Publisher's Note
The publisher has gone to great lengths to ensure the quality of this reprint but points out that some imperfections in the original copies may be apparent.

British Library Cataloguing-in-Publication Data
A catalogue record for this book is available from the British Library

Library of Congress Cataloging-in-Publication Data
A catalog record for this title has been requested

ISBN 13: 978-1-03-209490-8 (pbk)
ISBN 13: 978-1-138-85952-4 (hbk)

Typeset in Times New Roman
by Swales & Willis Ltd, Exeter, Devon, UK

Contents

List of illustrations ix
List of acronyms x
List of contributors xii

1 Rewiring the circuitry of audiovisual translation: introduction 1
  Luis Pérez-González

PART I
Audiovisual translation in action **13**

2 History of audiovisual translation 15
  Carol O'Sullivan and Jean-François Cornu

3 Subtitling on the cusp of its futures 31
  Marie-Noëlle Guillot

4 Investigating dubbing: learning from the past, looking to the future 48
  Charlotte Bosseaux

5 Voice-over: practice, research and future prospects 64
  Anna Matamala

6 Subtitling for deaf and hard of hearing audiences: moving forward 82
  Josélia Neves

7 Respeaking: subtitling through speech recognition 96
  Pablo Romero-Fresco

8 Audio description: evolving recommendations for usable, effective and enjoyable practices 114
  Elisa Perego

Contents

9 Surtitling and captioning for theatre and opera 130
   Alina Secară

10 Game localization: a critical overview and implications
   for audiovisual translation 145
   Minako O'Hagan

11 Film remakes as a form of translation 160
   Jonathan Evans

PART II
Theoretical perspectives in audiovisual translation studies **175**

12 Mediality and audiovisual translation 177
   Henry Jones

13 Spoken discourse and conversational interaction in
   audiovisual translation 192
   Silvia Bruti

14 Psycholinguistics and perception in audiovisual translation 209
   Louise Fryer

15 Narratology and audiovisual translation 225
   Jeroen Vandaele

16 Pragmatics and audiovisual translation 242
   Louisa Desilla

17 Multimodality and audiovisual translation: cohesion in
   accessible films 260
   Aline Remael and Nina Reviers

18 Sociolinguistics and linguistic variation in audiovisual translation 281
   Wai-Ping Yau

19 Gender in audiovisual translation studies: advocating
   for gender awareness 296
   Luise von Flotow and Daniel E. Josephy-Hernández

PART III
Research methods in audiovisual translation studies   313

20 Corpus-based audiovisual translation studies:
    ample room for development   315
    Maria Pavesi

21 Multimodal corpora in audiovisual translation studies   334
    Marcello Soffritti

22 Eye tracking in audiovisual translation research   350
    Jan-Louis Kruger

23 Audiovisual translation and audience reception   367
    David Orrego-Carmona

24 Ethnographic research in audiovisual translation   383
    Dang Li

PART IV
Audiovisual translation in society   399

25 Minority languages, language planning and audiovisual
    translation   401
    Reglindis De Ridder and Eithne O'Connell

26 Audiovisual translation and popular music   418
    Rebecca Johnson

27 Audiovisual translation and fandom   436
    Tessa Dwyer

28 Audiovisual translation and activism   453
    Mona Baker

29 Audiovisual translator training   468
    Beatriz Cerezo Merchán

30 Audiovisual translation in language teaching and learning   483
    Laura Incalcaterra McLoughlin

31 Accessible filmmaking: translation and accessibility
   from production   498
   Pablo Romero-Fresco

32 Technologization of audiovisual translation   516
   Panayota (Yota) Georgakopoulou

Index   *540*

Illustrations

Figures

16.1	Text evokes Context	251
31.1	Subtitling production process in Cole's film *The Colours of the Alphabet*	507

Tables

8.1	Key adjectives used to define AD	119
17.1	Multimodal transcription	264
20.1	Extract from the Pavia Corpus of Film Dialogue displaying various types of data	320
20.2	Concordances of *amico* in the translational component of the Pavia Corpus of Film Dialogue	321
20.3	Concordances of 'smiles' plus adverbs in *–ly* from the audio description of *The English Patient*	321
20.4	Bilingual concordances for 'sorry' and *¿Qué pasa?* from the CORSUBIL corpus	322
21.1	Elements to be labelled in monolingual, dialogical multimodal audiovisual material	343
29.1	Suggested sequencing of course materials in dubbing courses	474

Acronyms

AAE	African American English
AAVE	African American Vernacular English
AD	Audio Description
ASR	Automatic Speech Recognition
AVT	Audiovisual Translation
CAT	Computer-Assisted Translation
CBAVT(S)	Corpus-based Audiovisual Translation (Studies)
CBTS	Corpus-based Translation Studies
CC	Closed Captioning
CORSUBIL	Corpus de Subtítulos Bilingües Inglés-Español
CP	Cooperative Principle
cps	characters per second
ECR(s)	Extralinguistic Cultural References
EEG	Electroencephalogram
EFL	English as a Foreign Language
ESA	Entertainment Software Association
ESRB	Entertainment Software Ratings Board
FPS	First Person Shooter
FTA(s)	Face-threatening Act(s)
GDC	Game Developers Conference
GILT	Globalization, Internationalization, Localization and Translation
HCI	Human-Computer Interaction
L1	First language (mother tongue)
L2	Second language
LPP	Language Planning and Policy
LSP(s)	Language Service Provider(s)
MLM	Minority Language Media
MMC	Multimodal Corpora
ms	milliseconds
MT	Machine Translation
NES	Nintendo Entertainment System
NMT	Neural Machine Translation
PBSMT	Phrase-Based Statistical Machine Translation
PCFD	Pavia Corpus of Film Dialogue
QC	Quality Control
RBMT	Rule-Based Machine Translation

ROM	Read Only Memory
RPG	Role Playing Game
SDH	Subtitling for the Deaf and Hard of Hearing
SEO	Search Engine Optimization
SPA	Software Publishers Association
TCS	Truth Conditional Semantics
TIWO	Television in Words
TM(s)	Translation Memor(ies)
TMS(s)	Translation Management System(s)
TQA	Translation Quality Assessment
TTS	Text to Speech
UCT	User-centred Translation
VIP(s)	Visually Impaired Person(s)
VoB	Video Object
VoD	Video on Demand
VR	Virtual Reality
WMM	Windows Movie Maker
wpm	Words per minute

Contributors

Mona Baker is Professor Emerita of Translation Studies at the Centre for Translation and Intercultural Studies, University of Manchester, author of *Translation and Conflict: A Narrative Account* (Routledge 2006), editor of *Translating Dissent: Voices from and with the Egyptian Revolution* (Routledge 2016) and co-editor of the series *Critical Perspectives on Citizen Media* (Routledge).

Charlotte Bosseaux is Senior Lecturer in Translation Studies at the University of Edinburgh. She has worked on literary translation and point of view, and her current focus is on voice, performance and characterization in audiovisual material. She is the author of *How does it Feel: Point of View in Translation* (2007) and *Dubbing, Film and Performance: Uncanny Encounters* (2015).

Silvia Bruti is Associate Professor of English Language and Linguistics at the University of Pisa, Italy. Her current research focuses on intercultural pragmatics and audiovisual translation, with particular emphasis on the translation of compliments, conversational routines and terms of address in interlingual subtitles and dubbed interaction.

Beatriz Cerezo Merchán is Lecturer of Translation and English Language at the Department of English and German Philology, Universitat de València, Spain. Her current research focuses on audiovisual translation, the didactics of translation, and audiovisual translation as a tool in foreign language acquisition.

Jean-François Cornu is a professional translator specializing in subtitling and the translation from English into French of books on cinema and art. A former Senior Lecturer at the University of Rennes-2, France, he is also an independent film researcher. In 2014, he published *Le doublage et le sous-titrage: histoire et esthétique* (Presses universitaires de Rennes). He is a member of the Association des Traducteurs Adaptateurs de l'Audiovisuel (ATAA) and co-editor of its e-journal *L'Écran traduit*.

Reglindis De Ridder conducted doctoral research at Dublin City University between 2011 and 2015. Her PhD investigates the use of marked Belgian Dutch and marked Netherlandic Dutch lexis in subtitles produced by VRT, the Dutch-language public service broadcaster in Belgium. She is currently pursuing a postdoctorate at Stockholm University. Her research interests include audiovisual translation, sociolinguistics and corpus linguistics.

Louisa Desilla is Assistant Professor of Translation and Intercultural Studies at the Aristotle University of Thessaloniki, Greece. Her research interests reside in the pragmatics of intercultural communication and audiovisual translation, and in the reception of subtitled/ dubbed films. She was Co-investigator on the AHRC funded networking project 'Tapping the Power of Foreign Films: Audiovisual Translation as Cross-cultural Mediation'. She has published in international journals in the fields of linguistics and translation.

Tessa Dwyer is Lecturer in Film and Screen Studies at Monash University, Melbourne and president of the *Senses of Cinema* journal. She has published widely on the language politics of screen media, including her monograph *Speaking in Subtitles: Revaluing Screen Translation* (2017). Tessa is also co-editor of *Seeing into Screens: Eye Tracking the Moving Image* (2018).

Jonathan Evans is Senior Lecturer in Translation Studies at the University of Portsmouth, UK. He is the author of *The Many Voices of Lydia Davis* (2016) and co-editor of *The Routledge Handbook of Translation and Politics* (2018).

Louise Fryer is one of the UK's most experienced describers. As well as describing for the UK's National Theatre and for the audio description charity VocalEyes, she is a teaching fellow at University College London (UCL) and a partner in the research project ADLAB PRO (http://www.adlabproject.eu/).

Panayota (Yota) Georgakopoulou holds a PhD in translation and subtitling from the University of Surrey. A seasoned operations executive with 20 years of experience in the subtitling industry, Yota has held varied positions in the field. Most recently, she has led research in language technologies and tools, and their application in subtitling workflows at a prominent multinational language service provider.

Marie-Noëlle Guillot is Professor of Intercultural Communication and Translation Studies at the University of East Anglia (Norwich, UK). Her research has two strands, cross-cultural pragmatics and translation studies, and two domains of application: FL interactional pragmatic development, and cross-cultural representation through translation, in subtitling/ dubbing and museum translation specifically.

Laura Incalcaterra McLoughlin is Senior Lecturer in the School of Languages, Literatures, and Cultures at the National University of Ireland, Galway. Her main research area is applied linguistics, particularly in connection with audiovisual translation, language technologies and e-learning. She has published widely in these fields and participated in many related national and international projects.

Rebecca Johnson is an independent researcher. She holds a PhD in Translation and Intercultural Studies from the University of Manchester. Her research concerns the interface between protest and the arts in the post-9/11 context, with a particular focus on the genres of hip hop and comedy.

Henry Jones is a Post-Doctoral Research Associate at the University of Manchester's Centre for Translation and Intercultural Studies. His research interests include online translation communities, media theory and corpus-based translation studies. He is currently working as part of a multi-disciplinary team on the *Genealogies of Knowledge* project (www.genealogiesofknowledge.net/).

Daniel E. Josephy-Hernández holds a PhD in Translation Studies from the University of Ottawa. He has taught translation and translation theories in Costa Rica, Canada and China. His research concentrates mostly on gender and audiovisual translation in *anime*, focusing on critical analyses of hegemonic gender portrayals in this medium, and the censorship and distribution of *anime*. He has published work on video game translation, translation in Wales and film censorship in Iran.

Jan-Louis Kruger is Associate Professor and Head of Department in the Department of Linguistics at Macquarie University. He also holds an extraordinary professorship in the School of Languages at North-West University in South Africa. His current research focuses on the cognitive processing of subtitles, including aspects such as psychological immersion and cognitive effort.

Dang Li is a Post-doctoral Research Fellow at the School of Foreign Languages, Shanghai Jiao Tong University, and a member of the Baker Centre for Translation and Intercultural Studies. She holds a PhD in Translation and Intercultural Studies from the University of Manchester. Her research interests lie mainly in audiovisual translation, non-professional subtitling, and corpus-based translation studies.

Anna Matamala is Senior Lecturer at Universitat Autònoma de Barcelona. Her current research focuses on audiovisual translation and media accessibility, with a special interest in dubbing, voice-over, audio description and audio subtitling, as well as translation technologies.

Josélia Neves is Full Professor in the College of Humanities and Social Sciences, Hamad bin Khalifa University, Qatar, where she teaches in the MA in Audiovisual Translation. She is a member of the TransMedia Research Group and a board member of the European Association for Studies in Screen Translation. She collaborates with various European Universities both as a visiting professor and a researcher.

Eithne O'Connell was, until her retirement in 2016, Associate Professor in Translation Studies in the Centre for Translation and Textual Studies at Dublin City University. Her research interests include audiovisual translation and minority languages, with particular reference to the Irish language, children's literature and translation for children.

Minako O'Hagan is Associate Professor in the School of Cultures, Languages and Linguistics at the University of Auckland, New Zealand. Her main research interest lies in the intersection between translation and technology with her current work focused on ethics of technologies and research methodologies involving new technologies.

David Orrego-Carmona is Lecturer in Translation Studies at Aston University (UK) and a Research Associate at the Department of Linguistics and Language Practice at the University of the Free State (South Africa). His research explores the production and reception of professional and non-professional translations, as well as the impact of the democratization of technologies on the consumption of translations.

Carol O'Sullivan is Director of Translation Studies in the School of Modern Languages at the University of Bristol. Her research interests include audiovisual translation, translation history and literary translation. She is the author of *Translating Popular Film* (2011). Her current project is on the history of screen translation in the silent and early sound periods, and she is the co-editor with Jean-François Cornu of a volume in preparation on this topic. She is Editor-in-Chief of the journal *Translation Studies*.

Maria Pavesi is Professor of English Language and Translation at the Department of Humanities, Section of Theoretical and Applied Linguistics, of the University of Pavia. Her current research interests include audiovisual translation with a focus on the language of dubbing and audiovisual input in second language acquisition.

Elisa Perego is Associate Professor of English Language and Linguistics at the University of Trieste, Italy. Her research focuses on audiovisual translation accessibility and reception; subtitling and audio description; and empirical and cross-national research methodology. She is currently the coordinator of the European project ADLAB PRO (2016–2019) on audio description.

Luis Pérez-González is Professor of Translation Studies and Co-director of the Centre for Translation and Intercultural Studies at the University of Manchester, UK. He is a Co-investigator on the AHRC-funded project *Genealogies of Knowledge: The Evolution and Contestation of Concepts across Time and Space* (2016–2020). Former editor of the *Interpreter and Translator Trainer*, he is also author of *Audiovisual Translation: Theories, Methods and Issues* (Routledge 2014) and co-editor of Routledge's *Critical Perspectives on Citizen Media* book series.

Aline Remael is Professor of Translation Theory, Interpreting and Audiovisual Translation at the University of Antwerp (TricS research group). Her main research interests and publications are in AVT/media accessibility, including audio description, live subtitling with speech recognition. She leads a national Flemish project on accessible theatre (2017–2019) and is currently a partner in three Erasmus+ projects: ACT (Accessible Culture and Training), ADLAB PRO and project ILSA (Interlingual Live Subtitling for Access).

Nina Reviers has recently completed her PhD research in the field of media accessibility at the University of Antwerp (TricS research group). She helped develop Flemish guidelines for the audio description of live-events as a member of the Transmedia Benelux Research Group. She has collaborated in the European projects ADLAB, ADLAB PRO and is a member of the editorial board of the newly established *Journal of Audiovisual Translation*.

Pablo Romero-Fresco is a *Ramón y Cajal* grant holder at Universidade de Vigo (Spain) and Honorary Professor of Translation and Filmmaking at the University of Roehampton (UK). He is the author of the books *Subtitling through Speech Recognition: Respeaking* (2011) and *Accessible Filmmaking* (forthcoming) and leader of the research centre GALMA (Galician Observatory for Media Accessibility), for which he is coordinating the EU-funded projects Media Accessibility Platform and ILSA (Interlingual Live Subtitling for Access).

Alina Secară is Lecturer in Translation Studies at the Centre for Translation Studies, University of Leeds, and holds a PhD in Audiovisual Translation from the same institution.

Her research interests also include computer-assisted translation technology and translator training. She is also a freelance theatre captioner.

Marcello Soffritti is Professor in German Linguistics and Translation at the Department of Interpreting and Translation of the University of Bologna. His current research focuses on multimedia translation, German for Special Purposes and language contact.

Jeroen Vandaele, previously Professor of Spanish at the University of Oslo, now teaches Literary Translation, Hispanic Literatures, and Theory of Style in Translation at Ghent University. His research focuses on translation, ideology, censorship, and comedy. In 2015 he published *Estados de gracia: Billy Wilder y la censura franquista.*

Luise von Flotow is Director of the School of Translation and Interpretation at the University of Ottawa. Her research interests include feminism and gender issues in translation, cultural diplomacy and translation, transnational feminist interests in translation studies and audio-visual translation. She is the author of *Translation and Gender. Translation in The Era of Feminism* (1997) and co-editor and translator of a range of volumes.

Wai-Ping Yau is Associate Professor in the Department of English at Hong Kong Baptist University. His research interests include audiovisual translation, film adaptation, literary translation, and Chinese film and fiction. He is also a translator of Chinese fiction and poetry.

1
Rewiring the circuitry of audiovisual translation
Introduction

Luis Pérez-González

It is customary for introductions to new publications on audiovisual translation (AVT) to start by drawing the reader's attention to various signs of its vitality. The nature and significance of developments witnessed over the last decade, however, has generated a raft of sophisticated indicators to measure the vibrancy of AVT. No longer limited to the growing number of thematic collections and monographs, specialized conferences and dedicated training programmes, the growing prominence, diversity and clout of AVT studies is now also signalled by the inception of collective research projects funded by international stakeholders, the formation of transnational research groups, and the participation of AVT scholars and trainers in successful programmes of collaboration with industry partners.

Crucially, this sense of buoyancy and expansiveness poses its own risks. As a self-standing area of scholarly enquiry within a wider discipline whose short history has been often accounted for in terms of successive, occasionally spasmodic, twists, AVT has recently attempted to foreground its growing maturity through the trope of the 'turn'. Remael's cautiously hedged claim that '[t]he 21st century well may see the advent of the "audiovisual turn" in T[ranslation] S[tudies]' (2010: 15) is now routinely repeated like a mantra in the literature, albeit devoid of the caveats and presentational nuances that moulded the original statement (see, for example, McLaughlin 2014: 380) and/or diluted by a trivializing understanding of 'turns' as little more than relatively self-standing research themes. Jiménez-Crespo's (2017: 5) premise that developments in the study of crowdsourced translation are 'inspired by the "technological turn" (Cronin 2010; O'Hagan 2013), the "sociological turn" (Wolf 2007; Angelelli 2012), and the "audiovisual turn" (Remael 2010)' is a case in point. Troping the history of a discipline, by acknowledging that an assemblage of turns could potentially co-exist at any given point, somewhat erodes the scholarly significance of the research domain that the term 'turn' sought to foreground in the first place. A mechanistic adoption of the logic of turns can be interpreted as an endorsement of 'commodification, superficiality and transitory (and thus flimsy) commitments' (Straw 2016: 2), where contributions are valued only inasmuch as they point 'to a direction in which we want to go now, largely because we see so many others going there as well' (*ibid*: 3). Ultimately, any attempt to appraise the vitality of a given research domain in terms of its competitive positioning within the knowledge regime in which it is embedded is bound to be 'sutured with neoclassical assumptions of neoliberalism, the prevailing political economy of the modern academy, which promotes accumulation and quantitative growth above other values' (Keeling 2016: 317). Apart from these ethical risks, troped disciplinary narratives can also have other unintended consequences—potentially even frustrate attempts to gauge that discipline's capacity to set its own research agenda, develop new methodological directions and facilitate advances in cognate areas of research. Recent views on the state of AVT studies articulated by scholars in the wider translation studies community suggest that qualitative appraisals should be prioritized at this point in the construction of the field. As Baker (2014: xiv) notes, for all its vibrancy,

> most of the literature published by scholars of audiovisual translation, while unquestionably useful and welcome, has failed to engage other disciplines and lay the foundation for interdisciplinary research and critical theorizing. Understandably, perhaps, the priority has been to address practical needs, with training manuals and descriptive accounts of professional practice dominating the field.

The need for AVT research to move beyond what has traditionally been regarded as its core remit is more pressing than ever before. In the digital culture, the instantaneity and global reach of audiovisual content flows has undermined the homogeneity of national audiences and the internal coherence of the markets that once thrived around them—which has, in turn, begun to erode the dominance of specific AVT modalities within individual countries. Technological advances also mean that we are becoming increasingly exposed to audiovisual content that facilitates new forms of interaction between the producers and consumers, amid the gradual shift of cultural and creative industries towards participatory forms of organization—thus challenging existing means of analysis and critique. Crucially, AVT is under pressure to develop in seemingly opposing directions. On the one hand, it is increasingly envisioned and funded to play a socially inclusive role by fostering the integration of sensory impaired members of the community within mainstream society, as far as their access to cultural commodities and venues is concerned. On the other hand, it is at the heart of various initiatives and projects to optimize revenue generation through new technologization processes driven by corporate players.

The impact of these developments—prompted by the ever more complex technology-mediated interplay between verbal and visual semiotics, complete with its industrial and social dimensions—is beginning to resonate beyond the confines of AVT and attract attention from scholars who have not been traditionally associated with this field of scholarly enquiry. Tymoczko (2005), for example, has acknowledged the potential of AVT processes to effect change in the wider field of translation, possibly requiring the re-theorization of fundamental concepts of translation studies. The two-way dialogue between AVT studies and the broader discipline, however, could be hampered by the lack of comprehensive reference works showcasing the scope of the research undertaken by AVT scholars.

Indeed, the body literature on AVT comprises a significant number of encyclopedia or companion entries—see, for example, Baker and Hochel (1998), Gottlieb (1998), O'Connell (2007), Pérez-González (2009), Chiaro (2009), Díaz Cintas (2010), Díaz Cintas and Orero (2010), Remael (2010), Remael (2012), Díaz Cintas (2013), Chaume (2013), Gambier (2013), Taylor (2013), and Yau (2014); practical textbooks specializing in a single AVT modality—examples include, but are not limited to Díaz Cintas and Remael (2007), Franco et al. (2010), Romero-Fresco (2011), Chaume (2012); and relatively wide-ranging collections—an indicative non-exhaustive list would encompass, for example, Orero (2004), Chiaro et al. (2008), Anderman and Díaz Cintas (2009), Díaz Cintas (2007), Díaz Cintas et al. (2007), Díaz Cintas

(2009), Remael *et al.* (2012), Orrego-Carmona and Lee (2017). The publication rate of special journal issues covering a specific research theme within AVT—e.g. Agost *et al.* (2012), Baños *et al.* (2013), Díaz Cintas (2012)—or the field as a whole—Gambier (2003), Gambier and Ramos Pinto (2016)—has accelerated in recent years, as has that of monographs specializing in one AVT modality. Until the recent publication of *Audiovisual Translation: Theories, Methods, Issues* (Pérez-González 2014), however, there was no volume in English that systematically charted and critiqued influential concepts, research models and methodological approaches in AVT studies, or theorized recent developments and trends. But while this recent volume fills a gap and provides a solid foundation for new researchers in the field, a single monograph written by one author cannot possibly be expected to capture the diverse and vigorous developments that are currently shaping every corner of AVT.

The Routledge Handbook of Audiovisual Translation therefore aims to deliver the sort of comprehensive survey of state of the art research that the field currently needs. Its four sections engage, respectively, with (i) the evolving practices associated with both consolidated and emerging AVT modalities; (ii) key theoretical models that have informed and continue to drive scholarly advances in the area; (iii) methodological approaches supporting traditional and innovative ways of interrogating data sets; and (iv) key themes revealing the impact of AVT on various aspects of social life. Through its thirty-two chapters, the Handbook seeks to rewire the circuitry of this scholarly domain, bringing to the fore current and potential avenues for scholarly interaction and mutual engagement across individual practices, theories, methods and themes—both among members of the AVT research community and with scholars working across a range of disciplines.

Part I: Audiovisual translation in action

Part I consists of ten chapters focusing on established and emerging modalities of AVT. These contributions examine key terms and practices, explore the changing contexts in which these modalities have been and continue to be used, provide an indication of their future trajectory, and intervene in the debates arising from the evolving contexts of production and consumption for each of these forms of interlingual, intersemiotic and intercultural mediation. All chapters in this part identify key debates at the heart of these areas, thus contributing to set the research agenda for years to come.

In Chapter 2, **Carol O'Sullivan** and **Jean-François Cornu** deliver a chronological overview of the technological developments and socio-cultural changes that shaped the birth and evolution of audiovisual translation—inextricably associated, during its formation years, with film as the first form of mass entertainment. Taking a look at the interplay between changing translation practices, technical processes and marketing strategies, the authors identify a range of important issues that remain uncharted territory in the history of AVT, as research conducted to date has tended to concentrate on the same AVT modalities and filmic cultures and/or industries. The authors' call for more research on how film translation practices have evolved throughout the twentieth century and their impact on their reception by audiences resonates with similar recommendations in other chapters focusing on the contemporary AVT scene, including Chapters 3, 4, 22 and 23.

In her forward-looking contribution to this Handbook, Chapter 3, **Marie-Noëlle Guillot** looks at one of the most widely studied AVT modalities from a refreshingly original perspective, structuring her chapter around three main aspects: the constraints and opportunities informing subtitling practices, the means and modes—understood as the range of semiotic resources—that lend themselves to manipulation during the subtitling process, and the research models and methods informing scholarship in subtitling studies. In addition to a rigorous overview of traditional research foci in this area, the reader is presented with a stimulating critique of the role that subtitling plays in the new cultural regime unleashed by digitization. Guillot's treatment of the creative specificities and potential of subtitling and subtitles, the implications of emerging co-creative subtitling models involving professionals and amateurs, and the impact of these new practices on the negotiation of intercultural differences in a global context brings into sharp relief the extent to which these issues have come to take centre stage in subtitling studies.

Echoing Chapter 2's call to take action against dominant Eurocentric perspectives, **Charlotte Bosseaux** identifies additional priorities for the development of dubbing studies in Chapter 4. One of the most established research topics within AVT studies, dubbing, is examined here from new angles that are not yet widely represented in the extant body of literature. In keeping with her own interest in the prosodical dimension of dubbing, Bosseaux advocates the relevance of multimodal theory as a new research avenue for dubbing scholars. Other suggested angles pertain to the technologization of dubbing—both in terms of the involvement of amateurs in the practice of this activity and the transformation of the dubbing workflow through the use of voice-synthesizing tools—and the development of 'accessible dubbing', a concept that Bosseaux models after Romero-Fresco's notion of 'accessibility' in AVT, as elaborated in Chapter 31.

Voice-over, an AVT modality that has been relatively neglected by translation scholars to date, takes centre stage in **Anna Matamala**'s Chapter 5. The fact that voice-over is prevalent in audiovisual markets where subtitling and dubbing have not traditionally had a significant presence is reflected in the geographical origin of a substantial part of the experiments and studies that this chapter reports on. And yet, the impact of technological advances on voice-over practices and the need to conduct more research on the reception of voiced-over commodities also emerge here as challenges to be tackled in connection with this AVT modality. The circuitry of AVT is thus being rewired through the emergence of research agendas that cut across individual AVT modalities, as they evolve to cater for the niche audiences that digitization has empowered.

But nowhere is the need to question and reconceptualize current professional practices—and the body of scholarship that these conventions have informed—more pressing than in assistive subtitling, an AVT modality that **Josélia Neves** surveys and interrogates in Chapter 6. Drawing on the premise that technological affordances have the potential to enhance the quantity, quality and diversity of the current provision of subtitles for the deaf and hard of hearing, Neves advocates a change in the paradigm of mediation at the heart of this field. The shift towards an 'enriched (responsive) subtitles' model that does not regard ableism as the benchmark against which disabilities are to be defined will enable access to personalized subtitle formats on demand, first on web-based platforms and then via traditional broadcast media. As Neves notes, this should not represent the end of subtitling for the deaf and hard of hearing, but the upgrading of this AVT modality to serve the needs and expectations of wider constituencies in the era of bespoke media content.

Being a born-digital form of AVT, respeaking has been informed since its inception by assumptions, tools and methods that other modalities of audiovisual transfer see as shaping their future. In Chapter 7, **Pablo Romero-Fresco** chronicles the institutionalization of respeaking within European higher education providers and delineates a unique domain of research where academics have spearheaded important industrial developments from the start. But the informational society that has fuelled the growth and recognition of respeaking is placing ever more challenging demands on this AVT modality, with automation poised to play a central role in delivering more and better intralingual and interlingual respoken output, both for fictional and factual media content.

As was also the case with subtitles for the deaf in Neves' contribution, **Elisa Perego** places traditional audio description practices under close scrutiny in Chapter 8. Driven by the insight that users of this assistive form of audiovisual transfer do not constitute the homogeneous constituency that current professional guidelines assume, the author shows how former norms are being superseded by new user-centred and flexible recommendations. Readers are presented here with a thorough account of key debates in the field, pertaining to the need for research on the reception of audio descriptions by different user groups, and the place that the describers' personal interpretation of media content should have, if any, in the narrations they deliver. Audio description, as surveyed in this chapter, emerges as a key node in the circuitry of AVT, as it would appear to be serving as a productive testing ground for the refinement of corpus-based and eye-tracking research methods, that are explored in more depth in Chapters 20 and 22, respectively.

Together with subtitling for the deaf and hard of hearing, and respeaking and audio description, surtitling and captioning for theatre and opera have benefited from a heightened awareness, on the part of various administrations and legislative bodies, of the extent to which assistive forms of audiovisual transfer can facilitate the integration of individuals with sensory impairments as members of mainstream audiences. Unsurprisingly, Chapter 9, where **Alina Secară** explores the origin and expansion of surtitling practices, intersects with the previous three chapters in various and productive ways. Again, the importance of undertaking research on the reception of surtitles by different user groups, the challenges posed by the growing ubiquity of on-demand services and the impact of automation on the production of surtitles emerge as drivers for change and innovation.

The centrality of user-experience and the relationship between content producers and the user base is also a central concern for the future of research on game localization, as **Minako O'Hagan** contends in Chapter 10. Although key players in the game industry failed to grasp the importance of translation quality until relatively not long ago, ongoing research is drawing on ever more sophisticated methods to gauge and enhance the contribution that localization makes to the immersive experiences that contemporary games deliver. Using eye-tracking technology and collecting biometric data—such as facial expressions, galvanic skin response or heart rates, to give but a few examples—are helping researchers to gain a better understanding of users' behaviour and preferences. But the emphasis of game localization research on user-experience issues should also address the social dimension of the gaming phenomenon, including the formation and evolution of participatory fan and crowdsourcing communities—another recurring thread traversing other chapters in this Handbook.

The shift of AVT practices towards customization, based on available data about the end-users' preferences and expectations, also features in the final contribution to Part I. In Chapter 11, **Jonathan Evans** explores a form of audiovisual transfer whose translational dimension has been primarily acknowledged by film scholars. Remakes, whether they are official or unofficial, interlingual or shot in the same language as the original film, are conceptualized here as intertextual assemblages made, in many cases, for a 'knowing audience'. Unlike other AVT modalities, where the ubiquity of relevant technologies allows viewers to produce their own translated versions as a form of self-mediation, remakes are still undertaken mainly by the industry. However, the central place accorded to the reception of the adapted film by target viewers in the production of remakes—the ultimate and arguably most creative form of translation—warrants their inclusion in this volume.

Luis Pérez-González

Part II: Theoretical perspectives in audiovisual translation studies

The second part of this Handbook consists of eight chapters exploring the interface between AVT and a range of theoretical models that have proved particularly productive in terms of their capacity to inform research on various forms of audiovisual transfer. Some of these models are associated with disciplines that have long intersected with AVT and the wider discipline of translation studies, e.g. pragmatics, sociolinguistics and spoken discourse analysis. Other conceptual networks examined here, however, correspond to (sub)disciplines that are only now beginning to make their presence felt in the AVT literature.

In Chapter 12, **Henry Jones** sets out to heighten our awareness of various theorizations of mediality, arguing that they have the capacity to facilitate our understanding of the material dimension of audiovisual texts. Crucially, the evolving materiality of audiovisual content has played a significant role in shaping a range of practices to accommodate various types of constraints, including but not limited to the spatio-temporal type. The set of notions explored here is not commensurate with a single conceptual network or disciplinary domain, but Jones' sophisticated overview manages to weave complementary, sometimes clashing, accounts of transformative technological shifts from across the ages—most of which have not been sufficiently explored in AVT scholarship. Neither should AVT scholars overlook the key notion of narrativity. Although professional translators routinely operate in a narrative *milieu*, they rarely reflect on the implications of their mediation for narrativity in the work they produce. **Jeroen Vandaele**'s contribution, in Chapter 15, paves the way for future research work on the narrative mechanisms and devices that drive most audiovisual texts, under the medial constraints at play in each case. The tendency for professionals to focus on a single, often short, segment of language at a time could interfere with the narrative configuration of the source text in terms of its intended clarity and opacity, as realized through carefully placed elements of suspense, curiosity, surprise and character-oriented focalization. The generative power of mediality and narrativity cannot be underestimated by researchers in our field, as the growing interest in multimodal theory (Chapter 17) and research methods like eye tracking (Chapter 22) confirms.

As **Silvia Bruti** shows in Chapter 13, one of the most established strands of research on the impact of medial constraints on AVT pertains to the study of translated interaction as an idiosyncratic communicative event. Using concepts drawn from discourse and conversation analysis, Bruti illustrates the changes in interpersonal dynamics and characterization that subtitling and dubbing conventions often entail. Bruti's wide-ranging chapter traces the evolution of scholarly work in this area, from the older structuralist approaches to more recent contributions where fictional dialogue, as defined by its markers of orality, is conceptualized as a genre in its own right, or where the translation of conversation is understood as part of a wider process of multimodal meaning-making. In Chapter 16, **Louisa Desilla** further gauges the extent to which AVT may tamper with the suprasegmental organization of the source dialogue. The author shows how established notions drawn from various strands of pragmatics, like speech acts, politeness and implicature, can assist researchers in identifying and relaying filmmakers' creative intentions, as expressed through the characters' speech. Should translations spell out what directors chose to express in the source conversation using indirect language, for example, they may be altering the perception of certain characters and the coherence of the plot—all of which might be detrimental in terms of reception and enjoyment by the target audience.

Unlike the theories surveyed in some of the chapters that I have just outlined, the models of psycholinguistics and cognitive perception that **Louise Fryer** surveys in Chapter 14 are still under-represented in the AVT literature. Audio description is chosen here by the author to illustrate how a raft of concepts relating to perception and presence, as defined in the field of cognitive perception, can help AVT scholars explain systematically how professional audio describers go about making content selection choices, i.e. how they decide which elements of the multimodal text to include in their descriptions. Structured as a constellation of themes, the main body of this chapter provides abundant food for thought for AVT scholars working on the very concept of accessibility (Chapter 31) and the multiple modalities of assistive AVT explored in this Handbook. Audio description and describers' decisions on how to make audio-visual texts accessible to viewers with sensory impairments are also at the heart of Chapter 17, where **Aline Remael** and **Nina Reviers** use the social semiotic strand of multimodal theory to examine how meaning emerges from the interplay between different types of meaning-making resources or modes. Patterns of multimodal cohesion observed in the original text may be altered in the describers' versions, which could in turn undermine the overall coherence of the multimodal ensemble presented to viewers. The authors illustrate their argument with a detailed case study that shows how multimodal cohesion is construed in the original text and relayed in audio description and subtitles for the hard of hearing. Both Chapters 14 and 17 show how cognitive perception models and multimodal theory provide AVT scholars with new and sound conceptual tools to articulate evidence-driven accounts of decision-making processes, and their consequences, in assistive forms of audiovisual transfer.

The social dimension of AVT, on the other hand, is brought into sharp relief in Chapters 18 and 19. In the first of these, **Wai-Ping Yau** reflects on the role that the presence of linguistic variation in audiovisual texts plays in the construction and representation of individual and collective identities. Idiolects, sociolects, and dialects—and the connotations that these all carry—make a significant contribution to the overall quality of films, in terms of characterization and plot development. Yau's chapter gauges the extent to which mainstream AVT strategies tamper with the intended function of linguistic variation, as envisaged by the creators of the source text, and influence the reception by the target audience of the different identities at play. Ultimately, translated audiovisual texts tend to neutralize the diversity of identities represented in their original versions, thus preventing target language viewers from identifying and making sense of the social tensions and power differentials that creators portrayed in the source text. On the other hand, in Chapter 19 **Luise von Flotow** and **Daniel Josephy-Hernández** zoom in on the representation of gender-based identities and struggles. Their chapter explores how scholars from across disciplines in the Humanities have theorized the influence of feminism on the way language is used to represent and perform gender in audiovisual products. Drawing on a carefully chosen set of examples, von Flotow and Josephy-Hernández illustrate, for example, the difficulties that Romance languages encounter in trying to recreate genderlects and queer references that originated in Anglo-American audiovisual products; they also show that—contrary to widely held assumptions about its open-mindedness and flexibility—English also finds it difficult to recreate gender-aware features emerging in European and Asian languages. Ultimately, the authors conclude, the linguistic realization of sexual difference and derivative gendered behaviour remains a sensitive issue across languages and cultures that AVT scholars should approach from new angles.

Part III: Research methods in audiovisual translation studies

The third part of this Handbook seeks to flag up a range of research methods—whether these are fully established within AVT, e.g. corpus-based and eye-tracking studies; evolving into more robust approaches, as is the case with reception studies or multimodal corpora; or relative newcomers to the field, e.g. ethnography.

Corpus-based translation studies, the focus of **Maria Pavesi**'s contribution in Chapter 20, shows how large computer-held collections of carefully selected texts can facilitate quantitative analyses of dubbed dialogue—and enable comparisons between its idiosyncratic features and those of fictional conversation written originally in the source and target languages of the combination under scrutiny. The generalizability of the insights yielded by the analysis of corpus data, typically operationalized in the form of frequency lists and the search for discernible usage patterns around individual lexical items or whole phrases, has allowed researchers to address important questions pertaining to the prevalence of specific translation strategies in dubbing, and the construction of conversational authenticity and naturalness in film dialogue, which is held to play a pivotal role in shaping the audience's perception of a film's quality. While computer-based translation studies share many premises and tools with the wider research domain of corpus-based translation studies, working with multimodal corpora places specific demands, as **Marcello Soffritti** explains in Chapter 21. The development of databases comprising parallel sets of multimodal texts calls for complex annotation protocols and unwieldy query interfaces that are difficult to set up and manage by small research teams or individual scholars. So while multimodal corpora have a great contribution to make to enhance our understanding of AVT, in terms of their capacity to extend the generalizability of current insights derived from qualitative tools such as multimodal concordances, their viability will be ensured only if and when advances in automation can assist with the design, compilation, processing and maintenance of these corpora.

The use of eye-tracking technology to gain new insights into the processing of audiovisual texts by viewers has seen its popularity rise on the back of technological advances in recent years—as borne out by the references to this methodology in most chapters included in Part I of this Handbook. As **Jan-Louis Kruger** shows in Chapter 22, eye tracking helps researchers understand the impact that formal and mechanical aspects of AVT practices have on the viewers' experience, but also how specific attributes of audience members influence the way in which they distribute their visual attention among the various semiotic resources they are presented with. The experimental dimension of eye-tracking research has been hailed as a game changer in the trajectory of AVT scholarship; as Kruger argues, the rigour of its various measurements and its perceived scientific status mean that it has now become indispensable for any study of text and image processing in the context of an audiovisual text. In Chapter 23, **David Orrego-Carmona** casts his net wider, looking at reception studies in a more general sense—not necessarily confined to the use of quantitative or experimental methods, such as eye tracking. Based on a comprehensive survey of previous research, the author advocates the importance of methodological triangulation for the future development of reception studies. Through the combination of quantitative and qualitative perspectives, Orrego-Carmona argues, reception research can meaningfully contribute to the study of very different topics, ranging from the amount of cognitive effort involved in processing certain forms of audiovisual stimuli and their translations, to the social impact of certain translation practices.

Part III finishes with Chapter 24, where **Dang Li** explores one of the most exciting methodological developments in our field, i.e. the advent of ethnographic and, more specifically, netnographic approaches to the study of AVT. In an ever more participatory media landscape where certain types of audiovisual texts are increasingly translated by communities of citizens pursuing different agendas, the involvement of researchers in such groups—not only in translation-related activities, but also in the discharge of community management or editorial roles—is bound to shed light on the motivations and aspirations of prosumers, as well as the collaborative workflow within these, mostly virtual, communities. Drawing on her own netnographic fieldwork, Li delivers an overview of the main methodological challenges she encountered, including the compilation and management of her digital data set, and the development of a personal rapport with the community members. Crucially, netnographers should be willing to explore, develop an awareness of, and manage their own digital identity across various fieldsites and platforms, even once their project has been completed.

Part IV: Audiovisual translation in society

The eight chapters included in Part IV of the Handbook address a range of themes pertaining to the place of AVT in society. Some of the chapters focus on the professional and economic trajectories in the expansion of AVT, primarily in terms of institutionalization, academization and technologization. Other contributions, however, explore the social impact of AVT as a force for social change, with particular emphasis on subtitling as the type of audiovisual transfer that ordinary citizens without specific training in (audiovisual) translation find more easy to take on, either individually or as part of a collectivity.

Chapter 25, by **Reglindis De Ridder** and **Eithne O'Connell**, revolves around minority language AVT and the language planning implications of studies undertaken by scholars in the field. In a global media marketplace dominated by English as the main source language, AVT has typically been used to foster the interests of the industry. As a result, in terms of their relative positioning within global media flows, small (and even some major) languages have been minoritized against English. The authors engage with the complexity of the issues at stake here by drawing on different examples of minority languages from across the world, and examining their idiosyncratic sociolinguistic fabric, the directionality of translation flows into and out of minority languages and the impact that the latter have on language planning decisions.

In Chapter 26, **Rebecca Johnson** examines the links between popular music and AVT—a relatively unexplored area of research due to, among other reasons, the perceived low symbolic capital of the music genres discussed in this chapter. The industry has tended to overlook the translation of popular music lyrics, but motivated prosumers are now capitalizing on the affordances of digital technologies to mediate lyrical content across linguistic and cultural boundaries, either as members of communities of fandom or activism. Their participation, the author argues, is widening the range and scope of translational interventions in popular music through the generalization of remakes or parodies that are quickly eroding the status of the music video as *the* medium used by the industry to distribute popular music globally.

Fandom, one of the contexts of media content production and consumption surveyed in the previous contribution, is the main focus of Chapter 27. In her piece, **Tessa Dwyer** focuses mainly on fansubbing, although fandubbing and game translation hacking also feature in this critique of the interplay between fandom and AVT over the span of several decades. Starting with the emergence of Japanese *anime* fandom, and fansubbing, in the US, Dwyer goes on to chronicle the shifting configuration of fandom communities into prosumer and crowdsourcing agencies. Dwyer's account of the centrality of the citizen-turned-translator complements the accounts of evolving subtitling and dubbing practices provided in Chapters 3 and 4, and foregrounds the role that affect and performance play in today's amateur AVT in the context of the digital culture.

Unlike the communities examined in the previous chapter, the activist subtitling collectivities that **Mona Baker** discusses in Chapter 28 resort to AVT in order to effect social and political change. After surveying the small body of literature that has so far addressed the interface between activism and audiovisual translation, the author articulates a number of priorities for the theorization of activist AVT and illustrates the main difficulties associated with the study of this type of data. Drawing on the findings of her own research on activist subtitling during the 2011 Egyptian Revolution, Baker identifies a number of activist subtitling strategies and presents the reader with an insightful overview of various issues influencing the production of such translations, including but not limited to the constraints posed by the technology used to distribute subtitled media content, the prefigurative dynamics at play within the subtitling groups examined here, and perceptions of agency and visibility in these communities.

The following two chapters bring to the fore the growing presence of AVT in academic settings, whether in the form of audiovisual translator training programmes, or through the contribution that AVT makes to foreign language learning. In Chapter 29, **Beatriz Cerezo Merchán** charts recent developments in AVT training. After presenting recent advances in translation pedagogy, the author proposes a competence-based approach to the training of audiovisual translators. Both general and specific competences required in this field of professional practice are identified and illustrated, and practical guidelines for the development of subtitling and dubbing courses are articulated—in terms of suggested contents, pedagogical resources, task-based projects and assessment tools—to bolster the development of said competences. For her part, in Chapter 30 **Laura Incalcaterra McLoughlin** shifts the focus towards the benefits that can accrue from the incorporation of (mainly) subtitling activities in the foreign language classroom. After accounting for the effectiveness of traditional training scenarios involving the student's exposure to subtitled audiovisual material, Incalcaterra McLoughlin draws on recent studies to argue that AVT tasks where learners are actively involved in the production of subtitles and the completion of different preparatory activities yield more successful pedagogical outcomes and are generally more enjoyable for students. The author shows the extent to which research in this area of study is currently informed by different disciplines—including, but not limited to, second language acquisition, cognitive psychology and translation pedagogy—and ends by suggesting future avenues of research to mainstream active AVT tasks, on account of their capacity to boost learners' linguistic and intercultural proficiency.

The last two contributions to this Handbook are forward-looking chapters laying the foundations for new developments in AVT. In Chapter 31, **Pablo Romero-Fresco** proposes and articulates the 'accessible filmmaking' approach, under which the translation of films under production—whether through general or assistive forms of audiovisual transfer— should receive serious consideration and be held to scrutiny during the pre-production or production stages, rather than during the post-production or distribution stage, as is almost invariably the case now. Crucially, the integration of discussions on translation in earlier stages of the film production process is bound to prompt collaboration between filmmakers and translators. Romero-Fresco surveys the history of accessible filmmaking, delivers a blueprint for the integration of this approach within translator training programmes and explores scholarly developments on the study of this transfer approach, led by the application of ethnographic and eye-tracking methods.

In Chapter 32, the final contribution, **Panayota Georgakopoulou** addresses the impact of technological change on the AVT industry, foregrounding the extent to which translation practices are influenced by the technological tools and infrastructure available at any given point— thus offering a contemporary counterpoint to the argument that Jones rehearses in Chapter 12. Significantly, Georgakopoulou's wide-ranging chapter conceptualizes digitization and crowd-sourcing as past milestones in the historical evolution of the AVT industry. In the author's view, the present state of the field is being shaped by the migration of tools to the cloud and the growing incorporation of machine learning into AVT workflows. Speech recognition and synthesis and machine translation are posited as potential paradigm-changing language technologies with the capacity to disrupt the traditional configuration of the AVT industry.

This reference work provides substantial evidence that AVT has now reached, to borrow part of Guillot's chapter title, 'the cusp of its futures'. Its evolving practices are channelling the theoretical vitality and methodological vibrancy of scholarly research in the field, but they also signal their ambition to have an ever deeper and more meaningful impact on social life. It is hoped that this Handbook will give AVT the voice it needs to make its presence felt within the Humanities research landscape; and scholars from other disciplinary backgrounds a useful tool to appreciate and benefit from what AVT scholarship has to offer.

References

Agost, R., P. Orero and E. Di Giovanni (eds) (2012) 'Multidisciplinarity in Audiovisual Translation'. Special issue of *MonTI* 4.

Anderman, G. and J. Díaz Cintas (eds) (2009) *Audiovisual Translation: Language Transfer on Screen*, Basingstoke: Palgrave Macmillan.

Angelelli, C. (2012) 'The Sociological Turn in Translation and Interpreting Studies. Introduction', *Translation and Interpreting Studies* 7(2): 125–128.

Baker, M. (2014) 'Preface', in L. Pérez-González, *Audiovisual Translation: Theories, Methods, Issues*, London & New York: Routledge, xiv–xv.

Baker, M. and B. Hochel (1998) 'Dubbing', in M. Baker (ed.) *Routledge Encyclopedia of Translation Studies*, 1st edition, London & New York: Routledge, 74–76.

Baños, R., S. Bruti and S. Zanotti (eds) (2013) 'Corpus Linguistics and Audiovisual Translation: In Search of an Integrated Approach'. Special issue of *Perspectives: Studies in Translatology* 21(4).

Chaume, F. (2012) *Audiovisual Translation: Dubbing*, Manchester: St Jerome.

Chaume, F. (2013) 'Research Paths in Audiovisual Translation: The Case of Dubbing', in C. Millán-Varela and F. Bartrina (eds) *The Routledge Handbook of Translation Studies*, London & New York: Routledge, 288–302.

Chiaro, D. (2009) 'Issues in Audiovisual Translation', in J. Munday (ed.) *The Routledge Companion to Translation Studies*, London & New York: Routledge, 141–165.

Chiaro, D., C. Heiss and C. Bucaria (eds) (2008) *Between Text and Image: Updating Research in Screen Translation*, Amsterdam & Philadelphia: John Benjamins.

Cronin, M. (2010) 'The Translation Crowd', *Tradumàtica* 8. Available online: http://www.fti.uab.es/tradumatica/revista/num8/articles/04/04central.htm [last access 20 December 2017].

Díaz Cintas, J. (ed.) (2007) *The Didactics of Audiovisual Translation*, Amsterdam & Philadelphia, John Benjamins.

Díaz Cintas, J. (ed.) (2009) *New Trends in Audiovisual Translation*, Bristol, Buffalo & Toronto: Multilingual Matters.

Díaz Cintas, J. (2010) 'Subtitling', in Y. Gambier and L. van Doorslaer (eds) *Handbook of Translation Studies*, Volume 1, Amsterdam & Philadelphia: John Benjamins, 344–349.

Díaz Cintas, J. (2012), 'Présentation', in J. Díaz Cintas (ed.) 'La manipulation de la traduction audio-visuelle/The Manipulation of Audiovisual Translation'. Special issue of *Meta* 57(2), 275–278.

Díaz Cintas, J. (2013) 'Subtitling: Theory, Practice and Research', in C. Millán-Varela and F. Bartrina (eds) *The Routledge Handbook of Translation Studies*, London & New York: Routledge, 285–299.

Díaz Cintas, J. and P. Orero (2010) 'Voiceover and Dubbing', in Y. Gambier and L. van Doorslaer (eds) *Handbook of Translation Studies*, Volume 1, Amsterdam & Philadelphia: John Benjamins, 441–445.

Díaz Cintas, J., P. Orero and A. Remael (eds) (2007) *Media for All. Subtitling for the Deaf, Audio Description and Sign Language*, Amsterdam & New York: Rodopi.

Díaz Cintas, J. and A. Remael (2007) *Audiovisual Translation: Subtitling*, Manchester: St Jerome.
Franco, E., A. Matamala and P. Orero (2010) *Voice-over Translation: An Overview*, Bern: Peter Lang.
Gambier, Y. (ed.) (2003) 'Screen Translation'. Special issue of *The Translator* 9(2).
Gambier, Y. (2013) 'The Position of Audiovisual Translation Studies', in C. Millán-Varela and F. Bartrina (eds) *The Routledge Handbook of Translation Studies*, London & New York: Routledge, 45–59.
Gambier, Y. and S. Ramos Pinto (eds) (2016) 'Audiovisual Translation. Theoretical and Methodological Challenges'. Special issue of *Target* 28(2).
Gottlieb, H. (1998) 'Subtitling', in M. Baker (ed.) *Routledge Encyclopedia of Translation Studies*, 1st edition, London & New York: Routledge, 244–248.
Jiménez-Crespo, M. A. (2017) *Crowdsourcing and Online Collaborative Translations: Expanding the Limits of Translation Studies*, Amsterdam & Philadelphia: John Benjamins.
Keeling, D. M. (2016) 'Of Turning and Tropes', *Review of Communication*. Special issue entitled 'Figures of Entanglement' 16(4): 317–333.
McLaughlin, M. (2014) 'Translation Studies', *French Studies* 68(3): 377–385.
O'Connell, E. (2007) 'Screen Translation', in P. Kuhiwczak and K. Littau (eds) *A Companion to Translation Studies*, Clevedon, Buffalo & Toronto: Multilingual Matters, 120–133.
O'Hagan, M. (2013) 'The Impact of New Technologies on Translation Studies: A Technological Turn?', in C. Millán-Varela and F. Bartrina (eds) *Routledge Handbook of Translation Studies*, London & New York, Routledge, 503–518.
Orero, P. (ed.) (2004) *Topics in Audiovisual Translation*, Amsterdam & Philadelphia: John Benjamins.
Orrego-Carmona, D. and Y. Lee (eds) (2017) *Non-Professional Subtitling*, Newcastle upon Tyne: Cambridge Scholars Publishing.
Pérez-González, L. (2009) 'Audiovisual Translation', in M. Baker and G. Saldanha (eds) *The Routledge Encyclopedia of Translation Studies*, 2nd edition, London & New York: Routledge, 13–20.
Pérez-González, L. (2014) *Audiovisual Translation: Theories, Methods, Issues*, London & New York: Routledge.
Remael, A. (2010) 'Audiovisual Translation', in Y. Gambier and L. van Doorslaer (eds) *Handbook of Translation Studies*, volume I, Amsterdam & Philadelphia: John Benjamins, 12–17.
Remael, A. (2012) 'Media Accessibility', in Y. Gambier and L. van Doorslaer (eds) *Handbook of Translation Studies*, volume 3, Amsterdam & Philadelphia: John Benjamins, 95–101.
Remael, A., P. Orero and M. Carroll (eds) (2012) *Audiovisual Translation and Media Accessibility at the Crossroads*, Amsterdam & New York: Rodopi.
Romero-Fresco, P. (2011) *Subtitling through Speech Recognition: Respeaking*, Manchester: St Jerome.
Straw, W. (2016) 'Twists and Turns: Splits, Snowballs and Tweaks in Cultural Theory', *Etopia: Canadian Journal of Cultural Studies*. Special issue entitled 'Intersections | Cross-Sections Re: Turns': 1–11.
Taylor, C. (2013) 'Multimodality and Audiovisual Translation', in Y. Gambier and L. van Doorslaer (eds) *Handbook of Translation Studies*, volume 4, Amsterdam & Philadelphia: John Benjamins, 98–104.
Tymoczko, M. (2005) 'Trajectories of Research in Translation Studies', *Meta* 50(4): 1082–1097.
Wolf, M. (2007) 'Introduction: The Emergence of a Sociology of Translation', in M. Wolf and A. Fukari (eds) *Constructing a Sociology of Translation*, Amsterdam & Philadelphia: John Benjamins, 1–36.
Yau, Wai-Ping (2014) 'Translation and Film: Dubbing, Subtitling, Adaptation and Remaking', in S. Bermann and C. Porter (eds) *A Companion to Translation Studies*, Oxford: Wiley-Blackwell, 492–503.

Part I
Audiovisual translation in action

2
History of audiovisual translation

Carol O'Sullivan and Jean-François Cornu

Introduction

Audiovisual translation studies has been experiencing a resurgence in interest in historical approaches since the early 2010s. This has followed a more general growing interest in translation history since the late 1990s. These developments require the researcher to look simultaneously at translation practices, technical processes and marketing strategies that are all intertwined, especially in the early years of film translation. We say 'film translation' here since this phrase is widely used in the pre-TV era, though as is explained elsewhere in this volume, a number of different terms have been used over the years. This chapter takes, broadly speaking, a chronological approach. It begins by looking at the translated intertitles and film explainers of the silent era. It goes on to look at the transition to sound, at the short-lived multilingual versions and then at the development of subtitling and dubbing. The question of translation into English and the cultural position of the 'foreign film' is briefly dealt with. The chapter ends by outlining current issues and new debates in film translation history, touching on a couple of significant methodological contributions in this area.

Audiovisual translation in the silent period

In the pre-sound era, films were silent, but not speechless: mouths could be seen speaking on the screen and title cards conveyed narration and the gist of dialogues actually or seemingly spoken by the actors. The translation of silent film is one of the biggest gaps in audiovisual translation (AVT) research. AVT researchers have tended to write off this field on the grounds that the translation of silent film is unproblematic, at least by comparison with the problems which accompanied the coming of sound. For instance, Jan Ivarsson and Mary Carroll observe that intertitles were simply 'removed, translated... filmed, and re-inserted' (1998: 9). Tessa Dwyer has insightfully noted, however, that 'the internationalism and supposed universalism of the silent era was in fact underwritten by a vast array of translation practices' (2005: 301). These could include the presence of live narrators (see below), the reorganization of intertitles, and the modification of storylines, including the provision of alternate endings (the so-called 'Russian endings'; see Cherchi Usai 2000: 12). Markus Nornes, one of the few scholars to have looked in any detail at the translation of silent film, has identified one typical workflow as involving the shipping of a list of titles from Hollywood to the various distributors, who would translate the titles and send these 'flash titles' back to the studio (Nornes 2007: 97–98). This negatively affected the quality of the titling, e.g. when technicians without language expertise were reshooting the titles. Thereafter, these titles were dispatched along with the print so that the distributor could have more control over the translation and reinsertion of the titles (*ibid.*: 98). Paratranslation was also important; for example 'each Famous Players-Lasky film was also accompanied by fifty or so other items that required translation and printing in the target languages' (*ibid.*). Error-ridden English titles written by non-native speakers in the film's country of origin were also a source of complaints. Title cards could be quite elaborately ornamented ('art titles') and this ornamentation was often lost from recreated titles. Barry Salt (1992: 109) sees a link between a reduction in film export (e.g. during the First World War) and an increased use of illustrated title cards; in periods where overseas markets accounted for a lot of trade, illustrated title cards were less favoured because they were more challenging to translate. Such links between film style and translation are key to audiovisual translation history.

Dwyer concludes that 'the degree of translation required to preserve the myth of universalism [of silent film] was phenomenal' (2005: 301). She draws on Ruth Vasey's film-historical study *The World According to Hollywood 1918–1939*, which pays considerable attention to the textual instability of film, and the ways in which this facilitated the sale of films across national borders. As Vasey (1997: 64) notes, '[s]ilent movies were themselves never so precisely fixed as their talkie descendants'. This is well illustrated by Joost Broeren's study of the Dutch context and the Desmet collection of silent films, which includes useful details on their localization. Broeren argues that cinema of the 1910s 'is fluid, changeable, malleable; there is no original because every print could be different, and thus every print was an original—or no print was' (Broeren 2008: 65). An example of a heavily localized silent film can be found in Nornes (2007: 101): the Dutch version of *Where are my Children* (1916) was extensively recut and censored for exhibition in the Netherlands. Another manifestation of translation which shows the extent to which silent film was indebted to translation and translation-like processes was the 'translating dissolve' (see O'Sullivan 2011: 45–50) which developed as a way of negotiating differences between the language of the diegesis and the language of narration.

Although the area remains almost completely undiscussed by translation scholars (see Díaz Cintas and Remael 2007: 26), we must consider the translation of film in the silent period as a holistic process involving the translation of title cards, the omission or addition of title cards, film editing and paratranslation.

Benshis, bonimenteurs and other film explainers

From the very early years of cinema (late 1890s, early 1900s), there were people whose task was to explain and comment on what was happening on the screen. When title cards were introduced, they would read out or explain their content for the benefit of illiterate audience members. Such 'film explainers' were active in the United States and Europe until the mid- or late 1910s (Boillat 2007: 132, Barnier 2010: 264). In France and Quebec they were called *bonimenteurs* ('yarn spinners') and *conférenciers* ('lecturers') (Barnier 2010: 89–119, Lacasse 2000, Lacasse, Bouchard and Scheppler 2009). They were also popular in Japan where *benshis* were sometimes stars in their own right and lasted into the early sound years. Of all the film explainers, the *benshis* have probably been the most studied, given their cultural profile in Japan and the Japanese historiographical tradition (Nornes 2007: 110–119).

Film explainers sometimes translated foreign films. In the early 1900s in the USA, 'titles were read from the screen aloud and translated into a dozen languages' (Brownlow 1973: 11). Very few researchers have commented upon the role of film explainers as translators. Boillat (2007: 124–129) develops this aspect of their activity in a sense that goes beyond the need to translate a foreign language, and has to do with wider processes of 'image-reading' and 'cultural translation.' In this broader sense, film explaining may thus be considered a form of intralingual, interlingual and intersemiotic film translation. The translation aspect of film explaining occasionally reappeared after the transition to sound, for example in René Clair's *Man About Town*, the American version of his *Le Silence est d'or* (1947), in which actor and singer Maurice Chevalier summarizes the narration and dialogue in English at regular intervals, while the original French sound-track remains unchanged (Cornu 2014: 26–27). Film explaining itself does continue, in a way, via interpreting at film festivals (see Razlogova 2015 for a historical approach).

Audiovisual translation and the transition to sound

Although, as previously mentioned, languages were not totally absent from silent films, the talkies ushered multilingualism into cinema on a worldwide scale. Synchronized speech was first introduced in American films, and solutions quickly needed to be devised to successfully maintain the worldwide distribution of Hollywood product. Because of the prevalence of the English language in the early talking period, the situation was quite different in English-speaking and non-English-speaking countries.

The first talking film to be released internationally was Warner Brothers' *The Jazz Singer* (Crosland 1927). Although mainly a silent film with a musical sound-track and only a few 'live' talking scenes, it heralded the talking era and continues to be perceived as its starting point to this day. Information is oddly scarce as to how this film was shown to non-English-speaking audiences around the world. It remains unclear how or whether it was translated at all when it reached continental Europe in 1929. It seems that in France the film was shown with intertitles in French, with written translations of the spoken scenes, projected onto an adjacent screen like slides (Anon. 1929: 24, Thompson 1985: 158–159).

With the increasing number of talking films released outside their original linguistic region, one of the early translation strategies consisted in *not* translating them (see e.g. Low 1985: 91). In 1929–1930, dubbing processes had not yet begun to be devised, and subtitling as we know it today was rare. Because audiences outside America quickly resented having to sit through English-speaking films, Hollywood producers and foreign distributors resorted to 'synchronized' films, i.e. silent versions of talkies with music as their only sound, and inserted intertitles similar to silent title cards (Cornu 2014: 27–28, Freire 2015: 194–203). This practice was used in Italy, for example, where an ordnance of 22 October 1930 forbade speech on film in languages other than Italian (Quargnolo 2000: 19). Only songs were permitted in the foreign language. Quargnolo observes that more than 300 films were exhibited with title cards in the place of dialogue, 'which more or less explained the dialogue spoken by the actors in the original film, but which weighed down its rhythm and limited and fragmented the flow of images' (our translation). Some films ended up with huge quantities of title cards: up to 200 or even 250 title cards per film (*ibid.*: 20). Another strategy eschewing translation as such consisted in reshooting close-ups containing spoken dialogue with a local cast, and keeping the speechless long shots of the original films to avoid having to shoot the whole film again (Cornu 2014: 28–29). These practices were short-lived, as was the strategy of making bilingual or multilingual films in order to avoid the need for translation. Notable examples include *Kameradschaft/La Tragédie de la mine* (Pabst 1931), *Niemandsland* (Trivas 1931) and *Allô Berlin? Ici Paris* (Duvivier 1931) (Rossholm 2006: 66).

Simultaneously and in different parts of the world, processes and methods were developed which broadly fall into two categories: adding written texts in the form of titles superimposed onto the film or projected on an adjacent screen; or replacing the original dialogues with lines spoken in languages that could be understood by local audiences. Adding titles that could be read simultaneously with hearing the characters speak became known as subtitling. Changing the spoken language of the film was achieved through two main strategies: the ill-fated multilinguals and the much more enduring dubbing process.

With multilinguals, the same story and dialogue would be shot in a number of languages, using the same technical crew, but changing the cast for each different language. Dubbing consisted of replacing the original dialogue and actors' voices with new lines in the languages of the countries where the film was to be released. Both methods are further developed in specific sections below.

In the early 1930s, a small number of major Hollywood studios bet on the dubbing method to reconquer the territories they had temporarily lost with the introduction of speech in films. Audiences throughout Latin America and Europe enjoyed the novelty but soon resented the fact that the films spoke English. Making their films heard in Spanish, French and other major European languages seemed to be the solution for Hollywood to keep film markets that were essential to recoup production costs and increase profits. In Asia, Hollywood companies preferred to use subtitling, which took the form of projecting titles on a secondary screen located beside the main image screen, particularly in Japan and China. A similar practice obtained in the Middle East (Cornu 2014: 230).

Outside America, in the late 1920s and early 1930s, Germany was the country that produced the highest number of films, both for local consumption and export. To maintain distribution beyond its borders as well as feeding its theatres with foreign talking films, Germany also turned to dubbing. However, the overall control of the German film industry by the Nazis from 1933 brought about a decline in the export of films to the rest of the world.

The Hollywood domination of worldwide film distribution made English the main language used in the new talking films. However, during the early transition years, talkies from non-English-speaking countries also started to circulate in Anglophone countries. These mainly came from France and Germany. Intertitles were briefly used to translate foreign-language dialogue, e.g. in *Westfront 1918* (Pabst 1930) as they had been used to translate incidental foreign-language dialogue in Hollywood product as well, in films such as *Hell's Angels* (Hughes 1930) and *Seas Beneath* (Ford 1931). The Film Society in Britain also used intertitles, having tried such techniques as 'printing a synopsis of the story on translucent paper which the audience read by holding up their copies to the light from the screen', as Thorold Dickinson recalls (quoted in Mazdon and Wheatley 2013: 27). In a few cases, films were provided with some English-speaking sequences for release in English-speaking territories, for instance, René Clair's *Le Million* (1931). According to reviews at the time, the opening sequence of this film was apparently reshot with altered dialogue; instead of all characters speaking French, two observers in the opening scene are transformed into an Englishman and his friend who interprets the French dialogue of the other characters for him. Extra scenes featuring these two characters were also introduced at intervals, in order that the action of the film could be interpreted for an English-speaking audience. In some ways this could be considered a kind of 'pre-recorded' form of film explaining.

Multilingual versions

Much of the research on the transitional period between the late 1920s and early 1930s has focused on Hollywood's multilingual versions (Vincendeau 1988, Ďurovičová 1992). The first multilingual film may have been E.A. Dupont's *Atlantic* (1929) for British International Pictures, which was shot in English in July 1929, in German and French later in 1930 (Low 1985: 92–93, Barnier 2002: 124, Wahl 2016: 56, 79–80). The film consisted of sequences that could be used in all versions, and dialogue sequences which needed to be reshot in each language. It was shot over a period of several months in 1929 and 1930, making it a cross between a multilingual version (which was, in its archetypal version, shot simultaneously on a single set in shifts) and a remake. The boundary between multilingual versions, remakes and screen translations is very fuzzy, as with Augusto Genina's *Prix de beauté* (1930) and its mixture of a multilingual live sound recording with an early form of dubbing (Pozzi 2003), and the French version of Fritz Lang's *M* (1931) (Albera *et al.* 2013).

The great ferment of multilingual versions in Hollywood took place from 1930 to 1931. As scholars such as Colin Gunckel (2008) have shown, one of the great stumbling blocks was the poor linguistic choices made by the production companies; Gunckel looks at Spanish-language films in Hollywood and shows how the primitiveness of the sound technologies was exacerbated by the non-native or regionally inappropriate accents of the characters. As Martin Barnier shows (2004: 201–202), French language filming in California and Europe lasted several years beyond the heyday of the multilingual versions; French musical comedies were shot as late as the mid-1930s by Paramount, Fox and MGM. The last British International Pictures multilingual version was shot in 1931 (Low 1985: 93).

Whereas the production of multilingual versions principally happened over just two years in Hollywood (Barnier 2002: 119–124; Cornu 2014: 29–30), in Europe, they were made over a longer period, with three main production centres, London, Paris and Berlin. The Tobis company, a Dutch-German-Swiss concern, epitomized the pan-European multilingual production of the early 1930s by making such films in all three cities (Barnier 2002: 124–125).

Determined to compete on European ground, Paramount created a state-of-the-art Hollywood-style production centre outside Paris. Opened in 1929, the Saint-Maurice-Joinville studios produced multilingual versions on a large scale in most European languages. Paramount employed the best screenplay and dialogue writers, theatre and film actors and directors who churned out polyglot versions day and night. According to Ginette Vincendeau, at Paramount films could be shot in up to 14 different language versions (1988: 26). Like the Hollywood-made multilinguals, these eventually failed to be commercial hits and Paramount stopped making them in mid-1932 (Barnier 2002: 121–122).

As the biggest European film-producing country equipped with the best sound stages (Wolfgang Jacobsen quoted in Kreimeier 1996: 181), Germany was to become the largest multilingual producer, through the Tobis company and its rival, the huge Ufa film conglomerate. Berlin was the main centre of this production, which consisted largely of light comedies and operettas. As in Hollywood and Joinville, entire casts were hired to work in shifts on the same set, playing the same scenes each in their own languages. Some polyglot actors could play in several versions of a film, like the Anglo-German actress Lilian Harvey who was fluent in three languages and starred in the famous *Der Kongress tanzt* (Charell, 1931) shot in German, French and English (Barnier 2002: 126–128). Ufa was the company which produced multilinguals for the longest time in the early sound period, from 1929 to 1939 (Wahl 2016). In Italy such versions continued to be made in Italian, Spanish and

German for another few years, from 1939 to 1943, uniting the three fascist powers on screen (Heinink 2013: 115).

Although generally short-lived, multilinguals have been well documented (Ďurovičová 2004; Bock and Venturini 2005; Pitassio and Quaresima 2005). Some of these films were specific experiments in early sound practices and are evidence of the quick and creative adaptation of directors and technicians to the new constraints of sound recording (Barnier 2002). Such interesting outcomes of the research on multilinguals for the history of early sound recording and reproduction practices have inspired a similar perspective on early sound practices in dubbing (Cornu 2014). Although they may not be considered 'translated films' in their own right, unlike dubbed and subtitled versions, multilinguals involve translation operations which have not been investigated: in particular, screenplays and dialogue had to be translated from the main language into a varying number of other languages. Yet very little evidence and few accounts, if any, survive about how such translation was done and by whom.

History of subtitling in the sound period

The subtitles of the early talking films are sometimes considered a direct legacy of silent intertitles. Yet their function is different (Cornu 2014: 223–229). The title cards in silent films were used to convey both narrative information and dialogue, and they were inserted between shots (except towards the end of the silent era when intertitles could be superimposed on the picture of films such as F. W. Murnau's *Sunrise* and Alfred Hitchcock's *The Ring*, both 1927). The subtitles of talking films only translate dialogue, and written information such as shop signs, newspaper headlines, etc. They appear as lines of text horizontally superimposed in the lowest part of the image in most languages, although they can be vertically positioned on either side of the image in Asian languages (see e.g. Nornes 2007: 150–151). However, there is a technical link between intertitles and early subtitles in the photographic process used to add text to image in the very early talking years (and see above for a few examples of films where intertitles were used with a translating function).

Because the first talking films distributed worldwide were overwhelmingly American productions, subtitling was initially mainly done out of English into other languages. As the main markets for Hollywood productions were European countries, various subtitling processes were developed mostly in Europe at first. In the early years, the photographic printing process was widely used both in America and Europe, but it was poorly legible when the white letters of subtitles 'melted' in the white areas of the image (see, for example, the French subtitling of G. W. Pabst's *Kameradschaft* or Leontine Sagan's *Mädchen in Uniform*, both 1931). Methods to improve readability were devised in Hungary, Sweden and France (Ivarsson and Carroll 1998: 9–11). The most enduring ones were chemical subtitling (from 1933 to the early 1990s) and laser subtitling (from 1988 to the late 2000s), whereby subtitles were 'burnt' into the film strip. A fine black line circling each letter made the subtitles easier to read, but they could still occasionally disappear in deep white backgrounds. This problem was solved with the advent and expansion of digital subtitling which guarantees perfect legibility in all areas of the image (Cornu 2014: 230–239, 266–272). All these processes have been used for the theatrical release of films. Electronic subtitles were introduced in the 1970s, first for television. Computer-generated texts were created and incorporated within the electronic TV image. This method was consequently applied to video releases of films on VHS tapes, and then to DVDs that now use digital systems. It is also used in film festivals, with subtitles being projected below or within the image.

AVT developed rather differently on different continents. European countries with major film industries, such as Germany, Italy and France, tended to favour dubbing, a costly method for countries which had smaller film infrastructures. This is the main reason why Scandinavian countries, as well as the Netherlands, Belgium, Switzerland, Portugal and Greece opted for subtitling. In Latin America, dubbing became the preferred choice in Spanish-speaking countries after an initial period of acceptance of subtitles, while subtitling quickly imposed itself in Portuguese-speaking Brazil (Freire 2015). Levels of literacy and national bilingualism also played a part in the choice of dubbing. Although a major film-producing country favouring dubbing, France has contributed to the technical and commercial development of subtitling from the transition-to-sound period until today. This is partly due to an on-going cinephile tradition among viewers; subtitling never quite lost its foothold in the market.

Accounts of early translation practices applied to subtitling are scarce and it is often difficult to know how the pioneering subtitlers worked and who they were. Early talkies subtitled in and out of English seemed to have a very limited number of subtitles which were meant to convey the very gist of what was said on the screen. This is particularly true of films subtitled into English in the UK and the USA, and of Portuguese-subtitled films distributed in Brazil (Freire 2015: 191). Foreign films subtitled into French seem to have contained a larger number of subtitles sooner. According to Suzanne Chantal, a pioneer of French subtitling who worked throughout the 1930s, some translators were happy to keep to a limited number of concise subtitles, while others tried to translate all the dialogue and convey the subtleties it contained (1936: 42).

The first films to be subtitled in English in the UK were probably *Kameradschaft* (Pabst 1931) and *Mädchen in Uniform* (Sagan 1931) in the spring of 1932 (Low 1985: 100). However, Mazdon and Wheatley (2013: 28–19) report on a showing of the early French talkie *Le Collier de la reine* (1929) in June 1930 in Bristol with English subtitles, which may not have been on the film print itself, but separately projected on or near the screen. Early optical subtitling techniques in which 'the titles were set up in the lab, photographed and combined with the negative' (Low 1985: 100) gave poor results; later, more satisfactory mechanical and chemical methods were adopted (*ibid.*; Ivarsson and Carroll 1998: 13–15).

Subtitling may have begun in the United States with Herman Weinberg, who certainly claims credit for being the first working subtitler in New York; the first film he subtitled was *Zwei Herzen im 3/4 Takt* (Two Hearts in Waltz Time) by Géza von Bolváry in 1930, though subtitles took another year or two to catch on. Weinberg describes experimenting first with full screen titles 'giving the audience a brief synopsis of what they were going to see in the next ten minutes'; the invention of the Moviola sound editing machine allowed the timing of dialogue to be measured precisely enough for superimposed titles synchronized to the dialogue to be added to the film. Weinberg's account of the early experiments with subtitles (quoted in Nornes 2007: 149–150) shows how subtitles were very selective at first. This is borne out by the very low subtitle counts of the first films shown with subtitles in English, as well as by Nornes' own findings for the Japanese context (*ibid.*: 170–171). Films gradually became more densely subtitled, in the sense of having a greater number of subtitles, over the following decades.

History of dubbing

Strategies to overcome linguistic barriers during the transition to talking cinema were commercially motivated. Subtitling was restricted to limited audiences, and the multilinguals lacked the box-office potential of the original stars, who were replaced by lesser-known actors in the foreign versions. During the same period, a number of Hollywood studios worked on a method to maintain their commercial assets abroad. Substituting the original American voices with those of actors performing in other languages seemed promising. This would preserve the main appeal of American films for foreign audiences by allowing them to see the stars on the screen, while being able to understand what they said in the audiences' languages.

Such methods were initially developed in the USA and in Germany which, as the biggest European film-producing country, was interested in distributing its films internationally, throughout Europe and in America. There were experiments in substituting voices during the shooting, with a sort of 'live dubbing', but these were thwarted by problems in achieving the proper synchronization of the images of the screen actors and 'their' speech (Cornu 2014: 94–95, 96–103). With the development and improvement of the re-recording technique and multi-track sound mixing, dubbing became possible as a specific form of post-synchronization: it substituted the original voices after shooting, by recording the dialogue in other languages in a studio and matching the existing lip movements with the new vocal sounds as closely as possible.

From a technical point of view, two major methods proved relatively satisfactory. One consisted of actors learning the translated dialogue by heart before recording a scene or fragment of a scene, while watching the original film without sound. Dubbing actors had to deliver their lines while following the facial and lip movements as best as they could to give the illusion that their voices belonged to the characters on the screen. The challenge for them was to sound as natural as possible when performing under such constraints. The other method comprised a mechanical system which broke down all the lines into minute sections based on the lip movements. Such information was transcribed on a strip of paper or celluloid that ran simultaneously with the film, but at a lower speed, to maintain constant synchronicity. This strip was then used by translators endeavouring to write dialogue that would match the lip movements. The translated lines were transcribed in turn on a similar strip, called the *rhythmo-band* (London 1936: 115), which was projected in synchronization with the film, but on a separate screen. To make lip synchronization as accurate as possible, dubbing actors had to say their lines exactly as each syllable went past a vertical bar on the separate screen. The first 'empirical' method was used in some Hollywood studios and their dubbing facilities in France, and known as *doublage à l'image* ('image-guided dubbing'). Although invented in Germany, the *rhythmo-band* method was little used in its home country, but was commercially developed in France, along with a similar system invented by a French engineer. It became known there as *doublage à la bande* ('band-guided dubbing') (Cornu 2014: 103–124).

Prior to recording, the translation of dialogue was also a delicate stage of the dubbing process. In the early 1930s, translators of dubbed films would often be good writers, though not necessarily professional translators. The original dialogue of a film was fully translated by an anonymous translator, and then reworked or 'adapted' to the specific dubbing constraints by a dialogue writer (Cornu 2014: 144).

While commercial circumstances contributed to the development of dubbing, this translation method was also fostered by legal and political contexts. In Italy, dubbing was used as a weapon with which Mussolini's fascist regime consolidated its prohibition of foreign languages in cinemas. As part of this nationalist policy, a 1933 decree only allowed Italian-dubbed versions made in Italy for release (Mereu Keating 2016: 18, and see section above on 'Audiovisual translation and the transition to sound'). For similar reasons, from 1941 Francoist Spain also imposed dubbed versions as the only form of foreign films allowed on its screens, with a very limited opening to subtitled versions after 1946 (Garnemark 2012). In both countries, all foreign films were heavily censored.

The major market for Hollywood films in the early 1930s, France quickly introduced legislation making it compulsory for dubbed versions to be made on French territory as of 1932. This move abruptly stopped the making of French-dubbed versions in Hollywood. It is important to note that, unlike Italy and, later, Spain, the French authorities never attributed this policy to nationalist politics. They acted in response to pressure from the film industry itself, in particular the distribution and exhibition sectors (Cornu 2014: 58).

China offers another interesting situation where politics and ideology heavily interfered with the distribution of foreign films. Shortly after Mao's ascent to power in 1949, a limited number of foreign films started to be released, only in dubbed versions and after severe ideological intervention. They mostly came from other Communist countries or were Western European productions deemed 'progressive' by the Chinese regime, such as Vittorio de Sica's neorealist *Bicycle Thieves* (Chen 2014).

Today, dubbing continues to be a thriving section of the film industry in Italy, Spain, Germany and France. It is much less used in other European countries where subtitling was adopted at an early stage or where foreign films are less widely released, as in the UK. English-dubbed films are a rarity in English-speaking countries.

More expensive than subtitling, dubbing remains widely used in national film industries which can afford it. In countries such as Germany, Italy, Spain and France, it is not restricted to cinema, and television programming heavily depends on dubbed films. In Germany, viewers' attitudes and the strength of the dubbing industry have led to the virtual disappearance of subtitled films in cinemas. A similar trend can be observed in Austria and Switzerland (Boillat 2013: 145). However, the situation is somewhat special in France where distributors' marketing habits and viewers' behaviour still strongly favour dubbing, and yet the demand for subtitled films is relatively high.

Audiovisual translation and the 'foreign film'

Film translation into English invites us to adopt different methodological and interpretive frames; it is, after all, translation against the current of the film trade. The concept of the 'foreign film' is central here. We may define the 'foreign film' as a film that requires translation for the purposes of distribution or importation, usually from an Anglophone perspective. 'Foreign films' in the UK originally included imports from other English-speaking countries, but now it refers, more or less, to the body of films originally shot in a language that is not English. Considerable work has been done on international co-productions and the linguistic issues they raise (see e.g. Betz 2001; Jäckel 2003). Histories of the foreign film are marked by the challenges of distributing dubbed or subtitled films in English-language markets (see e.g. McDonald 2009). Key moments have been identified when foreign films enjoyed relative success at the UK and US box offices; these include the early years of sound (cf. Mazdon and Wheatley 2013: 31, Porter 2010) and the period immediately following the Second World War. This success was never more than relative; as Balio (2010: 301) points out, 'during the 1950s [a boom time for the importation of foreign films with English subtitles or (more rarely) dubbed dialogue] foreign films accounted for as much as 7 per cent of the total U.S. box office each year, whereas since 1970 they have accounted for around 2 percent on average.'

Current issues and new debates

The history of AVT is a very new field that links translation studies and film studies. It can fruitfully contribute to enrich our knowledge of how AVT evolved, and the impact it has had on distribution and reception. In recent years, a number of issues have been studied by translation studies specialists and film historians. Some of them concern the already mentioned multilinguals, ideological censorship and political issues (Danan 1991, 1999; Díaz Cintas 2012; Chomentowski 2014), the technological and commercial development of dubbing and subtitling (Danan 1996, Cornu 2014), and debates on the pros and cons of both methods as discussed in film magazines since the advent of sound cinema. Many of these issues need more in-depth studies, especially in regions of the world where they have not yet been researched. For example, the history of dubbing is becoming clearer in the European countries where it has been most in use (France, Italy, Spain), but we need to know more about its development in Germany, and in other countries and continents such as India and Latin America.

Future issues include the history of more recent practices such as voice-over translation, redubbing and resubtitling (the making of new dubbed and subtitled versions of older films). Studying reception is all the more crucial as data are scarce, regardless of the historical period. The impact of film and AVT on film style is also a fascinating aesthetic issue which has hardly been touched upon. Because of assumptions based on the 'speechless' nature of silent cinema, the history of translation practices in the silent era has been typically neglected. It covers a set of major issues which would help us understand better how films were circulated worldwide, how titled cards were translated or adapted outside the linguistic boundaries of the films, and who was responsible for the content and look of the translated titles.

The stumbling block for most of these research areas is the access to the films themselves as primary sources (see e.g. Ďurovičová 2004). Much material is lost or not properly identified in film archives (e.g. silent film prints; early sound dubbed and subtitled prints; television broadcast versions). Many silent films may exist only in languages other than their original language, which may make them difficult to identify. A key problem is that translated copies of films from the pre-digital period are, by definition, not usable as 'originals' and may be preserved neither by archives in the target culture nor in the source culture. Where prints survive, they may be physically fragile because of their nitrate film base, subject to shrinkage and potentially impossible to project. Many film copies in circulation are unapproved or illegal prints that can be difficult or impossible to authenticate.

The history of the early stages of AVT raises specific problems as researchers cannot just rely on the few films available on DVDs which often don't carry the dubbed or subtitled versions made for their initial theatrical release. This is where film archives have a major part to play, in cataloguing and giving access to the existing prints of such versions. The contributions of researchers, audiovisual translators, film archivists and curators are all vital if they are to uncover this period of audiovisual history. Among other difficulties, they face the decay and loss of prints; they have to authenticate the unapproved prints in which many of the early versions circulate; they must go against the low status audiovisual translation has had as a result of the 'auteur' emphasis of film history. Their findings and methodology will be essential to make the history of more recent periods and, indeed, future ones.

Primary sources also include 'non-film' material, such as reviews, distribution and publicity material, dubbed dialogue lists, subtitle lists, oral history, etc. This category of documents is enormously valuable, especially when prints are no longer extant or not yet identified. The Media History Digital Library (Media Library, n.d.), with its 'Lantern' platform, which at time of writing has scanned more than 1.3 million pages of media periodicals, is a major step forward from this perspective.

Much translation studies research depends on the availability of text pairs. The instability of the film medium, particularly in the silent period, means that it can be difficult, and in some contexts impossible, to establish pairs of film texts which can be shown to stand to each other in the relation of source text and target text. Paolo Cherchi Usai has commented that 'every copy of the same silent film is different, thanks to the intervention of time, storage conditions, projectionists, editors, colourists, thieves, producers, distributors, re-issuers, titlers, re-titlers, censors, overenthusiastic archivists, incompetent archivists, and practically everyone else who ever came in contact with it' (2000: xi). Versions for export could be physically different versions, shot on a second camera on the same set (*ibid.*: 11). Even though tampering with sound film is not as easily achieved, the presence of censorship, pressures of programme length and other factors mean that even in the sound period 'original' and translated film texts may not align.

- The lack of attribution of AVT means that tracking resubtitling, in particular, becomes more difficult. Critical interest has only recently begun to rise into the question of retranslation of film and television (see Zanotti 2015: 110), which may help to illustrate how the norms of censorship and attenuation, linguistic conventions and subtitle density have developed over time.
- It can be difficult to find detailed reception data. Press data is inevitably partial. Published or unpublished letters and diaries from professionals may contain some valuable data (see e.g. Chantal 1977, Eisenschitz 1999). Initiatives such as British Film Institute archivist Luke McKernan's 'Picturegoing' project (Picturegoing, n.d.) are to be welcomed, even if the data from such projects will inevitably remain at an anecdotal level.
- There is a not inconsiderable language barrier in research; much of the research in this area has been done in French, Italian, Spanish and German. More research published in English, or translated into English, would certainly widen the field at the international level. Translation initiatives such as that of Wahl (2009) are greatly to be encouraged in this regard.
- The overwhelming emphasis so far has been on fiction film. This parallels in interesting ways the predominant emphasis on literary translation in translation studies more widely, but there is a vast corpus of documentaries, educational films and industrial films which were also subjected to translation and which deserve study in their own right.
- A major need for research in this field is to explore to what extent the specificity of a given audiovisual translation is significant; in other words, to what extent it makes a measurable difference to the reception of a film. Jeremy Hicks (2005) has shown in relation to the early Soviet sound film *Chapaev* (Vasilyev Brothers, 1934) that the different translations in the UK, where the film was given title cards by Ivor Montague for the Film Society, and the US, where it was more conventionally subtitled, led to very different degrees of success for the film in the different markets. This fascinating study does not go into detail about the translations themselves, but there is no indication in Hicks' article that copies of the titled, or subtitled, prints of the period survive. Given the period of several years of experimentation during the transition to sound, when audiences' displeasure with the quality of translation was often relayed through press reports, it would be very interesting to consider how the reception of other films may have been directly affected by the quality of the translation.

Research methods

AVT history has taken rather an eclectic approach to research methods. One of the most interesting and scholarly approaches comes from film studies, with the work of Charles O'Brien (2005, 2010), who has also taken a quantitative approach through his Cinemetrics site (Cinemetrics, n.d.). Together with other researchers, O'Brien counts 'shots and time[s] film lengths to calculate the average shot lengths [and hence the cutting rate] of the films' (*ibid.*), which helps him explain patterns and changes in the rhythm of films.

Another interesting methodological approach is that of Ďurovičová who, with a number of colleagues, led a Spring School in film studies research on multiple-language versions at Gradisca in Italy (2003–2006) where multiple versions of the 'same' film were screened (Ďurovičová 2004). This gave rise to three volumes, mostly consisting of case studies, the usefully detailed nature of which is a tribute to a project based around public screenings, rather than comparisons of film prints on parallel viewing tables.

One of the methodological problems is that some of the most methodologically aware work in AVT history has not put translation to the fore. This gap in research and method remains to be filled.

Summary

The historiography of AVT is still a work in progress. Some periods and specific types of film translation are now more clearly defined. The multilingual versions made throughout the 1930s are perhaps the best example. However, multilinguals were produced again after the Second World War at least up to the 1950s, although on a much more limited scale, often within international co-production projects. These would need to be investigated more thoroughly. The silent era is another, crucial, unexplored period that has much to teach us about the emergence of translation practices in cinema. Dubbing and subtitling developed and expanded in very distinctive ways according to the period of film history and the linguistic and film-industrial areas, and must also be studied in relation to commercial strategies and ideological contexts. Many historical issues of AVT indeed remain uncharted territory. Researching the history of this particular form of translation may also contribute to a better understanding of what makes a film and how it is perceived.

Further reading

Cornu, J.-F. (2014) *Le doublage et le sous-titrage: histoire et esthétique*, Rennes: Presses universitaires de Rennes | *A comprehensive study of historical developments and aesthetic issues in dubbing and subtitling into French. It shows that film translation practices go beyond mere technical operations in their implications on the audiovisual content of a film and argues that the reception of films has always been dependent on the choice of translation mode.*

Danan, M. (1991) 'Dubbing as an Expression of Nationalism', *Meta* 36(4): 606–614 | *Seminal appraisal of the relationship between nationalist politics and dubbing since the advent of the talking film. It argues that the choice of an audiovisual translation mode is closely linked to questions of the cultural and linguistic identity of the target country.*

Ďurovičová, N. (1992) 'Translating America: The Hollywood Multilinguals 1929–1933', in R. Altman (ed.), *Sound Theory, Sound Practice*, New York & London: Routledge, 138–153 | *A standard reference on multiple-language versions by one of the pioneers in this research. Considers the multilinguals 'an effort to establish a feasible exchange rate between cost and national culture'.*

Hicks, J. (2005) 'The International Reception of Early Soviet Sound Cinema: *Chapaev* in Britain and America', *Historical Journal of Film, Radio and Television* 25(2): 273–289 | *A key step forward in showing how translation choices could have a direct influence on a film's reception in its target market. It compares the successful distribution of* Chapaev *in the United States with superimposed English titles with its relative lack of success in the UK with interpolated title cards.*

Nornes, A. M. (2007) *Cinema Babel*, Minneapolis: University of Minnesota Press | *An eclectic and pioneering combination of approaches to film translation history, including a provocative essay on subtitling and one of the most comprehensive available treatments of translation in silent film.*

O'Sullivan, C. and Cornu, J.-F. (forthcoming 2018) *The Translation of Films 1900–1950*, Oxford: Oxford University Press | *The first book-length study of the international history of audiovisual translation which includes silent cinema. It shows how audiovisual translation practices were closely tied to commercial, technological and industrial contexts.*

Related topics

3 Subtitling on the cusp of its futures
4 Investigating dubbing: learning from the past, looking to the future
11 Film remakes as a form of translation
12 Mediality and audiovisual translation
25 Minority languages, language planning and audiovisual translation
31 Accessible filmmaking: translation and accessibility from production

References

Albera, F., C. Angelini, and M. Barnier (2013) '*M/Le Maudit*, ses doubles et son doublage', *Décadrages* 23–24: 80–113; also published in German as '"M"/"Le Maudit" Doppelgänger und dubbing', in A. Boillat and I. Weber Henking (eds) (2014) *Dubbing: Die Übersetzung im Kino / La traduction audiovisuelle*, Marburg: Schüren, 65–114.

Anon. (1929) 'Talkies in France', *The New York Times*, 4 March, 24.

Balio, T. (2010) *The Foreign Film Renaissance on American Screens 1946–1973*, Madison: University of Wisconsin Press.

Barnier, M. (2002) *En route vers le parlant: Histoire d'une évolution technologique, économique et esthétique du cinéma (1926–1934)*, Liège: Céfal.

Barnier, M. (2004) *Des films français made in Hollywood: Les versions multiples 1929–1935*, Paris: L'Harmattan.

Barnier, M. (2010) *Bruits, cris, musiques de films: Les projections avant 1914*, Rennes: Presses universitaires de Rennes.

Betz, M. (2001) 'The Name above the (Sub)Title: Internationalism, Coproduction, and Polyglot European Art Cinema', *Camera Obscura* 46: 1–44.

Bock, H.-M. and S. Venturini (eds) (2005) 'Multiple and Multiple-language Versions II'. A special issue of *Cinema & Cie* 6.

Boillat, A. (2007) *Du bonimenteur à la voix-over*, Lausanne: Éditions Antipodes.

Boillat A. (2013) 'Versions originales ou doublées: Le contexte suisse de l'exploitation—Entretien avec Cédric Bourquard', *Décadrages* (23–24): 142–146.

Broeren, J. (2008) '*The titles are in Dutch—which makes it quite simple*': Intertitles as an Agent of Appropriation in the Netherlands, 1907–1916, Unpublished MA Dissertation, Utrecht University.

Brownlow, K. (1973) *The Parade's Gone By*, London: Abacus [1968].

Chantal, S. (1936) 'Sous-titres et adaptation française de . . . ' (1st part), *Cinémonde* 378, 16 January, 42.

Chantal, S. (1977) *Le Ciné-monde*, Paris: Grasset.

Chen, T. (2014) 'An Italian Bicycle in the People's Republic: Minor Transnationalism and the Chinese Translation of *Ladri di biciclette/Bicycle Thieves*', *Journal of Italian Cinema & Media Studies* 2(1): 91–107; also published in French as 'Une bicyclette italienne en République populaire de Chine: À propos de la version chinoise du *Voleur de bicyclette*', *L'Écran traduit* (2015) 4. Available online: http://ataa.fr/revue/archives/3667 [last access 20 December 2017].

Cherchi Usai, P. (2000) *Silent Cinema: An Introduction*. Basingstoke: Palgrave Macmillan.

Chomentowski, G. (2014) 'Du cinéma muet au cinéma parlant: La politique des langues dans les films soviétiques', *Cahiers du monde russe* 55(3): 295–320.

Cinemetrics (n.d.) 'Movie Measurement and Study Tool Database'. Available online: http://www.cinemetrics.lv/index.php [last access 20 December 2017].

Cornu, J.-F. (2014) *Le doublage et le sous-titrage: histoire et esthétique*, Rennes: Presses universitaires de Rennes.

Danan, M. (1991) 'Dubbing as an Expression of Nationalism', *Meta* 36(4): 606–614.

Danan, M. (1996) 'À la recherche d'une stratégie internationale: Hollywood et le marché français des années trente', in Y. Gambier (ed.) *Les Transferts linguistiques dans es médias audiovisuels*, Villeneuve d'Ascq: Presses universitaires du Septentrion, 109–130.

Danan, M. (1999) 'Hollywood's Hegemonic Strategies: Overcoming French Nationalism with the Advent of Sound', in A. Higson and R. Maltby (eds) *'Film Europe' and 'Film America': Cinema, Commerce and Cultural Exchange, 1920–39*, Exeter: University of Exeter Press, 225–248.

Díaz Cintas, J. (ed.) (2012) 'La manipulation de la traduction audiovisuelle/The Manipulation of Audiovisual Translation', *Meta* 57(2): 275–527.

Díaz Cintas, J. and A. Remael (2007) *Audiovisual Translation: Subtitling*. Manchester: St. Jerome.

Ďurovičová, N. (1992) 'Translating America: The Hollywood Multilinguals 1929–1933', in R. Altman (ed.) *Sound Theory, Sound Practice*, New York & London: Routledge, 138–153.

Ďurovičová, N. (2004) 'Multiple and Multiple-language Versions'. A special issue of *Cinema & Cie* 4.

Dwyer, T. (2005) 'Universally Speaking: Lost in Translation and Polyglot Cinema', *Linguistica Antverpiensia*. New Series 4: 295–310.

Eisenschitz, B. (1999) 'La parole écrite: Extrait des mémoires d'un traducteur', in Jacques Aumont (ed.) *L'Image et la parole*, Paris: Cinémathèque Française, 29–45.

Freire, R. L. (2015) 'The Introduction of Film Subtitling in Brazil', *Matrizes* 9(1): 187–211.

Garnemark, R. (2012) 'Ingmar Bergman, maternidad y Franquismo: Traducción y censura de *En el umbral de la vida*', *Meta* 57(2): 310–324; also published in French as 'Ingmar Bergman, maternité et franquisme: traduction et censure d'*Au seuil de la vie*', *L'Écran traduit* (2013) 3. Available online: http://ataa.fr/revue/archives/2104 [last access 20 December 2017].

Gunckel, C. (2008) 'The War of the Accents: Spanish Language Hollywood Films in Mexican Los Angeles', *Film History* 20: 325–343.

Heinink J. B. (2013) 'Multiple Versions After the Advent of Sound Films', in E. Riambau (ed.), *Multiversions*, Barcelona: Filmoteca de Catalunya, 110–115; also published in the same volume in Catalan as 'Les versions múltiples a partir de l'inici del sonor', 50–63.

Hicks, J. (2005) 'The International Reception of Early Soviet Sound Cinema: *Chapaev* in Britain and America', *Historical Journal of Film, Radio and Television* 25(2): 273–289.

Ivarsson, J. and M. Carroll (1998) *Subtitling*, Simrishamn: TransEdit HB.

Jäckel, A. (2003) 'Dual Nationality Film Productions in Europe after 1945', *Historical Journal of Film, Radio and Television* 23(3): 231–243.

Kreimeier, K. (1996) *The Ufa Story: A History of Germany's Greatest Film Company 1918–1945*, trans. by Robert and Rita Kimber, New York: Hill and Wang; English translation of *Die Ufa-Story: Geschichte eines Filmkonzerns* (1992).

Lacasse, G. (2000) *Le Bonimenteur de vues animées: Le cinéma muet entre tradition et modernité*, Québec & Paris: Nota Bene and Méridiens Klincksieck.

Lacasse, G., V. Bouchard and G. Scheppler (2009) 'Cinéma et oralité: le bonimenteur et ses avatars', *Cinémas* 20(1): 7–21.

London, K. (1936) *Film Music: A Summary of the Characteristic Features of its History, Aesthetics, Technique; and Possible Developments*, trans. from the German by E. S. Bensinger, London: Faber & Faber.

Low, R. (1985) *The History of the British Film 1929–1939: Film Making in 1930s Britain*. London: Allen & Unwin.

McDonald, P. (2009) 'Miramax, Life is Beautiful, and the Indiewoodization of the Foreign-language Film Market in the USA', *New Review of Film and Television Studies* 7(4): 353–375.

Mazdon, L. and C. Wheatley (2013) *French Film in Britain: Sex, Art and Cinephilia*. Oxford: Berghahn.
Media Library (n.d.) Media History Digital Library. Available online: http://mediahistoryproject.org/ [last access 20 December 2017].
Mereu Keating, C. (2016) *The Politics of Dubbing: Film Censorship and State Intervention in the Translation of Cinema in Fascist Italy,* Bern: Peter Lang.
Nornes, A. M. (2007) *Cinema Babel*. Minneapolis: University of Minnesota Press.
O'Brien, C. (2005) *Cinema's Conversion to Sound: Technology and Film Style in France and the United States,* Bloomington: Indiana University Press.
O'Brien, C. (2010) 'The "Cinematization" of Sound Cinema in Britain and the Dubbing into French of Hitchcock's *Waltzes from Vienna* (1934)', in L. Mazdon and C. Wheatley (eds) *Je t'aime . . . moi non plus: Franco-British Cinematic Relations*, Oxford: Berghahn, 37–49.
O'Sullivan, C. (2011) *Translating Popular Film*, Basingstoke: Palgrave Macmillan.
Picturegoing (n.d.) 'Picturegoing: Eyewitness Accounts of Viewing Pictures'. Available online: http://picturegoing.com/ [last access 20 December 2017].
Pitassio, F. and L. Quaresima (eds) (2005) 'Multiple and Multiple-language Versions III'. A special issue of *Cinema & Cie* 7.
Porter, V. (2010) 'The Exhibition, Distribution and Reception of French Films in Great Britain during the 1930s', in L. Mazdon and C. Wheatley (eds) *Je t'aime . . . moi non plus: Franco-British Cinematic Relations*, Oxford: Berghahn, 19–36.
Pozzi, D. (2003) '*Prix de beauté*: un titolo, due edizioni, quattro versioni', in A. Antonini (ed.) *Il film e i suoi multipli/Film and its multiples*, IX Convegno Internazionale di Studi sul Cinema, Forum, Udine, 67–76.
Quargnolo, M. (2000) 'Il doppiato italiano', in C. Taylor (ed.) *Tradurre il cinema: Atti del Convegno organizzato da G. Soria e C. Taylor 29–30 novembre 1996*, Trieste: Università degli studi di Trieste.
Razlogova, E. (2015) 'The Politics of Translation at Soviet Film Festivals during the Cold War', *SubStance* 44(2): 66–87
Rossholm, A. S. (2006) *Reproducing Languages, Translating Bodies: Approaches to Speech, Translation and Cultural Identity in Early European Sound Film,* Stockholm: Department of Cinema Studies.
Salt, B. (1992) *Film Style and Technology: History & Analysis*, second edition, London: Starword.
Thompson, K. (1985) *Exporting Entertainment: America in the World Market, 1907–1934*, London: BFI.
Vasey, R. (1997) *The World According to Hollywood 1918–1939*, Exeter: University of Exeter Press.
Vincendeau, G. (1988) 'Hollywood Babel', *Screen* 29(3): 24–39.
Wahl, C. (2009) *Sprachversionsfilme aus Babelsberg: Die international Strategie der Ufa 1929–1939*, Munich: Edition text + kritik.
Wahl, C. (2016) *Multiple Language Versions Made in Babelsberg: Ufa's International Strategy, 1929–1939 [translation of Wahl 2009]*, Amsterdam: Amsterdam University Press.
Zanotti, S. (2015) 'Analysing Redubs: Motives, Agents and Audience Response', in R. Baños and J. Díaz Cintas (eds) *Audiovisual Translation in a Global Context: Mapping an Ever-Changing Landscape*, Basingstoke: Palgrave Macmillan, 110–139.

Filmography

Allô Berlin? Ici Paris (1931) Julien Duvivier. IMDb entry: http://www.imdb.com/title/tt0134281/?ref_=fn_al_tt_1
Atlantic (1929) Ewald André Dupont. IMDb entry: http://www.imdb.com/title/tt0019658/?ref_=fn_al_tt_2
Bicycle Thieves (1948) Vittorio de Sica. IMDb entry: http://www.imdb.com/title/tt0040522/?ref_=fn_al_tt_1
Chapaev (1934) Sergei Vasilyev and Georgi Vasilyev. IMDb entry: http://www.imdb.com/title/tt0024966/?ref_=fn_al_tt_1

Der Kongress tanzt (1931) Erik Charell. IMDb entry: http://www.imdb.com/title/tt0022034/?ref_=fn_al_tt_1
Hell's Angels (1930) Howard Hughes. IMDb entry: http://www.imdb.com/title/tt0020960/?ref_=fn_al_tt_1
Kameradschaft (1931) Georg Wilhelm Pabst. IMDb entry: http://www.imdb.com/title/tt0022017/?ref_=fn_al_tt_1
Le Collier de la reine (1929) Tony Lekain and Gaston Ravel. IMDb entry: http://www.imdb.com/title/tt0198377/?ref_=fn_al_tt_1
Le Million (1931) René Clair. IMDb entry: http://www.imdb.com/title/tt0022150/?ref_=fn_al_tt_1
Le Silence est d'or/*Man About Town* (1947) René Clair. IMDb entry: http://www.imdb.com/title/tt0039823/?ref_=fn_al_tt_1
M (1931) Fritz Lang. IMDb entry: http://www.imdb.com/title/tt0022100/?ref_=nv_sr_7
Mädchen in Uniform (1931) Leontine Sagan. IMDb entry: http://www.imdb.com/title/tt0022183/?ref_=fn_al_tt_2
Niemandsland (1931) Victor Trivas. IMDb entry: http://www.imdb.com/title/tt0022204/?ref_=fn_al_tt_2
Prix de beauté (1930) Augusto Genina. IMDb entry: http://www.imdb.com/title/tt0021273/?ref_=fn_al_tt_1
Seas Beneath (1931) John Ford. IMDb entry: http://www.imdb.com/title/tt0022353/?ref_=fn_al_tt_1
Sunrise (1927) F. W. Murnau. IMDb entry: http://www.imdb.com/title/tt0018455/?ref_=fn_al_tt_1
The Jazz Singer (1927) Alan Crosland. IMDb entry: http://www.imdb.com/title/tt0018037/?ref_=nv_sr_2
The Ring (1927) Alfred Hitchcock. IMDb entry: http://www.imdb.com/title/tt0018328/?ref_=nv_sr_1
Westfront 1918 (1930) Georg Wilhelm. IMDb entry: http://www.imdb.com/title/tt0021542/?ref_=fn_al_tt_1
Where are my Children (1916) Phillips Smalley and Lois Weber (uncredited). IMDb entry: http://www.imdb.com/title/tt0007558/?ref_=fn_al_tt_1
Zwei Herzen im 3/4 Takt (Two Hearts in Waltz Time) (1930) Géza von Bolváry. IMDb entry: http://www.imdb.com/title/tt0021572/?ref_=fn_al_tt_1

3
Subtitling on the cusp of its futures

Marie-Noëlle Guillot

Introduction

Subtitling today is facing considerable opportunities and challenges, in practice and theory. This applies with particular acuteness to interlingual film subtitling, the written target language rendition(s) of source text speech in films that is the focus in this chapter (henceforth 'film subtitling' or 'subtitling' for short).

The practice itself is approaching its hundredth year. Subtitling as an academic discipline is young in research terms, barely twenty-five years old. It has been steadily firming up its foundations and developing its credentials as a research strand and area of professional specialization within the discipline of audiovisual translation (AVT). Since the mid-1990s, it has been busy identifying domains of concern, evolving methodologies, developing greater rigour in research, finding interdisciplinary partners to help it come to terms effectively with the multimodal nature of subtitling. In the midst of all that came the onset of fansubbing, and with it the ripple effect that has underpinned the explosion of amateur practices generally—subtitling by the people for the people. Together with its catalyst, the spectacular technological developments ongoing since then on a global scale, this explosion has radically changed what is at stake in subtitling. One of the most momentous changes for the practice since its inception may well turn out to be that technology has put it in the hands of the general public, literally at their fingertips, with the opportunity to shift from a passive role as viewers to active and activist roles as prosumers—producers and distributors of their own edited materials (Díaz Cintas 2013: 273, Pérez-González 2014). There is no aspect of subtitling, in practice or theory, that has not been and will not be affected by this phenomenon and its implications. Its long-term significance was heralded by a handful of scholars with early 'insights into the butterfly effect of globalization on audiovisual translation' (Pérez-González 2006 and above). The extent to which it would rock the foundations of subtitling even before they were fully established has only more recently begun to be more fully appreciated.

The aim of this chapter is to locate film subtitling at this crucial juncture between its recent past as a maturing practice and a young discipline, and the uncharted territories of its future, with the questions that it compels the field to revisit and the new ones that it raises.

Technological development is a main drive in the review of aspects and issues of subtitling in this perspective, as a platform to project in what lies ahead, but also to revisit the past and reassess its achievements, and its oversights. There are urgent themes to be addressed and re-addressed at this interface of past and future, and of professional and amateur practice in film subtitling. These include the creative specificities and potential of subtitling and subtitles; the question of quality in the sharing of the AVT sphere by professionals and amateurs; and the sociocultural aspects of film subtitling and linguistic and cultural impact in increasingly cross- and intercultural global contexts.

These themes are the canvas for the three sections in this chapter, entitled 'Processes and evolutions, constraints and opportunities', 'Means and modes of meaning in subtitling' and 'Research and methodologies'.

Processes and evolutions, constraints and opportunities

Today a standard PC with subtitling software is all that is needed for subtitlers to complete a film subtitling project, and synthesize the processes involved in subtitling that before digitization were carried out separately, normally by several individuals, and with less flexibility, or reliability.

We are a long way away from subtitles' post-silent films intertitles debuts, generally traced as subtitling's historical platform (Díaz Cintas and Remael 2007: 26, Pérez-González 2014: 35–43), and a long way from the timecoded VHS tapes of the 70s and 80s. The tasks involved were then laboriously sequential: transcribing and analyzing source dialogue lines, identifying their exact location, defining units of text to be subtitled, spotting (or cueing or time-coding), i.e. setting the times for subtitles to come in and out of frame and the duration of on-screen display (not too short, to avoid flashing effects, nor too long, to avoid viewers getting distracted), producing a spotting list synthesizing this information, with subtitle numbers for ease of reference and, at best, explanations about unusual words or phrases (e.g. idioms or colloquialisms) and culture-specific references, producing subtitles conforming to accepted guidelines, at least for mainstream subtitling, checking and editing. While the technical processes of transferring subtitles to films have evolved considerably since the early days, from mechanical and thermal subtitling to laser engraving and superimposition electronic techniques today (Ivarsson and Carroll 1998: 12–19, Díaz Cintas 2010a), these basic procedures have not to a great extent. What has changed, significantly, is that, thanks to increasingly sophisticated subtitling software applications readily available to professionals and non-professionals, some free on the Internet, these steps can be integrated and subtitles produced online, by almost anyone with a modicum of IT expertise. The sharing out of subtitling space between producers and consumers heralded in the 80s with the subtitling by fans of Japanese *anime*, then with cumbersome videotapes, now from readily shared digital files, is today almost unimpeded, technically speaking at least. And there is more on the technical horizon, with respeaking and voice recognition software (Romero-Fresco 2011) already extensively deployed in live intralingual subtitling for news or sports programmes in the UK, for example, and tested for interlingual practices in combination with computer assisted translation tools.

These developments are recapitulated in updates and syntheses by regular commentators in AVT (Díaz Cintas 2013, Gambier 2013, O'Hagan 2013, Pérez-González 2014, Taylor 2013, Yau 2014 in the past few years, for example; Chiaro 2009, Díaz Cintas 2010b, Gottlieb 1998, O'Connell 2007, Pérez-González 2009, Remael 2010 before then). Core definitions of subtitling have themselves changed little over the years, but show signs of mutation. They are practically the same in Gambier's introduction to the 2003 landmark special issue of *The Translator* on screen translation, when technology's impact was beginning to get more broadly recognized, and in his account ten years later in another benchmark handbook, when it had become an integral feature in AVT:

> moving from the oral dialogue to one/two written lines and from one language to another, sometimes to two other languages.
>
> *(2003: 172)*

vs.

> moving from oral dialogues in one or several languages to one or two written lines.
>
> *(2013: 50)*

Change is signposted in Gambier's description of the processes involved, as carried out 'by the same person (translating and spotting) or by a translator and a technician spotting and timing the subtitles' (2003: 172) and, ten years later, 'more and more frequently . . . by the same person: translating, spotting (or cueing, time-coding) and editing, thanks to *ad hoc* software' (2013: 50).

Definitions are identical in Díaz Cintas and Remael's 2007 staple academic reference manual for subtitling, and Díaz Cintas in a later 2013 handbook entry. In both, subtitling is accounted for in greater detail as

> a translation practice that consists of presenting a written text, generally on the lower part of the screen, that endeavours to recount the original dialogue of the speakers, as well as the discursive elements that appear in the image (letters, inserts, graffiti, inscriptions, placards and the like) and the information that is contained on the soundtrack (songs, voices off).
>
> *(2007: 8; 2013: 274)*

There is a telling departure from these benchmark accounts in Pérez-González, also a leading subtitling scholar, from 2009 (*Encyclopedia of Translation Studies* entry) to 2014 (AVT monograph). In the 2009 entry, interlingual subtitles are said to

> provide viewers with a written rendition of the source text speech, whether dialogue or narration, in their own language.
>
> *(2009: 14)*

References to number of lines, explicit in Gambier, and spatial positioning at the bottom of the screen, identified as common in Remael and Díaz Cintas, are present in Pérez-González's 2009 entry. In his generic account of subtitling/subtitles, Pérez-González notes that 'subtitles composed according to widely accepted parameters contain a maximum of two lines of text'/'normally near the bottom of the frame' (2009: 15, 14), while acknowledging that other alternatives are possible. They are absent from the 2014 version:

> snippets of written text superimposed on visual footage that convey a target language version of the source speech.
>
> *(2014: 15–16)*

Spatial considerations and number of lines are discussed later in Pérez-González's volume, of course. The contrast with other definitions for subtitling is still significant. It is an index of the underlying tensions between practices imposed in mainstream subtitling and the film industry, with strict sets of guidelines and the 'accepted parameters' flagged above in Pérez-González, and their perversion by fans and amateur subtitling. It embodies the debates, in practice and in theory, that have pitted accessibility, a main longstanding theme in subtitling, against creativity, in its challenge of the diktats of medial constraints—objectivized in the industry and relativized outside of it. Are accessibility and creativity incompatible? This is a main debate for the twenty-first century.

With digitization, subtitling has become faster and cheaper, already a trademark of subtitling by comparison with dubbing. There are now added pressures: expectations of almost instant availability via a range of distribution channels and platforms, on mobile/hand-held devices or catch-up and on-demand television, with growing flexibility in viewing options: multiple language but also text fonts, size, colours. *A la carte* menus fully individualizing options are just round the corner, emulating and superseding types of subtitles that already make standard use of the interplay of different typographical resources (subtitles for use by the deaf and hearing impaired, for example, or 'closed' subtitles that are not part of the programme, unlike the 'open' subtitles of cinema, and can be turned on and off), and, imminently, of individual viewing devices in cinemas (e.g. subtitle glasses with titles projected on lenses). With greater control in one or fewer hands, textual reliability is also arguably easier to safeguard, with fewer opportunities for mishaps, like textual slips from editing decisions not involving translators commonly reported on in the literature for commercial subtitling. By the same token, there is greater scope for the layout and textual resourcefulness and boldness that has been a trademark of amateur subtitling.

Technically speaking, innovation is pushing the boundaries of the possible at a rate unimaginable just a few years ago—simplifying, automatizing, speeding up and diversifying processes and options, and has become one of the most extensively reported-on topics in syntheses of AVT and subtitling developments, including those just cited (Díaz Cintas 2013, Gambier 2013, also O'Hagan 2013, etc.). Basic technical and other challenges themselves have not gone away. But they are getting modulated, and acquiring a different spin with fresh reviews of longstanding assumptions, relating to interlingual subtitling's medial features.

Interlingual subtitling is characterized by the interplay of three distinct but interdependent components, routinely identified as baseline in definitions, as in the set above: source text speech, written text, visual footage. The interaction of the visual, the auditory, text and images has unique features and has been a main locus of attention for subtitling studies from their earliest days. Three types of phenomena are usually identified, all fundamental in their impact on the core activity for interlingual subtitling: representation through language, in cross-cultural mode.

Top of the list are the spatial and temporal factors that earned subtitling its label as 'constrained translation' in the early days (Titford 1982). Where subtitles should be positioned on the screen, how much space they should occupy, how long they should be displayed on screen so as not to impinge on viewing experience have been prime concerns for mainstream practices and guidelines, with their standard edicts. The number of characters per line is one (normally 36–40 maximum including spaces and punctuation), with also the number and positioning of lines (2 maximum at any one time, bottom of the screen). Others include temporal synchronicity with utterances, display time (one to six seconds maximum, no longer than is needed for subtitles to be read, but not so short that the text should flash and not register), with adaptations as required depending on languages (e.g. Japanese and vertical display). Ivarsson and Carroll's (1998) code of subtitling practices is an early influential embodiment of recommendations to the profession, and a platform for subsequent streamlined versions (e.g. Díaz Cintas and Remael 2007).

Readability has been the main drive with unobtrusiveness, for these and other recommendations about text itself: fonts (usually sans serifs types, white on dark background), but also punctuation conventions, like the use of ellipsis/triple dots to indicate that a subtitle is carried over the next subtitle/s, segmentation into syntactically and semantically self-contained units avoiding demanding lexical or other items (e.g. acronyms), etc.

Guidelines are underpinned by assumptions about various factors: audiences' reading speeds and strategies, their cognitive capacity to process fragmented text sequentially, since subtitles appear one after the other on their own, and to respond at the same time to non-verbal visual and aural signs, risks of perceptual disorientation in case of double takes or related mishaps, expectations. Capacities and expectations are highly variable, as variable as target audiences are diverse—socioculturally, in terms of age, status, education, viewing and processing habits, themselves in a state of flux as audiences get more adept at processing text on screen in semiotically complex contexts in the age of online multimedia. Empirical backup has been technically challenging to secure, and limited, with few dedicated experimental investigations initially, though see d'Ydewalle *et al.* 1987 and De Linde and Kay 1999, for example. It is now building up with studies harnessing cutting-edge technology to research (e.g. eye trackers, as elaborated below). These more recent studies look set to prompt reviews of the one-size-fits-all approaches ubiquitous in mainstream subtitling, but already challenged in fansubbing by unfettered practices putting paid to the normative and to the expectations it creates. Technology itself is making some of these practical limitations a thing of the past. Professional subtitling programmes now use pixels and have moved from mono- to non-monospaces fonts, for example, allowing for greater rationalization of space and flexibility in the numbers of characters used, particularly in Internet subtitling (Díaz Cintas 2013: 274–275). Digital manipulation of images and embedded text is likewise becoming commonplace.

A second routinely prominent concern with space and time is the shift from speech to writing, to which subtitling owes its categorization as a 'diasemiotic' or 'intermodal' form of translation (Gottlieb 1998). How can the aural in speech be expressed in writing, how can the expressive in voice quality, intonation, orality, accents and other sociocultural markers or paralinguistic features like pausing be conveyed in written mode? We normally speak faster than we read, so these conundrums are compounded by space and time limitations, notably in mainstream practice. Without the straitjacket of imposed standards, there has been, here too, scope for creative representation, including with techniques used in closed subtitles for viewers with no or limited access to sound, and capitalized on in amateur subtitling: variations in the use of colour, harnessed to speaker-coding in SDH, of typography and punctuation to convey aurally expressed shifts in tone and loudness, emotions (e.g. larger fonts for anger) (in static writing), as well as animated writing and in text or pop-up hypertext notes, etc. Speech in source dialogues is itself a far cry from naturally occurring speech, to which it is at times misguidedly assimilated: it is written-to-be-spoken, shaped by audience design and narrative efficiency, diegesis and the need to keep overhearing audiences in the loop. It is stylized in all respects, with pre-planned continuity, coherence and cohesion, artificially conveying speech naturalness and orality in what Chaume describes for dubbing as 'prefabricated orality' (2004). For subtitling the representational leap and suspension of linguistic disbelief is even greater. The inventiveness of amateur practices and viewers' responses are an index of our capacities to generate make-belief with text, and to respond to it. They are a test for mainstream practices, but also an invitation to (re)appraise them by contrast in their stylized distinctiveness (see next section).

Multimodality is a third core aspect. Text in films does not work on its own. It is just one of their meaning-making resources, with other visual and aural modes: images, perspective, sounds and music, etc. Nor does it simply co-exist with other semiotic codes. They all mesh together in ways orchestrated by film directors and editors to 'achieve coherence, intentionality, informativity, intertextuality, relevance and the maxims of conversation' (Gambier 2013: 47), in narrative wholes that are greater than the sum of their parts. Modes and their submodes (e.g. typography, font, etc. for writing and the core mode of language) clarify, add, contradict or enhance one another (Taylor 2013, Pérez-González 2014). Their relationship impacts on what can or should be translated in subtitles, and how, in an additional layer of information that is also an integral part of the equation. By multiplying the signifying codes that can be harnessed to produce meaning in films or relied on in their interpretation, and by diversifying their uses, technology in this case has, if anything, made things even more complex for our understanding of the tension between creativity and accessibility.

A fourth significant but underrepresented aspect will be just flagged at this point. It relates to 'cultural a-synchrony' (Manhart 2000), i.e. source/target linguistic and cultural mismatches, always present, rarely addressed explicitly, and raises issues of linguistic and cultural representation and audience responses taken up in subsequent sections.

Digitization has not removed perennial challenges. It has in some respects added to their intractability and also produced new ones. One such challenge is coping with, and responding to, the diversification of practices and (constantly changing) expectations that it is proliferating (vs. the one-size-fits-all of their mainstream embodiments). Another challenge is acknowledging the evolving audiences' viewing capacities and receptivity to multimedial products, now also systematically available for repeated consumption online. There is also increasing individualization of practices, e.g. to particular communities of viewers with shared needs and group-specific expectations engaging in participatory practices (fans of film or TV series, for example) (Pérez-González 2014), and increasing pressure to deliver subtitling at ever shorter notice, both within these communities (e.g. for immediate access to new episodes) and in the industry. Fast turnover has knock-on effects on quality, but these are as conceptual and the result of paradigm shifts as they are practical and the by-product of tight deadlines, or working conditions for professional subtitlers. With the proliferation of practices defying accepted norms, the long undisputed ideals of top down representational accuracy, fidelity, and authenticity in mainstream film and cultural products are being called into question with bottom-up amateur/collaborative practices, in which affectivity, subjectivity and social engagement are the main drivers (Pérez-González 2012, 2014), heralding fundamental change.

Means and modes of meaning in subtitling

With the unbound creativity of fansubbers and amateur subtitling in their reaction to the linguistic and cultural standardization of industry products, subtitling has been given public licence to shake off the shackle of some of its most constraining practices, and the opportunity to review their ideological implications. By the same token, transformational practices are an incentive for subtitling to re-evaluate its specificities as an expressive medium: do we have the full measure of textual stylization, the inevitable by-product of medial constraints in mainstream practices and their greatest bane, but paradoxically perhaps also their greatest gift?

Fansubbing emerged in the 1980s as a reaction against the neutralization in US productions of Japanese animated films of anything linguistically and culturally Japanese. With their freer uses of colours, typefaces, typography, variable length of subtitle text, siting on screen, and novel uses of notes and glosses superimposed on visuals to provide explanatory comments about what is seen and heard ('thick translation', a notion critiqued in Hermans 2003), fansubbers are circumventing accepted practices and conventions with deeply held principles at their core. Standard recommendations that subtitles should attract as little attention as possible, and interfere as little as possible with the processing of other semiotic resources are of little import to them.

There are well documented typologies of subtitling issues and strategies for dealing with them in line with these and other desiderata, relating to either medial constraints (space/time/textual fragmentation), or to aspects of linguistic and cultural mis-mappings across languages, as synthesized in Díaz Cintas and Remael 2007, for example. Two main strategies are generally identified in the field to deal with medial constraints: text reduction—with omission, condensation and/or reformulation, at word or phrase level—and syntactic adaptations to minimize the pressure of coping with text displayed sequentially in stand-alone segments; simple lexis is also preferred, likewise to ease the cognitive load.

Linguistic and cultural encoding encompass a range of other features or aspects. Chief among them as an issue in interlingual transfer are culture-bound terms and references, or 'extralinguistic cultural references' (ECRs) (Pedersen 2007, 2010) referring to people, places, customs, institutions, units of measurement, to give but a few examples, that are unknown and/or unintelligible to target viewers and candidates for glosses in amateur practices. Translation strategies in mainstream subtitling range from literal translations to complete recreations and omissions (Agost Canós 2004, Gottlieb 2009, Katan 1999/2004, Ramière 2010, Tomaszkiewicz 2001, Wyler 2003 among others). Humour and non-standard language are related and frequently focused on aspects. Like ECRs, they are more or less taxing depending on the cultural specificity of their manifestations, including puns, play on words, etc. (Vandaele 2002); and the degrees of acceptability for non-standard tokens—e.g. greater or lesser offensiveness of swear, curse or vulgar words. These are argued in the field to be more offensive and less well tolerated in the shift from evanescent speech to more enduring writing, and so prone to levelling (e.g. Lambert 1989). Amateur practices by contrast retain, gloss, make visible—inconspicuousness is not a concern, acculturation is. Is the polarization inevitable, in practices themselves, and in the conceptualization of issues?

How to represent in writing the oral in source dialogues has been another recurrently addressed challenge, and raises similar questions. Accents and colloquial or other traits that mark speakers out geographically and/or socioculturally seldom find a match across languages, causing a difficult tug in practices between 'incoherent localisation' with ill-adapted local varieties or 'banalising neutralisation' eschewing representation altogether (Ranzato 2010: 109). This extends to presence/absence in the representation of orality features that give source dialogues the feel of everyday conversation—filled and unfilled pauses, hesitations, discourse markers denoting particular verbal habits and other features of interpersonal verbal exchanges—and likewise play narratively significant functions in characterization. Like greetings, leave-takings and other pragmatic features of everyday communicative practices and verbally enacted phenomena like politeness tend to be first to go as non-essential when space is at a premium, and equivalence is an issue in any case—with at times significant implications for the depiction of, and response to, characters and interpersonal relationship (Hatim and Mason 1997, Remael 2003). Multilingualism, epitomized in its functions as a narrative tool in Tarantino's *Inglourious Basterds*, for example (Mingant 2010, O'Sullivan 2011) is a further aspect at the centre of representational practices debates.

In all, 'loss' has never been far from the surface as a driving theme. Indeed, it is an easy bone to pick when text is taken at its face value in constrained contexts, and has therefore found an easy echo in equally literal public overt responses. With the creativity of non-mainstream practices as a counterpoint, there is scope to revisit loss assumptions from fresh perspectives, and to explore alternative views. Has the emphasis in film subtitling on the inevitable by-products of reduction and vicissitudes of cross-linguistic transfer come in the way of giving it due credit for its potential as a meaning-resource on its own terms? In other words, have so-called 'constraints' on subtitling and linguistic difference and how to deal with them masked just how creative and expressive subtitling can be in its own right? This, too, is a debate for subtitling for the twenty-first century, with a root in perennial translation studies dichotomies/tensions, and implications for accessibility/creativity arguments.

In the tussle for producing meaning in the multimodally rich but spatially constrained film context of mainstream professional subtitling, priority is given overall to the communicative intentions of source dialogues over textual and semantic detail, in a process argued to foster cultural and linguistic neutralization and standardization by suppressing non-mainstream identities (Fawcett 2003, Díaz Cintas 2005, Gambier 2013; Pérez-González 2009, 2014). The extent to which target texts should mirror source text practices, and are, can or should be adapted to target practices, communicative preferences and expectations—i.e. 'domesticated' for target audiences, a basic dilemma in translation studies—is a moot point in subtitling. Gambier documents domesticating practices as part of accessibility (2003). It amounts to giving audiences what they are used to, and conforming to the framework of target languages and their cultural codes—adapting *Harry Potter* to foreign markets by erasing all reference to the idiosyncratic UK public school system and language features associated with it, for example. Nornes denounces domestication as 'corrupt' and advocates instead a subtitling that avoids the erasure of difference and strives 'to intensify the interaction between the reader and the foreign' (Nornes 2007: 178–9—chapter 5 was first published in 1999). 'Abusive subtitling', mainstay of fansubbing by choice and by dint of fansubbers keeping close to original text, with wordier, more word-for-word subtitles (Gambier 2013: 53–4), brings to the fore the transgressive nature of Nornes' preferred strategies. Whether it is subscribed to or not, his radical take is an incentive to engage with questions of linguistic and cultural representation, to this day still comparatively neglected. They have produced some debates, in practice and theory, as just noted. Oddly in view of the unprecedented exposure to AVT-mediated cultural products worldwide, the impact on audiences of AVT-mediated cross-cultural representations, and of the cultural mismatch noted earlier in shaping them, has been barely looked into, with only brief mentions in updates on AVT developments. It is signposted as raising questions, about 'the power of subtitling in the dissemination and entrenchment of certain concepts and realities in other cultural communities' in Díaz Cintas (2013: 278), for example. It is beginning to attract more attention, with input from cross-cultural pragmatics considered in the next section.

Mainstream subtitling cannot ever fully emulate source dialogues, let alone naturally occurring speech. Nor is it necessarily desirable, or defendable, as foregoing debates suggest. The specificities and intrinsic expressive potential of subtitles as text have rarely been a feature in these debates, however. The language choices and strategies that are a by-product of constraining factors (textual condensation, synthesis, modulation, etc.) give subtitles conspicuous formal, linguistic and pragmatic/sociocultural distinctiveness. Their syntactic simplicity, paratactic nature, additive build-up of meaning sequentially in stand-alone units affiliates them more to speech than to writing (Halliday 1987), for example. The extent to which such differentiating features have a role in generating meaning, in their own terms and in their interaction with other semiotic resources, has tended to be obscured in face-value textual comparisons highlighting what subtitles miss out. Subtitles' capacity to generate their own sets of internal linguistic and pragmatic settings, and harness to this end the stylized interplay of features like punctuation, register shifts, lexical and other contrasts heightened by omission and reduction, has become a feature in a growing number of studies, explicitly or implicitly (De Meao 2012 [representation of dialects], Guillot 2007, 2008, 2010 [orality, punctuation, interpersonal address], Longo 2009 [dialects], Ranzato 2010, 2011 [dialects, stylistic specificities, non-standard language]). They are conspicuous for shifting the perspective away from the relationship between source and target to subtitling as a meaning-making resource on its own terms, and an in-built cognitive dimension recognizing in text the capacity to trigger types of experience on the basis on a few integrated cues—e.g. of orality, in line with Fowler's theory of mode (1991); see Guillot 2010, 2012a, 2012b for applications to subtitling. This stance finds corroboration in professional subtitlers' accounts of their own practices, and trust in audiences' capacity to respond to representational conventions established internally within film and their subtitles (Bannon 2009/2013, for example). It is a key feature in emergent debates about cross-cultural representation, and their linguistic drive to acknowledge AVT as generating distinctive language varieties and registers, and subtitling as endowed with a greater capacity to mean in its own right, within its broader multimodal context and together with it, than it has generally been credited for in mainstream practices.

Amateur practices are concurrently argued more and more to assume a non-representational function, and to eschew the referential for the affective with forms of translation that showcase the expression of subjective spectatorial experience (Pérez-González 2014). Debates about representation and creativity in mainstream subtitling may seem almost paradoxical in this sense. If, on the other hand, the productivity of subtitling as a construct able to generate its own system of in-text multimodal representation rests not with a capacity to achieve sameness, but with 'a capacity to diversify the dialectics of difference' (Guillot 2012b: 118), as such debates also make room to contend, they produce an interesting counterpoint for the creativity perspectives of transformational practices.

Research and methodologies

There is 'a danger that future research could be tempted to focus primarily on new technological advances and the possibilities they offer, to the detriment of the linguistic, pedagogical, cultural, commercial and political issues that continue to lie at the heart of screen translation in its various forms' warns O'Connell in a 2007 overview of screen translation (2007: 132).

AVT research has matured in the last ten to fifteen years, all the while having to keep pace with technological developments inconceivable just a decade or two ago, and reshaping the world of subtitling in ways that are immeasurably complex to account for. Doing justice to the linguistic and cultural spheres as well as the technical dimension remains a leitmotiv, now with ever more explicit calls for a plurality of standpoints and for the interdisciplinarity of approaches that the breadth of the field requires (Díaz Cintas 2013, Gambier 2013, Pérez-González 2014).

There have been recurrent themes: achieving a less fragmented, more coherent field of research paying due heed to multimodality and the complementarity of different meaning-making semiotic codes and a better empirical understanding of reception processes is a main one still, for screen translation and for subtitling. They are central in Gambier's 2003 mapping of the field, and in his 2013 update. His recurrent admonitions to move beyond the text and fully engage in the study of the interplay of the verbal and non-verbal modes, are an index of how exacting multimodality has been to account for, despite the development of multimodal transcription tools to capture the various elements involved and characterize their dynamic interaction in their joint meaning-making processes (Thibault 2000, Baldry and Thibault 2006, with applications in Taylor 2003 and Desilla 2009 for example). The same sense of demandingness is manifest in his renewed call for experimental studies on viewer's processing habits, reading strategies and receptions patterns, and the three Rs: response, reaction and repercussion—referring, respectively, to perceptual decoding (lisibility), psycho-cognitive issues (readability) and attitudinal issues (viewers' preferences and habits, and the sociocultural in the broader non-diegetical contexts that influences the receiving process) (Gambier 2013: 57). In his 2009 encyclopedia entry for AVT, Pérez-González warns against piecemeal anecdotal approaches, prescriptivism, and lack of theorization. These are recurrent themes in his 2014 state of the art volume on theories, methods and issues in AVT, where they share centre stage with amateur/participatory subtitling practices as agents of change, in practice and theory.

Un(der)-specified theoretical context, un(der)-specified methodology, un(der)-specified research questions, anecdotal observations, conclusions and generalizations on the basis of limited evidence and small decontextualized text segments in micro-level fragmented analyses, insufficient consideration of the interdependence of linguistic choices and narrative/filmic structure and modes, and concurrent neglect of macro-perspectives in approaching subtitle text may all have a good deal to answer for in perpetuating debates about limitations and loss, to some extent unhelpfully.

The field has evolved all the same and moved on. Like AVT generally, film subtitling is at a turning point and is embracing the new sets of challenges that will establish it fully as a discipline, for which technology has given it new tools. In reception, for example, cutting-edge equipment like eye trackers has spurred a spate of research updates on past studies, with trail-blazing empirical work on untested assumptions about reading and psycho-cognitive responses in mainstream subtitling practices, in line with Gambier's calls. The work also extends to the impact on processing of new features like the 'pop-up' hypertext notes common in amateur subtitling, and now finding their way in mainstream practices and popularized in non-subtitled media products like the recent *Sherlock* BBC1 series in the UK (2010, 2012, 2014) (Bairstow 2011, Caffrey 2008, Künzli and Ehrensberger-Dow 2011, Kruger 2012, Rajendran *et al.* 2013). With other methods of data collection (e.g. consecutive questionnaires, corpus groups) they are giving the field scope to develop a better understanding of viewers' responses and needs, and of their processing potential. Digitization and text processing software are facilitating data collection, storing and analysis, and more systematic corpus-based work supplementing the case study approaches that have been a main methodology for subtitling studies from their early days. Dubbing is ahead of the game with corpus work (see Baños *et al.* 2013, for example), but it is building up for subtitling (Sotelo Dios 2011, Sotelo Dios and Guinovart 2012, Tiedemann 2007, Tirkkonen-Condit and Mäkisalo 2007). Copyrights, software compatibility, methodological harmonization, and access remain key concerns in both. Digitization is also promoting cross-fertilization at a conceptual, methodological and technical level, giving AVT the benefits of the interconnectedness of the research world.

While technology has been a boost to subtitling research, it is also getting further insights from harnessing the tools of other disciplines, including linguistics and the study of communicative practices and preferences across languages and cultures in cross-cultural pragmatics. The models and approaches identified as contributing to AVT research bear witness to the variety of angles that have informed it (psycholinguistic, cognitive, neurolinguistics pragmatic for process models; shift-based and corpus driven for comparative models; systems and norm-based, discourse and ideological for causal models, as documented in Pérez-González 2014). Cross-cultural pragmatics has been surprisingly untapped until recently, and is critical for addressing an overarching, largely uncharted and increasingly topical question for film subtitling: its cross-cultural impact on audiences, and related unresolved issues of description and representation. The question encapsulates just about every aspect of subtitling and is complex. It is sketched out below from the points of view of description and reception by way of final synthesis of lesser catered-for aspects of subtitling.

From an AVT research point of view, we are beginning to understand better how subtitling simulates spoken language within the multimodal polysemiotic film context and the constraining factors that make subtitle text linguistically, pragmatically and socioculturally distinctive. What is central for description, however, and research in cross-cultural representation, is documenting the extent to which subtitling texts bear the pragmatic imprint of source dialogues, and of naturally occurring speech, and how: is it literal, or conveyed through idiosyncratic expressive means that produce language varieties or registers in their own right? This is a recent domain of research in AVT. Pavesi has led the way for dubbing, with corpus-based work that highlights dubbing's creative specificity, and the capacity of selected target language features to convey pragmatic meaning and sociolinguistic variation symbolically and non-randomly (e.g. as privileged carriers of orality, markers of otherness in pronominal address, sites of cross-linguistic variation in demonstratives; Pavesi 2009a, 2009b, 2009c, 2014). Similar mimetic processes have been identified in case study work for subtitling, and situated pragmatic indexing across a range of features and communicative practices—including pronominal address, greeting/leave-takings, phonings (Guillot 2010, 2016). Other relevant findings are building up in studies with an explicit pragmatics focus and methodological framework—e.g. on politeness, speech acts like advice requests, apologies or compliments, greetings, swearing, implicatures (Bruti 2009a, 2009b; Desilla 2012, Greenall 2011, Mubenga 2015, Pinto 2010), and studies with an incidental pragmatics dimension, explicit or implicit, simply by virtue of their dealing with language use—e.g. dialects, humour (Longo 2009, Ranzato 2010). Results of these studies need to be collated in order to acquire critical mass, and be more robustly accounted for and harmonized methodologically.

In reception, the cross-cultural dimension of subtitling has been largely by-passed, except for a few studies of humour (e.g. Fuentes Luque 2003) and one empirical study of comprehension of implicit meaning across cultures (Desilla 2014). Issues from a cross-cultural angle relate to distinctive features of the reception process for audiences: suspension of linguistic disbelief, and the cultural mismatch between the foreign seen on screen (e.g. Chinese, French, Spanish, etc.) and pragmatic expectations and perceptual frames triggered by (stylized) subtitled text in their own language (e.g. English and how politeness is enacted in English, in greetings, requests, disagreements, etc.). The extent to which this discrepancy impacts on viewers' responses to foreign language films is untested. Does AVT produce misperceptions and promote linguistic stereotyping (e.g. rudeness for Spanish in Spanish-to-English subtitling as argued by Pinto 2010), or can it override stereotypical responses by activating its own interpretative modes, with selected features indexing particular pragmatic values (Guillot's and Pavesi's stance)? There is no empirical evidence for either position, or any other, and research is overdue. It is complex and requires cross-disciplinary input. There is expertise relevant to a cross-cultural approach in audience and reception research—including of audience profiling in film and television studies, and of perceptual and psycho-cognitive aspects in the audiovisual accessibility research referred to above. There is also empirical know-how from research at the interface of cognitive linguistics and translation (Rojo 2015). How this expertise can be harnessed to the specific challenges of assessing subtitling's impact on audiences' perceptually mediated cross-cultural response and literacy is a pending question. It is an important step for subtitling research, in itself and to boost further the educational value of subtitling, already acknowledged for foreign language learning (Gambier *et al*. 2015), and to give it and AVT generally its proper place as a tool for cross-cultural exchange.

Accessibility has from the early days been a central theme for film subtitling and subtitling research, and a normative drive in the industry with repercussions on every aspect of the practice. With digitization and the opportunities it has produced for subtitling to move out into the public sphere and the hands and practices of consumers-turned-prosumers, creativity has become an increasingly defying force. For Pérez-González, the self-mediation practices that are already having an influence on the production and translation of commercial media content offer 'a unique opportunity to learn about how audiovisual translation can be done, rather than simply represent how the industry wants it done' (2014: 230). What lies ahead for subtitling is the thrilling prospect of reconceptualizing itself through this exploration, in practice and in theory, and from within, as a distinctive and powerful medium of intercultural exchange in a global context.

Related topics

2   History of audiovisual translation
6   Subtitling for deaf and hard of hearing audiences: moving forward
7   Respeaking: subtitling through speech recognition
13 Spoken discourse and conversational interaction in audiovisual translation
14 Psycholinguistics and perception in audiovisual translation
15 Narratology and audiovisual translation
16 Pragmatics and audiovisual translation
18 Sociolinguistics and linguistic variation in audiovisual translation
20 Corpus-based audiovisual translation studies: ample room for development
22 Eye tracking in audiovisual translation research
23 Audiovisual translation and audience reception
30 Audiovisual translation in language teaching and learning

Further reading

Bannon, D. (2009/2013) *The Elements of Subtitles: A Practical Guide to the Art of Dialogue, Character, Context, Tone and Style in Film and Television Subtitling*, Blackstock: Translation Studies Press | *A practical guide to dialogue, character, context, tone and style in film and television subtitling, offering a professional perspective on subtitling in practice and original insights into its various aspects.*

Díaz Cintas, J. and A. Remael (2007) *Audiovisual Translation: Subtitling*, Manchester: St Jerome | *A staple subtitling handbook providing a comprehensive overview that combines subtitling research and professional expertise. Supplied with a DVD with WinCaps subtitling software, instructions for use and exercises.*

Nornes, A. M. (2007) *Cinema Babel: Translating Global Cinema*, Minneapolis: University of Minnesota Press | *A pioneering and provoking discussion of subtitling from a film/media perspective, within global cinema context. The volume includes (Chapter 5) 'For an Abusive Subtitling', Nornes' critical discussion of so-called 'corrupt' and 'abusive' practices first published in* Film Quarterly, *52(3), 17–34.*

Pérez-González, L. (2014) *Audiovisual Translation: Theories, Methods and Issues*, London & New York: Routledge | *Essential guide to audiovisual translation research and benchmark for the discipline to establish its authority in the twenty-first century.*

References

Agost Canós, R. (2004) 'Translation in Bilingual Contexts', in P. Orero (ed.) *Topics in Audiovisual Translation*, Amsterdam & Philadelphia: John Benjamins, 63–82.

Bairstow, D. (2011) 'Audiovisual Processing while Watching Subtitled Films: A Cognitive Approach', in A. Şerban, A. Matamala and J.-M. Laveur (eds) *Audiovisual Translation in Close-up: Practical and Theoretical Approaches*, Bern: Peter Lang, 205–217.

Baldry, A. and P. J. Thibault (2006) *Multimodal Transcription and Text Analysis*, London & Oakville: Equinox.

Bannon, D. (2009/2013) *The Elements of Subtitles: A Practical Guide to the Art of Dialogue, Character, Context, Tone and Style in Film and Television Subtitling*, 3rd edition, Blackstock: Translation Studies Press.

Baños, R., S. Bruti and S. Zanotti (eds) (2013) 'Corpus Linguistics and Audiovisual Translation: In Search of an Integrated Approach', Special Issue of *Perspectives: Studies in Translatology* 21(4).

Bruti, S. (2009a) 'The Translation of Compliments in Subtitles', in J. Díaz Cintas (ed.) *New Trends in Audiovisual Translation*, Clevedon: Multilingual Matters, 226–238.

Bruti, S. (2009b) 'Translating Compliments and Insults in the *Pavia Corpus of Film Dialogues*: Two Sides of the Same Coin?', in M. Freddi and M. Pavesi (eds) *Analysing Audiovisual Dialogue: Linguistic and Translational Insights*, Bologna: CLUEB, 143–163.

Caffrey, C. (2008) 'Using Pupillometrics, Fixation-Based and Subjective Measures to Measure the Processing Effort when Viewing Subtitled TV Anime with Pop-up Gloss', in S. Göpferich, A. Jakobsen and I. Mees (eds) *Looking at Eyes—Eye Tracking Studies of Reading and Translation Processing*, Copenhagen Studies in Language 36. Samfundslitteratur, Copenhagen, 125–144.

Chaume, F. (2004) *Cine y traducción*, Madrid: Cátedra.

Chiaro, D. (2009) 'Issues in Audiovisual Translation', in J. Munday (ed.) *The Routledge Companion to Translation Studies*, London: Routledge, 141–165.

De Linde Z. and Kay N. (1999) *The Semiotics of Subtitling*, Manchester: St Jerome.

De Meao, M. (2012) 'Subtitling Dialects: Strategies of Socio-cultural Transfer from Italian into English', in S. Bruti and E. Di Giovanni (eds) *Audiovisual Translation across Europe: An Ever-Changing Landscape*, Bern: Peter Lang, 79–96.

Desilla, L. (2009) *Towards a Methodology for the Study of Implicatures in Subtitled Films; Multimodal Construal and Reception of Pragmatic Meaning Across Cultures*, Unpublished Doctoral Thesis, University of Manchester.

Desilla, L. (2012) 'Implicatures in Film: Construal and Functions in *Bridget Jones* Romantic Comedies', *Journal of Pragmatics* 44(1): 30–35.

Desilla, L. (2014) 'Reading between the Lines, Seeing beyond the Images: An Empirical Study on the Comprehension of Implicit Film Dialogue Meaning across Cultures', *The Translator* 20(2): 194–214.

Díaz Cintas, J. (2005) 'Audiovisual Translation Today. A Question of Accessibility for All', *Translating Today* 4: 3–5.

Díaz Cintas, J. (2010a) 'The Highs and Lows of Digital Subtitles', in L. Zybatow (ed.) *Translationswissenschaft—Stand und Perspektiven. Innsbrucker Ringvorlesungen zur Translationswissenschaft VI*, Frankfurt am Main: Peter Lang, 105–130.

Díaz Cintas, J. (2010b) 'Subtitling', in Y. Gambier and L. van Doorslaer (eds) *Handbook of Translation Studies*, volume 1, Amsterdam & Philadelphia: John Benjamins Publishing, 344–349.

Díaz Cintas, J. (2013) 'Subtitling: Theory, Practice and Research', in C. Millán-Varela and F. Bartrina (eds) *The Routledge Handbook of Translation Studies*, London & New York: Routledge, 285–299.

Díaz Cintas, J. and A. Remael (2007) *Audiovisual Translation: Subtitling*. Manchester: St Jerome.

d'Ydewalle, G., J. V. Rensbergen and J. Polle (1987) 'Reading a Message when the Same Message is Available Auditorily in Another Language: The Case of Subtitling', in J. K. O'Regan and A. Lévy-Schoen (eds) *Eye Movements: From Psychology to Cognition*, Amsterdam & New York: Elsevier Science Publishers, 313–321.

Fawcett, P. (2003) 'The Manipulation of Language and Culture in Film Translation', in M. Calzada Pérez (ed.) *Apropos of Ideology*, Manchester: St Jerome, 145–163.

Fowler, R. (1991) *Language in the News: Discourse and Ideology in the Press*, London: Routledge.

Fuentes Luque, A. (2003) 'An Empirical Approach to the Reception of AV Translated Humour. A Case Study of the Marx Brothers' *Duck Soup*', *The Translator* 9(2): 293–306.

Gambier Y. (2003) 'Screen Transadaptation: Perception and Reception', *The Translator: Screen Translation* 9(2): 171–189.

Gambier Y. (2013) 'The Position of Audio-visual Studies', in C. Millán-Varela and F. Bartrina (eds) *The Routledge Handbook of Translation Studies*, London: Routledge, 45–59.

Gambier Y., A Caimi, and C. Mariotti, Cristina (eds) (2015) *Subtitles and Language Learning: Principles, Strategies and Practical Experiences,* Bern: Peter Lang.

Gottlieb, H. (1998) 'Subtitling', in M. Baker (ed.) *Routledge Encyclopedia of Translation Studies*, London and New York: Routledge, 244–248.

Gottlieb, H. (2009) 'Subtitling against the Current: Danish Concepts, English Minds', in J. Díaz Cintas (ed.) *New Trends in Audiovisual Translation*, Clevedon: Multilingual Matters, 21–43.

Greenall, A. K. (2011) 'The Non-translation of Swearing in Subtitling: Loss of Social Implicature?', in A. Şerban, A. Matamala, and J.-M. Lavaur (eds) *Audiovisual Translation in Close-up: Practical and Theoretical Approaches*, Bern: Peter Lang, 45–60.

Guillot, M.-N. (2007) 'Oral et illusion d'oral: Indices d'oralité dans les sous-titres de dialogues de film', *Meta* 52(2): 239–259.

Guillot, M.-N. (2008) 'Orality and Film Subtitling: The Riches of Punctuation', *The Sign Language Translator and Interpreter* 2(2): 127–147.

Guillot, M.-N. (2010) 'Film Subtitles from a Cross-cultural Pragmatics Perspective: Issues of Linguistic and Cultural Representation', *The Translator* 16(1): 67–92.

Guillot M.-N. (2012a) 'Stylization and Representation in Subtitles: Can Less be More?', *Perspectives Studies in Translatology* 20(4): 479–494.

Guillot, M.-N. (2012b) 'Film Subtitles and the Conundrum of Linguistic and Cultural Representation: A Methodological Blind Spot', in S. Hauser and M. Luginbuehl (eds) *Contrastive Media Analysis*, Amsterdam & Philadelphia: John Benjamins, 101–121.

Guillot, M.-N. (2016) 'Communicative Rituals and Audiovisual Translation—Representation of Otherness in Film Subtitles', *Meta* 61(3): 606–628.

Halliday, M. (1987) 'Spoken and Written Modes of Meaning', in R. Horowitz and S. J. Samuels (eds) *Comprehending Oral and Written Language*, London: Academic Press, 55–82.

Hatim, B. and I. Mason (1997) *The Translator as Communicator*, London: Routledge.

Hermans, T. (2003) 'Cross-cultural Translation Studies as Thick Translation', *Bulletin of the School of Oriental and African Studies* 66(3): 380–389.

Ivarsson, J. and M. Carroll (1998) *Subtitling*, Simrishamn: TransEdit.

Katan, D. (1999/2004) *Translating Cultures: An Introduction for Translators, Interpreters and Mediators*, 2nd edition, Manchester: St. Jerome Publishing.

Kruger, J.-L. (2012) 'Making Meaning in AVT: Eyetracking and Viewer Construction of Narrative', *Perspectives: Studies in Translatology* 20(1): 67–86.

Künzli, A. and M. Ehrensberger-Dow (2011) 'Innovative Subtitling: A Reception Study', in C. Alvstad, A. Hild and E. Tiselius (eds) *Methods and Strategies of Process Research: Integrative Approaches in Translation Studies*, Amsterdam & Philadelphia: John Benjamins, 187–200.

Lambert, J. (1989) 'La traduction, les langues et la communication de masse', *Target* 1(2): 215–237.

Longo, A. (2009) 'Subtitling the Italian South', in J. Díaz Cintas (ed.) *New Trends in Audiovisual Translation*, Clevedon: Multilingual Matters, 99–108.

Manhart, S. (2000) '"When worlds collide": Betrachtungen über fremde Kulturen im filmtranslatorischen Handlungsgefüge', in M. Kadric, K. Kaindl and F. Pöchacker (eds) *Translationwissenschaft: Festschrift für Mary Snell-Hornby zum 60. Geburtstag*, Tübingen: Stauffenburg Verlag, 167–181.

Mingant, N. (2010) 'Tarantino's *Inglourious Basterds*: A Blueprint for Dubbing Translators?', *Meta* 55(4): 712–731.

Mubenga, J. S. (2015) *Film Discourse and Pragmatics in Screen Translation*, Saarbrücken: Lambert Academic Publishing.

Nornes, A. M. (1999) 'For an Abusive Subtitling', *Film Quarterly* 52(3): 17–34.

Nornes, A. M. (2007) *Cinema Babel: Translating Global Cinema*, Minneapolis: University of Minnesota Press.

O'Connell, E. (2007) 'Screen Translation', in P. Kuhiwczak and K. Littau (eds) *A Companion to Translation Studies*, Clevedon, Buffalo & Toronto: Multilingual Matters, 120–133.

O'Hagan, M. (2013) 'The Impact of New Technologies on Translation Studies: A Technological Turn', in C. Millán-Varela and F. Bartrina (eds) *The Routledge Handbook of Translation Studies*, London: Routledge, 503–518.

O'Sullivan, C. (2011) *Translating Popular Films*, Basingstoke: Palgrave Macmillan.

Pavesi, M. (2009a) 'Dubbing English into Italian: A Closer Look at the Translation of the Spoken Language', in J. Díaz Cintas (ed.) *New Trends in Audiovisual Translation*, Clevedon: Multilingual Matters, 197–209.

Pavesi, M. (2009b) 'Referring to Third Persons in Dubbing: Is there a Role for Source Language Transfer?', in M. Freddi and M. Pavesi (eds) *Analysing Audiovisual Dialogue: Linguistic and Translational Insights*, Bologna: CLUEB, 125–142.

Pavesi, M. (2009c) 'Pronouns in Film Dubbing and the Dynamics of Audiovisual Communication', *VIAL—Vigo International Journal of Applied Linguistics* 6: 89–107.

Pavesi, M. (2014) '*This* and *That* in the Language of Film Dubbing: A Corpus-Based Analysis', *Meta* 58(1): 107–137.

Pedersen, J. (2007) 'Cultural Interchangeability: The Effects of Substituting Cultural References in Subtitling', *Perspectives: Studies in Translatology* 15(1): 30–48.

Pedersen, J. (2010) 'When Do You Go for Benevolent Intervention? How Subtitlers Determine the Need for Cultural Mediation', in J. Díaz Cintas, A. Matamala and J. Neves (eds) *New Insights into Audiovisual Translation and Media Accessibility: Media for All 2*, Amsterdam & New York: Rodopi, 123–136.

Pérez-González, L. (2006) 'Fansubbing Anime: Insights into the Butterfly Effect of Globalisation on Audiovisual Translation', *Perspectives: Studies in Translatology* 14(4): 260–277.

Pérez-González, L. (2009) 'Audiovisual Translation', in M. Baker and G. Saldanha (eds) *The Routledge Encyclopedia of Translation Studies*, 2nd edition, London: Routledge, 13–20.

Pérez-González, L. (2012) 'Amateur Subtitling and the Pragmatics of Spectatorial Subjectivity', *Language and Intercultural Communication* 12(4): 335–353.

Pérez-González, L. (2014) *Audiovisual Translation: Theories, Methods, and Issues*, London: Routledge.

Pinto, D. (2010) 'Lost in Subtitle Translations: The Case of Advice in the English Subtitles of Spanish Films', *Intercultural Pragmatics* 7(2): 257–277.

Rajendran D. J., A. T. Duchowski, P. Orero, J. Martínez and P. Romero-Fresco (2013) 'Effects of Text Chunking on Subtitling: A Quantitative and Qualitative Examination', *Perspectives: Studies in Translatology* 21(1): 5–21.

Ramière, N. (2010) 'Are you "Lost in Translation" (when Watching a Foreign Film)? Toward an Alternative Approach to Judging Audiovisual Translation', *Australian Journal of French Studies* 47(1): 100–115.

Ranzato, I. (2010) 'Localising Cockney: Translating Dialect into Italian', in J. Díaz Cintas, A. Matamala and J. Neves, *New Insights into Audiovisual Translation and Media Accessibility: Media for All 2*, Amsterdam & New York: Rodopi, 109–122.

Ranzato, I. (2011) 'Translating Woody Allen into Italian. Creativity in Dubbing', *JoSTrans: The Journal of Specialised Translation* 15: 121–41. Available online: http://www.jostrans.org/issue15/art_ranzato.pdf [last access 20 December 2017].

Remael, A. (2003) 'Mainstream Narrative Film Dialogue and Subtitling: A Case Study of Mike Leigh's *Secrets & Lies* (1996)', *The Translator* 9(2): 225–247.

Remael, A. (2010) 'Audiovisual Translation', in Y. Gambier and L. van Doorslaer (eds) *Handbook of Translation Studies*, volume 1, Amsterdam & Philadelphia: John Benjamins Publishing, 12–17.

Rojo, A. (2015) 'Translation Meets Cognitive Science: The Imprint of Translation on Cognitive Processing', *Multilingua* 34(6): 721–746.

Romero-Fresco, P. (2011) *Subtitling through Speech Recognition: Respeaking*, Manchester: St Jerome Publishing.

Sotelo Dios, P. (2011) 'Using a Multimedia Parallel Corpus to Investigate English-Galician Subtitling', in B. Maegaard (ed.) *Proceedings of the Supporting Digital Humanities Conference*, Copenhagen 17–18 November 2011. Available online: https://pdfs.semanticscholar.org/e8ad/d030828e650e20396f330d33ee12ef1105dc.pdf [last access 20 December 2017].

Sotelo Dios, P. and X. Gómez Guinovart (2012) 'A Multimedia Parallel Corpus of English-Galician Film Subtitling', in A. Simões, R. Queirós and D. da Cruz (eds) *Proceedings of the 1st Symposium on Languages, Applications and Technologies Slate* 2012, Schloss-Dagstuhl: OASIcs, 255–66. Available on-line http://drops.dagstuhl.de/opus/volltexte/2012/3527/pdf/20.pdf [last access 20 December 2017].

Taylor, C. (2003) 'Multimodal Transcription in the Analysis: Translation and Subtitling of Italian Films', *The Translator* 9(2): 191–206.

Taylor, C. (2013) 'Multimodality and Audiovisual Translation', in Y. Gambier and L. van Doorslaer (eds) *Handbook of Translation Studies* volume 4, Amsterdam & Philadelphia: John Benjamins Publishing, 98–104.

Thibault, P. (2000) 'The Multimodal Transcription of a Television Advertisement: Theory and Practice', in A. Baldry (ed.) *Multimodality and Multimediality in the Distance Learning Age*, Compobasso: Palladino Editore, 311–385.

Tiedemann, J. (2007) 'Building a Multilingual Parallel Subtitle Corpus', in P. Dirix, I. Schurman, V. Vandeghinste, and F. Van Eynde (eds) *Proceedings of the 17th Meeting of Computational Linguistics in the Netherlands*. Utrecht: Utrecht University, 147–162.

Tirkkonen-Condit, S. and J. Mäkisalo (2007) 'Cohesion in Subtitles: A Corpus-based Study', *Across Languages and Cultures* 8(2): 221–230.

Titford, C. (1982) 'Subtitling: Constrained Translation', *Lebende Sprachen* 27(3): 113–116.

Tomaszkiewicz, T. (2001) 'Transfert des références culturelles dans les sous-titres filmiques', in Y. Gambier and H. Gottlieb (eds) *(Multi)media Translation*, Amsterdam & Philadelphia: John Benjamins, 237–247.

Vandaele, J. (2002) '(Re-)Constructing Humour: Meanings and Means', *The Translator* 8(2): 149–172.

Wyler, L. (2003) '*Harry Potter* for Children, Teenagers and Adults', *Meta* 48(1–2): 5–14.

Yau, W.-P. (2014) 'Translation and Film: Dubbing, Subtitling, Adaptation and Remaking', in S. Bermann and C. Porter (eds) *A Companion to Translation Studies*, Oxford: Wiley-Blackwell, 492–503.

Filmography

Inglourious Basterds (2009) Quentin Tarantino. IMDb entry: http://www.imdb.com/title/tt0361748/?ref_=fn_al_tt_1

Sherlock (2010–) Mark Gatiss and Steven Moffat. IMDb entry: http://www.imdb.com/title/tt1475582/?ref_=fn_al_tt_1

4

Investigating dubbing

Learning from the past, looking to the future

Charlotte Bosseaux

Introduction

Dubbing, the process whereby the original dialogue track of an audiovisual text is replaced with a re-recorded version in the target language, has been practised for many years all over the world. From a semiotic perspective, dubbing is an example of 'isosemiotic' translation, where information is conveyed via the same semiotic channels in the source and target texts (Gottlieb 2005: 4). This chapter examines how dubbing has developed since it was first conceived and used, following the advent of sound in film, and is structured around three main sections. After outlining a brief history of dubbing, it moves on to deliver an overview of established research issues in dubbing studies, including the research methods used under each strand, and an account of the influence of technology on dubbing practice and scholarship. The third section focuses on future trajectories for dubbing studies and draws attention to new debates coalescing around those emerging scholarly trends.

A history of dubbing

The history of dubbing has been explored in some detail by Izard (1992) and Chaume (2012), to name but a couple of scholars, and the present volume also contains a chapter on the history of audiovisual translation (AVT) (Chapter 2). This first section should therefore be read in conjunction with Chapter 2 to gain a better understanding of how dubbing fits in and has developed within AVT.

Dubbing has been used and studied for many years all over the world, as documented by Chaume (2012: 6-10), who presents a 'global map of dubbing' in Europe, Asia, the Americas, Africa and Oceania. Dubbing—which is commonly used in Austria, Belgium, Brazil, China, the Czech Republic, Germany, France, Hungary, India, Iran, Italy, Japan, Korea, Peru, Slovakia, Spain and Turkey—is 'one of the oldest modes' of AVT whose 'origins can be traced back to the late 1920s' (*ibid.*: 1). Indeed, it is when 'written language on screen in silent movies' in the form of intertitles was introduced 'to accompany the iconic representation of images' that translation became 'essential to the full understanding of filmic narration' (*ibid.*: 10). In the late 1920s, dialogue began to be incorporated in films that became known as 'talkies'. However, even before the advent of sound, famous directors regarded translation as instrumental for the expansion of film as a global form of art and entertainment. For instance, 'as early as 1923, David W. Griffith noted that only 5 per cent of the world's population then spoke English and rhetorically wondered why he had to lose 95 per cent of his potential audience' (*ibid.*: 11).

Thus, the popularization of talkies prompted the need for different types of translation, from the provision of intertitles to dubbing and subtitling—initially into French, German and Spanish (Izard 1992). As noted in Chaume (2004a and 2012), foreign audiences did not react positively to these early forms of translation undertaken during the post-production process. In the 1930s, a new solution was explored in the form of multiple film versions, through which translation became an integral part of the production process. Multiple versions designates the process whereby the same director would make the same film in two or three different languages (e.g. French, German and Spanish) using the same actors, although on occasion the actors might be changed if additional languages were involved. One can imagine that such a venture proved very costly and after a few years, when dubbing and subtitling techniques had become more developed, the translation of films was once again relegated to the distribution process, where it has remained to this day. As will be elaborated below in a section on new debates and future research trajectories in dubbing, the fact that dubbing is currently part of the distribution process may be detrimental to the quality of translated audiovisual products and scholars are suggesting various alternatives to this state of affairs.

There are different reasons why dubbing has been preferred over subtitling in the different countries where it has taken root, although the situation is not monolithic and even 'dubbing countries' such as Brazil, France or India are increasingly using subtitling with fansubbing practices, for instance. Until recently there was a debate over whether subtitling is better than dubbing—as discussed for instance in the introduction of Luyken *et al.* (1991) and Díaz Cintas (2004)—but this discussion has now been dismissed by scholars for being obsolete, since the reasons for opting for one over the other are varied (including, but not limited to, economic, historical, and political factors). Crucially, advances in technology, as will be outlined below, have also evolved and are still changing the AVT landscape.

Going back to the reasons why certain audiovisual industries end up opting for specific AVT modes, the choice of dubbing has been often accounted for in terms of censorship and manipulation—in particular in relation to Spain, Italy and Germany (see, for instance, Danan 1991). On the other hand, it has also been argued that the strength and resilience of dubbing in certain audiovisual markets—including Spain, Germany, Italy and France—boil down to viewers' habits and expectations. So while in Spain, for instance, the imposition of dubbing under Franco's dictatorship sought to facilitate censorship and manipulation, this modality of AVT remains strong nowadays insofar as Spanish viewers have become used to dubbing and what it involves.

Research issues in dubbing studies

Various themes and challenges have attracted the attention of scholars who have contributed to the expansion of existing knowledge on dubbing in the last few decades. Specialists have addressed, for example, the impact of dubbing translational norms or conventions in the target culture. Consideration has also been given to the challenges that translators have to tackle when presented with ideologically loaded and culture-specific elements (e.g. Danan 1991, Agost 1999, Merino *et al.* 2005, Richart Marset 2012, Ballester 2001 and Ranzato 2011, 2012), humour (e.g. Zabalbeascoa 1996a, 1996b, 2005, Vandaele 2002, Chiaro 2006,

Martínez-Sierra 2008), as well as dialectal and linguistic variation (e.g. Di Giovanni *et al.* 1994, Dore 2009, Parini 2009).

Like other AVT modes, dubbing has been primarily studied using a descriptive translation studies framework—as illustrated by the work of Karamitroglou (2000) in the Greek context, Goris (1993) in the French context, Ballester (2001) and Sanz Ortega in Spain (2015), and Pavesi (2009) in Italy. These studies have been and still are important in terms of their capacity to shed light on the socio-historical contexts in which dubbing is performed, highlighting target text norms, the status of source and target cultures, and strategies used by translators. It should be noted, however, that most of these studies have been performed in Western Europe and dubbing research would greatly benefit from studies conducted outside of this region.

Insofar as space restrictions preclude a detailed exploration of these established research themes, the remainder of this section will focus on a selection of issues that have driven developments in the dubbing research landscape in the last few decades.

Synchronization

Dubbing is an example of constrained translation, insofar as it involves the mediation of texts that are made up of various forms of semiotics, namely both verbal and non-verbal meaning-making resources. It is therefore not surprising that much of the initial research into dubbing in the late 1980s predominantly emphasized medial constraints in dubbing, particularly synchronization—and, more specifically, lip-synchronization. Technical constraints linked to the different types of synchronization have been studied from a research angle in various subfields of AVT, including multimodality, sociolinguistics and linguistic variation.

When it comes to the constraints derived from the observance of dubbing conventions, Chaume (2012) distinguishes six aspects or 'priorities that must be taken into account in a standard dubbing with the concept of ideal receiver in mind' (2012: 15). These priorities include acceptable lip-sync, credible and realistic lines of dialogue, coherence between images and words, loyal translation, clear sound quality and acting standards. When researching this mode of AVT, many scholars have considered the constraints inherent to the dubbing process. As noted above, emphasis has been placed specifically on synchronization, which is defined in its most general sense as a process consisting of 'matching the target language translation and the articulatory and mouth movements of the screen actors and actresses, and ensuring that the utterances and pauses in the translation match those of the source text' (Chaume 2012: 68).

There are three types of synchronization. The first one, 'lip' or 'phonetic synchrony' (a term originally used by Fodor 1976), involves 'adapting the translation to the articulatory movements of the on-screen characters, especially in close-ups and extreme close-ups' (Chaume 2012: 68). The second one, kinesic synchrony, is 'the synchronisation of the translation with the actors' body movements' (*ibid.*: 69), while the third one, isochrony, corresponds to the 'synchronisation of the duration of the translation with the screen characters' utterances' (*ibid.*; drawing from Whitman-Linsen 1992: 28). These three dimensions of synchrony have been discussed at length by Agost 1999; Chaume 2004c, 2012; Chaves 2000, Fodor 1976, Goris 1993, Luyken *et al.* 1991, Mayoral *et al.* 1988, and Whitman-Linsen 1992. As far as lip-synchronization is concerned, Chaume (2012: 74) notes that phonetic equivalence takes precedence over semantic or pragmatic equivalence when dubbing close-up shots: the priority at that point is finding a word that will match the screen actor's mouth movements, rather than a term that has the same or similar meaning to the word being used in the original dialogue. When it comes to kinesic synchrony, body language may accompany the delivery of speech on screen in various ways, thus adding nuances to or complementing the meaning of the characters' lines. Finally, when trying to achieve isochrony, the dubbed dialogue may have to be shortened and certain words may have to be substituted by shorter ones or omitted altogether. Ideally, any changes in semantic meaning derived from efforts to secure maximum synchrony should not affect characterization, i.e. the way in which we perceive characters, or the overall meaning of an audiovisual product. One must bear in mind that certain vocabulary choices could end up having an impact on characterization if, for instance, they carry negative connotations in the target language that were not present in the source text. This may happen, for example, if a character were to use the work 'chick' instead of the more neutral 'girl' to designate a 'young woman' in the translated dialogue. Uttering the word 'chick' could thus be detrimental to the way a given character is perceived by the target language audience.

It should be noted, however, that synchronization is not merely a concern for dubbing; it is also an integral part of original audiovisual products, as part of what is typically referred to as sound post-synchronization. Sound in films is usually not natural, i.e. noises that can be heard in the background are usually recorded after the film has been shot. In most cases, this is done by 'foley artists', i.e. sound recordists who seek to recreate realistic ambient sounds using creative strategies, e.g. recording the sound of sizzling bacon to imitate rain and that of roaring lions for car engines. During the dubbing process, adapters and sound engineers are able to substitute part of the film's 'composite soundtrack', which combines a number of tracks where dialogue, music and sound effects are recorded separately. As Ranzato (2016: 155) explains, dubbing films into another language involves creating 'a new dubbing track' in the target language:

> An important technical element needed to prepare the local version of a film is the music and effects track (M&E track) also known as the international soundtrack, which joins together the separate tracks of sound effects and music. The M&E track contains all sound elements of the film except the dialogue, which comes in a separate track and is substituted by local distributors with a dubbed track in the native language. A skilful post-production handling of the mixing of this track containing music and sound effects with the new track containing the dubbed dialogue is of crucial importance for the creation of a good local version.

Another type of synchronization worth mentioning in relation to dubbing and the challenges it entails is 'character synchrony' (Whitman-Linsen 1992), which pertains to the target audience's expectations as to what the voice of a character should sound like. As Chaume notes, 'in general, a child actor cannot be dubbed by an older male voice; a woman's voice must sound feminine; and the "baddie" must sound grave and sinister' (2012: 69–70). However, abiding by these conventions may not always be practical or feasible in the industry—e.g. local legislation may not allow children to become involved in dubbing work. Very little has been written on this topic although, as elaborated below, Bosseaux's work on performance and characterization in dubbing (2015, 2018) provides insightful views on voice as an integral part of a character's identity and on the importance of choosing appropriate voices.

When discussing synchronization, it is also essential to mention the notion of genre. Indeed, the extent to which synchronization is achieved depends on the genre and type of audiovisual material the translator is working with. Chaume emphasizes that a 'thorough application of all synchronization types is required for the television series genre, although the degree of perfection is not as high as that demanded by the big screen' (2012: 76). Indeed, films require a high quality of all types of synchronization since mismatches could result in a dubbed film getting a negative reception and failing in terms of its box office performance. Cartoons are also 'more flexible because of their young audience, who are more likely to miss such aspects (Chaume 2004c: 46). Finally, it must be emphasized that lip-synchronization constraints are not solely the result of objective medial restrictions, but that they have been enforced by the film industry to impose the linear narrative patterns of Classical Hollywood cinema, as highlighted by Pérez-González (2007), who draws on the work of Mowitt (2004). It would be interesting to see other researchers exploring the interface between synchronization and narrative organization, for instance, along the lines of generic conventions—e.g. differences among cartoons, advertisements, films, television series and documentaries, as it has been commonly argued that different genres demand different levels of synchronization. On the whole, constraints have been discussed at length in the literature, but no alternative approaches have yet been articulated in terms of actual dubbing practice.

Dubbing process

This chapter now turns to consider the role that various agents play in the dubbing production chain, in order to draw attention to the complexity of the dubbing process and the challenges this represents for dubbing research. A dubbed film or TV programme is the result of the work of many people: translators, dialogue writers, dubbing directors, actors and sound engineers. According to Chaume, 'Western European dubbing workflows' follow a specific 'production chain' (2012: 29) that begins when translators are sent a script to produce a rough translation and, sometimes, also a first draft of the target language dialogue. When translating and dialogue writing is done by different professionals, dialogue writers are responsible for the following tasks: synchronizing the text to the screen characters' mouths; adding dubbing symbols, i.e. indications inserted in the translation that are meant to help actors to recreate a number of paralinguistic features of the original actors' voice and performance; segmenting the translation into 'takes'—i.e. units that play an important role in organizing the recording of voice talents and even setting the translators' fees, depending on the country; and making the translated dialogue sound like spontaneous speech. If all these tasks are not carried out by dialogue writers they are taken over by dubbing assistants.

The text then goes back to the dubbing company that is in charge of the artistic and technical side of the dubbed production. It is at this point that the dubbing director sets out to find suitable voice talents—namely dubbing artists or 'dubbers'. This is a particularly important stage in the process for, as Chaume emphasizes, the success of a dubbed product is contingent on the choice of the right voices (2012: 36). Despite the experience that dubbing directors have in making such creative decisions, viewers' reactions can be sometimes unpredictable, and it is not uncommon for them to level criticisms against dubbing voice choices online or in the press. Directors also assist actors throughout the dubbing process, e.g. by giving them acting directions and providing them with information about the overall film plot—it should be noted that voice talents only have access to the loops or takes they are involved in recording at any given point. They record their takes in a dubbing booth, usually working alone or in separate booths, and hence without necessarily engaging in live interaction with other members of the dubbing cast. As a result, the process is a 'continuous series of stops and starts, rather than a theatrical performance' (*ibid.*: 37). Once the recording has been completed, the sound engineers reassemble and edit the tracks that have been dubbed separately. They are responsible for synchronizing the new dubbed tracks with the international track and the original images. The text is then edited and ready to go back to the TV channel or to the commissioning film distributor. Voice talents and sound technicians or engineers thus work under the supervision of dubbing directors, who perform a similar role to that of a film, TV series or theatrical director, and they have the power to modify the initial translator's and dialogue writer's words as they see fit. However, dubbing actors may request to have certain lines of dialogue altered if they feel that they do not fit the style of their acting. Likewise, engineers also have their say when it comes to making changes to the translation. As this account reveals, dubbing involves many different agents who have the capacity to make changes to what the translators and dialogue writers have produced. This situation has an obvious impact on research and scholars ought to consider the whole of the production chain when proceeding to study dubbed products.

There have been a number of studies on the dubbing process in Europe, notably by Chaume (2007, 2012), who presents the chain of production in France, Italy, Germany and Spain, and Sanz Ortega (2015) who delivers a thorough account of the dubbing process in Spain as part of her study of the impact of dubbing on plot and characterization in polyglot films. Although Chaume concedes that the differences between countries are minimal (2012: 29–37), some of them are significant. For instance, France has developed a specific synchronization system called 'the *rhythmo-band* method' (see O'Sullivan and Cornu, Chapter 2, this volume); in Germany, rates are determined based on the number of words to be translated, whereas in Italy they are based on the number of translated reels. It would therefore be interesting to explore the impact that these varying working conditions in the industry have on dubbing products. We are lacking, for instance, studies on the status of translators, with the notable exception of Sanz Ortega (2015), dialogue writers and dubbing artists. We also need to know more about how dubbing is performed by professionals and fans in non-Western markets, particularly in Asia, Africa and Oceania, since different practices or traditions exist according to where dubbing is practised or performed.

Idiosyncrasy of dubbed language

Another prolific research angle in dubbing studies pertains to the idiosyncrasy of dubbed language. Chaume explains that 'what sets the linguistic code apart in audiovisual texts is that in films, television series, cartoons and certain advertisements, we are dealing with a written text that must seem oral and spontaneous' (2012: 100). As can be inferred from this quote, dubbing is considered to be a very specific type of discourse. Dubbed dialogue is a 'combination of linguistic features used both in spoken and written texts' (Chaume 2012: 81, drawing from Remael 2000; Chaume 2004a, Pérez-González 2007), although it can be conceptualized more specifically as a simulation of spontaneous speech (Franzelli 2008: 225) as it mimics speech by using false starts, repetitions, ellipsis, pauses and interruptions. However, this orality is an illusion; it is 'préfabriquée' (Tomaszkiewicz 2001: 381)—as it is 'actually planned, or as we might say feigned, false, prefabricated' (Chaume 2012: 82; see also Baños 2009 and Baños and Chaume 2009). This is because dubbed dialogue has its origin in a script that is 'written to be spoken as if not written' (Gregory and Carroll 1978: 42) or, as Remael (2003: 227) puts it, it is a form of 'secondary speech'.

Researchers have also emphasized that dubbed language has a specific sound to it; it does not sound like original dialogue. It 'does not correspond to the way normal people talk' (Whitman-Linsen 1992: 118) and, in some instances, characters have been described as 'speak[ing] like printing pages' (Assis 2001: 216). The term 'dubbese', first coined by Pavesi (1996), is now widely used to talk about dubbed language in particular as a 'culture-specific linguistic and stylistic model for dubbed texts' that is 'similar, but not equal to real oral discourse and external production oral discourse (i.e. original target-culture films, sitcoms, etc.)' (Chaume 2012: 87). Many other scholars have since followed Pavesi's lead, including Chaume (2004a), Baños (2009), Marzà and Chaume (2009) and Freddi and Pavesi (2009).

According to Chaume, (dubbed) dialogue writing must meet the following three requirements: 'creating the effect of natural, credible and true-to-life dialogue', 'complying with lip-sync' and 'promot[ing] a balance which avoids overacting and underacting when dubbing actors perform the dialogues (i.e. avoiding cacophonies, etc.)' (2012: 88). The fact that these three criteria are not always met, as a result of what Chaume refers to as the burden of dubbing, acknowledges that dubbing 'consolidated at a time when imitating real spoken language was completely unacceptable' (2012: 91). Nevertheless, as Caillé (1960) points out, dubbing should aim to realistically convey the 'content' of the human voice in order for it to be taken seriously by audiences. According to him, lip-synchronization should not be the aspect to consider when dubbing, as this is crucial only when dealing with close-ups; rather, the emphasis should be on recreating the rhythm, sensitivity, anger or tenderness conveyed by the original. Therefore, a dubbed version should endeavour to keep the 'savour' or taste of the original voice, since 'if the voices of actors are judiciously chosen, if the dubbed text is judiciously translated, if it moves or entertains, we have succeeded' (1960: 107, my translation). Caillé thus foregrounds that the choice of dubbing voices may be a crucial factor in terms of a film's audience appreciation.

Voice and prosody

Although there are studies positing that it is important to maintain the qualities of the voices of the original actors (e.g. Mingant 2010, Bosseaux 2015, 2018, and Sanz Ortega 2015) more reception studies are needed to ascertain what the actual impact of voice attribution is on dubbed products. According to Chion, the source of the sound is normally understood to be what is seen on screen—something which dubbing changes drastically. Drawing on Jean Renoir, Chion explains that 'accepting dubbing is like ceasing to believe in the oneness of the individual' (1985: 74, my translation). Indeed, in dubbing, the original body is separated from its original voice, even if dubbed films give the illusion that the voice and the body are working together. As Bosseaux points out, a dubbed voice 'changes pitch, articulation, class, regional context, colloquialisms, individual turns of phrase, timbre, educational levels and other suggestions of cultural positions and capabilities' (2015: 69). It is thus worth wondering to what extent viewers engage differently based on changes in voice.

On the whole, voice has generally been overlooked in dubbing research. A notable exception is Bosseaux (2015, 2018), whose work aims to understand the impact of dubbing on characterization and performance, with a strong focus on voice. Bosseaux explains for instance that, in the French context, it is not uncommon for actors' voices to change from film to film. For instance, the American actress Julianne Moore has had eleven French voices since the beginning of her career. One voice talent can also lend his or her voice to different foreign actors. For instance Isabelle Gardien, one of Moore's French voices, also gives her voice to Cate Blanchett, Emily Watson and Tilda Swinton. It is difficult, however, to comment on the significance of such changes in greater detail, since to this day no comprehensive experimental studies have been carried out to gain a good understanding of how audiences perceive voices, the impact of having an actor dubbed by different dubbing actors, or the effect of having the same voice talent lending his or her voice to numerous foreign actors.

There are also very enlightening studies investigating how geographic and social accents are dealt with in dubbing—all of which reveal the extent to which rendering those in the target language is a thorny endeavour. The collections edited by Armstrong and Federici (2006) and Federici (2009) illustrate the challenges involved in mediating regional, social and idiolectal varieties of language. Examples include the works of Parini (2009), who analyzes how Italian-speaking gangsters or *mafiosi* in American films such as *Goodfellas* (Martin Scorsese 1990) and *Donnie Brasco* (Mike Newell 1997) are sometimes dubbed into Sicilian in the Italian dubbed versions; Taylor (2006), who highlights that the different dialects and sociolects typically associated with the working class used in the films of British director Ken Loach are neutralized in the Italian dubbed versions; and Dore (2009), who discusses the target-culture approach adopted in the dubbing of the first series of *The Simpsons* and, in particular, the choice of Neapolitan and Sicilian to translate sociolects and dialects. Additionally, Mingant (2010) sets out to 'look at the codified relationship between a film and its audience, the issue of voice texture, and how dubbing may result in a loss of narrative and thematic construction' (2010: 713). Mingant emphasizes that dubbing involves a double suspension of disbelief, a pact with viewers whereby the audience 'tacitly accepts' (2010: 713) what is shown to them on-screen at face value. In the dubbed version, this suspension of disbelief is doubled as it 'requires that most of the characters should speak French' (*ibid.*: 715). She explains that 'spectators routinely accept to twice suspend their disbelief, passing over the discrepancy between nationality and language' (*ibid.*: 717). Indeed, if cinema creates an illusion, dubbing creates 'the illusion of an illusion' (Caillé 1960: 108, my translation). Mingant highlights that, when translating accents, there is a common strategy of neutralization in France and 'most Hollywood male actors tend to have the neutral voice of a man in his late thirties' (*ibid.*: 722). She mentions the example of Jean-Pierre Michaël, who gives his voice to Brad Pitt and has also dubbed Keanu Reeves, Michael Fassbender, Jude Law, Christian Bale, Ethan Hawke and Ben Affleck. What this means is that a French voice talent is hired to dub multiple American, English or Spanish actors, which could prove confusing for viewers. The dearth of reception studies about these cases represents an important research niche to be addressed in the future.

Intonation is another aspect that has received very little attention in dubbing, despite the relatively sizeable body of literature addressing the nature of dubbing as prefabricated discourse. Works by scholars such as Chaume (2012), Marzá and Chaume (2009), Whitman-Linsen (1992) and Baños and Chaume (2009) have all commented on the important role of prosody and paralinguistic elements; there remains, however, a lack of actual empirical studies on intonation. A notable exception is the work of Sánchez Mompeán (2012, 2016, forthcoming), the only scholar to have approached the study of prosody, i.e. patterns of stress and intonation, empirically to date. She analyzes paralinguistic as well as prosodic elements (tonicity, tone, tonality, pitch-direction, pitch-range, loudness and tempo) in the original and dubbed versions of a film, in an attempt to demonstrate the importance of pronunciation as a meaning-making strategy. Sánchez Mompeán explains that intonation is more often than not overlooked and emphasizes that dubbed versions are 'often depleted of the connotative richness transmitted through intonation in the original sitcom' (2016: 18). Sánchez Mompeán's work on the importance of intonation demonstrates the importance of investigating not only *what* people say, but also *how* they say it. In dubbing, we are not only dealing with words but also with paralinguistic elements and prosodic features such as intonation, rhythm, timbre and volume. Drawing on Perego and Taylor (2009), Sánchez Mompeán also highlights that the 'limited number of dubbing actors does not suffice to provide a colourful repertoire of tones, necessary to convey all kinds of voices and sound convincing' (2012: 2), a statement reflecting points made earlier in this chapter on the choice of voices.

Finally, in recent years, multilingualism has also become a much discussed topic (e.g. Corrius 2008, Díaz Cintas 2011, Martínez-Sierra *et al.* 2010, and de Higes Andino *et al.* 2013). The role of multilingualism, a rather new development in dubbing research, is elaborated on in the next section, which outlines future trajectories of dubbing scholarship and articulates the new debates with which scholars are engaging.

Future trajectory and new debates

The remainder of this chapter focuses on new research directions and debates that are already attracting significant attention from dubbing specialists.

Fan/fundubbing

To start with, it is important to consider new working practices that are expected to change the way we experience traditional dubbing. First of all, there is the development of fandubbing or fandubs which are 'home-made dubbings of television series, cartoons (particularly of Japanese *anime*) and trailers that have not yet been released in the target language country' (Chaume 2013: 111) and are broadcast on the web. Fandubs and fandubbing are also referred to as 'fundubs' or 'fundubbing' to emphasize the 'witty and humorous nature of this type of home-grown dubbing' (*ibid.*). Apart from Adobe Premiere, Windows Movie Maker is the most commonly used tool in the context of fandubbing: fans working from home translate, lip-sync and revoice the dialogues, record them in a new soundtrack and upload them back on the web. In addition to Windows Movie Maker, fandubbers also rely on Virtual Dub, an open-source freeware video capture and video processing utility that can also be used with Microsoft Windows. As far as commercial tools are concerned, two software applications developed by KIWA—VoiceQ ADR (Audio Dialogue Replacement) and VoiceQ DUB—are also popular. Given the growing ubiquity of fandubbing tools, it will be interesting to gauge the future impact of fandubbing practices on professional dubbing. Could these lead to the enforcement of alternative medial constraints derived from the varying synchronization conventions, across audiovisual genres and national industries? And could viewers' perception of these constraints and viewing habits change over time?

Technologization

Software is also being developed with the capacity to 'transfer[ing] the physical qualities of actors' voices across languages' (Pérez-González 2014: 23). Reel Voice system, developed by Voxworks, is a good example of voice-conversion technology that allows dialogues in the target language to be recorded and manipulated in various ways. Crucially, Reel Voice makes it possible to align the pitch of the target language voice with that of the original screen actor's voice. Another piece of software, Video Rewrite, can be used to 'automate the production of audiovisual footage' (*ibid.*), using existing footage to create a new clip of a 'person mouthing words that she did not speak in the original footage' (*ibid.*: 24). Both software applications may impact on future dubbing practices—although, apart from Chaume's

(2012) and Pérez-González's (2014) general accounts, these technological developments have not been so far explored in depth by dubbing scholars.

In sum, advances in technology, the role of the Internet, social media, and new software are not only changing the way dubbing is conducted, but also the way translation professionals and viewers think about dubbing and watch audiovisual material. However, there would seem to be very little ongoing research addressing these developments, and it is hoped that scholars will fill in this gap in the near future.

Film studies, multimodality and AVT

The first significant turn in dubbing research has been driven by a call from scholars such as Chaume (2004b and 2012) for a more fluid conversation between film studies and AVT by undertaking interdisciplinary research. Chaume's advocacy for a heightened convergence between these two disciplinary areas has been accompanied by a range of pioneering pieces of research on film dialogue, scriptwriting, screenwriting and screenplays by Remael (2000, 2004 and 2008), Cattrysse and Gambier (2008) and, more recently, Martínez-Sierra (2012), Sanz Ortega on polyglot films (2015), and Bosseaux on characterization and performance (2015). Indeed, it is fair to say that film studies scholars do not usually pay attention to the role and impact of translation in the film process, with the notable exception of Egoyan and Balfour (2004). This is a view also shared within film studies. In the early pages of *Cinema Babel*, for example, Nornes (2007: 3–4) reiterates that film studies scholars have for too long failed to consider the implications of translation.

Closely related to this push for interdisciplinarity are multimodal studies, which have been advocated by various scholars (e.g. Bosseaux 2015, Chaume 2012 and Pérez-González 2007). Generally, proponents of the relevance of multimodality to dubbing studies claim that, in order to get a full or better picture of the dubbing process and the impact of dubbing, we need to engage not only with the linguistic mode but also with the verbal and non-verbal (including visual and acoustic) semiotics of translated multimodal texts. Bosseaux (2015) for instance, proposes a multimodal model for the analysis of acoustic and visual aspects of performance in original audiovisual texts and their dubbed counterparts, in an attempt to reveal how dubbing may affect characterization. Through a careful analysis of visual (e.g. body movements, facial expressions), oral (vocal) and linguistic semiotics, Bosseaux demonstrates the extent to which dubbing alters the performance delivered in the original audiovisual text.

Film industry and AVT

Another new trajectory revolves around attempts to explore and develop research on the interface between AVT and the film industry. According to Lambourne (2012), only 0.1–1 per cent of a film's production budget is devoted to AVT translation (including accessibility), which represents a negligible share of the revenue generated by blockbusters worldwide. Drawing on various sources of box office data for the first decade of this century, Romero-Fresco (2013) highlights that:

> Best Picture Oscar-winning Hollywood films made between 2001 and 2011 came from foreign markets. Of this, more than three-quarters (80.4% and 76.3%, respectively) was from foreign countries where these films are subtitled or dubbed. The remaining revenue came from territories where the films are shown in English but where some viewers are likely to watch them with AD and especially SDH.

A paradox thus emerges: if translation generates so much of the revenue of a film, why is it so often left as an 'afterthought rather than a natural component of the film' (Sinha 2004: 174)? This is not only true of subtitling, the focus of Sinha's essay, but also of dubbing, with dubbed versions also 'suffer[ing] from a lack of resources at the post-production stage' (Lebtahi 2004: 409, my translation). Romero-Fresco (2013) explains that in order to make films that are more accessible, filmmakers need to be aware of the impact translation has on a finished product. He goes on to argue that, instead of being confined to the post-production stage, translation needs should be addressed during the pre-production and production stages, as part of what he calls 'accessible filmmaking'. Romero-Fresco (2013) defines this approach as:

> the consideration during the filmmaking process (and through collaboration between the translator and the creative team of the film) of some of the aspects that are required to make a film accessible to viewers in other languages and viewers with hearing or visual loss.

Extending the logic of Romero-Fresco's argument, industrial attention to dubbing should not be restricted to the distribution stage. Instead, it should feature at least during the post-production process, with directors ideally engaging in conversations with translators, as Stanley Kubrick, for instance, used to do (Zanotti, forthcoming). It is promising to see that changes are already taking pace in the film industry, in the form of creative subtitling (McClarty 2012) and 'part-subtitling' (O'Sullivan 2008) in multilingual films, e.g. in blockbusters like *Slumdog Millionaire* (2008) and *Inglourious Basterds* (2009), where 'subtitles take up as much as 70 per cent of the dialogue' (Romero-Fresco 2013).

Just as Romero-Fresco's accessible filmmaking is about encouraging more collaborative work between subtitlers and pre- and post-production teams, Bosseaux's work (2015)—which aims to raise awareness of the impact of dubbing on performance and characterization at a theoretical level—also has practical implications. It draws on the premise that characterization is contingent on the dubbing actors' mastery of their voices—e.g. Daniel Day Lewis in *Lincoln* (2012)—and raises concerns about the feasibility of recreating this important aspect of filmic creativity, given that dubbing crews and particular voice actors work under tight deadlines to come up with successful characterization strategies in dubbed films, in a context that demands a high degree of creativity at the best of times. Speaking about *Inglourious Basterds* (2009) on occasion of its premiere at the Cannes Film Festival, Quentin Tarantino is purported to have said that 'it does not make sense to dub this film' (quoted in Mingant 2010: 713). The fluid interaction between the various languages (English, German, French and Italian) spoken by characters in this film is reported to have driven Tarantino's artistic vision (O'Sullivan 2010, Mingant 2010, Sanz Ortega 2015). How can this creative feature be recreated when, as part of its international distribution process, the film has to be dubbed into French, Italian and Spanish? The reception enjoyed by these dubbed versions may have been warmer, if an effort had been made to contextualize the role of this linguistic interplay in the filmic narrative—e.g. by explaining where the characters come from or what their accents signal. Paying more attention to how films are dubbed would therefore represent the first step towards making them more 'accessible', to use Romero-Fresco's term.

Summary

Reading audiovisual products is a complex task. The visual and acoustic elements combine to generate meaning and there are many modalities to consider. Moreover, meaning is not fixed and can—and often will—vary from one audience to the next. Indeed, when audiovisual products travel in translation it is hard to know how they will be received or perceived, and it would be unrealistic to expect that perception to be the same for different linguacultures.

This chapter has shown that the various agents and technical dimensions involved make dubbing a rich and complex process. One of the most common objections to dubbing is that audiences do not get to hear the original voices. Indeed, as early as 1936, Jean Fayard, editor of the French journal *Pour Vous*, commented that audiences can only 'appreciate Wallace Beery, Katharine Hepburn or Clark Gable if they hear their original voice; their gestures, without the intonations that go with them, lose all their significance' (1936, my translation). What Fayard is highlighting is that, if audiences cannot hear the voices of actors, there will be a mismatch between what is seen and what is heard and the whole of the performance will cease to make sense. That is not to say that voice actors should mimic the intonation of the original, a practice that Chaves (2000) identifies in the Spanish context as 'la curva' and which was used with the first dubbed American films. As Sánchez Mompeán puts it, they should instead 'bear in mind the intended purpose and try to reproduce the same effect by making use of their own patterns, which could indeed coincide in both languages' (2012: 95).

It is fair to say that there are many interesting and valuable studies on dubbing but, as this chapter has tried to show, there is still room for further investigation with a focus on interdisciplinarity, multimodality, and more communication between researchers and practitioners. More importantly, it has been noted that dubbing research has been conducted almost exclusively by European scholars, and hence is running the risk of being viewed as Eurocentric. Since dubbing is used all over the world, knowing more about professional practices in non-Western countries with a dubbing tradition, or where dubbing practices are emerging, would represent an invaluable contribution to the internationalization of dubbing studies.

Further reading

Bosseaux, C. (2015) *Dubbing, Film and Performance: Uncanny Encounters*, Oxford: Peter Lang | *In this book, Bosseaux uses a multimodal, tripartite model that can be used to investigate how visual, acoustic and linguistic elements are combined for the purposes of characterization in original films and their respective dubbed versions.*

Chaume, F. (2012) *Audiovisual Translation: Dubbing*, Manchester: St Jerome Publishing | *This textbook presents an overview of dubbing research and practice. It includes various practical exercises that are useful to yield insights into the practice of dubbing.*

Pérez-González, L. (2014) *Audiovisual Translation: Theories, Methods and Issues*, London & New York: Routledge | *This book maps key developments in AVT with a focus on research models and methodological approaches. It covers all areas of AVT including dubbing and is an excellent companion to Chaume (2012).*

Related topics

2 History of audiovisual translation
5 Voice-over: practice, research and future prospects
6 Subtitling for deaf and hard of hearing audiences: moving forward
11 Film remakes as a form of translation
17 Multimodality and audiovisual translation: cohesion in accessible films
18 Sociolinguistics and linguistic variation in audiovisual translation
19 Gender in audiovisual translation: advocating for gender awareness

References

Agost, R. (1999) *Traducción y doblaje: Palabras, voces e imágenes*, Barcelona: Ariel Practicum.
Armstrong, N. and F. M. Federici (eds) (2006) *Translating Voices, Translating Regions*, Rome: Aracne.
Assis, R. A. (2001) 'Features of Oral and Written Communication in Subtitling', in Y. Gambier (ed.) *(Multi)Media Translation. Concepts, Practices and Research*, Philadelphia & New York: John Benjamins, 213–221.
Ballester, A. (2001) *Traducción y nacionalismo*, Granada: Comares.
Baños, R. (2009) *La oralidad prefabricada en la traducción para el doblaje. Estudio descriptivo-contrastivo del español de dos comedias de situación:* Siete Vidas *y* Friends, Unpublished Doctoral Thesis, University of Granada, Spain.
Baños, R. and F. Chaume (2009) 'Prefabricated Orality: A Challenge in Audiovisual Translation', *Intralinea* 6. Available online: http://www.intralinea.org/specials/article/Prefabricated_Orality [last access 20 December 2017].
Bosseaux, C. (2015) *Dubbing, Film and Performance: Uncanny Encounters*, Oxford: Peter Lang.
Bosseaux, C. (2018) 'The Case of French Dubbing: Deconstructing and Reconstructing Julianne Moore', Special Issue of *Perspectives* DOI: 10.1080/0907676X.2018.1452275.
Caillé, P.-F. (1960). 'Cinéma et traduction: le traducteur devant l'écran', *Babel* 6(3): 103–109.
Cattrysse, P. and Y. Gambier (2008) 'Screenwriting and Translating Screenplays', in J. Díaz Cintas (ed.) *The Didactics of Audiovisual Translation*, Amsterdam & Philadelphia: John Benjamins, 39–55.
Chaume, F. (2004a) *Cine y traducción*, Madrid: Cátedra.
Chaume, F. (2004b) 'Film Studies and Translation Studies: Two Disciplines at Stake in Audiovisual Translation', *Meta* 49(1): 12–24.
Chaume, F. (2004c) 'Synchronization in Dubbing: A Translational Approach', in P. Orero (ed.) *Topics in Audiovisual Translation*, Amsterdam & Philadelphia: John Benjamins, 35–52.
Chaume, F. (2007) 'Dubbing Practices in Europe: Localisation Beats Globalisation', *Linguistica Antverpiensia* 6, Special Issue: 'A Tool for Social Integration? Audiovisual Translation from Different Angles': 203–17.
Chaume, F. (2012) *Audiovisual Translation: Dubbing*, Manchester: St Jerome Publishing.
Chaume, F. (2013) 'The Turn of Audiovisual Translation', *Translation Spaces* 2: 105-123.
Chaves, M. J. (2000) *La Traducción cinematográfica: El doblaje*, Huelva, España: Universidad de Huelva Publicaciones.
Chiaro, D. (2006) 'Verbally Expressed Humour on Screen: Reflections on Translation and Reception', *JoSTrans: The Journal of Specialised Translation* 6. Available online: http://www.jostrans.org/issue06/art_chiaro.php [last access 20 December 2017].
Chion, M. (1985/1994) *Le son au cinéma*, Paris: Éditions de l'Étoile.
Corrius, M. (2008) *Translating Multilingual Audiovisual Texts. Priorities, Restrictions, Theoretical Implications,* Unpublished Doctoral Thesis, Universitat Autònoma de Barcelona, Spain.
Danan, M. (1991) 'Dubbing as an Expression of Nationalism', *Meta* 36(4): 606–614.
De Higes Andino, I., A. M. Prats, J. J. Martínez-Sierra and F. Chaume (2013) 'Subtitling Language Diversity in Spanish Immigration Films', *Meta* 58(1): 134–145.
Díaz Cintas, J. (2004) 'Dubbing or Subtitling: The Eternal Dilemma', *Perspectives* 7(1): 31–40.
Díaz Cintas, J. (2011) 'Dealing with Multilingual Films in Audiovisual Translation', in W. Pöckl, I. Ohnheiser and P. Sandrini (eds) *Translation, Sprachvariation, Mehrsprachigkeit*, Frankfurt: Peter Lang, 215–233.
Di Giovanni, E., F. Diodati and G. Franchini (1994) 'Il problema delle varietà linguistiche nella traduzione filmica', in R. Baccolini, R. M. Bollettieri Bosinelli and L. Gavioli (eds) *Il doppiaggio: trasposizioni linguistiche e culturali*, Bologna: Clueb, 99–104.
Dore, M. (2009) 'Target Language Influence over Source Texts: A Novel Dubbing Approach in The Simpsons, First Series', in F. Federici (ed.) *Translating Voices for Audiovisual*, Rome: Aracne, 134–156.

Egoyan, A. and I. Balfour (2004) (eds) *Subtitles: on the Foreignness of Film*, Cambridge, MA: MIT Press.

Fayard, J. (1936) 'Doublage . . . or not doublage', *Pour Vous* 372, 2 janvier. Available online: http://www.ataa.fr/blog/doublage-or-not-doublage/ [last access 20 December 2017].

Federici, F. (2009) (ed.) *Translating Voices for Audiovisual*, Rome: Aracne.

Fodor, I. (1976) *Film Dubbing: Phonetic, Semiotic, Esthetic and Psychological Aspects*, Hamburg: Helmut Buske.

Franzelli, V. (2008) 'Traduire la parole émotionnelle en sous-titrage: colère et identités', *Etudes de linguistique appliquée* 150: 221–244.

Freddi, M. and M. Pavesi (eds) (2009) *Analysing Audiovisual Dialogue. Linguistic and Translational Insights*, Bologna: Clueb.

Goris, O. (1993) 'The Question of French Dubbing: Towards a Frame for Systematic Investigation', *Target* 5(2): 169–190.

Gottlieb, H. (2005) 'Multidimensional Translation: Semantics Turned Semiotics', in H. Gerzymisch-Arbogast and S. Nauert (eds) *MuTra 2005 Conference Proceedings: Challenges of Multidimensional Translation*. Available online: http://www.euroconferences.info/proceedings/2005_Proceedings/2005_Gottlieb_Henrik.pdf [last access 20 December 2017].

Gregory, M. and S. Carroll (1978) *Language and Situation: Language Varieties and Their Social Contexts*, London: Routledge and Kegan Paul.

Izard, N. (1992) *La traducció cinematogràfica*, Barcelona: Publicacions de la Generalitat de Catalunya.

Karamitroglou, F. (2000) *Towards a Methodology for the Investigation of Norms in Audiovisual Translation*, Amsterdam & Atlanta: Rodopi.

Lambourne, A. (2012) 'Climbing the Production Chain', Paper presented at the *Languages & The Media, 9th International Conference on Language Transfer in Audiovisual Media*, Berlin, 21–23 November.

Lebtahi, Y. (2004) 'Télévision: Les artefacts de la traduction-adaptation', *Meta* 49(2): 401–409.

Luyken, G.-M., T. Herbst, J. Langham-Brown, H. Reid and H. Spinhof (1991) *Overcoming Language Barriers in Television. Dubbing and Subtitling for the European Audience*, Manchester: The European Institute for the Media.

Martínez-Sierra, J. J. (2008) *Humor y traducción. Los Simpson cruzan la frontera*, Castellón de la Plana: Servei de Publicacions de la Universitat Jaume I.

Martínez-Sierra, J. J. (2012) 'On the Relevance of Script Writing Basics in Audiovisual Translation Practice and Training', *Cadernos de Tradução* 29(1): 145–163.

Martínez-Sierra, J. J., J. L. Martí, I. de Higes Andino, A. M. Prats and F. Chaume (2010) 'Linguistic Diversity in Spanish Immigration Films. A Translational Approach', in V. Berger and M. Komori (eds) *Polyglot Cinema: Migration and Transcultural Narration in France, Italy, Portugal and Spain*, Vienna: LIT, 15–31.

Marzà, A. and F. Chaume (2009) 'The Language of Dubbing: Present Facts and Future Perspectives', in M. Freddi and M. Pavesi (eds) *Analysing Audiovisual Dialogue. Linguistic and Translational Insights*, Bologna: Clueb, 31–40.

Mayoral, R., D. Kelly and N. Gallardo (1988) 'Concept of Constrained Translation. Non-linguistic Perspectives of Translation', *Meta* 33: 356–367.

McClarty, R. (2012) 'Towards a Multidisciplinary Approach in Creative Subtitling', *MonTI* 4: 133–155.

Merino, R., J. M. Santamaría and E. Pajares (eds) (2005) *Trasvases culturales: Literatura, cine, traducción 4*, Vitoria: Universidad del País Vasco.

Mingant, N. (2010) 'Tarantino's "Inglourious Basterds": A Blueprint for Dubbing Translators?', *Meta* 55(4): 712–731.

Mowitt, J. (2004) 'The Hollywood Sound Tract', in A. Egoyan and I. Balfour (eds) *Subtitles. On the Foreignness of Film*, Cambridge, Mass. & London: The MIT Press, 382–401.

Nornes, A. M. (2007) *Cinema Babel*, Minneapolis, London: University of Minnesota Press.

O'Sullivan, C. (2008) 'Multilingualism at the Multiplex: A New Audience for Screen Translation?', *Linguistica Antverspiensia* 6: 81–97.

O'Sullivan, C. (2010) 'Tarantino on Language and Translation', MA Translation Studies News Blog, 21 February. Available online: http://matsnews.blogspot.co.uk/2010/02/tarantino-onlanguage-and-translation.html [last access 20 December 2017].

Parini, I. (2009) 'The Transposition of Italian American in Italian Dubbing', in F. Federici (ed.) *Translating Regionalised Voices in Audiovisuals*, Rome: Aracne, 157–178.

Pavesi, M. (1996) 'L'allocuzione nel doppiaggio dall'inglese all'italiano', in C. Heiss and R. M. Bollettieri Bosinelli (eds) *Traduzione multimediale per il cinema, la televisione e la scena*, Bologna: CLUEB, 117–130.

Pavesi, M. (2009) 'Dubbing English into Italian: A Closer Look at the Translation of Spoken Language', in J. Díaz Cintas (ed.) *New Trends in Audiovisual Translation*, Bristol: Multilingual Matters, 197–209.

Perego, E. and J. Taylor (2009) 'An Analysis of the Language of Original and Translated Film: Dubbing into English', in M. Freddi and M. Pavesi (eds) *Analysing Audiovisual Dialogue. Linguistic and Translational Insights*, Bologna: Clueb, 57–74.

Pérez-González, L. (2007) 'Appraising Dubbed Conversation. Systemic Functional Insights into the Construal of Naturalness in Translated Film Dialogue', *The Translator* 13(1): 1–38.

Pérez-González, L. (2014) *Audiovisual Translation: Theories, Methods and Issues*, London & New York: Routledge.

Ranzato, I. (2011) 'Translating Woody Allen into Italian: Creativity in Dubbing', *JoSTrans: The Journal of Specialised Translation* 15: 121–141. Available online: http://www.jostrans.org/issue15/art_ranzato.pdf [last access 20 December 2017].

Ranzato, I. (2012) 'Gayspeak and Gay Subjects in Audiovisual Translation: Strategies in Italian Dubbing', *Meta* 57(2): 369–384.

Ranzato, I. (2016) *Translating Culture Specific References on Television: The Case of Dubbing*, New York & London: Routledge.

Remael, A. (2000) *A Polysystem Approach to British New Wave Film Adaptation, Screen Writing and Dialogue*, Unpublished Doctoral Thesis, Leuven: Katholieke Universiteit Leuven.

Remael, A. (2003) 'Mainstream Narrative Film Dialogue and Subtitling', in Y. Gambier (ed.) *The Translator* 9(2): 225–245.

Remael, A. (2004) 'A Place for Film Dialogue Analysis in Subtitling Courses', in P. Orero (ed.) *Topics in Audiovisual Translation*, Amsterdam & Philadelphia: John Benjamins, 103–126.

Remael, A. (2008) 'Screenwriting, Scripted and Unscripted Language. What Do Subtitlers Need to Know?', in J. Díaz Cintas (ed.) *The Didactics of Audiovisual Translation*, Amsterdam & Philadelphia: John Benjamins, 57–67.

Richart Marset, M. (2012) *Ideología y traducción. Por un análisis genético del doblaje*, Madrid: Biblioteca Nueva.

Romero-Fresco, Pablo (2013) 'Accessible Filmmaking: Joining the Dots between Audiovisual Translation, Accessibility and Filmmaking', *JoSTrans: The Journal of Specialised Translation* 20: 201–223. Available online: http://www.jostrans.org/issue20/art_romero.pdf [last access 20 December 2017].

Sánchez Mompeán, S. (2012) *The Intonation of Dubbed Dialogue: A Corpus-based Study on the Naturalness of Tonal Patterns in the Spanish Version of* How I Met your Mother, Unpublished MA dissertation, University of Roehampton, UK.

Sánchez Mompeán, S. (2016) '"It's not What They Said; It's How They Said It": A Corpus-based Study on the Translation of Intonation for Dubbing', in A. M. Rojo López and N. Campos Plaza (eds) *Interdisciplinarity in Translation Studies. Theoretical Models, Creative Approaches and Applied Methods*. Bern: Peter Lang: 259–276.

Sánchez Mompeán, S. (forthcoming) 'More than Words Can Say: Exploring Prosodic Variation in Dubbing', in I. Ranzato and S. Zanotti (eds) *Reassessing Dubbing: Historical Approaches and Current Trends*, Amsterdam & Philadelphia: John Benjamins.

Sanz Ortega, E. (2015) *Beyond Monolingualism: A Descriptive and Multimodal Methodology for the Dubbing of Polyglot Films*, Unpublished Doctoral Thesis, University of Edinburgh, UK.

Sinha, A. (2004) 'The Use and Abuse of Subtitles', in A. Egoyan and I. Balfour (eds) *Subtitles: On the Foreignness of Film*, Cambridge, MA: MIT Press, 171–190.
Taylor, C. (2006) 'The Translation of Regional Variety in the Films of Ken Loach', in N. Armstrong and F. M. Federici (eds) *Translating Voices, Translating Regions*, London: Aracne, 37–52.
Tomaszkiewicz, T. (2001) 'La structure des dialogues filmiques: Consequences pour le sous-titrage', in M. Ballard (ed.) *Oralité et Traduction*, Arras: PU, 281–399.
Vandaele, J. (2002) '(Re-)Constructing Humour: Meanings and Means', *The Translator* 8(2): 149–72.
Whitman-Linsen, C. (1992) *Through the Dubbing Glass*, Frankfurt: Peter Lang.
Zabalbeascoa, P. (1996a) 'Translating Jokes for Dubbed Television Situation Comedies', *The Translator* 2(2): 252–257.
Zabalbeascoa, P. (1996b) 'La traducción de la comedia televisiva: implicaciones teóricas', in J. M. Bravo and P. Fernández (eds) *A Spectrum of Translation Studies*, Valladolid: Universidad de Valladolid, 173–201.
Zabalbeascoa, P. (2005) 'Humour and Translation. An Interdiscipline', *Humour* 18(2): 185–207.
Zanotti, S. (forthcoming) '(Dis)embodied Voices in Dubbed Auteur Films: An Archival Perspective', in I. Ranzato and S. Zanotti (eds) *Reassessing Dubbing: Historical Approaches and Current Trends*, Amsterdam & Philadelphia: John Benjamins.

Filmography

Donnie Brasco (1997) Mike Newell. IMDb entry: http://www.imdb.com/title/tt0119008/?ref_=fn_al_tt_1
Goodfellas (1990) Martin Scorcese. IMDb entry: http://www.imdb.com/title/tt0099685/?ref_=fn_al_tt_1
Inglourious Basterds (2009) Quentin Tarantino. IMDb entry: http://www.imdb.com/title/tt0361748/?ref_=fn_al_tt_1
Lincoln (2012) Steven Spielberg. IMDb entry: http://www.imdb.com/title/tt0443272/?ref_=fn_al_tt_1
Slumdog Millionaire (2008) Danny Boyle. IMDb entry: http://www.imdb.com/title/tt1010048/?ref_=nv_sr_1

Sitography

Virtual Dub: http://www.virtualdub.org/index.html [last access 20 December 2017].
VoiceQ ADR and DUB: https://www.voiceq.com/ [last access 20 December 2017].
Windows Movie Maker: http://www.windows-movie-maker.org/ [last access 20 December 2017].

5
Voice-over
Practice, research and future prospects

Anna Matamala

Introduction

Dubbing and subtitling have been the object of extensive research in audiovisual translation (AVT) (Chaume 2012, Díaz Cintas and Remael 2007) due to the popularity of these modalities in many countries. However, there is a third audiovisual transfer mode that has not been analyzed in such detail, but which nonetheless is extensively used in many audiovisual markets: voice-over. Sometimes termed the 'ugly duckling' of audiovisual translation (Orero 2006b), a 'damsel in distress' (Wozniak 2012: 211) or even an 'orphan child' (Bogucki 2013: 20), many academic and non-academic voices have drawn attention to the limitations of voice-over (Glaser 1991, Tomaszkiewicz 2006, Garcarz 2007), and have accounted for the fact that it continues to be used in some countries in terms of the low costs that it incurs. However, voice-over is a reality accepted by many audiences, and its academic study has increasingly captured the attention of translation scholars.

This chapter aims to define and categorize different varieties of voice-over, and see how this transfer mode is used in both fictional and non-fictional audiovisual genres. Beyond the realm of practice, attention will be paid to research issues in voice-over, focusing on synchronization constraints, aspects of linguistic and cultural mediation, manipulation and translator's visibility, the technologization of voice-over practices, voice-over training and reception research.

Defining voice-over

The term 'voice-over' is used in translation studies, on the one hand, and film studies and the film industry, on the other (Franco 2001a). Within the field of translation studies, Díaz Cintas and Orero (2006: 477) define voice-over as a 'technique in which a voice offering a translation in a given target language (TL) is heard simultaneously on top of the source language (SL) voice.' The authors also indicate that 'the volume [of the original programme] is reduced to a low level that can still be heard in the background when the translation is being read' (*ibid.*). They also highlight that it is 'common practice to allow the viewer to hear the original speech in the foreign language at the onset of the speech and to reduce subsequently the volume of the original so that the translated speech can be inserted' (*ibid.*). This translation, according to the same authors, 'usually finishes several seconds before the foreign language speech does, the sound of the original is raised again to a normal volume and the viewer can hear once more the original speech' (*ibid.*).

On the other hand, within the field of film studies, Kuhn and Westwell (2012: 446–447) define voice-over quite differently, as the 'voice of an offscreen narrator or a voice heard but not belonging to any character actually talking on screen' (*ibid.*). They indicate that in 'newsreels and documentary films a voice over will most commonly consist of a commentator (who may occasionally appear intermittently on screen) who provides third-person overview that orientates the viewer to what they are seeing (this kind of voice over is sometimes referred to as voice-of-God narration)' (*ibid.*). As for fiction films, according to the same authors, 'voice overs can take various forms', and may be used to 'convey the interior thoughts of a character seen on screen' (*ibid.*). They also point out that 'DVD releases are now often made available with directors, other creative players, or film scholars, providing a voice over that comments on the onscreen action' (*ibid.*). 'Voice-over' is also used in the expression 'voice-over artists', which is widely used in the industry to refer to voice talents or voice actors reading commercials, audiobooks or dubbing movies, to give but three examples.

Voice-over vis-à-vis other audiovisual transfer modes

Voice-over has been conceptualized as a type of revoicing (Luyken *et al.* 1991: 80, Chaume 2004: 35), a type of dubbing (Dries 1995: 309), and even a type of interpreting (Gambier 1996: 9). This chapter endorses Pérez-González's view (2014: 19) that whilst 'technically speaking, voice-over and lip-synchronized dubbing are types of revoicing, they are often dealt with and described separately.'

Voice-over and simultaneous interpreting share the use of a superimposed voice to deliver the translation on top of its original counterpart. However, interpreting is generally produced live, without drawing on a written translation of the original content. By contrast, in voice-over, the translator works from pre-recorded material to create a written translation that is then generally read aloud by a voice talent. It must be acknowledged, though, that voice-over may have its origins in the simultaneous interpreting of films. As explained by Franco *et al.* (2010: 48), interpreters were hired to translate Western films in closed-door screenings and also in open film festivals in the former Soviet Union. Later on, the interpreters' voices were recorded on tapes, and this is how voice-over was probably born. In fact, Burak (2011) suggests that pirate voice-over translation began to sweep the former Soviet Union when Russian *nouveau riches* hired them to watch the latest American movies. Translators generally worked at home and recorded their voice-over translations simultaneously while listening to the original soundtrack. One of the most famous translators was Andrewy Gavrilov, and this is probably why voice-over is often known in Russia as Gavrilov translation (Burak 2011). This Gavrilov translation is said to have inspired voice-over in Poland (Holobut 2014), as will be elaborated below. However, other sources point towards commentators in silent films (Hendrykowski 1984), newsreels (Garcarz 2007) or even subtitling (Joanna Klimkiewicz, personal communication, in Szarkowska 2009) as the origins of the modality. Indeed, voice-over has been linked to subtitling by researchers such as Espasa (2004) in that both transfer modes imply a co-presence of two linguistic codes (the original and the translation) and in many language pairs they both entail condensing the original dialogues.

Voice-over and dubbing, on the other hand, share the fact that they are oral renderings of audiovisual content that has been prepared in advance. However, synchronization constraints differ in each case: in dubbing the translation has the same duration as (isochrony) and matches the lip movements of (lip synchronization) the original dialogue, whilst in voice-over this is not the case, as will be explained below. It is worth noting at this point that voice-over has been referred to by some authors as 'partial dubbing' or 'half-dubbing'. Gambier (2004), for example, considers 'demi-doublage' (French for 'half-dubbing') a synonym for voice-over, whereas Chaume (2013: 108) considers half-dubbing a 'type of voice-over.' According to Chaume (2013: 108), in half-dubbing 'a male reader reads the leading male's dialogue in a film or series, a female reader reads the leading female's dialogues, and sometimes a third voice reads the dialogues of other main characters in the film.' Chaume explains that '[a]ttempts have been made to insert these target language dialogues into silences in the original film', but these have just been 'little more than experiments … and have had no significant impact.' Chaume's approach to half-dubbing has probably been inspired by Hendrickx's short tentative paper on 'partial dubbing' (also termed by the author 'concise synchronization'), where he proposes to 'make full use of the silent passages in the original dialogues', and suggests that the dialogue 'may possibly even be replaced—partly or entirely—by a (shorter) description of what is going on, or it may simply be reproduced in indirect speech' (Hendrickx 1984: 218). Hendrickx considers partial dubbing an easy and economical transfer mode that would involve 'adding to the original soundtrack a spoken text giving the necessary information in the target language without providing a full translation of the dialogue' (*ibid*: 217). However, Hendrickx acknowledges his proposal is subject to further testing, because many questions pertaining to the number of actors or the intonation to be used remain unanswered.

A trickier relationship is that of voice-over with two additional transfer modes that are usually bundled together under the category 'revoicing', i.e. narration and (free) commentary, which share the absence of lip synchronization (Pönniö 1995). Narration has been defined as 'simply a kind of voice-over, where the translation has been summarized' (Chaume 2012: 3) or as 'an extended voice-over' used in monologues (Luyken *et al.* 1991: 80), in contrast to voice-over, which is generally used for spontaneous speech (Gambier 1996). On the other hand, free commentary has been defined as 'a variation of voice-over and dubbing, where a comedian manipulates the translation for humoristic purposes and adds jokes or funny comments' (Chaume 2012: 4), generally in comedy or sports programmes in Europe (Chaume 2013: 110). Another definition of free commentary has been provided by Luyken *et al.* (1991: 80), who consider it as a means of adapting a programme for a new audience, totally replacing the original speech and only keeping synchronization with the image (Laine 1996). However, some authors have noticed that linking narration and free commentary to voice-over (either as a type of, or as a variation of the latter) can be confusing. First of all, voice-over in translation studies implies two superimposed voices, whilst very often in narration and in free commentary the original soundtrack disappears and only the target language voice is heard (Aleksonyte 1999: 6, Chaume 2013: 108). Secondly, 'narration' and 'commentary' seem more adequate terms to be used in film studies when referring to 'speech sequences by invisible speakers over programme images' (Franco *et al.* 2010: 40), rather than terms to be used when describing audiovisual transfer modes. This is why Franco *et al.* (2010) have proposed a new term, 'off-screen dubbing', to define a type of revoicing in which a translating voice replaces an off-screen voice from the original soundtrack. This off-screen dubbing—similarly to other types of AVT—can be either a faithful or a free version of the original, depending on the client's requirements, and often coexists with voice-over in non-fictional genres. For instance, it is often the case that, in a documentary, off-screen dubbing is used for the narrator (meaning that only the target language voice, rather than the original narrator, is heard), while voice-over is used to designate the interviewees' and other forms of spontaneous speech (meaning both voices overlap).

Voice-over types

Apart from situating voice-over within the taxonomy of audiovisual transfer modes and exploring its relationship with other transfer modes, some internal categorizations of this modality have been proposed.

Orero (2004) and Franco *et al.* (2010) examine how voice-over fits within the process of media content assembly and distinguish between voice-over for production and voice-over for post-production, depending on whether translators work from edited or non-edited content. In other words, whether they are given excerpts of audiovisual content that have not yet been converted into a full programme (voice-over for production) or they are given a fully-fledged audiovisual programme (voice-over for post-production). In the first scenario, the translator is often sent excerpts of audiovisual content (for instance, interviews), generally without a script or transcript, and has to deliver a written translation. Then, the excerpts are shaped into a full programme, and the relevant translation segments are voiced. In the second scenario, a finished product (for instance, a documentary), generally with a post-production script, is provided to the translator, who delivers a written document that will be used for the final recording in the target language. Although the final result in both scenarios is the same, a translation for voice-over, the process is different and has its own specificities in each of these varieties.

Other categorizations have been put forward in the literature. Grigaraviciute and Gottlieb (1999: 44) differentiate between first and third-person voice-over, the former being a direct voice-over and the latter a reported voice-over. The standard practice is to use first-person voice-over, meaning that the translation uses the same pronoun as the speakers in the original programme. For instance, if the speaker says 'I think . . .', the translation will keep the first person in the target language, making the translator more invisible. In a third-person or reported voice-over, the role of the mediator is more visible as the words of the speaker are reported in the third person. Examples of third-person voice-over have been provided by Franco (2000a: 238), who examines German versions of Brazilian documentaries in which the interviewees' answers are frequently converted into indirect speech.

The number of voices featuring in the translated version could be another categorization criterion, as it enables scholars to differentiate between single-voice voice-over and multiple-voice voice-over. An instance of the former would be television voice-overs in Poland, where only one voice is used for all characters. An example of the latter would be documentaries voiced-over in Spain, where various voices, both male and female, are used to revoice the original speakers. And also the Lithuanian voice-over of TV films (Grigaraviciute and Gottlieb 1999), in which the common patterns is to use two actors, a male and a female for all male and female actors, respectively.

Voice-over main features

Our initial definition of voice-over outlined its most distinctive feature: the presence of a translating voice overlapping with a translated voice; in other words, a voice delivering a translation in overlap with the original voice. However, voice-over presents other defining features.

First of all, voice-over involves the observance of various types of synchronies. Inspired by existing classifications in dubbing (Chaume 2004), Orero (2006a) and Franco *et al.* (2010) differentiate four types of synchronies:

- 'Voice-over isochrony' designates the constraining effect that the length of the original speech has on that of the translated text—given that the translation usually begins some words after the original utterance and finishes some words before the latter ends. This allows the original words at the onset and at the end of each voice-over utterance to be heard, in an attempt to arguably enhance authenticity. In some instances, especially in fictional genres with fast-paced dialogues, reaching voice-over isochrony is not possible, and the original and the translation may finish approximately at the same time. It can also occur that the translation finishes later. In order to account for the various scenarios, Sepielak (2016a) proposes to differentiate between full isochrony (when at least one word is heard at the beginning and at the end of the utterance), initial isochrony (where at least one word is audible only at the beginning), and final isochrony (where at least one word is heard only at the end of the utterance).
- 'Literal synchrony' is used by authors such as Luyken *et al.* (1991: 141), who favour literal translation when the original voice is heard without any overlapping from the voice providing the translation. By doing so, members of the audience who understand the language can relate the translation to the original (Kauffmann 2004). Voice-over professionals, however, consider that this strategy should only be deployed when a literal transfer would not result in an unnatural translation.
- 'Kinetic synchrony' refers to translations that are synchronized with the body language of the characters on screen. This means that when a linguistic expression is linked to a certain gesture made by one of the characters, the translation should match this gesture to avoid inconsistencies between the verbal and the visual.
- Finally, 'action synchrony' involves the synchronization of the translation with the images on screen. The order of the elements in a sentence may differ in the original and in the translation, whether because of systemic differences between languages or because of the rephrasing that voice-over isochrony often entails. Still, words should be synchronized with the visuals they correspond to, thus avoiding a mismatch between what the translation states and what audiences see on screen.

A key aspect of voice-over is that, contrary to the norm in dubbing, lip synchronization is not retained. While dubbing generates the illusion that the screen actors speak the language of the translation, in voice-over the viewer is constantly confronted with a version in which original and translation coexist. A practical consequence is that voice-over is cheaper and faster to produce.

Secondly, voice-over generally implies the preparation of a written translation which is delivered orally in a pre-recorded format. Typically, translators are provided with an audiovisual file (with or without a script or transcript) and are required to deliver a written translation, following the formatting requirements of the client. In some instances it is expected that the translator will provide a perfectly synchronized translation, ready to be recorded. In other cases, an editor revises the translation to check whether it meets the required standards (Kotelecka 2006, Szarkowska 2009: 190). The last steps in the production of voiced-over content are the recording of the translated version by a voice-over narrator or various voice talents, and the final revision of the audiovisual output.

In some cases hybrid scenarios can be observed. For instance, the voice-over of interview excerpts can sometimes be outsourced to freelance interpreters working from home with their own recording software. In these scenarios they are not requested to provide the commissioner with a written transcript of the translated version, but with a sound file where the voice-over synchronies have been recorded. In order to produce that deliverable, interpreters usually watch the original a few times, take notes when necessary, and finally record a voice-over version that comes to an end before that of its original counterpart. This process does not unfold as per the voice-over workflow described above, and it does not fully match standard interpreting practices either (insofar as, in this particular scenario, the interpreter is given the chance to watch the video files a number of times). It should be noted, however, that the final output complies with voice-over conventions in terms of synchrony.

Thirdly, the coexistence of the original and the target language, the interplay of the written translation with its oral delivery, the synchronization constraints as well as the involvement of various agents in the process (from the translator to the voice talent) affect the text, which suffers various transformations along the process. From a linguistic point of view, a key feature is that the original text is often rephrased to fit in the space available, but also to make it more comprehensible to the audience. For instance, when the original version contains spontaneous colloquial speech characterized by hesitations, false starts, repetitions and discourse markers, the original is reformulated and many spontaneous features disappear for the sake of comprehensibility.

Finally, the final output is generally delivered by one or more voices, either male or female, depending on the country's tradition, very often with a non-emphatic intonation. For instance, in Poland, filmic dialogue will always be read by a man, although in non-fictional genres both male and female voices can be heard, with a preference for female voice artists in cooking programmes and nature documentaries in some channels (Szarkowska 2009: 189). The intonation in Poland will always be flat, as discreet as possible so that the audience forgets the existence of the voice-over (Wozniak 2012: 215). In fact, as explained by Szarkowska (2009: 187), the term used by professional translators in Poland for voice-over is *szeptanka*, which literally means 'whispering.' Bogucki (2013: 20), on the other hand, notes that some professionals restrict the term 'voice-over' to non-fictional genres and prefer 'lectoring' to describe the practice in fiction films. By contrast, in countries such as Belarus, Bulgaria and the Ukraine, four or five actors imitating the emotions in the original version, providing a more emphatic intonation of voice-over for fictional genres, are used (Wozniak 2012: 215). Different voice talents with a non-emphatic pronunciation are also used in documentaries voiced-over in Spain, although prosody in reality shows is more and more emphatic.

Inextricably connected with delivery is the issue of accents in voice-over. Accents are generally standard, although foreign accents have been used in certain productions, especially in the UK (Fawcett 1996, Franco *et al.* 2010: 79). Díaz Cintas and Orero (2006: 478) state that sometimes, 'if the person on screen speaks Spanish, the voice-over narrator will read the translation in English with a clear foreign accent, showing characteristic inflexions that are associated with a Hispanic person speaking English.' However, they acknowledge that this practice 'lends itself to debate', as it could 'be interpreted as a sign of the inability of foreign people to speak English correctly' (*ibid.*: 478).

Voice-over practice

Although voice-over has also been used in radio broadcasting (Orero 2009: 133), the focus of this chapter is audiovisual content, where voice-over is deployed to mediate both fictional and non-fictional content. Non-fictional genres include documentaries, interviews, commercials, among others, whilst fictional genres encompass films, TV series, or animation series, to mention a few examples. Each of these genres poses specific challenges that have been addressed in the literature. Orero (2004) discusses the difficulties of interview voice-over, whilst Matamala (2009a, 2009b, 2010), Franco (2000a) and Espasa (2004) have explored in some depth the challenges of translating documentaries using voice-over. Díaz-Vegas (2012) and Permanyer (2012), for their part, approach reality shows, and Matamala (2005) and Kotelecka (2006) deal with professional aspects of voice-over in Catalonia and Poland, respectively, and draw a picture of diverging workflows and processes.

Whether voice-over is used to translate fictional or non-fictional audiovisual content depends on each country's tradition. Voice-over in fiction is limited to certain Eastern European countries such as Poland (on TV), Bulgaria, Russia and other former Soviet Union countries (Estonia, Latvia, Belarus, Lithuania) (Chaume 2013: 108). Voice-over in non-fiction is more widely used and encompasses not only voice-over countries but also traditionally dubbing and subtitling countries, as elaborated below:

- In Poland voice-over is used for both fictional and non-fictional content (Bogucki 2010) on television, although the new affordances of digitization allow some channels to choose between subtitling and voice-over. Szarkowska and Laskowska (2015) provide a summary of various studies on AVT trends in Poland, which show a preference for voice-over over subtitling. The results of a Canal Plus study undertaken in the 1990s showed that 52.2% of Poles preferred voice-over, with 8.1% of them preferring subtitles (Bogucki 2013). A BBC survey in the early 2000s revealed that 52% were in favour of voice-over, as opposed to 4.5% who were more partial to subtitles. A study about the Polish public broadcaster TVP found that 45% respondents were in favour of voice-over, with 45% in favour of dubbing and 4% opting for subtitling. A more recent poll by the same authors, however, hints at the emergence of new habits and views, with a strong preference for subtitles instead of voice-over (77.25% versus 6.88%, respectively)—thus challenging the widely held assumption that Poland is a stronghold of voice-over.
- In the Ukraine, voice-over translation is generally used for television broadcasting, except in programmes of Russian origin, which are either subtitled or left untranslated. Dubbing, though, is used for cinema releases, and DVDs usually contain Russian dubbing and Ukrainian subtitling (Stashkiv 2015). In Russia, voice-over is generally used for both fiction and non-fiction on television, cinema and DVDs, except for cinema films that may be dubbed (Burak 2011). Mixed scenarios can also be found: for instance, Krasovska (2004) explains that Latvian voice-over and Russian subtitles are combined in Latvian commercial TV channels.
- Older variations in voice-over practice have been documented in subtitling regions such as Scandinavia—as illustrated, for example, by the Swedish television versions of *Pippi Longstocking* and *Emil from Lönnenberg* (now available on DVD with dubbing). Both productions were broadcast on Danish television with a voice-over where the 'translating voice' superimposed on the original track reported what was said, but also provided other cues that were not obvious from the picture (Pedersen 2010, Olaf Loom 2011).
- In Spain, traditionally a dubbing country, documentaries (Matamala 2009a) are generally translated using a combination of voice-over rendering the interviewee's words and off-screen dubbing to convey the narrator's words. Each voice in the original is voiced-over by a different actor of the same gender. Voice-over is also used in reality

shows and in foreign language excerpts inserted in news programmes—although some TV news programmes, e.g. those aired by the public Catalan TV broadcaster—have recently moved to subtitling in the latter case.
- In subtitling countries such as Croatia, voice-over can also be combined with subtitling in non-fictional contents (K. Nikolic, personal communication, 07 September 2015).

Technological developments are likely to result in further variety and continue to shape viewers' preferences in different ways. For instance in Poland, young audiences may be moving towards subtitling (Bogucki 2010: 8) or even dubbing, although voice-over remains the preferred option in translated TV programmes (Chaume 2012). In dubbing countries, the voice-over market is increasing, as popular hybrid genres such as reality shows are generally voiced-over. Finally, there is an increasing number of advertisements and infomercials shown in television shopping channels that are translated using voice-over (Chaume 2013: 118). All in all, firm boundaries between clearly delineated camps may be a thing of the past, since technologies seem to move towards a greater empowerment of audiences, who will hopefully be able to choose the audiovisual transfer mode that is more suited to their personal needs—irrespective of what the national traditions and collective preferences are.

Research issues in voice-over

In what follows, this chapter surveys a range of issues related to voice-over that have been addressed from a research perspective. They have been grouped in seven categories, although some studies could be included in more than one sub-section.

Translation and synchronization techniques

In many language pairs, translating for voice-over implies condensing the original text, omitting or rephrasing information. Various researchers have dealt with this topic in fictional genres, often comparing voice-over with other transfer modes. For instance, Aleksonyte (1999) contrasts the level of reduction in the Lithuanian voice-over of the Danish Films *Breaking the Waves* (10% of information lost) against its Danish subtitling (14% of information lost). Similarly, Grigaraviciute and Gottlieb (1999: 71) analyze the Lithuanian voicing over of the Danish production *Charlot & Charlotte* in terms of amount of information and semantic content transmitted. Their research shows that full translation is prevalent (71%) in voice-over, followed by reduction (19%) and omission (10%).

Working with the English-Polish language pair, Wozniak (2012) studies the condensation of the original texts in the voice-over of *Star Trek*, as well as the degree of audibility of the original soundtrack, combining the analysis of translation strategies and synchronization strategies. Wozniak proposes to transform the voice-over of feature films into a voice-in-between, to allow for a better access to the original soundtrack and to information in the translation. This would mean that the voice providing the translation would not be over the original but would be placed between different utterances. In Wozniak's (2012: 216) words, 'the principle of superimposition should be replaced with that of juxtaposition.'

Also dealing with Polish fictional genres, Sepielak and Matamala (2014) analyze film voice-overs in terms of synchrony and translation strategies. They observe that elements are very often condensed or omitted for the sake of voice-over isochrony, and this type of synchrony cannot be kept in very short utterances or fast-paced dialogues, with anticipation emerging as a useful strategy. Their corpus shows no evidence of recurrent translation strategies being deployed to reach literal synchrony; on a related note, only a few excerpts that illustrate kinetic synchrony are found in the corpus.

A more in-depth analysis of the topic is found in Sepielak (2014, 2016a), who focuses on both translation and synchronization techniques in voiced-over multilingual feature movies in Polish. Sepielak (2014) applies Gottlieb's (1997) translation techniques to a corpus of four multilingual films voiced-over from English into Polish. Sepielak's aim is to research how the multilingual elements in the corpus are transferred in the voiced-over version. Sepielak's analysis shows that transfer, exposition, deletion and imitation are the most frequently used translation techniques. However, the researcher considers that imitation and exposition are the ones that most underline the multilingual aspect of the film. As indicated by Sepielak (2014: 269), imitation 'is based on the assumption that spectators understand an L3 element which is simply included in the translated version and read out by the voice-artist.' On the other hand, 'exposition', a term proposed by herself, refers to a special case of omission in which the multilingual element is not transferred into the target language but is still audible to the audience through the original soundtrack. In Sepielak's words (2014: 269), exposition 'assumes that spectators base their comprehension not only on the translated soundtrack but also on the original one.' Her analysis is interesting in that it views the translation as part of a wide semiotic process that exceeds linguistic transfer. In other words, she does not only study how a unit in a source language is translated into the target language (Polish in this case) but also analyzes how the original soundtrack contributes to the process of meaning-making. In Sepielak (2016a), this scholar goes a step further and, using the same corpus, links the translation techniques identified in previous work to voice-over synchronization strategies. She analyzes which synchrony types are kept, and what translation techniques are used to that end.

Linguistic aspects of voice-over

The language features of voice-over have also attracted the attention of researchers, who have sometimes criticized the standardization that voice-over entails. Drawing on a set of documentaries voiced-over in French, Kauffmann (2004) notes that language variation often disappears in favour of linguistic standardization, a situation also observed by Franco (2000b: 228). Remael (1995, 2007) attributes this practice to language policies prioritizing the educational function of public broadcasters, and recognizes this standardization is also applicable to other transfer modes.

Language policies undoubtedly impact on the language of the translation, but it is also worth highlighting that this deletion of oral features may be a feature inherent to voice-over. As Franco *et al.* (2010: 74) explain, many spontaneous features such as hesitations, repetitions, false starts or syntactic anomalies disappear in the voiced-over version for two main reasons: on the one hand, to reach voice-over isochrony and, on the other, to prioritize comprehension. Whilst in other transfer modes such as dubbing an effort is made to recreate credible dialogues, in voice-over transmitting information in a comprehensible way is prioritized. And this often means deleting language features which are typical of spontaneous colloquial language.

Another language-based research strand in voice-over pertains to the study of slang in voiced-over films (Garcarz 2007). For instance, Holobut (2011) presents a qualitative analysis of Ben Stiller's film *Zoolander* in which she compares how the Polish subtitled and the Polish voiced-over versions verbally portray the characters in the fashion world the film shows.

Holobut concludes that subtitles reconstruct lexical and phraseological idiosyncrasies of particular characters in the film and retain more metaphors and vulgarisms than the Polish voice-over, but they disregard pragmatic adequacy. By mixing slang expressions in complex grammatical structures typical of written language, characters appear to be inconsistent and '"over-voiced" (in the sense of being at times excessively expressive).' On the contrary, the voice-over version aims at maximal text reduction, avoids excessive interference with the original soundtrack, and disregards the stylistic idiosyncrasies of each character, but offers a more consistent portrayal of the fashion community. Characters therefore become 'under-voiced', 'i.e. devoid of individual stylistic identity', a strategy that combined with the reader's interpretative competence is considered to be successful.

In a more recent study, Holobut (2014) approaches slang in Polish voice-over focusing on a feature-length pilot episode of *Miami Vice*. In this study, though, the researcher adopts a diachronic perspective and compares a 1989 version and a 2008 version of the same episode. Her analysis stresses interesting changes in the voice-over practice linked to cultural aspects, moving from a source-oriented approach in the former version to a target-oriented approach in the latter. The 1989 version is more literal, with few omissions, and slang is transferred by means of cultural equivalents, paraphrases and calques, which are combined with terminology from law and commerce, making the characters speak an awkward mix of slang and 'bureaucatrese'. On the contrary, the 2008 version provides a free translation of the original message. Dialogues are reworked, and a more concise approach to the translation is taken, with slang terms being often omitted. When used, though, they sound natural and contribute to a better characterization of the characters. According to Holobut, these differences are due to diverging working flows: while in 1989 the translator provided a 'raw translation' that was reworked by an editor, in the 2008 version the professional translates and adapts at the same time. Holobut also attributes these changing practices to the fact that communist audiences needed assistance when facing foreign topics: explicitation was needed to make sure the viewers could appreciate the foreign reality. The 2008 version, on the contrary, addresses a post-communist society which is more familiar with American culture and fictional models. Therefore, the translation is more concise and consistent, and more independent stylistically from the original communicative patterns.

Cultural aspects of voice-over

A recurrent topic in most audiovisual transfer modes, the translation of cultural references has also been an object of research in voice-over. Franco (2001b) focuses on documentaries and, using a corpus of documentaries about Brazil voiced-over into French and German, she addresses the issue of foreignization or adaptation. Franco observes that a greater degree of exoticism or foreignization is 'almost inevitable in translated documentaries' (Franco 2001b: 177) although she considers that a balance must be reached so that this foreign flavour 'does not impair the target viewer's comprehension of the whole information' (*ibid*: 178). For her part, García Luque (2011) studies a science documentary translated from French into Spanish. Contrary to Franco's analysis, García Luque observes a clear domestication of cultural references, which, according to the author, aims to increase the end-user acceptance of and engagement with the documentary.

Analyses encompassing various non-fictional genres and language pairs are needed to shed light on the most established practices, and hence understand whether they are linked to the original genre, target audience preferences, or broadcasters' norms.

Authenticity, manipulation and the translator's visibility

Voice-over has often been said to contribute to the feeling of authenticity: the fact that the original is heard underneath has been claimed to create the illusion of reality. As Franco (2000a: 236) puts it, there is 'at least some consensus about the implicit function of this mode which, like subtitling, provides a kind of "authenticity illusion" through the simultaneous presence of the original counterpart.' This is enhanced when literal synchrony is kept, because viewers are assured that 'what is being said is exactly what is being told' (Luyken *et al.* 1991: 80). However, Mayoral (2001) voices a different view on this issue, noting that the coexistence of two auditory messages hinders comprehension.

Orero (2006c) explores the commonly held perception of voice-over as a form of translation that boosts authenticity by drawing on the concepts of simulacrum and hyper-reality. In the context of media studies, simulacrum is understood as a process in which significatory elements are combined to create a new reality. In the case of voice-over, the real is replaced by signs of the real and the effect is so powerful that it becomes a hyper-reality, i.e. 'more real than the real.' Orero illustrates the relationship between voice-over and the feeling of reality by analyzing aspects such as the delay effect (i.e. voice-over isochrony), the voice features, the format, and the visibility of the translator, a topic which she revisits in her later work. Darwish and Orero (2014), for example, reveal how content can be distorted through voice-over, that is, they show how a transfer mode associated with authenticity can in fact transfer information which does not correspond to the original. They also show how the voice-over translator may gain more visibility under certain circumstances. They illustrate their point by studying the translation of TV news through voice-over. More specifically, they use a real-life example from the BBC, namely a news item broadcast in 23 April 2006, in which a journalist delivers a news report followed by a Bin Laden audio tape. Whilst the voice of a male, supposedly Bin Laden speaking in Arabic, is heard on the background, the voice of a foreign man delivers the translation as a voice-over. The presence of the translator distinct from the journalist is not only made evident through the use of another voice, but also by the use of an on-screen caption which states 'voice of translator'. Darwish and Orero interpret this strategy as an attempt on the part of journalists to detach themselves from sensitive content, and hence shift the responsibility to translators. However, both the physical presence of an overlapping voice with a foreign accent and the explicit acknowledgement of the voice-over translator may break the illusion of reality often attributed to voice-over. Darwish and Orero's research also demonstrates that the original content of the news item under analysis does not match the voice-over. For instance, the BBC's English voice-over reads 'the enemy continues to murder our children, our women, the elderly, and destroy our homes', whilst in the original version there is not explicit mention of 'the enemy', 'our children', 'our women' or 'the elderly.'

Further manipulations of content in voice-over are also observed by Holobut (2012), who compares the voice-over version of the British series *The Saint* broadcast on Polish public television under the old regime and more recent ones. Holobut stresses the socio-cultural manipulation in the portrayals of Western reality and links her analysis to historical factors.

The reception of voice-over

Research on the reception of voice-over is still sparse. Polls on user preferences exist (see above), but empirical research in which users are confronted with voiced-over excerpts is almost non-existent. An exception is Sepielak (2016b), who compares the reception of voiced-over and subtitled content in terms of content comprehension and language identification in multilingual movies. A total of 113 participants volunteered to participate in the experiment and were randomly assigned to two different groups: the first one watched a 15-minute excerpt of the movie *Le Mépris* (1963) voiced-over into Polish, and the second one watched the same excerpt in its subtitled version. Results show that content comprehension was higher in the subtitled condition, but when asked to identify the number of languages spoken by a character, volunteers watching the voice-over version performed better. More research is undoubtedly needed in this field. Bogucki (2010: 6), for instance, states that 'dialogues involving several speakers are hard to follow when read by a single lector', that is, by a single voice artist, an aspect that lends itself to reception research.

Technologies in voice-over

Rehm and Uszkoreit (2012: 38), in the *Strategic Research Agenda for Multilingual Europe*, mention 'automatic voice-over' as an important research topic, and highlight that 'in 2020 we will see wide use of automatic subtitling and first successful examples of automatic voice over for a few languages.' However, research so far has been limited, to the best of our knowledge, to a small-scale project: ALST (Matamala 2015). This project has researched the implementation of speech recognition, machine translation, and speech synthesis in voice-over. Each of these technologies is seen as a key element in a semi-automatized workflow that could be implemented, although not exclusively, in voice-over. The process would involve three key steps, always followed by human revision or post-editing: the first step would be the generation of a script semi-automatically; the second step would be the machine translation of the script into the target language, and the final step would be the text-to-speech voicing of the output.

Matamala *et al.* (2017) compare the time and self-reported effort involved in three situations: manually transcribing a non-fictional excerpt in English to be voiced-over, respeaking it, and post-editing a transcript automatically generated by a speech recognition system. Their experiment shows the potential of respeaking when creating a transcript for a text that has to be voiced-over, and the willingness of professionals to embrace new transcription methods. On the other hand, Ortiz-Boix and Matamala (2015) research the effort involved in two situations: translating non-fictional content for voice-over from English into Spanish *versus* post-editing non-fictional content that has been machine translated. Comparing the effort involved in both tasks means comparing temporal effort (time spent on the tasks), technical effort (keystroke, mouse movements and clicks for each tasks), and cognitive effort (pause to word ratio, average pause ratio), in all cases through keylogging data. Results prove that post-editing requires less effort than translating, although results are not always statistically significant. However, Ortiz-Boix and Matamala (2016) are not only interested in the process but also in the final product. This is why they also carry out a three-level evaluation of the translated and post-edited voice-overs. In the first stage, expert lecturers and professionals evaluate the written output generated by translators and post-editors. In the second, these excerpts are recorded in a dubbing studio, where the recording director and voice talents also assess their quality. Thirdly, end-users blindly assess both post-edited and translated audiovisual excerpts, once recorded. Results show no significant differences between human translations and post-edited machine translations in the first level assessments, whilst human translation performs slightly better in the second and third levels.

The didactics of voice-over

Translating for voice-over is a field of professional practice in many countries, hence training is needed in this transfer mode. Matamala (2008) and Franco *et al.* (2010: chapter 5) describe the curricular design of a course on voice-over offered by the Universitat Autònoma de Barcelona within the MA in Audiovisual Translation, both in its face-to-face and its online modes of delivery. Their work explores the course structure, contents, methodology, and assessment; they also reflect on a range of challenges, and provide sample exercises, with an emphasis on non-fiction. Similarly, Chmiel (2015) discusses how voice-over is taught in Poland, more specifically in the Postgraduate Programme in Audiovisual Translation offered by the Department of Translation Studies (Adam Mickiewicz University). The course contents and assessment model are described, highlighting the specificities of Polish fiction voice-over.

New topics, new methodological approaches

Research on voice-over has increased in the last years, but still more research is needed. Some of the innovative approaches taken in other audiovisual transfer modes need to find their place in voice-over. Research issues that would merit more investigation are elaborated on in this section:

- First of all, basic descriptive research is much needed, not only focusing on case studies but also dealing with larger corpora. We do not know how voice-over is implemented in certain countries and what translation and synchronization strategies are followed in different language pairs. And this knowledge is lacking not only synchronically but also diachronically, from a historical perspective.
- Secondly, we do not know how users react to various voice-over strategies. Various methods could be used to this end: from traditional questionnaires to more innovative tools such as eye trackers (already used in the analysis of subtitles) or equipment monitoring physiological reactions (heart rate, galvanic skin response, electroencephalography). Apart from seeing how the final output is understood or enjoyed by audiences, more information on the process of creating voice-over should be sought, including analysis of workflows and guidelines governing this practice and also investigations researching the translation process. This can be achieved, for instance, by planning experiments in which the on-screen and keyboard activity are recorded.
- Thirdly, technological developments are likely to play an important role in this field over the next years. Wider research projects in which various technologies are implemented in the process of voice-over could shed more light on the feasibility of new workflows. Alternative processes such as amateur or fan voice-over are also under-researched.

Finally, an area in which incipient research is present but which undoubtedly will increase in the coming years is the relationship of voice-over with accessibility (Jankowska *et al.* 2015, Szarkowska and Jankowska 2012) around two particular foci: the integration of voice-over with existing access modes such as audio description, and the similarities/differences between voice-over and audio subtitles.

Conclusion

Voice-over is an active field of professional practice in many countries; it is used to mediate various genres and audiences generally welcome it. Although the body of research on voice-over is much smaller than that focusing on other modes of AVT, the volume of quality research on voice-over has increased considerably in the last few years. Voice-over researchers should learn from what has been done in other fields, join efforts and develop ambitious research agendas that go beyond self-contained case studies. Generating knowledge about old, current and new practices will allow us to better understand voice-over and will positively impact on the whole field of AVT.

Summary

Voice-over is a pre-recorded transfer mode in which a voice delivering the translation is heard on top of the original voice. Voice-over is used for non-fictional genres in certain Western European countries, and for fictional genres in many others. Voice-over is not constrained by lip synchronization but observes other types of synchronies: voice-over isochrony, literal synchrony, kinetic synchrony, and action synchrony. Voice-over implies the preparation of a written translation in which the language is often rephrased. Depending on the country's tradition and the genres, one or more voice talents deliver the voice-over, very often with a flat intonation. Research on voice-over has focused on translation and synchronization techniques, linguistic and cultural aspects, authenticity and manipulation, reception, technologies, and training, but new approaches are being developed.

Further reading

Franco, E., A. Matamala and P. Orero (2010) *Voice-over Translation: An Overview*, Bern: Peter Lang |
  This is the first academic book on voice-over, which provides both theoretical and practical insights into this transfer mode. It differentiates between voice-over for production and postproduction, and describes training experiences in the field. The book also includes the results of a global survey on voice-over.

Related topics

4   Investigating dubbing: learning from the past, looking to the future
8   Audio description: evolving recommendations for usable, effective and enjoyable practices

References

Aleksonyte, Z. (1999) *Comparative Analysis of Subtitles and Voice-over in Danish and Lithuanian Respectively as Compared to English (based on the Danish film* Breaking the Waves*)*, Vilnius: Faculty of Philology, University of Vilnius.
Bogucki, L. (2010) 'The Demise of Voice-over? Audiovisual Translation in Poland in the 21st Century', in B. Lewandowska-Tomaszczyk and M. Thelen (eds) *Meaning in Translation. Lodz Studies in Language*, Frankfurt: Peter Lang, 415–424.
Bogucki, L. (2013) *Areas and Methods of Audiovisual Translation Research*, Frankfurt: Peter Lang.
Burak, A. (2011) 'Some Like it Hot—Goblin-Style: Ozhibiliazh in Russian Film Translations', *Russian Language Journal* 61: 5–31.

Chaume, F. (2004) 'Synchronization in Dubbing: A Translational Approach', in P. Orero (ed.) *Topics in Audiovisual Translation*, Amsterdam & Philadelphia: John Benjamins, 35–52.

Chaume, F. (2012) *Audiovisual Translation: Dubbing*, Manchester: St. Jerome.

Chaume, F. (2013). 'The Turn of Audiovisual Translation. New Audiences and New Technologies', *Translation Spaces* 2: 105–123.

Chmiel, A. (2015) 'Teaching Voice-over in the Voice-over Land', in A. Jankowska and A. Szarkowska (eds) *New Points of View on Audiovisual Translation and Media Accessibility*, Frankfurt: Peter Lang, 129–147.

Darwish, A. and P. Orero (2014) 'Rhetorical Dissonance of Unsynchronized Voices: Issues of Voice-over in News Broadcasts', *Babel* 60(2): 129–144.

Díaz Cintas, J. and A. Remael (2007) *Audiovisual Translation: Subtitling*. Manchester: St. Jerome.

Díaz Cintas, J. and P. Orero (2006) 'Voice-Over', in K. Brown (editor-in-chief) *Encyclopedia of Language & Linguistics*, vol. 13, 2nd edition, Oxford: Elsevier, 477–479.

Díaz-Vegas, J. (2012) *El 'voice-over' en los 'reality shows'*, Unpublished BA Dissertation, Universitat Autònoma de Barcelona.

Dries, J. (1995) *Dubbing and Subtitling: Guidelines for Production and Distribution*, Düsseldorf: The European Institute for the Media.

Espasa, E. (2004) 'Myths about Documentary Translation', in P. Orero (ed) *Topics in Audiovisual Translation*, Amsterdam & Philadelphia: John Benjamins, 183–197.

Fawcett, P. (1996) 'Translating Film', in G. T. Harris (ed.) *On Translating French Literature and Film*, Amsterdam: Rodopi, 65–88.

Franco, E. (2000a) 'Documentary Film Translation: Aa Specific Practice?', in A. Chesterman, N. Gallardo and Y. Gambier (eds) *Translation in Context. Selected Contributions from the EST Congress*, Amsterdam & Philadelphia: John Benjamins, 233–242.

Franco, E. (2000b) *Revoicing the Alien in Documentaries. Cultural Agency, Norms and the Translation of Audiovisual Reality*, Doctoral thesis, Leuven: KUL. Available online: http://tede.ibict.br/tde_arquivos/1/TDE-2005-02-23T06:09:47Z-94/Publico/ElianaPCFranco.pdf [last access 20 December 2017].

Franco, E. (2001a) 'Voiced-over Television Documentaries. Terminological and Conceptual Issues for their Research', *Target* 13(2): 289–304.

Franco, E. (2001b) 'Inevitable Exoticism: The Translation of Culture-Specific Items in Documentaries', in F. Chaume and R. Agost (eds) *La traducción en los medios audiovisuales*, Castelló de la Plana: Publicacions de la Universitat Jaume I, 177–181.

Franco, E., A. Matamala and P. Orero (2010) *Voice-over Translation: An Overview*, Bern: Peter Lang.

Gambier, Y. (1996) 'La traduction audiovisuelle un genre nouveau?', in Y. Gambier (ed.) *Les transferts linguistiques dans les medias audiovisuels*, Villeneuve d'Ascq: Presses Universitaires du Septentrion, 7–12.

Gambier, Y. (2004) 'La traduction audiovisuelle: un genre en expansion', *Meta* 49(1): 1–11.

Garcarz, M. (2007) *Przeklad Slangu w Filmie: Polskie Przeklady Filmów Amerykanskich na Jezyk Polsi*, Krakow: Tertium.

García Luque, D. (2011) 'De cómo "domesticar" un documental de divulgación científica en el proceso de traducción. Estudio de la versión española de *L'Odyssée de l'espèce*', *Sendebar* 22: 235–263.

Glaser, G. (1991) 'Why Marilyn Monroe is a Polish Baritone', *New York Times*, 24 February. Available online: http://www.nytimes.com/1991/02/24/movies/film-why-marilyn-monroe-is-a-polish-baritone.html [last access 20 December 2017].

Gottlieb, H. (1997) *Subtitles, Translation and Idioms*, Unpublished Doctoral Thesis, University of Copenhagen.

Grigaraviciute, I. and H. Gottlieb (1999) 'Danish Voices, Lithuanian Voice-over. The Mechanics of Non-synchronous Translation', *Perspectives: Studies in Translatology* 7(1): 41–80.

Hendrickx, P. (1984) 'Partial Dubbing', *Meta* 29(2): 217–218.

Hendrykowski, M. (1984) 'Z Problemów Przekladu Filmowego', in E. Balcerzan (ed.) *Wielojezycznosc Literatury i Problemy Przekladu Artystycznego*, Wroclaw: Ossolineum, 243–259.

Holobut, A. (2011) 'Under-voiced and Over-voiced Characters in Film Translation', in A. Nizegoirodcew and M. Jodlowiec (eds) *Beyond Sounds and Words. Volume in Honour of Janina Aniela Ozga*, Krakow: WUJ, 164–184.

Holobut, A. (2012) 'Three Lives of *The Saint* in Polish Voiceover Translation', *Meta* 57(2): 478–495.

Holobut, A. (2014) 'Good Cops and Bad Cops in Polish Voice-over Translation', in E. Willim (ed.) *Continuity in Language. Styles and Registers in Literary and Non-Literary Discourse*, Krakow: AFM, 137–161.

Jankowska, A., M. Mentel and A. Szarkowska (2015) 'Why Big Fish Isn't A Fat Cat? Adapting Voice-over and Subtitles for Audio Description in Foreign Films', in Ł. Bogucki and M. Deckert (eds) *Accessing Audiovisual Translation*, Bern: Peter Lang, 137–148.

Kauffmann, F. (2004) 'Un exemple d'effet pervers de l'uniformisation linguistique dans la traduction d'un documentaire', *Meta* 49(1): 148–160.

Kotelecka, J. K. (2006) 'Traducción audiovisual para la television en Polonia: versión locutada. Entrevista con Barbara Rodkiewicz-Gronowska', *Trans. Revista de Traductología* 10: 157–168.

Krasovska, D. (2004) 'Simultaneous Use of Voice-over and Subtitles for Bilingual Audiences', *Translating Today* 1: 25–27.

Kuhn, A. and G. Westwell (2012) *A Dictionary of Film Studies*, Oxford: Oxford University Press.

Laine, M. (1996) 'Le commentaire comme mode de traduction', in Y. Gambier (ed.) *Les transferts linguistiques dans les médias audiovisuels*, Villeneuve d'Ascq: Presses Universitaires du Septentrion, 197–205.

Luyken, G. M., T. Herbst, J. Langham-Brown, H. Reid and H. Spinhof (eds) (1991) *Overcoming Language Barriers in Television: Dubbing and Subtitling for the European Audience*, Manchester: The European Institute for the Media.

Matamala, A. (2005) 'Freelance Voice-over Translation. Translating for Catalan Television', *JoSTrans: The Journal of Specialised Translation* 4: 45–48. Available online: http://www.jostrans.org/issue04/art_matamala.php [last access 20 December 2017].

Matamala, A. (2008) 'Teaching Voice-over Translation: A Practical Approach', in J. Díaz Cintas (ed.) *The Didactics of Audiovisual Translation*, Amsterdam & Philadelphia: John Benjamins, 231–262.

Matamala, A. (2009a) 'Main Challenges in the Translation of Documentaries', in J. Díaz Cintas (ed.) *New Trends in Audiovisual Translation*, Bristol: Multilingual Matters, 109–120.

Matamala, A. (2009b) 'Translating Documentaries: From Neanderthals to the Supernanny', *Perspectives. Studies in Translatology* 17(2): 93–107.

Matamala, A. (2010) 'Terminological Challenges in the Translation of Science Documentaries: A Case-study, *Across Languages and Cultures* 11(2): 255–272.

Matamala, A. (2015) 'The ALST Project: Technologies for Audiovisual Translation', in *Proceedings of Translating and the Computer* 37: 12–17.

Matamala, A., P. Romero-Fresco and L. Daniluk (2017) 'The Use of Respeaking for the Transcription of Non-fictional Genres: An Exploratory Study', *Intralinea* 19. Available online: http://www.intralinea.org/current/article/the_use_of_respeaking_for_the_transcription_of_non_fictional_genres [last access 20 December 2017].

Mayoral, R. (2001) 'El espectador y la traducción audiovisual', in F. Chaume and R. Agost (eds) *La traducción en los medios audiovisuales*, Castelló: Servei de Publicacions de la Universitat Jaume I, 33–48.

Nikolic, K. (2015) Personal communication.

Olaf Loom, P. (2011) *Making Television Accessible*, ITU report. Available online: http://g3ict.org/download/p/fileId_915/productId_192 [last access 20 December 2017].

Orero, P. (2004) 'The Pretended Easiness of Voice-over Translation of TV Interviews', *JoSTrans: The Journal of Specialised Translation* 2: 76–96. Available online: http://www.jostrans.org/issue02/art_orero.php [last access 20 December 2017].

Orero, P. (2006a) 'Synchronization in Voice-over', in J. M. Bravo (ed.) *A New Spectrum of Translation Studies*, Valladolid: Publicaciones de la Universidad de Valladolid, 255–264.

Orero, P. (2006b) 'Voice-over: The Ugly Duckling of Audiovisual Translation', *Proceedings of the Marie Curie Euroconferences MuTra 'Audiovisual Translation Scenarios'*, Saarbrücken 1–5 May 2006.

Orero, P. (2006c) 'Voice-over: A Case of Hyper-reality', in M. Carroll, H. Gerzymisch-Arbogast and S. Nauert (eds) *Proceedings of the Marie Curie Euroconferences MuTra 'Audiovisual Translation Scenarios', Saarbrücken 1–5 May 2006*. Available online: http://www.euroconferences.info/proceedings/2006_Proceedings/2006_Orero_Pilar.pdf [last access 20 December 2017].

Orero, P. (2009) 'Voice-Over in Audiovisual Translation', in J. Díaz Cintas and G. Anderman (eds) *Audiovisual Translation: Language Transfer on Screen*, Basingstoke: Palgrave Macmillan, 130–139.

Ortiz-Boix, C. and A. Matamala (2015) 'Quality Assessment of Post-edited versus Translated Wildlife Documentary Films: A Three-Level Approach', *Proceedings of WPTP4*.

Ortiz-Boix, C. and A. Matamala (2016) 'Post-editing Wildlife Documentary Films: A Possible New Scenario?', *JoSTrans: The Journal of Specialised Translation* 26: 187–210. Available online: http://www.jostrans.org/issue26/art_ortiz.pdf [last access 20 December 2017].

Pedersen, J. (2010). Audiovisual Translation—in General and in Scandinavia. *Perspectives. Studies in Translatology* 18(1): 1–22.

Pérez-González, L. (2014) *Audiovisual Translation. Theories, Methods and Issues*, London & New York: Routledge.

Permanyer, E. (2012) *A Hybrid Television Genre, a Hybrid Translation Mode? Voice-over Translation of Factual Entertainment in Spain*, Unpublished MA Dissertation, Roehampton University.

Pönniö, K. (1995) 'Voice over, narration et commentaire', in Y. Gambier (ed.) *Communication audio-visuelle et transferts linguistiques* (International Forum, Strasbourg, 22–24 June 1995). Special issue of *Translatio (FIT Newsletter/Nouvelles de la FIT)*, 303–307.

Rehm, G. and H. Uszkoreit (eds) (2012) *Strategic Research Agenda for Multilingual Europe*, Berlin: Springer.

Remael, A. (1995) 'From the BBC's *Voices from the Island* to the BRTN's *De President van Robbeneiland*: A Case Study in TV Translation', *Linguistica Antverpiensia* XXIX-XXX: 107–128.

Remael, A. (2007) 'Whose Language, Whose Voice, Whose Message? Different AVT Modes for Documentaries on VRT-Canvas Television, Flanders', *TradTerm* 13: 31–50.

Sepielak, K. (2014) 'Translation Techniques in Voiced-Over Multilingual Feature Movies', *Linguistica Antverpiensia New Series* 13. Available online: https://lans-tts.uantwerpen.be/index.php/LANS-TTS/article/view/69 [last access 20 December 2017].

Sepielak, K. (2016a) 'Synchronization Techniques in Multilingual Fiction Voiced-over Films in Poland', *International Journal of Communication* 10: 1054–1073. Available online: http://ijoc.org/index.php/ijoc/article/viewFile/3559/1578 [last access 20 December 2017].

Sepielak, K. (2016b) 'The Effect of Subtitling and Voice-over on Content Comprehension and Languages Identification in Multilingual Movie', *The International Journal of Sciences: Basic and Applied Research* 25(1): 157–165. Available online: http://gssrr.org/index.php?journal=JournalOfBasicAndApplied&page=article&op=view&path%5B%5D=4168 [last access 20 December 2017].

Sepielak, K. and A. Matamala (2014) 'Synchrony in The Voice-over of Polish Fiction Genres', *Babel* 60(2): 145–163.

Stashkiv, H. (2015) 'Audiovisual Translation as Power Play', in A. Jankowska and A. Szarkowska (eds) *New Points of View on Audiovisual Translation and Media Accessibility*, Frankfurt: Peter Lang, 21–30.

Szarkowska, A. (2009) 'The Audiovisual Landscape in Poland at the Dawn of the 21st Century', in A. Goldstein and B. Golubović (eds) *Foreign Language Movies—Dubbing vs. Subtitling*, Hamburg: Verlag Dr. Kovač, 185–201.

Szarkowska, A. and A. Jankowska (2012) 'Text-to-speech Audio Description of Voiced-over Films. A Case Study of Audio Described *Volver* in Polish', in E. Perego (ed.) *Emerging Topics in Translation: Audio Description*, Trieste: EUT, 81–98.

Szarkowska, A. and M. Laskowska (2015) 'Poland—A Voice-over Country No More? A Report on an Online Survey on Subtitling Preferences among Polish Hearing and Hearing-impaired Viewers', in Ł. Bogucki and M. Deckert (eds) *Accessing Audiovisual Translation*, Bern: Peter Lang, 179–197.

Tomaszkiewicz, T. (2006) *Przekład audiowizualny*, Warsaw: PWN.

Wozniak, M. (2012) 'Voice-over or Voice-in-between? Some Considerations about Voice-over Translation of Feature Films on Polish Television', in A. Remael, P. Orero and M. Carroll (eds) *Audiovisual Translation and Media Accessibility at the Crossroads*, Amsterdam: Rodopi, 209–228.

Filmography

Breaking the Waves (1996) Lars Von Trier. IMDb entry: http://www.imdb.com/title/tt0115751/fullcredits?ref_=tt_ql_1

Le Mépris (1963) Jean-Luc Godard. IMDb entry: http://www.imdb.com/title/tt0057345/?ref_=fn_al_tt_1

Miami Vice (2006) Michael Mann. IMDb entry: http://www.imdb.com/title/tt0430357/?ref_=nv_sr_2

Pippi Longstocking (1969) Olle Hellbom. IMDb entry: http://www.imdb.com/title/tt0366905/?ref_=fn_al_tt_2

The Saint (1962–1969) Various directors. IMDb entry: http://www.imdb.com/title/tt0055701/?ref_=fn_tt_tt_3

Zoolander (2001) Ben Stiller. IMDb entry: http://www.imdb.com/title/tt0196229/?ref_=fn_al_tt_1

6
Subtitling for deaf and hard of hearing audiences
Moving forward

Josélia Neves

Introduction

Any attempt to map subtitling for deaf and hard of hearing audiences (SDH) 50 years after its introduction on television will show that this audiovisual translation (AVT) modality has since come a very long way in terms of its acceptance, provision of services and research activity. Such subtitles are designed for people with hearing impairment because, in addition to rendering speech, they identify speakers and provide extra information about sound effects and music. Quite a novel concept to many Europeans only a few years ago, and an understudied topic even at the turn of the century, in recent years SDH has attracted the interest of regulators, professionals and academics, and particularly that of AVT researchers, who have contributed to raising awareness of its affordances and complexity. This has occurred through the study of SDH from numerous standpoints, the introduction of dedicated training at graduate and post-graduate levels, and the creation of research opportunities that bring together academics and professionals from different fields.

Most of the latest developments in SDH may be attributed to a bi-directional circular motion, whereby academia and the industry feed into each other and work together towards understanding and improving actual services. Further momentum for SDH has been provided by the opportunities and demands of a rapidly changing technological environment, in which convergence has allowed for the diversification of self-tailored services (e.g. streaming films on handheld devices that allow viewers to choose the subtitle language, size and positioning to suit their individual preferences). In addition, the recognition of the rights and needs of all individuals has shifted emphasis away from specific constituencies (e.g. people with disabilities) and focused instead on universal accessibility 'everywhere, everywhen, everyone' (Socol 2008).

The impact of such ongoing changes on SDH is manifold, as will be elaborated in this chapter. After delivering an overview of the conceptual frameworks and the terminology used in this field of professional practice and scholarly enquiry, and surveying a range of applications and norms in SHD, this chapter will gauge the potential to challenge current conventions, beliefs and practices.

Key terms and concepts in subtitling for deaf and hard of hearing

If we are to take the English language as a starting point, two terms are traditionally used to refer to the subtitles that were introduced on television in the 1970s (Ivarsson and Carroll 1998: 24) for the benefit of people with hearing impairment. Even though the services provided were substantially similar in remit, differences in the technology enabling the broadcast of these subtitles and in the intended audience dictated that 'teletext/closed subtitling' and 'subtitling for the deaf and hard of hearing' (SDH) be used in the UK, and '(closed) captioning' (CC) in the US. Influenced by the practices in these two leading countries, other countries followed suit in the provision of the service, adopting the techniques and finding equivalent terms in their different languages—a process that involved deciding whether the subtitle addressees would be referred to explicitly or omitted in the chosen terms (Neves 2008).

When first introduced, SDH and CC were 'same language' (intralingual) written renders of the screen dialogues and accounts of other aural components (sound effects and music) in audiovisual materials, to the extent that this type of audiovisual transfer designed specifically for the benefit of hearing impaired viewers was regarded as a form of 'transcription' or 'adaptation', rather than translation proper. This belief has remained unchanged in many circles, and both the terminology and the practices that they entail have found their way into other media and settings beyond television broadcasts. For instance, in the context of global distribution of media content, 'captioning' is the preferred term by the DVD industry; as far as the Internet is concerned, YouTube favours 'CC', while Netflix uses 'SDH'—in all cases, the subtitles reflect the language of the source text.

'Subtitling for the deaf and hard of hearing', commonly abbreviated as 'SDH' or 'SDHH' (Utray, Pereira and Orero 2009), has become the standard term in academic settings—perhaps as a reflection of the large number of European researchers working in the field. Politically and referentially inappropriate for grouping various audiences—d/Deaf and hard of hearing—under one label (Neves 2005, 2007a, 2008), the term has been nuanced to read as 'Subtitling for deaf and hard of hearing *audiences*' (Neves 2007b) or 'Subtitling for deaf and hard of hearing *viewers*' (Romero-Fresco 2009 and 2015). The later designation has been adopted in two large-scale European projects—Digital Television for All (DTV4ALL) and Hybrid Broadcast and Broadband TV for All (HBBTV4ALL)—and, hence, reinforced the understanding that a diverse constituency of hearing impaired viewers can be catered for through this service.

Despite the above-mentioned nuances, both CC and SDH fail to account for the full scope of this AVT modality. At present, there is a widely held consensus that SDH delivers intralingual or interlingual 'translation'; can take the form of burnt in (open) or superimposed (closed) subtitles; may be prepared beforehand or provided live; can be provided in an edited or (near) verbatim form; refers to verbal and non-verbal (acoustic) information; is meant to be used preferentially by people with hearing loss, although it is equally useful for people with intellectual or learning difficulties or with a lesser command of the spoken language (e.g. immigrants).

This range of options, which can be combined in various ways and with different purposes, raises questions about the adequacy of the terminology used in this field. 'Enriched (responsive) subtitling' would reflect more closely what SDH has become in the present technological age. At a time when 'enriched content' and 'responsive design' have become core concepts in digital environments, using new terminology to refer to what has now become a totally different reality would strip the 'old terms' from their biased connotations, and speak for a convergent and user-centred reality in which subtitles are part of a complex yet flexible multi-layered media landscape. 'Enriched' speaks for all the added elements that make subtitles relevant to specific users and 'responsive' for the standardized properties enabling subtitles to travel across platforms and media. The term also accounts for the growing interaction between the person and technology, at both ends of the process: production and reception. Significantly, the wealth of content presently rendered in the form of online subtitles has an ever-growing afterlife, beyond their immediate purpose, as they become searchable big data. For all these reasons, the adoption of a totally new term to designate this range of subtitling practices would definitely do away with much of the confusion and inaccuracy of the terminology that is presently in use, while removing the stigma of disability and allowing for developments already in progress.

In the meantime, while terms such as SDH or CC may soon lack currency, they are still productive in discussions of the basics of this AVT modality, as used in conventional settings, for the benefit of audiences with hearing impairments.

The road to acknowledgement

Presently, the reasonably established SDH/captioning mode is widely accepted as the most valuable means to provide hearing-impaired citizens with access to information and entertainment. Paramount to this acknowledgment has been the enforcement, on 3 May 2008, of the UN Convention on the Rights of Persons with Disabilities and its Optional Protocol (A/RES/61/106), 'the first comprehensive human rights treaty of the 21st century' (Enable, n.d.) that, by sporting 82 signatories to the Convention and 44 signatories to the Optional Protocol, has brought to the fore the rights of people with disabilities. Article 9 of the Convention places particular emphasis on providing people with disabilities with access to information and communication, as a means to allow them to 'live independently and participate fully in all aspects of life' (UN 2006: 9). This new socio-political environment has had a top down impact on services offered to people with disabilities at national level, through the enforcement of national laws and regulations on multiple spheres, including those pertaining to access to information and, in particular, to television and the Internet—the main platforms used for the universal distribution of information content. This contextual framework has obviously had a direct impact on the offer of accessibility services, such as subtitling, audio description and sign language interpreting, and has led to the introduction of SDH in a number of countries and an increase in the offer in many others.

As we stand today, the provision of SDH on audiovisual content—and particularly on television, still seen as the preferential platform for easy open access—is progressing at three quite distinct paces. Pioneering countries, such as the United States, Canada, the United Kingdom, France, Australia and Denmark, now sport close to 100 per cent of subtitled television programmes on their national open-to-air channels, with a spill over to their web-based video object (VoB) counterparts, using a mix of prepared and live subtitling methods (cf. Remael 2007, Romero-Fresco 2015, MAA 2015). Broadcasters, such as the BBC, are making a great effort to transpose the 100 per cent subtitling benchmark to their online video on demand (VoD) services. Having achieved their target quota on television, the BBC has now turned to improving the quality of its services, while working towards increasing subtitle availability on their VoD streaming platform. Once this has been accomplished, broadcast subtitles will be transferred to other media automatically through 'an audio fingerprinting algorithm to represent the broadcast content and web clips to speed up the search whilst providing sufficient temporal accuracy' (Armstrong *et al.* 2015: 4). This line of progression speaks of the dynamics of accessibility services in the fast-changing global context in which the first step still is 'to make available', then 'to increase quantity', and only then to truly address 'quality'. Once this is also in place, there will be a drive for 'diversity', whilst still improving on the previous two requirements: quantity and quality.

A second group of countries, including Italy, Spain, Portugal, Germany, Poland, Flemish-speaking Belgium, the Netherlands and Brazil, have been making steady progress towards implementing and increasing their offer across public and private channels and platforms. Such efforts, which began in the 1980s and 1990s, have been all the more successful when driven by lobbying forces and supported by research. This is the case of Spain, Portugal, Italy and Poland, for instance, where a significant body of applied research carried out in the last two decades has stimulated the development of accessibility services. Some of them have even experimented with new approaches. For example, the Portuguese national broadcaster TRP provides live subtitling through automatic speech recognition, doing away with the need for respeaking, while also providing live commentary subtitles on sports events, such as football matches. Another instance of 'newcomers' building upon other countries' practices is the Spanish UNE 153010 Standard (AENOR 2012), which moves away from established SDH norms in contexts with a longer tradition and advocates different colour and placement conventions.

A third scenario may still be sketched. However encouraging the outlook may be in Europe and in North America and Australia, large regions of the world remain uncharted, as far as SDH is concerned. Initial steps towards the introduction of SDH are taking place in South America, Asia, Southern Africa and the Middle East, where academia appears, again, to be driving change and developments in the industry. Even in the current context of global audiovisual flows, much remains to be done if deaf and hard of hearing communities all over the world are to be able to exercise their right to access information and entertainment, on a par with members of their respective wider communities.

Stakeholders for change

The contexts where accessibility services have become mainstream are those in which stakeholders—legislators, providers, producers, distributers and end-users—have combined efforts to support and effect change. Dynamic systemic environments where relationships of trust are built are more conducive to new developments. In the case of SDH, one particular group of stakeholders, the Deaf community, is 'making a difference' by enhancing the quantity and quality of services provided in their national contexts. With the recognition of sign languages in different countries and the increased provision of Deaf education in mainstream school systems, Deaf communities have become more engaged and have gained lobbying force. By taking a more active role in society, airing their views and needs and participating in collaborative R&D projects, hearing impaired individuals and their representative associations have contributed towards developing the subtitling services that are made available to them. In some cases, organizations are formally involved in working groups, writing policies and standards, such as the Canadian Closed Captioning Standard (CAB 2012) or the Spanish UNE 153010 standard. Deaf associations have also collaborated in national and international research projects—e.g. SAVAS (Sharing AudioVisual Language Resources for Automatic Subtitling), SUMAT (Online Service for Subtitling by Machine Translation), DTV4ALL and HBBTV4ALL. In some cases, individuals have contributed by filling in

Josélia Neves

surveys or taking part in specific case studies. Others have turned to social media in an effort to raise awareness—as illustrated by the campaign a young Portuguese deaf father launched through social media, demanding that Disney provide subtitles on their commercial releases, so that he and his family (and many other deaf families) could enjoy watching them together. The power of collective lobbying has also been felt in the action deaf viewers have taken against Netflix, Fox, Universal, Warner Bros and Paramount, accusing them of discrimination for not providing SDH on their streaming services. A protest that started in 2012 with petitions and lawsuits filed in the US, demanding the provision of subtitles in the English language, has since cascaded down to lesser-spoken languages, as is the case of Greek or Portuguese. These and similar actions prove that deaf communities are developing a heightened awareness of their rights and the will to exercise them.

This active stance is revealing of the important role that end-users play in the chain of subtitle supply. By becoming involved at the various levels of this systemic chain, deaf viewers are actively engaged in promoting quantitative and qualitative improvements. However, it should be noted that no service will ever be suitable for 'all' users: those who participate actively in these campaigns represent only some of the different constituencies of individuals requiring subtitling for access. Furthermore, by expressing their preferences, d/Deaf viewers are not necessarily providing proof of adequacy. This can only be achieved through objective data captured via eye trackers, magnetic resonance imaging (MRI) and electroencephalographies (EEG). As Romero-Fresco (2015: 10) puts it, 'what viewers think of SDH, how they understand these subtitles and how they view them' does not necessarily match.

Quality and standards

Achieving 'quality' appears to be the central aim of the now established providers of accessible content, who have contributed towards normalization by writing published and/or in-house standards and guidelines. These are mainly regulatory bodies, broadcasters or service providers, within contexts where acceptable 'quantity' levels in the provision of SDH have been attained. Among the best-known efforts, in the form of standards, one may list Ofcom's *ITC Guidance on Standards for Subtitling* (1999), the American DCMP *Captioning Key* (2017), the Spanish AENOR *UNE 153010* (2012), the Canadian *Closed Captioning Standards and Protocol for Canadian English Language Broadcasters* (CAB 2012) or the Australian *Broadcasting Services (Television Captioning) Standard* (ACMA 2013)—all focusing on television subtitling. There are other instruments pertaining to other platforms, including those listed in the *eAccess+* wiki or the ATVOD guidelines (2012), for instance. The outcomes of big-scale research projects, in the guise of deliverables, white papers or recommendations, or of smaller projects—often conducted by individual PhD researchers (e.g. Neves 2005, Kalantzi 2010, Arnáiz-Uzquiza 2013, Zárate 2014, Muller 2015, among others)—have also served to put forward recommendations to improve subtitle quality. These have served to harmonize subtitling practices in different countries, but have also served as 'inspiration' to those introducing subtitling services in new contexts. This speaks also of the important role these documents play in shaping practices at a global level, an added responsibility for anybody attempting to develop guidelines to be followed and taken as models for best practice. The importance of model standards and guidelines can be illustrated by the adoption of the BBC's approach to SDH by most equivalent SDH services around the world. This emphasizes the importance of issuing quality standards that are based on research, while remaining aware that no set of guidelines will ever manage to apply across all contexts and scenarios.

However useful practical standards and guidelines may be to those studying, working, wishing to work in the field, '[q]uality can be perceived very differently by those involved in the production and consumption of translated audiovisual products depending on their needs and expectations' (Baños and Díaz Cintas 2015: 4). Any attempt to understand the diversity of issues that contribute to the creation of effective subtitles, will need to take into account every step and stakeholder in the production chain, and most importantly, get to know the needs of the end-user—the ultimate beneficiary of the service. This interest in understanding reception by measuring cognitive load and attention through technological means has offered important insights into the way viewers engage their senses in response to audiovisual stimuli. Research on these issues shows that people's perception—as interrogated through questionnaires and interviews where people express their preferences—does not tally with effectiveness—measured objectively through physical reactions to stimuli. The notion of quality would thus appear to be subjective and difficult to capture through qualifiable and quantifiable monitoring. Understanding, readability and enjoyment may be contingent on external parameters such as time of day, state of mind, company and physical environment, as well as the degree of interest or previous knowledge in a topic. Multi-disciplinary large-scale collaborative research projects aiming 'to establish objective benchmarking for service quality' (HBB4ALL 2014) may lead to 'preferable' parameters, with the caveats that (i) 'quality is not a universal and unique measure, but one encompassing the many definition [sic] and metrics for quality from the perspectives of the key stakeholders in the value chain'; and (ii) 'too many stakeholders are involved when broadcasting media accessibility content to define one quality for all ... for all services; for all stakeholders; for all processes; for all countries; for all language conditions; for all budgets' (*ibid.*).

As far as quality considerations are concerned, it should be noted that the scope and spread of SDH is growing, with much of it happening beyond established contexts. The growing dynamics of volunteer subtitling or fansubbing, and its potential capacity to fill in the gaps in contexts where SDH is not available yet—as is the case described by Abe (2006), where volunteers are providing 'summarized captioning via Computer Assistance' in Japan—is bound to change the landscape. Of equally great importance is the growing use of SDH for educational purposes, in schools and in smaller communities, where products can be tailored to the specific needs of the groups they are intended for. Small-scale activities in relatively contained contexts will allow for the provision of fit-for-purpose solutions that may not have taken norms or guidelines into account. Non-professional subtitlers, such as teachers and educators, often work without previous training in subtitling, driven only by their wish to create an effective form of mediation, or an optimal learning or entertaining experience. This desire often allows for creativity and experimentation beyond regulated norms. In their attempt to find solutions that will prove useful and adequate to their specific circumstances, such individuals will often follow their intuition and their experiences as users. These *ad-hoc* practices could serve as inspiration for the enhancement of mainstream SDH, given that innovation often derives from the need to solve small but real problems. This may also mean that small-scale case studies end up informing guidelines with a broader scope and challenging conventional practices.

Norms and transgressions

In what appears to be a contradictory strategy, scholars are aiming to identify the 'Universals of SDH' (Romero-Fresco 2015: 14 and 350) by analyzing user preference and provider performance while, at the same time, technology is contributing to the fragmentation of audiences and offering new opportunities for individual viewership and tailoring. The growing offer of online catch-up services, cross-platform broadcasting—where someone can start watching a programme on one platform and seamlessly continue on a different one—and the proliferation of short-form video content are bound to impose new requirements on the way SDH is provided, so that it too can travel across platforms and formats. Standardization or unification, on the one hand, will guarantee transferability; but diversity will also be required if end-users are to be given a choice. This fragmented environment may require that such universals be found, for these 'do not have prescriptive force' (Chesterman 1993: 4) as norms do. However, understanding norms is still necessary to identify best practices and to 'regulate' the production of subtitles that will suit the relevant purpose in each setting. In the case of SDH, subtitles should provide viewers with supplementary information on non-verbal, acoustic information and allow for easy readability and comprehension.

Most of the norms in use, some of which take the form of the guidelines listed above, have been specifically created for teletext/closed captioning, and devised within the limitations that the 'old' systems imposed. Initially, analogue teletext technology allowed for very little diversity and its output was often difficult to read—a situation that has now changed, with digital teletext now providing better standards. Interestingly enough, even if digital technology is allowing for more diverse outputs, most standards in use are still close to those of teletext on analogue television, resembling the 'colours, font size, number of lines, subtitle position, paging, text division, subtitle speed, subtitle synchronization, spelling, grammar issues, subtitle editing, contextual information and information provided on teletext pages' (Bartoll and Martínez Tejerina 2010: 70). Although technology provides other options, traditional parameters are still relevant in many ways, for they have become engrained as 'expectancy norms' and become 'norm-models' (Chesterman 1997: 45) at various levels. In their current form, norms guarantee harmonization within specific contexts, e.g. guidelines used by subtitlers working for a particular company or broadcaster or imposed by regulators at national levels. But ongoing efforts to capture SDH universals to 'harmonize SDH practices across Europe' (Romero-Fresco 2015: 10) may come to prove that identifying practices that facilitate understanding and comfort is more important than normalizing.

While large-scale international collaborative projects are working towards establishing standards and harmonizing outputs, smaller-scale research by smaller groups or individuals is looking into creative approaches to SDH, by testing positioning in 'dynamic subtitles', visual imagery (e.g. emoticons, cartoon bubbles and creative typefaces) and haptic devices. Examples of these innovative trends are the work of the BBC Research and Development team (see Brooks and Armstrong 2014, Brown *et al.* 2015) exploring subtitle portability and dynamic subtitle placement; McClarty's (2012) experiments with creative subtitling; or the work carried out by Fels and her team on 'emotive subtitling' (Fels *et al.* 2005). Younger researchers, such as Sala Robert (2014) and Al Taweel (2015) have experimented with cartoon speech bubbles or emoticons to capture paralinguistic features of speech; and Nanayakkara and his team have tested a 'haptic chair' and a computer display of informative visual effects' to convey music to deaf viewers (Nanayakkara *et al.* 2013: 116).

These two apparently opposing approaches—the traditional and the innovative—are bound to converge, take advantage of the technological affordances of digital formats, and respond to user preferences—exceeding what were, at some point, fictional hypotheses about individuals being given the opportunity to tailor subtitles to their preferences and needs (Neves 2007c: 96–97). The introduction of pull-protocols to audiovisual content will demand for similarly 'pull-able' responsive subtitles, using cumulative information and adaptable formats. Research towards the provision of such 'adjustable' subtitles is ongoing and the BBC has taken the lead in implementing responsive subtitling for its online content. In 2015, the BBC implemented its responsive online design, providing a 'stream of video feature data' with 'subtitles that can be resized and reformatted on the fly in response to device orientation, screen size and user preference, without obscuring important features' (Brooks and Armstrong 2014).

The direction in which technology is taking the distribution of content, and that of subtitles, is bound to have an impact on the position these hold in the production workflow. Subtitling in the past has been perceived as an afterthought, an added 'nuisance' that interferes with the original text, covering important information, as well as an additional load of trouble and (rarely budgeted) extra expense. These creative approaches and even the user-centred options will make it necessary for subtitles, in general, and SDH in particular, to be integrated at an early stage—preferably while the original product is under development, as per Romero-Fresco's (2013) 'accessible filmmaking' approach, which is very much in line with practices in the videogame and localization industries.

It should be noted that the greater the freedom of choice that is given to the end-user, the more stable the standards of transmission and the more interchangeable the units of information (mostly subtitles) need to be. On the one hand, providing viewers with the capacity to personalize font sizes and colours, or subtitle positioning on a screen, may only require the availability of a set of predefined options that work within different screen sizes and types. The same applies to the addition of extra layers of information—e.g. giving audiences the means to activate tags for sound effects and music or alternative solutions such as the insertion of emoticons. However, other types of choices (e.g. verbatim vs. edited subtitles) might prove more difficult to implement. Manipulating the content to promote readability, understanding and enjoyment is the crux of ongoing research, and an important element in the very definition of quality in SDH.

Ongoing debates and research opportunities

The idiosyncrasy of SDH as a text-type can be accounted for in terms of presentation and content. Both these elements converge and interact, but content is the more complex of the two. By analyzing viewer preferences though questionnaires in triangulation with technology-based empirical research—using eye tracking, for instance—researchers can gauge the impact of different formats on the intake of audiovisual information (see Armstrong *et al.* 2015, Romero-Fresco 2015). But if we are to gain a better understanding of what 'quality' entails in the context of SDH, we will need to grasp what makes achieving readability and understanding major problem areas. A greater refinement of the ongoing research on reading speeds, chunking and comprehension and editing is vital to identify 'preferable' subtitling strategies or even variable subtitle types that allow for choice, as is done with text presentation on screen.

In truth, these issues are to be found in all types of subtitling, but they gain greater pertinence in SDH, given the profile of the intended end-users. For instance, hearing-impaired viewers may have little or no access to aural cues, may (or may not) rely on visual cues such as lip movement, and may read subtitles in what is their second language. These particularities will dictate requirements that are not found in subtitles for hearing viewers.

The equally longstanding debate over verbatim vs. edited subtitles is also far from being resolved. On the one hand, deafened and hard of hearing viewers, who rely on residual hearing and lip reading for accessing speech, show preference for verbatim subtitles—an approach that would appear to be endorsed by deaf associations and broadcasters (Jensema and Burch 1999, Schilperoord *et al*. 2005, Hersh 2013). On the other hand, scholars working in AVT and many others from deaf studies have repeatedly made a case for edited subtitles (Neves 2005, Romero-Fresco 2009, Kalantzi 2010). Some, as is the case of Ward *et al*. (2007), draw attention to the fact that each viewer's reading competence will be paramount in determining how effective different subtitle types are. As part of a study involving children, Ward *et al.* (2007: 27) conclude that 'research needs to focus on the comprehension elements of captions, in a manner similar to the research on reading print in texts'. It is therefore important to understand how deaf and hard of hearing people read in general for, only then, may we truly understand how subtitles should ba written and presented to boost their understanding and performance as readers.

It should be noted, however, that reading subtitles will always be quite different from reading static text on paper, or even on screen. As Kruger *et al*. (2015) explain, 'the reading of subtitles compete [sic] with the processing of the image, sometimes resulting in interrupted reading'; additionally, those temporal limitations regarding the presence of subtitles on the screen mean that 'readers have less time to reread or regress to study difficult words or to check information'. Gaining a better understanding of what might improve readability standards is particularly urgent, given that, as Bartoll and Martínez Tejerina (2010: 70) categorically put it, 'subtitles that cannot be read by deaf people or that are read with difficulty are almost as bad as no subtitles at all'.

Readability, as understood in this context, brings form and content together to create meaning and foster understanding. Although it may be possible to check how far people get through a subtitle by analyzing eye-tracking data, measuring understanding and identifying the variables that enable it is far more complex and requires detailed neuropsycholinguistic studies. Ongoing studies on the individual elements that contribute to enhancing subtitle readability and understanding seek to determine ideal reading speeds and subtitle presentation rates, two aspects on which academics do not seem to agree. While the outcomes of the DTV4ALL European projects tend to postulate a subtitling speed of 150 wpm as ideal for 'allowing the viewers to spend roughly as much time reading the subtitles as looking at the new image' (Romero-Fresco 2015: 341), other studies reported in Sandford (2015) contend that subtitles should follow the natural speed of speech, for 'the perceived rate of subtitles is not representative of the actual speed but is a symptom of technical issues and the overall natural feel of the programme' (Sandford 2015: 66). These discrepancies between studies informed by empirical research techniques and the input of significant numbers of informants confirm that further research is needed.

Equally challenging opportunities for research in SDH may be found in gauging the impact of subtitle chunking on comprehension. Early studies (Neves 2005) suggest that segmentation may play a very important role both in incrementing reading speed and in improving comprehension. The findings from the DTV4ALL project involving hearing subtitle readers (Rajendran *et al*. 2013) suggest there is no significant relation between segmentation and comprehension, but that good chunking contributes towards a better balance between subtitle reading and screen gazing. These scholars go on to suggest that, as happens in recorded subtitling, text chunking by phrase or by sentence be adopted in live subtitling 'by European subtitling broadcast services and media companies' (Rajendran *et al*. 2013: 19).

In addition, readable subtitles will result in a better overall experience that will facilitate understanding, and hence lead to enjoyment. Broadcasters are aware of how important it is for viewers to enjoy their programmes. For instance, Ofcom (2015: 1), clearly states that 'television service providers should promote the enjoyment and understanding of their services for people who are deaf or hard of hearing amongst other things'. In so doing they acknowledge that this segment of the population requires special attention, as they account for a significant share of regular television viewers.

As discussed in this section, the effectiveness of SDH revolves around three main criteria: readability, understanding and enjoyment. Achieving these will guarantee a fulfilling 'user experience'—a concept used in reference to human-computer interaction but that can also be applied to the active consumption of subtitled audiovisual content. This extension of the concept is particularly relevant at a time when subtitles are becoming part of the interactive online experience. When viewers are given the opportunity to become actively involved in the design of their own viewing parameters, there is bound to be yet another shift in the understanding of 'quality', for that will be measured on individual standards rather than on universals.

Conclusion

The present SDH landscape is undergoing rapid change. While VoD and web-based content is gaining momentum, attention still needs to be given to regular television broadcasting in conventional settings, as it is still a vital part of most people's everyday life—although, in some cases, television broadcasters are providing less SDH on their mainstream channels. As Muller (2012: 271) shows, in France 'two of the three public service channels that have been offering, albeit restricted, SDH, for nearly thirty years, are currently providing the least.'

Now that the switchover from terrestrial to digital TV is almost complete—with a move from conventional 4:3 PAL standard definition TV to 16:9 flat widescreen modern high definition TVs—and smart TVs are finding the way into the homes of most westerners, various access issues persist. Among these, technical constraints continue to make it difficult to zap between programmes without losing the subtitles, or impossible to receive subtitles through set top boxes or cable distribution, not to mention the difficulties in recording or reactivating such subtitles on catch-up TV, to name but a few.

Still lagging far behind, developing countries have very limited, if any, SDH on television, and web streaming is still irregular in places where Internet connectivity is still patchy. Furthermore, in gauging the potential for further development of online distribution, it should be noted that the current provision of SDH is predominantly in English, even though deaf and hard of hearing people all over the world will be wanting to read subtitles in their own languages.

As online connectivity continues to expand, and new commercial, ethical or statutory regulations come into force, the basic recommendations for all types of accessibility services for video on demand put forward by the Authority for Video on Demand (ATVOD 2012) apply also in the case of SDH online services. Such recommendations involve (1) publicizing the presence of SDH, (2) ensuring consistency of provision, in terms of continuity across programmes, (3) facilitating the activation of services and consistency across interfaces, (4) monitoring playout and checking for quality by meeting focus groups and collecting feedback and, finally, (5) consulting with stakeholders. This list provides a multifaceted framework for research that has to be undertaken to guarantee access in the present web-based environment.

Summary

As a field of professional practice and scholarly enquiry, SDH is currently traversed by multiple tensions and driven by attempts to enhance quantity, quality and diversity. Heightened general awareness, public demand and regulations will play a major role in increasing the provision of SDH, as shown by the experience of countries that have overcome the first stage in their implementation of accessibility services. Better quality requires a more refined understanding of the profile and needs of different audiences. Finally, quantity and quality will necessarily be driven by the ever-growing affordances of technology, which is fragmenting audiences, allowing for individualized user experience, and calling both for normalization and creativity—thus allowing for a variety of solutions on a broad spectrum of devices and platforms.

As user-centred technological environments become ever more ubiquitous, viewers will be able to choose specific formats that suit their personal needs. The traditional disability-oriented 'subtitling for the deaf and hard of hearing' paradigm will thus shift towards a more encompassing framework characterized by the use of 'enriched (responsive) subtitles'. Adopting a non-discriminating terminology will signal a greater degree of respect for diversity, consistent with the spirit of the 2001 UNESCO Universal Declaration on Cultural Diversity and the 2006 UN Convention on the Rights of Persons with Disabilities. This should not mark 'the end' of SDH, but rather the incorporation of SDH standards as a subtitling variety to be made available to every viewer on demand. Although this might take longer to achieve on traditional media (e.g. television or the cinema), it is certainly the way forward on versatile web-based platforms.

Further reading

Matamala A. and P. Orero (eds) (2010) *Listening to Subtitles. Subtitles for the Deaf and Hard of Hearing*, Bern: Peter Lang | *An interesting compilation of articles that account for various European research projects, covering topics such as subtitle formats, criteria for readable subtitles, SDH for children or sign language for access to television.*

Romero-Fresco, P. (ed.) (2015) *The Reception of Subtitles for the Deaf and Hard of Hearing in Europe*, Bern: Peter Lang | *A compilation of the main outcomes of the DTV4ALL project.*

Swarkowska, A. (2013) 'Towards Interlingual Subtitling for the Deaf and Hard of Hearing', *Perspectives: Studies in Translatology* 21(1): 68–81 | *This article examines interlingual subtitling for the deaf and the hard of hearing as a self-contained AVT modality. Although interlingual SDH shares some common ground with its elder siblings, i.e. standard interlingual subtitling for hearing viewers and monolingual subtitling for the deaf and the hard of hearing, it differs from them in terms of its text reduction, redundancy and editing conventions.*

Related topics

3 Subtitling on the cusp of its futures
7 Respeaking: subtitling through speech recognition
8 Audio description: evolving recommendations for usable, effective and enjoyable practices
9 Surtitling and captioning for theatre and opera
10 Game localization: a critical overview and implications for audiovisual translation
14 Psycholinguistics and perception in audiovisual translation
17 Multimodality and audiovisual translation: cohesion in accessible films
22 Eye tracking in audiovisual translation research
27 Audiovisual translation and fandom
31 Accessible filmmaking: translation and accessibility from production

References

Abe, N. (2006) 'Study on Summarized Captioning via Computer Assistance. The Case of City A', *Interdisciplinary Information Sciences* 12(1): 1–10.

ACMA (Australian Communications and Media Authority) (2013) *Broadcasting Services (Television Captioning) Standard*. Available online: https://www.legislation.gov.au/Details/F2013L00918 [last access 20 December 2017].

AENOR (Asociación Española de Normalización y Certificación) (2012) *Standard UNE 153010: Subtitulado para personas sordas y personas con discapacidad auditiva. Subtitulado a través del teletexto*, Madrid: Asociación Española de Normalización y Certificación.

Al Taweel, G. (2015) *Conveying Emotions in Arabic SDH: The Case of Pride and Prejudice*, Unpublished MA Dissertation, Hamad bin Khalifa University, Qatar.

Armstrong, M., A. Brown, M. Crabb, C. J. Hughes, R. Jones and J. Sandford (2015) *Understanding the Diverse Needs of Subtitle Users in a Rapidly Evolving Media Landscape*. BBC R&D White Paper (WHP 307). Available online: http://downloads.bbc.co.uk/rd/pubs/whp/whp-pdf-files/WHP307.pdf [last access 20 December 2017].

Arnáiz-Uzquiza, V. (2013) *Subtitling for the Deaf and Hard-of-hearing: Some Parameters and their Evaluation*, Unpublished Doctoral Thesis, Departament de Traducció i Interpretació, Universitat Autònoma de Barcelona, Spain.

ATVOD (Authority for Television On Demand) (2012) *Best Practice Guidelines for Access Services*. Available online: https://www.ofcom.org.uk/__data/assets/pdf_file/0018/82242/access_services_best_practice_guidelines_final_120912.pdf [last access 20 December 2017].

Baños, R. and J. Díaz Cintas (2015) 'Audiovisual Translation in the Global Context', in R. Baños and J. Díaz Cintas (eds) *Audiovisual Translation in a Global Context: Mapping and Everchanging Landscape*, Basingstoke: Palgrave Macmillan, 1–10.

Bartoll, E. and A. Martínez Tejerina (2010) 'The Positioning of Subtitles for the Deaf and Hard of Hearing', in A. Matamala and P. Orero (eds) *Listening to Subtitles. Subtitles for the Deaf and Hard of Hearing*, Bern: Peter Lang: 69–86.

Brooks, M. and M. Armstrong (2014) 'Enhancing Subtitles', *TVx2014 Short paper*. Available online: http://www.bbc.co.uk/rd/blog/2014–10-tvx2014-short-paper-enhancing-subtitles [last access 20 December 2017].

Brown, A., R. Jones and M. Crabb (2015) 'Dynamic Subtitles: The User Experience', TVx2015, June 2–5, 2015, Brussels, Belgium. Available online: http://www.bbc.co.uk/rd/publications/whitepaper305 [last access 20 December 2017].

CAB (Canadian Association Broadcasters) (2012) *Closed Captioning Standards and Protocol for Canadian English Language Television Programming Services*, 3rd edition. English-language Working Group on Closed Captioning Standards. Available online: http://www.cab-acr.ca/english/social/captioning/captioning.pdf [last access 20 December 2017].

Chesterman, A. (1993) 'From "Is" to "Ought": Laws, Norms and Strategies in Translation Studies', *Target* 5(1): 1–20.

Chesterman, A. (1997) *Memes of Translation*, Amsterdam & Philadelphia: John Benjamins.

DCMP (Described and Captioned Media Program) (2017) *Captioning Key*. Available online: http://www.captioningkey.org/about_c.html [last access 20 December 2017].

eAccess+ (2014) *Standards and Guidelines for Accessible Audiovisual Media in the United Kingdom*. Available online: http://hub.eaccessplus.eu/wiki/Standards_and_Guidelines_for_accessible_audio-visual_media_in_the_United_Kingdom [last access 4 November 2015].

Enable (n/d) *Convention on the Rights of Persons with Disabilities*, United Nations. Available online: https://www.un.org/development/desa/disabilities/convention-on-the-rights-of-persons-with-disabilities/convention-on-the-rights-of-persons-with-disabilities-2.html [last access 20 December 2017].

EU (European Union) (2010) *Audiovisual Media Services Directive*, Directive 2010/13/EU of the European Parliament and of the Council. Available online: http://eur-lex.europa.eu/legal-content/EN/TXT/PDF/?uri=CELEX:32010L0013&from=EN [last access 20 December 2017].

Fels, D., L. Daniel, C. Branje and M. Hornburg (2005) 'Emotive Captioning and Access to Television', *Proceedings 11th Americas Conference Information Systems*, 11–14 August; Omaha, Nebraska. Available online: http://pdf.aminer.org/000/239/965/towards_emotive_captioning_for_interactive_television.pdf [last access 20 December 2017].

HBB4ALL (2014) Quality Measures for TV Access (I). HBB4ALL Project Deliverable D2.6.1. Available online: http://pagines.uab.cat/hbb4all/sites/pagines.uab.cat.hbb4all/files/d2.6.2-uab_final-quality-metrics-for-tv-access_v1.00.pdf [last access 20 December 2017].

Hersh, M. (2013) 'Deaf People's Experiences, Attitudes and Requirements of Contextual Subtitles: A Two-country Survey', *Telecommunications Journal of Australia* 63(2): Article 406.

ITC (Independent Television Commission) (1999) *Guidance on Standards for Subtitling*. Ofcom.

Ivarsson, J. and M. Carroll (1998) *Subtitling*, Simrishamn: TransEdit HB.

Jensema, C. and R. Burch (1999) *Caption Speed and Viewer Comprehension of Television Programs: Final Report for Federal Award Number H180G60013*. Office of Special Education Programs, US Department of Education, Washington, District of Columbia.

Kalantzi, D. (2010) *Subtitling for the Deaf and Hard of Hearing: A Corpus-based Methodology for the Analysis of Subtitles with a Focus on Segmentation and Deletion*, Unpublished Doctoral Thesis, University of Manchester, UK.

Kruger, J.-L., A. Szarkowska and I. Krejtz (2015) 'Subtitles on the Moving Image: An Overview of Eye Tracking Studies', *Refractory* 25. Available online: http://refractory.unimelb.edu.au/2015/02/07/kruger-szarkowska-krejtz/ [last access 20 December 2017].

McClarty, R. (2012) 'Towards a Multidisciplinary Approach in Creative Subtitling', *MonTI* 4: 133–153.

MAA (Media Access Australia) (2015) *Access on Demand: Captioning and Audio Description on Video on Demand Services*. Media Access Australia Report Series. Available online: file:///Users/user/Downloads/Access_on_Demand_REPORT2_30Apr2015_01.pdf [last access 20 December 2017].

Muller, T. (2012) 'Subtitles for Deaf and Hard of hearing on French television', in S. Bruti and E. Di Giovanni (eds) *Audiovisual Translation across Europe*, Bern: Peter Lang, 257–273.

Muller, T. (2015) *A User-centred Study of the Norms for Subtitling for the Deaf and Hard-of-hearing on French Television*, Unpublished Doctoral Thesis, Universitat Autònoma de Barcelona, Spain.

Nanayakkara, S. C., L. Wyse, S. H. Ong and E. A Taylor (2013) 'Enchancing Musical Experience for the Hearing-impaired Using Visual and Haptic Displays', *Human-Computer Interaction* 28: 115–160.

Neves, J. (2005) *Audiovisual Translation: Subtitling for the Deaf and Hard-of-Hearing*, Unpublished Doctoral Thesis, University of Surrey Roehampton. Available online: http://roehampton.openrepository.com/roehampton/handle/10142/12580 [last access 20 December 2017].

Neves, J. (2007a) 'Of Pride and Prejudice: The Divide between Subtitling and Sign Language Interpreting on Television', *The Sign Language Translator & Interpreter* 1(2): 251–274.

Neves, J. (2007b) 'Subtitling Brazilian Telenovelas for Portuguese Deaf Audiences: An Action Research Project', *TRADTERM 13. Revista do Centro Interdepartamental de Tradução e Terminologia FFLCH/USP*: 121–134.

Neves, J. (2007c) 'A World of Change in a Changing World', in J. Díaz Cintas, P. Orero and A. Remael (eds) *Media for All. Subtitling for the Deaf, Audio Description and Sign Language*, Amsterdam & New York: Rodopi, 89–98.

Neves, J. (2008) '10 Fallacies about Subtitling for the d/Deaf and the Hard of Hearing', *JoSTrans: The Journal of Translation Studies* 10: 128–143. Available online: http://www.jostrans.org/issue10/art_neves.pdf [last access 20 December 2017].

Ofcom (2015) 'Measuring Live Subtitling Quality. Results from the Third Sampling Exercise'. Available online: https://www.ofcom.org.uk/__data/assets/pdf_file/0022/40774/qos_3rd_report.pdf [last access 20 December 2017].

Rajendran, D., A. Duchowski, P. Orero, J. Martinez, P. Romero-Fresco (2013) 'Effects of Text Chunking on Subtitling: A Quantitative and Qualitative Examination', *Perspectives: Studies in Translatology* 21(1): 5–21.

Remael, A. (2007) 'Sampling Subtitling for the Deaf and the Hard-of-hearing in Europe', in J. Díaz Cintas, P. Orero and A. Remael (eds) *Media for All. Subtitling for the Deaf, Audio Description and Sign Language*, Amsterdam & New York: Rodopi, 23–52.

Romero-Fresco, P. (2009) 'More Haste Less Speed: Edited vs. Verbatim Respeaking', *Vigo International Journal of Applied Linguistics* (VIAL) VI: 109–133.

Romero-Fresco, P. (2013) 'Accessible Filmmaking: Joining the Dots between Audiovisual Translation, Accessibility and Filmmaking', *JoSTrans: The Journal of Specialised Translation* 20, 201–223. Available online: http://www.jostrans.org/issue20/art_romero.pdf [last access 20 December 2017].

Romero-Fresco, P. (ed.) (2015) *The Reception of Subtitles for the Deaf and Hard of Hearing in Europe*. Bern: Peter Lang.

Sala Robert, E. (2014) *Creactive Subtitles. Subtitling for All*. Barcelona, Universitat Pompeu Fabra. Available online: http://www.tdx.cat/handle/10803/398140 [last access 20 December 2017].

Sandford, J. (2015) 'The Impact of Subtitle Display Rate on Enjoyment under Normal Television Viewing Conditions', *The Best of IET and IBC* 7: 62–67.

Schilperoord, J., V. de Groot and N. van Son (2005) 'Nonverbatim Captioning in Dutch Television Programs: A Text Linguistic Approach', *Journal of Deaf Studies and Deaf Education* 10(4): 402–416.

Socol, J. (2008) *What is Universal Accessibility?* 27 January, Blog Post. Available online: https://coffeeonthekeyboard.com/what-is-universal-accessibility-part-one-in-a-trilogy-66/ [last access 20 December 2017].

UN (United Nations) (2006) *Convention on the Rights of Persons with Disabilities and Optional Protocol*. Available online: http://www.un.org/disabilities/documents/convention/convoptprot-e.pdf [last access 20 December 2017].

UNESCO (2001) *Universal Declaration on Cultural Diversity*. Paris, 2 November. Available online: http://unesdoc.unesco.org/images/0012/001271/127162e.pdf. [last access 20 December 2017].

Utray, F., A. M. Pereira and P. Orero (2009) 'The Present and Future of Audio Description and Subtitling for the Deaf and Hard of Hearing in Spain', *Meta* 54(2): 248–263.

Ward, P., Y. Wand, P. Paul and M. Loeterman (2007) 'Near-verbatim Captioning versus Edited Captioning for Students who are Deaf or Hard of Hearing: A Preliminary Investigation of Effects on Comprehension', *American Annals of the Deaf* 152(1): 20–28.

Zárate, S. (2014) *Subtitling for Deaf Children. Granting Accessibility to Audiovisual Programmes in an Educational Way*, Unpublished Doctoral Thesis, University College of London.

Sitography

DTV4ALL (Digital Television for All): http://www.psp-dtv4all.org/ [last access 20 December 2017].

HbbTV4ALL (Hybrid Broadcast and Broadband TV for All): https://cordis.europa.eu/project/rcn/191771_en.html [last access 20 December 2017].

SAVAS (Sharing AudioVisual language resources for Automatic Subtitling) https://cordis.europa.eu/project/rcn/103572_en.html [last access 20 December 2017].

SUMAT (An Online Service for Subtitling by Machine Translation): http://www.fp7-sumat-project.eu/about-us/index.html [last access 20 December 2017].

7

Respeaking
Subtitling through speech recognition

Pablo Romero-Fresco

Definition and terminology

In broad terms, respeaking may be defined as the production of subtitles by means of speech recognition. A more thorough definition would present it as 'a technique in which a respeaker listens to the original sound of a (live) programme or event and respeaks it, including punctuation marks and some specific features for the deaf and hard of hearing audience, to a speech recognition software, which turns the recognized utterances into subtitles displayed on the screen with the shortest possible delay' (Romero-Fresco 2011: 1). Thus, in many ways, respeaking is to subtitling what interpreting is to translation, namely a leap from the written to the oral without the safety net of time. It is, in effect, a form of (usually intralingual) computer-aided simultaneous interpreting with the addition of punctuation marks and features such as the identification of the different speakers with colours or name tags. Although respeakers are normally encouraged to repeat the original soundtrack, and hence produce verbatim subtitles, the fast-paced delivery of speech in media content often makes that difficult. The challenges arising from high speech rates are compounded by other constraints. These include the need to incorporate punctuation marks through dictation while the respeaking of the original soundtrack is unfolding; and the expectation that respoken output will abide by standard viewers' reading rates. Consequently, respeakers often end up paraphrasing, rather than repeating or shadowing, the original soundtrack (Romero-Fresco 2009).

Although the term 'respeaking' seems established now, only a few years ago it was just one of many labels used to refer to this type of practice, alongside 'speech-based live subtitling' (Lambourne *et al.* 2004), (real time) 'speech recognition-based subtitling' and 'real-time subtitling via speech recognition' (Eugeni 2008b), as well as shorter alternatives such as 'speech captioning', 'shadow speaking' (Boulianne *et al.* 2009) or 'revoicing' (Muzii 2006). However, the status of this technique as the most common live subtitling method in the industry and a fast-growing area of academic research has helped to consolidate the term respeaking. Just as the ubiquity of the term 'audio-visual translation' has made the use of the hyphen redundant, 're-speaking' has also lost its hyphen on account of its growing visibility. The situation is different in other languages, where the respeaking technique was introduced much earlier than the terminology that designates it. As a result, there is still some inconsistency in the way the literature refers to what has sometimes been branded as a 'tâche sans nom' (Moussadek 2008), a trade without a name. It is for this reason that languages such as German and Italian have opted for the calque respeaking, whereas others like French and Spanish are using *sous-titrage vocal* and *rehablado*, respectively (Romero-Fresco 2008). As will be explained below, in some cases the different terms reflect not only a linguistic difference but also a different approach to the production of subtitles through speech recognition.

History

The origins of respeaking may be traced back to the experiments conducted in the early 1940s by US court reporter Horace Webb, who explains that 'the system was born in a Chicago courtroom. Its father was a pen shorthand reporter and its mother frustration' (NVRA 2008). Until then, court reporters used to take shorthand notes of the speech and then dictate their notes for transcription into typewritten form. Webb proposed to have the reporter repeat every word of the original speech into a microphone, using a stenomask to cancel the noise. The subsequent recording of the reporter's words would then be used for transcription (NVRA 2008). No speech recognition was used at the time and no live transcription was produced, but the basic principle of respeaking was already set. This was called 'voice writing' and may thus be seen as the precursor of respeaking, or 'realtime voice writing', as it is called in the US. Respeaking/realtime voice writing involves the same technique but uses speech recognition software for the production of TV subtitles and transcriptions in courtrooms, classrooms, meetings and other settings. The very first use of respeaking or realtime voice writing dates back to 1999, when court reporter Chris Ales transcribed a session in the Circuit Court in Lapeer, Michigan, with the speech recognition software Dragon Naturally Speaking.

In Europe, the origins of respeaking are linked to those of live subtitling for deaf and hard of hearing viewers. In 1982, the British channel ITV began to subtitle headlines of public events such as a visit of the Pope or the football World Cup using a standard keyboard (Lambourne 2006). This method proved too slow and in 1987 ITV started using the Velotype, a syllabic keyboard developed in the Netherlands that allowed subtitlers to produce between 90 and 120 words per minute (wpm) after a training period of 12 months. Also in 1987, ITV set up its own live subtitling unit for news programmes. A tandem method was tested whereby two subtitlers would share the workload in a given programme. This increased subtitling speed to somewhere between 120 and 160 wpm, much closer to the 175-wpm standard speech rate of news presenters in the UK (Ofcom 2015b).

In Flanders, the public broadcaster VRT also experimented with the QWERTY method in 1981 and broadcast its first live subtitles in 1982. Velotype was also tested in Flanders, but it never went into production. In 1990, the BBC set up its own live subtitling unit, resorting first to keyboards and then to stenography. Following what the National Captioning Institute had done in the US in 1982, the BBC hired professional stenotypists to increase the speed of the subtitles. The result was very satisfactory—live verbatim subtitles at up to 220–250 wpm, in other words, suitable for news programmes. The problem, however, was that the training required to become a stenotypist, between three and four years long, made this method particularly expensive. Following some experiments by Damper *et al.* (1985), who proposed the use of speech recognition combined with keyboards to change the colour and position of live subtitles, the BBC finally decided to test respeaking in April 2001 with the World Snooker Championship, just as it was being introduced in Flanders by VRT. In countries such as Spain, France and Italy, respeaking was not introduced until some years later (2004, 2007 and 2008, respectively), mostly due to 'new legislation or other forms of agreement brokered between governments and, for instance, public broadcasting channels, following constant pressure from the deaf and hard of hearing organisations' (Remael 2007: 25). This legislation often set subtitling quotas of 90% and even 100%, thus including subtitles for live programmes.

However, the consolidation of respeaking as an area of professional activity, initiated by the BBC (UK) and VRT (Flanders) in 2001, was not immediately followed by commensurate developments in terms of academic training provision or scholarly research activities. Under these circumstances, subtitling companies knew what they had to do (producing live subtitles) and what were the means available to do it (speech recognition software). In the absence of codes of good practice or other conventions, however, they went about doing it in different ways, as outlined in the next section.

Professional practice on TV

Although, on the whole, respeaking has overtaken stenography as the preferred method to produce live subtitles for TV around the world, the situation varies greatly depending on the country. In the US and Canada, most live captions (the term used to refer to subtitles in North America) are produced by stenotypists. Some US broadcasters also resort to real-time voice writers, but their numbers are still significantly lower than those of stenotypists. English-language Canadian broadcasters are now beginning to contemplate the possibility of using respeaking, which is however more common in French Canada (EBG 2014). Steno-made live subtitles for TV can also be found in other countries such as Italy, where they are still more common than respoken subtitles; Australia, where there is a 50/50 split between both methods; and the UK, where stenotypists are now only used to subtitle the most challenging programmes. Other countries such as Spain, Switzerland, Belgium and France resort almost exclusively to respeakers.

With the exception of a few respeakers working for public broadcasters such as TVE in Spain, most respeakers tend to work for subtitling companies, either in-house or on a freelance basis. Given the complexity of their job, they are not normally expected to work live for longer than one hour at a time, as longer slots are likely to have a negative impact on their performance. In-house respeakers will typically divide their working day into 3 or 4 live subtitling shifts, which are complemented by further time devoted to preparation and the production of pre-recorded subtitles.

As far as the setting and equipment are concerned, the ideal situation is to have soundproof booths for respeakers. Another possibility is to have soundproof rooms where several respeakers can work together, although this may lead to interferences between them. Respeakers usually have a computer and a TV screen in front of them. They wear headphones to listen to the original programme and they use a USB microphone, with or without a stand, to respeak into. As far as software is concerned, most respeakers use Dragon Naturally Speaking for speech recognition, a subtitling application to display the recognized utterances as subtitles on the screen and a newsroom application where they can access the list of contents of the programme they are going to respeak and, in some cases, even some of the scripts that are going to be used in the programme. Indeed, whereas a few years ago most respeakers would have no option but to respeak programmes live in their entirety, the situation has now changed. The pressure exerted by some regulators to prompt closer collaboration between broadcasters and subtitling companies (Ofcom 2103) has resulted in more scripts being available for respeakers before the start of a live programme and in the introduction of a hybrid mode of subtitling, combining live and pre-recorded subtitles for live programmes (Mikul 2014). For segments of the programme for which scripts are available before the start, respeakers will simply cue in live the subtitles that they have prepared beforehand, whereas non-scripted segments will be subtitled through live respeaking.

The above-mentioned set-up remains fairly consistent across countries, but there are also significant variations. In French-speaking Canada, for example, respeakers at TVA network use a joystick to include punctuation in the subtitles; their counterparts at the Italian company Colby, on the other hand, use a touch screen to introduce keywords that may crop up in the programme they are subtitling. One of the main differences across countries pertains to the way in which errors in the subtitles produced by respeakers are corrected. Indeed, the interplay between accuracy and delay constitutes an intrinsic part of live subtitling and is often described as a trade-off: launching the subtitles without prior correction results in smaller delays but less accuracy, while correcting the subtitles before cueing them on air increases accuracy but also delay. In the UK, the norm is to correct only some of the errors in the subtitles and only once they have been displayed on the viewers' screens so that the delay of the subtitles is kept to a minimum. The viewers will then see the error on the screen and, a few seconds later, a correction introduced by a double hyphen (--). In Spain, Switzerland and Belgium, respeakers often verify and, if necessary, correct errors in the subtitles before cueing them, thus favouring accuracy over the reduction of delay. This is taken to an extreme in France, where respeaking is approached in a collaborative manner with teams of three or four professionals: a respeaker, a corrector (who corrects the mistakes made by the speech recognition software before the subtitles are sent on air) and a whisperer, who suggests potential corrections to the corrector. Sometimes there is also a whisperer for the respeaker. Needless to say, this adds delay to the live subtitles but it also ensures a high accuracy rate.

A more extreme solution is the introduction of the so-called antenna delay, also known as broadcast delay or signal delay (Rander and Looms 2010). It consists of inserting a short delay in 'live' programmes in order to allow the subtitlers enough time to prepare, correct and synchronize the subtitles before they are displayed on screen to the viewers. This is common practice in the Netherlands, where a 60-second delay allows for the synchronization and correction of intralingual subtitles for fast-paced daily talk shows, and in Flanders (Belgium), where the antenna delay ranges from 5 to 20 minutes for intralingual subtitles and even longer for interlingual subtitles into Dutch (Ofcom 2015a). In the UK, Ofcom has proposed the use of this antenna delay to reduce the latency and improve the accuracy of subtitles for chat shows, which are notoriously problematic due to the presence of fast speech rates, overlapping speech and non-scripted content. A first successful test involved delaying the Welsh cookery programme *Coglinio Byw* by 30 seconds. However, broadcasters tend to oppose this method, arguing that the problems it causes (for example the fact that the viewers cannot use social media such as Twitter or online betting applications during the programme if it is delayed) outweigh the benefits it has for the viewers.

As will be explored below, both accuracy and delay currently constitute key topics of research and discussion, not least when it comes to finding methods to assess them and compare them. For the time being, suffice it to say that the average delay of live subtitles is around 0s-3s for subtitles produced with the hybrid mode, 3s-5s for steno-made subtitles, 5s-7s for respoken subtitles with on air corrections, 8s-10s for respoken subtitles with prior corrections and over 10s for respoken subtitles with prior corrections by more than one subtitler (Ofcom 2015a). Their accuracy depends largely on the model used to assess the errors.

At the moment, and in the case of the widely spread NER model, the minimum requirement is 98% (Romero-Fresco and Martínez 2015).

Other key features of respoken subtitles relate to their display mode, their edition rate (i.e. the degree to which the subtitles have been summarized as compared to the original audio) and the extent to which they include speaker identification, macros, sound effects and other distinctive features of subtitles for the deaf and hard of hearing (SDH). In the US and Canada, live captions are displayed in scrolling mode (and in capitals), whereas in Europe they may be displayed only in blocks (Spain, Switzerland, Belgium), only scrolling (France) or with a combination of scrolling for the live respoken parts and blocks for the scripted segments (the UK and Italy). The edition rate, one of the most controversial issues in SDH which is closely related to subtitling speed, varies depending on national traditions and practices, as well as on the chosen subtitling method. Steno-made subtitles require a low edition rate and can sometimes be near-verbatim, whereas respoken subtitles hardly exceed 180 wpm, which means that respeakers are forced to condense the soundtrack of the many programmes that feature speech rates over 180 wpm. In general, all live subtitles identify the speakers, which may be done with the use of a double chevron (Canada), colours (the UK) or labels with the speakers' names (Spain), and they may or may not include information about important sounds and music.

Finally, the rapid development of speaker-independent speech recognition technology (which, unlike speaker-dependent speech recognition, turns the original audio of a programme into subtitles without the need for a respeaker in between) is bringing about new approaches to live subtitling. In countries such as Japan (Imai *et al.* 2008), live subtitlers have become editors of automatically recognized subtitles that they correct and cue live, whereas in Portugal some broadcasters are showing live subtitles produced by automatic speech recognition without any editing or human intervention.

Respeaking in contexts other than TV

Over the past years, standard intralingual respeaking for live TV programmes and court reporting has expanded to other applications and contexts. In many companies, subtitlers are using respeaking to subtitle pre-recorded programmes in order to increase productivity. This technique, initially known as 'scripting' (Marsh 2006), allows respeakers to pause the original soundtrack if they wish, which brings this type of respeaking closer to consecutive interpreting than to simultaneous interpreting. Once the programme has been respoken, the subtitles are synchronized with the audio by another subtitler and/or with the help of specialized software. When pre-recorded subtitling is done manually, with no respeaking involved, the usual ratio of working time versus film duration is around 10:1 minutes. When done with respeaking, it can go down to 6:1. Furthermore, it allows subtitling companies to spread their work among different staff members and to prevent respeakers from spending their working day subtitling on air.

As well as on TV, respeaking is also being used in live public events such as conferences, talks, religious ceremonies, university lectures and school classes, and in private contexts such as business meetings and telephone conversations. In these contexts, respeakers may work on site or remotely and they may or may not have visual access to the speakers. Finally, interlingual respeaking, a technique that bridges the gap between audiovisual translation (AVT) and simultaneous interpreting, is also being used by some broadcasters such as VTM in Belgium and in public events, although not as extensively as intralingual respeaking.

Training

Even though respeaking was introduced in Europe as a profession in 2001, the provision of formal training at higher education level did not start until 2007. During this six-year period, and given the lack of research, codes of practice or even basic guidelines, companies had no option but to train their own staff. Preferred candidates would normally be graduates in languages and ideally postgraduates in subtitling, but the reality was that the first respeakers had very diverse qualifications, ranging from an MPhil in Medieval and Renaissance Literature to a BA in Swahili and African Culture (Romero-Fresco 2011). Depending on the company, candidates would be required to fill in an application form with a brief subtitling exercise and/or a knowledge test on current affairs, which would be followed by a series of increasingly complex respeaking tests.

Whereas courses and modules on subtitling and SDH have proliferated in Europe over the past decade, respeaking courses at university level are still few and far between. Some universities (such as the University of Leeds, in the UK) include introductory sessions on respeaking as part of their courses on AVT. More in-depth training options are provided by Universitat Autònoma de Barcelona (a three-month online module and a one-month face-to-face module in Spanish as part of an MA in Audiovisual Translation), the University of Antwerp (a six-month face-to-face course unit in Dutch, including an interlingual English-to-Dutch component), the University of Roehampton (a three-month face-to-face module in English, Spanish, French, Italian and German) and Universidade de Vigo (a three-month online module on intralingual respeaking in English, Spanish and Galician, and a pioneering three-month online module on interlingual respeaking in the same languages).

The training delivered by these institutions focuses on issues that are specific to respeaking (especially those related to the use of speech recognition software), but it also includes elements from both SDH and interpreting (Arumí Ribas and Romero-Fresco 2008). In terms of SDH, respeaker trainers draw on key aspects such as general subtitling skills, awareness of the needs of deaf and hard of hearing viewers and familiarity with subtitling software and conventions. As far as interpreting is concerned, the emphasis is often placed on the multitasking skills required to listen, comprehend and synthesize the source text and to reformulate it and deliver it live as a target text. Contrary to what it may seem, the multitasking involved in respeaking may be regarded as even more complex than that of interpreting. Activating immediate verbal agility and speed upon receiving the message, interpreters must listen to the source text and speak the target text at the same time, while they also listen to their own voice (the target text again) to monitor what they are saying. In turn, respeakers must also listen (to the source text), speak (the target text) and listen (to the target text), but their job does not finish there. Rather, it is passed on to the software, which means that respeakers also have to read (what is being displayed on the screen in case there are errors) and sometimes write or rather type (correcting the errors, changing the position of some subtitles, etc.). The complexity here does not only lie in the multiplicity of tasks, but in the fact that, although happening at the same time, these tasks do not overlap fully. Indeed, when correcting an error live, respeakers are expected to watch and correct an utterance said in the recent past, as they make an effort to listen to the audio in the present in order to respeak it in near the future. Whereas interpreters often speed up their delivery to catch up with the original when they are lagging behind, respeakers cannot afford to do this, as it could be detrimental to the accuracy of the voice recognition (Romero-Fresco 2011).

The wide range of skills required to work as a respeaker begs the question of what is the most suitable profile for the job and, in particular, of whether subtitlers or interpreters are better suited to this discipline. Although there is widespread agreement that respeaking combines interpreting (as far as the process is concerned) and subtitling (especially regarding the product and the context), it has been adopted from the beginning as a new modality of AVT, which may explain why most respeaking jobs are filled by subtitlers instead of interpreters and why it has been AVT scholars, and not interpreting scholars, who have conducted research in this area.

Research

Research on respeaking is still scarce considering the popularity and widespread use of this technique in the industry, its social impact and the increasing number of publications dealing with AVT and, more specifically, with media accessibility. A quick search on the translation and interpreting database BITRA shows that only 4% of the academic publications on accessibility and 0.8% of published outputs on AVT, respectively, deal with live subtitling and respeaking.

So far, research in this area has focused on the respeaking process, the training of respeakers, the analysis of respoken subtitles (including quality assessment), their reception by the users, and finally the application of respeaking for other purposes, such as transcription.

An excellent forum to gain an overview of the initial research on respeaking from the perspective of AVT was the *International Seminar on New Technologies in Real Time Intralingual Subtitling*, held in Forlì in 2006. Most of the contributions (Eugeni and Mack 2006) focused on the process and the professional practice of respeaking as implemented in different countries, while others dealt with stenotyping, the use of respeaking on the Internet or users' needs. The second edition of the conference, held three years later in Barcelona (Respeaking 2009, n.d.), focused on the reception of respoken subtitles and the strategies used by live subtitlers. Practical, professional and training experiences in Finland, Denmark and Italy were also presented, along with applied studies such as the use of real-time subtitling through speech recognition in education. The following conference in the series, held in Antwerp in 2011 (Respeaking 2011, n.d.), approached respeaking from the point of view of system developers, broadcasters and academics. Topics of interest included the issue of subtitling delay, live editing, new apps, working tools and error correction. Training provision and, specifically, the overlap between respeaking and interpreting was another key topic in the conference. The 2013 conference in Barcelona (Respeaking 2013, n.d.) featured the presentation of the Translectures project (Translectures, n.d.), which looked into the automatic transcription and translation of online video lectures. Discussions also revolved around respeaking in various contexts (radio, film festivals), quality measures, respoken subtitles and minor languages. Finally, the latest edition of the conference, held in Rome in 2015 (Respeaking 2015, n.d.), explored issues such as live subtitling quality on TV, respeaking by blind users, new technological solutions and experimental studies on the nature and reception of respeaking. The first international association of respeaking, onA.I.R (onA.I.R, n.d.), includes on its website information about all these conferences and more generally about respeaking projects and initiatives.

As far as academic publications are concerned, from its birth as an object of academic scrutiny in 2006 (Eugeni and Mack 2006), respeaking has been the focus of dissertations (Marsh 2004, González Lago 2011), theses (Eugeni 2009a), articles (Boulianne *et al.* 2009, Luyckx *et al.* 2013) and even a monograph (Romero-Fresco 2011). Early publications, including most papers in a special issue of *InTRAlinea* published in 2006, delivered general descriptions of respeaking (Eugeni 2006, Mack 2006, Lambourne 2006, Romero-Fresco

2008) and of how live subtitling and, more specifically, respeaking was first implemented in countries such as Italy (de Seriis 2006), Denmark (Baaring 2006), Taiwan (Chen 2006), Spain (Orero 2006), the Netherlands (de Korte 2006), Belgium (Remael and van der Veer 2006) and the UK (Marsh 2006). Other contributions focused on technological solutions for respeaking (Aliprandi and Verruso 2006) and its application to contexts such as speech reporting (Trivulzio 2006) and the university environment (Pirelli 2006).

The special issue of *InTRAlinea* also included the first academic reflections on how to train respeakers in the contributions by Muzii (2006) and especially by Remael and van der Veer (2006), who outline the main skills and exercises from subtitling and interpreting that are needed to train respeakers at higher education. The latter laid the foundations for the first respeaking module delivered at university level, in this case at the University of Antwerp in 2007. It was also the starting point of the first comprehensive pedagogical model for the training of respeakers, developed by Arumí and Romero-Fresco (2008), which was applied in the respeaking courses taught at Universidade de Vigo, Universitat Autònoma de Barcelona (Spain) and the University of Roehampton (UK). This model has been reviewed and expanded (Russello 2010) as well as updated on the basis of feedback obtained from students (Romero-Fresco 2012a), which has led to the above-mentioned discussion of whether interpreting or subtitling students are better suited to respeaking. Initial findings (Romero-Fresco 2012a) suggest that although interpreting students find it difficult to dictate punctuation marks and must pay attention to their diction and intonation when respeaking (which needs to be more controlled than in interpreting), they perform better in respeaking than subtitling students without prior interpreting training, who seem to struggle to perform different tasks simultaneously. In other words, when it comes to respeaking training, it seems easier to teach subtitling to interpreting students (adding some respeaking-specific skills and 'un-training' some aspects of interpreting such as intonation) than to teach interpreting to subtitling students, given that not all of them will necessarily have the multitasking skills required for respeaking.

However, these conclusions have recently been contradicted by the first findings obtained in the project Respeaking—Process, Competences, Quality (Respeaking Project, n.d.), conducted at the University of Warsaw and funded by the Polish National Science Centre for 2014–2017. The project uses screen casting, eye tracking, electroencephalography, and self-report questionnaires on cognitive load, as well as new models for the assessment of respoken subtitles, in order to measure the working memory capacity and paraphrasing, proofreading and respeaking skills of interpreters, translators and controls (bilinguals with no interpreting/translation background). The first three studies conducted as part of this project (Szarkowska *et al.* 2015, Chmiel *et al.* 2015 and Dutka *et al.* 2015) have found no significant differences in the performance of interpreters, translators and controls and no conclusive evidence that the former are better suited to respeaking. More research is needed in this area to ensure that the current pedagogical models used for the training of respeakers can be substantiated, modified or replaced on the basis of empirical evidence and with the help of new technological developments (Prazak *et al.* 2011). An empirical approach based on newly developed statistical analyses, keystroke logging and eye tracking is adopted by Van Waes *et al.* (2013) to observe the respeaking process. In their study, they draw conclusions on the causes and consequences of errors in live subtitling, the relationship between the correction of errors and the degree of editing of the source text, and the respeakers' reliance on visual input for the collection of information.

As well as the process of respeaking and the training of respeakers, research has also focused on the reception of respoken subtitles by the viewers. Eugeni (2008a), which includes data from 197 signing deaf on their reception of live subtitles for the news in Italy, is the first and, to this date, the largest reception study on live subtitling. The study explores the efficiency of syntactically and semantically edited live subtitles while balancing the needs of the deaf community and the main public broadcaster, RAI. It also offers a solution as a compromise to satisfy both: subtitles mirroring the grammar of Italian sign language while respecting the Italian grammatical rules. The first reception studies conducted in the UK (Romero-Fresco 2010, 2011 and 2012b) analyzed reception on the basis of the users' views, comprehension and perception on live subtitling. Users' concerns about the accuracy and delay of live subtitles, although partly determined by their unrealistic expectations about the accuracy of speech recognition technology, proved justified by the low scores obtained in an experiment testing the comprehension of live subtitled news programmes. The eye-tracking-based perception tests showed two potential reasons for these poor comprehension scores: the speed of the subtitles and their scrolling mode. The faster the subtitles, the more time the viewers spend reading them, as opposed to looking at the images, which has a negative impact on comprehension. This has recently been substantiated by eye-tracking data obtained across Europe (Romero-Fresco 2015), which shows that an average speed of 150 wpm tends to lead to an equal distribution of attention between subtitles and images (50%–50%). In contrast, subtitles at 180 wpm lead to a distribution of 60%–40% and subtitles at 200 wpm lead to 80%–20%, thus turning the viewers into subtitle readers.

As for the display mode, the results, corroborated by Rajendran *et al.* (2013), show that scrolling subtitles cause the viewers to spend significantly more time on the subtitles (and less on the images) than block subtitles. These findings have been used by countries such as Switzerland to replace their scrolling subtitles by block subtitles and by regulators such as Ofcom to require broadcasters to use block subtitles for their hybrid mode.

Finally, in France, Muller (2015) shows that the national policy of having a 4-people respeaking team in order to improve accuracy to the detriment of latency (CSA 2011) is not necessarily motivated by the users' preferences. In her study, most users prioritized the reduction of delay over the correction of errors, which would require a different approach to the one that has been adopted nation-wide. In general, reception studies in live subtitling are scarce and mostly limited to surveys commissioned by user associations (Matthews 2015). Useful as these may be, they must be complemented with more academic reception research to ensure that viewers are not just receivers but also, to some extent, participants in the decisions informing the guidelines on live subtitling.

An area that has been explored more thoroughly is the analysis of live subtitles and their main features, including accuracy, delay, speed, edition rate and display mode. The analyses come not only from academics (Jensema *et al.* 1996 in the US, Eugeni 2009b and Romero-Fresco 2009 in the UK, Luyckx *et al.* 2013 in Belgium, García Romero 2015 in Spain, and Bortone 2015 in Italy) but also from official reports elaborated by user associations (Apone *et al.* 2010 in the US), broadcasters (EBG 2014 in Canada) and regulators (Ofcom 2015a in the UK). Although the aim of these studies was initially to describe the main characteristics of live subtitles, the focus is now being placed on the assessment of live subtitling quality. This is arguably the most debated topic of discussion in this area and one in which the requirements of the industry and the users seem to have met the interest of many researchers in the field. Different models have been put forward to assess the quality of live subtitles, whether based on subtitling theory (Eugeni 2012), on the everyday practice of live subtitling (Dumouchel *et al.* 2011) or the automatization of quality assessment (Apone *et al.* 2010).

In Canada, for example, the Canadian Radio-television and Telecommunications Commission (CRTC) set up in 2012 a two-year project requiring broadcasters to analyze the quality of their live captions in 265 programmes using the so-called Verbatim Test (EBG 2014), which regards accuracy as the extent to which the captions match word for word the audio of a programme. Only 19% of the programmes monitored met the 95% threshold established by the Verbatim Test, which was criticized by the broadcasters for not being a reliable determinant of accuracy and for punishing captioners who achieve better quality through adept editing than through verbatim captions that may be too fast for the viewers to read. With a view to accounting for the possibility of correct and incorrect editing and for the presence of different types of errors in live subtitling, the NER model (Romero-Fresco and Martínez 2015) was created in 2012 and since then it has been adopted by universities, broadcasters, access service providers and regulators in countries such as the UK, Spain, France, Switzerland, Italy, South Africa and Australia. In the UK, Ofcom adopted the NER model to set up the largest study conducted so far on the quality of live subtitling, analyzing the accuracy, delay, speed and edition rate of 78,000 subtitles from all terrestrial TV channels in the country between 2013 and 2015 (Romero-Fresco 2016). The results show an overall accuracy rate of 98.4% (above the 98% threshold set by the NER model), an average delay of 5.4 seconds (exceeding the maximum of 3 seconds established by the Ofcom guidelines), an average subtitling speed of 140 wpm (exactly the same speed found by Jensema *et al.* in 1996 in their analysis of 205 US TV programmes) and an average edition rate of 22%.

It is difficult to know whether these findings can be extrapolated to other contexts given that accuracy and delay have still not been analyzed thoroughly in other countries and that all these features are largely dependent on the live subtitling method used, the display mode of the subtitles, the genre of the programme analyzed and the speech rates of the speakers in the programme. What remains consistent across countries is the debate regarding the speed and edition rate of live subtitles. Some access service providers and broadcasters argue that live subtitles should not have a maximum speed and should therefore be fully verbatim, including every word spoken in a programme (Sandford 2015). This would bring about a dramatic decrease in the time (and therefore the cost) involved in subtitling, but at the same time it would also result in subtitles that would be too fast for many readers to follow (EBG 2014, Romero-Fresco 2015).

Finally, alongside the above-mentioned studies on respeaking training, its process and the nature and reception of respoken subtitles, researchers are beginning to explore the use of respeaking for other purposes, such as transcription, where the efficiency of respeaking is being compared to that of manual transcription and of automatic speech recognition (Sperber *et al.* 2013, Bettinson 2013). In the medical field, and mostly in the US, researchers have looked into the feasibility of replacing manual transcriptions of patients' data with a semi-automatic approach based on respeaking (or voice writing, as this technique is known there). Al-Aynati and Chorneyko (2003) found speech- recognition-based transcription to be a viable tool to transcribe pathology reports but also more time consuming than manual transcription, given the extra time needed to edit the errors caused by the speech-recognition software. In turn, Zick and Olsen (2011) analyzed the accuracy, word-per-minute dictation time and turnaround time of speech-recognition-based transcription versus that of manual transcription for physician charting in emergency departments. They concluded that the former is nearly as accurate as traditional transcription, it has a much shorter turnaround time and is less expensive than traditional transcription.

In Europe, two EU-funded projects, Translectures and SAVAS, have explored the use of speech recognition and in some cases respeaking to improve the efficiency of transcription and subtitling. Translectures (Translectures Project, n.d.) aimed to develop tools for the automatic transcription and translation of online educational videos. In the studies conducted as part of the project, the automatic generation of subtitles through speech recognition plus a manual review process to eliminate errors proved considerably faster than the traditional manual production of subtitles (Valor Miró et al. 2015). The SAVAS project (SAVAS, n.d.) aimed to develop speech recognition technology in seven languages (Basque, Spanish, Italian, French, German, Portuguese and English) for the production of fully automatic and respeaking-based subtitles and transcriptions. As in the case of Translectures, the SAVAS technology showed very promising results both in terms of accuracy and efficiency when compared to manual transcriptions (Álvarez et al. 2015).

Taking into account the encouraging results obtained in the medical field in the US and in these two EU-funded projects, Matamala et al. (forthcoming) tested the efficiency of respeaking as a transcription tool for documentaries by comparing manual transcription (by far the most recurrent method used nowadays in the film industry) to respeaking and to the revision (or post-editing) of a transcript generated by automatic speech recognition. The results show that manual transcription was the most efficient method, which is not surprising given that the participants were professional manual transcribers with no experience or training in respeaking. However, it was respeaking that allowed the highest number of participants to finish the transcription in the time allocated for the task, especially for those who combined the use of hands and voice. This points to the need to further test the use of respeaking (combined or not with manual input) in the transcription industry, especially since most participants complained about the taxing and boring nature of their manual job and expressed their wish to start using this new technology.

Conclusion

As well as consolidating in most countries as the preferred method for the production of live subtitles for TV, respeaking is currently expanding to other live contexts, such as public events (conferences, talks, religious ceremonies, university lectures, school classes, etc.), business meetings and telephone conversations, with respeakers working on site or remotely and with or without visual access to the speakers. Off-line respeaking for the production of pre-recorded subtitles is also becoming more popular, as is the introduction of interlingual respeaking (Romero-Fresco and Pöchhacker 2017), which edges this technique closer to simultaneous interpreting. In the near future, the use of automatic speech recognition, which is turning some respeakers into editors of automatically generated subtitles and transcriptions, may become more widespread, as will perhaps the still controversial insertion of antenna delays, which allows time for teams of subtitlers to prepare fully synchronized, error-free intra- or interlingual subtitles for 'live' programmes.

However, despite this rapid growth, professional respeaking still has many gaps to bridge, especially with regard to other related industries such as the film industry. To mention but one example, the production of a documentary by a broadcaster typically involves the transcription of the audio once the footage has been filmed and before the film is edited. Nowadays, teams of professional transcribers are doing this transcription manually. This manual transcription is then used for the filmmaker and editor to edit the film into its final form. Once the film is finished, it is sent to a subtitling company for the production of SDH, which is often done by respeaking the audio into subtitles. At this stage, the speech-to-text work has been done twice, with and without technology and sometimes in the same building. Needless to say, if production companies were aware of the existence of respeaking and if they were in contact with access service providers, the original footage of the film could be transcribed by respeaking before the film is edited and this transcription could be sent to the subtitlers, who could use it as a basis for their subtitles.

Respeaking training is still not as prominent as it should be and certainly much more scarce than training in subtitling or interpreting. However, there are now several universities teaching respeaking modules in a range of formats (face-to-face and online, in one or multiple languages), which complements the in-house training that is still provided by many companies.

Successful as they have been, these universities must now adapt to the above-mentioned changes regarding new applications and technological developments in respeaking. In addition, the development of interlingual respeaking may help to arise the interest of the interpreting community in this area, which could result in new and much-needed professional opportunities for interpreters and in the introduction of respeaking as an element within interpreting training.

As for research in this area, it is still limited to a few enthusiastic and prolific authors who are making the most of the social importance of respeaking by leading national and international projects and setting up fruitful collaborations with access service providers and governmental regulators. Now that the quantity of live subtitles is beginning to be regulated, many countries are considering the introduction of measures to assess the quality of live subtitling. Research is thus more necessary than ever, not least because the imminent introduction of automatic speech recognition and automatic live subtitles (which are, by definition, fast and verbatim) will pose an important challenge for many viewers. Most models of assessment focus on accuracy instead of speed, which means that error-free automatic subtitles displayed at the speed of speech (often over 200 wpm) will be considered 100% accurate in terms of quality, even though they may not be accessible for many viewers. Following the example of Ofcom in the UK with the NER model, it may be necessary to include speed as one more factor to be measured regarding live subtitling quality (Romero-Fresco 2016).

To conclude, it is hoped that the increasing visibility of respeaking in the industry and its social importance will contribute to the creation of further training opportunities at university (not least in collaboration with the interpreting studies community, especially when it comes to interlingual respeaking) and to the increasing development of research in this area in order to ensure that the new guidelines on live subtitling are based on empirical evidence and that the new developments in the industry are not introduced at the expense of the viewers.

Summary

Respeaking may be defined as the production of subtitles by means of speech recognition. Respeakers listen to the original sound of a live programme or event and respeak it, including punctuation marks and some specific features for the deaf and hard of hearing audience, to a speech recognition software, which turns the recognized utterances into subtitles displayed on the screen with the shortest possible delay. Although respeakers are usually encouraged to repeat the original soundtrack in order to produce verbatim subtitles, the high speech rates of some speakers and the need to dictate punctuation marks and abide by standard viewers' reading rates means that respeakers often end up paraphrasing rather than repeating or shadowing the original soundtrack.

Originated in the US as a way to improve the efficiency of court reporting, respeaking was later on introduced in Europe as a means to provide live subtitles on TV, where it has consolidated over alternative methods such as stenography. Lately, the use of respeaking has expanded to other contexts such as pre-recorded subtitling for TV, live public events (conferences, talks, religious ceremonies, university lectures, school classes, etc.), business meetings and telephone conversations.

Although until recently training in respeaking was only provided by subtitling companies, some universities have developed respeaking courses, which normally focus on elements from interpreting, SDH and aspects that are specific to respeaking, mostly related to the use of speech recognition software. As far as research is concerned, it is relatively scarce, especially if compared to research in other related fields such as AVT and accessibility. Academic work on respeaking has so far focused on the process of respeaking, the training of respeakers (comparing, for example, the performance of interpreters and subtitlers) and the analysis and reception of respoken subtitles by the viewers. One of the most debated topics of discussion and research is quality assessment. This has prompted the introduction of models such as the NER model, which is currently used by universities, regulators and subtitling companies and provides a bridge between academia and the industry.

The future of respeaking is closely linked to the development of speech recognition technology, whether for the use of respeaking in interlingual contexts or for other uses, such as transcription in the film and medical industries. Likewise, the rapid development of speaker-independent speech recognition technology (which, unlike speaker-dependent speech recognition, turns the original audio of a programme into subtitles without the need for a respeaker in between) is bringing about new approaches to live subtitling. In this context, live subtitlers may become editors of automatically recognized subtitles that they correct and cue live or may disappear altogether if broadcasters decide to show live subtitles produced by automatic speech recognition without any editing or human intervention. Research on quality will thus be essential to ensure that these automatic subtitles meet the standards required by the viewers.

Further reading

Eugeni, C. (2008) 'Respeaking the News for the Deaf: For a Real Special Needs-oriented Subtitling', *Studies in English Language and Literature* 21, National Taiwan University of Science and Technology, Taipei | *This is the largest reception study conducted so far on live subtitling, including data from 197 signing prelingual deaf on their reception of live subtitles for the news in Italy. The study explores the efficiency of syntactically and semantically edited live subtitles while balancing the needs of the deaf community and the main public broadcaster, RAI. It finally offers a solution as a compromise to satisfy both.*

Romero-Fresco, P. (2011) *Subtitling through Speech Recognition: Respeaking*, Manchester: Routledge | *The first and so far only monograph on live subtitling and respeaking, this book covers the origins of live subtitling, the different methods used to provide live subtitles and the training and professional practice of respeaking around the world. It also features an in-depth respeaking course and a detailed analysis of the reception of respeaking, featuring information about viewers' preferences, comprehension and perception of respoken subtitles obtained with eye-tracking technology.*

Romero-Fresco, P. (2016) 'Accessing Communication: The Quality of Live Subtitles in the UK', *Language & Communication* 49: 56–69 | *The largest study conducted so far on the quality of live subtitles, it analyzes the accuracy, delay, speed and edition rate of 78,000 subtitles from 300 programmes broadcast on all five terrestrial TV channels in the UK.*

Romero-Fresco, P. and J. Martínez (2015) 'Accuracy Rate in Live Subtitling: The NER model', in J. Díaz Cintas and R. Baños (eds) *Audiovisual Translation in a Global Context: Mapping an Ever-changing Landscape*, Palgrave Macmillan, 28–50 | *This article presents the NER model currently used by universities, broadcasters, access service providers and regulators around the world to assess the quality of live subtitles. The article includes the background of quality assessment in live subtitling, a comparison with other models and examples of the application of the NER model in several languages.*

Van Waes, L., M. Leijten and A. Remael (2013) 'Live Subtitling with Speech Recognition: Causes and Consequences of Text Reduction", *Across Languages and Cultures* 14(1): 15–46 | *This article is an example of the research on live subtitling carried out in Belgium, using newly developed statistical analyses, keystroke logging and eye tracking to observe the respeaking process (including the causes and consequences of errors in live subtitling and the respeakers' reliance on visual input for the collection of information).*

Related topics

3   Subtitling on the cusp of its futures
6   Subtitling for deaf and hard of hearing audiences: moving forward
17 Multimodality and audiovisual translation: cohesion in accessible films
14 Psycholinguistics and perception in audiovisual translation
22 Eye tracking in audiovisual translation research
23 Audiovisual translation and audience reception
29 Audiovisual translator training
31 Accessible filmmaking: translation and accessibility from production
32 Technologization of audiovisual translation

References

Al-Aynati, M. and K. A. Chorneyko (2003) 'Comparison of Voice-automated Transcription and Human Transcription in Generating Pathology Reports', *Archives of Pathology and Laboratory Medicine* 127(6): 721–725.

Aliprandi, C. and F. Verruso (2006) 'Tecnologie del linguaggio naturale e sottotitolazione multilingue diretta', in C. Eugeni and G. Mack (eds) *Intralinea, Special Issue on Respeaking*. Available online: http://www.intralinea.org/specials/article/Tecnologie_del_Linguaggio_Naturale_e_sottotitolazione_multilingue_diretta [last access 20 December 2017].

Álvarez, A., C. Aliprandi, I. Gallucci, N. Piccinini, M. Raffaelli, A. del Pozo, R. Cassaca, J. Neto, C. Mendes and M. Viveiros (2015) 'Automating Live and Batch Subtitling of Multimedia Contents for Several European Languages', *Multimedia Tools and Applications* 75(18): 10823–10853.

Apone, T., M. Brooks and T. O'Connell (2010) *Caption Accuracy Metrics Project. Caption Viewer Survey: Error Ranking of Real-time Captions in Live Television News Programs*, Boston: WGBH National Center for Accessible Media. Available online: http://ncam.wgbh.org/invent_build/analog/caption-accuracy-metrics [last access 20 December 2017].

Arumí Ribas, M. and P. Romero-Fresco (2008) 'A Practical Proposal for the Training of Respeakers', *JoSTrans: The Journal of Specialised Translation* 10: 106–127. Available online: http://www.jostrans.org/issue10/art_arumi.php [last access 20 December 2017].

Baaring, I. (2006) 'Respeaking-based Online Subtitling in Denmark', in C. Eugeni and G. Mack (eds) *Intralinea, Special Issue on Respeaking*. Available online: http://www.intralinea.org/specials/article/Respeaking-based_online_subtitling_in_Denmark [last access 20 December 2017].

Bettinson, M. (2013) *The Effect of Respeaking on Transcription Accuracy*, Unpublished Honours Thesis, Melbourne: University of Melbourne.

BITRA (Bibliography of Interpreting and Translation) Available online: https://aplicacionesua.cpd.ua.es/tra_int/usu/buscar.asp?idioma=en [last access 20 December 2017].

Bortone, M. (2015) *Quality of Chat Shows in Italy: A Comparative Analysis of Respoken and Stenotyped Subtitles*, Unpublished MA Dissertation, London: University of Roehampton.

Boulianne, G., J.-F. Beaumont, M. Boisvert, J. Brousseau, P. Cardinal, C. Chapdelaine, M. Comeau, P. Ouellet, F. Osterrath and P. Dumouchel (2009) 'Shadow Speaking for Real-time Closed captioning of TV Broadcasts in French', in A. Matamala and P. Orero (eds) *Listening to Subtitles. Subtitles for the Deaf and Hard of Hearing*, Bern: Peter Lang, 191–207.

CSA (2011) *Charte relative à la qualité du sous-titrage à destination des personnes sourdes ou malentendantes*, Paris: Conseil Supérieur de l'Audiovisuel. Available online: http://www.csa.fr/Espace-juridique/Chartes/Charte-relative-a-la-qualite-du-sous-titrage-a-destination-des-personnes-sourdes-ou-malentendantes-Decembre-2011 [last access 20 December 2017].

Chen, S.-J. (2006) 'Real-time Subtitling in Taiwan', in C. Eugeni and G. Mack (eds) *Intralinea, Special Issue on Respeaking*. Available online: http://www.intralinea.org/specials/respeaking [last access 20 December 2017].

Chmiel, A., A. Lijewska, Ł. Dutka, A. Szarkowska, I. Krejtz and K. Krejtz (2015) 'Tapping the Linguistic Competence in the Respeaking Process. Comparing Intralingual Paraphrasing Done by Interpreting Trainees, Translation Trainees and Bilinguals', Paper presented at the *5th International Symposium on Respeaking, Live Subtitling and Accessibility*, 12 June 2015, Rome.

de Seriis, L. (2006) 'Il Servizio Sottotitoli RAI', in C. Eugeni and G. Mack (eds) *Intralinea, Special Issue on Respeaking*. Available online: http://www.intralinea.org/specials/article/Il_Servizio_Sottotitoli_RAI [last access 20 December 2017].

Damper, R., A. Lambourne and D. Guy (1985) 'Speech Input as an Adjunct to Keyboard Entry in Television Subtitling', in B. Shackel (ed.) *Proceedings Human-Computer Interaction—INTERACT'84*, Amsterdam: North Holland, 203–208.

Dumouchel, P., G. Boulianne and J. Brousseau (2011) 'Measures for Quality of Closed Captioning', in A. Şerban, A. Matamala and J.-M. Lavaur (eds) *Audiovisual Translation in Close-up: Practical and Theoretical Approaches*, Bern: Peter Lang, 161–172.

Dutka, Ł., A. Szarkowska, K. Krejtz and O. Pilipczuk (2015) 'Investigating the Competences of Interlingual Respeakers—A Preliminary Study', paper presented at the *5th International Symposium on Respeaking, Live Subtitling and Accessibility*, 12 June 2015, Rome.

English Broadcasters Group (EBG) (2014) *Report on Efforts to Improve the Quality of Closed Captioning*, Toronto: EBG. Available online: http://www.crtc.gc.ca/fra/BCASTING/ann_rep/bmt_cbc_rm_sm.pdf [last access 20 December 2017].

Eugeni, C. (2006) 'Introduzione al rispeakeraggio televisivo', in C. Eugeni and G. Mack (eds) *Intralinea, Special Issue on Respeaking*. Available online: http://www.intralinea.org/specials/article/Introduzione_al_rispeakeraggio_televisivo [last access 20 December 2017].

Eugeni, C. (2008a) 'Respeaking the News for the Deaf: For a Real Special Needs-oriented Subtitling', *Studies in English Language and Literature* 21, National Taiwan University of Science and Technology, Taipei.

Eugeni, C. (2008b) 'A Sociolinguistic Approach to Real-time Subtitling: Respeaking vs. Shadowing and Simultaneous Interpreting', in C. J. Kellett Bidoli and E. Ochse (eds) *English in International Deaf Communication*, Bern: Peter Lang, 357–382.

Eugeni, C. (2009a) *La sottotitolazione in diretta TV. Analisi strategica del rispeakeraggio verbatim di BBC News (Live Subtitling for TV. Strategic Analysis of Live Subtitling for BBC News)*, Unpublished Doctoral Thesis, Naples: Università degli Studi di Napoli Federico II.

Eugeni, C. (2009b) 'Respeaking the BBC News: A Strategic Analysis of Respeaking on the BBC', *The Sign Language Translator and Interpreter* 3(1): 29–68.

Eugeni, C. (2012) 'A Strategic Model for the Analysis of Respoken TV Subtitles', *US-China Foreign Language* 10(6).

Eugeni, C. and G. Mack (2006) (eds) *Intralinea, Special Issue on New Technologies in Real Time Intralingual Subtitling*. Available online: http://www.intralinea.org/specials/respeaking [last access 20 December 2017].

García Romero, A. J. (2015) *Measuring Accuracy, Delay, Errors and Speed in Live Subtitling: Revisiting the Application of the NER Model in the Spanish Television*, Unpublished MA Dissertation, London: University of Roehampton.

González Lago, M. D. (2011) *Accuracy Analysis of Respoken Subtitles Broadcast by RTVE, the Spanish Public Television Channel*, Unpublished MA Dissertation, London: University of Roehampton.

Imai, T., A. Kobayashi, S. Sato, S. Homma, T. Oku and T. Takagi (2008) 'Improvements of the Speech Recognition Technology for Real-Time Broadcast Closed-Captioning', *Proceedings of the Spoken Document Processing Workshop* 2: 113–120.

Jensema, C., R. McCann and S. Ramsey (1996) 'Closed-captioned Television Presentation Speed and Vocabulary', *American Annals of the Deaf* 141(4): 284–292.

de Korte, T. (2006) 'Live Inter-lingual Subtitling in the Netherlands', in C. Eugeni and G. Mack (eds) *Intralinea, Special Issue on Respeaking.* Available online: http://www.intralinea.org/specials/article/Live_inter-lingual_subtitling_in_the_Netherlands [last access 20 December 2017].

Lambourne, A., J. Hewitt, C. Lyon and S. Warren (2004) 'Speech-Based Real-Time Subtitling Services', *International Journal of Speech Technology* 7(4): 269–79.

Lambourne, A. (2006) 'Subtitle Respeaking', in C. Eugeni and G. Mack (eds) *Intralinea, Special Issue on Respeaking.* Available online: http://www.intralinea.org/specials/article/Subtitle_respeaking [last access 20 December 2017].

Luyckx, B., T. Delbeke, L. Van Waes, M. Leijten and A. Remael (2013) 'Live Subtitling with Speech Recognition. Causes and Consequences of Text Reduction', *Across Languages and Cultures* 14(1): 15–46.

Mack, G. (2006) 'Detto scritto: un fenomeno, tanti nomi', in C. Eugeni and G. Mack (eds) *Intralinea, Special Issue on Respeaking.* Available online: http://www.intralinea.org/specials/article/Detto_scritto_un_fenomeno_tanti_nomi [last access 20 December 2017].

Marsh, A. (2004) *Simultaneous Interpreting and Respeaking: A Comparison*, Unpublished MA Dissertation, London: University of Westminster.

Marsh, A. (2006) 'Respeaking for the BBC', in C. Eugeni and G. Mack (eds) *Intralinea, Special Issue on Respeaking.* Available online: http://www.intralinea.org/specials/article/Respeaking_for_the_BBC [last access 20 December 2017].

Matamala, A., P. Romero-Fresco and L. Daniluk (forthcoming) 'An Exploratory Study on the Use of Respeaking for The Transcription of Non-fictional Genres', submitted to *Meta*.

Matthews, L. (2015) *Getting the Full Picture? Viewers' Experiences of Television Subtitling*, London: AOHL (Action on Hearing Loss).

Mikul, C. (2014) *Caption Quality: International Approaches to Standards and Measurement*, Sydney: Media Access Australia.

Moussadek, M. (2008) 'Sous-titreur pour sourds à la TV, un nouveau métier en Suisse', *Intermittent'Sign* 140: 15.

Muller, T. (2015) 'Long Questionnaire on SDH in France', in P. Romero-Fresco (ed.) *The Reception of Subtitles for the Deaf and Hard of Hearing*, Berlin: Peter Lang, 163–189.

Muzii, L. (2006) 'Respeaking e localizzazione', in C. Eugeni and G. Mack (eds) *Intralinea, Special Issue on Respeaking.* Available online: http://www.intralinea.org/specials/article/Respeaking_e_localizzazione [last access 20 December 2017].

National Verbatim Reporters Association (NVRA) (2008) 'The Horace Web Story'. Available online: https://nvra.org/historical [last access 20 December 2017].

Ofcom (2013) 'Measuring the Quality of Live Subtitling'. Available online: https://www.ofcom.org.uk/__data/assets/pdf_file/0017/51731/qos-statement.pdf [last access 20 December 2017].

Ofcom (2015a) *Measuring Live Subtitling Quality: Results from the Fourth Sampling Exercise*, London: Office of Communications. Available online: https://www.ofcom.org.uk/__data/assets/pdf_file/0011/41114/qos_4th_report.pdf [last access 20 December 2017].

Ofcom (2015b) *Measuring Live Subtitling Quality: Results from the Third sampling Exercise*, London: Office of Communications. Available online: https://www.ofcom.org.uk/__data/assets/pdf_file/0022/40774/qos_3rd_report.pdf [last access 20 December 2017].

onA.I.R (n.d.) 'Respeaking onA.I.R'. Available online: http://www.respeakingonair.org/en/ [last access 20 December 2017].

Orero, P. (2006) 'Real-time Subtitling in Spain', in C. Eugeni and G. Mack (eds) *Intralinea, Special Issue on Respeaking.* Available online: http://www.intralinea.org/specials/article/Real-time_subtitling_in_Spain [last access 20 December 2017].

Pirelli, G. (2006) 'Le necessità dei sordi: la sottotitolazione in tempo reale all'università', in C. Eugeni and G. Mack (eds) *Intralinea, Special Issue on Respeaking*. Available online: http://www.intralinea.org/specials/article/Le_necessita_dei_sordi_la_sottotitolazione_in_tempo_reale_alluniversita [last access 20 December 2017].

Prazak, A., Z. Loose, J. Psutka and V. Radova (2011) 'Four-phase Re-speaker Training System', *SIGMAP, International Conference on Signal Processing and Multimedia Applications*, 217–220.

Rajendran, Dhevi J., A. T. Duchowski, P. Orero, J. Martínez and P. Romero-Fresco (2013) 'Effects of Text Chunking on Subtitling: A Quantitative and Qualitative Examination', *Perspectives: Studies in Translatology* 21(1): 5–21.

Rander, A. and P. Olaf Looms (2010) 'The Accessibility of Television News with Live Subtitling on Digital Television', *EuroITV '10. Proceedings of the 8th International Interactive Conference on Interactive TV & Video*: 155–160.

Remael, A. (2007) 'Sampling Subtitling for the Deaf and the Hard-of-Hearing in Europe', in J. Díaz Cintas, A. Remael and P. Orero (eds) *Media for All*, Amsterdam: Rodopi, 23–52.

Remael, A. and B. van der Veer (2006) 'Real-Time Subtitling in Flanders: Needs and Teaching', in C. Eugeni and G. Mack (eds) *Intralinea, Special Issue on Respeaking*. Available online: http://www.intralinea.org/specials/article/Real-Time_Subtitling_in_Flanders_Needs_and_Teaching [last access 20 December 2017].

Respeaking 2009 (n.d.) *Second International Seminar on Real-Time Intralingual Subtitling*, held at Universitat Autònoma de Barcelona, Spain, 19 June 2009. Available online: http://www.respeaking.net/barcelona_2009.html [last access 20 December 2017].

Respeaking 2011 (n.d.) *Third International Symposium on Live Subtitling with Speech Recognition. Exploring New Avenues and New Contexts: Live Subtitling and Other Respeaking Applications for (Media) Accessibility*, held at University of Antwerp, 21st October 2011. Available online: http://www.respeaking.net/antwerp%202011.html [last access 20 December 2017].

Respeaking 2013 (n.d.) *4th International Symposium on Live Subtitling: Live Subtitling with Respeaking and Other Respeaking Applications*, held at Universitat Autònoma de Barcelona, Spain, 12 March 2013. Available online: http://www.respeaking.net/barcelona%202013.html [last access 20 December 2017].

Respeaking 2015 (n.d.) *5th International Symposium on Respeaking, Live Subtitling and Accessibility*, held at Università degli studi Internazionali di Roma, 12 June 2015. Available online: http://www.unint.eu/it/component/content/article/8-pagina/494-respeaking-live-subtitling-and-accessibility.html [last access 20 December 2017].

Respeaking Project (n. d.) *Respeaking: Process, Competences, Quality*. Available online: https://avt.ils.uw.edu.pl/projekty/ [last access 20 December 2017].

Romero-Fresco, P. (2008) 'La subtitulación rehablada: palabras que no se lleva el viento', in Á. Pérez-Ugena and R. Vizcaíno-Laorga (eds) *ULISES: Hacia el desarrollo de tecnologías comunicativas para la igualdad de Oportunidades*, Madrid: Observatorio de las Realidades Sociales y de la Comunicación, 49–73.

Romero-Fresco, P. (2009) 'More Haste Less Speed: Edited vs. Verbatim Respeaking', *Vigo International Journal of Applied Linguistics* (VIAL) VI: 109–33.

Romero-Fresco, P. (2010) 'Standing on Quicksand: Viewers' Comprehension and Reading Patterns of Respoken Subtitles for the News', in J. Díaz Cintas, A. Matamala and J. Neves (eds) *New Insights into Audiovisual Translation and Media Accessibility*, Amsterdam: Rodopi, 175–195.

Romero-Fresco, P. (2011) *Subtitling through Speech Recognition: Respeaking*, Manchester: Routledge.

Romero-Fresco, P. (2012a) 'Respeaking in Translator Training Curricula. Present and Future Prospects', *The Interpreter and Translator Trainer* (ITT) 6–1: 91–112.

Romero-Fresco, P. (2012b) 'Quality in Live Subtitling: The Reception of Respoken Subtitles in the UK', in A. Remael, P. Orero and M. Carroll (eds) *Audiovisual Translation and Media Accessibility at the Crossroads*, Amsterdam: Rodopi, 111–133.

Romero-Fresco, P. (2015) 'Final Thoughts: Viewing Speed', in P. Romero-Fresco (ed.) *The Reception of Subtitles for the Deaf and Hard of Hearing*, Berlin: Peter Lang, 335–343.

Romero-Fresco, P. (2016) 'Accessing Communication: The Quality of Live Subtitles in the UK', *Language & Communication* 49: 56–69.

Romero-Fresco, P. and J. Martínez (2015) 'Accuracy Rate in Live Subtitling: The NER Model', in J. Díaz Cintas and R. Baños (eds) *Audiovisual Translation in a Global Context: Mapping an Ever-changing Landscape*, Palgrave Macmillan, 28–50.

Romero-Fresco, P. and F. Pöchhacker (2017) 'Quality Assessment in Interlingual Live Subtitling: The NTR Model', *Linguistica Antverpiensia* 16: 149–167.

Russello, C. (2010) 'Teaching Respeaking to Conference Interpreters', paper presented at the *2010 Intersteno Conference*. Available online: https://www.intersteno.it/materiale/ComitScientifico/EducationCommittee/Russello2010Teaching%20Respeaking%20to%20Conference%20Interpreters.pdf [last access 20 December 2017].

Sandford, J. (2015) 'The Impact of Subtitle Display Rate on Enjoyment under Normal Television Viewing Conditions', *The Best of IET and IBC 2015–2016*, The Institution of Engineering and Technology, 62–67.

SAVAS project (n.d.) Available online: https://cordis.europa.eu/project/rcn/103572_en.html [last access 20 December 2017].

Sperber, M., G. Neubig and C. Fügen (2013) 'Efficient Speech Transcription through Respeaking', *InterSpeech*, 1087–1091.

Szarkowska, A., Ł. Dutka, A. Chmiel, A. Lijewska, K. Krejtz, K. Marasek and Ł. Brockide (2015) 'Are Interpreters Better Respeakers? An Exploratory Study on Respeaking Competences', paper presented at the *5th International Symposium on Respeaking, Live Subtitling and Accessibility*, 12 June 2015, Rome.

Translectures Project (n.d.) 'Transcription and Translation of Video Lectures'. Available online: http://www.translectures.eu/ https://www.intersteno.it/materiale/ComitScientifico/EducationCommittee/Russello2010Teaching%20Respeaking%20to%20Conference%20Interpreters.pdf

Trivulzio, F. (2006) 'Natura non facit saltus', in C. Eugeni and G. Mack (eds) *Intralinea. Special issue on New Technologies in Real Time Intralingual Subtitling*. Available online: http://www.intralinea.org/specials/article/1690 [last access 20 December 2017].

Valor Miró, J. D., C. Turró, J. Civera, and A. Juan (2015) 'Evaluación de la revisión de transcripciones y traducciones automáticas de vídeos Polimedia', *Proceedings of I Congreso Nacional de Innovación Educativa y Docencia en Red (IN-RED 2015)* Valencia (Spain), 461–465.

Van Waes, L., M. Leijten and A. Remael (2013) 'Live Subtitling with Speech Recognition: Causes and Consequences of Text Reduction', *Across Languages and Cultures* 14(1): 15–46.

Verdeguer, S. (2012) *Quality in Live Subtitling: A Comparative Analysis of Respoken Subtitles in the UK*, Unpublished MA Dissertation, London: University of Roehampton.

Zick, R. G. and J. Olsen (2011) 'Voice Recognition Software versus a Traditional Transcription Service for Physician Charting in the ED', *The American Journal of Emergency Medicine* 19(4): 295–298.

8

Audio description

Evolving recommendations for usable, effective and enjoyable practices

Elisa Perego

Definition

Audio description (AD) is a form of assistive audiovisual translation, or inclusion service, designed to make (audio)visual products available to blind and visually impaired persons (VIPs). AD offers people who cannot see what others take for granted. Also known as 'video description', 'described video' (Piety 2004), and 'audio captions' (Snyder 2014), AD is a unique form of communication that captures and translates the visual elements of a source text into spoken words. When present, e.g. in audiovisual texts, these words combine—and yet do not interfere—with the existing auditory ensemble (consisting of dialogues, sounds, music, noise, silence, etc.) to form a new coherent text. AD enables VIPs to access, understand better and appreciate more fully products that are conceived primarily as visual, such as paintings or films. Therefore, it has an important social impact enabling VIPs to integrate in the cultural and social life they are embedded in.

AD can therefore be used to describe the visual aspects of any product, service or event that combines multiple semiotic modes to create meaning. In practice, this includes all static and dynamic arts—e.g. artworks in cultural venues, museums and heritage sites as well as television programmes, films and theatre plays—but also educational material, public meetings, sports or religious events, and ceremonies.

Despite the versatility of AD and the variety of uses it has been put to, this assistive service appears to be typically associated with the medium of film. Film AD is no doubt the most well-known, spread, established and researched AD type. However, more recent forms of AD (e.g. dance and concert AD) are gaining ground.

Depending on the nature of the product to be made accessible, AD has to fulfil different requirements (Remael *et al.* 2015). It can be prepared ahead and delivered in a pre-recorded form—as in the case of film or museum AD, or it can be performed live—as often happens in theatre performances (Holland 2009). In the case of museum exhibitions (Neves 2015), AD can be combined with tactile information. In those countries where subtitling is the dominant AVT modality, the subtitles are voiced (i.e. turned into audio subtitles) and they interweave with regular AD, which is added in the pauses between dialogues (Braun and Orero 2010). AD can also be preceded by an audio introduction (York 2007). Audio introductions are introductory notes that serve as a framework for the blind audience or provide information about the visual style of the product. Audio introductions have been used in the opera and theatre since the early days of AD, but they have been traditionally absent from AD for films and television, even though the idea of introducing them to these products has recently begun to gain currency (Fryer and Romero-Fresco 2014, Romero-Fresco and Fryer 2013).

The creation of AD entails the collaboration of several professionals: audio describers, voice talents or voice actors, sound technicians and, ideally, blind consultants. There is not yet a fixed template for the creation of AD, but even if each company follows its own in-house rules, the process generally starts with the analysis of the product, the writing, rewriting and editing of the description, the timing of the AD script—especially in film description, where it is necessary to map out the pauses between the dialogues—and its final editing. The latter step usually benefits both from teamwork, which can help to make the right lexical choices, and from the presence of a blind consultant, who can help to tailor the script to the real needs of end users by providing feedback and suggesting adaptations (Perego and Benecke 2014). Finally, rehearsing the AD enables professionals to make final changes before recording it with voice talents or synthetic voices and mixing it with the original soundtrack, if present (Remael *et al.* 2015: 12–13).

The whole process is time-consuming—it takes about 16 to 20 hours to write the descriptions for a 1-hour drama episode, and about 2 to 3 hours to record a 1-hour script (Cronin and King 1990: 503). The fact that the audio describer often has to spot the in and out times to insert ADs between dialogues in films only adds up to the already complex descriptive work. However, in spite of its technicalities and need for precision, AD is a highly creative process, even comparable to a kind of literary art form (Snyder 2008), that demands a thorough mastering of one's mother tongue.

Target audience

AD caters both for blind and visually impaired patrons. Indeed, professionals and scholars know well that the target audience for audio described content is varied. Significantly, official parameters used to define blindness vary across different countries, and the same AD might not suit all audience members to the same extent (ADLAB 2012: 6, Ofcom 2010: 9, Remael *et al.* 2015: 17). Each type of visual impairment affects differently an individual's ability to perceive the world and to conduct their daily routine activities independently or with various degrees of assistance. For example, people can suffer from moderate to severe visual impairment, or they can be completely blind. Furthermore, visual impairment may be congenital when it occurs during the process of foetal development, at birth or immediately following birth, i.e. before visual memory has been established at all—or adventitious—i.e. after having enjoyed a period of normal vision, which allows visual memory to remain at least partially (Project IDEAL 2013, WHO 2014). Consequently, 'some users will still rely on the visual information to some extent, whereas others might use the AD as a talking book' (Remael *et al.* 2015: 17).

Originally meant exclusively for VIPs (see, for example, Frazier 1975, Cronin and King 1990), AD is thought to be extremely useful for other sectors of the population too. Potential extended users include vulnerable audiences such as the mentally disabled, users with attention deficit hyperactivity disorder, new immigrants and older adults (ADLAB 2012, Dosch and Benecke 2004, Ofcom 2010, Morisset and Gonant 2008, Remael *et al.* 2015), but also regular users such as children, language learners or people who want to follow AV material while performing another task. However, in spite of the known benefits that AD delivers to VIPs, the impact of AD on sighted viewers is not yet fully understood. To date, empirical research on the effect of AD on sighted users is limited or incomplete. While a number of empirical studies would appear to confirm preliminarily that AD does not pose major challenges to regular audiences (Cronin and King 1990, Krejtz *et al.* 2012a, 2012b; Perego 2016), it is not yet possible to give a definite answer on whether AD would interfere with sighted viewers' comprehension, memory and enjoyment of the audio described product; another question that remains currently unanswered is whether the addition of a verbal stimulus to the film complex semiotic system may have a positive effect on viewers—e.g. helping them remember lexical items. Knowing whether sighted viewers are able to cope with AD, however, would help scholars open new theoretical and applied perspectives into the study of AD. Not only could it tell us, for instance, whether sighted viewers and VIPs can tolerate audio described films, but it would also shed light on the feasibility of extending the uses of AD beyond its original purpose and target audience.

History and development of audio description

AD has always been employed, more or less loosely, to verbalize visual material for the blind (Benecke 2004, Ofcom 2000, Snyder 2014). However, the first instance of its professional use was documented in the early 1940s: in Spain, after the Civil War, AD began to be provided weekly (Orero 2007).

The use of AD as a formalized means of enhancing entertainment for VIPs can be traced back to the 1980s, and attributed to Margaret and Cody Pfanstiehl, from the Metropolitan Washington Ear, who started to produce and promote AD for live theatre performances across the whole of the US (ADC 2013, Snyder 2014). By the end of the 1980s, over fifty establishments overseas were producing described performances. In Europe, the work of a small family-run theatre in Nottinghamshire paved the way for the regular provision of AD in British theatres (Ofcom 2000: 4). Today, the UK still is Europe's leading country in terms of number of venues that regularly offer audio described performances, with others (e.g. Spain) quickly catching up.

Back in the 1980s, cinema began to benefit from AD too. The first countries to employ regular descriptions using live script readers were Britain and France (Ofcom 2000: 4), but it was in the US that AD took off. A key figure in this respect was Gregory Frazier, a pioneer in the field and the founder of Audio Vision, a non-profit organization that has provided description services since 1989, and been the standard setter for descriptive services ever since. Today, Britain (followed by Spain and the Dutch-speaking areas of the Netherlands and the Flemish region) is a leading country in cinema AD; in most other European countries, the provision of AD is either confined to special screenings—often in the context of film festivals or one-off projects—or simply does not exist at all (ADLAB 2012).

The 1980s also witnessed the first instances of AD on television (ADLAB 2012, Ofcom 2000). Today, the service is offered in most countries, although there is wide variation in terms of availability and regulatory framework concerning the provision of assistive forms of translation, with the US and the UK leading the field. The reason for the scarcity of AD on television is that private broadcasters are still too reluctant to offer AD, given that it is not likely to deliver a substantial return on the investment required to deliver AD services (ADLAB 2012: 17). To make things worse, the scant offer of AD on television is not always compensated by the availability of audio described home video products. The production of DVDs and Blu-ray discs remains very limited, except in the English-speaking world, where AD is routinely included with other post-production extras. By contrast, in some European countries (e.g. Portugal, Italy and Flanders) the offer of audio described commercial DVDs and Blu-ray discs is almost negligible (ADLAB 2012).

Although its existence as an area of professional practice is widely acknowledged, AD is a relatively young academic discipline. Its inception dates back to the 1970s, when Gregory Frazier (1938–1996) developed the first set of AD principles as part of his master dissertation in the field of broadcasting (Frazier 1975). Since then, AD has been practised and studied all over the world, with different countries following different timeframes in terms of enforcement of legislation, provision of AD services, production of guidelines, as well as support for research and training initiatives (ADLAB 2012, ADLAB PRO 2017a, Perego 2014a, Rai *et al.* 2010).

In the academic world, AD has gained recognition and visibility mainly since the turn of the century—although some key studies were conducted much earlier (e.g. Lodge 1993, Peli *et al.* 1996). AD-specific events (e.g. the biannual *Advance Research Seminars on Audio Description* held in Barcelona, Spain) and thematic sessions within specialized conferences (*Media for All* and *Languages and the Media*) are being held on a regular basis, and the number of academic publications on different aspects of AD has significantly increased. The fact that AD-related papers are being published in a range of journals from various disciplinary areas (from translation studies to literary, medical and psychology periodicals) bears witness to the multi-faceted nature of AD and the relevance of multiple disciplines to the development of research on this specific AVT mode.

Audio description guidelines: past and present

Guidelines are sets of general rules, principles or pieces of advice seeking to streamline and harmonize particular processes, ultimately enhancing the quality of the final product. In the case of AD, guidelines (also known as standards or norms) have emerged from the need to establish reliable criteria and to homogenize AD scriptwriting practices—at least within each local context. Guidelines have also emerged to assist professionals lacking specific training in AD, as this is not always easy to find (ADLAB PRO 2017a).

Existing guidelines differ in terms of length, precision, theoretical orientation and general focus, and they do not adhere to a uniform structure (Vercauteren 2007, Rai *et al.* 2010, Bittner 2012), as they are often issued by different organizations. Ireland and the UK, for instance, have official guidelines compiled by television and broadcasting commissions, respectively. The Spanish guidelines have been developed and approved by a recognized standardization body, AENOR. The guidelines currently used in Germany and in Italy were formulated by professional service providers: Bayerischer Rundfunk and Senza Barriere. In France and French Belgium, the guidelines have been prepared by cultural associations or theatre companies, whereas in Flemish Belgium, Catalonia, Greece and Portugal they have been produced and developed by academics.

Guidelines have become available at different points in each country, which is indicative of varying national stances towards AD in particular, and towards inclusion services in general. Most guidelines have been issued since the turn of the century. The British standards can be traced back to the year 2000 (Ofcom 2000). The UK was followed by Germany (Dosch and Benecke 2004), Spain (AENOR 2005), Ireland (BCI 2005), Greece (Georgakopoulou

2008), France (Morisset and Gonant 2008), Catalonia (Puigdomènech *et al.* 2008), French-speaking Belgium (ABCD 2009, Audioscenic 2010) Poland (Szymańska and Strzymiński 2010), Dutch-speaking Belgium (Remael and Vercauteren 2011), Portugal (Neves 2011), and Italy (Busarello and Sordo 2011). Outside Europe, the countries with recognized guidelines are Australia (with guidelines inspired by their UK and the US counterparts) and the US (ADC 2009).

Most guidelines agree on key aspects of AD formulation (Bittner 2012, Rai *et al.* 2010). However, while they are all essentially prescriptive, some are more rigid in their expression of the rules and fail to consider that, in some cases, these rules can or even should be disregarded. So, instead of providing a general strategy that makes audio describers think about creative alternatives, they tend to restrict their sphere of action (Bittner 2012). Furthermore, however valid locally, most guidelines are rarely based on empirical research; instead, in most cases, they are informed by experience, common sense and personal preferences.

The growing awareness that the actual needs of blind users (as opposed to the intuition of sighted describers) should shape the norms governing AD formulation, and that reception research can facilitate the definition of usable translation standards and good practices (Chmiel and Mazur 2012) has shaped the remit of the European project ADLAB (*Audio Description: Lifelong Access for the Blind*). ADLAB (2011–2014) sought to draw reliable AD guidelines reflecting the preferences and needs of the visually impaired audience and ensure that they are usable throughout Europe. The idea of common European guidelines is not new (Vercauteren 2007), but it was not until 2011 that it became a reality under the framework of the ADLAB project.

The extensive research work and results of the empirical studies carried out by the ADLAB team produced the first set of accessible AD strategic guidelines or recommendations: *Pictures Painted in Words: ADLAB Audio Description Guidelines* (Remael *et al.* 2015). These guidelines (i) have been made available as an open source e-book with several accessibility features—so users can choose to read the book using text-to-speech or magnification; (ii) are strategic because they propose flexible strategies (vs. rigid norms) to face the most critical issues arising in the AD process; and (iii) reach out beyond the realm of film and television to cover areas such as theatre, museum and exhibitions. In the case of film AD, they emphasize the importance of having a deep understanding of the main narrative elements of the source material, thus highlighting the relevance of film and cinema studies to the practice of AD.

Instead of offering set solutions to AD problems, these recommendations show that there are several ways of dealing with difficulties in any given set of circumstances. The guidelines thus take the form of advice based on meticulous analysis and testing and they are organized under headings that flag up the most challenging areas in AD formulation (Maszerowska *et al.* 2014; Remael *et al.* 2015). Technically, each chapter revolves around a specific topic (e.g. text on screen, or wording and style) and it is divided into four parts: definition of the topic, analysis of the source text (e.g. film, play, audio introduction, etc.), suggestions on the production of the target text (based on the following model: 'once you have established whether ... make a decision on ... '), and examples of possible strategies taken from real ADs. The central idea is that it is necessary to adopt individual strategies instead of general across-the-board recommendations. As in any other type of translation, individual solutions are decided within each specific context and should be carefully considered by the decision-maker, i.e. the audio describer.

The language of audio description

Distinctive features

Language is an aspect of AD that has received much attention (Arma 2011, Maszerowska *et al.* 2014, Piety 2004, Rai *et al.* 2010, Salway 2007, Snyder 2008, Taylor 2015). After all, AD entails the transposition of images into words. Lexical, grammatical, syntactic and stylistic choices therefore become crucial to warrant that AD is at the same time usable, effective and enjoyable. Scholars and guidelines have therefore been trying to determine the most appropriate linguistic features of a good AD for some time. In order to designate these features, a wide range of adjectives has been employed. On the whole, though, the adjectives 'meticulous', 'concise', 'visually intense' and 'usable' (see below for definitions) seem to portray the distinctive and preferred features of AD language (Perego 2014a: 28–30) (see Table 8.1). There is no univocal definition for each term, and while no systematic research on these specific aspects of AD exists yet, it is possible to make some general observations. On the whole, 'meticulous' and 'visual intense' pertain mainly to the lexical domain of AD, whereas 'concise' and 'usable' are more closely related to the syntax.

These key features can be defined as follows:

- A *meticulous* AD provides detailed, accurate and precise descriptions through well-chosen, clear (vs. obscure, jargon-rich) vocabulary. A meticulous AD generates from the observational skills of the describer that should be able to analyze and understand the source text, select its most salient visual elements, and make the right word choice in a given context. However, not only do words have to be appropriate to the context: they should also engage the listener through long-lasting descriptions.

Table 8.1 Key adjectives used to define AD

Main features of AD	Common terms used in literature	Sources
Meticulous	detailed	Remael and Vercauteren 2011
	accurate	Ofcom 2010
	precise	AENOR 2005, Morisset and Gonant 2008
	well-chosen	ADP 2009
Concise	succinct	ADP 2009, Ofcom 2010, Snyder 2007
	concise	ADP 2009
Visually intense	imaginative	ADP 2009, Snyder 2007
	rich	Morisset and Gonant 2008
	descriptive	BCI 2005
	vivid	ADP 2009, Remael and Vercauteren 2011, Snyder 2007, Taylor 2015
	varied	Remael and Vercauteren 2011, Ofcom 2010, Busarello and Sordo 2011
Usable	simple	Ofcom 2010
	clear	ADP 2009, Taylor 2015

- *Visual intensity* refers to the depth and the force with which AD conveys visual details in words. The adjectives found in literature—e.g. 'imaginative', 'rich', 'descriptive', 'vivid', 'varied'—generally refer to visual intensity, a quality of AD that brings it closer to an art than a craft (Snyder 2008: 192).
- Given the needs of the target audience and the communicative purposes of AD, as well as its strict time limitations, the density of information conveyed through carefully selected words is not compatible with an equally dense, or intricate, syntax. *Concision* is therefore vital. Audio describers should learn to use no more words than necessary to convey ideas effectively, taking care not to omit important information.
- Concision is also a first step towards usable ADs that are easy to access and understand. In AD, *usability* is typically achieved through the use of plain syntax favouring short sentences and uncluttered constructions, as well as a logical organization of information (e.g. from known to new, from general to specific) facilitating text processing and visualization (Taylor 2015: 49–50).

Idiosyncratic features of a special language

Ideally, AD should be meticulous, concise, visually intense and usable. But how do ADs behave in reality? Only corpus-based investigations can answer this question and enable us to understand how AD works in practice. To date, corpus-based research in AD is limited (Arma 2011, Jiménez Hurtado *et al.* 2010, Piety 2004, Salway 2007). However, existing studies preliminarily indicate that AD *has* some idiosyncratic features. In other words, it would seem to be a language of its own, exhibiting features that are different from those characterizing general language.

Salway (2007), for instance, observed that, compared to general language, AD shows a higher rate of non-grammatical words; words referring to actions, especially in the form of troponyms—verbs that express a particular manner of doing something, e.g. spins, crawls, etc. (Salway 2007: 159); and unusual lexical combinations to describe, for example, characters' appearances ('woman/man in'; 'woman/man wearing') or aspects of their interaction with other characters (e.g. 'turns to', 'shakes hands', 'sit next to', etc.) (Salway 2007: 160–161). Salway's pioneering study is based on a large corpus (91 films), but the regularities he found can only be regarded as typical of English AD language—indeed other languages might behave differently. This has been initially demonstrated in a smaller-scale comparative study conducted on Italian vs. English by Arma (2011, 2012), which has identified some similarities in sentence structure that exist in both languages, but also a number of Italian-specific features, e.g. the tendency to overuse secondary embedded clauses despite recommendations against this practice (Busarello and Sordo 2011).

The existence of regularities in AD scripts, as documented in existing corpora, is both useful and encouraging. These findings might be of assistance to those who produce ADs and train audio describers (ADLAB PRO, n.d.). Drawing on other corpora might also yield insights into the idiosyncrasy of AD in other languages, and thus refine our understanding of the universal features of AD across languages—which could then be tested on VIPs to establish how the effectiveness of AD can be maximized (Salway 2007: 171).

The style of audio description

An important aspect of the language of AD pertains to style, i.e. the way in which vocabulary and grammar vary across different speech situations. The style of a text is aimed to produce certain effects and to evoke certain responses in AD users. It is determined by diction (the choice and use of words) and syntax (the sentence structure) (Leech and Short 1981). Closely related to such phenomena is the use of rhetorical devices, e.g. rhythmic patterns and sound effects, which are typical of poetry and verse-drama.

The style of AD is crucial: there is a widely held consensus (Rai *et al.* 2010) that it should match the style, tone and pace of the programme, scene or event that is being described, and be consistent throughout a film or across the various episodes of a television series. The information included in the description must also be appropriate for the target audience for a specific film (Rai *et al.* 2010: 7). The description should not stand out or draw attention to itself, but the describer should blend in seamlessly with the rest of the audio. To do so, the AD should respect the genre of the source text and its specificities (Georgakopoulou 2008, Ofcom 2000, Maszerowska *et al.* 2014, Rai *et al.* 2010, Remael *et al.* 2015). Accordingly, the AD for a dramatic black and white film will have to avoid colloquial or slang lexical choices, unconventional syntax, or a squeaky voice to narrate it.

On the other hand, AD for children favours a more intimate and expressive style, as well as the use of proper intonation and lexical choices. The description of Disney's *Dumbo* (1941), for example, includes items like 'big smile', 'Dumbo's little trunk' and 'two plump teardrops'. These are reflective of the greater simplicity of narratives aimed at children, but also of the 'cuteness' that drives some animation films (Ofcom 2000, AENOR 2005, BCI 2005).

Objectivity vs. subjectivity

Whereas it is easy to agree on the style that AD scripts should have, the question of interpretative vs. neutral descriptions is still open and the debate on objectivity vs. subjectivity remains unresolved. Interpretation is the 'subjective treatment of reality perceived by audio describers . . . and the equally subjective verbal expression of that reality' in AD (Mazur and Chmiel 2012: 173–174). Most early AD guidelines do not welcome subjective judgments and they openly favour objectivity as a way to avoid manipulation, spoon-feeding or a patronizing attitude towards the target audience (Mazur and Chmiel 2012, Rai *et al.* 2010). The ITC guidelines (Ofcom 2000: 15–16) warn their readers and prospective audio describers not to give personal opinions or interpret events, and stipulate that, in general, information must never give away the plot. In the same vein, the French Audio Description Charter dictates that embracing objectivity is important: by remaining objective, audio describers do not impose their feelings on viewers, aiming instead to stir the listener's (Morrisett and Gonant 2008: 2, Rai *et al.* 2010: 61). This is an uncompromising view that is shared, for instance, by the German (Dosch and Benecke 2004) and the Italian (Busarello and Sordo 2011) guidelines, and that is also fiercely endorsed by the American school: qualitative judgements are unnecessary, unwanted and unacceptable because they interpret subjectively (instead of describing objectively) and leave no interpretative space to users (Snyder 2007: 102).

From a practical point of view, formulating objective descriptions favours the use of factual adjectives ('tall', 'blond-haired'), rather than evaluative adjectives ('ugly', 'beautiful'), and specific descriptive adverbs ('arguably', 'characteristically', 'clearly', 'instinctively') are preferred over vague interpretative ones ('anxiously', 'brusquely', 'eagerly') (Ofcom 2000, Mazur and Chmiel 2012).

Instances of more flexible views on the use of interpretative language, however, do exist (Haig 2005, Mälzer-Semlinger 2012, Orero 2012, Udo and Fels 2009), especially in Europe and in Canada. These derive from a different conception of AD and of the work of the audio describer, based on the premise that a work of art such as a film—as is also the case with paintings or dance performances—needs to be fully understood, and its story needs to be reconstructed for the new audience, even when the reconstruction of the source text can open the way for the AD to incorporate inferences made by the describer (Udo and Fels 2009). According to the supporters of this view, interpreting is not a problem; on the contrary, it is sometimes the only means to give VIPs an experience that is comparable to that of sighted audiences.

Crucially, it is not always clear when judgments are subjective, or which interpretations are more objective, and hence more worthy of being included in AD (Mazur and Chmiel 2012: 174). This is the reason why it is difficult—almost impossible, despite the describer's effort—to be objective. In fact, audio describers are also viewers, and the story that they tell will always represent, to some extent, their own interpretation of seemingly factual contents (Remael et al. 2015: 17). The fact that any source text contains elements that are extremely difficult to describe objectively—e.g. gestures, facial expressions, or complex emotions (Dosch and Benecke 2004, Mazur and Chmiel 2012, Mazur 2014)—lends further credence to the idea that rigid norms governing AD are disruptive and can interfere with the quality and the effectiveness of the final product.

It is reassuring however to read that, in spite of the different views on the objectivity/subjectivity issue, 'the research revealed that there are many definitions of a successful audio description, not merely because describing styles differ, but because there are many fundamental differences in audience expectation, need and experience' (Ofcom 2000: 4). Current research seems to show that VIPs do not appreciate inflexible objectivity (Mazur and Chmiel 2012), which brings us back to the most crucial principles of AD formulation: (i) it is necessary to find the right balance between interpretation and objectivity, so that VIPs are always given enough room to develop their own interpretations; and (ii) the need to always favour the end users' preferences over sighted viewers' and audio describers' intuitions. Such preferences should provide orientation for professionals, and can be formalized through systematic audience research (ADLAB 2013, ADLAB PRO 2017b).

Reception studies

Given the relatively recent establishment of AD as a field professional practice, and a domain of scholarly enquiry and specialized training in higher education institutions, a substantial number of early studies on AD are descriptive and designed to identify the main features and technical developments pertaining to this form of audiovisual transfer (Benecke 2004, Snyder 2007). With the exception of those issued by ITC (Ofcom 2000) and the ADLAB project (Remael et al. 2015), guidelines are mainly based on the practitioners' experience, rather than on the real preferences of VIPs or their reactions to established AD solutions. However, unlike what happened with other forms of AVT, findings from survey-based and empirical research on AD (and, in particular, film AD) became available in the 1990s, that is, relatively early in the development of this discipline (Cronin and King 1990, Peli et al. 1996, Schmeidler and Kirchner 2001).

Both survey and empirical research rely on direct and indirect observation. Survey research involves asking questions to respondents, and it is often used to assess thoughts, opinions, and feelings. Empirical research is based on observation and interpretation of evidence and it is used, for instance, to gauge user experience. The challenges involved in formulating effective ADs for VIPs promptly raised the awareness of academics that it is crucial to assess the effects of AD on real users and produce user-oriented translations adhering to their actual needs. Despite the difficulties that both methodologies involve (Chmiel and Mazur 2012), reception studies (also known as audience studies) facilitate the direct involvement of VIPs in research, and deliver key insights into the processing and appreciation of AD (Fels *et al.* 2005, Chmiel and Mazur 2012, Mazur and Chmiel 2012, Perego 2016, Walczak and Szarkowszka 2012).

Reception research and VIPs

To date, the results of reception research have been able to confirm the advantages of film AD for VIPs. From the early stages of its introduction on television in the US, VIPs have displayed an overall positive reaction to the AD service. They do not perceive AD as obtrusive; instead, AD is regarded as an aid to increase their independence and understanding of key elements in the plot of a film, and a source of added enjoyment (Frazier 1975, Peli *et al.* 1996, Schmeidler and Kirchner 2001). Moreover, AD enhances the comprehension of VIPs, even when specific AD styles (i.e. cinematic vs. standard) or techniques (text-to-speech AD) are tested. Indeed, cinematic AD, a type of AD that uses filmic terms referring to editing, *mise-en-scène* and cinematography, is easily understood and appreciated, especially by frequent cinema-goers (Fryer and Freeman 2013), despite the sceptical attitude of most guidelines towards the use of jargon (Perego 2014b, Rai *et al.* 2010). Also the text-to-speech technique, whereby AD is narrated by a synthetic voice, does not seem to have a particularly negative impact on VIPs' perception of AD. While declaring to prefer human voices, VIPs seem to be very open to this cheaper alternative to traditional AD. Text-to-speech AD is therefore well accepted as an effective solution to increase the current number of accessible products on the market (Szarkowska and Jankowska 2012, Walczak and Szarkowska 2012). Recently, it has also been demonstrated that AD enhances the sense of immersion (strong emotional involvement and reactions toward media exposure) of VIPs because it helps them to experience the emotional content of audiovisual products (Fryer and Freeman 2013), thus making their experience closer to the experience of sighted viewers.

Several large-scale projects have exploited the benefits of survey and empirical research, too: the AUDETEL project (Lodge 1993) studied the requirements of the target audience in order to develop an innovative system designed to make television accessible to visually impaired people through AD. The Bollywood for All project (Rai 2009) explored whether a potential demand for audio described Bollywood films existed in the UK and India, and it investigated the target audience medium (TV/DVD/Cinema) and language preferences with respect to AD. The ADLAB project (ADLAB, n.d.) formulated new AD guidelines based on research and experiments involving real users in four different countries. The ITC Guidance on Standards for Audio Description resulted from a large survey conducted on blind and partially sighted people throughout the UK with the help of the Royal National Institute for the Blind (Ofcom 2000).

Reception research and sighted viewers

Besides focusing on VIPs, reception studies have also shown some of the effects that AD has on sighted viewers, although research in this field is limited and results are not yet conclusive. A survey of sighted viewers watching AD with their visually impaired families, covering their experience over one year, showed that they did not find AD obtrusive (Cronin and King 1990), which is confirmed by more recent research (Perego 2016). Besides tolerating AD well, sighted viewers seem to benefit from AD in some circumstances. In their eye-tracking studies conducted on children (8–9 years), Krejtz *et al.* (2012a, 2012b) showed that the addition of AD to educational films facilitates knowledge and vocabulary acquisition. In fact, AD positively guides the attention of viewers towards the described objects and provides them with specialized vocabulary presented in context, without interfering with the recognition of the film scenes. Similarly, Szarkowska *et al.* (2013) showed that teenagers (15 to 17 years) exposed to audio described works of art focused significantly longer on the described elements in the painting, which functioned as an aid to developing their visual literacy. For her part, Perego (2016) demonstrated that when AD is added to a film it does not negatively affect the cognitive aspects of film viewing (understanding and recognition of pictorial details) of young adults (15–28 years), nor does it dramatically affect its overall enjoyment. On the other hand, listening to AD without the visuals can pose some challenges to sighted viewers, who understand less in terms of film content, enjoy the film less, and have to struggle to integrate information delivered though only one semiotic channel.

Future reception research

Still in its infancy within the wider field of AVT studies, reception research remains a powerful tool to investigate best practices and produce usable ADs, but also to assess the possible benefits that sighted viewers can reap from AD.

More detailed knowledge and systematic research on the effects of AD on VIPs is still missing. We do not know, for instance, whether (i) their cognitive benefits and positive reaction to AD would be maintained irrespective of the film genre and complexity; (ii) groups suffering from different types of blindness (congenital vs. adventitious) would react differently to the same AD; (iii) blind children and older adults have specific processing difficulties; (iv) text-to-speech AD is effective with all film genres, if it combines well with all forms of audiovisual translation, if it is equally effective for all groups of users (younger/older, more/less familiar with text-to-speech AD), etc.

There is also a dearth of knowledge and research on the effects of AD on sighted viewers. For instance, we do not have sufficient evidence as to whether users without visual impairment could benefit from AD, e.g. in the contexts of language acquisition and literacy development for native speakers and immigrants, or as a support for vulnerable users, including those with reduced perceptual and cognitive abilities. A number of scholars and some guidelines endorse that such benefits exist (ADP 2009: 3–5, AENOR 2005, Rai *et al.* 2010: 14–15, 53, 60, Dosch and Benecke 2004, Rai *et al.* 2010: 53, Morrisett and Gonant 2008: 1, Rai *et al.* 2010: 60, Ofcom 2000: 9, 13, Remael and Vercauteren 2011: 1), but this has not been corroborated by systematic research. Future research developments should ensure that AD addresses the actual needs of its users, rather than take for granted that scholars are already aware of such needs.

The future of audio description

AD for the blind has come a long way in the past several years, both as an area of professional practice and as a domain of scholarly enquiry. Several countries in Europe and beyond have improved their AD practices and increased their service provision; more importantly, they have also demonstrated the advantages of letting research inform the re-definition of AD quality standards. There is little doubt that AD will continue to advance thanks to technological developments and research. There are still questions waiting to be answered, but the box of methodological tools that is now available to researchers is growing. Corpus-based studies, eye tracking and empirical research still have much to offer in order to gauge the real merits and limitations of existing ADs, but also to better understand what are the needs and preferences of VIPs, understood as a heterogeneous group of users.

Summary

This chapter has defined AD as an accessible form of AVT for the blind and visually impaired people, and explored the composition of its primary target audience, with particular emphasis on its heterogeneity and diversified needs. After outlining the history of AD both as a professional practice and as an academic discipline, it has focused on AD guidelines, showing the commonalities and the differences that exist between those already available on the market. It has also foregrounded the changes that have taken place over the last few years regarding the role of guidelines—as they move away from the former rigid norms that governed professional AD practices towards the formulation of new user-centred and flexible recommendations. The second half of the chapter has examined some of the most relevant aspects of the language of AD, including the qualities shaping its key lexical features (meticulousness, concision, visual intensity and usability) and other idiosyncratic trends (relatively high rate of content words and marked collocational structures) identified through corpus-based research. After looking at the stylistic properties of AD, the chapter has finally delved into the unresolved debate of description vs. interpretation in AD. The chapter closes with an overview of the most relevant findings of AD reception research involving both VIPs and sighted viewers.

Further reading

Remael, A., N. Reviers and G. Vercauteren (2015) *Pictures Painted in Words. ADLAB Audio Description Guidelines*, Trieste: EUT | *These innovative guidelines suggest strategies (rather than prescriptive rules) for dealing with common challenges in the process of AD writing. They do not offer set solutions to AD problems, but show creative and flexible approaches to deal with specific difficulties in particular circumstances. It uses examples of successful ADs.*

Maszerowska, A., A. Matamala and P. Orero (2014) (eds) *Audio Description: New Perspectives Illustrated*, Amsterdam & Philadelphia: John Benjamins | *This is the first academic volume on the topic addressing basic issues regarding AD strategies. It sets a robust practical and theoretical framework for AD. Not only is the book oriented towards the identification of the challenges that await the describer, but it also offers an insight into possible solutions.*

Snyder, J. (2007) 'Audio Description: The Visual Made Verbal', *The International Journal of the Arts in Society* 2: 191–198 | *A concise but comprehensive snapshot on AD practice seen by a professional.*

Related topics

14 Psycholinguistics and perception in audiovisual translation
15 Narratology and audiovisual translation
17 Multimodality and audiovisual translation: cohesion in accessible films
20 Corpus-based audiovisual translation studies: ample room for development
21 Multimodal corpora in audiovisual translation studies
22 Eye tracking in audiovisual translation research
23 Audiovisual translation and audience reception
29 Audiovisual translator training
30 Audiovisual translation in language teaching and learning
31 Accessible filmmaking: translation and accessibility from production

References

ABCD (Association Bruxelloise et Brabançonne des Compagnies Dramatiques ASBL) (2009) *Vademecum de l'audiodescription*, ABCD: Belgium.

ADC (Audio Description Coalition) (2009) 'Standards for Audio Description and Code of Professional Conduct for Describers'. Available online: http://audiodescriptionsolutions.com/the-standards/download-the-standards/ [last accessed 20 December 2017].

ADC (2013) 'A Brief History of Audio Description in the U.S.' Available online: http://audiodescriptionsolutions.com/about-us/a-brief-history-of-audio-description-in-the-u-s/ [last accessed 20 December 2017].

ADLAB (n.d.) 'ADLAB Project: Audio Description: Lifelong Access for the Blind'. Available online: www.adlabproject.eu [last accessed 20 December 2017].

ADLAB (2012) *Report on User Needs Assessment*. Available online: http://www.adlabproject.eu/Docs/WP1%20Report%20DEF [last accessed 20 December 2017].

ADLAB (2013) *Report on Testing*. Available online: http://www.adlabproject.eu/Docs/WP3%20Report%20on%20Testing [last accessed 20 December 2017].

ADLAB PRO (2017a) *Assessment of Current AD Training Practices. Project Report*. Available online: https://adlabpro.files.wordpress.com/2017/07/20170608_uam_io1_report.pdf [last accessed 20 December 2017].

ADLAB PRO (2017b) *Audio Description Professional: Profile Definition. Project Report*. Available online: https://www.adlabpro.eu/wp-content/uploads/2018/04/IO2-REPORT-Final.pdf [last accessed 20 December 2017]

ADP (Audio description Project) (2009) 'Guidelines for Audio Description (2010 Update)'. Available online: http://www.acb.org/adp/docs/AD-ACB-ADP%20Guidelines%203.1.doc [last accessed 20 December 2017).

AENOR (2005) *Norma UNE 153020. Audiodescripción para personas con discapacidad visual. Requisitos para la audiodescripción y elaboración de audioguías*, Madrid, AENOR.

Arma, S. (2011) *The Language of Filmic Audio Description: A Corpus-Based Analysis of Adjectives*, Unpublished Doctoral Thesis, Università degli Studi di Napoli Federico II.

Arma, S. (2012) '"Why Can't You Wear Black Shoes like the Other Mothers?" Preliminary Investigation on the Italian Language of Audio Description', in E. Perego (ed.) *Emerging Topics in Translation: Audio Description*, Trieste, EUT Edizioni Università di Trieste, 37–55.

Audioscenic (2010) *Audiodescription*. Available online: https://www.audioscenic.be/l-audiodescription/ [last accessed 20 December 2017].

BCI (Broadcasting Commission of Ireland) (2005) *BCI Guidelines on Audio Description*. Available online: http://www.bci.ie/codes/access_codes.html [last accessed 14 April 2013].

Benecke, B. (2004) 'Audio-Description', *Meta* 49(1): 78–80.

Bittner, H. (2012) 'Audio Description Guidelines: A Comparison', *New Perspectives in Translation* 20: 41–61.

Braun, S. and P. Orero (2010) 'Audio Description with Audio Subtitling: An Emergent Modality of Audiovisual Localization', *Perspectives: Studies in Translatology* 18(3): 173–188.

Busarello, E. and F. Sordo (2011) *Manuale per aspiranti audio descrittori di audiofilm per non vedenti*. Scurelle, Trento: Cooperativa Sociale Senza Barriere ONLUS.

Chmiel, A. and I. Mazur (2012) 'AD Reception Research: Some Methodological Considerations', in E. Perego (ed.), *Emerging Topics in Translation: Audio Description*, Trieste: EUT, 57–80.

Cronin, B. J. and S. R. King (1990) 'The Development of the Descriptive Video Service' *Journal of Visual Impairment and Blindness* 84(10): 503–506.

Dosch, E. and B. Benecke (2004) *Wenn aus Bildern Worte werden—Durch Audio Description zum Hörfilm*, Munich: Bayerischer Rundfunk.

Fels, D. I., J. P. Udo, P. Ting, J. E. Diamond, and J. I. Diamond (2005) 'Odd Job Jack Described—A First Person Narrative Approach to Described Video', *Journal of Universal Access in the Information Society* 5(1): 73–81.

Frazier, G. (1975) *The Autobiography of Miss Jane Pitman: An All-Audio Adaptation of the Teleplay for the Blind and Visually Handicapped*, Unpublished Masters Dissertation, San Francisco State University, USA.

Fryer, L. and J. Freeman (2013) 'Cinematic Language and the Description of Film: Keeping AD Users in the Frame', *Perspectives: Studies in Translatology* 21(3): 412–426.

Fryer, L. and P. Romero-Fresco (2014) 'Audiointroductions', in A. Maszerowska, A. Matamala and P. Orero (eds) *Audio Description: New Perspectives Illustrated*, Amsterdam & Philadelphia: John Benjamins, 11–28.

Georgakopoulou, Y. (2008) *Audio Description Guidelines for Greek: A Working Document*. English translation available in Rai, S., J. Greening and L. Petré (2010) *A Comparative Study of Audio Description Guidelines Prevalent in Different Countries*, London: RNIB, Annexe 5.

Haig, R. (2005) 'Audio Description: Art or Industry?', Blog entry, 5 August. Available online: http://www.rainahaig.com/pages/AudioDescriptionAorI.html [last accessed 20 December 2017].

Holland, A. (2009) 'Audio Description in the Theatre and the Visual Arts: Images into Words', in A. Gunilla and J. Díaz Cintas (eds) *Audiovisual Translation. Language Transfer on Screen*, Basingstoke: Palgrave Macmillan, 170–185.

Jiménez Hurtado, C., A. Rodríguez and C. Seibel (coord.) (2010) *Un corpus de cine. Teoría y práctica de la audiodescripción*, Granada: Tragacanto.

Krejtz, I., A. Szarkowska, K. Krejtz, A. Walczak and A. Duchowski (2012a) 'Audio Description as an Aural Guide of Children's Visual Attention: Evidence from an Eye-Tracking Study', in *ETRA '12, Proceedings of the Symposium on Eye Tracking Research and Applications*, New York: ACM, 99–106.

Krejtz, K., I. Krejtz, A. Duchowski, A. Szarkowska and A. Walczak (2012b) 'Multimodal Learning with Audio Description: An Eye Tracking Study of Children's Gaze during a Visual Recognition Task', in *Proceedings of the ACM Symposium on Applied Perception (SAP '12)*, New York: ACA, 83–90.

Leech, G. and M. Short (1981) *Style in Fiction—A Linguistic Introduction to English Fictional Prose*, Edinburgh: Pearson Education Limited.

Lodge, N. K. (1993) *The European AUDETEL Project—Enhancing Television for Visually Impaired People*, London: The Institution of Electrical Engineers.

Mälzer-Semlinger, N. (2012) 'Narration or Description. What Should Audio Description "Look" Like?', in E. Perego (ed.) *Emerging Topics in Translation: Audio Description*, Trieste: EUT, 29–36.

Maszerowska, A., A. Matamala and P. Orero (eds) (2014) *Audio Description: New Perspectives Illustrated*, Amsterdam & Philadelphia: John Benjamins.

Mazur, I. (2014) 'Gestures and Facial Expressions in Audio Description', in A. Maszerowska, A. Matamala and P. Orero (eds) *Audio Description: New Perspectives Illustrated*, Amsterdam & Philadelphia: John Benjamins, 179–198.

Mazur, I. and A. Chmiel (2012) 'Audio Description Made to Measure: Reflections on Interpretation in AD based on the Pear Tree Project Data', in A. Remael, P. Orero and M. Carroll (eds) *Audiovisual Translation and Media Accessibility at the Crossroads. Media for All 3*, Amsterdam: Rodopi, 173–188.

Morisset, L. and F. Gonant (2008) *La charte de l'audiodescription*. Available online: http://www.csa.fr/en../content/download/19660/329348/file/Charte+de+l%27audiodescription.+Principes+et+Orientations.pdf [last accessed 20 December 2017].

Neves, J. (2011) *Guia de audiodescrição. Imagens que se ouvem*, Leiria: Instituto Politécnico de Leiria.

Neves, J. (2015). 'Descriptive Guides: Access to Museums, Cultural Venues and Heritage Sites', in A. Remael, N. Reviers and G. Vercauteren (eds) *Pictures Painted in Words. ADLAB Audio Description Guidelines*, Trieste: EUT, 70–73.

Ofcom (2000) *ITC Guidance on Standards for Audio Description*. London: Ofcom. Available online: http://audiodescription.co.uk/uploads/general/itcguide_sds_audio_desc_word3.pdf [last accessed 20 December 2017].

Ofcom (2010) 'Code on Television Access Services (updated 2017)'. London: Ofcom. Available online: https://www.ofcom.org.uk/__data/assets/pdf_file/0020/97040/Access-service-code-Jan-2017.pdf [last access 20 December 2017].

Orero, P. (2007) 'Visión histórica de la accesibilidad en los medios en España', *Trans* 11: 31–43.

Orero, P. (2012) 'Film Reading for Writing Audio Descriptions: A Word is Worth a Thousand Images?', in E. Perego (ed.) *Emerging Topics in Translation: Audio Description*, Trieste: EUT, 13–28.

Peli, E., E. Fine and A. Labianca (1996) 'Evaluating Visual Information Provided by Audio Description', *Journal of Visual Impairment & Blindness* (90)5: 378–385.

Perego E. (ed.) (2014a) 'Da dove viene e dove va l'audiodescrizione filmica per i ciechi e gli ipovedenti', in E. Perego (ed.) *L'audiodescrizione filmica per i ciechi e gli ipovedenti*, EUT: Trieste, 15–46.

Perego, E. (2014b) 'Film Language and Tools', in A. Maszerowska, A. Matamala and P. Orero (eds) *Audio Description: New Perspectives illustrated*, Amsterdam & Philadelphia: John Benjamins, 81–101.

Perego, E. (2016) 'Gains and Losses of Audio Description for Sighted Viewers', *Target* 28(3): 424–444.

Perego, E. and B. Benecke (2014) 'Aspetti tecnici e procedurali dell'audiodescrizione. Il caso della Bayerischer Rundfunk', in E. Perego (ed.) *L'audiodescrizione filmica per i ciechi e gli ipovedenti*, Trieste: EUT, 121–126.

Piety, P. (2004) 'The Language System of Audio Description. An Investigation as a Discursive Process', *Journal of Visual Impairment and Blindness* 98(8): 453–469.

Project IDEAL (2013) *Visual Impairment*. Available online: http://www.projectidealonline.org/v/visual-impairments/ [last accessed 20 December 2017].

Puigdomènech, L., A. Matamala and P. Orero (2008) 'The Making of a Protocol for Opera Audio Description', *La traducción del futuro: mediación lingüística y cultural en el siglo* XXI(1), Barcelona: PPU, 381–392.

Rai, S. (2009) *Bollywood for All: The Demand for Audio Described Bollywood Films*, London: RNIB.

Rai, S., J. Greening and L. Petré (2010) *A Comparative Study of Audio Description Guidelines Prevalent in Different Countries*, London: RNIB.

Remael, A., N. Reviers and G. Vercauteren (2015) *Pictures Painted in Words. ADLAB Audio Description Guidelines*, Trieste: EUT.

Remael, A. and G. Vercauteren (2011) *Basisprincipes voor audiobeschrijving voor televisie en film. [Basics of Audio Description for Television and Film]*, Antwerp: Departement Vertalers & Tolken, Artesis Hogeschool.

Romero-Fresco, P. and L. Fryer (2013) 'Could Audio Described Films Benefit from Audio Introductions? An Audience Response Study', *Journal of Visual Impairment and Blindness* 107(4): 287–295.

Salway, A. (2007) 'A Corpus-based Analysis of Audio Description', in J. Díaz Cintas, P. Orero, A. Remael (eds) *Media for All: Subtitling for the Deaf, Audio Description and Sign Language*, Amsterdam: Rodopi, 151–174.

Schmeidler, E. and C. Kirchner (2001) 'Adding Audio Description: Does it make a Difference?', *Journal of Visual Impairment and Blindness* 95(4): 197–212.

Snyder, J. (2007) 'Audio Description: The Visual Made Verbal', *The International Journal of the Arts in Society* 2(1): 99–104.

Snyder, J. (2008) 'Audio Description. The Visual Made Verbal', in J. Díaz Cintas (ed.) *The Didactics of Audiovisual Translation*, Amsterdam & Philadelphia: John Benjamins, 191–198.

Snyder, J. (2014) *The Visual Made Verbal: A Comprehensive Training Manual and Guide to the History and Applications of Audio Description*, LLC: Dog Ear Publishing.

Szarkowska, A. and A. Jankowska (2012) 'Text-to-Speech Audio Description of Voiced-Over Films. A Case Study of Audio Described Volver in Polish', in E. Perego (ed.) *Emerging Topics in Translation: Audio Description*, Trieste: EUT, 81–98.

Szarkowska, A., I. Krejtz, K. Krejtz, and A. Duchowski (2013) 'Harnessing the Potential of Eye-Tracking for Media Accessibility', in S. Grucza, M. Płużyczka, and J. Zając (eds) *Translation Studies and Eye-Tracking Analysis*, Frankfurt: Peter Lang, 153–183.

Szymańska, B. and T. Strzymiński, T. (2010) *Standardy tworzenia audiodeskrypcji do produkcji audiowizualnych*. Available online: http://www.audiodeskrypcja.org.pl/index.php/standardy-tworzenia-audiodeskrypcji/do-produkcji-audiowizualnych [last accessed 20 December 2017].

Taylor, C. (2015) 'The Language of AD', in A. Remael, N. Reviers and G. Vercauteren (eds) *Pictures Painted in Words. ADLAB Audio Description Guidelines*, Trieste: EUT, 48–51.

Udo, J. P. and D. Fels (2009) 'Suit the Action to the Word, the Word to the Action: An Unconventional Approach to Describing Shakespeare's Hamlet', *Journal of Visual Impairment & Blindness* 103: 178–183.

Vercauteren, G. (2007) 'Towards a European Guideline for Audio Description', in P. Orero, and A. Remael (eds) *Media for All: Subtitling for the Deaf, Audio Description and Sign Language*, Amsterdam: Rodopi, 139–150.

Walczak, A. and A. Szarkowska (2012) 'Text-to-Speech Audio Description of Educational Materials for Visually Impaired Children', in S. Bruti and E. Di Giovanni (eds) *Audiovisual Translation across Europe. An Ever-changing Landscape*, Bern: Peter Lang, 209–233.

WHO (World Health Organization) (2014) *Visual Impairment and Blindness*, Fact sheet N° 282. Available online: http://www.who.int/mediacentre/factsheets/fs282/en/ [last accessed 20 December 2017].

York, G. (2007) 'Verdi Made Visible. Audio-introduction for Opera and Ballet', in P. Orero, A. Remael and J. Díaz Cintas (eds) *Media for All. Accessibility in Audiovisual Translation*, Amsterdam: Rodopi, 215–229.

Filmography

Dumbo (1941) Various directors. IMDb entry: http://www.imdb.com/title/tt0033563/?ref_=nv_sr_2

9
Surtitling and captioning for theatre and opera

Alina Secară

Article 27.1 of the Universal Declaration of Human Rights adopted by the United Nations General Assembly in Paris on 10 December 1948 states that '[e]veryone has the right freely to participate in the cultural life of the community, to enjoy the arts and to share in scientific advancement and its benefits' (United Nations 1948). It is within this general framework that the current chapter will introduce and discuss two access services, namely captioning and surtitling for theatre and opera.

The *Oxford English Dictionary* defines captions as 'appearing across the lower portion of a cinema screen, or of the frame of a television programme, video recording, etc., and typically supplying a translation of the dialogue, or a version of it for the benefit of the deaf or hard of hearing; (also) a similar caption provided for the audience of an opera or other stage performance'. Surtitles, on the other hand, are defined as 'caption[s] projected on to a screen above the stage during the performance of an opera, esp. to translate the libretto or explain the action' (Oxford English Dictionary, n.d.). In Low's (2002: 97) terms, a surtitle is 'a kind of caption displayed above the stage during a live performance, giving a written translation of the audible words—though not all of them—which are being sung at any given moment'. As the differences between these definitions may still leave space for confusion, this chapter will use the terms 'captions' and 'captioning' when referring to monolingual transfer, and 'surtitles' and 'surtitling' when discussing an interlingual product—usually, although not exclusively, in a live theatre or opera setting. Finally, the term 'titles' will be used to refer generally to the product generated in both of these scenarios.

Brief history of the field

It is well documented (Low 2002, Mateo 2007, Oncins 2015) that opera surtitling originated in Canada, with the Canadian Opera Company creating the first surtitled production in 1983. Burton (2009) acknowledges the presence of titles in an opera house in Hong Kong before that, in the early 1980s, but they do not fit the definition of sur- or subtitles, as they were displayed vertically on the side of the stage. Shortly afterwards, other opera companies around the world, including Covent Garden, began to provide this service.

The beginnings of captioning, and especially its growth, are closely linked to the approval and enforcement of legislation regarding provision of access services, for televised programmes in particular. The 2003 UK Communications Act specifically requires provision of subtitling, signing and audio description for TV products; it also sets quotas—80%, 5% and 10% of programmes, respectively, for each of these three audiovisual translation (AVT) modes—to 'be reached by the tenth anniversary of the relevant date for each channel, as well as a subtitling quota to be reached by the fifth anniversary (60%)' (Ofcom 2006: 1). At the European level, the Audiovisual Media Services European Directive on access services was introduced in 2009, and the EU Directive on Web Content Accessibility in 2015. Internationally, different strategies are gradually being put in place and it is clear that this sector is growing in visibility.

The presence of captions on TV, at cinemas and online has also brought a certain pressure to offer them as a default in theatres as well. To get a sense of the number of accessible performances today, using the UK as an example, it suffices to look at events delivered or supported by StageTEXT (StageTEXT, n.d.), a leading British organization dedicated to making theatre and culture accessible to deaf, deafened and hard of hearing audiences and readers. In 2013 alone, StageTEXT 'made nearly 400 events accessible to deaf, deafened and hard of hearing audiences' by working with 150 museums, galleries and arts venues across the UK (StageTEXT 2015: 11). The efforts are even more impressive if we look at the number of hours of captioned TV content, for example 100% of BBC1 output (Ofcom 2006, 2017). This is quite substantial if we consider that this is not a closely monitored sector, although arts organizations are legally required to make their events accessible to disabled patrons. This figure is particularly impressive if we also take into account that a little over two decades ago this service did not exist.

Audience

Action On Hearing Loss estimates that by 2031 'there will be 14.5 million people with hearing loss in the UK' (2011: 11). Deafness is often something that is experienced as people get older, so more than 70% of over 70-year-olds and 40% of over 50-year-olds have some form of hearing loss (*ibid.*). Many of these people would find it difficult to understand a play without support, so captions are invaluable for them.

For opera-goers, surtitles provide the translation needed to understand the text written originally in another language. Yvonne Griesel (2005: 6) talks about three possible target audiences for interlingual surtitles. Source language audiences, target language audiences and audiences with knowledge of both source and target languages. Interlingual surtitling can be therefore regarded as different from captions—even though, in essence, it also helps opera-goers to overcome language barriers.

However, this is not the whole picture when it comes to understanding the audience for these two types of services. One of the most exciting changes is the identification of an undeclared audience, i.e. individuals who appreciate surtitles and captions but are not necessarily recognized by theatres and operas as potential beneficiaries of the service. In our ever more globalized world, where large numbers of people have the language of their host communities as their second language (e.g. 4.9 million people in the UK speak English as their second language, according to StageTEXT 2015), the audience for captioning is changing. Theatres in the UK such as the New Wolsey and the West Yorkshire Playhouse ran surveys to assess the extent to which this undeclared audience exists. The results show a significant difference between those audience members who book access tickets and those who report to have found the service useful (Secară and Allum 2011). The surveys involved asking members of the audience to place a card in a designated box, on their way out at the end of the performance, if they had found the captions useful. The results were then compared to those who had specifically booked access tickets. In the New Wolsey case, out of 359 people in the audience, 29% reported to have found the captions useful while only 4% had booked access tickets. In the West Yorkshire Playhouse case, the figures were 18% and 3% for a 522 house. These two examples would seem to be indicative of the important potential of captions.

In bilingual contexts such as Canada, interlingual surtitles were reported to act as a bridge between official language communities, and hence as a vehicle for reaching new audiences. The translation of surtitles should therefore be regarded as different from existing translations of plays. In the former, the text of the surtitles needs to stay closer to the original, as both the source and target texts need to harmoniously coexist during the live performance. Moreover, in these bilingual situations surtitles can also introduce a new layer of interpretation. As Carlson (2006: 199, in Ladouceur 2014: 53) puts it, 'an additional "voice", especially in the case of multilanguage audiences, can use its inevitable difference from spoken text in more original and powerful ways, for the production of additional meanings'. For example, Marc Prescott's *Sex, Lies et les Franco-Manitobains* (2001) contains rap slang which, even in translation, can remain inaccessible to certain members of the audience. Due to this, Prescott added in the surtitles, 'If you don't understand what this guy is saying, don't worry—Neither does 50% of the rest of the audience' (Prescot, 2009: slide 602, in Ladouceur 2014: 53). Therefore the surtitles also become projections of the translators' opinions and thoughts, share the same space as the play, and become relevant to all the members of the audience.

Description of surtitles and captions and techniques

According to Mateo (2007), surtitling can be explored from a textual, ideological and technical perspective. The remainder of this section delivers an overview of both captioning and surtitling techniques structured around these three perspectives.

Textual implications

Some scholars have raised the question of what should be regarded as the source text for the production of surtitles: the full prose libretto, the singable version or even the original work on which the libretto is based. Irrespective of the source used, there are elements that require careful consideration. Relying on her experience as a librettist translator, Orero (in Orero and Matamala 2008: 263) underlines the importance of four elements when translating for the opera. Firstly, the translation should rely on the music score and follow the stage instructions; secondly, rhythm takes precedence over rhyme; poetical feeling should be prioritized, which effectively entails the need to avoid compensation by explanation; finally, all elements which convey a certain atmosphere—e.g. the use of an archaic tone, specialized vocabulary or register to mark social differences—should be recreated in the translation. The complexity of creating surtitles that engage with and prioritize these four aspects can be illustrated by the long—and yet, not exhaustive—list of issues and difficulties that Orero and Matamala (2008: 266) have identified based on previous research. These include 'condensation, ensembles, variation in the density of words, repetitions, melismas, poetic or overblown styles, archaism, synchronization, adaptation of cultural, humoristic and historical references, the need to create comprehensible surtitles that form a logical unit, the avoidance of previous translations and the avoidance of representing in writing both onomatopoeias and all sounds which are clearly recognisable by the public, since they may detract attention'.

While 'the aim of surtitles is to convey the meaning of what is being sung, not necessarily the manner in which it is being sung' (Burton 2009: 63), the aim of the captions is to provide both the meaning and the way in which the lines are being delivered. Moreover, identifying the source text for captions is less problematic, as it will always be the work as it appears on stage. As far as the text itself is concerned, the list of issues is also very specialized and the main potential challenges pertain to the use of dialect and non-standard varieties of language—which should be rendered in such a way that allows for an accessible reading experience; overlapping dialogue and decisions regarding the timing of different bits of speech; the density of words and repetitions; and the need to provide accurate and appropriate sound captions. Examples 1–4 below illustrate each of these aspects using titles from captioned plays. All the examples come from captions created by the author for plays performed at the West Yorkshire Playhouse theatre in Leeds, UK.

Firstly, the portrayal of dialect, non-standard language varieties and accents can be either rendered phonetically or a description can be inserted:

Example 1

The Secret Garden

MARTHA: Can't tha' dress thissen, Miss?

Privates on Parade

[AS DIETRICH] / [GERMAN ACCENT]

Overlapping dialogues are incredibly challenging as they affect the speed of the caption display. A lag can therefore be introduced if a decision is taken to include all the lines of the source text; alternatively, a label can be included to alert the audience to the existence of an overlap, which allows for the omission of the overlapping lines:

Example 2

Cat on a Hot Tin Roof

[GOODBYES ARE SHOUTED DOWNSTAIRS]

GOOPER: Big Mama!

BIG MAMA: Hold those people down there, don't let them go!

When repetitions occur, the captioner can either repeat the lines or simply resort to a label that indicates what is going on and gives the viewers more time to look at the stage, rather than at the caption unit:

Example 3

Crouch, Touch, Pause, Engage

ALL: [SHOUT] One, two, three, four, five.

ALFIE: Better.

[THEY REPEAT]

Sound captions need to be included only when they add to what is happening on the stage. If sounds have a purely decorative value, the captioner should resist the temptation of creating a caption. In the example below, the sound caption is absolutely necessary as there is a reference to the sound in the text:

Example 4

Caucasian Chalk Circle

[WATER DRIPS]

LAVRENTI: What's that dripping noise?

There are many aspects linking surtitles to television interlingual subtitling. Low (2002) provides a list of features that these two types of activities have in common. He notes that, insofar as both surtitles and interlingual subtitling provide a legible version of the verbal material, the presentation aspect is crucial in their reception by the target audience. Both are size- and time-constrained and therefore rely on condensation in order to achieve an optimal display, both from a formal and temporal perspective. Due to the relatively short time available to display surtitles, the target language version needs to be easy to process and therefore the translation choices need to take into consideration the readability factor. This is different from a traditional translation environment, where lexical and phraseological choices are not necessarily conditioned by temporal constraints. Due to this, ambiguity must be avoided and features which enhance the reading experience, such as grammatically accurate line breaks (Perego 2008), encouraged. Moreover, to enhance the reading experience, each title should represent one idea or unit of information, which may or may not be commensurate with one sentence. Punctuation follows normal rules, repetition is avoided, and all semiotic channels considered when deciding whether to include or exclude brief or ambiguous utterances whose meaning can be retrieved without actually including them in the text of the surtitle. Burton (2009) also calls for simplicity and highlights the importance of avoiding 'flowery or poetic turns' (*ibid.*: 62), musical repetitions and interjections such as 'Ah!' and 'Oh!'.

Captioning also shares some of these features, especially the need for legible and easily readable text, use of standard punctuation, reliance on all the semiotic channels to render meaning, use of line breaks and idea units. However, for captioning, the text is never altered and summarization is not an option. The script provided is very rarely modified and the titles are a verbatim representation of the original. In terms of differences between television subtitles and surtitles and captions, the one that stands out is linked to the timing aspect. In television subtitling timing is done in line with the target audience's reading speed. The BBC monolingual subtitling guidelines (BBC 2009), which follow recommendations from the UK media industry regulator, Ofcom, set 800 characters per minute as the preferred standard for the creation of monolingual English subtitles. Because of this, condensation is at times needed; on other occasions, a verbatim textual transfer is possible due to the editing of the TV material that may incorporate, for example, generous speech–pause ratios. However, in an opera or theatre scenario, back-to-back dialogues are more frequent, and therefore the display time for any given caption potentially much shorter. As text needs to be rendered verbatim and no condensation is possible, reading speed standards are not adhered to. Captions are simply timed following the exact rhythm of the live performance. This may seem counter-intuitive as, in most situations, the speech rates are higher than reading rates and therefore the delivery of a line spoken by a character will be usually faster than the time one would need to read it in written form.

It may be argued that synchronizing captions and surtitles with the rhythm of speech delivery may make them inaccessible to the target audience. Empirical studies on this issue are lacking but, as Burton and Holden note, 'live surtitles should be painted with a broader brush; the text should hang above the audience's heads as a guide to comprehension, not distracting their attention by cramming in too much text or by flashing past too quickly' (in Orero and Matamala 2008: 265). This may also apply in the case of captions, as the text displayed on the captioning units is at times used as an anchoring device that assumes a certain degree of residual hearing or familiarity with the play on the part of audience members, or simply that viewers will make use of other meaning-making resources conveyed by other semiotics of the multimodal text.

It is acknowledged that there should always be a link between the captions or the surtitles and the mise-en-scène. Indeed, Ladouceur (2014: 45) maintains that surtitles can actually act as an additional voice through which a second interpretation of the performance is possible. Drawing on an example of a bilingual theatre in Canada, she successfully argues that surtitle translation 'exceeds its primary function and takes on a creative role within the performance' (*ibid*.). She also contrasts the translation of plays with the translation done for surtitles and concludes that the latter needs to stay closer to the original as they co-exist in the delivery. Moreover, surtitles become the voice of the translator as their thoughts and opinions are superimposed on the translation. This is in total contrast to Burton's suggestion that 'the subtitler's aim should be transparency, or even invisibility' (2009: 63). For captioning, more recently, companies such as Ramps on the Moon made accessibility a central part of their thinking and aesthetics. This involves fully integrating access services—captioning, sign language and audio description—in every play performed by their disabled and non-disabled practitioners.

Another textual aspect worth mentioning at this point pertains to the need to comply with house styles when creating both captions and surtitles. Burton (2009) lists six categories of conventions that may vary depending on the specific technology used in a given assignment or the preference of the company commissioning the work.

1. Number of characters per line. As in the case of subtitling, where strict limits on the number of characters per line apply, each caption or surtitle contains on average up to a maximum of 40 characters. This depends on the size of the safe area where the lines are to be displayed, but also on the font and font size to be used. Preferred fonts are typically Arial, Courier New or Helvetica, with size set typically around 16.
2. In surtitling dashes may be used if a duologue occurs. In captioning, every character's line begins with a name label, identifying that character. A dialogue between Richard and Hastings in Richard III, will usually be depicted as illustrated in Example 5:

    Example 5

    Richard III

    HASTINGS: Good time of day onto my gracious lord.

    RICHARD: As much unto my good Lord Chamberlain.
3. The timing or cueing of the titles, as they are done live, need to keep with the rhythm and the pace of the performance. It is therefore crucial not to give away dramatic

punch-lines too early. It is also important to be aware of the possibility that actors may skip lines at any point, which would make it necessary to quickly adapt the titles to the actual performance.

4 Italics are only used in surtitling and indicate that the voice is off-stage or are used for emphasis. In captioning italics are not used and emphasis is signalled with the help of punctuation or the use of all capitals.

5 Quotation marks are used for reported speech and brackets may identify an aside, although a label such as ASIDE may be used in captioning for this purpose.

6 Titles are usually centred or left aligned. However, just as in subtitling, alignment can follow the position of the characters on the stage. This can be useful especially if two characters' lines overlap and therefore their renditions can be presented simultaneously. This aspect goes hand in hand with that of mobility, 'whether or not the text moves synchronically with its emission by the actor (i.e. scroll up) or whether it instead appears on the screen in blocks and remains fixed' (Oncins 2015: 53). In captioning, scrolling up is used more frequently, whereas in surtitling a blocking style is favoured.

Social implications

Low (2002) points out that the advent of surtitling in the late 80s is linked to a change in the way opera started to be viewed. He suggests that an ever-growing need to make opera accessible in the audience language, long supported by composers such as Wagner and Puccini, played a part in the uptake of this service. As opera had started to alienate audiences, especially younger generations, due to a certain lack of intelligibility, the advent of surtitling brought a solution not only in terms of provision of a more 'audience-friendly' performance but also one which could potentially lead to financial gains by an increase in the number of patrons attracted by this service. Low also highlights a third, interesting aspect. Surtitling has made possible a revitalizing of the programming of opera houses: lesser-known works can now be performed, as lack of familiarity with or understanding of the sung original is no longer an impediment.

By providing accessible captioned performances, opera and theatre houses benefit from an increased diversity in their audience. With more than ten million people who are deaf or hard of hearing in the UK alone, this is a population segment which can no longer be ignored.

The use of surtitles or captions also marks a change in our consumption preferences. In a text-dominated society, our expectations and abilities to manipulate and use text are rather different now. As Burton (2009: 61) argues, '[n]o longer do we sit in the dark for hours at a time, listening to whole acts of Wagner or Richard Strauss with only the dimmest idea of what is actually going on. Surtitles are now largely a necessity and there are likely to be complaints if they are not provided'. Moreover, the presence of surtitles can highlight specific functions of the original text. For example, the humour in Papageno's opening lines from Mozart's *Magic Flute* could potentially be lost to an English-speaking audience, if presented only with the original German. This also brings pressure on directors and actors to remain faithful to the original form of the performance.

Technical implications

Captions and surtitles should allow opera- and theatre-goers—some of whom are deaf, deafened or hard of hearing people—to access the words and formal aspects of a performance. From a practical point of view, the text is usually presented on one or several display units that are located on, near the set or close to the audience members. A professional captioner or surtitler, sitting in the control box or in a dedicated area, but always in line of sight of the stage and the units, cues the lines of the pre-prepared script in sync with the live performance.

There is no standard system implemented across the world at the moment for providing surtitling and captioning, as the needs of every venue may be different. Display scenarios can vary from a relatively uncomplicated one, where slides are projected on a screen using a digital projector, to settings equipped with complex LED screens, hand-held devices or intelligent glasses. The reminder of this section explores a number of these options and provides an insight into the advantages and disadvantages of each of these systems.

In many venues, projecting slides on a screen located at the top of the proscenium, or on a TV usually situated at the side(s) of the stage, is the only display option available. This usually involves pre-preparing the text using an off-the-shelf general software application such as MS PowerPoint and live cueing the text using the same tool. The simplicity and affordability of this set-up has a number of additional advantages, as it allows professionals to customize text positioning, colour, font and alignment. Moreover, it allows for a block display of text, which has been shown to be more user-friendly than scrolling text (Romero-Fresco 2012). With the help of eye-tracking technology, this research shows that reading patterns are influenced by the way in which the text is displayed. However, notwithstanding its advantages, it is relatively difficult in such a context to handle unexpected situations, such as actors skipping lines, as ideally, when this occurs, the captioner should be able to navigate fast in the script and jump to the point that might require the removal of a caption. Also, text may be washed out by stage lighting—unless the venue is equipped with a high-specification projector.

The second type of 'open captioning' environment is represented by large LED display screens used in the set or at the side of the stage. These dedicated special units allow captions to be visible to everyone, while allowing a great deal of customization when it comes to brightness and display of the text. These units make text very readable from a distance, can be customized to display a letterbox shape, and usually come with dedicated software which allows for easy live navigation within the script; crucially, they are reliable and visible under stage lighting conditions and outdoors in the sunshine (Secară and Allum 2010). However, they are expensive, sometimes perceived as unattractive, and are heavy and cumbersome to transport.

'Closed captions' implementations, where personal devices are employed, is the third scenario to be considered in relation to the delivery of surtitles and captions. Matamala and Orero (2007) provide an example of the Gran Teatre del Liceu in Barcelona where Thin Film Transistor screens installed at the back of every seat provide a customized experience for audience members. They can choose between Catalan, Spanish or English input. Soon after the introduction of these systems, hand-held devices followed. These rely on SD cards or apps for each receiver with text already uploaded or transmitted via wireless technology. Most of these scenarios involve pre-cueing, meaning that the presence of a live captioner is no longer needed, and they may also allow patrons live navigation through the text. This type of closed captioning equipment has the advantage of being unobtrusive and therefore not interfering with the look of the show, which is important for the director. Moreover, if automated, it works from any seat in the house and can be used in all performances. However, they can be expensive to install, the automated timing may not be very accurate and they can cause eye strain as the viewer is exposed to different depths of field, i.e. reading close but looking far away at actors and the stage (Secară and Allum 2010).

In terms of software, a wide variety of tools is available. From PowerPoint to Figaro, Vicom, Naoteck, Supertitles, Opera Voice and Jayex all have been used in surtitling or captioning of live performances. For a comparison of their features, including information on text positioning, typography, format and brightness, see Oncins (2015).

New developments in technology in general, and captioning technology in particular, have revolutionized the way captioning is created in venues where accessibility services are available. Although there are significant differences from one context to another, common trends in the way technology is used in the provision of captioning can be observed. From the point of view of creation and delivery, new tools and technologies are now being combined.

From the point of view of reception, technological developments linked to caption display mechanisms now mean that physical access to surtitles can take a completely new form. In April 2012, the announcement of the new Google Glasses (Forbes 2012) opened the door to a new way of presenting captions. In 2015, winners of the European Living Lab prize brought multilingual surtitles using smart glasses to the internationally acclaimed Avignon theatre festival. As the festival organizers noted, '[t]his glasses project fits the Avignon Festival because it offers a way to share cultures in a simple fashion, to make the "others" accessible to a very diverse public. It brings us the surtitling solution for which we have been searching for years: individualized, comfortable and adjustable, without interfering with the overall show' (Rondin 2015). Therefore, similar to a trend observed in TV broadcasting a few years ago (Byford 2008), we are moving towards solutions which provide viewers with a customized experience and diversify the way in which information is presented to an ever more segmented and discerning audience. At Avignon, two shows were multilingually surtitled: Shakespeare's *King Lear* was surtitled into French, English and Mandarin, while *Return to Berratham* by Angelin Preljocaj was rendered into English, French, German, Italian and Polish. The users were able to customize the colour, size, position and brightness of the text and therefore were in control of the viewing experience. The user could also take control of the timing and what text got projected on the glasses. One of the advantages of this set-up, when compared with the traditional captioning context with display units near the stage, is that viewers enjoy a certain freedom to view the performance and text from whatever seats they choose. By contrast, in traditional caption-unit settings, opera and theatre houses, the seats available to ticket holders requiring accessibility services have been confined to areas of maximum visibility. Moreover, when using the glasses, viewers reported that the physical reading experience was enhanced by having text displayed in an easier to access format (Rondin, *ibid.*). They preferred this display option over traditional methods, where captions and surtitles are displayed on open screens or at the top of the proscenium. However, while promising, the results reported by the organizers were not scientifically proven and therefore more research is needed to gauge the real impact of using these new technological advances in the cultural sector.

For delivery, speech recognition tools such as *Dragon Naturally Speaking* are also being tested, especially for remote captioning of live events and for captioning of Q&A sessions at the end of a play or opera. Speech recognition tools are therefore used when a pre-prepared script is not available. In terms of process, the captioner respeaks into a microphone the lines being uttered on stage and the tool, previously trained to recognize the speech patterns of the captioner, uses a customized language model to turn the respoken content into lines of text. These then become available on the display tool of choice, whether these are traditional units and TVs of hand-held devices.

A similar speech recognition tool was used in a recent project carried out by StageTEXT and a variety of other partners. The project, called CaptionCue (CaptionCue

Project, n.d.), looked into the possibility of using speech technology and other triggers from the sound and lighting desk to automatically cue and display pre-prepared captions or surtitles. The project also tested the advantages and disadvantages of different display methods, with captions displayed 'on an LED screen integrated into the seat, on two LED screen at the side of the stage and on tablets resting on holders for viewers sitting in the balcony' (StageTEXT 2015: 7). Their findings suggest that the volunteer audience was generally happy with the quality of automatically cued captions even if they were not always synchronous with the speech. Following from that, the National Theatre in London announced the launch in 2017 of its Open Access Smart Capture initiative to revolutionize accessibility in its theatre performances. Its first phase, the ProFile project, enables deaf and hard of hearing audiences to access automatically cued captions via speech technology on smart glasses. The system, which 'enables users to see captions projected onto lightweight smart glasses', has been developed by Epson. With this new software application, 'the captions are automatically cued [and] users can personalise the position, font and background colour of the captions' (VocalEyes 2017). In terms of display, in the CaptionCue project the context allowing viewers to spend 'the most time watching the stage and the least time on captions were screens on the side, followed by the integrated screen and, worst of all, tablets' (*ibid.*: 8). It is clear that the way in which surtitles and captions are produced and then displayed does have an influence on their reception by the target audience. With more solutions being offered on the market today, and with technological advances continuing apace, it is important to continue investigating and testing different solutions and suggesting scenarios for various contexts that may contribute to maximizing the viewers' experience.

Reception of surtitles and captions

To understand the importance of the linguistic and technical factors described above, we shall now discuss briefly the reception of surtitles and captions by target viewers. We will take inspiration from the words of Riitta Virkkunen who considers that 'surtitling has a very specific function: The audience uses the surtitles for communicating with other symbolic modes used in the performance for creating meanings. In practice this means that surtitles mostly serve as a medium for the verbal content but also help to comprehend music and acting' (2004: 93).

The titles should therefore first and foremost facilitate comprehension and convey meaning. It is thus unfortunate that current captioning display solutions are not ideal from a reception point of view. Indeed, surtitles 'forcing spectators to shift their focus, even if momentarily, away from the stage, are much more disruptive, since they are directly competing with other stimuli to the visual channels, leaving unimpeded the auditory channel' (Carlson 2006: 197). Oncins points out that 'no reception studies have been undertaken to evaluate user satisfaction according to the various positions and presentations' (2015: 47). Although we can now refer to the StageTEXT study mentioned in the previous section to shed some light on this topic, further studies are needed. In particular, we can draw inspiration and gain significant insights from the multitude of studies carried out in the fields of subtitling and the arts using eye-tracking technology.

We already know that the reading style of every individual will adapt to the situation in which the reading takes place. We should however bear in mind that when reading a multimodal dynamic text such as captions or surtitles, the reading style will adjust to the pace imposed by the display of the information, as long as the resulting strain is not disproportionate.

In these contexts, reading competes with other types of information processing, such as listening and visual search, and may therefore lead to significant cognitive load. In a multimodal context 'the viewer has to not only manage cognitive resources across different sources of information (verbal and nonverbal, visual and auditory) but also do so without having control over the speed of presentation, unlike in static reading of written or some multimedia texts' (Kruger and Steyn 2013: 106). Reading in a multimodal environment therefore assumes the management of various simultaneous sources of information that compete for attention. Nevertheless, in a coherently constructed product that needs to be processed, these sources are not to be seen as obstacles but rather as elements that are very frequently used successfully to disambiguate information. This interactive account of language comprehension was documented by Trueswell (2008), who shows that, in linguistically complex situations, the readers' syntactic parsing decisions are made using the visual referent world. Adults use the visual context to guide their initial interpretation of an ambiguous phrase (Trueswell 2008). In a surtitling and captioning environment, for example, this means that time will be distributed proportionately, depending on their perceived centrality, across the channels delivering linguistic and non-linguistic information, both of which are crucial to the understanding of the intended message.

However, our attention span is known to be limited, and therefore conducting competing strenuous activities is difficult and, sometimes, impossible. For this reason, it is essential to ensure that the way in which we present captions—in terms of font, brightness, display, cueing—is in sync with the needs and abilities of our target viewers. For example, results from research looking into the perception of art works may teach us where to place captioning display units. These studies tell us that, when viewing paintings, fixations made by different groups of people tend to cluster in so-called regions of interest, thus forming areas of maximum fixation on a fixation map. Wooding's (2002) analysis of the eye movement patterns of different individuals concludes that most people seem to focus on similar zones of interest or centres of interest, even if the viewing order and eye trajectory are different. This seems to be supported by experiments carried out by film editors to determine 'predicted gaze position[s]' with a view to incorporate their findings into video coding processes (Peli *et al.* 2005). In their experiments, using different clips with varying levels of motion, shown on monitors of standard size, Peli *et al.* (*ibid.*: 4) report that '1/2 time the gaze of more than 15 subjects (out of 20) was contained within an area that was less than about 13% of the movie scene or about 5% of the screen for 4 subjects'. They also report differences between patterns within age and gender groups, whereby 'the older and male observers' COIs [centres of interest] were more tightly grouped than the younger and female observers' (*ibid.*). If we regard the stage as a canvas or a screen on which a story is projected, it would seem logical to present captions in those areas in or surrounding the stage where our spectators' visual attention will focus, given the amount of action or volume of information that is being presented there. It could then be argued that, by integrating the captions in an area where the attention of the spectators is maintained, eye strain (Carlson 2006) would be limited if not completely eliminated.

A recent subtitling study, Fox (2014) manipulates the positioning of the subtitles to follow the centres of interest where the visual attention is naturally concentrated during a film scene and shows that viewers' processing speed is enhanced when presented with subtitles which change position following visual centres of interest in the programme watched. In theatre captioning, this type of integrated captioning has been used by the UK based company Graeae. With accessibility a recognized characteristic of their productions, Graeae is 'committed to pioneering and evolving the "aesthetics of access", continually exploring new ways to weave in layers of accessibility and communication (such as BSL interpretation and audio description)' (Graeae 2015).

The StageTEXT (2015) study mentioned earlier in this section shows that attention when watching captions is efficiently and evenly distributed between the stage and the captioning display unit. Attention while watching captions displayed on LED screens at the side of the stage was divided as follows: 43% of the viewers' attention focused on the captions and 56% on the actors. In the case of the stage integrated LED, the distribution was 45% and 51% for captions and actors, respectively. Finally, when exposed to captions displayed on the mobile devices, 52% of the viewers' attention focused on the captions, with the remaining 43% on actors. These findings suggest that the newer display technology proved the most problematic. At any rate, even if the differences between these three display methods were statistically significant, the distribution of attention in all three display environments was deemed efficient for the overall aim of the service.

Looking to the future

According to Laura Arends, former Director of Communications at StageTEXT, the main obstacles to providing captioning services include the lack of 'awareness that they exist, the scarcity of resources, both financial and in terms of staff time; the fact that there isn't a good awareness in the arts and culture sector of the number of people who would benefit from the service; and the perception that hearing audiences will find captioning distracting and complain' (personal communication). Arends also acknowledges the central role technology plays in the provision of captioning services. As she puts it;

> when we started, we used displays that we bought over from America and had to be mended in France. They had far fewer LEDs, so they couldn't show any special characters, and the software was really hard to use. We collaborated with a UK-based software and LED company and created our own bespoke software and displays, which are much better. We've really benefitted from the development of technology recently. In particular, the rapid development of *Dragon Naturally Speaking* software means that we can now use a re-speaker for some events; cheaper Android tablets and the rise in WiFi and SSIS technology have boosted the adoption of hand-held captioning and live subtitles for tours. Moreover, live streaming has improved and is much more able to deal with larger amounts of data, which means we can now offer live subtitling of streamed events. And while GoogleGlass hasn't transferred into the mainstream, we are now seeing the development of Sony Eyeglasses and other personal captioning technology that could really change captioning in the future.

When asked about the future of captioning, Arends mentions the CaptionCue project aiming to automate captioning in cultural venues, and expects to see more open captioned performances in more theatres—including amateur and all the corners of the country that have not been reached yet. Captioning on demand is an aim for the future. For VocalEyes (2017), the automatic captioning implementation at the National Theatre brings the potential for a new ambitious initiative to automate audio description. Speech technology will be central to that project as well, as various speech models will need to be tested, developed and implemented to deliver the description.

Research questions

A great deal of research has already been carried out in this area. This has involved documenting the history of the field, identifying the translation difficulties the source text poses, as well as the techniques for dealing with those challenges. However, many areas remain unexplored. For example, we are quite some way away from designing and undertaking a sound reception study to assess the way in which titles are read and processed by end users under different experimental conditions—primarily various presentation settings and types of venue. It would also be necessary to carry out a study addressing the evolving needs of title users, and the extent to which their changing needs are met by the services they are being provided with. Conducting a comprehensive evaluation of existing technological tools and exploring the potential integration of new tools in the workflow—e.g. speech recognition for post-show discussions or computer-assisted translation tools for text segmentation and pre-processing—would also pave the way to gain a better understanding of this field and deliver a better service for those who need and enjoy surtitling and captioning. Finally, as we move towards on-demand services, options available to offer surtitling and captioning should also be explored.

Summary

This chapter has provided definitions of surtitling and captioning for theatre and opera and examined the history of these practices. It has surveyed the key features of surtitling in the opera, where surtitling originated as a service, before moving the focus of the discussion to theatre captioning, which enables productions to reach different types of audiences. After discussing the textual, social and technical aspects of surtitling and captioning in these contexts, the chapter also explores the growing formal experimentation driven by technological advancements in the industry.

This chapter has attempted to show that surtitling and captioning services are not to be regarded as 'un mal necessaire' ('a necessary evil') (Marleau 1982), emerging instead as practices that are nowadays enjoyed and demanded by various groups of people, and even included as an integral element in various theatre companies' performances. It has been argued that this is possible due to the ever-changing target audience needs and expectations (Secară and Allum 2011, Dewolf 2001), as well as the general enthusiasm surrounding these types of services and the wider opportunities they offer.

Further reading

StageTEXT (n.d) 'Making Theatre and Culture Accessible to Deaf, Deafened and Hard of Hearing People'. Available online: http://www.stagetext.org/ [last accessed 20 December 2017] | *StageTEXT offers a wealth of information on recent research and practical guidelines for access service provision.*

Şerban, A. and R. Meylaerts (eds) (2014) 'Multilingualism at the Cinema and on Stage: A Translation Perspective', Special Issue of *Linguistica Antverpiensia* 13 | *This special issue contains a number of articles on translating for the stage.*

Dragon Naturally Speaking (n.d.) 'Dragon Speech Recognition Software'. Available online: http://www.nuance.co.uk/dragon/index.htm [last accessed 20 December 2017].

Subtivals (n.d.) 'Live Subtitling Made Easy'. Available online: http://subtivals.org/ [last accessed 20 December 2017].

Related topics

3   Subtitling on the cusp of its futures
6   Subtitling for deaf and hard of hearing audiences: moving forward
7   Respeaking: subtitling through speech recognition
8   Audio description: evolving recommendations for usable, effective and enjoyable practices
17 Multimodality and audiovisual translation: cohesion in accessible films
22 Eye tracking in audiovisual translation research
31 Accessible filmmaking: translation and accessibility from production

References

Action On Hearing Loss (2011) *Taking Action on Hearing Loss in the 21st Century*. Available online: http://www.actiononhearingloss.org.uk/ [last accessed 20 December 2017].

BBC (2009) 'Online Subtitling Editorial Guidelines'. Available online: http://www.bbc.co.uk/guidelines/futuremedia/accessibility/subtitling_guides/online_sub_editorial_guidelines_vs1_1.pdf [last accessed 20 December 2017).

Burton, J. (2009) 'The Art and Craft of Opera Surtitling', in J. Díaz Cintas and G. Anderman, (eds) *Audiovisual Translation: Language Transfer on Screen*, Basingstoke: Palgrave Macmillan, 58–70.

Byford, M. (2008) *News at When? Broadcast Journalism in the Digital Age*, Public Lecture, University of Leeds, 29 February.

CaptionCue Project (n. d.) 'CaptionCue'. Available online: https://www.accessibletheatre.org.uk/technical/digital-technology/captioncue/ [last accessed 20 December 2017].

Carlson, M. (2006) *Speaking in Tongues: Language at Play in the Theatre*, Ann Arbor, MI: The University of Michigan Press.

Dewolf, L. (2001) 'Surtitling Operas', in Y. Gambier and H. Gottlieb (eds) *(Multi)Media Translation: Concepts, Practices, and Research*, Amsterdam & Philadelphia: John Benjamins, 179–188.

Forbes (2012) 'Google Glasses Sound as Crazy as Smartphones and Tablets Once Did'. Available online: https://www.forbes.com/sites/greatspeculations/2012/04/05/google-glasses-sound-as-crazy-as-smartphones-and-tablets-once-did/#2bc9a5c81342 [last accessed 20 December 2017].

Fox, W. (2014) 'Film Identity, Reception, Aesthetics and Information Flow: Integrated Titles and Other Possible Improvements', Paper presented at the *Languages & The Media, 10th International Conference on Language Transfer in Audiovisual Media*, Berlin, 5–7 November.

Graeae (2015) 'Our Artistic Vision'. Available online: http://www.graeae.org/about-us/ [last accessed 20 December 2017].

Griesel, Y. (2005) 'Surtitles and Translation towards an Integrative View of Theatre Translation', in H. Gerzymisch-Arbogast and S. Nauert (eds) *MuTra 2005—Challenges of Multidimensional Translation*, Conference Proceedings, Saarbrücken. Available online: http://www.euroconferences.info/proceedings/2005_Proceedings/2005_Griesel_Yvonne.pdf [last accessed 20 December 2017].

Kruger, J. L. and F. Steyn (2013) 'Subtitles and Eye Tracking: Reading and Performance', *Reading Research Quarterly* 49(1): 105–120.

Ladouceur, L. (2014) 'Bilingual Performance and Surtitles: Translating Linguistic and Cultural Duality in Canada', *Linguistica Antverpiensia* 13: 45–60.

Low, P. (2002) 'Surtitles for Opera. A Specialised Translating Task', *Babel* 48(2): 97–110.

Marleau, L. (1982) 'Les sous-titres . . . un mal necessaire', *Meta* 27(3): 271–295.

Matamala, A. and P. Orero (2007) 'Accessible Opera in Catalan: Opera for All', in J. Díaz Cintas, P. Orero and A. Remael (eds) *Media for All: Subtitling for the Deaf, Audio Description and Sign Language*, Amsterdam: Rodopi, 201–214.

Mateo, M. (2007). 'Surtitling Nowadays: New Uses, Attitudes and Developments', *Linguistica Antverpiensia* 6: 135–154.

Ofcom (2006) *Television Access Services. Review of Code and Guidance*. Available online: http://tinyurl.com/qjq7pzw [last accessed 20 December 2017].

Ofcom (2017) *Ofcom's Code on Television Access Services*. Available online: https://www.ofcom.org.uk/__data/assets/pdf_file/0020/97040/Access-service-code-Jan-2017.pdf [last accessed 20 December 2017].

Oncins, E. (2015) 'The Tyranny of the Tool: Surtitling Live Performances', *Perspectives: Studies in Translatology* 23(1): 42–62.

Orero, P. and A. Matamala (2008) 'Accessible Opera: Overcoming Linguistic and Sensorial Barriers', *Perspectives: Studies in Translatology* 15(4): 262–277.

Oxford English Dictionary (n.d.) *Oxford English Dictionary*. Available online: http://www.oed.com/ [last accessed 20 December 2017].

Peli, E., R. B. Goldstein and R. L. Woods (2005) 'Scanpaths of Motion Sequences: Where People Look when Watching Movies', *Computers in Biology and Medicine* 37(7): 957–64.

Perego, E. (2008) 'Subtitles and Line-breaks: Towards Improved Readability', in D. Chiaro, C. Heiss and C. Bucaria (eds) *Between Text and Image. Updating Research in Screen Translation*, Amsterdam & Philadelphia: John Benjamins, 211–223.

Prescott, M. (2001) *Big; Bullshit; Sex, Lies et les Franco-Manitobains*, SaintBoniface, MB: Les Éditions du Blé.

Prescott, M. (2009) *Sex, Lies et les Franco-Manitobains*. Produced by Théâtre au Pluriel, Edmonton, November 5–6.

Romero-Fresco, P. (2012) 'Quality in Live Subtitling: The Reception of Respoken Subtitles in the UK', in A. Remael, P. Orero and M. Carroll (eds) *Audiovisual Translation and Media Accessibility at the Crossroads*, Amsterdam: Rodopi, 111–133.

Rondin, Paul (2015) 'Multilingual Surtitles on Augmented Reality Glasses'. Available online: http://www.theatreinparis.com/avignon-2015.html [last accessed 20 December 2017].

Secară, A. and T. Allum (2010) 'Enabling Access to Live Cultural Events through Captioning and Speech Recognition Technologies', Paper presented at the *Languages & The Media, 8th International Conference on Language Transfer in Audiovisual Media*, Berlin, 6–8 October.

Secară, A. and T. Allum (2011) 'The Potential of Variety in Theatre Captioning'. Paper presented at the *Media for All* Conference, London, 29 June–1 July.

Şerban, A. and R. Meylaerts (eds) (2014) 'Multilingualism at the Cinema and on Stage: A Translation Perspective', Special Issue of *Linguistica Antverpiensia* 13.

StageTEXT (n.d) 'Making Theatre and Culture Accessible to Deaf, Deafened and Hard of Hearing People'. Available online: http://www.stagetext.org/ [last accessed 20 December 2017].

StageTEXT (2015) 'StageTEXT: CaptionCue. Research and Development Report'. Available online: http://tinyurl.com/pghryw3 [last accessed 20 December 2017].

Trueswell, J. C. (2008) 'Using Eye Movements as a Developmental Measure within Psycholinguistics', in I. Sekerina, Eva M. Fernández and H. Clahsen (eds) *Developmental Psycholinguistics: On-line Methods in Children's Language Processing*, Amsterdam & Philadelphia: John Benjamins, 73–96.

United Nations (1948) The Universal Declaration of Human Rights. Available online: http://www.un.org/en/universal-declaration-human-rights/index.html [last accessed 20 December 2017].

Virkkunen, R. (2004) 'The Source Text of Opera Surtitles', *Meta* 49(1): 89–97.

VocalEyes (2017) 'VocalEyes to Partner on Transformational New Theatre Access Technology'. Available online: http://vocaleyes.co.uk/vocaleyes-to-partner-on-transformational-new-theatre-access-technology/ [last accessed 20 December 2017].

Wooding, D. S. (2002) 'Eye Movements of Large Populations: II. Deriving Regions of Interest, Coverage and Similarity Using Fixation Maps', *Behaviour Research Methods, Instruments & Computers* 34(4): 518–28.

10
Game localization
A critical overview and implications for audiovisual translation

Minako O'Hagan

Introduction

In his study on Nintendo games, Altice (2015: 3) asserts that 'translation takes place between circuits, codes, and cathode rays just as it does between human actors'. This statement sets the tone for this chapter, which examines game localization as a relatively new practice and research domain in relation to audiovisual translation (AVT). Game localization cannot be discussed without considering the technological dimension of games as digital media. As a major digital entertainment sector in the twenty-first century, the video game industry has become a competitive global business with significant revenues drawn from international markets (Chandler and Deming 2012). Behind the global expansion of the game industry lies game localization, which plays a key role in distributing digital games in markets beyond the country of origin of the product (O'Hagan and Mangiron 2013). Digital games can be considered specialized software and therefore game localization has much in common with software localization: it involves technical, cultural and linguistic adjustments to the original software. Yet, there are aspects that are unique to the former, arising from the specific characteristics of games as digital interactive entertainment. Modern games are high-tech multimedia products with a non-linear structure, comprising different types of assets (i.e. the different components of a game), including full-fledged movies (known as cut-scenes in the industry), which commonly form part of today's mainstream console games. Furthermore, video games still occupy a contested space (Egenfeldt-Nielsen *et al.* 2013) in public perception, often associated with crime and violence, compared to other established art forms. All games are subject to age ratings that are country-specific and may also be subject to censorship. Game localization deals with artefacts which are not only technically complex but also culturally challenging. In addition, in contrast to utilitarian business software, games seek user engagement, which extends to users' affective responses (Juul 2005). In particular, high-budget 'AAA' console games offer user entertainment tailored for specific key target markets with the localized game aiming to pass as if it was originally made for the given market. Such requirements sometimes warrant extended leeway being applied during the localization process, with the end justifying the means. But game localization, understood as a set of industrial processes applied to the digital medium, also involves restrictions, as discussed later in this article. In this way, the underlying technological nature and socio-cultural contexts of games give rise to both freedom and constraints, shaping a dynamic and unique translation practice.

Despite the persistent reluctance of society to fully embrace games and gaming as a respectable activity, some game studies scholars consider that video games have become pervasive enough to constitute a 'social norm' (Juul 2010). Indeed, games are today played by family members across broad age groups and by both sexes (ESA 2017) and are designed to cater for all tastes and preferences. Accordingly, modern games are more varied and playable on different platforms. Furthermore, certain properties of game design that aim to engage users can now also be observed in 'serious games' which are developed with specific didactic purposes in mind. Their application in the military and, increasingly, in education fields aims to exploit the concept of gamification, whereby game design elements provide an effective mechanism to enhance learner engagement in a given task (Gee 2003).

The game industry stands at the cutting edge of technology, which is applied in different ways in both game hardware and software. Among recent trends promoted by the infrastructural shift to Web 2.0 are the growth of a user-centred, participatory culture and the building of user communities. The game industry has long embraced user 'co-creation' (Dovey and Kennedy 2006) by deliberately allowing user input to be incorporated into a game. For example, the widespread practice known as 'modding' refers to game users modifying a game to their liking, while 'emergent play' designates the discovery by end users of a new way of playing a game, unintended by the designer—the latter often involving the exploitation of technical glitches in the software (O'Hagan and Mangiron 2013). Similarly, fan translators have emerged among the most highly engaged users of video games: fan translators take localization into their own hands, as part of what is known as 'ROM hacking', a process in which tech savvy gamers gain access to the game's Read Only Memory (ROM) files (Muñoz-Sánchez 2009). Once ROM files are obtained, the language of the ROM data can be changed by fan translators through small programs known as 'patches' in a practice known as 'translation hacking' (*ibid.*). Furthermore, fan participation has been extended through crowdfunding, with some fans offering free localization of their chosen games (Tomala 2014). These practices in turn can be linked to fan translation, one of the most hotly debated topics in AVT research (Pérez-González 2014).

Seeking to locate game localization in the context of AVT research, this chapter provides a critical overview of game localization as a practice and a concept. The next section outlines the historical development of game localization practices, followed by a description of their key features. After covering the fundamentals of game localization, the chapter outlines a research agenda for the field. It then moves on to examine various game localization research methodologies, most of which remain under-developed. By way of conclusion, the article brings into focus the impact of technological advances, against the background of the broader technologization of translation, as a meaningful anchor point to frame game localization.

For the purposes of this chapter, the terms 'video games' and 'digital games' are used interchangeably. For further discussion on the terminology and definition of video games in the context of game localization research, readers are referred to O'Hagan and Mangiron (2013: 63–66).

Historical background

Digital games reportedly had their origin in the USA, where the game industry was first developed in the early 1970s, at a time when it was dominated by the game company Atari.

In the mid-1980s, Japanese companies entered the American market and a number of major milestones followed suit, including the demise of Atari and the release of the Nintendo Entertainment System (NES). Both countries remain to date among the world's biggest game producing and consuming nations, although the make-up of the game industry is in a state of flux. For example, Korea and China are becoming increasingly important, especially in the area of online games.

In contrast to the well-chronicled history of video games, the history of game localization is hazy, especially in the academic literature—which might be regarded as indicative of the limited interest in localization in game studies. From a game industry perspective, Hasegawa (2009) divides the historical development of game localization into different stages: early phase (prior to mid-80s); growth phase (to mid-90s); development phase (to late 90s); maturing phase (2000 to 2005) and advanced phase (after 2005).

In broad terms, both practitioners and researchers of game localization agree that it was only in 2000 that game localization began to be streamlined into a systematic industrial process (O'Hagan and Mangiron 2013). It is worth highlighting that game localization was initially developed independently of software localization. For example, the industry body, Software Publishers Association (SPA), initially represented primarily the interests of business software publishers, with game publishers being relatively marginalized (Kent 2001: 469). This foregrounds the separate paths followed by the otherwise closely associated practices of software and game localization. The former came into existence with the advent of personal computers in the 1980s, prompting the need for the computer industry to distribute mainly US-made software in international markets (Esselink 2000). The term 'localization' was introduced to designate the process whereby a given digital product or content is made available for the target region by translating and adapting it in the local language and conventions (Esselink, *ibid.*). As well as translating texts for the user interface of software applications and adapting country-specific formats such as date, time and currency, it was also necessary to enable software itself to process user input in the user's language, which required the involvement of software engineers. The idea behind game localization is similar, yet with some differences, as explained below.

In the early days, the amount of text being used within games that required translation tended to be relatively small. This, combined with a lack of awareness in the game industry of the need for professional input, was the main reason why professional translators were not involved in game localization. For example, it was common for Nintendo games to be first translated by Japanese game engineers from Japanese into English, and then to be edited by an English native speaker (Uemura *et al*. 2013: 171). Furthermore, it was commonly assumed that any game that happened to be successful in its home country was likely to appeal to other markets, regardless of translation availability and quality (Kohler 2005). During the 1980s and into the 1990s, the practice evolved largely on a trial and error basis; although this often resulted in poor translations, it was not always necessarily detrimental for sales (Kohler, *ibid.*). The correlation between the localization quality and game sales has never been clear-cut (O'Hagan and Mangiron 2004) and this remains the case today. Over and above the lack of professional input, other earlier stumbling blocks which affected translation included the game technology itself, in the form of limitations in memory and processing capacities of the game console hardware (Altice 2015). Such constraints often led to the need to drastically reduce the amount of the target text in English, at times as much as halving it, as recalled by English translators of Japanese games working at the time (e.g. Ted Woolsey, cited in Kohler 2005: 226). This very point marks one of the fundamental differences between localization and other types of translation which are not bound by the constraints of an electronic medium.

Many games were being localized by the mid-1990s, but the quality of localization continued to be inconsistent. It was then that games began to evolve from being heavily text-based, and hence without graphics, to include full-fledged multimedia elements. It was also a time when computer-synthesized voices were the mainstay, in contrast to today's mainstream games which are usually voiced by humans. The use of human voice led to audio localization, involving re-voicing by professional actors into the target language. Its evolution over time shows the extent to which the development of games and their localization have been dictated by technology (Altice 2015); pragmatic solutions have been sought to tackle technological limitations while exploiting growing capability—from arcade games to 16-bit consoles, CD-ROM and DVD to today's game systems that comprise high-spec computers.

Game localization has also given rise to unique cultural issues that have to be addressed in translation. Prior to the establishment of age ratings boards—e.g. the US Entertainment Software Ratings Board (ESRB)—in 1994, issues relating to age suitability of game content as well as to cultural sensitivity in different regions were brought into focus during the localization process. This is demonstrated by the strict self-regulatory process enforced by Nintendo of America on NES games. Their 'NES Game Standards Policy' covered a broad range of rules to address any aspects that could be considered potentially unsuitable for the target users or offensive in the target market, including violence, sexual innuendo, nudity and religious references (O'Hagan and Mangiron 2013: 225). These internal rules, which were strictly applied to NES games localized from Japanese to be sold in the North American region, exemplify the self-regulation and self-censorship exercised at the time by game companies, largely in response to the public perception of games as less savoury entertainment unsuitable for minors (Sheff 1993). Such self-restraint has been largely replaced and formalized today by territory-specific age ratings boards established in key regions such as North America, Europe and Japan, with Germany, Australia and China imposing particularly strict regulations (Chandler and Deming 2012: 35–42).

One of the unique features typically attributed to digital games, in contrast to productivity software, is that games are designed to expand users' imagination, thus exceeding the utilitarian goal of the latter (Uemura *et al*. 2013). This foregrounds the 'affective' dimension that arises from intense user engagement in the game medium and, concomitantly, the importance of handling cultural issues during the localization process in such a way that games are able to cross national borders. Crucially, the increased use of audiovisual content and sophisticated multimedia story-telling has led to the creation of games that sometimes raise complex cultural issues. These may include a wide spectrum of issues such as sexuality, religion and political views, which differ across cultures. As a result, 'culturalization' has emerged as a significant mechanism both in the practice and research of game localization to address factors contributing to 'intercultural dissonance' (Edwards 2012: 25). Edwards considers culturalization to be the solution to problems associated with 'geographics', a term used in game development to refer to the location of the player (Novak 2012: 95). This focus highlights the impact of the broad cultural dimensions affecting the player's response to the game, as is further elaborated below.

Into the 2000s, as games continued to grow in complexity and timelines continued to shrink to enable the simultaneous shipment ('sim-ship') of the original and the localized games, previous *ad hoc* approaches to localization became unsustainable. This led to the systematization of game localization with an increasing use of computer-based tools to facilitate the process. Just as the software localization became a well-established industrial process through various initiatives launched by the industry, the game industry began to promote a better awareness of localization issues. This is demonstrated by the establishment of the

Game Localization Special Interest Group in 2008 under the umbrella of the International Game Developers Conference (GDC) series, which ultimately led to the compilation of Best Practices for Game Localization (Honeywood and Fung 2012). It is now acknowledged by the software localization sector, through the adoption of the acronym GILT (Globalization, Internationalization, Localization and Translation), that considerations of localization should take place during the game development phase. GILT puts the traditionally downstream activities of localization and translation upstream as part of the whole globalization process, and encourages an integrated approach to the development of a product that has translation in mind from the start. In this way, game localization practices have become gradually approached in a more stable and systematic manner (Hasegawa 2009), with the concept of internationalization increasingly at the heart of this new model (Chandler and Deming 2012). The next section discusses what game localization practices actually entail.

Game localization in practice

The key concept behind localization is 'locale', whose original meaning was a 'small area' or 'vicinity', but in this field has come to designate the combination of 'region, language and character encoding' (Esselink 2000: 1). For example, Simplified Chinese must be used for Mainland China, whereas Traditional Chinese is used for Hong Kong and Taiwan, each of which, in turn, must be represented and mapped by correct character sets and encoding systems (a process that, in the case of non-Roman scripts such as Chinese, Japanese and Korean has become easier after the adoption of the international standard Unicode). The concept of locale allows the version of the product to be tailored for a specific region in the relevant language variety as well as linked to other information associated with the target locality, such as date formats, units of currency and so forth (O'Hagan and Mangiron 2013: 88). The more recent definition of locale includes information on cultural, technical and geographical conventions beyond languages (European Quality Standard EN 1508, cited in Jiménez-Crespo 2013: 12–13). This highlights the inherent characteristic of localization as operating at the intersection between language, culture and digital medium.

Another key concept developed in the localization industry is the afore-mentioned framework captured by the acronym GILT. In particular, the internationalization process has become essential to efficiently enable the one-to-many distribution of an electronic product (Pym 2010). It is increasingly applied to game localization, as part of the globalization processes and strategies required to release a game product in various markets. From a technical perspective, game localization is closely linked to game development, as illustrated in the expression 'localization-friendly game development' (Chandler and Deming 2012)—which essentially points back to internationalization.

In a localization context, internationalization means to prepare a given product or content to be localization-ready to avoid costly retrofitting. Chandler and Deming (*ibid.*: 4–8), for example, maintain that well-internationalized games are relatively easy to localize. Internationalization involves technical considerations such as developing a game's code base to support all the intended target languages, and separating translatable elements from the software code. This allows for an easy extraction and re-integration of the software strings (texts) once they have been translated. Other internationalization considerations include (i) making allowance for text expansions to avoid target text being cut off (commonly known as 'truncations') if the space allocated on screen, based on the space required by the source language, is insufficient; and (ii) some cultural aspects involving non-verbal elements, such as the suitability of icons, graphics or the layout. In sum, the process of internationalization is designed to ensure that no major changes will be required during the subsequent localization process for a specific target market.

Similar to software localization, there are in-house and outsourcing models which determine the subsequent workflow. Also, localization may be based on either a post-gold model—where a localized version is released after the elapse of a certain period of time from the release of the original game—or on sim-ship. Most major AAA games and their various locales are now sim-shipped or distributed with shorter intervals, following the release of the original games. Historically, Japanese games tended to be released using a post-gold model. However, as illustrated in the cases of major Japanese publishers such as Nintendo and Square Enix, a sim-ship model is being increasingly used (O'Hagan and Mangiron 2013). The actual localization work process differs according to the model used, but typically localization begins by extracting assets (i.e. elements in the game) that are subject to translation and preparing them for localization as part of 'localization kits'—which ideally include clear instructions and sufficient context for the fragmented texts. Once relevant assets are translated, they need to be compiled back into the software and tested, as is also the case in the context of software localization. This testing is essential to ensure that a localized product functions as expected (functional testing) and also to verify that a given translation fits the context (linguistic testing). The latter is necessary due to the fact that translators typically work on extracted strings from software which are often provided without a context. This creates a major challenge for translators, which is further compounded by the non-linear structure of games and the fact that translators are not able to access the finished game in sim-ship environments. The problem is further exacerbated if translators are not familiar with games in general (Dietz 2006).

To understand the broader context of game production, including localized games, it is worth highlighting the specific make-up of the game industry. It consists of game developers, game publishers who often finance the game development and, in the case of console games, console manufacturers—i.e. Nintendo, Microsoft and Sony. The decision-making process concerning game localization reflects these industry structures and the hierarchy of the key actors. For example, publishers are typically in the most powerful position and determine which regions are to be served by localized versions; what degree of localization (i.e. full versus partial) should be put in place for each locale; and what release timeframe (sim-ship versus post-gold) will be adopted. The localization process for console games is linked to the console manufacturer through the mandatory process of 'submission' of games, whereby the relevant game manufacturer verifies localized games according to pre-published criteria. This procedure aims to ensure that the localized games load and play properly on the given platform through adherence to the manufacturer-approved use of key terminology, among other things—hence the critical demonstration of translation as an embedded element in a technical system. Furthermore, insofar as games are commercial and highly competitive products, it is often the publisher (and its marketing department) who makes certain localization-related decisions from a strategic business perspective. Other business decisions pertain to the legal obligations relating to licensing agreements, something particularly important in the case of transmedia franchise titles where games are made based on movies (e.g. *Star Wars*), TV series (e.g. *Simpsons*), books (e.g. *Harry Potter*) or comics (e.g. *Watchmen*). Game localization practices are ultimately shaped by the business interests of the game industry, and the degree of discretion bestowed on the localizers will depend on corporate interests. In recent years, however, these industry-driven processes are being affected by developments such as crowdfunding, including free localization by communities of fan users.

Compared to productivity software, games tend to have a greater variety of assets. These include in-game text assets, art assets (such as text in images), audio and cinematic assets, printed assets (manuals and packaging in addition to marketing and legal documents) and other collateral (associated assets such as web materials, TV commercials etc). Furthermore, video games incorporate a broad range of genres, including action adventure games, role playing games (RPG), First Person Shooter (FPS), sports games, and hybrid games (a mixture of different genres), to give but some examples—a diversity that has important implications, as it would require a certain degree of subject specialization on the part of the translator. For example, unauthentic use of terminology in specialized games, such as the flight simulation ones, is likely to break the suspension of disbelief for any user who is familiar with the domain (Dietz 2006). From this perspective, translating games can be similar to translating technical texts featuring subject-specific terminology. The same would apply, for instance, in games revolving around sports, music, cooking or military combat scenarios. Some RPG games are narrative-driven and may require skills akin to those of literary translators; some dialogues, for example, might have to be translated in a specific style and register, whether contemporary or archaic. Due to the great variety of games that are now being produced, it is increasingly difficult to discuss game translation strategies in terms of one common translation approach (Fernández Costales 2012). The sheer variety of games and diverse approaches used in game localization seems to have delayed the adoption by the game localization sector of computer-aided translation (CAT) tools—compared with the ubiquity of these technologies in the field of software localization practices. However, today their use is on the increase. This includes tools that are specifically developed in-house with game localization in mind, and machine translation (MT) applications are also on the horizon (O'Hagan and Mangiron 2013: 142–146).

Depending on the size and importance of the target market, games may be fully localized—in which case the cinematic audio asset will be dubbed (a process referred to as 'voice-over' or VO in game localization) as well as subtitled—or partly localized—i.e. only subtitled (Chandler and Deming 2012: 9–10). While the application of these language transfer modes places game localization under the umbrella AVT, game localization does not generally follow AVT norms (Mangiron and O'Hagan 2006). For example, interlingual subtitles used in game cut-scenes are usually translated verbatim, with little consideration for legibility on screen or the recipient's reading speed. In most mainstream games, VO is performed by professional voice actors; each speaking part will normally be recorded separately, rather than in actual interaction with other game characters. Both subtitle and dubbing scripts tend to be organized according to each game character, which results in a certain de-contextualization that can sometimes prove detrimental to high quality translation. This approach to the translation of the cinematic asset in games signals that such assets (and their translation) are not normally regarded as the main feature or reason why gamers are attracted to the particular game. Gamers are often eager to focus on the actual interactive gameplay action, so non-interactive cut-scenes are normally perceived as not particularly engaging (Egenfeldt-Nielsen *et al*. 2013). The way in which VO is handled in video games is arguably indicative of the secondary importance that cinematics has for many gamers (Newman 2004). Nevertheless, full localization is becoming ever more common as a mechanism to enhance gamer immersion (Schliem 2012).

Current and future debates

While game localization research is beginning to mature, the field is far from well-established, and many gaps are yet to be filled in the theorization of this dynamic practice. In *Introducing*

Translation Studies: Theories and Applications Munday positioned 'video game translation' under new media and translation, marking it as one of the important developments derived from technological progress. In particular, he identifies this practice as a 'site for transcreation' (Munday 2016: 286–287), highlighting the creative dimension of the practice. Mangiron and O'Hagan (2006) first made use of this term to conceptualize game translation as the transfer of the gameplay 'experience' from the source to the target text. In their discussion of the translation of some weapon names and the use of regional accents in VO for cut-scenes in the major Japanese RPG *Final Fantasy* series, Mangiron and O'Hagan illustrated how translators focused on recreating 'the overall gameplay experience' (*ibid.*: 15), while retaining the 'look and feel' of the game. For example, the original naming of a sword called '花鳥風月' [a classical Chinese idiom literally meaning 'flower, birds, winds and moon' that generally refers to the beauty of nature] was translated as 'Painkiller' in the North American version of the game. This was justified by the translator on the basis of the weapon's powerful qualities—indeed, characters using the 'Painkiller' had a major advantage, as they could skip painful grinds and earn points more quickly. Importantly, the translation of the weapon's name also manages to convey a touch of ironic humour (see Alex O. Smith, cited in O'Hagan and Mangiron 2013: 191, for an in-depth discussion). As is also the case in AVT contexts, humour in game localization is often an important element that serves various functions—not least relieving tension—and calls for creative solutions (Mangiron 2010).

The applicability of transcreation in game localization has been explored by a number of authors. For example, Bernal-Merino (2006) has observed how, in contemporary contexts, the concept is now used by a new generation of translation companies that aim to 'distance themselves from traditional translation firms'. In this emerging context, transcreation foregrounds the creativity involved in translation, and positions itself as a value-added service (*ibid.*: 32). In keeping with this development, the localization sector uses the term transcreation to describe some game localization strategies involving a transformative approach (e.g. Wood *et al.* 2010). For his part, Fernández Costales (2012) discussed examples of transcreation strategies in Spanish translations of games originally released in English, and analyzed such strategies in terms of the genre each game belongs to. Fernández Costales found evidence of transcreation strategies being deployed more often in text-heavy RPGs and adventure games, although the link between the game genre and the specific strategies was found to be somewhat tenuous. By contrast, drawing on auteurism theory, Pettini (2015) discovered that a creative emphasis was not always the translator's preferred strategy. Interestingly, translators resorted to a literal approach in those cases where the signature style of a high-profile game designer was discernible. Pedersen (2014), on the other hand, conducted a meta-analysis of the concept of transcreation in the context of advertising and marketing translation—although he also covered other areas such as localization, internationalization and adaptation—in search of a clear definition of the concept. Pedersen's study revealed that the concept lent itself to various interpretations and concluded that the term transcreation primarily serves to draw attention to a range of characteristics that, while inherent to translation, are not explicit in the term 'translation'. On the whole, in the context of game localization, the use of the term transcreation is associated with the ludic dimension of the game and the importance of preserving the 'gameplay experience'; furthermore, it is to be considered in relation to culturalization.

Culturalization refers to a broad range of operations in game localization covering verbal as well as non-verbal transformations of game elements during the localization process. It can verge on censorship, typically self-censorship, by the publishers of the games themselves.

The Western release of the Japanese game *Fire Emblem Fates* (Nintendo 2015) is a case in point. Immediately after its distribution in Japan, a major controversy erupted on social media platforms, mainly among Western gamers outside Japan, because of a scene depicting a drink being spiked with a 'magic powder'. The drink in question was meant to serve as a cure for a female soldier character who wished to overcome her nervousness when meeting attractive female characters. The debate concerned the potentially homophobic intention of this aspect of the plot as well as what some regarded as the promotion of a form of anti-social behaviour such as drugging. The intensity of the debate, which began before the official localized versions were released, prompted fans to post versions of the Japanese original scene on social media with their own translation. The ensuing controversy forced Nintendo to issue an announcement to fans, explaining how they would handle the said scene during the localization process, and noting that the offending scene would be localized 'to make it appropriate for [each] particular territory' (cited in Sato 2016). When the localized US version eventually came out, the scene in question had been largely recontextualized.

It is relevant to point out that not all bilingual fans agreed on the interpretation of the scene, with some of them pleading not to change the original content in subsequent localized versions (Kain 2016). The interpretation of certain aspects of a game typically requires a broad understanding of relevant cultural and social aspects of the country where the game originates, in addition to gaming knowledge. For example, sexually ambivalent characters, who often feature in Japanese games, are not normally intended to make statements on sexuality; likewise, the presence of magic potions is fairly common in fantasy games aimed at young children. Ultimately, the issue at stake in the previous example was the company's response to users, which led to the adoption of self-censorship on the part of the publisher. Significantly, this case illustrates the challenging milieu in which game localizers and game publishers find themselves in the era of social media, where word about games may spread rapidly across the world even before the official localized versions have been released. It also shows how, in this context, localizers and publishers run the risk of alienating long-standing fans, particularly if the final decision on the localization strategy adopted in each case appears to be dictated by the most vocal users—who may not always represent *bona fide* fans. This suggests that the availability of multiple communication channels and the heightened visibility of game users may act as a two-edged sword in colouring the reception of localized games.

As game localization research matures, there will be more studies exploring the transformative nature of translation, as encapsulated in the concept of transcreation. Game localization is often accounted for in functionalist terms, i.e. as driven by the ultimate purpose (*skopos*) of the game—that is, entertaining the end-user. This resonates with the 'user-centered translation' (UCT) approach proposed by Suojanen *et al.* (2015), which makes explicit the widely tacit assumption that translators are familiar with the potential users of the translation (*ibid.*: 144). Positioned at the intersection between usability studies and human-computer interaction (HCI), UCT can make a significant contribution to the study of modern video games as immersive digital environments.

Furthermore, UCT implies a shift in the focus of translation quality assessment (TQA) towards users' perspectives—in keeping with the long-perceived need for reception studies in AVT research (Gambier 2009). TQA is a complex matter in the context of video game localization, where even major translation blunders can be tolerated (see Kohler 2005 for examples) as long as the core game experience is maintained in the eyes of the end users; however, in some cases, one misplaced word can prompt the recall of a localized game—as illustrated in O'Hagan and Mangiron 2013: 178). Game fans are diverse, as is often evident in their response to elements pertaining to the socio-cultural context of the game. Insofar as games are affective media fostering the users' emotional engagement, it would be justifiable for translators to aim squarely at users modelled around the 'personas' or 'implied readers' they have in mind when translating (Suojanen et al. 2015). A UCT-based approach with formative user feedback may therefore play an important role in recreating software-mediated cultural experiences (O'Hagan 2015). In particular, such an approach will help resist the *ad hoc* adoption of self-censoring decisions that tamper with the game experience delivered in the localized versions of the game.

Game localization is a dynamically evolving practice driven by the needs of the game industry and the users' demands. As has been elaborated on, this scenario enhances the relevance of a UCT-based approach to game translator training (Mangiron 2006, Granell 2011, Bernal-Merino 2014). Research on game localization is helping to identify the competences that the industry is demanding from game localizers, whether they take the form of personal traits and skills, subject-specific knowledge or professional self-awareness (e.g. O'Hagan and Mangiron 2013: 243–275). The development of training opportunities will also enable the integration of CAT tools in this area of professional practice, as explained below.

Common research methods

Game localization is a site of research whose impetus comes from practices that have evolved in response to market demands. As an area of translation firmly grounded in industry practices, initial descriptive studies drawing on practitioner insights have provided a solid platform to launch this area of research in translation studies (see Mangiron 2017 for an overview of game localization research). Sources such as industry reports and fan discussion forums continue to provide access to insider and user information which may otherwise be difficult to obtain. These sources help researchers gain an understanding of the 'how' and 'what' questions concerning the practice. However, more in-depth research seeking detailed answers to the 'why' question may require the collection of additional primary data.

In terms of methodological innovation, game localization lags behind the cognate field of AVT, which has witnessed major developments in recent years. Confined within the product-oriented paradigm, case studies focused on translation strategies dominate the literature in the field (e.g. Mangiron and O'Hagan 2006, Fernández Costales 2012, Mangiron et al. 2014). There are also studies focused on practitioners, whether they are based on small samples of interviews (e.g. Jayemanne 2009) or a more extensive ethnographic study (e.g. Mandiberg 2015). Mandiberg conducted in-person interviews with 40 localization industry personnel working in different roles in the US, Holland and Japan over the period 2010–2013. Frustratingly, Mandiberg's attempt at conducting workplace observations was hampered by non-disclosure agreement clauses—a challenging factor in game localization research (O'Hagan and Mangiron 2013), in contrast with the increasing number of workplace-based studies now being conducted in other areas of translation (e.g. Ehrensberger-Dow and Massey 2014).

The need for empirically based reception studies has been stressed by scholars in AVT for some time (e.g. Gambier 2003) and this plea has resulted in an increasing number of viewer studies, for example, using eye tracking (e.g. Caffrey 2009, Kruger and Faans 2014). Given the particularly strong interest in users within the field of game localization, eye tracking has become a fast-developing research method. For example, in the area of accessibility of cut-scenes in localized games, Mangiron (2016) used eye tracking to test reception of same-language subtitles by deaf and hard of hearing players vis-à-vis their hearing counterparts. This study involved the manipulation of the subtitles and associated elements to throw light on the differences in visual attention by participating subjects, as measured by fixation durations. The study found that, when long two-line subtitles were displayed, deaf and hard of hearing subjects showed a significantly longer fixation duration, indicating that subtitle reading represented a greater cognitive load for them. By combining the data with a pre-test questionnaire, Mangiron was able to suggest a set of preliminary guidelines for game companies to consider subtitling approaches geared for better accessibility.

As far as research methods seeking to obtain game player data are concerned, O'Hagan and Mangiron (2013: 312–318) and O'Hagan (2016) reported on an explorative study on player experience. The study involved native speakers of English, German and Japanese playing a game in its original English version and its respective German and Japanese locales. The study experimented with a number of data streams, including eye-tracking, galvanic skin response and heart rates as well as facial expressions, combining them with subject interviews and play trajectories. Even though it was conceived as a pilot study, it served to point to an emerging research method deploying a range of user biometric data. As technological tools such as portable mobile sensors continue to improve, an empirical player experience approach has scope to provide objective data, and hence complement subjective data gathered through player interviewers and surveys.

The influence of technology on game localization

The ever-growing number of studies on the impact of technology on translation and the translation industry undertaken in recent years has widened the scope of research within the field of translation studies, and paved the way for the emergence of new research foci, including the conceptualization of translation as human-computer interaction (O'Brien 2012). In light of these advances, investigating the impact of technology on game localization is bound to provide a significant stimulus to the development of the field as an area of scholarly enquiry. However, there is very little research available on the use of CAT tools, and their impact on the localization process and the finished game products. Primarily, this is because, unlike other localization sectors, the use of CAT tools such as translation memory and terminology management systems on an enterprise-wide level is a relatively recent development in game localization. Leaving CAT tools aside, other in-house tools are currently being developed to cater for the specific needs of the sector. These include applications (i) enabling the accurate tracking of multiple story lines; (ii) providing translators with fuller contexts for the translation of movie scripts through the use of screenshots as a solution to the recurrent lack of context for these game components; and (iii) facilitating a consistent management of terminology within a game and across game series. The ubiquity of non-disclosure agreement clauses in the video game industry is likely to continue hindering workplace-based research, but it is hoped that the growing recognition of the benefits derived from this type of research will eventually outweigh closed attitudes within this competitive industry, particularly from well-established game companies. Indeed, independent ('indie') game companies are generally more open to facilitate workplace-based research and thrash out new ideas for collaboration. This may allow the researcher to access user data collected in-house, for example, to develop and apply a UCT approach. Similarly, the ever more popular video streaming sites such as 'Twitch TV', that contain gameplay trajectory clips with added commentary by gamers, may provide new research data—as long as the ethical issues involved in the use of such data can be cleared.

More recently, the industry has been drawing on the concept of brain-machine interface to develop new experimental games where brain waves directly interact with the game, giving rise to neurogaming. As demonstrated in the Digital Games Research Association

Conference held in May 2015 (DiGRA 2015), UK filmmaker Karen Palmer has been exploring the use of wearable sensors to design new interactive narratives using the brain-machine interface concept. In her Syncself and Syncself2 video installations, the game is over when the player's sensor device detects loss of concentration. Similarly, her more recent work such as Riot (Palmer, n.d.) allows the player emotion to drive the game in real time through facial recognition software and AI. Such directions of interactive storytelling build on biofeedback games in which the individual gamer's physiological response is fed back into the game system in real time (e.g. Dekker and Champion 2007).

Further developments are being driven by the use of head-mounted virtual reality (VR) units to increase players' sense of immersion in the game world. According to the ESA report (ESA 2017: 9), 63% of the most frequent gamers are already familiar with VR and this technology is expected to redefine the gaming experience. PlayStation VR is the first VR headset designed to work with a specific game console, and Microsoft has released HoloLens to promote augmented reality (AR) applications using holographic images (The Year of VR 2016). Significantly, VR technology is likely to make important contributions in terms of enhancing accessibility, for example, by delivering an immersive playing experience to users with certain physical disabilities. The last two areas of study are turning game localization research into a multi-disciplinary area of study, further contributing to the broadening of the research basis and opportunities for innovation, both within game localization and AVT.

Conclusion

Research on game localization is inherently linked to AVT scholarship and has the potential to serve as a catalyst pushing the boundaries of current translation studies research. In the process of game localization, translation takes place within an interactive digital medium which is dynamically pushing towards further enhanced user engagement: through VR units, game players enter the immersive multimodal environment to experience the virtual world. This is likely to add further complexity to any potential application of a UCT approach to the study of game localization, although some elements of the immersive experience may not be directly related to localization issues.

This chapter has shown that game localization has widened the remit of translation concepts to focus on the user experience of a game world that demands all-encompassing culturalization. Yet, there needs to be a balance between preserving the original gameplay experience and taking steps to harness the voices from the heterogeneous user base. Indeed, one of the most unpredictable yet potentially significant developments regarding game users concerns the evolution of user communities around activities such as fan translation and translation crowdsourcing in the ever more participatory and collaborative digital landscape. Collecting big data from such communities will likely help researchers gain a fresh understanding of user behaviour and preferences concerning game localization strategies. However, access to user data entails the caveat of research ethics concerning data privacy and disclosure. These are some of the key challenges shared with AVT researchers who are attempting to make sense of dynamic and changing contexts of practice and research.

Further reading

Chandler, H. and S. O. Deming (2012) *The Game Localization Handbook*, 2nd edition, Sudbury, MA, Ontario & London: Jones & Bartlett Learning | *A comprehensive practical handbook explaining all aspects of game localization from a practitioner's perspective. Each chapter of the book contains an interview with industry experts and is an informative source bringing into light the practical dimension of game localization.*

Dovey, J. and H. W. Kennedy (2006) *Game Cultures: Computer Games as New Media*, Berkshire: Open University Press | *This is a well thought-through introduction to many dimensions of game culture with a detailed analysis of its complexity. While localization is not specifically discussed it provides a relevant background for game localization researchers who are particularly interested in cultural aspects of this process.*

Egenfeldt-Nielsen, S., J. H. Smith and S. P. Tosca (2013) *Understanding Video Games: Essential Introduction*, 2nd edition, New York & London: Routledge | *Written by game studies scholars, the book is an accessible scholarly introduction to video games and provides relevant background information on games and analytical frameworks used in game studies.*

O'Hagan, M. and C. Mangiron (2013) *Game Localization: Translating for the Global Digital Entertainment Industry*, Amsterdam & Philadelphia: John Benjamins | *A comprehensive monograph on game localization written with translation scholars in mind to locate the subject domain in translation studies. Also drawing on game studies literature, the book conceptualizes game localization by applying translation theory.*

Related topics

22 Eye tracking in audiovisual translation research
23 Audiovisual translation and audience reception
27 Audiovisual translation and fandom
29 Audiovisual translator training
32 Technologization of audiovisual translation

References

Altice, N. (2015) *I am Error: Nintendo Family Computer/Entertainment System Platform*, Cambridge, Mass. & London: MIT Press.

Bernal-Merino, M. (2006) 'On the Translation of Video Games', *JoSTrans: The Journal of Specialised Translation* 6: 22–36. Available online: http://www.jostrans.org/issue06/art_bernal.php [last access 20 December 2017].

Bernal-Merino, M. (2014) *Translation and Localisation in Video Games*, New York & London: Routledge.

Caffrey, C. (2009) *Relevant Abuse? Investigating the Effects of an Abusive Subtitling Procedure on the Perception of TV Anime Using Eye Tracker and Questionnaire*, Unpublished Doctoral Thesis, Dublin City University.

Chandler, H. and S. O. Deming (2012) *The Game Localization Handbook*, 2nd edition, Sudbury, MA, Ontario & London: Jones & Bartlett Learning.

Dekker, A. and E. Champion (2007) 'Please Biofeed the Zombies: Enhancing the Gameplay and Display of a Horror Game Using Biofeedback', *Proceedings of DiGRA 2007: Situated Play*, 550–558. Available online: http://www.digra.org/wp-content/uploads/digital-library/07312.18055.pdf [last access 20 December 2017].

Dietz, F. (2006) 'Issues in Localizing Computer Games', in K. J. Dunne (ed.) *Perspectives in Localization*, Amsterdam & Philadelphia: John Benjamins, 121–134.

DiGRA (2015) *Digital Games Research Association Conference: Diversity of Play—Games, Cultures*, Identities held at Leuphana University, 14–17 May, 2015. Lüneburg, Germany. Available online: http://projects.digital-cultures.net/digra2015/ [last access 20 December 2017].

Dovey, J. and H. W. Kennedy (2006) *Game Cultures: Computer Games as New Media*, Berkshire: Open University Press.

Edwards, K. (2012) 'Culturalization of Game Content', in H. Chandler and S. O. Deming (eds) *The Game Localization Handbook*, 2nd edition, Sudbury, MA, Ontario & London: Jones & Bartlett Learning, 19–34.

Egenfeldt-Nielsen, S., J. H. Smith and S. P. Tosca (2013) *Understanding Video Games: Essential Introduction*, 2nd edition, New York & London: Routledge.

Ehrensberger-Dow, M. and G. Massey (2014) 'Cognitive Ergonomic Issues in Professional Translation', in J. W. Schwieter and A. Ferreira (eds) *The Development of Translation Competence: Theories and Methodologies from Psycholinguistics and Cognitive Science*, Newcastle upon Tyne: Cambridge Scholars Publishing, 58–86.

ESA (Entertainment Software Association) (2017) *Essential Facts About the Computer and Video Game Industry*. Available online: http://www.theesa.com/wp-content/uploads/2017/04/EF2017_FinalDigital.pdf [last access 20 December 2017].

Esselink, B. (2000) *A Practical Guide to Software Localization*, revised edition, Amsterdam & Philadelphia: John Benjamins.

Fernández Costales, A. (2012) 'Exploring Translation Strategies in Video Game Localisation Multidisciplinarity in Audiovisual Translation', *MonTI* 4: 385–408.

Gambier, Y. (2003) 'Screen Transadaptation: Perception and Reception', *The Translator* 9(2): 171–190.

Gambier, Y. (2009) 'Reception and Perception of Audiovisual Translation: Implications and Challenges', in H. C. Omar, H. Haroon and A. A. Ghani (eds) *The Sustainability of the Translation Fields*, Kuala Lumpur: Malaysian Translators Association, 40–57.

Gee. J. (2003) *What Videogames Have to Teach us about Learning and Literacy*, New York: Palgrave.

Granell, X. (2011) 'Teaching Video Game Localization in Audiovisual Translation Courses at University', *JoSTrans: The Journal of Specialised Translation* 16: 185–202. Available online: http://www.jostrans.org/issue16/art_granell.pdf [last access 20 December 2017].

Hasegawa, R. (2009) 'ゲームローカライズの歴史とこれから [Game Localization History and Future]', in デジタルコンテンツ制作の先端技術応用に関する調査研究報告書 [Study Report on Advanced Technology Applications for Developing Digital Content], 121–132. Tokyo: JKA. Available online: http://www.dcaj.or.jp/project/report/pdf/2009/dc_09_03.pdf [last access 20 December 2017].

Honeywood, R. and J. Fung (2012) *Best Practices for Game Localization*. Available online: http://c.ymcdn.com/sites/www.igda.org/resource/collection/2DA60D94–0F74–46B1-A9E2-F2CE-8B72EA4D/Best-Practices-for-Game-Localization-v22.pdf [last access 20 December 2017].

Jayemanne, D. (2009) 'Generations and Game Localization: An Interview with Alexander O. Smith, Steven Anderson and Matthew Alt', *The Journal for Computer Game Culture* 3(2): 135–147.

Jiménez-Crespo, M. (2013) *Translation and Web Localization*, London & New York: Routledge.

Juul, J. (2005) *Half-real: Video Games Between Real Rules and Fictional Worlds*, Cambridge, Mass. & London: MIT Press.

Juul, J. (2010) *Casual Revolution: Reinventing Video Games and their Players*. Cambridge, Mass. & London: MIT Press.

Kain, E. (2016) "'Fire Emblem Fates' and the Curious Case of Localization Gone Terribly Wrong', *Forbes*. Available online: http://www.forbes.com/sites/erikkain/2016/02/29/fire-emblem-fates-and-the-curious-case-of-localization-gone-terribly-wrong/#625ace467fe1. [last access 20 December 2017].

Kent, S. L. (2001) *The Ultimate History of Video Games: From Pong to Pokémon and Beyond: The Story Behind the Craze that Touched our Lives and Changed the World*, New York: Three Rivers Press.

Kohler, C. (2005) *Power-up: How Japanese Video Games Gave the World an Extra Life*. Indianapolis: Brady Games.

Kruger, J. L. and S. Faans. (2014) 'Subtitles and Eye Tracking: Reading and Performance', *Reading Research Quarterly* 49(1): 105–120.

Mandiberg, S. (2015) *Responsible Localization: Game Translation Between Japan and the United States*, Unpublished Doctoral Thesis, University of California, San Diego.

Mangiron, C. (2006) 'Video Games Localisation: Posing New Challenges to the Translator', *Perspectives: Studies in Translatology* 14(4): 306–317.

Mangiron, C. (2010) 'The Importance of Not Being Earnest: Translating Humour in Video Games', in D. Chiaro (ed.) *Translation, Humour and The Media*, London: Continuum: 89–107.

Mangiron, C. (2016) 'Reception of Game Subtitles: An Empirical Study', *The Translator* 22(1): 72–93.

Mangiron, C. (2017) 'Research in Game Localisation: An Overview', *The Journal of Internationalization and Localization* 4(2): 74–99.

Mangiron, C. and M. O'Hagan. (2006) 'Game Localisation: Unleashing Imagination with a "Restricted Translation"', *JoSTrans: The Journal of Specialised Translation* 6: 10–21. Available online: http://www.jostrans.org/issue06/art_ohagan.pdf [last access 20 December 2017].

Mangiron, C., P. Orero and M. O'Hagan (eds) (2014) *Fun for All: Translation and Accessibility Practices in Video Games*, Bern: Peter Lang

Munday, J. (2016) *Introducing Translation Studies: Theories and Applications*, 4th edition, New York & London: Routledge.

Muñoz-Sánchez, P. (2009) 'Video Games Localization for Fans by Fans: The Case of Rom Hacking', *The Journal of Internationalization and Localization* 1(1): 168–185.

Newman, J. (2004) *Videogames*, London & New York: Routledge.

Novak, J. (2012) *Game Development Essentials: An Introduction*, Clifton Park, N.Y.: Delmar Cengage Learning.

O'Brien, S. (2012) 'Translation as Human-computer Interaction', *Translation Spaces* 1: 101–122.

O'Hagan, M. (2015) 'Game Localisation as Software-mediated Cultural Experience: Shedding Light on the Changing Role of Translation in Intercultural Communication in the Digital Age', *Multilingua* 34(6): 747–771.

O'Hagan, M. (2016) 'Game Localisation as Emotion Engineering: Methodological Exploration', in M. O'Hagan and Q. Zhang (eds) *Conflict and Communication: A Changing Asia in a Globalizing World: Language and Cultural Perspectives*, New York: Nova, 123–144.

O'Hagan, M. and C. Mangiron (2004) 'Games Localization: When Arigato Gets Lost in Translation', in *Proceedings of New Zealand Game Developers Conference Fuse 2004*, Dunedin: University of Otago, 57–62.

O'Hagan, M. and C. Mangiron (2013) *Game Localization: Translating for the Global Digital Entertainment Industry*, Amsterdam & Philadelphia: John Benjamins.

Palmer, K. (n.d.) 'Syncself 1 and 2'. Available online: http://karenpalmer.uk/portfolio/syncself-one/ [last access 20 December 2017].

Pedersen, D. (2014) 'Exploring the Concept of Transcreation—Transcreation as "More Than Translation"?', *Cultus. Journal of Intercultural Mediation and Communication* 7: 57–71.

Pérez-González, L. (2014) *Audiovisual Translation*, London & New York: Routledge.

Pettini, S. (2015) 'Auteurism and Game Localization. Revisiting Translational Approaches: Film Quotations in Multimedia Interactive Entertainment', *Translation Spaces* 4(2): 268–288.

Pym, A. (2010) *Exploring Translation Theories*, London & New York: Routledge.

Sato (2016) 'Nintendo Responds to Changes to Fire Emblem Fates' Western Localization', *Siliconera*. Available online: http://www.siliconera.com/2016/01/21/nintendo-responds-changes-fire-emblem-fates-western-localization/ [last access 20 December 2017].

Schliem, A. (2012) 'GDC 2012 [March 5–9] Increases Localization Focus', *Multilingual* 23(4): 8–9.

Sheff, D. (1993) *Game Over: Nintendo's Battle to Dominate an Industry*, London: Hodder & Stoughton.

Suojanen, T., K. Koskinen and T. Tuominen (2015) *User-Centered Translation*, London & New York: Routledge.

The Year of VR (2016) *Gameinformer* 73: 21–51.

Tomala, A. M. (2014) 'Using the Crowd in Game Development', *Multilingual* 25(4): 39–41.

Uemura, M, K. Hosoi and A. Nakamura (2013) ファミコンとその時代 [Famicom and Its Era], Tokyo: NTT Shuppan.

Wood, V, Krauss, S. and F. Ravetto (2010) 'Behind the Curtains of Buzz', Presentation delivered at the *Localization Summit, International Game Developers Conference 2010*, 10 March, San Francisco.

11
Film remakes as a form of translation

Jonathan Evans

How often have you come away from a remade movie or TV show comparing it to the original or wondering what the original was like? Films and TV shows are remade all the time, often crossing linguistic and cultural borders. The phenomenon of Japanese horror remakes, with American films such as *The Ring* (2002) remaking Japanese movies (in this case, Hideo Nakata's *Ringu/Ring* from 1998), is a well-known example. But there are also American remakes of British TV shows, such as *The Office* (2001–2003) and its American counterpart *The Office* (2005–2013), where differences in cultures, rather than differences in languages, had to be negotiated by the producers. Remakes have been around in the cinema ever since George Méliès' *Une partie de cartes/Card party* (1896), which was a remake of Louis Lumière's *Partie d'écarté/Card game* (1896). In other words, remakes are almost as old as cinema itself.

This chapter focuses on film remakes as a form of translation. This may sound contentious, especially as remakes are seldom included in overviews of translation theory such as *The Routledge Encyclopedia of Translation Studies* (Baker and Saldanha 2008) or Jeremy Munday's *Introducing Translation Studies* (2012). Even in some overviews of work on audiovisual translation (AVT) (e.g. Chiaro 2009 or O'Connell 2007) remakes are not mentioned. In other cases, remakes are briefly mentioned but the text focuses mainly on other audiovisual modalities such as subtitling and dubbing (examples of this include Delabastita 1990, Gambier 2003, 2004, O'Sullivan 2011). In the last few years, there have been a number of articles in translation studies that have worked towards redressing this balance (Wong 2012, Evans 2014a, 2014b, Yau 2014). In addition, Henrik Gottlieb (2007) and Stephen Mandiberg (2008) both argue that remakes are a form of translation as they replace the signs of the source text, in other words, as they replace the units of meaning in one language with units of meaning in another language.

Interestingly, scholars working in film studies have often used translation as a way of discussing remakes. Jennifer Forrest and Leonard Koos, for example, use the traditional categories of free and literal translation (which translation studies has generally moved away from) to suggest ways in which remakes might be conceptualized (2002: 15). Other scholars have similarly used translation as a metaphor for the remaking process (Aufderheide 1998, Wills 1998, Grindstaff 2001, Leitch 2002, Booth and Ekdale 2011). While these scholars compare remakes to translations, there is work that more specifically reads remakes through translation theory. Lucy Mazdon, for instance, uses Lawrence Venuti's concept of 'foreignizing translation' in her *Encore Hollywood* (2000) and elsewhere (Mazdon 2004) to explain her approach to remakes as a 'site of difference' (Mazdon 2000: 27). Yiman Wang (2008) also borrows from Venuti in her analysis of how Hong Kong remakes inscribe foreignness. Taking a slightly different approach, Laurence Raw (2010) uses skopos theory to discuss Michael Winner's remake of *The Big Sleep* (1978). These scholars demonstrate the relevance of translation theory to film remakes, even when they are discussing, as Raw does, a remake in the same language. However, many of the mentions of translation in work on remakes tend to be equivocal, simultaneously giving remakes the status of translation and also revoking it (Evans 2014a: 301–303). A good example of this is Abé Mark Nornes' statement that Hollywood 'eschew[s] translation for the remaking of perfectly wonderful foreign films—the ultimate free translation' (2007: 8). Here Nornes simultaneously says that remakes are translations and contrasts them to translation; for if one eschews translation for remaking, then remaking cannot be translation. There persists a certain discomfort in according remakes the status of translation in other scholars' work (e.g. Wehn 2001, Grindstaff 2001) that could be explained by the perception that translation solely acts on language. This perception is one that is also shared by the localization industry, where it is felt that translation is the 'replacement of natural-language strings' (Pym 2004: 52). Much recent work in translation studies has focused on the multimodal aspects of translation (e.g. O'Sullivan and Jeffcote 2013, Pérez-González 2014, Bosseaux 2015) and there is a wealth of work that argues that translation goes beyond just replacing strings of natural language, as Anthony Pym (2004: 52) points out. Remakes are a multimodal form of translation (Evans 2014a) where more than just language is translated and they may therefore trouble traditional perceptions of translation.

This chapter will focus on interlingual remakes, that is, remakes where the source films were created in another language. There are many remakes where the language is not changed, and these have been discussed in film studies (see e.g. Horton and McDougal 1998, Verevis 2006, Zanger 2006). While such remakes require a similar recontextualization of the film to translation, due to a change in audience over time or, in the case of American remakes of British productions, for a different culture, the interlingual focus of this chapter places remakes more comfortably into what Roman Jakobson called 'translation proper' (1959: 233), that is, the translation of a text from one language to another, highlighting similarities with other forms of translation.

The chapter explores the history of remakes before moving onto the theoretical aspects of remakes as a form of translation. The first section, 'Multiple-language versions and early remakes', focuses on the early remakes and multiple-language versions made in the early sound period (1929–1933). The second section, 'Recent American remakes', analyzes the sorts of remake most people will be familiar with, that is, American remakes of productions from elsewhere in the world. This sort of remake is often at the root of negative approaches to remakes which see them as 'a less than respectable Hollywood commercial practice' (Forrest and Koos 2002: 2). There is considerably less work on remakes into other languages, which form the focus of my third section, Remakes around the world. In this section, I look at local versions of American movies as well as remakes that do not travel via English, such as the Korean remake of *Ringu, Ring/The Ring Virus* (1999). In the final section, Remakes and translation theory, I discuss how remakes can be conceptualized as translations and discuss theoretical issues such as audience recognition, legal acknowledgement and remaking as industrial process.

Multiple-language versions and early remakes

The arrival of sound film caused a disturbance in the various global film industries (Williams 1992: 132). Despite Hollywood's position of power, films were being produced throughout the world in the early twentieth century (Shohat and Stam 1994: 28). Silent cinema had seldom been silent, with musical accompaniment and lecturers, or *benshi* as they were known in Japan, reading out intertitles and giving commentary on the film (Nornes 2007: 89–122). Text was often limited to intertitles, which could be translated. Both intertitle translation and lecturers/*benshi* allowed for a reasonably global distribution of films, although Hollywood was the main exporter of texts: various countries installed quotas to limit the importation of American cinema in the 1920s (Ďurovičová 1992: 140).

Sound complicated this arrangement. Not only did cinemas have to be refitted for sound film, studios had to learn how to record sound and produce synchronized dialogue, actors' voices could now be heard, which had consequences for non-native speakers of English working in Hollywood (as dramatized in the 2011 movie *The Artist*). In Europe, the arrival of sound film led to the demise of French Impressionist and German Expressionist cinema as well as vastly affecting avant-garde cinema (Williams 1992: 135).

Sound, as you might imagine, brought the element of language to the fore in film. Up until then, silent cinema had been constructed around sequences of moving images with speech represented as text in intertitles. With the arrival of sound, it became possible to hear the voices of actors on screen. This made it impossible to continue with the previous methods of translation, as intertitles became much less common and the audience wanted to hear the recorded sound as part of the film. Given the high percentage of profits due to world sales by American studios, which could be up to 40 percent (Ďurovičová 1992: 139), Hollywood invested in finding a way of selling sound films to non-English-speaking locations. A number of solutions were tried before the forms of subtitling and dubbing, as they are understood today, became the dominant forms of AVT. These early, short-lived solutions included removing the dialogue and replacing it with intertitles (Cornu 2014: 27), replacing scenes of dialogue filmed in English with scenes of dialogue filmed in the language of distribution (*ibid.*: 28) and making multiple-language versions of films (Ďurovičová [1992: 139] uses the term 'foreign language version' to refer to these films). These latter are the focus of this section as they are, effectively, remakes made at the same time as the films themselves.

There were also a number of silent films remade into sound films throughout the 1930s, but my focus here is on the multiple-language versions of films as they can be understood as a form of translation. They have typically not been studied in translation studies, though short sections can be found on them in the work of Nornes (2007: 137–141), Jean-François Cornu (2014: 29–30) and Luis Pérez-González (2014: 215–217). Scholars in film studies have paid a little more attention to them, though, as Ginette Vincendeau (1988: 24) notes, there are numerous archival issues involved in the research on multiple-language versions, leading to difficulties researching them. It is worth pausing to reflect that, because of the central status of the original, often English-language film, the foreign language remakes are seen as secondary products and may not have been archived and preserved in the same way as the English-language version of the film. Vincendeau argues that many of these multiple-language versions are seen as aesthetic failures (*ibid.*) and so have been ignored by film scholars, with a few exceptions by *auteur* directors such as G.W. Pabst's 1931 *Die 3 Groschen Oper/The Threepenny Opera*, which was also released in 1931 in a French version known as *L'opéra de quat'sous*. The combination of languages makes Pabst's

The Threepenny Opera an exceptional case in more ways than one. Recent home-viewing technologies, such as Blu-ray and DVD, have made access to some of these multilanguage versions easier, as the BFI DVD release of *The Threepenny Opera*, for example, contains both versions. These releases suggest an interest in these early multiple-language versions among the contemporary audience.

Multiple-language versions flourished for a brief moment in the period 1929 to 1933. As Nataša Ďurovičová notes, '[the] brevity of the phenomenon is taken as proof of its insignificance' (1992: 139), leading many film scholars to overlook them. Yet even if multiple-language films were, ultimately a failure, due to being too expensive, they also represent a moment in film history where the translation of film became of key significance.

Multiple-language versions are more similar to literary translation than other forms of AVT. In subtitling and dubbing, the focus of the translation is on the verbal elements of the text. Subtitling adds a written (and often condensed) translation of the verbal elements of the film, while dubbing replaces the audio elements in the source language with audio elements in the target language. Multiple-language versions replace the whole of the source film with the target film, just like other remakes (Evans 2014a: 310), but where they differ from other remakes is that they are supposed to offer a trustworthy representation of the source film, following what Andrew Chesterman has called an 'ethics of representation' (2001: 139–140). Yet it is also clear that multiple-language versions did more than just copy the source texts: they add to and alter the narratives in various ways. Pérez-González (2014: 215–217) discusses the differences between the English, French and Spanish versions of the Laurel and Hardy vehicle, *Blotto* (1930). He notes that there were 'a number of scenes ... that were too risqué for the American audience', such as cabaret scenes, which were extended in the Spanish and French versions (*ibid.*: 216). In fact, the French and Spanish versions were one reel longer than the English version (*ibid.*: 217), demonstrating significant expansion of the text. Nornes (2007: 139) notes that differences in representation of sexuality were common in multiple-language versions. In the German version of *Anna Christie* (1930), Greta Garbo 'wore sexier costumes, and her character's sexual past was more explicit' (*ibid.*). These changes represent the different national standards of censorship and attitudes to the female body at the time.

One of the most written about examples of a multiple-language version is *Drácula*, the Spanish-language version of Tod Browning's *Dracula*, directed by George Melford. Both films were produced in 1931 by the same company; the English-language version was shot on the sets during the day, the Spanish-language version was shot by night (Nornes 2007: 137), as was common practice at the time (Lénárt 2013). Melford's version is substantially longer than Browning's, running for an extra 30 minutes. András Lénárt (2013) argues that this is due to the interference of the producers in Browning's version, compared to the freedom given to Melford. However, Melford's budget was also significantly smaller (*ibid.*). The Spanish-language version used actors from multiple Spanish speaking countries, in an effort to delocalize the connotations of the Spanish accents, but the effect has been called 'infelicitous' (Barrenechea 2009: 228). However, there are aspects of the film that are considered more successful than the English-language version. Antonio Barrenechea (2009: 229) argues that the plot feels more developed; the extra half hour allows for extended scenes. He also argues that the cinematography in Melford's version offer a 'nightmarish ambiance' (*ibid.*: 230) which is suitable to the story. Nornes also states that 'people familiar with the Spanish *Dracula* prefer its luscious photography and racy atmosphere' (2007: 137). *Drácula* suggests that the multiple-language versions could offer more variation from their source texts than commonly expected of them. Their use as a common form of translation, however, lasted only a few years, before dubbing and subtitling became standard. However, Hollywood did not stop making remakes, either of American or foreign movies.

Recent American remakes

This section looks at more recent interlingual remakes made in America. I have already mentioned the wave of J-Horror remakes from the early 2000s, such as *The Ring* (2002) or *The Grudge* (2004), but Hollywood has consistently remade films from other countries, as well as remaking American movies. Many of the interlingual remakes' source films come from France: Lucy Mazdon (2000: 152–156) lists 60 remakes from French during the period 1936–1999. As such, much of the critical attention on remakes has focused on remakes of French films (e.g. Durham 1998; Mazdon 2000). There have been remakes from other countries, such as *Vanilla Sky* (2001) which remade the Spanish film *Abre los ojos/Open Your Eyes* (1997) (see White 2003), but numbers are smaller by country. Mazdon argues that France is the second largest source of films to be remade other than America itself (2000: 2). There are a number of factors that have contributed to the popularity of French film as a source for remakes, from the perception of French culture as prestigious (*ibid.*: 21) and the relatively healthy state of the French film industry (*ibid.*: 23) to the proactive stance of French production companies trying to sell remake rights (*ibid.*: 25).

The popular perception of American remakes is somewhat negative. In an article in British newspaper *The Guardian*, Andrew Pulver argues that remakes show that 'Hollywood is bereft of original ideas' (2010), though he also provides examples of good remakes, such as *The Ring* and *Down and Out in Beverly Hills* (1986), which remade Jean Renoir's *Boudu sauvé des eaux/Boudu Saved from Drowning* (1932). The (re)use of foreign films by Hollywood has been described as 'imperialistic' (Leitch 2002: 56) and Hollywood filmmakers as 'colonizers' (*ibid.*). In this reading, Hollywood remakes take a successful, or well-regarded, foreign film and use the prestige that it already has to try and make more money: 'the remake has long been seen as indexical signifier [*sic*] of Hollywood greed' (Rolls and Walker 2009: 186). Films that are already successful represent less of a risk than new, original movies (Mazdon 2000: 14). There is no doubt that remaking is a commercial process in many cases, but there are also non-commercial remakes, made by independent or experimental filmmakers which aim to recreate older experimental movies, such as Perry Bard's *Man with a Movie Camera: The Global Remake* (2008-ongoing), which recreates Dziga Vertov's *Chelovek s kino-apparatom/Man with a Movie Camera* (1929). As Jaimie Baron (2012) notes in this case, Bard's film encourages the viewer to explore the viewing process and always points to the source movie.

The scholarship on interlingual remakes generally tries to overcome the image of remakes as a 'purely commercial venture' (Mazdon 2000: 21), focusing on issues such as national identity and gender (Vincendeau 1993, Durham 1998, Mazdon 2000) or the relationship between art and commercial cinemas (Falkenberg 1985). These approaches all look beyond the commercial aspect of remakes to discuss them as a form of artistic practice.

There are certain patterns that have been observed across American remakes. Almost all relocate the action to America, which leads to a number of cultural adaptations. As Vincendeau notes, American cinema tends to rely on 'clear-cut motivation' whereas European art cinema prefers ambiguity (1993: 23). The remakes that she is discussing tend to 'streamline' (*ibid.*) their material in order to make it more accessible and clearer. Michael Harney (2002: 73–75) also notes that American remakes tend to amplify their material, making characters wealthier and their problems more complex. Again, this could be seen as a tendency to clarify and make explicit motivation; such tendencies are also seen in written translation, where texts are often made syntactically more explicit or in other ways made less implicit than their source texts, a process sometimes called 'explicitation' (see Blum-Kulka 1986; Berman 2012 takes a critical approach).

Jim McBride's *Breathless* (1983), which remakes Jean-Luc Godard's *À bout de souffle/ Breathless* (1959), has been discussed by many scholars (Falkenberg 1985, Wills 1998, Durham 1998: 49–69, Mazdon 2000: 79–88, Verevis 2006: 165–170, Evans 2014a). In some ways, *Breathless* is iconic of Hollywood remakes: it takes a successful French film and recreates it in an American setting. Unlike other remakes, however, its source film is very well-known in the USA and viewers would be likely to compare the two movies. While the remake was made by a Hollywood studio (Orion) and featured Richard Gere as its star, McBride had a background in underground, non-commercial film (such as his 1967 film *David Holzman's Diary*) and it is difficult to read the film as solely a commercial appropriation. There is also an element of homage in the film, seen in careful reconstructions of certain scenes. In addition, Mazdon argues that *Breathless* transgresses some of the norms of Hollywood production, with its unresolved ending and its portrayal of sex (2000: 84). Scholarly work on *Breathless* has tended to focus on comparative readings of the movie with its source film, in a manner similar to translation analysis. Yet, where translations are supposedly for an audience who cannot access the source text (as it is in another language), *Breathless* can be most fruitfully read in relation to *À bout de souffle* as an intertextual work.

Another way of reading remakes is through Walter Benjamin's concept of the text's afterlife (1999: 72), as Dorothy Wong (2012) does. The idea of a translation or remake as an afterlife—or survival as it is also translated (Benjamin 2009: 31)—suggests that the target text will differ in many ways to the original, while still resembling it. Wong connects the afterlife to ghosts and haunting (2012: 24–25), offering another fecund metaphor for the relationship between remake and source film and linking it to wider work on spectralities in cultural theory (see Blanco and Peeren 2013). The connection to ghosts is apt in relation to the wave of Asian horror films that were remade in the early 2000s (see Lim 2007). Both Bliss Cua Lim and Wong see these horror remakes as ultimately 'deracinating' (Lim 2007: 113), that is, removing the original context of the source film. This is a common complaint about remakes, which overlooks that remakes do not aim to present a foreign film as such (subtitled versions could do this), but rather adapt a film for a new audience. The issue remains, however, that American films are sold around the globe and remakes are sold back to the locations where the source film was made. Lim notes that the remake of *Ringu/Ring* made more money in Japan than the original film (*ibid.*: 125).

The position of American remakes is somewhat problematic. American remakes can be seen as appropriations from other cultures, taking something that is successful, repackaging it and reselling it with the intention of making more money. Remakes represent a form of transcultural adaptation, which is never quite as predictable as the source culture would like (Appadurai 1996: 174). Yet, in an age where more and more movies are available for home viewing, remakes can also encourage viewers to find the foreign original. The fact that there is an American remake of a film may mean that the original becomes available on DVD or Blu-ray. Movies are no longer solely distributed in the cinema and there are multiple ways the public can access them. Equally, some remakes may offer new ways of looking at old movies, encouraging viewers to go back to those sources.

Remakes around the world

America is not the only country that produces remakes: they are produced all around the world. This aspect of remaking has received much less critical attention than American remakes. There are several possible reasons for this. Film studies has been criticized for Eurocentrism which overlooks film production elsewhere (Shohat and Stam 1994), though this has been changing over the last twenty years. However, there still remains a problem of access to films from some places, often in Africa and Asia, as they are not distributed globally (Andrew 2006: 26). Iain Robert Smith (2008: 8) reports only being able to find a CD-R bootleg of the Turkish film *Turist Ömer Uzay Yolunda/Tourist Ömer in Star Trek* (1974), which suggests limited distribution, though video sharing sites like Youtube and Vimeo are making it easier to see such films, as well as a number of small DVD distributors.

A number of remakes made outside of America are remakes of American movies, such as the Turkish *Star Trek* remake discussed by Smith (2008), with other remakes being made in Turkey, India and East Asia (see Smith 2016, Wright 2009, O'Thomas 2010). In India, for instance, over 70 films since 2000 were remakes (Wright 2009). Chinese cinemas (including Hong Kong, Taiwan, PR China and Singapore) also have strong remaking traditions (Aufderheide 1998, Wang 2008, 2013; Evans 2014b). One of the key issues with these films is how they relate to Hollywood. As Smith (2008) and Evans (2014b) argue, remade films may both celebrate and criticize their source films. *Turist Ömer Uzay Yolunda/Tourist Ömer in Star Trek*, for instance, celebrates *Star Trek*, which is the setting that it appropriates, but at the same time it offers a commentary on the TV show from a Turkish perspective (Smith 2008). There is a hybridity in the film that comes from connecting two cultures; this becomes more obvious when the viewer has access to the source film. Neelam Sidhar Wright (2009) similarly argues that there is a combination of resistance and innovation involved in Bollywood (Indian) remakes of American movies. Here the relationship between source and target cultures is different, as the remaking film industry is normally smaller, less well-funded and less well-distributed. The power relations (industrial, economic, political) between countries are implicated in any discussion of remakes.

Like American remakes, remakes out of English also tend to relocate their narratives and consequently make adaptations for the local culture. In *San qiang pai an jing qi/A Woman, A Gun and A Noodle Shop* (2009), the action and narrative of *Blood Simple* (1984) are relocated from Texas to the Chinese Gobi desert in the pre-Qing (pre-1644) period. Beyond the obvious linguistic change from English to Mandarin Chinese, the Chinese film uses brighter colours than its source. There is also a more obvious strand of humour (Evans 2014b: 290) in the film. Interestingly, like many American remakes, it also makes motivation more explicit (*ibid*.: 292), suggesting that this is not just a feature of American remakes. However, the source film was an independent movie, which did not follow Hollywood conventions. *A Woman, A Gun and A Noodle Shop* also differs from many non-American remakes in that its director (Zhang Yimou) was internationally known, meaning that it received a wider distribution than many other Chinese films.

Not all remakes involve an English source. There are a number of Korean remakes of Japanese films and television, such as the Korean version of *Ring, The Ring Virus* (1999). One reason for this is the ban on Japanese media in South Korea until 2004 (Byrne 2014: 186), following the legacy of Japanese imperialism. The Korean version uses a very similar narrative to the Japanese film, but differs in gender presentation, which becomes more fluid in the Korean version (*ibid*.), as well as how it presents the horror aspects, as the Korean version focuses more on the mystery (*ibid*.: 187). James Byrne argues that *The Ring Virus* draws from a tradition of Korean melodrama (*ibid*.: 188). The Korean remake, then, adapts the narrative to Korean traditions but also adapts the presentation of character, exploring the source material of the novel both films are based on (Suzuki 2007) in a different way.

Remakes from around the world question the perception of remakes as 'overwhelmingly, a Hollywood practice' (Rolls and Walker 2009: 186). The strategies of cultural adaptation often remain the same, as the remakes localize the narrative and adapt the film to the local audience. More research is needed into the multitude of remakes around the world, especially between cultures where English is not spoken.

Remakes and translation theory

In this final section, I discuss how remakes have been and can be conceptualized as translations, as well as the issues they raise for translation theory. There are numerous attempts to taxonomize remakes, including Thomas Leitch's (2002: 45–50) four-part model, which includes 'readaptations', which are based on the same literary work as the film they are remaking; 'updates', which tend to transpose a narrative to the present; 'homages', which are respectful in their treatment of the earlier film; and 'true remakes', which try to replace the earlier film. Hans Maes (2005) offers a fifteen-part classification, which includes 'pornographic remakes' (i.e. a pornographic version of a film or TV show) and remakes that deny their status as remakes. These taxonomies show the variety of approaches taken in remakes and the variety of relationships between source and target texts in remade films. The approach of, for example, *Twelve Monkeys* (1995) to its source *La Jetée* (1962) is very different from the American remake of *Funny Games* (2007) to the Austrian version (1997). The former is very adaptive and expands on the narrative of the source while ignoring its formal experimentation; the latter is very similar to its source.

The distinction between official remakes and unofficial remakes is productive theoretically. The former of these acknowledge their source film paratextually, in the credits, or they may be advertised as a remake (as was the case of *A Woman, A Gun and A Noodle Shop*). The latter would not officially acknowledge their sources, as Forrest and Koos (2002: 5) argue that many remakes do not. Official remakes, then, are like other forms of translation (especially literary translation) as they acknowledge their source texts and are sanctioned by copyright agreements (Evans 2014a: 305). Unofficial remakes complicate the relationship between copyright and the status of a text as a remake. As Thomas Leitch (2002: 38–39) explains, films are based on a property, which can be an unpublished story or a published piece of fiction or, sometimes, reportage (in the case of films 'based on a true story'). The producers of the film need to pay for the right to produce derivative works based on that property. This is normally acknowledged in the credits somewhere, as, for example, 'based on a story by'. Most narrative films are, then, a form of adaptation, even if the public never has access to the original property. Constantine Verevis (2006: 14–16) argues that some remakes are based on the earlier film and consequently pay adaptation fees to the owners of that film. If we accept that films are based on a property, these original films are actually adaptations of a text that is owned by the producers of the film. Given these prior texts, films are a form of intersemiotic translation (Jakobson 1959), where a text in one medium is adapted for another. Remakes are therefore a form of intersemiotic retranslation (Evans 2014a: 303), as they adapt a property that has already been adapted once again. As Leitch notes, remakes have a triadic structure of reference (2002: 39), referring at once to an earlier film and a source text or property.

Leitch's triadic structure helps explain the legal and industrial background to remakes, but it does not account for the audience experience of the film. Audiences may just read the remake as relating to the earlier film, as a translation of that film. Given that many properties, that is, original stories, never become available to the public, many remakes are experienced in this way. Here remakes are like other forms of translation, as they represent a version of the source text that may be compared to it. Furthermore, in cases where the source film has not been made available in the remaking country (as happened in many cases [Mazdon 2000: 4]), remakes may be the only version of the film in circulation and the comparison between the two versions would be impossible to make. This is how most written translations are experienced, as readers seldom have access to the source text. In other forms of AVT, the source text sound may be present (as in subtitling) or replaced (as in dubbing), but it is hard to know how much of the audience can understand the source language, meaning that in many cases the translated text is the way that viewers experience the film.

Remakes problematize the perception that translations should produce target texts which are equivalent to their source texts (see Pym 1995, 2014 for discussion of equivalence). As we have seen, remakes often vary significantly from their source texts, adding or removing parts and generally adapting the text for the target location (although they may be later watched in other locations). Even in the case of the early Hollywood remakes, or multiple-language versions, the translated text is markedly different from its source. Remakes seldom aim to give access to the source film, but rather recreate the film in a new way. Remakes may therefore productively be thought of as a 'creative misuse' of a foreign text, which is how Koichi Iwabuchi (2002: 40) describes the way that texts are negotiated when they travel across cultural borders. The interest in watching remakes, for most viewers (and most scholars), is actually in the productive difference they show from their source film. The Spanish *Drácula* offers an interesting rethinking and recontextualization of the script of Browning's *Dracula*. Even the two versions of *Funny Games*, which are supposed to be very similar, offer interesting differences. As such, many remakes, and particularly recent remakes, feel like translations made for a knowing, rather than an unknowing, audience. Their relation with their source films can often be similar to what Linda Hutcheon (2000) calls 'parody'. Like the parodies Hutcheon discusses, remakes are often double-coded, pointing both back to the source film and to themselves. This is why they so often feel ambiguous, both in the tension between appropriation and homage in many American remakes and in the tension between celebration and critique in many remakes into other languages.

The notion of the unofficial remake further complicates theories of remaking and translation. For example, *Angst essen Seele auf/Fear Eats the Soul* (1974) is often discussed as a remake of *All that Heaven Allows* (1955) (Mulvey 1989: 75), but there is no paratextual acknowledgement. In this example, the audience perception of the remake is stronger than the copyright relationship. Are unofficial remakes still remakes? They can certainly still be read as remakes and comparing *Fear Eats the Soul* and *All that Heaven Allows* reveals a similar plot of an older woman chastised for falling in love with a man outside of her social circle but ultimately accepted again by her family and friends. There are also clearly differences and adaptations that address the local audience. There is a risk that 'remake' can be used to describe any repeated sequence in cinema (Verevis 2006: 21), making 'remake' too wide a category and most scholars would try to limit remakes to something more concrete; Verevis notes that acknowledgment and narrative repetition are usually present in remakes (*ibid.*) while Mazdon argues that they are films 'based on an earlier screenplay' (2000: 2). 'Translation' may be used in a similarly metaphorical way to refer to various forms of 'mediation, change or confrontation with difference' (Sturge 2007: 13), while there is also a more specific practice of written translation, as it is commonly understood.

Remakes also differ from many other forms of translation as they require many people and a lot of resources to make. They are part of a large industrial process, which means that there are a lot of different influences on the final product. Studying remakes, then, requires taking into account these industrial processes as well as the product itself. In addition, as we have seen throughout, remakes form part of the cultural flows of globalization (Appadurai 1996), which means that there are constantly questions of negotiation and recontextualization in their production and reception. These aspects are present in other forms of translation, but are highlighted by remakes.

Summary

The chapter began by discussing the neglected position of remakes in translation studies and how film studies has often compared remakes to translations. It then moved on to the multiple-language versions, produced between 1929 and 1933 as an early form of film translation. While supposedly offering a trustworthy representation of the source film, these remakes tended to differ in various ways, particularly in relation to the representation of sexuality. While these films have traditionally been difficult to access, they are becoming more available on home-viewing formats. The next section has focused on Hollywood remakes, which are often regarded as commercial exploitation. American remakes are often culturally relocated and adapted for the new target audience, including for example making characters' motivation more explicit. Yet when reading the films, there is often a more complex relationship with the source film than the idea of remakes as appropriation supposes. In some cases, such as McBride's *Breathless*, it may be worth considering the remake as an intertextual work, or, as Wong (2012) suggests, an 'afterlife' of the source film. The third section has discussed remakes into other languages, which also relocate and adapt the movies they are remaking. Here the relationship between source and target is often ambiguous, both celebratory and critical. The chapter has discussed remakes of Hollywood films, as well as remakes that did not have an English source, such as the Korean version of *Ringu/ Ring*. These films challenge the perception of remakes as solely a Hollywood practice. The final part of the chapter has explored the difference between official and unofficial remakes. Official remakes make clear their source text in paratexts, but unofficial ones do not. This leads to audience perception of the remake being stronger than the copyright relationship. The chapter has also argued that remakes are translations made for a knowing audience and so question the idea of translations as a form of a reliable substitute for the source text, presenting instead intertextual rewritings. Finally, remakes have been presented as an industrial process involving many people.

Further reading

Forrest, J. and L. R. Koos (eds) (2002) *Dead Ringers: The Remake in Theory and Practice*, Albany: State University of New York Press | *An excellent collection of essays on remaking, including many on transnational remakes. Includes useful essays on* Trois hommes et un couffin, La Femme Nikita, *and other American remakes of French films.*

Mazdon, L. (1996) 'Rewriting and Remakes: Questions of Originality and Authenticity', in G. T. Harris (ed.), *On Translating French Literature and Film*, Amsterdam: Rodopi, 47–63 | *This chapter uses Lefevere's idea of 'rewriting' to discuss remakes as a form of translation, helping to develop a translational framework for understanding film remakes.*

Smith, I. R. and C. Verevis (eds) (2017) *Transnational Film Remakes*, Edinburgh: Edinburgh University Press | *This book offers a collection of essays on transnational remakes and is edited by two key figures in the field. The introduction offers an excellent overview of the literature on remakes in film and media studies.*

Related topics

2 History of audiovisual translation
3 Subtitling on the cusp of its futures
4 Investigating dubbing: learning from the past, looking to the future

References

Andrew, D. (2006) 'An Atlas of World Cinema', in S. Dennison and S. H. Lim (eds) *Remapping World Cinema: Identity, Culture and Politics in Film*, London & New York: Wallflower Press, 19–29.
Appadurai, A. (1996) *Modernity at Large: Cultural Dimensions of Globalization*, Minneapolis: University of Minnesota Press.
Aufderheide, P. (1998) 'Made in Hong Kong: Translation and Transmutation', in A. Horton and S. Y. McDougal (eds) *Play it Again, Sam: Retakes on Remakes*, Berkeley: University of California Press, 191–199.
Baker, M. and G. Saldanha (eds) (2008) *The Routledge Encyclopedia of Translation Studies*, 2nd edition, London: Routledge.
Barrenechea, A. (2009) 'Hemispheric Horrors: Celluloid Vampires from the "Good Neighbour" Era', *Comparative American Studies* 7(3): 225–237.
Baron, J. (2012) 'The Experimental Film Remake and the Digital Archive Effect: A Movie by Jen Proctor and Man with a Movie Camera: The Global Remake', *Framework* 53(2): 467–490.
Benjamin, W. (1999) *Illuminations*, trans. by H. Zohn, London: Pimlico.
Benjamin, W. (2009) *One Way Street and Other Writings*, trans. by A. Chaudhuri, London: Penguin.
Berman, A. (2012) 'Translation and the Trials of the Foreign', trans. by L. Venuti, in L. Venuti (ed.) *The Translation Studies Reader*, 3rd edition, Abingdon: Routledge, 240–253.
Blanco, M. and E. Peeren (eds) (2013) *The Spectralities Reader: Ghosts and Haunting in Contemporary Cultural Theory*, London: Bloomsbury.
Blum-Kulka, S. (1986) 'Shifts of Cohesion and Coherence in Translation', in J. House and S. Blum-Kulka (eds) *Interlingual and Intercultural Communication: Discourse and Cognition in Translation and Second Language Acquisition Studies*, Tübingen: Narr, 17–35.
Booth, P. and B. Ekdale (2011) 'Translating the Hyperreal (Or How *The Office* Came to America, Made Us Laugh, and Tricked Us into Accepting Hegemonic Bureaucracy)', in C. Lavigne and H. Marcovitch (eds) *American Remakes of British Television: Transformations and Mistranslations*, Lanham, MD: Lexington Books, 193–210.
Bosseaux, C. (2015) *Dubbing, Film and Performance: Uncanny Encounters*, Bern: Peter Lang.
Byrne, J. (2014) 'Wigs and Rings: Cross-cultural Exchange in the South Korean and Japanese Horror Film', *Journal of Japanese and Korean Cinema* 6(2): 184–201.
Chesterman, A. (2001) 'Proposal for a Hieronymic Oath', *The Translator* 7(2): 139–154.
Chiaro, D. (2009) 'Issues in Audiovisual Translation', in J. Munday (ed.) *The Routledge Companion to Translation Studies*, London: Routledge, 141–165.
Cornu, J.-F. (2014) *Le doublage et le sous-titrage: Histoire et esthétique*, Rennes: Presses Universitaires de Rennes.
Delabastita, D. (1990) 'Translation and the Mass Media', in S. Bassnett and A. Lefevere (eds), *Translation, History & Culture*, London: Cassell, 97–109.
Durham, C. A. (1998) *Double Takes: Culture and Gender in French Films and Their American Remakes*, Hanover, NH: University of New England Press.

Ďurovičová, N. (1992) 'Translating America: The Hollywood Multilinguals 1929–1933', in R. Altman (ed.) *Sound Theory, Sound Practice*, London: Routledge, 138–153.
Evans, J. (2014a) 'Film Remakes, the Black Sheep of Translation', *Translation Studies* 7(3): 300–314.
Evans, J. (2014b) 'Zhang Yimou's *Blood Simple*: Cannibalism, Remaking and Translation in World Cinema', *Journal of Adaptation in Film and Performance* 7(3): 283–297.
Falkenberg, P. (1985) '"Hollywood" and the "Art Cinema" as a Bipolar Modeling System: *À bout de souffle* and *Breathless*', *Wide Angle* 7(3): 44–53.
Forrest, J., and L. R. Koos (2002) 'Reviewing Remakes: An Introduction', in J. Forrest and L. R. Koos (eds) *Dead Ringers: The Remake in Theory and Practice*, Albany: State University of New York Press, 1–36.
Gambier, Y. (2003) 'Introduction: Screen Transadaptation: Perception and Reception', *The Translator* 9(2): 171–189.
Gambier, Y. (2004) 'La Traduction audiovisuelle: un genre en expansion', *Meta* 49(1): 1–11.
Gottlieb, H. (2007) 'Multidimensional Translation: Semantics Turned Semiotics', in H. Gerzymisch-Arbogast and S. Nauert (eds) *Proceedings of the Marie Curie Euroconferences MuTra 'Challenges of Multidimensional Translation' Saarbrücken 2–6 May 2005*. Available online: http://www.euroconferences.info/proceedings/2005_Proceedings/2005_Gottlieb_Henrik.pdf [last access 20 December 2017].
Grindstaff, L. (2001) 'A Pygmalion Tale Retold: Remaking La Femme Nikita', *Camera Obscura* 16 (2): 133–175.
Harney, M. (2002) 'Economy and Aesthetics in American Remakes of French Films', in J. Forrest and L. R. Koos (eds) *Dead Ringers: The Remake in Theory and Practice*, Albany: State University of New York Press, 63–87.
Horton, A. and S. Y. McDougal (eds) (1998) *Play it Again, Sam: Retakes on Remakes*, Berkeley: University of California Press.
Hutcheon, L. (2000) *A Theory of Parody: The Teachings of Twentieth-Century Art Forms*, Urbana and Chicago: University of Illinois Press.
Iwabuchi, K. (2002) *Recentering Globalization: Popular Culture and Japanese Transnationalism*, Durham, NC: Duke University Press.
Jakobson, R. (1959), 'On Linguistic Aspects of Translation', in R. A. Brower (ed.) *On Translation*, New York: Oxford University Press, 232–239.
Leitch, T. (2002) 'Twice Told Tales: Disavowal and the Rhetoric of the Remake', in J. Forrest and L. R. Koos (eds) *Dead Ringers: The Remake in Theory and Practice*, Albany: State University of New York Press, 37–62.
Lénárt, A. (2013) 'Hispanic Hollywood. Spanish-Language American Films in the 1920s and 1930s', *Americana: E-journal of American Studies in Hungary* 9(2). Available online: http://americanaejournal.hu/vol9no2/lenart [last access 20 December 2017].
Lim, B.C. (2007) 'Generic Ghosts: Remaking the New "Asian Horror Film"', in G. Marchetti and T. S. Kam (eds) *Hong Kong Film, Hollywood and the New Global Cinema*, London & New York: Routledge, 109–125.
Maes, H. (2005) 'A Celestial Taxonomy of Remakes?', *Cinemascope. An Independent Film Journal* 1(2): 1–11.
Mandiberg, S. (2008) *Remakes as Translation: Cultural Flow*, Unpublished MA Dissertation, New York University. Available online: http://www.stephenmandiberg.com/wp-content/uploads/2009/05/mandiberg_remakes_as_translation.pdf [last access 20 December 2017].
Mazdon, L. (2000) *Encore Hollywood: Remaking French Film*, London: BFI Publishing.
Mazdon, L. (2004) 'Introduction', *Journal of Romance Studies* 4(1): 1–11.
Mulvey, L. (1989) *Visual and Other Pleasures*, Basingstoke: MacMillan.
Munday, J. (2012) *Introducing Translation Studies: Theories and Applications*, 3rd edition, Abingdon: Routledge.
Nornes, A. M. (2007) *Cinema Babel: Translating Global Cinema*, Minneapolis: University of Minnesota Press.

O'Connell, E. (2007) 'Screen Translation', in P. Kuhiwczak and K. Littau (eds) *A Companion to Translation Studies*, Clevedon: Multilingual Matters, 120–133.

O'Sullivan, C. (2011) *Translating Popular Film*, Basingstoke: Palgrave Macmillan.

O'Sullivan, C. and C. Jeffcote (eds) (2013) *Translation Multimodalities*. Special Issue of *Journal of Specialised Translation* 20. Available online: http://www.jostrans.org/issue20/issue20_toc.php [last access 20 December 2017].

O'Thomas, M. (2010) 'Turning Japanese: Translation, Adaptation, and the Ethics of Transnational Exchange', in C. Albrecht-Crane and D. Cutchins (eds) *Adaptation Studies: New Approaches*, Madison/Teaneck: Fairleigh Dickinson University Press, 46–60.

Pérez-González, L. (2014) *Audiovisual Translation: Theories, Methods and Issues*, London & New York: Routledge.

Pulver, A. (2010) 'The Girl with the Dragon Tattoo Director Lashes out at US Remake', *The Guardian*, 9 November. Available online: http://www.guardian.co.uk/film/2010/nov/09/girl-dragon-tattoo-american-remake [last access 20 December 2017].

Pym, A. (1995) 'European Translation Studies, *Une science qui dérange*, and Why Equivalence Needn't Be a Dirty Word', *TTR* 8(1): 153–176.

Pym, A. (2004) *The Moving Text: Localization, Translation and Distribution*, Amsterdam & Philadelphia: John Benjamins.

Pym, A. (2014) *Exploring Translation Theories*, 2nd edition, London: Routledge.

Raw, L. (2010) 'The Skopos of a Remake: Michael Winner's *The Big Sleep* (1978)', *Adaptation* 4(2): 199–209.

Rolls, A. and D. Walker (2009) *French and American Noir: Dark Crossings*, Basingstoke: Palgrave Macmillan.

Shohat, E. and R. Stam (1994) *Unthinking Eurocentrism: Multiculturalism and the Media*, London: Routledge.

Smith, I. R. (2008) '"Beam Me Up, Ömer": Transnational Media Flow and the Cultural Politics of the Turkish *Star Trek* Remake', *The Velvet Light Trap* 61: 3–13.

Smith, I. R. (2016) *The Hollywood Meme: Transnational Adaptations of American Film and Television*, Edinburgh: Edinburgh University Press.

Sturge, K. (2007) *Representing Others: Translation, Ethnography and the Museum*, Manchester: St Jerome.

Suzuki, K. (2007) *Ring*, trans. by R. B. Rohmer and G. Walley, London: Harper.

Verevis, C. (2006) *Film Remakes*, Edinburgh: Edinburgh University Press.

Vincendeau, G. (1988) 'Hollywood Babel', *Screen* 29(3): 24–39.

Vincendeau, G. (1993) 'Hijacked', *Sight and Sound* NS3(7): 22–25

Wang, Y. (2008) 'The "Transnational" as Methodology: Transnationalizing Chinese Film Studies through the Example of *The Love Parade* and Its Chinese Remakes', *Journal of Chinese Cinemas* 2(1): 9–21.

Wang, Y. (2013) *Remaking Chinese Cinema: Through the Prism of Shanghai, Hong Kong, and Hollywood*, Honolulu: University of Hawai'i Press.

Wehn, K. (2001) 'About Remakes, Dubbing and Morphing: Some Comments on Visual Transformation Processes and Their Relevance for Translation Theory', in Y. Gambier and H. Gottlieb (eds) *(Multi)Media Translation: Concepts, Practices, and Research*, Amsterdam & Philadelphia: John Benjamins, 65–72.

White, A.M. (2003) 'Seeing Double? The Remaking of Alejandro Aménabar's *Abre los ojos* as Cameron Crowe's *Vanilla Sky*', *International Journal of Iberian Studies* 15(3): 187–196.

Williams, A. (1992) 'Historical and Theoretical Issues in the Coming of Recorded Sound to the Cinema', in R. Altman (ed.) *Sound Theory, Sound Practice*, London: Routledge, 126–137.

Wills, D. (1998) 'The French Remark: *Breathless* and Cinematic Citationality', in A. Horton and S. Y. McDougal (eds) *Play it Again, Sam: Retakes on Remakes*, Berkeley: University of California Press, 147–161.

Wong, D. (2012) 'The Remake as a Translation': Localism, Globalism and the Afterlife of Horror Movies', *Translation Quarterly* 66: 21–30.
Wright, N.S. (2009) '"Tom Cruise? Tarantino? E.T.? . . . Indian!": Innovation and Imitation in the Cross-cultural Bollywood Remake', *Scope* 15. Available online: http://www.scope.nottingham.ac.uk/cultborr/chapter.php?id=15 [last access 20 December 2017].
Yau, W-P. (2014) 'Translation and Film: Dubbing, Subtitling, Adaptation, and Remaking', in S. Bermann and C. Porter (eds) *A Companion to Translation Studies*, Chichester: Wiley Blackwell, 492–503.
Zanger, A. (2006) *Film Remakes as Ritual and Disguise: From Carmen to Ripley*, Amsterdam: Amsterdam University Press.

Filmography

À bout de souffle (Breathless) (1959) Jean-Luc Godard. IMDB entry: http://www.imdb.com/title/tt0053472/
Abre los ojos (Open Your Eyes) (1997) Alejandro Amenábar. IMDB entry: http://www.imdb.com/title/tt0259711/
All That Heaven Allows (1955) Douglas Sirk. IMDB entry: http://www.imdb.com/title/tt0047811/
Angst essen Seele auf (Fear Eats the Soul) Rainer Werner Fassbinder. IMDB entry: http://www.imdb.com/title/tt0071141/
Anna Christie (1930) Jacques Feyder. IMDB entry: http://www.imdb.com/title/tt0020642/
Blood Simple (1984) Joel Coen. IMDB entry: http://www.imdb.com/title/tt0086979/
Blotto (1930) James Parott. IMDB entry: http://www.imdb.com/title/tt0020698/
Boudu sauvé des eaux (Boudu Saved from Drowning) (1932) Jean Renoir. IMDB entry: http://www.imdb.com/title/tt0022718/
Breathless (1983) Jim McBride. IMDB entry: http://www.imdb.com/title/tt0085276/
Chelovek s kino-apparatom (Man with a Movie Camera) (1929) Dziga Vertov. IMDB entry: http://www.imdb.com/title/tt0019760/
David Holzman's Diary (1967) Jim McBride. IMDB entry: http://www.imdb.com/title/tt0062864/
Die 3 Groschen-Oper (The Threepenny Opera) (1931) G.W. Pabst. IMDB entry: http://www.imdb.com/title/tt0021818/
Down and Out in Beverly Hills (1986) Paul Mazursky. IMDB entry: http://www.imdb.com/title/tt0090966/
Dracula (1931) Tod Browning. IMDB entry: http://www.imdb.com/title/tt0021814/
Drácula (1931) George Melford. IMDB entry: http://www.imdb.com/title/tt0021815/
Funny Games (1997) Michael Haneke. IMDB entry: http://www.imdb.com/title/tt0119167/
Funny Games (2007) Michael Haneke. IMBD entry: http://www.imdb.com/title/tt0808279/
La Jetée (1962) Chris Marker. IMDB entry: http://www.imdb.com/title/tt0114746/
L'opéra de quat'sous (The Threepenny Opera) (1931) G.W. Pabst. IMBD entry: http://www.imdb.com/title/tt0022235/
Man with a Movie Camera: The Global Remake (2008-ongoing) Perry Bard. Available online: http://dziga.perrybard.net/ [last access 20 December 2017].
Partie d'écarté (Card game) (1896). Louis Lumière. IMDB entry: http://www.imdb.com/title/tt0000026/
Ring (The Ring Virus) (1998) Dong-Bin Kim. IMDB entry: http://www.imdb.com/title/tt0289424/
Ringu (Ring) (1998) Hideo Nakata. IMDB entry: http://www.imdb.com/title/tt0178868/
San qiang pai an jing qi (A Woman, A Gun and A Noodle Shop) Zhang Yimou. IMBD entry: http://www.imdb.com/title/tt1428556/
The Artist (2011) Michel Hazanavicius. IMDB entry: http://www.imdb.com/title/tt1655442/
The Big Sleep (1978) Michael Winner. IMDB entry: http://www.imdb.com/title/tt0077234/

The Grudge (2004) Takaski Shimizu. IMDB entry: http://www.imdb.com/title/tt0391198/
The Office (2001–2003). IMDB entry: http://www.imdb.com/title/tt0290978/
The Office (2005–2013). IMDB entry: http://www.imdb.com/title/tt0386676/
The Ring (2002) Gore Verbinski. IMDB entry: http://www.imdb.com/title/tt0298130/
Turist Ömer Uzay Yolunda (Tourist Ömer in Star Trek) (1974) Hulki Saner. IMDB entry: http://www.imdb.com/title/tt0182503/
Twelve Monkeys (1995) Terry Gilliam. IMDB entry: http://www.imdb.com/title/tt0114746/
Une partie de cartes (Card party) (1896) Georges Méliès. IMDB entry: http://www.imdb.com/title/tt0000132/
Vanilla Sky (2001) Cameron Crowe: IMDB entry: http://www.imdb.com/title/tt0259711/

Part II
Theoretical perspectives in audiovisual translation studies

12
Mediality and audiovisual translation

Henry Jones

Introduction

The significance of the relationship between humans and technology is illustrated perhaps nowhere more strikingly than in the prelude to Stanley Kubrick's iconic film *2001: A Space Odyssey* (1968). Having discovered in a thrilling 'eureka' moment the radically transformative potential of using an animal bone as a weapon, both for hunting prey and for defending the social group from predators and competitors, the prehistoric ape-man on which the first 25 minutes of the drama have focused jubilantly tosses his newfound tool high into the air (Ambrose 2001: 1748). The camera tracks its ascent as it twists and turns before morphing, in a perfectly timed jump-cut, into a 21st-century spaceship gliding serenely in orbit above the Earth below. What Kubrick's scene seeks to show is that it is our use of technology that has made us who we are today, that has enabled us to become not simply the dominant species on the planet, but the only species to have left our home planet and to have set foot on another world.

Indeed, while the long-established myth holding our genus *homo* to be the only tool-makers and -users in the animal kingdom has now been dispelled, research in palaeoanthropology has made it increasingly clear that technology is inarguably more central to our evolutionary development than for any other creature on the planet (Ambrose 2001: 1748). As specialists in this field have demonstrated, the increase in brain capacity, population size and geographical range that has defined *homo sapiens* can be linked directly to a series of specific technological advances made by our prehistoric ancestors (*ibid.*). For example, the production and use of even the most basic tools such as hand-axes, clothing and containers have been shown to represent the single most important factor in having enabled humans to 'wrong foot' the biological principles of 'the survival of the fittest'—principles, that is, which would ordinarily lead to the extinction of a physically frail and vulnerable species such as our own (Taylor 2010). As Cronin (2013: 10) summarizes, technology is 'fundamental to a sense of what it is to be human', and the tools we use are not merely an 'extrinsic' outcome of our development but 'intrinsic' to our very existence, capable of shaping us just as much as we shape them (Cronin 2013: 10).

Importantly, however, it is not just primitive, primordial technologies that can be said to hold a particular determining influence in the development of human society and culture. Rather, the significance of this relationship has been shown to extend across the ages to any of the tools humans employ for whatever purpose. Most notably for our purposes here, this includes the 'media tools' we use for the storage and transmission of thoughts and ideas (Littau 2011), from the most fundamental (e.g. spoken language) to the most advanced computer-based tools of the twenty-first century, able to archive vast quantities of data and send it thousands of miles at the click of a mouse. In this chapter, our focus is on audiovisual translation as an act of communication which is necessarily mediated by such tools and consequently shaped by the particular characteristics (or 'mediality') that define each media form.

While ever since the pioneering work of Harold Innis and Marshall McLuhan in the 1950s and 1960s discussion of media and mediality has featured prominently in research based in a number of disciplines from across the Humanities, within translation studies this issue has only very recently begun to attract any serious attention. Little mention is made for instance in James S. Holmes' (1972/2000: 178) famous 'map' of the discipline and, as Michael Cronin (2013: 25) notes, the notion of medium has traditionally been construed simply as 'a kind of classificatory aid, a way of expressing how contents are differently transmitted'. This poses problems for a chapter seeking to give a short overview of the 'state of the art' in this area of study because 'Mediality and audiovisual translation' does not refer to a distinct and well-established domain with a long history of research or a widely accepted set of methodologies, questions and objectives. Rather, it is the case that a small but growing number of translation scholars have come, over the last few years, to reflect on this issue from a range of different perspectives to serve a variety of aims and interests.

That is not to say that the question of media and mediality does not warrant extensive investigation from within this academic discipline. In fact, it can be argued that quite the opposite is true. As Karin Littau (2011: 261) has recently suggested, understanding the role that different media have played and continue to play in the history of translation in all its forms is now more important than ever before: amid the turbulent socio-cultural and political upheavals of the current so-called 'digital renaissance' (Jenkins 2001), it is of paramount importance for (audiovisual) translation studies to come to terms with the media environment in which translators are situated, and the ways in which the rapid transformations that are currently occurring in the world of technology are affecting translation practice.

This chapter aims therefore to help promote a greater awareness of mediality in audiovisual translation studies and to demonstrate its rich potential as a productive angle of enquiry with which to proceed within this field. It will start in the following section with a discussion of Marshall McLuhan's influential work on media as environments and the ways in which these shape our experience of the world. The explanatory power of his philosophy of technology will be illustrated with a pertinent example drawn from Karen Littau's more recent work on media-induced transformations in reading, writing and translation practices. The following section (The pitfalls of technological determinism) will then deal with the criticisms that have been made with respect to this line of thought and the importance of placing (media) tool use in its social context will be emphasized. Finally, the second half of this chapter (Mediality and audiovisual translation) will demonstrate how these ideas can and have been applied specifically with regard to the study of audiovisual translation, tracing the changes in the technological environment over time as a means of shedding light on the gradual shift towards a 'democratization' of this activity.

The medium is the message

While scholars had naturally been aware of the fact that, throughout history, different civilizations in different parts of the world had made use of different media tools, until the 1950s and 1960s it had largely been assumed (with a few notable exceptions—Friedrich

Nietzsche and Ernst Kapp, for instance) that these communication technologies were essentially neutral instruments (Tremblay 2012: 571). Broadly speaking, hand-written papyrus scrolls, mass-printed books and live television were considered passive conduits for the transmission of information and/or inert containers for its storage. It was thought that they had little influence over social and cultural practice, and as a result that they were more or less interchangeable, 'suitable for all purposes and in all circumstances' (Tremblay 2012: 571). As Gaëtan Tremblay (2012: 563) notes for example, with the advent of the television in the 1950s, 'researchers had only been interested in specific effects of different types of messages (for the purposes of propaganda or advertising), and public debate about the media was obsessed with the morality of the programs that were broadcast'.

Particularly influential in questioning this assumption was Canadian theorist Marshall McLuhan. In a book entitled *Understanding Media* (McLuhan 1964: 19), he famously declared that the prevailing fixation with the content of media was the 'numb stance of a technological idiot'. Instead, he sought to prove that 'the medium is the message', that it is the media technology by which that content is stored and/or transmitted that has the most significant consequences for society and culture, and that truly deserves our attention (McLuhan 1964: 7). With respect to the television therefore, the relative morality of the programmes being broadcast, McLuhan (1964: 20) argued, paled into insignificance when compared with the broader implications of the arrival of this new technology into sitting-rooms the world over. As Cronin (2013: 22) summarizes, 'the ability to beam images from around the globe into people's private homes within hours and eventually within microseconds of the events actually happening was infinitely more important in its effect (the creation of imagined global communities of spectatorship) than what was actually shown in the images'. Like all new media forms, television was proving itself as a powerful agent of change, affecting all aspects of how we experience the world, interact with each other and use our physical senses (Gordon 2010: 107).

Drawing on the work of his compatriot and mentor Harold Innis (1950/1972), McLuhan's most important contribution then as a 'pioneer' of media and communication studies was to suggest that media technologies should instead be thought of in terms of the 'environments' they engender (Tremblay 2012: 562). As McLuhan explained, these environments are not 'passive wrappings' but 'active processes' that impose their own pervasive structure by means of their distinctive set of 'groundrules' (McLuhan and Fiore 1967/1996: 68). Understood in this sense, media technologies not only have the power to 'shape and control the scale and form of human association and action' (McLuhan 1964: 9). Because they each have their own 'intrinsic technological logic' (Winthrop-Young and Wutz 1999: xiv), their own unique array of possibilities and constraints, any change in the technological landscape of a civilization will necessarily engender significant 'personal, political, economic, aesthetic, psychological, moral, ethical and social consequences' (McLuhan and Fiore 1967/1996: 26).

McLuhan provides several examples to support this argument, but his philosophy of technology is perhaps most convincingly illustrated in Karin Littau's (2006, 2011) more recent work on the history of reading and the ways in which advances in media technology have impacted upon the production, consumption and indeed translation of written texts. In considering the effect of the invention of wood-based paper pulp in the mid-nineteenth century in Western Europe on the 'translation ethos' of the time, for example, Littau (2006: 21; 2011) explains that, prior to this invention, books were generally printed on a kind of paper made from recycled linen or cotton rags. Although higher quality and more durable, this 'rag paper' and the books into which it was made remained relatively expensive. The development of a wood-fibre-based product in the 1980s provided a much more abundant raw material which meant that books—and secular literature in particular—could be mass-produced on an unprecedented scale and sold to the public at a fraction of the price. As a direct consequence, Littau (2006) asserts that reading practices underwent a 'revolutionary shift' in European society: before, when books were expensive and comparatively rare, most families might have owned only one volume (invariably the Bible); now with the rapid expansion of the market, an ever broader readership was able to buy and consume literature, meaning more people could read not only for moral and religious instruction, but for pleasure and leisure too. Indeed, with the invention of pulp, the novel soon emerged 'as the period's most popular form of escape from the drudgeries of everyday life' (Littau 2006: 19). Most significant however is the fact that not only were Europeans now reading *more*, but that they were also reading *differently*. Because books were suddenly so much cheaper and more readily available, they came to be considered no longer 'as artefacts to be preserved', but as 'affordable products' to be consumed rapidly and then discarded (Littau 2006: 21). As a result, readers increasingly read 'many a novel superficially, rather than re-reading the Word in depth' (Littau 2006: 20).

This change from what Littau (2006: 19), following Rolf Engelsing (1974), terms 'intensive' reading practices to 'extensive' ones caused major transformations in the way in which literature was translated. On the one hand, printing on pulp paper increased the demand for translation, with works that had proved popular abroad often being translated 'with great speed' to feed the insatiable appetite of the home culture (Littau 2011: 245). Furthermore, because these translations were aimed at a wider and no longer necessarily highly educated audience, they tended to favour fluency-creating strategies. Foreign culture-specific references, loyalty to the source-language word order or, in short, anything that might prevent the reader from being able to 'fly through three or four pages and never stumble once . . . [as if] on a smooth-planed board', would consequently tend to be excised from the translated text and replaced by immediately intelligible and readable language (Littau 2011: 275). Indeed, as Lawrence Venuti (1995) has argued at length, this 'domesticating' translation strategy has never since ceased to dominate, at least in the English-speaking world.

The pitfalls of technological determinism

When following this line of thought, it is important to be aware of a number of the criticisms that have been launched at such media-focused analysis. In a now famous attack on McLuhan's philosophy of technology as an agent of socio-cultural change, the cultural theorist Raymond Williams (1974/1990) argued that this 'technological determinism' represented in itself a dangerous misrepresentation of the relationship between human beings and their tools. If the medium is the message, if technological change is the determining factor or 'cause' of social change, Williams (1974/1990: 127) argued that 'all other causes, all that men ordinarily see as history, are at once reduced to effects'. Indeed, as Gaëtan Tremblay (2012: 565) notes, when McLuhan discusses for example the homogenization of human culture in the age of globalization and the development of (to use McLuhan's much used phrase) the 'Global Village', social-economic factors such as the expansion of mass culture and of the capitalist system are made to seem of little relevance. Instead, for the Canadian theorist, this homogenization 'is basically the product of print culture made possible by the invention of the printing press' (Tremblay 2012: 565).

What is more, if the effect of the medium is the same 'whoever controls or uses it, and whatever apparent content he may try to insert', Williams (1974/1990: 128) writes, 'then we can forget ordinary political and cultural argument and let the technology run itself'. In other words, not only would McLuhan's technological determinism seem to limit the possibility of individual free will, but it would seem to excuse the uneven distribution of wealth and the gaping social inequalities that characterize the modern world, making them seem the inevitable product of a certain technological environment. As such, 'it is hardly surprising that this conclusion has been welcomed by the 'media-men' of the existing institutions' (Williams 1974/1990: 128).

In sum, it is important to recognize that 'in each stage, . . . a technology is always, in a full sense, social' (Williams 1981: 227). Media and their use are necessarily embedded in a network of complex and variable social relations (Williams 1981: 227). The tools we use cannot be 'abstracted' from society and their use must always be placed within its socio-cultural context. Or, as Mark Deuze (2006: 65; emphasis added) neatly puts it, we must examine technology starting from the assumption 'that humans and machines are *implicated in one another*, rather than one influencing or directing the other'. To return to the example given by Littau (2006, 2011), while there can be no doubt that the invention and proliferation of wood pulp-based paper and the consequent explosion of the book market was certainly instrumental to the dramatic change in reading habits and translation practices that occurred during the second half of the nineteenth century, it must also be recognized that the development and effects of this new technology went hand in hand with the social changes of the period (Littau 2006: 19). Indeed, it cannot be overlooked that this technological advance did not simply spring 'out of thin air', and that the need to produce cheaper, more widely accessible books came as a result of social demand. Specifically, we must note that the expansion of the capitalist system in the seventeenth and eighteenth centuries had given rise to a new and ever more dominant middle class. As Littau (2006: 19) describes, this rapidly growing section of society was experiencing a much clearer demarcation between work and free time, higher levels of education (and of literacy) and labour was increasingly divided within the family between the roles of the male 'breadwinner' and his housewife. Many more members of European society (and women in particular) consequently had the time, ability and desire to read, and the economic potential of this burgeoning market created a powerful incentive for technological change.

Mediality and audiovisual translation

Having outlined the theoretical foundations on which this area of study is based, we can now turn to focus on how an understanding of mediality can inform research into audiovisual translation. To do so, this second half of the chapter will use a media-based perspective to explore and explain the gradual shift away from a once-dominant top-down industry-controlled mode of audiovisual translation practice towards today's more open and 'participatory' field (Pérez-González 2014: 233). It will argue that while technological change is by no means the sole factor influencing this development, we can only achieve a full understanding of the ongoing 'democratisation' (Pérez-González 2014: 233) of the audiovisual translation marketplace by taking into consideration the changing affordances of the different technologies involved. This section seeks to trace the shifting contours of the technological landscape in which audiovisual translation activity has been situated, examining the specific constraints and possibilities opened up by each new environment, from film and television to the networked digital technologies of the twenty-first century.

Film

An oft-cited anecdote regarding the impact of early cinema on contemporary audiences concerns the Lumière brothers' (1895) short film *L'arrivée d'un train en gare de La Ciotat*

('The arrival of a train into La Ciotat station'). Faced with the on-screen approach of a large railway engine, the story goes that many members of the audience were filled with 'fear, terror, even panic' (Karasek 1994, cited in Loiperdinger 2004: 90) and leaped from their chairs, convinced that the train 'could plunge off the screen and onto them' (Loiperdinger 2004: 90). Although the exact details of this tale are almost certainly the result of journalistic rumour-mongering and exaggeration, its persistence as one of the 'founding myths' of the cinema demonstrates the extent to which this popular legend about the power of the medium is to a certain extent almost believable.

Indeed, there can be no doubt that, for contemporary spectators, film presented a vastly more immersive, and 'realistic' experience than anything they had known before (McLuhan 1964: 314). As Marshall McLuhan (1964: 314) notes in his chapter on 'The Movies', this was because—even during the so-called 'silent era' of early cinema—film had the capacity to store and convey a far greater quantity and quality of information than any of its precursors. Compared with the printed page, painted magic lantern slides or even photography, here was a recording technology *par excellence*, a medium whose 'high-definition' moving images could take just an instant to present, for example, 'a scene of landscape with figures that would require several pages of prose to describe' (McLuhan 1964: 314). It is easy to imagine that, on encountering this revolutionary new media form for the first time, viewers might have been so entranced with the bewitchingly lifelike pictures being projected onto the screen that they could lose themselves in its illusion, forget their 'conscious self', and react instinctually and 'bodily' to its content (Littau 2006: 50).

It is worth noting then that, as Charles Musser's (1991) insightful account of the early cinema makes clear, it was primarily this almost hallucinatory characteristic of film as an exhilarating new technology that initially accounted for its rapid rise in popularity and unprecedented success as a medium of mass entertainment. 'Audiences . . . were tremendously impressed by [the] animated photographs projected on the screen,' writes Musser (1991: 63–4), citing a critic of the time who, after watching Robert Paul's film *Rough Sea at Dover*, declared '[t]he thing was altogether so realistic and the reproduction so absolutely accurate, that it fairly astounded the beholder. It was the closest copy of nature any work of man has ever yet achieved'. It was the 'magical' nature of this new technology that the general public flocked in their thousands to experience, turning film production into a 'big business' industry and film products into often hugely profitable consumer commodities (Musser 1991: 45). As the cinema rapidly expanded and became increasingly commercialized, and given the dominance of the industrial, 'mass-culture' logic of the capitalist societies from which film technology emerged, it was perhaps unsurprising that this media form came to be governed by a distinctly linear, 'top-down' model of production and distribution. We must, in other words, acknowledge that the socio-economic context in which the movie industry developed was a significant force in promoting the centralization of work processes within the production companies and the emergence of industry-controlled patterns of distribution and translation for film products.

Nevertheless, we can also argue that it is equally important to recognize the ways in which the particular characteristics of the cinema technology simultaneously favoured the development and initial entrenchment of this elite-controlled model. Indeed, we should note to begin with that, despite the widespread enthusiasm for this new media form amongst the general public, it was not just anyone that could engage in the production and distribution of motion pictures. This was, as Musser's (1991) book highlights, a highly technical mode of communication in which participation not only required a certain level of expert knowledge and training, but also a significant financial investment, given that many of the raw materials and pieces of specialist equipment were both in themselves far from cheap and aggressively protected by strict patent laws. In the United States, for instance, Thomas Edison employed a team of lawyers to ensure the virtual monopoly he enjoyed over the film-making technologies he had developed was upheld in the patent courts, and in doing so effectively put many of his primary competitors out of business (Musser 1991: 12). For many years, no-one in the US was able to create motion pictures without first paying Edison a hefty licence fee. This allowed the businessman-inventor to hold absolute power over much of the fledgling film industry and to maximize his individual profits by safeguarding the scarcity, and thus economic value, of the film products his studios were producing. Most ordinary citizens, by contrast, had little opportunity to intervene in and contribute to the course and content of the film-making process, instituting a rigidly structured and highly defined 'break' between the film producers and their audiences (Thompson 1995: 29).

The nature of the media technology meant that every aspect of the reception of film products too was largely determined according to this 'top-down' model. This was principally because, for most members of society, movies could only be viewed in certain public spaces—in cinemas, theatres and other specially-adapted venues—and at specific predetermined times set outside of their direct control: without the financial or technological capacity to access the filmic texts on their own terms, audiences could not for instance choose to watch a film that had been produced and distributed a few years previously or which was not being shown in cinemas in their own town, country or language. As Thompson (1995: 25) notes, they could of course still attempt to influence the market decisions of the movie industry—either by writing letters expressing their opinions and desires, or simply by 'voting with their feet' and demonstrating their likes and dislikes through their purchasing power—but the fact remains that this was nevertheless a 'fundamentally asymmetrical' relationship in which consumers were forced to assume a comparatively passive role.

The inaccessibility of motion picture texts and technologies to the average spectator, combined with the fact that celluloid film was costly and technically difficult to manipulate (Ivarsson 2004), also meant that translation practices were essentially the sole preserve of professional translators employed and directly controlled by the production and distribution companies (Kayahara 2005). This was true both for the so-called 'intertitle' slides that were inserted between scenes from around 1903 onwards in order to facilitate the viewer's comprehension of the ever more complex on-screen action (Nornes 2007: 95), and for the interlingual subtitles and dubbed voice-tracks which would later be used to translate the spoken dialogue of the 'talkies' (Pérez-González 2014: 43). In the media environment of film, therefore, the views and desires of the audience with respect to translation were subordinated to the commercial interests of the movie industry. Translations would generally only be commissioned for films and overseas markets that were deemed economically viable (Kayahara 2005), and translation strategies would often be adopted which either—in the case of intertitles—pared these down to a bare minimum, shortening the films and saving the producers money, or heavily 'domesticated' the source text so that it might be as immediately comprehensible and unobtrusive to the target spectator as possible (Nornes 2007: 100). The film-makers' concerns with producing easily accessible, broad appeal products which, by maintaining an 'efficient, purposeful and uninterrupted flow of narrative information' (Berliner 1999: 6), would require little 'filling in' or subjective interpretation in order to deliver their affective charge thus took precedence over providing the audience access to the cultural richness and depth of meaning present in the source film (Mowitt 2004: 398, Sinha 2004: 175).

Television

From a certain perspective, it could be argued that the arrival of television in the 1950s did little to change this state of affairs in terms of the producer–consumer relationship. After all, the production of audiovisual content was still very much controlled by the media corporations, and distribution and translation too remained processes over which ordinary citizens could have very little influence. If we consider the impact of television from a more indirect point of view however, it becomes clear that the invention of this new media technology engendered a number of subtle changes to the media landscape, changes with regard to which it is important to be aware when considering more recent developments.

For a start, television brought the consumption of audiovisual media products into the domestic sphere of the home and family life. Whereas previously, as noted above, motion pictures could only be accessed in the public space of the cinema or theatre, people were now able to view such content in the privacy of their own living rooms. Initially, of course, this was a technology that only the wealthier sections of society could afford, but the costs involved were soon sufficiently lowered that watching television could gradually become part of the ordinary routines of most individuals and families across the developed world (Thompson 1995: 40). In this way—by allowing the images to be beamed directly into people's homes—not only did this new technology greatly expand the general public's exposure to and consumption of audiovisual material, with programmes (eventually, if not initially) being broadcast almost every hour of every day, but it also dramatically altered the way in which audiences engaged with the audiovisual text. Put simply, viewing a movie in the cinema was (and still is) an event: we *go to watch a film*, that is, we take time outside of our normal schedules, travel to a specific location, queue up, buy a ticket and give the product our whole and undivided attention, sitting in silence in a darkened room with the screen filling our field of vision, absorbing the images 'in psychological solitude like the silent book reader' (McLuhan 1964: 318). Television encourages an altogether different mode of viewing activity: integrated within the practical context of the domestic setting, it has much less to do with notions of spectacle and occasion, and becomes more associated with the basic activities of normal everyday life. Television meant that audiovisual content could be watched in an increasingly flexible, consumer-determined manner. As Thompson (1995: 40) notes, it could even be viewed 'casually', i.e. accorded only our intermittent consideration, perhaps while we carry out other day-to-day actions, such as cooking, cleaning or socializing.

In sum, television 'set the stage' in many ways for the shift which would later become much more prominent, beginning with the emergence of home video technologies and continuing in the digital era, towards greater consumer control over the processes involved in audiovisual text production, distribution, consumption and indeed translation. It began to erode the position of absolute power that the film producers had once held in determining the reception of their products, giving audiences more choice in deciding how they engaged with this form of media content. What is more, by expanding the quantity of audiovisual texts on offer and greatly facilitating spectators' access to them, television also rendered the consumption of this audiovisual material a routine everyday activity, creating habitual viewing practices and paving the way for the astonishing ubiquity of audiovisual content that has come to characterize the modern age.

Home video technology

The defining feature of VHS (Video Home System) and VCR (Video Cassette Recording) technologies was that, for the first time in the history of audiovisual media, they provided the average consumer with the possibility of obtaining their own individual 'copy' of the film or television series (Hills and Sexton 2015: 2). This was an important step forward in that it endowed viewers with a much greater degree of freedom over what they watched and when: with the ability to purchase or rent an official VHS cassette version, or record media content directly from a live television broadcast with VCR, the general public were no longer subordinated to the 'temporal order' imposed by the broadcasting organizations, cinemas or distribution companies (Thompson 1995: 40). Rather, they could create personal archives of their favourite films and shows, and access such content whenever they wished as part of the ordinary routines of their lives (Hills and Sexton 2015: 2).

In this media context, as Matt Hills and Jamie Sexton (2015: 2) note, the notion of a 'national' or 'mass' audience quickly began to lose relevance as the audiovisual market place became more and more fragmented: with a far larger pool of audiovisual products suddenly on offer to the consumer at any one moment, the viewing public was no longer necessarily watching the same things at the same time. Individuals had much freer rein to explore the audiovisual landscape on their own terms, to view only content that interested them most. Moreover, they now had the capacity, if they wished, to 'pore' over it—watch and re-watch using the pause, fast-forward and rewind functions of their video player—to gain a much deeper knowledge or 'mastery' of the television series or film in question (Hills and Sexton 2015: 2). This 'fandom' was further fuelled by the fact that VHS technology also allowed producers to begin to include additional 'extras'—such as 'bloopers', deleted scenes, 'making of' documentaries or actor interviews—at the beginning or end of the main feature. By watching this paratextual content, interested consumers could thus learn more about the processes of production as well as gain a deeper understanding of the story world of the film product being presented. In this way, VHS technologies opened the way for the creation of smaller-scale, more 'proactive' consumer groups and networks that Xiaochang Li (2009: 9, cited in Pérez-González 2014: 73) terms 'audienceships'. Importantly, these informal networks were brought together much less on the basis of such top-down categories as nationality or market demographic, but more on the basis of their own shared enthusiasm for or interest in a certain genre or type of audiovisual content (Hills and Sexton 2015: 2).

Through advances in VHS and VCR technology, and the development of such fan groups, consumers were also able to begin to establish alternative, more 'horizontal' patterns of distribution (Hills and Sexton 2015: 2). Unlike the highly linear model engendered within the environment of film and television, with the arrival of the videocassette, consumers were now able to obtain, copy and share content between themselves, circulating official or 'bootlegged' versions of television shows and films through dynamic, peer-to-peer structures which had much less to do with the rigid, top-down influence of the state and media industries. Indeed, Hill and Sexton (2015: 2–3) discuss the emergence of the so-called 'video nasty' phenomenon in 1970s Britain as an example of such groups: as the film scholars explain, home video technologies gave rebellious, countercultural individuals the capacity to obtain, duplicate and circulate copies of these obscenely violent (hence 'nasty') horror films through informal cult cinema networks, despite their being officially banned by the government and media institutions of the time.

Within this technological environment, the language barrier did however remain a significant obstacle to the expansion and impact of such alternative distribution networks (Cubbison 2005: 48). After all, as with film, VHS and VCR technologies were still analogue media forms whose content was not easily manipulated or annotated (Thompson 1995). Thus when it came to the circulation of foreign-language texts such as, for instance, Japanese *anime* cartoons, the vast majority of non-Japanese-speaking fans were still essentially dependent on the professional industry-controlled translations of the major distribution companies (Pérez-González 2007: 69). The 'top-down' logic of the media industry continued to govern many aspects of their consumer activity, limiting the number of shows available to feed their growing appetite, and allowing them access only to the highly domesticated 'mass-appeal' target-language versions that the profit-focused corporations released onto the market (Cubbison 2005: 51). Indeed, while a select few consumer groups, having become dissatisfied with commercial modes and strategies for translation, did manage to begin to engage in the subtitling of *anime* in the early 1980s, they were able to do so only by exploiting commercial computer-based editing software—i.e. technologies which were then both expensive and not yet readily accessible to most ordinary citizens (Ivarsson 2004, Newitz 1994). What is more, their operations remained relatively small in scale, given that distribution within the network still required the subtitling team to actively duplicate and send physical tapes via the postal system. As we will see in the next section, it was not until the late 1990s and early 2000s, when digital technologies became more widespread and affordable on the mass market, and the Internet developed into an accessible tool for ordinary citizens, that fan-led translation activity would truly be able to rival mainstream practices.

Digital technologies and the Web 2.0

To understand what it is about the nature of digital technologies that sets them apart from their analogue precursors and that can account for their transformative potential, it is useful to start by considering these new media tools as essentially 'translation technologies' (Cronin 2013: 105), able to 'translate' and transform any media object into the universal language of mathematics, into a 'standardised series of digital numbers' (Kittler 1999: 1). This most basic principle of 'numerical representation' has two major implications for our purposes here. First, it renders digital media content intensely 'spreadable' (Jenkins *et al.* 2013: 3). By translating a photograph, film or piece of music into a string of numbers, we convert it into a dematerialized form of abstract information. Unlike an analogue photograph, film or musical recording this pure mathematical data is ultimately separable from its physical 'hardware' and, for this reason, can be both infinitely reproduced and more or less instantaneously transmitted between any number of nodes within a network (Schiwy *et al.* 2011: 2). In this way, digital technologies have enabled the development of the Internet, the 'network of networks' that now provides the possibility to anyone with a connection of exchanging digitized content with potentially billions of other users worldwide.

The second implication of numerical representation is that, again unlike analogue media objects, digitized materials are necessarily 'modular' or 'fractal' in their structure (Manovich 2001: 51). That is to say, because they are represented by numbers, computer-mediated productions can be approached as a collection of 'discrete samples' or 'bits' of quantified information which, even when assembled into larger-scale objects, 'maintain their separate identity' (Manovich 2001: 51). This modularity means that digital content is inherently 'variable' as each constituent part can be individually handled without affecting the integrity of the whole (Manovich 2001: 56). Thus, '[a] new media object is not something fixed once and for all', Manovich (2001: 56) writes, 'but can exist in different, potentially infinite, versions'. In comparison with 'old' media, digital content almost invites customization and manipulation, given that these processes are now neither difficult nor expensive. Indeed, many of the most time-consuming aspects involved can to a large extent be automated, realized at the click of a button by the algorithms programmed into the relatively cheap and easy-to-use personal computers and editing software that have flooded onto the consumer market from the late 1990s onwards (Manovich 2001: 49).

The advent of digital media has gone hand in hand with the so-called 'rise of the volunteer' (Pym 2011: 5), with the massive increase in the participation of non-professional, untrained individuals in the production and circulation of media products (Chouliaraki 2010: 227). Of course, as Mark Deuze (2006: 66) rightly insists, we must not lose sight of the fact that the growing desire among ordinary citizens to become more engaged in the meaning-making processes of modern society—as active agents rather than simply passive consumers—also has its roots in a more general sea-change in socio-political attitudes towards the established structures of the state, the media and democracy. But it is nevertheless the case that the technological developments of the last 60 years or so—beginning with television and VHS— have played a significant role in enabling and encouraging this shift, and that the arrival of these new digital tools has finally succeeded in all but removing many of the obstacles that once prevented the average viewer from producing or appropriating, manipulating and then circulating audiovisual material for themselves (Pérez-González 2014: 240). Indeed, in today's media environment, the previously steadfast distinction between producers and consumers has become increasingly blurred, as those who were once excluded from the processes of media production and distribution now have the means to become co-producers (or 'prosumers' as they are known) of content themselves and share this worldwide.

It is no coincidence then that translation too in this context has become 'no longer a special task left for special people' (Pym 2011: 5). In other words, thanks at least in part to these new technologies, it is no longer the sole preserve of paid, highly trained professionals, but an activity in which many individuals from a range of professional and socio-cultural backgrounds, armed with just a modicum of technical know-how, can and do engage (Pérez-González 2014: 233). Consequently, recent years have seen a huge proliferation in highly motivated fan cultures and other 'communities of interest' (Pérez-González 2007) who, by organizing themselves into collaborative work structures, produce and circulate subtitles or even dubbed voice-tracks to a wide array of different audiovisual texts. These groups include, for instance, the modern-day 'descendants' of the VHS-era *anime* clubs who, by means of the Internet and transnational peer-to-peer ('p2p') file sharing platforms such as *BitTorrent*, are now able not only to access a far greater selection of original Japanese source texts, freed from the profitability constraints of the mainstream distribution channels, but also to allow their own translated versions to be downloaded and consumed by millions of fellow fans across the globe.

Finally, the arrival of digital technologies has coincided with an unprecedented wave of (often prosumer-led) innovation, with new modes of audiovisual translation emerging into the field which harness the unique affordances of today's media tools to develop more 'visually harmonious' and 'interactive' experiences for viewers (Pérez-González 2014). For instance, having become frustrated with the narrow limitations of the industry-approved 'ground rules' for translation, a number of subtitling teams have embraced the modularity and variability of digital content to experiment with the colour, size, direction, font and shape of their titles, sometimes even using animation effects or dynamic writing in an attempt to increase the affective impact on the viewer (Pérez-González 2007: 77; 2014: 204). Perhaps even more strikingly, as Laurie Cubbison (2005) and Melek Ortabasi (2006) have both discussed, translators are increasingly willing and able in this media environment to explore the possibility of inserting 'hyperlink capsules' or 'optional pop-ups' into their target texts, rather than presenting translated films in an exclusively linear fashion. By clicking on these links or pressing the 'enter' button on their remote control, viewers (or users, as we might better call them in this context) are able to pause the progression of the narrative to access additional, extra-diegetic information about the historical, cultural and social 'intertextualities' of the source film (Ortabasi 2006: 288). As Cubbison (2005: 51) argues, not only do these extra features thus give the viewer much more control over their interaction with the translation, allowing them to choose the level of depth with which they engage with the source culture, but they also allow subtitlers to better 'compensate for the cultural barriers between fans from one nation and a text from another'. In other words, whereas previously the industry-imposed restrictions on the number of characters permitted in a subtitle meant that many of the non-verbal semiotic cues present in the source text were left untranslated (with the translator having to concentrate primarily on condensing the source dialogue into the target language), these 'pop-ups' allow for the development of a 'thicker' form of translation which better takes into account the multimodal nature of the cinematic text (Ortabasi 2006: 287).

Summary

Due to the space constraints of this chapter, the account provided above has necessarily been a rather simplified outline of what is in fact an intensely complex and geographically variegated reality. For example, not only has it glossed over some of the more subtle, and at times contradictory, changes in the media environment, but it has also focused exclusively on the history of audiovisual media production and translation in Europe and North America, and has thus done little to correct a significant bias towards the Western world that exists in the academic English-language literature on this subject. Nevertheless, it is hoped that by presenting some of the most influential and transformative technological shifts in this part of the world from across the ages, this chapter has demonstrated the extent to which a greater awareness and appreciation of mediality is able to provide invaluable insights with regards to the study of audiovisual translation practice. It has shown for instance how the media environment of film limited the extent to which ordinary citizens could participate in the meaning-making processes associated with the production of audiovisual texts (including translation), and set out the ways in which successive technological advances have gradually empowered individuals in an ongoing process of democratization. Consequently, it remains just to conclude that while the medium might not be the (only) message, it is certainly one that we cannot afford to ignore.

Further reading

Cronin, M. (2013) *Translation in the Digital Age*, London & New York: Routledge | *Cronin's insightful book explores the consequences of the proliferation of computer-based media for the world of translation. Of particular interest are the sections on the interaction between language and technology, on amateur translation and on the rise of 'indicative' or 'gist' translation in the network age.*

Deuze, M. (2006) 'Participation, Remediation, Bricolage: Considering Principal Components of Digital Culture', *The Information Society* 22: 63–75 | *Defining culture as the 'shared norms, values, practices and expectations of a group of people' (2006: 63), Deuze's paper investigates the principal components of the emerging 'digital culture' that has come to dominate the developed world. Arguing that these components have their roots in the offline world and to a large extent predate the invention of new media technologies, he emphasizes the need to situate the influence of technology in its socio-cultural context.*

Littau, K. (2011) 'First Steps towards a Media History of Translation', *Translation Studies* 4(3): 261–281 | *Although this paper does not deal specifically with audiovisual translation, Littau provides fascinating insights into the ways in which changes in the media environment have shaped translation practice. Taking a historical approach, she examines the dominant 'translation ethos' at different stages in Western history, from the oral culture of the Ancient Greeks to the digital culture of the modern age, and demonstrates how an awareness of mediality is essential to any study of human society and culture.*

Manovich, L. (2001) *The Language of New Media*, Cambridge, MA & London, UK: MIT Press | *Manovich's much cited book has become a key text in the study of the new digital media age. In a clear and persuasive style, he explores the properties of computer-based technology and explains how these can account for the radical socio-cultural transformations of the modern day.*

McLuhan, M. (1964) *Understanding Media*, London & New York: Routledge | *This work is now recognized as representing the first true exploration of the effects of media change on society. While his 'mosaic' style can be off-putting to many readers, the book is filled with ground-breaking perceptions which have changed the way we think about technology forever.*

Related topics

2   History of audiovisual translation
3   Subtitling on the cusp of its futures
4   Investigating dubbing: learning from the past, looking to the future
15 Narratology and audiovisual translation
16 Pragmatics and audiovisual translation
18 Sociolinguistics and linguistic variation in audiovisual translation
31 Accessible filmmaking: translation and accessibility from production

References

Ambrose, S. (2001) 'Paleolithic Technology and Human Evolution', *Science* 291(5509): 1748–1753.

Berliner, T. (1999) 'Hollywood Movie Dialogue and the 'Real Realism' of John Cassavetes', *Film Quarterly* 52(3): 2–16.

Chouliaraki, L. (2010) 'Self-mediation: New media and citizenship', *Critical Discourse Studies* 7(4): 227–232.

Cronin, M. (2013) *Translation in the Digital Age*, London & New York: Routledge.

Cubbison, L. (2005) 'Anime Fans, DVDs, and the Authentic Text', *The Velvet Light Trap* 56: 45–57.

Deuze, M. (2006) 'Participation, Remediation, Bricolage: Considering Principal Components of Digital Culture', *The Information Society* 22: 63–75.

Engelsing, R. (1974) *Der Bürger als Leser: Lesergeschichte in Deutschland 1500–1800*, Stuttgart: Metzler.

Gordon, W. T. (2010) *McLuhan: A Guide for the Perplexed*, New York & London: Continuum.

Hills, M. and J. Sexton (2015) 'Cult Cinema and Technological Change', *New Review of Film and Television Studies* 13(1): 1–11.

Holmes, J. S. (1972/2000) 'The Name and Nature of Translation Studies', in L. Venuti (ed.) *The Translation Studies Reader*, London & New York: Routledge, 172–185.

Innis, H. (1950/1972) *Empire and Communications*, Toronto: University of Toronto Press.

Ivarsson, J. (2004) 'A Short Technical History of Subtitles in Europe'. Available online: http://www.transedit.se/history.htm [last access 20 December 2017].

Jenkins, H. (2001) 'Convergence? I Diverge', *Technology Review* 93. Available online: http://web.mit.edu/cms/People/henry3/converge.pdf [last access 20 December 2017].

Jenkins, H., S. Ford and J. Green (2013) *Spreadable Media: Creating Value and Meaning in a Networked Culture*, New York: New York University Press.

Kayahara, M. (2005). 'The Digital Revolution: DVD Technology and the Possibilities for Audiovisual Translation Studies', *JoSTrans: The Journal of Specialised Translation* 3. Available online: http://www.jostrans.org/issue03/art_kayahara.php [last access 20 December 2017].
Kittler, F. (1999) *Gramophone, Film, Typewriter*, trans. G. Winthrop-Young and M. Wutz, Stanford, CA: Stanford University Press.
Li, X. (2009) 'Dis/Locating Audience: Transnational Media Flows and the Online Circulation of East Asian Television Drama', Unpublished MA dissertation, Massachusetts Institute of Technology.
Littau, K. (2006) *Theories of Reading: Books, Bodies and Bibliomania*, Malden, MA & Cambridge, UK: Polity Press.
Littau, K. (2011) 'First Steps towards a Media History of Translation', *Translation Studies* 4(3): 261–281.
Loiperdinger, M. (2004) 'Lumière's Arrival of the Train: Cinema's Founding Myth', trans. by B. Elzer, *The Moving Image* 4(1): 89–118.
Manovich, L. (2001) *The Language of New Media*, Cambridge, MA & London, UK: MIT Press.
McLuhan, M. (1964) *Understanding Media*, London & New York: Routledge.
McLuhan, M. and Q. Fiore (1967/1996) *The Medium is the Message*, London: Penguin.
Mowitt, J. (2004) 'The Hollywood Sound Tract', in A. Egoyan and I. Balfour (eds) *Subtitles: On the Foreignness of Film*, Cambridge, MA & London, UK: MIT Press, 382–401.
Musser, C. (1991) *Before the Nickleodeon: Edwin S. Porter and the Edison Manufacturing Company*, Berkeley: University of California Press.
Newitz, A. (1994) 'Anime Otaku: Japanese Animation Fans outside Japan', *Bad Subjects* 13: 1–12.
Nornes, A. M. (2007) *Cinema Babel: Translating Global Cinema*, Minneapolis: University of Minnesota Press.
Ortabasi, M. (2006) 'Indexing the Past: Visual Language and Translatability in Kon Satoshi's *Millennium Actress*', *Perspectives: Studies in Translatology* 14(4): 278–291.
Pérez-González, L. (2007) 'Intervention in New Amateur Subtitling Cultures: A Multimodal Account', *Linguistica Antverpiensia* 6: 67–80.
Pérez-González, L. (2014) *Audiovisual Translation: Theories, Methods and Issues*, London & New York: Routledge.
Pym, A. (2011) 'What Technology Does to Translating', *The International Journal for Translation and Interpreting Research* 3(1). Available online: http://trans-int.org/index.php/transint/article/viewFile/121/81 [last access 20 December 2017].
Schiwy, F., A. Fornazzari and S. Antebi (2011) 'Introduction' in F. Schiwy, A. Fornazzari and S. Antebi (eds) *Digital Media, Cultural Production and Speculative Capitalism*, London & New York: Routledge, 1–6.
Sinha, A. (2004) 'The Use and Abuse of Subtitles', in A. Egoyan and I. Balfour (eds) *Subtitles. On the Foreignness of Film*, Cambridge, MA & London: The MIT Press, 172–190.
Taylor, T. (2010) *The Artificial Ape: How Technology Changed the Course of Human Evolution*, London: Palgrave Macmillan.
Thompson, J. (1995) *The Media and Modernity: A Social Theory of the Media*, Cambridge: Polity Press.
Tremblay, G. (2012) 'From Marshall McLuhan to Harold Innis, or from the Global Village to the World Empire', *Canadian Journal of Communication* 37: 561–575.
Venuti, L. (1995) *The Translator's Invisibility. A History of Translation*, London & New York: Routledge.
Williams, R. (1974/1990) *Television: Technology and Cultural Form*, London & New York, Routledge.
Williams, R. (1981) *Culture*, London: Fontana.
Winthrop-Young, G. and M. Wutz (1999) 'Translators' Introduction', in F. Kittler (1999) *Gramophone, Film, Typewriter*, trans. G. Winthrop-Young and M. Wutz, Stanford, CA: Stanford University Press.

Filmography

2001: A Space Odyssey (1968) Stanley Kubrick. IMDb entry: http://www.imdb.com/title/tt0062622/?ref_=fn_al_tt_4

L'arrivée d'un train en gare de La Ciotat (1896) Auguste Lumière and Louis Lumière. IMDb entry: http://www.imdb.com/title/tt0000012/

Rough Sea at Dover (1896) Robert Paul. IMDb entry: http://www.imdb.com/title/tt0000030/?ref_=fn_al_tt_1

13

Spoken discourse and conversational interaction in audiovisual translation

Silvia Bruti

Spontaneous vs. planned conversation

Although linguistics has, until recently, focused on the study and description of written language, the turn of the century has witnessed a shift to the study of spoken language as a domain of research in its own right. Significantly, for the purposes of this chapter, 'research into the features of faked casual conversation in audiovisual conversation has . . . begun to surface' as a particularly productive research theme within the field of audiovisual translation (Valdeón 2011: 224). Back in the 70s, Gregory and Carroll were the first to recognize that, while dialogues in audiovisual texts are scripted in nature, they are 'written to be spoken as if not written' (Gregory and Carroll 1978: 42). In doing so, they paved the way for the debate on the authenticity of film language when they argued that this is a genre of its own, where naturalness is the result of detailed planning. Today, much of the current research on audiovisual translation (AVT) touches upon the comparability between filmic dialogue and spontaneous dialogue, and consequently also translated dialogue (in particular, dubbing).

Indeed, the growing interest in the colloquial features of original and dubbed filmic dialogue stems from concerns over the quality of audiovisual products, and, consequently, their translation, including their potential contribution to the acquisition of a second language on the part of the viewers (see, among many, Pavesi 2012; Bruti 2015). The pervasiveness of orality in multimodal texts, including films, has certainly favoured the interest in the nature of filmic dialogue that, while far from a perfect replica of spontaneous conversation, represents a convenient register to use as a source of input in a second language for, as Moreno Jaén and Pérez Basanta (2009: 288) rightfully note, 'teachers cannot teach conversation, which is by nature multimodal, with monomodal materials'.

Further to this applied research agenda, an ever-growing range of recent interdisciplinary studies has revealed that scriptwriters—and subsequently audiovisual translators—tend to achieve a certain degree of conversational naturalness by replicating specific features of spontaneous speech that are widely accepted and identified as such by their audience. The selection of such features is crucial, as credibility is singled out by professionals and scholars alike as one of the most important requirements for audiovisual products to succeed commercially. Chaume (2012) coined the expression 'prefabricated orality' (Baños and Chaume 2009) to designate this 'combination of features deriving from both oral and written texts' (Chaume 2012: 81). This is because while filmic speech requires a certain degree of spontaneity, it is bound by medial constraints, genre conventions, stylistic rules (e.g. standardization, censorship, patronage) dictated by television authorities and broadcasting companies, as well as the strong link that exists between images and words. For these reasons, Chaume (2012: 82) suggests using an integrated approach to analyze original and translated filmic speech that takes into account the 'multiple semiotic codes operating simultaneously'. From a similar standpoint, Pavesi (2012) acknowledges that scripted conversation aims to replicate real, or plausible, face-to-face communication, but it does so under specific situational and interactional constraints that differ significantly from those shaping spontaneous spoken language. In Pavesi's own words, screen dialogue is the result of a 'multilayered structure in which several addressers—the film maker, the script-writer, the actors, etc.—interact among themselves but also communicate with the silent audience watching the screen and listening to the dialogues' (2012: 158). The most striking difference with spontaneous conversation is that, although the audience is the final addressee of all exchanges, it is not a party to the interactional context and cannot participate fully in the latter.

Other scholarly strands have gauged the comparability of fictional dialogue with spontaneous conversation from various perspectives, sometimes with contrasting results. Several studies have pointed out how and to what extent features of spontaneous conversation have been used in original and translated filmic dialogue, starting from the seminal studies by Gottlieb (1998), Hatim and Mason (1997), Blini and Matte Bon (1996), Díaz Cintas and Remael (2007) on subtitling; and Chaume (2004), Baños and Chaume (2009), and Freddi and Pavesi (2009) on dubbing. More specialized studies like those by Quaglio (2009a; 2009b) and Forchini (2012), both of which are based on Biber's (1988) multidimensional analysis, highlight a number of similarities between the interpersonal dimension in both types of interaction (Biber 1988). However, the analysis of more specific features, such as vague language (Quaglio 2009b), shows that changes do not only have to do with frequency of use; they are also dictated by the need for audiovisual texts to be clear and able to attract a sizeable audience. Other corpus-based studies comparing screen dialogue (drawing on a collection of film transcripts) and real-life conversation (British National Corpus) by Rodríguez Martín and Moreno Jaén (2009) and Rodríguez Martín (2010) have similarly concluded that filmic dialogue employs a wide range of conversational strategies and devices, especially those that are closely connected with the dialogic nature of interaction (e.g. personal pronouns, turn-taking management devices). On the whole, it can be safely argued that narrative requirements and industrial constraints have a direct bearing on the choice of the mechanisms that normally lend discourse a natural flavour. Translated conversation tends to deploy fewer conversational features (e.g. discourse markers, interjections, hesitations, dysfluencies, false starts, etc.) and neater turn-taking mechanisms. In this chapter the focus is placed on structural and expressive aspects of conversation.

Conversational features in subtitling

Studies on subtitling unanimously point out that some conversational features are eliminated from subtitles because this modality of audiovisual translation involves a transfer from oral to written discourse—which, in turn, entails the need for a significant amount of text reduction.

The turn-taking system is thus often altered to follow more closely the rules of written language; as a result, subtitled conversation features more homogeneous turns and a neater sequencing (e.g. with little overlapping). Likewise, many indexes of the unplanned nature of discourse that are present in original dialogues—in an attempt to reproduce naturalness—are also drastically reduced.

The following two subsections focus on the structural and organizational aspects of conversation, and examine how expressive and orality markers are rendered in subtitling.

The structural organization of conversation in subtitling

The structural elements of conversation, mainly turn-taking rules, are sometimes manipulated in subtitles to follow the rules of written rather than spoken language. Audiovisual narratives favour smooth transitions between turns at talk, and this is further emphasized in subtitling because of the spatio-temporal constraints that subtitlers operate under. The emphasis on narrative linearity has also been found to result in streamlined, more compact narratives—as subtitlers often condense or even suppress the nonconformist voice of secondary characters (Remael 2003, Pérez-González 2007, Zabalbeascoa 2012). Translating lengthy exchanges through short subtitles, however, can be detrimental in terms of audience perception. As Díaz Cintas notes, overtly condensed dialogue can 'raise suspicion, as would laconic dialogues channelled into expansive subtitles' (2012: 277).

Drawing on dialogic theories of communication, Remael (2003) emphasizes that film interaction is always characterized by a dynamic of 'dominance'. From a quantitative point view, powerful characters deliver the highest number of turns or words; from a semantic perspective, dominant characters choose and suggest topic changes throughout the conversational exchange; interactionally, dialogue is often asymmetric, with powerful characters managing turn-taking; and finally, and most importantly, strategically speaking, dominant characters are allotted the most important moves in the exchange—i.e. those that push the plot forward and are responsible for the most crucial narrative nuclei. Remael's study reveals that the majority of 'dominance' patterns found in original filmic dialogue are either replicated or even enhanced in their subtitled counterparts. Cases of inversion of dominance are relatively few and far between but they happen and, when they do, they have an impact on the narrative dynamics of the film. For instance, quantitative 'dominance' on the part of one character may be redressed in the subtitled version by levelling out the unbalanced turns at talk in the original filmic dialogue. A more balanced outcome can be reached by allotting an equal number of lines and words to characters, as illustrated by the following examples.

In Example 1 (*Match Point*, Allen 2005), the changes entailed by the subtitling process affect mainly the interactional and quantitative dimension of the original dialogue between the two characters' distinctive speech styles: brilliant, upper-class Tom, and his scheming, lower-class tennis instructor Chris. Tom is rather verbose and, from the moment he meets Chris, he employs a friendly, colloquial style to reduce the social distance that exists between them. By contrast, Chris, who aspires to be part of Tom's glamorous world, is exceptionally gentle and more formal, although concise (artfully so, as he is much more articulated when talking to his peers). As shown in the example, Tom is the one who chooses topics, manages conversation and speaks the most, so the decision of reducing and altering his turns creates a more symmetrical exchange.

Example 1 (my transcription; back-translation in italics)

Original dialogue	Italian subtitles
TOM Yeah, well, the olds say thank you very much for the lovely flowers, they said it was very thoughtful, and totally unnecessary, but, off the record, well done, A+, 'cause they love that sort of thing.	TOM Beh, i vecchi dicono 'Grazie infinite per i bellissimi fiori'. *The old folks say* *'Thank you so much for the wonderful flowers'.* 'Un gesto premuroso e totalmente non necessario'. *A thoughtful gesture* *and totally unnecessary.* Ma . . . un vero colpo da maestro! Adorano questo genere di cose! *But . . . a real masterstroke!* *They love this sort of things!*
CHRIS Oh, they're lovely people. And your sister's very bright.	CHRIS Oh, sono molto simpatici e tua sorella è molto intelligente! *Oh, they are very nice* *and your sister is very bright.*

In particular, what gets lost in Example 1 is the attribution of the statement 'it was a thoughtful but unnecessary gesture'—which can be ascribed in the subtitled version to Tom instead of his parents. Conversely, some elements that are distinctive about Tom's attitude—such as 'off the record' and 'well done', with only the latter being condensed into 'A+' in the expression 'un colpo da maestro' (*a masterstroke*)—are eliminated.

In other cases, as illustrated in Example 2 from the *The King's Speech* (2010), changes affect more evidently the strategic dimension of interaction. Modifications in this extract pertain to the character of Elizabeth, the future King's wife, who meets Lionel Logue, an unconventional speech therapist, and attempts to persuade him to treat her husband's heavy stuttering.

Example 2 (my transcription; back-translation in italics)

Original dialogue	Italian subtitles
ELIZABETH No, look, erm . . . My husband has seen everyone to no avail. Awfully for him, he's given up hope.	ELIZABETH No, sentite. Ehm . . . Mio marito si è rivolto a tutti, senza successo. *No, listen. Erm . . . my husband has turned* *to everybody, without success.* – Temo stia perdendo ogni speranza. *I'm afraid he is losing every hope.*
LIONEL He hasn't seen me.	LIONEL – Non si è rivolto a me. *He hasn't turned to me.*

(continued)

(continued)

Original dialogue	Italian subtitles
ELIZABETH You're awfully sure of yourself.	**ELIZABETH** Molto sicuro di voi stesso. *Very self-confident.*
LIONEL Well, I'm sure of anyone who wants to be cured.	**LIONEL** Sono molto sicuro di chiunque voglia essere curato. *I very much trust anyone who wants to be treated.*
ELIZABETH Of course he wants to be cured. My husband is, erm . . . he's required to speak publicly.	**ELIZABETH** Certo che vuole essere curato. *Of course he wants to be treated.* A mio marito si . . . si richiede di parlare in pubblico. *My husband is . . . is requested to speak in public.*
LIONEL Perhaps he should change jobs.	**LIONEL** Forse dovrebbe cambiare lavoro. *Maybe he should change his job.*
ELIZABETH He can't.	**ELIZABETH** Non può. *He can't.*
LIONEL Indentured servitude?	**LIONEL** Un contratto di apprendista? *Is he an apprentice?*
ELIZABETH Something of that nature. Yes.	**ELIZABETH** Una cosa del genere, sì. *Sort of, yes.*
LIONEL Well, have your hubby pop by . . . ah . . . Tuesday would be good . . . he can give his personal details, I'll make a frank appraisal and we'll take up from there.	**LIONEL** Bene, il maritino dovrà fare un salto qui. *Well, the dear husband will have to pop here.* Martedì andrebbe bene. *Tuesday would be fine.* Mi darà i suoi dettagli personali, *He will give me his personal details,* io farò una valutazione schietta e poi partiremo da lì. *I will make a frank assessment and then we will start from there.*
ELIZABETH Doctor . . . forgive me, I do *not* have a "hubby". We don't "pop". And nor do we ever talk about our private lives. No, you must come to us.	**ELIZABETH** Dottore, perdonatemi . . . *Doctor, forgive me . . .* Io non ho un maritino, non facciamo un salto *I haven't got a dear husband, we don't pop here* e non vogliamo mai parlare

> della nostra vita privata.
> *and we never want to discuss*
> *our private life.*
> No, voi dovete venire da noi.
> *No, you must come to us.*

The first instance, 'awfully for him', is rendered with the Italian equivalent of 'I'm afraid he's losing every hope', which shifts the speech focus from Prince Albert's plight to his wife's viewpoint. This shift contributes to presenting her as even more powerful—indeed, in this excerpt she is trying to arrange medical treatment for her husband without his consent. Similar remarks apply to her last turn in the extract featured in the example, where she uses a formal and emphatic marked construction 'nor do we . . .' that is lost in the subtitles. This is significant in comparison with Lionel's previous turn, which undergoes neutralization in the Italian subtitles. In the original dialogue, Logue employs extremely colloquial forms, such as 'hubby' and 'pop by', both of which are criticized by Elizabeth as inappropriate. *Maritino*, the Italian term used to subtitle 'hubby', is an endearment obtained through the deployment of the diminutive suffix *–ino*. Although it is typically employed in affective or light-hearted settings and retains the humorous tone of the original, it is not associated with a lower and inappropriate register in Italian—which is also the case with the choice of *fare un salto* to subtitle the English expression 'pop by'.

On the whole, even though these changes do not abound, they occasionally have a severe impact on interpersonal dynamics and 'prove detrimental to the dynamics of dramatic characterization envisaged by the creator of the original audiovisual text' (Pérez-González 2014: 16).

Expressive and orality markers in subtitling

Manipulative behaviour in subtitling can also result in the cleaning up of expressive markers of various types. Some of them impinge more directly on the interpersonal dimension, as they contribute to the illocutionary force of an utterance and represent a sort of socio-pragmatic reflection of the forces at play. Among them are most notably vocatives, interjections, tag questions, expressive and phatic speech acts, politeness devices such as mitigation, understatement and the like (see, among many, Hatim and Mason's (1997) chapter on Pragmatics).

Some other elements that may be downgraded or removed in subtitling are instead manifestations of the unplanned nature of spontaneous spoken discourse, through which film creators seek to make their scripted dialogues more 'natural'. They include elements that underline the online dimension of speech, such as hesitations, fillers, repetitions and redundancies (Blini and Matte Bon 1996, Kovačič 1996, Taylor 2002, Bussi Parmiggiani 2002), and also some discourse markers that help speakers organize their talk. If they are omitted, the structure of the story is not seriously compromised, as denotative meaning is always preserved, but the narrative development of the film can be altered to a greater or lesser extent (Díaz Cintas and Remael 2007: 165–166). When repetitions or hesitations are expunged from a shy or insecure character's speech, for instance, the original interpersonal dynamics may be significantly altered, and viewers of the subtitled version may no longer perceive those characters in the same way.

This is exemplified in Example 3, which features an extract from *Green Street* (Alexander 2005), a film about football hooliganism. Matt's first turn rejects an invitation in a dubious and tentative manner, as signalled by the opening discourse marker 'well' and the approximator 'sort of'; however, his rejection is presented as strongly assertive in the subtitles. In Pete's turn, instead, other elements are toned down. This is the case with the swearing 'fuck you'—which is not meant to cause offence, but used as an in-group marker—and the familiarizer 'mate'—replaced here by the addressee's first name Matt, which happens to be phonetically similar to the replaced element. In most cases, providentially, the 'inter-semiotic redundancy' of subtitling (Gottlieb 1998: 247) allows the audience to correctly decode the message by accessing images (in particular gazes and gestures) and paralinguistic features (e.g. loudness, pitch, contour), both of which reveal much about the characters' relationships.

Example 3 (my transcription; back-translation in italics)

Original dialogue	*Italian subtitles*
MATT	MATT
Well, I sort of have plans with Shannon this afternoon, so . . .	Ho preso un impegno con Shannon, per oggi pomeriggio. *I have made a commitment to Shannon for this afternoon.*
PETE	PETE
All right, fuck you, then. We'll have a beer later, yeah?	Come non detto. Ci prendiamo una birra più tardi. *Forget what I just said. We have a beer later on.*
MATT	MATT and PETE
Yeah, yeah, see you at the pub!	– Sì, ci vediamo al pub.
PETE	– A dopo, Matt.
All right, mate! (leaves)	– *Yes, see you at the pub.*
	– *See you later, Matt.*

Similar remarks hold for the extract from *Sliding Doors* (Howitt 1998) presented in Example 4. The exchange involves Gerry, an unaccomplished novelist, and Russell, one of his closest friends. Gerry often confides his love troubles to Russell, but in this scene he wants to share with him the news that he has completed his novel. He strengthens his utterance through repetition and the use of 'bloody' as an intensifying adverb, but in the Italian subtitled version both elements are reformulated as *Sono un mago* ('I'm a wizard'). Russell reacts with positive appreciation, which is more condensed in Italian, while appearing to be puzzled because he probably expected Gerry to talk about his love troubles. After Gerry's second turn, Russell acknowledges that he has understood but expresses his surprise with an exclamation and a discourse marker ('oh' and 'well'), and his affection through the familiarizer 'mate'. All these elements are expunged from the subtitle, which thus becomes a strong but more impersonal statement.

Example 4 (my transcription; back-translation in italics)

Original dialogue	Italian subtitles
GERRY I've done it, Russell. I've bloody done it!	GERRY Ce l'ho fatta, Russell. Sono un mago. *I made it, Russell. I'm a wizard.*
RUSSELL Excellent. Congratulations. Done what?	RUSSELL Congratulazioni! A fare cosa?! *Congratulations! To do what?!*
GERRY I've finished it.	GERRY Sono arrivato alla fine. *I arrived at the end.*
RUSSELL Oh, the book. Oh, well, great, mate, that's great.	RUSSELL Del libro? È grandioso. *Of the book? It's fantastic.*

Formulaic language in subtitling

One further element that deserves attention is the use of formulaic language. In spontaneous speech, prefabricated items are quite well spread, especially in the form of set phrases and collocations, because they are memorized and retrieved as chunks. As Conklin and Schmitt report on the basis of several experimental studies, 'normal discourse, both written and spoken, contains large (but not yet fully determined) percentages of formulaic language. . . . Overall . . . formulaic language makes up between *one third* and *one half* of discourse' (Conklin and Schmitt 2012: 46, *my emphasis*).

Within the class of formulaic expressions, conversational routines—i.e. a series of speech acts such as greetings, congratulations, thanks, apologies—are important strategies for the negotiation and control of social identity and relationships between participants in an exchange. Sometimes they are mainly used to smoothen interaction, but contribute little factual information. This depends on the trade-off between a whole series of parameters: the unwritten rules of behaviour of a lingua-cultural community, the intimacy among speakers, the formality of the situation of utterance, the purposes of communication and so on. In everyday conversation, when speakers are very close or the situation of utterance is relaxed, these elements may often be dispensed with. If, instead, speakers are more distant, phatic talk is needed as a social lubricant (Bonsignori *et al.* 2011; Bonsignori *et al.* 2012; Bonsignori and Bruti 2014a). However, in fictional filmic dialogue—a genre where speech is scripted and rehearsed in advance—social chit-chat is seldom just social chit-chat; given the spatio-temporal constraints at play, anything that is uttered by characters must respond to specific narrative aims.

As Guillot has aptly shown (2012, 2016), the use and frequency of routines need therefore to be relativized and subordinated to their diegetic function. Furthermore, the nature of audiovisual texts also strongly conditions translation. Thus if routines are used in the original dialogues to accompany corresponding images on screen, they have to be reproduced in subtitles (and in dubbing, albeit for different reasons, as elaborated in the next section). Translation is only 'a matter of modulating words, but adherence to the image must in any case be pursued' (Bonsignori and Bruti 2014a: 77). Good wishes, for instance, have been shown to be quite widely used in TV series, as they accompany family celebrations such as birthday or Thanksgiving parties (Bonsignori and Bruti 2014a). Consequently, although they are concentrated in a few episodes, they are very 'image-related' and hence always prioritized in the subtitles.

Silvia Bruti

An isolated but very significant feature that has been observed in TV series, in line with Guillot's findings (2012, 2016), is that some characters occasionally perform social rites with unusual phrasing. In an episode of American TV series *Brothers and Sisters* (see Example 5), Holly Harper utters a wish before taking leave. The children of her former lover tried to deceive her upon finding that their father left her a legacy of 10 million dollars. So the place typically occupied by conventional expressions such as 'goodbye' or 'see you' is here replaced by a biting and ironic wish, which sanctions sarcastically the end of the encounter.

Example 5 (my transcription; back-translation in italics)

Original dialogue	*Italian subtitles*
HOLLY HARPER Enjoy your bankruptcy.	HOLLY HARPER Godetevi la bancarotta *Enjoy the bankruptcy.*

In addition, some situation-bound and rapid routines may turn into strategic instruments to deliver information for the audience's benefit. For example, the closing of an interactional encounter may contain a reference to the moment in which two characters made each other's acquaintance, and that had not previously been shown to the audience. This represents 'a very economical way of condensing essential diegetic information' (Bonsignori and Bruti 2014a: 87) and can be easily translated in the subtitles, as illustrated in Examples 6 and 7 from *Brothers and Sisters*.

Example 6 (my transcription; back-translation in italics)

Original dialogue	*Italian subtitles*
WARREN Pleasure to meet you.	WARREN Piacere. *Pleasure.*
KITTY Nice to meet you.	KITTY Il piacere è mio. *The pleasure is mine.*

Example 7 (my transcription; back-translation in italics)

Original dialogue	*Italian subtitles*
PROF. HARRIS It was very nice meeting you. ((handshake))	PROF. HARRIS È stato un piacere. *It has been a pleasure.*
RORY Same here. ((handshake)) Pleasure to meet you.	RORY Anche per me. *For me too.*

By way of summary, it must be observed that the dissatisfaction with some of the limitations and features of professional subtitling on the one hand, and the exponential growth of popularity of audiovisual products on the other, have favoured the spread of community translation practices such as fansubbing. Over the last decades, the phenomenon has rocketed, because it has pursued the aim of achieving a translation that makes up for the 'cultural insensitivity' (Pérez-González 2014: 17) often displayed by official commercial translations. Fansubbers tend in fact to adhere to the source text closely (preserving many of the features that are focused upon in these paragraphs) not as a mere imitation strategy, but in order to render adequately both style and register (Massidda 2015). In so doing, they prioritize narrative and affective functions (Bruti and Zanotti 2012, 2013) through a series of different formal conventions, thus meeting the audience's tastes and expectations.

Conversational features in dubbing

In dubbing many expressive and orality markers are also deleted, although for different reasons from the ones at play in subtitling. These are not only related to lip synchrony constraints, as plenty of studies in the last decades have thoroughly demonstrated (Pérez-González 2014: 22), but to translation universals (Mauranen and Kujamäki 2004) and to typical features of dubbed speech that have somehow crystallized through repetition (Pavesi 2005: 48).

The structure of conversation and the distribution of turns at talk in dubbed interaction is bound by less strict constraints than subtitled speech, given that quantitative synchronism requires the length of turns in the original and dubbed dialogues to match (Herbst 1994). As Valdeón argues in relation to other related aspects of orality (e.g. interruptions and unfinished utterances, as elaborated below), the structure of dubbed conversation remains very similar to the original because 'the constraints imposed by the multimodal text might prevent any changes in the target texts, for instance isochrony' (Valdeón 2011: 227). The following two subsections will therefore focus on expressive and orality markers and formulaic language, respectively.

Expressive and orality markers in dubbing

It has been noted that the dialogues of contemporary Anglophone audiovisual texts are carefully crafted to depict realistic contemporary life (Taylor 1999). Dysfluencies are thus used more commonly than in older films and TV programmes, which sought to construct informality through other means, notably the use of a lower register and the deployment of a range of discourse markers (Quaglio 2009a, Valdeón 2009, Valdeón 2011).

As hinted at above, interruptions and unfinished utterances are the most frequently preserved forms of dysfluency for reasons of isochrony. Conversely, repeats—i.e. recurrent segments, not necessarily entire words—are rendered in different ways, although not all of them achieve the same pragmatic effect as the original dialogue. Valdeón (2011), for example, has explored the implications of retaining and eliminating repeats. In some cases, repetitions are voluntary and confer more illocutionary strength on speech; in other cases, repeats are involuntary and betray a wide range of emotions, including uncertainty, surprise and nervousness. Consequently, it is the overall characterization of the protagonists, and not only the local stretch of discourse containing the dysfluency in question, that is altered. These choices, however, are the result of a trade-off between the tendency to imitate speech in its spontaneous nuances and the need for audiovisual fiction to be comprehensible and entertaining—while complying with rules imposed by the market and production companies (Romero-Fresco 2009). Of note is the fact that some elements are more difficult to alter because they are utterance-initial or final, and hence more clearly foregrounded through the linguistic code and other semiotic modes. Instead, those that occur within a turn can be more easily manipulated, either by deletion or replacement (Valdeón 2011: 231).

The majority of studies on this aspect of dubbing have until now dealt mainly with hesitation markers (Romero-Fresco 2009), interjections (Cuenca 2006, Bruti and Pavesi 2008) and discourse markers (Romero-Fresco 2006, Cuenca 2008, Forchini 2010, Baños 2014, Freddi and Malagori 2014).

Hesitators and gap-filling elements have different preferred realizations across languages. In Spanish, for example, hesitation can be expressed thanks to lengthened vowels, repeated syllables, or also unintelligible sounds (Valdeón 2009). Also in dubbed Spanish, the most common way to signal uncertainty is deletion (*ibid.*: 138), followed by strategies involving the use of pauses or lexical items—e.g. discourse markers or repeated items. In Italian too, hesitation is communicated with filled pauses like *mmm* and *ehm*, but a wide array of other expressions are available to perform this function, including elongated vowels and gap-filling words like *ma, allora, non so, forse, praticamente*, or *cioè*.

In *Notting Hill* (Michell 1999), a film analyzed in Valdeón (2009), the hesitation marker *er* and its nasalized version *erm* occur 105 and 87 times, respectively (see Bonsignori 2009 for more information on the various options available to transcribe these items and the way in which they are used in English). A look at the dubbed dialogue suggests that these hesitations—which signal the awkwardness of some situations and, in particular, the clumsiness of the male protagonist in this film—are not always retained in the target language. The fragment of dialogue featured in Example 8 shows that, when they are,

Example 8 (my transcription; back-translation in italics)

Original dialogue	Italian dubbing
ANNA to WILLIAM I will take this one.	ANNA to WILLIAM Prendo questo qua. *I take this one.*
WILLIAM Oh, right, right. So, er, well, on second thoughts, uhm, maybe it's not that bad after all. Actually, it's a sort of classic, really. None of those childish kebab stories you find in so many books these days. And um, I tell you what, I'll throw in one of those for free. Useful for, er, lighting fires, wrapping fish, that sort of thing ...	WILLIAM Oh, certo certo! In fondo, eh, bè, ripensandoci, dopo tutto, non è così male. A dire il vero, è un po' classico. Niente storie sul kebab. Infantilismi che trovi sui libri di oggi. E ehm, facciamo così, le do uno di questi gratis. È utile per . . . accendere il camino, incartare il pesce, quelle cose lì ... *Oh, right, right! In sum, er, well, thinking back again, after all, it's not so bad. To tell the truth, it's a classic. No stories about kebab. Childish things you find in contemporary books. And uhm, let's do this, I give you one of these for free. It's useful to . . . light the fire, wrap fish, that sort of thing . . .*

Italian uses a wider repertoire of items, in some cases to enhance the naturalness of the dubbed interaction.

In this extract Anna, a famous American actress, visits William Thacker's bookshop in Notting Hill. William, excited and embarrassed at the same time, comments on the book she has picked up. Many hesitation markers, such as *er, um* and *uhm*, feature in the dialogue (*uh* and *um* are used 19 and 16 times, respectively, in the whole film). Apart from these, there are other elements that also signal difficulty in planning one's speech and are associated with spontaneity and naturalness. These include pauses, repetitions (e.g. 'Right, right!'); forward-pointing phrases like 'I tell you what'; or fillers such as 'well' and 'actually'. In the dubbed version, only two out of the four original hesitation markers are used: *eh* and *ehm*. Instead, other resources have been relied upon to convey the same effect. Filling phrases signalling uncertainty (*in fondo, bè, a dire il vero*), for example, are consistent with dubbing practices in Spanish (Valdeón 2009: 138–139).

Interjections in dubbed language (Bruti and Pavesi 2008, Valdeón 2009) are generally less frequent and less assorted than in non-fictional spontaneous conversation. Sometimes they are turned into other exclamatory items (Valdeón 2009: 124) because they sound more natural in the target language. A study on interjections in dubbed Italian (Bruti and Pavesi 2008) shows that the pattern differs considerably from that of interjections in spontaneous speech, partly because many occurrences are modelled on the source text, thus producing awkward expressions in some cases. The interjections that find a similar counterpart in English 'tend to be over-represented in dubbing, whereas interjections which are specific and restricted to Italian tend to be under-represented' (*ibid.*: 220)—a fact that confirms the Unique Item Hypothesis put forward by Tirkkonen-Condit (2004), which states that the absence of certain linguistic stimuli in the original text strongly conditions the translating process, even when the target language is rich in those elements.

Discourse markers have been quite extensively analyzed in fictional dialogue and dubbing. Even though translation choices are informed by a number of interrelated factors, such as the position of the discourse marker and its place within the overall multimodal ensemble of the audiovisual text, specialists agree that what often gets lost in translation is interpersonal meaning. Choices also seem to depend on the genre of the film, as the same dialogue adapter tends to choose different alternatives for the same discourse markers in different film genres (Romero-Fresco 2009, Freddi and Malagori 2014: 205).

In *Love Actually* (Curtis 2003), for example, discourse markers are extensively employed, as the plot of the film is based on a series of interweaving conversations revolving around lovers, friends and acquaintances. Phrasal markers such as 'you know' and 'I mean' are both utilized on 16 and 10 occasions, respectively. As Deborah Schiffrin points out (1987: 267), 'you know' is a marker of 'metaknowledge of what speaker and hearer share, and . . . about what is generally known', whereas 'I mean', although interactional, is more clearly speaker-centred and betrays the intention of expanding one's speech or explaining one's intentions (*ibid.*: 296). In the Italian dubbed version, 'you know' is omitted 8 times, translated 6 times as *sai* ('you know'), and once as *sa* ('you know', polite form) and *sai . . . allora*. 'I mean' is omitted altogether 3 times or translated as *insomma* (3 times), *voglio dire* (2 times), *cioè* (once), and once as *un momento* ('one moment'). Essentially, when 'you know' is translated, it is always rendered literally. By contrast, 'I mean' is translated using different pragmatic equivalents attending to the context in which the utterance is delivered—as illustrated in the extract featured in Example 9.

Silvia Bruti

Example 9 (my transcription; back-translation in italics)

Original dialogue	Italian dubbing
SARAH It's my brother. He's not well. He calls a lot.	SARAH Era mio fratello. Non sta bene. Mi chiama spesso. *It was my brother. He's not well. He often calls me.*
KARL I'm sorry.	KARL Mi dispiace. *I'm sorry.*
SARAH No, it's fine. It's fine. I mean, it's not really fine, it is what it is and there being no parents now and us being over here, it's my job to keep an eye over him. I mean not my job, obviously, I'm glad to do it . . .	SARAH No, va bene. Va bene. Cioè, in realtà non va bene. Le cose stanno come stanno e poi visto che non abbiamo più i genitori e adesso ha solo me, è mio dovere tenerlo d'occhio. Insomma, non sarebbe un mio dovere. Ovviamente sono contenta di farlo . . . molto. *No, it's ok. It's ok. That is, it's not ok. Things are the way they are and given that we no longer have parents and now he has only me, it's my duty to keep an eye on him. In short, it wouldn't be my duty. Of course I'm happy to do it. . . very happy.*

In the extract above the meta-discursive function of 'I mean' is quite evident. It allows conversation to flow and bestows dubbed language with an air of naturalness and spontaneity (Romero-Fresco 2009: 45). However, discrepancies in the dubbing of discourse markers are relatively frequent; ultimately, viewers watching dubbed content agree to suspend disbelief, and hence make occasional compromises to enjoy their 'diegetic experience' (Romero-Fresco 2009: 57).

Formulaic language in dubbing

Along with Guillot (2016), several studies on social rituals in films and TV series and their Italian dubbed versions (Bonsignori *et al.* 2011, 2012; Bonsignori and Bruti 2014b, 2015) have revealed that conversational routines are strategically employed in audiovisual dialogue and tend to be translated in most cases. Specifically, corpus-based analyses have confirmed that routines play an important role in the pragmatic construction of orality both in original and dubbed dialogue, although they have also acknowledged that discrepancies in linguistic mapping across languages do occur. These often result in socio-pragmatic shifts, neutralization or omissions. In the case of greetings, for example, shifts entail changes from one time expression to another, or from phatic expressions to vocatives. Familiarizers—which are more numerous in English (e.g. 'mate', 'dude', 'pal' and the like) than in Italian—are often omitted, and stylistic variations between different levels of formality often occur.

Based on the findings of a small corpus-based study of original Italian films (Bonsignori *et al.* 2011; Bonsignori *et al.* 2012), the representation of greetings and leave-takings would appear to be handled in similar ways in original and dubbed films, both in English and Italian—thus confirming the role that these items play as key markers of orality in both. Comparison of dubbed and original cinematic Italian shows that *ciao* is the most frequent greeting in both registers. Differences are found when looking at the second most frequent greeting in these two varieties (i.e. *salve* in dubbed Italian and *buongiorno* in its original filmic counterpart). For leave-takings, *ciao* appears to be also the most frequently employed formula in both modes, but *ci vediamo*, which is quite frequent in dubbing, never occurs in Italian filmic speech. The same results apply also in dubbed television series, 'possibly because [*salve* and *ci vediamo*] obliterate class, gender, age, and formality differences, acting as a kind of *passe-partout* form' (Bonsignori and Bruti 2015: 109). These results tie in with Pavesi's idea that the language of dubbing follows 'the third norm' (1996: 128), i.e. dubbese adheres neither to the source nor to the target language, but to a third language that strengthens formulaic language and translational clichés.

Summary

This chapter has discussed the main features of spoken discourse and conversational interaction in audiovisual dialogue and translation. The organizational structure of conversation proves to be more complex to mediate in subtitling where, due to space constraints, it is frequently altered—with inevitable and serious consequences in terms of the way in which interpersonal dynamics and characterization in the subtitled version may differ from the original film.

The number of expressive and orality markers is reduced in both subtitling and dubbing, although in distinct ways and for different reasons. In subtitling, their meaning can sometimes be retrieved thanks to the other semiotic channels, whereas in dubbing they are preserved when used in turn initial and turn final position, even though this does not necessarily result in natural-sounding translations.

Formulaic speech acts like greeting, parting, and wishing-well routines are used strategically in audiovisual diegesis as keys to orality. They are always translated, although they may sometimes result in differences between the representation of power relationships and relative closeness between interactants in the original and translated dialogues.

Further reading

Baños, R. (2014) 'Orality Markers in Spanish Native and Dubbed Sitcoms: Pretended Spontaneity and Prefabricated Orality', *Meta* 59(2): 406–435 | *This article discusses the idiosyncratic features of audiovisual dialogue in translated and non-translated texts, drawing on corpus-based results—a relatively under-represented methodology in AVT.*

Guillot, M. N. (2016) 'Communicative Rituals and Audiovisual Translation. Representation of Otherness in Film Subtitles', *Meta* 61(3): 606–628 | *Representation of spontaneity is a concept used here to explore how conversational routines are constructed in fictional dialogue vis-à-vis translated conversational interaction.*

Remael, A. (2003) 'Mainstream Narrative Film Dialogue and Subtitling', in Y. Gambier (ed.) 'Screen Translation', special issue of *The Translator* 9(2): 225–247 | *This paper delivers an original study of the impact that the structural organization of fictional conversation (and its translation) has on the narrative dynamics of filmic texts.*

Valdeón, R. A. (2011) 'Dysfluencies in Simulated English Dialogue and Their Neutralization in Dubbed Spanish', *Perspectives: Studies in Translatology* 19(3): 221–232 | *Three different types of dysfluencies (interruptions, unfinished sentences and repeats) are examined to gauge their contribution to the representation of orality in English TV series and their Spanish dubbed versions.*

Related topics

3   Subtitling on the cusp of its futures
4   Investigating dubbing: learning from the past, looking to the future
16 Pragmatics and audiovisual translation
18 Sociolinguistics and linguistic variation in audiovisual translation
20 Corpus-based audiovisual translation studies: ample room for development

References

Baños, R. (2014) 'Orality Markers in Spanish Native and Dubbed Sitcoms: Pretended Spontaneity and Prefabricated Orality', *Meta* 59(2): 406–435.
Baños, R. and F. Chaume (2009) 'Prefabricated Orality. A Challenge in Audiovisual Translation', in M. G. Marrano, G. Nadiani and C. Rundle (eds) *The Translation of Dialects in Multimedia*, special issue of *Intralinea*. Available online: http://www.intralinea.org/specials/article/Prefabricated_Orality [last access 20 December 2017].
Biber, D. (1988) *Variation across Speech and Writing*, Cambridge: Cambridge University Press.
Blini, L. and F. Matte Bon (1996) 'Osservazioni sui meccanismi di formazione de sottotitoli', in C. Heiss and R. M. Bollettieri Bosinelli (eds) *Traduzione multimediale per il cinema, la televisione, la scena*, Bologna: Clueb, 317–332.
Bonsignori, V. (2009) 'Transcribing Film Dialogue: From Orthographic to Prosodic Transcription', in M. Freddi and M. Pavesi (eds) *Analysing Audiovisual Dialogue. Linguistic and Translational Insights*, Bologna: Clueb, 185–200.
Bonsignori V. and S. Bruti (2014a) 'Across Lingua-Cultures: Introductions and Wishes in Subtitled TV Series', in B. Garzelli and M. Baldo (eds) *Subtitling and Intercultural Communication. European Languages and Beyond*, Pisa: ETS, 77–100.
Bonsignori V. and S. Bruti (2014b) 'How People Greet Each Other in TV Series and Dubbing', in M. Pavesi, M. Formentelli and E. Ghia (eds) *The Languages of Dubbing. Mainstream Audiovisual Translation in Italy*, Bern: Peter Lang, 89–111.
Bonsignori V. and S. Bruti (2015) 'Conversational Routines across Languages: The Case of Greetings and Leave-takings in Original and Dubbed Films', in J. Díaz Cintas and J. Neves (eds) *Audiovisual Translation: Taking Stock*, Newcastle upon Tyne: Cambridge Scholars Publishing, 28–44.
Bonsignori V., S. Bruti and S. Masi (2011) 'Formulae across Languages: English Greetings, Leave-takings and Good Wishes in Dubbed Italian', in A. Serban, A. Matamala and J. M. Lavaur (eds) *Audiovisual Translation in Close-up. Practical and Theoretical Approaches*, Bern: Peter Lang, 23–44.
Bonsignori V., S. Bruti and S. Masi (2012) 'Exploring Greetings and Leave-takings in Original and Dubbed Language', in P. Orero and A. Remael (eds) *Audiovisual Translation and Media Accessibility at the Crossroads*, Amsterdam & New York: Rodopi, 357–379.
Bruti, S. (2015) 'Teaching the Use of Pragmatic Routines through Audiovisual Material', in B. Crawford Camiciottoli and I. Fortanet-Gómez (eds) *Multimodal Analysis in Academic Settings. From Research to Teaching*, London & New York: Routledge, 213–237.
Bruti, S. and M. Pavesi (2008) 'Interjections in Translated Italian: Looking for Traces of Dubbed Language' in A. Martelli and V. Pulcini (eds) *Investigating English with Corpora. Studies in Honour of Maria Teresa Prat*, Monza: Polimetrica, 207–222.
Bruti, S. and S. Zanotti (2012) 'Orality Markers in Professional and Amateur Subtitling: The Case of Vocatives and Address Pronouns', in C. Buffagni and B. Garzelli (eds) *Film Translation from East to West. Dubbing, Subtitling and Didactic Practice*, Bern: Peter Lang, 167–192.
Bruti, S. and S. Zanotti (2013) 'Frontiere della traduzione audiovisiva: il fenomeno del *fansubbing* e i suoi aspetti linguistici', in C. Bosisio and S. Cavagnoli (eds) *Atti del XII Congresso internazionale AItLA, Comunicare le discipline attraverso le lingue: prospettiva traduttiva, didattica, socioculturale*, Perugia: Guerra, 119–142.

Bussi Parmiggiani, E. (2002) 'Forme di attenzione e pluricodicità nel film sottotitolato', in A. Caimi (ed.) *Cinema: Paradiso delle lingue. I sottotitoli nell'apprendimento linguistico*, special issue of *Rassegna italiana di linguistica applicata* 34(1–2): 177–198.

Chaume, F. (2004) *Cine y traducción*, Madrid: Cátedra.

Chaume, F. (2012) *Audiovisual Translation: Dubbing*. Manchester: St. Jerome.

Conklin, K. and N. Schmitt (2012) 'The Processing of Formulaic Language', *Annual Review of Applied Linguistics* 32: 45–61.

Cuenca, M. J. (2006) 'Interjections and Pragmatic Errors', *Meta* 51(1): 20–35.

Cuenca, M. J. (2008) 'Pragmatic Markers in Contrast: The Case of *Well*', *Journal of Pragmatics* 40(8): 1373–1391.

Díaz Cintas, J. (2012) 'Subtitling. Theory, Practice, Research', in C. Millan and F. Bartrina (eds) *The Routledge Handbook of Translation Studies*, London & New York: Routledge, 273–287.

Díaz Cintas, J. and A. Remael (2007) *Audiovisual Translation: Subtitling*, Manchester, St. Jerome.

Forchini, P. (2010) '"Well, uh no. I mean, you know". Discourse Markers in Movie Conversation', in L. Bogucki and K. Kredens (eds) *Perspectives on Audiovisual Translation*, Bern: Peter Lang, 45–59.

Forchini, P. (2012) *Movie Language Revisited. Evidence from Multi-dimensional Analysis and Corpora*, Bern: Peter Lang.

Freddi, M. and C. Malagori (2014) 'Discourse Markers in Audiovisual Translation', in A. Maiorani and C. Christie (eds) *Multimodal Epistemologies: Towards an Integrated Framework*, London: Routledge, 191–209.

Freddi, M. and M. Pavesi (eds) (2009) *Analysing Audiovisual Dialogue. Linguistic and Translational Insights*, Bologna: Clueb.

Gottlieb, H. (1998) 'Subtitling' in M. Baker (ed.) *Routledge Encyclopedia of Translation Studies*, London & New York: Routledge, 244–248.

Gregory, M. and S. Carroll (1978) *Language and Situation: Language Varieties and their Social Contexts*, London: Routledge and Kegan Paul.

Guillot, M. N. (2012) 'Stylisation and Representation in Subtitles: Can Less Be More?', *Perspectives: Studies in Translatology* 20(4): 479–494.

Guillot, M. N. (2016) 'Communicative Rituals and Audiovisual Translation—Representation of Otherness in Film Subtitles', *Meta* 61(3): 606–628.

Hatim, B. and I. Mason (1997) 'Politeness in Screen Translating', in L. Venuti (ed.) *The Translation Studies Reader*, London & New York: Routledge, 430–445.

Herbst, T. (1994) *Linguistische Aspekte der Synchronisation von Fernsehserien. Phonetik, Textlinguistik, Übersetzungstheorie*, Niemeyer: Tübingen.

Kovačič, I. (1996) 'Subtitling Strategies: A Flexible Hierarchy of Priorities', in C. Heiss and R. M. Bollettieri Bosinelli (eds) *Traduzione multimediale per il cinema, la televisione, la scena*, Bologna: Clueb, 297–305.

Massidda, S. (2015) *Audiovisual Translation in the Digital Age*, London: Palgrave.

Mauranen, A. and P. Kujamäki (eds) (2004) *Translation Universals: Do they Exist?*, Amsterdam & Philadelphia: John Benjamins.

Moreno Jaén, M. and C. Pérez Basanta (2009) 'Developing Conversational Competence through Language Awareness and Multimodality: The Use of DVDs', *ReCALL* 21(3): 283–301.

Pavesi M. (1996) 'L'allocuzione nel doppiaggio dall'inglese all'italiano', in C. Heiss and R. M. Bollettieri Bosinelli (eds) *Traduzione multimediale per il cinema, la televisione e la scena*, Bologna: Clueb, 117–130.

Pavesi, M. (2005) *La traduzione filmica. Aspetti del parlato doppiato dall'inglese all'italiano*, Roma: Carocci.

Pavesi, M. (2012) 'The Potentials of Audiovisual Dialogue for Second Language Learners', in P. Alderete-Díez, L. Incalcaterra McLoughlin, L. Ní Dhonnchadha and D. Ní Uigín (eds) *Translation, Technology and Autonomy in Language Teaching and Learning*, Bern: Peter Lang, 155–174.

Pérez-González, L. (2007) 'Appraising Dubbed Conversation. Systemic Functional Insights into the Construal of Naturalness in Translated Film Dialogue', *The Translator* 13(1): 1–38.

Pérez-González, L. (2014) *Audiovisual Translation: Theories, Methods, and Issues*, London & New York: Routledge.

Quaglio, P. (2009a) *Television Dialogue: The Sitcom* Friends vs. *Natural Conversation*, Amsterdam & Philadelphia: John Benjamins.

Quaglio, P. (2009b) 'Vague Language in the Situation Comedy *Friends* vs. Natural Conversation', in M. Freddi and M. Pavesi (eds) *Analysing Audiovisual Dialogue. Linguistic and Translational Insights*, Bologna: Clueb, 75–91.

Remael, A. (2003) 'Mainstream Narrative Film Dialogue and Subtitling', in Y. Gambier (ed.) 'Screen Translation', special issue of *The Translator* 9(2): 225–247.

Rodríguez Martín, M. E. (2010) 'Exploring Conversational Grammar through Films in the ELT Classroom: A Corpus-based Approach', in M. Moreno Jaén, F. Serrano Valverde and M. Calzada Pérez (eds) *Exploring New Paths in Language Pedagogy. Lexis and Corpus-based Language Teaching*, London: Equinox, 245–258.

Rodríguez Martín, M. E. and M. Moreno Jaén (2009) 'Teaching Conversation through Films: A Comparison of Conversational Features and Collocations in the BNC and a Micro-corpus of Movies', *International Journal of Learning* 16(7): 445–458.

Romero-Fresco P. (2006) 'The Spanish Dubbese: A Case of (Un)idiomatic *Friends*', *JoSTrans: The Journal of Specialised Translation* 6: 134–151. Available online: http://www.jostrans.org/issue06/art_romero_fresco.php [last accessed 20 December 2017].

Romero-Fresco P. (2009) 'Naturalness in the Spanish Dubbing Language: A Case of not-so-close *Friends*', *Meta* 54(1): 49–72.

Schiffrin, D. (1987) *Discourse Markers*, Cambridge: Cambridge University Press.

Taylor, C. (1999) 'Look who's Talking. An Analysis of Film Dialogue as a Variety of Spoken Discourse', in L. Lombardo, L. Haarman, J. Morley and C. Taylor (eds) *Massed Medias. Linguistic Tools for the Interpreting Media Discourse*, Milano: Led, 247–278.

Taylor, C. (2002) 'The Subtitling of Film Dialogue: An Economic Use of Language', in G. Iamartino, M. L. Bignami and C. Pagetti (eds) *The Economy Principle in English: Linguistic, Literary and Cultural Perspectives*, Milano: Unicopli, 278–288.

Tirkkonen-Condit, S. (2004) 'Unique Items: Over or Under-represented in Translated Language?', in A. Mauranen and P. Kujamäki (eds) *Translation Universals: Do They Exist?*, Amsterdam & Philadelphia: John Benjamins, 177–184.

Valdeón, R. A. (2009) 'Imitating the Conversational Mode in Audiovisual Fiction: Performance Phenomena and Non-clausal Units', in C. Amador and A. Nunes (eds) *The Representation of the Spoken Mode in Fiction*, New York: Edwin Mellen, 197–221.

Valdeón R. A. (2011) 'Dysfluencies in Simulated English Dialogue and their Neutralization in Dubbed Spanish', *Perspectives: Studies in Translatology* 19(3): 221–232.

Zabalbeascoa, P. (2012) 'Translating Dialogues in Audiovisual Fiction', in J. Brumme and A. Espunya (eds) *The Translation of Fictive Dialogue*, Amsterdam: Rodopi, 63–78.

Filmography

Brothers and Sisters (2006–2011) Jon Robin Baitz. IMDb entry: http://www.imdb.com/title/tt0758737/?ref_=nv_sr_1

Green Street (2005) Lexi Alexander. IMDb entry: http://www.imdb.com/title/tt0385002/?ref_=fn_al_tt_1

Love Actually (2003) Richard Curtis. IMDb entry: http://www.imdb.com/title/tt0314331/?ref_=nv_sr_1

Match Point (2005) Woody Allen. IMDb entry: http://www.imdb.com/title/tt0416320/?ref_=fn_al_tt_1

Notting Hill (1999) Roger Michell. IMDb entry: http://www.imdb.com/title/tt0125439/?ref_=nv_sr_1

The King's Speech (2010) Tom Hooper. IMDb entry: http://www.imdb.com/title/tt1504320/?ref_=nv_sr_1

Sliding Doors (1998) Peter Howitt. IMDb entry: http://www.imdb.com/title/tt0120148/?ref_=nv_sr_1

14
Psycholinguistics and perception in audiovisual translation

Louise Fryer

Introduction

This chapter explores audiovisual translation (AVT) in relation to models of psycholinguistics and cognitive perception. It introduces the concept of media accessibility as embracing various types of translation—namely sign language interpreting, subtitling for the deaf and hard of hearing (SDH) and audio description (AD) for people who are blind or partially sighted—that enable users with a sensory disability to access audiovisual media content. It focuses on the subjective nature of perception, and addresses Gambier's (2009) concerns about loss in AVT, demonstrating how language and other forms of knowledge can compensate for the loss of information in sensory modes that cannot be perceived directly by the user. It argues that access modes of AVT such as AD and SDH are no less prone to loss or subjectivity than lexical modes of translation. It also discusses how the concept of immersion or presence can be of use in measuring the efficacy of AD and SDH and how Gibson's (1979) concept of affordances and an understanding of visual perception can help describers make choices in content selection. This chapter therefore addresses Vermeer's (1989) concern as to how translators choose between different translation options that may appear to be equally possible and appropriate.

Media accessibility

Most AVT modes are interlingual, translating the foreign source language into a different target language so that viewers who do not speak the former will be able to understand the dialogue by means of subtitles, dubbing or voice-over. However, the access modes of AVT are not only intralingual, but also intermodal. They translate information from one sensory mode to another, leaving the target language unchanged. For this reason, some scholars have wondered whether access modes are really translations at all. Gambier (2009) for example suggests these types of translation may be better thought of as adaptation, manipulation, transfer or remake. However, since the 1970s, people who are D/deaf or who have impaired hearing have been able to access the audio component of an audiovisual product through visually presented words via subtitling and sign language interpreting. Since the mid-1990s, the visual elements have been made audible for people who are blind or whose vision is impaired through AD. Accessibility is now acknowledged as an umbrella term that encompasses all modes of translation for minorities with sensory disabilities (Díaz Cintas and Anderman 2008).

It is also recognized that the access modes go beyond their primary purpose. They are useful not only for people with specific needs but also more broadly for anyone in a disabling situation who is unable to access the full AV content. For example, hearing people trying to listen in a noisy environment might welcome subtitles and sighted people might wish to listen to an AD version of a film while driving. Young children acquiring language, migrants or other non-native speakers might benefit also from the added context and rich vocabulary that AD provides. Equally, non-native speakers might find the dialogue easier to follow if they watch the same language subtitles (captions) as they watch a television programme or a film. Yet, if much of the research in the field of media accessibility has been concerned with discovering ways in which to maximize the media experience for people previously excluded, it has also shed light on the way media are experienced by people who are able to access both audio and visual channels.

Current debates

In his book *Enforcing Normalcy* (1995), Lennard Davis examines how cultural assumptions govern our conception of people with disabilities and drive the proliferation of 'ableist' discourses in society. '[N]ormalcy', Davis argues, 'is constructed to create the "problem" of the disabled person' (1995: 1) and boundaries between the abled and the disabled are constructed and maintained through a process of cultural construction. Ultimately, understanding disability requires a deep understanding of the 'able' or 'normal'. Against this background, a recent survey by the Erasmus-plus-funded research project ADLAB PRO (2017) sampled tutors and trainers of 192 AD courses and found that 'knowledge of the needs of the visually impaired' was ranked as the third most important competence that should be taught to trainee describers. Following Davis's logic, in order to understand blindness, it is necessary to expand our understanding of sight. Snyder (2005) urges describers to develop their powers of observation, while Fryer (2016: 60) advocates 'that describers should reflect the casual observation of the average member of the sighted audience but develop their writing skills and grasp of language so as to be able to convey that visual information effectively.' In order to do so, it is important that describers have a model of how 'normal' sight works.

Audio description as constrained translation

AD is a form of constrained translation (Mayoral *et al.* 1988). Users cannot rely exclusively on the description, and need to make use of other types of information that they receive directly from the source text. Crucially, the AD must fit within the time constraints of the source soundtrack: descriptions can only be incorporated at those points where they do not cause overlap with the other channels on the soundtrack, especially the dialogue. In screen modes such as TV and film, this means that the describer should generate 'in times' and 'out times' in their script to tie the descriptions to particular moments in the soundtrack. In live AD modes—e.g. theatre, opera and sport—this timing is not absolute, but relative and putative. The describer will select two cues usually from the dialogue, but sometimes from non-verbal sound effects or visual cues, such as lighting; it should be noted, however, that the describer should be prepared to improvise, should the timing change. The fact that describers need to maintain synchrony with the source text in various ways means that they will have less freedom than lexical translators.

Unsurprisingly, in light of these constraints, much of the literature on AD has focused on the process through which describers decide which of the many elements in the visual array should be selected or omitted from their description (Rai *et al.* 2010, Greening and Rolph 2007, Remael and Vercauteren 2007). Writing about interlingual lexical translation, Vermeer notes that '[w]e still know too little about the functioning of the brain, and hence of culture and language, to be able to rely on much more than intuition when choosing between different variants which may appear to the individual translator to be equally possible and appropriate' (1989: 231). Recent advances in neuroscience, however, mean that much more is now known about the brain, although there is still a long way to go before we are able to fully understand how language is processed (Feldman 2008). Access modes of AVT, in particular, have raised questions about user reception. Although the translator and the target audience are 'part of the same speech community' (Piety 2004), AD and SDH users may have no direct sensory experience of what is being subtitled or described. Consequently, neuroscientists, psychologists and translators are beginning to recognize that the audio and visual components of AV media do not function independently; instead, the meaning conveyed through each of these communicative channels influences and interacts with the other.

Multisensory integration

Humans are skilled at combining different sensory codes of meaning into a coherent whole through a process known as multisensory integration. The effect on people with no sensory impairment is thought to be cumulative, such that each sensory mode adds an extra level of understanding. For example, in the struggle to hear comments of an individual against the background chatter of a cocktail party, watching the speaker's lips moving corresponds to an increase in the volume of the sound of interest of 15–20 decibels (Sumby and Pollack 1954). However, there is a hierarchy amongst the senses. Sight is prioritized over sound, such that auditory information is misattributed to a visual stimulus within a certain temporal window. For example, the 'ventriloquist effect' (e.g. Choe *et al.* 1975, Bertelson 1998) occurs when we mistakenly attribute the speech we hear as coming from the mouth we see moving, that is the mouth of the dummy rather than from the motionless mouth of the ventriloquist. In other words there is a visual bias of auditory location. A more complex explanation of the process thought to underlie multisensory integration is given below.

Temporal simultaneity is important for audiovisual binding to take effect, such that the audio and visual signals are recognized as belonging to the same event. It has been recently discovered that semantic congruency—loosely understood as the harmony or agreement between the meanings of several stimuli—also plays a role (Laurienti *et al.* 2004) in facilitating this recognition. We are more likely to recognize that a sound and an image are part of the same event if it makes sense that they should be so. For example if we hear a gun and see a body crumple, we will infer that the person has been shot, especially if we are watching a Western, the victim is a bank robber and the gunman a sheriff.

Eramudugolla *et al.* (2011: 60) have shown that speech is a particularly important example of multisensory integration because of its behavioural relevance to humans and the existence of specific brain regions that appear to be specifically tuned to auditory speech and lip gestures. Most modes of AVT are concerned with translating speech, and that is, to some extent, also the case with some of the access modalities. As Kruger explains, '[a]udio description . . . is substantially different from other AVT modes like dubbing and subtitling, primarily because the focus in other modes is on dialogue' (2012: 232).

Yet, because AD is delivered orally and is a text to be listened to, rather than read, it shares many qualities with speech—as will be further elaborated below.

Context

Translation of any kind and, in particular, AVT, does not exist in a vacuum, but occurs within a given context. The context might be physical, as is the case with AD taking place in a cinema, museum, theatre or sports stadium, and will vary along technical and social lines according to the medium being described:

- AD in a cinema is pre-recorded, mixed with the soundtrack, and closed—i.e. the user chooses to hear it via headphones or an application on his or her mobile phone. By contrast AD on TV is pre-recorded and mixed with the soundtrack and can be open—such that, when selected, it is heard by everyone in the room. AD in UK theatres is usually live, closed and received via a headset that does not fully cover the ears, so that the sounds from the stage are heard naturally, whereas in French theatres, it may be recorded but triggered live by a technician to keep it in synchrony with the dialogue. Finally, AD in a museum might be delivered live and heard naturally by anyone within earshot.
- The context might also vary along social lines. AD users might be attending a play with friends, watching TV at home with their family or via video on demand (VoD) on their computer, alone. Users might know the describer personally—as happens often in the theatre—or not—in the case of film or TV AD that, in many countries, is delivered by a voice talent.

At any rate, context is important because it is a 'cognitive phenomenon' (Aijmer and Simon-Vandenbergen 2004: 1783). The user's understanding of the AD message will be affected not only by what the describer says, but also by 'the mental states (what is known or believed)' (*ibid.*) that the user brings to the experience.

Mental models

Psychologists (Schubert *et al.* 2001, Jones 2007, Pinchbeck and Stevens 2005) have postulated that data is organized in the brain through schemata. A schema is a shortcut by which the brain groups together everything a person has discovered, either directly through their senses (bottom up) or indirectly through their intellect (top down), about a person, place or object. The notion of *Umwelt* (von Uexküll 1940), understood as the perceptual world in which an organism exists and acts as a subject, usefully captures the influence of our environment on our experiential understanding and, ultimately, the expectations that individuals derive from the latter. Attending a Shakespeare tragedy, for example, AD users would not expect to laugh; should laughter feature in a performance of *Hamlet*, for example, it would be harder to process because it would be unexpected.

Schemas are said to create a reference frame into which we can slot the incoming data. They also present us with scripts (Schank and Abelson 1975), which activate for us a set of words we are likely to hear in that context. This can, for example, ease the potential confusion that polysemous words that have multiple meanings would have otherwise presented. In a written translation these will be homographs: words that look the same, but sound different, such as 'tear' (as in a drop of fluid excreted from the lacrimal gland when we weep) and 'tear' (as in the verb to rip or pull apart). In a description, which is orally delivered, confusion may more likely stem from homophones that sound the same even if written differently. In a forest setting we might climb a 'beech'. We are unlikely to climb a 'beach' even at the seaside. In the absence of a description of the location we may struggle to understand the word 'beech', upsetting the effectiveness of the translation by delaying or obstructing our ability to process it.

Congruency

One of the reasons why mental models are important is because the AD must be congruent with the context. Bearing this in mind can help describers select which elements to prioritize in their AD. For example, the AD of a horror film should prioritize ingredients essential to the horror genre in appropriate language. To describe a 'witch's familiar' as a pussycat would be incongruent and conflict with the user's expectation. But schemata can also save the describer valuable time. For example, the soundtrack of a horror film will convey scary audio information through the music, the creaking of floorboards, the hooting of an owl, the amplified heartbeat of the protagonist, that may need little explanation from the describer, while contributing tension (Fryer 2010). This may be because the user fills in the missing associated visual information from their *Umwelt*.

AD and emotion

Research by Ramos (2015) demonstrated that sound was able to induce symptoms of fear (measured by increase in heart rate) in blind participants, supporting research by Rickard (2004), which showed that music and sound cues in horror films increase galvanic skin response (sweating) in sighted participants. Rickard cites this as evidence supporting Schachter and Singer's (1962) cognitive theory of emotion, according to which the type of emotion is determined cognitively, while the strength to which that emotion is felt is determined by bodily arousal. In the same way Fryer and Freeman (2014) found that blind people were able to state which emotion a film clip was trying to induce, even with no AD, but they only actively *felt* that emotion when listening to the film clip with AD. However, this was not the case for films designed to induce disgust. Ramos (2015), who has conducted relevant research on this issue, argues that 'disgust-evoking scenes are not associated with any film genre in particular, and therefore lack concrete sound cues' (2015: 83). It could therefore be said that viewers exposed to this type of scene lack specific scripts and schemata.

Fryer and Freeman (2014) further showed that AD users were more likely to feel frightened if the AD for a horror film was delivered by a human voice than by a synthesized voice. A human voice was able to add another layer of meaning beyond the semantic, through prosody.

Prosody

Wildgruber *et al.* (2006) point out that information about emotional states is generally given through non-verbal signals. These may be apprehended visually, as is the case with facial expression, eye-gaze, gesture, body posture and relative spatial position between two or more characters (for example, facing each other or turned away). Non-verbal signals may also be apprehended aurally—e.g. through intonation, inflection, pitch and pace, namely prosody. AD users can use prosody to understand a character's emotional frame of mind, not simply from the dialogue but also from the cadences that the describer or voice talent uses to deliver the AD. Although some research has already highlighted the importance of prosody in oral forms of translation (Malmkjær 2005, Kübler and Volanschi 2012), recent research in neuroscience (Leonard and Chang 2014) has highlighted its importance in our cognitive architecture by identifying specific groups of neurons that are primed to be activated by changes in a speaker's tone. These particular neurons—which respond to relative shifts in pitch, either upwards or downwards—are located in the superior temporal gyrus of the brain together with other neurons that are believed to process context-dependent aspects of speech. It is clear then, that audio describers should pay as much attention to the oral as to the lexical-semantic aspect of the AD message, as a series of words can have its meaning completely reversed by a change of inflection. Take for example a small boy who wants to eat some brightly coloured sweets. His parents tell him that he cannot have the blue ones because they make him cross. The little boy thinks for a moment, then he says: 'It's not HAVING the blue sweets that makes me cross; it's NOT having the blue sweets that makes me cross'. This illustration further feeds into this analysis of mental models, psycholinguistics and AVT from its reference to colour.

Colour and cognition

AD guidelines in different countries diverge on several points (Rai *et al.* 2010) but all agree that describing colour is important. This may seem curious for a translation mode primarily aimed at people with little or no visual perception. Bertrand Russell (1917) distinguished between 'knowledge by description' and 'knowledge by acquaintance' arguing there is no way of going from one to the other. It is a question fundamental to psychology and philosophy (and to AVT) whether propositional and experiential knowledge are of equal value. As Hayhoe (2017) points out in his discussion of blind people's experiences in museums, the importance of art—which I extend here to include the visual element of AV material—goes beyond the directly perceptual to include personal, cultural and symbolic meanings from which blindness need not automatically exclude, providing that the same information is presented in a different (i.e. verbal) mode. Although a person who has been blind since birth cannot know what red looks like, they may still understand that culturally red is associated with heat, passion and danger. It would be important to know if, for example, a character was wearing a red dress. Yet the meaning of red would depend on the cultural context of the film as red is associated with good luck in Asian cultures but with the communist revolution in Russia.

These cultural variations of colour have been of particular interest to psycholinguists. The Sapir-Whorf hypothesis (see Kay and Kempton 1984 for a review) which is also known as 'the doctrine of linguistic relativity' (*ibid.*: 65) proposes that language is culturally determined and even our very thought processes are constrained by the sounds or visual appearance of the words with which we think. For example, the Western categorization of colour into the 'seven colours of the rainbow' is not universal but culturally determined: Isaac Newton, the seventeenth-century English scientist who viewed the spectrum of light waves through a prism, chose to divide it into seven because that was regarded as a 'magic' number at the time. The number of colours 'seen' in a rainbow varies today across cultures. People in the Baltic States 'see' a rainbow as having two colours, red and blue, while in China a rainbow is considered to have five colours (Oldfield and Mitchinson 2013). Other studies argue for universal colour categories (e.g. Berlin and Kay 1969, Regier *et al.* 2015). Interestingly, Gilbert *et al.* (2006) found that the speed of identification of a green or blue square positioned with others of the alternate colour, was dependent on whether the square was presented in the left or right half of the visual field. The researchers concluded that people 'view the right (but not the left) half of their visual world through the lens of their native language' (2006: 489). Roberson *et al.* sought to 'shed light on whether language and cognition are coupled or separable in the domain of color categorization and perception' (2005: 4). By presenting different coloured stimuli to participants and asking them to name them, they showed that the Himba in Northern Namibia have five basic colour terms which more or less equate to the English terms red, white (including beige and yellow) black, blue (although these overlap) and green (including colours in the blue/green/purple range). They noted that the Himba's ability to discriminate, or at least the number of terms they have available to describe different hues is severely reduced. The researchers also found a relation between colour vocabulary and memory performance. Comparing speakers of different languages, they found that participants were more likely to remember stimuli that were most consistently named in their own language. Roberson *et al.* conclude that '[w]hat appears to be universal, in this case, is the tight link between naming and memory' (2005: 21).

Visual and verbal meaning

Some scholars (e.g. Braun 2008) have argued that translating images into words is more problematic than unimodal, lexical translation. However, as more is understood about psycholinguistics that position seems increasingly untenable. Mental models make clear the extent to which all translation users and translators are individual. As we each build up our own schemata based on our personal interactions and experiences, each of us develops our own mental lexicon. Jean Aitchison (2012) has argued cogently against what she calls the fixed meaning assumption: the idea that each word has a single uncontested meaning that is universally agreed. This contention is consistent with the views of American film critic, James Monaco: focusing on the relationship between pictures and meaning, Monaco advocates the iconicity of images, noting that whereas 'a picture bears some direct relationship with what it signifies, a word seldom does' (Monaco 2009: 176). However, that is not to say that an image has a single uncontested meaning. Monaco considers the image of a rose and explores the way its connotations vary depending on how it is shown by the filmmaker, whether it is in crisp or soft focus, with its thorns hidden or on display. A red rose has a particular meaning in Western culture where it is usually associated with love but in a historical film about the English Wars of the Roses, the colour of the rose would have a different connotation—a red rose being associated with the House of Lancaster which was at war with the House of York, whose own emblem was a white rose. The audio describer would need to focus on the colour rather than any other aspect of the rose, although they would not be expected to go into a long explanation regarding the socio-historical implication of the rose which may or may not be understood by every member of the audience, whether sighted or blind. The argument here is that the audiovisual translator, just as the translator of any other type of text, cannot control the reception of their translation. It is not possible to guarantee that the meaning one person attaches to specific words and phrases will be the same as another's, not now and certainly not over time, as meanings drift and associations change. This is not, however, unique to receivers of audiovisual translations. Even audiences of the original will create their own personal variant of the film they are watching based on their knowledge, prejudices and assumptions (Remael 2012).

Perception

Perception is how we synthesize the multiple inputs we receive from our senses in order to, literally, make sense of the world. In the nineteenth century Hermann von Helmholtz (1977) defined perception as an active way of drawing unconscious inferences from the data we take in through our eyes, ears, mouth, nose and skin. Bruner and Postman (1949) and Neisser (1976) developed the theory of perceptual hypothesis, according to which we make assumptions based on our experiences and test them against our sensory data. For example, if we see steam coming from a cup of coffee we hypothesize that it is too hot to drink. If we touch the cup, and a burning sensation on the pads of our fingers conveys confirmatory data, this reinforces the hypothesis. Next time, if we touch the cup, we will do so more carefully and perhaps blow on the liquid before taking a sip. Experience refines our hypothesis, such that we emphasize some aspects of the data (e.g. the density of the steam) and minimize others (e.g. the colour of the coffee). This function of filtering is designed to reduce cognitive load. Sensory data is inherently unstable and we constantly compare it against the permanent representations that are stored in the brain to allow us to infer and anticipate. The psychologist J. J. Gibson recognized that, despite our access to multiple sources of data, '[p]erception may or may not occur in the presence of information' (1979: 56). In other words, although the information is there, we do not necessarily notice it.

Visual perception: the importance of affordances

Gibson concentrated on visual perception and developed what he called an 'ecological' approach (1979) in recognition of the fact that we are part of our environment. We do not exist in a bubble, nor are we passive recipients of sensory data. Our pupils dilate and we look longer at things that we like. If we do not like what we see, we close our eyes or turn our heads or even walk away. Gibson distinguished between the qualities of objects (e.g. colour, texture, composition, size, shape, mass, elasticity, rigidity and mobility) and their 'affordances', i.e. what objects and environments enable us to do with them. He argues that our perception of things can be judged to be 'true' if we are able to engage with them successfully. For example, we may be able to describe to a blind person the qualities of a chair and tell them it is made of mahogany, with an ornate carved backrest and a seat upholstered in red brocade, when what they really want to know is whether or not anyone is sitting on it and whether it looks strong enough to take their weight, i.e. whether it affords them the opportunity to sit down.

Support for Gibson's model of visual perception comes from brain-anatomy studies (Gawande 2008) showing that 80 per cent of fibres that connect to the primary visual cortex come from brain regions associated with higher function such as memory; only 20 per cent come direct from the retina. This relates to a newer model of perception referred to as the 'brain's best guess' theory of perception (Gregory 2009), that likens the brain to a radio receiver as 'the mind integrates weak, rudimentary signals from a variety of sensory channels, information from past experiences, and hard-wired processes, and produces a sensory experience full of brain-provided colour, sound, texture, and meaning' (*ibid.*: 30). Gawande, like Gibson, concludes that 'perception is inference' (*ibid.*). Describers should therefore seek to give users the type and quantity of information such that they can infer and anticipate.

In line with the best-guess hypothesis, Kruger (2017) argues that when watching a film, viewers with no sensory impairment co-create the narrative using the same cognitive architecture by which they create their perception of reality. They 'fill in the gaps, predicting and assuming continuities even when absent' (Kruger 2017). This is clear from the developing language of film. Directors no longer show a tracking shot, following a visitor's progress as they step up to a door, knock on it and wait for it to be opened by the host, before the visitor steps in over the threshold. They simply show the guest approaching the door then cut to the guest indoors with the host. The audience fills in the rest. Furthermore, viewers identify with characters and indulge in embodied simulation such that they map a character's actions onto their own sensorimotor and neural representations (Gallese and Guerra 2012).

Audio description and the ecological approach to visual perception

Guidelines produced by the American organization Audio Description International (ADI) propose that the 'first rule of description' is to 'describe what you see' (Rai *et al.* 2010, Annexe 4). Too often, the focus in AD is on the visual. From Snyder's (2005) perspective, describers should make decisions on what to narrate on the basis of what can be seen around them, based on a WYSIWYS ('What You See Is What You Say') approach. According to blind academic Georgina Kleege (2015), this standpoint reveals what she calls a 'severe visual dependency', which is not unusual amongst the sighted given the extent to which our perceptual systems are dominated by our vision (see Posner *et al.* 1976 for a review). Yet Fryer (2010) and others (Remael 2012, Szarkowska and Orero 2014) have argued that 'sound as much as vision influences choices in AD' (Fryer 2010: 205). Although the goal of AD is to compensate verbally for the missing visual information, concentrating on what we see with our eyes may paradoxically not be the best way to do it. This raises the question of how to recognize the best way.

Using Gibson's concept of affordances, it is worth asking what audiovisual products afford. They might offer us the chance to become immersed in another world (e.g. a sci-fi film), to find out about another country (a documentary), to examine our own world more closely (a nature documentary); or just sit back and enjoy ourselves (a light comedy). Beyond the global question addressed to the audiovisual product as a whole, the same question might be then applied to the visual elements of each scene. For example, the magnified image of a venomous spider on a fingertip might make us wonder at the impact of the creature in relation to its size. Following Gibson, the AD can be deemed to be 'true' if the user is able to engage with the AD product successfully. That is, to respond to it in the same way as an audience member with no visual impairment.

Assessing impact

For a translation to be successful it must deliver 'an equivalent intended effect' (Lee 2008: 168). The difficulty comes in deciding how that equivalence should be assessed. The studies by Ramos (2015) and Fryer and Freeman (2014) cited above reflect attempts to introduce a scientific method for assessing impact, with AVT catching up with the moves made towards 'scientific' investigation of translation in the 1960s (e.g. Nida 1964). Use of existing psychological measures such as the Emotion Elicitation Scale (Gross and Levenson 1995) and the ITC Sense of Presence Inventory (Lessiter *et al.* 2001) allows the impact on audiences with and without sensory disabilities to be directly compared (Fryer and Freeman 2013). These measures rely on questionnaires and have been complemented by physiological measures such as heart rate and galvanic skin response in order to circumvent the limitations of post-hoc questionnaires—that have been criticized for being subjective and dependent on the user's memory. More complex measures that track psychophysiological responses in real time have also been explored. For example, Jan Louis Kruger and his colleagues (2016) have turned to neurophysiological signals using an electroencephalogram (EEG) that measures electrical activity in the brain. Specifically, they draw on a paradigm that discriminates between those who were more emotionally involved and those who were less so, as distinguished by the levels of coherence in electrical signals between the prefrontal cortex and posterior parietal cortex of the brain. The significance of those brain areas is that activity in the prefrontal cortex is associated with executive function (attention) and regulation of emotions while the posterior parietal cortex is associated with the imagination, particularly when we imagine ourselves to be someone else. Increased levels of coherence suggest greater control or increased inhibition in response to emotive stimuli resulting in suppression of the emotional response, while decreased coherence is associated with increased immersion (less suppression of emotional response).

Functional neural networks

Models of the way the brain works have moved from the idea of specialist regions dedicated to the processing of unique types of sensory data in favour of functional networks. These temporary links are thought to arise from the synchronous firing of neurons, increasing the probability that different modes of sensory data bind. This is the mechanism believed to underlie cognitive processes such as multisensory integration described above. Recent thinking suggests that this electrical brain activity reflects an evaluation of whether incoming data from different sensory channels is complementary and thus deserving of attention, or is redundant and should be suppressed (Senkowski et al. 2008). Brain regions are linked via a network of connected pathways that communicate through synchronized electrical activity. Oscillations in neuronal electrical activity are categorized into five frequency bands: delta (0.5–3.5 Hz), theta (4–7 Hz), alpha (8–12 Hz), beta (13–30 Hz) and gamma (>30Hz), (Gray et al. 1989). Imaging techniques, such as EEG, can show coherent frequencies suggesting that two or more regions are connected (Singer and Gray 1995). Measuring such activity allows us to 'see' how the synchrony or coherence changes according to cognitive tasks. Increased coherence in the beta band of the electrical signal is linked to less emotional involvement, because it implies the activation of the amygdala, a brain structure associated with attention that can limit emotional response. Reiser et al. (2012) argue that decreased functional coherence between the prefrontal cortex and posterior structures indicates a decoupling of the amygdala, in other words, a disconnection of the top-down control that prevents us becoming emotionally involved. The more loose the connection, the less inhibited our response to emotion-stimulating data will be.

Beta-coherence therefore is believed to decrease with immersion and increase with less emotional involvement (Reiser et al. 2012). Kruger et al. (2016) found that beta-coherence was lower for students watching a subtitled than an unsubtitled film clip, suggesting that the subtitled version was more affective. This is in line with self-report measures used in other studies (e.g. Wissmath et al. 2009). The benefit of physiological measures is that they are continuous and can measure changing emotional states over the course of a film. They are also thought to be objective, as responses cannot be faked to please the researcher. The disadvantages are that physiological measures are complex to administer, analyse and interpret.

Tim Smith (2013, 2015) has used eye tracking to try to understand how our eyes engage with the moving image and eye tracking has been seized on by members of the AVT research community, such that translations can reflect more accurately the 'natural' process of visual perception (Orero and Vilaró 2012, Di Giovanni 2014). However, as Di Giovanni herself points out, eye tracking can help to identify which parts of the screen to focus on, but not how much of that information to convey. Her participants reacted most positively to the ADs that included the most detail, which were those constructed in line with the eye-tracking analysis. However it has also been argued that too much detail can overburden the user, contributing too much to their cognitive load. While eye tracking may have a role to play in guiding some describer decisions, it cannot compare the impact of original and translated versions on people with and without sight.

Presence

Instead both types of audience can and have been compared using another measure borrowed from psychology. One that is based on 'presence' or a feeling of immersion that is so strong that we forget that what we are witnessing is a mediated experience (Lombard and Ditton 1997). It is presence that is disrupted by any form of incongruence discussed above. Presence was developed as a measure to test the efficacy of virtual environments. Much like those who doubt the efficacy of the access modes of AVT, early presence researchers (e.g. Zelter 1992) assumed that the more sensory channels a virtual environment replicated, the more immersed the consumer of that environment would be. However, they discovered that there was no direct linear relationship. In what is known as 'the book problem', Gysbers *et al.* (2004) point out that even low-immersion media such as TV or books can induce a sense of presence (Bracken 2010, Bracken 2005, Jones 2007, Wirth 2007). This has been shown to be the case, for both SDH and AD, where levels of presence were higher for people with a sensory impairment watching the target text compared with people with no sensory impairment watching its original counterpart (Wissmath *et al.* 2009, Fryer and Freeman 2013).

Linguistic compensation

In 2006, Yves Gambier wrote about the widely held view among specialists that AVT involves a certain degree of loss, and goes on to state that, should that loss exist, '[i]t cannot be restricted to verbal elements. Is there not a certain loss in the meaning of pictures when one reads subtitles?' (2006: 3). He particularly bemoans 'language hypertrophy' or the prioritizing of linguistic over non-verbal communication modes including 'camera moves, viewing angles, editing, soundtrack, tone of voices, facial expressions, gestures, gazes, body movements, all of which are also meaningful' (*ibid.*). In response to Gambier, Heyns (2009: 131) talks of the 'serendipitous gain' of translation, those happy accidents that arise from expressing a phrase differently, such that the new phrase brings its own associations (scripts and schemata). It could be further argued that language hypertrophy is deserved (particularly for spoken language with its additional channels of prosodic information) especially because research that shows that the primary visual cortex, i.e. the part of the brain devoted by the sighted to vision, is recruited by blind individuals for memory, verbal and auditory processing tasks and speech (Bedny *et al.* 2011, Collignon *et al.* 2011, Ricciardi and Pietrini 2011).

As this overview has shown, language is essential to the integration of sensory input and therefore to perception. Thus, speech replaces visual input for people with a visual impairment, and written text replaces audible speech for those who are hearing impaired. Fryer (2013: 43) has proposed a 'linguistic compensation hypothesis' that underpins the accessibility practices in AVT, suggesting that a missing sensory channel need not necessarily be replaced by another sensory mode, but can be effectively replaced with words. Unfortunately speech does not save us from the treacherous waters of translation with its subjective mental lexicons and culture-bound meanings, but it does at least put us all, regardless of sensory loss, in the same boat.

Conclusion

This chapter has drawn on models of visual perception in order to provide a framework for AD as an example of the access modes of AVT. It has shown that by understanding the interaction between the audio and the visual and by drawing on concepts relating to perception and presence, we are indeed able to rely on much more than intuition when choosing between different variants that may appear to the individual translator to be equally possible and appropriate. The interconnection between arts and science disciplines has contributed useful research methods, resulting in reception studies using scientific methods that have moved translators away from measuring meaning (i.e. comprehension) to measuring experience, broadening our understanding of the purpose of translation.

Further reading

Cattaneo, Z., and T. Vecchi (2011) *Blind Vision: The Neuroscience of Visual Impairment*, Cambridge MA: MIT Press | *In this book, psychologists Cattaneo and Vecchi discuss what is known about blindness in terms of neuroscientific research. They discuss spatial cognition, mental imagery and the 'tyranny of the visual'.*

Hull, J. M. (2013) *Touching the Rock: An Experience of Blindness*, London: SPCK Pub. | *A moving autobiographical memoir. These short reflections on John Hull's experience of losing his sight, were the inspiration for the BAFTA award-winning film* Notes on Blindness *(Middleton and Spinney 2016)*

Maszerowska, A., A. Matamala, and P. Orero (eds) *Audio Description: New Perspectives Illustrated*, Amsterdam & Philadelphia: John Benjamins | *One of the best introductions to the complexities of AD, this book takes Tarantino's film* Inglourious Basterds *as a starting point and discusses all the decisions an audio describer would need to take in order to make it accessible to audiences with a visual impairment.*

Sacks, O. (2010) *The Mind's Eye*, Alfred A. Knopf Publishers | *The renowned neuroscientist Oliver Sacks uses his own failing eyesight as a spur to discuss case studies illustrating different types of blindness. Eminently readable and eye-opening.*

Related topics

8   Audio description: evolving recommendations for usable, effective and enjoyable practices
15 Narratology and audiovisual translation
17 Multimodality and audiovisual translation: cohesion in accessible films
18 Sociolinguistics and linguistic variation in audiovisual translation
22 Eye tracking in audiovisual translation research
23 Audiovisual translation and audience reception

References

ADLAB PRO (2017) 'Report IO1 on Assessment of current AD Training Practices'. Available online: https://adlabpro.wordpress.com [last access 20 December 2017].

Aijmer, K. and A. Simon-Vandenbergen (2004) 'A Model and a Methodology for the Study of Pragmatic Markers: The Semantic Field of Expectation', *Journal of Pragmatics* 36(10): 1781–1805.

Aitchison, J. (2012) *Words in the Mind: An Introduction to the Mental Lexicon*, London: John Wiley & Sons.

Bedny, M., A. Pascual-Leone, D. Dodell-Feder, E. Fedorenko and R. Saxe (2011) 'Language Processing in the Occipital Cortex of Congenitally Blind Adults', *Proceedings of the National Academy of Science, U.S.A.* 108(11): 4429–4434.

Berlin, B. and P. Kay (1969) *Basic Color Terms: Their Universality and Evolution*, Berkeley & Los Angeles: University of California Press.

Bertelson, P. (1998) 'Starting from the Ventriloquist: The Perception of Multimodal Events', in M. Sabourin, F. Craik and M. Robert (eds) *Advances in Psychological Science: Vol. 1. Biological and Cognitive Aspects*, Hove, UK: Psychology Press, 419–439.

Bracken, C. (2005) 'Presence and Image Quality: The Case of High Definition Television', *Media Psychology* 7: 191–205.

Bracken, C. (2010) 'Sounding out Small Screens and Telepresence: The Impact of Audio, Screen Size and Pace', *Journal of Media Psychology* 22(3): 125–137.
Braun, S. (2008) 'Audiodescription Research: State of the Art and Beyond', *Translation Studies in the New Millennium* 6: 14–30.
Bruner, J. S. and L. Postman (1949) 'On the Perception of Incongruity: A Paradigm', *Journal of Personality* 18: 206–223.
Cattaneo, Z. and T. Vecchi (2011) *Blind Vision: The Neuroscience of Visual Impairment*, Cambridge MA: MIT Press.
Choe, C., R. Welch, R. Gilford and J. Juola (1975) 'The "Ventriloquist Effect": Visual Dominance or Response Bias?', *Perception & Psychophysics* 18: 55–60.
Collignon, O., A. Vandewalle, P. Voss, G. Albouy, G. Charbonneau, M. Lassonde and F. Lepore (2011) 'Functional Specialization for Auditory-spatial Processing in the Occipital Cortex of Congenitally Blind Humans', *Proceedings of the National Academy of Sciences* 108(11): 4435–4440.
Davis, L. J. (1995) *Enforcing Normalcy: Disability, Deafness and the Body*, London & New York: Verso.
Díaz Cintas, J. and G. Anderman (eds) (2008) *Audiovisual Translation: Language Transfer on Screen*, Basingstoke: Palgrave Macmillan.
Di Giovanni, E. (2014) 'Visual and Narrative Priorities of the Blind and Non-blind: Eye Tracking and Audio Description', *Perspectives: Studies in Translatology* 22(1): 136–153.
Eramudugolla, R., R. Henderson and J. Mattingley (2011) 'Effects of Audio-visual Integration on the Detection of Masked Speech and Non-speech Sounds', *Brain and Cognition* 75(1): 60–66.
Feldman, J. (2008) *From Molecule to Metaphor: A Neural Theory of Language*, Cambridge MA and London: MIT Press.
Fryer, L. (2010) 'Audio Description as Audio Drama. A Practitioner's Point of View', *Perspectives: Studies in Translatology* 18(3): 205–213.
Fryer, L. (2013) *Putting It Into Words: The Impact of Visual Impairment on Perception, Experience and Presence*, Unpublished Doctoral Thesis, Goldsmiths, University of London.
Fryer, L. (2016) *An Introduction to Audio Description: A Practical Guide*, London: Routledge.
Fryer, L. and J. Freeman (2013) Visual Impairment and Presence: Measuring the Effect of Audio Description, *Proceedings of the 2013 Inputs-Outputs Conference: An Interdisciplinary Conference on Engagement in HCI and Performance*, 1–4.
Fryer, L. and J. Freeman (2014) 'Can you Feel What I'm Saying? The Impact of Verbal Information on Emotion Elicitation and Presence in People with a Visual Impairment', *Proceedings of the International Society for Presence Research*, 99–107.
Gallese, V. and M. Guerra (2012) 'Embodying Movies: Embodied Simulation and Film Studies', *Cinema: Journal of Philosophy and the Moving Image* 3: 183–210.
Gambier, Y. (2006) 'Multimodality and Subtitling', in M. Carroll, H. Gerzymisch-Arbogast and S. Nauert (eds) *Proceedings of the Marie Curie Euroconferences MuTra: Audiovisual Translation Scenarios*, Copenhagen 1–5 May 2006. Available online: http://www.euroconferences.info/proceedings/2006_Proceedings/2006_proceedings.html [last access 20 December 2017].
Gambier, Y. (2009) 'Challenges in Research on Audiovisual Translation', in A. Pym and A. Perekrestenko (eds) *Translation Research Projects* 2, 17–25. Available online: http://www.intercultural.urv.cat/media/upload/domain_317/arxius/TP2/TRP_2_may_3.pdf#page=23 [last access 20 December 2017].
Gawande, A. (2008) 'The Itch', *The New Yorker, 30 June*. Available online: http://cdn.journalism.cuny.edu/blogs.dir/422/files/2014/02/Scratching-an-itch-through-the-scalp-to-the-brain-The-New-Yorker.pdf [last access 20 December 2017].
Gibson, J. J. (1979) *The Ecological Approach to Visual Perception*, 3rd edition, Boston: Houghton Mifflin.
Gilbert, A., T. Regier, P. Kay and R. Ivry (2006) 'Whorf Hypothesis is Supported in the Right Visual Field but Not the Left', *Proceedings of the National Academy of Sciences* 103, 489–494.
Gray, C. M., P. König, A. K. Engel and W. Singer (1989) 'Oscillatory Responses in Cat Visual Cortex Exhibit Inter-columnar Synchronization which Reflects Global Stimulus Properties', *Nature* 338(6213): 334–337.

Greening, J. and D. Rolph (2007) 'Accessibility: Raising Awareness of Audio Description in the UK', in J. Díaz Cintas, P. Orero and A. Remael (eds) *Media for All: Subtitling for the Deaf, Audio Description and Sign Language*, Amsterdam & Philadelphia: John Benjamins, 127–138.

Gregory R. L. (2009) *Seeing Through Illusions*, Oxford: Oxford University Press.

Gross, J. and R. Levenson (1995) 'Emotion Elicitation Using Films', *Cognition and Emotion* 9: 87–108.

Gysbers, A., C. Klimmt, T. Hartmann, A. Nosper and P. Vorderer (2004) 'Exploring the Book Problem: Text Design, Mental Representations of Space, and Spatial Presence in Readers', in M. A. Raya and B. R. Solaz (eds) *Seventh Annual International Workshop: Presence 2004*, Universidad Politècnica de València, 13–19.

Hayhoe, S. (2017) *Blind Visitor Experiences at Art Museums*, Lanhma, Maryland: Rowman & Littlefield.

Heyns, M. (2009) 'Irreparable Loss and Exorbitant Gain: On Translating Agaat', *JLS/TLW* 25(3): 124–135.

Hull, J. M. (2013) *Touching the Rock: An Experience of Blindness*, London: SPCK Pub.

Jones, M. (2007) 'Presence as External versus Internal Experience: How Form, User, Style, and Content Factors Produce Presence from the Inside', *Proceedings of the Tenth Annual International Meeting of the Presence Workshop*, Barcelona, Spain, 115– 126. Available online: https://astro.temple.edu/~lombard/ISPR/Proceedings/2007/Jones.pdf [last access 20 December 2017].

Kay, P. and W. Kempton (1984) 'What Is the Sapir-Whorf Hypothesis?' *American Anthropologist* 86(1): 65–79.

Kleege, G. (2015) 'Blind Self Portraits', Plenary paper presented at Blind Creations Conference, Royal Holloway College, June, University of London.

Kruger, J. (2012) 'Making Meaning in AVT: Eye Tracking and Viewer Construction of Narrative', *Perspectives* 20(1): 67–86.

Kruger, J. (2017) 'Beta Coherence as Objective Measure of Immersion', Paper presented at *Advanced Research Seminar in Audio Description* (ARSAD), 16 March, Barcelona. Available online: http://grupsderecerca.uab.cat/arsad/sites/grupsderecerca.uab.cat.arsad/files/kruger_arsad_2017.pdf [last access 20 December 2017].

Kruger, J. L., M. T. Soto-Sanfiel, S. Doherty and R. Ibrahim (2016) 'Towards a Cognitive Audiovisual Translatology: Subtitles and Embodied Cognition', in R. Muñoz (ed.) *Reembedding Translation Process Research*, Amsterdam & Philadelphia: John Benjamins, 171–194.

Kübler, N. and A. Volanschi (2012) *Semantic Prosody and Specialised Translation, or How a Lexico-grammatical Theory of Language can Help with Specialised Translation*, Amsterdam & Philadelphia: John Benjamins.

Laurienti, P., R. Kraft, J. Maldjian, J. Burdette and M. Wallace (2004) 'Semantic Congruence is a Critical Factor in Multisensory Behavioral Performance', *Exp. Brain Res.* 158: 405–414.

Lee, J. (2008) 'Rating Scales for Interpreting Performance Assessment', *The Interpreter and Translator Trainer* 2(2): 165–184.

Leonard, M. and E. Chang (2014) 'Dynamic Speech Representations in the Human Temporal Lobe', *Trends in Cognitive Sciences* 18(9): 472–479.

Lessiter, J., J. Freeman, E. Keogh and J. Davidoff (2001) 'A Cross-media Presence Questionnaire: The ITC Sense of Presence Inventory', *Presence: Teleoperators, and Virtual Environments* 10(3): 282–297.

Lombard, M. and T. Ditton (1997) 'At the Heart of It All: The Concept of Presence', *Journal of Computer-Mediated Communication* 3(2). Available online: http://onlinelibrary.wiley.com/doi/10.1111/j.1083–6101.1997.tb00072.x/full [last access 20 December 2017].

Malmkjær, K. S. (2005) *Linguistics and the Language of Translation*, Edinburgh: Edinburgh University Press.

Maszerowska, A., A. Matamala and P. Orero (eds) *Audio Description: New Perspectives Illustrated*, Amsterdam & Philadelphia: John Benjamins.

Mayoral, R., D. Kelly and N. Gallardo (1988) 'Concept of Constrained Translation. Non-linguistic Perspectives of Translation', *Meta* 33(3): 356–367.

Monaco, J. (2009) *How to Read a Film*, 4th edition, Oxford: Oxford University Press.
Neisser, U. (1976) *Cognition and Reality. Principles and Implication of Cognitive Psychology*, San Francisco: Freeman.
Nida, E. A. (1964) *Toward a Science of Translating: With Special Reference to Principles and Procedures Involved in Bible Translating*, Leiden: Brill.
Oldfield, M. and J. Mitchinson (2013) 'Some Quite Interesting Facts about Rainbows', *Daily Telegraph*, 28 May. Available online: http://www.telegraph.co.uk/men/the-filter/qi/10076379/QI-some-quite-interesting-facts-about-rainbows.html [last access 20 December 2017].
Orero, P. and A. Vilaró (2012) 'Eye Tracking Analysis of Minor Details in Films for Audio Description', *MonTI* 4: 295–319.
Piety, P. (2004) 'The Language System of Audio Description: An Investigation as a Discursive Process', *Journal of Visual Impairment & Blindness* 98(08): 453–469.
Pinchbeck, D. M. and B. Stevens (2005) 'Presence, Narrative and Schemata', in *Proceedings of Presence 2005: The 8th International Workshop on Presence*, 221–26. Available online: https://astro.temple.edu/~lombard/ISPR/Proceedings/2005/Pinchbeck%20and%20Stevens.pdf [last access 30 August 2017]
Posner, M. I., M. J. Nissen and R. M. Klein (1976) 'Visual Dominance: An Information-processing Account of Its Origins and Significance', *Psychological Review* 83(2): 157–171.
Rai, S., J. Greening and L. Petré (2010) *A Comparative Study of Audio Description Guidelines Prevalent in Different Countries*, London: RNIB.
Ramos, M. (2015) 'The Emotional Experience of Films: Does Audio Description Make a Difference?', *The Translator* 21(1): 68–94.
Regier, T., C. Kemp and P. Kay (2015) 'Word Meanings across Languages Support Efficient Communication', in B. MacWhinney and W. O'Grady (eds) *The Handbook of Language Emergence*, Chichester, UK: Wiley-Blackwell, 237–263.
Reiser, E. M., G. Schulter, E. M. Weiss, A. Fink, C. Rominger and I. Papousek (2012) 'Decrease of Prefrontal–posterior EEG Coherence: Loose Control during Social-emotional Stimulation', *Brain and Cognition* 80(1): 144–154.
Remael, A. and G. Vercauteren (2007) 'Audio Describing the Exposition Phase of Films: Teaching Students What to Choose', *TRANS* 11: 73–94.
Remael, A. (2012) 'For the Use of Sound. Film Sound Analysis for Audio-description: Some Key Issues', *MonTI* 4: 255–276.
Ricciardi, E. and P. Pietrini (2011) 'New Light from the Dark: What Blindness can Teach us about Brain Function', *Current Opinion in Neurology* 24(4): 357–363.
Rickard, N. S. (2004) 'Intense Emotional Responses to Music: A Test of the Physiological Arousal Hypothesis', *Psychology of Music* 32(4): 371–388.
Roberson, D., J. Davidoff, I. R. Davies and L. R. Shapiro (2005) 'Color Categories: Evidence for the Cultural Relativity Hypothesis', *Cognitive Psychology* 50(4): 378–411.
Russell, B. (1917) *Mysticism and Logic*, London: George Allen & Unwin Ltd.
Sacks, O. (2010) *The Mind's Eye*, Alfred A. Knopf Publishers.
Schachter, S. and J. Singer (1962) 'Cognitive, Social and Physiological Determinants of Emotional State', *Psychological Review* 69(5): 379–399.
Schank, R. and R. Abelson (1975) *Scripts, Plans and Knowledge*, New Haven: Yale University.
Schubert, T., F. Friedmann and H. Regenbrecht (2001) 'The Experience of Presence: Factor Analytic Insights', *Presence: Teleoperators and Virtual Environments* 10(3): 266–281.
Senkowski, D., T. R. Schneider, J. J. Foxe and A. K. Engel (2008) 'Crossmodal Binding through Neural Coherence: Implications for Multisensory Processing', *Trends in Neurosciences* 31(8): 401–409.
Singer, W. and C. M. Gray (1995) 'Visual Feature Integration and the Temporal Correlation Hypothesis', *Annual Review of Neuroscience* 18: 555–586.
Smith, T. (2013) 'Watching you Watch Movies: Using Eye Tracking to Inform Film Theory', in A. P. Shimamura (ed.) *Psychocinematics: Exploring Cognition at the Movies*, New York: Oxford University Press, 165–191. Available online: http://eprints.bbk.ac.uk/12588/1/9%2BSmith_psychocinematics_inpress.pdf [last access 20 December 2017].

Smith, T. (2015) 'Read, Watch, Listen: A Commentary on Eye Tracking and Moving Images', *Refractory: A Journal of Entertainment Media* 25(9). Available online: http://eprints.bbk.ac.uk/12583/1/Refractory_commentary_timjsmith_accepted.pdf [last access 20 December 2017].

Snyder, J. (2005) 'Audio Description: The Visual Made Verbal', *International Congress Series* 1282: 935–939.

Sumby, W. and I. Pollack, (1954) 'Visual Contribution to Speech Intelligibility in Noise', *Journal of the Acoustical Society of America* 26: 212–215.

Szarkowska, A. and P. Orero (2014) 'The Importance of Sound for Audio Description', in Maszerowska, A., A. Matamala and P. Orero (eds) *Audio Description. New Perspectives Illustrated*, Amsterdam & Philadelphia: John Benjamins, 121–139.

Vermeer, H. J. (1989) 'Skopos and Commission in Translational Action', trans. by A. Chesterman, in L. Venuti (ed.) *The Translation Studies Reader*, London: Routledge, 221–232.

von Helmholtz, H. (1977) 'The Facts in Perception', in R. Cohen and E. Yehuda (eds) *Hermann Von Helmholtz: Epistemological Writings*, Netherlands: Springer 115–185.

von Uexküll, J. (1940) *Bedeutungslehre*, Leipzig: Johann Ambrosius Barth, trans. by B. Stone and H. Weiner as 'The Theory of Meaning', *Semiotica* 42(1): 25–87.

Wildgruber, D., H. Ackermann, B. Kreifelts and T. Ethofer (2006) 'Cerebral Processing of Linguistic and Emotional Prosody: FMRI studies', *Progress in Brain Research* 156: 249–268.

Wirth, H. J. (2007) 'Schismatic Processes in the Psychoanalytic Movement and their Impact on the Formation of Theories', *International Forum of Psychoanalysis* 16(1): 4–11.

Wissmath, B., D. Weibel, and R. Groner (2009) 'Dubbing or Subtitling? Effects on Spatial Presence, Transportation, Flow and Enjoyment', *Journal of Media Psychology: Theories, Methods, and Applications* 21(3): 114–125.

Zelter, D. (1992) 'Autonomy, Interaction and Presence', *Presence: Teleoperators and Virtual Environments* 1(1): 1275–132.

Filmography

Notes on Blindness (2016) Peter Middleton and James Spinney. Official film website: http://www.notesonblindness.co.uk

15
Narratology and audiovisual translation

Jeroen Vandaele

Introduction

The term *narratology* was coined by Todorov (1969: 10) to designate an emerging discipline envisioned as the 'science of narrative'. Narratology, however, has come to be perceived as a 'humanities discipline' that articulates concepts and models 'widely used as heuristic tools' for the study of narrative (Meister 2014). Originally oriented towards the study of literary texts, many of narratology's analytic advances have proven useful for narrative film analysis, including translation research driven by the insight that 'the reason for making a film is to tell a story' (Zabalbeascoa, Izard and Santamaría 2001: 109). The present chapter begins by exploring the classical concepts of narratology as developed in literary theory, before proceeding to consider to what extent such concepts apply to audiovisual narrative. The bulk of this chapter then examines the relevance of narratology to the study of audiovisual narrative in translation, and discusses a variety of narratological insights that bear on narratives conveyed across media, subtitling, dubbing and audio description: action, plot, narration, description, narrativity, focalization and characterization. The focus is on narrative film fiction, that is, narrative films about a fictional story world.

Basics of narratology

Narrative is often defined as a communication form among other existing forms—such as 'descriptive', 'argumentative', 'explanatory' or 'instructive' communication (see e.g. Chatman 1978, Fludernik 2000, Herman 2008). The identity of narrative communication among the other forms mentioned, claims Ryan, 'resides on the level of the signified' (Ryan 2004: 8), that is in the kind of meaning that is communicated. A text is narrative, from this perspective, if its meaning is to 'create a world' and 'populate it with characters'; if that world and characters 'undergo changes of state' caused by 'accidents' or 'deliberate actions'; and if the text—understood here in a broad, cross-medial way—produces in the reader or audience an interpretation of that world in terms of 'goals, plans, causal relations, and psychological motivations' (*ibid.*: 8–9). A narrative, in this sense, is a text about a world with a plot, that is with 'events and characters' actions' arranged in 'causal and temporal patterns' (Kukkonen 2014).

Following this line of thought, Quentin Tarantino's feature film *Pulp Fiction* (1994) is narrative communication because it is about a world (and it is moreover narrative *fiction* as it *creates* that world) and features (brutal) characters such as the hitmen Jules (Samuel Jackson) and Vincent (John Travolta) and their boss Marsellus Wallace. Also, throughout this instance of narrative communication viewers are presented with a multitude of actions—as when, early in the film, Jules and Vincent kill a pair of young, out-of-their-league suburbanites for reneging on a deal with Marsellus; with plenty of accidents—as when Jules and Vincent happen to be present at a diner held up by two amateurish robbers; and with many dramatic changes of state—as when Jules and Vincent miraculously escape being killed themselves, leading Jules to think things over and announce his imminent retirement from gangster life. Audiences try to make sense of the narrative in terms of chronology (which is not so easy, given the film's non-linear structure), goals (the purposes of gangsters and others), causal relations (accidents and plans), and psychological motivations (e.g. desired retirement from gangster life). The focus of Ryan and others on the signi*fied* of narrative communication therefore involves the analysis of the story worlds, the characters and their motivations, and the chronology and causality of actions, states of affairs, dramatic changes and coincidences.

Since Russian Formalism, however, narratology has time and again stated that a narrative is not just an evolving story world (i.e. a related series of situations, actions and events lived by characters), but also, and fundamentally, the gradual *communication*—sign after sign—of that story world to the audience. Cohn (1990: 777) usefully lists the various terms used for this distinction, although each of them may have slightly different connotations for each narratologist (Vercauteren 2012: 212–5). Terms frequently used to refer to the action world are *fabula* (Russian Formalism), 'story' (Chatman 1978), 'story world' or 'story logic' (Herman 2002), 'the told' (Sternberg 2009: 460), 'intradiegetic world' (Genette 1972), 'action logic', or just 'actions' and 'events' as part of the 'plot'. As said, the inferable chronology of events is considered an important logic here. Bordwell, for example, defines the *fabula* as 'the story's state of affairs and events' but also as the 'spatio-temporal realm in which the action unfolds in chronological order' (2008: 98, 110). The inferable causality between events is also considered an important structuring principle (Ryan 2004: 8–9), hence the term 'action logic'—which has ties with the philosophy of action (see Doležel 1998) and cognitive science (Schank and Abelson 1977, Sternberg 2009: 485). Terms frequently used to refer to the *communication* of the story world are the *sjuzhet* (Russian Formalism), the 'telling' (Sternberg 2009), the 'extradiegetic communication' (Genette 1972), the 'narrating' (Prince 1982), 'narration' (Bordwell 1985), 'discourse' (Chatman 1978), and 'text' (Bal 1985).

Narrative theorists including Sternberg (1978, 2010) and Bordwell (1985, 2008) argue—against positions such as Ryan's—that narrative communication cannot be adequately characterized by privileging the signified, however named and defined (whether event, *fabula*, plot, or so forth). Bordwell (2008: 110), for example, notes that 'we have access to the *fabula* only by means of narration', which means that 'narration isn't simply a window through which we watch a pre-existing story that we might see from elsewhere'. Instead, narration is 'the very force that conjures the *fabula* into being' (*ibid.*). As Sternberg has shown, Bordwell (2008: 100) argues, narrative concepts 'must be gauged in relation to their capacities to create distinctive effects on the perceiver. For example, a flashback isn't just an abstract rearrangement of story incidents. Its function is to trigger interest in finding out what led up to what we see'. The telling (or narration, or discourse) is emotionally crucial here, if we understand this term as *how* a story world and its characters are gradually communicated to the reader or audience.

Pulp Fiction equally illustrates how narration—conspicuously non-chronological in this case—is not an abstract theoretical structure but the very communication process that enables the production of narrative effects. First, consider the film's opening, the initial diner scene (Filmography: 'Nobody ever Robs Restaurants' clip). This scene is the beginning of the film discourse but *not* the beginning of the story (or *fabula*, or plot). Whereas some films narrate their story *ab ovo* ('here is character A, and here is what next happens to A and why so'), *Pulp Fiction*'s filmic narration has an *in medias res* quality ('here is what is happening to characters'): the characters are unknown to the viewer, and so are their precise circumstances, yet we plunge in the middle of the action. The narration has the camera on a young couple, Pumpkin (Tim Roth) and Honey Bunny (Amanda Plummer); it registers their conversation (they suddenly come up with the idea of robbing the diner) and the start of their improvised action (they start shouting and pointing guns). The communication then freezes the images in mid-action, superposes the title sequence on the frozen images, and lets a furious guitar riff kick in. The film narration thus triggers questions—narrative knowledge gaps—yet leaves them unanswered for the time being. Who are these romantic robbers? Will they get away with their violent behaviour? Given their degree of improvisation and violence, will something go horribly wrong for them or other clients? These are central narrative effects—'curiosity' and 'suspense gaps'—impossible to explain without reference to the narration, that is to how and when aspects of the *fabula* are disclosed (the improvisation, the start) and withheld (the outcome).

Consider now the end of the film narration, i.e. the final diner scene. Here the audience watches Vincent and Jules reflecting on life—their own good fortune, divine intervention, and the relative cleanliness of pigs and dogs. Although the camera is on the gangsters throughout the scene, much of the not-so-busy diner is seen in the background. A new narrative effect, 'narrative surprise', is produced when the registering of their dialogue is briefly interspersed with a shot of an action that the viewer had already seen from another angle in the *in medias res* beginning of the film—namely Pumpkin shouting '*Garçon*! Coffee!' to the waitress. The diner that formed the décor of the opening scene, it now transpires, is much like the diner where Jules and Vincent are talking about pigs and life. The audience is suddenly able to anticipate what the amateurish robbers are about to do; and it realizes that Vincent and Jules—who have been thoroughly characterized as ruthless killers by virtue of their actions throughout the film—are among the other clients. The suspense of this narrative situation could not have been attained early in the discourse. The narrative power of discourse-story interaction is fully appreciated at this point, and further exploited in the scene. The opening and final diner scenes of *Pulp Fiction* thus illustrate suspense, curiosity and surprise.

The examples also show how these 'big three' narrative emotions (Bordwell 1985: 101) depend on specific discourse-story interactions: (i) chronological or noticeably delayed communication of future action causes suspense, as dominantly in thrillers; (ii) noticeably delayed communication of past actions causes curiosity, as dominantly in detective stories; and (iii) *un*noticeably delayed communication of critical information causes surprise when that information is finally disclosed. As for (i), Sternberg (1978) adds that narration, especially in fiction, can enhance suspense in artful or 'aesthetic' (i.e. less synchronous or 'mimetic') ways by artificially delaying the communication of the action development. A 'cliffhanger', as illustrated by *Pulp Fiction*'s opening scene, is the creation of narrative suspense by stopping the communication in mid-action. As for the difference between (i) and (ii), 'suspense derives from a lack of desired information concerning the outcome of a conflict', while 'curiosity is produced by a lack of information that relates to the narrative past' (1978: 65). Who are these people? What background do they have? In what situation are they? How have they landed in such a situation? As for (iii), 'narrative surprise' differs from (i) and (ii) because it does *not* signal a gap or suppressed information (e.g. the fact that the two amateurish robbers are there with Jules and Vincent), so that the sudden disclosure throws new, surprising light on the narrated world. The more these narrative effects dominate our response to a text, the higher the text's narrativity as a 'felt quality' (Porter Abbott 2014).

Two more heuristic concepts should be added at this point: 'characterization' and 'focalization'. As for characterization, Aristotle's famous idea that a tragedy, or perhaps a narrative in general, consists mainly of characters and plot, with the greatest weight on plot, requires qualification in two ways. The most classical objection is that some narratives are more plot-driven, with characters as servants, while others are more character-oriented, with some plotting as a servant. As Remael and Vercauteren put it (2007: 79), 'some films are driven by character, some by action'. Less classically, yet no less importantly, the narrative meaning of a character depends on ongoing character*ization* in discourse, much like the narrative meaning of plot, or the narrated action, depends on its narrat*ion*, or discourse. Characters are not just 'what they do' (Aristotle paraphrased by Cattrysse and Gambier 2008: 48), but what they appear to be and do at time t in the discourse. The unfolding characterization—narration's twin, the gradual disclosure of character traits—fully interacts with narrativity: since narrativity is about 'framing and testing hypotheses' as triggered and constrained by the film discourse (Bordwell 1985: 37, 39), characterization is involved as it steers hypothesis formation about possible actions, intentions, evaluations and emotions of characters. At the end of *Pulp Fiction*, for instance, we are much more interested in the dénouement of the diner scene because at that point we *know* something about the robbers (their amateurism and improvisation), we know much about Jules and Vincent (they are professional killers, though one has an identity crisis and is thinking of retiring). As a result, we *suspect* trouble for the robbers, yet we do *not* know what is about to happen.

Focalization, for its part, was coined by Genette (1972) as he realized that literary 'perspective', if left unanalyzed, creates confusion between two very different questions: 'Who is the character whose point of view orients the narrative perspective?' and 'Who is the narrator?' (1972: 241). Genette called the former kind of perspective 'focalization', while the latter kind refers to the 'narration'. A narrator can tell (parts of) a story focalized through the minds of several characters, or through her own mind as a kid, to give but two examples. Bal (1985) argued next that there are basically two ways in which the narration (or narrator) can select or filter story-world information for the audience: the narration can provide audiences with information not filtered by a character, or it can suggest that it restricts the information to what a character is perceiving in the story world. In more technical terms, Bal's proposal is that 'a focalizer can be either "external" (a narrator) or "internal" (a character)' (*ibid*.) and 'most narratologists today follow' this view (Jahn 2005). In this model, Genette's two types of literary narrative perspective, i.e. narration and focalization, are thus related in the following way: the ongoing narration of a story world (i.e. the speech acts delivered by the narrator) can choose a certain focalization (i.e. by adhering to the perspective of a narrator and/or characters). Moreover, it can choose to explicitly signal or leave implicit the kind of focalization chosen (e.g. 'The car was green' may mean either 'As a narrator I assert that the car was green' or 'As a narrator I report that the character-focalizer saw that the car was green'). Indeed, the narrational instance is always in command and selects the information; hence, it may always decide to restrict the information to what a character perceives/thinks or to what it wants to communicate.

Narration may choose a certain focalization so as to produce narrative perspective and hence narrative effects. These include curiosity about characters, because it tells little about their antecedents; suspense when we see characters together, because it has given insight in their conflicting agendas; or surprise, as it reveals that they are together in the same room. Focalization exists in film too, though with some modifications.

Narratology across media

Narratology has been 'conceived from its earliest days as a project that transcends disciplines and media', Ryan explains (2004: 1) with reference to Bremond's famous statement that story 'is independent of the techniques that bear it along. It may be transposed from one to another medium without losing its essential properties' (Bremond 1964: 4, translated by Chatman 1978: 20). The crucial thing to bear in mind—the one on which the possibility of narrativity hinges—is the capacity for a medium to sequentially provide cues of information about an action world and its characters. Since narrativity depends on narrative perspective, since narrative perspective depends on gradual narration, and since gradual narration exists both in words and moving images, both words and images are able to produce narrative perspective and hence narrativity (Chatman 1999: 436).

Indeed, any sequentially organized semiotic channel of communication can withhold and gradually disclose information for narrative effect. As it restricts information, it does something to our minds: either we want answers, because we are curious or in suspense, and the mind abhors a vacuum; or we are surprised by secretly delayed information. As we confront this flow of gaps and partial and full disclosures, we may want to 'motivate'—conjure up a reason for—its restrictive communication. We may, for example, infer that the narration mimics the mind of a character and therefore restricts its communication to what a character's minds perceives, feels and thinks. (Technically, the narration is then 'figural' or 'internally focalized', through a focalizing character that filters the information, and the narration or motivation is 'mimetic'.) Or we may for example feel that the narration takes responsibility for playing with our minds. (Technically, the narration may remain 'author-like' or 'externally focalized', not filtered by a character's mind, and the motivation is 'aesthetic'.)

In terms of narrative effect, the grand narratological theme of focalization thus boils down to the mechanisms of gapping and disclosure in discourse time (Do we know more, as much, as little, or less than a character at time t in the discourse?) and to the motivation we ascribe to these epistemic discourse moves. Regarding figural narration, Wilson points out that there are very few good movies 'in which *every* shot of the film (or of a lengthy segment of the film) represents the field of vision of the central character' (1986: 86, 128; emphasis in original). As we will now see, however, narration can still remain functionally figural—that is figural for the purposes of narrativity—in a broader sense.

A first mainstream cinematic way of employing constrained narration is to 'let properties of the way in which the fictional world looks to us on the screen *stand in for* properties of the way in which that world is experienced by the character', even though 'the action is only partially, if at all, seen from his or her physical point of view' (Wilson 1986: 87, emphasis in original). For instance, as Jules and Vincent are about to enter the apartment of the soon-to-be-bumped-off 'business partners' of Marsellus Wallace, there is a difference between the visual perspective of the two hitmen and that of the audience: the former stand facing a closed door, while the latter only see the back of the hitmen's upper bodies as they face this door. But what is most important for narrativity is that we know as little as they do about what exactly to expect behind that door—and this creates feelings of curiosity and suspense, mixed with the incongruous hilarity of their dialogue (about risky foot massages). Notice, actually, that this 'behaviouristic' restricted narration of cinema constrains our knowledge even more than typical figural prose narration, which as a mindreading activity not only selects *what* characters perceive but also verbalizes *how* they perceive it as well as other *non-perceptual* activity that is going on in their minds. In the film, as in real life, our only window into the minds of others is their behaviour and words. Yet we manage to handle this situation in real life (Goffman 1969), so we can handle this in film too (Wilson 1986: 90). This is particularly the case in mainstream film, a form of communication that automatically draws attention to the relevance of its cues (Sperber and Wilson 1986), and even tends to simplify those cues (Bordwell 1985).

A second less mainstream cinematic way of employing constrained narration is precisely to imitate the gapped, i.e. incomplete and interrupted, nature of real-life perception more fully, also with narrative effects (Wilson 1986: 89–95). In the mockumentary TV series *The Office* (2001–2003), for instance, the camera of the fictional 'documentary makers' sometimes manages to capture images of characters seemingly colluding, while the team's microphone is unable to register what the characters are up to (suspense) or what they have possibly done (curiosity).

Cinematic or audiovisual narration does not have to constrain its information flow with reference to characters, however. Like novels, filmic narration can also decide to produce narrative perspective by restricting and distributing information without motivating it as internal focalization (hence 'mimetic' narration). In that vein, Tarantino contrasts the traditional use of flashbacks as a narrative strategy articulating a 'personal perspective' in film, with the 'narrative perspective' that flashbacks set out to deliver in *Reservoir Dogs* (1992):

> Novels go back and forth all the time. You read a story about a guy who's doing something or in some situation and, all of a sudden, chapter five comes and it takes Henry, one of the guys, and it shows you seven years ago, where he was seven years ago and how he came to be and then like, *boom*, the next chapter, *boom*, you're back in the flow of the action. Flashbacks, as far as I'm concerned, come from a personal perspective. These [in *Reservoir Dogs*] aren't, they're coming from a narrative perspective. They're going back and forth like chapters.
>
> *(Tarantino, quoted in Bordwell 2006: 91)*

The parallelisms between prose narration and audiovisual narration thus suggest that translation, even of the intersemiotic kind, should be able to preserve narrativity and its basic mechanisms. Ryan (2004: 1–2), however, brings into sharp relief the role that medium-specific considerations play in the narration process:

> the question of how the intrinsic properties of the medium shape the form of narrative and affect the narrative experience can no longer be ignored . . . Even when they seek to make themselves invisible, media are not hollow conduits for the transmission of messages but material supports of information whose materiality, precisely, 'matters' for the type of meanings that can be encoded.

Bearing in mind that *medium* is a tricky concept (Ryan 2004: 16ff.), our question here can be formulated as follows: Does the medium of communication—that is the chosen technology of narration, the sensory tracks it addresses (vision, hearing), and the sign systems it exploits (verbal, non-verbal)—after all modulate the possibility to produce narrative effects?

Surprisingly perhaps, given his insights into the possibilities of cinematic restricted narration, Wilson's reply is plainly affirmative: 'since verbal telling and cinematic showing are such very different narrational procedures, the issues that get raised in each case are not at all identical' (1986: 100). Though a medium's ability to show and restrict information is what makes narrativity possible, verbal telling and audiovisual narration differ to some extent in ways that pertain to narration and audiovisual translation. Two important issues are (1) simultaneity in narration and (2) the illusion of non-narration (Vercauteren 2012: 210).

As for the first problem, Neira Piñeiro (2003: 177–8) argues, audiovisual narrative discourse can communicate more information *simultaneously* than purely verbal narrative. Indeed, the description of an image is never saturated by one or even a few sentences (Chatman 1999: 438); the look of a character is more quickly visualized as a whole and scanned than told and read; images can at once show a character simultaneously engaged in multiple action and intentionality—as will be elaborated on in the audio description section below; images can at once show several characters engaged in action and intentionality (*ibid*); split-screen narration can multiply these problems; audiovisual narration simultaneously works with several channels that may interact, namely moving images, dialogue and the rest of the soundtrack. Sometimes the interaction will produce 'redundancy', but other times there will be mutual dependence between channels ('anchoring') (Marleau 1982: 274, Díaz Cintas and Remael 2007: 50).

As far as the second problem is concerned, it is worth noting that, while the narration of verbal narrative is always uttered ('enunciated') and therefore tends to suggest the presence of a narrator, film narration has a predominantly 'mimetic' effect, effacing the figure of the narrator (Gaudreault and Jost 1990: 40). Some important scholars have therefore gone so far as to reject the existence of filmic narrators (e.g. Bordwell 1985, Wilson 1986: 136). In terms of impression, an illusion of story-world autonomy—the fourth-wall effect—is indeed often created in mimetic narrative (Gaudreault and Jost 1990: 39–40, Vandaele 2010: 765–73). Thus, Bordwell (1985), invoking Occam's razor, speaks of filmic narrat*ion* and does away with the filmic narrat*or* unless there happens to be a person who verbally narrates and whom the viewer either hears (e.g. a voice-over narrator outside the narrative world) or both sees and hears (e.g. the character-narrator Walter Neff in Billy Wilder's *Double Indemnity* [1944]). In terms of analysis, however, narration without a narrator seems quite impossible, about as spooky as any other action posited to exist without any executing agent (Gaudreault and Jost 1990: 61). When Bordwell defines narration as 'the organization of a set of cues for the construction of a story' (1985: 62), one may wonder if this 'organization' is not organized by anybody, not even a group of agents (screenwriter, shooter, editor) (see also Currie 1995: 248). For Chatman (1984: 5), it does not matter if we call this agency the film's 'silent narrator', or 'principle of construction', or 'implied director', or 'whatever you may want to name the narrating instance'. Chatman (1999: 439–40), however, also admits that film narration differs from verbal narration in important ways, as will be elaborated below.

Translating narrativity: action doubles as narration

Though Bordwell and Wilson oppose the idea of a filmic narrator or communicator, there is an enormous difference between the immediate perception of the real world and the mediated perception of communicative film. Fiction films that are ostensibly written, shot and edited for communication with audiences indeed carry the constant presumption, like all human communication, that the viewers should be looking for relevant audiovisual information all the time (Sperber and Wilson 1986). Narrative film does not usually allow us to 'dwell' much on its 'plenitude of visual details' (Chatman 1999: 438–9), so it invites us to look for the narratively relevant.

This means, first, that all the 'action'—verbal, para-verbal and non-verbal—always doubles as narration. The action we seem to 'witness' is in fact action we are *told about*. As Remael (2003: 233) writes, 'film dialogue is not just "dialogue", it is also narrative', and this is so all the time, even though 'mimetic' audiovisual narration does not usually present a visible speaker, that is a verbalizing ('diegetic') narrator. Action, dialogue included, is the orientation of the characters within and towards their own world, the so-called '*intra-diegetic*' story world, and *at the same time* the action is the signified that the narration directs towards the spectators, who seek to understand its relevance (informativeness) for their understanding of the action world.

Second, this also seems to mean that in narrative texts the 'situation'—of characters—doubles as a description for audiences. This is a complicated matter, however. For starters, many narratologists (e.g. Bremond, Chatman, Sternberg, or Herman) have pointed out that descriptive parts tend to become servants of narrative texts (see also Orero and Vilaró 2012: 313). Descriptions are narrativized, as when we are gradually told in *Pulp Fiction* who should count as clients in the diner scenes; this signals the narrative relevance of descriptions and hence reduces the importance of the narration-description distinction as a means to discriminate between the narratively relevant and the less relevant. In film, moreover, the distinction is anyway much harder to make than in verbal narrative (Chatman 1984: 441).

In light of this theoretical discussion, how do audiences, translators and translation analysts go about finding narrative relevance in the source film? In narrative discourse, we constantly look for cues that allow us to produce degrees of narrative 'clarity' (Pérez-González 2014: 51) yet also narrativity-inducing degrees of temporary 'opacity' (Sternberg 2009: 460, 500). As for narrative clarity, or 'cohesion' (Chaume 2004), we are on the outlook for cues to construct and interpret chronology, causality and coincidence related to characters and their world. As for temporary opacity, we want to look for cues that produce interpretive gaps, possibly suggest hypothetical answers, overtly delay answers, and disclose covertly delayed information that throws new light on the situation. Audio describers should thus find, select and verbalize the visuals that are narratively relevant in this sense. Subtitlers for hearing audiences should find, select and render such narratively relevant cues in dialogue, with a focus on their verbal aspects rather than the para-verbal ones (such as intonation), while subtitlers for hearing-impaired people should also include narratively relevant cues in the rest of the soundtrack (e.g. Dick Dale's guitar riff 'Misirlou' that kicks in just when *Pulp Fiction*'s opening scene freezes in mid-action).

Subtitling: dialogue doubles as narration

To begin this section on interlingual subtitling for hearing audiences, consider the '*Garçon! Coffee!*' exclamation uttered in the opening and closing diner scenes of *Pulp Fiction*. As a speech act and action, this is a one-time event, as part of a dialogue between two characters in the story world (Pumpkin and the waitress); yet the narration registers the act and communicates this registration (a multimodal quote) to the audience on two different discourse moments (first in the opening diner scene and then in the concluding diner scene). The one-time speech act thus becomes part of two radically different narrative acts carried out by the narration. What changes between the first and the second mention, is the narrative meaning of '*Garçon!* Coffee!' as produced by the narration and its sequencing: the first time it characterizes and also keeps us in mid-action; the second time it surprises. When it is first uttered, and on a microlevel, an 'anchoring' between image and speech may be going on: *'Garçon!'* further determines the gesturing of Pumpkin and, to the extent that *'Garçon!'* is odd for Americans, they may have to interpret the images (and 'Coffee!') to understand *'Garçon!'* as an appellative. Yet here already the narration makes sure that it shows the waitress, who critically picks up the word and tartly comments that *'Garçon* means "boy" in French', so that any possible opacity and anchoring suddenly shift to action-logical redundancy, salience and memorability. The *narrative* relevance of this redundancy and salience becomes apparent in the second mention, at the end of the film discourse. The upshot for subtitling is that it here is narratively relevant to also draw attention to the appellative and its specific wording—against the tendency of subtitles to consider appellatives and other 'procedural' or 'interactional' communication not action-relevant and hence to be sacrificed, given the subtitle's limited space and time. The question for subtitling is always whether the action—any action, appellation included—is relevant for the narration (e.g. surprise-preparing).

Relevant dialogue beyond the plot: narration

One way of answering the question of relevance is by saying that speech acts by characters may be either plot-relevant 'dialogue' or plot-irrelevant 'conversation', as Cattrysse and Gambier suggest with reference to screenwriting theory (2008: 52). Following this reasoning, subtitles will have to translate plot-relevant 'dialogue' lines for the sake of narrative clarity, as when Vincent indicates just before the start of the robbery that he needs to go to the toilet; the preceding pigs-and-dogs discussion, by contrast, is 'conversation', irrelevant for narrative clarity. However, as said, narrative relevance (narrativity) stems not only from plot (*fabula*) but also from opaque and retardatory narration (the *garçon* scene) and characterization. Regarding narration, the supposedly plot-irrelevant pigs-and-dogs conversation does have narrative relevance since it relaxes and distracts the audience before disclosing *where* they are conversing—a narrative surprise that produces further suspense. 'Conversation' may thus be narratively relevant while—or even by—suggesting plot-irrelevant comic relief.

Relevant dialogue beyond the plot: characterization

Regarding characterization, Díaz Cintas and Remael (2007: 172, 174) and Remael (2003) show that dialogue has an impact on characterization, which in turn has an impact on narrative relevance—not just when a narrative is character-oriented (*pace* Aristotle) but also because characterization guides our narrative response. The so-called 'primacy effect', or cognitive salience of first impressions, allows the narration to later stage the surprising 'fall of early impressions' (Sternberg 1978). For instance, it takes little time for the discourse in *Pulp Fiction* to show Jules as a ruthless killer, yet in the end Jules refrains from killing Pumpkin and Honey Bunny (Filmography: 'BMF Wallet' clip). The so-called 'recency effect', or cognitive salience of the latest impressions we received, somewhat counteracts the primacy effect in this example: Jules had just told Vincent that he wanted to quit gangster life, which lends some credibility to Jules' nevertheless surprisingly merciful stance (surprising since Pumpkin has just pointed a gun squarely at his face).

Furthermore, as Remael shows, mainstream film subtitles have a tendency to make characters come across as more abrupt, less idiosyncratic and more standardized, and to reduce the speech of already quite silent and possibly dissenting characters (2003: 236–240; also Kruger 2008: 81). Again, this is not only important for character-oriented narrative, it may also change the audience's perception of characters, their traits and motivation, the causalities that we hypothesize, and our time- and information-governed answers to curiosity and suspense gaps. When Jules and Vincent are let into the apartment, for instance, Jules' first words ('Hey kids. How you boys doin'? Hey, keep chillin'!') seem to imply an exaggerated sense of closeness as well as Jules' self-confident identity and condescension, especially given the suspenseful situation (Filmography: 'Big Kahuna Burger' clip). It is possible that the stiffer, more standardized language of for example the Norwegian Netflix subtitles produces a partly different characterization and hence narrative situation: *Hei unger. Hvordan har dere det? / Ta det med ro.* ('Hello, kids. How are you doing? / Take it easy.'). Less standardized and more slangy, the Dutch Netflix subtitles do capture more meanings that are also narratively relevant: *Hallo jongens, hoe gaat het met jullie? / Chill . . .* ('Hello boys, how's it going with you? / Chill . . .). The use here of the one-word 'chill' also shows how timing in subtitling (synchrony with speech onset and duration of appearance) may have effects on narrativity beyond its function to establish which character is being heard and translated. Thanks to its concision, 'Chill . . .' can stay on the screen somewhat longer than needed for comprehension and thus draw attention to Jules' way of speaking and behaving, with effects on characterization ('Who is he?') and suspense ('What will he do?').

Audio description: verbalizing images that double as narration

Audio description (AD) is meant to help visually impaired audiences find narrative relevance in films and TV programmes, despite partial or total lack of access to the images (Vercauteren 2012: 209). It is a 'spoken commentary added to film soundtracks' ideally 'supplementing the information that is already available from character dialogue and other parts of the soundtrack' (Palmer and Salway 2015: 126). On the one hand, all images are potentially relevant in the sense that they may provide clarity and relevance for *fabula* construction, or at least communicate the *presumption* of relevance for *fabula* construction, or perceptibly or imperceptibly sidestep a coherent *fabula* construction at time t in the *sjuzhet*. On the other hand, as with subtitles, the time available for inserting verbalizations between dialogues is limited, so the first question will be '*What* do we select?' (Marzà Ibáñez 2010, Vercauteren 2012).

Narratively relevant images: detection and selection

First, as for cues that produce clarity (coherence or relevance for *fabula* construction), AD has to select those images that necessarily contextualize *fabula*-relevant aspects of the dialogue. For example, as the hitmen find themselves outside the building where the apartment hit is about to take place, Vincent's highly deictic 'How many up there?' is soon specified by the image of the building in question. Significantly, AD also has to select those images that speak for themselves—as happens in this scene, when Jules and Vincent enter that building (see Vercauteren 2012: 225–227 on what to include for coherence).

Second, in terms of cues that produce narrativity through opacity (presumed or covert relevance for *fabula* construction), AD ideally selects as many images as possible that suggest what the dialogue does not suggest. To that effect, audio describers can learn to recognize their narrative states of mind—suspense, curiosity and surprise—and become aware of the discursive cues that trigger those mental states. In that respect, 'eye behavior is central to understanding human action, both onscreen and offscreen' (Bordwell 2008: 327). The gaze of characters may indicate what one or several characters have in mind—quite literally taken—when saying something: any visually present referent of a verbal item, any other character, any element that constitutes an 'affordance' for some character (Gibson 1979), i.e. an opportunity for an action at some point.

Of note is the fact that the narratively relevant visual cues may be small, i.e. not quite screen-filling and easily overlooked (Vandaele 2012). As they approach the apartment, for instance, the gaze of characters Jules and Vincent suggests that they are repeatedly performing one type of mute action—checking out the safety of an apartment block before their encounter with potentially armed targets—even though their dialogue is about their boss, his wife Mia, how the boss severely maimed a guy who gave her a foot massage, or whether foot massages are really such a big deal.

The scene prior to the gangsters' arrival outside the flat introduces us to Jules and Vincent, who are featured in a car talking about differences between the US and Europe, mainly Amsterdam and Paris (Filmography: 'Royale with Cheese' clip). When they arrive at the apartment building, they start discussing the business at hand:

Jules: We should have shotguns for this kind of a deal. [*Gun loading sound.*]
Vincent: How many up there?
Jules: Three or four.
Vincent: That's counting our guy?
Jules: Not sure.
Vincent: So that means it could be up to five guys up there?
Jules: It's possible.
Vincent: We should have fuckin' shotguns. [*Part of car is slammed shut.*]
Vincent: What's her name?
Jules: Mia.

The British audio description below reduces narrativity—suspense—by not selecting the two hitmen's ongoing visual checks (at least ten) before they knock on the apartment door. The following paragraph features the description that has been inserted in the audio described dialogue:

> They enter an apartment block ... Jules and Vincent get into the old-style elevator. They stare unemotionally ahead. Vincent looks puzzled [*in reaction to what Jules says*] ... The men in matching black suits, white shirts and thin black ties step from the lift into the hallway. Jules leads Vincent further down the corridor. They pause by a window ... They return to pause by the door where they'd paused a moment ago. ... Jules mimes a gun [*in reaction to what Vincent says*]. Jules shakes his head. ... He has a *jheri* curl hairdo and sideburns. Vincent has shoulder-length hair and twinkling blue eyes.
> *(AD file available on http://progressive.ifdnrg.com/ streams/yourlocalcinema/PulpFictionCLIP.mp3)*

Despite including the initial dialogue about what awaits them in the apartment, the AD thus shifts the original's suspense-laden comedy or comic suspense (Vandaele 2010) towards pure comedy about the dangers of foot massage. This is because the narrativity (in this case, the narrative suspense) here hinges on those visual cues that continuously remind us, during the incongruous dialogue or in minute alternation, that there is also imminent danger. Also lost, for the same reason, is the characterization of both men as witty and relaxed even under pressure, with a possible gun fight ahead.

Given such problems of detection or selection, Orero and Vilaró (2012) suggest using eye-tracking methodology for investigating the visual attention that audiences pay to characters; and eye-tracking research by Kruger (2012: 67) seems to confirm that 'visually peripheral elements' which play a 'covert' role in narrative are important and compete for attention with more 'overt' visual elements. Vandaele (2012) draws attention to the following visual cues besides gaze: available objects of perception, apparent non-perception, sharedness of (non-)perception, and passive reactions of characters (non-reaction as action).

Narratively relevant images: aspects of verbalization

In the previous scene there was narratively relevant simultaneity in communication—dialogue and safety checks—but there were in principle sufficient opportunities for verbal compensation. The problem was one of detection and/or selection. Beyond this problem, however, the opportunity for speech may sometimes be too limited to compensate for the audiovisual narration's simultaneity (Vercauteren 2012: 220–221). Moreover, even when there is an opportunity for speech, the verbal narration of two actions will suggest the relevance of both asserted actions, while film narration can show two actions without actually communicating that both should count as relevant actions (Chatman 1999: 440, Vercauteren 2012: 210).

In the Coen brothers' *No Country for Old Men* (2007) (Filmography: 'The Deputy' clip), simultaneous audiovisual narration thus suggests that the gaze of one character-in-action is *not* directed toward something that is important to him: a sheriff does not realize that the criminal Anton is approaching. To enter in a narrative state, audiences need information (or disinformation) about affordances. Any description that 'the sheriff has his back turned to Anton' and 'remains calm' will therefore be an important part of the verbal narration. However, audio narration cannot achieve simultaneity; so when it *asserts*, as it has to, that (a) the sheriff is on the phone (b) with his back to Anton (c) who is approaching, it communicates the presumption of relevance of all three asserted facts, whereas the filmic narration may suggest this overall relevance somewhat more gradually.

Taking their cue from Wittgenstein, Palmer and Salway (2015: 131) advise audio describers to assess where the verbal expressions available are situated on what they call the action-thought continuum: 'They are *standing* behind the curtain' is closer to the behavioural pole (action), while 'They are *hiding* behind the curtain' is closer to the mindreading pole (thought). To see that this choice may modulate though not make or break suspense, consider for the sheriff scene the choice between thought-reading narration (e.g. 'The sheriff does not see that Anton is approaching') and behaviourist narration (e.g. 'The sheriff has his back turned to Anton, who is approaching'). Insofar as film narrative seldom engages in mindreading, and since the explicit verbal expression of causality ('because', 'therefore', 'in order to') has no counterpart in image sequences (Ryan 2004: 11), what Palmer and Salway (2015) call behaviourist narration is often preferred by audio description specialists. Palmer and Salway also point out that expressions are often located between the poles of the continuum. Indeed, to what extent are expressions like 'She smiles' or 'She hesitates' behaviourist descriptions or renderings of a character's emotive-mental point of view (*ibid.*: 134)? Furthermore, given the links between narrative force and hypothesis formation, I suggest that modalizing expressions may sometimes be useful ('He *seems* to'), though one should not cognitively 'overburden' the audience (Pérez-González 2014: 26).

Narratively relevant images: The timing of characterization

Visual communication is able to present information simultaneously (Remael and Vercauteren 2007: 75), while purely verbal narrative communication is radically sequential—word after word, proposition after proposition. We have just seen how this difference may affect the micro-dynamics of narrativity; yet it may also affect the dynamics of characterization. The audio description for *Pulp Fiction* quoted above, for instance, waits to give certain details about the physical appearance of Jules, such as his *jheri* curl hairdo and sideburns, until they have left the car and entered the building—instead of delivering that information when Jules first makes his appearance in the film. Some insights by Chatman (1999: 450) are almost of *verbatim* relevance here: no member of the audience will actually formulate in so many words that Jules was black, had a *jheri* curl hairdo and sideburns, and so on; we may have a profound sense of Jules' presence as incarnated by Samuel Jackson but not of the assertion of those details as such, nor in the order given by the verbal narration. Yet the AD, when it has the chance, may need to single out and assert some aspects for character construction. Regarding Jules, the audio describer should ask which aspects impinge on later hypothesis formulation by non-impaired audiences: does this image communicate something *relevant soon* for hypothesis formation about this character's behaviour in future situations—e.g. the hallway scene, the apartment scene and the diner scene?

Dubbing

Narrative and synchrony

The best-known constraint of translation for dubbing, i.e. lip synchrony, should not be problematic for the development of narrative. Experts in semiotic coherence (e.g. Chaume 2008; cf. also Schwarz 2011: 400) indicate one caveat regarding narrative clarity: lip synchrony should not come at the cost of 'kinesic' *a*synchrony, where facial expressions and body movements would not cohere with the dubbed dialogue, as when a character shakes her head but says *sí* ('yes') in Catalan (Chaume 2008: 133). In order to test if lip synchrony can be married with overall semiotic coherence, including narrative clarity, Chaume presents his readers with a case from *Pulp Fiction* that is interesting for its narrative meanings. Vincent has just arrived at his boss' home to pick up Mia (Uma Thurman), who, unseen by Vincent, talks to him over an intercom microphone 'with a striking close-up of her lips' (2008: 138). She says, 'Go make yourself a drink, and I'll be down in two shakes of a lamb's tail.' As a speech action, it is an instruction as well as a promise. As a part of narration, it characterizes Mia as a mysterious and elusive person—open to mind games, verbally creative, and perhaps somewhat dominant. As such, the scene harks back to the earlier conversation Vincent and Jules had about her, and builds curiosity as well as suspense. What is she like? Will Vincent be able to resist her? Is he in danger of going too far, like the unfortunate foot massager?

Existing translations show that aspects of synchrony need not hinder narrative clarity or emotions. A Spanish dubbing from Netflix Mexico—*Prepárate una copa y bajaré en menos de lo que te imaginas* ('Prepare a drink and I will come down in less than you imagine')—complies with three noticeable lip closings and most narrative functions, though not the verbal creativity of *two shakes of a lamb's tail*. The corresponding French dubbing from Netflix France—*Faites comme chez vous. J'en ai pour deux secondes. Le temps d'un battement de cil.* ('Act as if you're at home. I need two seconds. The time it takes to bat an eyelash.')—also retains three noticeable lip closings and most narrative functions, though not the explicit drinking instruction, which is relegated to the next scene where Mia speaks off-screen, which in French includes the instruction *Servez-vous à boire* ('Serve yourself a drink').

Narrative and synchrony

Besides lip and kinesic synchrony, there is one more aspect of dubbing to be mentioned in the context of narrative fiction. As often happens in translation, there is a standardization tendency in the dubbing of dialogue—sometimes a consequence or legacy of explicit ideology (Vandaele 2015: 173). Quite parallel to what Remael (2003) says about mainstream subtitling, Pérez-González (2014: 128) notes that dubbing translates less the characterization-enhancing aspects of the original film dialogue (its 'appraisal telos') than aspects that propel the narrative (its 'mood telos'); and Bosseaux (2015) relates neutralizing characterization to aspects of performance in dubbing (e.g. range of vocabulary, voice characteristics, and so on).

Summary

This chapter has focused on the production and translation of narrativity in audiovisual texts. Action (in the story) should always be analyzed as the narration of action; and the narration of action (and action situations) produce narrative clarity (coherence) as well as degrees of opacity (conspicuous and hidden information gaps). As for clarity, narrativity of course depends on comprehensible scene construction, so the identification of setting, participants, action and interaction is basic. As for opacity, the chapter has focused on 'the big three' narrative effects—suspense, curiosity and surprise (Bordwell 2008: 101). These narrative effects are produced through character-oriented focalization as well as the narrating instance's decision to tell things selectively and in a certain order. This is possible across media but each medium of narration does have special possibilities and constraints. Audiovisual translators, moreover, often have to cope with additional constraints of space and time. Their translation solutions, however, can at the very least be grounded in a profound understanding of narrativity, its mechanisms and devices, and the extent to which it depends on medium-specific narration.

Further reading

Bordwell, D. (1985) *Narration in the Fiction Film*, Madison: University of Wisconsin Press.
Bosseaux, C. (2015) *Dubbing, Film and Performance*. Oxford: Peter Lang.
Díaz Cintas, J. and A. Remael (2007) *Audiovisual Translation. Subtitling*, London: Routledge.
Gaudreault, A. and F. Jost (1990) *Le récit cinématographique*, Paris: Nathan.
Palmer, A. and A. Salway (2015) 'Audio Description on the Thought-Action Continuum', *Style* 49(2): 126–148.

Related topics

3   Subtitling on the cusp of its futures
4   Investigating dubbing: learning from the past, looking to the future
6   Subtitling for deaf and hard of hearing audiences: moving forward
8   Audio description: evolving recommendations for usable, effective and enjoyable practices

12 Mediality and audiovisual translation
13 Spoken discourse and conversational interaction in audiovisual translation
16 Pragmatics and audiovisual translation
17 Multimodality and audiovisual translation
22 Eye tracking in audiovisual translation research
23 Audiovisual translation and audience reception

References

Bal, M. (1985) *Narratology: Introduction to the Theory of Narrative*, Toronto: University of Toronto.
Bordwell, D. (1985) *Narration in the Fiction Film*, Madison: University of Wisconsin Press.
Bordwell, D. (2006) *The Way Hollywood Tells It: Story and Style in Modern Movies*, Berkeley: University of California Press.
Bordwell, D. (2008) *Poetics of Cinema*, New York: Routledge.
Bosseaux, C. (2015) *Dubbing, Film and Performance*, Oxford: Peter Lang.
Bremond, C. (1964) 'Le message narratif', *Communications* 1(4): 4–32.
Cattrysse, P. and Y. Gambier (2008) 'Screenwriting and Translating Screenplays', in J. Díaz Cintas (ed.) *The Didactics of Audiovisual Translation*, Amsterdam: John Benjamins, 39–55.
Chatman, S. (1978) *Story and Discourse: Narrative Structure in Fiction and Film*, Ithaca, NY: Cornell University Press.
Chatman, S. (1984) 'What Is Description in the Cinema?' *Cinema Journal* 23(4): 4–11.
Chatman, S. (1999). 'What Novels Can Do That Films Can't and Vice Versa', in L. Braudy and M. Cohen (eds) *Film Theory and Criticism: Introductory Readings*, New York & Oxford: Oxford University Press, 435–451.
Chaume, F. (2004) *Cine y traducción*, Madrid: Cátedra.
Chaume, F. (2008) 'Teaching Synchronisation in a Dubbing Course: Some Didactic Proposals', in J. Díaz Cintas (ed.) *The Didactics of Audiovisual Translation*, Amsterdam: John Benjamins, 129–40.
Cohn, D. (1990) 'Signposts of Fictionality: A Narratological Perspective', *Poetics Today* 11(4): 775–804.
Currie, G. (1995) *Image and Mind: Film, Philosophy and Cognitive Science*, Cambridge: Cambridge University Press.
Díaz Cintas, J. and A. Remael (2007) *Audiovisual Translation. Subtitling*, London: Routledge.
Doležel, L. (1998) *Heterocosmica: Fiction and Possible Worlds*, Baltimore: Johns Hopkins University Press.
Fludernik, M. (2000) 'Genres, Text Types, or Discourse Modes? Narrative Modalities and Generic Categorization', *Style* 34(2): 274–92.
Gaudreault, A. and F. Jost (1990) *Le récit cinématographique*, Paris: Nathan.
Genette, G. (1972) *Figures III*, Paris: Seuil.
Gibson, J. J. (1979) *The Ecological Approach to Visual Perception*, Boston: Houghton Mifflin.
Goffman, E. (1969) *The Presentation of Self in Everyday Life*, London: Penguin.
Herman, D. (2002) *Story Logic: Problems and Possibilities of Narrative*, Lincoln: University of Nebraska Press.
Herman, D. (2008) 'Description, Narrative, and Explanation: Text-Type Categories and the Cognitive Foundations of Discourse Competence', *Poetics Today* 29(3): 437–472.
Jahn, M. (2005) *Narratology: A Guide to the Theory of Narrative*. Cologne: English Department, University of Cologne. Available online: http://www.uni-koeln.de/~ame02/pppn.htm [last access: 20 December 2017].
Kruger, J. L. (2008) 'Subtitler Training as Part of a General Training Programme in the Language Professions,' in J. Díaz Cintas (ed.) *The Didactics of Audiovisual Translation*, Amsterdam: John Benjamins, 71–87.
Kruger, J. L. (2012) 'Making Meaning in AVT: Eye Tracking and Viewer Construction of Narrative', *Perspectives* 20(1): 67–86.

Kukkonen, K. (2014) 'Plot', in P. Hühn, J. Pier, W. Schmid and J. Schönert (eds) *The Living Handbook of Narratology*. Available online: http://www.lhn.uni-hamburg.de/article/plot [last access: 20 December 2017].

Marleau, L. (1982) 'Les sous-titres... un mal nécessaire', *Meta* 27(3): 271–85.

Marzà Ibáñez, A. (2010) 'Evaluation Criteria and Film Narrative. A Frame to Teaching Relevance in Audio Description', *Perspectives* 18(3): 143–153.

Meister, J. Ch. (2014) 'Narratology', in P. Hühn, J. Pier, W. Schmid and J. Schönert (eds) *The Living Handbook of Narratology*. Available online: http://www.lhn.uni-hamburg.de/article/narratology [last access: 20 December 2017].

Neira Piñeiro, M. del R. (2003) *Introducción al discurso narrativo fílmico*, Madrid: Arco Libros.

Orero, P. and A. Vilaró (2012) 'Eye Tracking Analysis of Minor Details in Films for Audio Description', *MonTI* (4): 295–319.

Palmer, A. and A. Salway (2015) 'Audio Description on the Thought-Action Continuum', *Style* 49(2): 126–148.

Pérez-González, L. (2014) *Audiovisual Translation: Theories, Methods and Issues*, London & New York: Routledge.

Porter Abbott, H. (2014) 'Narrativity' in P. Hühn, J. Pier, W. Schmid and J. Schönert (eds) *The Living Handbook of Narratology*. Available online: http://www.lhn.uni-hamburg.de/article/narrativity [last access: 20 December 2017].

Prince, G. (1982) *Narratology. The Form and Functioning of Narrative*, The Hague: Mouton.

Remael, A. (2003) 'Mainstream Narrative Film Dialogue and Subtitling', *The Translator* 9(2): 225–247.

Remael, A. and G. Vercauteren (2007) 'Audio Describing the Exposition Phase of Films: Teaching Students What to Choose', *TRANS* (11): 73–94.

Ryan, M. L. (2004) *Narrative across Media: The Languages of Storytelling*, Lincoln: University of Nebraska Press.

Schank, R. C. and R. P. Abelson (1977) *Scripts, Plans, Goals, and Understanding: An Inquiry into Human Knowledge Structures*, Hillsdale: Lawrence Erlbaum.

Schwarz, B. (2011) 'Translation for Dubbing and Voice-Over', in K. Malmkjær and K. Windle (eds) *The Oxford Handbook of Translation Studies*, Oxford: Oxford University Press, 394–409.

Sternberg, M. (1978) *Expositional Modes and Temporal Ordering in Fiction*, Baltimore: Johns Hopkins University Press.

Sternberg, M. (2009) 'Epilogue: How (Not) to Advance Toward the Narrative Mind', in G. Brône and J. Vandaele (eds) *Cognitive Poetics*, Berlin: Mouton de Gruyter, 455–532.

Sternberg, M. (2010) 'Narrativity: From Objectivist to Functional Paradigm', *Poetics Today* 31(3): 507–659.

Sperber, D. and D. Wilson (1986) *Relevance: Communication and Cognition*, Oxford: Blackwell.

Todorov, T. (1969) *Grammaire du Décaméron*, The Hague: Mouton.

Vandaele, J. (2010) 'Narrative Humor (I): Enter Perspective', *Poetics Today* 31(4): 721–785.

Vandaele, J. (2012) 'What Meets the Eye: Cognitive Narratology for Audio Description', *Perspectives* 20(1): 87–102.

Vandaele, J. (2015) *Estados de Gracia. Billy Wilder y la censura franquista (1946–1975)*, Leiden & Boston: Brill.

Vercauteren, G. (2012) 'A Narratological Approach to Content Selection in Audio Description: Towards a Strategy for the Description of Narratological Time', *MonTI* 4: 207–231.

Wilson, G. M. (1986) *Narration in Light: Studies in Cinematic Point of View*, Baltimore: Johns Hopkins University Press.

Zabalbeascoa, P., N. Izard and L. Santamaría (2001) 'Disentangling Audiovisual Translation into Catalan from the Spanish Media Mesh', in Y. Gambier and H. Gottlieb (eds) *(Multi)Media Translation*, Amsterdam & Philadelphia: John Benjamins, 101–12.

Filmography

Double Indemnity (1944) Billy Wilder. IMDb entry: http://www.imdb.com/title/tt0036775/?ref_=fn_al_tt_1

No Country for Old Men (2007) Ethan Coen and Joel Coen. IMDb entry: http://www.imdb.com/title/tt0477348/?ref_=nv_sr_1

No Country for Old Men (clip) 'The Deputy': https://www.miramax.com/watch?v=Y0aTVuYTqUmu_BDKlAXt9niW_A4NjGFr

Pulp Fiction (1994) Quentin Tarantino. IMDb entry: http://www.imdb.com/title/tt0110912/?ref_=nv_sr_1

Pulp Fiction (clip) 'Big Kahuna Burger': https://www.miramax.com/watch?v=ExMjlvYToStXO4a_C_Vx0D2ZzNZGG1Ql

Pulp Fiction (clip) 'BMF Wallet': https://www.miramax.com/watch?v=lpNHRuYzr1Vc3apQBydQ9cJMXgUjjZCj

Pulp Fiction (clip) 'Nobody ever Robs Restaurants': https://www.miramax.com/watch?v=ZvaG1wYTr1njYTXQTiK91qsASFjxf0SC

Pulp Fiction (clip) 'Royale with Cheese': https://www.miramax.com/watch?v=FmM3NvZTor5ZSe5SOQC5N3udTwFBJYQn

Reservoir Dogs (1992) Quentin Tarantino. IMDb entry: https://www.imdb.com/title/tt0105236/

The Office (2001–3) Ricky Gervais and Stephen Merchant. IMDb entry: http://www.imdb.com/title/tt0290978/?ref_=nv_sr_2

16
Pragmatics and audiovisual translation

Louisa Desilla

What is pragmatics?

Successful communication undoubtedly presupposes, but does not automatically derive from, the mere recognition of the dictionary meanings of the words uttered. A constellation of other factors are involved in utterance interpretation, jointly determining what is referred to as 'interpersonal meaning', 'meaning in context' or 'meaning in interaction' (Thomas 1995). These include the situational context in which the utterance is produced, sociocultural and encyclopaedic knowledge as well as cognitive and conversational principles. Thus, the field of semantics with its rather restricted focus on meaning within the language system, namely the sense of words and the propositions expressed by sentences (Hurford and Heasley 1983: 1–3), fails to account for interpersonal meaning in its totality. The field traditionally associated with the study of meaning in interaction is pragmatics. As Thomas explains (1995: 22; emphasis added):

> This [definition of Pragmatics as meaning in interaction] reflects the view that meaning is not something which is inherent in the words alone, nor is produced by the speaker alone, nor by the hearer alone. Making meaning is a dynamic process, involving the *negotiation* of meaning between speaker and hearer, the context of utterance (physical, social and linguistic) and the meaning potential of an utterance.

Despite early attempts to define pragmatics in contrast to semantics, most modern approaches argue for a complementary relationship between the two. For proponents of the latter stance, pragmatics exploits propositional meaning in elucidating the expression (by the speaker) and the recognition (by the hearer) of communicative intentions (Dascal 2003: 6–10). However, the comprehension of interpersonal meaning is not always straightforward; quite often, propositional meaning diverges considerably from the speaker's communicative intention and this will become evident in the following section where specific pragmatic phenomena are explored.

Pragmatics as a field has bloomed over the second half of the twentieth century. Several trends have emerged and developed, such as philosophical pragmatics (Austin 1962, Searle

1969 and Grice 1975), cognitive pragmatics (Sperber and Wilson 1986/1995 and Blakemore 1987, 1992), interactive pragmatics (Thomas 1995) and societal pragmatics or pragmalinguistics (Mey 1993). As evident from the names of the various subfields, pragmaticians have not hesitated to implement insights from other fields, often adopting an interdisciplinary perspective.

Translation and interpreting activities have increasingly provided a rich source of data for pragmatic research, with an entire special issue of the *Journal of Pragmatics* (Baker 2006) dedicated to this field, as well as an edited volume already dedicated to *The Pragmatics of Translation* (Hickey 1998). At the same time, intercultural pragmatics and cross-cultural pragmatics have made significant contributions to the field of intercultural communication (Jackson 2014: 36). Contrary to the established close collaboration between pragmatics and intercultural studies and their reciprocal development pathways, it can be claimed that pragmatic research in audiovisual translation (AVT) is still in its infancy. Although scholars have often highlighted the importance of sensitizing audiovisual translators to the pragmatics of multimodal texts (e.g. Hatim and Mason 1997, Mason 2001, Remael 2004), there is very little data on the way pragmatic meaning is actually treated in the different AVT modalities or indeed understood by target audiences. Few rigorous attempts have been made to critically apply pragmatic models to the analysis of audiovisual texts, while the potential synergies between the two fields remain largely unexplored (Desilla 2014).

Pragmatic phenomena and AVT

This section examines three salient pragmatic phenomena, namely speech acts, politeness and implicature, and explores their relevance to the analysis of audiovisual texts. The subsections will follow the same structure for the sake of reader-friendliness: first, each phenomenon will be introduced by means of an example. The way this phenomenon has been approached within pragmatics will be presented and any concepts/theories will be briefly explained. By referring to a selection of key studies that have explored this phenomenon in the context of AVT, it will be shown how the relevant theoretical insights and methodological tools can be applied in practice. At the same time, the discussion in each subsection will tease out the potential ramifications of mishandling the relevant aspects of pragmatic meaning for the comprehension and enjoyment of audiovisual texts. Before embarking upon each phenomenon, we should always bear in mind that as opposed to the single layer of naturally occurring interaction between at least two participants, communication in audiovisual texts usually unfolds on two layers or levels: in films, for instance, the communication among the film characters takes place on the horizontal level while on the vertical level lies the communication between the filmmakers and the audience (Vanoye 1985: 99–118). As will be illustrated in the following sections, it is precisely this double-layeredness (Kozloff 2000) and complex audience design, in tandem with the multimodal nature of audiovisual material, that render the aforementioned pragmatic phenomena particularly worthy of investigation in the context of AVT.

Speech acts

Actions may speak louder than words but, interestingly, speakers use language to do a variety of things on a daily basis. Consider the following utterances:

Examples 1–5

1   I'll come back, I promise.

2   Don't copy what I say!

3   Sweet dreams!

4   You should eat sunflower seeds, as they are rich in iron.

5   Sharp scratch!

Speech Act Theory, which has played a pivotal role in the development of pragmatics, emerged in the early 1960s as a reaction against the logical positivism of Truth Conditional Semantics (TCS) (Thomas 1995: 28). In the paradigm of TCS, sentences are essentially statements representing a state of affairs in the external world and, hence, can be evaluated in terms of truth or falsity (*ibid.*: 30). In other words, TCS was firmly based on the premise that the sole purpose of language is to describe some state of affairs, known as the descriptive fallacy (Hurford and Heasley 1983: 21). Austin, a philosopher of language, in his 1962 seminal publication entitled *How to Do Things with Words* brought into sharp relief that language does not merely reflect reality; it also creates reality, a belief that has been ever since shared by all the approaches developed within pragmatics. As evident in the examples above, people not only describe the world but crucially perform actions via language, such as promising (1), reproaching (2), leave-taking (3) and advising (4).

According to Austin, a speech act consists of three different layers or sub-acts: the *locution*, i.e. what is uttered, the *illocution* or (*illocutionary*) *force*, i.e. the speaker's communicative intention and the *perlocution*, i.e. the effect of the illocution upon the addressee(s), which can be manifested by means of a verbal or nonverbal reaction (Thomas 1995: 49). For instance, the locution of (5), which is very often said by nurses before a blood test or an injection, would be 'sharp scratch', the illocution would be that of a warning, and the perlocution might be that the patient looks the other way. Austin's work is very important as it is with his Speech Act Theory that communication ceases to be considered simply a process of linguistic encoding-decoding and starts to involve intentions. Quite often, though, an utterance may have two illocutions simultaneously. The adjacency pair in Example 6 is a good case in point:

Example 6

[*The following talk exchange takes place at the dinner table*]

Mum: Can you pass me the salad, please?

Daughter: There you go.

In essence, Mum's utterance is an indirect request. Like all indirect speech acts, it has two distinct but complementary illocutions: (a) a direct illocution, which arises when the grammatical form and the linguistic expressions of the sentence uttered are interpreted literally, and (b) an indirect illocution which is any additional communicative force the utterance may have (Searle 1979: 30–32). Hence, the direct illocution of 'Can you pass me the salad, please?' is an enquiry about her daughter's ability to pass the salad, while its indirect illocution is a request that her daughter pass the salad. The addressee is able to capture the indirect illocution by virtue of the conventionality of this utterance; certain linguistic expressions such us 'can you', 'could you (possibly)' lead to standard requestive interpretations and are generally considered polite. On this basis, Example 6 illustrates *conventional indirectness* (Blum-Kulka 1989: 68, *cf.* Blum-Kulka 1987: 141). Language indirectness and, in particular, *non-conventional indirectness* (*ibid.*), will be examined in detail below.

One of the first researchers to show interest in the handling of speech acts in AVT is Bruti (2006, 2009). Bruti (2006) focuses specifically on compliments, which she treats as 'culturally constrained speech acts', and examines them in subtitled films from English into Italian. In a more recent publication (Bruti 2014), she compares the translation of compliments in professional subtitling to that in fansubbing. Moreover, Bonsignori *et al.* (2012) explore how English greetings, leave-takings and good wishes are dubbed into Italian (*cf.* Bonsignori and Bruti 2015). In Somwe Mubenga (2009) speech acts feature as the core units of meaning in the research methodology for film discourse put forward by the author under the name of 'multimodal pragmatic analysis'. Finally, Pedersen (2008) proposes a model of subtitle quality assessment that is largely based on aspects of speech act theory and, in particular, on the importance of conveying the speaker's illocution to the target audience.

Politeness

As Pinker (1994: 230) aptly remarks, 'when we put words into people's ears we are impinging on them and revealing our own intentions, honourable or not, just as surely as if we were touching them'. Jack's utterance addressing Alice he has just met in a club (Example 7), epitomizes this quite clearly:

Example 7

Jack: So, your place or mine?

Being polite, in the broadest sense, means to show consideration towards the feelings of others by making appropriate verbal, paraverbal and nonverbal choices in a given sociocultural context (Sifianou 2001: 116). Although we all have an idea of what is polite and are able to recognize behaviour that deviates from the norm, politeness is a very complex notion and has been variously defined and approached within linguistics. At the most basic level a distinction needs to be made between deference and politeness as a pragmatic phenomenon. *Deference* can be described as 'the respect we show to other people by virtue of their higher status, greater age, etc.', which is construed in the grammar (e.g. the choice between *tu/vous* in French, *du/Sie* in German, *tu/Lei* in Italian *tú* vs. *Usted* in Spanish and so on) and/or lexicon of languages (e.g. address forms and honorifics, such as Doctor, Professor and Sir/Madam) (Thomas 1995: 150–151). As such, deference is very close to the common perception of 'politeness' and has been mainly studied within sociolinguistics. Pragmatics, on the other hand, is not interested *per se* in 'any moral or psychological disposition towards being nice to one's interlocutor' (*ibid.*: 178) but rather in politeness as 'a strategy (or a series of strategies) [deliberately] employed by the speaker to achieve a variety of goals' which include, but are by no means limited to, 'promoting harmonious relations' (*ibid.*: 157–158). Several theories have been proposed for politeness as a pragmatic phenomenon, e.g. Lakoff (1973), Brown and Levinson (1978/1987), Leech (1983) and Fraser (1990). In the present volume, the focus will be exclusively on Brown and Levinson's 'face management' approach, which is perhaps the most influential paradigm, quite popular among AVT scholars, as well.

Brown and Levinson's (1978/1987) politeness theory is built around *face* referring to every person's feeling of self-worth or self-image, which can be maintained, enhanced or damaged through interaction. Face is twofold: *positive face* is reflected in our desire to be liked and approved of by others and *negative face* encapsulates our desire to have the freedom to act as we choose and not to be imposed upon. Accordingly, there are *face-threatening acts* (FTAs), namely speech acts that can threaten the addressee's negative face (e.g. requests, orders, threats, warnings, offers, promises, compliments) or his/her positive face (e.g. expressions of criticism/disapproval/contempt, complaints, disagreements, challenges). Similarly, there are FTAs that pose a threat to the speaker's negative face (e.g. expressing thanks, accepting apologies/offers, excuses, unwilling promises and offers) or his/her positive face (e.g. apologies, acceptance of compliments, admissions of guilt/responsibility).

If a speaker decides to actually perform an FTA, there is a range of strategies to choose from based on his/her assessment of the size of the FTA in question, which can be calculated by taking into account the power and distance between the interlocutors as well as the rating of the imposition (Brown and Levinson 1978/1987). This selection of strategies includes: performing the FTA without any redress (bald on-record), performing the FTA with redress using positive politeness, performing the FTA with redress using negative politeness and performing the FTA with off-record politeness.

Speakers tend to opt for performing the FTA with no redressive action, namely speaking directly without any mitigation whatsoever, in Examples 8–11 (Thomas 1995: 170–171):

Examples 8–11

8 In an emergency: e.g. 'Help me out of here'

9 When the FTA is perceived as being in the addressee's interest: e.g. 'Have a chocolate'

10 When the power differential is great: e.g. 'You are to stand to attention every time the door is opened'

11 When the speaker has chosen to be deliberately offensive: e.g. [*Mr Tam Dalyell, MP, in the House of Commons on 29 October 1986, referring to the then Prime Minister, Margaret Thatcher*] 'I say that she is a bounder, a liar, a deceiver, a crook'.

When performing the FTA with positive politeness, the speaker appeals to the addressee's positive face by using in-group identity markers, expressing interest in him/her and/or claiming common ground (Sifianou 2001: 129):

Example 12

I know you are a gem. Give me just a few more days to return the book.

Alternatively, if the context warrants it, negative politeness may be employed by means of deference markers, hedging, admitting/apologizing for the imposition, and/or being thankful or indebted, as illustrated below (adapted from Thomas 1995: 172):

Example 13

[*From a student's email to his lecturer*]

Dear Prof. X, I would be grateful if we could perhaps meet on Thursday to discuss my essay. Many thanks.

Using off-record politeness would be another possibility when performing FTAs. More specifically, the speaker can give hints, resort to metaphors/irony/sarcasm, and/or be ambiguous/vague. For instance, the speaker may say:

Example 14

Gosh, I'm out of cash. I forgot to go to the bank.

Here, as Sifianou (2001: 129–130) explains,

> the exact interpretation is left to the addressee, because it is not clear whether a statement or a request has been made. Thus if the addressee understands it as a request and says something like 'I would like to help you but I'm out of cash myself', the speaker could still say 'Oh! I didn't mean I wanted you to lend me money'. This strategy is used when the risk of loss of face is judged as great.

Off-record politeness options can be intimately linked with the generation of implicatures that will be discussed below, along with their communicative advantages.

One of the main criticisms articulated against Brown and Levinson (1978/1987) is that they seem to suggest that positive and negative politeness strategies are mutually exclusive. In everyday conversation, however, the speaker can employ both in a single utterance (Thomas 1995: 176):

Example 15

Do me a favour—piss off!

In a similar vein, it is not always easy to identify the precise strategy used: for example, although Jack's utterance addressing Alice in Example 7 is an indirect invitation to spend the night together, thus potentially illustrating off-record politeness, due to the easily recognizable sexual associations it tends to carry as a fixed expression it could be also regarded as a bald on-record FTA in this context.

Hatim and Mason (1997) were the first AVT scholars who drew attention to politeness in subtitling, expressing the concern that this aspect of interpersonal meaning may suffer in the target text due to the physical constraints intrinsic to this AVT modality. Indeed, limitations of time and space necessitate the reduction of the original which often involves changing (indirect) requests into direct imperatives as well as omitting hedging and indicators of modality: for instance, when faced with rather strict constraints, the subtitler might be tempted to render 'I was wondering if you could give me a lift' as 'Give me a lift'. As Díaz Cintas and Remael (2007: 155) advise, these reformulations 'must be undertaken with care' because they 'can make a character come across more abrupt, more decisive or less polite' and, therefore, not as intended by the filmmakers, who have voiced criticism of such distortions (Pérez-González 2014). The narrative ramifications of politeness shifts in subtitling are discussed in more depth in Mason (2001) and Remael (2003). In addition, Yuan's (2012) investigation of audience response to politeness representations in Chinese>English subtitling sheds some light on how the impression of a character's personality, attitude and intentions can differ between source- and target-viewers. Notwithstanding the risk for characterization posed by certain forms of text condensation, it should be recognized that pragmatic meaning in audiovisual texts can also be recovered, if only partly, from body language and/or prosody, as viewers systematically draw on them in the meaning-making process, rather than relying solely on the subtitles (Desilla 2014). The study by Gartzonika and Şerban (2009) explores the treatment of FTAs in the English subtitles of the Greek film *Loaf and Camouflage* (1984) and reveals some interesting cases where offensive language has been, quite surprisingly, added in the target text for the sake of effect.

Implicature

In Example 6, Mum's indirect request was considered an instance of *conventional indirectness* (Blum-Kulka 1989: 68). Now consider the following exchange which exemplifies *non-conventional indirectness* (adapted from Blum-Kulka 1989: 39):

Example 16

[*This conversation takes place at a grocery store between a 5-year-old boy, his father and his grandmother*]

Boy (pointing to an item on a shelf):	What's that?
Father (waiting in the queue):	We can't buy up the whole shop.
Grandmother:	He wasn't asking you to buy anything. He only wanted to know what it is. He's a good boy.

Here, the addressees do not agree on a specific interpretation (Blum-Kulka 1989: 39). As opposed to the grandmother, the father interprets the boy's utterance as conversationally implying a request (*ibid.*). Contrary to Mum's utterance in Example 6 where both illocutions are valid simultaneously, the boy's utterance can be interpreted either as a request or as an information-seeking question but not both (*ibid.*). The locution 'What's that?' does not conventionally (i.e. in any context) convey a requestive intention. Thus, it appears that the indirect meaning in Example 16 is recovered taking primarily context into account. Indeed, as the term suggests, non-conventional indirectness is more context-bound than conventional indirectness. It is also worth noting that owing to their relatively wide range of possible interpretations, instances of non-conventional indirectness are presumably riskier and demand more processing effort than instances of conventional indirectness (*cf.* Weizman 1989, Dascal 1983).

In the present chapter, implicature is treated as a sub-type of non-conventional indirectness. The two most influential pragmatic approaches to implicature are subsequently presented. First, Grice's pioneering study of implicature is outlined. Then, the focus is shifted to the cognitive psychological perspective of Relevance Theory (Sperber and Wilson 1995, Wilson and Sperber 2004). Particular emphasis is placed upon the relevance-theoretic model of utterance comprehension, which accounts for both implicit and explicit meaning. It is also shown how this model has formed the basis for the pragmatic analysis component of a methodology proposed for the investigation of implicatures in AVT.

If indirectness can be costly and put smooth communication in peril, then why do speakers indulge in it anyway? As Lee and Pinker (2010) point out, the answer resides in its important pay-offs. Various explanations have been proposed for the universal phenomenon of indirectness, such as the regard for politeness described above, the desire to intensify the force of one's message and/or to make one's language more interesting and appealing (Brown and Levinson 1978/1987, Leech 1983). In the aforementioned explanations, the use of indirectness seems to help the speaker obtain some communicative advantage or avoid some undesirable effect (Thomas 1995: 122). In Example 17, let us revisit Jack's indirect invitation to Alice (originally featured in Example 7), this time accompanied by her response:

Example 17

[*This talk exchange takes place in a club. The interlocutors have just met. Jack, who is overconfident, flirts with Alice who does not seem interested*]

Jack: So, your place or mine?

Alice: I'd rather eat chocolate!

In what follows, it will be demonstrated how Alice's reply to Jack's indirect invitation to spend the night together, and in particular, the implicatures it evokes can be catered for within both the Gricean and Relevance Theory frameworks.

The essence of Grice's account of conversation and implicature resides in one of the William James lectures he gave at the University of Harvard in 1967 (Atlas 2005: 45), which was published in 1975 in a paper entitled 'Logic and Conversation'. As the title suggests, conversation is treated here as a manifestation of rational behaviour. Grice claims that communication does not occur in a haphazard, accidental way, and that conversations are rule-governed, cooperative exchanges (1975/1991: 306). In the course of everyday communication, interlocutors are assumed to observe the Cooperative Principle (CP), which is formulated as follows:

Cooperative Principle: Make your conversational contribution such as is required, at the stage at which it occurs, by the accepted purpose or direction of the talk exchange in which you are engaged.

(Grice 1975/1991: 307)

The CP is intended to encapsulate the rational, cooperative, goal-oriented nature of communication and gives rise to the following maxims of conversation (Grice 1975/1991: 308–309):

Quantity

- Make your contribution as informative as is required (for the current purposes of the exchange)
- Do not make your contribution more informative than is required

Quality

- Do not say what you believe to be false
- Do not say that for which you lack adequate evidence

Relation

- Be relevant

Manner

- Avoid obscurity
- Avoid ambiguity
- Be brief
- Be orderly

As Grice observes, the maxims are not always adhered to; speakers often fail to observe them for various reasons (1975/1991: 310). Nevertheless, communication can proceed smoothly and, thus, be successful regardless of whether speakers adhere to the maxims or not, since addressees always entertain the assumption that (at least) the CP is observed (Marmaridou 2000: 229–230). Although there are various types of maxim non-observance, only one is characteristically associated with the generation of what Grice calls *particularized conversational implicatures*, namely *maxim flouting* or *exploitation*. In floutings speakers blatantly fail to adhere to a maxim in order to exploit it for communicative purposes (Grice 1975/1991: 310). At first glance, Alice's response seems completely irrelevant thus flouting the maxim of Relation. However, based on Grice, there is no reason to assume that Alice is not a rational cooperative speaker. To maintain this assumption and be able to decipher Alice's utterance, Jack needs to activate his background knowledge and, more specifically, that idea of chocolate as a substitute for sexual pleasure. Given this piece of information, one would be able to infer the implicature that Alice rejects Jack's invitation and in quite a derisive manner, for that matter.

Grice's CP 'shook the world of language studies in the past century' (Mey 2002: 911). The CP and maxims of conversation have been applied to different fields, including AVT (e.g. Zabalbeascoa 2005, Skuggevik 2009). He was one of the first to acknowledge the importance of inference in linguistic communication, and his pioneering work on implicature paved the way for future approaches. However, to the best of my knowledge, there are no studies specifically on implicatures in AVT from a Gricean perspective.

Having the Gricean programme as its point of departure, Relevance Theory set out to shed more light upon human communication, while attempting to answer some of the issues not satisfactorily addressed by Grice (Wilson 1994: 55–57). According to its proponents, the pivotal role of inference is not securely established in his theory, while the CP and maxims of conversation themselves pose additional problems: the rationale behind their postulation remains hazy and the maxim of Relation is neglected (Sperber and Wilson 1995: 35–37, *cf.* Wilson 1994: 56).

Relevance Theory has been described as a cognitive psychological theory; in the authors' own words, '[the] aim is to identify the underlying mechanisms, rooted in human psychology, which explain *how* humans communicate with one another' rather than to define communication *per se* (Sperber and Wilson 1995: 32; emphasis added). One of the fundamental tenets of Relevance Theory is that 'every aspect of communication and cognition is governed by the search for relevance' (Wilson 1994: 46). People tend to pay attention to information that they expect to be relevant to them at a given moment (*ibid.*). It is stressed that relevance is not an absolute concept but is achieved in varying degrees (Wilson and Sperber 2004: 609). Interactants select a specific input not simply because it is relevant but because it is the most relevant input available to them on a particular occasion (*ibid.*).

Along with foregrounding the role of relevance in verbal communication, Sperber and Wilson have revamped the notion of context. For them, context is not merely restricted to the immediate socio-physical context and co-text in which an utterance is produced; instead, it is conceptualized as potentially encompassing a whole range of assumptions that the hearer entertains about the world, such as encyclopaedic information, memories, cultural assumptions, beliefs about the speaker and so on (Sperber and Wilson 1995: 16–17). Interestingly, in this framework, context is not determined *a priori*, as many pragmatic theories including Grice would have it, but is construed during interpersonal communication (Sperber and Wilson 1998: 374). Relevance Theory is equipped with the conceptual tools for understanding context selection (Hill 2006: 3). One such tool is the coinage *cognitive environment* (Sperber and Wilson 1995: 30). A cognitive environment consists of all the facts or assumptions that one may perceive or infer; it encompasses anything available to us through senses, memory, culture and communication (*ibid.*; Hill 2006: 3). The relationship between cognitive environment and context can be schematically represented in Figure 16.1 below:

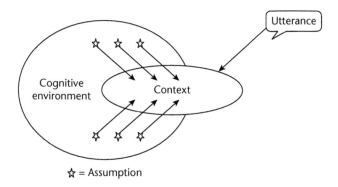

Figure 16.1 Text evokes Context (adapted from Hill 2006: 14).

As Hill (2006: 14) explains, '[an] utterance does not evoke the audience's entire cognitive environment. It only evokes certain assumptions, and these form the context in which the utterance is processed'.

At the same time, as part of the comprehension process, the addressee needs to construct appropriate hypotheses about both the explicit and the implicit meaning of an utterance or, in relevance-theoretic terms, the *explicature*(s) and *implicature*(s) respectively. Implicatures are defined as contextual assumptions or implications derived by the speaker's intention and the hearer's expectation that the utterance of the former is optimally relevant (Sperber and Wilson 1995: 194–195). Two different kinds of implicature are recognized, namely implicated premises and implicated conclusions (*ibid.*: 195). On the one hand, *implicated premises* are mainly retrieved from the addressee's background knowledge and memory (*ibid.*). Such assumptions are identifiable by virtue of guiding the addressee towards an interpretation consistent with the principle of relevance and being the most readily accessible assumptions to this end (*ibid.*). *Implicated conclusions*, on the other hand, are deduced from the context and the explicatures of an utterance processed together (*ibid.*). Such conclusions are identifiable as implicatures based on the speaker's expectation that the addressee will recover them, as the former intends his/her utterance to be relevant to the latter (*ibid.*). Hence, both implicated premises and implicated conclusions are included in the first interpretation complying with the principle of relevance (*ibid.*). Furthermore, the implicatures of an utterance can have varying degrees of strength: an implicature may be strong, i.e. highly predictable, or weak, i.e. not easily determinable (*ibid.*: 199).

In the light of the above, the inferential tasks that Jack would presumably undertake in order to understand Alice's reply in Example 17 can be described as follows: Jack assumes that Alice's utterance is optimally relevant to him; since what he wants to know (taking largely for granted that Alice would like to spend the night with him) is whether she prefers them to spend the night at his or her place, he assumes that Alice's utterance will achieve relevance by replying to his question. This expectation of relevance may be satisfied by the assumption that chocolate is considered as a substitute for sexual pleasure, which is drawn from Jack's cognitive environment. This assumption will be the implicated premise of Alice's utterance that, together with the explicature—i.e. that Alice would rather eat chocolate than spend the night with Jack—can yield the implicated conclusion that Alice refuses to spend the night with Jack because she prefers a substitute of sexual pleasure instead. In turn, the strongly implicated conclusion processed together with background knowledge might generate a series of weak implicatures—i.e. that Alice is not attracted to Jack, she is irritated by his coarse flirting, etc. The surplus processing effort required by Alice's indirect answer is compensated for by surplus cognitive effects, namely the strongly communicated implicature, and possibly the aforementioned weakly communicated implicatures. One should also add to the extra effects the tones of mockery and sarcasm conveyed by Alice's utterance.

Emerging when speakers mean much more (or something completely different from) what they actually say, implicatures are prevalent not only in everyday communication but also in film dialogue (Kozloff 2000, *cf.* Desilla 2012). According to Desilla (2012: 35), 'particularly, the concept of *implicated premise* acquires a very interesting dimension when applied to film communication, as it can flexibly include knowledge available from previous films', thus catering for *intertextuality* (Stafford 2007: 83–84), which is very often achieved indirectly through dialogue, the visuals, music, cinematography, editing or combinations of the above.

Drawing on Relevance Theory, as well as multimodality and film studies, Desilla (2009, 2012, 2014), designed a methodology that sheds light upon the construal, cross-cultural relay and comprehension of film dialogue implicatures by filmmakers, translators and audiences, respectively, in an attempt to address the scarcity of studies of implicit meaning in AVT. More specifically, Desilla proposed a cognitive pragmatic definition of implicature—where relevance-theoretic concepts are adapted accordingly to cater for the semiotic complexity of subtitled films—that is worth quoting at length (Desilla 2014: 195):

> Implicature in film can be defined as any assumption intended by the filmmakers which is implicitly and non-conventionally communicated in the film dialogue. Audiences can infer the intended implicatures via the selection and the joint processing of the most relevant elements from their cognitive environment. The cognitive environment potentially includes information entertained by the viewers themselves as well as information conveyed (perceived or inferred) by the various semiotic resources deployed in the film being viewed. The former may consist, *inter alia*, of encyclopedic and sociocultural

knowledge, as well as personal experience. The latter may be retrieved via the components of the *mise-en-scène*, cinematography, editing and soundtrack. In the case of subtitled films, the cognitive environment of the target audience obviously includes the subtitles which are added onto the visual image. The appropriate selection and exploitation of some of the aforementioned elements comprising the cognitive environment actually forms the particular context for the recovery of implicated conclusions. The utterance(s) that trigger the implicature(s) are intended by the filmmakers to evoke a specific context: background knowledge will be triggered in the form of implicated premises while the information readily conveyed via the film's image and sound will be selected as immediate contextual premises.

Desilla's methodology for investigating implicatures in films comprises three stages: multimodal transcription, pragmatic analysis and empirical testing of implicature comprehension by source- and target-audiences. Multimodal transcription (Baldry and Thibault 2006) was selected as a means of identifying the contribution of verbal and nonverbal semiotic resources to the construal of implicatures and the creation of overall meaning by the filmmakers, and was complemented by a pragmatic analysis of the utterances evoking implicatures and their target-language counterparts in the light of Relevance Theory (Wilson and Sperber 2004) (for analysis of specific examples see Desilla 2012, Pérez-González 2014). Featuring as the final stage of this methodological apparatus, the experimental component was designed to probe implicature comprehension by a sample of source- and target-viewers, while essentially testing the extent to which the intuitive pragmatic analysis undertaken represents a realistic account of implicature understanding by source- and target-audiences (for a more extended account of the experimental design and discussion of findings see Desilla 2014).

The proposed methodology was applied to a case study of implicatures in *Bridget Jones's Diary* (2001), *Bridget Jones: The Edge of Reason* (2004) and their Greek subtitled versions available on DVD. The comparison and contrast of source text and target text in terms of their constitutive explicatures and implicatures revealed three types of implicature relay: preservation (i.e. implicature into same implicature), explicitation (i.e. implicature into explicature), and modification (i.e. implicature into different implicature) (Desilla 2009). It was observed that the vast majority of the instances of implicature identified in the two romantic comedies are preserved in the subtitles, while explicitation (partial or total) is only occasionally opted for. Interestingly enough, half of the cases of explicitation concern instances of implicatures triggered by what translation studies scholars have called *culture-specific items* (Newmark 1988, Ramière 2004) or, more recently, *extralinguistic culture-bound references* (Pedersen 2005). Nevertheless, most implicatures belonging to this category were found to be kept implicit in Greek, with the translator resorting to explicitation only when the intact preservation of an extralinguistic culture-bound reference in the subtitles would highly jeopardize comprehensibility (Desilla 2009). The possible explanations considered for the low frequency of explicitation revolve around factors like subtitle mechanics, practices in the DVD subtitling industry, film polysemiosis, audiences' needs and expectations, as well as distinctive characteristics of implicatures such as open-endedness (*ibid.*). In particular, it was suggested that spelling out implicatures in the subtitles can be both impossible—for example, due to strict physical constraints—and undesirable because of the audience's expectations of target text faithfulness and/or the filmmakers' preference for indirect communication in a given scene fragment. In addition, it was argued that explicitation is less urgent, or even redundant, whenever information easily retrievable from sound and/or image can help the target audience recover the intended implicatures.

Indeed, the majority of implicatures identified in the two films are multimodally construed, often serving a comedic function and, therefore, spelling them out in the subtitles would not only be superfluous but could lead to significant loss of effect. Kovacic (1994), who was the first to promote the concept of relevance as a criterion for source text reduction in subtitling, argues that information readily accessible from context is a highly likely candidate for omission, so that viewers are not overloaded with processing (*cf.* Bogucki 2004). Put differently, the relevance and, ultimately, the effectiveness of the subtitled text decreases as the audience's processing effort increases (Gambier 2003: 185).

Last but not least, it would seem that the narrative functions—intimately linked to plot and characterization—served by a number of implicatures in the two films seem to dictate, more or less strongly, their cross-cultural preservation (Desilla 2009). One of the major narrative functions of implicatures resides in their contribution to the creation of intimacy (sexual and emotional) between the protagonists, a finding that is in accord with research in the language of intimates (e.g. Joos 1967, Tannen 1989, Terkourafi 2011). In this light, explicitation, especially if practised extensively on the part of the translator, can, hypothetically, affect this aspect of characterization. In other words, the target audience might perceive the protagonists as less intimate than intended by the filmmakers (Desilla 2009). At the same time, explicitation is likely to have its gravest consequences when applied to implicatures which are at the services of plot; certain implicatures in the two romantic comedies are skilfully employed for 'misleading' the viewers and keeping them in suspense. Spelling out these implicatures would automatically lead to the resolution of the ambivalence deliberately pursued by the filmmakers. Consequently, explicitation would disrupt the filmmakers' control of the audience's knowledge while simultaneously depriving the audience of the pleasure of searching for that knowledge, as well as of all the suspense experienced in the meantime (*ibid.*).

On the whole, from Desilla's case study, it emerges that implicatures invite the audience to join the game of meaning making by operating at both the horizontal and the vertical levels of filmic communication. In Sperber and Wilson's (1995: 207) terms, 'style is the relationship'; the fairly large number of implicatures in the film dialogue reflects a high degree of closeness not only between the main characters but also between the filmmakers and the viewers. Hence, frequent explicitation in the subtitles may ultimately skew the target audience's perception of the relationship between the filmmakers and the source-audience (*cf.* Hill 2006: 73). Given that the aim of subtitles is to make the film experience comprehensible but no less enjoyable, it seems that explicitation should be applied with caution, since it could significantly lower the degree of engagement of the target audience.

New research avenues

As shown above, pragmatic phenomena have an instrumental role in the comprehension and enjoyment of audiovisual texts. AVT is an excellent environment for both intercultural and cross-cultural pragmatic research (Guillot 2010, 2012), as illustrated by the work of *Tapping the Power of Foreign Language Films: Audiovisual Translation as Cross-cultural Mediation*, an AHRC-funded research network seeking to collate research on the pragmatics of AVT and foster stronger cross-disciplinary collaborations (Tapping the Power, n.d.). From an intercultural pragmatics stance, one can investigate how aspects of interpersonal meaning, such as speech acts and implicature, are handled in the target text and understood by target viewers. From a purely cross-cultural pragmatics perspective, it could be tested whether politeness norms in different cultures (e.g. the positive and negative politeness orientations in Europe as presented in Hickey and Stewart 2005) actually govern the audiovisual translator's behaviour.

As evidenced by the regrettably small number of studies on the pragmatics of AVT cited in this chapter, very little is known about the way pragmatic phenomena travel across modes and cultures. To begin with, there has been a restricted emphasis on films with far too little attention paid to other genres which have been translated for years and could offer interesting data, like sitcoms, reality television, talk-shows, etc. Also, most scholars have so far focused on interlingual subtitling, while other AVT modalities have been rather neglected. For instance, it would be worth looking at FTAs in dubbing and speech acts in surtitling. On a similar note, to date there has hardly been any research on the pragmatics of amateur subtitling, despite the growing body of literature on the nature and particularities of what Pérez-González (2014) discusses under *cybercultures of collaborative AVT*. In both *political subtitling* and *aesthetic subtitling*, translators boldly and innovatively resort to long explicative glosses within brackets and also notes at the upper part of the screen (Díaz Cintas and Muñoz Sánchez 2006, Pérez-González 2014: 256). Such *contextual adjustment material* (Hill 2006)—which is normally absent from the translator's arsenal in mainstream professional subtitling mainly due to physical constraints and, if used, may cause frustration among mainstream viewers—is, by contrast, expected and appreciated by fansub audiences. Thus, studies on the treatment of implicatures in the context of amateur subtitling are likely to yield different findings to those of existing work on official DVD subtitles.

Last but not least, there have been extremely few empirical investigations of the understanding of pragmatic phenomena by actual audiences with scholars so far largely relying on their own intuitions about how film dialogue would be presumably interpreted. It is high time that research in the pragmatics of AVT systematically followed developments in the field of experimental pragmatics, which has been testing pragmatic hypotheses for over a decade now. As Sperber and Noveck point out (2004: 8), 'experimental data can be used together with intuition . . . to confirm or disconfirm hypotheses'. New studies on the reception of pragmatic meaning utilizing methodologies from psycholinguistics and/or experimental psychology would significantly enhance our understanding of the way target audiences comprehend audiovisual texts in comparison to source audiences (Desilla 2014).

Summary

In line with the scope and aims of this volume, the present chapter has provided an overview of three salient pragmatic phenomena, i.e. speech acts, politeness and implicature, teasing out their significant role in the construal, translation and reception of audiovisual texts. An attempt has also been made to familiarize readers with some key studies on the pragmatics of AVT and highlight future trajectories in under-researched modalities and practices. The very fact that AVT allows for the opportunity to tamper with pragmatic meaning as intended by the filmmakers (e.g. through spelling implicatures out in the subtitles or changing a direct request into an indirect one in the dubbed text) renders pragmatic phenomena particularly worthy of investigation in this multimodal context. Indeed, it has been demonstrated that the double-layeredness of film communication *per se* necessitates the careful relay of pragmatic meaning across cultures as any mishandlings may affect character perception, plot development and/or viewer enjoyment. Ultimately, this chapter aspires to sensitize readers to the pragmatics of audiovisual texts and, hopefully, inspire some of them to come up with new research ideas in this fascinating area.

Further reading

Bruti, S. (2006) 'Cross-cultural Pragmatics: The Translation of Implicit Compliments in Subtitles', *JoSTrans: The Journal of Specialised Translation* 6: 185–197. Available online: http://www.jostrans.org/issue06/art_bruti.php [last access 20 December 2017] | This article brings together speech act and politeness considerations focusing on the subtitling of implicit compliments. It discusses data from films belonging to various genres.

Desilla, L. (2014) 'Reading Between the Lines, Seeing Beyond the Images: An Empirical Study on the Comprehension of Implicit Film Dialogue Meaning Across Cultures', *The Translator* 20(2): 194–214 | This article reports on the first attempt to explore the comprehension of film dialogue implicatures by actual source and target viewers, drawing on insights from cognitive (experimental) pragmatics, film-studies and AVT.

Hatim, B. and I. Mason (1997) 'Politeness in Screen Translating', in B. Hatim and I. Mason (eds) *The Translator as Communicator*, London: Routledge, 65–80 | The first scholars to draw attention to the way politeness is relayed in subtitling. One of the greatest strengths of this work pertains to its particular emphasis on audience design.

Remael, A. (2003) 'Mainstream Film Dialogue and Subtitling', *The Translator* 9(2): 225–247 | A refreshing approach to the pragmatics of audiovisual translation, which moves beyond the micro-level analysis bringing into sharp relief the narrative ramifications of politeness shifts in subtitling. Importantly, the article does justice to the semiotic complexity of films, taking into account the role of the visuals.

Thomas, J. (1995) *Meaning in Interaction. An Introduction to Pragmatics*, London: Longman | Although written over 20 years ago, this book remains an excellent introduction to pragmatics, covering all the key pragmatic phenomena and relevant theories. Its uniquely accessible and entertaining style, as well as its plethora of examples from real-life interactions, make it ideal for beginners in the field.

Related topics

13   Spoken discourse and conversational interaction in audiovisual translation
17   Multimodality and audiovisual translation: cohesion in accessible films
18   Sociolinguistics and linguistic variation in audiovisual translation
23   Audiovisual translation and audience reception

References

Atlas, J. D. (2005) *Logic, Meaning, and Conversation: Semantic Indeterminacy, Implicature, and their Interface*, Oxford & New York: Oxford University Press.
Austin, J. L. (1962) *How to Do Things with Words*, Oxford: Oxford University Press.
Baker, M. (ed.) (2006) 'Translation and Context', special issue of *Journal of Pragmatics* 38(3).
Baldry, A. and P. Thibault (2006) *Multimodal Transcription and Text Analysis. A Multimodal Toolkit and Coursebook*, London: Equinox.
Blakemore, D. (1987) *Semantic Constraints on Relevance*, Oxford: Blackwell.
Blakemore, D. (1992) *Understanding Utterances*, Oxford: Blackwell.
Blum-Kulka, S. (1987) 'Indirectness and Politeness in Requests: Same or Different?', *Journal of Pragmatics* 11: 131–146.
Blum-Kulka, S. (1989) 'Playing it Safe: The Role of Conventionality in Indirectness', in S. Blum-Kulka and J. House (eds) *Cross-cultural Pragmatics: Requests and Apologies*, New Jersey: Ablex Publishing, 37–70.
Bogucki, Ł. (2004) 'The Constraint of Relevance in Subtitling', *JoSTrans: The Journal of Specialised Translation* 1: 71–88. Available online: http://www.jostrans.org/issue01/art_bogucki_en.php [last access 20 December 2017].

Bonsignori, V., S. Bruti and S. Masi (2012) 'English Greetings, Leave-takings, and Good Wishes in Dubbed Italian', in A. Şerban, A. Matamala and J. M. Lavaur (eds) *Audiovisual Translation in Close-Up*, Bern: Peter Lang, 23–44.

Bonsignori, V. and S. Bruti (2015) 'Conversational Routines across Languages: The Case of Leave-takings and Greetings in Original and Dubbed Films', in J. Díaz Cintas and J. Neves (eds) *Audiovisual Translation: Taking Stock*, Newcastle upon Tyne: Cambridge, 28–45.

Brown, P. and S. Levinson (1978/1987) *Politeness: Some Universals in Language Usage*, Cambridge: Cambridge University Press.

Bruti, S. (2006) 'Cross-cultural Pragmatics: The Translation of Implicit Compliments in Subtitles', *JoSTrans: The Journal of Specialised Translation* 6: 185–197. Available online: http://www.jostrans.org/issue06/art_bruti.php [last access 20 December 2017].

Bruti, S. (2009) 'Translating Compliments in Subtitles', in A. Baldry, M. Pavesi, C. Taylor Toresello and Christopher Taylor (eds) *From Didactas to Ecolingua: An Ongoing Research Project on Translation and Corpus Linguistics*, Trieste: Edizioni Università di Trieste, 91–110.

Bruti, S. (2014) 'Compliments in Fansubs and in Professional Subtitles: The Case of *Lost*', *Rivista Internazionale di Technica della Traduzione (International Journal of Translation)* 16: 13–34.

Dascal, M. (1983) *Pragmatics and the Philosophy of Mind I: Thought in Language*, Amsterdam & Philadelphia: John Benjamins.

Dascal, M. (2003) *Interpretation and Understanding*, Amsterdam & Philadelphia: John Benjamins.

Desilla, L. (2009) *Towards a Methodology for the Study of Implicatures in Subtitled Films: Multimodal Construal and Reception of Pragmatic Meaning Across Cultures*, Unpublished Doctoral Thesis, University of Manchester.

Desilla, L. (2012) 'Implicatures in Film: Construal and Functions in Bridget Jones Romantic Comedies', *Journal of Pragmatics* 44(1): 30–5.

Desilla, L. (2014) 'Reading Between the Lines, Seeing Beyond the Images: An Empirical Study on the Comprehension of Implicit Film Dialogue Meaning Across Cultures', *The Translator* 20(2): 194–214.

Díaz Cintas J. and P. Muñoz Sánchez (2006) 'Fansubs: Audiovisual Translation in an Amateur Environment', *JoSTrans: The Journal of Specialised Translation* 6. Available online: http://www.jostrans.org/issue06/art_diaz_munoz.pdf [last access 20 December 2017].

Díaz Cintas, J. and A. Remael (2007) *Audiovisual Translation: Subtitling*, Manchester: St. Jerome.

Fraser, B. (1990) 'Perspectives on Politeness', *Journal of Pragmatics* 14(2): 219–236.

Gambier, Y. (2003) 'Screen Transadaptation: Perception and Reception', *The Translator* 9(2), in Y. Gambier (ed.) 'Screen Translation'. Special issue on Audiovisual Translation: 171–189.

Gartzonika, O. and A. Şerban (2009) 'Greek Soldiers on the Screen: Politeness, Fluency and Audience Design in Subtitling', in J. Díaz Cintas (ed.) *New Trends in Audiovisual Translation*, Clevedon: Multilingual Matters, 239–250.

Grice, H. P. (1975/1991) 'Logic and Conversation', in P. Cole and J. Morgan (eds) *Syntax and Semantics 3: Speech Acts*, New York: Academic Press, 41–58. Reprinted in S. Davis (ed.) (1991) *Pragmatics: A Reader*. Oxford & New York: Oxford University Press, 305–315.

Guillot, M. (2010) 'Film Subtitles from a Cross-cultural Pragmatics Perspective: Issues of Linguistic and Cultural Representation', *The Translator* 16(1): 67–92.

Guillot, M. (2012) 'Stylization and Representation in Subtitles: Can Less be More?', *Perspectives: Studies in Translatology* 20: 479–494.

Hatim, B. and I. Mason (1997) 'Politeness in Screen Translating', in B. Hatim and I. Mason (eds) *The Translator as Communicator*, London: Routledge, 65–80.

Hickey, L. (ed.) (1998) *The Pragmatics of Translation*, Clevedon: Multilingual Matters.

Hickey, L. and M. Stewart (eds) (2005) *Politeness in Europe*, Clevedon: Multilingual Matters.

Hill, H. (2006) *The Bible at Cultural Cross-Roads: From Translation to Communication*, Manchester: St. Jerome.

Hurford, J. R. and B. Heasley (1983) *Semantics: A Coursebook*, Cambridge: Cambridge University Press.

Jackson, J. (2014) *Introducing Language and Intercultural Communication*, London & New York: Routledge.
Joos, M. (1967) *The Five Clocks of Language*, New York: Harcourt Brace.
Kovacic, I. (1994) 'Relevance as a Factor in Subtitling Reductions', in C. Dollerup and A. Lindegaard (eds) *Teaching Translation and Interpreting 2*, Amsterdam & Philadelphia: John Benjamins, 244–251.
Kozloff, S. (2000) *Overhearing Film Dialogue*, California: University of California Press.
Lakoff, R. T. (1973) *The Logic of Politeness; Or Minding your P's and Q's*, Chicago: Chicago Linguistics Society.
Lee, J. J. and S. Pinker (2010) 'Rationale for Indirect Speech: The Theory of the Strategic Speaker', *Psychological Review* 117(3): 785–807.
Leech, G. N. (1983) *Principles of Pragmatics*, London: Longman.
Marmaridou, S. (2000) *Pragmatic Meaning and Cognition*, Amsterdam & Atlanta: John Benjamins.
Mason, I. (2001) 'Coherence in Subtitling: The Negotiation of Face', in F. Chaume Varela and R. Agost (eds) *La traducción en los medios audiovisuales*, Castelló de la Plana: Servei de Publicacions de la Universitat Jaume I, 19–32.
Mey, J. (1993) *Pragmatics: An Introduction*, Oxford: Blackwell.
Mey, J. (2002) 'To Grice or Not to Grice', *Journal of Pragmatics* 34: 911.
Mey, J. (2006) 'Translation and Context', *Journal of Pragmatics* 38(3): 315–316.
Newmark, P. (1988) *A Textbook of Translation*, Hemel Hempstead: Prentice Hall.
Pedersen, J. (2005) 'How is Culture Rendered in Subtitles?', in S. Nauert (ed.) *Proceedings of the Marie Curie Euroconferences MuTra Challenges of Multidimensional Translation, Saarbrücken, 2–6 May 2005*. Available online: http://www.euroconferences.info/proceedings/2005_Proceedings/2005_Pedersen_Jan.pdf [last access 20 December 2017].
Pedersen, J. (2008) 'High Felicity: A Speech Act Approach to Quality Assessment in Subtitling', in D. Chiaro, C. Heiss and C. Bucaria (eds) *Between Text and Image: Updating Research in Screen Translation*, Amsterdam & Philadelphia: John Benjamins, 101–115.
Pérez-González, L. (2014) *Audiovisual Translation: Theories, Methods and Issues*, London & New York: Routledge.
Pinker, S. (1994) *The Language Instinct: How the Mind Creates Meaning*, New York: Harper Perennial Modern Classics.
Ramière, N. (2004) 'Reaching a Foreign Audience: Cultural Transfers in Audiovisual Translation', *JoSTrans: The Journal of Specialised Translation* 6. Available online: http://www.jostrans.org/issue06/art_ramiere.php [last access 20 December 2017].
Remael, A. (2003) 'Mainstream Film Dialogue and Subtitling', *The Translator* 9(2): 225–247.
Remael, A. (2004) 'A Place for Film Dialogue Analysis in Subtitling Courses', in P. Orero (ed.) *Topics in Audiovisual Translation*, Amsterdam & Atlanta: John Benjamins, 103–126.
Searle, J. R. (1969) *Speech Acts: An Essay in the Philosophy of Language*, Cambridge: Cambridge University Press.
Searle, J. R. (1979) *Expression and Meaning: Studies in the Theory of Speech Acts*, Cambridge: Cambridge University Press.
Sifianou, M. (2001) *Discourse Analysis: An Introduction*, Athens: Leader Books.
Skuggevik, E. (2009) 'Teaching Screen Translation: The Role of Pragmatics', in J. Díaz Cintas and G. Anderman (eds) *Audiovisual Translation: Language Transfer on Screen*, Basingstoke: Palgrave Macmillan, 197–213.
Somwe Mubenga, K. (2009) 'Towards a Multimodal Pragmatic Analysis of Film Discourse in Audiovisual Translation', *Meta* 54(3): 466–484.
Sperber, D. and D. Wilson (1986/1995) *Relevance: Communication and Cognition*, 2nd edition, Oxford: Blackwell.
Sperber, D. and D. Wilson (1998) 'Mutual Knowledge and Relevance in the Theories of Comprehension', in A. Kasher (ed.) *Pragmatics: Critical Concepts, Volume V: Communication, Talk in Interaction, Discourse*, London & New York: Routledge, 369–384.

Sperber, D. and I. A. Noveck (2004) 'Introduction', in I. A. Noveck and D. Sperber (eds) *Experimental Pragmatics*, Basingstoke: Palgrave Macmillan, 1–22.
Stafford, R. (2007) Understanding *Audiences and the Film Industry*, London: British Film Institute.
Tannen, D. (1989) *Talking Voices: Repetition, Dialogue and Imagery in Conversational Discourse*, Cambridge: Cambridge University Press.
Tapping the Power (n.d.) 'Tapping the Power of Foreign Language Films: Audiovisual Translation as Cross-cultural Mediation'. Available online: www.filmsintranslation.org [last access 20 December 2017].
Terkourafi, M. (2011) 'The Puzzle of Indirect Speech', *Journal of Pragmatics* 43(11): 2861–2865.
Thomas, J. (1995) *Meaning in Interaction. An Introduction to Pragmatics*, London: Longman.
Vanoye, F. (1985) 'Conversations publiques', *Iris* 3(1): 99–188.
Weizman, E. (1989) 'Requestive Hints', in S. Blum-Kulka and J. House (eds) *Cross-cultural Pragmatics: Requests and Apologies*, New Jersey: Ablex, Norwood, 71–95.
Wilson, D. (1994) 'Relevance and Understanding', in G. Brown, K. Malmkjær, A. Pollitt and J. Williams (eds) *Language and Understanding*, Oxford: Oxford University Press, 35–58.
Wilson, D. and D. Sperber (2004) 'Relevance Theory', in L. R. Horn and G. Ward (eds) *The Handbook of Pragmatics*, Oxford: Blackwell, 607–632.
Yuan, X. (2012) *Politeness and Audience Response in Chinese-English Subtitling*, Oxford: Peter Lang.
Zabalbeascoa, P. (2005) 'The Curse of Conflicting Norms in Subtitling: A Case Study of Grice in Action', in J. D. Anderson (ed.) *Research on Translation for Subtitling in Spain and Italy*, Alicante: Universidad de Alicante, 29–36.

Filmography

Bridget Jones's Diary (2001) Sharon McGuire. IMDb entry: http://www.imdb.com/title/tt0243155/?ref_=fn_al_tt_1
Bridget Jones: The Edge of Reason (2004) Beeban Kidron. IMDb entry: http://www.imdb.com/title/tt0317198/?ref_=fn_al_tt_4
Loaf and Camouflage [Λούφα και Παραλλαγή] (1984) Nikos Perakis. IMDb entry: http://www.imdb.com/title/tt0123976/?ref_=fn_al_tt_1

17
Multimodality and audiovisual translation
Cohesion in accessible films

Aline Remael and Nina Reviers

Introduction

Multimodality is fast becoming the main conceptual framework for the study of audiovisual texts, i.e. texts that create meaning through the use of multiple semiotic modes, such as films. Individual semiotic modes include the aural-verbal mode (dialogues and lyrics); the aural, non-verbal mode (music and sound effects); the visual-verbal mode (various types of text on screen); and the visual, non-verbal mode (images) (Delabastita 1989, Remael 2001, Zabalbeascoa 2008). Multimodality examines how these individual modes function and how they can be combined into a unified whole. All the modes have a role to play in the creation of meaning in a text, but their importance will vary: in some films or film scenes music may be dominant; in others, the images may carry the story forward. What is more, combining different modes creates supplementary meaning, on top of the meanings conveyed by the individual modes. This is what Baldry and Thibault (2006) refer to as the 'resource integration principle'. What matters, however, is 'how they [the semiotic modes] all add up and combine with each other so that viewers can interpret them in certain ways' (Zabalbeascoa 2008: 25). To guide users' interpretations, filmmakers insert different types of implicit and explicit links between modes, which serve as cues for the users to reconstruct a coherent end product. In this chapter, multimodal texts are seen to work through multimodal cohesion, which is accomplished through different cross-modal ties between the different semiotic modes. We pragmatically define multimodal cohesion as any instance of implicit or explicit 'sense-relation' between two or more signs, from the same or different modes, within a given text that helps the viewer create a coherent textual semantic unit (for an overview of key concepts in multimodal theory, see the publications listed in the Further Reading section, at the end of this chapter).

Multimodality and multimodal cohesion in audiovisual texts remain complex issues that have been addressed from different angles. The challenge of multimodal research today involves designing a systematic framework for the analysis of multimodal texts and their cohesion, especially in the context of film and film translation. To date, three different approaches have been deployed to do so. In *Introducing Social Semiotics* (2005: 179), van Leeuwen approaches multimodality from the perspective of social semiotics and puts forward four concepts that guide the integration and co-occurrence of different kinds of semiotic resources: rhythm, composition, information linking and dialogue. Rhythm is seen to provide coherence and meaningful structure to events that develop over time, whereas composition does the same within a spatial dimension. The concept of information linking is used to refer to the cognitive connections between items of information in time and to refer to the temporal or causal links between words and images in space-based multimodal texts. Finally, for van Leeuwen, dialogue is a broad term that encompasses the structures of dialogic exchanges (i.e. not only human dialogue) and musical interaction in multimodal texts and communicative events. However, these terms remain open to interpretation when applied in different contexts, as do the relations between them. As formulated by van Leeuwen, this set of concepts does not constitute, nor is it meant to be regarded as a systematic analytical framework.

Many scholars have built on van Leeuwen's pioneering work trying to come up with a more specific conceptualization of co-occurrence and cohesion across different semiotic signs. One of them is Royce (2007), who accounts for the co-occurrence of different semiotic modes in terms of the linguistic concept of lexical cohesion. From this standpoint, the integration across modes is based on reference, repetition, synonymy, collocation and part-whole relations—including meronymy (the semantic relationship that holds between a car steering wheel and the car) and hyponymy (the semantic relationship between a spoon and the wider category of cutlery that includes it). Royce uses these linguistic concepts to name the cohesive ties that exist between non-verbal modes. For example, a shot of a woman's hand writing a letter prompts the viewers to link the hand to a woman they have seen in a previous scene (*The Hours* 2002)—in what could be analyzed as an example of meronymic relationship.

However, we have found that these categories do not necessarily cover all instances of co-occurrence in filmic texts, because some instances are driven primarily by implication (based on the mental models that viewers bring to their spectatorial experience) and dialogic interaction (comparable to van Leeuwen's concept of dialogue). 'Complementarity' is thus suggested as an additional concept that builds on van Leeuwen's concept of information linking. It is meant to designate the relationship between two signs that simply co-occur or appear in each other's immediate textual environment. For example, a man interrupting his telephone conversation and saying 'hold on', as a reaction to mumbling and shouting in the streets outside his office (*Süskind* 2012). This concept can enable subtle distinctions, as the difference between lexical cohesion and complementarity can be a matter of degree (see Reviers and Remael 2015).

Chiao-I Tseng (2013) has recently made an interesting contribution to this discussion. Her work builds on the social semiotics tradition and makes an initial attempt to bring together the above-mentioned concepts under a systematic analytical model. Tseng (2013: 153) states that 'viewer's comprehension of film narrative is premised on the meaning patterns they have constructed somewhere else, either from their previous film viewing experiences or from other life experiences'. In this sense her approach is akin to the theory of mental models developed by Johnson-Laird (1983) and regularly applied in narratology, which contends that readers and viewers processing narratives construct mental representations of such narratives (see, for instance, Herman 2009). Similarly, Tseng (2013: 1) demonstrates that film viewers attend to four elements to construct a coherent film narrative—characters, objects, settings and action—that she uses as her starting point to analyze filmic cohesion. Based on insights from social semiotics and systemic functional linguistics, she argues that 'the structure of identification, namely, how relevant people, places and things are actually tracked, highlight the unity of a particular text' (*ibid.*: 39). In other words, viewers track the identities of characters and objects by constructing cohesive chains that guide their narrative interpretation. Tseng's approach is particularly relevant to audiovisual translations (AVTs). Our own, admittedly limited, research on cohesion in AVT (Reviers and Remael 2015) suggests that cohesion is not only created through the use of, for instance, explicit references and lexical cohesion, but also by more implicit sense-relations that become apparent by tracking characters, their actions and behaviour. In short, the ease with which the basic, narratological building blocks (characters, setting and time) can be identified by users across audiovisual texts seems to be a crucial manifestation of cohesion between such texts and their translations, and is therefore an appropriate starting point for the present study.

Research problem

Multimodal cohesion constitutes a particular challenge in AVT and media accessibility. In AVT one mode is altered/translated and, as a result, the explicit or implicit interaction between the translated mode and the other modes may also be altered, sometimes unintentionally. Translators of audiovisual texts must therefore be cautious not to break down the multimodal cohesion of the source text and recreate a coherent and cohesive end product. This is particularly true for assistive forms of audiovisual translation such as audio description (AD) and subtitling for the deaf and hard of hearing (SDH).

The aim of the present chapter is to discuss and illustrate how multimodal cohesion is maintained or (re)created in an accessible film clip with AD for the blind and visually impaired and SDH using Tseng's model. AD makes audiovisual products accessible for blind and visually impaired users by translating the visual mode of, for instance, fiction films (this chapter's topic) into an aural-verbal narration that makes use of the original verbal-aural and non-verbal-aural modes of the film—i.e. its dialogues, sound effects and music—to produce a new coherent, purely aural target text. SDH translates the aural-verbal dialogues as well as narratively relevant sounds and music into subtitles, a visual-verbal mode that also involves the use of colours or other methods for speaker identification. In both assistive forms of AVT, one mode is entirely replaced by another and the end product should also function mono-modally for the target audience (visually in the case of SDH and aurally in the case of AD). The analysis presented below pays particular attention to the role of sound in AD and SDH, as this aspect has not received sufficient attention to that, even though several authors have acknowledged the importance of sound in both assistive modalities. Neves (2010), for instance, tackles the challenge of incorporating music in SDH, proposing strategies to move beyond the current verbal and symbolic renderings typically used in SDH; Igareda (2012), on the other hand, illustrates the importance of music and lyrics in audio described films. For her part, Fryer (2010) provides valuable insights into the importance and functions of sound in AD.

Analysis

This section delivers a detailed analysis of a short clip from *Nights in Rodanthe* (Wolfe 2008). The film tells the story of Dr Paul Flanner, a (plastic) surgeon who retreats to the tiny coastal town of Rodanthe in the Outer Banks of North Carolina, where he stays at an inn run by Adrienne Willis. As Paul arrives, a major storm is forecast. With the storm closing in, they turn to each other for comfort and begin an intense romance. The selected scene features Paul, just after his arrival at the inn, jogging along the beach, thinking back to a surgery he performed a few weeks earlier. *Nights in Rodanthe* was selected because it was available with both AD and SDH. This specific scene was chosen because it stands on its own as a coherent unit, features all semiotic modes and has important sound and music elements, which are bound to be impacted in the accessible versions. Table 17.1 features a multimodal transcription of the clip.

Methodology

The social semiotic strand of multimodal theory, and in particular the work of van Leeuwen, Baldry and Thibault, has developed a method for film analysis known as multimodal transcription. Together with the development of multimodal corpora, this sort of transcription has become a much-used methodological tool in multimodal research (see e.g. Pérez-González 2014: 165; 295 and Baldry and Thibault 2006). Multimodal transcription is a method that supports the detailed and empirical analysis of the functioning and interplay of all the components of audiovisual texts. This methodology, initially developed for film analysis, has been applied to the analysis of translated film by several authors, including Taylor (2004a, 2004b). The idea is to segment the text into its smallest constitutive units in order to facilitate an objective and empirical analysis. In brief, the transcription consists of a column-based table, in which the visual and auditory components of the film clip are transcribed on the basis of logical, semantic units. Significantly, '[t]he number and ordering of the columns included in the transcription, the range of modes and sub-modes covered in the analysis, and the set of notation conventions used for coding purposes depend on the specific needs of the individual project' (Pérez-González 2014: 295). The transcription for the purpose of this study is available in Table 17.1, and consists of six columns: unit number, transcription of the AD, coding of the visual image and kinesic action, transcription of the sound and music, transcription of the dialogue and, finally, transcription of the SDH. Each unit largely corresponds to one shot delineated by a clear cut. Items listed in the same row occur simultaneously. The length of cells within columns signals continuity.

Theoretical framework

As indicated above, Tseng focuses on the process of identification that filmic texts use to ensure that viewers can track the identity of participants (i.e. characters, settings and objects) and their cumulative development, across sequences. The framework for the analysis of filmic cohesion that she develops contains four analytical tools, which constitute the basic building blocks of our analysis: the presenting system, the presuming system, the comparative system and the system for the direction of identity retrieval.

Characters can be presented on the basis of three parameters. First, they can be presented as generic (e.g. as a teacher, member of a larger group of teachers) or as specific individuals (e.g. a teacher who is named or known). However, the distinction must be seen as a continuum that is subject to change, as generic characters can evolve into named individuals while the narrative unfolds. Second, both a generic and a specific presentation can be realized mono-modally or cross-modally, by two or more modes simultaneously. Third, Tseng's framework is based on the analysis of the most salient elements of the narrative. Participants can acquire salience immediately or gradually. In the case of a gradual presentation process, the options are either a dynamic or a static method. In a dynamic introduction a participant becomes more salient gradually, e.g. through different shot types. In the case of a gradual but static introduction, the film makes use of a prelude (for instance, the sound of a car is heard,

Table 17.1 Multimodal transcription

No.	Audio Description	Visual Image + Kinesic Action	Sound + Music	Dialogue	SDH
1	[FEMALE VOICE THROUGHOUT] Dawn. Dressed in a **hooded sweat top**, Paul descends the <u>steps</u> from his . . .	Horizontal, median, stationary shot from the <u>back end of a wooden balcony</u> overlooking the <u>ocean on the horizon</u>. **Paul, in jogging suit, slowly walks from the left of the screen to the edge of the balcony in the middle of the frame, with his back to the camera** (from close to medium shot distance). Low-key lighting and grey colours.	**Footsteps** on wooden stairs and slow <u>ocean waves</u> in the background.		
2	. . . <u>balcony</u> to the <u>beach</u>. **He** begins to jog, then race along <u>it</u>. **He** walks along a <u>hospital corridor</u> accompanied . . .	Cut to a tracking shot starting <u>underneath the balcony stairs and moving right towards the beach</u>. The visual focus moves from **Paul's feet** on the stairs (close distance), to **Paul in the centre of the image on the beach running** (long shot distance). Tempo of the kinesic action moves from slow walking to running, then racing. Low-key lighting and grey colouring continue.	<u>Slow ocean waves</u> and **footsteps** on the <u>sand</u> gradually going faster. As the **footsteps go faster**, up-tempo piano music joins in (building up from low to high-pitched notes). Ocean waves gradually make place for **rhythmic, fast, loud breathing**.		
3	. . . by a team of people.	Cut to a medium (tracking) shot of **Paul's face and upper body**. He is gazing into the distance along the <u>beach</u>. Low-key lighting and colouring continue. The tempo of the kinesic action remains high.	**Breathing** and up-tempo piano music continue.		
4		Cut to a close-up of **Paul's running feet** <u>on the beach</u> (high-angle, tracking shot). Low-key lighting and colouring continue. Tempo kinesic action remains high.			
5		Cut to a close-up of **Paul's face and upper body**, against <u>the ocean in the background</u>. (Identical to shot 3).			

6	Cut to a low-angle, tracking shot of **Paul** walking quickly **in doctor's suit** along a brightly lit (high-key lighting), brightly coloured hospital corridor, surrounded by nurses. **Paul** is filmed **from the front**, reading a chart a nurse is holding in front of him. Another doctor cuts across the screen to quickly shake Paul's hand, then walks off screen.	Up-tempo piano music continues.	[PAUL'S VOICE]: Any problems with anaesthesia? [NURSE'S VOICE]: no problems. [PAUL'S VOICE]: absolutely not, you're sure? [DOCTOR'S VOICE]: Paul. [PAUL'S VOICE]: Hi John.	– Any problems with anaesthesia? WOMAN: No problems. – Absolutely none? You sure? WOMAN: yes.
7	Cut to a close-up shot of **Paul's face and upper body** as he is running along the beach (identical to shot 3 and 5).	Up-tempo piano continues, fast, rhythmic **breathing joins in again.**		
8	Cut to Paul **in the hospital corridor**: low-angle, tracking shot, following **Paul** (right) turning left towards a nurse and walking past her, disappearing through electronic doors opening on the far left of the screen, followed by the group of nurses. On the door is written: 'operating room 1'. High-key lighting, bright colours and high tempo kinesic action.	Up-tempo piano music continues.	[NURSE'S VOICE]: Miles Davis again, **doctor Flanner**? [PAUL'S VOICE]: Bach, today, Bach!	– Miles Davis again, **Dr. Flanner**? – Bach today. Bach.
	He's in . . .			
9	Cut to tracking shot of **Paul** on the beach again; identical **close-up of his face and upper body** (shot 3, 5 and 7).	Up-tempo piano continues, fast, rhythmic **breathing joins in again.**		
10	Stationary, slightly low-angled shot of **Paul** (median close-up) **in the middle of the frame**, in the operating room **in scrubs**. Contrast lighting created by a bright overhead light in the top right corner of the image.	Up-tempo piano music continues.		
	. . . theatre, preparing a patient's face for surgery.			

(continued)

Table 17.1 (continued)

No.	Audio Description	Visual Image + Kinesic Action	Sound + Music	Dialogue	SDH
11	Bright overhead...	Cut to a **low-angle shot of Paul** in the operating room **in his scrubs**. Visual focus on Paul's hand in close-up at the bottom of the screen, his head right above and four bright lights surrounding his head, creating contrast lighting. The tempo of the kinesic action (hands moving) is high.			
12	...lights blaze...	Cut to a top-shot of a patient lying on Paul's table. Visual focus on the patient's face lit by a bright light, surrounded by **hands**, green cloth, and surgical material in darker light. Kinesic tempo of the hands remains high.			
13	...behind **him**.	Cut to a close-up, top-shot of the patient's brightly lit face, half covered by green sheets and **two hands** measuring a scar on the patient's face, and giving an injection. Kinesic action remains high.			
14	**Paul** races along the beach. The patient's....	Cut to a low-angle shot of **Paul in scrubs**, surrounded by four bright overhead lights (contrast lighting continues). As he bends forward, his headlight blinds the camera. Kinesic action of hand movements is median.	Up-tempo piano music continues and when Paul bends towards the camera, ocean waves mix in.		
15	...heartbeat flat lines.	Cut to a median close, tracking shot of **Paul's face and upper body** again on the beach (identical to shots 3, 5, 7 and 9)	Up-tempo piano music continues, ocean waves become louder and rhythmic **breathing joins in.**		
16		Cut to a low-angle, **medium close-up of Paul in scrubs** in the operating room, looking up alarmed (gazing at something off-screen to the left). Contrast light created by a big overhead light next to Paul's head.	Loud, high-pitched beeping and low (unclear) voices. Up-tempo piano continues.		
17		As **Paul further turns his head**, a cut follows to a shot of a heart monitor and other screens behind Paul. The camera quickly zooms in on the flat line on the heart monitor. Contrast lighting continues.	Loud, high-pitched beeping and muffled voices. Up-tempo piano continues.		[EKG BEEPING RAPIDLY]

18		Cut to a high-angle, overview shot of the operating room. Visual focus is on the brightly lit patient in the middle, **surrounded by doctors, nurses,** and the equipment in darker shadows.	Beeping sound of charger and beeping of heart monitor. Up-tempo piano continues.	[FEMALE VOICE]: the patient's gone. [MALE VOICE]: charging.	WOMAN: charge. MAN: Charging.
19		Cut to an extreme close-up of the heart monitor.			
20		*Cut to the close-up of Paul's face on the beach (identical shot 3, 5, 7, 9 and 15)*	Loud beeping and up-tempo piano music continue.	[PAUL'S VOICE]: Talk to me.... [PAUL'S VOICE]:...come on now. Three, four...	Talk to **me**! Come on, now!
21		Cut to a **close shot of Paul** in the operating room, looking down.			
22		Cut to a high-angle, medium close shot of **Paul in his scrubs performing heart massage.** Paul is high up in the frame, the patient's brightly lit face is visible in the lower left corner. Kinesic tempo is high.			Three, four five, six...
23		Cut to a medium, horizontal shot of a man standing behind the operating room door. Contrasting light turns him into a dark silhouette.		[PAUL'S VOICE]:.... five, six.	
24	As **Paul**...	Cut to a medium-close, horizontal shot of **Paul doing heart massage** in his scrubs (identical shot to 21)	Loud beeping and up-tempo piano music continue.		
25	...pumps **his** patient's chest...	Cut to a close-up of the man's face behind the operating room door.		Soft voice.	...seven, eight, nine, 10, 11....
26	...**he** looks over **his** shoulder	Cut to a horizontal, medium shot of **Paul doing heart massage** in his scrubs (identical shot to 21 and 24). He looks over his shoulder to the right, while continuing heart massage.	Up-tempo piano music goes faster.	Soft voice continues.	
27	...and sees Mark watching anxiously.	Cut to a close-up of the man's face behind the operating room door, slowly looking down.		Soft voice continues.	

Legend: **bold** = character identification chain| underlined = setting(s) identification chain| *italics* = present time period | regular print = flashbacks.

and then the car appears). Again, all these operations can be performed mono-modally or through a combination of different film modes. In the clip under analysis, the most salient element moving the story forward is the protagonist. Different camera techniques coded in the transcription gradually present Dr Flanner as the most salient element and he remains central throughout the clip (see, for instance, rows 1 to 3 in Table 17.1). Our analysis will therefore focus on the identity tracking of Dr Flanner. Next it will examine the tracking of the settings and a few specific objects in them that are closely associated with the character.

The second notion of cohesion in the framework is that of identity tracking through the presuming system (*ibid.*: 60). Tseng explains that 'the presuming systems set out features that bring about the re-identification and tracking of filmic participants *after* [our emphasis] they are presented in a film'. Characters, settings and objects are presented gradually throughout the film and each scene contributes new elements to the previously constructed mental model of that participant. Characters, objects or settings are not presented only once; instead, they normally reappear. As our analysis shows, however, the processes of presentation and reappearance (presuming) of participants often overlap. Elements can reappear explicitly (either mono- or cross-modally) or implicitly, e.g. when some physical parts of a visual participant reappear in different shots.

Next, there is the comparative system. Filmic comparative elements can indicate a relation of similarity or difference between two shots of a participant, through attributes of quantity (generic participants presented in groups or as individuals) or of quality, such as tempo and volume in the audio mode or colour and lighting in the visual mode. There is an obvious connection here with van Leeuwen's concepts of rhythm and composition.

The final step in the framework is determining the direction of the identity retrieval. The identity of a participant can be determined endophorically (from the text itself) or exophorically (from the context of situation/culture). According to Tseng, cohesion is normally concerned with endophora only. But while endophoric links are primarily derived from within the text, they are also articulated by mental models that rely both on the viewing experience and the viewers' knowledge of the world. For Tseng such endophoric cohesion includes 'indirectly retrievable' information, based on implicational relations—more specifically lexical relations such as synonymy, hyponymy and meronymy, similar to Royce's interpretation of intersemiotic complementarity presented earlier. This type of cohesion, that she calls 'bridging' (*ibid.*: 70), occurs when the link needs to be inferred. Bridging, which can be cued mono-modally or cross-modally, resembles complementarity in our original terminology, as it designates instances where two signs complement each other semantically simply by co-occurring in each other's immediate textual environment. When analyzing links between non-verbal filmic modes, cohesive relations based on juxtaposition are achieved through film editing and it is the viewer who retrieves the relevant links by implication.

Presenting and tracking characters and settings

We now turn to our clip to identify the consecutive semiotic signs that trace the identification of the character and the setting, thereby forming a cohesive chain. For details relating to the multimodal narrative into which the chains fit as well as details about camera positions and film techniques, readers are referred to the numbered units in the transcription available in Table 17.1. The clip consists of two interrelated scenes, which also represent two sub-chains insofar as the identity tracking of participants is concerned: one that tracks participants in a past time period and setting, and one that tracks participants in a present time period and setting. After analyzing the source text in detail, we examine the same identity chains in the accessible versions of the film with AD and SDH.

Tracking the character in the original clip

Dr Paul Flanner, the film protagonist, is known to the viewers because he has already been presented. Therefore the scene builds on the mental model the audience has of Paul as a person, meaning he is depicted here as a specific (not a generic) person. Hence the discussion below focuses on the 'presuming system'—i.e. the reappearances of Paul that together form a cohesive chain—which allows viewers to keep identifying Paul as Paul and the 'comparative system' to indicate similarity or differences between the ways in which he reappears. Overall, Paul's identity is tracked cross-modally. The input of the visual mode is predominant and is supported by two aural modes: sound and minimal dialogue.

In **unit 1** Paul makes an explicit visual reappearance as a specific, known character: he can be seen walking into the scene and ending up in the middle of the frame. He is thereby identified as salient. Like in all the following units, this reappearance works anaphorically, as it points backwards to the referent that was introduced earlier in the film. His identity can be retrieved directly, as we can see his whole figure and directly recognize him as Paul. His reappearance is expressed cross-modally since it is accompanied by the sound of footsteps on a wooden balcony. **Unit 2** features a shot change to a close-up of Paul's feet. His character makes an implicit visual reappearance, accompanied by an explicit acoustic reappearance of the sound of footsteps, and audiences have to infer that the feet refer to the same referent by an anaphoric, meronymic cohesive relation (i.e. bridging). In the same unit, there is a second reappearance of Paul, when his whole figure gradually becomes visible while he walks further away from the camera and starts running. Here he makes an explicit visual reappearance, as he can be directly recognized as the same Paul we saw in unit 1. His identity is tracked cross-modally again, as the sound of footsteps reappears, this time implicitly; in other words, the sound of the footsteps refers to the same referent, but the audio quality (comparative system) is different, as the feet now walk on sand. Simultaneously, another cross-modal identification cue is added: loud breathing. The next three alternating units in the character identification chain are all linked anaphorically and meronymically (implicit reappearance through bridging): a close-up of Paul's face (**unit 3**), one of his running feet (**unit 4**) and another close-up of his face, identical to the previous one (**unit 5**), all simultaneously cued aurally as well by the sound of footsteps and breathing. It must be noted that the identification of Paul in units 1, 2, 3, 4 and 5 is supported by the comparative system, as there is a clear similarity between the reappearances expressed through quality attributes in the different modes: Paul is wearing the same jogging-outfit in all implicit and explicit reappearances and low-key lighting, colour and mise-en-scène are the same in the different units. The music in these units also contributes to the relation of similarity between the reappearances, more specifically through the system of quality (non-diegetic): the rhythm and tempo of Paul running along the beach (footsteps and breathing) are mirrored in the rhythm and tempo of up-tempo piano music, creating a strong cohesive relation between the different visual and aural modes in this sequence.

In **unit 6** the camera gradually moves from a long shot of Paul in a white doctor's coat to a medium shot with a frontal view of Paul down to his waist. The character makes an explicit, visual reappearance, and can be directly identified. The identification is again cross-modal, as dialogue kicks in with a voice linked anaphorically and aurally to Paul through previous scenes of the film, but also linked to him through the visual mode—since dialogue and the visual sign of Paul in doctor's coat coincide and are linked to him through the content of the dialogue (they are discussing an upcoming surgery). However, the comparative mode here suggests that the Paul identified in this specific unit occurs in a different time period, as he is presented as a different person through the quality attributes of clothing, i.e. a doctor's coat (diegetic) and through the different, high-key lighting and bright colours in the hospital corridor (partly diegetic, partly non-diegetic). Another important cross-modal cohesive element in this unit that is expressed through the comparative system is the music: the up-tempo piano music resembles the fast tempo of the kinesic action (fast walking) and of the dialogue (fast talking). What is more, it is the same piano music as in the previous unit where Paul was on the beach (sound-bridge), creating a cohesive link with earlier reappearances of Paul in the identity chain. As one can see in the transcription, this cohesive role of the music continues along the whole identity chain.

In **unit 7** we return to Paul running on the beach. He makes an explicit, directly retrievable reappearance that is tracked cross-modally: we see a close-up of his face and we hear his breathing. These cues have a clear filmic similarity (comparison) to the previous elements in the chain, as their quality is the same (lighting, colour, tempo, rhythm) as in units 1 to 5. At the same time they create a relation of difference with the directly preceding cue in unit 6, where lighting, colour, tempo and clothing of the character were different. The continuing piano music again creates a cohesive link of similarity across all the chain elements.

Unit 8 cuts back to Paul at the hospital with an explicit visual reappearance that is directly retrievable. The relation to previous elements in the identity chain is again cued through the comparative system (lighting, clothes, rhythm, tempo). Paul's identification is supported here by the aural mode, as we can hear his voice, and a cue from the dialogue, as a secondary character calls him by his name. In **unit 9** we briefly return to Paul on the beach, where he is identified cross-modally in the same way as in unit 7.

Units 10–14 depict Paul in the operation room preparing a patient for surgery. The tracking of Paul is achieved visually here, through a quick follow-up of implicit and explicit visual appearances: we see Paul's face, upper body and then his hands (which are linked through meronymy) and we see Paul wearing green scrubs (which can be linked to the cueing of Paul in white doctor's coat earlier through hyponymy since a white doctor's coat and green scrubs are both part of the larger category 'clothes hospital personnel wear'). What stands out when we look at the non-verbal cueing in this series of units is that there are no sound-effects (only the piano music continues) until unit 14 when the sound of waves is heard faintly in the background—even though visually we are still in the operating room. Even though the sound of waves has no co-referential relation to Paul's identity, it can be seen as part of his identity chain, as it serves as a *leitmotif* on the one hand (the sound of waves was heard earlier in unit 1 when we saw Paul on the beach and is possibly linked in the mental model of the audience to the identity of the jogging Paul), or it can be seen as a prelude, since in the subsequent unit (**unit 15**) this recognizable sound of waves becomes louder and is combined with a visual shot of Paul on the beach, tracked in the same cross-modal way as in units 7 and 9.

Units 16 to 27 depict Paul during surgery in the OR, intertwined with one flashback to the same beach scene (unit 20). Paul in the hospital is cued by a series of explicit, visual reappearances that are directly retrievable of his face and upper body in scrubs (units 16, 17, 20, 21, 22, 24 and 26). The comparative system creates a relation of similarity with previous appearances in the operating room and a relation of difference with the identity cues of Paul on the beach. One cue of the identity chain in this sequence stands out: in unit 18 a top-shot of the operating room depicts a patient in the middle of the frame surrounded by a group of doctors and nurses in similar green scrubs. There is a co-referential link in this shot to Paul's identity chain that is indirect (bridging) and can be established through hyponymy: in the mental model of the audience, Paul has been identified as an individual, being part of the larger generic group of 'doctors and nurses'. This identification through hyponymy is supported by the comparative system: there is a similar relation (through the quality system), namely the green scrubs they all wear, but also a difference relation in terms of the quantity system, Paul is now seen as part of a larger group.

These visual reappearances are expressed cross-modally: we can hear Paul's voice in units 20, 21 and 23. Since audiences have heard his voice earlier in the film, this is an explicit reappearance. However, there is a relation of difference with previous verbal cues as well, as he is now shouting and distressed, which translates into a very different voice quality. Moreover, the verbal cues referring to Paul are interrupted: after unit 21 'Come on now, three, four' there is a brief interruption (unit 22) in the verbal-aural mode, then the count picks up again with 'Five, six', referring anaphorically to the first part of the enumeration, and continuing the aural-verbal link identifying Paul in his doctor's coat, across the brief interruption. The interruption in the aural identity chain of Paul is due to the brief appearance of another character chain (his son Mark is watching closely from behind the operating room door). After this dialogue turn, there are no other manifestations of the aural mode that can be used to track Paul's identity chain.

Finally, the cohesion and identity tracking in this sequence (units 16 to 27) is supported cross-modally by the sounds and music. Even though the sounds and music here have no relation of co-referentiality to Paul's identity and are not strictly part of Paul's identity chain (but part of the setting or non-diegetic), the high volume of the sound (beeping of a heart monitor) and music (still the same piano music) put the aural mode into a salient position in the narrative. Especially the increased tempo and rhythm (attributes of the comparative system) again mirror the tempo and rhythm of the kinesic actions of Paul. What is more, the beeping and piano music continue across all 12 units—even over shot 20 where Paul is on the beach and no longer in the operating room—tightening the cohesive link between both sub-chains (past and present) of Paul's identity chain. What is remarkable is that the piano music in this sequence is largely non-diegetic (it is added as a sound effect during post-production to serve as a sound-bridge), but in unit 8 it is suddenly identified as diegetic, since Paul asks the nurse to play Bach in the operating room during surgery. This links the music more tightly to Dr Flanner as a kind of leitmotif.

Tracking the setting in the original clip

In the previous section we have focused on the detailed discussion of how the protagonist Dr Flanner can be tracked in a selected clip of *Nights in Rodanthe*. However, it became clear during the analysis that it is not always possible to separate the tracking of the character from that of other elements in the narrative, namely objects and settings, since they interact on several occasions. To paint a more complete picture of the scope of the cohesive links operating in this clip, we now move on to briefly discuss the setting identity chain. Parallel to the two sub-chains in the identity chain of Paul (present and past), there are two related sub-chains in the setting chain: the beach setting and the hospital setting.

The beach setting in this scene is re-presented as a specific setting in the first few units (units 1 to 5), by a combination of explicit and implicit visual reappearances through shots of a balcony, the beach, the ocean and the grey sky above; these are all identities that can be retrieved directly or indirectly through meronymy. The setting is rendered cross-modally, as it is accompanied by the sound of waves in the background. The comparative system also contributes to the cohesion in this chain, as the qualitative attributes (colour, mise-en-scène, lighting) of the different reappearances resemble each other.

The cohesive strategies described above are repeated throughout the clip to support the identification and reappearance of the beach setting in units 7, 9, 15 and 20 (explicit and implicit visual reappearance though meronymy, supported by the sound of waves and the repetition of qualitative filmic comparison techniques such as lighting and colour). However, two particular units stand out: unit 14 contains a prelude (see description character chain) and in unit 20 the beach is visible but there is no sound of waves (the sounds of the hospital setting accompany the visuals of the beach).

The second sub-chain re-presented in this clip is the hospital where Dr Flanner works. The hospital has been presented before in the film and is part of the mental model of the audience by now. Two separate locations in the hospital reappear in this sequence: a hospital corridor (units 6 and 8), and an operating room (units 10–14; 16–19; 21–17). The setting chains consist of a series of implicit, visual reappearances, whose identities can be established indirectly through meronymy: both the corridor and the operating room can be inferred to be part of the larger already known identity of the hospital. In the same way, the setting identification is supported by close-ups of particular parts of objects and characters in the settings that are part of the overall hospital and operating room setting: the chart a nurse is carrying in unit 6, the patient's face under green cloth in units 12, 13, 18, 22, Paul's headlight in unit 14, the heart monitor visible in units 17 and 19, the green scrubs and face mask of Dr Flanner and the nurses, and the equipment Paul is using in units 12 and 13. We would like to highlight here that the identity chains of the participants are highly intertwined in film: secondary objects and characters (of which one could also analyze the individual identity chain), are here seen to be part of the identity chain of the setting, based on their salience and their meronymic/hyponymic relations.

The identities of the two settings are expressed cross-modally, as the visuals are supported by sound effects: the almost inaudible voices and mumbling of the operating room staff in unit 18 and the beeping of the heart monitor across units 16 to 24. Specifically, the operating room is also cued by a visual-verbal sign (anaphoric reference), namely diegetic on-screen text in unit 8, where 'operating room 1' is written on the electronic doors. The comparative system also contributes to the identity tracking and cohesion of the setting, more specifically through the bright colours and high-key lighting that characterizes all the reappearances of the hospital setting and that contrast with the low-key lighting and soft colours of the beach setting.

As was also the case with the character chain, the piano music plays a cohesive role in the setting chain. The piano music forms a sound-bridge between the alternating settings, suggesting a sense of unity between them. This is supported by the tempo and rhythm of the music that mirrors the tempo of the character's kinesic action, and is also mirrored in the high tempo editing of this clip.

Tracking the participants in the version with AD

AD focuses on replacing the visual mode of the narration by a succinct verbal description and therefore relies on different items from the presenting, presuming and comparative systems to track the identities of the participants. But in contrast to 'traditional' verbal discourse, analyzed by Tseng (2013: 31–36) in terms of cohesive reference and identification and conceptualized by Halliday and Hasan (1976) and Martin (1992) in more depth, the descriptions have to co-exist with the non-verbal and verbal-aural modes of the audiovisual product and are therefore timed to create links with the sound effects, music and dialogue. It is through this careful timing and the judicious selection of verbal cues that now replace the visual mode that it creates cross-modal aural cohesive links and manages to produce a simplified version of the original identity chains while remaining largely, but not entirely, synchronous with the chronology of the narration. In the next paragraphs we have a close look at the identity chains in the AD. We discuss the character and setting chain together, since we have argued in the previous section that they are highly fused, and that is no different for the AD version.

In **units 1 and 2** the AD presents Paul as a specific (not generic) and 'known' person by using anaphoric references (his proper name 'Paul' and the personal pronouns 'his' and 'he'). The AD adds a time indication, namely 'Dawn'. This more explicitly links the present scene to the temporal development of the film than the film's visual mode, which works through implication, i.e. here through the juxtaposition of the previous scene in the inn, which we are not discussing here, and the beach scene, which follow each other chronologically, and through the indication of time by way of its visual use of light and colour, among other things (as we have seen when analyzing the use of the comparative system in the previous section). The verbal-aural rendering of the AD makes the anaphorical link to the passing of time explicit and replaces the visually rendered morning light.

In **units 1 and 2** the identity chain of the setting is tracked by the use of anaphoric reference through lexical cohesion, namely the repetition of the nouns 'balcony' and 'beach', part of the setting that has been presented/described earlier in the film. The chains in the AD are expressed cross-modally and create a direct cohesive link with the aural, non-verbal modes, i.e. the ocean waves, Paul's footsteps on the beach and the sand and simultaneously—in an indirect *verbal prelude*—with the increasingly rhythmic sound of Paul's breathing. It must be noted that the aural non-verbal cues of the identity chains are, indeed, accessible to the new target audience. However, the AD partially covers these sounds, so they are less redundant, since they are not available equally long.

What the AD does not render are the meronymic relationships (bridging) of the subsequent shots in the visual character identity chain or the visual details of the setting identity chain provided by the filmic images in **units 3, 4 and 5**—which 'show' more than linearly ordered words in an AD can 'tell'. Overall there are fewer 'reappearances' of both Paul and the two main settings in the accessible version of the film, which works on the implied understanding that if the AD does not specify that characters leave or that a setting changes, they will still be assumed to be present (this is also the case for units 7, 9 and 20, for instance, where short reappearances to Paul on the beach are not explicitly described, as we will discuss later). Since there are fewer reappearances in the accessible version, the 'comparative' links associated with these reappearances are also less redundant and more succinct than in the original version. For instance, low-key lighting and colour (that express a relation of difference with the other setting in the clip) are subsumed under the description 'dawn'. The AD does explicitly include the quality attribute of Paul's jogging suit (see description unit 1). Mentioning the jogging suit provides a lexical link to the action Paul is performing and the setting in which he is performing it, the beach, thereby creating a mental model combining character-action-setting in the minds of the listeners through cross-modally functioning tracking. Another cohesive element of the comparative system highlighted in the analysis of the original clip and recreated in the AD is the rhythm and tempo of the music that mirrors the rhythm of the action. The careful timing of the AD ('He begins to jog, then race along it') is timed right before the up-tempo music starts and the fact that the AD leaves a small pause for the sounds (for a brief moment the piano music, the quick footsteps and the breathing can be heard rhythmically interacting) potentially creates a comparable cohesive link across all chain elements as in the original clip.

In **unit 6**, the visual identity chain of Paul switches to the hospital setting. The AD describing unit 6 has anticipated this switch at the end of unit 2 where it already refers to 'a hospital corridor', identifying Paul in it with an anaphoric reference (personal pronoun 'he'). Paul's breathing, connected to the beach scene, is still briefly audible in unit 6 but is soon overtaken by the up-tempo piano music which, as we indicated above, contributes to the relation of similarity between Paul's reappearances in different settings and creates a sound-bridge between the character chains of Paul in the two settings. In other words, the identity chain in the AD ('He walks along a hospital corridor accompanied by a team of people') makes use of the aural modes as well: the bridging music mixed with the gradually fainter sound of Paul's breathing, in order to skip the meronymic visual shots of Paul on the beach in units 3, 4 and 5, and render the character and setting chains of unit 6, in the hospital corridor, instead. This is a necessary and common AD strategy, often referred to as 'foreshadowing', since in unit 6 dialogue kicks in leaving no room for description. A similar tactic is used for the intrusions of the visuals and sounds of the beach identity chains in **units 7 and 9**. Once the hospital identity chain becomes the dominant narration, the beach chain intrudes by association only through the rhythmic mix of breathing and music, whereby the salience of one or the other sometimes varies. Meanwhile, in unit 6 the dialogue confirms the AD, indicating that the character chain of Paul is now developing in a hospital setting and that the atmosphere in this setting is hectic, as the music and breathing suggest. This time the AD does not mention the quality attribute of Paul's different outfit (the doctor's coat) nor the high-key lighting and bright colours, reducing the visual redundancy of the cross-modal storytelling of the original clip.

More redundancy is lost as the AD of units **8 and 9** also skips a brief return to the hospital corridor, taking its target audience straight to the operating theatre where Paul is now preparing a patient for surgery. In other words, the identity chain in the AD counts fewer cues. However, the essence from the character and identity chains is rendered briefly in the AD (Paul is identified anaphorically by 'he' and the hospital setting is activated in the audience's mind via meronymy by mentioning the noun 'theatre' and 'surgery'). In addition, it is supported cross-modally by aural non-verbal cues as well as the dialogues. The up-tempo music creates a sound-bridge, but is here also identified in the dialogue as diegetic ('Bach today, Bach!') and the rhythmic breathing intrudes in the hospital soundtrack, in the way the shots to the beach intrude on the visual image in the original clip. Overall, the visual mode is pared to its essence in its verbal rendering and the aural modes are called to the rescue. The cohesive link between breathing and beach-jogging or the comparative link between the character chain on the beach and the character chain at the hospital becomes less explicit as it becomes less repetitive. What does remain is the generally hectic rhythm of both settings, which still provides the required link in support of the AD.

This implied connection is further enhanced by information the AD then selects for the description in **units 11, 12, 13** in the operating room: the identity chain of the setting is maintained but reduced to the glaring lights of the operating room ('bright overhead lights blaze') in which the presence of Paul ('him') is also confirmed. The more subtle differences in lighting colour and dress between the beach scene and the operating scene expressed through the comparative system in the original clip are lost.

Nevertheless, the contrasting relation between the two settings is then restored more explicitly by the AD in **units 14 and 15.** It juxtaposes, in two subsequent sentences, the character chain of 'Paul' racing along the beach, and the chain of Paul in the hospital, which implicitly reappears through lexical cohesion, i.e. by repeating the noun 'the patient', who had been introduced as part of the hospital setting in the AD of unit 9: 'Paul races along the beach. The patient's heartbeat flat lines'. In other words, the cohesive link between the two chains is created by implication and is supported cross-modally in the AD: the combined working of the AD and the non-verbal-aural mode, more specifically, its alternation with as well as its mixing of the rhythmic piano music (identified as operating music but also rhythmically connected to Paul's stressed breathing), the sound of Paul's breathing itself and the sound of waves. The AD at this point again provides a *verbal prelude* (or foreshadowing) to the telling sound that is heard a fraction later in **unit 16**: the beeping of the heart monitor. Subsequently, from units 16 to 23 the AD leaves the tracking of character and setting entirely up to the aural mode: the increasingly loud beeping sound of the instrument it has identified indirectly as a heart monitor (the audience needs to infer that the beeping comes from a heart monitor, based on the information that the patient's heartbeat flat lines), the rhythmic piano music and the dialogues which confirm through the voices of medical personal (previously identified by the AD in unit 3 as 'a team of people') that the patient (first mentioned in unit 9) has passed away.

The AD then picks up Paul's identity chain in **unit 24**, saying that he tries heart massage ('As he pumps his patient's chest . . .'), which is confirmed by the dialogue spoken by Paul himself. As the rhythm of the piano music also grows more hectic, the AD links the character chain of Paul to that of the man looking in through the OR's glass door: 'he looks over his shoulder and sees Marc watching anxiously'. The implicit link provided through juxtaposition in the visual mode, which implies that Paul sees the other character looking in through editing, is rendered more explicit in the verbal rendering of the AD which actually states that Paul ('he') 'sees Mark', who has been identified in the film (and the AD) earlier. All in all, some of the redundancy used in the original tracking of identity and setting chains is lost, while the tracking itself remains intact—supposing that the target audience can make good use of the aural clues provided to reconstruct the story and the mental models of the narrative they have constructed based on previous parts of the film.

Tracking the participants in the version with SDH

The challenges for SDH are quite different from those described above: all aural modes become inaccessible and must be rendered visually, including music, as demonstrated by Neves (2010). However, that is something SDH hardly ever seems to achieve today, as SDH often does little more than identify speakers or state that music can be heard (for more on SDH see Further Reading section). The scene under analysis is a case in point. It contains an abbreviated version of the verbal-aural mode in units 6, 8, 18, 20–21, 22 and 25, and only one reference to the specific sound produced by the heart monitor in unit 14.

The SDH banks on the fact that the target audience has access to the visual mode and hence to the visual character and setting identity chains as described under previous subsections and can use the subtitles to supply the information given through the dialogues, even if they can no longer access the aural non-verbal mode of sounds and music. For the identity chains on the beach this means: the sound of Paul's footsteps, of the ocean waves, Paul's breathing, and the rhythmic piano music, as well as the varying rhythms of breathing /piano and the way they alternate and/or are mixed. For the identity chains in the hospital this means: the same piano music and its intensifying rhythm in units 26–27, the beeping of the medical instruments and its growing intensity (unit 16), the muffled voices of the medical staff surrounding Paul and the aforementioned sounds accompanying the cuts to the beach scene, linking the temporally distinct but thematically connected identity chains of character and setting.

All the same, the SDH does manage to salvage the basic participant identity chains of the film and is helped in doing so by the visual non-verbal and limited visual-verbal modes already present in the film. The SDH thereby continues to track the participant identity chains of character and setting/objects cross-modally to some extent. It renders the essence of all aural-verbal modes in writing and thereby provides cohesive links cross-modally with the visual non-verbal mode. Paul is not identified explicitly in the subtitles (by for instance mentioning his name) since he is on screen when he talks, but the other speakers at the hospital are identified as 'man' or 'woman' (see units 6 and 8), whereas the visuals convey that they are medical personnel. In unit 6 the subtitled dialogue sets the stage for the operation: in unit 8 it indicates that Bach will be played during the operation and the words 'operating room 1' on the hospital door name the specific setting explicitly through the film's own visual-verbal mode. In unit 18 the subtitles summarize the dialogue stating that the patient has passed away and that a defibrillator is being used to revive him or her, and in units 21, 22 and 25 Paul's subtitled counting indicates in a simultaneous cohesive link with the visual mode that he is performing heart massage.

One sound effect is explicitly subtitled: an explicit and direct presentation of the beeping sound of the heart monitor in the subtitles with unit 16 (direct identification of the source of the sound through a noun 'EKG' and mentioning of the fast tempo). This functions as a *verbal-visual prelude* for the dialogue subtitled in unit 18, granted that the beeping is only mentioned once, briefly, while the beeping sound actually continues until the end of the clip. Then, in unit 25 the visual-verbal mode provides an explicit cross-modal cohesive link between the verbal and non-verbal visual modes since the subtitle renders the continuation of Paul's counting, whereas in the aural-verbal mode, the muffled voices are hardly discernible at this stage.

It is also important to remember that filmic sounds (see Remael 2012, referred to earlier in the paper) are produced by specific diegetic sources, the people as well as the settings and objects in the film. They have a visual as well as an aural rhythm and the target group of SDH can see them. While in this clip the aural rhythm is not rendered accessible (with the exception of unit 16), the accompanying visual rhythm reflected in the kinesic action and editing remains accessible. In the beach chain, visual rhythm is provided through the movement of Paul's feet, the ocean waves and the meronymic close-ups of Paul breathing heavily. In the hospital chain, Paul and colleagues are marching along the corridor or moving hectically about the operating room. The different meronymic shots of the glaring operating room spotlights have their own spatial rhythm as they frame the figure of Paul. Moreover, the meronymic close-up of his fast-moving hands while operating, the shot of the heart monitor and its flat line, the way Paul turns his head in alarm, and the return to the visual rhythm of his run along the beach leave little to the imagination. What is more, the audience also has access to Paul's visual expressions, the alarmed look on the face of the character behind the hospital door (units 25 and 27), and Paul's awareness of him as he looks over his shoulder (unit 26). To what extent the effect of the visually accessible 'sounds' and other visual information can compensate for the lack of access to the aural non-verbal modes is hard to determine.

The main losses are the tonality of the voices and sounds (intonation, pitch, loudness), which contribute to the atmosphere of the scene and the hectic piano music, which as a structural element is linked to the setting of the hospital scene only by the SDH and no longer links the participant chains across time. Considering the way in which this loss is compensated, it is fair to hypothesize that the tracking of all participant chains remains intact, even if the added excitement that is the domain of sound and music accompanying the images is lost.

Concluding remarks

This chapter aimed to introduce the main concepts used for the analysis of multimodal or cross-modal cohesion in film today and to illustrate how they can be used to analyze AVTs. More concretely, we have demonstrated how filmic multimodal or cross-modal cohesion functions and investigated to what extent such cohesion is recreated in the accessible versions of a clip taken from a film with AD and SDH, while testing the usefulness of the said concepts.

The discussion of the theoretical framework underlined that research into multimodal cohesion is still in its infancy, and much conceptualization and theorizing remains to be done. Indeed, a truly systematic and comprehensive analytical model is not yet available for our research domain, whereas existing concepts and terminologies often overlap. Nevertheless, we have combined a number of these concepts in our analysis, in a bid to propose a first 'inventory' of the ways in which cohesion can be created in AD and SDH. We feel that Tseng's model shows great potential for unravelling the intricate ways in which the different modes and sub-modes of audiovisual texts *and* their translations interact to create a cohesive audiovisual product.

The analysis of the original clip of *Nights in Rodanthe* highlighted the most salient elements that are at the disposal of viewers to track the identity of the most narratively relevant participants, a basic condition for cohesion. The subsequent discussion in sections showed that the identity tracking of participants remains intact in the accessible versions of this clip, even if the chains work differently, and sometimes rely on different modes or use the presenting-presuming-comparative system differently.

Whether these 'shifts' in the identity chains of the accessible versions of the clip with AD and SDH lead to a loss of cohesion and alter the reception of the narrative, cannot be determined by text analysis alone. Other methodologies, such as reception studies, should be used to corroborate text analytical findings. However, we have indicated that the 'gaps' or losses incurred in one mode, visual or aural, do not necessarily have to be problematic. The analysis of the original clip revealed how redundant the filmic medium is (the same information is conveyed more than once, through multiple modes), and one of these modes remains accessible to the new audiences of the accessible versions. The visually impaired audience extracts information from the soundtrack and music, the deaf and hard of hearing audience makes use of the visuals. This process of information retrieval works in combination with the process of mental model building, briefly mentioned in the opening section. Both target audiences are aware of the information that is not accessible to them and they actively apply compensation strategies, also relying on external sources such as their knowledge of the world. As the analysis has illustrated on several occasions, the loss of redundancy in the cross-modal cues leads to slimmer identity chains, a greater need for reconstruction through implication and hence, possibly, to a greater cognitive effort for our two specific audiences. On the other hand, less redundancy, succinct description and focused subtitling may also shield the blind and deaf audiences from information overload and help them grasp the most narratively salient information.

We must conclude by indicating that on the one hand, the potential of the Tseng model has not been fully exploited in our analysis and that there is room for more research, but also that the model has its limits. Tseng underlines the importance of actions and action chains in film, which can be analyzed through the transitivity system (2013: 108–145), but adding more details to the analysis was beyond the scope of the present chapter. Conversely, she admits that tracking participants yields one type of information but that '[t]o provide a complex description . . . further analytical methods accounting for other dimensions still need to be developed, such as methods for describing filmic resources which manipulate emotions of different camera uses which affect and constrain information concerning characters' (*ibid.*: 109). The same can be said for music and sounds. We have analyzed how the presence of music and sound can support the identification of characters on the textual level, but these aspects of film contribute to the production's (connotative) meaning level as well. Moreover, they are not only employed to convey the characters' emotions, but also manipulate the audience's emotional involvement in the film. In order to chart the effect of, say, shifts or losses in textual redundancy, theoretical and text analytical approaches to the study of audiovisual texts should be complemented with experimental and cognitive studies taking on a cognitive and experimental view to analyzing the reception of audiovisual texts and their translations.

Summary

Multimodal productions, which make use of verbal, visual and aural modes to create a coherent message, need to fulfil basic textual requirements, one of which is that of textual cohesion, in this case multimodal cohesion. This chapter analyzes the challenges involved when such texts are made accessible for visually or aurally impaired audiences (e.g. through AD and SDH), since in such texts the original multimodal cohesion is altered. This chapter first defines and discusses the concept of multimodality, multimodal cohesion and cross-modal interaction. It discusses the analytical tools for multimodal analysis developed to date within social semiotics on the basis of seminal publications by van Leeuwen (2005), Royce (2007) and Tseng (2013). The chapter goes on to explore how these concepts and, in particular, the concept of 'cohesive chains' developed by Tseng, can be applied in the analysis of accessible multimodal texts. This is exemplified in a detailed multimodal transcription and analysis of a scene from the film *Nights in Rodanthe*. It illustrates and evaluates the above-mentioned analytical tools and inventorizes the ways in which multimodal cohesion is established in AD and SDH—thus paving the way for the development of new multimodal research methods within AVT.

Further reading

Baumgarten, N. (2008) 'Yeah: That's it!: Verbal Reference to Visual Information in Film Texts and Film Translations', *Meta* 53(1): 6–25 | *This article delivers an introduction to cross-modal linking and multimodal cohesion in audiovisual texts.*

Halliday, M. A. K. (2004) *Introduction to Functional Grammar*, New York: Routledge | *This volume explores key concepts of systemic functional grammar, on which multimodal theory is based.*

Kress, G. and T. van Leeuwen (1996). *Reading Images: The Grammar of Visual Design*. New York: Routledge | *This is an innovative and seminal work exploring the grammar of images, based on Halliday's social semiotic approach to meaning-making in language.*

Matamala, A. and P. Orero (2010) *Listening to Subtitles. Subtitles for the Deaf and Hard of Hearing*, Berlin: Peter Lang | *This book is a useful introduction to key SDH concepts and issues.*

Maszeroska, A., A. Matamala and P. Orero (eds) (2014) *Audio Description: New Perspectives Illustrated*, Amsterdam & Philadelphia: John Benjamins | *This book is based on research carried out in the framework of the European ADLAB project (www.adlabproject.eu) and provides a comprehensive overview of the challenges of AD and research in this field.*

O'Halloran, K. (2011) 'Multimodal Discourse Analysis', in K. Hyland and B. Paltridge (eds) *Companion to Discourse*, London & New York: Bloomsbury, 120–137 | *This work provides a definition of multimodal discourse and demonstrates how multimodal texts can be analyzed.*

Pérez-González, L. (2014) *Audiovisual Translation: Theories, Methods, Issues*, London & New York: Routledge | *This work is a comprehensive overview of practice and research in AVT and contains a chapter on multimodal theory.*

Related topics

6   Subtitling for deaf and hard of hearing audiences: moving forward
8   Audio description: evolving recommendations for usable, effective and enjoyable practices
13 Spoken discourse and conversational interaction in audiovisual translation
14 Psycholinguistics and perception in audiovisual translation
21 Multimodal corpora in audiovisual translation studies
22 Eye tracking in audiovisual translation research
23 Audiovisual translation and audience reception
31 Accessible filmmaking: translation and accessibility from production

References

Baldry, A. and Thibault, P. J. (2006) *Multimodal Transcription and Text Analysis: A Multimodal Toolkit and Coursebook with associated Online Course*, London: Equinox.

Delabastita, D. (1989) Translation and Mass-communication, *Babel* 35(4): 193–218.

Fryer, L. (2010) 'Audio Description as Audio Drama. A Practitioner's Point of View', *Perspectives: Studies in Translatology* 8(3): 205–213.

Halliday, M. A. K. and R. Hasan (1976) *Cohesion in English*, London: Longman.

Herman, D. (2009) *Basic Elements of Narrative*, Oxford: Wiley-Blackwell.

Igareda, P. (2012) 'Lyrics against Images: Music and Audio Description', *MonTI* 4: 233–254.

Johnson-Laird, P. N. (1983) *Mental Models: Toward a Cognitive Science of Language, Inference and Consciousness*. Cambridge, MA: Harvard University Press.

Martin, J. R. (1992) *English Text: Systems and Structure*, Amsterdam & Philadelphia: Benjamins.

Neves, J. (2010) 'Music to my Eyes . . . Conveying Music in Subtitling for the Deaf and the Hard of Hearing', in Ł. Bogucki and K. Krzysztof (eds) *Perspectives in Audiovisual Translation, Lódz Studies in Language 20*, Frankfurt am Main: Peter Lang GmbH, 123–145.

Pérez-González, L. (2014) *Audiovisual Translation: Theories, Methods, Issues*, London & New York: Routledge.

Remael, A. (2001) 'Some Thoughts on the Study of Multimodal and Multimedia Translation', in Y. Gambier (ed.) *(Multi)Media Translation*, Amsterdam & Philadelphia: John Benjamins, 13–22.

Remael, A. (2012) 'For the Use of Sound', *MonTI* 4: 255–276.

Reviers, N. and A. Remael (2015) 'Recreating Multimodal Cohesion in Audio Description: A Case Study of Audio Subtitling in Dutch Multilingual Films', *New Voices in Translation Studies* 13: 50–75.

Royce, T. (2007) 'Intersemiotic Complementarity: A Framework for Multimodal Discourse Analysis', in T. B. Royce (ed.) *New Directions in the Analysis of Multimodal Discourse*, Mahwah, NJ: Lawrence Erlbaum, 63–109.

Taylor, C. (2004a) 'The Language of Film: Corpora and Statistics in the Search for Authenticity. *Notting Hill* (1998)—A Case Study', *Miscelanea: A Journal of English and American Studies* 30: 71–85.

Taylor, C. (2004b) 'Multimodal Text Analysis and Subtitling', in E. Ventola, C. Charles and M. Kaltenbacher (eds) *Perspectives on Multimodality*, Amsterdam & Philadelphia: John Benjamins, 153–172.

Tseng, C.-I. (2013) *Cohesion in Film. Tracking Film Elements*, Basingstoke: Palgrave Macmillan.
Van Leeuwen, T. (2005) *Introducing Social Semiotics*, London & New York: Routledge.
Zabalbeascoa, P. (2008) 'The Nature of the Audiovisual Text and its Parameters', in J. Díaz Cintas (ed.) *The Didactics of Audiovisual Translation*, Amsterdam & Philadelphia: John Benjamins, 21–37.

Filmography

The Hours (2002) Stephen Daldry. IMDb entry: http://www.imdb.com/title/tt0274558/?ref_=fn_al_tt_1

Nights in Rodanthe (2008) George C. Wolfe. IMDb entry: http://www.imdb.com/title/tt0956038/?ref_=fn_al_tt_1

Süskind (2012) Rudolf van den Berg. IMDb entry: http://www.imdb.com/title/tt1609159/?ref_=fn_al_tt_1

18
Sociolinguistics and linguistic variation in audiovisual translation

Wai-Ping Yau

Introduction

This chapter examines audiovisual translation (AVT) from the perspective of sociolinguistics, with an emphasis on linguistic variation, i.e. the ways in which language is used differently in different places by different people in different situations. Special attention will be paid to issues arising from the growing awareness of the importance and implications of the different forms of language that are used in different social contexts. To explore these issues, this chapter will rely on a range of key sociolinguistic concepts that are defined and critiqued in the next section.

Key concepts in sociolinguistics

Sociolinguistics is usefully defined by Spolsky (1998: 3) as 'the field that studies the relation between language and society, between the uses of language and the social structures in which the users of language live'. A basic premise of sociolinguistics is that 'a language— any language—is full of systematic variation, variation that can only be accounted for by appealing, outside language, to socially relevant forces and facts' (*ibid.*: 4). Sociolinguistics seeks to 'map linguistic variation on to social conditions' in order to find out how language varies synchronically (at a particular period) and diachronically (through time) (*ibid.*). Sociolinguistics, as Spolsky stresses (*ibid.*: 24), is therefore 'concerned with language *in situ* and *in vivo*, alive in its geographical and social setting and space'.

In its attempt to understand linguistic variation, sociolinguistics focuses attention on the ways in which members of a 'speech community' communicate by drawing on a 'repertoire' comprising 'a set of language varieties' as well as 'a set of norms for using them' (*ibid.*: 25). This approach is capable of wide, flexible application, with 'no theoretical limitation on the location and size of a speech community' (ibid.). Thus, depending on the purpose of study, a speech community can be located at, below or above the national level, and may refer to, for example, a neighbourhood, a city, a region, a country, or a transnational, digitally linked network. Moreover, the concept of 'variety', which can be broadly defined as 'any identifiable kind of language' (*ibid.*: 6), allows patterns of linguistic variation to be studied in terms of a wide range of categories including dialect, style, register, genre, sociolect, diglossia, and code-switching. A discussion about these categories will be useful to analyze audiovisual translation from a sociolinguistic perspective.

A *dialect* can be defined as a 'variety of language used recognizably in a specific region' (Spolsky 1998: 122). The first point to note is that, important as they are, geographical differences alone may not fully explain linguistic variation; social factors may come into consideration. Thus, in Britain, the same term 'headache' will be used, and pronounced with the educated accent, by those from the top social class, whereas 'speakers from the lowest class will use *skullache, headwarch, sore head*, and other forms, in a variety of pronunciations, depending on where they are from' (Crystal 1997: 39; emphasis in the original). This example also illustrates the extent to which dialects may be stigmatized as 'sub-standard varieties of a language, spoken only by low-status groups—implicit in such comments as "He speaks correct English, without a trace of dialect"' (Crystal *ibid*.: 24). Indeed, as Spolsky (1998: 30) notes, dialectal differences 'are regularly transformed into powerful mechanisms for asserting and recognizing social differences'. But the dichotomy between dialect and language is problematic, not least because dialects form a linguistic continuum that can be broken by political factors into languages. For example, with the dissolution of Yugoslavia, the dialect continuum of Serbo-Croatian split into Serbian and Croatian as separate languages (*ibid*.). In fact, in sociolinguistics, 'all languages are analysed into a range of dialects', and 'everyone speaks a dialect—whether urban or rural, standard or non-standard, upper class or lower class' (Crystal 1997: 24).

The process and attendant problems of creating a standard language are often discussed by sociolinguists under the heading of 'standardization'. Standardization may involve selecting a regional variety as the official medium of communication. The standard variety, codified in grammars, dictionaries and works of literature, will then be taught in schools, used in the media and other institutions, and considered to be the correct form of the language. As Wardhaugh and Fuller (2015: 37) note, 'the standard variety of any language is actually only the preferred dialect of that language', although it is often seen as 'the natural, proper, and fitting language of those who use—or should use—it' (*ibid*.: 34). This popular perception promotes what Wardhaugh and Fuller refer to as 'the standard language ideology', i.e. the fact that '[p]eople tend to think of a language as a legitimate and fixed system which can be objectively described and regard dialects as deviations from this norm' (*ibid*.: 33). Because command of the standard variety confers power and prestige, standardization may be resisted on the grounds that the standard variety 'enhances the powerful position of those who speak it, while diminishing all other varieties, their speakers, and any possible competing norms' (*ibid*.: 35). As will be discussed below, researchers of audiovisual translation have paid increasing attention to the interaction of social and geographical factors in linguistic variation, as well as the ideological implications of the use of dialect.

Whatever the dialect they use, speakers can choose different styles, registers and genres that they consider suitable for different social contexts. Wardhaugh and Fuller (2015: 52) use the term *style* to refer to the level of formality adopted in speech or writing, which can be affected by a variety of factors, including the type of occasion, the level of intimacy between the participants, and their differences in terms of, for example, age and social class. It is also worth noting that shifts in levels of formality can be indicated by switching between the standard language and a non-standard variety. As Crystal (1997: 42) explains, a 'Berlin business manager may use standard German at the office and lapse into local dialect on returning home'.

Register, on the other hand, denotes 'specific ways of speaking associated with particular professions or social groups' (Wardhaugh and Fuller 2015: 52). Speakers acquire different registers through interaction with different social groups, and can use a register to 'construct an identity at a specific time and place' (*ibid.*: 53). In particular, a sense of group identity can be created or upheld by using the associated jargon. As Spolsky (1998: 34) notes, '[g]angs and other closed peer groups often develop their own forms of jargon to serve as markers of group membership and also to make their speech less intelligible to outsiders.' Of particular interest to the remit of this chapter is 'slang', which Spolsky (1998: 35) defines as 'a kind of jargon marked by its rejection of formal rules, its comparative freshness and its common ephemerality, and its marked use to claim solidarity'. With its frequent use of taboo expressions (such as 'fuck' and 'shit'), slang may be indicative of liberation, subversion or dissent. Unsurprisingly, as Spolsky notes, '[s]lang is a feature of the speech of the young and the powerless' (*ibid.*: 36).

Genre also connects linguistic analysis to the context of use, but differs from style and register in its emphasis on 'the conventional structures used to construct a complete text within the variety' (Biber and Conrad 2009: 2). The genre of humour, which has attracted considerable attention in the study of audiovisual translation, is especially amenable to analysis from a sociolinguistic perspective. Humour 'frequently plays on stereotypes' (Chiaro 1992: 7) and makes extensive use of cultural signs such as 'institutions, attitudes, beliefs, typical practices, characteristic artefacts, etc.' (Nash 1985: 9). These references provide humour with an effective means of creating a sense of self and community. As Nash (*ibid.*: 9) notes, '[h]umour is not for babes, Martians, or congenital idiots. We share our humour with those who have shared our history and who understand our way of interpreting experience.' Researchers of audiovisual translation have long been preoccupied with translation problems concerning humour, jargon, slang, taboo expressions, different levels of formality, and stylistic shifts between a standard and a non-standard variety, but conceptualizing such issues from a sociolinguistic perspective encourages a closer scrutiny of the connection between these linguistic forms and the social contexts in which they are used.

Sociolect (also called social dialect) 'describes a language variety that is characteristic for a socially defined group' (Bussmann 1996: 439). Factors involved in defining a social group may include 'occupation, place of residence, education, income, "new" versus "old" money, racial or ethnic category, cultural background, caste, religion, and so on' (Wardhaugh and Fuller 2015: 42). There seems an obvious correspondence between social and linguistic differences in such cases as the British public-school sociolect (*ibid.*). But analysis of sociolect may in fact involve complex issues, some of which are illustrated by research on 'Kiezdeutsch', a sociolect spoken by 'multiethnic groups of urban youths in Germany' (*ibid.*: 43). To start with, while non-standard sociolects are often negatively perceived ('lazy, sloppy, and degenerate' are some common adjectives used to describe these varieties), it has been argued that features of Kiezdeutsch 'are part of normal language development and variation, not a bastardization through foreign influence' (*ibid.*). Furthermore, it has been argued that speakers of Kiezdeutsch are not limited to 'socially marginalized youths of immigrant background', but also include monolingual German speakers (*ibid.*). This suggests that a sociolect is acquired through social interaction, and that 'the identification with a group is a key element in the development of a social dialect' (*ibid.*: 45). In recent years, as will be discussed below, issues of power relations and sense of identity concerning the use of sociolects have been brought to the fore in the study of audiovisual translation.

Diglossia refers to 'a situation in which there are two distinct codes with clear functional separation' (Wardhaugh and Fuller 2015: 90). Used originally to refer to varieties of the same language, the term has been extended to cover speech communities where two or more languages perform distinct functions. In a diglossic community, a high (H) variety is used for formal speech and serious written communication, and the low (L) variety is used for daily conversation and informal written communication. The L variety is acquired naturally and spoken at home, while the H variety is learned at school and associated with a prestigious written tradition. This functional separation has ideological consequences: 'The H variety is the prestigious, powerful variety; the L variety lacks prestige and power' (*ibid.*: 92). The H variety is felt to be 'more "beautiful," "logical," and "expressive" than the L variety', and thus 'deemed appropriate for literary use, for religious purposes, and so on' (*ibid.*). This view of the 'natural superiority' of the H variety is 'reinforced by the fact that a considerable body of literature will be found to exist in that variety and almost none in the other' (*ibid.*). In a diglossic society, the H variety 'is likely to be used over a wider region and thus can serve some unifying purpose', whereas the L varieties 'are more localized and show dialectal variation and the tendency to change of unwritten dialects' (Spolsky 1998: 64). Problems may arise, as will be discussed below, 'when there is a desire to decrease regional and/or social barriers, or when a need is seen for a unified "national" language' (Wardhaugh and Fuller 2015: 93).

The strict separation of the H and L varieties in terms of function and status sets diglossia apart from other forms of bilingualism, where a function can be performed by either or both of the varieties, and where varieties are mixed. *Code-switching* is a common form of bilingualism where a speaker switches from one language or regional variety to another between or within sentences. Code-switches come in different forms and serve different purposes. Bilinguals may shift between languages depending on the topic, because 'a speaker's vocabulary will develop differently for different topics in the two languages' (Spolsky 1998: 50). Speakers may start a sentence in one language variety and finish it in another simply because they are 'upset, tired, or otherwise distracted' (Crystal 1997: 365). A code-switch may also suggest 'the speaker's attitude towards the listener—friendly, irritated, distant, jocular, and so on' (*ibid.*). In particular, in a conversation between two bilinguals, a switch to the lesser used language is 'bound to create a special effect': for example, if a child disobeys instructions given in the usual language, a mother may switch to another language, 'thereby showing her stronger emphasis or displeasure' (*ibid.*). Significantly, a switch to a minority language can be used to shut out those who do not speak the language, or to signal 'solidarity with a social group' (if the listener also shifts to the minority language, then 'a degree of rapport is established') (*ibid.*). Indeed, a language 'becomes a virtual guise for the bilingual speaker, who can change identity as easily as changing a hat' (Spolsky 1998: 50). Code-switching, understood as a way of creating identities, exemplifies the constructivist approach that considers identities as 'fluid, multiple, and culturally constructed' (Wardhaugh and Fuller 2015: 103). It is important to note that 'there is no one-to-one correspondence between language choice and social identity', in that, depending on the context, language choice may relate to different identities: not only 'macrosocial categories, such as age, gender, or social class', but also aspects of personal identity (*ibid.*). From a constructivist perspective, code-switching also shows how speakers 'use language to position themselves vis-à-vis their interlocutors' in matters such as 'social values and ideologies about language, speakers, and social norms' (*ibid.*). Code-switching and other issues concerning audiovisual translation in bilingual or multilingual contexts will be discussed below.

But before exploring audiovisual translation from a sociolinguistic perspective further, a note about terminology. The definitions of terms such as style and register adopted here are widely used by sociolinguists, but scholars of audiovisual translation may employ such terms in slightly different ways depending on the theoretical frame of reference. For example, register is used by Hatim and Munday (2004: 347) within a functional systemic framework to refer to 'variation in context, relating to the language user (geographical dialect, idiolect, etc.) and/or language use (field or subject matter, tenor or level of formality and mode or speaking vs writing)', so that register analysis covers regional dialect, sociolect as well as level of formality. It should be noted that such tools of analysis, as used in functional systemic linguistics, are compatible with a sociolinguistic approach to the study of audiovisual translation, because in sociolinguistics, as noted above, social and geographical factors often come into consideration in the study of linguistic variation, and terms such as style, register and genre overlap in meaning. The remainder of this chapter discusses different issues of audiovisual translation from a sociolinguistic perspective, but it is worth remembering that these issues are in fact interrelated.

Subtitling and dubbing of linguistic variation

Medial constraints

Problems of translating dialect, slang, taboo expressions, and different levels of formality have been much researched, with special attention given to medium-specific and other constraints facing the audiovisual translator. Audiovisual translation differs from literary translation in one crucial aspect: an audiovisual text is directed at both hearing and sight. Whether it is dubbing or subtitling, the translation of dialogue is directly affected by the mise-en-scène, music and written signs on the screen. In professional practice, the dubber faces the challenge of lip synchronization, while the subtitler must fit the subtitles into the available space on the screen, follow the rhythm of the original dialogue, and ensure sufficient time for the viewer to read the subtitles.

These medium-specific constraints are discussed by Pettit (2005) in connection with translation problems concerning levels of formality. Pettit examines a range of examples from the dubbed and subtitled versions of three films—Wayne Wang and Paul Auster's 1995 films *Smoke* and *Blue in the Face*, and Jane Campion's 1993 film *The Piano*—to determine whether and why levels of formality are retained or not. The sample shows an interesting diversity: *Smoke* and *Blue in the Face* are set in 1990s Brooklyn and characterized by the frequent use of colloquialisms, whereas in *The Piano*, set in mid-nineteenth century New Zealand, 'the mode of expression tends to be more formal, in keeping with Victorian conventions of the era' (Pettit 2005: 53). This sample is studied in order to 'establish the extent to which coherence is secured in relation to verbal, non-verbal, audio and visual signs of the audiovisual text' (*ibid.*: 51). In *Smoke*, for example, the shopkeeper Auggie makes a compliment to his regular customer Paul for becoming a contributor to *The New York Times*: 'That's a feather in your cap, man.' In both the dubbed and subtitled versions, this idiomatic expression is translated as the colloquial *Tu devrais être fier comme un pou* ('You must be as proud as a peacock'), in coherence with the characters' demeanour and mode of communication on the screen (*ibid.*: 54). In *The Piano*, on the other hand, we hear the mute Ada's inner thought about her fiancé: 'Were it good he had God's patience.' In both the dubbed and subtitled versions, this sentence is translated literally as *Il serait bon qu'il ait une patience divine*, so as to 'fit the eloquent style of the character' (*ibid.*: 56). In each of these examples, the level of formality is maintained in both the dubbed and subtitled versions.

But retaining the style of the original dialogue may prove difficult, and Pettit's analysis of stylistic shifts yields useful findings. First, lip synchronization often causes a shift in the level of formality and a reduction in the coherence of the dubbed dialogue with narrative elements such as characterization. In *Smoke*, Auggie suggests to Paul: 'You'll never get it if you don't slow down, my friend.' The first part of that sentence is rendered as *Tu ne verras pas* ('You won't see [the point]') in the dubbed version, probably in order to achieve partial synchronization between 'you'll never' and *tu ne verras*, thus resulting in a loss of the familiar tone of the original dialogue. This informal style, however, is more successfully reproduced as *Tu ne pigeras pas* in the subtitled version, 'in keeping with Auggie's easygoing character and the informal setting of the sequence' (Pettit 2005: 57).

Second, a colloquial expression in the original dialogue may be deleted or substituted with a more formal expression if a shorter subtitle is required. In *Smoke*, the black teenager Rashid says, 'If the guy from the check-cashing place hadn't run off screaming bloody murder, he would have shot me.' The subtitler leaves out 'screaming bloody murder' and uses the more formal term *employé* ('employee') for the sake of condensation, whereas the dubbed dialogue displays a colloquial vividness with the additions of *le gars* ('the bloke') and *hurlant comme un malade* ('yelling like a madman')' (*ibid.*: 58).

Third, in the absence of an equivalent expression in the target language, the dubber or subtitler may focus on the denotative meaning at the expense of the speaker's stylistic identity. In *The Piano*, Morag is a middle-aged immigrant from England with racist views about the Maoris, and 'upholds British traditions and etiquette at every occasion' (Pettit 2005: 59). Referring to Ada's wedding dress, Morag says, 'Careful, the lace is most fragile.' Here, the use of the term 'most', in the sense of 'very', suggests a formal style that is 'indicative of social class and formal setting' (*ibid.*). The dubber translates 'most' as 'très', while the subtitler leaves out the term and uses an exclamation mark 'to portray the pedantic nature of the speaker' (*ibid.*). Both translations miss the social and cultural connotations of the English term.

Finally, the dubber or subtitler may use an expression which is more colloquial than the original one in order to enhance characterization, or to compensate for failing to reflect the informal style elsewhere. In *Blue in the Face*, the 'man with unusual glasses' (played by Lou Reed) says, 'And if there was probably a childhood trauma that I had . . .' Here, the dubber uses a more colloquial term *gosse* ('kid'), because the character usually 'talks about various events in a relaxed, informal manner' (Pettit 2005: 60). In this connection it is worth noting that 'the voice of the dubbing actor can compensate, to a certain extent, for meaning which been changed or lost' (*ibid.*: 62).

Censorship

In addition to medium-specific constraints, the audiovisual translator also works under the constraint of censorship concerning the use of slang and taboo expressions. According to Rittmayer (2009: 6), the 'biggest problem for translating slang is censorship—either performed willingly by the translator, or imposed by some outside body', because censorship 'can greatly alter the impact a text has in the target language, especially if the use of slang is important to character development or plot development'. This point is illustrated by an example drawn from Catherine Breillat's 1999 film *Romance*. In one scene, the central character Marie 'is shown making out with, and being groped by Paolo, the stranger she met at a bar the night before', and at one point Paolo asks, *Est-ce que tu veux me faire une pipe?* ('Do you want to give me a blowjob?') (Rittmayer 2009: 7). In French, using 'une pipe', which is 'technically a slang term', is 'the most polite way of referring to fellatio', and the term is used by Marie several times in the scene. Marie's 'openness in talking about sex' is successfully brought out in the English subtitles, which 'consistently use the term "blowjob" as a translation' (*ibid.*). In the dubbed version, however, 'the voice actor demands "Blow me baby", so that Paolo becomes more vulgar or masculine' (*ibid.*). At the same time, Marie 'becomes much more polite' and 'much more reserved about sexuality', as she mentions 'blowing' only once and 'euphemistically refers to "*that*"' throughout the scene (*ibid.*). Moreover, in the original dialogue, Paolo—played by the Italian-born porn star Rocco Siffredi—speaks French with an Italian accent, and is portrayed as '"*l'étranger*"—both the stranger and the foreigner, and very much an "Other" to Marie' (*ibid.*). In the dubbed version, the accent is gone, and with it, the 'dual notion of stranger/foreigner' (*ibid.*).

Taboo expressions

Apart from censorship and medium-specific limitations, Fernández Fernández (2009) identifies two other important issues involved in the translation of taboo expressions. The first concerns the use of the standard language in audiovisual translation. Using the standard accent for dubbing means excluding regional expressions and pronunciations, such that 'the translation of swearwords tends to be watered-down and generalised' (*ibid.*: 213). In Spain, this 'imperative' to use the standard language for dubbing comes as a consequence of economic constraints, insofar as 'it allows film-makers to commercialise the same film throughout the Spanish-speaking market, reducing costs in marketing and distribution' (*ibid.*). The second issue concerns excessive literalism, which leads Fernández Fernández to caution against the potential pitfalls of the strategy of foreignization, as advocated by Venuti (1995). By 'allowing cultural and linguistic differences to stay intact in the translation', the audiovisual translator risks rendering the dialogue unnatural (Fernández Fernández 2009: 213). Examples include *maldita sea* ('damn it') and *hijo de perra* ('son of a bitch') (*ibid.*: 212). From a sociolinguistic perspective, it is important to situate the word of caution offered by Fernández Fernández in the context of the sharp differences of power between countries: 'not only do we imitate America's way of life, we also transfer America's way of speaking to the Spanish language' (*ibid.*). In response to excessive literalism, Fernández Fernández (*ibid.*: 213) recommends that the strategies of domestication and foreignization 'be applied in a balanced way according to specific situations'.

Greenall (2012), on the other hand, uses Alan Parker's 1991 film *The Commitments* as an occasion for reflection on the target audience as a determinant of translation strategy concerning the use of taboo expressions. Of the 274 instances of swearing, only 148 appear in the Norwegian subtitled version (*ibid.*: 53). This radical reduction in swearing is unlikely to be the result of censorship or the constraints of screen time and space, so Greenall (*ibid.*: 57) concludes that probably 'the subtitler is operating on the assumption that the swearing that is missing in the subtitles should somehow be available to the audience by virtue of the larger context'. Furthermore, Greenall (*ibid.*: 58) notes that 'in Norway today, a large part of the audience of a film such as *The Commitments* will be fairly fluent in English'. Thus Greenall (*ibid.*) suggests that researchers of audiovisual translation critically reflect on the common assumption that 'the audience has no knowledge of the source language, and hence is completely at the mercy of the translator or subtitler' (*ibid.*). Hjort (2009: 6) revisits another common assumption about the audience of audiovisual translation, namely that 'swearwords are stronger when written than when spoken'. Hjort's research in Finland shows that viewers 'are tolerant of swearwords and expect to see them rendered as faithfully to the original as possible in terms of harshness' (*ibid.*). Studies such as these suggest that assumptions about the audience of audiovisual translation need to be tested to establish the extent to which they are valid across societies and cultures.

Dialect

Dubbing or subtitling dialect presents particular problems. It seems reasonable to retain the use of dialect if it plays an important part in the original dialogue, but one of the thorny problems facing the audiovisual translator is that dialects carry social and cultural connotations. Thus there is unlikely to be a one-to-one correspondence between dialects in the source and target languages. Moreover, transcribing dialectal speech may make the subtitles difficult to read. Furthermore, dialogue dubbed or subtitled into a local dialect may not be intelligible or acceptable to a wide audience. These problems have led many audiovisual translators to adopt the standard language in preference to a dialect-for-dialect approach. As Chiaro (2009b: 181) notes, audiovisual translators tend to follow the norm of 'replacing non-standard forms in the S[ource]L[anguage] with standard forms, typical of the written language, in the target version'. Following Sternberg (1981), Chiaro (*ibid.*: 181) describes this norm for translating dialect as the 'homogenizing convention'. But Chiaro (*ibid.*) suggests that 'non-standard language can also be connoted through the insertion of linguistic features common in colloquial speech, such as fillers and discourse markers (e.g. *like; you know; I mean*, etc.) as well as deliberate mistakes'. This norm for translating dialect is studied by Goris (1993) with reference to dubbing in France. Goris (*ibid.*: 174) notes that dialectal features are left out, and distinctive characteristics of spoken language drastically reduced 'to the point that they are not even considered ungrammatical or even specifically oral anymore'. Standardization is often accompanied by *naturalization*. For example, 'ten inches' becomes *vingt-cinq centimetres* ('25 centimetres'); 'a girl with typical Brooklyn tact' is rendered as *une petite banlieusarde sans tête* ('an empty-headed little suburban girl'); and 'I know we're not selling California' is rendered as *[c]'est pas l'Eldorado ce terrain, mais . . .* ('this land is not El Dorado, but . . .') (*ibid.*: 177–178). The removal of such socio-cultural references, Goris argues, aims 'to give the impression that the French translations are in fact originals' (*ibid.*: 178).

The problems of standardization are discussed by Herbst (1997) in the context of dubbing in Germany. Herbst (*ibid.*: 294) notes that the extensive use of the standard language results in 'a certain unnaturalness' of the dubbed dialogue. In his view (*ibid.*: 295), standardization is 'inevitable', given that 'no regional or social accent (apart from the standard language) can be used as a target variety in translation without producing a comical or strange effect'. As a result of standardization, there is a loss of 'social meaning', as well as a lack of contrast between different 'speech styles' (*ibid.*). For example, accent contrasts between British and American varieties of English cannot be reproduced in the German dubbed version, because 'all varieties other than the standard language are regionally marked within the target culture' (*ibid.*). An additional problem is that 'in the German-speaking world the standard accent *Hochdeutsch* is hardly ever used in natural speech; at least not in informal conversation' (*ibid.*). Thus German dubbed films are characterized by 'the use of a regionally neutral pronunciation (in situations where it would not normally be expected)' (*ibid.*).

While the above discussion focuses attention on the economic imperative (Fernández Fernández 2009) and the quality of translation in terms of features of orality and dialectal variation (Goris 1993 and Herbst 1997), Erkazanci-Durmuş (2011) argues that standardization should be resisted on ideological grounds. Erkazanci-Durmuş (*ibid.*: 21–22) discusses 'how language perpetuates inequitable social relations and why different varieties of language have unequal access to social power', paying special attention to 'the power relations between the standard language and such varieties of language as dialects, ethnolects, sociolects, and so on'. In particular, Erkazanci-Durmuş (*ibid.*: 23) argues that standardization promotes 'the ideology of legitimate language', which 'may close off the target language to any kind of variation' and 'force the translator to adopt an "authoritative plain style"'. Standardization enforces a form of 'social governance', to the extent that 'the use of a non-standard variety where the standard variety is expected constitutes a violation of communicative competence rules' (*ibid.*). Because of its 'taken-for-granted superiority', the standard variety acts as a 'sociolinguistic dogma' that places translators 'in the hierarchies of language and social success' (*ibid.*: 24). This ideology, Erkazanci-Durmuş postulates, permeates institutions such as 'the media, literature, translation, art, and music' (*ibid.*). In Turkey, for example, an official broadcasting policy is put in place to preserve the standard language as a tool of 'national unity and integrity' against encroachment by non-standard varieties (*ibid.*: 26). Consequently, 'dialects, sociolects, ethnolects and other varieties of language in numerous source texts have been systematically translated into perfectly standard Turkish' (*ibid.*: 27). An example is Aziz Üstel's 2001 Turkish translation of Anthony Burgess's 1962 novel *A Clockwork Orange*. This translation, which seeks conformity with standard Turkish and 'systematically avoids re-lexicalization, over-lexicalization, and the Russian effect on language', was awarded The Best Translation Prize (*ibid.*: 28). Against 'systematic standardization', Erkazanci-Durmuş argues for a critical sociolinguistic approach to the study of translation that addresses linguistic variation as a vehicle for 'marginal voices' (*ibid.*: 21).

Longo (2009: 107) discusses how marginal voices are expressed through a 'dialectization' of the standard language in the subtitling of two films shot predominantly in dialect. Alessandro Piva's 2000 film *LaCapaGira* and Daniele Ciprì and Franco Maresco's 1998 film *Totò che visse due volte* are part of a wave of films depicting characters 'living on the margins of society' in the Italian south (Longo 2009: 99). Both films explore 'a new way for the south to see itself, to become the subject of its own way of thinking as opposed continuing to be determined and constructed by others' (*ibid.*). Longo stresses that the 'predominance of the local dialect', which plays a crucial part in this 'process of self-discovery', is 'enhanced' by the subtitles. In both films, 'subtitles combine with the visuals and the soundtrack to create different layers of signification' (*ibid.*: 100). The dialogue is subtitled into standard Italian in a way that prompts viewers 'to penetrate the dialect and its culture' (*ibid.*: 107). In other words, the subtitles provide 'a key to understand dialect rather than a tool to transpose it' (*ibid.*: 101). This is achieved in two ways. First, the subtitles are minimal, with just sufficient details for the audience to 'follow the plot'; viewers 'are asked to concentrate, without switching off, on the language spoken on the screen', on the assumption that, though difficult, dialect as a variety of the language can be understood (*ibid.* 100). Second, idiomatic expressions said in dialect are often translated literally or left untranslated, so that standard Italian is 'foreignised' (*ibid.*). In *LaCapaGira*, for example, the dialectal expression *fare tum e tum* (meaning 'being noisy' and/or 'not being able to keep silent') is transcribed in the subtitle: *fare* (literally, 'make') combines effectively with the onomatopoeic *tum e tum* to suggest the 'puerility' of 'the characters of the film who seem like grown up children' (*ibid.*: 104). It is important to understand that there has been discrimination against southern dialects since Italy achieved unification in 1861. In *Totò*, however, it is standard Italian that is parodied, put to ridicule, and presented as 'the Other' (*ibid.*: 102). In the film, standard Italian is spoken only by a prostitute (whose escapism is encapsulated by her 'saccharine Italian') and a gay couple (whose 'mannered Italian' smacks of '1950s popular fiction');

standard Italian is 'strongly stereotyped and limited in its use' (*ibid*.: 103). In *LaCapaGira*, on the other hand, the 'inexpressive stiltedness' of standard Italian used in 'a badly dubbed soap opera' contrasts sharply with 'the lively and vibrant dialect' used by the characters. In both films, the parodic impulse combines with the subtitling strategy to create a cultural vision: the dialects 'bear witness to the rich and varied linguistic and cultural traditions of the south which, as the subtitling of these films show, can also be understood by the rest of the country' (*ibid*.: 106).

Problems of translating sociolect are discussed by Jäckel (2001) with reference to the English subtitled version of Mathieu Kassovitz's 1995 film *La Haine*. The film presents France as a 'multicultural and divided society' through the portrayal of three protagonists speaking a sociolect typical of young people living in housing estates (*ibid*.: 223). This sociolect 'offers an almost perfect example of every possible deviation from standard French: sloppy language, bad grammar, misuse of words, use of local colloquialisms, slang, *verlan* (back-slang), Americanisms, Arabic, and all this intermingled with funk rhythm' (*ibid*.: 224). These features represent a 'reaction against the standard modern French language used by a largely middle-class French society'. For its users, this sociolect serves as 'a way of asserting their right to be different and to challenge authority' (*ibid*.). This sociolect functions as a form of protest against social exclusion: '[f]eeling excluded from mainstream society, people develop their own mechanisms of exclusion, in this instance, a verbally aggressive language mainly comprehensible to peers' (*ibid*.). The subtitles are, in the words of one critic, 'frankly geared towards the American market' (*ibid*.: 227). Referring to the use of African American English in the subtitles, one critic notes that the characters 'Vinz and Hubert talk as if they were *homeboys* in the *hood*' (*ibid*.; italics in the original). But this sociolect-for-sociolect approach is problematic in several ways. To start with, slang terms carry social and cultural connotations and may not be applicable to other contexts. In the case of *verlan*, the subtitlers 'could not hope to be understood if they borrowed or invented American back-slang', and therefore 'opted instead for simplicity'; for example, 'keuf' ('cop') becomes 'pig' (*ibid*.). But 'pig' has different associations and lacks the linguistic creativity and 'ludic' character of verlan, which 'functions as caricature' of standard French and its values (*ibid*.: 229). The preference for simplicity, along with the limitations of screen time and space, also leads to a loss of the idiosyncratic features of speech. For example, the 'verbosity' of those with an imperfect command of French is not reflected in the subtitles (*ibid*.: 228). Moreover, the adoption of African American English is accompanied by what Goris (1993: 177) calls 'naturalization'. For example, *Astérix* becomes 'Snoopy'; *Les Schtroumpfs* (the Smurfs) becomes 'Donald Duck'; and *Darty* becomes 'WalMart' (Jäckel 2001: 229). Added to this loss of cultural specificity is the decision not to subtitle the lyrics of two sampled songs—*Non, je ne regrette rien* ('No, I have no regrets') and *Nique la Police* ('Fuck the Police')—which combine to create 'a sense of community at a time of disillusionment and economic hardship' (*ibid*.: 230).

The sociolect-for-sociolect approach is explored by Queen (2004) in the context of German dubbing. Queen is aware of the problems arising from the lack of a one-to-one correspondence between sociolects, but argues that 'ideas about language as an index to social groupings are transferrable to the degree that the ideas overlap in the cultures in question' (*ibid*.: 515). Queen stresses that scholars and practitioners of audiovisual translation should pay attention to 'the socio-cultural and specificity of translation, particularly in terms of target cultural norms and expectations' (*ibid*.: 518–519). Queen refers to the history of German translations of Mark Twain's novel *Huckleberry Finn* as an example to illustrate the importance of awareness about the ideological consequences of choices made by translators.

Whereas the earliest translations use 'a more or less L2 [second language] or pidgin-like model for portraying [the African American character] Jim's speech', more recent translations adopt 'a colloquial variety depicted primarily through non-standard spelling', thus corresponding to a 'rise in anti-racist and anti-discriminatory discourses in Germany' (*ibid.*: 518). Queen notes that, given the difficulty of matching dialects, the practice of dubbing into standard German is common and understandable, even though this may 'erase most linguistic variation, especially regional variation' (*ibid.*: 520).

Queen's sample of study 'provides a broad range of A[frican]A[merican]E[nglish] usage that includes variation based on age, socio-economic class, region, gender and other sorts of affiliations, especially affiliations with a local, urban "street" culture' (*ibid.*: 518). AAE is usually dubbed into standard German, but Queen notes that a sociolect-for-sociolect approach has been adopted in some contexts. In particular, in films 'set in urban contexts', African American English may be rendered in an 'urban dubbing style', which shows linguistic features 'linked to general informality, *Jugendsprache* ('youth language'), and the urban working class' (*ibid.*: 521). Queen explains that most features of this style 'are not regionally specific and index the generally colloquial varieties of German known as *Umgangsprachen* and the youth-based register known as *Jugendsprache*' (*ibid.*: 522). 'The ideologies concerning these varieties of German and their relationships to one another', Queen argues, 'represent the backdrop against which the urban dubbing style may be interpreted' (*ibid.*). Features of the urban dubbing style are 'generally associated with the German industrial working class' and 'particularly with working-class males' (*ibid.*: 521). In other words, 'this style helps align AAE speakers with speakers of German urban varieties and in so doing constitutes them ideologically along similar lines' (*ibid.*: 522–523).

Berthele (2000: 607, quoted in Queen *ibid.*: 523) observes that '[t]his solution gives the German parallel to A[frican]A[merican]V[ernacular]E[nglish] a clear proletarian overtone.' For example, Queen's analysis of the dubbed version of the film *Boyz N the Hood* shows that 'the primary linguistic marker of the street affiliation of the characters occurs with the use of an informal, youth-marked variety of German rather than with an ethnically marked variety'. Several patterns emerge from the use of the urban dubbing style. First, characters dubbed in this style use its features 'relatively infrequently' (*ibid.*: 527). Second, related to the first, the dubbed version shows a sharp contrast between 'a character who is strongly street-oriented' and 'a character with weaker ties to the street', as opposed to the 'gradient differentiation' in the source text (*ibid.*: 529). Third, the urban dubbing style is never used 'to distinguish female speakers of AAE from non-speakers', even 'in films that feature primarily female casts' (*ibid.*: 531). Fourth, the urban dubbing style is also used for 'urban, working-class characters who are not African American English speakers', but not for characters from 'an urban, African American middle or upper middle class' (*ibid.*). In other words, 'the different ethnic links (African American, Italian American, Irish American) indexed in the originals are elided while the class-based indexes remain' (*ibid.*: 533). In fact, Germany has a sociolect involving 'more recent migrant populations, particularly those from Turkey and other parts of the Mediterranean', who 'share many of the characteristics of urban African American populations in the U.S.' (*ibid.*: 531). But this sociolect may not be suitable for dubbing African American English, because 'the sociolinguistic indexes for these migrant populations primarily involve non-nativeness rather than ethnicity specifically' (*ibid.*). Queen's findings are useful for exploring an alternative to standardization, one that attends to both overlaps and differences between dialects, whether regional or social, and to the ideological consequences of the translator's choices.

Humour

The genre of humour provides a fascinating site for the study of audiovisual translation from a sociolinguistic perspective: because humour depends on verbal inventiveness as well as on stereotypes and other socio-cultural references, how well humour travels is a telling indication of social uses of language in both source and target cultures. Researchers have concentrated on the problems presented by 'the close interplay of visuals and acoustics combined with words', the strategies for solving these problems, and the effects of the strategies adopted (Chiaro 2009a: 163).

Armstrong's (2004) case study of the voicing of the American television animation *The Simpsons* from English to French serves as a useful example. Armstrong analyzes the ways in which accents are used for three characters in *The Simpsons* and the dubbed version to makes references to stereotypes and other socio-cultural signs that help to create humour. First, Bart, voiced in a Cockney accent, is shown in an episode using the archaic slang terms 'noggin' (head) and 'peepers' (eyes), whose 'old-fashioned flavour' works with the low-class accent to create associations with *Oliver Twist* and *My Fair Lady*: 'the attribution to Bart of a stretch of archaic Cockney is meant to reinforce our perception of the "Artful Dodger" side of his character' (*ibid.*: 102). In the absence of a parallel dialect pattern, the French dubbed version can only use slang for Bart's dialogue. Second, 'Monty' Burns, who is 'almost always represented negatively, as a heartless, grasping megalomaniac', is given 'a pronunciation that shares characteristics of a UK English accent and the anglicised, upper-class US New England accent' (*ibid.*: 104). This strategy follows 'a long US tradition that gives movie villains an English or anglicised accent' (*ibid.*). In the French version, 'Monty' Burns is voiced in 'an upper-class accent sometimes referred to as "seizième", referring to the prosperous sixteenth district of Paris' (*ibid.*). Thus, in the French version, 'Monty' Burns is voiced in a way that 'attributes to him superiority but not otherness, or only to a lesser degree' (*ibid.*: 108). Finally, 'Diamond' Joe Quimby, the major of 'Springfield', is 'portrayed as a populist, corrupt womaniser' by being voiced in a Boston accent in a way that is 'designed to refer to the speech of John F. Kennedy, and perhaps the male members of the Kennedy "clan" more generally' (*ibid.*: 104–105). In the French version, Quimby is given 'a deep and harsh, "gravely" voice quality' and 'the accent of a small-time crook, an unsuccessful gangster of the type featured in films like those by Tarantino' (*ibid.*: 105). Armstrong's analysis shows how 'social identity is mediated through social-regional accents' (*ibid.*: 97).

Diglossia

Problems arising from the functional separation of language varieties in a diglossic society are discussed by Yau (2012) in the context of audiovisual translation in Hong Kong. In Hong Kong, standard Chinese (the H variety) has traditionally been used for subtitles, but since the 1990s Cantonese (the L variety; a Chinese dialect spoken by most people in Hong Kong) has been increasingly used to translate slang and taboo expressions. For example, Chen (2004) advocates the use of Cantonese subtitles as the most effective means to translate swearing. But Yau (2012: 565) argues that this approach reinforces the 'social stigma attached to written Cantonese' and confines it to a 'linguistic ghetto'. For example, in the subtitled version of Michael Winterbottom's 2004 film *9 Songs*, slang terms and taboo expressions are subtitled into Cantonese, whereas standard Chinese is 'reserved for a public form of communication such as lyrics of songs performed by established music groups' (*ibid.*: 567). This subtitling strategy in fact 'reinforces the rigid boundaries between the H and the L variety', so that 'the asymmetrical power relations inscribed in this dichotomy remains unaltered' (*ibid.*).

Yau argues that to use Cantonese subtitles for the Cockney English in *My Fair Lady* would be 'to treat Cantonese as inferior, deficient, ungrammatical—in other words, as bad Chinese' (*ibid.*: 567). But it is possible to use the L variety 'as a means of stressing the subcultural status of a marginal group' (*ibid.*: 568). In the subtitled version of Curtis Hanson's 2002 film *8 Mile*, for example, the 'angry, defiant lyrics' of the protagonist's freestyle rap are 'rendered with a locally marked vocabulary of colloquialisms, slang terms and swear words', in such a way that the use of Cantonese subtitles 'stresses a sense of alienation from the dominant culture, underlines rap as a form of articulating identity against a specific social background, and at the same time calls attention to the status of Cantonese as a marginalised discourse' (*ibid.*: 569). Moreover, Yau argues that it is possible to create a 'hybrid language' that 'dissolves the dichotomy between the standard and the non-standard variety' (*ibid.*: 570). In the subtitled version of Woody Allen's 2005 film *Match Point*, for example, formal and colloquial expressions in both Cantonese and standard Chinese combine to create a prose that is different from the spoken form of either Cantonese or standard Chinese and yet still intelligible (*ibid.*: 571). In this way, the subtitles 'acquire a thickness that is not quite opacity' (*ibid.*: 572). The audience is asked to read the subtitles 'not mimetically as a transparent medium, but rather rhetorically as textual practice that provides possibilities for' constructing identities and transforming power relations (*ibid.*). This subtitling practice suggests a form of code-switching that provides a way of creating identities and exploring alternatives to diglossia.

Summary

In the study of audiovisual translation, problems concerning linguistic variation have often been discussed with a view to finding ways to create coherence, to secure intelligibility, and to synchronize dubbing and subtitling with original speech. Increasing attention is paid to issues of identity, otherness, relations of power between different cultural constituencies, and the social contexts in which audiovisual translation is produced and received. This chapter has discussed significant research trends such as: studying audiovisual translation in terms of the relation between language and identity; examining the ideological implications of strategies for translating dialect, sociolect, style, register and other forms of linguistic variation; interrogating strategies of domestication that risk removing the traces of the other; exploring innovative strategies for creating identities and transforming power relations. These trends reflect an increasing awareness of the need to recognize the heterogeneity of language use across communities, social groups and individuals, and to investigate the consequences of the translator's choices. A sociolinguistic perspective with an emphasis on linguistic variation will be useful for examining audiovisual translation in a wide range of contexts (to avoid overlap, research on translating linguistic variation in areas such as gender and non-professional practices of audiovisual translation have not been discussed here). Research within a sociolinguistic framework is likely to continue to play an important role in the study of audiovisual translation.

Further reading

Erkazanci-Durmuş, H. (2011) 'A Critical Sociolinguistic Approach to Translating Marginal Voices: The Case of Turkish Translations', in F. Federici (ed.) *Translating Dialects and Languages of Minorities: Challenges and Solutions*, Bern, Peter Lang, 21–30 | *This essay argues that language standardization should be resisted on ideological grounds.*

Longo, A. (2009) 'Subtitling the Italian South', in J. Díaz Cintas (ed.) *New Trends in Audiovisual Translation*, Bristol, UK: Multilingual Matters, 99–108 | *This essay shows how marginal voices can be expressed through a 'dialectization' of the standard language in the subtitling of two films shot predominantly in dialect.*

Queen, R. (2004) '"Du hast jar keene Ahnung": African American English Dubbed into German', *Journal of Sociolinguistics* 8(4): 515–537 | *This essay explores the dialect-for-dialect approach in the context of German dubbing.*

Sternberg, M. (1981) 'Polylingualism as Reality and Translation as Mimesis', *Poetics Today* 2(4): 221–239 | *This essay discusses the 'homogenizing convention' as one option in a range of strategies for the verbal rendering of situations involving different languages or different varieties of a language. The examples, though drawn mainly from literary works, are of clear relevance to audiovisual translation.*

Yau, W.-P. (2012) 'Power, Identity and Subtitling in a Diglossic Society', *Meta* 57(3): 564–573 | *This essay explores how subtitles can interrogate the power relations inscribed in the dichotomy between the standard and the non-standard variety in diglossic contexts.*

Related topics

3 Subtitling on the cusp of its futures
4 Investigating dubbing: learning from the past, looking to the future
19 Gender in audiovisual translation: advocating for gender awareness
25 Minority languages, language planning and audiovisual translation
28 Audiovisual translation and activism

References

Armstrong, N. (2004) 'Voicing "The Simpsons" from English into French: A Story of Variable Success', *JoSTrans: The Journal of Specialised Translation* 2: 97–109. Available online: http://www.jostrans.org/issue02/art_armstrong.php [last access 20 December 2017].
Berthele, R. (2000) 'Translating African-American Vernacular English into German: The Problem of "Jim" in Mark Twain's Huckleberry Finn', *Journal of Sociolinguistics* 4: 588–613.
Biber, D. and S. Conrad (2009) *Register, Genre, and Style*, Cambridge: Cambridge University Press.
Bussmann, H. (1996) *Routledge Dictionary of Language and Linguistics*, London: Routledge.
Chen, C. (2004) 'On the Hong Kong Chinese Subtitling of English Swearwords', *Meta* 49(1): 135–147.
Chiaro, D. (1992) *The Language of Jokes: Analyzing Verbal Play*, London: Routledge.
Chiaro, D. (2009a) 'Issues in Audiovisual Translation', in J. Munday (ed.) *The Routledge Companion to Translation Studies*, London: Routledge, 141–165.
Chiaro, D. (2009b) 'Dialect Translation', in J. Munday (ed.) *The Routledge Companion to Translation Studies (Glossary of Key Terms)*, London: Routledge, 181.
Crystal, D. (1997) *The Cambridge Encyclopedia of Language*, 2nd edition, Cambridge: Cambridge University Press.
Erkazanci-Durmuş, H. (2011) 'A Critical Sociolinguistic Approach to Translating Marginal Voices: The Case of Turkish Translations', in F. Federici (ed.) *Translating Dialects and Languages of Minorities: Challenges and Solutions*, Bern, Peter Lang, 21–30.
Fernández Fernández, M. J. (2009) 'The Translation of Swearing in the Dubbing of the Film *South Park* into Spanish', in J. Díaz Cintas (ed.) *New Trends in Audiovisual Translation*, Bristol, UK: Multilingual Matters, 210–225.
Goris, O. (1993) 'The Question of French Dubbing: Towards a Frame for Systematic Investigation', *Target* 5(2): 169–190.

Greenall, A. (2012) 'The Non-translation of Swearing in Subtitling: Loss of Social Implicature?', in A. Serban, A. Matamala and J. M. Lavaur (eds) *Audiovisual Translation in Close-up: Practical and Theoretical Approaches*, Bern: Peter Lang, 45–60.

Hatim, B. and J. Munday (2004) *Translation: An Advanced Resource Book*, London: Routledge.

Herbst, T. (1997) 'Dubbing and the Dubbed Text—Style and Cohesion: Textual Characteristics of a Special Form of Translation', in A. Trosborg (ed.) *Text Typology and Translation*, Amsterdam: John Benjamins, 291–308.

Hjort, M. (2009) 'Swearwords in Subtitles', *inTRAlinea*. Available online: http://www.intralinea.org/specials/article/Swearwords_in_Subtitles [last access 20 December 2017].

Jäckel, A. (2001) 'The Subtitling of *La Haine*: A Case Study', in Y. Gambier and H. Gottlieb (eds) *(Multi) Media Translation: Concepts, Practices and Research*, Amsterdam: John Benjamins, 223–235.

Longo, A. (2009) 'Subtitling the Italian South', in J. Díaz Cintas (ed.) *New Trends in Audiovisual Translation*, Bristol, UK: Multilingual Matters, 99–108.

Nash, W. (1985) *The Language of Humour*, London: Longman.

Petitt, Z. (2005) 'Translating Register, Style and Tone in Dubbing and Subtitling', *JoSTrans: The Journal of Specialised Translation* 4: 49–65. Available online: http://www.jostrans.org/issue04/art_pettit.php [last access 20 December 2017].

Queen, R. (2004) '"Du hast jar keene Ahnung": African American English Dubbed into German', *Journal of Sociolinguistics* 8(4): 515–537.

Rittmayer, A. (2009) 'Translation and Film: Slang, Dialects, Accents and Multiple Languages', *Comparative Humanities Review* 3(1). Available online: http://digitalcommons.bucknell.edu/chr/vol3/iss1/1 [last access 20 December 2017].

Spolsky, B. (1998) *Sociolinguistics*, Oxford: Oxford University Press.

Sternberg, M. (1981) 'Polylingualism as Reality and Translation as Mimesis', *Poetics Today* 2(4): 221–239.

Venuti, L. (1995) *The Translator's Invisibility. A History of Translation*, London: Routledge.

Wardhaugh, R. and J. Fuller (2015) *An Introduction to Sociolinguistics*, 7th edition, Hoboken, NJ: John Wiley & Sons Inc.

Yau, W. P. (2012) 'Power, Identity and Subtitling in a Diglossic Society', *Meta* 57(3): 564–573.

Filmography

8 Mile (2002) C. Hanson. IMDb entry: http://www.imdb.com/title/tt0298203/?ref_=nv_sr_1

9 Songs (2004) M. Winterbottom. IMDb entry: http://www.imdb.com/title/tt0411705/?ref_=fn_al_tt_1

Blue in the Face (1995) P. Auster and W. Wang. IMDb entry: http://www.imdb.com/title/tt0112541/?ref_=fn_al_tt_1

Boyz N the Hood (1991) J. Singleton. IMDb entry: http://www.imdb.com/title/tt0101507/?ref_=fn_al_tt_1

La Haine (1995) M. Kassovitz. IMDb entry: http://www.imdb.com/title/tt0113247/?ref_=fn_al_tt_1

LaCapaGira (2000) A. Piva. IMDb entry: http://www.imdb.com/title/tt0241657/?ref_=fn_al_tt_1

Match Point (2005) W. Allen. IMDb entry: http://www.imdb.com/title/tt0416320/?ref_=fn_al_tt_1

Romance (1999) C. Breillat. IMDb entry: http://www.imdb.com/title/tt0194314/?ref_=fn_al_tt_1

Smoke (1995) W. Wang and P. Auster. IMDb entry: http://www.imdb.com/title/tt0114478/?ref_=nv_sr_3

The Commitments (1991) A. Parker. IMDb entry: http://www.imdb.com/title/tt0101605/?ref_=fn_al_tt_1

The Piano (1993) J. Campion. IMDb entry: http://www.imdb.com/title/tt0107822/?ref_=fn_al_tt_1

The Simpsons (1989-) Various directors. IMDb entry: http://www.imdb.com/title/tt0096697/fullcredits?ref_=tt_ql_1

Totò che visse due volte (1998) D. Ciprì and F. Maresco. IMDb entry: http://www.imdb.com/title/tt0144646/?ref_=fn_al_tt_1

19
Gender in audiovisual translation studies
Advocating for gender awareness

Luise von Flotow and Daniel E. Josephy-Hernández

Feminist theorization and activism are the precursors to gender studies. This chapter on gender and audiovisual translation (AVT) therefore begins with an overview of those feminist ideas that entered translation studies from the 1980s onward, and helped develop this new interdiscipline. While feminist theory and criticism first addressed the study of literary translations, a focus that continues to drive research in the field, the application of gender-focused theories to AVT studies has been developing only since the early 2000s. Progress has been slow—particularly if compared with developments in the domains of media and communications studies, which have been producing feminist and/or gender-aware ideas for decades (Carter 2012).

Questions connecting feminism and media studies were first raised in the 1960s and 1970s, and focused on the skewed representation of women's lives in the media. Friedan (1963, cited in Gallagher 2013: 24), for example, noted that media tended to show a glamourized version of how women's lives should be lived. In an essay published in 1978, Gaye Tuchman rehearsed a similar argument, contending that the mass media largely ignore women or portray them in stereotypical roles of victim and/or consumer, thereby symbolically annihilating them. Laura Mulvey ([1975] 1999: 62), for her part, pointed out the sexualization and intrinsic 'to-be-looked-at-ness' of the female body on the screen, presented by and for a 'determining male gaze that [in narrative film] projects its phantasy onto the female figure, which is styled accordingly', i.e. to meet and respond to these fantasies. Other critics noted the media's systematic resistance to—even backlash against—the women's movement from the 1960s onward, and their tendency to discredit, isolate and undercut women, cultivating images that fit 'the established structure of social relations' (Gerbner 1978: 46–48). Margaret Gallagher (2003) aptly summarizes the implications of these views, noting that 'early analyses found the media to be deeply implicated in the patterns of discrimination operating against women in society'. This stance would later be endorsed by critical media studies documenting the construction, dissemination and popularization of various other gender stereotypes through film and advertising, pointing to the construction of clichés of masculinity and heteronormativity (Gallagher 2003: 24). In the early 2000s, critical studies of the representations of Muslim women in the Western media drew attention to how political ideologies focus on women as 'a site on which wider, public meanings are inscribed' (Gallagher 2003: 25, also Macdonald 2006). Anglo-American scholars and other media critics noted the proliferation of images of Muslim women clothed in chadors, burqas and veils, a phenomenon that conveniently served politicians as an emotional justification for the illegal US invasions of Afghanistan and Iraq (Stabile and Kumar 2005). While the use of sexualized or veiled female bodies for commercial or political purposes has not necessarily declined, some public awareness of the gendered nature of contemporary audiovisual products has doubtless been raised as a result of critical media studies.

One noteworthy invention in regard to the reception of audiovisual products is the so-called Bechdel test. It sharply reveals the impact of feminist awareness and criticism and shows how reasoned ideological criticism can work to popular effect, well beyond the academic sphere. The Bechdel test is named after American cartoonist Alison Bechdel, in whose comic strip *Dykes to Watch Out For* it first appeared in 1985. Two women debate which film to go see that evening. The more radical black woman says she will only see a film that fulfils three basic requirements:

1 The movie has to have at least two women in it,
2 who talk to each other,
3 about something besides a man.

No such film is available that evening, and so the two friends spend the evening at home.

This cartoon and the feminist socio-cultural and political requirements it delineates have been widely applied by film critics and viewers alike. It is used to both assess audiovisual products from a feminist perspective and explain the failure of certain products from that same point of view. Dean Spade and Craig Willse's entry on 'Norms and Normalization' in the *Oxford Handbook of Feminist Theory* (2016: 551–572), for example, notes that the test is 'a popular critical tool and commentary on how media representations enforce harmful gender norms', since it shows how conventional fiction and media represent women only in their relationships to men. Interestingly, certain commercial film and media outlets have recognized the value of the Bechdel test, with the Scandinavian cable television channel Viasat Film incorporating it into some of their ratings in 2013, and the European cinema fund Eurimages following suit in 2014, making it part of its submission mechanism in an effort to collect information about gender equality in its projects. It now requires 'a Bechdel analysis of the script to be supplied by the script readers' (EWA Network, n.d.). Finally, a Bechdel 'movie list' now exists on the Internet (Bechdel Test Movie List, n.d.) that features hundreds of films with a Bechdel rating, provides a historical account of the development of this instrument, and invites viewers to add a film, criticize a rating, and include articles and explanations. The extensive references to the Bechdel test that can be found today through a very simple Internet search corroborate the fact that Bechdel has become a 'household name' for informed audiences, providing them with a simple but concrete frame of reference to assess, criticize and potentially boycott the 'way the unconscious of patriarchal society has structured film form' (Mulvey [1975] 1999: 833).

In what follows, the development of the more academic *feminist critique of film* will be reviewed briefly with reference to three important names: Mulvey, Silverman and De Lauretis. Their work provides separate but related examples of early gender-conscious criticisms of the audiovisual products that continue to drive cultural and socio-political representations of gender, where gender is considered as the socio-cultural behaviour that performs or demonstrates a certain sexual identity; it is behaviour that is learnt through repetitive practice, training, and mechanisms of social control. In a second segment, existing research that brings questions of gender into the study of translated audiovisual products will be reviewed, and a third section will briefly explore single initiatives in the field, and suggest further areas of academic research.

First, however, it is wise to consider the problematic meaning of the term 'gender'. Joan Scott (von Flotow and Scott 2016) has shown that in English—and in other languages that translate from or refer to English—the meaning of the term can vary substantially. For example, in a world that does not necessarily welcome feminist ideology, the term gender is often used by academics, journalists and cultural theorists to disguise the fact that their focus is, in fact, feminist and centred on women (Schwartz 2017). In mainstream journalistic publications, the term gender often refers only to women's demands for equality and justice, leaving other gender identities aside. In documents produced by institutions such as the United Nations, gender terminology—such as gender-mainstreaming—also refers largely to women, though that is changing as discussions around heteronormative language and attitudes begin to take hold. Even English-language dictionaries note the uncertainties around the word and cite examples where gender is simply equated with 'sexual difference', rather than referring to the contextual, cultural and behavioural differences that come with sexual difference, which is what the original feminist use of the term meant (Scott 1999). In other words, since its inception in the 1970s the term has been put to many different uses, in popular culture, international organizations such as the United Nations or the World Health Organization, in NGOs, in policy-making, news reporting, cultural politics and academic theorizing. Von Flotow and Scott (2016: 358) shows how diverse its meanings have become in the following terms:

> Adapted—not without controversy—by English and American feminists from the writings of American medical doctors, it [the term gender] resonated around the globe—again, not without controversy—in the wake of Second Wave feminism. Often used (whether by scholars or policy analysts) simply to indicate attention to the situation of women (the discrimination they face, the inequalities they experience), it soon acquired the status of theory for its advocates and critics alike. Recently it has received a great deal of publicity as a result of its denunciation by religiously-inspired opponents of gay marriage.

Scott argues that academics who regularly use the term may work with 'gender studies', 'theories of gender', 'social constructions of sex', or seek to analyze 'relations of domination based on sex'. And what about 'queer', writes Scott, 'is this a version of gender theory or is it antithetical to it?' (*ibid.*: 355). It seems difficult to pin down a stable meaning for the term, and since the management and representation of sexual difference always raise sensitive questions, gender in any translation situation will always be complicated by cultural politics.

Given the difficulties in defining 'gender', this chapter will use the term to refer first and foremost to the fact that biological sexual differences exist and are culturally managed and represented in many audiovisual products. Secondly, in recognition of the important questions raised by 'gender trouble' (Butler 1990) in academia, the term will also be used in regard to differences in sexual orientation, and their representation and translation in audiovisual products. However, since the focus of this chapter is on *translation*, we deliver a critique of scholarly work that explores how these sexual differences and gendered orientations are represented through the *language* of audiovisual products, and not through their visuals.

Gender in feminist film studies

Gender criticism entered film studies in the 1970s through feminist analyses of mainstream narrative film. The work of Laura Mulvey ([1975]/1999), Kaja Silverman (1988) and Teresa de Lauretis (1987) will be discussed briefly as examples.

In her article 'Visual Pleasure and Narrative Cinema', first published in 1975, Mulvey mobilizes a political use of psychoanalysis to explore and explain how the dual aspect of scopophilia—a term used and developed by Freud, which refers to the 'voyeuristic' pleasure in looking and the 'narcissistic' pleasure in being looked at—has played out for women in conventional narrative film. It has coded 'the erotic into the language of the dominant patriarchal order' (*ibid.*: 835), Mulvey asserts, with sexual imbalance in the world maintained through active/male and passive/female 'pleasure in looking' (*ibid.*: 837). In Mulvey's analysis, narrative film is structured to respond to and further fuel the dominant order, reinforcing 'pre-existing patterns of fascination already at work within the individual subject and the social formations that have moulded him' (*ibid.*: 833). Her use of the pronoun 'him' in the preceding sentence makes it clear that this human subject addressed by mainstream narrative film, is primarily male—and that the 'male gaze' rules such film, thus maintaining and re-asserting the *status quo* of male power over the female, where male producers and audiences of film can revel in the pleasures of voyeurism and vicarious power, reducing the female film figures to passive body parts, and where female audiences are expected and trained to learn the joys of 'being-looked-at-ness' through an eroticized focus on these body parts.

In *The Acoustic Mirror* (1988), Kaja Silverman centres her work on women's voices and speech in conventional narrative film, asserting that the *sound* of conventional cinema plays an important role in assigning behavioural traits to sexual difference, where 'the female voice is as relentlessly held to normative representations and functions as is the female body' (1988: viii). These normative functions underscore the spectacle that women become in these audiovisual products, a spectacle that is reinforced by women's voices, presented as '"thick with body"—for example, crying, panting, or screaming . . . but with little or no authoritative voice in the narrative' ([1984]1990, cited by Chaudhuri 2006: 45). In fact, Silverman characterizes women's speech in such film as 'unreliable, thwarted, or acquiescent', noting that it is always synchronized with the spectacle that the female body is reduced to. Women's healthy, sane, authoritative voices are almost never present, and certainly not used in voice-over, where the disembodied male 'voice-of-God', which connotes trustworthiness and authority to the general public, prevails. Silverman's interest in voice is of particular interest to AVT, where both script and *sound* are adapted to the new culture, while the image is seldom touched. The question so far hardly addressed in AVT research is how gendered voices are made to sound in translation.

Teresa de Lauretis (1987) moves away from the male/female binary of earlier feminist analyses to develop work on lesbian desire and its representation in film; she explores the differences and tensions between actual, real women, and questions the viability of any universally valid 'image of Woman' that conventional cultural productions might claim to disseminate. Instead, she posits an eccentric female subject that does not locate itself within the institution of heterosexuality, and she seeks to articulate the specificity of representing lesbian sexuality in film. Her coining of the expression 'queer theory' in 1990 leads to its use as an umbrella term for a wide range of non-binary gendered behaviours, identities and cultures, all of which have since been reflected in film and in film studies (Hanson 1999). As Jane Gaines (1997) puts it in a review of *Deviant Eyes, Deviant Bodies* (Staayer 1996), the 'queering' of feminist film and film theory has meant recognizing sexual variegation and gender indeterminacy, and has set an 'infinite continuum of sexes' against the straitjacket of binarism: work by film directors such as Patricia Rozema and Léa Pool, who are interested in lesbian women's lives and language, is exemplary in this regard.

While these theorists paved the way for a plethora of studies on different gender questions in film, relatively little attention has been paid to questions of gender in the *language* of audiovisual products, which is, after all, what is translated, and what translation studies research needs to focus on. Does this language corroborate the stereotypes that film critics such as Mulvey, Silverman and De Lauretis identify? And if so, how? And how are neologisms and cultural references deployed in audiovisual products to evoke or imply gendered identities and behaviours, and then translated?

Gender as a topic in audiovisual translation studies

Currently, there seem to be three main approaches to studying questions of gender in audiovisual products. All three derive from the critical feminist thinking of the 1970s and display a certain advocacy: the first focuses on feminist materials in Anglo-American audiovisual products and their translation into Romance languages; the second studies the differences between subtitled and dubbed versions of Anglo-American source texts; and the third looks at gay and queer source text materials and their treatment in translation. These three tendencies are discussed below.

The first, and most developed, approach examines translated audiovisual materials for the accuracy with which they reflect feminist content and nuance. The source films under discussion are exclusively English films or TV series, many of them referred to as 'chick flicks', such as the US American *Sex and the City* (1998–2004), *Ally McBeal* (1997–2002), or *Buffy the Vampire Slayer* (1997–2003), and the British *Bridget Jones's Diary* (2001). The language in the source films tends to emphasize the assertive, sexualized, and supposedly feminist language of relatively strident young heroines, whose stories are marketed as 'socially realistic and relevant' (Feral 2011a: 183), and whose non-traditional female sexuality not only represents a liberatory feminist achievement but is also a selling point. Academic studies that reflect this focus include Delia Chiaro (2007), Diana Bianchi (2008), Anne-Lise Feral (2011a, 2011b), Marcella De Marco (2006, 2012) and Alessandra De Marco (2013); they work from English originals to French, Italian or Spanish translations.

Feral's work elaborates on French dubbers' tendencies to eliminate or strongly modify and undermine 'textual elements that pose[d] the greatest threat to patriarchal notions of female sexuality' (2011a: 197) and instead, impose the 'dominant popular ideology and culture of France where socially constructed knowledge of femininity and sexuality are inseparable from images of the courtesan and the prostitute' (*ibid.*). Feral systematically extracts and comments on examples from these dubbed 'chick text' products that bolster her argument, which she then parallels with contemporary sociological studies of gender perceptions in France. One telling example is extracted from a *Sex and the City* (1998–2004) episode entitled 'The Power of Female Sex' (season 1, episode 5), where a group of educated young women is discussing the politics of power:

Example 1

Samantha: Women have the right to use every means at their disposal to achieve power.

Miranda: Short of sleeping their way to the top.

In French, the dubbed version (*comme coucher avec des mecs pour arriver au sommet*) expresses the exact opposite ('such as sleeping with guys to get to the top') of what Miranda says in English—thus proposing that having sex with one's employer/manager is a viable way to gain promotion. In Feral's view, this coincides with ongoing French ideas about '*promotion canapé*' (literally 'promotion via the sofa') (*ibid.*: 187) and, more generally, with the view that women need to be sexually appealing in order to succeed. She concludes that this social ambiance may account for the French translations of chick texts that 'so obviously create "courtesans" where there are none in English' (*ibid.*: 188).

Diana Bianchi's study of the Italian dubbing of *Buffy the Vampire Slayer* (1997–2003), a US American TV series whose heroine Buffy has been seen as a symbol of 'female agency' because she escapes the traditional portrait of women as victims and passive receivers of male help and protection, and because she also 'often saves "males in distress"' (2008: 184) describes similar findings. The sexually active, creative, and enterprising young woman Buffy is dubbed down into stereotypical notions around Italian female sexuality, where women are either sexually passive and proper, or consumed by a wild irrational passion. Her deliberate exploitation of men, her sexual stamina and energy are 'tamed and normalized' (*ibid.*: 191 ff). Bianchi suggests that this censorship serves to clean up the text and in so doing meets the requirements of network producers. Network demands and profits are also mentioned in an earlier study by Chiaro, who suggests that if risqué audiovisual products are not censored through the efforts of dubbers, they are limited to late night viewing, with smaller audiences, and therefore smaller profit margins. Prime time screening is compromised by language considered to be too aggressive, vulgar or rude (2007: 257). Of course, the definition of taboo language—or taboo ideas—is always relative, and contingent on cultural norms, audience expectations, profit margins, and practical, on-the-spot decisions made by dubbing actors and directors as much as by translators.

The second, related, line of research addresses the differences between the subtitled and dubbed versions of these same, or similar, audiovisual products. This research compares the subtitled and dubbed versions of the same English source text, and draws conclusions about how these products have been prepared for different target audiences.

Feral's comparative study (2011b) of the French subtitling and dubbing of *Sex and the City* explores how AVT conforms to distributors' assumptions about the intended audience's gender beliefs and values. Positioning France as a country where 90 per cent of all foreign audiovisual products are dubbed—with the intention of serving mass audiences rather than the intellectual minority that prefers subtitles—Feral shows how dubbing adapts the audiovisual text to these audiences, filtering and selecting the elements that will reach viewers and naturalizing them according to what they are deemed to understand or want. Feral's findings reveal that the subtitled versions maintain most of the US feminist references and attitudes, while the dubbed products not only weaken or completely eliminate the feminist content of the US productions, but also make important changes in the text itself. For example, references to women in public positions of authority are downplayed, a woman's post-graduate university degree is reduced to a French *baccalaureat* ('high school diploma'), and women characters' ambitions, interests and achievements are consistently undermined. The question raised here is the following: why is the majority of French viewers expected to prefer 'humbler female voices to those of the high-flying career women [in the source materials] who flaunt their academic and professional excellence and ambition?' (2011b: 399). Yet again, Feral draws a parallel between this situation and the history, status, and representation of feminism in France more generally, arguing that these dubbing practices reveal to what extent feminism in France has been marginalized in mainstream audiovisual practices and even turned into a weapon against women.

A third approach to the study of gender issues in AVT (Lewis 2010, Ranzato 2012, Chagnon 2016) examines non-binary sexual orientations and their linguistic representation in/through translation. Again, the source texts tend to be mainly English, which is described as having developed an abundant and colourful vocabulary for queer sexualities. Both Lewis and Ranzato find that the terminology available in Italian or Spanish for 'queer' ways of being and expressing oneself is either non-existent or weak, and often simply erased and replaced with more conventional language. Another problem revolves around the ambiguity of English and, more specifically, its capacity to play with the neutral grammatical gender of words such as 'friend', 'lover', or 'partner.' The Romance languages that these academics study have grammatical gender, and translators must decide whether the 'lover' or 'friend' is male or female: *un amant* or *une amante* in French, *un amigo* or *una amiga* in Spanish. The danger is that queer or non-binary implications are lost, or worse, rendered heteronormative. There seem to be fewer options for a translated text to 'queer' a script (Lewis 2010), and not only for reasons of grammar or terminology. Both Lewis and Ranzato speculate on the possibility that some translators may not even recognize queer references or moments of sexual ambiguity. They may not be aware of the censorship they are inflicting when they neglect or erase gay or camp references.

Lewis, for instance, explains that just like people in everyday life, characters in film are assumed to be heterosexual until they are proven queer (2010: 3). This assumption must impinge upon translators', publishers' or producers' capacities to perceive, recognize, valorize, and render queer content. They automatically privilege heteronormative elements, easily translating scripts into a conventional binary form. Lewis' case for 'queer translation' contests this 'heteronormative hegemony in order to give queer people a voice and greater visibility' (*ibid.*: 11). Her case study of the subtitled versions of *Gia* (1998), a film based on the life of a queer model, focuses on one small segment where Gia introduces her female love interest to her mother, who does not know or chooses not to know that Gia is a lesbian. Here, the focus is on the terms 'girlfriend', meaning lesbian lover, and 'boyfriend', a straight, binary boyfriend. Gia's attempt to let her mother know that she has a 'girlfriend' and her mother's willingness to overhear this is the crux of the matter (Example 2), and Lewis discusses to what extent the subtitled versions render this subtlety:

Example 2

English: This is my, uh, girlfriend, Linda.

Spanish: Esta es mi amiga, Linda.

French: Voici ma copine: Linda.

Italian: Questa è la mia amica, Linda.

Portuguese: Esta é minha amiga, Linda.

In Lewis' assessment the Spanish, Italian and Portuguese versions occult the possibility of a 'queer reading' of this exchange through the use of the term 'amiga/amica' which does not imply any romantic interest; the French (*Voici ma copine* rather than *Voici une copine*) does, and so demonstrates that a translation sensitive to the ambiguity of the text is indeed possible. Lewis concludes that many translations avoid recognizing this type of sexual ambiguity, and simply translate into heteronormative directions. She argues for and demonstrates the possibility of more nuanced approaches and suggests various solutions to the ongoing problem of audiovisual translators not recognizing gender difference.

On the question of dubbing English 'gayspeak' into Italian, Irene Ranzato (2012) cites Keith Harvey (2000) to underline the notion of gay speech communities as an important element in the creation of what she considers the 'fictional scripted language of fictional homosexuals portrayed . . . in usually stereotypical ways, often through the use of "camp"' (*ibid.*: 371). Her study identifies a number of problems facing Italian dubbers of gay film/gay-speak. First, the gay lexicon in English is far richer and broader than in Italian, which has often just borrowed, or calqued English words. Secondly, the campy references that gay Anglo-American characters might make to film heroines such as Marlene Dietrich, Judy Garland or other long-dead film divas who are supposedly fetishized by a sector of the gay community are simply unavailable or meaningless for Italian audiences: a problem of cultural references, which always defy easy translation. Faced with these challenges, and doubtless also for cultural reasons, Italian dubbing often cuts the references to such figures from popular culture, generalizes queer terms (removing the differences between 'butch' and 'dyke', for instance), and turns homosexual terms into heterosexual ones. As an example, Ranzato opens her article with a reference to the first Hollywood use of the word 'gay' to mean homosexual, in the comedy classic *Bringing Up Baby* (1938), where Cary Grant—wearing a frilly woman's bathrobe at a chaotic moment in the film—reputedly responds to the question about why he is dressed in this outfit: 'Because I just went gay all of a sudden!'. The Italian dubbed version, entitled *Susanna*, provides the translation *Perché sono diventato pazzo, ecco perché!* ('Because I've gone mad, that's why!') (*ibid.*: 370). Ranzato presents this as an early example of a general tendency in Italian dubbing to render homosexual content with references to madness or illness (*ibid.*: 380), a tendency that in her estimation has not diminished. In Italian dubbing, homosexuality is apparently erased, or attenuated, changed by translations that remove allusions as well as precise terms and replace homoerotic references with terms that render homosexuality as some kind of illness.

In Canada, on the other hand, where US American audiovisual products are often dubbed into French for Quebec, certain translations would appear to deliberately enhance or emphasize gay aspects of a product. A study of the TV shows *Queer as Folk* (2000–2005) and *The L Word* reveals (2004–2009) that the dubbed versions have systematically emphasized the show's gay phrases and vocabulary (Chagnon 2016). The language of these shows is 'gayed' and focused on the homosexual aspects of the script, which results in exaggerated stereotypes of gays and lesbians being created for the sole purpose of obtaining a larger viewership. Unlike Ranzato's (2012) work, which points to the erasure of gay in Italian dubbed products, Chagnon's points to the sales factor as an important element driving the tendency she observes.

Less advocacy-driven work

Other individual articles focus on more disparate topics in the area of gender-aware criticism of AVT. They include three contemporary studies that discuss translation *into English*: Asimakoulas (2012) describes the language of transsexual identity, and its translation in the Greek film *Strella* (2009); Hiramoto (2013) studies scripted gender stereotyping in the Japanese *anime* series *Cowboy Bebop* (1998–2003) and its US versioning; and Daniel E. Josephy-Hernández (2017) researches the portrayal of gender in the subtitled and dubbed versions of Kon Satoshi's film *Perfect Blue* (1997). Two other studies, by Nicole Baumgarten (2005) on the German dubbing of James Bond movies and Charlotte Bosseaux (2008) on the meaningfulness of voice quality point in the direction of broader gender questions in AVT studies. They are addressed below.

The three studies of audiovisual products translated into English are descriptive rather than advocative, acknowledging the challenges translations face in dealing with the gender focus of their respective source texts. Asimakoulas, for example, presents queer and 'trans' aspects of *Strella*, a Greek film about a man who, having just been released from prison after 15 years, begins searching for his long-lost son—only to end up falling for a young transsexual girl who turns out to be his son. Drawing on Butler (1990), Asimakoulas focuses his analysis on the language of 'non-normal subject positions where ambiguity prevails', and where queer characters take subversive and playful stances toward established ideas. He casts his discussion of the film and its English subtitles in terms of four types of language subversion that Harvey (2000) theorized in relation to 'gayspeak'—i.e. the variety of language used by gay men to identify themselves to each other. These uses of language, which Asimakoulas sees as undermining the dominant order, include a playful, disruptive attitude to language, a reversal of the expected order of language/dialogue, the use of paradox through the juxtaposition of contradictory ideas, and parody of other cultural manifestations. By classifying instances of gay/queer language found in the film according to these categories, Asimakoulas shows how diverse, locally situated, and culturally bound this film language is; likewise, he draws attention to the challenges that are bound to hinder any attempt to render such linguistic features into anything vaguely equivalent in English. His work does not set out, however, to attack or criticize the work of the English subtitlers; instead, it explores and charts an area that has been so far untouched in translation studies—the language of transgender. In so doing, Asimakoulas elaborates on issues of ambiguity that have a significant impact on 'translation proper'.

Hiramoto, similarly, recognizes the difficulties faced by the English dubbing world when confronted with the forms of the Japanese language that are used to reinforce 'hegemonic masculinity' in an *anime* series aimed at young adult males. The 'hero and babe characters' in the series entitled *Cowboy Bebop* (1998–2003) not only have exaggerated physical characteristics to mark their binary genders, but also make use of exaggerated language that connotes very male or very female traits (Hiramoto 2013: 53). Gender markers in Japanese are specific, but also ubiquitous. They are found in first and second person pronouns, in sentence final particles, and throughout one form of the language referred to as JWL (Japanese Women's Language)—a hyper-feminine form of speech used exclusively in constructed fictional dialogue (*ibid.*: 74), i.e. in scripts (see also Inoue 2003, Furukawa 2017). The English dubbing has much to contend with since English does not mark first and second person pronouns for gender or add gender indications at the end of sentences; nor does a specific form of women's speech exist in English. It can, therefore, not meet the extremes of the Japanese forms, and can only maintain the 'simplistic models of gendered language' in English, which fosters what Hiramoto calls a 'black-and-white interpretation of male and female characters' identities' (*ibid.*: 74). An example that seems to contradict his conclusion, however, concerns the characterization of the main 'babe', Faye, whose profoundly feminine use of language in Japanese would appear to clash with her robust personality. In the English dubbed version, this feminine aspect is diluted and her toughness is accentuated through the use of 'unladylike expletives and challenging tag questions' (*ibid.*: 71)—which could arguably cause her to come across as tomboyish. In other words, English viewers' perceptions of this character as asexual or simply rough are predicated on translations that cannot recreate the deeply feminine aspect that the Japanese script assigns to her.

Josephy-Hernández's work (2017), on the other hand, uncovers the unexpected effects of a relatively literal set of US American subtitles of Kon Satoshi's *anime* film *Perfect Blue* (1997), which maintain and even enhance the strong, forceful language used by Mima—a female idol and the film's main character—throughout the film. The literalism of the subtitling underlines her less-than-feminine language, a phenomenon Josephy-Hernández views as a perhaps unwitting emphasis of the film's critique of the female idol in Japanese popular culture. Here, the adoption of a literal rather than an adaptive approach to translation reflects some of the strongly gendered aspects of Japanese in the English version, thereby also serving to reinforce the underlying message.

These three studies raise an interesting issue that engages with the 'advocacy' studies critiqued in the previous section: they undermine claims about English being *the* language of flexible, inventive, adaptable and neologistic gender-bender possibilities. In fact, they show that many other languages are just as innovative in this area of sexual representation, and can prove equally challenging to render in translation. The fact that English does no better as a translating language confirms what researchers working on questions of gender are likely to find in their work: gender is a sensitive, culturally specific topic—in *all* its manifestations. And since AVT never occurs in a gender vacuum, the outcome of the translation process will be affected by (i) the attitudes of the translators working with audiovisual texts in their perceived or assumed roles as moral gate-keepers; (ii) the translators' experiences of and exposure to 'gender' as a discursive socio-cultural element affecting any language; and (iii) the agendas of specific broadcasting networks, involving assumptions about audience expectations—that will determine how much time and money is invested in translations.

The work by Nicole Baumgarten (2005) and Charlotte Bosseaux (2008) points to other gender-aware directions in AVT studies. While Baumgarten's study is perhaps of particular interest to audiovisual translators interested in downplaying or eliminating gratuitous sexist language in audiovisual products, Bosseaux's will resonate with those who are more concerned with the meaningfulness of voice and sound as part of the translation. Her contention that voice is an integral part of characterization, and that voice actors must recreate characters to avoid a disconnect between their visual and aural representations on-screen gels with Silverman's focus on voice, and is a topic that warrants further development in AVT.

Baumgarten (2005) eschews the current academic climate of advocacy in regard to gender representation and describes what seem to have been accidental findings. Having set out to discover how the translation of various types of texts from English to German have affected contemporary German language use, Baumgarten describes turning to an analysis of James Bond movies in order to examine 'linguistic features of "spoken" text production' (2005: 56). She hypothesizes that the affect of personal closeness may make the German language more vulnerable to taking on and exhibiting influences from English (*ibid.*) What she finds is that the German dubbing of *From Russia with Love* (1963) actually *removes* gratuitous sexist/misogynist references in the English script and uses the space that is freed up to reinforce plot development. Her work explores what she cautiously terms 'shifts in communicative preferences' (*ibid.*: 54) as the German dubbing tones down derogatory commentary on women. She proposes several explanations for these shifts in preferences: first, a 'normalizing' tendency that any translation might show to remove items that are 'unwelcome in the target culture'; second, a greater focus in German on the event structure, i.e. the content of a text, rather than on gratuitous asides that express subjective attitudes about women. This study of a dubbing approach that effectively counters the blatant sexism of the source material provides a certain relief from the more predictable work focused on advocacy and brings to mind an earlier text by Antje Ascheid (1997), which also argued that German dubbing shows strong creative tendencies.

Bosseaux's (2008) article centres on voice quality in the dubbing of film songs. She is one of the very few to explore what Pérez-González (2014: 199–200) has termed the 'semiotic potential of the para-verbal', involving the deployment of intonation, accent/phonetics of linguistic variation, voice quality, rhythm, speed and pausing. The 'aural' aspects of dubbing and the meaning conveyed by the sound of a voice could/should be of great interest in regard to the effects of dubbing: how are male/female/other voices made to sound not only in the scripted dialogues of the source cultures, but in the dubbed versions? Does the sound of a voice change across languages? And if so, what does this mean or indicate? For example, how is what Silverman describes as the 'prattle, bitchiness, sweet murmurings, maternal admonitions' ([1984]1990: 309, cited in Chaudhuri 2006) that is typical of the mainstream US female film subjects made to *sound*, first in English, and then in other languages? And to what effect? Bosseaux studies the question in regard to a dubbed song in one episode of *Buffy the Vampire Slayer* (1997–2003), the very successful and much-translated US chick-flick TV series. She compares the nasal, monotonous voice of the English-language protagonist to the French dubbed version, where Buffy has a more 'mature voice, with more depth and variation' (2008: 56). The voice in the source text ostensibly reflects Buffy's condition of boredom and depression at that point while the French voice implies sophistication and a certain ease in life. According to Bosseaux, this difference interferes with and disengages from the character's personality and emotions, causing confusion among viewers. While Bosseaux's analysis is not outright gender-conscious, it points the way toward studies that take into account questions of authority and power. Since voice provides important information about a character's age, social standing, authority, self-awareness, confidence, and sexual orientation, more research on this topic could lead to valuable insights into how gender is represented through sound.

Future areas of development

A substantial amount of research ground remains to be charted at the interface between gender studies and AVT. Descriptive, historical analyses that focus on gender issues are virtually non-existent in this area of scholarly enquiry. How are the divas, heroes or villains (Italian, German, US and others) of the 1930s, 1940s and 1950s presented in translation? And how is that handled in Russian, Chinese, Indian, Middle-Eastern or African cinema? While contemporary work proceeds largely from a position of advocacy in its study of almost exclusively mainstream US films or TV series, more historical research might descriptively trace how earlier work has laid the groundwork for today's practices.

The question of voice—pitch, tone, timbre—is emerging as another potentially fruitful research area. If questions of authority and power are indeed tied to voice, as Bosseaux asserts, then feminist, queer and gender-aware approaches to AVT would do well to explore this.

Similarly, the potential differences that reportedly exist between dubbing for mainstream (and therefore more conservative) audiences versus subtitling for the (educated and liberal) elite could do with further examination in regard to gender questions. After all, the so-called elite of many a society include the business interests that drive film-making, and therefore the representation of gender: they are involved. Does the conventional view of dubbing as a 'dumbing down' of cinema, a way of catering to and manipulating the masses, also pertain in regard to gender awareness? And if so, does this apply beyond the bounds of Hollywood productions?

The media as a force involved in creating and implanting gender-based neologisms (such as gayspeak, or more recently 'trans-language') in a culture would appear to constitute another pertinent research topic. In light of the last 40 years of activism on feminist and other gender fronts, research into the question of gender-related neologism and its translation—which is touched on in some of the studies critiqued earlier in this chapter—could provide strong evidence of media influence as well as media backlash. The treatment of these currents and counter-currents in translation would provide interesting avenues of comparative cultural studies in reception.

Finally, recurring hints about the conservatism of dubbing and also subtitling when compared to indigenous/local productions are intriguing: are local productions, created in the local language with its specific regionalisms, accents and levels of sound and meaning more likely to be gender-aware and innovative than translated materials? Are manifestations of gender representation more extreme or daring when they are local? Is translation of any kind always more likely to be proper and conservative—in other words 'orthonymic'—and to clean up a foreign work for local audiences?

The different approaches to gender awareness in the industrial and commercial aspects of dubbing, subtitling and broadcasting of translated audiovisual products also deserve more attention: How far are distributors, networks and other business interests involved in recognizing or even caring about questions of gender in translation? Clues (in Chiaro 2007) that Italian broadcasters can be more liberal in their translations if they broadcast at night, and references to blacklisted terms would seem to raise interesting questions for research in this regard. Do these restrictions apply elsewhere (other languages, cultures and/or sociopolitical moments)? And finally, what is the 'gender awareness' quality and effect of the many forms of fansubbing and fandubbing that circulate on the Internet? Here, translation beyond institutional control could provide a foil for the more official versions of gender in AVT. Since fansubbing is not constrained by the rules and regulations of the industry, is there such a thing, or should there be something like 'feminist' or 'queer' fansubbing?

Finally, to date, little or no work seems to be available on gender issues in localization of any sort. This is a promising area for future development, as the globalization of audiovisual products expands worldwide, often accompanied by marketing materials that tend to mobilize strongly gendered content. One translation example in this field comes from the videogame *Fire Emblem*, where the Japanese-to-English translation of specific types of warriors has elided the binary gender. Instead of having a class of 'swordsmen' or 'swordswomen', both obviously gendered terms, for the Japanese 剣士 (*Bureido*, 'blade'), the translation creatively uses the term 'myrmidon', borrowed from Greek mythology, for both male and female sword users. Questions one might ask here include whether this English translation 'queers' the text by avoiding the categorization by binary biological sex, or whether it neutralizes it, or whether it simply saves space. There is such a dearth of work on gender and language in videogame localization that such questions and many others remain purely speculative.

Conclusion

Scholarly work on gender issues in AVT dates back only to the early years of the twenty-first century. Yet the underlying questions around the use of language in audiovisual products for the purposes of gender stereotyping, and collaterally, as a sales technique have been present for decades—first and foremost through feminist critiques of media that date from the 1970s. The application and expansion of feminist ideas into the study of audiovisual products with a focus on gender awareness in the *language* of the translations has taken some time to develop, perhaps due to the power and distractive qualities of the images in audiovisual content. In any case, the most productive work in the field is currently being done in regard to Romance languages where scholars study how these products largely fail to take on the Anglo-American genderlects, which are constructed for, produced, and disseminated through film and television. This approach criticizes the refusal or inability of French, Spanish or Italian dubbing industries to match the neologisms and the blatantly queer references of the source materials, and advocates for attitudes and work methods that are gender-aware.

A less developed, but still promising, research strand addresses the English translations of audiovisual products from Greece and Japan, and shows how English translations also struggle and fail to render genderlects and neologisms from these languages. They thereby undermine the implied view that English is more liberal, or open-minded as far as gender terminology is concerned.

In fact, what we see over and over again is that the language for sexual difference and derivative gendered behaviours is always sensitive and often political, in every culture and at every social level. As this chapter has shown, in AVT this is borne out in each of the analyzed texts.

Further reading

Anderson, H. and M. Daniels (2016) 'Film Dialogue from 2000 Screenplays, Broken Down by Gender and Age'. Available online: https://pudding.cool/2017/03/film-dialogue/index.html [last access 20 December 2017].
Balirano, G. and D. Chiaro (2016) 'Queering Laughter? It was just a joke!', *Degenere* 2: 1–9.
Callahan, V. (ed.) (2010) *Reclaiming the Archive: Feminism and Film History*, Detroit: Wayne State University Press.
Corrius, M., M. de Marco and E. Espasa (2016a) 'Situated Learning and Situated Knowledge: Gender, Translating Audiovisual Adverts and Professional Responsibility', *The Interpreter and Translator Trainer* 10 (1): 59–75.
Corrius, M., M. de Marco and E. Espasa (2016b) 'Gender and the Translation of Audiovisual Non-profit Advertising', *Revista de Lenguas para Fines Específicos* 22(2): 31–61.
De Marco, M. (2016) 'The 'Engendering' Approach in Audiovisual Translation', *Target* 28(6): 314–325.

Related topics

3 Subtitling on the cusp of its futures
4 Investigating dubbing: learning from the past, looking to the future
10 Game localization: a critical overview and implications for audiovisual translation
23 Audiovisual translation and audience reception
24 Ethnography in audiovisual translation studies
27 Audiovisual translation and fandom

References

Anderson, H. and M. Daniels (2016) 'Film Dialogue from 2000 Screenplays, Broken Down by Gender and Age'. Available online: https://pudding.cool/2017/03/film-dialogue/index.html [last access 20 December 2017].
Ascheid, A. (1997) 'Speaking Tongues: Voice Dubbing in the Cinema as Cultural Ventriloquism', *Velvet Light Trap* 40: 32–41.

Asimakoulas, D. (2012) 'Dude (Looks Like a Lady): Hijacking Transsexual Identity in the Subtitled Version of "Strella" by Panos Koutras', *The Translator* 18(1): 42–75.

Balirano, G. and D. Chiaro (2016) 'Queering Laughter? It was just a joke!', *Degenere* 2: 1–9.

Baumgarten, N. (2005) 'On the Women's Service? Gender-Conscious Language in Dubbed James Bond Movies', in J. Santaemilia (ed.) *Gender, Sex and Translation. The Manipulation of Identities*, Manchester: St. Jerome Publishing, 53–70.

Bechdel Test Movie List (n.d.) Available online: http://bechdeltest.com/ [last access 20 December 2017].

Bianchi, D. (2008) 'Taming Teen-language. The Adaptation of *Buffyspeak* into Italian', in D. Chiaro, C. Heiss and C. Bucaria (eds) *Between Text and Image. Updating Research in Screen Translation*, Amsterdam & Philadelphia: John Benjamins, 181–193.

Bosseaux, C. (2008) 'Buffy the Vampire Slayer: Characterization in the Musical Episode of the TV Series', *The Translator* 14(2): 343–372.

Butler, J. (1990) *Gender Trouble*, London & New York: Routledge.

Callahan, V. (ed.) (2010) *Reclaiming the Archive: Feminism and Film History*, Detroit: Wayne State University Press.

Carter, C. (2012) 'Sex/Gender and the Media. From Sex Roles to Social Construction and Beyond', in K. Ross (ed.) *The Handbook of Gender, Sex and Media*, Chichester: Wiley-Blackwell Publishers, 365–382.

Chagnon, K. (2016) 'Télé, traduction, censure et manipulation: Les enjeux politiques de la réception du discours queer', Presentation at *15ᵉ édition de l'Odyssée de la traductologie*, Concordia University, Montréal.

Chaudhuri, S. (2006) *Feminist Film Theorists. Laura Mulvey, Kaja Silverman, Teresa de Lauretis, Barbara Creed*, London & New York: Routledge.

Chiaro, D. (2007) 'Not in front of the Children? An Analysis of Sex on Screen in Italy', *Linguistica Antverpiensa* 6, Available online: https://lans.ua.ac.be/index.php/LANS-TTS/issue/view/10 [last access 20 December 2017].

Corrius, M., M. de Marco and E. Espasa (2016a) 'Situated Learning and Situated Knowledge: Gender, Translating Audiovisual Adverts and Professional Responsibility', *The Interpreter and Translator Trainer* 10 (1): 59–75.

Corrius, M., M. de Marco and E. Espasa (2016b) 'Gender and the Translation of Audiovisual Non-profit Advertising', *Revista de Lenguas para Fines Específicos* 22 (2): 31–61.

De Lauretis, T. (1987) *Technologies of Gender: Essays on Theory, Film, Fiction*, Bloomington: University of Indiana Press.

De Marco, A. (2013) 'Translating Gender on Screen across Languages: The Case of *Transamerica*', in E. Federici and V. Leonardi (eds) *Bridging the Gap between Theory and Practice in Translation and Gender Studies*, Newcastle-upon-Tyne: Cambridge Scholars Publishing, 122–132.

De Marco, M. (2006) 'Audiovisual Translation from a Gender Perspective', *JoSTrans: The Journal of Specialised Translation* 6, 167–184. Available online: http://www.jostrans.org/issue06/art_demarco.php [last access 20 December 2017].

De Marco, M. (2012) *Audiovisual Translation through a Gender Lens*, New York: Rodopi.

De Marco, M. (2016) 'The "Engendering" Approach in Audiovisual Translation', *Target* 28(6): 314–325.

EWA Network (n.d.) (European Women's Audiovisual Network 2015) 'Gender Equality within Eurimages: Current Situation and Scope for Evolution'. Available online: http://www.ewawomen.com/en/eurimages-news.html [last access 20 December 2017].

Feral, A.-L. (2011a) 'Sexuality and Femininity in Translated Chick Texts', in L. von Flotow (ed.) *Translating Women*, Ottawa: University of Ottawa Press, 183–201.

Feral, A.-L. (2011b) 'Gender in Audiovisual Translation: Naturalizing Feminine Voices in the French *Sex and the City*', in *European Journal of Women's Studies* 18(4): 391–407.

Furukawa, H. (2017) 'De-Feminizing Translation: To Make Women Visible in Japanese Translation', in L. von Flotow and F. Farahzad (eds) *Translating Women. Different Voices and New Horizons*, London & New York: Routledge, 76–89.

Gaines, J. (1997) *'Deviant Eyes, Deviant Bodies*. Queering Feminist Film Theory'. Available online: http://www.ejumpcut.org/archive/onlinessays/JC41folder/DeviantEyesBodiesRev.html [last access 20 December 2017].

Gallagher, M. (2003) 'Feminist Media Perspectives', in A. Valdivia (ed.) *A Companion to Media Studies*, Malden USA: Blackwell, 19–39.

Gallagher, M. (2013) 'Media and the Representation of Gender', in C. Carter, L. Steiner and L. McLaughlin (eds) *The Routledge Companion to Media and Gender*, Florence US: Routledge, 23–35.

Gerbner, G. (1978) 'The Dynamics of Cultural Resistance', in G. Tuchman, A. K. Daniels, and J. Benet (eds) *Hearth and Home: Images of Women in the Mass Media*, New York: Oxford University Press, 40–46.

Hanson, E. (ed.) (1999) *Out Takes. Essays on Queer Theory and Film*, Durham & London: Duke University Press.

Harvey, K. (2000) 'Gay Community, Gay Identity, and the Translated Text', *TTR. Traduction, Terminologie, Rédaction* 13(1): 137–165.

Hiramoto, M. (2013) 'Hey, You're a Girl?: Gendered Expressions in the Popular Anime, *Cowboy Bebop*', *Multilingua* 32(1): 51–78.

Inoue, M. (2003) 'Speech without a Speaking Body: 'Japanese Women's Language' in Translation', *Language & Communication* 23: 315–330.

Josephy-Hernández, D. E. (2017) *Reflections on the Subtitling and Dubbing of Anime: The Translation of Gender in* Perfect Blue, *a Film by Kon Satoshi*, Published Doctoral Thesis, University of Ottawa. Available online: https://ruor.uottawa.ca/handle/10393/36596 [last access 20 December 2017].

Lewis, E. S. (2010) '"This is my Girlfriend, Linda". Translating Queer Relationships in Film: A Case Study of the Subtitles for *Gia* and a Proposal for Developing the Field of Queer Translation Studies', *In Other Words*, British Centre for Literary Translation 36: 3–22.

MacDonald, M. (2006) 'Muslim Women and the Veil. Problems of Image and Voice in Media Representations', *Feminist Media Studies* 6(1): 7–23.

Mulvey, L. ([1975] 1999) 'Visual Pleasure and Narrative Cinema', *Screen* 16(3): 6–18. Reprinted as 'Visual Pleasure and Narrative Cinema', in L. Braudy and M. Cohen (eds) *Film Theory and Criticism: Introductory Readings*, New York: Oxford University Press, 833–844.

Ranzato, I. (2012) 'Gayspeak and Gay Subjects in AVT', *Meta* 57(2): 369–384.

Schwartz, A. (2017) 'Yes, The Handmaid's Tale is Feminist', *The New Yorker*, 27 April. Available online: http://www.newyorker.com/culture/cultural-comment/yes-the-handmaids-tale-is-feminist?mbid=nl_TNY%20Template%20-%20With%20Photo%20(161)&CNDID=49743945&spMailingID=10906714&spUserID=MTk0MTgwNzEzMzUzS0&spJobID=1142191530&spReportId=MTE0MjE5MTUzMAS2 [last access 20 December 2017].

Scott, J. W. (1999) 'Some Reflections on Gender and Politics', in M. Ferree, J. Lorber and B. B. Hess (eds) *Revisioning Gender*, Thousand Oaks, London, New Delhi: Sage Publications, 70–98.

Silverman, K. (1988) *The Acoustic Mirror: The Female Voice in Psychoanalysis and Cinema*, Bloomington: Indiana University Press.

Silverman, K. ([1984]1990) 'Dis-embodying the Female Voice', in P. Erens (ed.) *Issues in Feminist Film Criticism*, Bloomington: Indiana University Press, 309–329.

Spade, D. and C. Willse (2016) 'Norms and Normalization', in L. Disch and M. Hawkesworth (eds) *The Oxford Handbook of Feminist Theory*, Oxford: Oxford University Press: 551–572.

Staayer, C. (1996) *Deviant Eyes, Deviant Bodies*, New York: Columbia University Press.

Stabile, C. A. and D. Kumar (2005) 'Unveiling Imperialism: Media, Gender and the War on Afghanistan', in *Media, Culture and Society* 27(5): 765–82.

Tuchman, G. (1978) 'The Symbolic Annihilation of Women in the Mass Media', in G. Tuchman, A. K. Daniels and J. Benet (eds) *Hearth and Home: Images of Women in the Mass Media*, New York: Oxford University Press, 3–38.

von Flotow, L. and J. W. Scott (2016) 'Gender Studies and Translation Studies. Entre Braguette: Connecting the Transdisciplines', in L. van Doorslaer and Y. Gambier (eds) *Border Crossings: Translation Studies and Other Disciplines*, Amsterdam & Philadelphia: John Benjamins, 349–374.

Filmography

Ally McBeal (1997–2002) David E. Kelley. IMDb entry: http://www.imdb.com/title/tt0118254/?ref_=fn_al_tt_1

Bridget Jones's Diary (2001) Sharon Maguire. IMDb entry: http://www.imdb.com/title/tt0243155/?ref_=nv_sr_1

Bringing Up Baby (1938) Howard Hawks. IMDb entry: http://www.imdb.com/title/tt0029947/?ref_=nv_sr_1

Buffy the Vampire Slayer (1997–2003) Joss Whedon. IMDb entry: http://www.imdb.com/title/tt0118276/?ref_=nv_sr_1

Cowboy Bebop (1998–2003) Shinichirō Watanabe. IMDb entry: http://www.imdb.com/title/tt1332125/?ref_=fn_al_tt_1

From Russia with Love (1963) Terence Young. IMDb entry: http://www.imdb.com/title/tt0057076/?ref_=nv_sr_1

Gia (1998) Michael Cristofer. IMDb entry: http://www.imdb.com/title/tt0123865/?ref_=fn_al_tt_1

Perfect Blue (1997) Kon Satoshi. IMDb entry: http://www.imdb.com/title/tt0156887/?ref_=fn_al_tt_1

Queer as Folk (2000–2005) Ron Cowen and Robert Lipman. IMDb entry: http://www.imdb.com/title/tt0262985/?ref_=nv_sr_1

Sex and the City (1998–2004) Darren Star. IMDb entry: http://www.imdb.com/title/tt0159206/?ref_=nv_sr_1

Strella (2009) Panos Koutras. IMDb entry: http://www.imdb.com/title/tt1332125/?ref_=fn_al_tt_1

The L Word (2004–2009) Various creators. IMDb entry: http://www.imdb.com/title/tt0330251/?ref_=nv_sr_1

Part III
Research methods in audiovisual translation studies

20
Corpus-based audiovisual translation studies
Ample room for development

Maria Pavesi

A history of the area

This chapter describes the development and use of corpora within audiovisual translation (AVT), exploring the methodological, theoretical and descriptive insights that corpora have originated in the field. In recent years researchers have become increasingly aware that large and principled electronic collections of audiovisual dialogue and computer-assisted methods of analysis are needed to carry out empirically validated investigations of AVT (e.g. Heiss and Soffritti 2008, Freddi and Pavesi 2009a, Baños *et al.* 2013, Pavesi *et al.* 2014). Corpus-based articles, monographs and doctoral theses have proliferated, drawing on both lower-scope data collections and larger databases that bring corpus-based research on AVT into line with other areas of Corpus-based Translation Studies (CBTS). This general approach to research on translation can be placed at the intersection between the theoretical and methodological frameworks of Descriptive Translation Studies and Corpus Linguistics since it responds to the call to look for distinctive features, patterns, norms and universals in translated texts by relying on extensive authentic data. Launched at the beginning of the 1990s by Baker's seminal work (Baker 1993, 1996), CBTS embody an empirical, intersubjective as well as descriptive, rather than prescriptive, viewpoint on translation as developed in Toury's (1995/2012) target-oriented polysystemic theory (Laviosa 2011).

There are sound methodological, theoretical and applied reasons to create and exploit corpora of AVT. The first one derives from the need to provide reliable generalizations and achieve descriptive adequacy by moving beyond the limited scope of single case studies, while overcoming the failures and inconsistencies of introspection and intuition. Corpora therefore allow the researcher to reveal cumulative effects that would not emerge through the examination of individual translations. These incremental effects, arising from the repetition of the same patterns across texts, account for the uniqueness of AVT registers by pinpointing their typicalities. They can also unveil evaluative and ideological meanings that prevail in different cultures and in different translation types (*cf.* Baker 2006: 13). In addition, corpus analysis can highlight areas that are recurrently problematic while developing translators' awareness about 'hidden' linguistic and stylistic regularities in translated and domestic screen dialogue. In this way, corpus analysis can ultimately be exploited to improve the translation quality of audiovisual products (see Freddi 2012: 382).

Two main foci of attention have been observed in corpus-based audiovisual translation studies (CBAVTS) since the beginning: (i) the description and explanation of the relationships between translated texts and original/non-translated texts and (ii) the description and explanation of the relationships between source texts and target texts. CBAVTS thus adopt both a target-oriented and source-oriented comparative approach, with investigations typically looking for similarities and contrasts within and between corpora and sub-corpora. Different emphases, however, have characterized research on the different modalities of dubbing, subtitling and audio description (AD), as will be shown in the remainder of this chapter.

Analysts in the field often work with translation-driven corpora compiled or assembled for a specific purpose or to investigate a specific class of phenomena, such as discourse markers, cultural references and pragmatic routines. More rarely, AVT corpora are multi-purposed, self-standing, flexible resources suitable to address a wide range of research questions. In most cases, these databases are monomodal written or spoken corpora, the latter comprising transcriptions of spoken dialogues at different levels of granularity and detail that can be further enriched with linguistically encoded paralinguistic and nonverbal information. As a result, spoken corpora crucially differ from speech corpora or multimodal corpora, in which the audio alone or in combination with the visual is also available (Adolphs and Carter 2013). In terms of division of labour, whereas spoken corpora inevitably present a partial picture of the dialogic exchange, they provide a good basis for large-scale investigations leading up to quantitative generalizations about the linguistic configuration of audiovisual dialogues. By contrast, speech and multimodal corpora are most appropriate for in-depth qualitative analyses centring on the interactions between the various signifying codes co-deployed on screen (Heiss and Soffritti 2008, Valentini 2008, Soffritti this volume).

Main issues in corpus-based audiovisual translation studies

Corpus compilation: types of corpora and construction criteria

Corpora come in different sizes but in AVT, due to the difficulties and economic costs of creating spoken corpora, they tend to be small do-it-yourself collections. Following Zanettin (2012), we can distinguish three main types of translation-driven corpora: monolingual comparable corpora, bilingual comparable corpora and parallel corpora. Monolingual comparable corpora are made up of two sets of texts in the same language, chosen using similar design criteria. Whereas the first set contains translations into a target language, and for this reason is also called translational corpus, the second set contains comparable domestic texts. By contrast, bilingual comparable corpora bring together non-translated texts belonging to different languages but sharing similar conceptual domains as well as discoursal and pragmatic functions. Lastly, parallel corpora include a principled set of source language texts together with their translations into a given target language. Monolingual comparable corpora are suitable to study the unique features of translated vis-à-vis non-translated varieties of the same language, while with parallel corpora researchers can address issues such as functional equivalence, translation shifts and translation strategies. Bilingual comparable corpora, in turn, allow the researcher to carry out preliminary contrastive analyses (Toury 1995/2012). At best, corpus-based research draws on a combination of corpus resources and uses both comparable and parallel components to formulate more accurate and reliable hypotheses about translated language (Saldanha and O'Brien 2013: 69). In CBAVT, researchers also resort to reference corpora, i.e. representative corpora of the source, target or translated language, functioning as baselines for comparison.

CBTS have identified various methodological issues in corpus building whose relevance extends to corpora of AVT. Such issues include representativeness, size, comparability, transcription conventions, annotation and corpus alignment. When constructing a corpus, audiovisual products should be chosen to be as representative as possible of the population at large or of specific genres or product types (e.g. audio described films, subtitled documentaries, TV series for adolescents). Related to representativeness are the issues of size, selection criteria and sampling, balance and homogeneity. In general, larger corpora have a better chance of being representative of the target population, although this advantage tends to tail off when the corpus exceeds a certain size. Moreover, whereas big corpora enable the scrutiny of a wide range of phenomena, including infrequent vocabulary items and spoken pragmatic features, they may generate unmanageable amounts of data that call for laborious sorting and further sampling. A smaller, specialized corpus may hence be preferred if we move from restricted and well-formulated hypotheses. It should be finally pointed out that corpora compiled to be general corpora need to be much larger and entail more careful design criteria than specialized corpora (Zanettin 2012: 41), as most of those used in AVT research.

Regardless of size, clear selection and sampling criteria are required to make sure that the corpus is representative and balanced. This means that it should contain an adequate coverage of the products under investigation without being skewed in favour of any specific generic or textual category. Uniformity is also required and items should be included that belong to the same category that researchers aim to investigate.

In CBAVT research, another important criterion is given by comparability between the different components of the corpus or, to a different extent, between the corpus and the reference corpora used. Comparability should be weighed up vis-à-vis factors including completeness of the audiovisual texts and date of release, but also composition and genre, so as to obtain corpus components that are modelled one over the other (Olohan 2004: 42, Zanettin 2012: 48). But there is also a trade-off between comparability and representativeness as different countries privilege different audiovisual genres in both films and TV series, often varying in terms of type and amount of audiovisual productions.

Specific to spoken corpora, and hence to many AVT corpora, is the issue of transcription. As a graphic representation of talk, transcription first requires the researcher to interpret data by considering the prosodic, gestural, textual, and environmental elements that interact with speech and constitute communicative exchanges in a multimodal context. The process, however, forcibly entails a selection and a reduction of the data that will be visualized graphically in the transcript (Adolphs and Carter 2013). Based on the aims of the project, decisions thus have to be made on how detailed the transcript can or has to be (Bonsignori 2009), although to allow the smooth electronic processing of the data, spoken corpora in AVT typically use some form of standardized orthographic transcription. For this reason, most sociolinguistic variation is necessarily levelled out, and can only be re-introduced through some form of annotation. Despite the centrality of transcription in spoken corpora, few published AVT studies explicitly state the rules and the procedures followed in managing spoken data.

Finally, as copyright clearance must be required for both original and translated audiovisual products, copyright issues are a major stumbling block in corpus building, slowing down the process or even halting it, and seriously limiting accessibility. In addition, these issues can easily hamper the representativeness of the corpus if the final compilation of audiovisual products relies on the clearances obtained.

Maria Pavesi

Three corpora of audiovisual translation

Not many AVT publications offer a fully fledged description of how the corpora used for analysis were built and even fewer, if any, make it explicit whether clearances from copyright holders were received. However, a few corpora are available or are being created that can exemplify the methodological choices carried out before and during corpus compilation. The TIWO (Television in Words) Audio Description Corpus (Salway 2007) was built to investigate the language of AD, starting from the hypothesis that this special language is characterized by the prevalence of features directly related to its communicative functions. More precisely, the analysis to be carried out through a corpus-based methodology was intended to 'identify and describe a special language in terms of statistically significant differences between linguistic features in a corpus of [audio description] scripts and a general language sample' (Salway 2007: 154). The TIWO is thus implicitly a monolingual comparable corpus, whose internal component is made up of 91 British English AD film scripts, totalling 618,859 words. To obtain a corpus representative of the translation modality, scripts were included that covered different ways of carrying out AD in Britain: action, children's animation, children's live action, comedy, dark, period drama, romantic, thriller and miscellaneous. The TIWO Audio Description Corpus includes complete scripts directly obtained from three major producers of AD, a fact that pre-empts copyright issues.

The Pavia Corpus of Film Dialogue (PCFD) is a parallel and comparable spoken corpus built to investigate original audiovisual dialogue and its dubbing translation (Pavesi 2014; PCFD, n.d.). The parallel component is made up of 24 orthographically transcribed American and British film dialogues and their dubbed Italian translations (about 500,000 word tokens). This component is unavoidably unidirectional owing to the translation policies pursued in Anglophone countries (which subtitle rather than dub foreign audiovisual products). The corpus also currently contains a comparable component of 24 Italian original films (about 220,000 word tokens). Constructed to research the representation of spokenness in film language and AVT, the PCFD alone and in combination with reference corpora of English and Italian can be used to address a wide array of sociolinguistic and pragmatic issues so as to eventually delineate a profile of contemporary dubbed Italian. The films to be included in the corpus were therefore chosen to be representative of mimetic audiovisual products, that is products that portray naturalistic language use, in compliance with a series of sampling criteria (Pavesi 2014: 37). Films had to:

(i) be set in contemporary times, representing contemporary dialogue;
(ii) present a prevalence of situations that in real life elicit free and bidirectional spontaneous spoken language;
(iii) have been released at regular intervals within a fixed time span (from 1996 to 2009);
(iv) have been successful, both with the critics and the general public.

The broad selection of films enhanced the representativeness of the corpus with the aim of offering a wide range of represented settings, situations, topics and characters, and generating variation along the portrayed sociolinguistic parameters. However, due to copyright issues, a compromise had to be reached between representativeness and availability, which meant that a few previously selected films had to be excluded from the final sample (Pavesi 2014).

As for alignment and systematic interrogation, the PCFD was converted into a relational database (Freddi and Pavesi 2009b, Freddi 2013), which permits users to carry out queries beginning from either the original or the translated components. Several parameters were added to the database: textual and contextual variables, i.e. character speaking, scene type and linguistic event (e.g. on the phone, on television), together with individual variables including accents (e.g. French accent, Spanish accent), accompanying paralinguistic behaviour (e.g. whispering, shouting, giggling), and salient non-linguistic behaviour (e.g. waving, kissing). Table 20.1 shows some of the parameters instantiated during the search of 'you know?' in the database.

The biggest monomodal corpus envisaged so far within a corpus-based approach to AVT is CORSUBIL (Corpus de Subtítulos Bilingües Inglés-Español): a bilingual corpus made up of English and Spanish subtitles, both meant for mainstream viewers, extracted from significant American movies, aiming at 18 million words, 9 million for each sub-corpus (Rica Peromingo 2014, Rica Peromingo *et al.* 2014). The considerable dimensions of the corpus are needed to address the wide goals of the project, both descriptive and applied, as the corpus is intended to provide data relevant for bilingual lexicology and lexicography, language teaching and language learning. Since among the functions of film dialogues we find the simulation of orality, one specific aim of research on CORSUBIL is the creation of bilingual lists of conversational routines in English and Spanish, allowing the analysis, for example, of polite speech-act formulas and discourse markers in translation and cross-linguistically. Differently from smaller corpora, the representativeness of the corpus is warranted by the very broad and principled selection of the most important movies in American film history, from the beginning of the talking movies onwards up to the twenty-first century. The equal division into five periods will permit researchers to have a general overview of the language of American film subtitles and the corresponding Spanish translations together with a diachronic and more time-specific perspective on audiovisual dialogue.

Tools for corpus analysis

The most common tools for corpus analysis in AVT research are frequency counts, monolingual concordances and bilingual or aligned concordances. Both individual words and clusters of words can be searched and frequency counts may be compared across corpora or sub-corpora to examine the differences between the source and the target texts or between the translated texts and comparable texts in the same target language (Freddi 2009, 2012; Romero-Fresco 2009, 2012). To test the hypothesis about the specificity of the language of AD, Salway (2007: 158–159), for instance, calculated the ratio between the relative frequency of words in the TIWO corpus and the relative frequency of the same words in a sample of the British National Corpus, thus obtaining a list of items that typify AD. In turn, Bonsignori *et al.* (2012) compiled frequency lists of greeting and leave-taking formulas in a DIY corpus of Anglophone films and their Italian dubbing translations both to compare the levels of formality and naturalness in source and target texts and infer the motivations that underlie recurrent translation choices. In both studies, frequencies pertained to the words contained in raw (un-annotated) corpora. Like other corpora, however, AVT databases can also be enriched with tags that allow the computing of specific phenomena. In Pavesi's (2013) investigation of demonstratives in the PCFD, all 1,678 English pronouns were manually annotated for syntactic role, pragmatic function and translation strategy into Italian. The annotated texts were then searched with the program AntConc 3.2.1w to gather information on the frequency of the various translation strategies, which was found to depend on the subject or object function of the demonstrative

Table 20.1 Extract from the Pavia Corpus of Film Dialogue displaying various types of data.

Title	Cue	Character	Scene	Attitude	Text	Translations
Lost in Translation	406	JOHN		kisses	Yeah, call those guys, you know and I-I- I'm gonna be back on Sunday and I-I love you, **you know?** Okay?	Sì, chiamali, è una buona idea! E poi, io, io, io torno domenica e- e- e . . . ti amo, lo sai. Okay.
Match Point	407	NOLA		clears throat	Erm . . . I thought he was very handsome. **You know?** And I told you I was just . . . I was overwhelmed with attention. So what about you and Chloe?	Em . . . bè, lo trovavo molto attraente. Inoltre, te l'ho detto, sono stata . . . sopraffatta dalle sue attenzioni. E la cosa fra te e Chloe?
The Holiday	18	IRIS		sighs	I was head over heels, **you know?** Everyone knew.	Ero innamorata cotta, lo sai? Lo sapevano tutti.
Two Lovers	1061	MICHELLE	Michelle's window	on the phone	I never saw you either. I could feel you, **you know?** I could really feel you.	Neanch'io ti ho mai visto. Ma ti ho sentito, credimi, ti ho sentito tantissimo.
Two Lovers	1166	REUBEN (VOICE)	pouring some wine	Hebrew accent	You know, we celebrate . . . we celebrate the New Year twice a year, **you know?** Because at Rosh Hashanah and . . . All right	Sì, noi festeggiamo . . . noi festeggiamo il nuovo anno due volte l'anno. La prima è Rosh Hashanah . . . e adesso. Ecco.

Table 20.2 Concordances of *amico* in the translational component of the Pavia Corpus of Film Dialogue.

---

sono rotto le palle! Ma che cazzo fai? Quello è **amico** mio. Ma perché non te ne vai?
egne saltate per settimane. Che significa, Eric? **Amico** mio, che ti succede? Oh, non è.
Un misero cazzone pelle e ossa. Tu hai tutto, **amico** mio, hai tutto. Tu pensi che i
cordarsene. Che cosa voleva da te? Chi? Quel tuo **amico** in macchina. Niente. È bravo. È
inciare con le conclusioni assurde. Dacci dentro, **amico** mio. Eric vede Lily . . . oh! Falla
ccio la donna. Dai. Tu fai la donna? Uo, aspetta, **amico**, mi sa che la cosa qui sta
donna matura con le mani di fata. Porca troia, **amico**. Io pensavo qualche basso,
io soprannome? No. Il Profeta. Io vedo il futuro, **amico**. E ora vedo che te ne tornerai
olo film che hai interpretato oggi insieme al tuo **amico**. . . Eh? Una parola a Ryan . . . e
to lì. Con il tuo pacchettino da frocetto, il tuo **amico** coglione e tutti che ridono del

---

and its deictic role in the dialogue. More recently, other frequency measurements have been used to investigate corpora of AVT, such as type/token ratios and lexical density (Formentelli 2014, see below).

Whereas frequency lists unveil overall patterns in audiovisual texts, monolingual concordances are suitable for in-depth analyses of word patterning. When extracting concordances in a corpus, all the lines containing the searched word, or node, are displayed together in a vertical list, hence providing in one go access to the various contexts in which lexical units and clusters occur. Table 20.2 displays the KWIC (Key Word In Context) concordances for *amico* 'friend', a recurrent lexical item in Italian dubbese where it often functions as a sociolinguistically marked vocative (Pavesi 2005: 50). The concordance lines are extracted from the PCFD.

The research potentials of concordancing are many. With a view to uncovering how much information AD conveys about characters' thoughts as opposed to actions, Palmer and Salway (2015) inspected the concordances of individual items that had turned out to be very frequent in the specific discourse. Starting from *–ly* adverbs and their combinations with the forms 'looks' and 'walks' in the TIWO corpus, the analysts discovered that, although each action verb has a different set of preferred adverb collocates, most of these add information about mental states (Palmer and Salway 2015: 142–143). *Looks*, for instance, is shown to be followed by 'directly' ($f = 9$), 'anxiously' ($f = 8$), 'sadly', 'steadily', 'thoughtfully' ($f = 7$), 'nervously' ($f = 6$), 'fearfully', 'grimly', 'longingly', 'quizzically' ($f = 4$). By carrying out a closer analysis of the concordances of the high-frequency verb form 'smiles' (see Table 20.3), it became clear that several recurrent word combinations give insight into characters' thoughts (Palmer and Salway 2015: 139).

Table 20.3 Concordances of 'smiles' plus adverbs in *–ly* from the audio description of *The English Patient* (Palmer and Salway 2015: 137).

Katherine **smiles** awkwardly.
She **smiles** benignly.
Lady Hammond **smiles** delightedly as Katherine crossed the courtyard.
Almasy **smiles** faintly.
She **smiles** fondly at the man with the melted face.
He **smiles** ruefully and lowers his head, looking pensive.

With bilingual concordances the researcher can explore the correspondences for given expressions starting from either the source or the target texts in parallel corpora, in this way examining cross-linguistic correspondences and checking whether given translation shifts are systematic. Rica Peromingo (2014) compared phraseological units in source and target texts by examining the bilingual concordances in a small sample of CORSUBIL. These show that as a rule there are no direct or one-to-one translations for the English discourse markers transferred into Spanish. Rather, one-to-many correspondences obtain in both directions: the same English expression has various renderings in Spanish, whereas the same Spanish phraseological unit translates different English formulas, as illustrated in the bilingual, aligned concordances for 'sorry' and *¿Qué pasa?* in Table 20.4.

Bilingual and monolingual concordances can in fact be combined when researchers draw on parallel and reference corpora simultaneously. In a study aimed to map out register shifts in racist discourse, at the outset Mouka *et al.* (2015) annotated for categories of appraisal a small corpus of Anglophone films subtitled into Greek and Spanish. The intensifying or neutralizing effect of translation choices was then assessed by inspecting the bilingual context of the negative expression. Such contextual interpretation was later checked against monolingual concordance lines and collocates for the same expression in reference corpora. In Example 1 below, the weakening of the negative evaluation implicit in 'border jumpers' is first indexed by the omission of the vulgar adjective in the Greek translation.

Table 20.4 Bilingual concordances for 'sorry' and *¿Qué pasa?* from the CORSUBIL corpus (Rica Peromingo 2014: Tables 1 and 2).

English subtitles	Spanish subtitles
21 00:02:42,640→00:43, 960 **Sorry.**	21 00:02:42,640→00:02:43,960 Perdón.
601 01:01:38,800→01:01:41,520 **Sorry**, but you will have to leave.	563 01:01:38,800→01:01:41,520 Lo siento. Tiene que irse.
948 01:49:09,600→01:49:11,360 Come on. **Sorry.**	848 01:49:09,600→01:49:11,360 Desde luego, perdona.
33 00:06:52,454→00:06:54,331 I'm **sorry**. I'm **sorry**, sir.	31 00:06:52,454→00:06:54,331 Perdóneme, señor, perdóneme.

77
00.07:48,880→00:07:51,280
  – What's the matter?
  – it's Michael
	72
	00:07:40,413→00:07:43,211
	  – *¿Qué pasa?*
	  – Michael no está.

513 00:52:34,200→00:52:25,680 What is it?	459 00:52:24,200→00:52:25,680 *¿Qué pasa?*
886 01:37:45,280→01:37.46,280 What's wrong?	806 01:41:27,568→01:41:29,661 *¿Qué pasa?*

Example 1

[en] And now some fucking Korean owns it who fired these guys and is making a killing because he hired 40 fucking **border jumpers**.

[el] Τώρα το 'χει ένας Κορεάτης, που απέλυσε τους δικούς μας και θησαυρίζει επειδή προσέλαβε **λαθρομετανάστες**.

[Back translation] Now a Korean owns it who fired our guys and is making a killing because he hired **illegal immigrants**.

The analysis of the concordance lines for 'border jumper' in the English reference corpus enTenTen12 further unveiled that the expression in the source linguaculture is 'used almost exclusively in a negative and highly disparaging sense (*border jumpers want our wealth; drug smugglers, human traffickers, border jumpers and other assorted criminals; border jumpers are slapping those legal criminals*)' (Mouka *et al.* 2015: 58). This highly negative colouring is not shared by its subtitled translation *λαθρομετανάστες* 'illegal immigrants', a more neutral expression belonging to standard and authoritative Greek.

The patterns emerging from these research analyses are all relevant to the identification of systematic linguistic and translational behaviour in source, target and reference texts as will be illustrated in the following sections.

Approaches to corpus analysis

Quantitative and qualitative corpus analyses in AVT research can be carried out following both a semasiological (form-to-function) and an onomasiological (function-to-form) approach. By pursuing a semasiological approach, researchers start from individual words or sequences of words to uncover underlying patterns of meaning and regularities. By contrast, with an onomasiological approach, the analyst starts from a given meaning and looks for features, constructions and patterns that express that meaning. In her study of compliments in dubbed dialogues, Bruti (2009), for instance, has argued for a procedure that integrates the retrieval of pragmatically loaded words such as 'nice' with the onomasiological analysis of the speech acts identified by scanning the corpus manually. In addition corpora can be annotated by the analyst for functional categories such as speech acts, humour and metaphors by adding 'special marks making the token "visible" to the corpus software' (Mikhailov and Cooper 2016: 11) to ease retrieval, inspection and quantification. This is however a lengthy procedure, feasible only with small corpora. As a result, most quantitative research in CBAVTS has adopted a semasiological approach, whereby researchers formulate some specific hypotheses and check on the translational behaviour of previously identified grammatical, lexical, discoursal or pragmatic features.

Starting from a now well-established corpus linguistic approach, AVT researchers have an additional analytical procedure at their disposal. Evidence of variation and regularity patterns can be collected inductively as it emerges from the data without the constraints deriving from hypotheses formulated in advance. A successful application of such corpus-driven analysis is Freddi's (2009, 2012) study of phraseology in both original and dubbed film language. By generating frequency lists with the software program Wordsmith Tools, the author first extracted the top word clusters in the English dialogues and then checked to which degree and with which functions the formulaicity detected in the original texts transferred to the Italian dubbing. High-frequency formulas like 'Oh my God' were rendered with the same formulas (in this case, *Oh mio Dio*, 'Oh my God') in translation, while other repeated clusters such as 'you know what' were dubbed with more varied and hence creative translations: *la sai una cosa, sai che ti dico, facciamo così*, all meaning 'you know what', together with *senti* ('listen') and *okay* ('okay'). By combining a corpus-based and a corpus-driven approach, Forchini (2013) tackled the translation of English vocatives, a phenomenon that has proved to be problematic in Italian dubbing. The researcher first selected a group of frequent familiarizers in English conversation ('man', 'guys', 'buddy' and 'dude') to later retrieve the frequency of these lexical items, their collocations (i.e. recurrent juxtapositions of words) and cluster combinations in a small diachronic corpus of original Anglophone films dubbed into Italian. The combination of the various computer-assisted analyses contributed to the definition of a usage profile for each vocative while highlighting how translational norms in Italian dubbing have evolved in time towards pragmatic equivalence.

A close-up on applications in corpus-based audiovisual translation studies

Naturalness and the register-specificity of audiovisual translation

CBAVTS have focused on key research questions that are connected to the nature of audiovisual texts and the different AVT modalities. The issue of spokenness or naturalness is strictly pertinent to screen dialogue, which represents a type of 'scripted/constructed dialogue' (Bednarek 2010: 63) or language 'written to be spoken as if not written' (Gregory 1967: 191–192). It is no surprise, therefore, that the issue of naturalness has taken centre stage in many investigations of the language of dubbing and its alignment or disalignment with spontaneous conversation though the study of a wide array of linguistic phenomena. These include discourse markers, greetings and leave takings, general extenders, word clusters, intensifiers, interjections, hesitations, marked word orders, personal and demonstrative pronouns, questions, slanguage and vocatives. To address the issue of naturalness, the most reliable target-oriented approach involves the comparisons between dubbed language and spontaneous spoken language, on the one hand, and between dubbed dialogue and domestic dialogue, on the other hand. Starting from a definition of naturalness as '*nativelike selection of expression in a given context*' (Romero-Fresco 2009: 51, italics in the original), Romero-Fresco (2009, 2012) displayed the full potentialities of such a comparative methodology by delving into the behaviour of a group of intensifiers (*en serio, de verdad* and *de veras*, 'really'), discourse markers (*veamos, vamos a ver* and *a ver*, 'let's see'), and transition markers ((*muy*) *bien* and *bueno*, 'so'/'okay'/'well') in dubbed Spanish. In his investigations, the author made use of three different corpora:

(1) a parallel corpus of transcripts of the American TV series *Friends* and their dubbed Spanish versions, totalling about 300,000 words;
(2) a comparable corpus consisting of the dubbed *Friends* dialogues and the original, *Friends*-inspired Spanish sitcom *Siete Vidas*, totalling about 300,000 words;
(3) the section of colloquial conversation in the reference Spanish corpus CREA (Corpus de Referencia del Español Actual), featuring about 12 million words (Romero-Fresco 2009: 52).

Results show that there is a close proximity in the frequency of the features investigated between Spanish original audiovisual dialogue and spontaneous spoken language. By contrast, the language of dubbing exhibits traits of unnaturalness and shifts towards the written and formal pole of variation, in part due to the adherence to internal dubbing norms as well as to the calquing from the English original texts. Interestingly, by comparing the occurrence of *de veras* in the Latin American and European components of CREA, Romero-Fresco argues that the unnatural frequency of the intensifier in dubbed Spanish is a vestige of *español neutro*, a standardized form of Spanish used when products were first dubbed in Latin America for all Spanish-speaking audiences.

Following a similar, predominantly target-oriented approach, Pavesi (2008, 2009a) examined the alignment between translated dialogues and spontaneous spoken language in her study of five syntactic and pragmatic phenomena in Italian dubbing. By comparing the frequency of features such as the conjunction and pronoun *che* 'that' and personal pronouns in a small corpus of dubbed Anglophone films and in the LIP (a reference corpus of spoken Italian), the author argues that naturalness is conveyed to viewers metonymically by giving priority to 'privileged carriers of orality' (Pavesi 2008: 79; 2009a: 209). Pavesi (2009b) widened this comparative approach in a follow-up study on the distribution and function of personal pronouns in the PCFD. Besides contrasting translated dialogue with spontaneous conversation and with original Italian films in the Forlixt1 corpus (Valentini 2008, Heiss and Soffritti 2008), the author compared the frequencies in the PCFD sub-corpus of original English dialogues with data extracted from a reference corpus of English conversation. These multiple comparisons revealed that the influence of English patterns on the translated dialogues is genre-specific and promotes the overrepresentation of second person pronouns in the language of dubbing.

As already highlighted by Romero-Fresco (2009, 2012) and Pavesi (2008, 2009a, 2009b), corpus analysis is indeed more informative when both translated and domestic screen dialogues are systematically compared to the language variety they are meant to approximate: spontaneous spoken language. The approach is thoroughly illustrated by Baños (2014a) in her target-oriented investigation of a broad selection of major spoken features belonging to the phonological, morphological, syntactic and lexical levels in a few episodes of the Spanish dubbed version of *Friends* and the domestically produced Spanish sitcom *Siete Vidas*. The results suggest that domestic products align more with colloquial conversation than do comparable dubbed products. This finding is shared with other corpus studies on dubbing including Rossi's (1999) pioneering research on more than 100 spoken features in neo-realistic films in Italian and Matamala's (2009) investigation of the interjections contained in sitcoms dubbed and originally shot in Catalan. If it is true that only corpus data can reveal systematic similarities and differences between original/domestic and translated audiovisual products, the results obtained in the above-mentioned investigations will need to be validated by means of bigger corpora that contain more varied selections of audiovisual products.

Corpus-based studies of subtitling have also addressed the typicalities of the specific translation modality, instantiated in this case by brevity and the representation of speech in writing (Tirkkonen-Condit and Mäkisalo 2007, Mattsson 2009). More specifically, according to Tirkkonen-Condit and Mäkisalo (2007), since the language of AVT is a type of translated language, the alignment between it and other translated languages is worth investigating to assess the impact of the specific medium and modality of transfer. In particular '[t]here are reasons to expect . . . that subtitle language might differ from other varieties of translated language in its exploitation of such cohesive devices that contribute to brevity and conciseness' (Tirkkonen-Condit and Mäkisalo 2007: 222). The research starts from a subtitle corpus totalling about 100 million words, the Finnish Broadcasting Corpus (FBC), and the comparable Corpus of Original and Translated Finnish (CTF), developed at the University of Savonlinna and counting up to 10 million words. From these sources three sub-corpora were used in the study:

(1) all the Finnish subtitles contained in the FBC with reference to the year 2004 (5.9 million words);
(2) the Translated Finnish sub-corpus of the CTF (5.9 million words);
(3) the Original Finnish sub-corpus of the CTF (3.8 million words) (Tirkkonen-Condit and Mäkisalo 2007: 223).

Clitic particles and cohesive devices were chosen to test the hypotheses about the specificity of subtitle language. Among them, *-kin* is a brief and multifunctional particle conveying several rhetorical relations of addition, elaboration and contrast, while *-hAn* is a multifunctional discoursal device carrying an implication of shared information. Results showed that those cohesive devices that are short, dialogic and unique to Finnish are more frequent in subtitled Finnish than in translated Finnish and occasionally non-translated Finnish as well. In other words, the brevity and colloquiality of the cohesive devices acquire functional priority in the language of subtitling, thus overruling the Unique Item Hypothesis (Tirkkonen-Condit 2004), according to which target-language-specific items will be less frequent in translated language owing to the lack of a translational stimulus in the source language. For example, *-kin* is more frequent in subtitled Finnish than in translated Finnish, while *-hAn* occurs more frequently in subtitled Finnish than in both translated and original Finnish. These results corroborate the authors' hypothesis that the language of subtitles is an autonomous variety of the target language.

Finally, the language of AD is different from the language of other modalities of AVT since it is not built to simulate spoken dialogue. The corpus-based study of AD has in fact concentrated on the language of description and narration, given the specific functions this intersemiotic translation performs within audiovisual texts. Plot-propelling elements such as characters' appearances and events must be represented linguistically to become accessible to blind and visually impaired spectators. Through frequency counts, Salway (2007) found that AD is characterized by nouns referring to characters, body parts and concrete entities (e.g. 'man', 'head', 'door' and 'room'), as well as by verbs of actions conveying 'manner' (e.g. 'hurries', 'leans', 'walks', 'smiles', 'watches', 'grabs'). The higher than average frequency of these forms sheds light onto the focus of AD, whose function is to provide concise 'information about events in cause-effect relationships occurring in space and time, and about the characters involved in the events and their emotional states' (Salway 2007: 154). The higher than expected frequency in the TIWO corpus of the verbs 'stops', 'starts', 'begins' and 'finishes' additionally shows the relevance of temporal transitions in this AVT modality, while the phrases 'looks at', 'looks up at', 'looks down at' and 'looks around' introduce information about characters' centre of attention (Salway 2007: 160).

All these corpus studies empirically support the autonomy and register-specificity of the languages of AVT in the main modalities in which they are realized and have been so far investigated.

Translation tendencies: norms and universals in audiovisual translation

Corpus-based investigations of AVT have also been concerned with the search for translational norms and translation universals to suggest generalizations on the language of AVT and infer the processes underlying translation outcomes. Through quantifications allowed by corpus analysis, a few studies have explored the role of standardization, interference and simplification (Laviosa 2009), together with routinization vis-à-vis creativity (Pavesi 2016), in defining genre- or register-specificity.

Formentelli (2014) investigated whether lexical simplification impinges on dubbed language both affecting the transfer from source to target texts, and applying to the comparison between translated and non-translated dialogues in the same language (*cf.* Chesterman 2004). Simplification was defined along several parameters that allowed the researcher to explore the complexity and variability of vocabulary choices. Four randomized samples were extracted from the PCFD and were annotated so as to allow a variety of frequency measurements. Results suggest that lexical simplification does not occur during the process of translation from English into Italian. By contrast, lexical simplification emerges from the analysis of core vocabulary: that is, non-translated Italian dialogues contain numerous instances of non-standard and regional terms that do not occur in the Italian dubbed dialogues.

The role of interference, on the other hand, was explicitly tested in a study on primary interjections in the PCFD translational component supporting the Unique Item Hypothesis (Bruti and Pavesi 2008). Italian interjections that exhibit a degree of similarity with English ones (e.g. *oh*, 'oh'/ 'ah') tend to be over-represented in dubbing, whereas those that are specific and restricted to Italian tend to be under-represented (e.g. multifunctional *eh* 'hm'/'oh'/ etc.). Related to the law of interference (Toury 1995/2012) are also a few corpus-based studies that deal with translational routines, i.e. reiterated translation solutions generating recurrent strings in the target texts. Pavesi (2005, 2008) looked at such stock translations as the marked, non-standard but spoken constructions that repeatedly render English spoken constructions in dubbed Italian, whereas Freddi (2009, 2012) examined the extent to which routinization in the PCFD was carried over from the source into the target language when translating naturalistic versus plot-developing formulas. Confirmation of the productivity of translational routines in dubbing comes from Zanotti's (2014) study of general extenders like 'or something' and 'and stuff' in a DIY corpus of American series dubbed into Italian.

A closer look at translation strategies and overall distributions

By means of bilingual concordances and corpus annotation, researchers have further shed light on translation strategies and shifts both in dubbing and subtitling (e.g. Tirkkonen-Condit and Mäkisalo 2007, Baños 2013, Matamala 2009, Pavesi 2013, Mouka *et al.* 2015). These studies have focused on typical features of orality such as discourse markers and vocatives (e.g. Rica Peromingo 2014, Forchini 2013) to identify translation regularities in translation operations, among which omission, equivalence and substitutions. A good example of corpus-based research on translation strategies is Formentelli and Monti's (2014) investigation of the translation strategies used in transferring slanguage from English into Italian. The study confirms the trend towards standardization and neutralization of informal and taboo vocabulary in dubbing. Of the 1,219 instances of English slang words, dirty words and swear words extracted from the PCFD, almost half are rendered by functional equivalence in Italian, whereas the greatest share (54 per cent) are either downgraded or omitted. Further evidence of neutralization or standardization is provided by an investigation on the dubbing of intensifiers from English (e.g. 'so', 'really', 'very') into Spanish (Baños 2013). In this case, however, the search of the parallel corpus made up of 10 episodes of *Friends* showed that most of the standardized choices in dubbing mirrored the structure of the source text, presumably for reasons of synchronization, giving rise to more conventional syntactic combinations of intensifier + adjective, e.g. *muy importante*, 'very important'. In the translations, however, there were also instances of more colloquial devices like morphological augmentation (e.g. *feísimo*, 'very ugly') and lexico-semantic resources, which selectively contributed to the naturalness of the translated audiovisual product. The tendency to naturalization in dubbing was in turn substantiated by the analysis of the operations carried out in the translation of English demonstratives into Italian (Pavesi 2013). In keeping with the optionality of the grammatical subject in Italian, English demonstratives in the PCFD were deleted most frequently when in subject position, with 42 per cent of subjects 'this' and 'that' disappearing from the dubbed Italian component. Substitutions (22 per cent of all translations) also contributed to bringing the target texts in line with target language preferences, while compensation strategies unveiled equivalent resources available in Italian speech. Cumulatively, these strategies were found to radically change the representation of deixis in the target dialogues. Whereas in English demonstratives signpost salient entities in the scene and in narration, in Italian access to the same entities must occur directly without the mediation of verbal language, as exemplified by '**This** is the only thing you got?' translated with a subjectless clause in Italian: *È l'unica cosa che hai?* 'Is the only thing that you have?' (Pavesi 2013: 109).

While parallel corpora are clearly necessary to investigate translation strategies, they can also be fruitfully used to make comparisons between the overall distributions of features in source and target texts. A series of investigations on greetings, leave takings, introductions and good wishes (e.g. Bonsignori *et al.* 2012, Bonsignori and Bruti 2015) explored the role of these conversational routines in audiovisual products from a pragmatic, filmic and cross-cultural perspective. The comparisons between frequency lists (see above) brought to the fore the Italian formulas that are systematically favoured in dubbing and in subtitling to express the same functions as the English ritualistic speech acts. Focusing instead on dialogue-structuring syntactic phenomena, Ghia (2014) studied interrogatives contrastively in English and dubbed Italian dialogue. All direct questions in a sample of both the original and translated components of the PCFD were tagged for form and function, distinguishing among categories of *wh-* vs. *yes-no* interrogatives, and information-seeking vs. pragmatic questions typically used to challenge the interlocutor (e.g. 'What are you doing?'). Like the original English dialogue, dubbing was found to be typified by a high frequency of interrogatives, in particular those that foster conflict and contribute to plot development. By contrast, on a syntactic level, questions in translation align with the target language and reproduce typical patterns of Italian conversation.

The studies reported above corroborate the usefulness of CBAVTS in identifying general trends in translated texts. Through such corpus findings, AVT is confirmed to result from several thrusts co-present during the transfer process. This means that the search for general tendencies and the study of translation strategies in AVT are inevitably interconnected with each other, whilst both impinge on the definition of naturalness. It also means that a major methodological difficulty in corpus-based research is isolating and separating the various components that shape AVT and its language.

Future trajectories

Corpus-based studies are a powerful approach to explore the dynamics of the process and the nature of the product of AVT both systematically and in-depth. There is, however, ample room for development in the field as less orderly work has been carried out in AVT in comparison to other areas of CBTS. Among the methodological weaknesses of current CBAVT research we find limited corpus size, partial comparability between sub-corpora and partial exploitation of the potentials of computer-assisted analysis. Researchers need to address these limitations to guarantee more reliable and representative datasets as well as more varied and conclusive research findings. The lack of bidirectionality in available parallel corpora represents an additional drawback when we attempt to establish cause-effect relationships in corpus analysis. Moreover, bilingual parallel corpora, which only have one source language (mostly English) and few target languages (mainly Italian and Spanish) limit the investigation of features that are specific to translated texts (Saldanha and O'Brien 2013: 68), thus hindering the search for translation universals in AVT. Hence, more source and target language pairs need to be involved and multilingual corpora should be compiled in order to gain data from a larger set of source language-target language combinations. The broader implementation of diachronic corpora would be an additional asset to research allowing analysts to probe challenging questions including how translational norms become established and how they evolve in time in different linguacultural settings and across spatial divides.

As for the phenomena investigated, there is still a lack of major quantitative investigations providing overall profiles of translated languages in all transfer modalities (*cf.* Pérez-González 2014: 117). Researchers thus need to move beyond limited descriptions of individual features to tackle the wider picture of AVT. The more systematic reliance on corpus-analytical resources and statistical measurements is also necessary to validate the significance of the findings, gain new ones and extend them to various aspects that have been so far under-investigated in CBAVT research. These include evaluation and ideology, which can be profitably explored by such means as semantic and pragmatic annotation, keyword lists, semantic prosody and sentiment analyses, as exemplified in Mouka *et al.* (2015). Not to be neglected are unsolved copyright issues as they jeopardize corpus creation itself and seriously compromise access to corpora, a limitation hampering the sharing of resources and replicability of results. At the same time, new technological applications should be envisaged including the larger use of research innovations that allow automated dialogue transcription, tagging and synchronization between text files, as well as between text files and audio or video files (Baños 2014b) in the transformation of monomodal corpora into multimodal corpora.

Besides representing instruments for descriptive and explanatory advancement in AVT studies, translation-driven corpora are liable to more extensive applications in various areas of the wider field, among which quality assessment and most importantly translator training, as shown in Sotelo Dios (2015). They can also be exploited in related research areas comprising Contrastive Linguistics, Intercultural Pragmatics and Conversation Analysis, together with Second Language Acquisition and Foreign Language Teaching (Rica Peromingo *et al.* 2014). These far-ranging applications additionally testify to the ample potentialities of CBAVTS and deserve to be explored in further enquiries in the field.

Maria Pavesi

Summary

A corpus is a principled collection of texts stored electronically to be analyzed quantitatively and qualitatively by using computer-assisted techniques. In this chapter we have shown that CBAVTS belong to the wider approach of CBTS whose premises and methodological tools they share. Spoken and written corpora of AVT can be systematically searched to obtain generalizations about the make-up of translated texts and the process of translation by investigating frequencies, recurrent word combinations and collocations, along with cross-linguistic and cross-cultural correspondences. This approach has allowed researchers to address several important issues including the naturalness of translated screen dialogue, translation strategies, general tendencies and variation in translational behaviour, thus proving to be a powerful epistemological resource in AVT worthy of continual development and refinement.

Further reading

Olohan, M. (2004) *Introducing Corpora in Translation Studies*, London & New York: Routledge | *This is a classic reference textbook on corpora in Descriptive Translation Studies, balancing theoretical issues with practical applications.*
Saldanha, G. and S. O'Brien (2013) *Research Methods for Translation Studies*, London & New York: Routledge | *This volume provides an updated and critical overview of methodology in translation studies including excellent sections on corpus-based approaches.*
Baños R., S. Bruti and S. Zanotti (eds) (2013) 'Corpus Linguistics and Audiovisual Translation: In Search of an Integrated Approach'. Special issue of *Perspectives: Studies in Translatology* 21(4) | *This the first journal issue dedicated to Corpus-Based Audiovisual Translation Studies with innovative articles on different languages and translation modalities.*
Pavesi M., M. Formentelli and E. Ghia (eds) (2014) *The Languages of Dubbing. Mainstream Audiovisual Translation in Italy*, Bern: Peter Lang | *This collection mostly contains corpus-based research articles tackling the same language of dubbing from insightful and complementary perspectives.*

Related topics

3   Subtitling on the cusp of its futures
4   Investigating dubbing: learning from the past, looking to the future
8   Audio description: evolving recommendations for usable, effective and enjoyable practices
13 Spoken discourse and conversational interaction in audiovisual translation
18 Sociolinguistics and linguistic variation in audiovisual translation
21 Multimodal corpora in audiovisual translation studies
22 Eye tracking in audiovisual translation research

References

Adolphs, S. and Carter, R. (2013) *Spoken Corpus Linguistics. From Monomodal to Multimodal*, London & New York: Routledge.
Baker, M. (1993) 'Corpus Linguistics and Translation Studies: Implications and Applications', in M. Baker, G. Francis and E. Tognini-Bonelli (eds) *Text and Technology: In Honour of John Sinclair*, Amsterdam & Philadelphia: John Benjamins, 233–250.
Baker, M. (1996) 'Corpus-based Translation Studies: The Challenges that Lie Ahead', in H. Somers (ed.) *Terminology, LSP and Translation. Studies in Language Engineering in Honour of Juan C. Sager*, Amsterdam & Philadelphia: John Benjamins, 175–186.

Baker, P. (2006) *Using Corpora in Discourse Analysis*, London: Continuum.

Baños, R. (2013) '"That is so Cool": Investigating the Translation of Adverbial Intensifiers in English-Spanish Dubbing through a Parallel Corpus of Sitcoms', *Perspectives: Studies in Translatology* 21(4): 526–542.

Baños, R. (2014a) 'Orality Markers in Spanish Native and Dubbed Sitcoms: Pretended Spontaneity and Prefabricated Orality', *Meta* 59(2): 406–435.

Baños, R. (2014b) 'Corpus Linguistics and Audiovisual Translation', *EST Newsletter* 45, 10–11.

Baños, R., S. Bruti and S. Zanotti (eds) (2013) 'Corpus Linguistics and Audiovisual Translation: In Search of an Integrated Approach'. Special issue of *Perspectives: Studies in Translatology* 21(4).

Bednarek, M. (2010) *The Language of Fictional Television. Drama and Identity*, London: Continuum.

Bonsignori, V. (2009) 'Transcribing Film Dialogue: From Orthographic to Prosodic Transcription', in M. Freddi and M. Pavesi (eds) *Analysing Audiovisual Dialogue. Linguistic and Translational Insights*, Bologna: CLUEB, 185–200.

Bonsignori, V. and S. Bruti (2015) 'Translating Introductions and Wishes in Audiovisual Dialogues. Evidence from a Corpus', in M. Ji (ed.) *Empirical Translation Studies. Interdisciplinary Methodologies Explored*, Sheffield: Equinox, 180–209.

Bonsignori, V., S. Bruti, and S. Masi (2012) 'Exploring Greetings and Leave-Takings in Original and Dubbed Language', in A. Remael, P. Orero and M. Carroll (eds) *Audiovisual Translation and Media Accessibility at the Crossroads. Media for All 3*, Amsterdam: Rodopi, 357–379.

Bruti, S. (2009) 'Translating Compliments and Insults in the *Pavia Corpus of Film Dialogue*: Two Sides of the Same Coin?', in M. Freddi and M. Pavesi (eds) *Analysing Audiovisual Dialogue. Linguistic and Translational Insights*, Bologna: CLUEB, 143–163.

Bruti, S. and M. Pavesi (2008) 'Interjections in Translated Italian: Looking for Traces of Dubbed Language', in A. Martelli and V. Pulcini (eds) *Investigating English with Corpora*, Milano: Polimetrica, 207–222.

Chesterman, A. (2004) 'Beyond the Particular', in A. Mauranen and P. Kujamäki (eds) *Translation Universals. Do they Exist?* Amsterdam & Philadelphia: John Benjamins, 33–49.

Forchini, P. (2013) 'A Diachronic Study of Familiarizers ('Man', 'Guys', 'Buddy', 'Dude') in Movie Language', *Perspectives: Studies in Translatology* 21(4): 504–525.

Formentelli, M. (2014) 'Exploring Lexical Variety and Simplification in Original and Dubbed Film Dialogue', in M. Pavesi, M. Formentelli and E. Ghia (eds) *The Languages of Dubbing. Mainstream Audiovisual Translation in Italy*, Bern: Peter Lang, 141–166.

Formentelli, M and S. Monti (2014) 'Translating Slanguage in British and American Films', in M. Pavesi, M. Formentelli and E. Ghia (eds) *The Languages of Dubbing. Mainstream Audiovisual Translation in Italy*, Bern: Peter Lang, 169–195.

Freddi, M. (2009) 'The Phraseology of Contemporary Filmic Speech: Formulaic Language and Translation', in M. Freddi and M. Pavesi (eds) *Analysing Audiovisual Dialogue. Linguistic and Translational Insights*, Bologna: CLUEB, 101–123.

Freddi, M. (2012) 'What AVT Can Make of Corpora: Some Findings from the Pavia Corpus of Film Dialogue', in A. Remael, P. Orero and M. Carroll (eds) *AVT and Media Accessibility at the Crossroads. Media for All 3*, Amsterdam: Rodopi, 381–407.

Freddi, M. (2013) 'Constructing a Corpus of Translated Films: A Corpus View of Dubbing', *Perspectives: Studies in Translatology* 21(4): 491–503.

Freddi, M. and M. Pavesi (eds) (2009a) *Analysing Audiovisual Dialogue. Linguistic and Translation Insights*, Bologna: CLUEB.

Freddi, M. and M. Pavesi (2009b) 'The *Pavia Corpus of Film Dialogue*: Methodology and Research Rationale', in M. Freddi and M. Pavesi (eds) *Analysing Audiovisual Dialogue. Linguistic and Translational Insights*, Bologna: CLUEB, 95–100.

Ghia, E. (2014) '"That is the Question": Direct Interrogatives in English Film Dialogue and Dubbed Italian', in M. Pavesi, M. Formentelli and E. Ghia (eds) *The Languages of Dubbing. Mainstream Audiovisual Translation in Italy*, Bern: Peter Lang, 57–88.

Gregory, M. (1967) 'Aspects of Varieties Differentiation', *Journal of Linguistics* 3(2): 177–198.

Heiss, C. and M. Soffritti (2008) 'Forlixt 1—The Forlì Corpus of Screen Translation: Exploring Microstructures', in D. Chiaro, C. Heiss and C. Bucaria (eds) *Between Text and Image. Updating Research in Screen Translation*, Amsterdam & Philadelphia: John Benjamins, 51–62.

Laviosa, S. (2009) 'Universals', in M. Baker and G. Saldanha (eds) *Routledge Encyclopedia of Translation Studies*, second edition, London & New York: Routledge, 306–310.

Laviosa, S. (2011) 'Corpus-based Translation Studies: Where Does it Come from? Where is it Going?', in A. Kruger, K. Wallmach and J. Munday (eds) *Corpus-Based Translation Studies. Research and Applications*, London: Bloomsbury, 13–32.

Matamala, A. (2009) 'Interjections in Original and Dubbed Sitcoms in Catalan: A Comparison', *Meta* 54(3): 485–502.

Mattsson, J. (2009) 'The Subtitling of Discourse Particles. A Corpus-based Study of *Well, You Know, I Mean*, and *Like*, and their Swedish Translations in Ten American Films', Unpublished Doctoral Thesis, University of Gothenburg, Sweden.

Mikhailov, M. and R. Cooper (2016) *Corpus Linguistics for Translation and Contrastive Studies*, London & New York: Routledge.

Mouka, E., I. E. Saridakis and A. Fotopoulou (2015) 'Racism Goes to the Movies: A Corpus-driven Study of Cross-linguistic Racist Discourse Annotation and Translation Analysis', in C. Fantinuoli and F. Zanettin (eds) *New Directions in Corpus-based Translation Studies*, Berlin: Language Science Press, 35–70.

Olohan, M. (2004) *Introducing Corpora in Translation Studies*, London & New York: Routledge.

Palmer, A. and A. Salway (2015) 'Audio Description on the Thought-action Continuum', *Style* 49(2): 126–148.

Pavesi, M. (2005) *La traduzione filmica. Tratti del parlato doppiato dall'inglese all'italiano*, Roma: Carocci.

Pavesi, M. (2008) 'Spoken Language in Film Dubbing: Target Language Norms, Interference and Translational Routines', in D. Chiaro, C. Heiss and C. Bucaria (eds) *Between Text and Image. Updating Research in Screen Translation*, Amsterdam & Philadelphia: John Benjamins, 79–99.

Pavesi, M. (2009a) 'Dubbing English into Italian: A Closer Look at the Translation of Spoken Language', in J. Díaz Cintas (ed.) *New Trends in Audiovisual Translation*, Bristol: Multilingual Matters, 197–209.

Pavesi, M. (2009b) 'Pronouns in Film Dubbing and the Dynamics of Audiovisual Communication', *VIAL* 6: 89–107.

Pavesi, M. (2013) '*This* and *That* in the Language of Film Dubbing: A Corpus-based Analysis', *Meta* 58(1): 107–137.

Pavesi, M. (2014) 'The *Pavia Corpus of Film Dialogue*: A Means to Several Ends' in M. Pavesi, M. Formentelli and E. Ghia (eds) *The Languages of Dubbing. Mainstream Audiovisual Translation in Italy*, Bern: Peter Lang, 29–55.

Pavesi, M. (2016) 'The Space of Italian Dubbing: From Naturalness to Creativity in Fictive Orality', in M. Canepari, G. Mansfield and F. Poppi (eds) *Remediating, Rescripting, Remaking. Language and Translation in the New Media*, Roma: Carocci, 13–30.

Pavesi M., M. Formentelli and E. Ghia (eds) (2014) *The Languages of Dubbing. Mainstream Audiovisual Translation in Italy*, Bern: Peter Lang.

PCFD (n.d.) 'Pavia Corpus of Film Dialogue'. Available online: http://studiumanistici.unipv.it/?pagina=p&titolo=pcfd [last access 20 December 2017].

Pérez-González, L. (2007) 'Appraising Dubbed Conversation. Systemic Functional Insights into the Construal of Naturalness in Translated Film Dialogue', *The Translator* 13(1): 1–38.

Pérez-González, L. (2014) *Audiovisual Translation: Theories, Methods, Issues*, London & New York: Routledge.

Rica Peromingo, J. P. (2014) 'La traducción de marcadores discursivos (DM) inglés-español en los subtítulos de películas: Un estudio de corpus', *JoSTrans: The Journal of Specialised Translation* 21: 177–199. Available online: www.jostrans.org/issue21/art_rica_peromingo.php [last access 20 December 2017].

Rica Peromingo, J. P., R. Albarrán Martín and B. García Riaza (2014) 'New Approaches to Audiovisual Translation: The Usefulness of Corpus-based Studies for the Teaching of Dubbing and Subtitling', in E. Bárcena, T. Read and J. Arús (eds) *Languages for Specific Purposes in the Digital Era*, Berlin: Springer-Verlag, 303–322.

Romero-Fresco, P. (2009) 'Naturalness in the Spanish Dubbing Language: A Case of Not-so-close Friends', *Meta* 54(1): 49–72.

Romero-Fresco, P. (2012) 'Dubbing Dialogues... Naturally: A Pragmatic Approach to the Translation of Transition Markers in Dubbing', *MonTI* 4: 181–205.

Rossi, F. (1999) *Le Parole dello Schermo. Analisi Linguistica del Parlato di sei Film dal 1948 al 1957*, Roma: Bulzoni.

Saldanha, G. and S. O'Brien (2013) *Research Methods for Translation Studies*, London & New York: Routledge.

Salway, A. (2007) 'A Corpus-based Analysis of Audio Description', in J. Díaz Cintas, P. Orero and A. Remael (eds) *Media for All. Subtitling for the Deaf, Audio Description and Sign Language*, Amsterdam: Rodopi, 151–174.

Sotelo Dios, P. (2015) 'Using a Multimedia Corpus of Subtitles in Translation Training. Design and Applications of the Veiga Corpus', in A. Leńko-Szymańska and A. Boulton (eds) *Multiple Affordances of Language Corpora for Data-driven Learning*, Amsterdam & Philadelphia: John Benjamins: 245–266.

Tirkkonen-Condit, S. (2004) 'Unique Items—Over- or Under-represented in Translated Language?', in A. Mauranen and P. Kujamäki (eds) *Translation Universals—Do they Exist?*, Amsterdam & Philadelphia: John Benjamins, 238–264.

Tirkkonen-Condit, S. and J. Mäkisalo (2007) 'Cohesion in Subtitles: A Corpus-based Study', *Across Languages and Cultures* 8(2): 221–230.

Toury, G. (1995/2012) *Descriptive Translation Studies and Beyond*, Amsterdam & Philadelphia: John Benjamins.

Valentini, C. (2008) 'Forlixt 1—The Forlì Corpus of Screen Translation: Exploring Macrostructures', in D. Chiaro, C. Heiss, and C. Bucaria (eds) *Between Text and Image. Updating Research in Screen Translation*, Amsterdam & Philadelphia: John Benjamins, 37–50.

Zanettin, F. (2012) *Translation-driven Corpora. Corpus Resources for Descriptive and Applied Translation Studies*. Manchester: St. Jerome.

Zanotti, S. (2014) '"It Feels like Bits of me are Crumbling or Something": General Extenders in Original and Dubbed Television Dialogue', in M. Pavesi, M. Formentelli and E. Ghia (eds) *The Languages of Dubbing. Mainstream Audiovisual Translation in Italy*, Bern: Peter Lang, 113–140.

Sitography

AntConc 3.2.1w: www.laurenceanthony.net/software/antconc/ [last access 20 December 2017].
Wordsmith Tools: www.lexically.net/wordsmith/ [last access 20 December 2017].

21
Multimodal corpora in audiovisual translation studies

Marcello Soffritti

Introduction

Since the 1990s, corpus-based research has been the drive behind key methodological advances—not least the development of techniques to quantitatively interrogate large computer-held collections of texts—in the neighbouring fields of linguistics, lexicography and translation studies, to name but a few examples. Corpora have become powerful and reliable tools to compile representative samples of authentic texts pertaining to various language varieties and genres, test hypotheses regarding the frequency and regularity of certain linguistic patterns that cannot be verified by the researcher's intuition, and support the generalization of linguistic findings. Effectively, corpora expose the limitations of linguistic research based on made-up examples and the analyst's subjective judgement.

This chapter examines how multimodal corpora (MMC) can be exploited for the purposes of AVT research. It discusses the architecture of these resources, consisting of audiovisual texts and their translations, and explores various aspects pertaining to the design, compilation, processing and maintenance of these corpora. After examining some of the difficulties that are endemic to MMC, the chapter ends by suggesting different avenues for the development of such computer-held resources in terms of their contribution to AVT research.

Types of corpora in translation research and practice

There are some obvious differences in the way translation researchers and practitioners generally use corpora. Translation practitioners are result-oriented and concerned with working out appropriate translation solutions for real life problems, often bound by a range of technical and organizational constraints. For them corpora are chiefly tools to carry out professional assignments under defined conditions, often in combination with a number of other tools, to enhance their productivity as translators. Dedicated corpora for the translation industry often take the form of translation memories (TMs), i.e. databases typically consisting of aligned sets of previously translated (source and target) text segments that translators can retrieve and edit as they translate new texts bearing a varying degree of resemblance with those stored in the database. TMs can be considered as parallel corpora whose representativeness is limited to mostly technical and professional domains, and whose relevance to the translator's work is maintained through continuous refinements and enlargements of the database every time new validated translations are added to the memory. In spite of sharing some fundamental characteristics with parallel corpora, TMs are not particularly helpful for research in translation, because they do not generally enable researchers to identify and explore strategic and methodological issues of scholarly and pedagogical relevance. Instead, translation scholars have benefited from the compilation of large annotated corpora, whether monolingual or bilingual, general or specialized.

Recent trends in translation theory and multimodality (Pérez-González 2014) call for a more systematic study of the contribution that non-verbal semiotics make to the overall meaning of texts combining written/spoken language, sounds and images. Just as linguistics and translation theory have capitalized on the growing availability of corpora, research in multimodality has become increasingly dependent on corpus-based evidence to verify and refine its own basic assumptions and statements (Bateman *et al.* 2002). Against this backdrop, this chapter explores the current and potential capacity of MMC to yield new insights into AVT. In contrast to their unimodal counterparts, multimodal corpora contain texts made up of both verbal and non-verbal meaning-making modes, and hence encompass the same kind of texts that lie at the heart of the AVT process. Ultimately, MMC are required because setting up 'a database or a corpus of film dialogues and their subtitles, with no pictures, and still pretend to study screen translation' would be pointless (Gambier 2006: 7).

The emergence of MMC can be traced back to the turn of the century, although calls to include audiovisual components in electronic corpora date back even earlier. A list of multimodal databases in López-Cózar Delgado and Araki (2005: 229–231), very likely out-of-date at the time of writing, quotes about 20 instances, not all of which are available on the Internet. Their number has probably increased since it was first published, although it will certainly remain negligible when compared with the number of unimodal corpora available to language scholars.

As multimodality establishes itself as a new qualitative dimension in the compilation of corpora, by incorporating non-written and non-verbal material, the written representation of language loses its primacy. The increasing number of communication channels represented in such corpora and technological platforms required to access them also add to the variety of multimodal data to be collected and stored (Knight 2011: 405). In the case of MMC consisting of audiovisual texts and their translations, corpus design is particularly challenging, because they must include multimodal content in both the source and target languages. The advent of digitization has, however, expedited the compilation process: AVT corpora can now be built more easily due to the greater availability of digital materials, the widespread availability of tools to compress digital data, and the growing ubiquity of suitable storage devices and online platforms for the exchange and distribution of audiovisual material. Another important factor to bear in mind in the era of social media is the willingness of users and communities to contribute materials in numerous ways—even though the quality and relevance of crowd-sourced materials are often questionable, and hence have to be carefully checked before they are included in the corpus.

Mining the Internet for multimodal corpora

Quite a different situation emerges if one looks at trends in mainstream web-based communication. Countless web pages are multimodal to varying degrees, in that they include at least visual elements conveying meaning, such as static pictures, graphics, symbols, icons, menu bars in different colours. In addition, various sounds (music, sound effects, and even human or animal voices) are often deployed in combination with written or visual elements. Acoustic information is sometimes available in separate files for retrieval. The same applies to motion videos: recordings of people, objects, events and locations can be integrated into websites, sometimes as constitutive components of the wider text, sometimes as autonomous items for purchase, practical use or simply as complementary information—whether it can be accessed directly or via a dedicated link.

The translation of webpages, as defined above, raises important questions that do not apply in other text types. Are translations of webpages to be considered as a form of AVT? And to what extent are they amenable to being included into a corpus of sorts? A good reason for including them in this discussion lies in the fact that, in many websites, versions of certain pages are readily available in other languages. Indeed, in some cases these translations exhibit changes in content vis-à-vis the original, as they are tailored to the needs of different audiences in the target locales. As a general principle, MMC informing language and translation research should consist of couplets of existing source products and their existing validated translations. Multilingual versions of webpages are therefore potentially relevant and could be considered for mining and inclusion in MMC. Wikipedia articles in different languages, including both verbal and non-verbal meaning-making resources, are a case in point.

On a different quality level, Internet browsers now feature a (machine) translation function that can be directly applied to most standard webpages. Translated web pages are thus the output of a corpus-based process, where the translation solutions are extracted from a corpus 'hidden in the cloud'. Specifically, they are generated by machine translation engines that process huge collections of parallel text segments, feeding on millions of webpages and owned by leading companies (Google Translate, Google Translator Toolkit, and some others in the recent past), in what represents the most prominent example of corpus-based translation supported by large-scale harvesting of parallel texts. Neural computation, statistical power and more or less conscious crowd involvement in an ever-ongoing process of engine refinement are the basis for this largely non-linguistic corpus building methodology. To a considerable extent, web-based machine translation is capitalizing on the growing reliability and ubiquity of special tools developed under the umbrella of existing language corpora (e.g. lemmatizers, parsers, part-of-speech taggers), and the qualitative output of automatic translation engines is increasingly appreciated by both average and specialized end-users. Crucially, the growing involvement of the crowd in the generation of data is likely to enhance and refine the amount of validated translations within such parallel 'corpora'.

In order to decide whether, and to what extent, machine translations of webpages can be regarded as MMC, one must take a closer look at the objects and processes at stake. MT-processed texts feature within webpages that also contain non-verbal elements, i.e. meaningful visual and/or acoustic content. However, only the written text within those multimodal ensembles is processed by MT engines, since the underlying corpus consists exclusively of segments of written language. Similar or even stronger limitations would appear to apply in most tools used to localize video games. It goes without saying that the new generation of such tools is unlikely to remain bound by such technological constraints.

More complex operations of the same kind take place when we look at another mainstream translation process involving multimodal material, i.e. the automatic translation of subtitles available for a growing number of YouTube clips. Subtitles available in this context are ever more frequently being produced automatically, i.e. with the help of speech recognition applications that manage to covertly perform written transcriptions of spoken words in real time. The output of speech recognition software is then promptly processed by MT applications that generate target language subtitled versions. Speech recognition and MT, both of which are based on a combination of statistically arranged data and increasingly sophisticated conversion rules, work in hand-in-hand.

Both MT engines and speech recognition software intersect with the definition of MMC presented in this chapter. Although the role played by textual corpora is more evident in the case of MT, speech recognition is probably closer to multimodal analysis, in that it applies segmenting and combining rules that are based on large inventories of spoken documents. These have been filtered so that they are representative of as many phonetic and acoustic elements as possible, which are in turn interwoven with rules of orthographic transcription. The deployment of two consecutive automatic processes of content conversion obviously entails a higher risk of error chains caused by the incorrect decoding of inaccurate or unclear pronunciation of the source words, along with a number of other imponderable shortcomings that can occur in later stages of the process. User satisfaction is still low and probably will remain so as long as the accuracy of automatically generated target subtitles remains below 90 per cent. However, insofar as this service is free and it is likely to improve, at least for some of the most widely used languages, this form of translation is not likely to disappear any time soon.

Some scholars will have reservations about the fact that machine translated webpages rely on procedures applied to simple text chunks and, as a result, the relationship between these mechanically produced target versions and the audiovisual material embedded in the text may be seriously disrupted. Still, the translation is not necessarily completed after a single iteration of this process. Rather, it can undergo one or more subsequent stages of validation; crucially, motivated end users can optimize these results in terms of the overall multimodality of the end product—if it is still required.

In sum, large-scale processes of translation driven by big data tend to rely on unimodal tools resembling ever growing parallel corpora, even for multimodal webpages. This simplified but highly effective approach to translation cannot be ignored nor hastily dismissed by cooperatively minded AVT practitioners. There are strong reasons to share methods or experiences: multimodal products, corpora and AVT are highly interdependent and more pervasive and, given their flexible boundaries and degree of overlap, they cannot be considered as separate fields.

Multimodal corpora

Foster (2007: 1) defines MMC as 'a recorded and annotated collection of communication modalities such as speech, gaze, hand gesture, body language, generally based on recorded human behaviour'. This definition obviously draws on the classical definition of multimodal texts as those 'whose meanings are realized through more than one semiotic code' (Kress and van Leeuwen 1996: 183, but see also Allwood 2008: 207 ff.). On the other hand, the term 'multimedia corpus' is used to designate 'a systematic collection of language resources involving data in more than one medium' that normally 'consists of a set of digital audio and/or video data and a corresponding set of textual data (the transcriptions and/or annotations of the audio or video data)' (Schmidt et al. 2014: 1). Given their shared conceptual core, this chapter will treat both terms as synonyms and will henceforth refer to both as MMC, thus reflecting the growing tendency to adopt an enhanced notion of multimodality (Bednarek 2015: 65).

The scholars cited in the preceding paragraph conceptualize MMC as monolingual collections enabling research on the complexity of meaning-making activities—mostly in dialogic settings, but also in human–machine interactions—through a growing range of advanced multimodal user interfaces (see Abuczki and Esfandiari 2013 or, for a more comprehensive charting of this area of research, the range of papers published in the *Journal on Multimodal User Interfaces*). Most of these interfaces contain and display annotated textual records of spoken communication consisting of sound recordings, video-streaming (as these interactional encounters are made with purposefully arranged cameras and microphones) and (written) transcriptions of the verbal content. Annotation is carried out in each of the three channels that run simultaneously when the user examines an extracted sample. It addresses not only classical features of syntax, vocabulary, morphology and style (on the written channel), but also intonation, pronunciation, pitch, pauses, and para-verbal signals (on the acoustic channel), as well as facial expressions, gaze, body movements and camera shots (on the visual channel). All annotated units are equally relevant, and they should all be ideally available when the corpus is being interrogated, although text search probably remains the quickest and most efficient way of locating contents in a corpus.

Hits generated in response to specific search queries are generally presented as multimodal concordances, which deliver a comprehensive overview of which meaning-making elements concur in a single segment of the dialogue (see, for instance, Baldry and Thibault 2008). Another key source of information lies in the statistical values generated by relevant aspects of the database architecture. These include quantitative information about annotated elements and the combinations, patterns and profiles that they are part of; comparisons between MMC data and data from general purpose corpora; and many more findings that can significantly enhance our knowledge of how communication works in different settings and how it can be best analyzed. Even research on the interaction between humans and technical devices in controlled situations can benefit from the interrogation of MMC: gestures, facial expressions and the emotional state of humans can be modelled and ultimately simulated so as to build artificial agents with the capacity to 'understand' and speak sensibly to human partners, or to assist impaired persons.

Being mostly monolingual, these MMC are only tangentially relevant to AVT because they do not feature comparable data in two or more languages—although Navarretta *et al.* (2011) present a rare instance of comparable MMC for some Nordic languages. To facilitate AVT research, corpora must contain source and target language multimodal texts. In other words, AVT-relevant MMC should include most features of monolingual MMC plus bilingual or multilingual aligned language data, together with a facility to run various query modalities in the user interface. In corpus linguistics terminology, these MMC of audiovisual texts and their translations should ideally be parallel. By embracing original audiovisual products together with their translated counterparts in one or more additional languages, these MMC respond to the definition of parallel corpora as collections in which 'two or more components are aligned, that is, are subdivided into compositional and sequential units (of differing extent and nature) which are linked and can thus be retrieved as pairs (or triplets, etc.)' (Fantinuoli and Zanettin 2015: 4). AVT translation is also heavily dependent on comparable corpora—typically a pair of corpora in two different languages which come from the same domain but are not translations of each other. However, given the notorious difficulties entailed in determining the optimal composition of comparable corpora (Fantinuoli and Zanettin 2015: 4), this chapter focuses exclusively on parallel corpora.

Contrary to what happens in unimodal and monolingual corpora, in MMC the target element of an original-translated couplet is processed not only in terms of its verbal components, but also in terms of its acoustic and/or visual ones, occasionally shortening or stretching the length of translated sequential units in comparison to their sources. On the other hand, like unimodal and monolingual corpora, multilingual MMC can differ significantly according to their intended use. Corpora can be used as a resource to inform scholarly research (e.g. research in AVT methodology, applied AVT, certain aspects of intercultural communication, semiotics of translation, etc.) or as a semi-practical tool in professional AVT training, e.g. as a repository of possible solutions to translation problems. The latter use is relevant to dubbing/subtitling in contexts where teamwork, standardization and reusability of the validated solutions are required.

Multimodal corpora for audiovisual translation studies

Unlike webpages, audiovisual products are generally identifiable as such in that they can totally or largely dispense with written components. They are made to be viewed and listened to, rather than read. Audiovisual texts also differ from webpages in that they are not necessarily located on the Internet, as they can be generated, distributed and used offline. Prototypical audiovisual products are also the outcome of traditional and autonomous industries and activities such as cinema, TV programmes, pedagogical publishing, theatre, and advertising. Newer and widespread audiovisual textualities include videogames, tutorials, documentation for technical and professional purposes, product information, and more. And since this list does not yet account for genres or distribution modalities, additional distinctions between classes of products may become necessary according to the translation modality (e.g. written, intersemiotic, dubbing, subtitling, voice over) used in each case. Accordingly, MMC for translation generally need to take into consideration a large number of different factors.

Multimodal corpora for translation

Unlike their general counterparts, parallel corpora used by translation scholars are not fully representative of general categories, such as genre, subject, or time period. Building a parallel corpus to the British National Corpus (BNC), for example, would involve finding validated translations for every text held in it. Even if this were possible, that parallel corpus of translated texts would not meet the requirements to be regarded as representative of the target language in question. Parallel corpora are at best coherent and homogeneous subsets of texts chosen to serve specific scientific, pedagogical or professional purposes, and these intrinsic limitations are particularly acute in the case of MMC consisting of audiovisual texts and their translations.

In this light, the appropriateness and usability of parallel corpora will depend on whether they are meant to support research on speech functions and translation quality, to give but two examples, or alternatively they are expected to provide operational support to translation process, translator training or even translation quality assessment. These factors are decisive in optimizing the design, expansion and modes of exploitation of parallel corpora. As a general requirement, however, parallel corpora conceived to assist translation scholars with their research should hold two language versions of the same text along with some sort of alignment function. Alignment, however, might not always be an option. Although visual data tend to remain the same in most translations of texts combining language and non-verbal meaning-making resources, some webpages may undergo processes of adaptation or localization to ensure that the visual and/or acoustic content is adapted to the needs or expectations of particular target groups. Likewise, movies, TV programmes, ads and other forms of audiovisual content may require structural changes during the translation process (Gambier 2006). Should a deep reshaping be required on all channels, these audiovisual texts may become impervious to alignment as found in unimodal parallel corpora.

MMC can hold certain types of audiovisual texts that are (or are to be) translated. Along with films, several TV genres (e.g. documentary films, cartoons, reports, interviews etc.), theatre performances (including opera and musicals), videogames, interactive virtual assistants, pedagogical materials and audio books are likely to be of commercial or political interest, and hence likely to be translated. In the case of MMC consisting of audiovisual texts and their translations, current corpus standards dictate that non-digital objects and data be stored in a digital format. Additionally, a written transcription should be provided and added to the audiovisual material, to make verbal elements of speech readily retrievable.

Aspects of multimodal corpus design, building, and exploitation

To develop an MMC that supports AVT research, general management protocols (Hunston 2009) and guidelines for the processing of specific components or features of the corpus are required. A detailed and critical description of the general tasks involved in corpus building is available in Lüdeling and Kytö (2008–2009). What follows is a selection of the main points to be considered specifically in the case of MMC made up of audiovisual texts and their translations. These points will be presented without delving into the technicalities of database architecture, application design, operating systems or browser requirements. Instead, the main focus of this overview concerns what is typically needed to build parallel MMC of original and translated audiovisual texts to assist with translation analysis and, to some extent, with quality assessment. This reflection on the specific complexity of MMC of audiovisual texts and their translations will foreground a range of fundamental methodological issues and enhance awareness of the peculiarities, opportunities and limitations arising in related empirical research.

Among the specific problems concerning parallel corpora for AVT, representativeness is the first to be tackled in the planning stage. The representativeness of MMC for AVT must be established on the basis of a larger array of parameters than the one informing the compilation of unimodal or monolingual corpora. Large institutional corpora of written language are considered as representative when their size exceeds 100 million words (the BNC consists of 100 million words, the DWDS corpora holds more than 2 billion words, while DeReKo exceeds 25 billion words). Institutional corpora of (transcribed) spoken language, on the other hand, are much smaller and none can claim to be fully representative of a given language. This inadequacy of spoken language corpora is obviously due to the amount of time and resources required for transcription and annotation, but also to various difficulties pertaining to the gathering of sufficient speech recordings. Applying the same representativeness criteria to MMC is not feasible: the structural complexity and manifold alignment problems associated with MMC would require an unmanageable volume of material and amount of data processing. Besides, parameters of representativeness should first be set for the various semiotic resources represented in audiovisual texts, including visual, acoustic, kinetic and generally non-verbal information, as described by multimodality theoreticians. But even assuming that the multimodal coverage of an entire given language could be plausibly planned and then seriously attempted, building a corpus meeting these specifications may still not be viable, given the need for huge storage space and potentially uneven quality of the recordings included in the collection. Finally, an MMC supporting research in audio-visual texts and their translations is only as good as the amount of parallel couplets it contains. Insofar as such couplets are rare and often difficult to gather, the goal of achieving representativeness moves definitely out of reach.

MMC for AVT should therefore aim not at general, but simply at achievable representativeness, and consequently restrict the scope of the projected collection to subsets of entities selected by kind of object, genre, time span, cultural impact, seminal potential, etc. Selecting this audiovisual material to be included in a corpus also implies opting for one or more types of multimedia products together with their translated version(s); establishing the number of source or target languages; and choosing one or more types of translation, i.e. subtitling, dubbing, voice-over, etc.

As most projects involving the development of MMC for AVT aim to rigorously document multimodal communication in translation, they should be fed exclusively by multimodal texts and their existing translations, rather than purposefully commissioned ones. Even if such translations are available on the Internet, they often have commercial relevance and are subject to copyright restrictions. The feasibility of including them in a corpus should therefore be carefully examined, and careful consideration should also be given to any other relevant regulations concerning access to and use of the corpus by third parties.

Other tasks concerning data acquisition and maintenance (purchase, web crawling, manual or automatic transcription, spectrographic analysis, exchange of already processed documents, testing and validation rounds, etc.) would deserve more space than this chapter allows. Instead, the remainder of this section focuses on the pre-processing, segmentation, annotation and alignment of data, since the way in which these aspects are managed in the context of MMC differs significantly from unimodal and/or monolingual corpora.

Complex activities such as the acquisition, storage and processing of data generally require special interfaces, particularly when it comes to handling different electronic formats, segmentation, time code allocation, alignment and file annotation. These steps, important as they are, remain hidden to end users and can be performed with one or more dedicated tools such as ELAN, PRAAT, ANVIL, EXMARaLDA, XTrans, etc.—see Schmidt *et al.* 2014. Choosing and adapting such data entry interfaces to handle audiovisual texts requires very accurate planning. In most cases, these tools not only enable the pre-processing of the multimodal files to be entered in the corpus, but they directly facilitate matching query functions once the corpus has been established (see for example Knight *et al.* 2008, Kipp 2014). Regardless of the applications chosen, staff responsible for data entry must be already skilled and/or especially trained not only in the use of these tools, but also in the handling of tags and labels.

The transcription of spoken texts and the internal segmentation of multimodal documents are additional tasks to be performed during the pre-processing of MMC. At a macro-level, the segmentation of texts included in an MMC for AVT obviously concerns generally video files and text files. Inside video files, sound and spoken words may be treated as separate data, extracted and stored in audio files, and represented as spectrograms or other speech waveforms. Text files are obtained through manual transcription, the purchase of original scripts, or with the help of speech recognition software applications, and they can be structured either according to official transcription guidelines for spoken language, or simply by conforming to standard orthography (Bonsignori 2009). Segmentation applies insofar as the components of the source subcorpus must be matched with their target counterparts in the translated versions.

At a lower level, documents contained in a corpus are generally composed of smaller sections and parts, which must be used as reference points when it comes to locating significant elements. Many written documents are already segmentable on the basis of their own internal structure (e.g. summary, introduction, chapters, etc.), and additional segmentation can be performed automatically at paragraph, sentence and even phrase level. This is not possible if the document is a video file: segmentation criteria must be then set by the project manager, e.g. from one camera shot to the next, from one setting to the next, etc.—for an instance of segmentation in a small corpus of subtitled films, see Sotelo Dios 2011: 253. In sound track files, segments can extend from a longer pause in conversation to the next, but other criteria can also be adopted. At all levels, time codes play a decisive role, because after corpus interrogation users will need their 'hits' to be modally complete, i.e. they should bundle (in temporal alignment) all visual, acoustic and written information pertaining to retrieved segments of the multimodal content. Unlike written corpora, in which a query renders its hits inside chunks of text of a pre-defined size, an MMC for AVT is bound to render chunks taken from video and/or audio tracks as well. How to optimize segmentation according to such constraints and requirements is still an open question for MMC designers.

The next distinctive feature of parallel MMC to take care of is alignment: between linguistic data, between linguistic and acoustic/visual data, between linguistic data and spectrograms, between scenes and subtitles, etc. On the temporal axis, alignment normally means synchronizing separate sound and video tracks with the help of time codes, attaching in a separate frame the corresponding lines of written text. Alignment between source and target elements requires both sets to have been previously chunked in the same way, so that source chunks are unequivocally linked to target chunks. Structural analogies to commercial TMs are clear, but this more complex kind of alignment needs dedicated applications. These must ensure that source and target elements can be simultaneously viewed by the user. Of course, peculiar alignment problems arise when target products have been changed with an increase or loss of footage in audiovisual components ('parallelism holes'). Such crucial spots must be handled separately and properly marked.

Annotation is the basis for effective and satisfactory data retrieval, since only annotated features of corpus materials can be specified and extracted in queries. And, of course, only on such a basis is it possible to identify statistical and distributional patterns of retrievable entities efficiently and reliably. There are several layers of annotation, depending on the analysis methodology, nature of documents, scientific or professional approach, previous conventions, existing norms, manual vs. automatic annotation, critical quantities of annotations, sustainable variety of annotation, etc.).

Annotation involves marking up segments of the corpus according to an organized set of tags and labels, each of which delimits the places where a defined feature is found. As a rule, annotation must identify whole documents belonging to the corpus, stating relevant information on, for example, textual genre, author(s), provenance, time of creation, keywords, person or entities involved and much more. This requirement must be met to ensure that references and macro-categories are correctly attributable to lists and samples extracted from the corpus. Many of the labels relating to structure and content of documents can be assigned automatically or semi-automatically, but at lower levels, manual processing by skilled operators is quite often needed. This is one of the most crucial points in the pre-processing of MMC for AVT. Their low-level annotation must deal with more distinctive and fine-grained linguistic, stylistic, thematic, visual or acoustic features than is the case in unimodal corpora. These features are located in the objects at different distances from one another and on different semiotic dimensions. This makes annotation in MMC a crucial task to organize and requires a specific methodology, whose standards are not yet fully developed (for an example of tag used in film audio description, see Jiménez Hurtado and Soler Gallego 2013: 583).

Most importantly, annotation in MMC for AVT may have to be performed on a parallel basis as well, i.e. managing diverging sets of features for source and target elements. Actually, separate linguistic annotation of source and target elements should be performed for written and spoken components of the corpus, since different texts in different languages are involved. This means that, even using a common tag set, a source text chunk would be linguistically and acoustically tagged in a certain way, and its matching target chunk in quite a different way. Furthermore, couplets of matching elements belonging to source and target audiovisual texts may also be visually different, depending on how radically the visual information has been handled in the translation process. The more the visual elements are modified in the target version, the bigger the divergences will be in the annotation of the visual channel. Modifications of the video track are normally kept to a minimum in the case of expensive film or videogame productions, and are likely to consist mostly of the addition or subtraction of available footage. But there are other cases in which they occur more frequently, for instance in multilingual versions of news or documentaries broadcast by internationally acting corporations (e.g. BBC, Euronews, DW, Al Jazeera and the like). When such differences affect both visual and spoken information above a given threshold, there may be doubts as to whether it is still a parallel corpus.

Tags and labels must be planned in advance not only according to norms and conventions. They must also conform to general standards of solidity and consistency, because the

Table 21.1 Elements to be labelled in monolingual, dialogical multimodal audiovisual material.

1	ACOUSTIC CHANNEL
1.1	Spoken language
	1.1.1 Para-verbal signs (not what is said, but how it is said)
	1.1.2 Voice qualities, cadence, inflection, or rate of speech.
	1.1.3 Distinctive sociolinguistic features and their connotations
1.2	Non-verbal acoustic signs
	1.2.1 Music
	1.2.2 Special effects
	1.2.3 Sound arrangements
2	VISUAL CHANNEL
2.1	Iconographic code
	2.1.1 Symbols and icons
2.2	Photographic code
	2.2.1 Colour
	2.2.2 Camera angles and variations
	2.2.3 Focal length of the lenses
	2.2.4 Directorial editing choices
	2.2.5 Luminance and contrast patterns
2.3	Mobility code
	2.3.1 Proxemic and kinesic issues

processing of corpus data takes place through one or more underlying databases, whose internal settings are pre-established and not changeable. With cautious database planning, adding labels at the end of a label tree may be allowed, if they should unexpectedly emerge after the start of the annotation activities. In any case, hierarchy, names and number of labels are governed by strict allocation rules (see e.g. several instances of annotation graphs in Schmidt *et al.* 2014).

Annotation of audiovisual texts in an MMC is in many regards tentative and experimental. One way to plan it could involve merging annotation schemes normally adopted for texts, audio and video documents, including suggestions from recent contributions by multimodality scholars (see Abuczki and Esfandiari 2013 for multimodal dialogue analysis; Maszerowska 2012 and Pérez-González 2014 in translation studies). Table 21.1 features a list of aspects to be labelled, as required for the analysis of 'simple' monolingual, dialogical multimodal material.

This already complex inventory is undoubtedly insufficient for full-fledged annotation. Other sets of labels and tags are equally important for the retrieval and analysis of the verbal components (lexemes, phrases, sentences, paragraphs, but also formulas, phrasemes, word collocations, n-grams, functional units in written and spoken communication, speech acts, puns, idiolects, dialects, regional varieties, fragments in foreign languages, and much more), and can be taken from classical corpora of written and spoken language.

Still more labels and tags are necessary for the management of relevant information concerning situations, contexts, temporal and spatial embedding, locations, cultural entities, or particular objects. It is extremely difficult to establish which and how many visual entities are actually relevant for the analysis of translation processes and the evaluation of translation quality, particularly when a corpus includes classes of visual products as news, fiction, documentaries, etc. Moreover, additional layers of tags may be required by particular translation processes of relevance to the corpus. When, for instance, dubbing or subtitling are involved, dedicated corpora may need mark-up of segments of video-shots in which lip movements are visible, or moments in which more than one person is speaking in the same subtitle frame.

Overall, the total number of tags to be taken into consideration easily goes into the hundreds (for descriptions of very rich tag sets in film corpora see Valentini 2009, Jiménez Hurtado and Soler Gallego 2013). Only a limited number can be handled automatically or semi-automatically, and the vast majority must inevitably be inserted by trained staff according to guidelines issued by the project managers. In projects involving more than one tagging person, intersubjective consistency in tagging non-linguistic entities is often difficult to achieve, given that definitions of numerous relevant phenomena are fuzzy, controversial or incomplete. Consistency among different projects would be even more difficult to guarantee. Tagging films or documentaries, for instance, implies taking note of countless entities, situations and events, distributed across different historical periods, geographical areas and cultural frames. So far, there has been no interdisciplinary agreement on how to code classes of visual objects (other than human figures) that may feature in audiovisual products to be translated. Even suggestions concerning the relevance of visual information in films are still to be transferred into precise tagging schemes. The same applies to classes of situations, interactional encounters between people as well as between persons and other entities, etc. All these elements are potentially relevant, and therefore require tagging, when it comes to checking regularities, constraints and quality in translation decisions and translated products (for examples and discussion of the methodological implications of complex AVT corpora interrogation enabled by rich tagging, see Valentini 2009).

Peculiarities of interrogation interfaces and result visualization will finally be considered briefly. Interrogation procedures generally empower users to specify as many combinations as possible among manually annotated categories together with automatically definable parameters. Since in an MMC there are numerous, heterogeneous annotated entities, particular care must be taken to allow flexible and transparent specifications of data to be retrieved, regardless of how complex a query can become. Extracting information from a richly annotated MMC is a crucial task in different regards. First, for every channel there are specific state-of-the art procedures for displaying query results. New applications developed for large linguistic corpora, for instance, present a significant volume of important linguistic information distributed in many different windows, each of which may contain a table, a diagram, a graph or a word cloud. As seen in current interface models for unimodal monolingual corpora, interrogation can be often refined, narrowed, enlarged and re-structured in subsequent steps. Most importantly, relevant correlations between newly extracted data can be assumed, tested and established at different levels, including statistical distribution, syntactic and semantic patterns, and every kind of collocation or n-gram. These otherwise inaccessible, invaluable findings are frequently made possible by the availability of several windows at the same time. Second, this already wide range of linguistic data in different windows should be managed in light of additional requirements posed by a parallel, i.e. at least bilingual architecture, in which query results should be ideally displayed in parallel windows. Given the physical limitations of computer screens, such simultaneous visualization becomes a very difficult task, if one chooses to accommodate as many interrogation modalities as in state-of-the-art applications (AntConc, ConcGram, Sketch Engine) or reference monolingual corpora (BNC, DWDS and others). Again, such decisions shall be made according to general priorities concerning the intended use of a corpus, so that certain windows displaying translated chunks of verbal and/or visual material may be privileged for simultaneous visualization, and others displaying further information would be presented only on demand or after scrolling down. Third, a query on an MMC shall additionally refer to categories of non-linguistic data, as established in the annotation system. Depending on how many visual and acoustic labels are available, additional display options must be planned and accommodated in dedicated windows. Current multimodal concordances are a first step in this direction, but appropriate solutions for visualizing all these elements are still lacking.

Future trajectory and new debates

As their very low number clearly indicates, building usable MMC for solid empirical research in AVT is undoubtedly more complex and challenging than building unimodal corpora. Many methodological issues still require additional reflection, and acceptable solutions will probably only arise after additional trial-and-error rounds of pilot projects. However, even small and only partially annotated MMC for AVT have proved to be useful as an empirical basis for very many contributions, especially by Spanish and Italian scholars. They can be expected to become a starting point in the future for new and original investigations, beyond the traditional notion of 'screen translation'. They could also be usefully exploited to calibrate to some extent new experimental procedures and tools of automatic annotation, along a path of mutual improvements in an interacting chain between intensive manual and extensive algorithm-driven operations.

Undoubtedly, methodological uncertainty and dependence on time-consuming manual operations put strong constraints on short-term enhancements. Most AVT researchers are well aware of these limitations and are likely to stick to limited multimodal translation corpora for clear-cut purposes (including research on translation quality in specialized domains, advanced training in academic courses, or vocational training for companies and institutions).

Small existing MMC could in turn be assembled in bigger ones, but this option still faces unsolved methodological, technical and financial problems. To name just one, there are few (in some cases, not even one) parallel MMC available for several combinations of widespread languages, so no developments are likely to take place in the near future. Materials for comparable MMC would be easier to find, e.g. resorting to some multilingual TV-channels (as reported in Afli *et al.* 2014), but their usability would be limited to preliminary translation (or adaptation) steps.

Consolidating small MMC into bigger entities also raises issues of consistency. To achieve consistency and uniformity within a single corpus project, a very high price must be paid in terms of working hours, costs and overall control procedures. Consistency among different projects may even prove to be impossible to achieve, because the annotating effort required by academic investigation lies far beyond both the commercial and cooperative assets currently available. To deal with these limitations, it is probably inevitable to reduce the number of tagging operations in which interpersonal subjectivity is most critical, and try to rely as much as possible on automatic procedures. Also in this regard, large and consistent MMC should be developed through academic research in collaboration with big data owners, taking advantage of jointly developed automatic annotation. For now, however, there is a significant clash between what would be desirable to conduct rigorous multimodal analyses and what can realistically be performed manually and/or automatically. Considering the wealth of insights and serendipity that the advent of large corpora unleashed, the consolidation of small MMC into bigger ones would be highly desirable and allow for solid generalization of finding within several fields of descriptive linguistics. A new generation of large(r) MMC, apt to support AVT translation, may arise under certain conditions from vast collections of already available multimodal objects, harvested with advanced crawling techniques that are able to detect appropriate or necessary AV products in web-based repositories. These collections could in the future be made searchable and become at least partially usable as components of MMC for AVT as soon as automated speech recognition and automatic translation (for suitable audiovisual material) are so reliable as to not require extensive editing. Studies in event detection as described e.g. in the Aladdin Project are also expected to provide substantial support for advanced indexing and annotation in MMC.

Summary

This chapter has explored different avenues to enhance MMC for the purposes of AVT research. Until now, research on multimodality has been mostly restricted to face-to-face interaction, without much consideration of visual or acoustic elements in the surrounding situation. From the point of view of AVT and related research, however, it is necessary to consider a very large amount of visual and acoustic element of the situations represented in the objects to be translated. It has therefore been proposed to enhance the notion of multimodality (and MMC) in order to accommodate all translation-relevant audiovisual products. Another kind of enhancement would involve shaping parallel corpus architectures. Unfortunately, multimodality and parallelism dramatically increase the complexity of corpora in a number of respects. In particular, annotation schemes may quickly become unmanageable and query interfaces too complicated. Future multimodal corpora for translation purposes will probably evolve into two types: small corpora for scholarly research, and larger ones for more general purposes. Larger corpora will be dependent on substantial progress in automatic annotation, and probably will have to restrict their annotation schemes to automatically identifiable features.

Further reading

Abuczki, Á. and B. G. Esfandiari (2013) 'An Overview of Multimodal Corpora, Annotation Tools and Schemes', *Argumentum* 9: 86–98. Available online: http://argumentum.unideb.hu/2013-anyagok/kulonszam/01_abuczkia_esfandiari_baiat.pdf [last access 20 December 2017] | *This paper provides a rich and insightful overview of most issues concerning monolingual MMC.*

Lüdeling, A. and M. Kytö (eds) (2008–2009) *Corpus Linguistics. An International Handbook*, 2 volumes. Berlin: Mouton de Gruyter | *This publication focuses on key aspects of corpus building and exploiting.*

Related topics

12 Mediality and audiovisual translation
13 Spoken discourse and conversational interaction in audiovisual translation
17 Multimodality and audiovisual translation: cohesion in accessible films
20 Corpus-based audiovisual translation studies: ample room for development
32 Technologization of audiovisual translation

References

Abuczki, Á. and B. G. Esfandiari (2013) 'An Overview of Multimodal Corpora, Annotation Tools and Schemes', *Argumentum* 9: 86–98. Available online: http://argumentum.unideb.hu/2013-anyagok/kulonszam/01_abuczkia_esfandiari_baiat.pdf [last access 20 December 2017].

Afli, H., L. Barrault and H. Schwenk (2014) 'Multimodal Comparable Corpora for Machine Translation', 7th Workshop on Building and Using Comparable Corpora, *Building Resources for Machine Translation Research*, Reykjavik. Available online: https://comparable.limsi.fr/bucc2014/6.pdf [last access 20 December 2017].

Allwood, J. (2008) 'Multimodal Corpora', in A. Lüdeling and M. Kytö (eds) *Corpus Linguistics. An International Handbook*, Berlin: Mouton de Gruyter, 207–225. New version 2010 available online: https://gupea.ub.gu.se/bitstream/2077/23244/1/gupea_2077_23244_1.pdf [last access 20 December 2017].

Baldry, A. and P. J. Thibault (2008) 'Applications of Multimodal Concordances', *Hermes—Journal of Language and Communication Studies* 41: 11–43.

Bateman, J., J. Delin and R. Henschel (2002) *Multimodality and Empiricism: Methodological Issues in the Study of Multimodal Meaning-making*. GeM project report 2002/01. Available online: www.purl.org/net/gem [last access 20 December 2017].

Bednarek, M. (2015) 'Corpus-assisted Multimodal Discourse Analysis of Television and Film Narratives', in P. Baker and T. McEnery (eds) *Corpora and Discourse Studies*, Basingstoke & New York: Palgrave Macmillan, 63–87.

Bonsignori, V. (2009) 'Transcribing Film Dialogue: From Orthographic to Prosodic Transcription', in M. Freddi and M. Pavesi (eds) *Analysing Audio-visual Dialogue. Linguistic and Translational Insights*, Bologna, CLUEB: 187–200.

Fantinuoli, C. and F. Zanettin (2015) 'Creating and Using Multilingual Corpora in Translation Studies', in C. Fantinuoli and F. Zanettin (eds) *New Directions in Corpus-based Translation Studies*, Berlin: Language Science Press, 1–11.

Foster, M. E. (2007) Issues for Corpus-Based Multimodal Generation. Available online: http://citeseerx.ist.psu.edu/viewdoc/summary?doi=10.1.1.106.125 [last access 20 December 2017].

Gambier, Y. (2006) 'Multimodality and Audiovisual Translation' in *MuTra 2006—Audiovisual Translation Scenarios: Conference Proceedings*. Available online: http://euroconferences.info/proceedings/2006_Proceedings/2006_Gambier_Yves.pdf [last access 20 December 2017].

Hunston, S. (2009) 'Collection Strategies and Design Decisions', in A. Lüdeling and M. Kytö (eds) *Corpus Linguistics. An International Handbook*, Berlin: Mouton de Gruyter, 154–168.

Jiménez Hurtado, C. and S. Soler Gallego (2013) 'Multimodality, Translation and Accessibility: A Corpus-based Study of Audio Description', *Perspectives: Studies in Translatology* (21)4: 577–594.

Journal on Multimodal User Interfaces. Available online: http://link.springer.com/journal/12193 [last access 20 December 2017].

Kipp, M. (2014) 'ANVIL The Video Annotation Research Tool', in G. Durand, U. Gut and G. Kristoffersen (eds) *Handbook of Corpus Phonology*, Oxford: Oxford University Press. Preprint available online: DOI: 10.1093/oxfordhb/9780199571932.013.024 [last access 20 December 2017].

Knight, D. (2011) 'The Future of Multimodal Corpora. O futuro dos corpora modais' *RBLA* (11) 2: 391–415.

Knight, D., S. Adolphs, P. Tennent and R. Carter (2008) 'The Nottingham Multi-Modal Corpus: A Demonstration'. Available online: http://www.cs.nott.ac.uk/~axc/DReSS/LRECw08.pdf [last access 20 December 2017].

Kress, G. and T. van Leeuwen (1996) *Reading Images: The Grammar of Visual Design*, London: Routledge.

López-Cózar Delgado, R. and M. Araki (2005) *Spoken, Multilingual and Multimodal Dialogue Systems: Development and Assessment*, Hoboken: John Wiley & Sons, 229–231. Available online: http://onlinelibrary.wiley.com/doi/10.1002/0470021578.app2/pdf [last access 20 December 2017].

Lüdeling, A. and M Kytö (eds) (2008–2009) *Corpus Linguistics. An International Handbook*, 2 volumes. Berlin: Mouton de Gruyter.

Maszerowska, A. (2012) 'Casting the Light on Cinema. How Luminance and Contrast Patterns Create Meaning', *MonTI* 4: 65–85.

Navarretta, C., E. Ahlsén, J. Allwood, K. Jokinen and P. Paggio (2011) 'Creating Comparable Multimodal Corpora for Nordic Languages', in B. Sandford Pedersen, G. Nešpore and I. Skadiņa (eds) *NODALIDA 2011 Conference Proceedings*, 153–160. Available online: http://dspace.utlib.ee/dspace/bitstream/handle/10062/17302/0Navaretta_Ahlsen_Allwood_etal_33.pdf?sequence=1 [last access 20 December 2017].

Pérez-González, L. (2014) 'Multimodality in Translation and Interpreting Studies', in S. Bermann and C. Porter (eds) *A Companion to Translation Studies*, Chichester: Wiley-Blackwell, 119–131.

Schmidt, T., K. Elenius and P. Trilsbeek (2014) *Multimedia Corpora (Media Encoding and Annotation)*. Available online: http://www.exmaralda.org/files/CLARIN_Standards.pdf [last access 20 December 2017].

Sotelo Dios, P. (2011) 'Using a Multimedia Parallel Corpus to Investigate English-Galician Subtitling'. Available online: http://sli.uvigo.es/arquivos/sdh2011.pdf [last access 20 December 2017].

Valentini, C. (2009) *Creazione e sviluppo di corpora multimediali. Nuove metodologie di ricerca nella traduzione audiovisiva*, Unpublished Doctoral Thesis, Alma Mater Studiorum Università di Bologna. Available online: http://amsdottorato.unibo.it/2125/ [last access 20 December 2017].

Sitography

Aladdin Project: http://multimedia.icsi.berkeley.edu/video-content-analysis/aurora-an-aladdin-project/ [last access 20 December 2017].

AntConc | Freeware corpus analysis toolkit for concordancing and text analysis: http://www.laurenceanthony.net/software/antconc/ [last access 20 December 2017].

ANVIL | Video annotation research tool: http://www.anvil-software.org/ [last access 20 December 2017].

British National Corpus (BNC) | http://www.natcorp.ox.ac.uk/ [last access 20 December 2017].

ConcGram | Phraseological search engine: https://benjamins.com/#catalog/software/cls.1/main [last access 20 December 2017].
DeReKo | Das Deutsche Referenzkorpus: http://www1.ids-mannheim.de/kl/projekte/korpora/ [last access 20 December 2017].
DWDS | Das Wortauskunftssystem zur deutschen Sprache in Geschichte und Gegenwart: https://www.dwds.de/ [last access 20 December 2017].
ELAN | Linguistic annotator: http://www.mpi.nl/corpus/html/elan/index.html [last access 20 December 2017].
EXMARaLDA | Werkzeuge für mündliche Korpora: http://exmaralda.org/en/ [last access 20 December 2017].
PRAAT | Doing phonetics by computer: http://www.fon.hum.uva.nl/praat/ [last access 20 December 2017].
Sketch Engine | Corpus manager and text analysis software: https://www.sketchengine.co.uk/ [last access 20 December 2017].
XTrans | Multi-platform, multilingual, multi-channel transcription tool: https://www.ldc.upenn.edu/language-resources/tools/xtrans [last access 20 December 2017].

22
Eye tracking in audiovisual translation research

Jan-Louis Kruger

Introduction

The object of study in research on audiovisual translation (AVT), the audiovisual text, is a complex polysemiotic text where information is presented simultaneously in a number of semiotic codes (i.e. verbal and non-verbal, visual and auditory codes). The processing of this text involves a variety of cognitive processes. It is therefore understandable that research in this field is very much concerned with the reception of the audiovisual text by various audiences with different needs.

The primary (but not exclusive) goal of all subfields within AVT is to provide or improve access to audiovisual texts to audiences who are either excluded from one or more of the auditory or visual codes, or who only have partial access to these codes. These audiences and their needs are by no means always easy to define. Let us take the example of audio description (AD). Blind audiences only have access to the soundtrack containing the auditory codes, and have to be given access to those elements in the image relevant to their understanding and enjoyment of the text. However, in considering what is relevant in the visual code, and how to present this to the audience, the audio describer has to consider the fact that the audience is made up of individuals with a range of needs. Some have been blind from birth (congenital blindness), whereas others may have lost their sight later in life, significantly impacting on their frames of reference. Congenital blindness, for example, means that an individual would have no memory of sight or colours, whereas, depending on the age of the onset of blindness, other blind individuals may have some memories to draw on in interpreting a scene. Furthermore, significant proportions of the user groups of AD are not totally blind, and have varying degrees of sight.

In the case of subtitling, the user groups who rely on or can benefit from the subtitles range from Deaf viewers (again spanning viewers who lost their hearing at different ages and who have varying levels of reading skills), to hard of hearing viewers (with varying degrees of hearing loss), to viewers who do not understand the language of the original text (in varying degrees), to viewers who have none of these barriers, but who could benefit from same-language subtitles to improve literacy or comprehension. Dubbing is the only form of AVT that really only benefits one group, namely those who cannot understand the language in the original text.

When we are therefore interested in the processing of audiovisual texts, we have to understand how the texts create meaning, and how they are processed by different audiences. The focus of this chapter will be on the processing of the visual codes, in other words both verbal (e.g. text on screen) and non-verbal (e.g. camera angles, editing, objects, etc.) visual elements in these texts, with a particular focus on how an investigation of eye movements can yield valuable information that is relevant to most fields within AVT. For example, in subtitling, the viewer has to divide his or her attention between the subtitles and the rest of the screen, and the meaning is created through a combination of information from the subtitles, the soundtrack and the image (or only the subtitles and the image in the case of Deaf viewers). The main emphasis will be on eye movements during the processing of subtitles, but some reference will also be made to the use of eye tracking for AD.

Eye tracking, or the study of eye movements, is a well-developed research methodology in reading research, psycholinguistic research, translation process research, and also in the field of AVT. In the case of AVT, eye-tracking research became established in the context of subtitle processing even before it had gained prominence within translation studies in the late 1990s.

Eye tracking

According to Findlay (1985: 101–102), '[v]ision is the primary human sense modality. The quantity of information passed along the optic nerve is far greater than that in any other pathway of special sense, and a large percentage of the posterior part of the cerebral cortex is primarily concerned with the analysis of this message'. Given the importance of this modality, it is understandable that researchers have been interested in gaining insights into the human cognitive system, by looking at how people attend to scenes and texts, for more than a century. In the past half a century, eye tracking has become an important experimental method in psycholinguistic research in the study of reading (*cf.* Keating 2014: 69, Rayner 1998), and it is particularly in this research that we find some of the most useful information and methodologies for understanding the processing of subtitles.

Eye tracking, at a basic level, concerns the study of eye movements. In particular, the eye movements that can be detected by an eye tracker provide us with a window on the internal systems of the mind (*cf.* Marchant *et al.* 2009). But applying eye tracking to dynamic scenes such as film is not without problems. On the one hand, the objects being fixated are constantly moving (*cf.* Papenmeier and Huff 2010). On the other hand, any text that appears in film (e.g. subtitles), is on screen for a limited period of time, forcing the reader to adopt reading strategies that differ slightly from those in the reading of static text where the reader is much more in control of the pace of reading (*cf.* Kruger and Steyn 2013).

Information is taken in by the eye in a process that allows light in through the pupil and projects it (upside down) onto the retina (the back of the eyeball). Importantly, we only have full visual acuity in a very small area in our field of vision (the fovea, which comprises less than 2 degrees of the visual field), which means that we constantly have to change the position of our eyes to focus on (or foveate) specific elements of the visual scene (for more details, see Holmqvist *et al.* 2011: 21–24, Liversedge *et al.* 2013). Eye movements consist of short periods of relative inactivity (fixations), followed by rapid movements (saccades) to the next point of fixation. During fixations, visuospatial processing occurs—the eyes collect and take in information. During saccades, however, the eyes do not take in any information, although cognitive processing continues in the brain (see Irwin 2004, Holmqvist *et al.* 2011).

The typical duration of a fixation is between 200 and 300 milliseconds (ms), and that of a saccade between 30 and 80ms (Holmqvist et al. 2011: 23), although there is much more variance than these averages suggest. Rayner (2009), for example, reports differences in fixation duration during different visual activities: the mean fixation duration during reading ranges from 225–250ms during silent reading, to 275–325ms during reading aloud, 260–330ms when looking at a scene (scene perception), and 180–275ms when looking for something specific in a scene (visual search). According to Holmqvist et al. (2011: 382), the difference in fixation duration during different tasks indicates 'functional links between what is fixated and cognitive processing of that item—the longer the fixation, the 'deeper' the processing'. More specifically, the more complicated the task, the longer the fixations become. Likewise, the number of fixations in a particular area tends to increase as the task becomes more complicated (cf. Holmqvist et al. 2011). But even these qualities of fixations have to be approached with caution as different activities require different visual behaviour. Reading, for example, elicits specific patterns of fixations and saccades in a particular order that differ substantially from the more random patterns associated with scene perception and visual search. It is therefore important not to generalize across activities.

By studying the eye movements (including number of fixations and duration of fixations) of viewers watching any form of audiovisual media, researchers can therefore gain an understanding of, or at least glimpses into, the workings of the mind of the audience. However, there has been growing evidence that these two processes (fixating and processing cognitively) are not fully synchronous—often our visual attention precedes the position of our eyes by a fraction of a second, meaning that the eye does not provide a direct window onto our cognitive processes (cf. Irwin 2004). To overcome the fact that knowing where and how viewers look does not always provide direct evidence of their cognitive processing, eye tracking is increasingly used in combination with other data such as comprehension measures, physiological measures like heart rate, retrospective protocols, and even electroencephalography (EEG), which involves the measurement of electrical activity in the brain by means of contacts on the scalp (see, for example, Kruger and Doherty 2016). Together these data are providing us with a picture of human cognitive processing, also in the field of AVT research.

Eye tracking remains a reliable source of information on what viewers look at, and more importantly, how they look at it (how long, in what patterns, with what pupil dilation—all providing pieces to the puzzle of cognitive processing and cognitive load). This chapter will therefore attempt to provide a basic introduction to the principles that underlie this type of research. In particular, the aims will be to give an overview of important trends in studies using eye tracking in the context of AVT, and also to identify the areas that will benefit most from the use of this technology. In striving to reach these aims, the chapter will also discuss the limitations of eye tracking and identify typical pitfalls in the use of eye tracking in terms of scientific rigour related to experimental design, sampling, and statistical analysis. It is just as important to know when to use eye tracking as it is to know when not to use it.

Overview of the use of eye tracking in audiovisual translation research

In the field of AVT, eye tracking gained prominence with the substantial body of work generated in Belgium by Gery d'Ydewalle and colleagues from the 1980s (see, for example, d'Ydewalle et al. 1985, d'Ydewalle et al. 1987, d'Ydewalle and Van Rensbergen 1989, d'Ydewalle et al. 1991, d'Ydewalle and Gielen 1992, d'Ydewalle and Van de Poel 1999, d'Ydewalle and De Bruycker 2007). Since 2010 a number of new studies have appeared using eye tracking in the context of AVT, particularly in subtitling—some of these are Perego *et al.* 2010, Szarkowska *et al.* 2011, Caffrey 2012, Ghia 2012, Bisson *et al.* 2014, Perego 2012, Moran 2012, Krejtz *et al.* 2013, Kruger 2013, Kruger *et al.* 2013, Rajendran *et al.* 2013, Winke *et al.* 2013, Fernández *et al.* 2014, Kruger and Steyn 2014, Kruger *et al.* 2015, Fox 2016, Szarkowska *et al.* 2016, Kruger 2016. Among these, the contributions to the volume on eye tracking and AVT edited by Perego (2012) are significant, and in particular the chapter on the impact of translation strategies on subtitle reading by Ghia, the chapter on the effects of linguistic variation on subtitle perception by Moran, and Caffrey's chapter on using eye tracking to investigate experimental subtitling procedures used in fansubbing.

A number of studies also used eye tracking to investigate the processing of audiovisual texts by sighted viewers in order to inform the field of AD (e.g. Igareda and Maiche 2009, Kruger 2012, Orero and Vilaró 2012, Krejtz *et al.* 2012, Di Giovanni 2014).

The early studies: attention distribution

The bulk of the studies involving eye tracking and AVT in the 1980s and 1990s were conducted in Belgium by Gery d'Ydewalle and colleagues. In the first studies, the main interest was on attention allocation. Findings included that participants fixate only one or two words per subtitle (d'Ydewalle *et al.* 1985), that participants look at the subtitles for about 30 per cent of the presentation time (d'Ydewalle *et al.* 1987), and that genre has an impact on the amount of time spent looking at subtitles with children spending less time looking at subtitles when watching action film than animation (d'Ydewalle and Van Rensbergen 1989). In the latter study, the assumption that reading behaviour is elicited automatically when text appears on screen is introduced, an assumption that is tested and confirmed in later studies. For example, in d'Ydewalle *et al.* (1991) the authors found that participants still read redundant subtitles (L1 subtitles on a film with an L1 soundtrack) 20 per cent of the time.

Slightly later, Jensema and colleagues conducted a rather small-scale research project on the eye movement strategies used by six Deaf viewers when watching captioned television (Jensema *et al.* 2000b), as well as a slightly larger study on the time spent by twenty-three Deaf viewers viewing captions at different speeds (Jensema *et al.* 2000a). Strangely, neither of these studies took any cognisance of the work done in Belgium by d'Ydewalle and colleagues, and both studies are severely limited in terms of the number of participants and the duration of the clips studied. However, since the studies engage with the reception of the users of subtitles it is perhaps useful to note the conclusions. In the first study (2000b), the findings include that people who view a particular video segment have similar eye movements, that adding captions turns the viewing process into more of a reading process (i.e. little time is spent looking at the image), and that higher captioning speed results in an increase in the time reading the captions. In the second study, they find that viewers looked at the captions 84 per cent of the time, at the picture 14 per cent of the time, and outside of the picture 2 per cent of the time. The very high percentage of time spent on the captions in these studies could very well be ascribed to the experimental design where Deaf viewers would have to try to process extremely short video clips without any other contextual or co-textual information.

As the technology and software for analyzing eye movement data improves, the amount of data obtained from eye tracking and the complexity of the research questions have increased. In more recent studies, the attention of researchers has shifted to matters related to the content of subtitles and away from a mere descriptive investigation of viewing behaviour in the presence of subtitles. Furthermore, most studies in the past decade in this area have turned to the use of inferential statistics and away from mere descriptive statistics to make sense of the eye-tracking data.

Subtitles, translation and language

The 2007 study by d'Ydewalle and De Bruycker takes eye-tracking research in AVT to the next level. Again confirming the automatic processing of subtitles, the authors find that 'even when the task does not require linguistic processing of text [e.g. in reversed subtitling where the L1 audio is subtitled into a foreign language], looking at words is almost obligatory' (2007: 203). However, reversed subtitles were skipped more often than standard subtitles (21 per cent vs. 4 per cent), were fixated less (0.59 fixations per word vs. 0.91 fixations per word), and elicited less gaze time (26 per cent vs. 41 per cent of presentation time), indicating significant differences in processing. Furthermore, two-line subtitles elicited more regular reading than one-line subtitles, were skipped less often, and elicited more fixations and fewer regressions (when the viewer makes a saccade back to an earlier location against the direction of reading).

Bisson *et al.* (2014) conducted a similar study, looking at the difference in the processing of standard subtitles (from a foreign language into the first language of the viewer), reversed subtitles (from the first language into a foreign language), and intralingual, or same-language, subtitles. As in d'Ydewalle and De Bruycker's (2007) study, they found that participants read the subtitles regardless of the subtitle condition, but that the participants displayed more regular reading behaviour in the standard condition when they did not understand the language of the soundtrack and had to rely on the subtitles. Bisson *et al.* (2014) found no statistically significant differences between the standard and intralingual conditions in terms of fixation duration, number of fixations, number of skipped subtitles, or number of consecutive fixations in the subtitle area, although the intralingual condition did elicit more attention to the image than the standard condition.

It is perhaps surprising that not many eye-tracking studies have focused on more micro-level processing of the linguistic features of subtitles. Notable exceptions are two studies in Perego's collection on eye tracking in AVT, namely the study by Ghia (2012) who investigated the impact of translation strategies on subtitle reading, and that by Moran (2012) on the effect of linguistic variation on the reception of subtitles. Ghia (2012) looks at the reading behaviour of Italian intermediate learners of English when watching a clip subtitled from English into Italian using either a literal or a non-literal translation strategy. In this study, the main focus was on attention dynamics when viewers look at subtitled film—a particularly complex issue due to the constantly changing image and the resultant changes in the importance of different sources of information. Ghia makes the obvious but long overdue link between eye-tracking studies of reading in the context of static texts, and the reading of subtitles. She calls attention to psycholinguistic studies on reading that have shown that 'saccades and fixations are affected by a series of both linguistic and contextual factors', including 'linguistic variables such as word class, length, and morphological complexity', and 'semantic-pragmatic features of texts' (Ghia 2012: 158). In order to investigate the impact of translation strategies on subtitle reading she considers regressions, and deflections (i.e. shifts between the subtitle and the image vertically). In terms of regressions, she did not find any significant difference between the two translation strategies, although linguistic features such as word length and frequency did result in increased regressions as is the case in static reading. However, she did find significantly more deflections in the presence of non-literal translation. In other words, non-literal language caused the readers to switch their visual attention more often between the subtitle text and the image, indicating a degree of confusion. On this basis she concludes that subtitle reading is indeed affected by translation and translation-specific features (2012: 177).

Moran's study (2012) focuses on the effects of word frequency and lexical cohesion on the cognitive effort required by the viewer to process the text as a whole. By showing that variables of low frequency (i.e. words that the typical reader would encounter less frequently) and low cohesion within the subtitle (in spite of co-occurring with shorter subtitle length) result in higher processing effort, she therefore finds a contradiction of the subtitling norm of condensing the dialogue and reducing the characters during subtitling. Cohesion in particular is an important consideration due to the fact that during subtitle reading, unlike during static reading, the viewer cannot refer back to earlier parts of the text to establish cohesion. Her measures included mean fixation duration as an indication of cognitive effort (finding longer mean fixation durations on subtitles in the presence of low-frequency words as well as low-coherence subtitles). Although this study was limited in terms of the number of participants, it explains the limitations of word frequency and cohesion thoroughly, and identifies global trends that can be investigated in more detail as methodologies are refined to allow for the investigation of individual words or linguistic features in a more robust manner across large numbers of subtitles without having to revert to manual inspection.

Audience and language

Winke *et al.* (2013) turn their attention to the impact of different relations between the language of the film and that of the audience on subtitle viewing, particularly in the context of language learning. Their study takes eye-tracking research in the context of static reading as the starting point for a discussion of the reading of different languages, building on the small number of eye-tracking studies that have investigated foreign language processing (*cf.* Winke *et al.* 2013: 257–258). Their study in particular responds to d'Ydewalle and De Bruycker's (2007) study and that of Bisson *et al.* (2014), with the difference that they are less interested in the difference between standard (FL audio with L1 subtitles), reversed (L1 audio with FL subtitles) and intralingual (L1 audio with L1 subtitles) subtitling, and more in the difference between the processing of subtitles in different L2 languages by studying the eye movements of learners of these languages. In addition to finding a high percentage of time spent reading subtitles (68 per cent), they find significant differences between the time learners of Arabic spent reading subtitles and that spent by learners of Russian or Spanish. Learners of Chinese spent less time on the subtitles when the content was familiar. On the whole, learners of Russian and Spanish and learners of Arabic and Chinese displayed different reading behaviour, indicating the influence of the distance between the L1 and the L2 on reading, with the time spent processing subtitles increasing as the distance between L1 and L2 increases. Limitations of the study acknowledged by the authors include the fact that the time it takes to acquire languages further from the L1 (e.g. English students learning Chinese and Arabic in this study), inevitably means that the levels of language proficiency were rather different. Also, the different alphabets and characters make it harder to make comparisons between the languages. Unfortunately, the study does not report on fixation durations, as that may have yielded more useful information, and furthermore, the fact that saccades are not considered in spite of the authors identifying the fact that saccadic movements differ between the reading of these languages, also leaves a number of unanswered questions.

Subtitle presentation rate

The speed at which subtitles are presented (normally measured in words per minute or wpm, or in characters per second or cps) has been the subject of a few studies, not least because this has significant implications for the amount of reduction that has to be done to allow sufficient display time. Although Jensema *et al.* (2000b) found only a marginal difference in the amount of time allocated by Deaf viewers to the subtitle area when subtitles were presented at a rate of 100wpm (82 per cent) and when subtitles were presented at 180wpm (86 per cent) this remains an area that warrants more attention.

In their study, Szarkowska *et al.* (2011) found that Deaf viewers spent just under 70 per cent of the time reading verbatim subtitles, which drops to around 60 per cent for standard subtitles and 50 per cent for edited subtitles (a much higher range in low to high presentation speed than in the earlier study). They found a similar range in the hard of hearing group from around 60 per cent in the verbatim condition to under 50 per cent in the edited condition, but very little difference between the three conditions for the hearing audience. In terms of the dwell time on the subtitles, they find that the edited subtitles were relatively the easiest to comprehend for all groups with the least dwell time, but that the deaf group had significantly longer dwell time on the verbatim subtitles than hearing participants (but no longer than hard of hearing participants). For all three groups the verbatim subtitles elicited significantly more fixations. Interestingly, they found that Deaf viewers displayed different reading behaviour with more fixations and fewer deflections between subtitle and image than the other groups.

In a later study (Szarkowska *et al.* 2016), they again investigated the difference between verbatim and edited subtitles, but this time they found no significant difference within groups between verbatim and edited subtitles, although the difference between groups on verbatim and edited subtitles remained. In this study they only offered subtitles at two presentation rates, namely 12cps and 15cps (or around 140wpm and 180wpm respectively), and found no significant differences within any of the three groups (deaf, hard of hearing and hearing) between the two rates in dwell time.

In spite of the apparent inconsistencies in the findings, which should signal that more studies are required to establish the impact of presentation rate more comprehensively, broadcasters sometimes abuse preliminary findings—indicating that verbatim subtitles do not pose any additional cognitive effort and can be processed effectively. What we have to bear in mind is that film is a polysemiotic text, and even if viewers can read the subtitles at a higher rate, this does not mean that they have sufficient time also to explore the primary visual information in the image.

Romero-Fresco (2015) specifically refers to the notion of viewing speed, as opposed to presentation speed or reading speed, which also takes into account the time for processing the other semiotic signs in the audiovisual material. He based his findings on an extensive eye-tracking experiment and found that at a speed of 120wpm, viewers spent approximately 60 per cent of the viewing time on the image and 40 per cent on the subtitle. At 150wpm viewers divided their attention equally between image and subtitles. When the speed was increased to 180wpm, viewers started spending less time on the image (between 30 per cent and 40 per cent), and more on the subtitles (between 60 per cent and 70 per cent). At 200wpm, viewers only spent 20 per cent of their viewing time looking at the image.

Subtitle rules and cognitive processing

Other than presentation rate, the rules, conventions and guidelines for subtitling can also be interrogated by using eye tracking to study viewers' eye movements. One such study was done by Perego *et al.* (2010), who investigated, among other things, the impact of line segmentation on eye movements and comprehension. They compared the fixation count, total fixation time and mean fixation duration as well as the number of shifts between the subtitle area and the image when participants viewed well-segmented subtitles to when they viewed ill-segmented subtitles. Although they found no differences between the two conditions in terms of fixation count, total fixation duration and shifts, they did find that participants' fixations were statistically significantly longer in the ill-segmented condition. Although the authors do not consider this difference to be particularly important due to the small magnitude of the difference (around 12ms), the impact of poor line segmentation does therefore induce significantly higher cognitive load. A limitation of the study is that a very small number of subtitles was investigated (28 in total), and that the line segmentations were manipulated only within subtitles (i.e. the subtitles still largely contained sense units, and did not split sense units between successive subtitles). The study primarily investigated the cognitive effectiveness of subtitle processing by testing not only comprehension, but also the processing of visuals in the presence of subtitles, and concludes that the cognitive processing of subtitles is effective.

Investigating different types of line segmentation or text chunking produced in live subtitling created through respeaking (i.e. using speech recognition software), Rajendran *et al.* (2013) compared no segmentation (where words keep appearing until the subtitle area is full before the next subtitle starts the same process), chunking by phrase (phrases appearing one by one on a single line), word-by-word presentation, and chunking by sentence. Looking at gaze points (using more lenient algorithms than conventionally used to define fixations) as well as 'saccadic crossovers' or revisits, they found that the word-by-word condition elicited more gaze points and also resulted in more vertical shifts to the image than the other conditions. The limitations of this study include the very short video clips used as well as the fact that the subtitles were displayed without sound to hearing participants.

Krejtz *et al.* (2013) investigated another subtitling rule, namely that subtitles should not remain on screen over a shot change, as it will induce re-reading of the subtitle which will be perceived as having changed with the image. Although they find that most viewers do not re-read the subtitles after the shot change, they did establish that about 3 per cent of viewers did re-read the subtitles, and about 30 per cent of viewers returned their gaze to the beginning of the subtitle after the shot change even if they soon realized that it was the same text and then resumed their reading. They also found that shifts from the subtitle to the image were significantly higher after a shot change than before, which seems to suggest that the reading process was interrupted, even if it did not result in re-reading. Another indication of the increased cognitive cost associated with subtitles that stay on screen over shot changes, is the fact that the first fixation duration after a shot change for those who returned to the beginning of the subtitle was significantly longer.

Breaking the rules

But of course not all subtitles adhere to the norms and conventions. The rise of fansubbing which employs many experimental techniques and routinely break with conventions, as well as other examples of films that test the boundaries of conventions has resulted in attention to such deviations from scholars using eye tracking. A handful of eye-tracking studies investigate viewing behaviour in the presence of non-standard subtitles. Caffrey (2012), for example, draws on the dependent variables used by d'Ydewalle and De Bruycker (2007), namely percentage skipped subtitles (i.e. subtitles that were not looked at), percentage gaze time in subtitles (i.e. the time viewers looked at the subtitles as a percentage of the time the subtitle was displayed), mean fixation duration, and word fixation probability (the probability that any individual word would be fixated at least once, calculated by dividing the number of fixations in the subtitle by the number of words in the subtitle), and adds median pupil size for pupillometric data. Pupil size has been established as a measure of cognitive effort, with larger pupil size indicating more effort. His study focuses on the impact of pop-up glosses used in the fansubbing of Japanese *anime* subtitled into English. His findings include that the presence of a pop-up gloss resulted in a higher number of skipped subtitles, and a lower percentage gaze time in the subtitle area, lower mean fixation duration, and lower word fixation probability. Similar to d'Ydewalle and De Bruycker's findings in 2007, Caffrey finds that one-line subtitles are significantly more likely to be skipped in the presence of pop-up glosses. His use of pupillometric data yields findings that suggest higher cognitive effort when both two-line subtitles and pop-up glosses are on screen, although this measure is notoriously unreliable in reading as well as in texts where the luminosity varies since the pupil may respond to the intensity of the light by contracting, which is not related to cognitive effort.

Fox (2016) investigates the processing of integrated titles, a form of subtitling where the titles are placed on the screen in positions that would require less effort from the viewer to process, such as close to where their eyes would naturally be such as the current speaker, and also integrating the titles more aesthetically with the image. In her study she addresses the questions whether individual placement and design of (sub)titles have an impact on reading time, time on the image, saccade length between titles and focal points, and overall viewing experience. Her study also uses eye tracking to identify focal points in a film in order to locate the optimal position for title placement, thereby adding another process element to the use of eye tracking. She finds statistically significantly shorter reading time for the integrated titles when compared to the reading time for traditional subtitles, and also statistically significantly more time for exploring the image in the presence of integrated titles. The study provides empirical support for an innovative form of integrated titles where the titles are placed in such a way that they complement the image, and minimize the effort required of the viewer.

Eye tracking and audio description

Eye tracking can also yield valuable information in the field of AD. The main challenge in AD is to understand how sighted viewers make sense of what they see—what they look at on screen in what sequence and in what manner, and how that relates to their interpretation of the film, to allow for better AD. Vilaró *et al.* (2012), for example, investigate the impact of sound on visual attention distribution, finding that the manipulation of the soundtrack influences where people look, and therefore also presents an important source of information to be taken into account in AD.

Likewise, Kruger (2012) combines the use of eye tracking with an analysis of viewer constructions of the narrative to provide information that could be beneficial in determining what should be included in AD. Using dwell time, fixation count and glance counts to specific areas of interest, and comprehension scores, he found a positive correlation between higher comprehension scores and glances to specific areas that were central to an understanding of the narrative, but were not very visually salient. In particular, this study points to the importance of top-down cognitive processes where viewers direct their eyes at particular areas on the screen to get narrative information, as opposed to bottom-up cognitive processes where the eyes are drawn to areas on the screen because of factors external to the viewer. Orero and Vilaró (2012), in a similar vein, use eye tracking to investigate whether viewers attend to minor details, and whether these details should therefore be audio described. They find that all participants look at the same regions in the same order, but their results concerning the importance of minor details are inconclusive. Taken together with the study by Kruger (2012), the study could, however, be seen as adding evidence that minor details only become important to AD when they are important to the central narrative of the film. Again, like the previous two studies, Di Giovanni (2014) uses eye tracking to identify visual priorities of sighted individuals, but then goes further to use these to inform the audio description. When comparing the visual-priority-derived AD to conventional AD, she finds significant benefits.

In the context of AD, eye-tracking research to date tended to use predominantly qualitative data obtained from heat maps although some of the studies mentioned also use quantitative data. The complexity of the visual information presented in film, however, makes eye-tracking data extremely difficult to interpret if the goal is to obtain information on the cognitive processing of the image. It is very tempting to use heat maps (visualizing where the majority of fixations were made by using shades of red and orange and yellow, providing very convincing red blots on the screen where most viewers attended) or focus maps (that do the same except that they blur those areas of the screen that did not receive much attention and bring into focus areas that received more attention). However, these maps can be misleading as they tend to be an accumulation of eye-tracking data across a number of frames visualized on the last frame. This is confirmed by the fact that studies comparing eye-tracking data to comprehension data often produce inconclusive results, signalling that current conventions in AD to focus on the description of visually salient elements may need to be revisited.

What further complicates the use of eye-tracking data for AD is the fact that there are many features in film that elicit visual attention automatically (i.e. bottom-up visual attention that is not under the cognitive control of the viewer), such as contrast, movement, faces (specifically eyes and mouths in close-up shots), and text on screen. In other words, viewers will be looking at these features involuntarily, making it very hard to distinguish between automatic viewing behaviour and viewing behaviour that is under the cognitive control of the viewer (or top-down attention). Nevertheless, eye tracking can give many important insights into the processing of audiovisual texts, insights that will doubtlessly be sought increasingly with this methodology in years to come.

Eye-tracking measures used in audiovisual translation research

As should be evident from the discussion above, different eye-tracking studies utilize slightly different measures that will be summarized in this section. As this methodology becomes more commonplace in the field of AVT research, it is important to start using standardized methodologies and terminology. Most eye-tracking measures relate to fixations, although there are a few measures that also include saccades. Since qualitative measures obtained through the use of heat maps and focus maps really only provide the starting point for more rigorous quantitative work, they will not be discussed here. In the next paragraphs, I will discuss some of the most common eye-tracking measures that have been used in studying the processing of subtitles beyond the mere distribution of attention between the subtitle area and the image area.

The valuable contributions made by d'Ydewalle and colleagues provided the first attempts at investigating the way in which subtitles are processed by viewers. The 2007 study discussed above identified some of the most important measurements in eye-tracking research in this field that remain the mainstay of this methodology for investigating eye movement in the presence of subtitles. In particular, d'Ydewalle and De Bruycker identify the following variables:

- percentage of skipped subtitles (i.e. the percentage of subtitles that did not receive any fixations or were not looked at by a viewer);
- latency time (i.e. the time between the appearance of the subtitle and the first fixation in the subtitle);
- percentage time in subtitles (also called percentage dwell time including fixations and saccades, i.e. the total time spent in the subtitle as a percentage of the time the subtitle was displayed—also called percentage dwell time in other studies);
- word fixation probability (i.e. the probability that a word would be fixated at least once);
- saccade amplitude in degrees and characters (also called saccade length, i.e. the distance between two consecutive fixations);
- percentage regressive eye movements (i.e. the percentage of times the saccades between consecutive fixations went against the direction of reading namely from right to left);
- number of back and forth shifts (also called revisits to the subtitle area, and referring to the number of times the participant shifted their gaze back and forth between subtitle and image).

D'Ydewalle and De Bruycker point out that they could not compute a measure of gaze for the simple reason that 'eye-movement data could not be mapped onto the individual words, but only onto the subtitle area as a whole' (2007: 199). This drawback means that it is not possible to calculate reading statistics when investigating subtitles because the subtitle text is part of the image rather than text that can be chunked automatically into individual words. In the study of static reading, by contrast, software has been developed to chunk words automatically into individual areas of interest and then to calculate various reading statistics. The fact that this software cannot be used for subtitles, means that eye-tracking research on subtitle processing has traditionally been a particularly time-consuming task, or could not really move beyond the study of the subtitle area as opposed to the words in the subtitle.

In her doctoral thesis, Specker (2008) investigates subtitle reading by looking at fixation counts, mean fixation duration and successive fixations before inspecting the fixation plots for individual subtitles. This methodology yields very rich data, taking into account the multimodal nature of the text, but still does not give a useful method for investigating the reading of a large number of subtitles as it relies on the manual inspection of scan fixation plots or scan paths. Ghia (2012) looks at regressions in the subtitle area and deflections to the subtitle area to study subtitle reading, whereas Moran (2012) focuses primarily on mean fixation duration, again not really relating the eye movements to the reading process.

Bisson *et al.* (2014) investigate the processing of subtitles in different conditions by looking at the following eye-tracking measures in the subtitle area:

- total fixation duration (i.e. the sum of the duration of all the fixations in the subtitle area);
- number of fixations (i.e. the sum of all the individual fixations in the subtitle area);

- average fixation duration (i.e. the total fixation duration divided by the number of fixations);
- number of skipped subtitles (as explained above);
- proportion of consecutive fixations (i.e. the percentage of fixations that were preceded by another fixation in the subtitle area).

The last measure in particular is intended to be a measure of reading behaviour based on the assumption that a higher proportion of consecutive fixations would indicate a higher degree of (continuous) reading, whereas the word fixation probability of d'Ydewalle and De Bruycker (2007) rather measures the probability that all the words in the subtitle were fixated. Although both these measures provide a useful quantification of reading behaviour, they lack nuance for investigating the actual reading of specific subtitles.

Winke *et al.* (2013) use a variation on the percentage time in subtitles (used by d'Ydewalle and De Bruycker 2007 and d'Ydewalle *et al.* 1991) or percentage dwell time (used by Kruger and Steyn 2014), namely the total fixation duration as percentage of the time the subtitle was displayed. Although they say that this measure is used in order to compare their results with that of d'Ydewalle and colleagues rather than the percentage of number of fixations on the areas of interest used in other studies, they do not, like the three studies mentioned above, include saccade duration, somewhat undermining the comparison. They also look at mean fixation duration as many of the other studies discussed here.

This brings us to the 2014 study by Kruger and Steyn which introduces a reading index for dynamic texts (RIDT). This measure makes it possible to determine the extent to which a subtitle was read by presenting an index of the reading that takes place in individual subtitles based on the following:

- Number of unique fixations per standard word. Unique fixations exclude those fixations that are so close to previous fixations that they could not be considered to add to the processing but are rather refixations, as well as excluding fixations following regressions where the eyes moved back to a word that has already been processed previously. Standard words use a standardized word count calculated from the number of characters in the subtitle divided by the average number of characters per word across the video as a whole.
- Average forward saccade length as a function of the standard word length—excluding saccades between refixations and also saccades that are so long that words between successive fixations were skipped. This index provides a way to obtain large-scale data on the reading of subtitles over extended text using eye-tracking measures. It must be noted, however, that all eye tracking yields a large volume of data.

Depending on the research question, the most useful eye-tracking measures for research in AVT can therefore be summarized as follows:

- Mean fixation duration: This measure provides a useful index of the processing effort, but should be used only to compare similar activities (e.g. reading of different types of subtitles and not reading to scene perception due to the fact that the eyes behave very differently when reading, which is a structured activity, than when exploring a visual scene).
- Dwell time: This provides a measure of the total time viewers spent looking at a particular area of interest, including both fixations and saccades, and is therefore a useful measure of attention allocation.

- Number of fixations per word: This is particularly useful when an attempt is made to measure the extent to which subtitles were processed, although a more nuanced measure would take into account refixations and regressions.
- Average forward saccade length: Like the number of fixations per word, this measure makes it possible to determine whether viewers performed regular reading or whether they skipped words.
- Glance count: This measure gives an indication of the number of times viewers shifted their eyes between different areas on the screen (e.g. between the image and the subtitles).
- Number of skipped subtitles: This is a fairly rough indication of how many subtitles were not even noticed by viewers, but should be considered together with other measures.
- RIDT (reading index for dynamic texts): This measure provides a useful quantification of the extent to which subtitles were read.

Using these measures, researchers can investigate a wide range of issues such as:

- the impact of linguistic and translation features on the processing of subtitles;
- the impact of user-specific qualities such as language proficiency, educational level, degree of hearing, etc. on subtitle processing;
- the impact of subtitle-specific qualities such as presentation speed, layout or line division, font size and style, position, and other subtitling guidelines such as the position of subtitles in relation to visual boundaries such as shot changes on the processing of subtitles.

Future trajectories

In the next decade the attention in AVT is bound to shift from research questions concerned with the impact of subtitles on comprehension, cognitive load, and attention distribution (as well as questions on the attention distribution of film viewers for AD), to research questions that are more aligned with research in other fields such as psycholinguistics and cognitive science. By now it is becoming evident that the basic questions have been answered, and the full potential of eye-tracking methodologies should be harnessed to interrogate various aspects associated with subtitling and AD conventions and guidelines, and with the utilization of subtitles and AD in education, therapy and other fields.

In the case of AD, subtitling has already yielded a wealth of information on the way sighted audiences view audiovisual texts, and where they get the most relevant visual information that can be utilized in creating AD that better produces an equivalent experience to blind and partially sighted audiences. With early indications that both subtitling and AD can be beneficial in focussing the attention of viewers with specific cognitive disorders, eye tracking in this domain will certainly gain momentum. Likewise, although many studies have shown that subtitles can be beneficial in terms of literacy, language proficiency, comprehension, and therefore in various educational contexts, future research will need to engage with a deeper understanding on which qualities of language and of the language of subtitles contribute to these benefits. Eye tracking will remain an important tool in this regard. However, due to the fact that eye tracking only offers an indirect indication of cognitive processing, methodologies employing eye tracking will have to be combined with methodologies such as EEG that could yield valuable online information on cognitive processing, particularly when combined with eye tracking.

As technology improves and becomes more user friendly and more affordable, eye-tracking studies are set to increase in the coming decades. In particular, with more sophisticated algorithms and more powerful computers, it is already becoming possible to perform much more large-scale eye-tracking studies with bigger numbers of participants resulting in more robust findings. However, there is also a need for researchers to use standardized methodologies and terminology and to report their experimental design in sufficient detail to allow for the replication of studies that will move the field closer to scientifically responsible and robust findings.

Summary

Using eye tracking in AVT research provides a powerful methodology for understanding how audiences process the audiovisual text. Particularly in subtitling, eye tracking can yield very detailed information on whether or how thoroughly viewers read the subtitles, which words or segments they looked at more, and how they switched their attention between the subtitles and the image. For this reason, eye tracking has become an indispensable tool in experimental research on AVT.

As an objective instrument for measuring visual attention distribution when viewers process the various visual signs contained in an audiovisual text, eye tracking can yield valuable information on how text and image are processed. It can help researchers determine how text-specific qualities such as subtitle style, presentation speed and line division impact on the effective processing of subtitles. It can also help us to understand how viewer-specific qualities such as language proficiency and hearing impact on subtitle processing. Also in the case of AD, eye tracking holds tremendous potential for helping us understand how sighted viewers process different visual codes, which could be used in decisions on which parts of the visual code are more important for AD.

In this chapter an overview is given of the most prominent studies in the field of AVT that have used eye tracking to look at attention distribution, language and translation of subtitles, the language of the audience, the presentation speed and other rules and conventions in subtitling, non-standard subtitles that break with conventions, and also AD. From these studies it becomes clear that eye-tracking research is becoming much more rigorous and provides a scientific tool that has become almost indispensable to AVT researchers. The chapter concludes with a summary of the most important eye-tracking measurements that are used in AVT research before sketching a few future trajectories in this approach.

Further reading

Holmqvist, K., M. Nyström, R. Andersson, R. Dewhurst, H. Jarodzka and J. van de Weijer (2011) *Eye Tracking: A Comprehensive Guide to Methods and Measures.* Oxford: Oxford University Press | *This is a definitive book on eye-tracking methodology with detailed discussions not only of the more technical aspects of eye tracking, but also of experimental design, equipment and data analysis.*

Irwin, D. E. (2004) 'Fixation Location and Fixation Duration as Indices of Cognitive Processing', in J. M. Henderson and F. Ferreira (eds) *The Interface of Language, Vision, and Action: Eye Movements and the Visual World*, New York, NY: Psychology Press, 105–133 | *This chapter provides a valuable discussion of the difference between attention allocation and cognitive processing.*

Doherty, S. and J. L. Kruger (2018) 'The Development of Eye Tracking in Empirical Research on Subtitling and Captioning,' in T. Dwyer, C Perkins, S. Redmund and J Sita (eds) *Seeing into Screens: Eye Tracking and the Moving Image*, New York: Bloomsbury, 46–64 | *This chapter charts the development of the usage of eye tracking in the context of empirical research on subtitling and captioning, including foreign and same-language subtitling and captioning. It forms a critique of the eye-tracking measures and methodologies in this field of research.*

Liversedge, S. P., I. D. Gilchrist and S. Everling (eds) (2013) *The Oxford Handbook of Eye Movements.* Oxford: Oxford University Press | *Like Holmqvist et al. (2011), this handbook provides valuable and comprehensive background information on eye-movement research.*

Perego, E. (ed.) (2012) *Eye Tracking in Audiovisual Translation,* Rome: Aracne | *This is a collection of groundbreaking studies in AVT using eye tracking.*

Related topics

5 Voice-over: practice, research and future prospects
6 Subtitling for deaf and hard of hearing audiences: moving forward
8 Audio description: evolving recommendations for usable, effective and enjoyable practices
14 Psycholinguistics and perception in audiovisual translation
17 Multimodality and audiovisual translation: cohesion in accessible films
23 Audiovisual translation and audience reception
31 Accessible filmmaking: translation and accessibility from production
32 Technologization of audiovisual translation

References

Bisson, M. J., W. Van Heuven, K. Conklin, and R. Tunney (2014) 'Processing of Native and Foreign Language Subtitles in Films: An Eye Tracking Study', *Applied Psycholinguistics* 35(2): 399–418.

Caffrey, C. (2012) 'Using an Eye-Tracking Tool to Measure the Effects of Experimental Subtitling Procedures on Viewer Perception of Subtitled AV Content', in E. Perego (ed.) *Eye Tracking in Audiovisual Translation*, Rome: Aracne, 223–258.

Di Giovanni, E. (2014) 'Visual and Narrative Priorities of the Blind and Non-Blind: Eye Tracking and Audio Description', *Perspectives: Studies in Translatology* 22(1): 136–153.

Doherty, S. and J. L. Kruger (2018) 'The Development of Eye Tracking in Empirical Research on Subtitling and Captioning,' in T. Dwyer, C Perkins, S. Redmund and J. Sita (eds) *Seeing into Screens: Eye Tracking and the Moving Image*, New York: Bloomsbury, 46–64.

d'Ydewalle, G. and W. De Bruycker (2007) 'Eye Movements of Children and Adults while Reading Television Subtitles', *European Psychologist* 12: 196–205.

d'Ydewalle, G. and I. Gielen (1992) 'Attention Allocation with Overlapping Sound, Image, and Text', in K. Rayner (ed.) *Eye Movements and Visual Cognition: Scene Perception and Reading*, New York: Springer-Verlag, 415–427.

d'Ydewalle, G. and M. van de Poel (1999) 'Incidental Foreign-Language Acquisition by Children Watching Subtitled Television Programs', *Journal of Psycholinguistic Research* 28: 227–244.

d'Ydewalle, G. and J. van Rensbergen (1989) 'Developmental Studies of Text-Picture Interactions in the Perception of Animated Cartoons with Text', in H. Mandl and J. R. Levin (eds) *Knowledge Acquisition from Text and Pictures*, North-Holland: Elsevier, 233–248.

d'Ydewalle, G., P. Muylle and J. van Rensbergen (1985) 'Attention Shifts in Partially Redundant Information Situations', in R. Groner, G. W. McConkie and C. Menz (eds) *Eye Movements and Human Information Processing*, North-Holland: Elsevier, 375–384.

d'Ydewalle, G., C. Praet, K. Verfaillie and J. van Rensbergen (1991) 'Watching Subtitled Television: Automatic Reading Behavior', *Communication Research* 18: 650–665.

d'Ydewalle, G., J. Van Rensbergen and J. Pollet (1987) 'Reading a Message when the Same Message is Available Auditorily in Another Language: The Case of Subtitling', in J. K. O'Reagan and A. Lévy Schoen (eds) *Eye Movements: From Physiology to Cognition*, Amsterdam: Elsevier Science Publishers B.V., 313–321.

Fernández, A., A. Matamala and A. Vilaró (2014) 'The Reception of Subtitled Colloquial Language in Catalan: An Eye-Tracking Exploratory Study', *Vigo International Journal of Applied Linguistics* 11: 63–80.

Findlay, J. M. (1985) 'Saccadic Eye Movements and Visual Cognition', *L'année psychologique* 85(1): 101–135.

Fox, W. (2016) 'Integrated Titles—An Improved Viewing Experience?', in S. Hansen-Schirra and S. Bruca (eds) *Translation: Computation, Corpora, Cognition* 4(1): 5–30.

Ghia, E. (2012) 'The Impact of Translation Strategies on Subtitle Reading', in E. Perego (ed.) *Eye Tracking in Audiovisual Translation*, Roma: Aracne Editrice, 155–182.

Holmqvist, K., M. Nyström, R. Andersson, R. Dewhurst, H. Jarodzka and J. van de Weijer (2011) *Eye Tracking: A Comprehensive Guide to Methods and Measures*, Oxford: Oxford University Press.

Igareda, P. and A. Maiche (2009) 'Audio Description of Emotions in Films Using Eye Tracking', *Proceedings of the Symposium on Mental States, Emotions and their Embodiment*, 6–9 April 2009, Edinburgh, Scotland.

Irwin, D. E. (2004) 'Fixation Location and Fixation Duration as Indices of Cognitive Processing', in J. M. Henderson and F. Ferreira (eds) *The Interface of Language, Vision, and Action: Eye Movements and the Visual World*, New York, NY: Psychology Press, 105–133.

Jensema, C., R. S. Danturthi, and R. D. Burch (2000a) 'Time Spent Viewing Captions on Television Programs', *American Annals of the Deaf* 145: 464–468.

Jensema, C. J., E. I. Sharkawy, R. S. Danturthi, R. Burch and D. Hsu (2000b) 'Eye Movement Patterns of Captioned Television Viewers', *American Annals of the Deaf* 145: 275–285.

Keating, G. D. (2014) 'Eye-tracking with Text', in J. Jegerski and B. Van Patten (eds) *Research Methods in Second Language Psycholinguistics*, London & New York: Routledge, 69–92.

Krejtz, K., I. Krejtz, A. Duchowski, A. Szarkowska and A. Walczak (2012) 'Multimodal Learning with Audio Description: An Eye Tracking Study of Children's Gaze During a Visual Recognition Task', *Proceedings of the ACM Symposium on Applied Perception* (SAP'12), ACM, New York, NY, USA, 83–90.

Krejtz, I., A. Szarkowska and K. Krejtz (2013) 'The Effects of Shot Changes on Eye Movements in Subtitling', *Journal of Eye Movement Research* 6(5): 1–12.

Kruger, J. L. (2012) 'Making Meaning in AVT: Eye Tracking and Viewer Construction of Narrative', *Perspectives: Studies in Translatology* 20(1): 67–86.

Kruger, J. L. (2013) 'Subtitles in the Classroom: Balancing the Benefits of Dual Coding with the Cost of Increased Cognitive Load', *Journal for Language Teaching* 47(1): 29–53.

Kruger, J. L. (2016) 'Psycholinguistics and Audiovisual Translation', *Target* 28(2): 276–287.

Kruger, J. L and S. Doherty (2016) 'Measuring Cognitive Load in the Presence of Educational Video: Towards a Multimodal Methodology', *Australasian Journal of Educational Technology* 32(6): 19–31.

Kruger, J. L. and F. Steyn (2014) 'Subtitles and Eye Tracking: Reading and Performance', *Reading Research Quarterly* 49(1): 105–120.

Kruger, J. L., E. Hefer and G. Matthew (2013) 'Measuring the Impact of Subtitles on Cognitive Load: Eye Tracking and Dynamic Audiovisual Texts', *Proceedings of Eye Tracking South Africa*, 29–31 August 2013, Cape Town.

Kruger, J. L., A. Szarkowska and I. Kretj (2015) 'Subtitles on the Moving Image: An Overview of Eye Tracking Studies', *Refractory: A Journal of Entertainment Media* 25. Available online: http://refractory.unimelb.edu.au/2015/02/07/kruger-szarkowska-krejtz/ [last access 20 December 2017).

Liversedge, S. P., I. D. Gilchrist and S. Everling (eds) (2013) *The Oxford Handbook of Eye Movements*, Oxford: Oxford University Press.

Marchant, P., D. Raybould, T. Renshaw and R. Stevens (2009) 'Are You Seeing What I'm Seeing? An Eye-Tracking Evaluation of Dynamic Scenes', *Digital Creativity* 20: 153–163.

Moran, S. (2012) 'The Effect of Linguistic Variation on Subtitle Reception', in E. Perego (ed.) *Eye Tracking in Audiovisual Translation*, Rome: Aracne, 183–222.

Orero, P. and A. Vilaró (2012) 'Eye-Tracking Analysis of Minor Details in Films for Audio Description', *MonTI* 4: 295–319.

Papenmeier, F. and M. Huff (2010) 'DynAOI: A Tool for Matching Eye-movement Data with Dynamic Areas of Interest in Animations and Movies', *Behavior Research Methods* 42: 179–187.

Perego, E. (ed.) (2012) *Eye Tracking in Audiovisual Translation*, Rome: Aracne.

Perego, E., F. Del Missier, M. Porta and M. Mosconi. (2010) 'The Cognitive Effectiveness of Subtitle Processing', *Media Psychology* 13(3): 243–272.

Rajendran, D. J., A. T. Duchowski, P. Orero, J. Martínez and P. Romero-Fresco (2013) 'Effects of Text Chunking on Subtitling: A Quantitative and Qualitative Examination', *Perspectives: Studies in Translatology* 21(1): 5–31.

Romero-Fresco, P. (ed.) (2015) *The Reception of Subtitles for the Deaf and Hard of Hearing in Europe*, New York: Peter Lang

Rayner, K. (1998) 'Eye Movements in Reading and Information Processing: 20 Years of Research', *Psychological Bulletin* 124: 372–422.

Rayner, K. (2009) 'Eye Movements and Attention in Reading, Scene Perception, and Visual Search', *The Quarterly Journal of Experimental Psychology* 62(8): 1457–1506.

Specker, E. A. (2008) 'L1/L2 Eye Movement Reading of Closed Captioning: A Multimodal Analysis of Multimodal Use', Unpublished Doctoral Thesis, Tucson: University of Arizona.

Szarkowska, A., I. Krejtz, Z. Kłyszejko and A. Wieczorek (2011) 'Verbatim, Standard, or Edited? Reading Patterns of Different Captioning Styles Among Deaf, Hard of Hearing, and Hearing Viewers', *American Annals of the Deaf* 156(4): 363–378.

Szarkowska, A., O. Pilipczuk, Ł. Dutka, I. Krejtz and J. L Kruger (2016) 'The Effects of Subtitle Presentation Rate on the Comprehension and Reading Patterns of Subtitles Among Deaf, Hard of Hearing and Hearing Viewers', *Across Languages and Cultures* 17(2): 183–204.

Vilaró, A., A. T. Duchowski, P. Orero, T. Grindinger, S. Tetreault and E. Di Giovanni (2012) 'How Sound is the Pear Tree Story? Testing the Effect of Varying Audio Stimuli on Visual Attention Distribution', *Perspectives: Studies in Translatology* 20(1): 55–65.

Winke, P., S. Gass, and T. Syderenko (2013) 'Factors Influencing the Use of Captions by Foreign Language Learners: An Eye Tracking Study', *The Modern Language Journal* 97(1): 254–275.

23
Audiovisual translation and audience reception

David Orrego-Carmona

Introduction

Although descriptive translation studies (Toury 1995) has paid significant attention to the study of the target culture in translational encounters, studies on the reception of translations are still scarce within our discipline (Suojanen *et al.* 2015). Audiovisual translation (AVT) has shown relatively more interest in the study of users and the conditions in which translations are used and enjoyed. Still, we need to know more about how people make sense of translated audiovisual products, and how said products affect their lives. Admittedly, the last few years have witnessed important developments on this front. However, most experiments tend to concentrate on case studies, and are restricted to one mode of AVT, so their contribution to knowledge remains limited.

The contribution of reception studies to AVT has been acknowledged since the inception of empirical research in the 1990s. As early as in 1995, Kovačič highlighted the importance of understanding how viewers receive subtitled content. She argued that subtitlers normally work with a non-existent ideal viewer on their minds—a viewer who differs from the actual individuals who will eventually consume audiovisual programmes. Although her discussion was restricted to subtitled content, she argued that this premise also applies to other AVT modalities, for all translational decisions are constrained by the profile of the viewers that translators have in mind. It is thus necessary to build that viewer's profile with evidence-based insights gathered through empirical studies. The construction of this profile can be informed by (i) how viewers process translated content; (ii) the way in which translation affects their comprehension process; and (iii) the social dimension of the translated material, understood as the effects of translated content on audiences and their preferences. But, as Gambier (2003: 184) notes almost one decade later in a publication that continues to inspire most studies on reception, 'we continually make reference to readers, viewers, consumers, users, etc.' even though '[v]ery few studies have dealt with the issue of reception in screen translation, and even fewer have looked at it empirically' (*ibid.*).

The lack of terminological consensus among scholars working on translation reception prompted Chesterman (2007) to propose an agreed set of terms. Chesterman recognizes that translations act as *causes* and produce *effects* which can be best studied within the receiving culture. Similarly to Kovačič (1995), Chesterman further argues that translations cause *reactions, responses* and *repercussions*. This *3 Rs* model informs Gambier's (2006) proposed framework to study the reception of translated audiovisual products at three different levels: *reactions* on the psycho-cognitive level; *responses* on the perceptual level; and *repercussions*, understood both as attitudinal issues pertaining to the viewer's preferences and habits, as well as to the wider sociocultural dimension of the context in which the products are received (Gambier 2006, 2009). This model is often quoted by scholars specializing in the study of reception in AVT studies (e.g. Caffrey 2009, Tuominen 2012, Orrego-Carmona 2015).

This chapter surveys the significant growth that reception studies have experienced during the last decade, driven by the popularization of eye tracking as a research method and the scholarly community's growing interest in accessibility, which is widely supported by research funding schemes. Despite such advances, more efforts are still needed to equip ourselves with relevant theoretical frameworks and to fine-tune the methods available for the study of reception, if we are to come up with reliable findings in this research domain.

Research methods for audience reception in translation studies

Translation studies scholars have resorted to an array of methods to collect data on reception: questionnaires and eye tracking have probably become the most common ones, although interviews, direct observation, and focus groups have also been applied (Suojanen *et al.* 2015). De Linde and Kay (1999: 35) propose a typology of methods to investigate the reception of subtitling, which involve different degrees of control on the research design on the part of the analyst:

- survey methods elicit viewers' responses to questions about their experience of subtitled television;
- semi-controlled experiments examine viewers' responses to different sets of pre-categorized subtitles;
- controlled experiments place constraints on 'both medium and viewer in order to gain precise behavioural information about how particular subtitle characteristics are received' (*ibid.*).

Semi-controlled and controlled experiment methods have been more popular among translation studies scholars. In the former, researchers identify specific features of the audiovisual product or translation they are interested in, and set out to gauge the effects those features have on viewers. This method differs from the survey method in that it maintains the same conditions for all participants. Apart from restricting the input in various ways, controlled experiments also record the viewers' 'actual motor behaviour' (*ibid.*: 37). De Linde and Kay refer specifically to recording eye movements, but there are other biometric indicators such as heart rate, skin conductance and electroencephalogram (EEG) measurements. These methods are normally combined with questionnaires, which are very time-efficient, to elicit viewers' reactions and opinions.

Each data collection method has its own strengths and weaknesses. For example, questionnaires enable the collection of big amounts of information in a relatively short period of time, but often yield unreliable self-reported data. For its part, eye tracking yields useful insights into attention distribution, but offers little information on the causes of viewers' behaviour. Additionally, eye-tracking equipment is expensive and the data collection process is technically demanding, as it produces large amounts of data that require specific knowledge to be processed, interpreted and presented. Interviews, on the other hand, are more time consuming than questionnaires because they require a longer preparation and transcription time. Finally, direct observation and focus groups provide vast qualitative data, but rely significantly on the researchers' subjectivity and the participant's self-reporting. While they make data transcription and processing more time consuming, these methods allow participants to behave more naturally.

Although there are single-method projects, mainly those revolving around questionnaires or interviews, using a combination of methods to allow for data validation is ever more common. Mixed-methods approaches make it possible to confront results secured through different methods, thus producing higher quality and more comprehensive data. Judging by recent publications and projects under development, it is safe to assume that, as far as reception studies in AVT are concerned, triangulation and mixed methods are becoming the norm.

Reception studies in AVT

In what follows, I will introduce empirical reception studies that have been conducted within AVT. As will become evident, it is common for this type of studies to test the reception of more than one aspect of the translation and involve a combination of methods. The categorization adopted here is therefore meant for presentation purposes only.

Subtitling studies using eye tracking

Eye-tracking methods have featured in AVT research since the inception of this area of scholarly enquiry. Some of the first and most influential studies on the reception of subtitles were carried out by cognitive psychologist d'Ydewalle and his colleagues at the Katholieke Universiteit Leuven. Since 1985, d'Ydewalle and his group have been concerned with the study of subtitle reading and its implications for language learning. D'Ydewalle et al. (1985: 381) found evidence to suggest that subtitle reading differs from typical reading behaviour. Instead of reading the subtitles in their entirety, the participants in their study 'first look[ed] at the visual image, jump[ed] quite accurately to the keywords of the subtitle (i.e., the words conveying the most important parts of the conversation) and then [went] back to the visual image.' If there happened to be any time left, some participants would return to the subtitle area and read the entire subtitles. Subsequent studies (d'Ydewalle et al. 1987), however, found subtitle reading to be 'a more or less' automatic behaviour. Contrary to what the 1985 study indicated, d'Ydewalle et al. (1987) found that viewers cannot avoid reading subtitles, even when they understand the source language of the audiovisual text they were presented with. None of these publications provides a complete description of the experiment: the lack of specific information on the number of participants or the translated audiovisual product complicates the interpretation of the results. Nevertheless, their findings—which laid the foundations for subsequent studies—demonstrated that the reaction of viewers of subtitled programmes react to this form of visual input in a somewhat automated manner, with the degree of automation varying according to other factors. These findings informed the formulation of new hypotheses to be tested in other experiments. Following an experiment with children, d'Ydewalle and van Rensbergen (1989) show that subtitle reading behaviour depends on the type of content presented to the viewer and is not fully automatic. When watching cartoons with dense dialogue, for example, children's gaze patterns resembled those of adult viewers; by contrast, they relied less on the subtitles when they watched action-oriented content.

In yet another study, d'Ydewalle et al. (1991) tested the use of intralingual subtitles—i.e. subtitles in the same language as the soundtrack dialogue—by English native speakers who were not used to viewing subtitled content, and Dutch native speakers who were. Both groups spent a considerable amount of time viewing the subtitles, which seemed to indicate that participants who are used to subtitling also look at the area of the frame where subtitles are featured, even if they understand the spoken language, and regardless of their familiarity with subtitles as a form of AVT. However, on this occasion, the researchers found there was a degree of control in subtitle reading that, admittedly, coexists with the more dominant automatic behaviour. Using news broadcast as input for their experiment, d'Ydewalle and Gielen (1992) showed that viewers look longer at the subtitle area when the audiovisual product conveys a significant amount of information in a short period of time. The participants viewed the subtitles during longer periods and at a faster pace, even when the news broadcast was in their own language.

Koolstra et al. (1999) also drew on eye tracking to investigate empirically the rationale for the industry's adherence to the 'six-second rule'. In their experiment, subtitles were shown at three different speeds (6, 8 and 10 seconds per subtitle). They found that the longer the subtitles remained on the screen, the longer viewers, in this case children, would spend looking at the subtitle area. Poorer readers spent only around 30 per cent of the time looking at the six-second subtitles (much less than other participants), but dedicated more time to reading ten-second subtitles. It was concluded that viewers with poorer reading skills were put off by the faster subtitles, but were more willing to make an effort to process the slower subtitles.

The studies surveyed so far have mostly focused on attention allocation. However, d'Ydewalle and de Bruycker (2007) have examined other aspects of reception, studying the reading behaviour of children and adults when watching videos with interlingual subtitles (subtitles that translate the foreign speech into the viewers' native language) and reversed subtitling (i.e. foreign language subtitles conveying the content of the native language soundtrack). Participants presented with interlingual subtitles skipped fewer of them and spent more time viewing the subtitle area. The focus on the actual reading of the subtitles, rather than the distribution of attention between the subtitle and the image area, was also addressed by Kruger and Steyn (2014) who explored the reception of interlingual subtitles in subtitled academic lectures that are offered within English-medium learning environments.

With the exception of Kruger and Steyn (*ibid.*), all the previous studies assess the reception of translated audiovisual products from a psycholinguistic perspective. In recent years, however, eye tracking has been employed ever more frequently by translation studies scholars in productive ways. In a study measuring performance and analyzing eye movements, Perego et al. (2010) assessed viewers' reactions to subtitle segmentation while watching a subtitled excerpt of a Hungarian film. The subtitles were created specifically for their experiment. The control condition involved the use of subtitles that followed professional subtitling standards, while subtitle segmentation in the treatment condition failed to adhere to those standards. Findings suggest that participants spent an average of 67 per cent of the time looking at the subtitle area. On the whole, subtitled segmentation was not found to have an effect on cognitive processes—as all participants performed well in the recognition of subtitles and scenes.

In order to test the effects of condensation in subtitles, Ghia (2012) compared the reception of literal and non-literal Italian subtitles for an English soundtrack. Gaze data revealed that non-literal translation caused more deflections (i.e. eye movements when the viewer first looks at the subtitle, then focuses on the image before returning to the subtitle area again) from the participants. The higher number of deflections occurred with condensed subtitles, which indicates that viewers' behaviour can be affected by different translation strategies. This might also imply that participants were following and comparing the English dialogue with the Italian subtitles.

Another study exploring specific characteristics of subtitling—in this case, word frequency and cohesion—is presented in Moran (2012). Intuitively, the findings of the study indicate that the presence of high-frequency words in the subtitles facilitates subtitle reading. The group of participants who watched the subtitles with the high-frequency words had 'significantly lower fixation durations associated with reading the subtitle, spent significantly more time viewing the image and scored better in the post-experiment questionnaire' (*ibid.*: 215). The subtitles in the high-cohesion condition also prompted better results and allowed the participants to spend more time on the image, which might be considered as a strong argument against reduction in subtitling—crucially, subtitles featuring high cohesion and high-frequency words contained more characters than their alternative conditions. Moran suggests that instead of focusing on character count, subtitling should be looking more at facilitating reading.

Exploring a different application of subtitles, Kruger *et al.* (2013b) assessed the benefits of using intralingual subtitles in education. Their purpose was to gauge the cognitive load that students had to manage while watching academic lectures with and without intralingual subtitles. The authors used a wide range of data collection methods in their study: eye tracking (pupil dilation), EEG, self-reported ratings and performance measures. The study showed that subtitles proved to be beneficial in these circumstances: they helped students by facilitating the processing and comprehension of the lecture. Further, the students who watched the subtitled version operated under a lower cognitive load than those who watched the non-subtitled version. Additionally, Kruger (2014) found that subtitles are not only cognitively effective, but also have a positive impact on immersion and enjoyment. The study included 88 university students with different mother tongues (English, Chinese, Japanese and Korean) who watched an excerpt with or without intralingual subtitles.

Eye tracking has also served to test experimental uses of subtitles. Bucaria and Chiaro (2007), for example, found that there are sociocultural gaps in the encyclopaedic knowledge of viewers which obscure comprehension, and suggested the possibility 'for screen translation to be integrated with extra information to make up for possible gaps in the sociocultural context' (*ibid.*: 115). Other subtitling studies have explored the viewer's reaction to this additional explanatory text on the screen. Caffrey (2009) makes use of eye tracking and questionnaires to study the cognitive effort required from participants who watch *anime* subtitled in English, both with and without additional pop-up glosses explaining culturally marked elements that feature in the audiovisual material at the centre of the study. The results suggest that increased processing effort is required when a pop-up gloss is on screen, which results in less processing time allocated to the subtitle and a greater number of skipped subtitles. However, the study did find that participants had a better understanding of culturally marked items when they watched the videos with pop-up glosses, even though their presence gave participants in the treatment condition the impression that the subtitles were too fast. Interestingly, and in line with the findings of other studies (d'Ydewalle and Gielen 1992, de Linde and Kay 1999), Caffrey found that, when there was more information on the screen (subtitles plus glosses), the participants read the subtitles faster.

Künzli and Ehrensberger-Dow (2011) studied the audience's response to standard subtitles and standard subtitles combined with surtitles, i.e. snippets of text that appear at the top of the screen and offer metalinguistic information on specific cultural references mentioned in the subtitles. They concluded that the material using the combination of standard subtitles and surtitles incurred a higher cognitive load, but 'participants' performance in terms of retention of various verbal and visual elements in the movie excerpts was identical in the two conditions' (2011: 197). Additionally, since the participants' reception capacity was not affected, Künzli and Ehrensberger-Dow (*ibid.*) argued that viewers are able to process a larger amount of information than previously conceived without compromising their comprehension or enjoyment, but warned that using surtitles for an entire film could yield different results, such as fatigue and/or reduced reception capacity. Künzli and Ehrensberger-Dow also stress that viewers' acceptance of innovative subtitling might be contingent on the age and literacy level of individual users. However, a similar experiment using Portuguese surtitles to gloss cultural items mentioned in the Portuguese subtitled version of a Finnish film (Ramos Pinto 2013) found some of the viewers made deliberate decisions on whether or not to follow the surtitles and thus achieved greater surtitle processing efficiency.

Focusing on young audiences, Orrego-Carmona (2015) analyzed whether there were any differences between the reception of subtitled audiovisual products produced by professional and non-professional subtitlers. The study, which was was carried out in Spain and involved 52 young participants, found no differences in terms of reception. Orrego-Carmona also looked at whether and how the viewers' knowledge of the source language of the audiovisual content affects subtitle-reading behaviour. Results indicate that, while participants with a low level of proficiency are highly dependent on the subtitles, the behaviour of those viewers with a higher level of proficiency is variable and results in different viewing experiences.

Advances in the study of reception have paved the way for studies that are not necessarily confined to material subtitled during post-production. Romero-Fresco (2013) advocates that AVT and accessibility should be given serious consideration as early as in the pre-production stage of filmmaking. Likewise, Fox (2016) has developed the concept of 'integrated titles' to designate subtitles that are not confined to the bottom of the screen, but can feature in any region of the frame instead. Fox's study begins by identifying the natural focus point of the visual composition by tracking the eye movements of native speakers. Then, she proceeds to place the integrated subtitles around the focal areas of the image, as delineated by the viewing patterns. Results suggest that viewers invest less time reading integrated subtitles than their regular counterparts, and are more likely to return faster to the focal points in the image.

Reception of humour and culture-specific items

The translation of humour and cultural references in general has also been studied from a reception-based perspective. Fuentes Luque (2003) used direct observation to explore the reception of translated humour from English into Spanish. The data collection involved the direct observation of participants' reactions during the screening of a dubbed film, the completion of a questionnaire by the experiment participants, and a brief interview with the participants. The cohort of 30 participants was divided into three different experiment conditions. The original English film, the dubbed Spanish version, and the subtitled Spanish version were thus watched by ten viewers each. Fuentes Luque's study—based on a small sample of participants with ages ranging from 16 to 64—found that participants watching the translated versions showed a less positive reception of humour elements than that of viewers who watched the original version in English.

The University of Bologna-Forlì (Italy) is home to a cluster of researchers studying the reception of humour and cultural references in audiovisual content subtitled and dubbed into Italian. Chiaro (2004) used questionnaires to collect data on the perception of verbally expressed humour dubbed into Italian. Antonini (2005) used an adapted humour-appreciation test involving a sample of 32 participants to study the reception of verbally expressed humour, visual humour and satire. The results show participants had problems understanding subtitled verbal humour although, surprisingly, participants were able to recreate puns that were not present in the subtitles. Antonini suggests this could be prompted by the canned laughter in the material used in this study, which raises questions as to whether, and to what extent, the original soundtrack influences viewers' behaviour and comprehension.

The composition of the sample used in Bucaria and Chiaro (2007) to study end user perception of Italian dubbing included cinema and TV experts, linguists, dubbing practitioners, and members of the general audience. The findings suggest that, as Italian audiences become more familiar with foreign cultures, they are more tolerant of 'dubbese'—which designates, in this case, the variety of Italian used by the dubbing industry to transpose both fictional and non-fictional foreign TV and cinema productions—and makes it more difficult for the audience to differentiate between 'what is and is not *real* spoken Italian' (Bucaria and Chiaro 2007: 115). In another study about dubbese, Antonini (2008) uses an online questionnaire to test the participants' understanding of translated content. This study reports that most of the participants' declared understanding differs greatly from their actual understanding of the translated content: while more than 60 per cent of the respondents declared they understood the cultural references through the Italian translation, in 70 per cent of the cases they did not actually understand them. This raises concerns about the reliability of self-reported comprehension methods and accentuates the need for triangulation. Other studies on the Italian audience's perception of dubbese (Antonini and Chiaro 2009) found that the features of dubbese language are recognized as such by respondents, and that this phenomenon is understood and accepted as a special variety of Italian.

Chiaro (2007) also explores the reception of humour and culture-specific references in the context of AVT. This study sets out to examine how audiences perceive verbally expressed humour comparing the reaction of 34 Italian viewers and 22 British informants to original, dubbed or subtitled content. A small disparity can be observed in the results, with British participants giving higher scores to verbally expressed humour than their Italian counterparts—which lends support to Fuentes Luque's (2003) suggestion that the reception of humour is culture-specific.

Accessibility studies

Intralingual and interlingual subtitling for the deaf and hard of hearing (SDH) has become a prolific area of reception-related scholarship. While the United Kingdom and the USA have conducted research in this area since the 1990s, SDH is now receiving more scholarly attention in Spain, Poland, Italy, Portugal, and Belgium, against the background of growing public support to accessibility. Indeed, in recent years, a wide range of countries, including but not restricted to EU member states, have passed legislation that requires TV channels and distributors to comply with a quota of accessible content in their programming.

Gottlieb (1995) relied on a 'protest button' to elicit the reactions of 123 deaf or hard-of-hearing viewers to subtitled material. Interestingly, he found that participants did not react to subtitles that were faulty according to professional standards; instead, subtitles that had been condensed in compliance with industrial conventions were perceived as faulty subtitles. This study demonstrated that participants' views of subtitling quality do not necessarily lend support to practices informed by professional subtitling standards. Admittedly, asking participants to assess the subtitles while they are watching audiovisual content could have affected the ecological validity of the experiment. Apart from having to divide their attention between the image and the subtitles, participants also had to be aware of the button and remain alert to judge the translations, which results in a non-natural viewing experience.

De Linde and Kay (1999) present a series of experiments testing a range of features that are of relevance to accessibility: subtitle rate, onset of speech, shot changes, and subtitle editing. Their analysis relies mostly on eye-movement measurements but also on the participants' comprehension of the content. In all cases, the sound of the clips was off, so that participants (10 hearing and 10 deaf participants) would have to rely solely on the subtitles for verbal information. While this experiment enabled the study of the hearing participants' performance under the same conditions as deaf participants, its findings do not lend themselves to comparison with the findings of other studies involving hearing participants with access to the soundtrack. Similarly to d'Ydewalle and Gielen (1992), de Linde and Kay (1999) found that subtitle pace affects reading speed: the faster the subtitles, the faster people read them. They also observed that slow subtitles induce re-reading, proving that both extremes, slow and fast subtitles, have a direct impact on viewers' behaviour. Interestingly, deaf viewers seemed to rely more on the image as a source of information, which suggests that impaired viewers engage differently with images.

In one of a series of studies on SDH undertaken in the USA (Jensema 1998), a sample of 578 participants consisting of deaf, hard of hearing and hearing viewers reported that 145 words per minute was a comfortable subtitle-reading speed—although they adapted well to an increased presentation rate of up to 171 words per minute. Jensema, Danturthi and Burch (2000) found the presence of subtitles drastically changed the behaviour of the six participants in their study and turned the viewing process into a reading activity. When watching subtitled content, subtitle reading takes over as the primary activity, while viewing the action becomes secondary. In a larger study (Jensema, el Sharkawy *et al.* 2000) collected eye-movement data from 23 participants watching subtitled television programmes. The results indicated that participants spent 84 per cent of their time looking at the subtitles, and there was little variation (82 per cent-86 per cent) when the subtitle speed increased from 100 to 180 words per minute. Additionally, this experiment revealed that age and sex did not have an impact on viewers' behaviour—thus contradicting the findings of other studies (d'Ydewalle *et al.* 1987, de Bruycker and d'Ydewalle 2003). Although the education level of participants seemed to be a significant variable, the size of the data set was too small to allow for robust conclusions on this matter.

Szarkowska *et al.* (2013) report on a series of experiments conducted to test SDH and audio description (AD). In one of the studies, they tested three different types of subtitles: edited (simplified and reduced) subtitles, standard subtitles and verbatim subtitles. The group of 40 participants in the study included deaf, hard of hearing and hearing people. Edited subtitles were found to allow participants to look at the image for longer, while their verbatim counterparts received better comprehension scores. However, it was also in this version that the participants fixated on the subtitles the most. The authors draw attention to various contradictory findings: most participants' preferred translation mode was not the one that produced the best comprehension scores.

As noted above, research on accessibility has been stimulated by growing financial and institutional support. The cross-national project DTV4ALL (2010–2013) funded by the European Commission aimed to explore the quality of SDH on three areas: 'what viewers think about SDH, how they understand these subtitles and how they view them' (Romero-Fresco 2015: 10). The project involved completing a questionnaire to learn about the preferences of 1,365 SDH respondents and conducting an eye-tracking experiment with 103 deaf, hard of hearing and hearing viewers in four of the participating countries (Spain, Poland, Italy and Germany). The results of the questionnaire reveal a very heterogeneous SDH landscape in Europe. While in countries such as Denmark and the UK coverage is not really an issue, in other countries (e.g. Poland, Spain, Germany) there is room for further legislation and more ambitious programming quotas. In terms of subtitle reception, the results of the eye-tracking tests indicate that deaf participants spend more time looking at the subtitles than their hearing or hard of hearing counterparts. This is in sharp contrast with the fact that deaf participants achieved lower scores in terms of average comprehension of the subtitles, although they scored better than participants in other groups on the comprehension of the image tests. As Romero-Fresco puts it, 'deaf viewers make up for their poor reading skills with a particularly good visual perception comprehension' (2015: 352).

Another area of accessibility that is attracting more attention is AD. The booming of this relatively recent AVT modality has made it possible for researchers to rely on viewers' feedback in order to propose standards and guidelines (Chmiel and Mazur 2012). Although there have been sound reception studies conducted in this area, they tend to be small-scale experiments involving few participants and relying mostly on self-reporting questionnaires and interviews. A study exploring the preferences of AD users in Belgium, Germany, Italy, Poland, Portugal and Spain was carried out as part of the ADLAB: Lifelong Access for the Blind project. Chmiel and Mazur (2016) report that the study included 80 visually impaired participants and 77 sighted participants. Two AD versions (narrative and descriptive) of a 20-minute excerpt were translated from English into all the languages of the participating counties, and questionnaires were used to elicit the participants' preferences and comprehension. The findings do not show significant differences in terms of preferences between the two types of AD.

The subtitling/dubbing debate

The comparison between subtitling and dubbing, one of the longstanding debates in AVT (Koolstra *et al.* 2002), has also attracted empirical research. Bairstow and Lavaur (2012) report on a study comparing dubbing and subtitling. In total, four conditions are included in this experiment: original version in English, dubbed version in French, original version with French subtitles, and a reversed condition (dubbed version with English subtitles). When it comes to the comprehension of dialogue, the dubbed versions score highest, but the degree of comprehension enabled by the version with French subtitles is almost as good. The original version scored the lowest results, due to the participants' low proficiency in English. For its part, the comparison between subtitling and dubbing conducted by Perego *et al.* (2015) revealed that subtitling does not affect the viewer's enjoyment and appreciation of the film when compared to dubbing. However, subtitling provides better support for 'the lexical aspects of performance', i.e. 'the ability to remember face–name associations and specific expressions of dialogues' (*ibid.*: 8)

Subtitling, language learning and proficiency in foreign languages

The potential of subtitles to enhance linguistic abilities is one of the reasons why researchers in psychology and education have become interested in exploring the reception of subtitles.

There are two main areas of enquiry in this branch of reception studies. Researchers in the first of such areas have tackled the issue of incidental learning of foreign language with subtitled content, in most cases with a special interest in vocabulary acquisition. Scholars working in the second area have explored how proficiency in the source language of the audiovisual content affects reception.

The incidental educational potential of subtitling is one of the reasons why subtitling is sometimes considered superior to dubbing. In a longitudinal study carried out by Koolstra *et al.* (1997) 1,050 Dutch elementary school children were tested over a period of three years to analyze the effects of television viewing on their decoding skills. The findings indicate that watching subtitled content on television actually stimulates the development of linguistic decoding. Again, the research group at the Katholieke Universiteit Leuven has been prolific in testing the benefits of subtitling for language learning. D'Ydewalle and Pavakanun (1995) tested the reception of cartoons with regular and reversed subtitles and found that they helped with vocabulary learning, although they were relatively less useful for grammar and syntax. D'Ydewalle and van de Poel (1999) obtained promising results when testing students who watched audiovisual content with subtitles and with subtitles and soundtrack. The findings also indicate that participants who watched the content with reversed subtitles outperformed those who watched content with regular subtitles. In an experiment conducted in the United States with beginner learners of Russian as L2, Sydorenko (2010) found that, apart from vocabulary acquisition, subtitles can also improve word-form meaning association—which would seem to indicate that subtitles help in the recognition of written word forms, as well as in the acquisition of word meaning.

In France, based on the findings of Lavaur and Nava (2008), which indicate that subtitles could have a detrimental effect when they are not necessary for viewers, Lavaur and Bairstow (2011) carried out two questionnaire-based studies to test to what extent viewers' knowledge of the foreign language featured in the soundtrack makes subtitles redundant. Bairstow (2011), on the other hand, reports on an experiment with monolingual and bilingual participants watching a clip in its original version with English soundtrack or with French subtitles. The results suggest that subtitles have a facilitating effect for monolinguals but constitute a distracting element for bilinguals. Of note is the fact that the subtitled version appeared to help monolinguals to understand visual information, and not only to access verbal information in the foreign language. These findings are consistent with those of Taylor's experiment, where participants who watched condensed subtitles were able to better complement their viewing experience with information from other semiotic modes (Taylor 2003).

Bairstow and Lavaur (2012) argue that participants classed as monolinguals in these studies may have some knowledge of the source (foreign) language—which may influence their engagement with subtitles. This insight prompted Lavaur and Bairstow (2011) to conduct a follow-up experiment testing the same conditions as in the previous study (original English version and interlingual subtitled version in French) but adding an intralingual subtitled version (in English). The high-school students participating in this experiment were divided into three groups depending on their proficiency in English (beginners, intermediate and advanced). The findings confirm that subtitles act as a distraction from visual meaning, but they also help viewers with a low proficiency in the source foreign language to retrieve linguistic information. The three groups of participants showed very different patterns of behaviour. The beginners' attention to visual semiotics dropped with the presence of English subtitles, and even more with the French subtitles. However, subtitles appeared to significantly facilitate dialogue comprehension. Intermediate participants processed the dialogue better than visual information in all three conditions, while advanced participants obtained the best results when viewing the original version.

Tuominen (2012) approached this issue from a different angle in an experiment involving focus groups in Finland. In contrast to the studies surveyed above, Tuominen set out to test whether the participants' formal training in translation influenced their reception of subtitles. The participants were divided into three groups: near-experts (consisting of students majoring in English or translation), and two groups of non-experts. Her results revealed that members of the near-expert group relied heavily on the subtitles and were able to recall them during the focus group discussions. This indicates that participants with the highest proficiency in the source language decided, probably consciously, to read the subtitles as they watched the programme chosen for this experiment. Tuominen also found that all participants, regardless of the variety in their level of proficiency in English, were able to watch the film comfortably and enjoyed it. In Tuominen's view, the fact that subtitles would not appear to play a distracting role may be due to the familiarity of Finnish audiences with subtitling as a mainstream form of AVT.

Dimensions of reception

As noted in the introduction, the reception of translated audiovisual content has an *individual* and a *social dimension*. At the individual level, which has received significantly more scholarly attention, reception studies have explored the responses and reactions of individual viewers when presented with (primarily) dubbed and subtitled programmes. The social dimension, on the other hand, pertains to the collective decisions through which each community favours one mode of AVT over others.

The limited access to resources and the difficulties involved in reaching large audiences have significantly constrained the type and scale of research that translation studies scholars interested in the social dimension of reception studies have been able to conduct so far. Thus, what de Linde and Kay (1999) label as 'the survey methods' have been carried out almost exclusively by government agencies, national TV channels, distributors and audiovisual market providers. Some examples could be the Audetel project on AD undertaken in the early 1990s (UK), the reports on subtitling quality and viewers' opinions published on a regular basis by Ofcom (UK), or the studies on the dubbing and subtitling industry and on the use of subtitling in Europe, which the Media Consulting Group carried out for the European Commission (2007, 2011). Apart from the VTB4All Project (Romero-Fresco 2015), most studies in AVT reception draw on relatively small samples of participants and tend to focus on the expectations and preferences of specific groups.

The study of reception at a social level, however, focuses on the impact of translated products on society and social preferences, and hence falls under what Gambier (2006) labels as *repercussions*. This dimension of reception concerning national and regional preferences is bound to develop as an important area of research in the near future, thanks to the affordances of big data and the empowerment of audiences, who are making an ever-bigger use of participatory technologies to express their views on (translated) media content. There is emerging evidence that digital technologies and the changing habits of media consumption that digitization has brought about are blurring traditional distinctions between subtitling and dubbing countries. TV channels and audiovisual markets are exploring new translation modalities and audiences are becoming used to other options (Chaume 2013). The availability and cohabitation of different modalities is bound to alter the reception of translated content over time, as audiences can now decide, and even demand, how they want to watch it (Orrego-Carmona 2014).

What is next?

Research on the reception of AVT encompasses a wide range of translation modalities, both established and emerging ones. Against this backdrop, some of the areas of scholarly research where reception studies are likely to feature more prominently in the future can be summarized as follows:

- Although reception studies have so far focused overwhelmingly on subtitling, they are likely to widen their scope and explore the extent to which dubbing, voice-over, AD and other translation modalities are able to improve the comprehension of, engagement with or immersion in translated audiovisual content.
- Some of the variables underpinning reception studies (e.g. the size and composition of participant samples) will receive further consideration. Likewise, the interplay between participants' ages and experience with specific AVT modalities could yield important advances in our understanding of how media content is received. Participants' ages may influence their perceptions of certain types of translation; consequently, it is necessary to gauge the extent to which being raised in a traditionally dubbing or subtitling country, or living in said country for an extended period of time, moulds one's expectations or influences one's reception of translated content in different ways.
- Evidence gathered through methodological triangulation and various experiments suggests that participants' stated (and hence, subjective) preferences are not necessarily consistent with those same viewers' performance, as measured by researchers through different indicators. Studies will need to explore how this misalignment between preferences and behaviour affect engagement and enjoyment.
- Experiments on subtitling reception have tended to measure the participants' use of subtitles by exposing them to audiovisual content whose original language is not known to them. Real viewers, however, often have some knowledge of the foreign language(s) they are presented with. Even if they do not, it is safe to assume that the original soundtrack influences their viewing experience. Indeed, viewers are always exposed to the paralinguistic aural input available in the original content and are simultaneously accessing this information while reading the subtitles. The interplay between the aural and the other media codes in translated products is another area that requires attention.
- As audiences become more responsive and willing to express their views through various social media platforms, big data might shed more light on the reception of translated content in the future. For instance, as shown by Orrego-Carmona (2014), tweets could provide valuable information for scholars seeking to map audience preferences and reactions.
- In order to study how subtitles are actually read, AVT scholars often have to resort to labour-intensive and time-consuming tools and resources. Neighbouring scholarly areas, such as machine learning and data mining, could make the analysis of data more manageable and would allow the exploration of larger data sets.
- Cognitive studies are quickly gaining ground within AVT, with some scholars (Kruger et al. 2013a, Chmiel and Mazur 2016) advocating the use of such approaches to gauge the amount of cognitive effort involved in viewing translated content, and hence to ensure that translation practices do not result in the audience's cognitive overload.

Summary

Reception studies stands out as a fast-growing area of research within AVT. Although most studies to date have focused on subtitling, other modalities of translation are beginning to receive more attention as users gain more exposure to them. This chapter has delivered an overview of research methods used to study reception and a range of experiments that have been conducted within AVT studies. Traditionally, the most popular methods have been questionnaires and eye tracking, but interviews, focus groups and direct observation have also been used. As in most other areas of translation studies, methodological triangulation is bound to yield particularly sound findings.

In the case of interlingual subtitling, reception studies have been more concerned with empirically testing established professional standards; in less established AVT modalities, such as AD, reception studies have facilitated the development of guidelines and standards. A number of future research avenues for reception studies in the context of AVT are sketched in the final part of the chapter. Future studies could draw on translation sociology to assess the social impact of AVT, and adopt a cognitive perspective to become better acquainted with the cognitive effort involved in processing translated media content.

Further reading

Chmiel, A. and I. Mazur (2016) 'Researching Preferences of Audio Description Users—Limitations and Solutions', *Across Languages and Cultures* 17(2): 271–288 | *This paper offers a comprehensive account of previous research on the reception of AD, suggests ways of overcoming its limitations, and explores avenues for future research in the field.*

Kruger, J. L., A. Szarkowska and I. Krejtz (2015) 'Subtitles on the Moving Image: An Overview of Eye Tracking Studies' *Refractory: A Journal of Entertainment Media* 25. Available online: http://refractory.unimelb.edu.au/2015/02/07/kruger-szarkowska-krejtz/ [last accessed 20 December 2017] | *Starting with an overview of eye-tracking studies in subtitling, the authors analyze how subtitling processing has been measured. The authors call for a more fine-grained analysis of how subtitles are actually read and cognitively processed.*

Suojanen, T., K. Koskinen and T. Tuominen (2015) *User-centered Translation*, London & New York: Routledge | *This book includes a chapter that draws links between reception studies and user-centred translation research.*

Related topics

 3 Subtitling on the cusp of its futures
 6 Subtitling for deaf and hard of hearing audiences: moving forward
22 Eye tracking in audiovisual translation research
31 Accessible filmmaking: translation and accessibility from production
32 Technologization of audiovisual translation

References

Antonini, R. (2005) 'The Perception of Subtitled Humor in Italy', *Humor: International Journal of Humor Research* 18(2): 209–225.

Antonini, R. (2008) 'The Perception of Dubbese: An Italian study', in D. Chiaro, C. Heiss and C. Bucaria (eds) *Between Text and Image: Updating Research in Screen Translation*, Amsterdam & Philadelphia: John Benjamins, 135–148.

Antonini, R. and D. Chiaro (2009) 'The Perception of Dubbing by Italian Audiences', in J. Díaz Cintas and G. Anderman (eds) *Audiovisual Translation: Language Transfer on Screen*, Basingstoke: Palgrave Macmillan, 97–114.

Bairstow, D. (2011) 'Audiovisual Processing while Watching Subtitled Films: A Cognitive Approach', in A. Şerban, A. Matamala and J. M. Lavaur (eds) *Audiovisual Translation in Close-up: Practical and Theoretical Approaches*, Bern: Peter Lang, 205–219.

Bairstow, D. and J. M. Lavaur (2012) 'Audiovisual Information Processing by Monolinguals and Bilinguals: Effects of Intralingual and Interlingual Subtitles', in A. Remael, P. Orero and M. Carroll (eds) *Audiovisual Translation and Media Accessibility at the Crossroads*, Amsterdam: Rodopi, 273–293.

Bucaria, C. and D. Chiaro (2007) 'End User Perception of Screen Translation: The Case of Italian Dubbing', *Tradterm* 13(1): 91–118.

Caffrey, C. (2009) *Relevant Abuse? Investigating the Effects of an Abusive Subtitling Procedure on the Perception of TV Anime Using Eye Tracker and Questionnaire*, Unpublished Doctoral Thesis, Dublin City University. Available online: http://doras.dcu.ie/14835/1/Colm_PhDCorrections.pdf [last accessed 20 December 2017].

Chaume, F. (2013) 'The Turn of Audiovisual Translation: New Audiences and New Technologies', *Translation Spaces* 2: 105–123.

Chesterman, A. (2007) 'Bridge Concepts in Translation Sociology', in M. Wolf and A. Fukari (eds) *Constructing a Sociology of Translation*, Amsterdam & Philadelphia: John Benjamins, 171–183.

Chiaro, D. (2004) 'Investigating the Perception of Translated Verbally Expressed Humour on Italian TV', *ESP Across Cultures* 1(1): 35–52.

Chiaro, D. (2007) 'The Effect of Translation on Humour Response', in Y. Gambier, M. Shlesinger and R. Stolze (eds) *Doubts and Directions in Translation Studies*, Amsterdam & Philadelphia: John Benjamins, 137–152.

Chmiel, A. and I. Mazur (2012) 'AD Reception Research: Some Methodological Considerations', in E. Perego (ed.) *Emerging Topics in Translation: Audio Description*, Trieste: Edizioni Università di Trieste, 57–80.

Chmiel, A. and I. Mazur (2016) 'Researching Preferences of Audio Description Users—Limitations and Solutions', *Across Languages and Cultures* 17(2): 271–288.

de Bruycker, W. and G. d'Ydewalle (2003) 'Reading Native and Foreign Language Television Subtitles in Children and Adults', in R. Radach, J. Hyona and H. Deubel (eds) *The Mind's Eye: Cognitive and Applied Aspects of Eye Movement Research*, Amsterdam: Elsevier Science, 671–684.

de Linde, Z. and N. Kay (1999) *The Semiotics of Subtitling*, Manchester: St. Jerome.

d'Ydewalle, G. and W. de Bruycker (2007) 'Eye Movements of Children and Adults while Reading Television Subtitles', *European Psychologist* 12(3): 196–205.

d'Ydewalle, G. and I. Gielen (1992) 'Attention Allocation with Overlapping Sound, Image, and Text', in K. Rayner (ed.) *Eye Movements and Visual Cognition: Scene Perception and Reading*, New York, NY: Springer, 415–427.

d'Ydewalle, G. and U. Pavakanun (1995) 'Acquisition of a Second/Foreign Language by Viewing a Television Program', in P. Winterhoff-Spurk (ed.) *Psychology of Media in Europe*, Wiesbaden: VS Verlag für Sozialwissenschaften, 51–64.

d'Ydewalle, G. and M. van de Poel (1999) 'Incidental Foreign-language Acquisition by Children Watching Subtitled Television Programs', *Journal of Psycholinguistic Research* 28(3): 227–244.

d'Ydewalle, G. and J. van Rensbergen (1989) 'Developmental Studies of Text-Picture Interactions in the Perception of Animated Cartoons with Text', in H. Mandl and J. R. Levin (eds) *Knowledge Acquisition from Text and Pictures*, Amsterdam: Elsevier Science, 233–248.

d'Ydewalle, G., P. Muylle and J. van Rensbergen (1985) 'Attention Shifts in Partially Redundant Information Situations', in R. Groner, G. McConkie and C. Menz (eds) *Eye Movements and Human Information Processing*, Amsterdam: Elsevier Science, 375–384.

d'Ydewalle, G., C. Praet, K. Verfaillie and J. van Rensbergen (1991) 'Watching Subtitled Television: Automatic Reading Behavior', *Communication Research* 18(5): 650–666.

d'Ydewalle, G., J. van Rensbergen and J. Pollet (1987) 'Reading a Message when the Same Message is Available Auditorily in Another Language: The Case of Subtitling', in J. K. O'Regan, and A. Lévy-Schoen (eds) *Eye Movements from Physiology to Cognition*, Amsterdam: Elsevier Science, 313–321.

Fox, W. (2016) 'Integrated Titles: An Improved Viewing Experience?', in S. Hansen-Schirra and S. Grucza (eds) *Eyetracking and Applied Linguistics*, Berlin: Language Science Press, 5–30.

Fuentes Luque, A. (2003) 'An Empirical Approach to the Reception of AV Translated Humour', in Y. Gambier (ed.) *Screen Translation*, special issue of *The Translator* 9(2): 293–306.

Gambier, Y. (2003) 'Introduction', in Y. Gambier (ed.) *Screen Translation*, special issue of *The Translator* 9(2): 171–189.

Gambier, Y. (2006) 'Multimodality and Audiovisual Translation', in M. Carroll, H. Gerzymisch-Arbogast and S. Nauert (eds) *Audiovisual Translation Scenarios*: Proceedings of the Marie Curie Conferences MuTra, Copenhagen 1–5 May. Available online: http://www.euroconferences.info/proceedings/2006_Proceedings/2006_Gambier_Yves.pdf [last accessed 20 December 2017]

Gambier, Y. (2009) 'Challenges in Research on Audiovisual Translation', in A. Pym and A. Perekrestenko (eds) *Translation Research Projects 2*, Tarragona, Intercultural Studies Group: 17–25.

Ghia, E. (2012) 'The Impact of Translation Strategies on Subtitle Reading', in E. Perego (ed) *Eye Tracking in Audiovisual Translation*, Roma: Aracne Editrice, 155–182.

Gottlieb, H. (1995) 'Establishing a Framework for a Typology of Subtitle Reading Strategies—Viewer Reactions to Deviations from Subtitling Standards', *Translatio (FIT Newsletter)* 14(3–4): 388–409.

Jensema, C. J. (1998) 'Viewer Reaction to Different Television Captioning Speeds', *American Annals of the Deaf* 143(4): 318–324.

Jensema, C. J., R. S. Danturthi and R. Burch (2000) 'Time Spent Viewing Captions on Television Programs', *American Annals of the Deaf* 145(5): 464–468.

Jensema, C. J., S. el Sharkawy, R. S. Danturthi, R. Burch and D. Hsu (2000) 'Eye Movement Patterns of Captioned Television Viewers', *American Annals of the Deaf* 145(3): 275–285.

Koolstra, C. M., A. L. Peeters and H. Spinhof (2002) 'The Pros and Cons of Dubbing and Subtitling', *European Journal of Communication* 17(3): 325–354.

Koolstra, C. M., T. H. A. van der Voort and G. d'Ydewalle (1999) 'Lengthening the Presentation Time of Subtitles on Television: Effects on Children's Reading Time and Recognition', *Communications* 24(4): 407–422.

Koolstra, C. M., T. H. A. van der Voort and L. J. T. van der Kamp (1997) 'Television's Impact on Children's Reading Comprehension and Decoding Skills: A 3-Year Panel Study', *Reading Research Quarterly* 32(2): 128–152.

Kovačič, I. (1995) 'Reception of Subtitles. The Non-existent Ideal Viewer', *Translatio (FIT Newsletter)* 14(3–4): 376–383.

Kruger, J.-L. (2014) *The Impact of Subtitles on Psychological Immersion*, paper presented at *Languages and the Media 2014 Conference*, Berlin.

Kruger, J.-L. and F. Steyn (2014) 'Subtitles and Eye Tracking: Reading and Performance', *Reading Research Quarterly* 49(1): 105–120.

Kruger, J.-L., E. Hefer and G. Matthew (2013a) 'Attention Distribution and Cognitive Load in a Subtitled Academic Lecture: L1 vs. L2', *Journal of Eye Movement Research* 7(5): 1–15.

Kruger, J.-L., E. Hefer and G. Matthew (2013b) 'Measuring the Impact of Subtitles on Cognitive Load: Eye Tracking and Dynamic Audiovisual Texts', *Proceedings of Eye Tracking South Africa*, Cape Town, August 29–31: 62–66.

Kruger, J.-L., A. Szarkowska and I. Krejtz (2015) 'Subtitles on the Moving Image: An Overview of Eye Tracking Studies' *Refractory: A Journal of Entertainment Media* 25. Available online: http://refractory.unimelb.edu.au/2015/02/07/kruger-szarkowska-krejtz/ [last accessed 20 December 2017].

Künzli, A. and M. Ehrensberger-Dow (2011) 'Innovative Subtitling: A Reception Study', in C. Alvstad, A. Hild and E. Tiselius (eds) *Methods and Strategies of Process Research: Integrative Approaches in Translation Studies*, Amsterdam & Philadelphia: John Benjamins: 187–200.

Lavaur, J. M. and D. Bairstow (2011) 'Languages on the Screen: Is Film Comprehension Related to the Viewers' Fluency Level and to the Language in the Subtitles?', *International Journal of Psychology* 46(6): 455–462.

Lavaur, J. M. and S. Nava (2008) 'Interférences liées au sous-titrage intralangue sur le traitement des images d'une séquence filmée', *Actes du colloque du Congrès 2007 de la Société Française de Psychologie*, Nantes.

Media Consulting Group and Peacefulfish (2007) *Study on Dubbing and Subtitling Needs and Practices in the European Audiovisual Industry. Final Report*, Paris, London, MCG, Peacefulfish. Available online: http://ec.europa.eu/translation/LID/index.cfm?fuseaction=main.PublicationDetail&PBL_ID=480&theme_selector=normal [last accessed 20 December 2017].

Media Consulting Group (2011) *Study on the Use of Subtitling: The Potential of Subtitling to Encourage Foreign Language Learning and Improve the Mastery of Foreign Languages EACEA/2009/01. Final Report*. Available online: http://www.mcu.es/cine/docs/Novedades/Study_on_use_subtitling.pdf [last accessed 20 December 2017].

Moran, S. (2012) 'The Effect of Linguistic Variation on Subtitle Reception', in E. Perego (ed.) *Eye Tracking in Audiovisual Translation*, Roma: Aracne Editrice, 183–222.

Orrego-Carmona, D. (2014) 'Subtitling, Video Consumption and Viewers: The Impact of the Young Audience', *Translation Spaces* 3: 51–70.

Orrego-Carmona, D. (2015) *The Reception of (Non)professional Subtitling*, Unpublished Doctoral thesis, Universitat Rovira i Virgili, Tarragona, Spain.

Perego, E., F. del Missier and S. Bottiroli (2015) 'Dubbing versus Subtitling in Young and Older Adults: Cognitive and Evaluative Aspects', *Perspectives* 23(1): 1–21.

Perego, E., F. del Missier, M. Porta and M. Mosconi (2010) 'The Cognitive Effectiveness of Subtitle Processing', *Media Psychology* 13: 243–272.

Ramos Pinto, S. (2013) *How Accessible are Audiovisual Products: A Reception Study of Subtitled Film*, paper presented at the *5th International Conference Media for All: Audiovisual Translation, Expanding Borders*, Dubrovnik.

Romero-Fresco, P. (2013) 'Accessible Filmmaking: Joining the Dots between Audiovisual Translation, Accessibility and Filmmaking', *JoSTrans: The Journal of Specialised Translation* 20: 201–223. Available online: http://www.jostrans.org/issue20/art_romero.pdf [last accessed 20 December 2017].

Romero-Fresco, P. (2015) *The Reception of Subtitles for the Deaf and Hard of Hearing in Europe: UK, Spain, Italy, Poland, Denmark, France and Germany*, Bern: Peter Lang.

Suojanen, T., K. Koskinen and T. Tuominen (2015) *User-centered Translation*, London & New York: Routledge.

Sydorenko, T. (2010) 'Modality of Input and Vocabulary Acquisition', *Language Learning & Technology* 14: 50–73.

Szarkowska, A., I. Krejtz, K. Krejtz and A. T. Duchowski (2013) 'Harnessing the Potential of Eyetracking for Media Accessibility', in S. Grucza, M. Pluzyczka and J. Zajac (eds) *Translation Studies and Eye-Tracking Analysis*, Bern: Peter Lang, 153–183.

Taylor, C. J. (2003) 'Multimodal Transcription in the Analysis, Translation and Subtitling of Italian Films', in Y. Gambier (ed.) 'Screen Translation', special issue of *The Translator* 9(2): 191–205.

Toury, G. (1995) *Descriptive Translation Studies and Beyond*, Amsterdam & Philadelphia: John Benjamins.

Tuominen, T. (2012) *The Art of Accidental Reading and Incidental Listening: An Empirical Study on the Viewing of Subtitled Films*, Unpublished Doctoral Thesis, University of Tampere, Finland.

24
Ethnographic research in audiovisual translation

Dang Li

Introduction

Over the last two decades, research in audiovisual translation (AVT) has been thriving. Yet, it has often been limited to the technical and linguistic constraints at play in the different audiovisual translation modes, the production process, and the quality of the translated work (Gambier 2006). So far, the people who actually make use of the translated content seem to have been largely overlooked by AVT scholars. As Gambier (2009: 52) notes, '[v]ery few studies have dealt with the issue of reception in AVT, and even fewer have looked at empirically [*sic*], even though we continually make references to readers, viewers, customers, users, etc'.

Undoubtedly, recent eye-tracking-based audience studies (e.g. Künzli and Ehrensberger-Dow 2011) have yielded important insights into the cognitive efforts required from viewers to process audiovisual material, thus opening up new avenues for quantitative research on reception studies. Nevertheless, the issue of reception in AVT is not confined to knowing about or catering for the cognitive capacity of end-users. This view would be too restrictive, considering that there are a wide range of sociological and audiovisual variables (e.g. age, gender, education, class, reading habits, audiovisual genre, broadcasting time and channel) that affect viewers' attitudes and their opinions on what they watch (Gambier 2001).

This is particularly true in the twenty-first-century media environment, where the digitization of media content and the convergence of media platforms overwhelm audiences with abundant and diverse media outlets; allow them to choose among various devices to access audiovisual material whenever and wherever they want; divide large audiences into smaller niche groups by tailoring target content to their specific needs; and allow (and often require) interactions between audiences and those who produce media content (Jenkins 2006). Moreover, the proliferation of communication technologies has made it possible for increasing audiences to promote their own media experiences by appropriating, translating (subtitling, in particular) and circulating a variety of audiovisual products on a collaborative and voluntary basis. This phenomenon, often known as 'community translation' (Fernández Costales 2012) or 'participatory audiovisual translation' (Pérez-González 2014), has in turn problematized traditional conceptualizations of viewers as passive information consumers, as well as our view of the very process of AVT, defined as 'the loss with very little intervention by the translator' (Gambier 2013: 54). Recent research on communities of amateur mediators suggests that the nature of these communities with 'permeable and porous' boundaries (Baker 2013: 25) makes them a new powerful *locus* of collective identity formation, which has the potential to challenge the 'narratives circulated by the media elites and the sociopolitical structures they represent' (Pérez-González 2010: 271).

Against this backdrop of fast changes in the current media landscape, such as the proliferation of media sources, the fragmentation of audiences, and the new forms of engagement of audiences with the information that comes their way, it is more important than ever before to undertake research on audiovisual translation from the point of view of end-users in their real-life settings, in order to gain a better understanding of the role of AVT in their daily lives. This requires scholars to move beyond traditional (predominantly quantitative) approaches to audience studies, and embrace new methodological developments that enable explorations into how specific audience groups, such as those engaged in collaborative and community-based translation, respond to, and appropriate, audiovisual texts; and shed light on the range of contexts, circumstances, and purposes driving those processes of engagement, collaboration and appropriation. This chapter argues that ethnography can serve as a useful research method in the context of AVT because it represents 'an epistemological shift' that 'forc[es] its practitioners to empathise with participants and adopt their standpoint' (Ladner 2014: 73), so as to 'secure an up-close, first-hand, intimate understanding of the social world, issues, and/or processes of interest, particularly as they are experienced and understood by the individuals studied' (Snow 1999: 98).

The fact that we are making use of an ever-growing and more mobile set of digital technologies to engage in the experience and co-creation of audiovisual texts inevitably presents several challenges for an ethnographic approach to AVT. For instance, how can we define the locus of users' activities, when they are geographically dispersed and interact through various types of online platforms (e.g. blogs, wikis and social networking sites)? If we are to investigate such multi-sited online communities, how should we present ourselves and build relationships with participants? How should we monitor and gauge the authenticity and truthfulness of the information provided by participants, given that it would be easy for them to provide researchers with false or inaccurate information, or even fabricate an online identity? Which fieldwork tools should we choose to capture, archive and analyze various forms of digital data (e.g. text images, audio and video) gathered from online fieldsites? Without the thorough technical, social and cultural knowledge required to fully participate in technology-mediated social settings, we are likely to be reduced to 'covert participant observers' who 'shape the digital fieldsite in sometimes unfamiliar ways' (Murthy 2008: 849).

This chapter sets out to address these important issues and presents 'netnography' or 'Internet ethnography' (Kozinets 2010)—a form of ethnographic research 'adapted to the unique contingencies of various types of computer-mediated social interaction' (*ibid.*: 20)—as a productive method to study how media consumers, particularly amateur mediators such as fansubbers and activist subtitlers, interact with audiovisual products and form communities based on their collaborative media consumption experiences. I then draw on my own experience as a netnographer investigating a multi-sited online community of Chinese fansubbers, and explain how netnographic fieldwork is conducted—with special attention to issues encountered during the fieldwork and the strategies developed to tackle them. Ultimately, this chapter shows how AVT researchers can manage effectively the sort of methodological challenges that are likely to arise when studying these sites of AVT activity.

Netnography

Netnography derives its name from the aggregation of 'net' (as in 'the Internet') and 'ethnography'. As the meanings of its constitutive morphemes—'ethno' (people) and 'graphy' (describing)—denote, ethnography involves a detailed or 'thick' description (Geertz 1973) of the culture of a group of people with unique, though often shared, patterns of behaviour, beliefs and values. This entails the need for prolonged periods of participant observation and/or researchers' immersion into the daily lives of the study subjects. By 'watching what happens, listening to what is said, [and] asking questions' (Hammersley and Atkinson 1995: 1), researchers gather representative data to inform their interpretations of the cultural issues under scrutiny. This relatively open approach allows the researcher to identify unforeseen events that emerge while conducting fieldwork as important and worth pursuing; it also helps researchers to make sense of these events based on their interaction with cultural members; information pertaining to the immediate environment where the activities under investigation take place; and the wider social context in which community members and their activities are embedded (Bryman 1998). From this perspective, the researcher's self-reflexivity and experience in the fieldsite is crucial for the construction of ethnographic knowledge, which is, in principle, dialogical and intersubjective (Hammersley and Atkinson 1995).

In the Digital Age, 'geography can no longer be the defining framework for culture' (Boyd 2009: 27), as people create cultures and communities on the Internet through digital media technologies. These online cultures and communities have opened up opportunities for researchers to apply traditional ethnographic principles (e.g. thick description, immersion, and self-reflexivity) to the study of Internet-based culture-sharing groups. As Murthy (2008: 838) notes, 'as ethnography goes digital, its epistemological remit remains much the same. Ethnography is about telling social stories'. Whether it is used for studying offline or online social phenomena, ethnography is about representing the social reality of others through the researcher's analysis of his/her own experience in the world of these 'others'.

In an effort to adapt the traditional ethnographic approach to the study of the complex world of the Internet and other technologically mediated communications, scholars have coined and applied different neologisms to describe their research methods: 'technography' (Richardson 1992), 'online ethnography' (Markham 1998), 'virtual ethnography' (Hine 2000), and 'digital ethnography' (Murthy 2008), to name just a few. Kozinets (2010: 5) points out that, terminological issues aside, there is a lack of clarity and consistency in terms of the 'specific procedural guidelines' that a researcher can follow when conducting online ethnography. To fill this gap, Kozinets (*ibid.*) proposes a method, namely netnography, with a set of procedures—planning for fieldwork, entering the online fieldsite of a community, collecting and analyzing data, and ensuring strict adherence to ethical standards—designed to facilitate the study of communities and cultures on the Internet.

In keeping with traditional ethnographical principles, netnography is context-specific, immersive, descriptive, and multi-method (Kozinets 2010). Unlike traditional ethnography, however, netnography 'uses computer-mediated communications as a source of data to arrive at the ethnographic understanding and representation of a cultural or communal phenomenon' (*ibid.*: 60). Netnography therefore often involves the collection of three different types of data: (i) 'archival data', i.e. pre-existing computer-mediated communications and other digital artefacts created by research participants; (ii) 'elicited data', namely data co-created by the researcher and the participants through personal and communal interactions; and (iii) 'fieldnote data', that is notes written by the researcher regarding his/her own observations and participation experiences of the research community (*ibid.*). Using the term 'netnography' in one's research project signals 'the importance of computer-mediated communications in the lives of cultural members', and acknowledges that 'netnography has its own uniquely adapted set of practices and procedures that set it apart from the conduct of face-to-face ethnography' (*ibid.*: 60).

A key advantage of netnography is, therefore, that through its engagement with the Internet and related digital media technologies, it not only allows researchers to connect with participants from communities that do not exist, or would be difficult to access, in the offline world, but also enables the exploration of the ways in which participants deploy digital media technologies to construct and share meaningful experiences and identities online. Nevertheless, it is this convenient access to private aspects of participants' lives that creates new ethical dilemmas about the implications of conducting covert/overt online research, the public/private nature of online interactions, and the need to anonymize/credit research participants, among other key issues.

Some scholars (e.g. Langer and Beckman 2005) maintain that a covert approach allows researchers to observe participant behaviour in an unobtrusive way, and thus can reduce the risk of distorting data gathered from the online fieldsites. By contrast, Kozinets argues, netnography 'is *a participative approach* to the study of online culture and communities' (2010: 74, emphasis in original). Removing the researcher's participative role from netnography also removes the opportunity to experience 'embedded cultural understanding' (*ibid.*). Without the experience and knowledge of the cultural context, the researcher is forced to interpret unfamiliar cultural meanings from an outsider's perspective; and since the researcher is not a participant in the online community under study, s/he has no one in that community to turn to in order to validate or dispute his/her interpretation. Consequently, the researcher is likely to provide a superficial analysis of the content that s/he manages to collect from the online fieldsite.

In order to adopt a participative role in the online community they would like to study, researchers should follow good netnographic research ethics. According to Kozinets (2010), such ethics dictate that the researcher should: (i) gain permission to study the community from its members; (ii) openly and accurately describe the research purpose for interacting with community members; and (iii) openly and accurately identify oneself, even though faking identities is common on the Internet. Kozinets (*ibid.*) also recommends that netnographers set up a dedicated webpage providing a more detailed explanation of their research focus and interests, and perhaps share the research findings with community members at different stages of the fieldwork.

When it comes to whether interactions on the Internet should be treated as if they took place in a public or a private space, Kozinets (2010: 141) argues that 'only certain kinds of Internet experiences can be described in spatial terms'. These include interactions in chatrooms and emails, which are forms of communication taking place in guarded places with expectations of privacy, and thus should never be recorded without gaining explicit permission. Oftentimes, however, community members use the Internet as a type of publishing medium; in these cases, they are aware that their content is available publicly, and hence likely to be observed by strangers (*ibid.*). This does not necessarily mean that posting on blogs, online forums and other social networking sites should automatically be regarded as a public activity, since community members may not expect or even react with anger if their remarks were to be read by people outside their communities. Drawing on Walther (2002), Kozinets (2010: 142) argues that anyone using publicly accessible communication systems on the Internet should be aware that these systems are 'mechanisms for the storage, transmission, and retrieval of comments'. He concludes that archives/communications that are gathered from publicly accessible online venues are usable by researchers, as long as they have properly considered the potential embarrassments or risks that might come from exposing participants' identities in the write-up, and the rights of participants to receive credit for their accounts and intellectual work (*ibid.*).

This leads to another ethical dilemma about whether to credit or anonymize participants' accounts and other creative work (e.g. photos, music and videos). On the one hand, much of their work can be considered to have 'semi-published' (Kozinets 2010) qualities and the content creators may be public figures. Researchers should therefore give the creators credit for their work, and ask them if they would like to have their real names, pseudonyms or both mentioned in the final research write-up. On the other hand, if the study is about a stigmatized, marginalized or illegal group, revealing participants' real names or pseudonyms is not appropriate, since 'pseudonyms are often traceable to real names, and people often care about the reputation of their pseudonyms' (*ibid.*: 153). Consequently, when studying vulnerable groups, researchers should explain at the beginning of their research projects the risks that their projects may entail for participants, and note that the latter have been anonymized. This decision, as emphasized by Kozinets (*ibid.*), must be made by researchers and their institutions, rather than by the participants themselves.

A related issue to the crediting of the study subjects is whether or not it is necessary to interact with them in the offline world in order to verify the authenticity of their identities and the information contained in their personal profiles. Kozinets (2010) believes that the virtual worlds are legitimate sites of culture, and therefore it is not always necessary to combine netnography with real-life research or verification. If a study is focused on phenomena that are directly related to online communities and online culture itself, or to one or more of their particular manifestations or aspects (e.g. online identity, online cultural artefacts, relationships, and other social interactive elements emerging through computer-mediated communications), then netnography can be used as a stand-alone method. In other words, 'pure' netnography can be conducted by using data gathered exclusively from online or other technology-mediated communications (*ibid.*). Rather than their offline demographics, in pure netnographic studies the primary concern for researchers is the personal information and the profiles that community members choose to make available online, as these are the only indication that members have of each other's identities and circumstances. If a study looks at members of a community whose activities extend well beyond their online interactions (e.g. *Star Trek* fans), then a 'blended ethnography/netnography' (*ibid.*: 65) would be more useful. Such blended studies, that combine online information with data gathered via traditional ethnographic techniques (e.g. in-person participant observation and face-to-face interviews) would be more helpful in yielding a general understanding of the experiences of the cultural members under scrutiny. A collection of their offline demographic data (e.g. age, gender, ethnicity, class, and so forth) would therefore be necessary in order to reveal how their specific circumstances affect the ways they behave in both offline and online contexts.

As Kozinets (2010) notes, whether a netnography based solely on online data is sufficient depends entirely on the research focus and questions that the researcher seeks to investigate. Furthermore, he questions the distinction between online and offline social worlds, arguing that 'the two have blended into one world: the world of real life, as people live it. It is a world that includes the use of technology to communicate, to commune, to socialise, to express, and to understand' (*ibid.*: 2). This means that when we come to topics such as the world of fansubbing communities, activist subtitlers and amateur mediators, our cultural portrayals would be extremely limited without detailed reference to various forms of technology-mediated communication that increasingly make these collectivities possible. Drawing on my own netnographic fieldwork on Chinese fansubbers' deployment of digital media technologies to facilitate their daily subtitling activities, the next section illustrates how fieldwork is conducted in this environment, draws attention to the challenges encountered during the fieldwork and discusses the strategies used to manage them.

A netnography of a fansubbing group

My netnographic fieldwork focused on a group of Chinese fansubbers based on the blog publishing platform WordPress. The group, anonymized here for reasons of confidentiality, has been engaging in fansubbing activities over 10 years, working voluntarily around the clock to translate and circulate a variety of foreign audiovisual content, which had been either banned or extensively re-edited by Chinese censors, as part of the government's fight against 'vulgar' content that usually features politically and sexually explicit material. Dodging Chinese censors and media regulators, the fansubbing group has developed into a well-established organization with over 1,000 members geographically dispersed across China and abroad. In order to uncover the subtle and precise ways in which group members make use of technology to facilitate their collaborative consumption of foreign audiovisual content and create shared meanings based on their membership of a fansubbing group, a netnography was conducted between March and December 2013.

Locating and entering the fieldsite

Since my study focused primarily on a community that was forged and interacted only online, a 'pure' netnography was chosen to investigate the textually mediated virtual world of community members. In order to gain direct experience of community membership, I decided to adopt a participative stance, and hence become grounded or embedded as much as possible in the online fieldsite.

The next step, then, was to gain permission to study the fansubbing group from its participants. After becoming acquainted with the history, genre speciality and membership requirements of the group via its blogging site on WordPress, I sent an exploratory email to the group's public email address, introducing myself and the research project I was planning to undertake. My introductory email was informed by the following strategies:

- *being genuine*—I fully disclosed my motivation to join the group and expressed my wish to be one more of the community members, taking care to avoid using too many academic expressions in the message;
- *being humble*—drawing on the premise that members of the fansubbing group must know much more about their own culture, I concluded that humility was a must-have attitude on my part, as that would encourage more sincere input from group members;
- *working towards the values cherished by the group*—based on the group's slogan (i.e. 'share the fun of creation and appreciate the beauty of subtitles'), I decided to contribute my own knowledge and skills to the betterment of the group, and made sure that this intention was clearly signalled in my first email to the group;
- *abiding by the group's codes of conduct*—I declared in the email that I was willing to follow the rules and norms of the group.

These strategies proved to be effective, as its gatekeepers granted me permission to join the group. The first thing they asked me to do was to introduce myself to the rest of the community in a chatroom called 'newbies camp' set up through Tencent QQ (i.e. China's most popular instant messenger that integrates file transfer, QQ mail, QQ blog, and other Tencent services such as games and music). When entering the chatroom, I introduced myself by describing my research project and revealing my real name, in order to let group members know my identity as a researcher-participant. The following are some of the replies I received at that point:

Reply 1: [Is Dang Li] your real name?!

Reply 2: A-drop-of-sweat-on-a-face emoticon [to acknowledge the embarrassment that revealing my real name would have caused].

Reply 3: So, there are indeed some cute newbies who introduce themselves by telling us their real names. Smiley face emoticon.

Reply 4: Let us know your pseudonym, please!

At that point, I realized that it was the group's norm to use pseudonyms to address each other; the norm was so strongly adhered to that, even when they met someone like me, members would rather not ask for/know my real name. Another thing that struck me as interesting was that no one in the chatroom seemed to be interested in my research project. Instead, they could not wait to find out what I looked like and urged me to upload a picture of myself. The first picture I uploaded was not approved, on the grounds that I was wearing a pair of sunglasses which blocked half of my face.

As an approved group member, I was warmly addressed through my pseudonym, or terms such as 'dear sis', and 'MM' (an Internet slang term pronounced as '*mei mei*' in Chinese, which usually refers to 'little sister'). In order to know more about me, some members asked which foreign language(s) I spoke or which audiovisual genres were my favourite; some looked for overlaps between the personal information featured in our QQ profiles, such as birthday, zodiac sign, horoscope, blood type, and geographical location. And there were others who seemed to be more interested in filling me in on who was who (e.g. group leaders and senior members) in the chatroom and their personalities. Such conversations were visible to everyone in the chatroom, making it easy for anyone interested in the topics being discussed to initiate further conversations. In this way, both newcomers, such as me, and existing members were able to quickly bond and form close relationships.

It soon became clear that the group's activities were not confined to its blogging site; the community operated across digital platforms as diverse as QQ instant messenger, Sina Weibo (the most popular microblog service in China), Douban (a Chinese social networking site popular among media fans who form or join fan groups to review their favourite media products), and a password-protected forum set up through File Transfer Protocol (FTP) servers that hosted the group's collection of foreign media content. This posed a challenge in terms of defining the boundaries of the fieldsite for my project. I turned to advice from previous scholars (e.g. Olwig and Hastrup 1997: 8), who pointed out that, when conducting netnography on a community whose members interact over multiple platforms, the researcher might still start from a particular digital site, but should 'follow connections which were made meaningful from that setting'. Other scholars also argued that, instead of conceptualizing the online fieldsite as a 'site', it might be more useful to view it as a network that 'incorporates physical, virtual, and imagined spaces' (Burrell 2009: 1) or as a set of relations that the netnographer traces between people, artefacts, and (physical and/or virtual) places (Hine 2009).

Consequently, I decided to allow my fieldwork to be fluid and based on the networks in which my participants embedded themselves. To do this, I did not identify any particular 'sites' as pre-existing places for my fieldwork; instead, I anchored it in my participants' connections. By doing this, I was able to keep track of their activities, while engaging in constant interaction with them across all possible platforms. This comprehensive participation was crucial for me to gain a more nuanced understanding of the group's social processes, since participants attuned their behaviour and interactions according to the communication functions provided by these platforms.

For instance, the open source blogging site WordPress and other social networking platforms (e.g. Sina Weibo and Douban) were mainly used by the group to publish its translated subtitles (saved as .srt files) for the public to download, promote its ethos, and attract potential participants. On the other hand, the group's online forum was used to make group-wide announcements, publish guidelines on members' codes of conduct, and provide members with instructions on the use of subtitling software applications and the subtitling conventions specified by the group (e.g. formatting standards, punctuation conventions, and the subtitling of off-screen voices). Supported by FTP technology, the forum also provided members with a safe and organized file-sharing environment, where they must provide their unique IDs and passwords to log into specified file-sharing spaces to upload or download the raw material (i.e. the video files of the original foreign films or TV programmes) for their subtitling projects. By separating what was given away (i.e. the translated subtitles) from what was retained (i.e. the original video content), the group managed to shield itself from potential government sanctions on large-scale unauthorized video distribution. Viewers outside the group who wanted to get their hands on the video content could still do so through other P2P networks (e.g. *The Pirate Bay*). However, compared to the video files hosted on such networks, the video files stored on the group's forum were much smaller: they were compressed by the group's 'compression team' to facilitate video-sharing within the group.

Taking advantage of QQ's communication functions (e.g. real-time text messaging, audio/video chat, and file transfer), members of the fansubbing group created various chatrooms for sub-teams in charge of different tasks (e.g. raw material, compression, timing, translation, and proofreading) involved in the subtitling process. Members belonging to different sub-teams who were involved in subtitling the same video content often set up a temporary chatroom to discuss problems they encountered during the subtitling project. As a result, the scope of members' activities expanded from one chatroom to several chatrooms, from interacting with only a few individuals in the same chatroom to doing so with a wider group of members from different chatrooms. In this sense, the instant messaging application QQ was used by members as a shared workspace, where multiple individuals were able to access, create and interact around a shared digital artefact; and where all group members were able to be present in multiple chatrooms at the same time and engage in multiple discussions and collaborations simultaneously.

While the 'opening point' of my fieldwork was the blogging site of the fansubbing group, the fieldsite kept evolving and expanding as my fieldwork progressed. This indicates that, rather than a particular website or platform, what holds an online assembly of individuals together as a community is its membership and members' shared practices on different digital platforms. Consequently, following and participating in these practices help researchers delineate the boundaries of their online fieldsite. In other words, it is the researcher's engagement with the research community that creates and defines a netnographic fieldsite.

Building research relationships

During the initial state of my fieldwork, I gained approval to study the fansubbing group from its gatekeepers as well as full access to the group's members-only forum and QQ chatrooms. This, however, did not guarantee a sustained, community-wide acceptance of my presence. As noted by Hine (2005: 20), 'establishing one's presence as a bona fide researcher and trustworthy recipient of confidences is not automatic, and varies depending on the cultural context under investigation'. If the researcher failed to form trusting relationships with research participants, they could remain suspicious or even hostile towards the researcher, who could be treated as an inconvenience, or worse, an intruder to their normal activities. Further exacerbating the doubts of my participants about their role in and potential contribution to my research project was the fact that they were operating at the mercy of Chinese censors, who could invoke censorship or copyright laws to suppress their subtitling activities. Participants could suspect me of having an ulterior motive to collect their personal information that could put them at the risk of copyright and censorship sanctions. Moreover, since I was not physically co-present with my participants while conducting fieldwork, I could remain invisible to them without getting myself involved in their daily online interactions.

In order to make myself visible and credible to my participants, I sought to follow some of the guiding principles common to ethnographic studies, including the need for the researcher to 'establish a large degree of ordinary sociability and normal social intercourse' with research participants (Walsh 1998: 253); and 'a commitment to try and view the object of enquiry through attempting some kind of alignment with the perspective of those who participate in the research' (Horst and Miller 2006: 167). To put these principles into practice, I followed the most common practice for self-presentation and communication in the fansubbing group, i.e. pseudonymity—as explained above, group members, by default, used pseudonyms to address and interact with each other across their forum, chatrooms, and other social networks. I also followed another norm, i.e. using an array of endearment terms (e.g. 'brother', 'sister', and 'sweetie') traditionally reserved for close family members or friends, rather than online contacts, when interacting with participants, as this appeared to be a widely held practice in the group. While most participants used avatars (e.g. cute animals or cartoon characters) as their profile pictures, I always posted a face picture in all my profiles on the platforms I used to interact with my study subjects.

I also found it useful to highlight my academic background and experience in (audiovisual) translation in my personal profiles, since doing so conveyed to my participants that I shared similar interests and experiences in subtitling. In fact, most of my participants were not interested in my academic identity as a researcher in translation studies. Instead, they were most interested in my future potential role as a valuable contributor who may assist them with their subtitling projects and other organizational activities. A typical day spent with my participants involved me engaging in tasks such as timing, translating or proofreading subtitles, using the group's subtitling software application on my computer, and having multiple conversations with group members who were engaged in the same subtitling project(s) that I was working on.

Our conversations usually unfolded in QQ chatrooms created to facilitate the coordination of specific projects. We often started out informing each other about the progress of our own tasks, and then discussed the problems we had encountered and came up with ideas to solve them. Quite often, we also discussed our viewing experiences of the content being subtitled, which opened up further conversations on various topics, ranging from mundane topics such as weather, pets and hobbies, to more intimate or sensitive ones, pertaining to love relationships, sexuality, pornography, and domestic politics. During such discussions, I never forced or cajoled my participants to reveal sensitive information about themselves. Neither was I judgemental about the views they shared on sensitive topics. I always 'listened' intently before typing my own views, and shared as much about myself as they shared about themselves in order to be as relatable to them as possible.

By following the normative practices regarding self-presentation and interaction in the fansubbing group, blending in through genuine and respectful communications, and being as relatable as possible, my presence in the group was normalized. In doing so, I also developed closer relationships with my participants. Nevertheless, despite the efforts I made towards building rapport with group members, it was they themselves who ultimately formed their impressions of me—not just about me as a researcher, or a participant, or a netnographer—but as a person. Knowing that digital media technologies provided research participants with an opportunity to access and learn more about various aspects of my digital self that I presented on my social media sites (e.g. my QQ blog and Sina Weibo account), I considered whether I should tighten my privacy settings on these sites to limit participants' access to parts of my profiles that were only visible to my family and close friends. In the end, I chose to open up my digital identity. My online profiles and the content posted in them (e.g. photos, and comments) that were available to my friends and family became also accessible to my participants, in order to convey the degree of openness that I expected from them.

During my fieldwork, members of the fansubbing group frequently visited my social media sites, leaving comments on my newly added pictures or blog posts. I also 'liked' or commented on their latest updates. Such interactions granted us more opportunities for social exchange and mutual investigation. Through this interaction, I amassed a significant number of QQ friends and Sina Weibo followers from the fansubbing group. These connections became useful, not only as a way to form a genuine bond with group members in the context of virtual settings, but also as a way to secure their sincere responses in an online questionnaire that I conducted about their sense of shared identity, as well as a high participation rate—40 out of 56 potential participants submitted a completely finished questionnaire.

Of particular significance in conducting this online questionnaire was to explore, from the point of view of participants, the meanings they attached to their experiences as members of the fansubbing group. The nature of that experience can be illustrated by the following extracts from some participants' responses to one of the questions in the questionnaire (both the question and answers were originally in Chinese and have been translated here by the author):

Question: How would you describe your relationship(s), if any, with other members (i.e. do you know them through certain social media platforms or in other contexts, e.g. offline, work, school, or other organizations)?

Participant 1 Response: People tend to distinguish themselves from the crowd based on how they label each other. Instead of labelling ourselves as 'a fansubbing group', I want to use 'sharing, fun, caring and supporting' to label our group. It is not just a virtual group, but a group formed by real people. Although I only know the pseudonyms of my fellow members, their selfless dedication to the group's fansubbing activities is the source of my sense of belonging. They are the reason why I am still in the group.

Participant 2 Response: Under this sky [the fansubbing group], there are numerous battles [subtitling projects] being fought [carried out by group members] every day. During such processes, our friendships are strengthening day by day. I like to call my fellow members comrades-in-arms. 'Selfless dedication', 'free sharing', and 'unconditional love'—these are things that are hard to find in our society. Several years ago, I joined the group to pursue my dreams. Fortunately, I met a group of people sharing the same dreams and beliefs. More fortunately, these dreams still remain the same until now, although a lot of people keep joining and leaving the group. For me, all fellow members are my dear friends and comrades from the moment they join the group.

Participant 3 Response: In the [Chinese] film *My Brothers and Sisters*, the father tells his children: 'We are snowflakes falling from the sky. As soon as we fall to the ground, we melt into water and freeze together, we will never be separated'. All my brothers and sisters in the fansubbing group are just like snowflakes falling from the sky, and the group is the place where we melt together.

These extracts show how a semi-structured questionnaire equipped me with an in-depth understanding of participants' perspectives and accounts of their technology-mediated socialization experiences that are often not amenable to observations. The intimate connection experienced by participants regardless of their spatial and temporal distances resonated with Anderson's (2006) 'imagined communities', a term designating virtual groupings whose members do not have to meet face-to-face in order to feel connected to each other. In the case of the fansubbing group, metaphors such as 'battlefield', 'sky', or 'snowflakes melting together' were used by group members to describe their mental images of mutual affinity. All these expressions illustrated how computer-mediated communications can '[dissolve] distances by reembedding social relationships that are disembedded in space-time' (Fuchs 2005: 15). By combining my own participation experience with members' accounts, I was able to produce a detailed description of the lived experience of a group of Chinese media audiences engaging in collaborative and community-based translation of foreign media products.

Fieldwork tools

Although the Internet and other related communication technologies allowed me to connect with the fansubbing group at all times from any location, I was faced with problems to decide which tools I should use to capture and manage various forms of digital data across multiple sites, and how to add reflective notes and insights while capturing digital data—so that the data, e.g. a particular message or image, could be adequately contextualized and interpreted. As far as these issues are concerned, Kozinets (2010) recommends a range of dedicated computer programs facilitating the qualitative research, such as NVivo, which allows researchers to capture, store and analyse digital data, while adding reflective field-notes along the way.

After spending a considerable amount of time becoming familiar with NVivo, I decided not to use this complex software application, as it could actually get in the way of my data collection and analytical processes. During my fieldwork, I used different tools to document my observations on participants' behaviour. I relied heavily on the note-taking software application Evernote to organize my archival and fieldnote data. Evernote, along with other social media applications (e.g. WordPress, QQ and Sina Weibo) used by my participants, were installed on the devices that I used to conduct my fieldwork. Evernote Web Clipper was further added as an extension tool for the desktop browser (Chrome) that I used to visit the group's blogging site, online platform, and other social networking sites (Sina Weibo and Douban) popular among group members. This application allowed me to capture any digital artefact (e.g. text, posting, image, or other multimedia files) that I found interesting on a webpage that I was browsing. The captured web clips were saved as they appeared on the original pages and as notes in my Evernote account, together with the URLs of the pages those clips were taken from. This means that I could always go back to the original pages to gain a sense of the situational contexts of captured data.

With Evernote, I was able to add my own comments in each clipped note. The comments usually referred to the nature of the clipped material, the meaning of the material to participants, my interpretation of the material, and an analysis of the material. All the fieldnotes created and saved in my Evernote account were indexed with titles and tags, which thus became searchable and filterable. This provided me with keyword-based search results that could inspire or remind me of any other related notes stored in Evernote. Besides, the sync feature of Evernote meant that notes stored in my Evernote account could automatically be synchronized between my laptop and smartphone when they were connected to the Internet. Even when I did not have my laptop with me, I could still visit my fieldsite, and add or edit notes through the Evernote app installed on my phone. Combining a traditional computer with a smartphone allowed me to immerse myself fully in the daily life of the fansubbing group.

Apart from asynchronous communications on multiple social networking sites, participants also stayed connected using the QQ real-time messaging service, which was the primary social space for them to engage not only in group discussions about issues and problems encountered while carrying out their subtitling projects, but also in spontaneous conversations about a variety of non-translation related topics—as elaborated above. Simply by logging into my QQ account via my computer or smartphone, I could check, search, and export the group's chat records through the Message History function provided by QQ. Compared to asynchronous messages posted on the group's forum and other public online sites, conversations unfolding in the group's QQ chatrooms were more private and intimate, and could easily border on being politically sensitive or socially transgressive. Insofar as collecting communications from chatrooms could breach ethical standards, recordings were immediately transferred to an encrypted hard drive and deleted from my devices (laptop and phone). Care was also taken to ensure that the identifying details (e.g. QQ accounts, pseudonyms and real names) of participants were removed when their QQ messages were directly quoted in my final report.

The tool used to conduct the online questionnaire was the web-based survey software application SelectSurvey.Net. The security level was set as 'force anonymous' in configuring the questionnaire to avoid potential breaches of participants' privacy. This means that all my respondents' personal details (e.g. email address) were removed from and became untraceable in their responses. To further minimize digital traces of our interactions, responses were exported as an Excel file (as allowed by the software) to an encrypted hard drive, and deleted from my SelectSurvey.Net account and my computer.

Summary

Under the impact of media convergence, audiences are increasingly migrating online to seek out and promote their own media experiences by engaging in various forms of media co-creative practices, such as participatory AVT. This makes it more important than ever to examine how audiences utilize media content for their own agendas, and how this in turn feeds back to the AVT industry and informs commercial AVT practices. Although the phenomenon of participatory AVT has not passed unnoticed by AVT scholars, methodological innovation has not kept pace, resulting in studies that often focus on the textual features of amateur outputs or the collaborative workflow models of amateur AVT. Little attention, however, has been paid to amateur mediators themselves, their perspectives, motivations and experiences of their involvement in participatory AVT. This is largely due to the fluid and often transient processes in which audiences deploy and interact with digital media, which make them difficult to study, but also make them compelling objects of ethnographic inquiry.

In this chapter, netnography has been presented as a useful method for studying the phenomenon of participatory AVT. As a specialized form of ethnography in the social spaces of online environments, netnography involves an active approach that seeks to engage and connect with members of a community that manifests itself through computer-mediated communications, with the aim to obtain a detailed and embedded understanding of the cultural meanings of that community. Utilizing this method, it is possible for us to identify, select, analyze and aggregate the particularities in networked forms of AVT performed by consumers, in order to gain first-hand and authentic insights into their collaborative consumption experiences. Such insights can be used as the basis for developing effective AVT services tailored to the real needs and expectations of media consumers.

Through a reflexive account of the author's netnographic fieldwork, this chapter has examined strategies developed by the author to overcome methodological challenges encountered during her fieldwork, which mainly include defining the boundaries of a multi-sited community; building relationships with participants in virtual contexts; and using fieldwork tools to manage digital data. While the strategies developed by the author are in relation to her personal experience in an online community formed by Chinese fansubbers, these strategies could provide some useful clues for researchers who may find themselves in similar situations.

More importantly, this chapter has attempted to show that a netnographic fieldwork is a continuous, self-reflexive experience constantly negotiated between the researcher, research participants, and the research context. As illustrated by the author's fieldwork, multiple online sites and identities have been navigated during the research process, sometimes as an outsider of the research community; sometimes as a peripheral participant on the way to full participation; and sometimes as an insider participating in the practices of the community. This indicates that (i) the fieldsite for the study of an online community can no longer be conceptualized as a single site or platform that the researcher enters and inhabits, but rather as the outcome of the researcher's trajectories in following and engaging with participants' practices across different online venues; and (ii) the notion of 'insider vs. outsider' is not fluid enough to truly reflect the experience of conducting online fieldwork as researchers reposition themselves within and across various platforms at various times throughout the research process. Hence, how researchers present and manage their digital identity can significantly influence their ability to gain access to the research community, forge trusting research relationships, collect good quality data, and construct netnographic knowledge. The author would therefore encourage other scholars to 'acknowledge and critically (though not necessarily negatively) engage with the range of possibilities of position, place and identity' (Coffey 1999: 36), so that we can continually be aware of our netnographic self and understand its relevance in the situations that we are studying.

Further reading

Hine, C. (2000) *Virtual Ethnography*, London: SAGE | *This book shows how ethnographic methods can be adapted creatively to research into computer-mediated forms of communication. Internet is conceptualized here as both a site for cultural formations and a cultural artefact which is shaped by users' understandings and expectations.*

Kozinets, R. V. (2010) *Netnography: Doing Ethnographic Research Online*, London: SAGE | *This book provides step-by-step procedural guidelines for the accurate and ethical conduct of netnography. It uses examples of netnographic studies of the blogosphere, videocasting, podcasting, social networking sites and virtual worlds to illustrate techniques, methods and tools used during netnographic fieldworks.*

Pérez-González, L. (2014) *Audiovisual Translation: Theories, Methods and Issues*, London & New York: Routledge | *Among other issues, this book delivers a thorough exploration of emerging new trends in AVT, such as amateur subtitling and other participatory subtitling practices in networked mediascapes.*

Related topics

19 Gender in audiovisual translation: advocating for gender awareness
23 Audiovisual translation and audience reception
27 Audiovisual translation and fandom
28 Audiovisual translation and activism

References

Anderson, B. (2006) *Imagined Communities*, New York: Verso Books.
Baker, M. (2013) 'Translation as an Alternative Space for Political Action', *Social Movement Studies* 12(1): 23–47.
Boyd, D. (2009) 'A Response to Christine Hine: Defining Project Boundaries', in A. N. Markham and N. K. Baym (eds) *Internet Inquiry: Conversations about Method*, London: SAGE, 26–32.
Bryman, A. (1998) *Quantity and Quality in Social Research*, London: Unwin Hyman.
Burrell, J. (2009) 'The Field Site as a Network: A Strategy for Locating Ethnographic Research', *Field Methods* 21(2): 181–199.
Coffey, A. (1999) *The Ethnographic Self: Fieldwork and the Representation of Identity*, London: SAGE.
Fernández Costales, A. (2012) 'Collaborative Translation Revisited: Exploring the Rationale and the Motivation for Volunteer Translation', *Forum—International Journal of Translation* 10(1): 115–142.
Fuchs, C. (2005) 'Knowledge and Society from the Perspective of the Unified Theory of Information (UTI) Approach', in *Proceedings of FIS 2005: Third Conference on the Foundations of Information Science*. Available online: http://www.mdpi.org/fis2005/F.24.paper.pdf [last access 20 December 2017].
Gambier, Y. (2001) 'Les traducteurs face aux écrans: Une élite d'experts', in F. Chaume and R. Agost (eds) *La traducción en los medios audiovisuales*, Castelló: Servei de Publicacions de la Universitat Jaume I, 91–114.
Gambier, Y. (2006) 'Multimodality and Audiovisual Translation', in *MuTra 2006—Audiovisual Translation Scenarios: Conference Proceedings*. Available online: http://www.translationconcepts.org/pdf/2006_Gambier_Yves.pdf [last access 20 December 2017].
Gambier, Y. (2009) 'Challenges in Research on Audiovisual Translation', in A. Pym and A. Perekrestenko (eds) *Translation Research Projects 2*, Spain: Intercultural Studies Group, 17–25.
Gambier, Y. (2013) 'The Position of Audiovisual Translation Studies', in C. Millán-Varela and F. Bartrina (eds) *The Routledge Handbook of Translation Studies*, London & New York: Routledge, 45–59.

Geertz, C. (1973) *The Interpretation of Cultures: Selected Essays*, New York: Basic Books.
Hammersley, M. and P. Atkinson (1995) *Ethnography: Principles in Practice*, London: Routledge.
Hine, C. (2000) *Virtual Ethnography*, London: SAGE.
Hine, C. (2005) 'Researcher Relationships and Online Relationships: Introduction', in C. Hine (ed.) *Virtual Methods: Issues in Social Research on the Internet*, London: Berg, 17–20.
Hine, C. (2009) 'How Can Qualitative Internet Researchers Define the Boundaries of Their Projects', in A. N. Markham and N. K. Baym (eds) *Internet Inquiry: Conversations about Method*, London: SAGE, 1–20.
Horst, H. and D. Miller (2006) *The Cell Phone: An Anthropology of Communication*, Oxford: Berg.
Jenkins, H. (2006) *Convergence Culture: Where Old and New Media Collide*, New York: New York University Press.
Kozinets, R. V. (2010) *Netnography: Doing Ethnographic Research Online*, London: SAGE.
Künzli, A. and M. Ehrensberger-Dow (2011) 'Innovative Subtitling: A Reception Study', in C. Alvstad, A. Hild, and E. Tiselius (eds) *Methods and Strategies of Process Research: Integrative Approaches in Translation Studies*, Amsterdam & Philadelphia: John Benjamins Publishing, 187–200.
Ladner, S. (2014) *Practical Ethnography: A Guide to Doing Ethnography in the Private Sector*, CA: Left Coast Press.
Langer, R. and S. C. Beckman (2005) 'Sensitive Research Topics: Netnography Revisited', *Qualitative Market Research* 8(2): 189–203.
Markham, A. N. (1998) *Life Online: Researching Real Experience in Virtual Space*, Walnut Creek, CA: Altamira Press.
Murthy, D. (2008) 'Digital Ethnography: An Examination of the Use of New Technologies for Social Research', *Sociology* 42(5): 837–855.
Olwig, K. F. and K. Hastrup (1997) *Sitting Culture: The Shifting Anthropological Object*, New York: Routledge.
Pérez-González, L. (2010) '*Ad-hocracies* of Translation Activism in the Blogosphere: A Genealogical Case Study', in M. Baker, M. Olohan, and M. Calzada (eds) *Text and Context: Essays on Translation and Interpreting in Honour of Ian Mason*, Manchester: St Jerome Publishing, 259–287.
Pérez-González, L. (2014) *Audiovisual Translation: Theories, Methods and Issues*. London: Routledge.
Richardson, L. (1992) 'Trash on the Corner Ethics and Technography', *Journal of Contemporary Ethnography* 21(1): 103–119.
Snow, D. (1999) 'Assessing the Ways in Which Qualitative/Ethnographic Research Contributes to Social Psychology: Introduction to the Special Issue', *Social Psychology Quarterly* 62(2): 97–100.
Walsh, D. (1998) 'Doing Ethnography', in S. Clive (ed.) *Researching Society and Culture*, London: SAGE, 217–232.
Walther, J. B. (2002) 'Research Ethics in Internet-Enabled Research: Human Subjects Issues and Methodological Myopia', *Ethics and Information Technology* 4(3): 205–2016.

Part IV
Audiovisual translation in society

25
Minority languages, language planning and audiovisual translation

Reglindis De Ridder and Eithne O'Connell

This chapter highlights often underestimated links between the fields of minority language (ML) media studies, sociolinguistics and translation studies. In doing so, it seeks to clarify key concepts relating to minority languages, language planning and policy (LPP) and audiovisual translation (AVT). It is hoped that drawing close attention to the past and current experience of minority languages will raise awareness of issues also of relevance to small, and many major languages, since they too are becoming *minoritized* in a world dominated by global English (Cronin 2003). The discussion is as wide-ranging as possible, within the inevitable space constraints, and draws on examples from around the world, while also addressing the European situation and the case of minority languages within the European Union. In an effort to avoid crude generalizations about minority languages and AVT, attention is drawn to the part played by such relevant variants as the asymmetry between individual language pairs; the implications of translation direction, i.e. translation *into* versus translation *from* a minority language; the relative language planning impact of various AVT modes and technologies; and the sociolinguistic needs of specific ML audiences.

Background

Thirty years ago, Gideon Toury (1985) drew attention to the links between minority languages and translation theory. He pointed out that translation could help to preserve and develop a minority language, but argued that too much translation activity *into* the minority language could have a negative effect. This was taken up by Michael Cronin who, while accepting that minority languages 'must translate continually in order to retain their viability and relevance as living languages' (1995: 89), warned that translation may endanger 'the very specificity of those languages that practice it' (*ibid.*). The relative advantages and disadvantages of minority language translation in both directions were explored with particular reference to scientific, literary and audiovisual texts by Eithne O'Connell and John Walsh (2006), who showed that while inward translation may invigorate a minority language and its culture, it may simultaneously challenge the language's ability to coin terminology corresponding to new concepts requiring translation.

Moreover, translations are considered classical language contact situations (Baumgarten and Özçetin 2008, Becher *et al.* 2009, Veiga Díaz 2012), which can trigger linguistic interference and may eventually also result in language change. An example of how this phenomenon (Antonini 2008, Herbst 1994) has also been identified in AVT is so-called *dubbese*. Three decades after Toury's remarks, issues relating to minority languages have still not moved into the mainstream of translation studies, although there has been a discernible growth in interest among scholars, over the last 20 years, particularly relating to the study of minority/ized languages, LPP and AVT (e.g. Antonini 2009, Armstrong and Federici 2006, Barambones *et al.* 2012, Bassols *et al.* 1995, Bueno Maia *et al.* 2015, De Ridder 2015, De Ridder and O'Connell 2018; Federici 2009, 2011; Fernández Torné and Matamala 2015, Folaron 2015, Kothari 1999, 2008; Kothari *et al.* 2004, Kruger and Rafapa 2002, Kruger *et al.* 2007, Lysaght 2010, Meylaerts 2011; O'Connell 1994, 1998, 2003; O'Connell and Walsh 2006, Remael and Neves 2007, Remael *et al.* 2008, Sanday Wandera 2015, Zabalbeascoa 2001).

Toury's point that too much unidirectional translation into a minority language may do more harm than good is well made. Yet, in the audiovisual industry, current post-production practices would suggest that the vulnerability of minority languages exposed willy-nilly to AVT is not generally understood. Take the example of the bilingual film *Kings* (2007). Although set in the UK, it tells the story of a group of Irish labourers, who converse with each other in their native tongue, Irish Gaelic. As O'Connell (2007a) has observed, having the main players speak their first language, which is a minority one even in their own country, is a useful filmic device to emphasize their cultural marginalization in the great colonial metropolis of London. Interestingly, the film in its original form incorporates English subtitles as an integral part from the outset. For Irish and English Anglophones, it may be attractively exotic to watch such a 'foreign' film made, unusually, in a neighbouring minority language.

One might think that integrating minority language translation into audiovisual productions such as this represents a win-win situation, certainly from the distributor's point of view: such works have a positive novelty value for major language speakers, while bolstering the self-image of the minority language speakers, who are so rarely portrayed in mainstream media. Be that as it may, it is unlikely that a sociolinguist, especially one interested in LPP, would see this bilingual phenomenon so positively. Certainly, minority languages benefit in terms of visibility from representation in prestigious audiovisual media such as film and television (see also Kruger *et al.* 2007 with regard to African minority languages). However, close scrutiny of the impact of the use of subtitles to translate from a minority language like Irish into a major language, such as English, shows that while the minority language viewers may enjoy their medium of expression achieving some prominence on the big screen, the benefit is simultaneously offset since the Irish language is overwritten once again by the dominant neighbouring language, in whose shadow and sphere of influence it continually struggles to survive. It is unlikely the decision to integrate English subtitles in *Kings* was motivated by anything more than the wish to reach a wider audience. Indeed, there is little evidence that the audiovisual industry as a whole has any particular interest in or understanding of the implications, either for major or minority languages, of the translation decisions it routinely makes. Audiovisual media, therefore, is a field where translation and sociolinguistics scholarship can make an important contribution by examining cause and effect and alerting both the industry and audiences to their findings.

Nor is it simply within the audiovisual industry that minority language translation and language planning issues and implications are frequently overlooked. As observed by Albert Branchadell (2011), most significant reference works in translation studies produced to date have not even thought of minority languages as a topic worthy of an entry or a substantial mention. Notable exceptions include Cronin's chapter 'Minority' in the second edition of Baker and Saldanha's *Routledge Encyclopedia of Translation Studies* (Cronin 2009) and the *Handbook of Translation Studies* (Gambier and Van Doorslaer 2011), in which Branchadell's piece on 'Minority Languages in Translation' appears. O'Connell (2007c) discusses minority languages in her chapter on AVT in Kuhiwczak and Littau's *The Companion to Translation Studies*. Also worth mentioning is the special issue of *The Translator* entitled 'Translation and Minority' (Venuti 1998). Ten years later in 2009, a new international translation studies journal, *mTm Journal*, was launched welcoming publications on translation from major into minor languages and vice versa, but also translation between minor languages. More recently, Debbie Folaron (2015) edited a special issue of the *Journal of Specialised Translation* entitled 'Translation and Minority, Lesser-used and Lesser-translated Languages and Cultures', which also includes papers on AVT.

Language planning is an area of study within sociolinguistics, which has also been slow to attract significant scholarly attention within translation studies. The term 'language planning' describes specific, deliberate interventions designed to provide linguistic support to a particular speech community, although it can be said that failing to intervene deliberately in practice also constitutes a language plan or policy of sorts. Such interventions may work either bottom-up, i.e. they may be community-generated, or top-down, i.e. when they are implemented by an authority such as a national body. The term in question has been expanded by Ricento (2000) into the more inclusive 'language planning and policy' (LPP). Policy, whether viewed as part of language planning or in addition to it, usually relates to more comprehensive measures intended to support or, in certain cases, restrict an individual language or set of languages and, as such, tends to be implemented by a government or other administrative body, i.e. top-down. Not surprisingly, LPP is frequently associated with languages so small and endangered that they, unlike world languages and some major languages, cannot rely on a *laissez-faire* approach to their speakers and linguistic resources to guarantee the continued existence and use of the language into the future.

For simplicity and convenience, overviews of LPP often focus on interventions relating to status, corpus and acquisition or usage (O'Connell and Walsh 2006). Research in minority language translation has shown that audiovisual media can impact on all types of language planning. Examples of how children's programmes in Basque were used in corpus planning, e.g. language standardization, have been provided by Barambones (2012), while Bassols *et al.* (1995) and Zabalbeascoa (2001) have described two contrasting approaches to minority language dubbing in Catalonia in the 1990s, each with different status, corpus and acquisition language planning implications. On the one hand, TVC, a Barcelona television station, acted as an agent promoting the Catalan standard recommended by the Institute of Catalan Studies (IEC), when translating the American children's animation series *The Flintstones* (1960–1966). On the other hand, Valencia-based Canal 9 avoided standardizing trends and chose to use children's informal street language as their linguistic guide when dubbing the same series.

Putting aside the socio-political tensions underlying the different approaches adopted in Barcelona and Valencia, it is clear, from a language planning perspective, how the two translation approaches enhanced the status of two different, potentially competing language varieties. By favouring one over the other, in each case, the dubbing teams also contributed to corpus development by favouring certain lexical and syntactic choices over others and, no doubt, accordingly influenced the language acquisition and usage of the respective audiences. This example is interesting because, for all that is written nowadays about globalization and multilingualism, many sociolinguists researching LPP investigate language *per se* while overlooking translation. Likewise, their colleagues in media studies may study print and audiovisual media while overlooking the LPP underpinning the media in its various forms and the AVT practices adopted. Yet, as Reine Meylaerts (2011: 744) points out, there is 'no language policy without a translation policy' and it is on that basis, and in an effort to attract more attention to the scope for interdisciplinary/multidisciplinary research linking minority languages, LPP and AVT, that this topic is the focus of this chapter.

Minority and minoritized languages

Minority languages

One possible explanation for the past reluctance of many translation and sociolinguistics scholars to engage meaningfully with the issue of minority languages is the problematic nature of the term 'minority language'. It may generally have negative and fixed connotations suggesting definitively that any given language either is, or is not a minority language and that minority languages, by definition, are disadvantaged and somehow inferior. Moreover, from a scholarly perspective, perhaps the greatest problem associated with the term 'minority language' is its lack of precision. Indeed, the phrase has multiple near-synonyms such as indigenous, aboriginal, autochthonous, minor and lesser-used language and, ironically, these terms together describe an estimated 90 per cent of the world's total of 7,000 languages (Folaron 2015: 16). It must be noted that a sociolinguist may have a very different understanding of minority languages from the European Union, for example, or the Council of Europe. Thus, in the European Charter for Regional or Minority Languages (1992), regional or minority languages are narrowly defined as those that are traditionally used within a given territory of a state by nationals of that state who form a group numerically smaller than the rest of the state's population; and different from the official language(s) of that state. The Charter explicitly excludes dialects and immigrant languages from its definition, presumably for political reasons, although from a linguistic perspective there can be many valid reasons to include them both. Furthermore, some definitions of minority languages include sign languages, while others do not.

Cronin (1995) has made a significant contribution to a reappraisal of the concept of minority by emphasizing that the asymmetric relationship between major and minority languages, expressed by the adjective 'minority,' is actually dynamic in nature. What many fail to appreciate is that, viewed across time, a minority language today may have been in the past, or become at some time in the future, a major language. Indeed, Irish Gaelic and English, which some hundreds of years ago enjoyed a similar status and number of speakers, are now located on opposite ends of the world/major/minority language continuum. English ranks as a world language with millions of mother tongue (L1) speakers and approximately as many again, who speak it as a second language (L2), while Irish is undisputedly an endangered minority language (O'Connell 2003). Similarly, what is deemed to be a minority language in one location may have a quite different status elsewhere at any time. Branchadell, drawing on Cronin's insight that the concept of minority expresses 'a relation not an essence' (Cronin 1995: 86), thus makes a terminological distinction between, on the one hand, an 'absolute minority language' (Branchadell 2011: 97), namely a language that is not a major/ity language in any state, and, on the other hand, one that is a major/ity language in one or more territory, but also functions as a minority language elsewhere, e.g. German in Germany versus German in Belgium.

Branchadell (*ibid.*) demonstrates that the concept of minority language must be understood, not as fixed, but rather as relative, and relative not just in numerical, but also in historical, geographical and, it could be added, political and ideological terms. Now this insight needs to be further developed in order to make an additional distinction within so-called 'absolute minority languages' between what might be considered fairly typical minority languages and less typical 'transitioning minority languages'. Typical minority languages are minority in relation to many key issues (e.g. small absolute numbers of speakers, limited domains of usage, etc.), while transitioning minority languages share only some of the typical characteristics of minority languages, as well as other characteristics more typical of small or major languages. A good example of the latter is Catalan, a language with more native speakers than the national language of another EU state, Denmark, and possibly destined to one day have its own independent national territory. In any case, the fundamental imprecision of the term 'minority language', coupled with the constantly changing dynamics of minority languages, whereby some are disappearing while others move towards greater official recognition, have not helped the development of a strong minority language focus within translation studies. Nevertheless, there is evidence of a significant growing interest in the topic over recent decades. It seems clear from a review of the literature within translation studies dealing with minority languages that current research, like this chapter, is firmly interdisciplinary, linking as it does minority/ized languages, LPP and AVT.

The renowned sociolinguist Joshua Fishman famously cautioned against the over-reliance of minority languages on the media (1991) and he accused some minority language activists of treating the mass media as a fetish (2001). To a certain extent, his point has been misunderstood: he believed that other foci, such as intergenerational transmission, were more important to the survival of minority languages than the media, not that media was of little importance. The year 1992 saw the publication of *Ethnic Minority Media* edited by Stephen Riggins, a collection of essays which drew attention to indigenous and minority languages, mainly in the Americas, and the positive role that modern media could play in their survival. More recently, scholars writing about media in languages as varied as Sami (Moring and Dunbar 2008) and Kashubian (Dolowy-Rybinska 2013) have grown in number, supporting each other's research and giving rise to the emergence of minority language media (MLM) as a field of study in its own right (Cormack 2004, 2013, Cormack and Hourigan 2007). This led to the publication of such pioneering works as *Minority Language Media: Concepts, Critiques and Case Studies* (Cormack and Hourigan 2007) and *Social Media and Minority Languages: Convergence and the Creative Industries* (Gruffydd Jones and Uribe-Jongbloed 2013). In the former, O'Connell (2007b) makes the case for closer scrutiny of the role of language and translation within MLM, since it is not enough to simply *use* a minority language in the media. She argues that one must also be clear about what kind of language and translation mode is being used and to what end, e.g. which national variety in the case of pluricentric languages, standard versus dialects, formal versus informal registers, translated versus original material, open versus closed subtitles, surtitles versus dubbing, etc. Failure to consider these issues and the attendant language planning implications, when a minority or minoritized language is used in the audiovisual media, is likely to result in unintended effects (O'Connell 2013).

Minoritized languages

It is important that studies of minority languages do not ignore the plight of any other minoritized language, regardless of relative size. As mentioned in the introduction, even major languages are now being minoritized in relation to English in an increasingly globalized world. For example, a numerically significant language such as Quechua, thought to have 13–14 million monolingual and bilingual speakers, is clearly minoritized in relation to Spanish in South America (Yataco 2015). This means that such languages are confronted with challenges, which are traditionally only associated with small or minority languages. Consequently, in minoritized language areas, the need is felt to engage in deliberate and focused language planning efforts such as, for example, deliberately creating terminology to correspond to foreign concepts (O'Connell and Walsh 2006), decreasing the exposure to foreign-language output in prime broadcasting time, and paying particular attention to the linguistic standard upheld in radio and television broadcasts (De Ridder 2015). Moreover, smaller languages must often rely on translation to supplement their linguistic, scientific and cultural resources, which is why language areas such as the Dutch and Scandinavian language areas, and indeed many minority language cultures are 'translation cultures *par excellence*' (Cronin 2003: 139).

More than half of the fiction published in such minoritized language areas, for instance, is imported foreign-language fiction translated into the minoritized language. By the same token, foreign-language films and television programmes are imported to supplement the original, native language output. As a result, language users in such language areas are generally exposed to more translations, and more specifically, modalities of audiovisual translation, such as interlingual subtitles, than to original, untranslated texts. This also implies a considerable exposure to translated language in general as well as the chosen linguistic standard of specific media. It follows that the linguistic decisions made by audiovisual translators may have implications for the ongoing development of such languages. This makes research into AVT particularly relevant from a sociolinguistic and language planning point of view.

AVT as a language planning tool

Before AVT began to emerge as a fully fledged discipline in the late 1990s, some research had already been conducted into the use of interlingual and intralingual subtitles as pedagogical tools in L2 acquisition in other fields (e.g. Price 1983, d'Ydewalle *et al.* 1991). Scholars such as Martine Danan (2004), Yves Gambier (2007), Robert Vanderplank (2010) and Eithne O'Connell (2011) provide overviews of this type of research. The literature suggests that the bimodal input (aural soundtrack and written subtitles) to which viewers are exposed in subtitled audiovisual material, proves particularly useful with regard to vocabulary acquisition, listening comprehension, and literacy development. Much of this research has focused mainly on L2 acquisition. However, there is some evidence that subtitled audiovisual material can also be used in L1 language and literacy development.

Kothari *et al.* (2004: 23), for instance, explored 'a simple and economical idea for infusing everyday television entertainment with reading and writing transactions', using intralingual subtitles in film songs in India. They emphasized that the potential of such subtitles, not only in India, but also elsewhere is 'enormous' (*ibid.*). Jan-Louis Kruger launched similar projects in South Africa to develop literacy (Kruger and Rafapa 2002) and to promote multilingualism (Kruger *et al.* 2007) with the help of intralingual subtitles. Thus, research to date indicates that subtitling effectively increases audience exposure to print from early childhood, improving L2 acquisition, but also L1 literacy. Similarly, subtitling can also be used as a useful language planning tool in L1 maintenance, as well as in language revitalization and language development within minority language cultures.

However, scholars have also investigated largely unintended effects of translation and particularly AVT, in recent decades. Research has provided evidence of some side effects of translation (e.g. Anderman and Rogers 2005, Becher *et al.* 2009) and, in particular, AVT on small as well as major languages. Henrik Gottlieb (2004, 2012a) conducted research into Anglicisms in Danish subtitles and their implications for the Danish language. In relation to the impact of English on other languages, Gottlieb claimed that 'there is no doubt that translations—not least those found in the popular media—constitute a driving force in what certain critics have seen as the corruption of domestic languages' (2005: 176). He corroborated this with examples of the influence of English on Finnish (Sajavaara 1991), Spanish (Lorenzo 1996), and German (Herbst 1994, 1995) AVT. From a sociolinguistic point of view, this evidence supports the need for the systematic analysis of both original and translated texts in minority and minoritized languages, so as to gauge the impact of (audiovisual) translation on language change. In the aforementioned examples, only two modes of AVT were mentioned: subtitling (in Danish, Dutch, and Finnish) and dubbing (in Spanish and German). Without doubt, other modes of AVT, such as voice-over (e.g. in Poland), but also website, software and game localization, for instance, are also worthwhile objects of sociolinguistic research in this regard. The linguistic choices translators make in AVT modes could trigger language change, but also the mere choice of a given linguistic standard, for instance in the case of pluricentric language areas, could affect the linguistic prestige and the status of national varieties.

Pluricentric language areas, in which different national varieties co-exist, must indeed also be considered in this chapter. As Michael Clyne (1992: 405) explains, '[a]lmost invariably, pluricentricity is asymmetrical, i.e. the norms of one national variety (or some national varieties) is (are) afforded a higher status, internally and externally, than those of the others'. This is also reflected in the linguistic standard to which text producers—whether authors or translators—adhere. This can result in the linguistic standard of the dominant national variety being used, thus minoritizing the non-dominant varieties. Luise von Flotow (2009) explains that major Hollywood productions usually are first dubbed into French in Canada and a few months later, once again in France, since France—by law—cannot import French translations from abroad. What is remarkable, however, is that this does not result in a Canadian dubbed version in Canadian French, even though the primary target audience are Canadian French speakers. The variety of French they use endeavours to be unmarked for geographic region and as a result is a rather artificial, 'International' French, *le synchronien*, which does not convey realistically the orality expected of this AVT mode (*ibid.*).

In literary publishing, usually only one translation is produced aiming at a whole pluricentric language area. In the whole Dutch language area, for instance, the Netherlandic Dutch standard is generally upheld in translation, which results in the publication of a single Netherlandic Dutch translation of foreign-language fiction. Unlike published fiction, however, several translated versions can be created, with relative ease, for audiovisual fiction in this language area, as films and television series are usually subtitled. This relatively cheap AVT mode facilitates the creation of separate Dutch subtitled versions on either side of the state borders to accommodate both Dutch and Belgian target audiences. Like most subtitling countries, however, dubbing is also a common AVT mode in the Dutch language area, although this AVT mode is reserved for children's films and series. Until the mid-1990s, the Netherlandic Dutch dubbed version of these audiovisual products was imported into Belgium. Thus, Dutch-speaking children in Belgium could only watch the 'foreign', Netherlandic Dutch dubbed version of children's animations and films. Nowadays, however, a separate Belgian Dutch ('Flemish') dubbed version is created and distributed for the Belgian market.

By contrast, a recent diachronic lexical analysis of interlingual television subtitles that specifically aimed at the Dutch-speaking Belgian audience, revealed that a higher number of marked Netherlandic Dutch lexis than marked Belgian Dutch lexis were found in this written text type (De Ridder 2015). This is in sharp contrast with the significantly higher number of marked Belgian Dutch lexis found in intralingual subtitles, in which, since the year 2000, Netherlandic Dutch is only used if it is heard in the soundtrack (*ibid.*). Thus, linguistic choices in translated audiovisual texts may affect the quality of the translation mode, in that they do not convey the orality of the spoken varieties with which the target audience is familiar. Similarly, they may also exert an influence on the already lower prestige of 'non-dominant' (Muhr 2012) national varieties and the status of their translators, while depriving the wider language area of its full linguistic richness.

It follows that, as smaller and minority language communities continue to be exposed to a considerable amount of AVT, translators and translation editors-in-chief, as well as AVT policy makers, may play a valuable role in status, corpus, and acquisition planning. Sociolinguistic research into AVT policy, but also in-depth analysis of authentic AVT texts and untranslated texts are important here. Daniel Nettle and Suzanne Romaine (2000) predicted that by the end of this century, 90 per cent of the world's languages will have vanished. Since, as András Kornai pointed out, less than 5 per cent of all languages today is represented in the digital world, this could mean language death will be hastened by 'digital language death' (Kornai 2013). Today, this importance of electronic online media is already reflected in the new subfield of e-sociolinguistics that investigates language use in these media (Danesi 2015). In brief, there is good reason to regard AVT as a frequently underestimated, but potentially significant language planning tool, particularly in smaller and minority language areas.

An indication of its future trajectory and new debates

As minority language AVT is a relatively new area of study, it offers many interesting topics worthy of future investigation. Given the recent advances in technology, especially in the digital area, it is likely that AVT will become much more commonplace than it currently is. For many years now, Europe has endeavoured, for both economic and cultural reasons, to strengthen and develop an indigenous audiovisual industry to offset USA dominance. This has resulted in generous support for cross-border and multilingual co-productions. In recent decades, even that great monolingual bastion, Hollywood, increasingly has integrated subtitling into films. There have been more bilingual, trilingual and, indeed multilingual productions, with many English-language films even featuring minority or minoritized languages: Sioux Indians in Kevin Costner's film *Dances with Wolves* (1990) spoke Lakota, which was subtitled into English, Dublin English in *The Commitments* (1991) and Glaswegian Scots in *Trainspotting* (1996). Mel Gibson's *The Passion of Christ* (2004) had Jesus and his disciples speaking Old Aramaic, the Jewish authorities speaking Hebrew and the Romans speaking Latin. The award-winning international co-production *Babel* (2006) broke all linguistic records by including Berber, Arabic, English, Spanish, French, Japanese and Japanese Sign Language. However, some of these linguistic escapades were not exactly kosher. For example, the form of Lakota taught by the *Dances with Wolves* dialogue coach was actually appropriate only for women, and the Jewish authorities featured in *The Passion of Christ*, having returned from Babylonian captivity speaking Aramaic, would only have used Hebrew for religious purposes.

Nevertheless, these examples are indicative of a trend towards increasing use of AVT within the mainstream film industry, which is likely to strengthen in coming years. Nonetheless, it is not just on the big screen that an increase in minority language AVT can be expected. In the past, before digital advances made AVT an affordable option, the high cost to minority language users of producing their own audiovisual material was often prohibitive. Now, it is possible to produce material, in the first instance for a small minority language audience, with the prospect of being able to offset some of the costs by selling on to a major language audience. An early example of this was the sale to NOS in the Netherlands of the Welsh soap opera *Pobol y Cym* (De Vallei) in 1991. The Welsh soundtrack was retained and subtitled into Dutch. In 2014, the Irish language Celtic Noir thriller series *An Bronntanas* (The Gift) was acquired by a major French international distribution company, Lagardère Entertainment (LE) Rights, so as to aim it at a worldwide audience (Murphy 2015). Another likely trend within the field will be increased use of AVT material to promote formal and informal minority language learning and literacy skills (O'Connell 2011). There is good reason to be optimistic about some of the pedagogical uses of subtitles, and indeed other AVT modes harnessed for similar purposes, e.g. using dubbing as a cost-effective way to provide children's programmes in a minority language, rather than having to make much more costly original programmes (O'Connell 2003, 2007b, 2010, 2011; O'Connell and Walsh 2006). An example of this is the popular television series, *Katie Morag*, commissioned by BBC's Cbeebies children's channel and later dubbed into Scottish Gaelic or *Gàidhlig* as *Ceitidh Mòrag* for broadcast in 2014 on BBC ALBA.

However, notwithstanding the fact that the exposure of the speakers of minority, minoritized or smaller languages to large volumes of audiovisual translations can bring educational benefits and commercial savings to their communities, the same phenomenon of AVT, depending on variables such as translation mode, language pair and direction, can also potentially constitute a real threat to the very linguistic sustainability of their own speech communities (e.g. O'Connell 2011). A contemporary example, also from Scotland, is the plight of minority language adult viewers of BBC ALBA, who frequently find themselves having to watch material with soundtracks in their L1, Gàidhlig, but accompanied by open interlingual subtitles which transform the programme into an unbalanced bilingual offering, with the written English subtitles requiring more cognitive processing and therefore having more impact than the minority language aural soundtrack (O'Connell 2011, 2013). This phenomenon recently resulted in Gàidhlig-speaking viewers organizing themselves via a bilingual website to lobby the broadcaster for more sociolinguistically sensitive arrangements (Gàidhlig TV 2015).

Common research methods associated with the particular area

Although authentic sets of translated texts and their corresponding source texts have already been used in translation studies and AVT analysis, the future use of more sizeable corpora will enable thorough study of recurring linguistic features in (audiovisual) translations (e.g. Freddi 2013). These corpora are specifically designed to systematically investigate and draw generalizations from the language used in the authentic data in such corpora. With the development of corpus linguistics, vast linguistic reference corpora have been built, but also other types of corpora, such as parallel translation corpora and monolingual comparable corpora are also used in translation research. Corpus linguistics techniques increasingly are applied in AVT. It is to be expected that further technological advances will soon significantly boost this field of research.

Minority and minoritized languages, in particular, benefit greatly from such valuable linguistic resources as corpora. A number have already been created, e.g. the Crúbadán corpora (Scannell 2007) covering texts in more than 2,000 smaller and minority languages extracted from the World Wide Web. Other examples are a 4.6-million-word corpus of twentieth-century Basque, the XX. Mendeko Euskararen Corpus, and the Scottish Corpus of Texts and Speech (SCOTS), a 4-million-word corpus of Scottish English and varieties of Scots with a multimedia component (Anderson and Corbett 2008). Nonetheless, specific AVT corpora of regional and minority languages, such as the 300,000 word English-Galician interlingual subtitle corpus, Veiga (Sotelo Dios 2011), are currently rather rare. The creation of such AVT corpora that are representative of AVT in minority and minoritized languages and provide valuable empirical evidence of what happens in the language of AVT, can reveal to what extent this AVT has an impact on the wider language.

Nevertheless, a few noteworthy AVT corpora have been compiled. One such corpus is the Forlì Corpus of Screen Translation (Valentini 2008). Its current version FORLIXT 3.0 contains source and target text transcriptions of almost one hundred films and allows users to scan transcribed film dialogues, as well as to stream the corresponding film sequences. It consists of the dubbed target texts, as well as the source text covering mainly French, German, and Italian. The 500,000 word Pavia Corpus of Film Dialogue (Pavesi *et al.* 2014) currently consists of a unidirectional parallel component of 24 English-language source texts alongside their dubbed Italian translations, as well as a component of transcribed original Italian film dialogues. The inclusion of such a component of untranslated, original material makes these corpora valuable resources, which also allow the study of translated language and how this differs from and affects the wider target language.

The Opus Corpus currently (OpenSubtitles2015) contains a substantial multilingual subtitle subset of almost 20 billion words in around 60 languages (Tiedeman 2012), many of which are smaller and minority languages. Parallel subtitle corpora have also been created for machine translation research (e.g. Armstrong *et al.* 2007). The SUMAT subtitle corpus (Petukhova *et al.* 2012) comprises some 20 million professional subtitles and was built to train Statistical Machine Translation systems to develop an automated subtitle translation service for nine European languages. It consists of intralingual subtitles and parallel subtitles. Yet, the importance of AVT is also reflected in the corpus design of balanced reference corpora. The 500-Million-Word Reference Corpus of Contemporary written Dutch (SoNaR) is a case in point. Reference corpora, which aim to be representative of the linguistic output of a given language area, cover a wide range of text types. The corpus builders of SoNaR included a total of 10 million subtitled words (Oostdijk *et al.* 2013), which illustrates that for such a corpus to be representative of the language of subtitling cultures like Dutch, it must include subtitles.

The influence of new technology on the area

Two examples of Audio Description (AD) corpora are the TIWO Corpus that consists of the English-language AD of 91 films (Salway 2007) and the Tracce Corpus (Jiménez and Seibel 2012, Jiménez Hurtado and Soler Gallego 2013), a Spanish-language AD corpus of some 300 films. Further development of information technology will enable even faster creation of such varied AVT corpora and a further refinement of corpus tools, allowing for quicker and more complex concordance searches. Searching soundtracks of dubbed material for specific pronunciation or intonation features could also reveal interesting changes in pronunciation in this audiovisual mode as opposed to non-translated dialogues. As information technology improves, it will also enhance the spread of more sophisticated multimodal corpora, in which users can scan concordance lines in the source or target text of AVT corpora and with a single mouse click have access to the corresponding section of the video file (Thompson 2010). This would be particularly useful in the lexical analysis of AVT to disambiguate polysemous words.

Large corpora are parsed and tagged automatically. A further refinement of such parsers and taggers would allow for more accurate lemma searches, which ideally also take into account geographical markedness. New statistical algorithms could automatically single out texts that are geographically marked. This means that no longer simply the country in which a given text is published is used to determine its origin, as this can be misleading (e.g. publishing houses may be located in one country but adhere to the linguistic standard of another country). Actual geographic markers present in the text can then determine its level of geographical markedness. Corpora that allow for 'batch' lemma searches of thousands of geographically marked lexical items or Anglicisms, which can be poured into the search engine would also be convenient to quickly investigate the geographic markedness of a given subset, or indeed the occurrence of Anglicisms.

In the 1980s and 1990s, eye movements were recorded to investigate reading behaviour in children and adults watching subtitled programmes (e.g. d'Ydewalle *et al.* 1991). In recent years, eye-tracking technology has improved considerably and eye trackers, although still expensive, have become easier to use. In translation studies, eye-tracking research methodology is applied to investigate translation processes and translator-computer interaction (O'Brien 2007, Saldanha and O'Brien 2013). By the same token, eye-tracking research has contributed to the study of the subtitle reading process and the processing effort involved (e.g. Kruger 2012, Kruger and Steyn 2013). Since subtitling is a common AVT method in minoritized languages, AVT research into subtitling using eye-tracking methods is a welcome development, as is clear from the contributions to a publication edited by Elisa Perego (2012) devoted entirely to this topic.

Conclusion

In conclusion, although the study of minority language AVT and, more particularly, its language planning implications have been relatively slow to attract scholarly attention, the research conducted to date indicates that the field is now recognized as worthy of much closer scholarly attention. As many major and small languages become increasingly minoritized in relation to English, and possibly other emerging global languages, linguists are likely to value more and more the experience of and strategies used by minority language communities to maintain and develop their languages. Their research efforts in the future will be greatly facilitated by advances in computational and corpus linguistics. Given the prevalence, penetration and continuing expansion of audiovisual media, AVT can reasonably be expected to play a pivotal role both within individual communities and in assisting them in their interlingual interactions with others. Furthermore, as audiovisual products continue to displace written sources of information and entertainment, both intralingual and interlingual subtitles will play an important part in developing both 'reading abilities and language skills' (Gottlieb 2012b: 64).

Further reading

Chiaro, D. (2009) 'Issues in Audiovisual Translation', in J. Munday (ed.) *The Routledge Companion to Translation Studies*, Oxon: Routledge, 141–165 | *A useful, entertaining discussion of current issues with examples from well-known films and television series.*

Cormack, M. and N. Hourigan (eds) (2007) *Minority Language Media: Concepts, Critiques and Case Studies*, Clevedon: Multilingual Matters | *A collection of essays marking the emergence of minority media studies as a discipline in its own right.*

Folaron, D. (2015) 'Translation and Minority, Lesser-used and Lesser-translated Languages and Cultures', *JoSTrans: The Journal of Specialised Translation* 24: 16–27. Available online: http://www.jostrans.org/issue24/art_folaron.pdf [last access 20 December 2017] | *A recent, comprehensive discussion of translation and minority languages.*

Kruger, J. and F. Steyn (2013) 'Subtitles and Eye Tracking: Reading and Performance', *Reading Research Quarterly* 49: 105–120 | *A recent overview and critical discussion of the use of eye-tracking in research on subtitling processing and the educational benefits of this AVT mode.*

Zuo, X. L. (2007) 'China's Policy towards Minority Languages in a Globalizing Age', *Transnational Curriculum Inquiry* 4(1): 80–91 | *An introductory overview of current Chinese minority language policies.*

Related topics

18   Sociolinguistics and linguistic variation in audiovisual translation
20   Corpus-based audiovisual translation studies: ample room for development
21   Multimodal corpora in audiovisual translation studies
22   Eye tracking in audiovisual translation research
30   Audiovisual translation in language teaching and learning

References

Anderman, G. and M. Rogers (eds) (2005) *In and Out of English: For Better, for Worse*, Clevedon: Multilingual Matters.

Anderson, W. and J. Corbett (2008) 'The Scottish Corpus of Texts and Speech: A User's Guide', *Scottish Language* 27: 19–41.

Antonini, R. (2008) 'The Perception of Dubbese', in D. Chiaro, C. Heiss and C. Bucaria (eds) *Between Text and Image*, Amsterdam & Philadelphia: John Benjamins, 135–147.

Antonini, R. (2009) 'The Role of the Media in the Standardization Process of the Irish Language', in F. M. Federici (ed.) *Translating Regionalised Voices in Audiovisuals*, Rome: Aracne, 71–93.

Armstrong, N. and F. M. Federici (2006) (eds) *Translating Voices, Translating Regions*, Roma: Aracne.

Armstrong, S., C. Caffrey, M. Flanagan, D. Kenny, M. O'Hagan and A. Way (2007) 'Leading by Example: Automatic Translation of Subtitles via EBMT', *Perspectives* 2007(14): 163–184.

Barambones, J., R. Merino, and I. Uribarri (2012) 'Audiovisual Translation in the Basque Country: The Case of Basque Television-Euskal Telebista (ETB)', *Meta* 57(2): 408–422.

Barambones Zubiria, J. (ed.) (2012) *Mapping the Dubbing Scene. Audiovisual Translation in Basque Television*, Bern: Peter Lang.

Bassols, M., M. Dolç, D. Paloma, A. Rico, L. Santamaria, M. Sagarra and A. M. Torrent (1995) 'Adapting Translation for Dubbing to the Customers' Requirements: The Case of Cartoons', in Y. Gambier (ed.) *Communication Audiovisuelle et Transferts Linguistiques/Audiovisual Communication and Language Transfer*, Sint-Amandsberg: FIT, 410–417.

Baumgarten, N. and D. Özçetin (2008) 'Linguistic Variation through Language Contact in Translation,' in P. Siemund and N. Kintana (eds) *Language Contact and Contact Languages*, Amsterdam & Philadelphia: John Benjamins, 293–316.

Becher, V., J. House and S. Kranich (2009) 'Convergence and Divergence of Communicative Norms through Language Contact in Translation', in K. Braunmüller and J. House (eds) *Convergence and Divergence in Language Contact Situations*, Amsterdam & Philadelphia: John Benjamins, 125–152.

Branchadell, A. (2011) 'Minority Languages and Translation', in Y. Gambier and L. Van Doorslaer (eds) *Handbook of Translation Studies*, Amsterdam & Philadelphia: John Benjamins, 97–101.

Bueno Maia, R., M. Pacheco Pinto and S. Ramos Pinto (2015) *How Peripheral is the Periphery? Translating Portugal Back and Forth*, Newcastle upon Tyne: Cambridge Scholars Publishing.

Chiaro, D. (2009) 'Issues in Audiovisual Translation', in J. Munday (ed.) *The Routledge Companion to Translation Studies*, Oxon: Routledge, 141–165.

Clyne, M. (1992) *Pluricentric Languages: Differing Norms in Different Nations*, Berlin: Mouton.

Cormack, M. (2004) 'Developing Minority Language Media Studies', *Mercator Media Forum* 7(1): 3–12.

Cormack, M. (2013) 'Concluding Remarks: Towards an Understanding of Media Impact on Minority Language Use', in E. H. Gruffydd Jones and E. Uribe-Jongbloed (eds) *Social Media and Minority Languages: Convergence and the Creative Industries*, Bristol: Multilingual Matters, 255–265.

Cormack, M. and N. Hourigan (eds) (2007) *Minority Language Media: Concepts, Critiques and Case Studies*, Clevedon: Multilingual Matters.

Cronin, M. (1995) 'Altered States: Translation and Minority Languages', *TTR* 8(1): 85–103.

Cronin, M. (2003) *Translation and Globalization*, New York: Routledge.

Cronin, M. (2009) 'Minority', in M. Baker and G. Saldanha (eds) *Routledge Encyclopedia of Translation Studies*, 2nd edition, London: Routledge, 169–172.

Danan, M. (2004) 'Captioning and Subtitling: Undervalued Language Learning Strategie', *Meta* 49(1): 67–77.

Danesi, M. (2015) *Language, Society, and New Media: Sociolinguistics Today*, New York: Routledge.

De Ridder, R. (2015) *'Arme rijke taal'. Audiovisual Translation and Minority Language Planning in Pluricentric Language Areas. A Case Study of Flemish Public Service Broadcasting*, PhD Doctoral Thesis, Dublin City University.

De Ridder, R. and E. O'Connell (2018) 'Using Audiovisual Translation to Track Language Planning Developments: Flemish Public Broadcasting Subtitles from 1995–2012', in J. Díaz Cintas and K. Nikolić (eds) *Fast-Forwarding with Audiovisual Translation*, Bristol: Multilingual Matters, 212–224.

Dolowy-Rybinska, N. (2013) 'Kashubian and Modern Media: The Influence of New Technologies on Endangered Languages', in E. H. Gruffydd Jones and E. Uribe-Jongbloed (eds) *Social Media and Minority Languages: Convergence and the Creative Industries*, Bristol: Multilingual Matters, 119–129.

d'Ydewalle, G., C. Praet, K. Verfaillie and J. V. Rensbergen (1991) 'Watching Subtitled Television: Automatic Reading Behavior', *Communication Research* 18(5): 650.

European Charter for Regional or Minority Languages (1992). Available online: http://conventions.coe.int/Treaty/Commun/QueVoulezVous.asp?CL=ENG&NT=148 [last access 20 December 2017].

Federici, F. M. (2009) (ed.) *Translating Regionalised Voices in Audiovisuals*, Rome: Aracne.

Federici, F. M. (2011) (ed.) *Translating Dialects and Languages of Minorities: Challenges and Solutions*, Bern: Peter Lang.

Fernández Torné, A. and A. Matamala (2015) 'Text-to-speech vs. Human Voiced Audio Descriptions: A Reception Study in Films Dubbed into Catalan', *JoSTrans: The Journal of Specialised Translation* 24: 61–88. Available online: http://www.jostrans.org/issue24/art_fernandez.pdf [last access 20 December 2017].

Fishman, J. (1991) *Reversing Language Shift: Theoretical and Empirical Foundations of Assistance to Threatened Languages*, Clevedon: Multilingual Matters.

Fishman, J. (2001) *Can Threatened Languages Be Saved?*, Clevedon: Multilingual Matters.

Folaron, D. (2015) 'Translation and Minority, Lesser-used and Lesser-translated Languages and Cultures', *JoSTrans: The Journal of Specialised Translation* 24: 16–27. Available online: http://www.jostrans.org/issue24/art_folaron.pdf [last access 20 December 2017].

Freddi, M. (2013) 'Constructing a Corpus of Translated Films: A Corpus View of Dubbing', *Perspectives: Studies in Translatology* 21(4): 491–503.

Gàidhlig TV (2015) Available online: http://www.gaidhlig.tv [last access 20 December 2017].

Gambier, Y. (2007) 'Sous-titrage et apprentissage des langues', in A. Remael and J. Neves (eds) *Tool for Social Integration? Audiovisual Translation from Different Angles*, Special Issue of *Linguistica Antverpiensia* 6: 97–114.

Gambier, Y. and J. Van Doorslaer (eds) (2011) *Handbook of Translation Studies*, Amsterdam & Philadelphia: John Benjamin.

Gottlieb, H. (2004) 'Danish Echoes of English', *Nordic Journal of English Studies* 3(2): 39–65.

Gottlieb, H. (2005) 'Anglicisms and Translation', in G. Anderman and M. Rogers (eds) *In and Out of English: For Better, for Worse*, Clevedon: Multilingual Matters, 161–184.

Gottlieb, H. (2012a) 'Old Films, New Subtitles, More Anglicisms?', in A. Remael, P. Orero and M. Carroll (eds) *Audiovisual Translation and Media Accessibility at the Crossroads*, Amsterdam: Rodopi, 249–272.

Gottlieb, H. (2012b) 'Subtitles—Readable Dialogue?', in E. Perego (ed.) *Eye Tracking in Audiovisual Translation*, Roma: Aracne, 37–81.

Gruffydd Jones, E. H. and E. Uribe-Jongbloed (eds) (2013) *Social Media and Minority Languages: Convergence and the Creative Industries*, Bristol: Multilingual Matters.

Herbst, T. (1994) *Linguistische Aspekte der Synchronisation von Fernsehserien: Phonetik, Textlinguistik, Übersetzungstheorie*, Tübingen: Max Niemeyer Verlag.

Herbst, T. (1995) 'People Do not Talk in Sentences. Dubbing and the Idiom Principle', *Translatio–FIT Newsletter* 14(3–4): 257–271.

Jiménez Hurtado, C. and S. Soler Gallego (2013) 'Multimodality, Translation and Accessibility: A Corpus-based Study of Audio Description', *Perspectives* 21: 577–594.

Jiménez, C. and C. Seibel (2012) 'Multisemiotic and Multimodal Corpus Analysis in Audio Description: TRACCE', in A. Remael, P. Orero and M. Carroll (eds) *Audiovisual Translation and Media Accessibility at the Crossroads*, Amsterdam: Rodopi, 409–425.

Kornai, A. (2013) 'Digital Language Death', *PLoS ONE* 8(10): http://journals.plos.org/plosone/article?id=10.1371/journal.pone.0077056 [last access 20 December 2017].

Kothari, B. (1999) 'Same-Language Subtitling: Integrating Post Literacy Development and Popular Culture on Television', *Media and Technology for Human Resource Development* 11(3): 111–117.

Kothari, B. (2008) 'Let a Billion Readers Bloom: Same Language Subtitling (SLS) on Television for Mass Literacy', *International Review of Education* 54(5–6): 773–780.

Kothari, B., A. Pandey and A. R. Chudgar (2004) 'Reading Out of the "Idiot Box": Same-Language Subtitling on Television in India', *Information Technologies and International Development* 2(1): 23–44.

Kruger, J. (2012) 'Making Meaning in AVT: Eye Tracking and Viewer Construction of Narrative', *Perspectives: Studies in Translatology* 20(1): 67–86.

Kruger, J. and L. Rafapa (2002) 'Subtitling, Literacy and Education in South Africa: Putting Audio-visual Media to Work in the Classroom', *Fourth Languages and the Media Conference*, Berlin.

Kruger, J. and F. Steyn (2013) 'Subtitles and Eye Tracking: Reading and Performance', *Reading Research Quarterly* 49: 105–120.

Kruger, J., H. Kruger and M. Verhoef (2007) 'Subtitling and the Promotion of Multilingualism: The Case of Marginalised Languages in South Africa', in A. Remael and J. Neves (eds) *Tool for Social Integration? Audiovisual Translation from Different Angles*, Antwerpen: Linguistica Antverpiensia, 35–49.

Lorenzo, E. (1996) *Anglicismos Hispánicos*, Madrid: Editorial Gredos-Biblioteca Románica Hispánica.

Lysaght, R. (2010) 'Teanga & Tikanga: A Comparative Study of National Broadcasting in Minority Language on Māori Television and Teilifís na Gaeilge', Unpublished Doctoral Dissertation, University of Auckland. Available online: https://researchspace.auckland.ac.nz/handle/2292/6729 [last access 20 December 2017].

Meylaerts, R. (2011) 'Translational Justice in a Multilingual World: An Overview of Translational Regimes', *Meta* 56(4): 743–757.

Moring, T. and R. Dunbar (2008) *The European Charter for Regional or Minority Languages and the Media*, Vol. 6, Strasbourg: Council of Europe.

Muhr, R. (ed.) (2012) *Non-Dominant Varieties of Pluricentric Languages. Getting the Picture*, Frankfurt am Main: Peter Lang.

Murphy, N. (2015) 'Irish Abroad: Tom Collins' *An Bronntanas* Seals Major International Distribution Deal'. Available online: http://www.scannain.com/teilifis/an-bronntanas-distribution-deal [last access 20 December 2017].

Nettle, D. and S. Romaine (2000) *Vanishing Voices: The Extinction of the World's Languages*, Oxford: University Press.

O'Brien, S. (2007) 'Eye-tracking and Translation Memory Matches', *Perspectives: Studies in Translatology* 14(3): 185–205.

O'Connell, E. (1994) 'Media Translation and Lesser-used Languages', in F. Eguiluz, F. Ortiz de Latierro, M. R. Merino Álvarez, V. Olsen Osterberg, E. Pajares Infante, and J. M. Santamaría López (eds) *Transvases Culturales: Literatura, Cine, Traduccion*, Vitoria: Facultad de Filología, 367–373.

O'Connell, E. (1998) 'Choices and Constraints in Screen Translation' in L. Bowker, M. Cronin, D. Kenny and J. Pearson (eds) *Unity in Diversity*, Manchester: St. Jerome Publishing, 65–71.

O'Connell, E. (2003) *Minority Language Dubbing for Children: Screen Translation from German to Irish*, Berlin: Peter Lang.

O'Connell, E. (2007a) 'The *Kings*'s Irish: Dialogue, Dialect and Subtitles in the Film *Kings*', in *Estudios Irlandeses* 3: 226–229. Available online: http://www.estudiosirlandeses.org/reviews/the-kings-irish-dialogue-dialect-and-subtitles-in-kings-2007/ [last access 20 December 2017].

O'Connell, E. (2007b) 'Translation and Minority Language Media: Potential and Problems. An Irish Perspective', in M. Cormack and N. Hourigan (eds) *Minority Language Media: Concepts, Critiques and Case Studies*, Clevedon: Multilingual Matters, 212–228.

O'Connell, E. (2007c) 'Screen Translation', in P. Kuhiwczak and K. Littau (eds) *A Companion to Translation Studies*, Clevedon: Multilingual Matters, 120–133.

O'Connell, E. (2010) 'Why Kermit and Harry Potter now speak Irish: Translating Minority Language Television for Children', in E. Di Giovanni, C. Elefante and R. Pederzoli (eds) *Writing and Translating for Children: Voices, Images and Text*, Bern: Peter Lang, 265–281.

O'Connell, E. (2011) 'Formal and Casual Language Learning: What Subtitles Have to Offer Minority Languages like Irish', in L. Incalcaterra McLoughlin, M. Biscio and M. A. Ní Mhainnín (eds) *Audiovisual Translation: Subtitles and Subtitling. Theory and Practice*, Oxford: Peter Lang, 157–175.

O'Connell, E. (2013) 'Towards a Template for a Linguistic Policy for Minority Language Broadcasters', in E. H. Gruffydd Jones and E. Uribe-Jongbloed (eds) *Minority Languages and Social Media: Participation, Policy and Perspectives*, Bristol: Multilingual Matters, 187–201.

O'Connell, E. and J. Walsh (2006) 'The Translation Boom: Irish and Language Planning in the 21st Century', *Administration: The Journal of the IPA* 54(3): 22–43.

Oostdijk, N., M. Reynaert, V. Hoste and I. Schuurman (2013) 'The Construction of a 500-Million-Word Reference Corpus of Contemporary Written Dutch', in P. Spyns and J. Odijk (eds) *Essential Speech and Language Technology for Dutch. Results by the STEVIN programme*, Heidelberg: Springer Verlag, 219–247.

OpenSubtitles2015 (2015) Available online: http://opus.lingfil.uu.se/OpenSubtitles2015.php [last access 20 December 2017].

Pavesi, M., M. Formentelli and E. Ghia. (2014) *The Languages of Dubbing: Mainstream Audiovisual Translation in Italy*, Bern: Peter Lang.

Perego, E. (ed.) (2012) *Eye Tracking in Audiovisual Translation*, Roma: Aracne.

Petukhova, V., R. Agerri, M. Fishel, S. Penkale, A. del Pozo, M. Maucec, A. Way, P. Georgakopoulou and M. Volk (2012) 'SUMAT: Data Collection and Parallel Corpus Compilation for Machine Translation of Subtitles', *LREC 2012 Conference Proceedings*, 21–28. Available online: http://www.lrec-conf.org/proceedings/lrec2012/pdf/154_Paper.pdf [last access 20 December 2017].

Price, K. (1983) 'Closed-captioned TV: An Untapped Resource', *Massachusetts Association of Teachers of Speakers of Other Languages Newsletter* 12(2): 1–8.

Remael, A. and J. Neves (eds) (2007) 'Tool for Social Integration? Audiovisual Translation from Different Angles'. Special Issue of *Linguistica Antverpiensia* 6.

Remael, A., A. De Houwer and R. Vandekerckhove (2008) 'Intralingual Open Subtitling in Flanders: Audiovisual Translation, Linguistic Variation and Audience Needs', *JoSTrans: The Journal of Specialised Translation* 10: 76–105. Available online: http://www.jostrans.org/issue10/art_houwer.pdf [last access 20 December 2017].

Ricento, T. (2000) 'Historical and Theoretical Perspectives in Language Policy and Planning', *Journal of Sociolinguistics* 4(2): 196–213.

Riggins, S. H. (1992) (ed.) *Ethnic Minority Media*, Newbury Park, CA: Sage Publishers.

Sajavaara, K. (1991) 'English in Finnish: Television Subtitles', in V. Ivir and D. Kalogjera (eds) *Languages in Contact and Contrast. Essays in Contact Linguistics*, Berlin: Mouton de Gruyter, 381–390.

Saldanha, G. and S. O'Brien (2013) *Research Methodologies in Translation Studies*, Manchester: St Jerome Publishing.

Salway, A. (2007) 'A Corpus-based Analysis of Audio Description', in J. Díaz Cintas, P. Orero and A. Remael (eds) *Media for All: Subtitling for the Deaf, Audio Description and Sign Language*, Amsterdam: Rodopi, 151–174.

Sanday Wandera, A. (2015) 'Evaluating the Acceptance and Usability of Kiswahili Localised Mobile Phone App in Kenya: A Case of M-Pesa App', *JoSTrans: The Journal of Specialised Translation* 2015(24): 112–128. Available online: http://www.jostrans.org/issue24/art_wandera.pdf [last access 20 December 2017].

Scannell, K. P. (2007) 'The Crúbadán Project: Corpus Building for Under-resourced Languages', *WAC 2007 Conference Proceedings*. Available online: http://borel.slu.edu/pub/wac3.pdf [last access 20 December 2017].

Sotelo Dios, P. (2011) 'Using a Multimedia Parallel Corpus to Investigate English-Galician Subtitling', *Proceedings of the SDH 2011 Conference: Supporting Digital Humanities*. Available online: http://sli.uvigo.es/arquivos/sdh2011.pdf [last access 20 December 2017].

Tiedemann, J. (2012) 'Parallel Data, Tools and Interfaces in OPUS', *LREC 2012 Conference proceedings*, 2214–2218. Available online: http://www.lrec-conf.org/proceedings/lrec2012/pdf/463_Paper.pdf [last access 20 December 2017].

Thompson, P. (2010) 'Building a Specialised Audio-visual Corpus', in A. O'Keeffe and M. McCarthy (eds) *The Routledge Handbook of Corpus Linguistics*, London: Routledge, 93–103.

Tiedemann, J. (2012) 'Parallel Data, Tools and Interfaces in OPUS', *LREC 2012 Conference Proceedings*, 2214–2218. Available online: http://www.lrec-conf.org/proceedings/lrec2012/pdf/463_Paper.pdf [last access 20 December 2017].

Toury, G. (1985) 'Aspects of Translating into Minority Languages from the Point of View of Translation Studies', *Multilingua—Journal of Cross-Cultural and Interlanguage Communication* 4: 3–10.

Valentini, C. (2008) 'Forlixt 1—The Forlì Corpus of Screen Translation: Exploring Macrostructure', in D. Chiaro, C. Heiss, and C. Bucaria (eds) *Between Text and Image: Updating Research in Screen Translation*, Amsterdam: John Benjamins, 37–50.

Vanderplank, R. (2010) 'Déjà Vu? A Decade of Research on Language Laboratories, Television and Video in Language Learning', *Language Teaching* 43(1): 1–37.

Veiga Díaz, M. T. (2012) 'Translators as Agents of Linguistic Change: Colour Terms in Medieval Literature Translated into Galician', in I. Carcía-Izquierdo and E. Monzó (eds) *Iberian Studies on Translation and Interpreting*, Oxford: Peter Lang: 191–208.

Venuti, L. (ed.) (1998) 'Translation and Minority', Special Issue of *The Translator* 4(2).

von Flotow, L. (2009) 'Frenching the Feature Film Twice: Or le synchronien', in J. Díaz Cintas (ed.) *New Trends in Audiovisual Translation*, Bristol: Multilingual Matters, 83–98.

Yataco, M. (2015) Facts about Quechua. Available online: http://www.ctmd.org/pages/enewsquechua0308.html [last access 20 December 2017].

Zabalbeascoa, P. (2001) 'Disentangling Audiovisual Translation into Catalan from the Spanish Media Mesh', in Y. Gambier and H. Gottlieb (eds) *(Multi)media Translation: Concepts, Practices, and Research*, Amsterdam & Philadelphia: John Benjamins, 101–111.

Zuo, X. L. (2007) 'China's Policy Towards Minority Languages in a Globalizing Age', *Transnational Curriculum Inquiry* 4(1): 80–91.

Filmography

An Bronntanas (2004) Tom Collins. IMDb entry: http://www.imdb.com/title/tt2792326/?ref_=nv_sr_1
Babel (2006) Alejandro G. Iñárritu. IMDb entry: http://www.imdb.com/title/tt0449467/?ref_=nv_sr_1
Dances with Wolves (1990) Kevin Costner. IMDb entry: http://www.imdb.com/title/tt0099348/?ref_=nv_sr_1
Katie Morag (2013-) Don Coutts. IMDb entry: http://www.imdb.com/title/tt3830024/?ref_=fn_al_tt_1
Kings (2007) Tom Collins. IMDb entry: http://www.imdb.com/title/tt0889136/?ref_=fn_al_tt_3
Pobol y Cwm (1974-) Various directors. IMDb entry: https://www.imdb.com/title/tt0240291/
The Commitments (1991) Alan Parker. IMDb entry: http://www.imdb.com/title/tt0101605/?ref_=nv_sr_1
The Flintstones (1960–1966) Joseph Barbera and William Hanna. IMDb entry: http://www.imdb.com/title/tt0053502/?ref_=nv_sr_2
The Passion of Christ (2004) Mel Gibson. IMDb entry: http://www.imdb.com/title/tt0335345/?ref_=fn_al_tt_1
Trainspotting (1996) Danny Boyle. IMDb entry: http://www.imdb.com/title/tt0117951/?ref_=nv_sr_1

26
Audiovisual translation and popular music

Rebecca Johnson

Introduction

The interface between audiovisual translation (AVT) and popular music is an area of study with increasingly—perhaps surprisingly—broad implications for contemporary global society and digital culture, as well as for the field of translation studies itself. In the introduction to the 2008 special issue of *The Translator* devoted to the translation of music, Susam-Sarajeva posits an explanation for the relative inattention afforded to music within translation studies, despite the deep emotional role that music plays in people's lives and its influence in wider societal construction, not to mention its ability to cross linguistic and cultural boundaries (2008: 188–190). She cites methodological and definitional difficulties relating to the nature of music as a form of expression, emphasizing the need for multidisciplinary approaches to address this lacuna.

With regard to popular music in particular—defined here in accordance with *The New Grove Dictionary of Music and Musicians* as music of any kind having wide popular appeal and distributed to large audiences by the music industry—Kaindl (2013a: 00:55) suggests that its perceived low symbolic capital as a non-canonized genre has led to its marginalization in the already limited body of theory on translation and music, as compared to, for example, opera surtitling. While popular music lyrics have long been used for pedagogical purposes in language learning (Hewitt 2000), this will usually involve the translation of transcribed song lyrics that are separated off from the music, as opposed to the synchronic translation of song lyrics while they are performed/consumed as part of a multimodal ensemble. Meanwhile, outside of translation studies, scholarship on popular music videos and other musical media will often overlook questions of translation. This, then, is an opportune moment for translation scholars with an interest in popular music culture. Indeed, the evolution of audiovisual translation since the rise of the Internet and digital media (Pérez-González 2014: 15), as well as the recent groundswell of theories and cross-disciplinary 'turns' that underline the socio-political import of aesthetic forms of expression previously side-lined by the epistemological norms of Western society (Bleiker 2009: 3), may endow the topic with a new momentum.

This chapter starts within the bounds of traditional understandings of translation, i.e. the interlingual transmission of meaning, as applied to song lyrics in audiovisual texts. This section looks first at the medium of the music video, and secondly at popular music in film and television. Following this, the scope of the discussion widens to incorporate different types of audiovisual music translation practice: the intralingual translation of song lyrics, and broader understandings of music and translation, e.g. the recycling (or re-appropriation) of popular music in different audiovisual contexts, the role of popular music in the 'translation' of cultures and identity, and the music video as a form of translation in itself. The final section sets out research methods in the study of popular music translation and suggests avenues for future research.

Interlingual translation of audiovisual popular music

Music video

As a 'key driver of popular culture' (Vernallis 2013: 437) in the digital era, music video is an exciting and evolving medium for popular music consumption. The format was ushered in with the arrival of MTV in the 1980s, and took off as an aesthetic form in its own right after Michael Jackson's $1 million budget, 14-minute long 'Thriller' video in 1983 (Hearsum and Inglis 2013: 485). During its reign, MTV acted as gatekeeper for both the content and quality of the music videos it aired, with few examples that did not conform to the desired (and somewhat limited) template (*ibid.*: 486). To cater for the wide diversity of markets across the globe, hundreds of separate MTV channels for popular music subgenres were rolled out across different countries, and the interlingual subtitling of lyrics within this setup was not provided for. To widen their appeal, artists would often release songs in other language versions—continuing our Michael Jackson theme, we might cite as an example his 1987 hit 'I just can't stop loving you', which was released in Spanish with the title *Todo mi amor eres tú*, and in French with the title *Je ne veux pas la fin de nous*.

Whilst some popular music artists still choose to do this, since the advent of the Internet—and in particular since the creation of YouTube in 2005—the music video scene has radically altered. YouTube, a participatory media platform (i.e. users can upload their own content and comment on videos published there), has replaced MTV as the primary alternative channel for audiovisual music consumption, evidenced by the fact that 75 per cent of the top 50 searches on the site are for music (Hearsum and Inglis 2013: 495). This scenario has led to (i) definitions of the medium being problematized due to minimal industrial control over quality and format and the ability of video producers to experiment; (ii) the globalization of audiovisual media flows, as compared to MTV's regionalization; (iii) the blurring of boundaries between producer and consumer (resulting in what is termed the 'prosumer') such that multiple amateur videos will usually exist for any given popular song—differentiated from the 'official video'—and music videos may be remediated by anybody who so desires, including the addition of subtitles by multilingual fans who wish to convey the meaning of popular song lyrics to foreign language audiences.

Comments posted by viewers in response to YouTube music videos attest to a high demand for the translation of lyrics. Sometimes translated lyrics are written in the information section underneath the video, but in cases where subtitles are added this alters the consumer experience by visually foregrounding the lyrics as they are heard in another language; also heightening the visibility of the subtitler as a cultural agent. Questions of quality have been raised regarding the production of YouTube videos due to its participatory nature (Hearsum and Inglis 2014: 488) and these apply equally to their subtitling, which is often of a low standard. However, the ability to comment underneath videos means that lyrical meaning in translation may be debated. This will perhaps be of lesser importance for the brand of commercial pop song containing few lyrics primarily formulated to pad out a beat; however, engaged subtitling will be extremely important for fans of recognized lyricists such as Canadian singer Joni Mitchell or French singer Edith Piaf, in which case questions of poetics will come into play (for an analysis of the latter see Kaindl 2013b). Also in question are the aesthetics of the subtitles themselves, and whether they add to or detract from the semiotic ensemble. In some cases, subtitles may entail the removal of the intended visual dimension altogether and its replacement with a blank screen filled with the translated lyrics. For some, demand for lyrical translation presents an opportunity for creativity. Rea Zuzume's (2015) Spanish subtitled version of British band Radiohead's 1997 single 'Paranoid Android' from the album *OK Computer*, illustrates the extent to which both the lyrics and the visual experience are key to the song's impact. In this instance, while the official video (an animated story) is lost, Zuzume attempts to recapture some of the Radiohead visual aesthetic by using imagery from the album cover as a backdrop, while the subtitles are placed in various locations around the screen in a font that blends with the backdrop. It is also evident that the subtitler has done his or her best to render the somewhat cryptic lyrics meaningfully into Spanish.

In contributing to the meaning and influence of a musical text as it travels and pluralizes, subtitlers underscore the hypertextual nature of cultural production in the digital age. As Littau puts it, this system 'generates a (foreign) text's productivity endlessly, and reconfigures the once distinct roles attributed to the author, the translator, or reader' (Littau 1997: 93), thereby challenging the widespread view of translation as secondary to the original. To exemplify the notion of the pluralized original, we might consider Peruvian-American rapper Immortal Technique's 2005 song 'Caught in a Hustle', which does not have an official video. Among the proliferation of amateur videos created for it online is one in which freestyle artist Joe Santos (n.d.) interprets the music by drawing a picture as the rap song plays. In the Spanish subtitled version of this (Santos 2007), the translator adds aesthetically presented subtitles in keeping with the artistic theme. This introduces a new layer of performativity to the evolution of the textual narrative, whose origins in the audiovisual format are already diffuse.

We might pause for a moment on hip hop, which as an internationalized genre of popular music is an interesting case, since historically its lyrics have been heavily coded in Black American slang, which tends to be impenetrable to the uninitiated outsider (Alim 2009a: 215). Being so lyric-heavy and its delivery often very fast-paced, it also demands the flouting of standard industry subtitling guidelines—yet the genre's global appeal remains indisputable both in its mainstream, commoditized manifestation and as an 'independent' underground music scene (Vito 2014: 397–398). An example of a hip hop 'fansubber' is Nightmare Theater—a person or collective seemingly based in Germany, who carries out the subtitling of French rap music videos into English on their YouTube channel created in 2006. Among the comments from appreciative viewers are requests for translations of new songs, recommendations of favourite hip hop acts, and offers of viewer contributions in different language combinations. This might be theorized as a transnational community of affinity 'clustered on the basis of mutual affinity and chosen affiliations' (Pérez-González 2014: 72). Such communities are premised on collective intelligence and genre knowledge (*ibid.*: 75) and are facilitated by the contemporary media landscape, which has broken through MTV's regionalization of the music industry, discussed above.

Beyond entertainment and social identity, hip hop's role in globalized political communities is also increasingly recognized (Alim 2009b: 3). In the case of activist (or 'conscious') hip hop, both the poetics and the content of the lyrics are key to its political function. Numerous localized hip hop movements have emerged in conflict zones such as the Middle East and Sudan (Taviano 2012), as well as in response to non-localized causes such as the Occupy movement. Evidently, lyrical translation is instrumental in raising awareness of the cause in hand, garnering empathy and audienceship through musical affect in a way that traditional political narratives, bound by nation state lines, will often fail to do. A salient example is Palestinian hip hop group DAM (n.d.), which began life on the Israeli hip hop scene rapping in Hebrew, but became politicized at the time of the second Intifada in 2000 and switched to Arabic. As the young rappers testify in the 2008 award-winning documentary film *Slingshot Hip Hop* (2008), this language choice was an act of dissent—one states, '[e]very time I speak Arabic I get stopped by a cop. They can't stand hearing our language' (Slingshot Hip Hop, n.d.). Another explains that she was fired from McDonald's for speaking in Arabic. Already a household name in the Middle East, the subtitling of DAM's music videos into English has been indispensable in raising their profile globally and cementing their place in the so-called Global Hip Hop Nation (Alim 2009b: 3), such that their official videos are now available with an English subtitles option as a matter of course.

While popular music artists are commonly pressured by the industry to learn and perform in English for sales purposes, the globalization of audiovisual media flows has led to higher visibility of artists for whom multilingualism is an important element of their image and appeal, and whose fan bases span different language communities. Examples include French-Spanish singer Manu Chao, Italian-Egyptian singer Dalida, and Greek singer Nana Mouskouri 'whose 60s-to-80s albums were mini-Berlitz courses' (Wilson 2014: 47). Music careers can be sustained, revived and furthered outside of industry channels—even posthumously as in Dalida's case—thanks to the relative freedom of today's dominant means of music consumption. In this context, music video fansubbers, especially in the case of non-English lyrics, might act as a counter force to widespread assumptions of the dominance of English in globalizing processes (Pérez-González 2012: 6). In sum, Vernallis' contention that '[s]uddenly music video has the right scale for today, and perhaps the right mode for a competitive global market (tied but loosely to language, it easily crosses national borders)' (2013: 463) might be reformulated in light of the linguistic opportunities that subtitling affords.

Film and television

The mid-1950s saw the beginning of the cinematic use of popular music (Boyce 2001), and nowadays there is significant crossover between the two arts or industries. Indeed, they could be said to enjoy a mutually beneficial relationship, since film may be a platform to raise the profile of a popular music artist, e.g. Québécois singer Céline Dion, whose career 'went viral when she stowed away on the ultimate planetary love boat, *Titanic*' (Wilson 2014: 41); equally, a popular music artist's involvement on a movie soundtrack will add value to the production, e.g. Manu Chao's soundtrack for León de Aranoa's 2005 film *Princesas* ('Princesses'), for which the track *Me llaman Calle* ('They Call Me Street')—a linguistic play on the protagonist's name Caye and her profession as a prostitute—earned a Goya nomination for Best Original Song.

While a film score is often viewed as supplementary to the story and can be universally appreciated for its nonverbal signifiers, the filmic appropriation of pre-existing popular music for its lyrical content may constitute an important narrative strand in itself, adding to the overall meaning of the film—thus heightening its relevance to AVT. Subtitling song lyrics in such cases is not technically difficult, and yet, since '[m]ost users or viewers are only dimly aware of the contribution that music makes to the semiotic fabric of audiovisual texts' (Pérez-González 2014: 208), they will oftentimes remain untranslated, and thereby pushed further into the background.

To illustrate the semantic and intertextual layers lent to a film by the adept integration of popular music into it—layers which risk being lost on a foreign audience—let us take a scene from Quentin Tarantino's *Kill Bill: Vol. 2* (2004). In this scene, the protagonist Beatrix (played by Uma Thurman) has been unexpectedly reunited with her young daughter, who was torn from her womb and whose existence was kept hidden from her by the child's father, Bill. As mother and daughter lie together on a bed watching the violent 1980 action movie *Shogun Assassin*, the diegetic audio of the young boy narrator's voice fades into the non-diegetic song 'About Her' (2004) by Malcolm McLaren, former manager of the Sex Pistols. The soulful soundscape evoked by the song sits in stark contrast to the world of cold-blooded murder tinged with dark humour that the characters inhabit. But there is more to it than the mood of the music itself. The first line of the song—'My man's got a heart like a rock cast in the sea'—is a looped sample of 'St. Louis Blues' performed by Bessie Smith in a 1929 short film (Who Sampled Website, n.d.). This is followed by the song proper, a cover of 'She's Not There' by The Zombies (1964), featuring the lines: 'Well no one told me about her, the way she lied / Well no one told me about her, how many people cried / But it's too late to say you're sorry / How would I know, how would I care?' These lyrics add to the complex emotions of trauma and joy contained within this scene; the sense of resolution and homecoming laced with adrenalin and unfinished business. Their deployment in this context also transforms the original narrative of the sampled songs, for example the line 'No one told me about her' appears now to refer to Beatrix and her missing daughter, and the man with a heart of rock could be Bill who stole her. The song choice, in its contemporary refashioning of historical popular music, also reminds us that

> In trying to understand how a piece of pop music works within a film one must also try to understand the kind of cultural codes that piece of music will bring with it . . . [I]t sometimes seems as if there is a never-ending set of references with which to deal with.
>
> *(Boyce 2001)*

Without subtitles, the chain of references here is unlikely to be triggered for the foreign viewer in the first place, risking the affective dimensions of the scene being flattened to a forgettable romanticism. Another, perhaps more immediately accessible example is cited in Desilla's comparative study of British and Greek viewers' grasp of implicature in *Bridget Jones's Diary* (2001); the latter group watching the Greek-subtitled version, in which the soundtrack lyrics are not subtitled. The scene in question features the strategic use of the classic hit 'Respect' by Aretha Franklin (1967), which plays at the moment the eponymous heroine delivers a triumphantly scathing remark to her boss upon resignation. Desilla states that

> The overwhelming majority of the British viewers recognised the song and were perfectly conscious of its function . . . As anticipated, the tune proved much more difficult to identify for the Greek audience. One [viewer] could provide the title of the song and a relevant explanation for its use.
>
> *(Desilla 2009, cited in Pérez-González 2014: 210)*

Compared to subtitling, dubbing song lyrics in films presents much more of a technical challenge, akin to the sung translation of opera instead of its surtitling. Not only is this the more expensive option, but it also involves questions of metre, rhyme and 'singability' (Bosseaux 2011: 186). In dubbing countries, therefore, film and television soundtracks with meaningful lyrics will usually be ignored, leading to a translational loss (Pérez-González 2014: 210). In the case of musical films, however—which sometimes boast the involvement of high profile popular music artists—one way or other lyrical translation must be addressed. Bosseaux notes that when foreign musical films are released in France, a mixed approach is adopted whereby dialogue is dubbed but songs are kept in the original and subtitled (2013: 81). Yet this solution is not always appropriate, such as in children's movies where everything including the songs must be dubbed over for the sake of the young audience. One fan of Disney's *The Lion King* (1994)—the soundtrack of which was famously composed by Elton John and remains the only animated movie soundtrack to be RIAA certified Diamond™, signifying 10,000,000 sales (RIAA Website, n.d.)—has compiled a blog detailing all language dubs of the movie that he/she has managed to acquire, including information about the translation of the songs (The Lion King Language Dubs Collection, n.d.). For example, the author lists the Farsi version as a non-official dub in which the song lyrics are subtitled; whereas it is the other way round for the Flemish version, in which the song lyrics are dubbed, not the rest of the film, and are included as a special feature to the Dutch DVD—testifying to the extreme popularity of Elton John's oeuvre. The fan also describes musical differences between different language versions, for example in the Zulu dub of the song 'I Just Can't Wait To Be King', he/she notes that 'a significant background choir has been added, which I believe is meant to be the animals singing'. Thus, while the soundtrack very much has Elton John's stamp on it—affording it global leverage—it also bows to requirements of 'fulfilling entertainment conventions in other parts of the world' (Wilson 2014: 48). This reveals how musical dubbing can go beyond lyrics as a vehicle for the hybridization—or 'creolization' (*ibid.*)—of cultures, running counter to widespread fears of Anglo-American cultural hegemony in the globalized era.

Aside from technical constraints, an important reason for not dubbing songs in musical films involving popular music artists might be recognition of unique artistic skill. A pertinent example is Lars von Trier's *Dancer in the Dark* (2000), starring Icelandic singer Björk, who also wrote most of the soundtrack (released the same year under the album title *Selmasongs*). This tragic drama revolves around the inner auditory world of blind factory worker Selma, played by Björk, whose imaginative musical 'journeys' are integral to the plot and character development. It is difficult to imagine how Björk's iconic voice could be divorced from her songs and replaced by another without effecting significant damage to the artistic value of the film. The loss would furthermore be immediately noticeable to viewers already familiar with her music and perhaps even drawn to the film precisely by her performance in it.

As regards television, there is comparatively less to say about the interlingual translation of popular music lyrics, given that, as discussed in the previous section, the medium has radically altered since the launch of MTV in the USA in 1981. Harrison explains that since the turn of the twenty-first century, music television has been disseminated across national channels, organized by genre, and that 'viewers go to music channels to fill a void left by the departure of programmes such as *Top of the Pops*—a BBC music chart television show broadcast weekly in the UK between 1964 and 2006. With the rise in popularity of new media, people want more music, sooner, faster and all the time' (Harrison 2013: 187). Harrison also notes that the target demographic for UK music channels is 16–34 year olds (*ibid.*: 192), which arguably suggests a commercial drive, rather than a cultural or pedagogical one that might place more importance on lyrics. While intralingual subtitling, discussed below, appears to be on the rise in music television, there is no indication of the same for interlingual subtitling, hence foreign language fans taking matters into their own hands and the proliferation of the practice online.

Even the Eurovision Song Contest, television's 'five-decade-old Cheeseball Olympics of pop music, the most watched ongoing musical event on Earth, with an annual audience estimated at 300 million' (Wilson 2014: 44), does not encourage the practice of lyrical subtitling. Indeed, the contest has generated controversy in recent years over its fluctuating language rules that have facilitated linguistic and cultural homogenization:

> Though it began with performers wearing local costume and singing in their native tongues, an 'international language' requirement was added in later years by the TV networks that administer it, to make it more commercially viable, so English and French songs predominate. (*ibid.*: 45)

One blogger inadvertently highlights Eurovision's missed opportunity by suggesting (rather optimistically, given the above observation) how his language-learning followers might take the initiative when watching the contest:

> Look up the lyrics to the songs (in your target language of course) and use the lyrics to reinforce new vocabulary or phrases that maybe [*sic*] useful later on. You can add these new words and phrases to an SRS like Anki, Mnemosyne, or even Memrise! It also gives you insight into how to write songs in your target language, slang, different dialects, political situations, vital grammatical point [*sic*] and even a little bit about their own culture.
>
> *(Koko the Polyglot 2015)*

The bigger picture notwithstanding, the interlingual translation of popular music is still occasionally found on television. One example found by the author is humorous: Australian music-themed comedy quiz show *Spicks and Specks* concluded one episode in June 2009 with a subtitled version, available on YouTube, of Belgian singer Plastic Bertrand's 1977 hit single *Ça plane pour moi* ('That works for me'), itself a pastiche of the punk genre featuring nonsense lyrics (*Spicks and Specks* Translates Plastic Bertrand 2009). The subtitles here function to increase the song's humour by foregrounding the lyrics and making them even weirder through their literal rendering. Interestingly, the same quiz show also features a game entitled 'Turning Japanese', in which contestants must guess the song by the lyrics, which have been translated into Japanese using an online translation tool and then translated back into English again. Future studies might explore further instances of the interlingual translation of popular music on television networks in different countries.

Intralingual translation of audiovisual popular music

Subtitling of popular music videos is often carried out intralingually. In this case, translational processes are wholly accounted for in terms of modes, understood as 'the visual and semiotic resources required to create and interpret audiovisual texts' (Pérez-González 2014: 192). More specifically, here we are looking at meaning transfer between two medial variants of the core mode of language: spoken/sung language to written language. Music subtitles in this context differ from the interlingual transfer of lyrical meaning, it is normal practice for the lyrics to be delivered verbatim (Harrison 2013: 188). Whether in a professional or non-professional setting, this form of subtitling may be carried out to enhance comprehension where the lyrical content is important, perhaps for poetic, pedagogical or political reasons; or for entertainment purposes, for example if consumers wish to sing along to a track or to perform it karaoke-style (YouTube is replete with such music videos, in which the vocal track may or may not be absent and the subtitles change colour to indicate when the lyrics should be sung). As with interlingual subtitling, foregrounding the written lyrics in a music video alters the affective experience of the music and, in most cases, constitutes a superimposition upon the intended visual dimension of the semiotic ensemble. As discussed earlier with reference to Littau (1997), this is characteristic of the hypertextual system of the digital age in which the pluralization of the original text becomes the norm.

The ability of music fans to participate in audiovisual media flows as co-creational 'prosumers' has seen intralingual subtitling and dubbing employed for creative and comic effect. A famous example is the literal video concept, a global Internet trend that is claimed to have originated with Current TV employee Dustin McLean's version of A-Ha's 'Take on Me' in 2008 (Dust Films Website, n.d.). Literal videos are parodies of official music videos that aim to 'narrow the yawning chasm of images-vs.-song lyrics-vs.-celebrity persona by simply inserting their own lyrics, which flatly reiterate or question whatever is happening onscreen' (Weeks 2008). For example, the literal version of British singer James Blunt's 2004 hit song 'You're Beautiful', uploaded by Simeon Bisas (2008), ridicules the artist's posturing in the video whereby he ill-advisedly removes his shirt in the middle of a snowstorm to reveal his bare chest and, sitting cross-legged, inexplicably organizes his shoes and the contents of his pocket into a line on the floor. This activity bears no apparent relation to the lyrical narrative, which recounts a fanciful encounter with an attractive woman on the subway. The 'literal' dubbed lyrics, accompanied by verbatim subtitles, are sung in an exaggeratedly effeminate voice and satirically exploit this narrative disjuncture, e.g. the opening lines become 'I fill the camera / Look of despair' to realign the lyrics with the visual narrative—a close-up of Blunt's melancholic face. Such practices might be theorized as a form of audiovisual interventionist approach (Pérez-González 2014: 58) that aims to undermine the commercial dominance of the popular music industry, an observation borne out by the fact that Bisas' video was initially removed from YouTube following a copyright complaint by Blunt's label EMI Music (Med Library Website, n.d.).

Another form of intralingual subtitling is for the deaf and hard of hearing on television. The provision of music subtitling for the deaf and hard of hearing may seem at first sight counter-intuitive; and yet, as scholar and practitioner at MTV Mark Harrison testifies, there is both consumer demand and scholarly interest:

> I am always asked, 'Why would anyone with a hearing impairment want to watch music on TV?' The fact is that the vast majority of subtitle users have lost their hearing gradually over time or later in life, leaving them missing music a great deal.
>
> *(2014)*

The fact that this demand is met is aided by the changing face of audiovisual music consumption in the digital age. In his illuminating study of subtitling for the deaf and hard of hearing for UK music channels, Harrison states that '[n]o genre of television has seen more diversification in order to maintain an audience than music television' (2013: 186). Here, subtitling practice is driven by principles of inclusion and accessibility, no matter how small the audience share of subtitle users, which amounts to less than 1 per cent for most music channels (*ibid.*: 192).

Unlike with YouTube music videos, this form of intralingual subtitling is conducted within an industrial setting, which means that strict guidelines must be adhered to (*ibid.*: 193). The # symbol is used at the beginning of each subtitle to indicate singing, and again at the end to indicate that the song is over. Punctuation is kept to a minimum and colour coding must be employed to reflect different singers/rappers/speakers. While usual conventions apply regarding line breaks and timings for intro/shot changes, a major difference from ordinary television subtitling is that, for copyright reasons as much as semantic ones, there can be no reduction, deletion or paraphrasing of lyrics—they must be 100 per cent verbatim, regardless of the language of the song, and sourced from an approved location (ideally the record label). As Harrison states, this makes things easier on the subtitler, but harder on the viewer, who must contend at times with more text than is comfortable to read in the allotted time (*ibid.*: 189). That said, genres often differ in this respect. As discussed below, hip hop songs contain many lyrics which at times require a reading speed of almost double the recommended rate; dance/electronic music, as well as jazz and easy listening, on the other hand, tends to be much lower in terms of lyrical volume (*ibid.*: 190).

From an AVT perspective, an intriguing aspect of music subtitling for the deaf and hard of hearing is that it demands the translation of not just linguistic but audio content as well. At present, this is a limited aspiration, since there is little available space for musical description given the higher number of subtitles, while specialist provision such as on-screen graphic representation of music, pitch and rhythm, or audio production enhancing rhythm and bass vibrations, does not exist (*ibid.*: 198). As such, the visual dimension comes into sharper focus within the musical ensemble in the form, for example, of instruments being played in live performances, facial expressions and/or dancing that displays the beat. Given that contemporary popular music has been increasingly subject to a commercial drive that entails 'a shift from active musical production to passive pop consumption, the decline of folk or community or subcultural traditions, and a general loss of musical skill' (Frith 2006: 231), paradoxically, perhaps, the development of audiovisual accessibility for the deaf and hard of hearing may help to reinstate awareness of the affective roots of the human musical experience.

Beyond subtitles—Alternative understandings of AVT and popular music

From an AVT perspective, popular music offers far more than just lyrics. Susam-Sarajeva argues that much can be gained in moving beyond conventional understandings of translational processes as applied to music (2008: 189). While several past studies have been conducted on the role of popular music in cross-cultural transfer, the contemporary audiovisual context opens up yet more avenues in this respect. Kaindl, for instance, traces the translation of not only the lyrics but also the visual dimension of the 1997 hit song 'Simarik' by Turkish singer Tarkan, as it moves, via several remakes, 'from ethnicity to globalization' (2005: 258). The song, which celebrates the emancipation of Turkish women from a male perspective, was first remade in Turkish for the international market, then covered twice in English with accompanying videos—first by Greek-American singer Stella Soleil in 2001, then in a highly stylized and sexualized manner by Australian singer Holly Valance in 2002. Kaindl notes that

Whereas the videos of the Turkish versions are constructed around a narrative, the English versions focus on the rhythmic dimension of the song, centered on dances with sexual connotations. The discursive element of the foreign song is visually eliminated and reduced to its mere motor-sensual aspects.

(ibid.: *259)*

In another case study involving the 2012 pop video 'Gangnam Style' by South Korean singer Psy—famously the first YouTube video ever to exceed one billion views (Rahman 2012)—we can observe intercultural remakes that sidestep the music industry (thus arguably non-commercially driven). The original song is culturally localized in that it mocks the residents of the wealthy Seoul neighbourhood of Gangnam, and yet it went viral, reached no. 1 in the UK Singles Chart, and was praised by UN Secretary General Ban Ki-Moon for its 'unlimited global reach' (Davies 2012). The music video spawned an array of lyrical-visual parodies in the months following its release, made by far-flung amateur prosumers online. These include 'Gandalf Style' by Angie Griffin and Chad Nikolaus (2012), which features a man in a wizard costume (supposedly Gandalf the Wizard from J.R.R. Tolkien's *Lord of the Rings*) dancing around an urban location to the bemusement of passers-by, singing new lyrics in English: 'I got a long grey beard / Keep it secret / Keep it safe' (referring to the eponymous ring). Another Gandalf version in German swiftly followed, uploaded by online comedy trio Y-Titty (2012). This version, staged in a similar way, albeit in a rural environment, has Gandalf complaining that he is underrated, arguing with Frodo the Hobbit, and insulting hobbits in general. Neither version attempts to capture the lyrical semantics of the source text; instead the phonetic semblance of Gangnam/Gandalf allows for the humorous visual and acoustic mood of the original video to be domesticated into the target culture.

Kaindl asserts that popular genres are always part of a cultural system or tradition, whether they are reflective of or reacting against that system, and that when they travel they become part of a new one (2013a: 18:05). AVT scholars can benefit greatly from other disciplines in this area, and vice versa. From a communication studies perspective, for example, Hanke (2006) explores processes of transculturalization and hybridization on the level of genre in music television. Focusing on the Latin American branch of MTV (MTV Latino), he observes a fusion of musical styles within the ostensible context of Euro-American homogenization and commodification, describing the production of music videos in particular as 'an aesthetic, expressive practice of translating the infinite possibilities of mutating, hybrid sounds into images that travel across time and space' (*ibid.*: 325). Hanke's account of hybridization parallels rock critic Wilson's 'creolization' of popular culture mentioned earlier, with both emphasizing the existence of a reciprocal cultural influence on the West that undermines claims of capitalist cultural hegemony. Wilson adds that such claims ignore 'how commercial music is redeployed in everyday life for people's own purposes' (2014: 49). He cites a Jamaican 'roughneck' attempting to explain why it is that the saccharine Céline Dion is so beloved of the nation's gangster underclass, to the extent that guns are fired into the air when she is played in clubs alongside reggae and ska music: 'Bad man have fi play love tune fi show 'dat them a lova too' (Bad men have to play love songs to show that they are lovers too) (*ibid.*: 50). Future AVT-based studies might investigate additional possibilities for hybridization afforded by media convergence and participatory culture, taking into account the visual dimension as well as the acoustic/verbal.

Considering hybridization on the level of medium, we might also seek to incorporate translation theory into media studies assessments of what Korsgaard terms 'wild new forms'

(2013: 501) of music video. These 'transgress traditional borders' by problematizing definitive characteristics of the medium such as brevity, and the music preceding the visuals (*ibid.*: 507), while retaining the core functions of showcasing musical features and marketing the song (*ibid.*: 517). Drawing on two case studies (Björk's 2011 app album *Biophilia*, and Arcade Fire's interactive video for the 2010 track 'We Used to Wait'), Korsgaard groups these experimental forms into five categories: participatory/interactive, user-generated content, remakes/remixes (including new language versions, literal videos and parodies discussed above), alternate lengths, and hi/low definition (*ibid.*: 502). In proposing 'that music videos are intermedial and remediational by nature and that music video continually defines itself by stretching beyond its own territory' (*ibid.*: 517), Korsgaard effectively theorizes the evolving medium of the music video in translational terms. He thus complements Kaindl's description of the medium as a complex audiovisual form weaving sound, language and image together in a functional relationship, and of the transfer between aural and visual codes in a music video which can be understood according to Jakobson's notion of intersemiotic translation, as follows:

> The key to understanding the mechanisms of such an intersemiotic transfer lies in the analysis of reciprocal dependencies and potential relations between the various elements. Such an approach was developed by Goodwin (1993), who views pop songs in terms of their narratives.
>
> *(Kaindl 2005: 252)*

Mention of narratives brings us back to the symbiotic relationship between film and popular music, since many movie directors 'give music its due as the stimulus that sets off a train of mental images' (Romney and Wootton 1995: 122). The narratives of popular music however are not just lyrical or visual and contained within the song itself, but are also bound up in the identity of the artist and/or a certain temporal period. As such, a song's inclusion in a film is sometimes not for its lyrical content at all, but for the broader socio-cultural narratives it represents. There may be a translational aspect to a musical text's 'relocation' in a film, be it from a certain temporal context or a certain social scene to another; notably when there is an element of challenge through which new meaning is produced. One example is the use of Britney Spears' 2004 single 'Everytime'—a simple and sad break-up song penned for her ex-boyfriend Justin Timberlake—in the 2012 black comedy film *Spring Breakers*, in which America's violent and morally vacuous underbelly comes to the fore. In the relevant scene, the three anti-heroines (played by Vanessa Hudgens, Ashley Benson and Rachel Korine), who are on spring break in Florida, gather round a piano holding guns and wearing pink balaclavas. Seated at the piano is their new 'friend'—a local rapper and drug dealer named Alien (played by James Franco). The song begins diegetically as an off-key sunset sing-along, but the real song eventually takes over non-diegetically, alongside slow-motion footage of the four wreaking carnage together:

> When Britney Spears's 'Everytime' floods the speakers, it's so gorgeous and alluring, the inherent sadness of the song subverted by playing it over horrific, dreamlike images of empowerment ... the sweetness of 'Everytime' does not compute with the violence of *Spring Breakers*.
>
> *(Turner 2014)*

The subversion of Spears' pop princess image here acts to renarrate the American dream as a whole into a nihilistic vision of aimless consumerism and feminism-gone-wrong. If we look at this from a translational perspective, perhaps as a form of intracultural meaning transfer, we might perceive how aesthetic texts can draw upon affective levels of experience that go beyond language, in order to bridge discrepancies between public narratives (e.g. what is sold by economic power structures) and the reality of people's lived experience. Since the stories of capitalism are internationally disseminated via the entertainment industry, this has wide-ranging socio-political implications. Bleiker indeed outlines how contemporary international relations theory might benefit from scholars sensitized to questions of translation in exploring music-based forms of expression:

> [C]an we gain political insight through music that other sources of knowledge, such as texts or visual arts, cannot provide? And if so, how can these forms of knowledge be translated back into language-based expression without losing the very essence of what they seek to capture and convey? . . . We might then be able to appreciate what we otherwise cannot even see: perspectives and people excluded from prevailing purviews, for instance, or the emotional nature and consequences of political events.
>
> *(2009: 1–2)*

Perhaps when seen in this light, AVT and popular music merits greater attention as an emerging field of study—of which this chapter has only sketched out the beginnings.

Research methods and avenues for future scholarship

Given the scarcity of existing scholarship on AVT and popular music, it seems reasonable to combine a discussion of current methodologies with ideas for new research directions in this section. In her overview of research methods in song translation as a whole since the 1990s, Bosseaux cites some key analytical tools borrowed from literary, poetic, stage and screen translation, such as semiotics and the notion of performability; and draws a major distinction between written (surtitling) and sung or 'singable' translation (2011: 184). Although the subtitling of music videos does not feature in this overview, Low's Skopos-inspired 'pentathlon' approach (2005) emerges as one of the few methodological frameworks devised for performative song translation that could equally be applied in an AVT context. This approach proposes five criteria that need to be balanced to produce a successful sung translation: 'singability, sense, naturalness, rhythm and rhyme' (*ibid.*: 185). While not all popular music translation aims towards a singable text, Low contends that this is the most difficult skopos due to its many constraints, and that the model's emphasis on function and purpose makes it versatile in helping a translator to ascertain which features to prioritize in a given case (*ibid.*: 186). A future study might seek to adapt Low's framework to incorporate the visual dimension beyond that of operatic performance and reassess his hierarchical view of the visual as 'a third code, ideally serving the auditory codes of language and music' (*ibid.*: 188).

Pitted against the bulk of song translation analysis to date, which has 'focused mainly on constraints, techniques and difficulties, with an emphasis on words and music' (2011: 194), Bosseaux acknowledges the broader socio-cultural or historical perspective of some popular music translation scholarship that is beginning to make waves. This looks beyond text and music to contextualize songs within their source and target cultures. Notable among proponents of this approach is Kaindl, introduced above, who uses polysystem theory (Even-Zohar 1997/1990, Toury 1995, Hermans 1999) to set out a 'socio-semiotic foundation for the translation of popular music' (2005: 242). Arguing that popular music can be structured as a system, and that translation in this context is a socially embedded and often fragmented practice, he views popular music (including videos) in terms of the 'mediated multiple text' (*ibid.*: 241), reflecting Littau's notion of translation as hypertext discussed above. Kaindl advocates the concepts of 'bricolage' (Lévi-Strauss 1966) and 'dialogics' (Bakhtin 1984) as analytical tools to explore the complexity of these systems. Bricolage refers to the appropriation of components including music, language, values and culture that a translator combines and connects 'in order to form a new, unified, signifying system'; while dialogics is the related idea that 'no text, discourse, genre, etc. exists alone but is part of a textual, discursive and generic network and stands in dialogic relationship with previous or future utterances' (*ibid.* 242). This foundation opens up a wealth of possibilities for future studies, with some preliminary ideas having been mooted in the previous section.

Multimodal theory is undoubtedly of immense value to studies of AVT and popular music. As discussed elsewhere in this handbook, multimodality is the combination of speech, writing, visualization and music, and—crucially—as a theoretical framework it 'does not prioritize language at the expense of other meaning-making modes' (Pérez-González 2014: 182). Whether translational processes are understood in the conventional sense or intersemiotically/intermodally, this approach will prove particularly useful in accounting for the complex range of modes and sub-modes that constitute the semiotic fabric of audiovisual popular music texts, and how they are brought to bear in translation.

Another fruitful methodological approach for future studies could be socio-narrative theory, first introduced to translation studies by Baker (2006), which views narratives in their various disparate forms as inherent to human cognition and constitutive (as opposed to representative) of social reality. Here, translational processes can be understood as processes of 'renarration' (Baker 2008: 16), which again might apply both in the conventional interlingual sense and/or in a broader sense. An advantage of the narrative framework over other sociological models is its emphasis on temporality, such that AVT studies might focus on temporal and not just spatial/cultural relocation. Socio-narrative furthermore permits us to extend our enquiry to questions of music and personal identity, i.e. how somebody might 'renarrate' themselves on an ontological (personal) level through music. An illustrative example here, taken from the author's own research, is the song/music video 'Enfants du désert' (2009) by French rapper Diam's (real name Mélanie Georgiades), whose 2006 album *Dans ma bulle* topped the French charts and reached Diamond™ status. In this text, available on YouTube, the artist aesthetically performs the inner process of her public conversion to Islam—an act for which she was widely condemned by fans and critics alike in the volatile French post-9/11 climate, and which led to her retirement from rapping in 2010. The song uses a variety of semiotic means—including an intertextual visual characterization of Diam's as *Forrest Gump* (Zemeckis 1994/Groom 1986)—to narrate the artist's ontological evolution (i.e. her characterological growth and change), a process which to her signifies an answer to the empty promises of fame and capitalist materialism, in a wider temporal context of global uneven development (Johnson 2017). Aligning religious conversion with translation here, through the concept of renarration, permits a richer understanding of the various affective, cultural and semiotic processes of meaning transfer involved in the text.

The above is by no means a definitive list of research methods in the growing study of AVT and popular music. Indeed, the gap in scholarship provides an exciting opportunity for new and creative approaches to keep abreast of developments such as the evolving nature and role of the music video, the rise of participatory translation practices in the digital era, and the increasing number of artists who are shunning commercial structures that have previously shaped production of and access to popular music, perhaps leading to a more truly universalized popular music experience.

Summary

Audiovisual translation and popular music remains an underexplored research subject, despite the significant role that music consumption plays in people's lives and identities and its evolution in the globalized digital era. This is in part due to popular music's perceived low symbolic capital, and in part to a need for interdisciplinary approaches that adequately capture the complexity of music as a form of expression. This chapter has provided an insight into existing scholarship on the topic and attempted to push the boundaries a little further to incorporate contemporary developments in both the music industry and the field of AVT, making a case for its relevance as a social, cultural and political force.

In considering the subtitling and dubbing of audiovisual popular music, we saw how music video has developed as a medium since the advent of YouTube to become more participatory in nature, enabling prosumers to facilitate access to lyrical content across linguistic boundaries, whether for poetic, pedagogical or political reasons, and calling into question notions of authorship. This was contrasted with the more industry-restricted media of film and television, where the interlingual translation of popular music lyrics is often overlooked; while conversely intralingual subtitling of music for the deaf and hard of hearing has become a priority for television producers fighting to maintain audience figures in the Internet age. In extending our understanding of translational practices, we then considered parodies, remakes, socio-cultural context, hybridization, and called into question the very definition of the medium of the music video. It is hoped that the overview provided here will serve as a springboard for the continued development of this highly enjoyable and fertile area of study.

Further reading

Gorlée, D. (ed.) (2005) *Song and Significance: Virtues and Vices of Vocal Translation*, Amsterdam: Rodopi | *This pioneering collection on the translation of song contains two chapters of particular value to studies of AVT and popular music. Kaindl's 'The Plurisemiotics of Pop Song Translation: Words, Music, Voice and Image' (p. 235–264) offers an invaluable analysis of the socio-cultural impact of popular music, drawing on different German versions (including video clips) of a French chanson. Meanwhile, Low's 'The Pentathlon Approach to Translating Songs' (p. 185–212) posits a functionalist framework applicable to vocal translation across a range of genres, including popular music.*

Minors, H. J. (ed.) (2013) *Music, Text and Translation*, London & New York: Bloomsbury | *This edited volume seeks to further develop research in music translation and includes contributions from several leading scholars in the field. A particular highlight with relation to AVT and popular music is Harrison's chapter 'Making Music Television Accessible to a Hard-of-Hearing Audience' (p. 187–198), offering a rare and extremely illuminating study from a practitioner in the field.*

Littau, K. (1997) 'Translation in the Age of Postmodern Production: From Text to Intertext to Hypertext', *Forum for Modern Language Studies* 33(1): 81–96 | *This article posits translation as the re-writing of the already pluralized original in the hypertextual system of the digital age. Setting out a robust theoretical grounding in questions of authorship (Barthes, Foucault, Derrida), it theorizes translation in terms of a convergence of postmodern literary theory and computer technology; in so doing the article offers an approach to audiovisual music consumption and related digital textualities that is framed within broader critical understandings of the concept of translation.*

Susam-Sarajeva, S. (2008) 'Translation and Music', *The Translator* 14(2): 187–200 | *This article is the introduction to the 2008 special issue of* The Translator *devoted to the translation of music. The article first seeks to account for the peripheral disciplinary position generally occupied by this area of study, and then provides an up-to-date, critical examination of existing research on the topic.*

Wilson, C. (2014) *Let's Talk About Love: Why Other People Have Such Bad Taste*, New York & London: Bloomsbury | *This book by a Canadian music critic provides a personalized insight into today's popular music industry. The humorous premise (the author's hatred of Québécois singer Céline Dion) is used as a springboard to interrogate the concept of taste from a cultural studies perspective. Chapter 3 'Let's Talk in French' and Chapter 4 'Let's Talk About World Conquest' are particularly noteworthy in regard to questions of translation and popular music in the globalized context.*

Related topics

3 Subtitling on the cusp of its futures
4 Investigating dubbing: learning from the past, looking to the future
6 Subtitling for deaf and hard of hearing audiences: moving forward
11 Film remakes as a form of translation
12 Mediality and audiovisual translation
17 Multimodality and audiovisual translation: cohesion in accessible films
24 Ethnography in audiovisual translation studies
27 Audiovisual translation and fandom
28 Audiovisual translation and activism

References

Alim, H. S. (2009a) 'Track 11: Creating an Empire within an Empire: Critical Hip Hop Language Pedagogies and the Role of Sociolinguistics', in H. S. Alim, A. Ibrahim and A. Pennycook (eds) *Global Linguistic Flows*, London & New York: Routledge, 213–230.

Alim, H. S. (2009b) 'Intro', in H. S. Alim, A. Ibrahim and A. Pennycook (eds) *Global Linguistic Flows*, London & New York: Routledge, 1–22.

Arcade Fire (2010) 'We Used to Wait', Interactive Video. Available online: http://www.thewildernessdowntown.com [last accessed 20 December 2017].

Baker, M. (2006) *Translation and Conflict: A Narrative Account*, London & New York: Routledge.

Baker, M. (2008) 'Ethics of Renarration', *Cultus* 1(1): 10–33.

Bakhtin, M. M. (1984) *Problems of Dostoevsky's Poetics*, trans. and edited by C. Emerson, Minneapolis: University of Minnesota Press.

Bisas, S. (2008) 'You're Beautiful (Literal Video Version)'. Available online: https://www.youtube.com/watch?v=YOlI5Qiq-9g [last accessed 20 December 2017].

Björk (2000) *Selmasongs*: Polydor.

Björk (2011) *Biophilia*: One Little Indian.

Bleiker, R. (2009) *Aesthetics and World Politics*, Palgrave Macmillan: Basingstoke.

Bosseaux, C. (2011) 'Song Translation', in K. Malmkjær and K. Windle (eds) *The Oxford Handbook of Translation Studies*, Oxford & New York: Oxford University Press, 183–197.

Bosseaux, C. (2013) 'Some Like it Dubbed: Translating Marilyn Monroe', in H. Julia Minors (ed.) *Music, Text and Translation*, London & New York: Bloomsbury, 81–92.

Boyce, L. (2001) '"I Didn't Know You Liked The Delfonics": How Does the Way Quentin Tarantino's Characters Talk about and React to Music Relate to the Manner in which that Music is Heard in his Films?', *Netribution Film Network*, September 7. Available online: http://www.netribution.co.uk/features/essays/quentin_tarantino_music.html [last accessed 20 December 2017].

DAM (n.d.) 'DAM Website'. Available online: http://www.damrap.com [last accessed 20 December 2017].
Davies, L. (2012) 'Rapper Psy brings Gangnam Style horseplay to United Nations', *The Guardian*, 24 October. Available online: http://www.theguardian.com/world/2012/oct/24/psy-gangnam-style-united-nations [last accessed 20 December 2017].
Desilla, L. (2009) *Towards a Methodology for the Study of Implicatures in Subtitled Films: Multimodal Construal and Reception of Pragmatic Meaning across Cultures*, Unpublished Doctoral Thesis, University of Manchester.
Dust Films (n.d.) 'Literal Videos'. Available online: http://www.dustfilms.com/literalvideos [last accessed 20 December 2017].
Even-Zohar, I. (1990) 'Polysystem Studies', Durham: Duke University Press, special issue of *Poetics Today* 11(1).
Even-Zohar, I. (1997) 'Factors and Dependencies in Culture: A Revised Outline for Polysystem Culture Research', *Canadian Review of Comparative Literature* 24(1): 15–34.
Frith S. (2006 [1988]) 'The Industrialization of Music', from *Music for Pleasure: Essays in the Sociology of Pop, Polity*. Reproduced in A. Bennett, B. Shank and J. Toynbee (eds) *The Popular Music Studies Reader*, London & New York: Routledge, 231–238.
Griffin, A. and C. Nikolaus (2012) 'Gandalf Style'. Available online: https://www.youtube.com/watch?v=M660rjNCH0A [last accessed 20 December 2017].
Groom, W. (1986) *Forrest Gump*, New York: Doubleday.
Hanke, B. (2006 [1998]) '" Yo Quiero Mi MTV!" Making Music Television for Latin America', in T. Swiss, J. Sloop and A. Herman (eds) *Mapping the Beat: Popular Music and Contemporary Theory*, Oxford: Blackwell, 219–45. Reproduced in A. Bennett, B. Shank and J. Toynbee (eds) *The Popular Music Studies Reader*, London & New York: Routledge, 317–325.
Harrison, M. (2013) 'Making Music Television Accessible to a Hard-of-Hearing Audience', in H. Julia Minors (ed.) *Music, Text and Translation*, London & New York: Bloomsbury, 187–198.
Harrison, M. (2014) 'Making Music TV Accessible to the Hard-of-Hearing Audience'. Interview published on website of *Languages & The Media: 10th International Conference on Language Transfer in Audiovisual Media*, November 5–7, Berlin. Available online: http://www.languages-media.com/press_interviews_2010_harrison.php [last accessed 17 September 2015].
Hearsum, P. and I. Inglis (2013) 'The Emancipation of Music Video: YouTube and the Cultural Politics of Supply and Demand', in J. Richardson, C. Gorbman and C. Vernallis (eds) *The Oxford Handbook of New Audiovisual Aesthetics*, Oxford: Oxford Handbooks Online, 483–500.
Hermans, T. (1999) *Translation in Systems. Descriptive and System-oriented Approaches Explained*. Manchester: St. Jerome.
Hewitt, E. (2000) 'A Study of Pop Song Translations', *Perspectives: Studies in Translatology* 8(3): 187–195.
Jackson, M. (1983) 'Thriller'. Available online: https://www.youtube.com/watch?v=sOnqjkJTMaA [last accessed 20 December 2017].
Jackson, M. (2012 [1987]) 'Todo mi amor eres tú'/'Je ne veux pas la fin de nous', available on *Bad 25* (reissue album): Epic, Legacy Recordings and MJJ Productions.
Johnson, R. (2017) *The Clash of Articulations: Aesthetic Shock, Multivalent Narratives and Islam in the Post-9/11 Era*, Unpublished Doctoral Thesis, University of Manchester.
Kaindl, K. (2005) 'The Plurisemiotics of Pop Song Translation: Words, Music, Voice and Image', in D. Gorlée (ed.) *Song and Significance: Virtues and Vices of Vocal Translation*, Amsterdam: Rodopi, 235–264.
Kaindl, K. (2013a) Video Interview on *Translating Music* Website. Available online: http://www.translatingmusic.com/styled-7/index.html [last accessed 20 December 2017].
Kaindl, K. (2013b) 'From Realism to Tearjerker and Back: The Songs of Edith Piaf in German', in H. Julia Minors (ed.) *Music, Text and Translation*, translated by L. Brodbeck and J. Page London & New York: Bloomsbury, 151–161.

Koko the Polyglot (2015) 'How to Use Eurovision to Learn Languages', *Koko the Polyglot Blog*, 10 March. Available online: http://kokothepolyglot.net/2015/03/10/how-to-use-eurovision-to-learn-languages/ [last accessed 13 March 2016].

Korsgaard, M. B. (2013) 'Music Video Transformed', in J. Richardson, C. Gorbman and C. Vernallis (eds) *The Oxford Handbook of New Audiovisual Aesthetics*, Oxford: Oxford Handbooks Online, 501–522.

Lévi-Strauss, C. (1966) *The Savage Mind*, anonymous translator, Chicago: University of Chicago Press [French original: *La pensée sauvage* (1962) Paris: Plon].

Littau, K. (1997) 'Translation in the Age of Postmodern Production: From Text to Intertext to Hypertext', *Forum for Modern Language Studies* 33(1): 81–96.

Low, P. (2005) 'The Pentathlon Approach to Translating Songs', in D. Gorlée (ed.) *Song and Significance: Virtues and Vices of Vocal Translation*, Amsterdam: Rodopi, 185–212.

Med Library website (n.d.) 'Literal music video'. Available online: http://medlibrary.org/medwiki/Literal_music_video [last accessed 20 December 2017].

Nightmare Theater (2006) 'Nightmare Theater YouTube Channel'. Available online: https://www.youtube.com/channel/UCOgDch8OS5Jlq4idINS3Bmw [last accessed 20 December 2017].

Pérez-González, L. (2012) 'Amateur Subtitling as Immaterial Labour in the Digital Media Culture', *Convergence: The International Journal of Research into New Media Technologies* 19(2): 157–175.

Pérez-González, L. (2014) *Audiovisual Translation: Theories, Methods and Issues*, London & New York: Routledge.

Psy (2012) 'Gangnam Style'. Available online: https://www.youtube.com/watch?v=9bZkp7q19f0 [last accessed 20 December 2017].

Rahman, R. (2012) 'PSY's "Gangnam Style" Becomes First YouTube Video to Earn a Billion Views', *Entertainment Weekly*, 21 December. Available online: http://www.ew.com/article/2012/12/21/psy-gangnam-style-billion-views-youtube [last accessed 20 December 2017].

RIAA website (n.d.) 'Diamond Awards'. Available online: http://riaa.com/goldandplatinum.php?content_selector=top-diamond-awards [last accessed 20 December 2017].

Romney, J. and A. Wootton (1995) *Celluloid Jukebox: Popular Music and the Movies Since the 50s*, London: British Film Institute.

Santos, J. (n.d.) 'The Battle Artist YouTube Channel'. Available online: https://www.youtube.com/user/BattleArts [last accessed 20 December 2017].

Santos, J. (2007) 'Immortal Technique—Caught in a Hustle (con subtítulos)'. Available online: https://www.youtube.com/watch?v=nia0_dMFfE4 [last accessed 20 December 2017].

Slingshot Hip Hop (n.d.) 'Trailer'. Available online: http://www.slingshothiphop.com/trailer/ [last accessed 20 December 2017].

Soleil, S. (2001) 'Kiss Kiss'. Available online: https://www.youtube.com/watch?v=rP1DdAA48dA [last accessed 20 December 2017].

Spicks and Specks Translates Plastic Bertrand (2009) 'Ça plane pour moi'. Available online: https://www.youtube.com/watch?v=945Zsz-b07M 20 December 2017].

Susam-Sarajeva, S. (2008) 'Translation and Music' *The Translator* 14(2): 187–200.

Tarkan (1997) 'Simarik'. Available online: https://www.youtube.com/watch?v=FkKShvCPrRc [last accessed 20 December 2017].

Taviano, S. (2012) 'Rezoulutionist Hip Hop: Translating Global Voices and Local Identities', *inTRAlinea* 14. Available online: http://www.intralinea.org/archive/article/rezoulutionist_hip_hop [last accessed 20 December 2017].

The Lion King Language Dubs Collection (n.d.) Blog. Available online: http://tlkdubs.weebly.com/ [last accessed 20 December 2017].

The New Grove Dictionary of Music and Musicians (2001), 2nd edition, Oxford: Oxford University Press.

Toury, G. (1995) *Descriptive Translation Studies—and Beyond*, Amsterdam & Philadelphia: John Benjamins.

Turner, K. (2014) 'Korine's Angels: The Ironic Harmony of "Everytime" and *Spring Breakers*', *Movie Mezzanine*, June 30. Available online: http://moviemezzanine.com/korines-angels-the-ironic-harmony-of-everytime-and-spring-breakers/ [last accessed 20 December 2017].

Valance, H. (2002) 'Kiss Kiss'. Available online: https://www.youtube.com/watch?v=6BGAryS37oo [last accessed 20 December 2017].

Vernallis, C. (2013) 'Music Video's Second Aesthetic?' in J. Richardson, C. Gorbman and C. Vernallis (eds) *The Oxford Handbook of New Audiovisual Aesthetics*, Oxford: Oxford Handbooks Online, 437–465.

Vito, C. (2014) 'Who Said Hip-Hop Was Dead? The Politics of Hip-Hop Culture in Immortal Technique's Lyrics', *International Journal of Cultural Studies* 18(4): 95–411.

Weeks, J. (2008) 'Literal-minded', November 3. Available online: http://www.artsjournal.com/bookdaddy/2008/11/literal-minded.html [last accessed 20 December 2017].

Who Sampled website (2015) 'About Her'. Available online: http://www.whosampled.com/Malcolm-McLaren/About-Her/ [last accessed 20 December 2017].

Wilson, C. (2014) *Let's Talk About Love: Why Other People Have Such Bad Taste*, New York & London: Bloomsbury.

Y-Titty (2012) 'PSY–Gangnam Style Parodie'. Available online: https://www.youtube.com/watch?v=Rh5g7KY0b9Y [last accessed 20 December 2017].

Zuzume, R. (2015) 'Radiohead—Paranoid Android (Sub Español)'. Available online: https://www.youtube.com/watch?v=g8GvKRO4Cag [last accessed 20 December 2017].

Filmography

Bridget Jones's Diary (2001) S. Maguire. IMDb entry: http://www.imdb.com/title/tt0243155/
Dancer in the Dark (2000) L. Von Trier. IMDb entry: http://www.imdb.com/title/tt0168629/
Forrest Gump (1994) R. Zemeckis. IMDb entry: http://www.imdb.com/title/tt0109830/
Kill Bill: Vol. 2. (2004) Q. Tarantino. IMDb entry: http://www.imdb.com/title/tt0378194/
Princesas (2005) F. Léon de Aranoa. IMDb entry: http://www.imdb.com/title/tt0434292/
Shogun Assassin (1980) R. Houston. IMDb entry: http://www.imdb.com/title/tt0081506/
Slingshot Hip Hop (2008) 'Trailer'. IMDb entry: http://www.imdb.com/title/tt1157718/
Spring Breakers (2012) H. Korine. IMDb entry: http://www.imdb.com/title/tt2101441/
The Lion King (1994) R. Allers and R. Minkoff. IMDb entry: http://www.imdb.com/title/tt0110357/
Titanic (1997) J. Cameron. IMDb entry: http://www.imdb.com/title/tt0120338/?ref_=nv_sr_1

27
Audiovisual translation and fandom

Tessa Dwyer

Introduction

Fan-based audiovisual translation (AVT) constitutes a relatively new entry in the broader discipline of translation studies, only emerging as a recognizable phenomenon during the 1980s and beginning to attract dedicated research from the late 1990s onward. Significantly, this timeline mirrors that of AVT studies itself that, as Pérez-González (2014: 2) notes, 'only began to gain traction after the surge of translation studies in the 1990s'. In this sense, these histories are conjoined. AVT 'proper' and its fan-based aberration developed contemporaneously. Nevertheless, within the discipline, fan AVT is typically identified as marginal, peripheral and 'improper'. It is not difficult to understand why. Fan AVT forms part of the broad sphere of non-professional translation (see Pérez-González and Susam-Saraeva 2012) and is largely amateur, free, unregulated and even illegal. Prone to errors and inconsistencies, such translation activity tends to pass under the radar of much academic and industry discourse and research.

Against these odds, fan AVT has risen to prominence nevertheless, in no small part due to its exponential global reach that has flourished off the back of networking technologies and file sharing protocols. Affixed in this way to technological shifts (see O'Hagan 2013), the growth of fan subtitling, dubbing and videogame translation registers another home truth about AVT as a whole: it is hostage to the winds of technological change. As both a field of practice and academic discipline, AVT must continually reinvent itself, shape-shifting in response to new media platforms and formats. This pressure reveals the key to fandom's success and ongoing significance for the field at large. If nothing else, fan practices distinguish themselves from other AVT types through their unauthorized and unregulated exploration of new technologies, with fans identified as particularly adept consumers or 'lead users' (Von Hippel 1986) that proactively mine new platforms and protocols in order to unlock emergent, often unforeseen, capabilities. Fans track how technological developments increasingly place media and the translation of media content in the hands of receivers. As Pérez-González (2014: 84) argues, discussion of such bottom-up practice 'brings to the fore the extent to which . . . audiovisual translation has now become a fluid and decentralized arena of unprecedented accessibility and diversity that is fast moving beyond existing means of analysis and critique'.

As Fernández Costales (2011) acknowledges, 'amateur or fan translation is a phenomenon that can hardly be avoided'. Assisted by Web 2.0 and peering technologies, fan AVT networks have spread their tentacles all around the globe, attracting huge user numbers and accounting for a large percentage of peer-to-peer traffic which, according to an Envisional (2011) report, represented 25 per cent of worldwide Internet usage in 2011, although this figure has lessened more recently (Cisco 2017). This chapter examines this phenomenon from a range of perspectives (historical, ethical, industrial) in order to establish how fandom connects with many of the dominant themes and challenges presently facing AVT, and thus gain a better understanding of the place it occupies within this domain of translation practice and research. Initially, the section entitled 'Historical overview' looks back at the emergence of fansubbing—the most ubiquitous and long-standing mode of fan AVT. The following section, 'Trending topics and debates', canvasses the growing diversity of fan AVT types and the numerous issues and debates they engender. This section reflects on trending topics that preoccupy fans and researchers alike, mapping key ways in which fan practices are discussed within AVT discourse. Specifically, it tests out the theory that fan translators constitute exemplary 'prosumers' who leverage the affordances of digital and networking technologies to actively shape and participate within contemporary global culture. The link between media fandom and 'participatory culture' is then explored in more detail in the section entitled 'Emergent trajectories: major/minor', as fan AVT becomes increasingly embroiled within industry practices and professional parameters. This final section develops a case study of fan-to-riches start-up Viki Global TV (Viki, n.d.) and considers new fan AVT debates resulting from industry shifts towards streaming and on-demand content delivery. Throughout the chapter, language hierarches within AVT flows and counter-flows are continually interrogated, linking the varied themes, topics and trends that characterize fan translation to broader questions around media and cultural access.

Currently, fan AVT encompasses a wide range of activities focused around three central practices: 'fansubbing' (fan subtitling), 'fandubbing' (fan dubbing) and videogame 'romhacking' (read-only memory hacking) or 'translation hacking'. The related practice of 'scanlation' (*manga* and comics scanning and translation) does not fall within the remit of AVT, while 'fanfic' (fan fiction), and fan parody, music and 'mashup' videos *can* but do not *necessarily* involve translation at all. Hence, scanlation and fanfic remain outside the scope of this chapter. While fansubbing constitutes the most established form of fan AVT, fandubbing actually developed at the same time yet on a smaller scale and has received scant scholarly attention to date (see Nord *et al.* 2015). Video game 'translation hacking' emerged later during the 1990s and 2000s and, although expanding, remains a relatively niche activity due to the high-level of technical skill required to 'reverse engineer' videogame code (Newman 2008, Mangiron 2012). The fans that practice fansubbing, fandubbing and romhacking are individuals and, naturally, no two are alike. Nevertheless, although some fan translators work in isolation (Svelch 2013; Dwyer 2012), media fandom necessarily involves some sense of collectivity, developing around shared cultural objects or phenomena. Just as media forms address publics *en masse*, so media fandom necessarily partakes in processes of socialization. Moreover, a fandom is larger than the sum of its individual constituents. It constitutes a *space* as much as any recognizable entity or activity—a space of interaction, not only between individuals that constitute the fandom but also between fans and their objects of attention. In this era of digital dissemination and Web 2.0, the interactive space of media fandoms foster 'supraterritorial' modes of interconnection (Pérez-González 2014: 73). And, although often derided as a form of passive or slavish devotion, fandom is anything but. Rather, it is reciprocal, performative and *transformative*, and has long constituted a decisive factor in the shaping of media industries, as film historian Donald Crafton (1999) explores in relation to early film and its associated, prolific fan press. It is for this reason that Paul Booth (2015) references previous sociological studies of fans to argue that fan identity is naturally hybrid and ambivalent, effortlessly careening between conformist consumerism and cultural resistance. It is important to recognize this hybridity as a residual characteristic of fandom in order to contextualize some of the claims repeatedly made in relation to fansubbing as 'participatory culture'.

Historical overview

While fansubbing today constitutes an increasingly heterogeneous practice that crosses diverse genres, countries and languages, its historical emergence was firmly tied to Japanese animation (known as *anime* outside Japan). Moreover, while *anime* fansubbing began in the late 1980s, it has an extensive prehistory that connects to earlier forms of informal and specialized translation practice such as live interpreting and diverse forms of titling and captioning. To date, these connections remain under-examined within AVT studies. In this section, I trace some of these historical threads while charting the seminal influence of *anime* subculture on the development of fan AVT broadly. This discussion necessarily begins in the US, as it was here that *anime* first found international success during the early 1960s (Deneroff and Ladd 1996, Mäntylä 2010).

Astro Boy (1963–66), *Gigantor* (1963–66) and *Kimba, the White Lion* (1965–66) constitute heavily adapted and revoiced re-workings of Japanese productions and they were broadcast by commercial US television network NBC with their cultural origins domesticated to such a degree that most viewers were unaware at the time that they were cultural imports (Hawkins 2013, Vanhée 2006, Cubbison 2005). After NBC inexpensively acquired *Tetsuan Atom* in 1963, Fred Ladd adapted it for the American market. His US adaptation *Astro Boy* proved a big hit and NBC sold it in syndication to 50 stations around the country (Deneroff and Ladd 1996). This success continued with *Gigantor, Kimba, The White Lion* and *Speed Racer (*1967–68). As its popularity grew in the American market in the early 1970s, *anime* began to be exported to numerous countries around the globe, where it would become a popular mainstay of local television programming (Gosling 1996, Mäntylä 2010, Vanhée 2006, Ruh 2010, Bryce *et al.* 2010, Tezuka qtd. in Schodt 1983). Germany led the way, broadcasting *Speed Racer* in 1971 before embarking upon a successful series of *anime* co-productions including *Vicky the Viking* (1974–75) and *Maya the Bee* (1975–80) (Mäntylä 2010). *Anime* also found early popularity in Italy and France from 1973 and 1974 onwards, culminating in the late 1970s with *UFO Robot Grandizer* (1975–77) known as *Goldrake* in Italy and *Goldorak* in France (Gosling 1996, Mäntylä 2010).

The mid-1970s, however, would prove to be a crucial turning point in the commercial fortunes of *anime* in the US. While viewers in diverse parts of the world happily tuned in to dubbed or revoiced *anime*, in the US audiences that had grown up on a steady diet of *anime* favourites suddenly found themselves bereft, as new titles were cancelled. US lobby groups like Action for Children's Television (see Furniss 1998) began to campaign against the perceived violence and sophisticated themes of some Japanese series and 'discouraged distributors dumped their cartoons on Japanese-language cable channels' (Jenkins 2006) where they tended to be shown with subtitles (Leonard 2005). It was to this subtitled *anime* that the newly formed Cartoon/Fantasy Organization (C/FO) then turned. Founded in 1977, and consisting of 16 members of the well-established Los Angeles Science Fantasy Society (LASFS), C/FO is regarded as the first US *anime* fan club (Patten 2004). Over the next few years, C/FO branches began to emerge dotted around the country. They capitalized on the affordances of early video recording technologies to tape the programmes and distribute them amongst their fan networks alongside other content sourced straight from Japan—often via US soldiers stationed at military bases or through fellow science-fiction fans and pen pals (Leonard 2005, Patten 2004). This is how 'fan distribution was born' (Mäntylä 2010: 8). The sudden cessation of *anime* programming on US broadcast television produced the conditions necessary to spawn a pro-active fandom willing to take access, distribution and translation into their own hands, using any means possible. These fans mobilized themselves to hunt down, exhibit, share and translate *anime* in direct response to the market gap and 'unsatisfied demand' (Mäntylä 2010: 24) that emerged following the industry's pulling of *anime* titles.

During the 1970s and up until the early 1980s, fans were not yet able to access the technology required to produce their own subtitles. Instead, they prepared translation booklets and synopses to accompany *anime* tapes and screenings. Containing line-by-line translations of the Japanese dialogue, these booklets were typically around 20 or 30 pages in length (Leonard 2004). Translation synopses, which simply summarized the main storyline and thereby enabled viewers to focus solely on the screen, rather than splitting attention between screen and page, were shorter (*ibid.*). These fan-produced materials recall some of the diverse methods used to translate films during the silent and early sound eras, when written synopses were often printed on the back of programmes or posted outside movie theatres or in their lobbies (Crafton 1999, Bowser 1990). Another type of informal fan translation practised in the early days of the C/FO involved live, spoken translation. When unsubtitled material was screened at *anime* conventions, it was often accompanied by a form of live, on-the-spot translation (Jenkins 2006), again echoing early cinema techniques of narrating and lecturing—traditions especially popular in Japan where *katsuben* (often referred to as *benshi*) accompanied both domestic and foreign film offerings, summarizing plots, translating intertitles, re-speaking dialogue and providing a particularly rich, performative layer of mediation that attracted huge followings (Anderson 1992). Such links between *anime* fandom and early modes of screen translation demonstrate significant continuities between fan, formal and informal modes of AVT. The varied techniques and traditions that feed into fansubbing and related activities suggest a role for informal practice in the development of translation culture broadly and especially in relation to AVT given the creativity required to transfer its complex multimodality.

According to Sean Leonard (2004, 2005), whose accounts of the fansubbing scene are based on numerous interviews with fansubbing and industry pioneers, the first fansub appeared in 1986. Yet it was not until 1989 that fansubs became widely accessible amongst the fan network. In 1986, Roy Black of C/FO Virginia added his own subtitles to an episode of *anime* title *Lupin III* that had been 'genlocked' to a Commodore Amiga PC. Consumer genlock ('generator locking') technology constituted the 'essential hardware' of the fansubbing movement (Leonard 2004: 10). Enabling the synchronization of two input signals simultaneously, genlocking made it possible for fans to superimpose subtitle tracks over video in real time. The results were then transferred onto videocassette tapes that were widely distributed across the fan network via fan-to-fan mail-order systems. Leonard estimates that in 1986, this technology would have cost around USD $4000 and notes it would have taken over a hundred hours of labour to produce a fansub. Such prohibitive costs were soon overcome as new, more accessible technologies emerged. In 1989, the 'earliest, widely-distributed' fansub was produced by Ranma Project (*ibid.*: 47) using laserdisc technologies that dramatically reduced the degradation of the image characteristic of VCR copies (Hawkins 2013). The following year and through the 1990s, fansubbing exploded in direct parallel with growth in Internet usage amongst fans. Through the Internet, fan interest and demand grew rapidly, while digital advances significantly improved the quality, speed and efficiency of fansubbing practices. Newly networked fans now enjoyed advances in digital and peering technologies, producing digisubs and utilizing bitTorrent protocol. Over this period fan AVT also expanded to include new formats, platforms and media types including videogames.

Interestingly, from the early days of *anime* fandom, dubbing practices have exerted a major influence over the community. In the USA as in most other international markets, initial exposure to *anime* occurred via dubbed television broadcasts and it was these dubs that hooked viewers. Pioneer USA *anime* distributor Streamline Productions distinguished itself from other early fan-led companies, eschewing fan preference for subtitles in an effort to reach the broadest audience possible. It is notable that many dedicated fans also prefer dubbing, as illustrated by the phenomenon of fandubbing. The German-language fandub group Crash Dub Studios (Crash Dub Studios, n.d.), for instance, has translated a range of titles from *Dragon Ball Z* (1989–96) (Hatcher 2005) to *Symphogear* or *Swan Song of the Valkyries* (2012) and Fighter4Luv Fandubs (Fighter4Luv, n.d.) has produced an English dub of *Sailor Moon* (1992–7) (Rodríguez 2014). Generally, dubbing is considered a better to approximate 'original' viewing experience and make *anime* more accessible for pre-teens, thereby matching the target demographic of most *anime* series in Japan. As *Anime News Network* columnist Ryan Mathews notes, '[t]he amazing truth is that watching a good dub brings you much closer to the original experience than a subtitle' (qtd. in Cubbison 2005: 49). Despite fandubbing's long history, however, it is significantly under-represented within AVT and fandom research.

Trending topics and debates

Getting up to speed

With the explosion in fansubbing facilitated via digitization and online networking, fan AVT entered its present post-*anime* phase characterized not by any dearth of *anime* content but rather by huge expansion into diverse genres, languages, countries and contexts. Fansub groups dedicated to South American telenovelas (Tauro 2002), Korean dramas (Hu 2010, Van Rossum 2015) and German soap operas (Hellekson 2012) are now commonplace. However, despite such signs of diversification, by far the majority of non-*anime* fansub activity now occurs around US television series, with fans around the world seeking up-to-date access to hit shows such as *Supernatural* (Warner Bros. 2005–) (Mendes Moreira De Sa 2015), *Big Bang Theory* (CBS 2007–) (Massidda 2015, Qiu 2010, Tian 2011), *Glee* (Fox 2009–2015) (Casarini 2015), *Californication* (Showtime 2007–2014) (Massidda 2015), *Lost* (ABC 2004–2010) (Massidda 2015, Bruti and Zanotti 2014, Vellar 2011, Hu 2014, Vandresen 2012), *Game of Thrones* (HBO, 2011–) (Svelch 2013), *True Blood* (HBO, 2008–2014) (Bold 2011, Tian 2011), *Prison Break* (Fox 2005–2017) (Wang 2014) and *CSI* (CBS, 2000–2015) (Tian 2011). Increasingly these days global fansubbing activity aims to bring subtitled US television content to fans in the shortest turnaround times possible, commonly within 24 hours of a show's first domestic airing, and prior to the appearance of a professionally subtitled version. When the first season of *Game of Thrones* (HBO, 2010-) premiered in the Czech Republic in 2011, for example, tens of thousands of viewers downloaded fansubs rather than waiting a further six hours for the professionally subtitled version to become available on HBO Czech Republic, merely one day after the episode's US debut (Svelch 2013). As Bold (2011) notes, 'passionate non-Anglophone fans refuse to be left behind when American TV channels release new episodes of their favourite shows'.

This 'need for speed' has often been discussed by scholars in disparaging terms. Rayna Denison (2011: 12), for instance, ponders whether the rise of 'speed subbing' groups indicates a 'shift in the fan culture from responsible to more profligate piracy'. Against this backdrop, fan demands for speedy access are often viewed negatively, and speed subbing is regarded as a superficial pursuit that prioritizes timing over quality (Denison 2011, Ito 2012). Such conclusions are too hastily drawn. Rather, fan demand for speed subbing needs to be contextualized in relation to notions of global connectivity and 'transworld simultaneity' (Scholte qtd. in Pérez-González 2014: 71). It also raises issues around global language politics and hierarchies. When fans demand instant access to the latest episode of an imported television series, they assert their rights as global citizens or 'netizens', with speed symbolizing a measure of equality. As Svelch (2013) and others have documented, fansubbers attract huge followings when they are able to circumvent windowed release strategies and other forms of geoblocking in order to provide timely access to recent releases. In this sense, 'getting up to speed' is about entering the conversation, speaking the same language (even if only metaphorically) and levelling the playing field.

Certainly, the need for speed speaks to fan interest in controlling both the means and manner of access—not just *what* but also *how, when* and *where*. As new technologies facilitate and indeed promote rhetoric about global connectivity and instant access, it should not come as a surprise to find that fans are utilizing new technologies to realize this ideal—mining the capabilities of networking to its full potential in order to partake in global culture as full citizens or netizens. In this way, speed subbing practices put to the test theories that extol the democratizing effects of new technologies (Pérez-González 2014), insisting upon the equitable distribution of global cultural content by reducing time lags. On the other hand, if so much current fansub activity and research revolves around timely access to US content, then what does this tell us about language politics and global screen dynamics more broadly? The manner in which speed subbing is increasingly coalescing around US television content in particular suggests the way in which informal modes of media distribution and translation can mirror, rather than disrupt, industry practices. How much is fan AVT contributing to translation flows that support US and Japanese entertainment giants, rather than helping to diversify content as well as language options? Perhaps with the current ascendancy of 'Quality TV' (Mittell 2015) dominated by US production powerhouses, fan AVT is facilitating cultural imperialism, ensuring the dominance of US media corporations on global television as well as the multiplex (González 2013). In this sense, informal fan AVT needs to be recognized for the part it is currently playing in replicating entrenched cultural hierarchies, contributing to the one-way nature of so much translation traffic from the US to the rest, as highlighted by Venuti (1995). According to Mattelart (2012: 746), informal modes of media distribution often buy into hegemonic power relations, and inequalities in access to pirated goods tend to echo those existing in relation to legal goods. To a degree, fansubbing bears out this theory as its reliance upon new technologies and high-speed Internet connections means it is only available to some. This idea that fansubbing might replicate rather than redress language inequalities is not without controversy, yet it is important to entertain this idea in order to counter the over-exuberant way in which fansubbing is sometimes linked uncritically to notions of grassroots 'people power' and forms of cultural opposition. Such approaches gloss over many of the social complexities and language politics that motivate and delimit fansubbing activity, as will be elaborated upon in the next section.

Participatory Prosumers

It has become commonplace to identify fansubbers as 'prosumers' who proactively contribute to the shaping and rewriting of cultural products and, by extension, the cultural sphere. This line of thought can be traced back to some of the earliest scholarship on fansubbing (Díaz Cintas 2005, Pérez-González 2006, Jenkins 2006). To effectively engage with this claim, it is necessary to first explain the terminology used and conceptual lineage from which it derives. Coined by futurist Alvin Toffler (1980), the term 'prosumer' constitutes a portmanteau that combines 'producer' and 'consumer' and, as Van Dijck and Nieborg (2009) explain, is commonly used to suggest that distinctions between the production and reception of cultural products have blurred so much so that consumers now actively participate in creation/production processes, constructing cultural products from scratch, shaping the course of their development, altering meanings and ultimately controlling their failure or success. The scholarly literature on this term and its varied applications is truly vast and I cannot hope to do justice to its breadth here. Instead, I will focus on the way in which this concept has become almost a preliminary for discussing fan interventions within AVT practice. This tendency can be interrogated somewhat by examining the Cultural Studies origins of Henry Jenkin's influential iterations of this concept in relation to 'participatory culture'. His discussion of participatory prosumers is, in turn, largely influenced by the concept of 'cultural poaching' developed by de Certeau in *The Practice of Everyday Life* (1984) to challenge then prevailing assumptions regarding the reception of mass media and popular culture. Significantly, both Jenkins and de Certeau refute the idea that media audiences are either passive or homogeneous and focus instead on the individual's role in constructing meaning.

Since the publication of Jenkins' *Textual Poachers* (1988a), discourse around media fandom has shifted considerably. When Jenkins first began writing about *Star Trek* fans and 'slash' fanfiction (1988b), this group of avid media consumers was virtually ignored by media scholars and tolerated at best by the media industry. Fans tended to be denigrated as excessive, obsessive, socially immature and even degenerate. Today, the situation is dramatically different, as fan audiences have moved from the margins to become 'the locus of television marketing and a major site of industrial strategy and practice' (Johnson 2007: 62). Industry promotion of popular media properties now regularly seeks to attract fan participation, inviting audiences to create mashup parodies, music videos and the like. Major US TV series support transmedia franchises that target fans' purchasing power as well as their free, promotional labour, sponsoring numerous fan contests and events like *Glee*'s 2009 'Who Is the Biggest GLEEk' contest (Casarini 2015: 217) while offering tie-in merchandising, books, videogames, Alternate Reality Games (ARGs), mobisodes, webisodes, podcasts, and wiki databases like *Lostpedia*. While transmedia tactics have long played a role in media marketing, transmedia extensions and storytelling that both cater to and generate a 'hungry fanbase' are becoming ever more ubiquitous (Mittell 2015).

Since Jenkins' ground-breaking study, media fandom scholarship (including later work by Jenkins) has become considerably more nuanced and cognisant of the many situated complexities and internal hierarchies that structure fan communities and practices. Drawing on a substantial body of fan scholarship from the 1990s, Booth (2015: 3) emphasizes fandom's hybrid nature, as it both 'lives off' and resists media industries at one and the same time. Despite often manifesting a culturally oppositional or resistant stance (brought to the fore in Jenkin's exploration of 'slash fanfic'), fandom cannot be entirely disentangled from the conservative impulses or mechanisms that drive capitalist modes of commodification, buoyed by the affective ties that bind fans to products (Booth 2015). For Booth, therefore, fans exist in a liminal state between resistance and complicity, while the increasing mainstreaming of fandom only adds to this ambivalence. In fact, fandom has become a key means by which 'cult' and 'niche' media are increasingly marketed to the masses.

Despite receiving little attention by media theorists to date, fan AVT constitutes one particular area of fandom aptly placed to tease out the possibilities and limitations of this hybrid double bind in relation to participatory culture. Fansubbing and other modes of fan AVT signal and engage with the geopolitics and language inequalities of the media industries and, in this way, broaden appreciation of the type of participation or intervention in which fans potentially engage. Fan AVT marks the absence or unsatisfactory nature of localized, translated versions of television shows, films, news reports and the like, demonstrating how media industries continue to be riven by language barriers and geographic borders despite the de-territorializing, transnational affordances of digital and networking technologies. In taking a do-it-yourself approach to screen translation, fansubbers defy the media industry's cultural and language hierarchies, typically eschewing legal parameters in the process (Rembert-Lang 2010). In this way, fan AVT is critical in its foundations. Nevertheless, at the same time fansubbing can enable certain inequalities to persist, and often ends up serving the interests of powerful media conglomerates, furthering the reach of Japan's globally dominant animation industry, for instance, or that of US television series. As so many fansubbers proudly insist, their DIY translations largely seek to 'spread the love' (Dwyer 2012: 218), advancing media titles and the commercial industries behind them by facilitating 'the demand formation phase necessary, but ancillary, to capitalist activity' (Leonard 2005: 283).

Hence, accounts that focus solely on the collaborative nature of fan AVT and empowerment of the audience/consumer require much qualification and contextualization. A body of recent scholarship shows that fan AVT practices often involve their own internal forms of social differentiation, exploitation and exclusion, either through instances of fan-to-fan piracy (Hemmungs Wirtén 2013), cultural gatekeeping (Schules 2014), generational differentiation (Vellar 2011) and technological barriers (Svelch 2013, Vellar 2011). Drawing upon the work of Pierre Bourdieu, Schules (2014) and Vellar (2011) pay close attention to the ways in which fansubbing accrues nuanced types of (largely social and subcultural) capital, thus drawing attention to the place that fansubbing plays in economic or market-based modes of cultural production. Along with Svelch (2013), Schules (2014) considers how quality issues add complexity to discussions of participatory culture and fansubbing. In his view, fansub headnotes or linear notes function on multiple levels, signalling the proficiency and cultural or genre expertise of the translator as much as facilitating the comprehension of source content. Indeed, he points out how these much-celebrated, interventionist notes (Pérez-González 2007) can function to conceal inaccuracies. Ultimately, by prioritizing the 'appearance of proficiency' over translation accuracy, headnotes enable translation errors to circulate unchallenged. Finally, both Schules (2014) and Svelch (2013) shift attention from fansub production to fansub reception, drawing attention to the subordinate position that fansub users occupy in relation to fansub producers—significantly impairing their ability to question, critique or participate on a meaningful level within translation processes or discourse.

Crowdsourcing

Perhaps crowdsourcing more than any other phenomenon signals the central importance of fan AVT within current cultural shifts and the ubiquity of mediated screen environments. Crowdsourcing is proving an essential tool in delivering media content to dispersed, linguistically diverse audiences and hence in providing global reach to news channels such as Al Jazeera (Pérez-González 2014), social media websites and eCommerce players such as LinkedIn (Kelly 2009), Facebook (DePalma and Kelly 2011) and Twitter (see McDonough Dolmaya 2011) as well as not-for-profit initiatives like Babels (Dimitroulia 2015) and TED Open Translation Project (O'Hagan 2011). The link between crowdsourcing and fansubbing is articulated by O'Hagan (2011: 31) who notes that 'crowdsourced translation legitimizes the concept of free translation', continuing that 'fan translation remains primarily "unsolicited" work whereas crowdsourced translation is "solicited" by its organisers'. She goes on to propose that crowdsourced translation operates via a 'top-down mechanism' whereas 'fansubbing is the result of a genuinely bottom-up formation of fans' grassroot efforts'. On the whole, these distinctions make sense and are widely accepted, despite the fact that they can't be applied as a blanket rule: some types of fansubs are more 'bottom-up' than others, for instance—as will be elaborated in the next section.

The distinction that O'Hagan draws between crowdsourced and fan translation is extrapolated further by Serenella Massidda (2015) who claims that the differing legal status of each practice relates inversely to their ethics. However, O'Hagan's own case study of TED.com's not-for-profit, crowdsourced subtitling exposes some overstatement within Massidda's claim. Crowdsourcing does not necessarily constitute a commercial strategy, despite its massive uptake by the business community. Additionally, whether profit-based or not, the ethics of crowdsourcing cannot be so summarily dismissed. As DePalma and Kelly (2011: 388) note, the commerce of crowdsourced translation tends not to concern cost-saving as much as market diversification and improved products or services. Facebook, they state, 'realized minimal or no cost savings; its large investment in technology offset most of what it saved from getting translations from its members'. In this regard, the ethics of commercial efforts to monetize the volunteer labour of translators, amateurs and fans is a complex, thorny issue that requires rigorous, ongoing debate, not dismissal. The central question is how ethics connects to piracy. More than 'legitimising' the free translation methods modelled by fansubbing (see O'Hagan 2011), crowdsourcing involves its *legalization*. In this way, crowdsourced AVT exposes the tenuous and shifting boundary between formal and informal modes and how 'over time, activities move in and out of the legal zone' (Lobato 2012). Once again, the concept of the 'lead user' is helpful for considering the relationship between crowdsourced and fan AVT, with fansubbers leading the way in exploring the collaborative potential of technological developments around language transfer—now being intensively mined for commercial purposes.

Emergent trajectories: major/minor

Fansubbing and fan AVT are currently experiencing mushrooming attention by media and translation scholars alike making it difficult to keep apace of the field. A major reason for this interest relates to fan AVT's central position in relation to media accessibility more broadly, globalization and technological interconnectedness. These are connections that global TV site Viki makes explicit through community campaigns and advocacy. Viki has sponsored a number of videos that showcase endangered languages and the role that AVT can play in their revival. In 2014, it launched two campaigns, partnering with the Living Tongues Institute of Endangered Languages to 'help save endangered and emerging languages' and with deaf actor Maree Maitlin to advocate on behalf of deaf and hard of hearing audiences, offering new tutorial videos specifically geared towards captioning (see Lawrence 2014, Fisher 2014, Dwyer 2016). It also initiated a Viki-managed 'Living Tongues' documentary channel. These initiatives serve to flag the importance of AVT for the future of linguistic and cultural diversity. As Kothari (2015) demonstrates, the same-language subtitling of Bollywood movie songs for local audiences has been shown to significantly improve mass reading and literacy levels in India. Popular screen content provides an invaluable means of reaching, engaging and educating global audiences and its translation can become a precious tool in the fight for literacy and language preservation alike. And, as Viki has recognized, the community-based nature of fansubbing makes it an ideal means for advancing such endeavours. Building language awareness from the bottom-up via fansubbing engages young people at the coalface of language revival and emerging technologies. DIY fansubbing harnesses affective ties to media content and in this way can promote local languages while also fostering global interconnections and social bonds, both online and off. As Viki reports on 'Official Viki Channel (Episode 20)', '[e]very two weeks, the last fluent speaker of an endangered language passes away'; '[t]oday less than 5% of the world's languages are available online'; '[f]or the other 95%, the Internet can be a path to extinction or revitalization'.

The vital links that Viki draws between AVT, media accessibility and language diversity position collaborative, participatory fan practices at the heart of global media and technological shifts (see Dwyer 2016, 2017). Viki presents an atypical mode of fansubbing. Some might even dispute its claim to represent fansubbing at all. Viki fansubs are legal and, as CEO Razmig Hovaghimian (2011) puts it, they are 'monetized' as part of a for-profit commercial service. Nevertheless, they remain voluntary and amateur: profits made do not flow back to the fansubbers themselves. Additionally, they confuse distinctions between top-down and bottom-up mechanisms. Fan AVT is solicited by Viki's open call for crowd participation, yet channels are mostly managed by contributors themselves and users can nominate new channels at any time, and advocate for language representation. While a case could be mounted that Viki's AVT is crowdsourced rather than fan-based, the entire project is underpinned by the fannish appreciation of particular media titles and genres—primarily Korean television drama: the site fosters affective community-building via its timed comments feature and by facilitating community discussion forums and private messaging between contributors who clearly identify as fans.

The ways in which Viki pushes and stretches definitions of fansubbing indicates an emergent trajectory in the field, as the blurring of commercial and community interests characteristic of much crowdsourcing becomes increasingly prevalent within media industry practices. Already, much overlap is surfacing between fan and professional AVT. Fansub groups like Dattebayo, for instance, have transformed themselves into professional distribution companies (see Schules 2014) while fansubs are inching their way onto a variety of commercial platforms, including TV broadcasting (Casarini 2014, Vellar 2011, Bourdaa 2013), DVDs and video-on-demand streaming services like Netflix (Ernesto 2012). Professional subtitling companies now hold fansub contests, with the aim of hiring winners (Di Giovanni and Spoletti 2011, Bold 2011), and adopt methods based upon fan strategies (Leong 2010, 65). Many professional game localizers such as Clyde Mandalin started as translation hackers and continue to moonlight as fan translators 'out of love', almost as a form of community service (see O'Hagan 2009, Parkin 2008). Additionally, the popularity of fansubbing is pushing networks towards more timely delivery of imported content

(Bold 2011) and encouraging them to offer both subtitled and dubbed options (Massidda and Casarini 2017, Casarini 2015). The other significant factor in Viki's approach to fansubbing is that overt commercialization of this grassroots practice does not necessarily trouble its ethics or result in de-politicization. Rather, Viki explicitly leverages its legitimate industry position to politicize fan AVT, using formal partnerships to establish clear links between fandom and broader media access issues in the digital, global age. In this way, Viki offers a 'big picture' perspective on fan AVT rarely entertained by individual fansub groups. This is not to suggest that the macro-politics advanced by Viki are ultimately more valid than those micro-politics that many fans proactively negotiate in their translation work—they are just different. Viki constitutes one particular example of commercialized fansubbing, and its politics need to be analyzed in this context specifically.

By shedding light on the ways that fansubbing is currently being reimagined and reshaped, Viki provides a segue for thinking about how fan translation itself is involved in a continual process of modification and revaluation. Fandubbing and videogame translation romhacking are two more 'minor' modes of fan AVT that illustrate the unpredictability and organic nature of the subcultural. Ultimately, it is here that much of the value of fan practice lies— in its unpredictability and innovation. One new trend in both fandubbing and romhacking reveals a particularly baroque logic of ceaseless inversion and enfolding: that is, the growing nostalgia for past AVT practices. This can involve fans actually recreating earlier forms of subtitling, dubbing or game localization in an act of homage (see O'Hagan 2009: 104). Rodríguez (2014), for example, explains how a recent fandub of *Sailor Moon* (1992–1997) explicitly seeks to honour the 'original' US dub made by DiC, casting actors with voices resembling those of the US dubbing cast, retaining the US theme song and character names, and 'even going so far as to editing it as if it were going to air on kids TV!'.

In the gaming community this type of nostalgic appreciation of past localization efforts extends to the professional realm and focuses more specifically upon translation errors, with clumsy or nonsense lines of translation being retained for comic effect (O'Hagan 2009, Mangiron 2012). AVT practices that were widely disparaged by fan communities when they first appeared are thus resurrected and lauded. Fandubbers in particular are now actively seeking to redeem 'bad' translation practices of the past. In doing so, they relativize and destabilize notions of value, authenticity and fidelity, demonstrating how modes of reception can engender claims to 'originality' that potentially threaten the authority of source texts and producers. As Booth (2015) notes, the concept of play is integral to fan practices and identities, unleashing a performative element within fan activities that is steeped in both nostalgia and novelty, at one and the same time. In fandom, Booth explains, 'semantic replications based in nostalgia . . . build to become a syntactic expression of novelty' (*ibid.*: 36). Nostalgia signals a finely calibrated appreciation of fandom and fan objects and 'it depends on feelings of affect generated by the original text but exceeds them', making connections to a new present via the past (*ibid.*; 167). It is the power of affective play that media industries are now seeking to capitalize upon via transmedia tie-ins, humorous or parodic 'funsubbing' (see Nord *et al.* 2015, Zhang 2013), crowdsourcing and other 'mutant' or underground forms of fan AVT. It is also this mode of play that keeps fans one step ahead.

Summary

This chapter has provided an overview of the growing interrelationship between media fandom and AVT practices, focusing on fansubbing, and extending the discussion towards the less established fields of fandubbing and video game translation hacking. Comprising three sections, it first traces the origins of fan AVT, exploring *anime* fandom in the US and beyond. Second, it reflects upon the predominant ways in which fan AVT discourse tends to be framed today, interrogating notions of 'participatory culture' and 'prosumer' intervention before examining how fan AVT is proximately placed in relation to the fast-developing phenomenon of crowdsourced translation. Third, the chapter considers emergent trajectories, presenting a case study of atypical fansubbing through global TV site Viki, suggesting that this example requires many assumptions about fan AVT to be rethought. Finally, it draws attention to playful, nostalgic practices amongst the fandub and gaming communities. The chapter proposes that fan translators constitute 'lead users' (von Hippel 1986) of new technologies, new collaborative AVT methods and unpredictable modes of affective, performative play. In this way, they are positioned at the centre of current developments in the AVT field.

Further reading

Dwyer, T. (2017) *Speaking in Subtitles: Revaluing Screen Translation*. Edinburgh: Edinburgh University Press | *This book includes two chapters on fansubbing while sketching a broader industry and conceptual context.*

Hatcher, J. S. (2005) '"Of Otakus and Fansubs": A Critical Look at Anime Online in Light of Current Issues in Copyright Law', *SCRIPT-ed* 2(4): 514–542 | *This early assessment of fansubbing in relation to US copyright law provides a useful, thorough overview of key issues and tensions.*

Jenkins, H. (1988a) *Textual Poachers: Television Fans and Participatory Culture*, New York & London: Routledge | *This seminal text introduces the widely influential concept of 'participatory culture' that has only become increasingly central to current cultural and industry practice in the years since publication.*

Leonard, S. (2005) 'Progress Against the Law: Anime and Fandom, with the Key to Globalization of Culture', *International Journal of Cultural Studies* 8(3): 281–305 | *Based on a series of interviews with fansubbing pioneers and early* anime *distributors, this article pieces together a largely firsthand account of the origins of the phenomenon.*

O'Hagan, M. (2009) 'Evolution of User-Generated Translation: Fansubs, Translation Hacking and Crowdsourcing', *Journal of Internationalisation and Localisation* 1: 94–121 | *Writing from an AVT perspective, O'Hagan joins the dots, uncovering points of interconnection between fansubbing and related shifts in the media and AVT landscape.*

Related topics

2 History of audiovisual translation
10 Game localization: a critical overview and implications for audiovisual translation
19 Gender in audiovisual translation: advocating for gender awareness
23 Audiovisual translation and audience reception
24 Ethnography in audiovisual translation studies
26 Audiovisual translation and popular music
27 Audiovisual translation and fandom
28 Audiovisual translation and activism
32 Technologization of audiovisual translation

References

Anderson, J. L. (1992) 'Spoken Silents in the Japanese Cinema; or, Talking to Pictures: Essaying the Katsuben, Contextualizing the Texts', in J. A. Nolletti and D. Desser (eds) *Reframing Japanese Cinema: Authorship, Genre, History*, Bloomington & Indianapolis: Indiana University Press, 259–311.

Barra, L. (2009) 'The Mediation is the Message: Italian Regionalization of US TV Series as Co-creational Work', *International Journal of Cultural Studies* 12(5): 509–525.

Bold, B. (2011) 'The Power of Fan Communities: An Overview of Fansubbing in Brazil', *Traduçao em Revista* 11(2). Available online: https://www.maxwell.vrac.puc-rio.br/18881/18881.PDFXXvm [last accessed 20 December 2017].

Booth, P. (2015) *Playing Fans: Negotiating Fandom and Media in the Digital Age*. Iowa City: University of Iowa Press.

Bourdaa, M. (2013) 'Fansubbing, a Cultural Mediation Practice', *INA Global*, October 15. Available online: http://www.inaglobal.fr/en/digital-tech/article/fansubbing-cultural-mediation-practice [last accessed 20 December 2017].

Bowser, E. (1990) *The Transformation of Cinema 1907–1915*, Berkeley, Los Angeles & London: University of California Press.

Bruti, S. and S. Zanotti (2014) 'Non-Professional Subtitling in Close-Up: A Study of Interjections and Discourse Markers', in R. Antonini and C. Bucaria (eds) *Non-Professional Interpreting and Translation in the Media*. Bern: Peter Lang.

Bryce, M., C. Barber, J. Kelly, S. Kunwar and A. Plumb (2010) 'Manga and Anime: Fluidity and Hybridity in Global Imagery', *Electronic Journal of Contemporary Japanese Studies* 10(1). Available online: http://www.japanesestudies.org.uk/articles/2010/Bryce.html [accessed 20 December 2017].

Casarini, A. (2014) 'Viewership 2.0—New Forms of Television Consumption and their Impact on Audiovisual Translation', *inTRAlinea* 16. Available online: http://www.intralinea.org/specials/article/viewership_2.0 [last access 20 December 2017].

Casarini, A. (2015) 'Chorus Lines—Translating Musical Television Series in the Age of Participatory Culture: The Case of *Glee*', in J. Díaz Cintas and J. Neves (eds) *Audiovisual Translation: Taking Stock*, Newcastle upon Tyne: Cambridge Scholars, 209–229.

Cisco (2017) 'Cisco Visual Networking Index: Forecast and Methodology, 2016–2021'. Available online: https://www.cisco.com/c/en/us/solutions/collateral/service-provider/visual-networking-index-vni/complete-white-paper-c11–481360.html#_Toc484813985, June 6 [last access 30 December 2017].

Crash Dub Studios (n.d.) Crash Dub Studios. Available online: www.crashdub.com [last access 20 December 2017].

Crafton, D. (1999) *The Talkies: American Cinema's Transition to Sound 1926–1931*, Berkeley, Los Angeles, London: University of California Press.

Cubbison, L. (2005) 'Anime Fans, DVDs, and the Authentic Text', *The Velvet Light Trap* 56: 45–57.

de Certeau, M. (1984) *The Practice of Everyday Life*, trans. S. Rendall, Berkeley: University of California Press.

Deneroff, H. and F. Ladd (1996) 'Fred Ladd: An Interview', *Animation World Magazine* 1.5, August. Available online: http://www.awn.com/mag/issue1.5/articles/deneroffladd1.5.html [last access 20 December 2017].

Denison, R. (2011) 'Anime Fandom and the Liminal Spaces between Fan Creativity and Piracy', *International Journal of Cultural Studies* 14(5): 449–66.

DePalma, D. A. and N. Kelly (2011) 'Project Management for Crowdsourced Translation: How User-Translated Content Projects Work in Real Life', in K. Dunne (ed.) *Translation and Localization Project Management: The Art of the Possible*, Philadelphia: John Benjamins, 379–407.

Díaz Cintas, J. (2005) 'Back to the Future in Subtitling', *MuTra 2005—Challenges of Multidimensional Translation*: Conference Proceedings. Available online: http://www.euroconferences.info/proceedings/2005_Proceedings/2005_DiazCintas_Jorge.pdf [last access 20 December 2017].

Di Giovanni, E. and F. Spoletti (2011) 'In Search of a Common Ground: Professional Visibility for Amateur Subtitlers', paper presented at *Media for All 4 International Conference*, June 2011, Imperial College London, UK.

Dimitroulia, T. (2015) 'Everyday Practices on the Internet and the Expansion of Crowdsourced Translation', in L. Yoka and G. Pashalidis (eds) *Semiotics and Hermeneutics of the Everyday*, Newcastle upon Tyne: Cambridge Scholars, 193–236.

Dwyer, T. (2012) 'Fansub Dreaming on Viki: 'Don't Just Watch But Help When You Are Free', in S. Susam-Saraeva and L. Pérez-González (eds) 'Non-professional Translation', special issue of *The Translator* 18 (2): 217–243.

Dwyer, T. (2016) 'Multilingual Publics: Fansubbing Global TV', in K. Lee, D. Marshall, G. D'Cruz, and S. Macdonald (eds) *Contemporary Publics*, Basingstoke: Palgrave Macmillan, 145–162.

Dwyer, T. (2017) *Speaking in Subtitles: Revaluing Screen Translation*. Edinburgh: Edinburgh University Press.

Envisional (2011) *Technical Report: An Estimate of Infringing Use of the Internet*, Cambridge: Envisional Ltd. Available online: http://documents.envisional.com/docs/Envisional-Internet_Usage-Jan2011.pdf [last access 20 December 2017].

Ernesto (2012) 'Netflix Caught Using "Pirated" Subtitles in Finland', *Torrent Freak*, 19 October. Available online: https://torrentfreak.com/netflix-caught-using-pirated-subtitles-in-finland-121019 [last access 20 December 2017].

Fernández Costales, A. (2011) '2.0: Facing the Challenges of the Global Era', *Tralogy I: Futures in Technology for Translation*. Available online: http://lodel.irevues.inist.fr/tralogy/index.php?id=120 [last access 20 December 2017].

Fighter4Luv Fandubs (n.d.). Available online: www.starsfandub.com [last access 30 December 2017].

Fisher, L. (2014) 'How Marlee Matlin Helped Force Streaming Video Closed Captions into Digital Age', *Good Morning America*, April 29. Available online: https://gma.yahoo.com/marlee-matlin-helped-force-streaming-video-closed-captions-091632770--abc-news-entertainment.html [last access 20 December 2017].

Furniss, M. (1998) *Art in Motion: Animation Aesthetics*. Sydney: John Libbey.

González, R. (2013) 'Emerging Markets and the Digitalization of the Film Industry: An Analysis of the 2012 UIS International Survey of Feature Film Statistics', *UIS Information Paper* 14. Available online: http://uis.unesco.org/sites/default/files/documents/emerging-markets-and-the-digitalization-of-the-film-industry-en_0.pdf [last access 20 December 2017].

Gosling, J. (1996) 'Anime in Europe', *Animation World Magazine* 1(5). Available online: http://www.awn.com/mag/issue1.5/articles/goslingeuro1.5.html [last access 20 December 2017].

Hatcher, J. S. (2005) '"Of Otakus and Fansubs": A Critical Look at Anime Online in Light of Current Issues in Copyright Law', *SCRIPT-ed* 2(4): 514–542.

Hawkins, A. (2013) *Piracy as a Catalyst for Evolution in Anime Fandom*, Unpublished Thesis, University of Michigan.

Hellekson, K. (2012) 'Creating a Fandom Via YouTube: *Verbotene Liebe* and Fansubbing', in B. Williams and A. Zenger (eds) *New Media Literacies and Participatory Popular Culture Across Borders*, Hoboken: Taylor and Francis, 180–192.

Hemmungs Wirtén, E. (2013) 'Swedish Subtitling Strike Called Off!: Fan-to-Fan Piracy, Translation and the primacy of Authorisation', in D. Hunter, R. Lobato, M. Richardson and J. Thomas (eds) *Amateur Media: Social, Cultural and Legal Perspectives*, London & New York: Routledge, 125–136.

Hovaghimian, R. (2011) 'Future of TV', *The Korea Times*, May 10. Available online: http://www.koreatimes.co.kr/www/news/tech/2011/05/129_86778.html [last access 20 December 2017].

Hu, B. (2010) 'Korean TV Serials in the English-Language Diaspora: Translating Difference Online and Making it Racial', *The Velvet Light Trap* 66: 36–49.

Hu, K. (2014) 'Competition and Collaboration: Chinese Video Websites, Subtitle Groups, State Regulation and Market', *International Journal of Cultural Studies* 17(5): 437–51.

Ito, M. (2012) 'Contributors versus Leechers: Fansubbing Ethics and a Hybrid Public Culture', in M. Ito, D. Okabe and I. Tsuji (eds) *Fandom Unbound: Otaku Culture in a Connected World*, New Haven & London: Yale University Press, 179–204.

Jenkins, H. (1988a) *Textual Poachers: Television Fans and Participatory Culture*, New York & London: Routledge.

Jenkins, H. (1988b) 'Star Trek Rerun, Reread, Rewritten: Fan Writing as Textual Poaching', *Critical Studies in Mass Communication* 5(2): 85–107.

Jenkins, H. (2006) 'When Piracy Becomes Promotion', *Reason Magazine*, November 17. Available online: http://reason.com/news/printer/116788.html [last access 20 December 2017].

Johnson, D. (2007) 'Inviting Audiences In: The Spatial Reorganisation of Production and Consumption on "TVIII"', *New Review of Film and Television Studies* 5(1): 61–80.

Kelly, N. (2009) 'Freelance Translators Clash with LinkedIn over Crowdsourced Translation', *Common Sense Advisory: Insight for Global Market Leaders* Blog, 19 June. Available online: http://www.commonsenseadvisory.com/Default.aspx?Contenttype=ArticleDetAD&tabID=63&Aid=591&moduleId=391 [last access 20 December 2017].

Kothari, B. (2015) 'Same Language Subtitling (SLS) on TV for Mass Literacy: A "Media for All" Perspective from India', paper presented at *Media for All 6th International Conference*, September 17, University of Western Sydney, Australia.

Lawrence, S. (2014) 'Viki and Actress Marlee Matlin launch "Billion Words March"', *SL First*, 29 April. Available online: http://slfirst.co.uk/entertainment/stage-theatre-tv/viki-actress-marlee-matlin-join-forces-to-launch-billion-words-march [last access 20 December 2017].

Leonard, S. (2004) 'Progress Against the Law: Fan Distribution, Copyright, and the Explosive Growth of Japanese Animation', *MIT Japan Program* 4(2). Available online: http://web.mit.edu/seantek/www/papers/progress-doublespaced.pdf [last access 20 December 2017].

Leonard, S. (2005) 'Progress Against the Law: Anime and Fandom, with the Key to Globalization of Culture', *International Journal of Cultural Studies* 8(3): 281–305.

Leong, J. (2010) 'Selling the Sweatdrop: The Translation of "Japaneseness" in Manga and Anime Fan Fiction', Unpublished Thesis, University of Western Australia.

Lobato, R. (2012) 'A Sideways View of the Film Economy in an Age of Digital Piracy', *NECSUS European Journal of Media Studies*. Available online: http://www.necsus-ejms.org/a-sideways-view-of-the-film-economy-in-an-age-of-digital-piracy-by-ramon-lobato [last access 20 December 2017].

Mangiron, C. (2012) 'The Localisation of Japanese Video Games: Striking the Right Balance', *Journal of Internationalisation and Localisation* 2: 1–20.

Mäntylä, T. (2010) 'Piracy or Productivity: Unlawful Practices in Anime Fansubbing', Unpublished MA Dissertation, Aalto University School of Science and Technology.

Massidda, S. (2015) *Audiovisual Translation in the Digital Age: The Italian Fansubbing Phenomenon*, Basingstoke: Palgrave Macmillan.

Massidda, S. and A. Casarini (2017) 'Sub Me Do—The Development of Fansubbing in Traditional Dubbing Countries: The Case of Italy', in Y. Lee and D. Orrego Carmona (eds) *Non-Professional Subtitling*, Newcastle: Cambridge Scholars Publishing, 63–83.

Mattelart, T. (2012) 'Audiovisual Piracy, Informal Economy, and Cultural Globalization', *International Journal of Communication* 6: 735–750.

McDonough Dolmaya, J. (2011) 'The Ethics of Crowdsourcing', *Linguistica Antverpiensia New Series* 10: 97–110.

Mendes Moreira de Sa, V. (2015) 'Piracy & Social Change| From Orkut to Facebook: How Brazilian Pirate Audiences Utilize Social Media to Create Sharing Subcultures', *International Journal of Communication* 9: 852–869.

Mittell, J. (2015) *Complex TV: The Poetics of Contemporary Television Storytelling*, New York: New York University Press.

Newman, J. (2008) *Playing With Video Games*, Florence: Taylor and Francis.

Nord, C., M. Hoshsaligheh and S. Ameri (2015) 'Socio-Cultural and Technical Issues in Non-Expert Dubbing: A Case Study', *International Journal of Society, Culture and Language* 3(2): 1–16. Available online: http://www.ijscl.net/article_11734_b9fac3605ffb0c68da832760430a527b.pdf [last access 20 December 2017].

O'Hagan, M. (2009) 'Evolution of User-Generated Translation: Fansubs, Translation Hacking and Crowdsourcing', *Journal of Internationalisation and Localisation* 1: 94–121.

O'Hagan, M. (2011) 'From Fan Translation to Crowdsourcing: Consequences of Web 2.0 User Empowerment in Audiovisual Translation', in A. Remael, P. Orero and M. Carroll (eds) *Audiovisual Translation and Media Accessibility at the Crossroads: Media for All 3*, New York: Rodopi, 25–41.

O'Hagan, M. (2013) 'The Impact of New Technologies on Translation Studies: A Technological Turn?', in C. Millán and F. Bartrina (eds) *The Routledge Handbook of Translation Studies*, London & New York, Routledge, 503–518.

Parkin, S. (2008) 'You Say Tomato: A Pro on Fan Translating Nintendo's Mother 3', *Gamasutra: The Art and Business of Making Games*, December 26. Available online: http://www.gamasutra.com/view/feature/132284/you_say_tomato_a_pro_on_.php [last access 20 December 2017].

Patten, F. (2004) *Watching Anime, Reading Manga: 25 Years of Essays and Reviews*, Berkeley, CA: Stone Bridge Press.

Pérez-González, L. (2006) 'Fansubbing Anime: Insights into the "Butterfly Effect" of Globalisation on Audiovisual Translation', *Perspectives: Studies in Translatology* 14 (4): 260–277.

Pérez-González, L. (2007) 'Intervention in New Amateur Subtitling Cultures: A Multimodal Account', *Linguistica Antverpiensia* 6: 67–80.

Pérez-González, L. (2014) *Audiovisual Translation: Theories, Methods and Issues*, London & New York: Routledge.

Pérez-González, L. and S. Susam-Saraeva (2012) 'Non-professionals Translating and Interpreting: Theoretical and Methodological Perspectives', in S. Susam-Saraeva and L. Pérez-González (eds) 'Non-professionals Translating and Interpreting', special issue of *The Translator* 18(2): 149–65.

Qiu, P. (2010) 'Audience Activity in the New Media Era: Chinese Fansubs of U.S. TV Shows', Unpublished MA Dissertation, University of Florida.

Rembert-Lang, L. (2010) 'Reinforcing the Tower of Babel: The Impact of Copyright Law on Fansubbing', *Intellectual Property Brief* 2(2): 21–33. Available online: http://digitalcommons.wcl.american.edu/cgi/viewcontent.cgi?article=1051&context=ipbrief [last access 20 December 2017].

Rodríguez, K. T. (2014) 'Hey Sailor Moon Fans: Did You Know There is a Sailor Stars Fandub and its Good?', *Examiner.com*, July 17. Available online: https://yeahstub.com/hey-sailor-moon-fans-did-you-know-there-is-a-sailor-stars-fandub-and-its-good/ [last access 28 September 2015].

Ruh, B. (2010) 'Transforming U.S. Anime in the 1980s: Localization and Longevity', *Mechamedia 5: Fanthropologies*, Minneapolis: University of Minnesota Press, 31–49.

Schodt, F. L. (1983) *Manga! Manga!: The World of Japanese Comics*, Tokyo: Kodansha International.

Schules, D. (2014) 'How to Do Things with Fan Subs: Media Engagement as Subcultural Capital in Anime Fan Subbing', *Transformative Works and Cultures* 17. Available online: http://journal.transformativeworks.org/index.php/twc/article/view/512/461 [last access 20 December 2017].

Svelch, J. (2013) 'The Delicate Art of Criticizing a Saviour: "Silent Gratitude" and the Limits of Participation in the Evaluation of Fan Translation', *Convergence* 19(3): 303–310.

Tauro, J. (2002) 'Anime Transform Landscape of Philippine TV'. Available online: http://ncca.gov.ph/about-culture-and-arts/in-focus/telenovela-anime-transform-landscape-of-philippine-tv/ [last access 20 December 2017].

Tian, Y. (2011) 'Fansub Cyber Culture in China', Unpublished MA Dissertation, Georgetown University.

Toffler, A. (1980) *The Third Wave: The Classic Study of Tomorrow*, New York, NY: Bantam.

Van Dijck, J. and D. Nieborg (2009) 'Wikinomics and its Discontents: A Critical Analysis of Web 2.0 Business Manifestos', *New Media and Society* 11(5): 855–874.

Vandresen, M. (2012), '"Free Culture" Lost in Translation', *International Journal of Communication* 6: 626–642.

Vanhée, O. (2006) 'The Production of a 'Manga Culture' in France: A Sociological Analysis of a Successful Intercultural Reception', paper presented at Mobile and Pop Culture in Asia, October 2006, University Hallym, Chuncheon, Korea.

Van Rossum, J. (2015) *Honorifics in Korean Drama: A Comparison of Translation Procedures Between Amateur and Professional Subtitlers*, Unpublished MA Dissertation, Leiden University.

Vellar, A. (2011) '"Lost" (and Found) in Transculturation: The Italian Networked Collectivism of US TV Series and Fansubbing Performances', in F. Colombo and L. Fortunati (eds) *Broadband Society and Generational Changes*, Oxford: Peter Lang, 187–200.

Venuti, L. (1995) *The Translator's Invisibility*, London & New York: Routledge.

Viki (n.d.) 'Viki Homepage'. Available online: www.viki.com [last accessed 20 December 2017].
Von Hippel, E. (1986) 'Lead Users: A Source of Novel Product Concepts', *Management Science* 32(7): 791–806.
Wang, F. (2014) 'Similarities and Differences between Fansub Translation and Traditional Paper-Based Translation', *Theory and Practice in Language Studies* 4(9): 1904–1911.
Zhang, X. (2013) 'Fansubbing in China', *MultiLingual*, July/August: 30–37.

Filmography

Astro Boy (*Tetsuwan Atomu*, 1963–66) Various creators. IMDb entry: http://www.imdb.com/title/tt0056739/?ref_=ttfc_fc_tt

Big Bang Theory (2007–) Chuck Lorre and Bill Prady. IMDb entry: http://www.imdb.com/title/tt0898266/?ref_=nv_sr_1

Californication (2007–2014) Tom Kapinos. IMDb entry: http://www.imdb.com/title/tt0904208/?ref_=nv_sr_1

CSI (2000–2015) Anthony E. Zuiker. IMDb entry: http://www.imdb.com/title/tt0247082/?ref_=nv_sr_1

Dragon Ball Z (*Doregan Boru*, 1989–96) Various directors. IMDb entry: http://www.imdb.com/title/tt0121220/?ref_=ttfc_fc_tt

Game of Thrones (2011–) Various directors. IMDb entry: http://www.imdb.com/title/tt0944947/?ref_=nv_sr_1

Gigantor (*Tetsujin28-go*, 1963–66) Mitsuteru Yokoyama. IMDb entry: http://www.imdb.com/title/tt0058807/?ref_=nv_sr_1

Glee (2009–2015) Various creators. IMDb entry: http://www.imdb.com/title/tt1327801/?ref_=fn_al_tt_1

Kimba, the White Lion (*Janguru Taitei*, 1965–66) Various directors. IMDb entry: http://www.imdb.com/title/tt0058817/?ref_=nv_sr_1

Lost (2004–2010) Various creators. IMDb entry: http://www.imdb.com/title/tt0411008/?ref_=nv_sr_2

Maya the Bee (*Die Biene Maja*/*Mitsubachi Māya no Bōken*, 1975–80) Seiji Endo and Hiroshi Saito. IMDb entry: http://www.imdb.com/title/tt0133295/?ref_=ttfc_fc_tt

Prison Break (2005–2017) Paul Scheuring. IMDb entry: http://www.imdb.com/title/tt0455275/?ref_=nv_sr_1

Sailor Moon (*Bishōjo Senshi Sērā Mūn*, 1992–7) Naoko Takeuchi. IMDb entry: http://www.imdb.com/title/tt0103369/?ref_=fn_al_tt_5

Speed Racer (*Mach GoGoGo*, 1967–68) Tatsuo Yoshida. IMDb entry: http://www.imdb.com/title/tt0061300/?ref_=fn_al_tt_2

Supernatural (2005–) Various directors. IMDb entry: http://www.imdb.com/title/tt0460681/?ref_=nv_sr_1

Symphogear (*Senki Zesshō Symphogear*, 2012) Tatsufumi Tamagawa. IMDb entry: http://www.imdb.com/title/tt2230531/?ref_=fn_al_tt_3

True Blood (2008–2014) Alan Ball. IMDb entry: http://www.imdb.com/title/tt0844441/?ref_=nv_sr_1

UFO Robot Grandizer (1975–77) Various directors. IMDb entry: http://www.imdb.com/title/tt0185070/?ref_=nv_sr_1

Vicky the Viking (*Wickie und die starken Männer*/*Chîsana baikingu Bikke*, 1974–75) Chikao Katsui and Hiroshi Saito. IMDb entry: http://www.imdb.com/title/tt0278855/?ref_=fn_al_tt_1

28
Audiovisual translation and activism

Mona Baker

Introduction

Activism and *activist* are emotive and ill-defined terms. They are claimed by any party wishing to project itself as a courageous, independent voice that speaks out against what it narrates as injustices, and in so doing place itself and its supporters at varying degrees of risk. The Zionist Organization of America, for instance, boasts that it is 'Always on the front lines of pro-Israel activism' (Zionist Organization of America, n.d.), just as the many groups opposed to Israel and documented on the Palestine Freedom Project website (Palestine Freedom Project, n.d.) refer to themselves and are referred to by others as activists. The terms themselves, according to Tymoczko (2010: 12), have only been in circulation since the middle of the twentieth century, and were initially associated with high profile initiatives that involve direct political action, such as the feminist demonstrations and anti-war rallies of the 1960s and 1970s.

Despite its inherent slipperiness, both activists and scholars tend to associate the concept with anti-establishment initiatives, and often with specific issues that exceed national and social boundaries, including the environment, campaigning for gay rights, and putting an end to injustices such as child abuse and torture (Martin 2007, Courington 1999, Permanent Culture Now n.d.). Today, *activism* is no longer understood to be restricted to the political field, nor to highly visible forms of protest. Nevertheless, in its many denominations—including social activism, cultural activism, art activism and aesthetic activism—the term tends to imply that whatever initiative activists engage in at least has the potential to challenge or undermine some aspect of the political establishment and/or the corporate culture that underpins it. Referring to cultural activism, Buser and Arthurs (2013: 2) suggest that whatever its focus, an activist intervention must 'challenge dominant interpretations and constructions of the world while presenting alternative socio-political and spatial imaginaries'. This assertion echoes a widely held assumption that an activist is essentially someone who poses a challenge to the mainstream values of the political, economic, cultural or social elite.

The increasingly global outlook of many activist movements today has placed audiovisual translation at the centre of all types of projects that work against the mainstream, especially those that involve political or aesthetic forms of intervention. The most common mode in this evolving context is subtitling, given the relative ease and speed with which subtitles can be added to an audiovisual product, and advances in technology that allow videos posted on the Internet to be simultaneously subtitled into different languages by activists located in different parts of the world. Unlike dubbing and voice-over, subtitling also has the advantage of requiring very little capital and resources, and of being impersonal. The latter is important in the context of high-risk activism, where the possibility of identifying voices in dubbed and voice-over products could have serious consequences for the individuals concerned.

Activism in translation studies

Translation scholars have been slow to address the phenomenon of activism, despite relatively early attempts by Tymoczko (2000) to reflect on the topic, and later to bring attention to it through a special issue of *The Massachusetts Review* titled *Translation and Activism* (Tymoczko 2006). The first international forum organized to debate the topic was held a year later, at the University of Granada, under the title 'Translation, Interpreting and Social Activism' (Translation and Activism, n.d.) and resulted in a collected volume published in the same year, under the same title (Boéri and Maier 2007). By 2008, scholars such as Guo (2008) were beginning to ask: 'what does the term "activism" refer to in translation studies?' and 'how can scholars conceptualize translators' activist practices?'. At the same time, David Katan revealed a persistent unease with and confusion over the issue among translation scholars when he argued in his introduction to the inaugural issue of *Cultus* that one of the contributors 'reclaims the translator's "activist" role in terms of what she sees as essential in improving quality: empirical/descriptive translation research and training which focuses on professional output' (2008: 9). Such uses of the term *activist* and *activism* arguably divest them of all meaning. Involvement in activist work is generally understood to come at a price, and while some translators and translation scholars may find the costs associated with activist work too high, the answer cannot be to either dismiss this vital dimension of translation or confuse it with important but non-activist work, and in so doing imply that what translators and translation scholars do has to be 'more activist than it is ... in order to be considered worthwhile at all' (Tymoczko 2007: 216). Apart from the costs associated with activism, be they physical or emotional, the inherently partisan nature of activist work is clearly at odds with the traditional discourse of neutrality that pervaded both the profession and the discipline until recently, and may have been a further factor in dissuading many translation scholars from engaging with the issue.

Boéri (2008: 22) offers a robust critique of slippery and restrictive uses of *activist* and associated terms in translation studies, with particular reference to the field of interpreting, specifically the work of the volunteer interpreting collective Babels. Her critique raises three important issues: the tendency of the rhetoric deployed in some of the literature to 'outstrip the actual power of social change that it assumes professional translators have at their disposal'; the exclusive focus on textual interventions and failure to address 'the broader role of the translator or interpreter as a social and political actor'; and the tendency 'to view the individual translator as the single motor of change, thus downplaying the collective dimension of both translation and activism'. While not denying the value of textual interventions or the contributions of individual activists, this critique—which addresses similar issues to those raised in Tymoczko (2000)—alerts us to important dimensions of activist work in translation that have traditionally been neglected in the discipline and are equally relevant in the context of audiovisual translation, as discussed later in this chapter.

Activism can assume different forms and involve divergent and opposing choices. While many might consider the task of translation to be fundamentally one of enabling communication and dialogue, others have argued that an activist stance can also 'involve blocking communication and refusing to transmit cultural information' (Tymoczko 2010: 230). Nornes (2007: 184) offers the example of Robert Gardner, who excluded subtitles from his ethnographic film *Forest of Bliss* (1986) in order to challenge the prevailing context of reception in which 'the ethnographic documentary renders other cultures transparent to a scientific gaze' and effect a new kind of relationship between spectators and the film's subjects. Alternatively, as Tymoczko argues, 'sometimes the fact of translation itself ... is the primary activist achievement' (2010: 229), especially in the context of censorship and repression. The work of the activist collective Translate for Justice (Translate for Justice, n.d.), recipient of the Elif Ertan New Voices in Translation Prize by the Translation and Interpreting Association of Turkey (2015) and the Hermann Kesten Incentive Award by the German PEN Centre (2016), is a good example. The collective has been extremely active since the 2013 Gezi protests in making suppressed news and documentation about violations of human rights in Turkey available at a global level.

Textual choices may also vary, and no specific textual strategy may be said to be activist per se, as extensively demonstrated by critics of Lawrence Venuti's influential work on foreignization (Tymoczko 2000, Boyden 2006, Baker 2007/2010, Shamma 2009, among many others). This issue is especially relevant in the context of audiovisual translation, where the related concept of abusive subtitling has not received the same level of critical attention.

Activism in audiovisual translation

Pérez-González (2014: 58) suggests that 'audiovisual translation, formerly a site of representational practice, is quickly becoming a site of interventionist practice'. Not all interventionist practices can be considered activist, however. Activism, as already explained, is understood to involve a degree of risk and to pose some form of challenge to mainstream values and the established social and political order. Hence, the type of interventions practised by the Guojiang Subtitle Group and discussed in Guo (2016) are arguably not activist. These included replacing 'China' with 'other countries' in the Chinese subtitles of Senator Rand Paul's critical remarks on Donald Trump: 'Trump says we ought to close that Internet thing. The question really is, what does he mean by that? Like they do in North Korea? Like they do in China?'. Such interventions reinforce the mainstream nationalist vision, and rather than incur risks are designed to ensure that the subtitlers avoid pressure and come to no emotional or physical harm.

In line with wider discussions of activism in the literature on fandom, Pérez-González's distinction between aesthetic and political activism (2014: 70) acknowledges the 'increasing similarities between fan cultures and contemporary mobilizations' (Brough and Shresthova 2012). The work of fansubbers and fandubbers poses two types of challenge to the established order. First, like other types of fan translation, 'it questions the current operation of global cultural industries by providing a new model of content distribution and its organization based on consumers' voluntary work' (Lee 2011: 1132). And second, it challenges the established global order by encouraging subtitlers to experiment with and develop innovative subtitling strategies that undermine restrictive conventions imposed by the industry (Pérez-González 2013: 10). Like the political subtitling initiatives discussed in Pérez-González (2010, 2014, 2016), Baker (2016), Mortada (2016) and Selim (2016), this form of aesthetic activism thus has the potential to undermine the prevailing world order, both corporate and political, given the overlap and interdependence of the two systems. Nevertheless, it is also important to note that fan projects in general, including those that involve audiovisual translation, are not inherently activist, that they can be simultaneously resistant and complicit, and that like other activist initiatives they are vulnerable to the same processes of co-optation that pervade all areas of political and social life. Their political significance, however, ultimately lies in their ability to reconfigure relations of power, at least temporarily, through the participatory culture they nurture (Brough and Shresthova 2012).

The nature and contexts of activist interventions in audiovisual translation are yet to be explored in sufficient detail, as are the distinctive restrictions and opportunities imposed on or afforded to activists in various venues and with different genres within this domain. For example, Boéri's (2008) concern over the literature's undue focus on the individual translator as the locus of activist intervention is less relevant to the subtitling of commercial audiovisual products disseminated through official channels. These are inherently collective and tightly controlled enterprises where, unlike literary translation, the names of subtitlers tend not to be declared, and which have therefore not been discussed in the literature from the perspective of activism or the individual agenda of a subtitler. At the same time, recent developments in technology mean that an individual activist such as Zorbec le Gras, who subtitled into English a largely unreported anti-austerity speech by French MEP Daniel Cohn-Bendit in May 2010 and disseminated it among some two million YouTube users (Pérez-González 2014: 59), can conceive, initiate and carry out an activist subtitling project largely on his own. The same is true of Sony Islam, whose work is used by Pérez-González as a leitmotif in discussing self-mediation in audiovisual translation. In the context of audiovisual translation then, such individual activist initiatives now merit closer scholarly attention to offset the almost exclusive focus on collective interventions, not only in the much researched area of fansubbing, but also in the political domain (Baker 2016, Mortada 2016, Pérez-González 2010, 2016, Selim 2016). Similarly, while activist interventions that take the form of manipulating or displacing text types and genres (Tymoczko 2010: 230) have received some attention in the wider discipline, this dimension of activism remains totally neglected by audiovisual translation scholars. Even Pérez-González's discussion of self-mediation, remediation and bricolage (2014: Chapter 7), which features several activist subtitling projects that involve generic shifts, does not explore the texts or initiatives analyzed from this perspective. The same is true of Baker's brief analysis of a subtitled political commercial and some of the parodies it elicited on the Internet (2014: 171–173), where the implications of the generic shift from political commercial to ludic parody are not addressed.

To date, the only sustained examination of subtitling in the context of political activism is Baker (2016). This study highlights other themes in the wider discussion of activism in translation studies that merit closer scrutiny in the context of audiovisual translation, including the visibility of individual activists and the level of agency they exercise within an activist initiative. Tymoczko (2007: 213) argues that '[e]ngaged translators are visible as subjects' and that '[p]olitical effectiveness is most likely if there is a group of visible translators with a common project or program'. Baker's study suggests otherwise, but also points to a more complex picture that requires a sustained research programme to unpack.

First, subtitlers working with activist collectives in the 2011 Egyptian Revolution, the context of Baker's study, seemed to lack visibility, and indeed not to be keen on even reflecting on the issue when it was raised in interviews. Unlike the film makers and other activists involved in the collectives examined (Mosireen and Words of Women from the Egyptian Revolution), they were never mentioned or quoted in national or international media, and did not give talks about the collectives at different venues. This meant that they were initially difficult to identify and could only be traced, for the purposes of arranging interviews, through the more visible film makers, journalists, urban planners and other activists connected with each collective. Their eschewing of visibility may be partly explained by entrenched attitudes to translation—including subtitling—as a secondary and derivative activity, but also by the contemporary culture of collaborative and collective activist work, where those involved are rarely interested in being credited as individuals. Mosireen videos acknowledge only collectives in the final credits, specifically Mosireen itself and occasionally another collective with which Mosireen collaborated in the production of a specific video. Film maker Philip Rizk explained in an unpublished interview with Baker that 'there was never any consideration . . . of any references made to individuals', including film makers, because 'Mosireen is . . . not a group that's celebrating authorship' (18 January 2014 [32:15, 38:20]). But for film makers, this eschewing of individual visibility did not extend to speaking about the collective to the media and in public venues, as it did in the case of the subtitlers. More importantly, the subtitlers were not only invisible to the outside world, but were also largely invisible within the collective itself. Philip Rizk acknowledged in the same interview that 'the most invisible participants are probably the translating team' [27: 20], and that most members of the collective did not know 'who the people are who are translating' nor 'why they're translating' [29: 50]. Another Mosireen film maker, Salma El-Tarzi, confirms that she had 'no idea' who translated the films she shot and edited for the collective, nor 'their names', nor 'what they look like' (2016: 90).

In terms of agency, and despite the vital work they undertook under intense pressure during a momentous period of history, the subtitlers interviewed tended to assume a largely passive role and '[did] not seem to think of themselves as an organic part of either collective, nor to be regarded as such by the film-makers' (Baker 2016: 16). Even the coordinator of the subtitling list of the larger of the two collectives, who had a long history of high-risk activism with other members of Mosireen, seemed to assume a largely subservient role in terms of subtitling, quite atypical of her character outside that context: 'I see myself, and I think a lot of people [i.e. subtitlers on the Mosireen list] see themselves as not being key people but just serving and supporting and doing what we can' (quoted in Baker 2016: 17). This choice of positioning within the larger collective has implications for the level of agency the subtitlers were willing to exercise. On the whole, subtitlers in both collectives were largely reluctant to intervene or make suggestions that could enhance the political message or even the legibility of the subtitles. None of them attempted, for instance, to alert film makers to the difficulty caused by placing background information in Arabic in the only space available for subtitling, at the bottom of the screen (Baker 2016: 16). In terms of subtitling strategies, examples of creative interventions that enhanced the political message turned out to have been introduced by the film makers, not the subtitlers (Baker 2016: 15). Perhaps, as Tymoczko asserts (2007: 216), 'radical manipulation of texts and . . . subordination of text to ideology . . . are inimical to translators whose primary orientation is to the integrity of texts themselves'. And yet, we know that in the field of audiovisual translation fansubbing has broken this taboo, and hence we might reasonably expect an even greater level of intervention from politically motivated subtitlers.

Beyond the question of visibility, the tendency to shy away from textual intervention, noted by Tymoczko, is not confined to the audiovisual field, nor to *ad hoc* groups of translators who do not have the time or luxury to reflect critically on their position within larger formations because of the high-risk nature of their activism. The broad distinction proposed by Guo (2008: 11) between activists who translate and activist translators may shed some light on this issue. Although activist groups dedicated to translation and interpreting, like Babels and Tlaxcala, make no distinction between professionals and non-professionals, and focus instead on a potential member's commitment to the political principles that inform the project (Boéri 2008: 32), they do define themselves as *translators* or *interpreters* 'and hence position themselves explicitly within the professional and scholarly world of translation' (Baker 2013: 26). In this respect they differ from fansubbing groups and members of activist collectives who do not identify as translators, such as the *Cuaderno de Campo* bloggers who subtitled George Galloway's 2006 interview into Spanish (Pérez-González 2014: 63–65). Positioning themselves specifically as translators seems to discourage activists from adopting bold interventionist strategies at the textual level, and at best confines their experimentation to the spaces around events and texts. Babels' foundational texts make reference to 'experimentation in linguistic activism', suggesting that the group does not view such interventions negatively. And yet, despite insisting that the group is a political actor rather than service provider for the Social Forum, Boéri confirms that 'there is no evidence to suggest that volunteers are expected or encouraged to intervene in the narratives they mediate once they are in the booth' (2008: 33).

Researching political activism in the audiovisual domain poses theoretical and methodological challenges that have not been discussed in the wider discipline. The most important of these are the loosely structured nature of the collectives that produce subtitled videos, and the fluidity of the data. Both are characteristic of contemporary social and political movements, which tend to be non-hierarchical, highly collaborative, and generally uninterested in exercising control over their output or maintaining a record of individual contributions to it. In the context of the Egyptian Revolution, while Mosireen did have a list of individuals whose task was to subtitle the videos shot by film makers, some of the film makers were also involved in subtitling some videos, especially those they considered particularly challenging, for instance because they featured stretches of poetry. Many of the film makers also revised videos after they had been uploaded to the collective's YouTube channel, without leaving a trace of what was revised, when, and by whom. At the same time, there was no attempt to control or document the subtitling of a collective's videos into languages not covered by the subtitling team. Co-founder of Words of Women from the Egyptian Revolution, Leil-Zahra Mortada, explained one pattern that reveals the fluidity and proliferation of subtitled versions on the Internet: 'I [typically] got a notification [from Amara/Universal Subtitles] that this person translated your video into whatever, Malaysian or Urdu or whatever. I didn't even upload it to YouTube' (unpublished interview by Baker, 27 February 2014 [44:50]). This level of fluidity and the absence of any trace of individual contributions and revisions have two implications for researchers interested in studying political activism in the context of audiovisual translation. First, textual and visual data, typically accessible through the Internet, need to be contextualized and supplemented by other sources, such as interviews and participant observation. Second, scholars need to formulate meaningful research questions that recognize the nature of the data and the movements that produce it, rather than attempt to address traditional questions that assume a stable, fixed and well documented set of outputs and discrete roles for those involved in producing them.

Finally, the few studies that have examined audiovisual translation collectives so far suggest that both aesthetic and political activism in this domain have been relatively modest in terms of scale, level of political awareness and impact on the profession and discipline. Whereas Boéri claims that 'Babels has inaugurated what we might call a "geopolitical turn" in conference interpreting' (2008: 23), and there is evidence to suggest that it has indeed shifted the debate in both profession and discipline (Baker 2018), nothing of this scale or theoretical sophistication has yet been witnessed in the area of audiovisual translation, especially where political activism is concerned. Fansubbing communities can be very large in size, and their work has had an acknowledged impact on the industry (Nornes 2007, Pérez-González 2014, among others) and attracted critical attention from a number of disciplines such as law and media studies (Leonard 2005, Lee 2011), but they have not shifted the debate in audiovisual translation scholarship in a similar way. Political activism in the audiovisual translation sphere, on the other hand, seems to be largely confined to work done by 'individuals working under their own steam' (Pérez-González 2014: 242) rather than collectives of the scale and complexity of Babels. And while fansubbing communities tend to be fairly stable networks with a relatively long-term agenda, most initiatives involving political activism are now carried out by what Pérez-González refers to as 'ad-hocracies' of amateur subtitlers: temporary constellations that come together to address a specific challenge and then disperse (2010, 2014: 243).

Activist textual strategies in audiovisual translation

Most discussions of activist textual strategies in the literature focus on subtitling, rather than other modes of audiovisual translation. Fansubbers as well as political activists have introduced a range of strategies that flout mainstream conventions, such as varying the size and colour of fonts, placing subtitles in different positions on the screen, adding non-diegetic subtitles to explain a pun or express sarcasm (Pérez-González 2014: 255–256), and replacing the original set of subtitles released with a film or video with another set that undercuts the original message or exploits the visuals to communicate a new one in a different context (Baker 2014: 171–173, Pérez-González 2014: 236–239). These strategies enhance the visibility of the mediator and the process of mediation, and some are adopted specifically to increase awareness of the foreign culture and encourage the viewer to engage with it on its own terms. Dwyer (2012: 229) suggests that the latter is the main goal of fansubbers, who are keen to challenge what she refers to, following Leonard (2005), as the 'culturally "deodorizing" function' of the industry.

To what extent these effects and the strategies intended to produce them serve activist goals depends on the context in which an audiovisual product is released and the nature of the fictional or non-fictional worlds mediated by the subtitles. More importantly, activist subtitlers may vary their strategies within the same audiovisual product, depending on the political goals they set out to pursue. Baker (2007/2010: 165–167, 126–128) demonstrates this with reference to the varying lexical choices adopted in subtitling *shaheed* into English in a Palestinian documentary about Israeli attacks on the Jenin refugee camp in 2002. Nornes (2007: 184–185) offers a more complex example of his own 'abusive translation' of a documentary by Sato Makoto about the impact on old people of mercury poisoning caused by the release of untreated toxic compounds into the Agano River basin. To encourage the English-speaking spectator to engage with aspects of the protagonists' humanity that even domestic viewers cannot appreciate through the rural and largely inaccessible dialect used by the people of Nigata, Nornes 'attempted to replicate the experience of an urban Japanese spectator by using sentence fragments, single words' and by adding his own comments in brackets as well as a subtitler's preface to explain the context and prepare the viewer 'to expect something strange and to read the subtitles with an open mind'. At the same time, '[w]here utterances were highly legible, the subtitles were no different than in any other film' (2007: 185).

Experimentation and creativity: abusive subtitling and/vs prefiguration

Nornes defines abusive subtitling as a practice that 'does not feign completeness' and 'does not hide its presence through restrictive rules' (1999: 28, 2007: 176). The abusive subtitler engages in 'experimentation with language . . . to bring the fact of translation from its position of obscurity' and to critique the 'imperial politics' that inform conventional industry practices, with a view to 'ultimately leading the viewer to the foreign original' (1999: 18, 2007: 176–177). Experimentation and creativity do not necessarily lead to an appreciation of the foreign, however, as O'Sullivan notes in her discussion of innovative subtitles in *Night Watch* (2004) and *Slumdog Millionaire* (2008), which 'serve to create an immersive experience for the target audience rather than to draw the viewers' attention to the foreignness of the film text' (2011: 152). Experimentation can also serve different activist goals, some of which have little to do with foregrounding the foreign or the fact of translation per se.

In the context of global movements of collective action, the question of foregrounding the foreign as such is of little interest. Indeed, commitment to solidarity—a key concept in contemporary political and social movements—calls for adopting practices that actively break down the binaries of foreign vs domestic and that place emphasis instead on actualizing values and principles which transcend individual cultures and partake of a global idiom of resistance (Baker 2016). As Pérez-González also notes, audiovisual translation is now a central element of the push to break down barriers in the media marketplace, where 'collaborative technologies are contributing to the formation of transnational networked collectivities, and hence re-defining the traditional boundaries of nation-based cultural and linguistic constituencies', ultimately raising awareness of the fluidity and complexity of cultural and national identities (2014: 61). In this context, activist subtitling cannot be defined purely in terms of foregrounding the foreign or the fact of translation as such, and scholars therefore need to explore concepts other than 'abusive subtitling' to make sense of emerging patterns of activist engagement with audiovisual products. Nornes predicted this as early as 1999, when he argued that what was once radical textual and visual experimentation was already becoming mainstream, and suggested that 'when abusive subtitling becomes normalized' scholars should 'think of other terms' (1999: 32, 2007: 187) that can offer more relevant insight into means and motives for breaking conventions in audiovisual translation.

Focusing on activist subtitling in the context of contemporary political movements, Baker (2016) borrows the concept of prefiguration from social movement studies, especially the work of Maeckelbergh (2009, 2011). Like abusive subtitling, where the main thrust of abuse 'is directed at convention' (Nornes 1999: 32), prefiguration privileges experimentation and involves challenging established patterns of practice. However, rather than foregrounding the foreign, the emphasis in prefigurative politics is on putting into practice the values and principles to which activists subscribe, and in so doing bringing the world they aspire to create into existence. The principles to be put into practice include a commitment to solidarity, diversity, non-hierarchy, horizontality and non-representational modes of practice. Activist film making and subtitling seek to actualize these principles rather than foreground the foreign or the fact of translation as such. The strategies used may appear similar on the surface, but the goals are different, to varying degrees and in different contexts. For instance, the collective Words of Women from the Egyptian Revolution deliberately reduced cutaway images 'to the bare minimum', opting to reveal cuts even though they 'could be perceived as "mistakes"', in order to be transparent about the unavoidable act of representation involved in shooting and editing any filmic product, rather than obscure it and lull the viewer into the illusion of a direct, unmediated experience of the women's voices (Mortada 2016: 132). This overlaps with the idea of bringing the fact of translation and mediation in general into light, but is informed by a subtly different political principle—rejection of representational practices—and is not restricted to translation. The same principle informs Philip Rizk's assertion that he is committed to resisting the act of representation even as he recognizes that he has to engage in it by speaking to the media about the Egyptian Revolution: 'I don't claim to be able to speak on behalf of a collective that is not uniform. The best I can do is . . . to spend time with the people that make up this revolution, to listen, to learn and speak in humility. In this act of speaking I do not attempt to "represent," I try to interpret, but representation is out of the question' (Rizk 2013). Well-educated activists like Rizk do not seek visibility as mediators: visibility is thrust on them by the dynamics of media practices and the unequal distribution of power. They accept it reluctantly and use it to give voice to others they know they cannot claim to 'represent'.

Another political principle, commitment to diversity, informs the strategy adopted by Words of Women in subtitling its interviews from Arabic into Spanish (Mortada 2016, Baker 2016). Mortada explains that it was important for the group to develop a gender-sensitive strategy that embraced 'people who do not identify as men or women, who adopt a queer politics' (2016: 134). This meant that rather than settle for the familiar activist strategy of replacing the masculine *o* and feminine *a* with @, which could be interpreted as a visual combination of both, the team opted to replace the gender marker with *x*, as in *amigx* and *deteniéndolxs*. This choice, Mortada explains, 'was felt to subvert the gender binary in the language' (2016: 134), to signal the collective's rejection of gender as a category that suppresses the diversity of human beings by forcing them into mutually exclusive choices within a rigid classificatory system. It is not a choice that aims to foreground the foreignness or otherwise of the women featured, nor specifically the mediator or act of mediation. As Baker notes, however, this innovative strategy which recognizes the space of subtitling as a medium of intervention turned out to be initiated by the film makers, not the subtitlers (2016: 15).

The pressures of a violent, revolutionary context impose certain constraints on activists' ability to adopt innovative practices that reflect their political principles. While a commitment to experimentation and breaking conventions is inherent in the logic of prefigurative politics (Yates 2015), as it is in abusive subtitling, this principle may be jettisoned for ethical reasons. Omar Robert Hamilton, a member of Mosireen interviewed by Baker, reflects on this issue from a film maker's perspective: 'you've got some father or mother crying over their kid who's been killed and they're saying how they're going to get their rights, and it's not the place for you to come in and video art and mess around . . . it's not your job to come in and make an Omar Hamilton film of their grief' (unpublished interview, 26 April 2014 [22:50]). What may appear in some activist work, including activist translation, as a tendency to shy away from experimentation and creativity may therefore have complex explanations.

Other constraints on adopting prefigurative practices are a facet of the inevitable tension between politics and logistics, and between different sets of political values. No activist initiative, within or outside the context of audiovisual translation, can achieve total coherence between political goals and actual practices (Yates 2015: 17), even in peaceful times. These difficulties are exacerbated during periods of turmoil and in the context of high-risk activism, and inevitably impact subtitling practices. Activist translation and interpreting initiatives like Tlaxcala and Babels, which are conceived and undertaken in stable, low-risk contexts, innovatively prefigure their commitment to linguistic and cultural diversity, solidarity and non-hierarchy by ensuring that they provide translations into and from languages such as Catalan, Greek, Hungarian, Persian, Tamazight and Turkish, in addition to the dominant English, French, German and Spanish, and by experimenting with layout and the ordering of languages on their website (Baker 2013). Mosireen and Words of Women from the Egyptian Revolution paid little attention to the prefigurative implications of their choice of subtitling languages, however. They typically put out calls on social media for volunteer subtitlers into English and Spanish, occasionally French and German, and circulated the odd call for subtitlers working into close regional languages such as Greek and Turkish. This practice undercuts the principle of solidarity because it does not support building South-South networks of communication and fails to recognize that 'solidarity is most desperately needed among activists located in areas of the world where the system of oppression is at its most brutal' (Baker 2016: 10). An attempt to engage subtitlers who can work into Kashmiri, Hindi, Kurdish and similar languages through calls on social media and other outlets could have proved rewarding, but the emotional and physical difficulty of documenting and disseminating information about harrowing events at great speed understandably left activists little time and energy for reflection and planning.

Another subtitling practice that undercut the collectives' commitment to prefiguration in the context of the Egyptian Revolution involved using English as a basis for subtitles into all other languages, rather than attempting to find volunteers who can subtitle directly from Arabic. This pattern replicated the practices of corporate media and the film industry and hence reproduced the structures of power that members of each collective are committed to challenging under normal circumstances. They also inadvertently allowed 'a colonial language that is deeply implicated in the processes of subjugation and misrepresentation' they were risking their lives to expose 'to function as a filter for values expressed by the diverse characters depicted in the videos' (Baker 2016: 10). This contrasts sharply with practices adopted by activist translators such as those involved in Tlaxcala, whose manifesto (Tlaxcala, n.d.) reveals awareness of the politics of language and their responsibility in 'de-imperializing' English and other dominant languages, disrupting linguistic hierarchies, and fostering networks of solidarity outside the North-South divide.

Despite the inevitable tensions and unavoidable compromises, prefigurative strategies in the context of revolutions and protests must ultimately aspire to enhance rather than undercut the political principles that inform contemporary global activism. Translational choices have to adapt the commitment to experimentation to the exigencies of the revolutionary moment, but should ideally be reflexive and demonstrate awareness of the political stakes involved. Some of the examples discussed in Baker (2016), such as lack of attention to code-switching and register variation in videos subtitled into Spanish and English, have the cumulative effect of streamlining the individual voices of speakers 'into the homogeneous voice of an articulate, educated representative of the Egyptian Revolution', and in so doing undercutting the commitment to diversity evident in the film-makers' decision to film a wide range of speakers and Mosireen's explicit invitation to subtitlers not to be afraid of 'street language' (2016: 13). Apart from the time constraints—specifically the need to get subtitled videos circulated on the Internet very quickly as events unfolded on the ground—and the emotional pressure involved, subtitlers' reluctance to break conventions and make bold decisions may be explained by the way they position themselves and are positioned within activist collectives, as already explained. This issue needs to be aired and debated within the discipline and among volunteer groups in order to ensure that audiovisual translation plays a positive role in supporting global networks of solidarity in future (Baker 2016: 18).

The impact of technology

Much has been written about the empowering impact of recent advances in technology in many areas of social and professional life, including translation. Pérez-González (2014: 233) suggests that audiovisual translation is experiencing a 'demotic turn', aided by the 'democratization of access to digital technologies' that have ended the monopoly exercised by the film and television industry. Advances in technology have indeed been instrumental in enabling the emergence of a vibrant, participatory culture that has benefited activist projects of both the political and aesthetic type. Platforms such as Amara provide tools that are 'free and open source and make the work of subtitling and translating video simpler, more appealing, and, most of all, more collaborative' (Amara website). Amara was used by the volunteer subtitlers and film makers of Mosireen and Words of Women.

While the empowering effect of such platforms is undeniable, it is also important to think critically about the political and aesthetic implications of increased reliance on them and an uncritical celebration of their liberatory potential. Amara is not as 'non-profit' and independent of the corporate world as it claims to be. Munday (2012: 332, fn 3) confirms that Amara (formerly Universal Subtitles), launched in 2010, had already received one million dollars in seed funding from Mozilla 'and was opening up to corporate clients' by 2012. Today, the Amara website features an entire section of 'Enterprise Solutions' that offers a variety of for-profit services for crowdsourcing and on-demand subtitling (Amara on Demand, n.d.). Many, though by no means all, contemporary activist initiatives strive to remain independent of the corporate world and its logic; they tend to use crowdfunding instead of corporate funding to support their work, and do not engage in for-profit activities. As Lievrouw explains, new social movements also favour small-scale projects and a micromedia, 'DIY aesthetic' that reflects their suspicion of 'supersized modern culture' (2011: 61). While this position may seem unrealistic to many, it is sensitive to the processes of appropriation evident in the history of many initiatives that straddle the activist and corporate worlds. One of the dangers posed by such mixed initiatives is that they perpetuate a pattern of dependency that gradually gives rise to an 'industry' of participatory and activist culture, one that quickly falls under the control of the monopolies of financial capitalism.

A related issue is that technology imposes its own restrictions on activists, some of which undercut their political and aesthetic agendas and block the commitment to experimentation emphasized in the literature on both abusive subtitling and prefiguration. And just as it opens up new spaces and opportunities for intervention by unaffiliated citizens, it creates the conditions for monopolies to emerge and control the form in which dissent may be expressed, as well as the parameters of innovation it can exercise. Attempts to experiment with the number and placement of subtitles in a Mosireen video entitled 'The Revolutionaries' Response to the Tahrir Monument' (Mosireen 2013) in November 2013 did not succeed, because YouTube compatible files have to be in .srt format, which does not support placing more than one subtitle per screenshot, or anywhere other than in the centre, at the bottom of the screen. Mosireen film maker Omar Robert Hamilton acknowledged that 'one's aesthetic sensibilities have to be put aside when it comes to using YouTube' (unpublished interview by Baker, 26 April 2014 [46:50]). Despite this, and the fact that YouTube places advertisements at the beginning of each video, some of which may be completely at odds with the political message being communicated, activist film makers and subtitlers have to accept it as 'a utilitarian space' [47.00] because 'there isn't anything close to another option' [48:30]. The most obvious alternative, Vimeo, does not have the same functionalities YouTube offers, including the ability to display soft subs and a means of selecting from a range of languages, and does not enjoy the same reach. Vimeo's restricted reach makes it of limited use in nurturing networks of solidarity across different national and subcultural communities.

In an ideal world, the tension between the logistics of any activist project and its political goals should be resolved in favour of politics, which means that logistical decisions should embody a commitment to autonomy from market relations and the profit-driven culture activists seek to challenge. In the real world, however, the best that activists can do in many cases is to reflect critically on how they position themselves within this tension rather than simply celebrate the emancipatory potential of the technology they opt to use at any moment. This is a theme that needs to be taken up in future research on activism in audiovisual translation, given the current tendency to celebrate the power of technology uncritically in both profession and discipline.

Summary

Recent technological advances and the increasingly global outlook of many activist movements today have placed audiovisual translation at the centre of various initiatives that seek to challenge the corporate and political order. This chapter has outlined a number of methodological challenges that complicate the study of activist audiovisual translation and called for a rethinking of research priorities and theoretical assumptions in this area of scholarship. The discussion has focused on political rather than aesthetic activism, and on subtitling as the most common mode of circulating activist audiovisual products on a global level. Issues discussed include the visibility and agency of subtitlers in political movements, activist textual strategies, abusive subtitling, prefiguration, the impact of technology, and the tension between politics and logistics. The arguments have been largely supported by examples from a study of subtitling during the 2011 Egyptian Revolution, including material drawn from unpublished interviews conducted by the author.

Related topics

19   Gender in audiovisual translation: advocating for gender awareness
26   Audiovisual translation and popular music
27   Audiovisual translation and fandom

Further Reading

Baker, M. (2016) 'The Prefigurative Politics of Translation in Place-based Movements of Protest: Subtitling in the Egyptian Revolution', *The Translator* 22(1): 1–21 | *Borrowing the concept of prefiguration from social movement studies, this study shows how activist film making and subtitling seek to actualize the principles of solidarity, diversity, non-hierarchy, horizontality and non-representational modes of practice, rather than foregrounding the foreign or the fact of translation as such.*

Mortada, L. Z. (2016) 'Translation and Solidarity in *Words of Women from the Egyptian Revolution*', in Mona Baker (ed.) *Translating Dissent: Voices* from *and* with *the Egyptian Revolution*, Abingdon and New York: Routledge, 125–136 | *This paper illustrates a range of activist subtitling practices by the collective Words of Women from the Egyptian Revolution.*

Nornes, A. M. (1999) 'For an Abusive Subtitling', *Film Quarterly* 52(3): 17–34 | *Nornes' concept of 'abusive subtitling', that Baker uses in this paper to make sense of emerging patterns of activist engagement with audiovisual products, was originally developed to account for fansubbing practices.*

Pérez-González, L. (2010) '"Ad-hocracies" of Translation Activism in the Blogosphere: A Genealogical Case Study', in M. Baker, M. Calzada Pérez and M. Olohan (eds) *Text and Context: Essays on Translation and Interpreting in Honour of Ian Mason*, Manchester: St. Jerome Publishing, 259–287 | *The term 'ad-hocracy' is used in this study to designate the sort of temporary communities of non-professional translators that are formed spontaneously to work on activist subtitling projects in the digital culture.*

Selim, S. (2016) 'Text and Context: Translating in a State of Emergency', in M. Baker (ed.) *Translating Dissent: Voices from and with the Egyptian Revolution*, Abingdon & New York: Routledge, 77–87 | *The author reflects on the process and experience of working as a subtitler for the Egyptian video collective Mosireen during 2012–2013.*

References

Amara on Demand (n.d.) 'Amara on Demand. Professionally Crafted Captions & Subtitles'. Available online: http://pro.amara.org/enterprise [last accessed 20 December 2017].

Amara website (n.d.) 'About Amara'. Available online: https://www.amara.org/en/about [last accessed 20 December 2017].

Baker, M. (2007/2010) 'Reframing Conflict in Translation', *Social Semiotics* 17(1): 151–169; reprinted in Mona Baker (ed.) *Critical Readings in Translation Studies*, London & New York, 113–129.

Baker, M. (2010) 'Resisting State Terror: Theorising Communities of Activist Translators and Interpreters', in J. Boéri and C. Maier (eds) *Compromiso Social y Traducción/Translation, Interpreting and Social Activism*, Granada: ECOS, traductores e intérpretes por la solidaridad, 25–27.

Baker, M. (2013) 'Translation as an Alternative Space for Political Action', *Social Movement Studies* 21(1): 23–47.

Baker, M. (2014) 'Translation as Renarration', in J. House (ed.) *Translation: A Multidisciplinary Approach*, Basingstoke: Palgrave Macmillan, 158–177.

Baker, M. (2016) 'The Prefigurative Politics of Translation in Place-based Movements of Protest: Subtitling in the Egyptian Revolution', *The Translator* 22(1): 1–21.

Baker, M. (2018) 'Narrative Analysis and Translation', in K. Malmkjær (ed.) *The Routledge Handbook of Translation and Linguistics*, London & New York: Routledge, 179–193.

Boéri, J. (2008) 'A Narrative Account of the Babels vs. Naumann Controversy', *The Translator* 14(1): 21–52.

Boéri, J. and C. Maier (eds) (2007) *Compromiso Social y Traducción/Translation, Interpreting and Social Activism*, Granada: ECOS, traductores e intérpretes por la solidaridad.

Boyden, M. (2006) 'Language Politics, Translation, and American Literary History', *Target* 18(1): 121–137.

Brough, M. M. and S. Shresthova (2012) 'Fandom Meets Activism: Rethinking Civic and Political Participation', *Transformative Works and Cultures* 10. Available online: http://journal.transformativeworks.org/index.php/twc/article/view/303/265 [last accessed 20 December 2017].

Buser, M. and J. Arthurs (2013) *Connected Communities: Cultural Activism in the Community*. Available online: http://www.culturalactivism.org.uk/wp-content/uploads/2013/03/CULTURAL-ACTIVISM-BUSER-Update.3.pdf [last accessed 20 December 2017].

Courington, C. (1999) '(Re)Defining Activism: Lessons from Women's Literature', *Women's Studies Quarterly* 27(3/4): 77–86.

Dwyer, T. (2012) 'Fansub Dreaming on ViKi: Don't just Watch but Help when you are Free', *The Translator* 18(2): 217–243.

El-Tarzi, S. (2016) 'Ethical Reflections on Activist Film-making and Activist Subtitling', in M. Baker (ed.) *Translating Dissent: Voices from and with the Egyptian Revolution*, London & New York: Routledge, 88–96.

Guo, T. (2008) 'Translation and Activism: Translators in the Chinese Communist Movement in the 1920s-30s', in P. Boulogne (ed.) *Translation and its Others, Selected Papers of the CETRA Research Seminar in Translation Studies* 2007, 1–25. Available online: https://www.arts.kuleuven.be/cetra/papers/files/guo.pdf [last accessed 20 December 2017].

Guo, O. (2016) 'Bringing U.S. Presidential Debates to a Chinese Audience', *The New York Times*, 3 January. Available online: http://www.nytimes.com/2016/01/04/world/asia/china-presidential-debates-trump-clinton.html?emc=edit_tnt_20160103&nlid=64183997&tntemail0=y&_r=0 [last accessed 20 December 2017].

Katan, D. (2008) 'Introduction', *Cultus* 1(1): 7–9.

Lee, H. K. (2011) 'Participatory Media Fandom: A Case Study of Anime Fansubbing', *Media, Culture & Society* 33(8): 1131–1147.

Leonard, S. (2005) 'Progress against the Law: Anime and Fandom, with the Key to the Globalization of Culture', *International Journal of Cultural Studies* 8(3): 281–305.

Lievrouw, L. A. (2011) *Alternative and Activist New Media*, Cambridge: Polity.

Maeckelbergh, M. (2009) *The Will of the Many: How the Alterglobalisation Movement Is Changing the Face of Democracy*, London & New York: Pluto Press.

Maeckelbergh, M. (2011) 'Doing Is Believing: Prefiguration as Strategic Practice in the Alterglobalization Movement', *Social Movement Studies* 10(1): 1–20.

Martin, B. (2007) 'Activism, Social and Political', in G. L. Anderson and K. G. Herr (eds) *Encyclopedia of Activism and Social Justice*, Thousand Oaks, CA: Sage, 19–27.

Mortada, L. Z. (2016) 'Translation and Solidarity in *Words of Women from the Egyptian Revolution*', in M. Baker (ed.) *Translating Dissent: Voices* from *and* with *the Egyptian Revolution*, Abingdon & New York: Routledge, 125–136.

Mosireen (2013) 'The Revolutionaries' Response to the Tahrir Monument'. Available online: http://mosireen.org/?p=1671 [last accessed 20 December 2017].

Munday, J. (2012) 'New Directions in Discourse Analysis for Translation: A Study of Decision-Making in Crowdsourced Subtitles of Obama's 2012 State of the Union Speech', *Language and Intercultural Communication* 12(4): 321–334.

Nornes, A. M. (1999) 'For an Abusive Subtitling', *Film Quarterly* 52(3): 17–33.

Nornes, A. M. (2007) *Cinema Babel: Translating Global Cinema*, Minneapolis & London: University of Minnesota Press.

O'Sullivan, Carol (2011) *Translating Popular Film*, Basingstoke: Palgrave Macmillan.

Palestine Freedom Project (n.d.) 'About us'. Available online: http://www.palestinefreedom.org/about [last accessed 26 July 2016].

Pérez-González, L. (2010) '"Ad-hocracies" of Translation Activism in the Blogosphere: A Genealogical Case Study, in M. Baker, M. Calzada Pérez and M. Olohan (eds) *Text and Context: Essays on Translation and Interpreting in Honour of Ian Mason*, Manchester: St. Jerome Publishing, 259–287.

Pérez-González, L. (2013) 'Co-creational Subtitling in the Digital Media: Transformative and Authorial Practices', *International Journal of Cultural Studies* 16(1): 3–21.

Pérez-González, L. (2014) *Audiovisual Translation: Theories, Methods and Issues*, London & New York: Routledge.

Pérez-González, L. (2016) 'The Politics of Affect in Activist Amateur Subtitling: A Biopolitical Perspective', in M. Baker and B. Blaagaard (eds) *Citizen Media and Public Spaces: Diverse Expressions of Citizenship and Dissent*, London & New York: Routledge, 118–135.

Permanent Culture Now (n.d.) 'Introduction to Activism'. Available online: http://www.permanentculturenow.com/what-is-activism/ [last accessed 20 December 2017].

Rizk, P. (2013) 'Interview with Philip Rizk by Shuruq Harb', *ArtTerritories*, 20 May. Available online: http://www.monabaker.org/?p=628 [last accessed 20 December 2017].

Selim, S. (2016) 'Text and Context: Translating in a State of Emergency', in M. Baker (ed.) *Translating Dissent: Voices* from *and* with *the Egyptian Revolution*, London & New York, 78–87.

Shamma, T. (2009) *Translation and the Manipulation of Difference: Arabic Literature in Nineteenth-Century England*, Manchester: St. Jerome.

Tlaxcala (n.d.) 'Tlaxcala's Manifesto'. Available online: http://www.tlaxcala-int.org/manifeste.asp [last accessed 20 December 2017].

Translate for Justice (n.d.) 'Welcome to Translate for Justice'. Available online: https://translateforjustice.com [last accessed 20 December 2017].

Translation and Activism (n.d.) 'Translation, Interpreting and Social Activism'. Available online: http://www.translationactivism.com [last accessed 20 December 2017].

Tymoczko, M. (2000) 'Translation and Political Engagement: Activism, Social Change and the Role of Translation in Geopolitical Shifts', *The Translator* 6(1): 23–47.

Tymoczko, M. (2006) (ed.) *Translation and Activism*, Special issue of *The Massachusetts Review* 47(III).

Tymoczko, M. (2007) *Enlarging Translation, Empowering Translators*, Manchester: Manchester: St. Jerome Publishing.

Tymoczko, M. (2010) (ed.) *Translation, Resistance, Activism*, Amherst & Boston: University of Massachusetts Press.

Yates, L. (2015) 'Rethinking Prefiguration: Alternatives, Micropolitics and Goals in Social Movements', *Social Movement Studies* 14 (1): 1–21.

Zionist Organization of America (n.d.) 'What is the ZOA'. Available online: http://zoa.org/about/ [last accessed 20 December 2017].

Filmography

Forest of Bliss (1986) Robert Gardner. IMDb entry: http://www.imdb.com/title/tt0093040/?ref_=fn_al_tt_1

Night Watch (2004) Timur Bekmambetov. IMDb entry: http://www.imdb.com/title/tt0403358/?ref_=fn_al_tt_2

Slumdog Millionaire (2008) Danny Boyle, Loveleen Tandan. IMDb entry: http://www.imdb.com/title/tt1010048/?ref_=nv_sr_1

29
Audiovisual translator training

Beatriz Cerezo Merchán

Introduction

Audiovisual translation (AVT) training was not incorporated into higher education translator training curricula until just over twenty years ago. Until then, professionals were trained in the workplace, outside educational institutions (Martínez Sierra 2008). This was primarily the case because of ever changing market needs, which required translators to learn new skills with urgency, but also because universities lacked the capacity to offer suitable training to cater for those emerging needs (Díaz Cintas 2008a: 3–4).

It is difficult to put a date on when and where the first courses were taught, but it would be safe to state that teaching in this area dates back to the late 1980s and 1990s. According to Gottlieb (1992: 161), the Université de Lille was the only institution offering courses in dubbing and subtitling in the late 1980s. This was followed by the University of Copenhagen (Københavns Universitet), which began delivering a subtitling course in the academic year 1990–1991. Since then, training in AVT has quickly found its way into university curricula, as a growing number of countries have felt the need to train future audiovisual translators. As part of this boom of audiovisual translation training, the original courses—focusing almost exclusively on inter-lingual subtitling—have become gradually complemented by others dealing with various AVT modes, such as dubbing, voice-over, subtitling for the deaf and hard of hearing (SDH), audio description (AD) for the blind, and video game translation—and even more recent developments such as respeaking.

Although a growing body of literature devoted to different aspects of this dynamically evolving discipline is already available, the teaching and assessment of the different types of audiovisual translation has received limited attention. Indeed, most of the studies published to date have focused on curricular structures, in particular institutions; the didactic potential of intra-lingual and inter-lingual subtitles in the learning of foreign languages; the teaching of subtitling and, to a lesser extent, the teaching of dubbing (Díaz Cintas 2008a: 3).

The consolidation of translation and interpreting as a professional and academic discipline, constant changes in the profession, and the transition towards new educational models that many countries are undergoing (Kim 2012: 106) have brought along renewed concerns over the suitability of current translation training practices. In the field of AVT, this has paved the way for the publication of studies with a more analytical approach to different aspects pertaining to AVT curricular design. These include Chaume (2003a), Santamaria (2003) and Matamala (2006) on the importance of new technologies in AVT training; Bartrina and Espasa (2003, 2005), Martínez Sierra (2008, 2012), and Díaz Cintas (2008b) on training methodologies in AVT; and Mayoral (2001), Moreno (2003), Chaume (2003b), Sponholz (2003), Díaz Cintas *et al.* (2006) and Cerezo Merchán (2012) on a wider range of curricular aspects related to the teaching and learning of AVT.

Audiovisual translators perform a wide range of tasks every day; these include, to name but a few, translating, dealing with technical issues relating to spotting/synchronization, proofreading translations, digitizing and encoding audiovisual material, dealing with other professionals, etc. Courses on any audiovisual translation mode should therefore seek to expose students to this wide array of tasks to differing degrees, depending on the level of specialization and the duration of their programme of study or the availability of specialized software, to mention but only a number of relevant parameters. In order to ensure that trainees in audiovisual translation develop the skills and competences required to gain professional proficiency, it is essential to design specialized curricula around specific learning objectives and competences, consider various teaching and learning approaches, ensure the availability of suitable contents and resources, design effective tasks, and identify reliable assessment methods.

Based on extant literature on translation and AVT training, this chapter will first present relevant pedagogical and methodological approaches to translation training that have influenced the way we understand AVT teaching and learning today. Next, it will draw on well-established curricular design models (Kelly 2005, Hurtado Albir 2015) to address selected key aspects of AVT training, namely audiovisual translator competences, content design, resources, tasks and assessment methods.

Pedagogical and methodological approaches to translation and AVT training

For a long time, trainers assumed that students learned to translate by imitating the teacher's model translation, often without being provided with any guidance on how to produce their translations (Kelly 2010: 389). During the last few decades, however, various pedagogical approaches to translation training have emerged, including the objective-based approach (Delisle 1980), the early profession- and learner-centred approach (Nord 1991), the process-centred approach (Gile 1995), the cognitive and psycholinguistic approaches (Kiraly 1995 and others), the situational approach (Vienne 1994, Gouadec 2003), the task-based approach (Hurtado Albir 1999, González Davies 2003, 2004), the induction-deduction-abduction approach (Robinson 1997, 2003), and the socio-constructive approach (Kiraly 2000, Kelly 2010)—which is currently endorsed by most translator training specialists. Competence-based training has gained significant ground in recent years. This model, which has its foundations in cognitive constructivist and socio-constructivist learning theories, is the logical continuation of objective-based learning and, as its very name signals, revolves around the notion of translation competence (Hurtado Albir 2015: 261).

As for methodological approaches, the main two models covered in the literature are the task- and project-based approaches. Also driven by constructivist principles, these approaches did not garner much consensus in the beginning. While specialists like Hurtado Albir (1999) favoured tasks as the basic organizational unit in the design of pedagogical materials, Kiraly (2000) endorsed the 'publishable translation project' for the same purposes. Over the years, however, González Davies (2004) and Hurtado Albir (2015) have stood up for eclectic approaches in which tasks and projects are combined. These new approaches involve the use of guided tasks, where the teacher's role is still essential at the beginning of the learning process; tasks are then followed by project-based work, where the teacher no longer occupies a central role. Following this approach, Hurtado Albir (2015: 263–264) advocates structuring the curriculum as a series of teaching units, each of which consists of preparatory tasks and a final task/project, informed by the relevant competences and learning objectives, contents, and assessment methods set for the course unit in question.

The small body of literature on audiovisual translation training that is currently available is primarily informed by the competence-based model, as will be elaborated in the next section. In terms of methodological approaches to audiovisual translator training, most specialists follow the task- and project-based approaches. A wide array of tasks and projects to be used in the AVT training classroom are proposed, for example, by Agost *et al.* (1999), Bartrina and Espasa (2003, 2005), Díaz Cintas and Remael (2007), Pereira and Lorenzo (2007), Díaz Cintas (2008b), Chaume (2012), Franco *et al.* (2010), Romero-Fresco (2011) and Martínez Sierra (2012).

The audiovisual translator's competences

According to the competence-based training model, the first step in the curricular design process is to set the objectives that are to be achieved. If we want to train professional audiovisual translators, the logical starting point is to identify the competences that make up the professional profile of translators of audiovisual texts.

The concept of translator competence has been defined as 'the underlying system of knowledge, abilities and attitudes required to be able to translate' (PACTE 2003). Hurtado Albir (1999, 2015), Mayoral (2001), Pym (2003), PACTE (2005), Kelly (2005), Kearns (2006), Göpferich (2009) or Kiraly (2013) have written about this notion, the interplay between competences and their respective constitutive sub-competences, and the development/acquisition of competences in formal educational settings. Specifically, Hurtado Albir's (2015) classification of translator training competences, which represents the first operationalization of PACTE's (2003) translation competence model, includes:

- methodological and strategic competences: applying the methodological principles and strategies required to work through the translation process effectively;
- contrastive competences: differentiating between the two working languages and monitoring any instance of mutual interference;
- extralinguistic competences: mobilizing encyclopaedic, bicultural and thematic knowledge to solve translation problems;
- occupational competences: performing successfully in the translation labour market;
- instrumental competences: managing documentary resources and an array of tools to solve problems;
- translation problem-solving competences: using optimal strategies to solve translation problems in different textual genres.

However, it should be noted that competence-based training does not only take into account specific (or discipline-related) competences, but also other skills required by the wider social context. In this sense, general (or transversal) competences, which apply to all disciplines, also play an essential role. The *Tuning Educational Structures in Europe Project* (González and Wagenaar 2003) identifies three types of general competences:

- instrumental competences, which encompass, among others, analysis and synthesis, information management, organization and planning, decision-making, problem-solving, IT skills;
- interpersonal competences, which include, but are not limited to, (self-)criticism skills, ethical behaviour, interpersonal skills, appreciation of diversity and multiculturalism, capacity for teamwork;
- systematic competences, which involve learning, creativity, working independently or project management, among others.

Various scholars have explored the relevance of this concept to audiovisual translator training, and attempted to gauge how/whether these differ from the (sub)competence(s) that apply in other fields of translation involving primarily the mediation of written texts (Kovačič 1998, James 1998, Klerkx 1998, Carroll 1998, Gambier 2001, Zabalbeascoa 1997, 2000, 2001; Agost *et al.* 1999, Bartrina 2001, Espasa 2001, Izard 2001, Chaume 2003b, Díaz Cintas 2006, 2008a; Matamala 2008, Neves 2008, Granell 2011, Cerezo Merchán 2012). Drawing on Hurtado Albir's (2015) translation competence model, the audiovisual translation competences identified by these scholars can be synthesized under the following headings:

- contrastive competences, which encompass (1) exhaustive knowledge of the target language—spelling, phonetic, morphological, syntactic and lexical dimensions; and (2) mastery of the source language—i.e. excellent written and oral comprehension, knowledge of colloquial varieties, dialects;
- extralinguistic competences, including (1) good knowledge of the cultures involved in the translation process; (2) exhaustive knowledge of the specific characteristics of the target audience; (3) film knowledge; (4) theatre knowledge; (5) familiarity with the language of film and visual semiotics; and (6) familiarity with various features of different audiovisual texts/genres;
- methodological and strategic competences, such as (1) theoretical knowledge of one or several AVT modes; (2) knowledge of software localization; (3) mastery of voicing techniques; (4) mastery of sign language techniques; (5) mastery of techniques to visualize text and image simultaneously; (6) capacity of synthesis—i.e. familiarity with techniques to streamline texts; (7) capacity to use creative language resources; (8) capacity to analyze various genres and reproduce their discursive features (e.g. false orality); (9) mastery of synchronization techniques, use of symbols and time-codes for dubbing and voice-over; and (10) mastery of synchronization and spotting techniques for subtitling;
- instrumental competences involve (1) mastery of AVT software—subtitling, dubbing, audio-description software, etc.; (2) mastery of specific software to digitize, codify and convert audiovisual files; (3) mastery of speech recognition programs; and (4) mastery of strategies to retrieve information and other resources;
- translation problem-solving competences, including (1) knowledge of translation strategies and techniques to translate different audiovisual genres; and (2) capacity to manage AVT projects (developing and organizing team projects).

It should be acknowledged that some of these competences could be listed under more than one of Hurtado Albir's (2015: 262) categories, as they are usually developed in combination with other competences. Also, it is worth noting that some of these competences are common to all forms of audiovisual translation, while others are more central to specific types.

Contents design

As Kelly (2010: 91) states, once the course learning objectives are set and these have been mapped on to the relevant competences, designers should proceed to plan the course content and structure. This involves dividing the course into units and sequencing the course contents.

Given the practical nature of audiovisual translation, the benefits of inductive teaching and learning approaches—in which a brief theoretical introduction at the beginning of the unit gives way to analytical and practical translation tasks, both inside and outside the classroom—are obvious. Indeed, there is widespread consensus that they encourage deeper learning (Díaz Cintas 2008a: 92). However, trainers should not overlook the fact that there will be differences in individual approaches to learning within any group of students—hence the need 'not to adopt one single strategy for all activities, and to adopt a flexible approach allowing different learners to apply their own personal styles' (Kelly 2005: 114). This can be, as proposed by Gentzler (2003: 13), best achieved by setting up an open-structured learning environment where 'theory, descriptive research, practice, and training productively interact with each other'.

Díaz Cintas (2008a: 92) suggests structuring the contents of a subtitling course around the following four dimensions: general considerations, technical considerations, linguistic considerations, and professional considerations. With some minor changes, this might be a valid template to structure the contents for any AVT course, since it allows for the development of the various AVT-specific competences presented above. For example, as part of the courses it offers to companies interested in receiving AVT training, the TRAMA research group at Universitat Jaume I (Spain) suggests a range of contents that can then be structured into units according to specific training needs and their associated objectives and tasks. Contents are suggested for different AVT modes:

- dubbing: general considerations on dubbing, the dubbing process, text segmentation (takes), symbols, types of synchronization, orality, software and tools and professional aspects;
- voice-over: general considerations on voice-over, text segmentation (takes), symbols, types of synchronization, orality, vulnerable translation, audiovisual genres characteristics, software and tools and professional aspects;
- subtitling: general considerations on subtitling, the process of subtitling, types of subtitles, spotting and speed of subtitles, subtitle formatting and segmentation, text reduction: strategies to synthesize information, ortho-typographic conventions, subtitling with templates, freeware and professional aspects;
- audio description (AD): general considerations on AD, visually impaired viewers, relevant legislation and industry standards, description of images, description of sounds, description of on-screen text, audio introduction, AD styles, AD scripts, and professional aspects;
- subtitling for the deaf and the hard of hearing (SDH): general considerations on SDH, hearing impaired viewers, relevant legislation and industry standards, subtitle formatting and positioning, speed of subtitles, linguistic code, identification

of characters, paralinguistic code (emotions and sounds), sound effects, music and songs, freeware, and professional aspects;
- video games: introduction to video game localization, video game market and industry, the process of video game localization, localization of video game components, translation of cinematic and audio elements, translation of on-screen text and textual graphics, web and multimedia localization, accessibility and video games, quality control assurance, and use of software.

Resources

Identifying and acquiring material, technical or human resources is essential to run any training programme (Kelly, 2010: 91). Due to length restrictions on this paper, only those resources relating to software and audiovisual material will be considered here:

- As freeware subtitling software (e.g. JACOsub, Aegisub or Subtitle Workshop) has become more ubiquitous, universities no longer need to buy expensive subtitling applications. An alternative to freeware involves using demo or low-cost versions of professional software (e.g. FAB, Spot or WinCAPS) that is made available to academic institutions at lower prices. Depending on the level of specialization of the course, the former option might suffice, as most applications follow the same principles (Kelly 2005: 75).
- As for dubbing (and, more widely, voice-over and AD), securing the relevant technical equipment and software is much more difficult (Chaume 2012: 43). Universities are normally reluctant to invest large sums of money in fully equipped dubbing booths, for example. Freeware applications such as Windows Movie Maker allow students to (1) gain a full understanding of the dubbing process by cancelling out the original soundtrack and recording their own translations on a new soundtrack; and (2) establish whether their dubbed dialogue is completely synchronized with and matches the original actors' mouth movements. The lack of low cost applications to systematize dubbing tasks has prompted some institutions to develop their own software. For instance, two programs called Dubbing and Dubbing2, based on Windows Movie Maker, have been developed at Universitat de Vic (Spain). Likewise, the research group TRAMA (Universitat Jaume I, Spain) has developed a template for Microsoft Word that runs with macros and allows formatting an audiovisual text in takes (Cerezo Merchán *et al.* 2016).
- As far as video game localization is concerned, the availability of dedicated software is a minor problem, as most translators work with text files, tables and spreadsheets (using, for instance, Microsoft Office or OpenOffice tools), commercial translation memories, such as SDL Trados, or free translation memories, such as Omega T.

In addition to programs that are of particular relevance to specific AVT modes, it is also necessary to make use of software applications that enable more general tasks, such as digitizing or encoding audiovisual material, merging videos and subtitle/voice files, or converting video formats (Cerezo Merchán 2012: 149).

In terms of the materials used in AVT training, specialists prioritize the use of real materials that expose students to the translation problems that they will deal with when they enter the job market (Chaume 2003b: 296). Although it has been traditionally difficult to access source language audiovisual texts (i.e. scripts, films, cartoons, series, documentaries, etc.), the advent of digitization and growing ubiquity of the Internet has made this aspect of the training process easier to manage. Trainers are now often able to use TV box sets equipped with hard drives to record programmes from terrestrial and digital TV channels, as well as software to copy and digitize DVD contents.

Some of the most common materials used in audiovisual translation training include audiovisual programmes, scripts and dialogue lists, templates, translations made for a different AVT mode (that can be used, for example, to convert dubbed dialogue into subtitles) or a different medium (subtitles for the cinema to be adapted to the requirements of the DVD format), localization kits, help tutorials, glossaries, and translation memories, to name but a few (Cerezo Merchán 2012: 151). As for audiovisual genres, some of the most commonly translated in the industry and, therefore, also in AVT training settings are movies, TV series, cartoons and documentaries (Chaume 2003b: 297).

Ensuring a sound pedagogical progression when sequencing materials is paramount. For instance, scripts, dialogue lists or templates are normally used at the beginning of the training process. Subsequent, more demanding tasks can be carried out without these materials, so that students also have to put in practice their aural comprehension skills. Progression is also important in selecting the audiovisual genres to be used at any given point. AVT courses are not structured in terms of the topic or the field to which the chosen texts belong; in other words, such courses do not necessarily move from thematically simpler to more complex texts, as is often the case in scientific or legal translation. Instead, trainers make sequencing decisions on the basis of the semiotic make-up of the genres at stake (Chaume 2003b: 296). In the case of dubbing, Chaume (2003b: 297–298) proposes the following progression based on the semiotic make-up of the texts: documentaries, cartoons, TV series and movies. In the same vein, Martínez Sierra (2012: 141) proposes the sequencing of learning materials in the dubbing process featured in Table 29.1.

Tasks

As outlined above, AVT specialists have embraced task- and project-based approaches and presented different activities that can be carried out as part of a course encompassing one or more AVT modes. Generally, these tend to be structured around four different phases, according to the type and level of competence to be acquired and developed by students.

Table 29.1 Suggested sequencing of course materials in dubbing courses (Martínez Sierra 2012: 141).

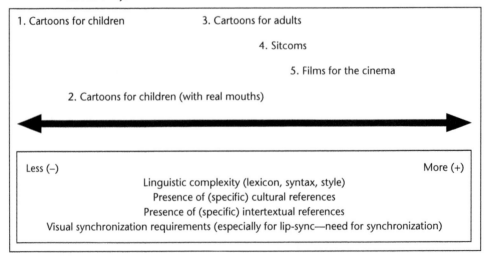

Phase 1: Introduction to AVT and/or different AVT modes

A general starting point for any AVT course is to help students to develop their declarative knowledge about AVT and/or different AVT modes, as well as some field-specific knowledge, so that they can situate AVT within translation studies; compare different AVT modes; look into the distinctive features, requirements and historical aspects of different AVT modes; focus on the semiotics of audiovisual texts and the priorities and constraints that apply in audiovisual translation, etc. Methodological and strategic competences, together with extralinguistic competences, are therefore crucial at this stage. Typical tasks to practise these competences include reading support texts, organizing debates, analyzing parallel source and target audiovisual texts, and completing questionnaires.

As examples of tasks used to develop these competences in the context of a subtitling course, Díaz Cintas (2008a: 93) cites the following: reading introductory papers or watching introductory videos on subtitling, analyzing different audiovisual products (series, cartoons, news, documentaries, etc.), exploring how a given product has been subtitled for different media (TV, DVD, cinema), and comparing different kinds of subtitles (by fans or professionals, for inter-lingual vs. deaf and hard of hearing audiences).

Phase 2: Pre-translation practice in AVT

During the second phase of any AVT course, students continue to develop their declarative knowledge on the linguistic and technical constraints and conventions at play in each AVT mode. This declarative knowledge should always be developed in combination with procedural knowledge. Indeed, students should be gradually exposed to pre-translation and translation tasks requiring the deployment of basic translation and methodological strategies. Contrastive, instrumental, methodological and strategic competences are activated at this stage through (1) tasks involving the acquisition of various types of knowledge—as illustrated in the previous section; (2) preparatory activities for the translation of texts; and (3) translations. Preparatory tasks may involve the analysis of source texts made up of one or several semiotic codes; reflecting on translation commissions; carrying out gist/extended translations; the student's familiarization with relevant translation software applications; conducting documentary and terminological searches; carrying out comparative translation analyses to identify correct solutions and errors; and revising translations. Translation tasks, sequenced along a continuum of growing difficulty, should aim to simulate professional working conditions.

Chaume (2012: 64–65; 79–80) proposes a number of pre-translation tasks in dubbing course units. These include developing students' familiarity with the use of conventions and symbols that signal various forms of dubbing synchrony; the translation of dialogue and its segmentation into takes that reflect the underpinning audiovisual narrative; inserting dubbing symbols within the translated dialogue; and recording translated dialogue using freeware applications to monitor the degree of lip-synchronization with the original conversation that students have managed to achieve.

For his part, Díaz Cintas (2008a) proposes a range of pre-translation tasks aiming to develop students' familiarity with basic methodological principles and strategies in the context of a subtitling course. These include improving the punctuation of a set of extant subtitles; correcting badly segmented subtitles; condensing a text by a set percentage or down to a certain number of words or lines; becoming acquainted with subtitled conventions stipulated by different companies; timing and subtitling clips with freeware applications; and writing reflective reports on subtitles carried out by fellow students.

Some interesting examples of pre-translation tasks are those focusing on the analysis of one or several of the semiotic codes deployed in audiovisual texts. According to Neves (2008: 184), watching clips without sound, or listening to dialogue without viewing the film should raise awareness of the importance of sound in SDH courses. Snyder (2008: 192), on the other hand, suggests listening to the soundtrack of a scene (audio only) to gauge the importance of the image in the AD process.

Once the students have used their methodological and strategic competences to address basic technical, linguistic and semiotic difficulties, the focus might be moved on to different translation problems derived from the use of complex terminology, the presence of culture-specific references or language variation (slang, accents or multilingualism), the centrality of humour, or the interplay between the dialogue and the songs featured in the soundtrack. Different types of scenes and genres can be used to tackle these problems separately at this preparatory stage, before several of them are presented as part of the same text. Matamala (2008: 126), for example, proposes tasks to solve the terminological difficulties that typically arise in voice-over projects involving specialized documentaries. Also in the context of voice-over, Matamala (2008: 125) suggests translating various short interviews and documentaries featuring a wide variety of accents and speeds.

Phase 3: AVT projects

Translation problem-solving competences, which feature prominently in this stage, are often developed by undertaking extended projects that involve the translation of texts pertaining to various audiovisual genres—normally accompanied by critical or reflective translation reports. According to Neves (2008: 187), projects constitute a stimulating educational strategy that brings together trainees, teachers/researchers, professionals, as well as translation providers and recipients. As far as SDH training is concerned, project work represents a unique opportunity to interact with the d/Deaf, test experimental solutions and secure feedback to improve current practices.

Phase 4: The profession

Although professional considerations can be explored at the beginning of the training process, before carrying out any practical translation tasks, students are more likely to assimilate them better once they have carried out practical work on one or various modes of AVT (Díaz Cintas 2008a: 101). Occupational competences are developed at this point, and students acquire declarative knowledge about the audiovisual translators' working environment, including the project workflow, the professionals involved in it, payment rates, requirements for professional association membership, and copyright restrictions. Chaume (2012: 44–45) suggests the following tasks to develop occupational competences in the context of a dubbing course: identifying dubbing companies and prospective employers, learning how to tailor one's CV and covering letter for the dubbing industry, providing an estimate for a hypothetical commission, or even gauging the volume of foreign TV content that a given channel has to translate.

Assessment methods

The assessment of any teaching and learning process should be aligned with its intended outcomes (Biggs 2003: 99). In competence-based learning approaches, assessment is a complex activity that encompasses a wide variety of approaches and instruments, beyond the traditional examinations in which students translate a text and the translation is graded (Kelly 2010: 92). Assessment can be, therefore, understood in a broad sense, given that tasks alone allow trainers to gather information on the students' learning process and acquisition of competences; identify students' needs; and improve their teaching competence (Galán-Mañas and Hurtado Albir 2015: 64).

Assessment proposals tailored for audiovisual translation training that are not restricted to the evaluation of translations are scarce. Kajzer-Wietrzny and Tymczyńska (2015) and Granell (2011), writing about the assessment of subtitling, voice-over, AD and video game localization courses, concur with Kelly (2010) that the development of translation competence is best evaluated through formative assessment; they also agree that summative assessment should be based on the students' performance in a number of projects carried out throughout a given course. However, they also acknowledge that curricular and institutional constraints often make it impossible to do without final examinations. In this context, it is therefore necessary 'to think about several assessment itineraries that fit into different institutional scenarios (i.e. formative assessment such as essay/test-based final examination, task-based continuous assessment, individual/group work, etc.)' (Granell 2011: 199).

As far as assessment criteria are concerned, Díaz Cintas (2001) and Kruger (2008) have published proposals for the assessment of subtitles. Although there are some differences between these models, they all provide sets of criteria based on the equally weighed assessment of linguistic and technical aspects. Following Brondeel (1994: 29), Díaz Cintas (2001: 41) distinguishes three assessment dimensions: (1) the informative dimension, pertaining to the completeness of information transfer, omission of information, or impact of such omissions, among other issues; (2) the semantic dimension, regarding the transfer of meaning and source text nuances; and (3) the communicative dimension, concerning the shift from an oral to a written medium. He also suggests incorporating an ortho-typographic dimension and a syntactic dimension—focusing on the preservation of coherence between the constitutive lines of a single subtitle and across individual subtitles. For his part, Kruger (2008: 85) also brings into the equation the assessment of translation and/or editing skills, subtitle segmentation, grammar, spelling and punctuation. As far as the technical parameters are concerned, Díaz Cintas (2001: 41) suggests assessing time coding, synchronization, formatting and line breaks, while Kruger (2008: 85) proposes cueing (duration and rhythm) and subtitle division.

Kajzer-Wietrzny and Tymczyńska (2015) examine various sets of market standards reported in the literature and proceed to develop detailed evaluation criteria for the grading of voice-over, subtitling and AD postgraduate exams in their institution. Under the heading of 'information transfer and language', they propose criteria to assess the choice of (1) content and translation strategies—i.e. selection of relevant information and skilful application of translation techniques in voice-over; careful observation and selection of relevant information, effective sequencing of information, appropriate inter-semiotic transfer strategies in audio description; selection of relevant information and skilful application of translation strategies in subtitling; and (2) linguistic means of expression—such as natural, concise and dynamic sentences; grammatical, semantic and pragmatic correctness, etc. in voice-over and subtitling; and precise, neutral and objective language, appropriate register, etc. in audio description. Under the heading of 'technical aspects', they include (1) formatting—i.e. correct spelling and punctuation, avoidance of consonant clusters, unpleasant sounds, unintended rhymes, transparent layout with clear directions for voice talent and time codes in voice-over and audio description; appropriate use of italics and capitalization, line breaks and number of lines and characters per line, in subtitling; and (2) synchronization—such as reading out with proper synchronization, intonation, and pronunciation when recording translations for voice-over and audio description; and temporal synchrony with characters' utterances, and appropriate duration audio adjusted to reading speed in subtitling.

Although they try to go beyond the evaluation of translation errors, and also gauge the students' attainment and deployment of specific translation competences, these assessment models illustrate what Waddington (2000: 233) calls 'analytical translation assessment methods', and hence differ from 'holistic translation assessment methods'. Studies such as Galán-Mañas and Hurtado Albir (2015) on assessment methods and instruments in general translator training courses, or De Higes Andino and Cerezo Merchán (in press) on assessment instruments in SDH training represent an application of this holistic method, as they link assessment tasks and competences. These authors advocate the use of a wide variety of instruments and tasks—including texts to translate, questionnaires, reflective diaries, reports, translation process recordings, student portfolio, and rubrics—to assess the learning process and the specific competences developed throughout the process. There is a lack of holistic studies proposing indicators and performance levels to assess audiovisual translation competences and linking them to translation assessment tasks, so the development of this strand of research in audiovisual translator training would be greatly beneficial.

Conclusions

This chapter has delivered an overview of recent literature on AVT training, surveyed current pedagogical and methodological approaches in this field of translational practice, and critiqued various aspects that lie at the heart of curricular design processes, such as competences, contents, resources, tasks and assessment. The importance of designing curricula informed by relevant competence-based models has been highlighted, and the benefits of translation task- and project-based approaches that allow for the integrated development of general and specific competences have been explored in some depth.

Further reading

Cerezo Merchán, B. (2012) 'La didáctica de la traducción audiovisual en España: Un estudio de caso empírico-descriptivo', Unpublished Doctoral Thesis, Universitat Jaume I, Castellón de la Plana. Available online: http://www.tesisenred.net/handle/10803/83363 [last access 20 December 2017] | *This doctoral thesis, informed by academic and professional insights on AVT in Spain, focuses on different curricular design parameters (objectives, competences, students' and teachers' profiles, contents, activities, resources, etc.) and makes suggestions to improve AVT training at university level.*

Chaume, F. (2003b) 'Teaching Audiovisual Translation: Some Methodological Proposals', in L. Pérez-González (ed.) *Speaking in Tongues: Language across Contexts and Users*, Universitat de València: Publicacions de la Universitat de València, 271–302 | *This paper provides a comprehensive overview of various aspects of curricular design in audiovisual translation training. Through a review of existing literature and his own experience, Chaume offers valuable ideas for the design and teaching of AVT courses.*

Díaz Cintas, J. (ed.) (2008) *The Didactics of Audiovisual Translation*, Amsterdam & Philadelphia: John Benjamins. *This collection is regarded as the first volume to focus exclusively on AVT training. It aims to offer AVT trainers a set of tools, ideas and activities for different AVT modes.*

Hurtado Albir, A. (2015) 'The Acquisition of Translation Competence. Competences, Tasks, and Assessment in Translator Training', *Meta* 60(2): 256–280 | *This article addresses key aspects of competence-based translator training. It features examples of translator training courses enabling the development and acquisition of competences, and highlights the need for new assessment methods under this training framework.*

Kelly, D. (2005) *A Handbook for Translator Trainers, A Guide to Reflective Practice*, Manchester: St. Jerome | *This handbook provides a step-by-step approach to curricular design for translator training courses. It provides practical guidance on how to identify learning objectives, outcomes and competences, develop course contents, design and sequence activities, and assessment.*

Related topics

30 Audiovisual translation in language teaching and learning
32 Technologization of audiovisual translation

References

Agost, R., F. Chaume and A. Hurtado Albir (1999) 'La traducción audiovisual', in A. Hurtado Albir (ed.) *Enseñar a traducir*, Madrid: Edelsa, 182–195.

Bartrina, F. (2001) 'La previsió del procés d'ajust com a estrategia de traducció per a l'ensenyament del doblatge', in R. Agost and F. Chaume (eds) *La traducción en los medios audiovisuales*, Castellón de la Plana: Publicacions de la Universitat Jaume I, 65–71.

Bartrina, F. and E. Espasa (2003) 'Traducción de textos audiovisuales', in M. González Davies (ed.) *Secuencias. Tareas para el aprendizaje interactivo de la traducción especializada*, Barcelona: Octaedro, 19–38.

Bartrina, F. and E. Espasa (2005) 'Audiovisual Translation', in M. Tennent (ed.) *Training for the New Millennium*, Amsterdam & Philadelphia: John Benjamins, 83–100.

Biggs, J. (2003) *Teaching for Quality Learning at University. What the Student Does*, Maidenhead: Open University Press.

Brondeel, H. (1994) 'Teaching Subtitling Routines', *Meta* 39(1): 26–33.

Carroll, M. (1998) 'Subtitler Training: Continuing Training for Translators', in Y. Gambier (ed.) *Translating for the Media*, Turku: University of Turku, 265–266.

Cerezo Merchán, B. (2012) *La didáctica de la traducción audiovisual en España: Un estudio de caso empírico-descriptivo*, Unpublished Doctoral Thesis, Universitat Jaume I, Castellón de la Plana. Available online: http://www.tesisenred.net/handle/10803/83363 [last access 20 December 2017].

Cerezo Merchán, B., X. Granell, J. L. Martí Ferriol, J. J. Martínez Sierra, A. Marzà, G. Torralba Miralles and F. Chaume (eds) (2016) *La traducción para doblaje en España: Mapa de convenciones*, Castellón de la Plana: Colección TRAMA, Servei de publicacions de la Universitat Jaume I.

Chaume, F. (2003a) 'Nuevas tecnologías y documentación en la enseñanza de la traducción audiovisual', in *VII Jornades de traducció a Vic. Interfícies: Apropant la pedagogia de la traducció a les llengües estrangeres*, Vic: Universitat de Vic.

Chaume, F. (2003b) 'Teaching Audiovisual Translation: Some Methodological Proposals', in L. Pérez-González (ed.) *Speaking in Tongues: Language across Contexts and Users*, Universitat de València: Publicacions de la Universitat de València, 271–302.

Chaume, F. (2012) *Audiovisual Translation: Dubbing*, Manchester: St Jerome.

De Higes Andino, I. and B. Cerezo Merchán (in press) 'Using Evaluation Criteria and Rubrics as Learning Tools in Subtitling for the D/deaf and the Hard of Hearing', in *The Interpreter and Translator Trainer*, special issue on *New Perspectives in Assessment in Translator Training* 12(1).

Delisle, J. (1980) *L'Analyse du discours comme méthode de traduction: Initiation à la traduction française de textes pragmatiques anglais: Théorie et pratique*, Ottawa: Éditions de l'Université d'Ottawa.

Díaz Cintas, J. (2001) 'Teaching Subtitling at University', in S. Cunico (ed.) *Training Translators and Interpreters in the New Millennium*, Portsmouth: University of Portsmouth, 29–44.

Díaz Cintas, J. (2006) *Competencias profesionales del subtitulador y el audiodescriptor*. Getafe: CESyA. Available online: http://www.cesya.es/sites/default/files/documentos/informe_formacion.pdf [last access 20 December 2017].

Díaz Cintas, J. (2008a) 'Teaching and Learning to Subtitle in an Academic Environment', in J. Díaz Cintas (ed.) *The Didactics of Audiovisual Translation*, Amsterdam & Philadelphia: John Benjamins, 89–103.

Díaz Cintas, J. (ed.) (2008b) *The Didactics of Audiovisual Translation*, Amsterdam & Philadelphia: John Benjamins.

Díaz Cintas, J. and A. Remael (2007) *Audiovisual Translation: Subtitling*, Manchester, St. Jerome.

Díaz Cintas, J., J. Mas López and P. Orero (2006) 'Reflexiones en torno a la enseñanza de la traducción audiovisual en España. Propuestas de futuro', in N. A. Perdu Honeyman, M. A. García Peinado, F. J. García Marcos and E. Ortega Arjonilla (coord.) *Inmigración, cultura y traducción: reflexiones interdisciplinares*, Almería: Universidad de Almería, 560–566.

Espasa, E. (2001) 'La traducció per al teatre i per al doblatge a l'aula: Un laboratori de proves', in R. Agost and F. Chaume (eds) *La traducción en los medios audiovisuales*, Castellón de la Plana: Publicacions de la Universitat Jaume I, 57–64.

Franco, E., A. Matamala and P. Orero (2010) *Voice-over Translation: An Overview*, Bern: Peter Lang.

Galán Mañas, A. and A. Hurtado Albir (2015) 'Competence Assessment Procedures in Translator Training', *The Interpreter and Translator Trainer* 9(1): 63–82.

Gambier, Y. (2001) 'Les traducteurs face aux écrans: Une élite d'experts', in R. Agost and F. Chaume (eds) *La traducción en los medios audiovisuales*, Castelló de la Plana: Publicacions de la Universitat Jaume I, 91–114.

Gentzler, E. (2003) 'Interdisciplinary Connections', *Perspectives: Studies in Translatalogy* 11(1): 11–14.

Gile, D. (1995) *Basic Concepts and Models for Interpreter and Translator Training*, Amsterdam & Philadelphia: John Benjamins.

González, J. and R. Wagenaar (eds) (2003) *Tuning Educational Structures in Europe. Final Report. Phase one*, Bilbao: Universidad de Deusto.

González Davies, M. (ed.) (2003) *Secuencias. Tareas para el aprendizaje interactivo de la traducción especializada*, Barcelona: Octaedro.

González Davies, M. (2004) *Multiple Voices in the Translation Classroom: Activities, Tasks and Projects*, Amsterdam & Philadelphia: John Benjamins.

Göpferich, S. (2009) 'Towards a Model of Translation Competence and its Acquisition: The Longitudinal Study TransComp', in S. Göpferich, A. L. Jakobsen and I. M. Mees (eds) *Behind the Mind: Methods, Models and Results in Translation Process Research*, Copenhagen: Samfundslitteratur, 12–38.

Gottlieb, H. (1992) 'Subtitling—A New University Discipline', in C. Dollerup and A. Loddegaard (eds) *Teaching Translation and Interpreting*, Amsterdam & Philadelphia: John Benjamins, 161–170.

Gouadec, D. (2003) 'Notes on Translator Training (Replies to a Questionnaire)', in A. Pym (ed.) *Innovation and E-Learning in Translator Training*, Tarragona: Universitat Rovira i Virgili, 11–19.

Granell, X. (2011) 'Teaching Video Game Localisation in Audiovisual Translation Courses at University', *JoSTrans: The Journal of Specialised Translation* 16. Available online: http://www.jostrans.org/issue16/art_granell.pdf [last access 20 December 2017].

Hurtado Albir, A. (1999) *Enseñar a traducir: Metodología en la formación de traductores e intérpretes*, Madrid: Edelsa.

Hurtado Albir, A. (2015) 'The Acquisition of Translation Competence. Competences, Tasks, and Assessment in Translator Training', *Meta* 60(2): 256–280.

Izard, N. (2001) 'L'ensenyament de la traducció audiovisual en el marc de la formació de traductors', in R. Agost and F. Chaume (eds) *La traducción en los medios audiovisuales*, Castelló de la Plana: Publicacions de la Universitat Jaume I, 73–76.

James, H. (1998) 'Screen Translation Training and European Co-operation', in Y. Gambier (ed.) *Translating for the Media*, Turku: University of Turku, 243–258.

Kajzer-Wietrzny, M. and M. Tymczyńska (2015) 'Devising a Systematic Approach to Examination Marking Criteria for Audio Visual Translation: A Case Study from Poland', *The Interpreter and Translator Trainer* 9(3): 342–355.

Kearns, J. (2006) *Curriculum Renewal in Translator Training: Vocational Challenges in Academic Environments with Reference to Needs and Situation Analysis and Skills Transferability from the Contemporary Experience of Polish Translator Training Culture*, Unpublished Doctoral Thesis, Dublin City University.

Kelly, D. (2005) *A Handbook for Translator Trainers. A Guide to Reflective Practice*, Manchester: St. Jerome.

Kelly, D. (2010) 'Curriculum', in Y. Gambier and L. van Doorslaer (eds) *Handbook of Translation Studies*, Amsterdam & Philadelphia: John Benjamins, 87–93.

Kim, M. (2012) 'Research on Translator and Interpreter Education', in C. Millán and F. Bartrina (eds) *Routledge Handbook of Translation Studies*, London & New York: Routledge, 102–116.

Kiraly, D. (1995) *Pathways to Translation: Pedagogy and Process*, Kent, Ohio: Kent State University Press.

Kiraly, D. (2000) *A Social Constructivist Approach to Translator Education: Empowerment from Theory to Practice*, Manchester: St. Jerome.

Kiraly, D. (2013) 'Towards A View of Translator Competence as an Emergent Phenomenon: Thinking Outside the Box(es) in Translator Education', in D. Kiraly, S. Hansen-Schirra and K. Maksymski (eds) *New Prospects and Perspectives of Educating Language Mediators*, Tübingen: Narr.

Klerkx, J. (1998) 'The Place of Subtitling in a Translator Training Course', in Y. Gambier (ed.) *Translating for the Media*, Turku: University of Turku, 259–264.

Kovačič, I. (1998) 'Language in the Media: A New Challenge for Translator Trainers', in Y. Gambier (ed.) *Translating for the Media*, Turku: University of Turku, 123–130.

Kruger, J. L. (2008) 'Subtitler Training as Part of a General Training Programme in the Language Professions', in J. Díaz Cintas (ed.) *The Didactics of Audiovisual Translation*, Amsterdam & Philadelphia: John Benjamins, 71–88.

Martínez Sierra, J. J. (2008) 'Hacia una enseñanza más completa de la traducción audiovisual', *Tonos: Revista electrónica de estudios filológicos*, 16(1). Available online: http://www.um.es/tonosdigital/znum16/secciones/estudios-11-Tradaudiovisual.htm [last access 20 December 2017].

Martínez Sierra, J. J. (2012) *Introducción a la traducción audiovisual*, Murcia: Editum.

Matamala, A. (2006) 'Les noves tecnologies en l'ensenyament de la traducció audiovisual', *X Jornades de Traducció i Interpretació a Vic: Tecnologies a l'Abast*, Vic: Universitat de Vic.

Matamala, A. (2008) 'Teaching Voice-over: A Practical Approach', in J. Díaz Cintas (ed.) *The Didactics of Audiovisual Translation*, Amsterdam & Philadelphia: John Benjamins, 115–128.

Mayoral, R. (2001) 'Campos de estudio y trabajo en traducción audiovisual', in M. Duro (ed.) *La traducción para el doblaje y la subtitulación*, Madrid: Cátedra, 19–45.

Moreno, L. (2003) *La traducción audiovisual en España: estado de la cuestión*, Unpublished Dissertation, Universidad de Granada.

Neves, J. (2008) 'Training in Subtitling for the d/Deaf and the Hard-of-hearing', in J. Díaz Cintas (ed.) *The Didactics of Audiovisual Translation*, Amsterdam & Philadelphia: John Benjamins, 171–189.

Nord, C. (1991) *Text Analysis in Translation: Theory, Methodology, and Didactic Application of a Model for Translation-Oriented Text Analysis*, trans. by C. Nord and P. Sparrow, Amsterdam: Rodopi. Translation from German into English of Nord, C. (1988) *Textanalyse und Übersetzen*, Heidelberg: Gross.

PACTE (2003) 'Building a Translation Competence model', in F. Alves (ed.) *Triangulating Translation: Perspectives in Process Oriented Research*, Amsterdam & Philadelphia: John Benjamins, 43–66.

PACTE (2005) 'Investigating Translation Competence: Conceptual and Methodological Issues', *Meta* 50(2): 609–619.

Pereira, A. and L. Lorenzo (2007) 'Teaching Proposals for the Unit "Subtitling for the Deaf and Hard of Hearing" within the Subject Audiovisual Translation (English>Spanish)', *Translation Watch Quarterly* 3(2): 26–36.
Pym, A. (2003) 'Redefining Translation Competence in an Electronic Age: in Defense of a Minimalist Approach', *Meta* 48(4): 481–497. Available online: https://www.erudit.org/revue/meta/2003/v48/n4/008533ar.pdf [last access 20 December 2017].
Robinson, D. (1997) *Becoming a Translator. An Accelerated Course*, London: Routledge.
Robinson, D. (2003) *Becoming a Translator: An Introduction to the Theory and Practice of Translation*, London: Routledge.
Romero-Fresco, P. (2011) *Subtitling Through Speech Recognition: Respeaking*, Manchester: St Jerome.
Santamaria, L. (2003) 'Les TIC i la didàctica de la traducció audiovisual', *VII Jornades de traducció a Vic. Interfícies: Apropant la pedagogia de la traducció a les llengües estrangeres*, Vic: Universitat de Vic.
Snyder, J. (2008) 'Audio Description. The Visual made Verbal', in J. Díaz Cintas (ed.) *The Didactics of Audiovisual Translation*, Amsterdam & Philadelphia: John Benjamins, 191–198.
Sponholz, C. (2003) *Teaching Audiovisual Translation. Theoretical Aspects, Market Requirements, University Training and Curriculum Development*, Unpublished Dissertation, Johannes Gutenberg-Universität Mainz. Available online: http://docplayer.net/6872781-Teaching-audiovisual-translation-theoretical-aspects-market-requirements-university-training-and-curriculum-development.html [last access 20 December 2017].
Vienne, J. (1994) 'Towards a Pedagogy of Translation in Situation', *Perspectives* 2(1): 51–59.
Waddington, C. (2000) *Estudio comparativo de diferentes métodos de evaluación de traducción general*, Madrid: Universidad Pontificia de Comillas.
Zabalbeascoa, P. (1997) 'La didáctica de la traducción: Desarrollo de la competencia traductora', in A. Gil de Carrasco and L. Hickey (eds) *Aproximaciones a la traducción*, Madrid: Instituto Cervantes. Available online: http://cvc.cervantes.es/lengua/aproximaciones/zabalbeascoa.htm [last access 20 December 2017].
Zabalbeascoa, P. (2000) 'From Techniques to Types of Solutions', in A. Beeby, D. Ensinger and M. Presas (eds) *Investigating Translation*, Amsterdam & Philadelphia: John Benjamins, 117–127.
Zabalbeascoa, P. (2001) 'La traducción de textos audiovisuales y la investigación traductológica', in R. Agost and F. Chaume (eds) *La traducción en los medios audiovisuales*, Castelló de la Plana: Publicacions de la Universitat Jaume I, 49–56.

30
Audiovisual translation in language teaching and learning

Laura Incalcaterra McLoughlin

Introduction

This chapter explores the use of Audiovisual Translation (AVT) in the field of language teaching and learning, focusing particularly on classroom and teacher-mediated environments where AVT tasks are performed by learners. It begins with a historical overview of the use of AVT in the language classroom and discusses the most relevant and recent contributions in this area, highlighting key research methods and scholarly research themes. It further discusses how technological developments and the availability of free resources are impacting on this area of research and concludes with indications for future directions and suggestions for further debate.

A history of the area

AVT has been used extensively in language teaching and learning ever since technology first enabled the projection of audiovisual material in combination with some form of translation, usually intra- and interlingual subtitles, and dubbing. Intralingual (or bimodal) subtitles are in the same language as that spoken on screen; interlingual ones, on the other hand, are presented in a language different from that spoken on screen and can be standard—i.e. audio in one's foreign language (L2) and written text in the mother tongue (L1) written text)—or reversed—L1 audio and L2 written text. Traditionally, especially in the earlier days, AVT was provided in a ready-made format to learners: the standard or reversed subtitled version of an audiovisual text was shown and complemented with a number of additional activities. More recently, however, learners have been involved in the AVT process itself, performing tasks such as subtitling, dubbing, and adding audio description (AD) or voice narration to video clips.

Subtitled material in language learning

Anecdotal evidence, empirical studies and scientific research on the impact of subtitled material on language learners have flagged up its beneficial effects not only on receptive skills and cultural awareness (Vanderplank 1988, Price 1983, Garza 1991, Winke *et al.* 2010, Abdolmanafi Rokni and Jannati Ataee 2014), but also on speaking skills (Borrás and Lafayette 1994) and learning strategies in general (Caimi and Mariotti 2015). Studies have also shown the effectiveness of subtitled videos and programmes in teaching and learning national languages, especially in countries with several indigenous languages, like Cameroon, South Africa or India, to name but a few, where subtitles have been linked with and advocated for the promotion of not just bilingualism but also multilingualism (Kothari *et al.* 2004, Kruger *et al.* 2007, Ayonghe 2009).

In an article published in 1988, describing one of the first studies on the effects of exposure to intralingual teletext subtitles, Vanderplank reported that initial reactions to the deployment of this new approach were not particularly supportive. Indeed, subtitles in language learning were seen as distracting and hampering the acquisition process, and it was felt that they could 'create a form of text dependency and lead to laziness' (1988: 272). Vanderplank's study however, showed otherwise: fifteen European exchange students of English as Foreign Language (EFL) who watched English language BBC programmes with teletext subtitles reported better understanding of fast speech and unfamiliar or regional accents, and feedback activities pointed to a high level of language retention and recall. At the same time, and in line with several subsequent studies, this research found that intralingual subtitles benefit learners with higher levels of language proficiency, rather than beginners and lower intermediate students. However, other variables also need to be considered in this respect, such as the length of the video, the occasional or systematic exposure to subtitles and, of course, the lexical and syntactical complexity of the text. Indeed, Talaván (2011) suggests that systematic exposure to short subtitled clips improves listening comprehension skills even among beginners.

Some doubts have been voiced as to whether improved comprehension of video material with intralingual subtitles is really due to good listening, rather than to good reading. Bird and Williams (2002) conducted two comprehensive experiments to verify the positive effects of this type of AVT on language learners. Although they found that the combination of auditory and visual (written) information seems to be beneficial only when there is ambiguity in the auditory input, they suggest that 'orthographic information can, under certain circumstances, have a significant facilitatory impact on long-term implicit and explicit learning of spoken word forms' (*ibid*.: 19).

Further concerns relate to the negative consequences of the redundancy effect studied under Cognitive Load Theory. Advocates of the use of what are commonly referred to as 'multimodal texts' (texts which convey information through different channels: auditory, visual, verbal) in language teaching often refer to the positive impact on cognition (and consequently on learning) of the combined delivery of verbal and visual information, as hypothesized in Dual Coding Theory—which will be discussed further in the next session. Conversely, Cognitive Load Theory maintains that the redundancy effect obtained when information is presented simultaneously through more than one channel increases the cognitive load, and therefore redundancy does not facilitate comprehension or learning. Indeed, studies comparing the impact of inter- and intralingual subtitles found that bimodal L2 subtitles (audio in L2 and subtitles in L2) were the least beneficial for lower levels of fluency, arguably because the cognitive load imposed on the learners hampered comprehension (Lambert and Holobow 1984). More recently, Kruger (2013) carried out an experiment with 21 students of North-West University in South Africa, delivering a 30-minute recorded lecture in Economics with intralingual subtitles. In order to establish whether presentation speed has an impact on cognitive load and comprehension, the students were divided into three groups, and three versions of the video of the lecture were prepared—with subtitle presentation speed of either 132 words per minute (wpm), 110wpm or 74wpm. Students then watched individually one of the versions of the lecture and answered questions. Whilst Kruger warns that generalization of his findings require further investigation with larger numbers of students, his initial results seem to support the redundancy effect theory: higher subtitle speeds carry higher cognitive load and impact negatively on the processing of subtitles. As he himself puts it, 'it would seem that a lower presentation rate results in a stronger relationship between comprehension and attendance to salient visual codes' (*ibid.*: 48). Significantly, as Kruger notes, 'subtitles, like any other teaching aid, cannot be used indiscriminately' (*ibid.*: 30), it is therefore necessary to gauge the audiovisual text and its translation accurately before engaging language students, considering not just the appropriateness of the linguistic and extra-linguistic content of the scenes for the level of proficiency of the students, but also the lexical density, syntactic linearity and presentation rate of subtitles.

Researchers working with interlingual subtitles have reported improved performance among learners of different ages with both low and high level of proficiency. However reversed subtitles appear to be the most beneficial, especially for beginners. Danan (1992) carried out a pilot and two experiments with learners of French at beginner and intermediate level, concentrating on active recall of lexical items following viewings with standard subtitles (L2-L1; pilot only), bimodal subtitles (L2-L2; experiments only), reversed subtitles (L1-L2) and audio with no subtitles. Danan consistently found that the reversed mode yielded the highest recall results and that bimodal input is to be preferred to standard.

The findings of a large longitudinal study (Mariotti 2015) involving nearly 2,000 participants (primary, secondary and tertiary teachers; secondary school and university students; adult learners with different educational backgrounds), carried out by the Subtitles in Language Learning research group, revealed that teachers find bimodal subtitles particularly suitable for intermediate and advanced learners. Students in general expressed a preference for interlingual combinations, but 'extremely motivated learners preferred L2-L2 subtitles' (*ibid.*: 140). Data collected confirmed the positive attitude to subtitles of students in formal and non-formal learning settings. Teachers' responses were equally positive, although some would like to see simplified subtitles for language learners. The same study revealed that students also raised concerns about the discrepancies between subtitle and audio, speed of subtitles and the inability to read and watch at the same time, showing the relevance of Cognitive Load Theory in this context.

Whilst most research has concentrated on vocabulary acquisition and listening comprehension, a number of studies have also explored the impact on L2 syntax acquisition showing that when exposure to subtitled material is short, there is no evidence of improvement (d'Ydewalle and Pavakanun 1997, van de Poel and d'Ydewalle 2001). By contrast, when the period of exposure is increased, positive results in the acquisition of L2 syntax have been noted (Ghia 2007, 2011, 2012).

Active AVT tasks in language learning

Discussing the findings of his 1988 study, Vanderplank wonders whether watching television can truly be considered as meaningful interaction (*ibid.*: 276), in the sense indicated by Krashen, i.e. interaction where speakers are active participants and concentrate on the communication act rather than the form of individual utterances (Krashen 1982: 1). As Vanderplank goes on to explain, watching television is 'a mainly passive activity' and '[f]or students to become proficient in the language, productive practice would also be necessary at various intervals' (Vanderplank 1988: 279). Whilst it could be argued that negotiating the intersemiotic connection between the various meaning-making modes at play in audiovisual texts—as realized in the verbal, visual and auditory channels—requires the activation of digital literacies and a number of cognitive strategies, the fact remains that watching and reading are, if not passive, certainly receptive skills.

Addressing these concerns, the most recent developments present AVT to students as an active task that requires their involvement in translating the verbal soundtrack and creating their own subtitled or revoiced version. Early investigations on the potential of this use of AVT date back to the late 1980s, but they developed further during the following decade for both dubbing (Duff 1989, Kumai 1996) and subtitling (Díaz Cintas 1995). Since then, researchers have examined its impact on mnemonic retention, pragmatic awareness, vocabulary acquisition, writing skills, specialist languages, pronunciation and intonation, autonomous learning and motivational factors as well as translation skills. Indeed it was the potential of AVT in translation courses that alerted researchers to the likely advantages of AVT performed by learners. In his 1995 article, Díaz Cintas laments the scarce attention afforded, until then, to the translation of audiovisual texts compared to literary and other written texts and argues that the need for reduction in subtitling forces students to distinguish between salient and redundant information and reflect on the coherence and internal cohesion of the target and source texts—which improves their understanding of the translation process and enhances their reflective and critical skills. Díaz Cintas also hints at the positive impact of the novelty of subtitling on language learners' motivation. Surprisingly, however, research has since then concentrated mainly on the active use of AVT in language acquisition, rather than on its implications for translator training. Neves' (2004) contribution is one of the few that looks at subtitling from both perspectives and describes how the various stages of the subtitling process in an undergraduate degree course on translation had a positive impact on advanced learners' receptive and productive skills. She also notes that, more generally, subtitling raised their language awareness in L1 and L2, and boosted their ability to extract information, infer opinions and attitudes, deduce meaning from context, as well as recognize discourse patterns and markers.

Another AVT mode which can be exploited in the context of language learning and applied linguistics is dubbing, which has so far received less attention than subtitling—possibly, as Danan (2010) points out, because the original soundtrack is replaced by its dubbed version. Yet, already in 1989 Duff highlighted the effectiveness of synchronization in translation training, as it raises awareness of various issues influenced by time and length constraints. Perhaps the most obvious application of dubbing in language learning pertains to the domain of phonetic and phonological training. Using inexpensive equipment and some ingenuity, Kumai (1996) introduced 'karaoke movies' to his Japanese students of English as a Foreign Language (EFL), who performed live dubbing of the movies paying attention to rhythm, intonation, emotion and speed. Indeed, Burston (2005: 81) argues that 'dubbing requires students to pay particular attention to timing, which fosters more native-like speech delivery', and notes that the images, facial expression and body language on the screen help students to empathize with the characters and their emotions. Burston adds that dubbing is a better option than role-plays because with the former students can listen to their own performance and improve it as many times as necessary. This view is consistent with the findings of other empirical studies. For example, Danan's (2010) comprehensive experiment involving 82 students of Dari, Pashto or Farsi between 2007 and 2010, showed the improvement of the participants' speaking skills and speed. On the other hand, Chiu's (2012) analysis of qualitative and quantitative data collected from 83 Taiwanese EFL students revealed that those participants who carried out dubbing activities significantly outperformed learners who had worked only with conversation; likewise, it showed that dubbing improves the use of intonation, reduces mispronunciation and improves the students' fluency and speech delivery rate. In a recent study, Talaván and Ávila-Cabrera (2015) have combined reversed subtitling with dubbing with a view to improving both oral and written production skills, as well as translation skills. Their findings suggest that, in the students' opinion, dubbing was more rewarding than subtitling, and that the former had contributed more significantly to the development of their translation skills.

Whilst earlier studies tended to rely mainly on qualitative data (students' and/or teachers' input and feedback), the next section surveys a range of pilot and case studies conducted towards the end of the last decade to further demonstrate the positive effects of AVT on language learning, gauge the extent of that improvement through the collection of quantitative and qualitative data, develop a theoretical framework for the use of AVT in language learning contexts, and propose strategies to integrate AVT in the syllabus.

Key theoretical perspectives

The theoretical framework underpinning the bulk of research on AVT and language learning is primarily informed by Paivio's Dual Coding Theory (1969, 1986), Mayer's Cognitive Theory of Multimedia Learning Channels (2005), Krashen's (1982) Theory of Second Language Acquisition, in particular the affective filter hypothesis, and a revised understanding of the role of translation in second language acquisition.

Paivio's Dual Coding Theory conceptualizes cognition as the dynamic association of representations from two independent systems. From this theoretical standpoint, it is argued that the association and interplay between the linguistic information stored in the verbal system and the imagery stored in the non-verbal system enhances memory. Research work informed by this theory therefore seeks to gain a thorough understanding of the intersemiotic processes through which verbal and non-verbal resources interact with and complement each other within multimodal texts.

Mayer's (2005) Cognitive Theory of Multimedia Learning Channels, on the other hand, draws attention to the limited capacity of those two information-processing systems to encode information by using only verbal or visual resources. In light of such limitations, it postulates that learning takes place through the co-deployment of verbal *and* visual representations, i.e. through a combination of words and pictures. This study builds on an earlier one (Mayer *et al.* 2001) that, apart from identifying the limitations exhibited by each channel, shows how the integration of verbal and non-verbal information demands a bigger cognitive effort from the text user. Specifically, the authors demonstrate that, when written text is superimposed on an animation film, 'learners must split their visual attention between the on-screen text and the animation, failing to adequately attend to some of the presented material' (*ibid.*: 190). Furthermore, their findings indicate that the amount of cognitive effort required from viewers increases when the audiovisual ensemble is presented to learners at a relatively fast pace and the text viewers cannot adjust the information delivery rate—as previously suggested by Kruger (2013). In instructor-mediated language learning settings, however, the simultaneous deployment of spoken and written language through different channels is not so cognitively taxing, as the learners' viewing experience is normally preceded by a range of preliminary activities seeking to manage and contextualize the learners' engagement with various aspects of the text, including the register and other conversational dynamics.

Apart from the theoretical models surveyed in this section, researchers who advocate the employment of active AVT tasks for language learning purposes tend to rely on the work of Cook (2010) and Laviosa (2014), who have recently spearheaded a revival in the use of translation as a pedagogical tool in the language learning classroom.

Research issues and methods

Current research in this area is prioritizing the systematic integration of AVT tasks in the language curriculum. By providing detailed guidance on how to achieve an optimal level of curricular integration, specialists aim to ensure that AVT tasks are no longer dealt with as isolated add-ons, but combined with an array of pre- and post-task activities to help learners elicit and recall information and assist trainers with the feedback delivery process (Talaván 2006; Incalcaterra McLoughlin and Lertola 2011, 2014). However, some of the most recent work in the fields of AVT and language learning involves the collection of quantitative data for statistical analysis, in an attempt to add an objective dimension to empirical observations. Pilot and case studies at the centre of this research strand tend to rely on relatively small cohorts of university students, including non-traditional students (adult and distance learners). Typically consisting of sets of pre-, post- and delayed tests for the experimental group and, in some cases, also a control group, these studies often rely on the triangulation of results and curves of statistical variations in relation to a number of hypotheses.

One of the first contributions to this research strand is Bravo's (2008) analysis of the impact of screen translation on foreign language learning based on three experiments with Portuguese learners of English. The first two make use of ready-captioned material, while the third combines the use of an L2-L2 intralingually subtitled text (English audio and English subtitles) with the subsequent creation of L2-L1 interlingual subtitles (English into Portuguese) by students. The aim of this study was to establish whether learners' understanding of idiomatic expressions would significantly improve after viewing and reading the L2 material, and gauge the extent to which this would allow them to re-use such expressions correctly in written production. Ten idiomatic expressions were identified in the audiovisual text and tests were administered before and after viewing the episodes, and then again after the completion of the subtitling activity. Students who initially appeared to understand the selected expressions correctly ranged from 0 to 50 per cent, with the comprehension of seven expressions below or at the 20 per cent mark. After viewing the episode, correct answers increased significantly to between 50 and 100 per cent (for one expression). Bravo (*ibid.*: 185) claims that:

> it was not the written input alone which made comprehension possible, as the expressions had previously been presented to the students in a written format. It was the correspondence between written text and spoken text, in the form of monolingual subtitles that transformed intersemiotic reception, using the two channels of visual perception of images and hearing, into multi-semiotic reception.

After completing the subtitling component of this task, the participants' correct answers increased even further to reach 75 to 100 per cent (for four expressions). In the written production test carried out three weeks later, 15 out of 20 students were able to use the English idioms correctly.

Possibly the first study involving a control group is Noa Talaván's (2010) experiment, which tested the listening comprehension skills of a cohort of 50 adult intermediate EFL learners divided into two groups. While only the experimental group carried out an active subtitling task, all participants—both in the experimental and the control groups—were exposed to a similar volume of L2 input. Members of both groups were presented with the same sequence of pre- and post-subtitling activities and viewed the video clip with bimodal subtitles. Results show that, while all students benefitted from the availability of bimodal subtitles, the experimental group members (who carried out the active subtitling task) returned statistically significant higher comprehension scores. These findings were corroborated by the result of other projects involving students with varying degrees of EFL proficiency. In an identical experiment involving students with lower EFL proficiency, Talaván (2011) found that 'there is an intrinsic relationship between subtitling as a task and LC [listening comprehension] improvement' (*ibid.*:209)—which is also reflected, from a qualitative perspective, in the participant's interest and willingness to take part in similar activities in the future. Finally, Talaván and Rodríguez-Arancón's (2014) study of the impact of subtitling activities on the listening comprehension skills of advanced EFL learners shows that subtitling has a very positive influence on the latter, as well as on the participants' perceived improvement of their writing skills and, more generally, their satisfaction with their involvement in the study.

Other specialists have chosen to concentrate on the interface between AVT and vocabulary acquisition and writing skills. Lertola (2012) describes an experiment consisting of small experimental and control groups made up of intermediate students of Italian as a foreign language. Lertola's starting hypotheses were that exposure to new vocabulary items through the viewing of audiovisual texts would improve incidental vocabulary retention, and that the addition of a standard interlingual subtitling task (L2-L1) would further increase such retention. Participants in both groups carried out tests before, immediately after and some time after the viewing component. The scores for each group showed that both hypotheses were correct; however, members of the experimental group (the only one that carried out an active interlingual subtitling task) returned statistically significant higher scores for vocabulary acquisition when tested some time after the completion of the subtitling task. For her part, Burczyńska's (2015) study of the impact of reversed subtitling on the writing skills of Polish EFL students found significant improvements in the spelling and grammar of her experimental group subjects, vis-à-vis their control counterparts, after completing only eight weeks' worth of reversed subtitling practice (twice a week for 45 minutes).

The impact of AVT on language learning has also been examined by specialists in the intercultural dimension of language pedagogy, who study how learners manage the opportunities for immediate cultural transfer afforded by the interplay between the various semiotic channels found in audiovisual texts. Borghetti and Lertola (2014) identify three types of opportunities to raise cultural and intercultural awareness within the context of a subtitling task presented to a group of intermediate learners of Italian. These can be found during or shortly after watching the videoclip, while subtitling, and during or shortly after class discussions. Borghetti and Lertola's analysis of the students' behaviour (questions and responses) at these junctures showed that they are more concerned about cultural issues—i.e. the (lack of) correspondence between the source and target cultures—than linguistic ones, which suggests that subtitling can 'elicit outward behaviour which might be a marker of awareness development (*ibid.*: 436). Specifically, Borghetti and Lertola (2014: 426) foreground the difficulty derived from having 'to take all information transmitted through different semiotic systems into account' and the need to 'reach beyond mere verbal communication', and conclude that the complexity of this task develops their decision-making skills and fosters their responsibility. It is worth noting that Borghetti and Lertola's study focuses on language learners rather than trainee translators, which might explain their 'conflicting findings' in relation to students' attitudes towards the source text and culture: participants tended to concentrate more on the target than the source. At any rate, the implications of this study are far reaching and pave the way for new approaches to the study of the translator's responsibility in training environments.

Against the background of growing interest in the interface between AVT and language learning, attempts have been made to facilitate the integration of AVT tasks in language learning curricula. Drawing on the premise that the longer the learners' exposure to subtitling practice, the bigger the boost for their language skills, Incalcaterra McLoughlin and Lertola (2014) advocate the introduction of subtitling modules within language degree programmes, for which they propose curricular templates and lesson plans.

In terms of the range of AVT modalities investigated in past and current research driven by a language teaching and learning agenda, the bulk of the literature has tended to focus on subtitling and dubbing. AD, however, has also received attention, both in relation to its impact on language acquisition (Clouet 2005, Martínez Martínez 2012, Ibáñez Moreno and Vermeulen 2013, 2015) and translation competence (Martínez and Gutiérrez 2009). These studies note that AD enables second language acquisition, and boosts learners' motivations, class cohesion and teamwork dynamics.

AD is normally used to make video material accessible to blind or visually impaired viewers, who are provided with a verbal 'translation' of the information conveyed through the visual channel, normally during pauses in the dialogue or other parts of the programme that do not feature any aural information. Audio describers need to be attentive observers and describe what they see in a precise and concise manner. For Ibáñez Moreno and Vermeulen (2013), these very requirements make AD a particularly interesting activity for language learners, and their experiment with 52 adult students of Spanish shows that this AVT mode can foster lexical and phraseological competence. In a later experiment testing the use of VISP (VIdeos for SPeaking), a mobile application for language learning that they developed to facilitate AD activities in class, Ibáñez Moreno and Vermeulen (2015) found that there is not sufficient evidence to demonstrate that AD contributes to the development of learners' lexical accuracy. As is also the case in other studies involving the use of AVT in the language classroom, participants in Ibáñez Moreno and Vermeulen's experiment recorded their interest enjoyment, thus confirming the motivational advantages of employing a task-based communicative approach based on audiovisual material—a very familiar and ubiquitous medium in students' everyday life.

Research on the use of AVT in translator training is still limited, with initial evidence pointing to the fact that the manipulation of the source text to respond to the space, time and synchronization constraints of AVT can contribute to improving trainees' skills and abilities on various levels (Klerkx 1998, Rundle 2000, Neves 2004; and Incalcaterra McLoughlin 2009, 2012, 2015). These articles do not focus primarily on the training of subtitlers, but on the effects that AVT can have on the development of the professional and linguistic skills of future translators. They also explore didactic strategies which expand students' understanding of what constitutes a text and stimulate reflection on different linguistic and extralinguistic elements of meaning, the implications of manipulating or adhering closely to the source text, various aspects pertaining to the translator's responsibility and visibility, as well as on the transfer process itself.

Specifically, Rundle's (2000) article reports on the use of a subtitling software application designed by the author within a course on translation into L2 that was not specifically focused on screen texts. Rundle identifies a number of fringe benefits for students, including the development of learners' transferable IT skills, students' exposure to professional tools, and the 'fun' element involved in subtitling practice. In addition, the author draws attention to the pedagogical benefits of creating 'self-contained, one-line units' in L2—insofar as students should construct such blocks 'according to the syntax of the target language', while ensuring that their subtitles meet conventional readability standards. Qualitative data from class discussions and students' written comments reveal the extent to which learners became involved in the process, with the challenge of physical constraints pushing them towards more courageous choices than they would have dared to take in the context of a written translation, and fostering a more critical approach to the source text.

Detailed lesson and module plans have been suggested to enhance the presence of AVT in translator training settings. These exploit and incorporate multimodal analysis techniques devised by Thibault (2000) and Taylor (2003) and adapt pre-subtitling tasks described by Díaz Cintas and Remael (2007). For her part, Incalcaterra McLoughlin (2009) proposes a revised model for multimedia analysis that prompts translation students to reflect on the signifying codes which make up the semantic web of an audiovisual text with a view to stimulating critical reflection on translation strategies and choices. In a later work, Incalcaterra McLoughlin (2012) shows how this approach can be operationalized through a lesson plan comprising of 5 stages: motivation, globality, analysis, synthesis and reflection. She also describes the structure of a whole subtitling course specifically aimed at trainee translators (2015). It is argued that pre-subtitling tasks such as transcription of the dialogue also have a role in sensitizing students to the peculiarities of speech acts, as the challenges of representing in writing salient elements such as tone of voice, repetitions, or emphatic traits, to give but a few examples, become immediately obvious. The case study presented in this article suggests that reflection on such challenges helps to enhance learners' translation skills.

A promising development at the interface between AVT and translator training is the recent creation of a substantial corpus of student subtitles thanks to the LeCoS Project (Learner Corpus of Subtitles), developed by Anna Bączkowska at the Kazimierz Wielki University in Bydgoszcz, Poland. The project allows for the analysis of translation students' subtitling behaviour and provides useful training material which can be utilized in different contexts.

The influence of new technologies

The availability of reasonably priced or even free technological tools has greatly impacted the shape of language teaching in the digital era and encouraged experiments with new and exciting methodologies, which enhance not only linguistic and (inter)cultural skills but also transferable IT skills. This is particularly true in the area of AVT, where expensive professional software is matched by freely downloadable programmes which are perfectly suitable for class use. Among the most widely used at the moment are Aegisub Advanced Subtitle Editor, DivXLand Media Subtitler and Subtitling Workshop. At the same time, well-known social networking sites such as YouTube have made subtitling possible at no cost and with little effort, and initiatives such as Lyrics Training make excellent use of this technique.

In addition, a number of projects funded by the European Union have provided free, easy-to-use captioning and revoicing tools and resources specifically designed for language teachers and learners. In 2006 the European Commission funded the Learning via Subtitling project, which resulted in the development of the LvS software application (the first subtitling application specifically designed for language learning that incorporates useful and intuitive feedback options) and a range of subtitling activities driven by a task-based approach. Evaluation questionnaires were distributed across 6 European countries to 104 students and 12 teachers of 8 different foreign languages. The results show that LvS tasks were well received, as 72 per cent of students found them very or quite interesting and 70 per cent of teachers reported higher participation by learners (Sokoli *et al.* 2011). One of the strengths of this project is the availability of highly structured and consistent lesson plans which facilitate inclusion of the tasks in the syllabus.

The success of this first venture inspired the development of a platform allowing users to perform AVT tasks online without the need to download any dedicated software application. The ClipFlair platform was therefore developed as part of a new project sponsored by the European Commission in 2011. ClipFlair goes beyond subtitling, as it allows for both captioning and revoicing in over 300 intralingual, interlingual, and multilingual activities in 15 European and non-European languages. As was the case for LvS, ClipFlair is also designed for language learning and each activity is accompanied by a description of learning objectives and the type of engagement expected from users, either repeating, rephrasing or reacting. The methodological framework (Zabalbeascoa *et al.* 2012) which underpins the project defines learner-types in terms of their degree of dependence on the instructor, and their reliance on e-learning, which allows for the matching between specific activities and learner-types.

These free projects and tools have facilitated the inclusion of AVT activities even in online language modules (Incalcaterra McLoughlin and Lertola 2015) and hence opened up new possibilities and trends in the use of AVT in language learning settings. However, commercial tools are now capitalizing on the benefits of these techniques, with apps like fleex.tv offering a subscription service for English language learners. Subscribers are able to watch videos in the original languages with a percentage of the dialogue subtitled in English and the remainder in their own language. The higher the level of English the learner has, the higher the percentage of English text used in the subtitles.

Future trajectories and new debates

Since the use of AVT in language learning contexts is a relatively new pedagogical trend, most researchers have concentrated on case studies focused, perhaps inevitably, on a limited number of language combinations and/or participant samples. Whilst these provide invaluable material and an excellent starting point for the consolidation of this training trend, a wider approach is now fast becoming necessary, with larger, international collaborations, integration and triangulation of data, sharing of corpora and the development of proficiency descriptors and transparent evaluation criteria. A broader cross-section of learners should also be considered, in terms of age, native language, geographic distribution and learning environment. Future research should also consider learners' degree of familiarity with AVT in general, and subtitling in particular as the ability to absorb information quickly is higher in subjects who are used to subtitles, while those who are not tend to spend more time shifting their attention from verbal to visual information and vice versa. This is likely to influence test results and could have a bearing on the degree of effectiveness of the various types of subtitles.

Furthermore, new research should also address the issue of cognitive load specifically in the context of second language acquisition. Data and suggestions emanating from these new perspectives would help turn AVT into a mainstream language teaching strategy. EU-funded programmes, like the ones mentioned earlier, go a long way towards achieving this objective by providing an archive of ready-made activities and freeing language teachers from the considerable time it takes to prepare suitable AVT tasks. However, they have limitations in terms of range and sequencing of activities and require additional effort in order for these activities to be incorporated in the syllabus. Certainly, the involvement of publishing houses specializing in language manuals would contribute greatly to widen the exploitation of AVT for language learning purposes, if AVT tasks were, for example, added as an integral part of textbooks and course material.

Studies have so far concentrated mainly on subtitling and, to a lesser extent, dubbing. Further research should therefore address the impact that other AVT modes can have on language learners and on teaching methodologies. In this respect, further quantitative data collected from learners of non-European languages would be particularly welcome. Also, the effect that subtitling and dubbing tasks can have on the professional training of future translators—as opposed to future subtitlers and dubbers—is still under-investigated, as is the impact of preparation of audio description and dialogue reduction for subtitling on writing skills and development of syntactic proficiency.

Recent progress on the use of smart subtitles (Kovacs 2013), which give students the opportunity to use dictionary features by hovering over certain words, point to exciting future possibilities for interactive AVT tasks. At the same time, new technologies, such as interactive television and the widespread use of social networking, point not only to new tools and approaches, but also to so far under-researched groups of learners such as independent adult learners operating outside the structure of a course and without the mediation of a teacher.

Finally, closer interdisciplinary collaboration between information technology and language teaching and learning scholars would certainly boost the pedagogical relevance of AVT in the language classroom, as would contribution from film studies scholars.

Summary

This chapter has explored the use of AVT in language teaching and learning settings. It has begun with a historical overview exploring the benefits of presenting language students with subtitled video material, and experimenting with different subtitle types: standard (audio in L2 and subtitles in L1), bimodal (audio in L2 and subtitles in L2) and reversed (audio in L1 and subtitles in L2). It has then moved on to focus more specifically on recent qualitative and quantitative studies involving the completion of active AVT tasks by learners, where AVT tasks and any other necessary preparatory activities are performed by students. Whilst subtitling is the most widely exploited AVT mode in the language classroom, this chapter has also shown that dubbing and AD have also been profitably and imaginatively applied in language teaching and learning contexts, and that, in some cases, two AVT modes have been combined in order to maximize their impact.

As far as research in this area is concerned, most students involved in pilot studies investigating different aspects of the interface between AVT and language learning are situated in face-to-face learning environments; however, participants enrolled in virtual learning environments have also participated in some trials. The theoretical framework underpinning these studies includes research into cognitive psychology, second language acquisition, translation studies and didactics of translation. Advances in technology and EU-funded projects have made AVT tools freely available to teachers and students and can facilitate the integration of AVT in language teaching curricula. Going forward, this chapter advocates a move towards mainstreaming active AVT tasks, which contribute not only to the linguistic and (inter)cultural development of language students, but also to the enhancement of learners' key digital skills and multimedia literacy. Research to be prioritized by specialists should take the form of large-scale international and longitudinal studies involving different languages and language combinations.

Further reading

Gambier, Y., A. Caimi and C. Mariotti (eds) (2015) *Subtitles and Language Learning. Principles, Strategies and Practical Experiences*, Bern: Peter Lang | *This collection of articles on the use of interlingual, intralingual and reversed subtitles in language teaching provides methodological guidance and scientific data for both researchers and teachers.*

Garzelli, B. and M. Baldo (eds) (2014) *Subtitles and Intercultural Communication*, Pisa: Edizioni ETS | *The second section of this book, entitled* Subtitling and Foreign Language Learning in Europe and Beyond, *explores the use of subtitles in foreign language teaching and in translator training, with a particular focus on intercultural communication.*

Ghia, E. (2012) *Subtitling Matters. New Perspectives on Subtitling and Foreign Language Learning*, Oxford: Peter Lang | *This book contains an extensive overview of use of subtitled material in second language acquisition and introduces two experimental studies on the acquisition of English syntax through subtitled texts.*

Related topics

3   Subtitling on the cusp of its futures
4   Investigating dubbing: learning from the past, looking to the future
8   Audio description: evolving recommendations for usable, effective and enjoyable practices
13 Spoken discourse and conversational interaction in audiovisual translation
16 Pragmatics and audiovisual translation
17 Multimodality and audiovisual translation: cohesion in accessible films
20 Corpus-based audiovisual translation studies: ample room for development
21 Multimodal corpora in audiovisual translation studies
29 Audiovisual translator training
30 Audiovisual translation in language teaching and learning
32 Technologization of audiovisual translation

References

Abdolmanafi Rokni, S. J. and A. Jannati Ataee (2014) 'The Effect of Movie Subtitles on EFL Learners' Oral Performance', *International Journal of English Language, Literature and Humanities* 1(5): 201–215.

Ayonghe, L. S. (2009) 'Subtitling as a Tool for the Promotion of Bilingualism/Multilingualism in Cameroon', in V. Tanda, H. K. Jick and P. N. Tamanji (eds) *Language, Literature and Social Discourse in Africa*, University of Buea: Departments of English and Linguistics, 106–120.

Bird, S. A. and J. N. Williams (2002) 'The Effect of Bimodal Input on Implicit and Explicit Memory: An Investigation into the Benefits of Within-Language Subtitling', *Applied Psycholinguistics* 23: 509–533.

Borghetti, C. and J. Lertola (2014) 'Interlingual Subtitling for Intercultural Language Education: A Case Study', *Language and Intercultural Communication* (14)4: 423–440.

Borrás, I. and R. C. Lafayette (1994) 'Effects of Multimedia Courseware Subtitling on the Speaking Performance of College Students of French', *The Modern Language Journal* 78: 61–75.

Bravo, M. C. (2008) *Putting the Reader in the Picture: Screen Translation and Foreign Language Learning*, Unpublished Doctoral Thesis, Universitat Rovira I Virgili, Spain. Available online: http://tdx.cat/bitstream/handle/10803/8771/Condhino.pdf [last accessed 20 December 2017].

Burczyńska, P. (2015) 'Reversed Subtitles as a Powerful Didactic Tool in SLA', in Y. Gambier, A. Caimi and C. Mariotti (eds) *Subtitles and Language Learning*, Oxford: Peter Lang, 221–244.

Burston, J. (2005) 'Video Dubbing Projects in the Foreign Language Curriculum', *CALICO Journal* 23(1): 79–92.

Caimi, A. and C. Mariotti (2015) 'Beyond the Book: The Use of Subtitled Audiovisual Material to Promote Content and Language Integrated Learning in Higher Education', in J. Díaz Cintas and J. Neves (eds) *Audiovisual Translation. Taking Stock*, Cambridge: Cambridge Scholars Publishing, 230–243.

Chiu, H. (2012) 'Can Film Dubbing Projects Facilitate EFL Learners' Acquisition of English Pronunciation?', *British Journal of Educational Technology* 43(1): E24–E27.

Clouet, R. (2005) 'Estrategia y propuestas para promover y practicar la escritura creativa en una clase de inglés para traductores', in J. Ramírez Martínez (ed.) *Actas del IX Simposio Internacional de la Sociedad Española de Didáctica de la Lengua y la Literatura, La Lengua Escrita*, Barcelona, 289–296.

Cook, G. (2010) *Translation in Language Teaching*, Oxford: Oxford University Press.

Danan, M. (1992) 'Reversed Subtitling and Dual-Coding Theory: New Directions for Foreign Language Instruction', *Language Learning* 42(4): 497–527.

Danan, M. (2010) 'Dubbing Projects for the Language Learner: A Framework for Integrating Audiovisual Translation into Task-Based Instruction', *Computer Assisted Language Learning* 23(5): 441–456.

Díaz Cintas, J. (1995) 'El subtitulado como técnica docente', *Vida Hispánica* 12: 10–14.

Díaz Cintas, J. and A. Remael (2007) *Audiovisual Translation: Subtitling*, Manchester: St Jerome.

Duff, A. (1989) *Translation*, Oxford: Oxford University Press.

d'Ydewalle, G. and U. Pavakanun (1997) 'Could Enjoying a Movie Lead to Language Acquisition?', in P. Winterhoff-Spurk and T. H. A. van der Voort (eds) *New Horizons in Media Psychology*, Opladen: Westdeutscher Verlag, 145–155.

Garza, T. J. (1991) 'Evaluating the Use of Captioned Video Materials in Advanced Foreign Language Learning', *Foreign Language Annals* 24: 239–258.

Ghia, E. (2007) 'A Case Study on the Role of Interlingual Subtitles on the Acquisition of L2 Syntax— Initial Results', in A. Baicchi (ed.) *Voices on Translation. Linguistic, Multimedia, and Cognitive Perspectives*, Special Issue of *RILA Rassegna Italiana di Linguistica Applicata* 1–2, Roma: Bulzoni, 167–177.

Ghia, E. (2011) 'The Acquisition of L2 Syntax through Audiovisual Translation', in A. Şerban, A. Matamala and J. L. Lavaur (eds) *Audiovisual Translation in Close-up: Practical and Theoretical Approaches*, Bern: Peter Lang, 95–112.

Ghia, E. (2012) *Subtitling Matters. New Perspectives on Subtitling and Foreign Language Learning*, Oxford: Peter Lang.

Ibáñez Moreno, A. and A. Vermeulen (2013) 'Audio Description as a Tool to Improve Lexical and Phraseological Competence in Foreign Language Learning', in D. Tsagari and G. Floros (eds) *Translation in Language Teaching and Assessment*, Newcastle upon Tyne: Cambridge Scholars Press, 41–59.

Ibáñez Moreno, A. and A. Vermeulen (2015) 'Using VISP (VIdeos for SPeaking), a Mobile App Based on Audio Description, to Promote English Language Learning among Spanish Students: A Case Study', *Procedia—Social and Behavioral Sciences* 178: 132–138.

Incalcaterra McLoughlin, L. (2009) 'Subtitles in Translators' Training: A Model of Analysis', *Romance Studies* 27(3): 174–185.

Incalcaterra McLoughlin, L. (2012) 'Subtitling and the Didactics of Translation', in S. Hubscher-Davidson and M. Borodo (eds) *Trends in Translator and Interpreter Training*, London: Continuum, 127–146.

Incalcaterra McLoughlin, L. (2015) 'Towards Translation Proficiency: Transcription and Subtitling', in A. Jankowska and A. Szarkowska (eds) *New Points of View on Audiovisual Translation and Media Accessibility*, Oxford: Peter Lang, 149–164.

Incalcaterra McLoughlin, L. and J. Lertola (2011) 'Learn through Subtitling: Subtitling as an Aid to Language Learning', in L. Incalcaterra McLoughlin, M. Biscio and M. A. Ní Mhainnín (eds) *Audiovisual Translation Subtitles and Subtitling*, Oxford: Peter Lang, 243–263.

Incalcaterra McLoughlin, L. and J. Lertola (2014) 'Audiovisual Translation in Second Language Acquisition. Integrating Subtitling in the Foreign Language Curriculum', *The Interpreter and Translator Trainer* 8(1): 70–83.

Incalcaterra McLoughlin, L. and J. Lertola (2015) 'Captioning and Revoicing of Clips in Foreign Language Learning. Using Clipfair for Teaching Italian in Online Learning Environments', in C. Ramsey-Portolano (ed.) T*he Future of Italian Teaching. Media, New Technologies and Multidisciplinary Perspectives*, Cambridge: Cambridge Scholars Publishing, 55–69.

Klerkx, J. (1998) 'The Place of Subtitling in a Translator Training Course', in Y. Gambier (ed.) *Translating for the Media*, Turku: University of Turku, 243–258.

Kothari B., A. Pandey and R. Chudgar (2004) 'Reading Out of the "Idiot Box": Same-Language Subtitling on Television in India', *Journal of Information Technologies and International Development* 2(1): 23–44.

Kovacs, G. (2013) 'Smart Subtitles for Language Learning', in *CHI 13. Extended Abstracts on Human Factors in Computing System*, New York: ACM, 2719–2724.

Krashen, S. D. (1982) *Principles and Practice in Second Language Acquisition*, Oxford: Pergamon.

Kruger, J. L. (2013) 'Subtitles in the Classroom, Balancing the Benefits of Dual Coding with the Cost of Increased Negative Load', *Journal for Language Teaching* 47(1): 55–71.

Kruger, J. L., H. Kruger and M. Verhoef (2007) 'Subtitling and the Promotion of Multilingualism: The Case of Marginalised Languages in South Africa', *Linguistica Antverpiensia* 6: 35–49.

Kumai, W. N. (1996) '*Karaoke* Movies: Dubbing Movies for Pronunciation', *Language Teacher* 20(9). Available online: http://jalt-publications.org/tlt/departments/myshare/articles/2049-karaoke-movies-dubbing-movies-pronunciation [last accessed 20 December 2017].

Lambert, W. E. and N. E. Holobow (1984) 'Combinations of Printed Script and Spoken Dialogues that Show Promise for Beginning Students of Foreign Language', *Canadian Journal of Behavioural Science* 16: 1–11.

Laviosa, S. (2014) *Translation and Language Education. Pedagogical Approaches Explained*, New York & London: Routledge.

Lertola, J. (2012) 'The Effect of the Subtitling Task on Vocabulary Learning', in A. Pym and D. Orrego-Carmona (eds) *Translation Research Project 4*, Tarragona: Intercultural Studies Group, Universitat Rovira i Virgili, 61–70.

Mariotti, C. (2015) 'A Survey on Stakeholders' Perceptions of Subtitles as a Means to Promote Foreign Language Learning', in Y. Gambier, A. Caimi and C. Mariotti (eds) *Subtitles and Language Learning*, Bern: Peter Lang, 83–104.

Martínez, S. and J. Gutiérrez (2009) 'Audio Description as a Didactic Tool: Exercises to Acquire Certain Translation Competences', paper presented at *Media for All 3 International Conference*, October 2009, Antwerp: Belgium.

Martínez Martínez, S. (2012) 'La audiodescripción (AD) como herramienta didáctica: Adquisición de la competencia léxica', in M. Del Pozo, A. Luna and A. Álvarez (eds) *Cruces. Traducir en la Frontera*, Granada: Atrio, 87–102.

Mayer, R. E. (2005) 'Cognitive Theory of Multimedia Learning', in R. E. Mayer (ed.) *The Cambridge Handbook of Multimedia Learning*, New York: Cambridge University Press, 31–48.

Mayer, R. E., J. Heiser and S. Lonn (2001) 'Cognitive Constraints on Multimedia Learning: When Presenting More Material Results in Less Understanding', *Journal of Educational Psychology* 93(1): 187–198.

Neves, J. (2004) 'Language Awareness through Training in Subtitling', in P. Orero (ed.) *Topics in Audiovisual Translation*, Amsterdam & Philadelphia: John Benjamins, 127–140.

Paivio, A. (1969) 'Mental Imagery in Associative Learning and Memory', *Psychological Review* 76(3): 241–263.

Paivio, A. (1986). *Mental Representations: A Dual Coding Approach*, Oxford: Oxford University Press.

Price, K. (1983) 'Closed-Captioned TV: An Untapped Resource', *MATSOL Newsletter* 12(2): 1–8.

Rundle, C. (2000) 'Using Subtitles to Teach Translation', in R. M. Bollettieri Bosinelli, C. Heiss and M. Soffritti (eds) *La traduzione multimediale. Quale traduzione per quale testo?*, Bologna: CLUEB, 167–181.

Sokoli, S., P. Zabalbeascoa and M. Fountana (2011) 'Subtitling Activities for Foreign Language Learning', in L. Incalcaterra McLoughlin, M. Biscio and M. A. Ní Mhainnín (eds) *Audiovisual Translation. Subtitles and Subtitling*, Oxford: Peter Lang, 219–242.

Talaván, N. (2006) 'Using Subtitles to Enhance Foreign Language Learning, *Porta Linguarum* 6: 41–52.

Talaván, N. (2010) 'Subtitling as a Task and Subtitles as Support: Pedagogical Applications', in J. Díaz Cintas, A. Matamala and J. Neves (eds) *New Insights into Audiovisual Translation and Media Accessibility*, Amsterdam: Rodopi, 285–299.

Talaván, N. (2011) 'Quasi-experimental Research Project on Subtitling and Foreign Language Acquisition', in L. Incalcaterra McLoughlin, M. Biscio and M. A. Ní Mhainnín (eds) *Audiovisual Translation. Subtitles and Subtitling*, Oxford: Peter Lang , 197–217.

Talaván, N. and J. J. Ávila-Cabrera (2015) 'First Insights into the Combination of Dubbing and Subtitling', in Y. Gambier, A. Caimi and C. Mariotti (eds) *Subtitles and Language Learning*, Bern: Peter Lang, 149–172.

Talaván, N. and P. Rodríguez-Arancón (2014) 'The Use of Interlingual Subtitling to Improve Listening Comprehension Skills in Advanced EFL Students', in B. Garzelli and M. Baldo (eds) *Subtitling and Intercultural Communication*, Pisa: Edizioni ETS, 273–288.

Taylor, C. (2003) 'Multimodal Transcription in the Analysis, Translation and Subtitling of Italian Films', *The Translator* 9(2): 191–205.

Thibault, P. (2000) 'The Multimodal Transcription of a Television Advertisement: Theory and Practice', in A. Baldry (ed.) *Multimodality and Multimediality in the Distance Learning Age*. Campobasso: Palladino Editore, 311–385.

Van de Poel, M. and G. d'Ydewalle (2001) 'Incidental Foreign Language Acquisition by Children Watching Subtitled Television Programs', in Y. Gambier and H. Gottlieb (eds) *(Multi)Media Translation, Concepts, Practices and Research*, Amsterdam: John Benjamins, 259–273.

Vanderplank, R. (1988) 'The Value of Teletext Subtitles in Language Learning', *ELT Journal* 42(4): 272–281.

Winke, P., S. Gass and T. Sydorenko (2010) 'The Effects of Captioning Videos Used for Foreign Language Listening Activities', *Language Learning & Technology* 14(1): 65–86.

Zabalbeascoa, P., S. Sokoli and O. Torres (2012) *ClipFlair Conceptual Framework and Pedagogical Methodology*. Available online: http://clipflair.net/wp-content/uploads/2014/06/D2.1ConceptualFramework.pdf [last accessed 20 December 2017].

Sitography

Aegisub Advanced Subtitle Editor: www.aegisub.org [last accessed 20 December 2017].
ClipFlair Platform: www.clipflair.net [last accessed 20 December 2017].
DivXLand Media Subtitler: www.divxland.org [last accessed 20 December 2017].
Fleex.tv: www.fleex.tv [last accessed 20 December 2017].
LvS software: http://levis.cti.gr [last accessed 20 December 2017].
Lyrics Training: http://lyricstraining.com [last accessed 20 December 2017].
Subtitling Workshop: www.subworkshop.sourceforge.net/ [last accessed 20 December 2017].

31
Accessible filmmaking
Translation and accessibility from production

Pablo Romero-Fresco

Introduction

The last decade has seen an exponential growth in audiovisual translation (AVT) services in general, and accessibility services in particular, around the world. This is being facilitated by new legislation and new accessibility guidelines that aim to increase both the quantity and the quality of subtitling for deaf and hard of hearing people (SDH) and audio description (AD) for blind and partially sighted people in countries such as Spain (AENOR 2012), France (MFP 2012) or the UK (Ofcom 2016). However, despite having achieved considerable visibility within translation studies and the translation industry, AVT and accessibility remain fairly invisible within film studies and the filmmaking industry.

Almost 60 per cent of the revenue obtained by the leading top-grossing films made in Hollywood in the last decade comes from the translated (subtitled or dubbed) or accessible (with subtitles for the deaf or AD for the blind) versions of those films, and yet only between 0.1 per cent and 1 per cent of their budgets is usually devoted to translation and accessibility (Romero-Fresco 2013). Relegated to the distribution stage as an afterthought in the filmmaking process, translators have to translate films in very limited time, for a small remuneration and with no access to the team behind creative filmmaking decisions. This may be seen as a profitable model for the film industry, but more than a decade of research in AVT has shown that it may also have a very negative impact on the quality and reception of translated films (Romero-Fresco 2017, 2018a). In fact, renowned filmmakers such as Ken Loach are now beginning to denounce that this model often results in the alteration of their film's vision and that, even more worryingly, they are not always aware of this (de Higes 2014).

Accessible filmmaking (Romero-Fresco 2018b, forthcoming) sets out to address these issues and integrate AVT and accessibility as part of the filmmaking process through collaboration between filmmakers and translators. Following a historical account of the origins and background of accessible filmmaking, this chapter will focus on how this relatively new initiative is being implemented from the point of view of research, training and professional practice to ensure that both translation and accessibility are taken into account at the (pre-)production and post-production stages of a film.

Background

The integration of AVT as part of the filmmaking process is not new. It goes back to the early days of cinema, before the introduction of sound. Silent films required the translation of the intertitles used by the filmmakers to convey dialogue or narration, which were 'removed, translated, drawn or printed on paper, filmed and inserted again in the film' (Ivarsson 1992: 15). This translation was done in the studios, as part of the post-production process of the film (Izard 2001). The introduction of partial or full audible dialogue in films such as *The Jazz Singer* (1927) and *The Lights of New York* (1928) brought about a new scenario and the need for a different type of translation. Some of these films (known as 'part-talkies' and 'talkies') used intertitles in the target language to translate the original audible dialogue. Others prompted the first attempts at dubbing and subtitling in French, German and Spanish, which were largely unsuccessful (Izard 2001). These three translation modes were part of the post-production process of the films.

Audience reactions to these translations were, however, largely negative, which led the film industry to opt for a different solution: the so-called multiple-language versions (Vincendeau 1999). Films were made and remade in two or three languages with the same director and sometimes in up to fourteen languages with a different director for each language version. This may be regarded as an extreme form of accessible filmmaking in which the need to make films accessible to foreign audiences was not just an element of post-production but rather a structuring principle of film production. The cost (usually 30 per cent of the total film budget) was, however, too high. As soon as dubbing and subtitling were fine-tuned, the studios opted for these modes, which helped reduce the cost of translations to around 10 per cent of the film budget. Increasingly outsourced and unsupervised by filmmakers, translations lost their status as part of the filmmaking process and were relegated to the distribution process, as is still normally the case now.

The heterogeneous and fragmented nature of filmmaking (in terms of time, locations, processes and technology) is likely to have facilitated this scenario, which remains unchanged after the introduction of accessibility services in the 1970s and 1980s. Regarded from the beginning as costly and catering to the needs of a very reduced and specific population (Stephanidis 2001), SDH was conveyed as a separate signal created outside the production process of the programmes. Whereas other types of translation such as videogame localization, which emerged as part of the distribution stage, have become a critical element in the development of videogames, AVT has taken the opposite direction. Having originated as an integral part of the post-production process of silent films, it came to occupy a central position in the production of multiple-language versions (which were effectively localized) but has since then become gradually consigned to the distribution process.

The invisibility of AVT in the film industry has also been reflected in the disciplinary curricula and research agendas. Some attempts have been made by AVT scholars (Chaume 2004, Mas and Orero 2005, Cattrysse and Gambier 2008, Fryer and Freeman 2012) and film scholars (Egoyan and Balfour 2004, Nornes 2007) to bridge the gap between these two disciplines but, up until now, they have been few and far between. As far as teaching is concerned, film(making) courses have traditionally disregarded translation and accessibility issues, and postgraduate programmes in AVT have not normally included film(making).

In an attempt to propose a different model, accessible filmmaking aims to integrate AVT and accessibility as part of the filmmaking process, which requires the collaboration between the translator and the creative team of the film. Accessible filmmaking thus involves giving consideration during the filmmaking process (and through collaboration between the translator and the creative team of the film) to the needs of viewers in other languages and viewers with hearing or visual loss, ultimately seeking to enhance their viewing experience.

The next sections will provide an overview of how the notion of accessible filmmaking is being applied in research, training and professional practice.

Research

From the point of view of research and training, accessible filmmaking entails an exchange between film(making) studies and AVT, where film scholars and film students learn about the aspects of AVT and accessibility that may have an effect on the nature and reception of (their) films, while AVT scholars and translation students explore the elements from filmmaking and film studies that can contribute to the theory and practice of translation and accessibility. The present overview of research in and around the notion of accessible filmmaking is divided accordingly into contributions originated from film and AVT.

Contribution from ethnographic film(making) to audiovisual translation

Although AVT is regarded as a vibrant research field, AVT scholars have traditionally not engaged actively with the (admittedly few) contributions from film studies that have explored the role played by translation in film, such as the volume edited by Egoyan and Balfour (2004) and the books by Nornes (2007) and Betz (2009). These contributions provide new and refreshing takes on AVT from the point of view of filmmaking (Egoyan and Balfour), history, culture, ideology and aesthetics (Nornes) and film studies and art cinema (Betz). Yet, if there is one area that has been largely ignored in AVT, this is ethnographic filmmaking, which encompasses the work of anthropologists and filmmakers such as David MacDougall. Their work contributes significantly to our understanding of the relationship between film and translation, but they are also the first examples of accessible filmmaking from the point of view of research and practice.

Up until the early 1960s, ethnographic documentaries such as those made by Jean Rouch had normally resorted to voice-over for translation. The pioneering use of subtitles by filmmakers John Marshall and Tim Asch in their documentaries at the beginning of that decade are regarded as a landmark in documentary filmmaking (Henley 2010). Indeed, it helped filmmakers to construct a closer relationship with their participants and it is also key for AVT, since it triggered some of the first theoretical reflections on the role played by translation in film.

Unlike in fiction films, subtitles in ethnographic films were regarded from the beginning as one of the creative ingredients of the filmmaking process, a 'dramatic component of visual anthropology' (Ruoff 1994) that required to be tackled collaboratively, often by filmmakers and non-professional translators (Lewis 2003), and from the editing stage (Henley 1996). All these elements—as well as the consideration by these filmmakers and scholars of the effect of subtitles upon the audience—account for the pioneering role played by ethnographic film studies in the research and practice of accessible filmmaking.

Subtitling is considered here as a linguistic, cultural and technical challenge, but one that encourages the creativity of the filmmakers and that allows them to develop new meanings and interpretations for their films (Zhang 2012). For MacDougall (1998), the main disadvantage in the use of subtitles is that the dialogue is packaged and acquires a somewhat prophetic nature, viewers lose freedom and become word-focused, and filmmakers have to go against the 'show, don't tell' formula that is traditionally recommended to enhance the visual nature of film. Yet, he points out that subtitles also present a great deal of benefits to filmmakers, as they can contribute to further the characterization of the participants in the film and can help filmmakers to recontextualize, focus or narrow down their ideas. Subtitles are a 'stamp of possession' (MacDougall 1998: 174) on a film, the 'textual eyes' (Zhang 2012: 447) that allow filmmakers to project their particular interpretation and to speak to the audience while the participants in the film are speaking to each other.

More specifically, many of these scholars reflect on the impact subtitling has on the filmmaking process. As far as production is concerned, and from a practical point of view, subtitling requires key changes in framing that must be planned before shooting (Henley 2010, Romero-Fresco 2013), whereas from a more theoretical standpoint subtitles are thought to act on the verbal level as the camera acts on a visual level 'to single out subjects and frame human relationships' (MacDougall 1998: 169). As far as editing is concerned, MacDougall also stresses the key role played by subtitles on the rhythm, cadence and tempo of the film. Rhythm in film is thus not only determined by the pace of the editing, an aspect that has been researched exhaustively by film scholars, but also by the pace at which the viewers read the subtitles. This is a consideration that has so far been overlooked in film studies and AVT alike. Thus, the density, speed, exposure time and complexity of the subtitles may be critical to determine the rhythm of a film, which may be different in its translated version. The following quote by MacDougall (1998: 168) sums up the role played by subtitling in ethnographic film:

> The writing and placing of subtitles involves considerable polishing and fine-tuning, but unlike the *ex post-facto* subtitling of a feature film, this remains part of the creative process, influencing the pacing and rhythm of the film as well as its intellectual and emotional content.

It would thus seem that just as the emergence of ethnographic filmmaking helped to give a voice to silent communities around the world through the use of subtitles, it also contributed to raising the visibility of translation amongst an admittedly small number of filmmakers and film scholars. Unfortunately, the obvious connection between ethnographic filmmaking and AVT studies has until now never materialized, as shown (to mention one example) by the absence of ethnographic filmmakers in AVT publications and conferences such as *Media for All* and *Languages and the Media* and by the fact that ethnographic conferences and panels such as the 2011 'Subtitling Ethnographic Films: Knowledge and Value in Translation' have so far fallen off the AVT radar. Given the current relevance of creative (McClarty 2012), integrated (Fox 2016) and abusive (Nornes 2007) subtitling, the use of, and reflection on, subtitling by ethnographic filmmakers is now more relevant than ever and it shows that it is possible to integrate AVT as a creative element within the filmmaking process through the collaboration of filmmakers and translators.

Contribution from audiovisual translation to film(making)

This section dwells on universal design, part-subtitling and creative subtitling as three concepts developed within AVT studies that may serve as a background to the notion of accessible filmmaking. This is followed by an overview of eye-tracking-based reception studies, one of the most fruitful lines of research in this area.

Adopting the term 'universal design' to the field of media accessibility, Udo and Fels (2009) conclude that neither SDH nor AD meet the criteria of universal design because they are designed after the fact, rather than at the beginning of the process; and the designer of the (audiovisual) product is not involved in the SDH/AD process at all. Udo and Fels propose a new structure to include audio describers and captioners in the film crew under the direction of a supervisor of accessibility services. Whereas this model may be regarded as an example of accessible filmmaking, it also presents a series of drawbacks, not least the need to apply the seven principles of universal design outlined by Connell *et al.* (1997), many of which are not relevant to media accessibility; significantly, there is also the fact that the model fails to include translation. It may be argued that if a new production model is to be successful in the film industry, it must be as cost-effective and wide-reaching as possible, involving not only viewers with hearing or visual loss, but also viewers in other languages.

Two other concepts that are related to accessible filmmaking and that may contribute to its development are part-subtitling and creative subtitling. Part-subtitling is usually discussed in the context of multilingual films and their translation, an emergent area of research within AVT (Baldo 2009, Corrius and Zabalbeascoa 2011, de Higes Andino *et al.* 2013, de Higes 2014, Díaz Cintas 2011, Heiss 2004, Mingant 2010, Sanz 2015, Şerban 2012, Zabalbeascoa and Voellmer 2014). According to O'Sullivan (2008), part-subtitles are those used in the original version of multilingual films for the benefit of their primary language audience. These subtitles are not an afterthought in the filmmaking process, but instead are considered at the pre-production stage, when the script is being developed, and are made during post-production by the scriptwriters and the filmmakers, often in collaboration with translators. As pointed out by Şerban (2012: 50), they are an artistic choice of the filmmaker to fulfil different roles, for 'they help tell the story, advance the plot, and as such they have a narrative function as well as a character portrayal role'. Part-subtitles are thus an example of accessible filmmaking that, given the increasing use of multilingualism in film in order to reflect today's globalized society, is bound to become an important element in the film industry and a very pertinent object of analysis and research.

As for creative subtitles, they are also gaining popularity among filmmakers and researchers, perhaps inspired by the innovation and creativity found in fansubs (O'Hagan 2009). Instead of abiding by a restrictive set of norms, creative subtitles—which are in line with Nornes' notion of abusive subtitling (2007)—fulfil both a linguistic and an aesthetic function, responding to the specific qualities of an individual film and giving the creative subtitler more freedom to create an aesthetic that matches that of the source text without being bound by standard font types, sizes and positions (McClarty 2012). Often produced with the collaboration of directors and editors to interact with the *mise en scène* in the original film, they stand as another example of accessible filmmaking. They do not only call for a collaborative approach, but also for an expansion of the subtitler's current role, who must be able to 'read' the film and understand how meaning is created through the use of film language and visual aesthetics.

Closely related to both part-subtitling and creative subtitles is the creative use of titles/on-screen text found nowadays in films and TV series such as Netflix's *House of Cards* and BBC's *Sherlock*. This device is described in the literature as TELOP (television optical projection), 'impact captioning' (Sasamoto 2014), 'decotitles' (Kofoed 2011), 'beyond screen text messaging' (Zhang 2014) or 'authorial titling' (Pérez-González 2012), and it allows filmmakers to integrate text coming from different sources into the *mise en scène*, without having to, for instance, show a close up of a mobile phone every time a message is received by one of the characters. According to Pérez-González (2012: 13), these authorial titles are an example of how the interventionism of fansubs or fan-made transformative subtitles and their reluctance to abide by standard guidelines has managed to 'shape the social semiotic practices of professional media producers working in the era of digital technologies'. In the case of *Sherlock*, the text acts as a cohesive signature for the series, 'as it aids in characterization, helps to progress the narrative, and binds the series as a whole' (Dwyer 2015), while remaining as an overtly post-production effect and prioritizing the communication between the filmmaker and the audience over that between the characters (Pérez-González 2012). Authorial titles combine the innovative nature of creative subtitles and the fact that, as part-subtitles, they are integrated in production. They are therefore a very interesting topic of research from the viewpoint of accessible filmmaking, not least to explore if and how they are made accessible to foreign, deaf and blind audiences, which requires the collaboration of the translator with the production team.

Finally, another fruitful line of research to explore accessible filmmaking is eye tracking-based reception research. Eye tracking was initially used in the field of psycholinguistics for the analysis of language comprehension processes with static texts (Rayner 1998). Over the past years, it has been increasingly applied to moving text and image, exploring the gaze behaviour of different types of viewers under different circumstances. The main findings from the analysis of original films so far show that the viewers' gaze is often focused on the central features of a traditionally composed film, with a particular bias on faces (where eyes are favoured over mouth) and moving objects (Smith 2013). This often creates an effect of attentional synchrony that brings together the viewers' gaze during many of the shots (Mital *et al.* 2011). The viewers' fixations at the beginning of a shot tend to be central and long, whereas there seems to be greater exploration of the screen and less attentional synchrony as the shot duration increases. However, the exploration of the screen is normally limited, as shown by the fact that viewers take in roughly 3.8 per cent of the total screen area during an average length shot. Peripheral processing is at play, but it is 'mostly reserved for selecting future saccade targets, tracking moving targets, and extracting gist about scene category, layout and vague object information' (Smith 2013: 168).

These findings are relevant not only for filmmakers and film scholars but also for translators and translation scholars, who can use them to ascertain how this typical reception of an original film may be modified when the translation of the film is read (subtitles) or heard (voice-over, dubbing, AD) by the target viewers. Surprisingly, eye-tracking studies on AVT are even more numerous than those conducted by film scholars. The most relevant studies carried out so far show, first of all, that the appearance of text on screen (whether subtitles or another type of on-screen text) draws the viewers' attention to it almost regardless of other factors such as the language in the soundtrack (d'Ydewalle and De Bruycker 2007). This is the type of finding originated in AVT studies that, within the collaborative framework of accessible filmmaking, provides filmmakers with proof that any on-screen text (part-subtitle, authorial title or standard subtitle, etc.) will normally take precedence over the images. Further studies have shown that experienced subtitle viewers watch subtitled programmes almost effortlessly (d'Ydewalle and De Bruycker 2007). They often start by reading the subtitles (Jensema *et al.* 2000), then shifting their visual attention between subtitles and images (de Linde and Kay 1999) and modulating their processing strategies according to the type of subtitled programme they are watching (Perego *et al.* 2010). Most viewers spend more time looking at the subtitles than at the images but the fixations on the images are longer (*ibid.*). In other words, once they have finished reading the subtitles, the viewers of a subtitled film use their remaining time to focus on the key parts of the image (often faces, when they are present) for as long as possible. Thus, they seem to explore the image less than the viewers of the original film without subtitles.

In general, the faster the subtitles and the more movement they present (for example, scrolling subtitles as opposed to subtitles displayed in blocks), the more time is spent reading them and the less time is left to look at the images (Romero-Fresco 2011, 2015). The latter study has made it possible to ascertain the average distribution of viewers' attention between text and image depending on the time the text is left on screen (Romero-Fresco 2015). Text displayed at a speed of 150 words per minute (wpm) leads to an average distribution of 50 per cent of the time on the subtitles and 50 per cent on the images. A faster speed of 180wpm yields an average of 60–65 per cent of the time on the subtitles and 40–35 per cent on the images, whereas 200wpm only allows 20 per cent of the time on the images. This provides filmmakers with empirical information as to how much time a part-subtitle or a Sherlock-style authorial title must be left on screen to ensure that viewers have time not only to read it but also to explore the rest of the screen. As for the difference in reception depending on the viewers' profile, the pan-European study presented in Romero-Fresco (2015) suggests that deaf viewers can find the subtitles on the screen more quickly than hearing viewers (perhaps because they rely on them heavily) but they take longer to read them than hearing viewers, which may be a sign of reading difficulties. However, despite having less time left to look at the images on the screen, the deaf viewers' visual comprehension is just as good as, and sometimes even better than, that of the hearing viewers. In other words, deaf viewers seem to make up for their sometimes substandard reading skills with a particularly good visual perception and comprehension.

As for the different translation modes, eye-tracking studies comparing dubbing and subtitling (Perego *et al.* 2014) suggest that general comprehension of film content and visual scene recognition are achieved equally with both translation modalities. They also point to a peculiarity of dubbing, the so-called dubbing effect: an unconscious strategy adopted by dubbing viewers to avoid looking at mouths in dubbing (particularly in close-ups), which prevails over the natural and idiosyncratic way in which humans watch reality and film (favouring eyes over mouths), and which allows them to suspend disbelief and be transported into the fictional world of the film (Romero-Fresco 2016a).

Finally, as well as exploring how reception research in AVT can contribute to film studies and vice versa, eye-tracking studies have recently engaged more directly with accessible filmmaking. Fox (2016) analyzes the reception of three versions of the film *Joining the Dots* (Romero-Fresco 2012): its original version with no subtitles, its translation with interlingual subtitles produced as an afterthought, and finally its translation with integrated subtitles created in collaboration with the filmmaker as part of the production process. These integrated subtitles were displayed in different positions within the shots on the basis of an established set of criteria regarding framing and *mise en scène*. The results of the experiment show that while viewers take a little more time to find integrated subtitles than standard subtitles, the overall reading time is reduced. With integrated subtitles, the viewers have more time available to watch and explore the images and they show very similar eye-movement patterns to the viewers of the original film with no subtitles. Furthermore, these integrated subtitles seem to increase the viewers' suspension of disbelief, producing an enhanced sense of presence in the fictional world of the film. These findings suggest that accessible filmmaking may bring about a degree of similarity in the way in which films are received by the source and target audience that is not normally found in films that are translated at the distribution stage. However, much more research is needed to investigate the impact that an accessible filmmaking approach can have on filmmakers, translators and viewers (of original and translated films).

Although eye-tracking research can be expected to reveal mainly what viewers see, rather than what they think, it has proven to be a useful tool for research in film and AVT, especially when combined with other measures such as comprehension, preferences and sense of presence. The latter measure is a recent addition to AVT studies that is beginning to show that, contrary to the traditional belief that subtitles draw viewers out of the film, they may maintain and sometimes even increase the target viewers' sense of presence and suspension of disbelief (Kruger *et al.* 2015, Romero-Fresco 2016b), which may be seen as one of the top priorities in fiction.

To conclude, in his overview of eye-tracking studies on film and AVT, Smith (2015) complains that film studies scholars cannot use translated films for their studies because the presence of subtitles 'invalidates the use of eye tracking as a way to measure how the filmmaker intended to shape viewer attention and perception'. The objective of accessible filmmaking is to present a framework where this is no longer the case and filmmakers are aware of, and involved in, the reception of their translated/accessible films. The next sections show how this is being implemented from the point of view of training and professional practice.

Training

Given the current prominence of industrial subtitling (Pérez-González 2012), carried out after the fact and with no communication with the creative team of the film, accessible filmmaking has so far been applied mainly at grass-roots level, and training has played a key role in its development. As mentioned above, film(making) courses have traditionally disregarded translation and accessibility issues and postgraduate programmes in AVT have not normally included film(making). This is beginning to change. Postgraduate courses in filmmaking such as the MA in Filmmaking at Kingston University (London), the Film Studies Masters at the University of Malta and the MA in Film Production at the ESCAC (Barcelona), the leading film school in Spain, now include classes on AVT and accessibility. The same goes for undergraduate and postgraduate film programmes at Universidad de Valladolid and the Central School of Speech and Drama (London). Likewise, AVT courses are beginning to open the door to film-related content, as shown by the MA in Audiovisual Translation at the Universitat Autònoma de Barcelona or the MA in Accessibility at the University of Macerata.

In some cases, accessible filmmaking is promoted not only through the exchange of content and modules between programmes but also through the collaboration between film students and AVT students. This is the case of a project set up by five students from the MA in Translation at the University of Antwerp who produced SDH and Italian subtitles for the award-winning film *De weg van alle vlees* (2013) in collaboration with, and under the supervision of, the Belgian filmmaker Deben Van Dam (RITS Film School, Antwerp). The film was broadcast by VRT, the main public broadcaster in Belgium, on 7 December 2014 with the SDH produced by the students and with their names included as part of the credits. A similar project was set up at the University of Roehampton in 2014 to produce French subtitles for Alvaro Longoria's film *Hijos de las Nubes* (2013), produced by Javier Bardem. The subtitles were created in collaboration with the filmmaker and were broadcast by the French TV channel Arte in February 2014. Following this project, the University of Roehampton launched in 2013 the first MA in Accessibility and Filmmaking, where students learn not only how to make films but also how to make them accessible to viewers in other languages and viewers with hearing and visual loss. The students graduating in this course are being employed both in the translation and the film industry and their first films have adopted an accessible filmmaking approach.

Furthermore, training in accessible filmmaking has also been made available to professionals in the industry through workshops and special courses. The workshops have taken place mainly at film festivals such as the International Edinburgh Film Festival (2013) and Venice Film Festival (2012 and 2013). As for the special courses, a case in point is the first official course on accessible filmmaking for documentary directors organized by Fondazione

Carlo Molo, the Torino Film Commission and Museo Nazionale del Cinema, which ran for three months between January and March 2016 and was taught jointly by film and AVT professionals and scholars.

Professional practice

As mentioned at the beginning of this chapter, accessible filmmaking was first applied in the film industry in silent films, where intertitles were produced as part of the post-production process (often supervised by the filmmakers), and also in multiple-language versions, where translation shaped the production process. In the following decades, this approach could only be found amongst the above-mentioned ethnographic filmmakers and some classic directors who were known for caring about every aspect of the filmmaking process, such as Kubrick, Fellini, Godard or Scorsese (Nornes 2007: 243). They made themselves available to translators and engaged with the reception of their films in other countries. In recent years, partly due to the emergence of multilingual films, more and more filmmakers are beginning to engage with translation from the production process and to collaborate with translators, as is the case of John Sayles (*Lone Star* 1996, *Men with Guns 1997*), Jim Jarmusch (*Mystery Train* 1989, *Night on Earth* 1991), Danny Boyle (*Slumdog Millionaire* 2008), James Cameron (*Avatar* 2009) and, more notoriously, Quentin Tarantino (*Inglourious Basterds* 2009) and Alejandro González Iñárritu (*Babel* 2006, *The Revenant* 2015), both of whom issued translation guidelines to their distributors in order to ensure that their vision for their films was maintained in the target versions (Sanz 2015).

However, given the inflexible nature of industrial subtitling, where distributors have the power to decide against the translation wishes of recognized filmmakers such as Ken Loach and Quentin Tarantino (Sanz 2015), independent filmmaking offers an ideal platform for accessible filmmaking to be developed. This is the case of recent films that have integrated translation and accessibility from an early stage, such as Michael Chanan's *Secret City* (2012), Enrica Colusso's *Home Sweet Home* (2012), Elisa Fuksas' *Nina* (2012), the above-mentioned *De weg van alle vlees* (Deben Van Dam 2013) and *Hijos de las Nubes* (Álvaro Longoria 2013) or the Emmy award-winning *Notes on Blindness* (Spinney and Middleton 2014), whose AD was produced by the AVT scholar and professional audio describer Louis Fryer in collaboration with the filmmakers.

In some cases, the commitment of these creators with accessible filmmaking turns them into activists and researchers, as they accompany their films with recommendations and reflections on how to ensure that the filmmaker's vision is maintained in translation and accessibility. In the UK, the visually-impaired filmmaker Raina Haig was the first to include AD as part of the production process in her award-winning debut film *Drive* (1997). Her website includes articles on disability and filmmaking and on how to integrate accessibility from production. In her view, in order to provide visually-impaired audiences with 'equitable commercial choices and artistic quality' the AD needs to be constructed 'in consultation or even collaboration with the filmmaker', thus regarding 'the job of audio description as a part of the film industry' (Haig 2002). This requires training in film studies for the audio describers to 'learn how to attune themselves to the filmmaker's vision' and in the basics of AD for filmmakers to be able to take decisions on how their film can be made accessible to a blind audience.

Also in the field of accessibility, filmmaker and artist Liz Crow founded in 2005 the production company Roaring Girl Productions, one of whose aims is 'to pioneer new approaches to film accessibility, working to make audio description, captioning and sign language (ACS) an integral part of the production process rather than an access 'add-on'. This is so that people with sensory impairments can participate fully as audience members and filmmakers' work can be accurately and sensitively conveyed' (Crow 2005b). In 'Making Film Accessible' (Crow 2005a) and 'A New Approach to Film Accessibility' (Crow 2005b), she provides detailed descriptions of how her films *Nectar* (2005), *Illumination* (2007) and *Resistance on Tour* (2008) were made accessible. For Crow, it is essential to avoid the prevailing template-based, one-size-fits-all approach to accessibility which results in AD and subtitles that are removed from the overall feel of the production:

> For the audience, the result is that the very methods designed to promote access can detract from the qualitative experience of the production. For the filmmaker, the access conventions available can misrepresent and undermine the vision they have worked so hard to create and communicate.
>
> *(Crow 2005c: 3)*

Crow's account of how accessibility was brought into the core of the creative process in the production of *Nectar* (2005) through experimentation with both aesthetic and technological solutions is particularly interesting and constitutes one of the first set of recommendations on accessible filmmaking. The subtitles, produced in collaboration with a deaf consultant, were not only based on traditional technical guidelines but also on aesthetic grounds. This helped to decide on the font, colour, speed and display mode of the subtitles on the basis of the visual identity, the *mise en scène* and the mood of the film. Reflecting on the whole process, Crow explains that this approach requires some extra time in post-production, which can be made possible by the inclusion of accessibility in the film budget and by its recognition as a budget line for funding bodies. Only in this way will filmmakers be able to keep control over the way in which their films are received by sensory-impaired audiences, with a degree of subjectivity (and collaboration with the translator) that is not possible within the rigid margins of standard industrial subtitling.

In the field of ethnographic documentary, a good example of accessible filmmaking is the filmography of award-winning director Alastair Cole. His latest film, *The Colours of the Alphabet* (2016), is a feature-length ethnographic documentary about multilingual

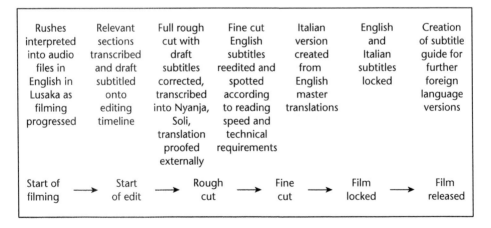

Figure 31.1 Subtitling production process in Cole's film *The Colours of the Alphabet* (2016).

education in Zambia in which he has used subtitles as 'an intrinsic part of the filmmaking process that can be planned and engaged with from the start of production, and embraced as a powerful tool for emphasizing perspective as well as forging characters and narratives' (Cole 2015: 134). Figure 31.1 (Cole 2015: 135) illustrates how subtitling was integrated in the filmmaking process:

Cole ensured that the subtitles were created before the film was locked edit, which allowed them to 'influence the pacing and emotional engagement of the film where necessary, and permitted the adjustment of any scene that would create significant problems in viewing with the subtitles' (Cole 2015: 138). Cole worked with a producer of language and accessibility (similar to the supervisor of accessibility services proposed by Udo and Fels (2009) but including, in this case, both translation and accessibility) to create a guide document for subtitlers. This document included the full original transcript, the translation into English, the English subtitles, the Italian subtitles and a section with comments for subtitlers regarding potential translation difficulties. The subtitlers of the various foreign versions of the film had the opportunity to contact the filmmaker, liaising first with the producer of language and accessibility.

In Cole's view, documentary filmmaking, and particularly ethnographic filmmaking (which has translation at its core), offers a unique context and a fruitful area of research to test new, creative and collaborative forms of translation and accessibility. Furthermore, he adds an essential ethical consideration to support the use of accessible filmmaking in this genre:

> The common, and often inevitable requirement to outsource the creation of various foreign language versions of films can result in removal of the director from any translation and subtitling debate, thus shifting ultimate responsibility for the translation and the representation of the characters involved in the film away from the person with whom the people in the film have entrusted their stories. Fully understanding the implications and procedures of subtitling, recognizing the key role of the director in any debate, and understanding one's own ideological perspective within the creation of the subtitles and the film as a whole is, I suggest, critical to mitigating the obvious dangers and harm mistranslation, and misrepresentation can entail.
>
> *(Cole 2015: 148)*

All these films, including the above-mentioned *Joining the Dots* (Romero-Fresco 2012), which has been shown at secondary schools in Switzerland and has been used by Netflix and the United Nation's ITU Focus Group on Media Accessibility as an example of good practice, show that accessible filmmaking can present a feasible alternative to the industrial model of translation and accessibility that currently prevails in the profession.

However, much work remains to be done in terms of research, training and practice in order to determine, for instance, what degree of collaboration between the creative team and the translators is required for a film to fulfil the standard of accessible filmmaking. After all, the films mentioned here include a wide range of options, from one or two meetings between filmmakers and translators (*Secret City, Home Sweet Home, Hijos de las Nubes*) to workshops (*De weg van alle vlees*) and much more thorough collaborations (*The Colours of the Alphabet, Joining the Dots, Nectar*). Romero-Fresco (2013: 215) provides a list of considerations to inform this collaboration at the different stages of the production:

Pre-production stage

- the provision of metadata for translators, including not only the script (in fiction) or the transcripts (in documentaries) but also any other information available, such as research material, the treatment, the storyboard and the shooting script, which may be very useful for the audio describer;
- attention to clothing colour if subtitles are to be used;
- collaboration between the subtitler and the creative team in pre-production if subtitles are to be used as part of the original film (part-subtitling).

Production stage

- attention to framing if subtitles are to be used. This is particularly important in the case of close ups with dialogue or narration.

Post-production stage

- collaboration between the translator and the post-production team;
- attention to on-screen titles (particularly in documentaries) and on-screen text when dialogue or narration is used over them. Unless the shot is extended, the viewers of the translated film may end up losing either the dialogue/narration or the translation of the text;
- access to the sound editors, or to the sound editing process, may prove very useful for SDH subtitlers. The experience could help them engage with and understand useful terms they need to describe the music, the special effects and the atmosphere for the deaf and hard of hearing viewers.

In order to avoid mere token gestures and consultations by filmmakers that do not result in effective collaboration with translators, further practical and theoretical work on this field could focus on a future set of minimum requirements for a film to obtain the standard of accessible filmmaking. This could include not only the provision of translation, SDH and AD, but also a degree (or different degrees) of collaboration between the creative team and the translators.

Conclusion

Accessible filmmaking is almost as old as cinema. It existed during the silent film era and was subsequently replaced by an industrialized model where translation and accessibility are relegated to the distribution stage, translators have no contact with the creative team and filmmakers have no control over the translated and accessible versions of their films. Profitable as this model may be, it has had a negative impact on the working conditions of translators and on the quality of translation, and is beginning to raise criticism by both filmmakers and translation scholars:

> Filmmakers must involve themselves in translation because the contribution of the translator is every bit as profound as that of the screenwriter, actor, or director . . . Thus, it behoves artists to understand the process and get involved if they care at all about their work. They should make themselves available to translators, demand the best, and participate in the process. After all, in an age when no film is complete until it crosses the frontier of language, it is the translator who has the last word. Global cinema is the translator's cinema.
>
> *(Nornes 2007: 243)*

Accessible filmmaking offers the possibility to implement this advice by integrating AVT and accessibility as part of the filmmaking process through collaboration between the translators and the creative team of the film. From the point of view of research, accessible filmmaking invites AVT scholars to explore the way in which film theorists and filmmakers have tackled the notion of translation, as in the case of ethnographic filmmaking and its consideration of subtitling as a dramatic component of visual anthropology. For film scholars, accessible filmmaking offers tools, developed in the field of AVT, to study the impact that translation and accessibility can have on the production and reception of film, such as the results of the eye-tracking reception studies conducted so far in this area. Some of these studies (Fox 2016) suggest that this model can help to produce in the target viewers an increased sense of presence and a degree of similarity in the way in which films are received by the source and target audience that is not normally found in films that are translated at the distribution stage.

Training-wise, accessible filmmaking offers an opportunity for AVT students to develop their creativity and knowledge of film(making), as well as their potential for employability, and for film students to collaborate with translators from their first productions. This has materialized in several initiatives at graduate and postgraduate level in countries such as Spain, Italy or Belgium that are beginning to bridge the gap between film and translation/accessibility training.

Finally, with the support of user associations, film commissions and the United Nation's ITU Focus Group on Media Accessibility, accessible filmmaking has also been implemented in the professional industry. Although still few and far between, some mainstream filmmakers such as Tarantino and Iñárritu are beginning to have a say in the way in which their films should be translated. But more importantly, an increasing number of independent filmmakers are embracing this approach and, in some cases, promoting it by producing guidelines and research to substantiate their practice.

Four years after the first article on the subject (Romero-Fresco 2013), accessible filmmaking is slowly but steadily developing, helped by the widespread recognition of accessibility as a key issue in audiovisual media and by the increasing presence of multilingualism and creative authorial titles in original films. Needless to say, it does not pose a threat to the deep-rooted industrialized model that relegates translation and accessibility to the distribution stage as an afterthought in the film industry. Instead, it sits quietly on the side, learning from the innovation and creativity of fan-made translation and offering an alternative model for those filmmakers who care about their foreign and sensory-impaired audiences as much as they do about their original viewers.

Summary

Despite a greatly increased volume of research over the past decade, AVT and media accessibility and its main services (dubbing, subtitling, SDH and AD for blind and partially sighted people) are still an afterthought in the filmmaking process. This results in a lack of investment in this area and a worrying decrease in quality and working conditions.

The present chapter focuses on the notion of accessible filmmaking as a way to tackle this problem by integrating AVT and accessibility during the filmmaking process through collaboration between filmmakers and translators. First, a historical account is provided of the origins and background of accessible filmmaking, from the silent film era and the multiple-language versions to the current invisibility of translation and accessibility in the film industry. This is followed by a section on research in this area, both from the point of view of (ethnographic) film and from AVT, with special emphasis on eye-tracking-based reception studies. The chapter concludes with a section on how accessible filmmaking is being implemented in training and professional practice at an international level as well as with a set of final conclusions.

Further reading

MacDougall, D. (1998) 'Subtitling Ethnographic Films', in D. MacDougall *Transcultural Cinema*, Princeton, NJ: Princeton University Press, 165-178 | *This is a seminal chapter covering the notion of translation (and, more specifically, subtitling) from the point of view of ethnographic filmmaking.*

Crow, L. (2005c) 'Nectar: A New Approach to Film Accessibility'. Available online: http://www.roaring-girl.com/wp-content/uploads/2013/07/Film-Accessibility.pdf [last access 20 December 2017] | *This is the first set of guidelines and recommendations on accessible filmmaking, published online by the filmmaker and artist Liz Crow and covering audio description, subtitling for the deaf and hard of hearing and sign language interpreting.*

Romero-Fresco, P. (2013) 'Accessible Filmmaking: Joining the Dots between Audiovisual Translation, Accessibility and Filmmaking', *JoSTrans: The Journal of Specialised Translation* 20: 201–223. Available online: http://www.jostrans.org/issue20/art_romero.pdf [last access 20 December 2017] | *This is the first academic article ever published on the notion of accessible filmmaking and it includes the link to the 2012 film Joining the Dots. Both the article and the film are hosted on the online site of the United Nation's ITU Focus Group on Media Accessibility as examples of good practice.*

Refractory, a Journal of Entertainment Media 25: Themed issue: *Eye-Tracking the Moving Image*. Available online: http://refractory.unimelb.edu.au/2015/02/06/volume-25-2015/ [last access 20 December 2017] | *The articles included in this issue, and especially the ones by Tim Smith and Kruger et al., provide a thorough and rigorous up-to-date overview of eye-tracking research in original and translated films.*

Related topics

2   History of audiovisual translation
3   Subtitling on the cusp of its futures
6   Subtitling for deaf and hard of hearing audiences: moving forward
8   Audio description: evolving recommendations for usable, effective and enjoyable practices
14 Psycholinguistics and perception in audiovisual translation
17 Multimodality and audiovisual translation: cohesion in accessible films
22 Eye tracking in audiovisual translation research
23 Audiovisual translation and audience reception
29 Audiovisual translator training

References

AENOR (2012) *Norma UNE 153010: Subtitulado para personas sordas y personas con discapacidad auditiva*, Madrid: AENOR.

Baldo, M. (2009) 'Dubbing Multilingual Films. La terra del ritorno and the Italian-Canadian Immigrant Experience', *Intralinea*. Special Issue: 'Multimedia Dialect Translation, The Translation of Dialects in Multimedia'. Available online: http://www.intralinea.org/specials/article/Dubbing_multilingual_films [last access 20 December 2017].

Betz, M. (2009) *Beyond the Subtitle: Remapping European Art Cinema*, Minnesota: University of Minnesota Press.

Cattrysse, P. and Y. Gambier (2008) 'Screenwriting and Translating Screenplays', in J. Díaz Cintas (ed.) *The Didactics of Audiovisual Translation*, Amsterdam & Philadelphia: John Benjamins, 39–57.

Chaume, F. (2004). *Cine y Traducción*. Madrid: Cátedra.
Cole, A. (2015) *Good Morning, Grade One. Language Ideologies and Multilingualism within Primary Education in Rural Zambia*, Unpublished Doctoral Thesis, University of Edinburgh.
Connell, B. R., M. Jones, R. Mace, J. Mueller, A. Mullick, E. Ostroff, J. Sanford, E. Steinfeld, M. Story and G. Vanderheiden (1997) 'The Principles of Universal Design', in M. Story, J. Mueller and R. Mace (eds) *The Universal Design File*, New York: New York State University Press.
Corrius i Gimbert, M. and P. Zabalbeascoa (2011) 'Language Variation in Source Texts and their Translation. The Case of L3 in Film Translation', *Target* 23(1): 113–130.
Crow, L. (2005a) 'Making Film Accessible'. Available online: http://www.roaring-girl.com/work/making-film-accessible/ [last access 20 December 2017]
Crow, L. (2005b) 'A New Approach to Film Accessibility'. Available online: http://www.roaring-girl.com/work/a-new-approach-to-film-accessibility/ [last access 20 December 2017]
Crow, L. (2005c) 'Nectar: A New Approach to Film Accessibility'. Available online: http://www.roaring-girl.com/wp-content/uploads/2013/07/Film-Accessibility.pdf [last access 20 December 2017].
de Higes Andino, I. (2014) *Estudio descriptivo y comparativo de la traducción de filmes multilingües: El caso del cine británico de inmigración contemporáneo*, Unpublished Doctoral thesis, Universitat Jaume I, Castelló de la Plana, Spain.
de Higes Andino, I., A. M. Prats Rodríguez, J. J. Martínez Sierra, F. Chaume (2013) 'Subtitling Language Diversity in Spanish Immigration Films', *Meta* 58(1): 134–145.
de Linde, Z. and N. Kay (1999) *The Semiotics of Subtitling*, Manchester: St. Jerome Publishing.
Díaz Cintas, J. (2011) 'Dealing with Multilingual Films in Audiovisual Translation', in W. Pöckl, I. Ohnheiser and P. Sandrini (eds) *Translation, Sprachvariation, Mehrsprachigkeit. Festschrift für Lew Zybatow zum 60*, Geburtstag, Frankfurt am Main/Berlin/Bern/Brussels/NewYork/Oxford/Vienna: Peter Lang, 215–233.
d'Ydewalle, G. and W. De Bruycker (2007) 'Eye Movements of Children and Adults while Reading Television Subtitles', *European Psychologist* 12: 196–205.
Dywer, T. (2015) 'From Subtitles to SMS: Eye Tracking, Texting and Sherlock', *Refractory: A Journal of Entertainment Media* 25. Available online: http://refractory.unimelb.edu.au/2015/02/07/dwyer/ [last access 20 December 2017]
Egoyan, A. and I. Balfour (2004) *Subtitles: On the Foreignness of Film*, Cambridge: MIT Press.
Fox, W. (2016) 'Integrated Titles—An Improved Viewing Experience? A Contrastive Eye Tracking Study on Traditional Subtitles and Integrated Titles for Pablo Romero-Fresco's *Joining the Dots*', in S. Hansen-Schirra and S. Grucza (eds) *Eyetracking and Applied Linguistics*, Open Access Book Series Translation and Natural Language Processing, Berlin: Language Science Press, 5–30.
Fryer, L. and J. Freeman (2012) 'Cinematic Language and the Description of Film: Keeping AD Users in the Frame', *Perspectives: Studies in Translatology* 21(3): 1–15.
Haig, R. (2002) 'Audio Description: Art or Industry?', interview originally published in *Dail* (Disability Arts in London Magazine) magazine, November 2002. Available online: http://www.rainahaig.com/pages/AudioDescriptionAorI.html [last access 20 December 2017].
Heiss, C. (2004) 'Dubbing Multilingual Films: A New Challenge?', *Meta* 49(1): 208–220.
Henley, P. (1996) 'The Promise of Ethnographic Film', Lecture given in honour of the late Professor Paul Stirling at the University of Kent at the 5th International Festival of Ethnographic Film.
Henley, P. (2010) *The Adventure of the Real. Jean Rouch and the Craft of Ethnographic Cinema*, Chicago: University of Chicago Press.
Ivarsson, J. (1992) *Subtitling for the Media. A Handbook of an Art*, Stockholm: Transedit.
Izard, N. (2001) 'Doblaje y subtitulación: una aproximación histórica', in M. Duro (ed.) *La traducción para el doblaje y la subtitulación*, Madrid: Cátedra, 189–209.
Jensema, C., S. E. Sharkawy, R. S. Danturthi, R. Burch and D. Hsu (2000) 'Eye Movement Patterns of Captioned Television Viewers', in *American Annals of the Deaf* 145(3): 275–285.
Kofoed, D. T. (2011) 'Decotitles, the Animated Discourse of Fox's Recent Anglophonic Internationalism', *Reconstruction* 11(1). Available online: http://reconstruction.eserver.org/ [last access 20 December 2017].

Kruger, J.-L., S. Doherty and M. T. Soto Sanfiel (2015) 'Psychological Immersion in a Foreign Language. The Effect of Same-language Subtitles on English Foreign Language Viewers', paper presented at the International Conference *Media for All 6*, 17 September.

Lewis, E. D. (2003) *Timothy Asch and Ethnographic Film*, London: Routledge.

MacDougall, D. (1998) 'Subtitling Ethnographic Films', in D. MacDougall (ed.) *Transcultural Cinema*, Princeton, NJ: Princeton University Press, 165–178.

Mas, J. and P. Orero (2005) 'La escritura de guiones: una asignatura a tener en cuenta para la enseñanza de la traducción audiovisual', in M. E. García García, A. González Rodríguez, C. Kunschak and P. Scarampi (eds) *IV Jornadas sobre la Formación y Profesión del Traductor e Intérprete*, Madrid: Universidad Europea de Madrid Ediciones [CD-Rom Edition].

McClarty, R. (2012) 'Towards a Multidisciplinary Approach in Creative Subtitling', *MonTI* 4: 133–155.

MFP (2012) *Le sous-titrage de référence pour sourds et malentendants*, Paris: MFP.

Mingant, N. (2010) 'Tarantino's *Inglourious Basterds*: A Blueprint for Dubbing Translators?', *Meta* 55(4): 712–731.

Mital, P. K., T. J. Smith, R. Hill and J. M. Henderson (2011) 'Clustering of Gaze during Dynamic Scene Viewing is Predicted by Motion', *Cognitive Computation* 3(1): 5–24.

Nornes, A. M. (2007) *Cinema Babel. Translating Global Cinema*, Minnesota: University of Minnesota Press.

Ofcom (2016) *The Quality of Live Subtitling: Measures Designed to Improve the Quality of Live Subtitling on UK TV to Benefit Deaf and Hard-of-hearing Viewers*, London: Office of Communications. Available online: http://stakeholders.ofcom.org.uk/consultations/subtitling/ [last access 20 December 2017].

O'Hagan, M. (2009) 'Evolution of User-generated Translation: Fansubs, Translation Hacking and Crowdsourcing', *Journal of Internationalisation and Localisation* 1: 94–121.

O'Sullivan, C. (2008) 'Multilingualism at the Multiplex: A New Audience for Screen Translation?', *Linguistica Antverpiensia* 6: 81–97.

Perego, E., F. del Missier, M. Porta and M. Mosconi (2010) 'The Cognitive Effectiveness of Subtitle Processing', *Media Psychology* 13: 243–272.

Perego, E., F. del Missier and S. Bottiroli (2014) 'Dubbing versus Subtitling in Young and Older Adults: Cognitive and Evaluative Aspects', *Perspectives: Studies in Translatology* 23(1): 1–21.

Pérez-González, L. (2012) 'Co-Creational Subtitling in the Digital Media: Transformative and Authorial Practices', *International Journal of Cultural Studies* 16 (1): 3–21.

Rayner, K. (1998) 'Eye Movements in Reading and Information Processing: Twenty Years of Research', *Psychological Bulletin* 124: 372–422.

Romero-Fresco, P. (2011) *Subtitling through Speech Recognition: Respeaking*, Manchester: Routledge.

Romero-Fresco, P. (2013) 'Accessible Filmmaking: Joining the Dots between Audiovisual Translation, Accessibility and Filmmaking', *JoSTrans: The Journal of Specialised Translation* 20: 201–223. Available online: http://www.jostrans.org/issue20/art_romero.pdf [last access 20 December 2017].

Romero-Fresco, P. (2015) *The Reception of Subtitles for the Deaf and Hard of Hearing in Europe*, Bern: Peter Lang.

Romero-Fresco, P. (2016a) 'The Dubbing Effect: An Eye-Tracking Study Comparing the Reception of Original and Dubbed Films', paper presented at *Linguistic and Cultural Representation in Audiovisual Translation*, Sapienza Università di Roma and Università degli Studi di Roma Tre, 11–13 February.

Romero-Fresco, P. (2016b) 'The Reception of Automatic Surtitles: Viewers' Preferences, Perception and Presence', paper presented at the Conference *Unlimited: International Symposium on Accessible Live Events*, 29 April 2016, University of Antwerp, Belgium.

Romero-Fresco, P. (2017) 'Accessible Filmmaking in Documentaries', in J. J. Martínez-Sierra and B. Cerezo Merchán (eds) *Building Bridges between Film Studies and Translation Studies*, Special Issue of *inTRAlinea*. Available online: http://www.intralinea.org/specials/article/accessible_filmmaking_in_documentaries [last access 20 December 2017].

Romero-Fresco, P. (2018a) 'Eye-tracking, Subtitling and Accessible Filmmaking', in T. Dwyer, C. Perkins, S. Redmond and J. Sita (eds) *Seeing into Screens: Eye Tracking and the Moving Image*, Bloomsbury, 235–257.
Romero-Fresco, P. (2018b) *Accessible Filmmaking Guide,* London: BFI.
Romero-Fresco, P. (forthcoming) *Accessible Filmmaking: Integrating Translation and Accessibility as Part of the Filmmaking Process*, London: Routledge.
Ruoff, J. (1994) 'On the Trail of the Native's Point of View', in *CVA Newsletter* 2: 15–18. Available online: https://www.dartmouth.edu/~jruoff/Articles/CVANewsletter.htm [last access 20 December 2017].
Sanz, E. (2015) *Beyond Monolingualism: A Descriptive and Multimodal Methodology for the Dubbing of Polyglot Films*, Unpublished Doctoral Thesis, University of Edinburgh.
Sasamoto, R. (2014) 'Impact Caption as a Highlighting Device: Attempts at Viewer Manipulation on TV', in *Discourse, Context and Media* 6: 1–10.
Şerban, A. (2012) 'Translation as Alchemy: The Aesthetics of Multilingualism in Film', *Multidisciplinarity in Audiovisual Translation, MonTI* 4: 39–63. Available online: http://repositori.uji.es/xmlui/bitstream/handle/10234/59924/MonTI_04_03.pdf?sequence=1 [last access 20 December 2017].
Smith, T. J. (2013) 'Watching You Watch Movies: Using Eye Tracking to Inform Cognitive Film Theory', in A. P. Shimamura (ed.) *Psychocinematics: Exploring Cognition at the Movies*, New York: Oxford University Press, 165–191.
Smith, T. (2015) 'Read, Watch, Listen: A Commentary on Eye Tracking and Moving Images', *Refractory: A Journal of Entertainment Media* 25. Available online: http://refractory.unimelb.edu.au/2015/02/07/smith/ [last access 20 December 2017].
Stephanidis, C. (2001) 'Adaptive Techniques for Universal Access', *User Modeling and User-Adapted Interaction* 11: 159–179.
Udo, J.-P. and D. Fels (2009) 'The Rogue Poster Children of Universal Design: Closed Captioning and Audio Description', *Ted Rogers School of Information Technology Management Publications and Research, Paper* 18, 1–32. Available online: http://digitalcommons.ryerson.ca/trsitm/18 [last access 20 December 2017].
Vilaró, A. and T. J. Smith (2011) 'Subtitle Reading Effects on Visual and Verbal Information Processing in Films', *Perception. ECVP Abstract Supplement* 40: 153. European Conference on Visual Perception, Toulouse, France.
Vincendeau, G. (1999) 'Hollywood Babel: The Coming of Sound and the Multiple-Language Version', in A. Higson and R. Maltby (eds) *'Film Europe' and 'Film America': Cinema, Commerce and Cultural Exchange 1920-1939*, Exeter: University of Exeter Press, 207–225.
Zabalbeascoa, P. and E. Voellmer (2014) 'Accounting for Multilingual Films in Translation Studies: Intratextual Translation in Dubbing', in D. Abend-David (ed.) *Media and Translation: An Interdisciplinary Approach*. London: Bloomsbury, 25–52.
Zhang, J. (2012) 'The Interaction between Visual and Written Ethnography in Subtitling', *Visual Anthropology*: Published in cooperation with the Commission on *Visual Anthropology* 25(5): 439–449.
Zhang, S. (2014) 'How Hollywood Figured out a Way to Make Texting in Movies Look less Dumb', *Gizmodo*, August 18. Available online: https://gizmodo.com/how-hollywood-figured-out-a-way-to-make-texting-in-movi-1623340285 [last access 20 December 2017].

Filmography

Avatar (2009) James Cameron. IMDb entry: http://www.imdb.com/title/tt0499549/?ref_=nv_sr_1
Babel (2006) Alejandro González Iñárritu. IMDb entry: http://www.imdb.com/title/tt0449467/?ref_=fn_al_tt_1
De weg van alle vlees (2013) Deben Van Dam. IMDb entry: http://www.imdb.com/title/tt3178340/?ref_=fn_al_tt_1
Drive (1997) Raina Haig.

Hijos de las Nubes (2013) Álvaro Longoria. IMDb entry: http://www.imdb.com/title/tt1661263/?ref_=fn_al_tt_1

Home Sweet Home (2012) Enrica Colusso. IMDb entry: http://www.imdb.com/title/tt2419712/?ref_=nm_knf_t3

Illumination (2005) Liz Crow.

Inglourious Basterds (2009) Quentin Tarantino. IMDb entry: http://www.imdb.com/title/tt0361748/?ref_=fn_tt_tt_1

Joining the Dots (2012) Pablo Romero-Fresco.

Lone Star (1996) John Sayles. IMDb entry: http://www.imdb.com/title/tt0116905/?ref_=fn_al_tt_1

Men with Guns (1997) John Sayles. IMDb entry: http://www.imdb.com/title/tt0119657/?ref_=fn_al_tt_1

Mystery Train (1989) Jim Jarmusch. IMDb entry: http://www.imdb.com/title/tt0097940/?ref_=fn_tt_tt_1

Nectar (2005) Liz Crow.

Night on Earth (1991) Jim Jarmusch. IMDb entry: http://www.imdb.com/title/tt0102536/?ref_=fn_al_tt_1

Nina (2012) Elisa Fuksas. IMDb entry: http://www.imdb.com/title/tt2261891/?ref_=fn_tt_tt_12

Notes on Blindness (2014) Peter Middleton and James Spinney. IMDb entry: http://www.imdb.com/title/tt3533352/?ref_=fn_al_tt_2

Resistance on Tour (2005) Liz Crow.

The Colours of the Alphabet (2016) Alastair Cole. IMDb entry: http://www.imdb.com/title/tt4368862/?ref_=fn_al_tt_1

The Jazz Singer (1927) Alan Crosland. IMDb entry: http://www.imdb.com/title/tt0018037/?ref_=fn_tt_tt_2

The Lights of New York (1928) Bryan Foy. IMDb entry: http://www.imdb.com/title/tt0019096/?ref_=fn_al_tt_2

The Revenant (2015) Alejandro Gómez Iñárritu. IMDb entry: http://www.imdb.com/title/tt1663202/?ref_=fn_al_tt_1

Secret City (2012) Michael Chanan. IMDb entry: http://www.imdb.com/title/tt2448704/?ref_=fn_al_tt_2

Slumdog Millionaire (2008) Danny Boyle. IMDb entry: http://www.imdb.com/title/tt1010048/?ref_=fn_al_tt_1

32
Technologization of audiovisual translation

Panayota (Yota) Georgakopoulou

Since the turn of our century, the Audiovisual Translation (AVT) industry has seen a period of transformation as a result of rapid technological change. This is only natural, as technology and AVT have always gone hand-in-hand. The very existence of AVT is a by-product of developments in film, video and broadcasting technologies, and as such it continues to change and evolve with them. In our digital, globalized world, an industry international by definition, with professionals working in different languages around the world, can expect trends such as the cloud, the crowd and big data to play a pivotal part in shaping its future course.

The beginnings of audiovisual translation

AVT started out as an art form originally interlinked with the video material itself as film-makers were experimenting with narrative in the early days of classical Hollywood cinema, e.g. intertitles in the silent film era (Thompson and Bordwell 1994: 39–40), or trying to cross the language barrier when sound made its appearance, e.g. by re-shooting a film in additional versions so as to cater for other languages (*ibid.*: 229–230). It became an add-on product to the film production process in the 1940s, when technology made it possible to separate the two and thus provide a financially viable way to translate film for foreign audiences. This led to the birth of subtitling and dubbing as the two main methods of audiovisual language transfer, which is still the case today.

AVT remained largely a manual craft through to the 1970s, with several professionals being involved in the process. Translators would work from a provided script to translate already spotted subtitles, or adapt film scripts for lip synchronization in the case of dubbing, but their skills were not considered sufficient for the more technical parts of the process. It was technicians and typists that transcribed the handwritten subtitles and cued them, while their insertion onto the film involved a variety of mechanical, thermal, photochemical and optical methods (see Ivarsson and Carroll 1998: 12–23).

The 1970s marked the first major milestone for the AVT industry, as the first open-captioned programmes were run on American TV. Line 21 of the broadcasting signal was reserved for the transmission of closed captions in the USA and teletext was invented in the UK, later to become an international standard adopted by the European Broadcasting Union (EBU).

Live closed-captioned broadcasts began in the 1980s, with the use of court stenographers, who were trained as stenocaptioners and utilized specially designed keyboards and short-forms to churn out captions at a speed similar to speech delivery in live broadcasts. Regular offline and live closed-captioning/teletext subtitling of television broadcasts for accessibility purposes became the norm from the 1980s onwards and its use increased as legislation was introduced in the decades that followed.

New technologies pushed the entertainment industry forward in the 1980s. The introduction of VHS in the late 1970s contributed to the rapid expansion of home video throughout the world, while the growth of cable and satellite channels in the 1980s boosted the volume of programming available and the need for AVT treatment. At the same time, the advent of the desktop computer revolutionized the translation process and, in particular, AVT. Dedicated subtitling software, originally DOS-based and linked to a TV monitor, caption generator and VHS player with jog shuttle, was developed, which allowed subtitlers to carry out the entire process from beginning to end, including the spotting, timing, translation of the dialogue and its adaptation to fit the length and time constraints of subtitles. This resulted in the definition of the job of a subtitler as a distinct profession in the market.

The digital revolution

Word processing, subtitling software, digital video, Web 1.0

The 1990s saw an increase in the pace of developments in the subtitling industry with concurrent technological advances. The rise in the use of Windows-type interfaces and word-processing programs was a turning point for the translation industry in its entirety, which evolved to the 'localization' industry as we know it today. Spell and grammar checkers were the first 'tools' translators ever used. Traditional translation agencies were transformed into Language Service Providers (LSPs), not simply translating, but localizing content, modifying it and adapting it to local requirements.

The subtitling industry also evolved as subtitling software became more sophisticated. More companies developing such software started appearing in the market to offer tools that simplified the subtitling task, mainly from a technical/timing aspect: FAB (Germany, 1996), SoftNI (USA, 1996), TitleVision (Denmark, 1996), CANVASs (Japan, 1997), Spot Software (Netherlands, 1997), Telestream (USA, 1998), Starfish Technologies (UK, 2000) and EZTitles (Bulgaria, 2002) came to compete with pioneers such as SysMedia (UK, 1974), Screen Systems (UK, 1976), Softel (UK, 1983) and Cavena (Sweden, 1989). These companies remained the world leaders until today in terms of products that allow the creation, repurposing, encoding, transcoding, insertion and transmission of subtitles. SysMedia was acquired by Screen Systems in 2011 (Screen Systems 2011), while Softel was taken over by Miranda in 2013 (Grass Valley 2013)—which sadly discontinued Softel's suite of products in 2018 (Grass Valley, n.d.).

Digital video formats in the 1990s made external VHS players used in subtitling workstations redundant. Films were digitized and stored on company servers, accessible from in-house subtitlers' workstations, or later copied onto DVD-Rs to be shipped to freelance workers. By the turn of the century, Digital Betacam machines were also discarded as clients began moving to entirely tapeless workflows. Not only was there no need to have expensive software and hardware in order to deliver subtitles to end clients, it was no longer necessary to be located in close proximity to them either.

The same was true of the majority of the workforce that was responsible for the creation of the subtitles. As an international industry by default, it was only natural that translators embraced technological advances and were counted among the early adopters of computers and dial-up modems. This led to an increase in homeworkers translating in text editors off-site and performing review and quality control only in dedicated subtitling workstations in the offices of subtitling localization providers. With the widespread adoption of the internet and the development of less costly subtitling software addressed to freelancers, this geographic proximity became even less of a necessity. At the same time, the introduction of basic keyword search on the web meant that translators no longer needed to rely on books and physical libraries for their research, making their geographical location almost irrelevant to their ability to offer their services to their clients.

DVDs and the template workflow in subtitling

The birth of DVD in the mid-1990s marked a new era for the AVT industry, in part because it boosted content volume further and made subtitling more prominent in traditional dubbing countries. It also posed a challenge for the industry, as it created demand for subtitling in a large number of languages within short turnaround times concurrently with two major issues for the Hollywood studios, namely piracy and costs. The result was the emergence of a new workflow for subtitling production, involving the use of already timed and spotted template files in the source audio language to be translated into all the target languages required in any film project (Georgakopoulou 2006), a workflow inspired by the early practices of Scandinavian subtitling companies which applied a similar methodology when working into more than one Scandinavian language simultaneously.

This separation of the act of translation from the more technical aspects of the craft of subtitling for the second time in AVT history had two important consequences. On the one hand, it solved the recruitment issue multilingual subtitling companies were faced with, as it automatically expanded the pool of freelance translation editors to include all available translators worldwide who, with little training in the principles of subtitling, could now become versed in this translation domain as well. On the other hand, an indirect consequence, the value of which would only become apparent much later, was the creation of a large volume of parallel subtitling corpora in multiple languages, which would eventually be used to further advance the technologization of the subtitling profession (Georgakopoulou 2012: 92). It also paved the way for the centralization and internationalization of the home entertainment AVT business in the hands of subtitling companies strategically located along the LA–London axis, in close proximity to their Hollywood client American and European headquarters (Carroll 2004).

First applications of language technologies in the translation industry

The 1990s were also the decade in which language technologies were introduced commercially on a large scale to enhance translators' productivity and consequently reduce project turnaround times and costs. Prime examples were the use of continuous dictation software, as well as technologies that offered the ability to reuse text, such as Translation Memories (TMs) and Machine Translation (MT).

With research dating back to the 1970s (Hidden Markov Model), and the n-gram language model of the 1980s, the Automatic Speech Recognition (ASR) field saw rapid improvements, which led to commercially successful applications in the 1990s, including the launch of continuous speech dictation software, such as IBM's ViaVoice (1997) and Dragon Systems'

NaturallySpeaking (1997), the latter being the most popular dictation package until recently. Dictation software has been used by professional translators as a means to increase their productivity. However, this is still primarily an individual choice rather than a workflow requirement enforced by LSPs. The practice dates back to the use of cassette tapes for dictating translation to then be transcribed, as a productivity enhancement tool by translators in the 1980s, before dictation software became available (Hendzel 2013).

The AVT industry took an interest in speech recognition as an alternative workflow for live captioning to replace the training- and cost-intensive workflows based on stenographers. Speech recognition was integrated in subtitling software and introduced to subtitlers via respeaking (or 'voice writing', as it is called in the States) around the turn of the century. The respeaking workflow consisted of professionals listening to the source audio and dictating it into a speech recognition engine, which transcribed it producing same language subtitles and captions. The practice was originally mocked for the incomprehensible, amusing or even insulting machine-made mistakes the use of this technology introduced (*Daily Mail Reporter* 2013). However, the improvements in speech recognition software, the enrichment of dictionaries used (including the use of crawling techniques to look for new named entities that appeared in the news for instance, so as to further enrich dictionaries), as well as the experience gained by respeakers themselves resulted in quality outputs similar to the ones achieved by stenographers, who are being phased out of the live subtitling profession. The practice of respeaking has recently also been implemented as an alternative way to produce real-time translation subtitles, which until now required the use of an interpreter in combination with a stenocaptioner, a process which resulted in high delays and costs, and was hence rarely practised. Interlingual respeaking workflows are slowly being implemented commercially (e.g. Red Bee Media Spain), while universities (e.g. Antwerp) are researching the possibility of cross-training interpreters into translation respeakers. The introduction of technology in live translation subtitling workflows and the resulting drastic reduction in cost will make it possible for real-time translation subtitling to become an everyday service in the years to come.

On the translation side, Computer Assisted Translation (CAT) tools became standardized and widespread, after being introduced in the workflows of LSPs specializing in the translation of technical texts. Shared glossaries evolved to fully blown terminology management systems, translation memories reduced the work of translators by providing the translation of previously translated chunks of text that to an extent matched the new source text, and quality assurance tools were integrated with text editors in translator workbenches. Rule-based machine translation (RBMT) was also commercially used for the first time, originally in controlled-language restricted-vocabulary domains, such as manuals, where the results were yielding significant accuracy to enhance translators' productivity. The AVT industry remained largely detached from these developments until the following century, mainly on the assumption that they were inappropriate for implementation in the entertainment domain, which provided the bulk of the material undergoing interlingual subtitling. However, significant developments in recent years, both in terms of content types that require AVT, as well as in the overall volume of content to be translated, have paved the way for experimentation with such technologies that are yielding promising results.

The broadband revolution: trends and debates

The impact of broadband Internet since the turn of the century has been much greater on the AVT industry than one could have envisaged.

Outsourcing

Broadband Internet access catalyzed the transformation of the translation industry into the globalized and centralized localization industry we know today. As the industry drew increasingly more on freelance translators and editors located anywhere in the world, the business was eventually outsourced to low-cost territories with multilingual capabilities. In the AVT industry, the outsourcing trend began at the turn of the century, when USA and UK companies had to find cheaper ways of producing English subtitling and captioning work: the volume of such work was increasing rapidly, while the prices offered for such services were steadily declining. Respeaking was the method implemented to achieve this in live captioning workflows, while outsourcing was used for offline workflows. Countries like India, Malaysia and the Philippines were selected as the low-cost alternative for producing transcripts of English source video due to the availability of a cheap workforce and its familiarity with the English language. Such outsourcing solutions offered further positive side effects, providing USA- and UK-based companies with the scalability and flexibility to cater for increases in workload, as well as the possibility of a round-the-clock subtitling service by taking advantage of the time difference between Asia and America/Europe.

This outsourcing of a flourishing skilled profession (i.e. English intralingual subtitling) to non-specialists that were unaccustomed to the slang, regional variations and cultural references used in filmic material, and viewed subtitling/captioning as just another type of transcription, originally met with strong opposition, especially in Europe—where verbatim transcriptions of the dialogue were avoided even for hard of hearing purposes. An increase in mishearings and comprehension errors were reported and professional unions condemned the practice (Nakata Steffensen 2007; Alberge 2007), but eventually workflows were ironed out and quality control measures by native subtitlers were put in place to correct such mistakes. Multinational subtitling companies took further control of the workflow by establishing their own offices in outsourcing countries, so that they controlled their operations best and made them fit their needs.

Translation management systems and the cloud

The creation of global enterprises posed a new set of challenges in working across cultures and time zones, and harmonizing tools and processes. Such enterprises had a vested interest in investing in technology, so as to deliver efficiencies of scale, maximize control of their operations and maintain their market position. This meant that Translation Management Systems (TMSs), an indispensable tool of LSPs since the 1990s, were widely being adopted by the AVT industry as well a decade or so later. Development of such systems has been ongoing, so as to accurately track, streamline and automate as much of the procedural translation management work as possible and, in some cases, TMSs are custom-built with development taking place internally in the aforementioned organizations. TMSs have been used to centrally manage the assets to be translated, such as videos, subtitle files, etc., control the languages into which translation is meant to take place, manage and select the translators to work on projects, allocate work, submit completed files, track payments, etc. Translators originally worked off desktop editors, not linked to their client TMS, while use of translation technology tools, such as TMs and MT, was still non-existent.

The proliferation of video formats in the twenty-first century and the explosion of an ever larger volume of audiovisual content online created another peak in demand for translation and accessibility services, while the timeframes for the provision of such services kept shrinking. Enter the cloud: it provided cost reduction through automation and avoidance of effort duplication, scalability and, more importantly, real-time access to and sharing of project information. It is now possible for global enterprises to become bigger than ever before and offer continuous localization services, which they can achieve by shifting from server-based TMSs to cloud-based ones: online editors, dashboards, automated work allocation, elimination of project handovers and much shorter turnaround times as a result. AVT companies further benefit from greater media security by adopting online editors, as video is streamed instead of downloaded to translators' workstations, while the download times disappear, speeding up the work of homeworkers. Additional efficiencies are made possible with the use of change management technology, tracking changes in source language content and mirroring them in all target language versions. Companies are now more inclined to integrate linguistic processing tools, such as terminology management tools and MT, to increase consistency and efficiency on the part of the translators. Increased quality control is made possible, metrics and performance indicators become available and clients have immediate access to the translated material for review and sign off. Such systems offer full project transparency, which has a hidden dynamic that could drastically change the visibility of translators in the supply chain of global LSPs, as they are now accessible by end clients who demand full disclosure of their vendors' processes.

Audiovisual content explosion

Broadband Internet also had a direct impact on the amount of video content that could be made available to consumers, unleashing unprecedented volumes of material. Broadcast TV and Internet access was integrated through a single set-top box at the turn of the century through IP delivery over ADSL, and Video on Demand (VOD) was launched as a commercial service (Wikipedia 2015), with Netflix being the prime example. The generalization and growing ubiquity of on demand audiovisual services have caused a dramatic increase in video consumption, and changed the ways audiences consume such content. 'Binge watching' and 'cord-cutting' are terms that characterize audience behaviour of late, while many refer to the next generation of viewers as the 'cord-nevers', i.e. viewers that will watch all of their content online, never resorting to pay-TV subscriptions (Rick 2014).

Moreover, the use of a multitude of devices to watch content has resulted in an increase of cloud-based TV services and the broadcast industry is embracing online delivery of content (McDonald 2015). Devices such as tablets and smartphones are also used as companion devices to the TV; they enhance the viewing experience by making it more interactive and allow, for instance, real-time chat during broadcasts. What became known as the 'second screen' phenomenon is now used among other things to deliver AVT services in a personalized manner to one's tablet or smartphone (e.g. the MovieReading App for synching subtitles and audio description tracks).

It is not only the term 'broadcast' that is being redefined in our days however. The term 'audiovisual content' has also taken on a whole new meaning, as communication itself in our century is becoming increasingly audiovisual. User Generated Content online is booming, largely promoted by social media sites such as Facebook, whereas 400 hours of audiovisual content are uploaded every minute on YouTube (Statista, n.d.), which boasts more than 1 billion users. Use of corporate video is also on the rise, as companies use video for their profiles, presentations and webinars, which they often share online. As a result, traditional LSPs are adding AVT services to their offering in order to satisfy their client needs, to the extent that support of subtitle formats is added in TM software used to ensure such subtitle translations are consistent with the clients' other printed and online material (Smith 2013). At the same time, the education sector is reinventing itself and Massive Open Online Courses (MOOCs) have become a global phenomenon, with universities expanding their repositories of video lectures and looking for ways to make them accessible. Coursera, a major MOOC provider, subtitles its courses in English and translates them online into more than 65 languages, by crowdsourcing translations through its Global Translation Community. In fact, translation is the platform's main selling point, as the provision of translated subtitles leads to increases in course enrolments by up to 200–300 per cent (Open Education Europa 2014).

For the first time in subtitling history, everyone is trying their hand at subtitling, in order to make this tsunami of videos accessible to a wider audience. Desktop subtitling and captioning software is mushrooming and becoming affordable for all types of budgets (e.g. Annotation Edit, Subtitle Translation Wizard, Movie Captioner), while open source subtitling software is now also available (e.g. Aegisub, Gaupol, Gnome Subtitles, Jubler, Subtitle Edit, Subtitle Editor, Subtitle Workshop). In addition, online subtitle interfaces are making their appearance, either proprietary ones (e.g. iMediaTrans, Plint, Sfera, ZOOsubs) or commercially available (e.g. MediaWen, OOONA's production tools), while companies like Amara, DotSub and Viki make use of online subtitle platforms to offer accessibility and translation services through a streamlined process of collaborative subtitling. While online subtitle platforms typically do not offer the standard of functionality found in high-end offline subtitle editors, they offer greater security to content owners via streaming videos, while simplifying the work of homeworkers. As such, we should expect their functionality to improve over time and eventually for them to completely take over from offline editors.

As the volume of content to be subtitled keeps increasing and the respective timeframes continue to shrink, companies are looking into new workflows in order to tackle their client demands, such as experimentation with respeaking for offline subtitle production, or the repurposing of live subtitle files into offline ones. At the same time, the notion of broadcast is redefined with Over The Top (OTT) offerings to a global audience, while non-entertainment video production is booming, creating new markets in which traditional subtitling/captioning enterprises compete against new types of companies offering alternative workflows based on technology and crowdsourcing.

Crowdsourcing

One of the most innovative trends that emerged as a side effect of moving to cloud-based enterprise offerings is crowdsourcing as the next level of corporate outsourcing. Not only have crowdsourcing models provided a levelling field for the supply and cost of labour, in the translation and AVT field, they have also provided solutions to issues such as speed, volume and resource availability, allowing the practice to flourish despite the attendant legality and quality issues.

Fansubbing

Crowdsourcing in AVT first appeared in the form of fansubbing, i.e. the creation of subtitle files for (popular) audiovisual productions by fans, in a fashion that breaks away from the established norms of subtitling practice. It started in the 1980s but has truly spread since the turn of the century, and it differs considerably from established forms of crowdsourcing in that the crowd maintains complete control over the translation process and the content to be translated, as opposed to 'managed' forms of crowdsourcing, where such control is maintained by the originators of the work (European Commission 2012). The creativity of solutions employed in fansubbing, which can be seen as a hybrid between traditional subtitling, subtitling for the hard of hearing and video game localization (Díaz Cintas 2005), has the potential to question established norms in the subtitling profession and influence subtitle production in the future.

Additionally, the very fact that such solutions are primarily provided by non-professionals, and are thus prone to translation errors and a presumed lower quality level, is likely to strengthen the argument of 'fit for purpose' translation. In this sense, crowdsourcing can help pave the way towards establishing a scale of translation quality levels for clients to choose from, depending on their budgets and the intended use of their translated content. Taking this a step further, Gambier (2006) argues that this could also strengthen the reasoning regarding the application of language technologies such as machine translation in subtitling, by 'viewing the output of machine translation programs . . . in a different light, in that they satisfy a certain number of users who are far from the illiterate but who do not need a polished, finely honed text'.

As the fansubbing phenomenon grows, the audience reception of amateur subtitles has been the focus of increasing academic research. Orrego-Carmona (2014, 2015) has shown that non-professional subtitles can provide a similar level of satisfaction to the audience as professional ones. The European Commission has also recognized the value of crowdsourcing by publishing a call for proposals (2015) focusing on innovative uses of crowdsourcing in order to strengthen the circulation of videos in lesser-used European languages through subtitling for VOD services, in cases where commercial subtitling services cannot be financially justified, as well as a call (2016) for the creation of an online tool to make subtitles easier to find and use.

Enterprise crowdsourcing

As opposed to fansubbing, what has come to be known as Enterprise Crowdsourcing in recent years (see Crow 2013; Deloitte Pixel n.d.; Lionbridge 2013; Matthews 2013) is an innovative approach to outsourcing by enterprises looking to benefit from ever ubiquitous and dependable Internet connections, the automation benefits of the cloud, and the billions of networked people around the globe. By putting to use their skills and availability, they are transforming them into an on-demand workforce that can complete from simple and repetitive to complex and creative tasks, for free or for a small fee. The benefits of such solutions are obvious: cost savings, scalability and better time-to-market through the simultaneous assignment of micro-tasks to a multitude of online workers, creating a dynamic for new business that is not viable with traditional models.

Solutions based on workflows powered by communities of amateurs are increasingly making their appearance in the translation market (Conyac, Gengo, Lionbridge Business Process Crowdsourcing, etc.). Amateur communities have attracted a lot of criticism, arising from concerns over their potential effect on the status of professional translation, the declining standards of translation quality and the ensuing blurring of the lines between professional and personal lives. By contrast, their positive impact is also duly noted when it comes to the strengthening of regional and minority languages (see European Commission 2012). In any case, crowdsourced translation companies are disrupting the marketplace, by offering much lower price points and higher throughput than traditional translation agencies. In some cases, they combine amateur crowd workers working alongside professional translators, who are mainly used to vet the amateur translators upon entry in the pool and edit their work so as to achieve higher quality output. By adding governance and a multi-layered quality control mechanism, Lionbridge (2014) coined the term 'Business Process Crowdsourcing' to refer to a cross of crowdsourcing with traditional Business Process Outsourcing, offering enterprises managed crowdsourcing solutions that combine the elasticity of the crowd with the quality assurance, security and performance management businesses require.

Prominent examples of crowdsourcing from the AVT sector are Amara and DotSub, which host both amateur and professional solutions, while serving the needs of diverse communities, from non-profits, educators and governmental organizations, to entertainment, media and corporate clients, as well as individuals. Crowdsourced subtitling services are also used by large streaming sites, such as Viki, 'the Hulu for foreign language content' (Lunden 2013), which uses its fan base to collaboratively subtitle videos wiki-style, with segments edited and re-edited on the fly, and the ones judged by the community as the most-accurate prominently displayed under the video player (Upbin 2010, cited in Dwyer 2012: 222). Finally, Amazon Mechanical Turk, the most widely known crowd marketplace for thousands of human intelligence tasks, lists translations and captions among them.

Mature language technologies are often used in crowdsourcing scenarios in order to maximize and capitalize on the skills of pools of distributed workers. Companies that offer transcription and captioning services, for instance, may employ speech recognition technology to produce preliminary transcripts of videos that their crowd then post-edits (e.g. Cielo24). Similarly, crowdsourced translation companies may use machine translation as the first draft of the translation their crowd workers are asked to work on (e.g. Unbabel). Crowdsourcing has also been researched recently as an alternative to offering real-time captioning services, by employing an algorithm for combining and aligning partial captions created by non-expert workers, with initial results showing that such output outperforms experienced captioners and ASR systems (Lasecki *et al.* 2012; Lasecki and Bigham 2014; Kazemi *et al.* 2014), thus opening up new possibilities in real-time captioning creation.

The influence of technology in the era of Big Data

The latest buzzword in our decade is 'big data'. It refers to data that is massive in volume, structured or unstructured, which, if processed, can help enterprises reach intelligent decisions. Subtitles are important metadata to help make videos searchable, so much so that, according to a Discovery Digital Networks study (Hammond 2014) conducted from January 2013 to April 2014, adding captions to videos led to increased viewings by 13.48 per cent, a lifetime increase of 7.42 per cent, significantly improved Search Engine Optimization (SEO) and also improved Return On Investment (ROI).

The use of statistical modelling in language technologies such as ASR and MT make them prime examples of technologies that harness the power of big data to yield useful results. Intralingual subtitles, together with the audio for which they provide timed transcripts, constitute big data used for the training of acoustic and language models that form the building blocks of ASR systems. When subtitle data are available in multiple languages for the same audio content, we talk of parallel data, which are of particular importance in the AVT field due to their applications in the training of Phrase-based Statistical Machine Translation (PBSMT) or Neural Machine Translation (NMT) systems. Subtitle files created with the template methodology are the ideal form of parallel data, already aligned at the subtitle level, and ready for use with very little effort invested in cleaning and pre-processing them. In other words, not only are subtitles important 'data' and 'meta-data', but they can also be used to improve the very tools that are used in their production; as such, they have appropriately been termed 'meta-tools' by Sánchez (2014).

Speech recognition

We have already seen how ASR has been used to transform the live captioning industry by implementing cost-effective workflows through the use of respeakers who, instead of typing, dictate the source language audio into specially designed subtitling software packages together with instructions relating to subtitle presentation and non-verbal audio elements that require descriptions for the benefit of hard of hearing audiences. Further progress has been made in ASR technology in the last 15 or so years since its first implementation in the AVT industry. Advances in the quality of ASR systems have made the training of respeakers faster and more affordable. The technology has also been making great strides towards speaker independent systems that require no training to the respeaker's voice, bringing us closer to a future reality where live intralingual captioning can be completely automated.

The current accuracy levels of raw ASR output for entertainment material are still far from human accuracy, though the advances are remarkable when it comes to broadcast domains involving studio-quality sound, no overlapping speakers, and restricted vocabulary, such as weather forecasts and broadcast news. Pioneering applications of the use of ASR for the automated live captioning of the news have been made by Voice Interaction (Meinedo *et al.* 2003) in collaboration with RTP, the public Portuguese broadcaster, and CRIM (Brousseau *et al.* 2003) and the TVA network, a Canadian broadcaster. Efforts towards improving ASR output for broadcast material have continued in research projects. Most recently, the Quaero, SAVAS and EU-Bridge research projects focused on developing ASR technology in several European languages for the broadcasting industry, while the project transLectures dealt with providing automated timed transcripts in caption format for educational video lectures. All projects reported improvements on previously state-of-the-art technology and produced reduced word error rates.

As a result of the SAVAS project, three software packages were developed which address operational issues of subtitle production, such as speech classification (i.e. speech, music and jingle detection), identification of speaker turns and speakers, text normalization for segmenting running text to words and sentences and putting words in a standard format, subtitle formatting and editing, as well as subtitle generation according to broadcaster specifications (Aliprandi *et al.* 2014). S.Live! was developed for automated production of live intralingual subtitles, S.Scribe! for offline subtitle production and S.Respeak! as a remote respeaking system scalable from single use to collaborative subtitling, available both in offline and live modes, with a fast post-editing component (*ibid.*). Other subtitling software solutions with integrated speaker independent ASR systems have also started appearing in the market. The PerVoice Subtitling Workstation is one such software package offering an alternative way of working for live subtitle production, by combining the benefits of raw ASR output with a touch-screen interface for post-editing and the ability to switch to a respeaking mode as needed. VoxcribeCC is yet another solution which works for offline caption creation, prepopulating an editor with ASR output for the user to post-edit. There are also speaker independent ASR-powered systems, such as EnCaption, that are addressed to broadcasters and promise to do away with the costs of human captioners altogether, by linking the system to a station's newsroom in order to access script information so as to build vocabularies and improve ASR performance. The Omnifluent Live Captioning Appliance is another such product available in a handful of languages, also addressed to broadcasters, which ensures high accuracy through customization of the ASR engines for speakers and language models based on domains, such as news, sports, etc. While none of these software packages have captured a large part of the market as yet and despite the fact that there are significant disagreements over the span of time it will take for the intralingual subtitling market to be overhauled by machines, there is no question that speaker independent ASR has the power to truly disrupt this market.

Another innovative application of ASR in the intralingual subtitling market is its use for aligning available transcripts to audio, so as to produce automated time-coded caption files. Automatic identification of speaker turns and speakers is achieved with high precision, however poor text segmentation reduces the benefits achieved by time-stamping to the word level to make the resulting file of human captioner quality. There are arguments though for considerable savings in captioning effort to warrant the use of such tools, especially in the case of single-talking-head video material, and a number of platforms have appeared offering such services, e.g. 3PlayMedia, AudioAlign, eCaption, EZ-Sync, SyncWords, etc.

ASR is also used for media monitoring purposes, to check for the presence of captions to go with the right video in the right language, as well as their accurate synchronization. As such, it is increasingly used by broadcasters as an automated quality control (QC) tool, helping them maintain their quality standards while controlling their costs. The Nexidia QC tool (TVTechnology 2013), for instance, claims to automatically highlight and correct caption synchronization issues, and also offers an automated QC solution for audio description streams by analyzing the primary and secondary audio programs against each other and providing a video description coverage score.

These rapid developments in recent years show that ASR certainly has the potential to revolutionize the AVT industry further through improvements and innovations in its use. It is difficult to predict what the future holds for captioners and subtitlers. Perhaps their role will shift from text generation to QC and to the 'arbiter of (human) taste and judgement' (Maxwell 2014) or to content curation, enhancing caption data with useful metadata as content owners discover new ways to make value from their content (Padmore 2015).

Machine translation

As translation is growing from luxury to utility due to globalization, emerging markets, online content and technological advances (TAUS 2013), and considerations of quality are shifting from publishable quality to 'fit for purpose' (typically for content types characterized by low longevity and expedited timeframes in which translation needs to be produced, and also defined by the demographics of the target audience), the demand for automation in translation technology is growing. PBSMT, introduced into every household by Google through its Translate service (which as of May 2013 supported over 100 languages and served the needs of over 200 million users daily, according to Wikipedia), is yielding interesting results and translation enterprises have begun introducing it in their localization workflows, applying it in increasingly more types of material. The recent breakthrough in the field with NMT, introduced by Google and Systran in 2016 (Le and Schuster 2016, Systran 2016) and followed by Facebook, Microsoft and an increasing number of adopters, is creating a buzz in the MT research community as many new research avenues are opening up and further improvements in MT quality seem tangible.

Early experiments in applying MT in subtitle workflows consisted in developing systems that would produce machine-translated subtitles for broadcast. The first reported attempt was an English-Japanese system for the translation of part of the World News program of NHK's satellite Channel 1 using the original news script (Sumiyoshi *et al.* 1995). Other such systems were developed later to translate closed captions. For over a decade now, TranslateTV (online) has translated US English captions into LA Spanish using RBMT technology. The KANT system (Nyberg and Mitamura 1997) was developed for English into German translation of captions, using example-based MT; the ALTo system for English to Spanish and Portuguese (Popowich *et al.* 2000; Turcato *et al.* 2000); CaptionEye/KE for Korean to English (Yang *et al.* 2001) and CaptionEye/EK for English to Korean (Seo *et al.* 2001); and cTranie for multilingual closed caption translation from Korean to English, Chinese and Japanese for digital television (Yuh *et al.* 2006). The best known application of MT for automated subtitling is of course the integration of Google Translate in YouTube (Google 2009).

A number of European research projects have also attempted to tackle the issue of MT in offline subtitle workflows with the use of post-editing. MUSA and eTITLE were two such projects that took place after the turn of the century. MUSA integrated both a translation memory component and a machine translation engine (Piperidis *et al.* 2005), while eTITLE (Melero *et al.* 2006) experimented with the integration of multiple state-of-the-art language technologies (ASR, text compression, TM and MT) in tools aimed to aid subtitlers. The results of the eTITLE project showed improved quality output when TMs were integrated with MT (*ibid.*). The feasibility of translating subtitles aided by MT was also examined by an Irish project in 2006 (Armstrong *et al.* 2006a), followed by a preliminary study by O'Hagan (2003) on the use of TMs and MT in subtitling. Further work went into experimenting with the type of corpus that would yield the best results in terms of the MT output; it was shown that a corpus of homogeneous data had a significant impact on translation quality (Armstrong *et al.* 2006b).

These projects paved the way for more research on the subject. The most recent projects dealing with subtitles, funded by the European Commission and focusing mainly on European languages, are SUMAT, transLectures and TraMOOC. Both transLectures and TraMOOC deal with the machine translation of academic video lectures in the form of subtitles, so as to serve the needs of millions of students worldwide. SUMAT examines the application of machine translation in the subtitling industry and specifically in the entertainment domain. This involves arguably some of the hardest video materials to be translated by machines, as they draw on extralinguistic and contextual information, are characterized by multiple speaker changes, slang and register variation, and include a variety of genres. The project was carried out by a consortium of nine companies, four being subtitle agencies which provided high-quality in-domain parallel subtitle data from their archives, to be used as training data for the training of MT systems in seven bidirectional language pairs. A full year of human and automated evaluation was performed to assess the quality achieved by the MT and the post-editing effort required to turn the raw MT output into subtitles of publishable quality.

As this is the most extensive evaluation to date of MT output by translator end-users in a subtitling scenario of entertainment material, its results are of large significance in terms of the usefulness of MT and so as to inform corporate decisions about its application in subtitle workflows. The genres tested were drama films and series, documentaries, magazine programs and corporate talk shows, and the evaluators were professional subtitlers. They were asked to evaluate the quality of the MT indicating the post-editing effort that would be required to turn raw MT output to subtitles of publishable quality, and found over 50 per cent of the machine-translated subtitles to require little to no post-editing effort. Unsurprisingly, they were not as positive in their assessment of MT when confronted with the potential of having to use it in their daily work, possibly because of their preference towards translation work, or their lack of previous experience with post-editing, which might have made their experience more cumbersome leading them to underestimate the benefits of MT (Etchegoyhen *et al.* 2014: 47–49; 52–53).

One of the most important parts of the evaluation was the timed experiments performed to assess the productivity gain translators would have when post-editing MT output versus translating the same material from a template file with no translation aid. The results varied considerably across different language pairs, even from translator to translator and from file to file within the same language pair, but the overall productivity result across all language pairs was a gain, with translators managing to produce approximately 40 per cent more subtitles than they would have in the same amount of time had they been translating from scratch (Etchegoyhen *et al.* 2014: 49–51). Post-editing effort in the MT of subtitles with respect to time was also investigated by Sousa *et al.* (2011) for the English–Brazilian Portuguese language pair, with results similar to the SUMAT findings. This is a significant finding in that it proves what many considered impossible: that MT can be of use in an open domain such as subtitles, even in the case of subtitles of varying genres of entertainment material.

Translator feedback during the SUMAT experiments indicated that the usefulness of the MT would be increased if combined with other CAT tools, such as TMs, and metrics indicating the expected MT quality, so that translators did not waste time dealing with MT output of substandard quality. Aside from the eTITLE project and O'Hagan's early study (2003), the application of TMs in subtitling was also researched by Flanagan and Kenny (2007), Flanagan (2009) and Pérez Rojas (2014), while Mejías Moreno (2010) worked on creating a CAT tool for subtitlers called CATSUBS. Even where the research did not show particularly positive outcomes from the application of TMs in subtitling (e.g. O'Hagan 2003), functions inherent to TMs, such as the concordance search which looks up specific words or phrases in the TMs and displays their translations in context, were shown to be of use to translators. Such results strengthen the argument that the way forward for increased subtitle production lies with the integration of both CAT tools and MT in subtitle editors and stresses the importance of monetization of these assets that are often largely underused, hidden in the vast subtitle archives of client and LSP repositories.

Aside from the use of Google Translate for the translation of YouTube subtitles, there are other commercial applications of MT in subtitling workflows. Such use cases were reported among Scandinavian language pairs and English by Volk and Harder (2007), Volk (2008) and Volk et al. (2010). The interest of subtitling companies in MT seems to be on the increase as evidenced from questions received on the SUMAT experiments. It is no coincidence that we are already seeing the first integrations of machine translation in subtitle editors: Jubler (Nicholson and Musicman 2009) and Subtitle Translation Wizard (Castro n.d.) both use Google Translate, while Subtitle Edit integrates both Google Translate and Microsoft Translator. At the same time, subtitle formats and functionalities of subtitle editors are added to CAT tools such as Star TransitNXT.

A commercial application that combines both ASR and MT has also been described by Sawaf (2012). Omnifluent Media, part of AppTek's suite of products, is a platform used for the creation of caption and subtitle files for live broadcast TV shows through the use of ASR and MT technologies, whilst keeping the human in the loop for quality assurance and optional post-editing purposes via a crowdsourcing workflow. A proof of concept of this system in the Arabic–English language pair reports results of throughput increase of transcribers and translators by a factor of 2 initially and 4 after training (*ibid.*). The product was implemented commercially in the Al Arabiya news channel in January 2014 (McLean 2014). Similarly, Omniscien's Language Studio combines ASR and MT technologies for the purposes of semi-automating subtitle creation and translation. Language Studio has been used most recently by iflix (Larrieu 2018) to localize their catalogue of video material in 22 language pairs, reporting a 60 per cent productivity gain in the transcription step and 56 per cent in the translation step, while use of MT was also extended from subtitling to the process of translating scripts for dubbing.

Speech synthesis

The last language technology influencing the future of the AVT industry is speech synthesis, i.e. the automated rendering of Text To Speech (TTS). The use of speech synthesis has long been established as a means of providing accessibility to the blind and visually impaired in the form of spoken electronic program guides, or assistive technologies such as screen readers. It is now also slowly being applied in AVT domains that use audio as a deliverable, i.e. dubbing, voice-over narration, audio description and audio subtitling.

Audio Description (AD) is an accessibility service catering to the needs of the blind and partially sighted population in a number of countries and a growing requirement for broadcasters, though its high production costs have been a hindrance to its greater adoption. Its production involves two main parts in the workflow, the script writing and the recording process, both of which are aided today by the use of specially designed software packages developed by companies that typically develop subtitling software. Such software aids in the script preparation process, while it also offers a streamlined process for the recording of descriptions with no more than the use of a good microphone and a soundproof room for the recording to take place.

As the use of synthetic voice has been finding applications outside the disability market (e.g. in the gaming industry, in public transport, in interaction with mobile devices), and the quality of speech has been continuously improving, experimentation with the use of speech synthesis for AD purposes was inevitable. Reception studies conducted by Kobayashi *et al.* (2010) in Japan and the USA, Szarkowska (2011) in Poland, and Fernández-Torné and Matamala (2015) in Catalonia showed that TTS would be acceptable to blind and partially signed patrons, even in cases where natural voices are still the preferred solution (*ibid.*). After all, according to Cryer and Home (2008), research studies suggest that blind and partially sighted people are likely to accept synthetic speech the more they are exposed to it and use it. Some may also prefer it if it helps them focus on the content of the text, while others would find it acceptable as a way of getting access to information faster, even if their preference lies with natural speech, (*ibid.*). A further factor to be taken into account when considering audience reception of synthetic speech is the maturity of the audience. In countries like the UK, where AD has been provided regularly with natural voices for over a decade now, it would probably prove harder for the audience to adjust and accept synthetic speech, as opposed to audiences that have not been conditioned to this type of service. The genre of the video material might also make a difference, as some productions might be more acceptable with 'flat' synthetic voices to sight impaired viewers than others.

Swiss TXT was one of the first companies to commission AD tracks with the use of text to speech. In an interview for the Languages and the Media 2012 conference, company representatives talked about their experience and stressed their belief that speech synthesis will become a standard component of AD in the years to come without being intrusive (Caruso and Linder 2012). SBS Discovery Media pioneered wide implementation of Speech Synthesis in their AD programming, and launched the SS AD service initially in Danish, Dutch, French, Italian, Polish and Swedish, and also in the UK in 2015 (Smith 2016). This has reportedly cut their AD costs by 56 per cent after initial equipment outlay (*ibid.*). Software providers, such as Cavena (Acapela 2014) and Screen Systems (2013) are also advertising integrated speech synthesis in their suite of products, offering it as an option to broadcasters both for AD and audio subtitling, the latter being used for additional accessibility purposes, mainly in countries where the dubbing practice is not widespread while subtitled foreign programming abounds.

The audio subtitling service in fact precedes the use of speech synthesis in AD, with the Dutch broadcaster NOS broadcasting audio subtitles with synthetic speech regularly since

2002 (Verboom *et al.* 2002), while the Swedish public broadcaster STV followed in 2005 (A-focus 2010, cited in Ljunglöf *et al.* 2012: 1). Audio subtitles are also in use in Finland since 2011 (European Federation of Hard of Hearing People 2011: 15) and currently offered for 100 per cent of Yle's programming and 50 per cent for other channels (Viestintävirasto 2016). Audio subtitles were introduced in Denmark in 2012 (Thrane 2013), while there are reports on experiments with audio subtitles in the Czech Republic (see Hanzlicek *et al.* 2008; Matušek and Vít 2012). Audio subtitles are also broadcast in Estonia in two channels (ETV and ETV2) as of June 2013 (Mihkla *et al.* 2014:21).

Could speech synthesis improve to such an extent that it could be used for voice-over narration and lip-sync dubbing as well? Some claim it can. The Dubbitron system by Speech Morphing was advertised a few years ago to offer language dubbing for entertainment material at a fraction of the cost, although the solution did not fly. MediaWen are now offering automated voice-over and dubbing by integrating IBM Watson's APIs in their STVHub platform. The company also partnered with XPERTEAM, an e-learning expert, to launch WBT VIDEO Learning, a collaborative video learning authoring software that makes use of language technologies such as speech recognition, translation memory, computer assisted translation and synthetic speech generation (Mediawen 2016). At the same time, Disney's Research team in collaboration with the University of East Anglia are developing a program of 'automated video redubbing strategies', which finds word sequences that can plausibly match the actors' speech motions, so speech redubbing is not obvious to the viewer (Choi 2015).

Conclusion

The second decade of the twenty-first century is defined by connectivity; information is accessible everywhere and it is increasingly audiovisual. TV is becoming yet another application on the Internet, with new OTT platforms announced almost every day (Huggers 2015), while the Federal Communications Commission is putting broadband policies in place. The AVT industry finds itself at a strategic inflection point, as both television and audiovisual content are being redefined, content volumes are growing exponentially, while the world is asking for access at all levels, immediately. Technology solutions are required that are able to transcribe, translate and index vast amounts of video content at the quality and speed that the market demands, and at costs it will support.

Cloud-based platforms are increasingly adopted by AVT enterprises, fansubbing is growing, subtitling is applied extensively to non-entertainment content, often with maximum flexibility as regards respect to the norms of the practice to date, while new entrants in the market feature managed crowdsourced solutions of amateurs and professionals. Meanwhile, experimentation with mature language technologies in the AVT market is flourishing and the promise to deliver solutions that make good use of valuable data and metadata hidden away in large content repositories is reinforced. Such developments have the potential to reshape subtitling workflows, client and LSP relationships, affect audience behaviour and challenge established norms, creating a paradigm shift in the industry. TAUS (2013) talks of a 'convergence era where technologies, such as speech, search and others will continue to be combined with machine translation to create new solutions'. Image recognition is an example of another technology whose value could be maximized if combined with speech recognition in videos, for instance. Could it be that the unveiling of Skype Translator (Skype Team 2015) by Microsoft and the idea of speech translation, i.e. the combination of ASR, MT and TTS to automatically translate audio from one language to another, is a sign of things to come in the future of AVT?

Further reading

Bywood, L., P. Georgakopoulou and T. Etchegoyhen (2017) 'Embracing the Threat: Machine Translation as a Solution for Subtitling', *Perspectives: Studies in Translatology* 25(3): 492–508 | *An overview of the SUMAT project and the year-long human evaluation performed on the quality of the machine translation output of the systems built. The paper analyzes the results in detail and makes suggestions for commercial applications of the technology.*

European Commission (2012) 'Crowdsourcing Translation', *Studies on Translation and Multilingualism*, May 2012. Available online: https://publications.europa.eu/en/publication-detail/-/publication/85558431-cfb4-4ff7-817d-5ad1338dc4b1/language-en/format-PDF/source-57847425 [last access 20 December 2017] | *An overview of the crowdsourcing phenomenon, complete with examples from different contexts as well as crowdsourced translation services, and an analysis of how it impacts the translation industry complemented with two interviews on the subject, one of which focuses on the AVT sector.*

Georgakopoulou, P. and L. Bywood (2014) 'MT in Subtitling and the Rising Profile of the Post-Editor', *Multilingual Computing*, January/February: 24–28 | *This article presents the SUMAT case study and its main findings regarding the application of machine translation in subtitling, and makes an initial attempt at detailing the profile of the post-editor, which is expected to be the next job profile in demand in the subtitling industry.*

Hearne, M. and A. Way (2011) 'Statistical Machine Translation: A Guide for Linguists and Translators', *Language and Linguistics Compass* 5(5): 205–226 | *This paper presents the basic principles underpinning Statistical Machine Translation, the dominant approach in machine translation research until recently, with multiple commercial applications, so that linguists better understand how their input is being used by researchers in building and improving SMT systems.*

TAUS (2017) The Translation Industry in 2022. Available online: https://www.taus.net/think-tank/reports/event-reports/the-translation-industry-in-2022 [last access 20 December 2017] | *A report outlining predictions (including the acceleration of automation) for the future of the translation industry over the following 5 years.*

Related topics

2 History of audiovisual translation
3 Subtitling on the cusp of its futures
6 Subtitling for deaf and hard of hearing audiences: moving forward
7 Respeaking: subtitling through speech recognition
8 Audio description: evolving recommendations for usable, effective and enjoyable practices
10 Game localization: a critical overview and implications for audiovisual translation
20 Corpus-based audiovisual translation studies: ample room for development
21 Multimodal corpora in audiovisual translation studies
23 Audiovisual translation and audience reception

References

A-focus (2010) *Utredning avseende TV-tillgänglighet för personer med funktionsnedsättning [Study on TV Accessibility for People with Disabilities]*, Myndigheten för radio och TV, December 2010, Stockholm, Sweden. Available online: http://www.mprt.se/Documents/Publikationer/Utredning%20avseende%20TV-tillg%C3%A4nglighet.pdf [last access 20 December 2017].

Acapela (2014) 'Audio Description: Worldwide Text-To-Speech Audio Description for Cavena with Acapela Voices', *Acapela news*, 9 November. Available online: http://www.acapela-group.com/audio-description-worldwide-text-to-speech-audio-description-for-cavena-with-acapela-voices [last access 20 December 2017].

Alberge, D. (2007) 'The Greatest Stories Ever Filmed (Mangled by Outsourced Subtitles)', *The Times*, 19 March. Available online: http://www.subtitlers.org.uk/docs/times19-03-2007art1.pdf [last access 20 December 2017].

Aliprandi, C., C. Scudellari, I. Gallucci, N. Piccinini, M. Raffaelli, A. del Pozo, A. Álvarez, H. Arzelus, R. Cassaca, T. Luis, J. Neto, C. Mendes, S. Paulo and M. Viveiros (2014) 'Automatic Live Subtitling: State of the Art, Expectations and Current Trends', *NAB Broadcast Engineering Conference Proceedings 2014 (NAB BEC)*, 7 April 2014. Available online: http://www.researchgate.net/publication/268069711_Automatic_Live_Subtitling_state_of_the_art_expectations_and_current_trends [last access 20 December 2017].

Armstrong, S., C. Caffrey and M. Flanagan (2006a) 'Translating DVD Subtitles from English-German and English-Japanese Using Example-Based Machine Translation', *MuTra 2006—Audiovisual Translation Scenarios: Conference Proceedings*, Copenhagen, Denmark, May 2006. Available online: http://www.mt-archive.info/MuTra-2006-Armstrong-1.pdf [last access 20 December 2017].

Armstrong, S., A. Way, C. Caffrey, M. Flanagan, D. Kenny and M. O'Hagan (2006b) 'Improving the Quality of Automated DVD Subtitles via Example-Based Machine Translation', *Translating and the Computer* 28, 16–17 November 2006, London: Aslib. Available online: https://www.researchgate.net/publication/228531663_Improving_the_Quality_of_Automated_DVD_Subtitles_via_Example-Based_Machine_Translation [last access 20 December 2017].

Brousseau, J., J. F. Beaumont, G. Boulianne, P. Cardinal, C. Chapdelaine, M. Comeau, F. Osterrath and P. Ouellet (2003) 'Automated Closed-captioning of Live TV Broadcast News in French', *Proceedings of the 8th European Conference on Speech Communication and Technology, EUROSPEECH 2003—INTERSPEECH 2003*, Geneva, Switzerland, 1–4 September 2003. Available online: http://www.researchgate.net/publication/221484988_Automated_closed-captioning_of_live_TV_broadcast_news_in_French [last access 20 December 2017].

Carroll, M. (2004) 'Subtitling: Changing Standards for New Media?', *Globalization Insider* XIII, 3(3), 14 September. Available online: http://www.translationdirectory.com/article422.htm [last access 20 December 2017].

Caruso, B. and G. Linder (2012) 'Speech Synthesis: A Technology that will Become Part of our Everyday Lives?', *Q&A, Languages and the Media 2012*, Berlin, November 2012. Available online: http://www.languages-media.com/press_interviews_2012_speech_synthesis.php [last access 28 September 2015].

Castro, P. (n.d.) 'Subtitle Translation Wizard', Editorial Review. Available online: http://subtitle-translation-wizard.software.informer.com [last access 20 December 2017].

Choi, C. (2015) 'Disney Does Better Dubbing', *IEEE Spectrum*, 21 April. Available online: http://spectrum.ieee.org/tech-talk/consumer-electronics/audiovideo/disney-makes-better-dubbing [last access 20 December 2017].

Crow, M. (2013) 'Looking to Outsource? Look First to the Crowd', *Wired*, June. Available online: https://www.wired.com/insights/2013/06/looking-to-outsource-look-first-to-the-crowd/ [last access 20 December 2017].

Cryer, H. and S. Home (2008) 'Exploring the Use of Synthetic Speech by Blind and Partially Sighted People', Literature review 2, Birmingham: RNIB Centre for Accessible Information (CAI).

Daily Mail Reporter (2013) 'End of "Ed Miller Band" and "Arch Bitch of Canterbury" Blunders as Ofcom Cracks Down on the Baffling TV Subtitles', *Mail Online*, 18 May. Available online: http://www.dailymail.co.uk/news/article-2326528/End-Ed-Miller-Band-Arch-bitch-Canterbury-blunders-Ofcom-cracks-baffling-TV-subtitles.html [last access 20 December 2017]

Deloitte Pixel (n.d.) 'How Can Enterprise Crowdsourcing Help You Harness the Power of the Crowd'. Available online: https://www2.deloitte.com/uk/en/pages/innovation/solutions/enterprise-crowd-sourcing.html [last access 20 December 2017].

Díaz Cintas, J. (2005) 'Back to the Future in Subtitling', *MuTra 2005—Challenges of Multidimensional Translation: Conference Proceedings*, Saarbrücken, 2–6 May 2005. Available online: http://www.euroconferences.info/proceedings/2005_Proceedings/2005_DiazCintas_Jorge.pdf [last access 20 December 2017].

Dwyer, T. (2012) 'Fansub Dreaming on Viki: 'Don't Just Watch But Help When You Are Free', in S. Susam-Saraeva and L. Pérez-González (eds) 'Non-professional Translation', special issue of *The Translator* 18 (2): 217–243.

Etchegoyhen, T., L. Bywood, M. Fishel, P. Georgakopoulou, J. Jiang, G. van Loenhout, A. del Pozo, M. Sepesy Maučec, A. Turner and M. Volk (2014) 'Machine Translation for Subtitling: A Large-Scale Evaluation', *Proceedings of the 9th International Conference on Language Resources and Evaluation (LREC)*, Reykjavik, Iceland, 26–31 May, 46–53. Available online: http://www.lrec-conf.org/proceedings/lrec2014/pdf/463_Paper.pdf [last access 20 December 2017].

European Commission (2012) 'Crowdsourcing Translation', *Studies on Translation and Multilingualism*, May 2012. Available online: https://publications.europa.eu/en/publication-detail/-/publication/85558431-cfb4-4ff7-817d-5ad1338dc4b1/language-en/format-PDF/source-57847425 [last access 20 December 2017]

European Commission (2015) 'Commission Launches €1 Million Preparatory Action to Crowdsource Subtitling to Increase the Circulation of European Works', Digital Agenda for Europe, 17 July. Available online: https://ec.europa.eu/digital-agenda/en/news/call-proposals-fostering-european-integration-through-culture-providing-new-subtitled-versions [last access 20 December 2017].

European Commission (2016) 'Call for Proposals to Develop an Online Tool Enabling the Tracking of Language Versions of Films', Digital Single Market, 26 July 2016. Available online: https://ec.europa.eu/digital-single-market/en/news/call-proposals-develop-online-tool-enabling-tracking-language-versions-films [last access 20 December 2017].

European Federation of Hard of Hearing People (2011) *State of Subtitling Access in the EU*, 2011 Report. Available online: http://ec.europa.eu/internal_market/consultations/2011/audiovisual/non-registered-organisations/european-federation-of-hard-of-hearing-people-efhoh-_en.pdf [last access 20 December 2017].

Fernández-Torné, A. and A. Matamala (2015) 'Text-To-Speech vs. Human Voiced Audio Descriptions: A Reception Study in Films Dubbed into Catalan', *JoSTrans: The Journal of Specialised Translation* 24, July: 61–88. Available online: http://www.jostrans.org/issue24/art_fernandez.pdf [last access 20 December 2017].

Flanagan, M. (2009) *Recycling Texts: Human Evaluation of Example-Based Machine Translation Subtitles for DVD*, Unpublished Doctoral Thesis, Dublin City University. Available online: http://doras.dcu.ie/14842/ [last access 20 December 2017].

Flanagan, M. and D. Kenny (2007) 'Investigating Repetition and Reusability of Translations in Subtitle Corpora for Use with Example-Based Machine Translation', in M. Davies, P. Rayson, S. Hunston and P. Danielsson (eds) *Proceedings of the Corpus Linguistics Conference CL2007*, Birmingham: University of Birmingham. Available online: http://ucrel.lancs.ac.uk/publications/CL2007/paper/129_Paper.pdf [last access 20 December 2017].

Gambier, Y. (2006) 'Multimodality and Audiovisual Translation', *MuTra 2005—Challenges of Multidimensional Translation: Conference Proceedings*, Saarbrücken, 1–5 May 2006. Available online: http://www.euroconferences.info/proceedings/2006_Proceedings/2006_Gambier_Yves.pdf [last access 20 December 2017].

Georgakopoulou P. (2006) 'Subtitling and Globalisation', *JoSTrans: The Journal of Specialised Translation* 6, July: 115–120. Available online: http://www.jostrans.org/issue06/art_georgakopoulou.php [last access 20 December 2017].

Georgakopoulou, P. (2012) 'Challenges for the Audiovisual Industry in the Digital Age: The Ever-Changing Needs of Subtitle Production', *JoSTrans: The Journal of Specialised Translation* 17, January: 78–103. Available online: http://www.jostrans.org/issue17/art_georgakopoulou.pdf [last access 20 December 2017].

Google (2009) 'Automatic Captions in YouTube', *Google Official Blog*, 19 November. Available online: http://googleblog.blogspot.gr/2009/11/automatic-captions-in-youtube.html [last access 20 December 2017].

Grass Valley (2013) 'Miranda Technologies Acquires Softel'. Available online: https://www.grassvalley.com/press/20130125-2763-miranda-technologies-acquires-softel/ [last access 20 December 2017].

Grass Valley (n.d.) 'Documentation Library'. Available online: https://www.grassvalley.com/cgi-bin/doc.pl?skin=jumpnav&super=broadcast&set=captioning&fmt=prodlist [last access 20 December 2017].

Hammond, M. (2014) 'Could Closed Captioning Increase Video Views, SEO and ROI?', *Business 2 Community*, 29 July. Available online: http://www.business2community.com/video-marketing/closed-captioning-increase-video-views-seo-roi-0959005#!bq41UO [last access 20 December 2017].

Hanzlicek, Z., J. Matoušek and D. Tihelka (2008) 'Towards Automatic Audio Track Generation for Czech TV Broadcasting: Initial Experiments with Subtitles-to-Speech Synthesis', *9th International Conference on Signal Processing (ICSP 2008)*, Beijing, China, November 2008. DOI: 10.1109/ICOSP.2008.4697710.

Hendzel, K. (2013) 'Professional-Quality Translation at Light Speed: Why Voice Recognition May Well Be the Most Disruptive Translation Technology You've Never Heard of'. Available online: http://www.kevinhendzel.com/professional-quality-translation-at-light-speed-why-voice-recognition-may-well-be-the-most-disruptive-translation-technology-youve-never-heard-of [last access 20 December 2017].

Huggers, E. (2015) 'The Perfect Storm?', *LinkedIn*, 9 February. Available online: https://www.linkedin.com/pulse/perfect-storm-erik-huggers [last access 20 December 2017].

Ivarsson, J. and M. Carroll (1998) *Subtitling*, Sweden: TransEdit HB.

Kazemi, M., R. Lavaee, I. Naim and D. Gildea (2014) 'Sliding Alignment Windows for Real-Time Crowd Captioning', *Proceedings of the 52nd Annual Meeting of the Association of Computational Linguistics (Volume 1: Long Papers)* (ACL 2014), Baltimore, June 2014. Available online: http://www.aclweb.org/anthology/P14–2039 [last access 20 December 2017].

Kobayashi, M., T. O'Connell, B. Gould, H. Takagi, and C. Asakawa (2010) 'Are Synthesized Video Descriptions Acceptable?', *ASSETS '10: Proceedings of the 12th International ACM SIGACCESS Conference on Computers and Accessibility*, New York: ACM, 163–170. Available online: http://dl.acm.org/citation.cfm?id=1878833 [last access 20 December 2017].

Larrieu A. (2018) 'iflix's Localization Journey—The Marriage of Human and Machine', *AI, MT and Language Processing Symposium*, Omniscien Technologies, 26–28 March 2018. Available online: https://omniscien.com/symposium/m3/ [last accessed 20 December 2017].

Lasecki, W. S. and J. P. Bigham (2014) 'Real-Time Captioning with the Crowd', *ACM Interactions* XXI(3), May–June. Available online: http://interactions.acm.org/archive/view/may-june-2014/real-time-captioning-with-the-crowd [last access 20 December 2017].

Lasecki, W. S., C. D. Miller, A. Sadilek, A. Abumoussa, D. Borrello, R. Kushalnagar and J. Bigham (2012) 'Real-Time Captioning by Groups of Non-Experts', *Proceedings of the ACM Symposium on User Interface Science and Technology* (UIST 2012), Boston, M.A. Available online: http://cs.rochester.edu/hci/pubs/pdfs/scribe.pdf [last access 20 December 2017].

Le Q. V. and M. Schuster (2016) 'A Neural Network for Machine Translation, at Production Scale'. Available online: https://research.googleblog.com/2016/09/a-neural-network-for-machine.html [last access 20 December 2017].

Lionbridge (2013) *The Crowd in the Cloud: Exploring the Future of Outsourcing*, White Paper, January 2013. Available online: http://info.lionbridge.com/enterprise-crowd-sourcing-blog.html [last access 20 December 2017].

Lionbridge (2014) *The Complete Guide to Business Process Crowdsourcing: Changing the Way Work Gets Done*, eBook. Available online: http://info.lionbridge.com/Business-Processing-Crowdsourcing-Guide.html?_ga=2.115694528.739831872.1496505877–1882480457.1445185987 [last access 20 December 2017].

Ljunglöf, P., S. Derbring and M. Olsson (2012) 'A Free and Open-Source Tool That Reads Movie Subtitles Aloud', *NAACL-HLT 2012 Workshop on Speech and Language Processing for Assistive Technologies (SLPAT)*, Montreal: Association for Computational Linguistics (ACL), 7–8 June 2012, 1–4. Available online: http://www.aclweb.org/anthology/W12–2901 [last access 20 December 2017].

Lunden, I. (2013) 'Viki, the Hulu for Foreign Language Content, Revamps Site, Upgrades Subtitling Tech to Scale Up Users', *TechCrunch*, 9 April. Available online: http://techcrunch.com/2013/04/09/viki-the-youtube-for-foreign-language-content-revamps-site-upgrades-subtitling-tech-to-scale-up-users [last access 20 December 2017].

Matthews T. (2013) 'The State of Enterprise Crowdsourcing 2013', *CrowdFlower Blog*, 13 November. Available online: https://www.crowdflower.com/the-state-of-enterprise-crowdsourcing-2013/ [last access 03 June 2017]

Matušek, J. and J. Vít (2012) 'Improving Automatic Dubbing with Subtitle Timing Optimisation Using Video Cut Detection', *IEEE International Conference on Acoustics, Speech and Signal Processing (ICASSP)*, March. Available online: https://www.researchgate.net/publication/261119065_Improving_automatic_dubbing_with_subtitle_timing_optimisation_using_video_cut_detection [last access 20 December 2017].

Maxwell, H. (2014) 'The Future of Pre-Recorded Subtitling', 22 April. Available online: https://www.redbeemedia.com/blog/the-future-of-pre-recorded-subtitling/ [last access 20 December 2017].

McDonald, A. (2015) 'Going Over the Top: Recent Developments in the OTT Space', *Digital TV Europe*, 11 May. Available online: http://www.digitaltveurope.net/365751/going-over-the-top/#.VbaswRE3k3s.mailto [last access 20 December 2017].

McLean, V. A. (2014) 'AppTek Provides Captioning and Subtitling to MBC's News Channel to Reach New Audiences', *PRWeb*, 26 January. Available online: http://www.prweb.com/releases/2014/01/prweb11521314.htm [last access 20 December 2017].

Mediawen (2016) 'Partnership Announcement: XPERTEAM and MEDIAWEN INTERNATIONAL Launch WBT VIDEO Learning by Mediawen', Press Release, Levallois, France, 20 January. Available online: https://mediawen.com/2016-WBTVIDEO-XPERTEAM-MEDIAWEN-en.pdf [last access 3 June 2017]

Meinedo, H., D. Caseiro, J. Neto, and I. Trancoso (2003) 'AUDIMUS.media: A Broadcast News Speech Recognition System for the European Portuguese Language', *Proceedings of PROPOR'2003*, Faro, Portugal.

Mejías Moreno, R. (2010) *Herramienta Para La Traducción Asistida En La Industria Audiovisual*, Unpublished Doctoral Thesis, Universidad Carlos III de Madrid, Spain.

Melero, M., A. Oliver and T. Badia (2006) 'Automatic Multilingual Subtitling in the eTITLE Project', *Proceedings of ASLIB Translating and the Computer 28*, London, England, November 2006. Available online: http://citeseerx.ist.psu.edu/viewdoc/download?doi=10.1.1.107.6011&rep=rep1&type=pdf [last access 20 December 2017].

Mihkla, M., I. Hein, I. Kiissel and T. Valdna (2014) 'A System of Spoken Subtitles for Estonian Television', in A. Utka (ed.) *Human Language Technologies—The Baltic Perspective*, September 2014, 19–26. Available online: http://ebooks.iospress.nl/publication/37998 [last access 20 December 2017].

Nakata Steffensen, K. (2007) 'Freelancers and the Crisis in British Subtitling', *ITI Bulletin*, May-June: 18–19. Available online: http://www.subtitlers.org.uk/docs/itibulletinma-ju07.pdf [last access 20 December 2017].

Nicholson, A. and L. Musicman (2009) 'Automatic Translation of Subtitles', FLOSS manuals, Jubler. Available online: http://en.flossmanuals.net/jubler/automatic-translation-of-subtitles [last access 20 December 2017].

Nyberg E. and T. Mitamura (1997) 'A Real-Time MT System for Translating Broadcast Captions', *Proceedings of the Sixth Machine Translation Summit*, San Diego, California, USA, 51–57. Available online: http://www.lti.cs.cmu.edu/Research/Kant/PDF/mts6.pdf [last access 20 December 2017].

O'Hagan, M. (2003) 'Can Language Technology Respond to the Subtitler's Dilemma?—A Preliminary Study', *Translating and the Computer 25*, November 2003, London: Aslib. Available online: http://mt-archive.info/Aslib-2003-OHagan.pdf [last access 20 December 2017].

Open Education Europa (2014) 'Top Coursera Courses Now Available in Multiple Languages Thanks to Global Translator Community', 5 May. Available online: http://www.openeducationeuropa.eu/en/news/top-coursera-courses-now-available-multiple-languages-thanks-global-translator-community [last access 08 October 2015].

Orrego-Carmona, D. (2014) 'Where Is the Audience? Testing the Audience Reception of Non-Professional Subtitling', in E. Torres-Simón and D. Orrego-Carmona (eds) *Translation Research Projects 5*, Intercultural Studies Group, Tarragona: Universitat Rovirai Virgili, 77–92. Available online: http://www.intercultural.urv.cat/media/upload/domain_317/arxius/TP5/06-Orrego-Carmona.pdf [last access 20 December 2017].

Orrego-Carmona, D. (2015) *The Reception of (Non)Professional Subtitling*, Unpublished Doctoral Thesis, Tarragona: Universitat Rovira I Virgili. Available online: https://www.academia.edu/12247046/The_Reception_of_Non_Professional_Subtitling_Doctoral_Thesis [last access 20 December 2017].

Padmore, D. (2015) 'Innovation in Speech Recognition and the Future of Closed Captioning', 14 April 2015. Available online: https://www.redbeemedia.com/blog/innovation-in-speech-recognition-and-the-future-of-closed-captioning/ [last access 20 December 2017].

Pérez Rojas, K. (2014) 'Automatically Building Translation Memories for Subtitling', in E. Torres-Simón and D. Orrego-Carmona (eds) *Translation Research Projects 5*, Intercultural Studies Group, Tarragona: Universitat Autònoma de Barcelona & University of Wolverhampton, 51–62. Available online: http://www.intercultural.urv.cat/media/upload/domain_317/arxius/TP5/04-Perez-Rojas.pdf [last access 20 December 2017].

Piperidis, S., I. Demiros and P. Prokopidis (2005) 'Infrastructure for a Multilingual Subtitle Generation System', *9th International Symposium on Social Communication*, Santiago de Cuba, Cuba, January 24–28. Available online: http://sifnos.ilsp.gr/musa/publications/Infrastructure%20for%20a%20multilingual%20subtitle%20generation%20system-final.pdf [last access 20 December 2017].

Popowich, F., P. McFetridge, D. Turcato, and J. Toole (2000) 'Machine Translation of Closed Captions', *Machine Translation* 15: 311–341. Available online: http://www.jstor.org/stable/20060451?seq=1#page_scan_tab_contents [last access 20 December 2017].

Rick, C. (2014) 'The State of Media and Entertainment Video 2014', *Streaming Media*, March. Available online: http://www.streamingmedia.com/Articles/ReadArticle.aspx?ArticleID=95386&PageNum=1 [last access 20 December 2017].

Sánchez, D. (2014) 'The Added Value of Subtitles', 14 September. Available online: https://www.redbeemedia.com/blog/the-added-value-of-subtitles/ [last access 20 December 2017].

Sawaf, H. (2012) 'Automatic Speech Recognition and Hybrid Machine Translation for High-Quality Closed-Captioning and Subtitling for Video Broadcast', *Proceedings of 10th Biennial Conference of the Association for Machine Translation in the Americas (AMTA)*, San Diego, California, 28 October-1 November 2012. Available online: http://www.mt-archive.info/10/AMTA-2012-Sawaf.pdf [last access 20 December 2017].

Screen Systems (2011) 'Screen Subtitling Acquires SysMedia'. Available online: https://subtitling.com/screen-subtitling-acquires-sysmedia/ [last access 20 December 2017].

Screen Systems (2013) *Spoken Subtitles—Audio for Accessibility*, White Paper, 26 September 2013. Available online: http://www.screensystems.tv/download/spoken-subtitles-whitepaper [last access 29 September 2015]

Seo, Y. A., Y. H. Roh, K. Y. Lee and S. K. Park (2001) 'CaptionEye/EK: English-to-Korean Caption Translation System Using the Sentence Pattern', *Proceedings of MT Summit VIII: Machine Translation in the Information Age*, Santiago de Compostela, Spain, 18–22 September, 325–329. Available online: http://www.eamt.org/events/summitVIII/papers/seo.pdf [last access 20 December 2017].

Skype Team (2015) 'Skype Translator Unveils the Magic to More People Around the World', Skype blog, 01 October 2015. Available online: https://blogs.skype.com/news/2015/10/01/skype-translator-unveils-the-magic-to-more-people-around-the-world/?eu=true [last access 20 December 2017].

Smith A. (2016) 'Localisation: Taking an Upstream View', *11th International Conference on Language Transfer in Audiovisual Media*, Berlin, Germany, 2–4 November.

Smith, S. (2013) 'New Subtitling Feature in Transit NXT', *STAR blog*, 11 November. Available online: http://www.star-uk.co.uk/blog/subtitling/working-with-subtitles-in-transit-nxt [last access 20 December 2017].

Sousa, S. C. M., W. Aziz, and L. Specia (2011) 'Assessing the Post-Editing Effort for Automatic and Semi-Automatic Translations of DVD Subtitles', *Recent Advances in Natural Language Processing Conference*, Hissar, Bulgaria. Available online: http://www.aclweb.org/anthology/R11–1014.pdf [last access 20 December 2017].Statista (n.d.) 'Hours of Video Uploaded to YouTube Every Minute as of July 2015'. Available online: https://www.statista.com/statistics/259477/hours-of-video-uploaded-to-youtube-every-minute/ [last access 20 December 2017].

Sumiyoshi, H., H. Tanaka, N. Hatada and T. Ehara (1995) 'Translation Workbench for Generating Subtitles for English TV News', *NHK Laboratories Note*, 435, Tokyo: NHK Science and Technical Research Laboratories, 1–8. Available online: http://cat.inist.fr/?aModele=afficheN&cpsidt=3614246 [last access 20 December 2017].

Systran (2016) 'SYSTRAN Announces the Launch of Its "Purely Neural MT" Engine, a Revolution for the Machine Translation Market'. Available online: https://globenewswire.com/news-release/2016/08/30/868116/10164884/en/SYSTRAN-announces-the-launch-of-its-Purely-Neural-MT-engine-a-revolution-for-the-machine-translation-market.html [last access 20 December 2017].

Szarkowska, A. (2011) 'Text-To-Speech Audio Description: Towards Wider Availability of AD', *JoSTrans: The Journal of Specialised Translation* 15, January: 142–162. Available online: http://www.jostrans.org/issue15/art_szarkowska.pdf [last access 20 December 2017].

TAUS (2013) *Translation Technology Landscape Report*. Available online: https://www.scribd.com/fullscreen/134651594?access_key=key-2hr0yyhsh8moed9i85yf&allow_share=true&escape=false&view_mode=scroll [last access 20 December 2017].

TAUS (2017) The Translation Industry in 2022. Available online: https://www.taus.net/think-tank/reports/event-reports/the-translation-industry-in-2022 [last access 20 December 2017] | *A report outlining predictions (including the acceleration of automation) for the future of the translation industry over the following 5 years.*

Thompson, K. and D. Bordwell (1994) *Film History: An Introduction*, London: McGrow-Hill, Inc.

Thrane, L. K. (2013) 'Text-to-speech on Digital TV—A Case Study of Spoken Subtitles on DR1Syn', *4th International Symposium on Live Subtitling*, UAB, Barcelona, 12 March. Available online: http://www.respeaking.net/Barcelona%202013/Lisbet%20Kvistholm%20Thrane%20-%20Text-to-speech%20on%20Digital%20TV%20-%20A%20Case%20Study%20of%20Spoken%20Subtitles%20on%20DR1Syn.pdf [last access 20 December 2017].

Turcato, D., F. Popowich, P. McFetridge, D. Nicholson and J. Toole (2000) 'Preprocessing Closed Captions for Machine Translation', in C. Van Ess-Dykema, C. Voss and F. Reeder (eds) *Proceedings of the Workshop on Embedded Machine Translation Systems*, Seattle, May.

TVTechnology (2013) 'Nexidia QC Automates Manual Processes', March 14, 2013. Available online: https://www.tvtechnology.com/news/nexidia-qc-automates-manual-processes [last access 20 December 2017].

Upbin, B. (2010) 'Viki Unlocks the Other 85% of Television', *Forbes*, Tradigital Blog, 8 December. Available online: http://blogs.forbes.com/bruceupbin/2010/12/08/viki-unlocks-the-other-85-of-television/ [last access 20 December 2017].

Verboom, M., D. Crombie, E. Dijk and M. Theunisz (2002) 'Spoken Subtitles: Making Subtitled TV Programmes Accessible', in ICCHP '02, 8th International Conference on Computers helping People with Special Needs, Linz, Austria. Available online: https://link.springer.com/chapter/10.1007/3-540-45491-8_62 [last access 20 December 2017].

Viestintävirasto Finnish Communications Regulatory Authority (2016) 'Obligation to Provide Audio Subtitles and Subtitles for TV Programmes', 29 September. Available online: https://www.viestintavirasto.fi/en/tvradio/programmes/audiosubtitlingandsubtitlingservices.html [last access 20 December 2017].

Volk, M. (2008) 'The Automatic Translation of Film Subtitles: A Machine Translation Success Story?', in J. Nivre, M. Dahllöf and B. Megyesi (eds) *Resourceful Language Technology: Festschrift in Honor of Anna Sågvall Hein*, Sweden: Uppsala Universitet, 202–214. Available online: http://uu.diva-portal.org/smash/get/diva2:131983/FULLTEXT01.pdf [last access 20 December 2017].

Volk, M. and S. Harder (2007) 'Evaluating MT with Translations or Translators: What is the Difference?', *Proceedings of MT Summit XI*, Copenhagen, Denmark, 499–506. Available online: http://www.zora.uzh.ch/20406 [last access 20 December 2017].

Volk, M., R. Sennrich, C. Hardmeier and F. Tidström (2010) 'Machine Translation of TV Subtitles for Large Scale Production', *Second Joint EM+/CNGL Workshop*, Denver, 4 November, 53–62. Available online: http://uu.diva-portal.org/smash/get/diva2:420760/FULLTEXT01.pdf [last access 20 December 2017].

Wikipedia (2015) 'Video on Demand'. Available online: https://en.wikipedia.org/wiki/Video_on_demand [last access 20 December 2017].

YouTube (n.d.) 'Statistics'. Available online: https://www.youtube.com/yt/press/statistics.html [last access 20 December 2017].

Yang, S. I., Y. K. Kim, Y. A. Seo, S. K. Choi and S. K. Park (2001) 'Korean to English TV Caption Translator: "CaptionEye/KE"', *Proceedings of the 6th Natural Language Processing Pacific Rim Symposium (NLPRS)*, Tokyo, Japan, 27–30 November, 639–645. Available online: http://www.afnlp.org/archives/nlprs2001/pdf/0172–01.pdf [last access 20 December 2017].

Yuh, S., K. Lee and J. Seo (2006) 'Multilingual Closed Caption Translation System for Digital Television', *IEICE Transactions on Information and Systems*, E89-D(6), June: 1885–1892. Available online: http://www.researchgate.net/publication/220234607_Multilingual_Closed_Caption_Translation_System_for_Digital_Television [last access 20 December 2017].

Sitography

3PlayMedia: http://www.3playmedia.com/ [last access 20 December 2017].
Aegisub: http://www.aegisub.org/ [last access 20 December 2017].
Amara: https://amara.org/en [last access 20 December 2017].
Amazon Mechanical Turk: https://www.mturk.com/mturk/welcome [last access 20 December 2017].
Annotation Edit: http://www.zeitanker.com/content/download/annotation_edit_demo/ [last access 20 December 2017].
AudioAlign: https://www.audioalign.com [last access 20 December 2017].
CANVASs: http://canvass.co.jp/global/corporate/index.html [last access 20 December 2017].
Cavena: http://www.cavena.com [last access 20 December 2017].
Cielo24: https://cielo24.com/ [last access 20 December 2017].
Conyac: https://conyac.cc/en [last access 20 December 2017].
Coursera Community: http://www.coursera.community [last access 20 December 2017].
DotSub: https://dotsub.com [last access 20 December 2017].
Dubbitron: http://www.innuva.com/projects/dubbitron/ [last access 20 December 2017].
eCaption: http://optispeech.com/ecaption/ [last access 20 December 2017].
EnCaption: http://www.enco.com/products/encaption4.html [last access 20 December 2017].
eTITLE Project: http://cordis.europa.eu/project/rcn/78351_en.html [last access 20 December 2017].
FAB: http://www.fab-online.com/ [last access 20 December 2017].
EU-Bridge: https://www.eu-bridge.eu [last access 20 December 2017].
EZ-Sync: http://www.lnts.com/about-ez-sync [last access 20 December 2017].
EZTitles: http://www.eztitles.com [last access 20 December 2017].
Gaupol: https://otsaloma.io/gaupol/ [last access 20 December 2017].
Gengo: http://gengo.com [last access 20 December 2017].
Gnome Subtitles: http://gnome-subtitles.sourceforge.net/ [last access 20 December 2017].
iMediaTrans: http://www.imediatrans.com/ [last access 20 December 2017].
Jubler: http://www.jubler.org/ [last access 20 December 2017].
KANT Project: http://www.lti.cs.cmu.edu/Research/Kant/ [last access 20 December 2017].
MediaWen: http://mediawen.com/#solution [last access 20 December 2017].
Movie Captioner: http://www.synchrimedia.com/#movcaptioner [last access 20 December 2017].

MovieReading App: https://itunes.apple.com/us/app/moviereading/id460349347?mt=8 [last access 20 December 2017].
MUSA Project: http://sifnos.ilsp.gr/musa/ [last access 20 December 2017].
Nexidia: http://www.nexidia.com/ [last access 20 December 2017].
Omnifluent Live Captioning Appliance: http://omnifluent.com/products/omnifluent-live-captioning/index.html [last access 14 October 2017].
Omnifluent Media: http://omnifluent.com/ [last access 23 August 2017].
Omniscien's Language Studio: https://omniscien.com/media-subtitling/ [last access 20 December 2017].
OOONA: http://ooona.net [last access 20 December 2017].
PerVoice Subtitling Workstation: http://www.pervoice.com/en/solutions/live-subtitling [last access 20 December 2017].
Plint: http://www.undertext.se/plint/ [last access 20 December 2017]
Quaero: http://en.www.quaero.org.systranlinks.net [last access 20 December 2017].
SAVAS: http://cordis.europa.eu/project/rcn/103572_en.html [last access 20 December 2017].
Screen Systems: https://subtitling.com/ [last access 20 December 2017].
Sfera: https://www.sferastudios.com [last access 20 December 2017].
Softel (now part of Miranda Technologies): https://www.grassvalley.com/press/20130125–2763-miranda-technologies-acquires-softel/ [last access 20 December 2017].
SoftNI: https://softni.com/about-us/ [last access 20 December 2017].
Spot Software: http://www.spotsoftware.nl [last access 20 December 2017].
Starfish Technologies: www.starfish.tv [last access 20 December 2017].
Star TransitNXT: https://www.star-group.net/en/products/translation-and-localization.html [last access 20 December 2017].
Subtitle Edit: http://www.nikse.dk/subtitleedit/ [last access 20 December 2017].
Subtitle Editor: http://home.gna.org/subtitleeditor/ [last access 30 April 2015].
Subtitle Translation Wizard: http://www.upredsun.com/subtitle-translation/subtitle-translation.html [last access 20 December 2017].
Subtitle Workshop: http://www.urusoft.net/products.php?cat=sw [last access 20 December 2017].
SUMAT: http://www.fp7-sumat-project.eu [last access 20 December 2017].
SyncWords: https://www.syncwords.com/ [last access 20 December 2017].
SysMedia (now part of Screen Systems): https://subtitling.com/screen-subtitling-acquires-sysmedia/ [last access 20 December 2017].
Telestream: http://www.telestream.net/captioning/overview.htm [last access 20 December 2017].
TitleVision: http://titlevision.dk/ [last access 20 December 2017].
TraMOOC: http://tramooc.eu [last access 20 December 2017].
TranslateTV: http://www.translatetv.com/ttv.php [last access 20 December 2017].
transLectures: http://www.translectures.eu/ [last access 20 December 2017].
Unbabel: https://unbabel.com [last access 20 December 2017].
Viki: http://www.viki.com [last access 20 December 2017].
VoxcribeCC: http://voxcribe.com/About%20Voxcribe.html [last access 20 December 2017].
ZOOsubs: http://www.zoodigital.com/platforms/zoosubs [last access 20 December 2017].

Index

Abe, N. 87
À bout de souffle/Breathless 165
Abre los ojos/Open Your Eyes 164
absolute minority languages 405
abusive subtitling 460–462, 502
accents 69
accessibility studies 373–375
accessible filmmaking 498–511
Acoustic Mirror, The (Silverman) 299
Action for Children's Television 438
action logic 226
Action on Hearing Loss 131
action synchrony 68
activism 453–464
'ad-hocracies' 459
ADLAB (Audio Description: Lifelong Access for the Blind) 118, 123, 210, 375
Affleck, B. 55
afterlife, text's 165, 169
age ratings boards 148
Agost, R. 50, 470
A-Ha 425
Aitchison, J. 215
Aladdin Project 346
Al-Aynati, M. 105
Aleksonyte, Z. 71
Ales, C. 97
aligned concordances 319
alignment 342
Allen, W. 293
Allô Berlin? Ici Paris 18
All that Heaven Allows 168
Ally McBeal 300
Al Taweel, G. 88
Altice, N. 145
Amara 463, 524
Amazon Mechanical Turk 524
An Bronntanas (The Gift) 409
Anderson, B. 393
Angst essen Seele auf/Fear Eats the Soul 168
anime 32, 185–186, 187, 303, 304–305, 358, 371, 438–440
Anna Christie 163

annotation 342–344
antenna delay 99
Antonini, R. 373
Araki, M. 335
Arends, L. 141
Aristotle 228
Arma, S. 120
Armstrong, N. 55, 292
arrivée d'un train en gare de La Ciotat, L' 181–182
Arthurs, J. 453
Arumi Ribas, M. 102
Asch, T. 500
Ascheid, A. 305
Asimakoulas, D. 303, 304
Astro Boy 438
Atlantic 19
attention allocation 370
attentional synchrony 503
attention distribution 353–354, 362
attitudinal issues 40
AUDETEL project 123
audience reception 367–379
audienceships 185
audio description (AD): description and discussion of 114–125; eye-tracking and 350, 358–359, 362; language learning and 490; multimodality and 262, 263, 272–275; narratology and 234–237; psycholinguistics and 209–211, 212–215; reception studies and 374, 375; technologization and 529; training for 472
audio introductions 114–115
Audiovisual Media Services European Directive 131
Audiovisual Translation: Theories, Methods, Issues (Pérez-González) 2
'audiovisual turn' 1
augmented reality (AR) 156
Auster, P. 285
Austin, J. L. 244
authenticity 74
automatic speech recognition 85, 100, 105, 106, 525–526, 528; *see also* speech recognition

automatic translation 336–337
automatic voice-over 75
Avignon Festival 138
Ávila-Cabrera, J. J. 487
Aziz Üstel 289

Babel 408
Babels 458–459, 461
Bączkowska, A. 491
Bairstow, D. 375, 376
Baker, M. 2, 315, 403, 430, 455, 456–457, 459, 460, 461, 462
Bal, M. 228
Baldry, A. 260, 263
Bale, C. 55
Balfour, I. 57, 500
Balio, T. 23
Ballester, A. 50
Ban Ki-Moon 427
Baños, R. 54, 55, 193, 325
Barambones, J. 403
Bard, P. 164
Bardem, J. 505
Barnier, M. 19
Baron, J. 164
Barrenechea, A. 163
Bartoll, E. 90
Bartrina, F. 469, 470
Bassols, M. 403
Baumgarten, N. 303–304, 305
Bechdel, A. 297
Bechdel test 297
Benjamin, W. 165
benshis 16–17, 162
Bernal-Merino, M. 152
Berthele, R. 291
beta-coherence 218
Betz, M. 500
Bianchi, D. 300, 301
Biber, D. 193
Big Bang Theory, The 440
Big Data, era of 524–530
Big Sleep, The 161
bilingual comparable corpora 316, 319
bilingual concordances 319, 322, 327
bilingualism 284
bimodal subtitles *see* intralingual subtitles
Bird, S. A. 484
Bisas, S 425
Bisson, M. J. 353, 354, 355, 360–361
Bjork 423
Black, R. 439
Blanchett, C. 54
Bleiker, R. 429
blind and visually impaired persons (VIPs) 114–125, 213–214, 350
Blini, L. 193

Blood Simple 166
Blotto 163
Blue in the Face 285–286
Blunt, J. 425
Boéri, J. 454, 456, 458
Bogucki, L. 69, 75
Boillat, A. 17
Bold, B. 441
Bollywood for All project 123
bonimenteurs 16–17
Bonsignori, V. 245, 319
'book problem' 219
Booth, P. 438, 443, 445
Bordwell, D. 226, 231
Borghetti, C. 489–490
Bosseaux, C. 51, 54, 57, 58, 238, 303–304, 305–306, 423, 429
Boudu sauvé des eaux/Boudu Saved from Drowning 164
Bourdieu, P. 443
Boyle, D. 506
Boyz N the Hood 291
brain-machine interface 156
'brain's best guess' theory of perception 216
Branchadell, A. 402–403, 404–405
Bravo, M. C. 488
Breaking the Waves 71
Breathless 165, 169
Breillat, C. 286–287
Bremond, C. 229
bricolage 430, 456
Bridget Jones's Diary 253–254, 300, 422
Bridget Jones: The Edge of Reason 253–254
bridging 268, 269
Bringing Up Baby 303
British National Corpus (BNC) 319, 339
broadband revolution 519–524
broadcast delay 99
Broeren, J. 16
Brondeel, H. 477
Brothers and Sisters 200
Brown, P. 245–246, 247
Browning, T. 163, 168
Bruner, J. S. 216
Bruti, S. 245
Bucaria, C. 371, 373
Buffy the Vampire Slayer 300, 301, 306
Burak, A. 65
Burch, R. 374
Burczyńska, P. 489
Burgess, A. 289
Burston, J. 486
Burton, J. 130, 134, 135, 136
Buser, M. 453
Business Process Crowdsourcing 523–524
Butler, J. 304
Byrne, J. 166–167

Caffrey, C. 353, 358, 371
Caillé, P.-F. 54
Californication 440
Cameron, J. 506
Campion, J. 285
Canadian Opera Company 130
CaptionCue 138–139, 141
captioning, for theatre and opera 130–142
Carlson, M. 132
Carroll, M. 15, 35
Carroll, S. 192
Cartton/Fantasy Organizaion (C/FO) 439
CATSUBS 528
Cattyrsse, P. 57, 233
causality 226, 232, 233–234
censorship 22, 49, 145, 286–287, 301, 302, 391
Cerezo Merchán, B. 469, 478
Chanan, M. 506
Chandler, H. 149
Chantal, S. 21
Chapaev 25
character, tracking 268–271
characterization 58, 228, 233–234, 235, 237, 248, 254
character synchrony 51
Charlot & Charlotte 71
Chatman, S. 231, 237
Chaume, F. 35, 48–57, 66, 193, 237, 469, 470, 474, 475
Chaves, M. J. 50, 59
Chelovek s kino-apparatom/Man with a Movie Camera 164
chemical subtitling 20
Chen, C. 292
Chesterman, A. 163, 367–368
Chiaro, D. 288, 300, 301, 371, 373
'chick flicks' 300
Chion, M. 54
Chiu, H. 486–487
Chmiel, A. 76, 375
Chorneyko, K. A. 105
chronology 226
chunking 90
cinema technology 181–183
Cipri, D. 289
Clair, R. 17, 18
ClipFlair platform 492
Clockwork Orange, A (Burgess) 289
closed captioning (CC) 83, 516–517
cloud 520–521
Clyne, M. 407
code-switching 284
Coen brothers 236
cognitive environment 251, 253
cognitive load/Cognitive Load Theory 362, 371, 372, 484, 485, 492

cognitive processing 358–359, 362
cognitive studies 378
cognitive theory of emotion 213
Cognitive Theory of Multimedia Learning Channels 487
cohesion 232, 262, 268, 277, 355
Cohn, D. 226
Cohn-Bendit, D. 456
Cole, A. 507–508
Collier de la reine, Le 21
colour 214–215
Colours of the Alphabet, The 507–508
Colusso, E. 506
Commitments, The 287, 408
community translation 383–384
competence-based training 469–472
complementarity 261
composition 261, 268
computer-aided translation (CAT) tools 151, 155
Computer Assisted Translation (CAT) tools 519
Conclin, K. 199
congruency 213
Connell, B. R. 502
content explosion 521–522
contextual adjustment material 255
continuous dictation software 518
conversational interaction 192–205
Cook, G. 488
Cooperative Principle (CP) 249–250
copyright 317, 329
Cornu, J.-F. 162
corpus-based audiovisual translation studies (CBAVTS) 315–330, 410–411
Corpus-based Translation Studies (CBTS) 315, 317
Corpus of Original and Translated Finnish (CTF) 326
CORSUBIL (Corpus de Subtítulos Bilingües Inglés-Español) 319, 322
Cowboy Bebop 303, 304
Crafton, D. 438
Crash Dub Studios 440
creative subtitling 502
Cronin, M. 177, 178, 179, 401, 403, 404
Crow, L. 506–507
crowdsourcing 444, 522–524
Cryer, H. 529
Crystal, D. 282
CSI 440
Cuaderno de Campo 458
Cubbison, L. 187–188
cultural a-synchrony 36
culturalization 148, 152–153
cultural poaching 442

cultural references 73
culture-specific items, reception of 372–373
curiosity 227–228

DAM 421
Damper, R. 97
Danan, M. 406, 485, 486
Dancer in the Dark 423
Dances with Wolves 408
Danturthi, R. S. 374
Darwish, A. 74
Dattebayo 445
Davis, Lennard 210
deaf and hard of hearing audiences:
  eye-tracking and 350, 353, 356;
  multimodality and 262; music subtitling for
  425–426; psycholinguistics and 209–210;
  respeaking and 100; subtitling and 82–92,
  101, 139, 154–155, 373–375, 472–473, 504;
  see also accessible filmmaking
De Bruycker, W. 354, 355, 357–358,
  360–361, 370
de Certeau, M. 442
decoding 376
deference 245
De Higes Andino, I. 478
De Lauretis, T. 297, 299
De Linde, Z. 35, 368, 374, 377
De Marco, A. 300
De Marco, M. 300
demi-doublage 66
Deming, S. O. 149
democratization 181
Denison, R. 441
DePalma, D. A. 444
de Sica, V. 23
Desilla, L. 252–253, 254, 422
Deuze, M. 181, 187
Deviant Eyes, Deviant Bodies (Staayer) 299–300
De weg van alle vlees 505, 506
dialects 55, 282, 288–291
dialogics 430
Diam 430
Díaz Cintas, J. 33, 37, 38, 49, 69, 70, 193, 194,
  233, 247–248, 469, 470, 472, 475,
  477, 486, 491
Dickinson, T. 18
dictation software 518–519
di Giovanni, E. 218, 359
digital games 145–156
digital language death 408
digital renaissance 178
digital revolution 517–519
digital subtitling 20
digitization 40, 377, 440, 474
diglossia 283–284, 292–293
discourse markers 197–198, 201, 202, 203

doctrine of linguistic relativity 214
domesticating practices 38, 73, 180
dominance patterns 194
Donnie Brasco 55
Dore, M. 55
DotSub 524
doublage à la bande 22
doublage à l'image 22
Down and Out in Beverly Hills 164
Dracula 163, 168
Drácula 163, 168
Dragon Ball Z 440
Dragon Naturally Speaking 97, 98,
  138, 141, 519
3 Groschen Oper, Die 162–163
Drive 506
DTV4ALL 373–375
Dual Coding Theory 484, 487
'dubbese' 54, 205, 373, 402
dubbing: beginnings of 18; compared to literary
  translation 163; conversational features
  in 201–205; for deaf and hard of hearing
  audiences 350; description and discussion of
  48–59; history of 21–23; language learning
  and 486–493; of linguistic variation 285–293;
  narratology and 237–238; software for
  473; subtitling versus 375, 504; training for
  468–478; voice-over and 66
Duff, A. 486
Dupont, E. A. 19
Ďurovičová, N. 26, 163
DVDs 518
dwell time 361
Dwyer, T. 15, 16, 459
d'Ydewalle, G. 35, 352, 353, 354, 355, 357–358,
  360–361, 369–370, 374, 376
Dykes to Watch Out For (Bechdel) 297

ecological approach to visual perception
  216–217
Edison, T. 183
Edwards, K. 148
Egoyan, A. 57, 500
Egyptian Revolution 456–457, 460–461, 462
Ehrensberger-Dow, M. 372
8 Mile 293
electroencephalography (EEG) 352, 362,
  368, 371
electronic subtitling 20
El-Tarzi, S. 457
emergent play 146
emotion, AD and 213
Emotion Elicitation Scale 217
emotive subtitling 88
Encore Hollywood (Mazdon) 161
Enforcing Normalcy (Davis) 210
Engelsing, R. 180

543

Index

enterprise crowdsourcing 523–524
Envisional 437
equivalent intended effect 217
Eramudugolla, R. 211
Erkazanci-Durmuş, H. 288–289
Espasa, E. 65, 70, 469, 470
Ethnic Minority Media (Riggins) 405
ethnographic film 500–501
ethnographic research 383–395
eTITLE 527, 528
EU Directive on Web Content Accessibility 131
Eugeni, C. 103–104
Eurovision Song Contest 424
Evans, J. 166
explication 165, 254
exploitation 250
expressive markers 197–199, 201–204
extralinguistic cultural references (ECRs) 37
eye tracking 154–155, 218, 236, 350–363, 368–372, 411, 503–505

fabula 226, 234
face management approach 245–246
face-threatening acts (FTAs) 246, 248, 255
familiarizers 204
fandom 436–447
fandubbing/fundubbing 56, 437, 455
fanfic 437
fansubbing 31, 36–37, 38, 87, 201, 357, 384, 387–395, 420, 437, 455, 459, 522–523
Fassbender, M. 55
Fayard, J. 59
Federici, F. M. 55
Fels, D. 88, 501–502
feminist critique of film 297–308
feminist theory and criticism 296–297
Feral, A.-L. 300–301
Fernández, A. 353
Fernández Costales, A. 152, 437
Fernández Fernández, M. J. 287
Fernández-Torné, A. 529
Fighter4Luv Fandubs 440
film archives 24
film explainers 16–17
filmmaking, accessible 498–511
film remakes 160–169
Findlay, J. M. 351
Finnish Broadcasting Corpus (FBC) 326
Fire Emblem 307
Fire Emblem Fates 153
Fishman, J. 405
fixations 351–352, 357–358, 359, 360–362
fixed meaning assumption 215
Flanagan, M. 528
Flintstones, The 403
focalization 228–230
focus maps 359

Fodor, I. 50
Folaron, D. 403
Forchini, P. 193, 324
foreign film, concept of 23
foreignizing translation 161
foreign language learning 42
Forest of Bliss 455
Forli Corpus of Screen Translation 410
formality 282, 286
Formentelli, M. 327
formulaic language 199–201, 204–205
Forrest, J. 160, 167
Foster, M. E. 337
Fowler, R. 39
Fox, W. 140, 353, 358, 372, 504
Franco, E. 65, 66, 67, 68, 70, 72, 73, 74, 76, 470
Franklin, A 422
Fraser, B. 245
Frazier, G. 116, 117
Freddi, M. 54, 193, 323–324, 327
free commentary 66
Freeman, J. 213, 217
freeware subtitling software 473
frequency counts 319, 321, 323
Freud, S. 299
Friedan, B. 296
Friends 324–325
From Russia with Love 305
Fryer, L. 210, 213, 217, 219, 262
Fuentes Luque, A. 372, 373
Fuksas, E. 506
Fuller, J. 282
functional neural networks 218
Funny Games 167, 168

Gaines, J. 299–300
Galán-Mañas, A. 478
Gallagher, M. 296
Galloway, G. 458
Gambier, Y. 33, 38, 40, 57, 66, 209, 219, 233, 367, 377, 383, 406, 523
game localization 145–156, 523
Game of Thrones 440–441
gap-filling elements 202–203
Garbo, G. 163
García Luque, D. 73
Gardien, I. 54
Gardner, R. 455
Gartzonika, O. 248
Gavrilov, A. 65
Gawande, A. 216
'gayspeak' 303, 304
gender 296–308, 461
Genette, G. 228
Genina, A. 19
genlocking 439
genre 51–52, 283

Gentzler, E. 472
geographics 148
geopolitical turn 458
Gere, R. 165
Ghia, E. 328, 353, 354–355, 360, 370–371
Gia 302–303
Gibson, J. J. 209, 216
Gielen, I. 370, 374
Gigantor 438
Gilbert, A. 214
GILT (Globalization, Internationalization, Localization and Translation) 149
Glee 440, 442
Godard, J.-L. 165
Goldorak 438
Goldrake 438
González Davies, M. 470
Goodfellas 55
Goodwin 428
Google Glasses 138
Google Translate 526, 527, 528
Göpferich, S. 470
Goris, O. 50, 288, 290
Gottlieb, H. 67, 71, 72, 160, 193, 373–374, 407, 468
Graeae 140–141
Granell, X. 477
Grant, C. 303
Greenall, A. 287
Green Street 198
greetings 204–205
Gregory, M. 192
Grice, H. P. 248–250, 251
Griesel, Y. 131
Griffin, A. 427
Griffith, D. W. 49
Grigaraviciute, I. 67, 71
Grudge, The 164
Guillot, M. N. 199–200, 204
Gunckel, C. 19
Guo, O. 455
Guo, T. 454, 457–458
Guojiang Subtitle Group 455
Gysbers, A. 219

Haig, R. 506
Haine, La 290
half-dubbing 66
Halliday, M. A. K. 272
Hamilton, O. R. 461, 463
Hanke, B. 427
Hanson, C. 293
Harder, S. 528
Harney, M. 164–165
Harrison, M. 423–424, 425–426
Harvey, K. 303, 304
Harvey, L. 19

Hasan, R. 272
Hasegawa, R. 147
Hatim, B. 193, 247, 285
Hawke, E. 55
Hayhoe, S. 214
heat maps 359
Hell's Angels 18
Hendrickx, P. 66
Herbst, T. 288
hesitation markers 202–203
Heyns, M. 219
Hicks, J. 25
Hijos de las Nubes 505, 506
Hill, H. 251
Hills, M. 185
Hine, C. 391
hip hop 420–421, 426
Hiramoto, M. 303, 304
history of AVT 15–26
Hjort, M. 287–288
Holden 135
Holmes, J. S. 178
Holmqvist, K. 352
Holobut, A. 72–73, 74
Home, S. 529
Home Sweet Home 506
home video technology 184–186
homographs 212
homophones 212–213
homosexuality 302–303
House of Cards 502
Hovaghimian, R. 445
Huckleberry Finn (Twain) 290–291
humour 283, 292, 372–373
Hurtado Albir, A. 469–470, 471–472, 478
Hutcheon, L. 168
hybridization 427
hyponymy 261

Ibáñez Moreno, A. 490
identity retrieval 268
idiomatic expressions 488
Igareda, P. 262
Illumination 507
illustrated title cards 16
imagined communities 393
Immortal Technique 420
implicated conclusions 251–252
implicated premises 251–252
implicature 248–254
Iñárittu, A. G. 506, 510
Incalcaterra McLoughlin, L. 490, 491
individual dimension of reception 377
information linking and dialogue 261
Inglourious Basterds 38, 58
Innis, H. 178, 179
integrated titles 358, 372

interjections 203
internationalization process 149–150
Internet ethnography 384
interpreting: respeaking and 103, 107; simultaneous 65
interrogation interfaces 345
intertextuality 252
intertitles 15, 18, 20, 162, 183, 499, 516
intonation 55, 59
intralingual subtitles 370, 371, 373, 406, 424–426, 483, 524
Introducing Social Semiotics (van Leeuwen) 260–261
Islam, S. 456
isochrony 50–51, 68
ITC Guidance on Standards for Audio Description 123
ITC Sense of Presence Inventory 217
ITU Focus Group on Media Accessibility 510
Ivarsson, J. 15, 35
Iwabuchi, K. 168
Izard, N. 48

Jäckel, A. 290
Jackson, M. 419
Jakobson, R. 161
James, W. 249
James Bond movies 303, 305
Jazz Singer, The 17, 499
Jenkins, H. 442
Jensema, C. 353, 356, 374
Jetée, La 167
Jiménez-Crespo, M. A. 1
John, E. 423
Johnson-Laird, P. N. 261
Joining the Dots 504, 508
Josephy-Hernández, D. E. 303, 305

Kaindl, K. 418, 426–427, 428, 429–430
Kajzer-Wietrzny, M. 477
Kameradschaft/Tragédie de la mine 18, 21
Karamitroglou, F. 50
'karaoke movies' 486
Kassovitz, M. 290
Katan, D. 454
Katie Morag 409
Kauffmann, F. 72
Kay, N. 35, 368, 374, 377
Kearns, J. 470
Kelly, D. 470, 472, 477
Kelly, N. 444
Kenny, D. 528
Kill Bill: Vol. 2 422
Kimba, the White Lion 438
kinesic synchrony 50–51, 68, 237–238
Kings 402
King's Speech, The 195–197

Kiraly, D. 469–470, 470
Kleege, G. 217
Kobayashi, M. 529
Kongress tanzt, Der 19
Koolstra, C. M. 370, 376
Koos, L. 160, 167
Kornai, A. 408
Korsgaard, M. B. 427–428
Kotelecka, J. K. 70
Kothari, B. 406, 445
Kovačič, I. 254, 367, 368
Kozinets, R. V. 385–387, 393
Krashen, S. D. 485, 487
Krasovska, D. 70
Krejtz, K. 124, 353, 357
Kruger, J.-L. 90, 211, 216, 217, 236, 353, 358, 359, 361, 370, 371, 406, 477, 484–485, 487
Kubrick, S. 58, 177
Kuhiwczak, P. 403
Kuhn, A. 65
Kumai, W. N. 486
Künzli, A. 372
KWIC (Key Word In Context) concordances 321
Kytö, M. 340

LaCapaGira 289–290
Ladd, F. 438
Ladouceur, L. 135
Lakoff, R. T. 245
Lambourne, A. 57
Lang, F. 19
language: AD and 119–122; eye-tracking and 355; minority 401–411; teaching and learning of 483–494
language hypertrophy 219
language learning 375–377
language planning 401–411
language planning and policy (LPP) 401, 403–404
language technologies 518–519
laser subtitling 20
Laskowska, M. 70
Lavaur, J. M. 375, 376
Laviosa, S. 488
Law, J. 55
lead user 436, 444, 447
Learning via Subtitling project 491
leave-takings 204–205
LeCoS Project 491
lectoring 69
Lee, J. J. 249
Leech, G. N. 245
le Gras, Z. 456
Leitch, T. 167–168
lemma searches 411
Lénárt, A. 163
Leonard, S. 439, 459

Lertola, J. 489–490
Levinson, S. 245–246, 247
Lewis, D. D. 58
Lewis, E. S. 302, 302–303
Li, X. 185
Lievrouw, L. A. 463
Lights of New York, The 499
Lim, B. C. 165
Lincoln 58
line segmentations 357
linguistic compensation 219
linguistic standardization 72
linguistic variation 281–293
Lionbridge 523–524
Lion King, The 423
lip-synchronization 50–51, 52, 54, 68, 201, 237–238, 285, 286
literal synchrony 68, 74
Littau, K. 178, 179–180, 181, 403, 420, 425, 430
'live dubbing' 22
live subtitling *see* respeaking
Living Tongues Institute of Endangered Languages 445
Loach, K. 55, 498, 506
Loaf and Camouflage 248
Longo, A. 289
Longoria, A. 505
López-Cózar Delgado, R. 335
Lorenzo, L. 470
Los Angeles Science Fantasy Society (LASFS) 439
Lost 440
Love Actually 203–204
Low, P. 130, 134, 136, 429
Lüdeling, A. 340
Lumière brothers 181–182
Lupin III 439
Luyken, G.-M. 49, 50, 66, 68
LvS software application 491
L Word, The 303
lyrics *see* music, popular

M 19
MacDougall, D. 500, 501
machine translation (MT) applications 151, 336–337, 518, 526–528
Mädchen in Uniform 21
Maeckelbergh, M. 460
Maes, H. 167
Maitlin, M. 445
Makisalo, J. 325–326
Makoto, S. 459
'male gaze' 299
Man About Town 17
Mandalin, C. 445
Mandiberg, S. 154, 160
Mangiron, C. 146, 152, 154–155, 155

manipulation 74
Manovich, L. 186
Man with a Movie Camera: The Global Remake 164
Maresco, F. 289
Marshall, J. 500
Martin, J. R. 272
Martínez Sierra, J. J. 57, 469, 470, 474
Martínez Tejerina, A. 90
Marzà, A. 54, 55
Mason, I. 193, 247
Massidda, S. 444
Massive Open Online Courses (MOOCs) 522
Matamala, A. 70, 71–72, 75, 76, 106, 132–133, 137, 325, 469, 476, 529
Match Point 194–195, 293
Mateo, M. 132
Mathews, R. 440
Matte Bon, F. 193
Mattelart, T. 441
maxim flouting 250
Maya the Bee 438
Mayer, R. E. 487
Mayoral, R. 50, 74, 469, 470
Mazdon, L. 21, 161, 164, 168
Mazur, I. 375
McBride, J. 165, 169
McClarty, R. 88
McKernan, L. 25
McLaren. M. 422
McLean, D. 425
McLuhan, M. 178, 179, 180–181, 182
media accessibility 209–210
Media History Digital Library 24
medial constraints 285–286
mediality 177–188
Mejías Moreno, R. 528
Melford, G. 163
mental models 212–213, 215
Mépris, Le 75
meronymy 261
Meylaerts, R. 404
Miami Vice 73
Michaël, J.-P. 55
Million, Le 18
Mingant, N. 55
minoritized languages 405–406, 409–410
minority languages (ML) 401–411
modding 146
mode, theory of 39
Monaco, J. 215
monolingual comparable corpora 316, 318
monolingual concordances 319, 321, 322
Montague, I. 25
Monti, S. 327
Moore, J. 54
Moran, S. 353, 354, 355, 360, 371

Index

Moreno, L. 469
Moreno Jaén, M. 192
Mortada, L.-Z. 455, 458, 461
Mosireen 457, 458, 461–462, 463
Mouka, E. 322–323, 329
Mowitt, J. 52
MTV 419, 420, 423, 427
Muller, T. 91, 104
multilingualism 37–38, 56
multilingual versions 18, 19–20, 49, 162–164, 499
multimodal corpora (MMC) 334–347
multimodality 36, 40, 57, 260–278, 335, 430, 484
multimodal transcription 253
multisensory integration 211–212, 218
Mulvey, L. 296, 297, 299
Munday, J. 152, 160, 285, 463
Murthy, D. 385
MUSA 527
music, popular 418–431
music and effects track (M&E track) 51
music videos 419
Musser, C. 182
Muzii, L. 102

Nanayakkara, S.C. 88
narration 66–67
narrative surprise 227–228
narratology 225–238
Nash, W. 283
naturalization 288, 290
naturalness 324–326
Nava, S. 376
Navarretta, C. 338
Nectar 507
Neiborg, D. 442
Neira Piñeiro, M del R. 231
Neisser, U. 216
NER model 105, 107
netnography 384–394
Nettle, D. 408
Neural Machine Translation (NMT) systems 524
neutralization 55, 238, 327–328
Neves, J. 262, 275, 476, 486
Newton, I. 214
n-gram language model 518
Niemandsland 18
Nightmare Theater 420
Nights in Rodanthe 262–278
Night Watch 460
Nikolaus, C. 427
Nina 506
9 Songs 292
Nintendo 147–148, 153
No Country for Old Men 236

norms 327
Nornes, M. 15–16, 16, 21, 38, 57, 161, 162, 163, 455, 459, 460, 500, 502
nostalgia 445
Notes on Blindness 506
Notting Hill 202–203
Noveck, I. A. 255

objectivity 121–122
O'Brien, C. 25–26
O'Connell, E. 39, 401–402, 403, 405, 406
Ofcom 90–91, 107, 134, 377
Office, The 230
off-screen dubbing 66–67
O'Hagan, M. 146, 152, 155, 444, 527
OK Computer (Radiohead) 420
Olsen, J. 105
Oncins, E. 139
onomasiological approach 323
opacity 232
Open Access Smart Capture 139
opera 114–115, 130–142
opéra de quat'sous, L' 162–163
Opus Corpus 410
orality markers 197–199, 201–204
Orero, P. 67, 68, 69, 70, 74, 132–133, 137, 236, 359
Orrego-Carmona, D. 372, 378, 523
Ortabasi, M. 187–188
Ortiz-Boix, C. 75
O'Sullivan, C. 460, 502
outsourcing 520
Over The Top (OTT) offerings 522

Pabst, G. W. 162–163
PACTE 470
Paivio, A. 487
Palmer, A. 236, 321
Palmer, K. 156
parallel corpora 316, 318–319, 334–335, 339, 410
paratextual content 185
paratranslation 16
Paremanyer, E. 70
Parini, I. 55
Parker, A. 287
parody 168
partial dubbing 66
participatory audiovisual translation 383–384, 395
participatory culture 437, 442
particularized conversational implicatures 250
part-subtitling 58, 502
Passion of Christ, The 408
Paul, R. 182, 455
Pavakanum, U. 376
Pavesi, M. 41, 50, 54, 193, 205, 319, 325, 327

Pavia Corpus of Film Dialogue (PCFD) 318–321, 325, 327, 328, 410
Pedersen, D. 152
Pedersen, J. 245
Peli, E. 140
pentathlon approach 429
perception 209–220, 215–216
perceptual decoding 40
perceptual hypothesis, theory of 216
Perego, E. 56, 124, 305, 353, 354, 357, 370, 375, 411
Pereira, A. 470
Pérez Basanta, C. 192
Pérez-González, L. 2, 33–34, 40, 42, 52, 57, 65, 162, 163, 238, 255, 306, 436, 455, 456, 459, 460, 463, 502
Pérez Rojas, K. 528
Perfect Blue 303
Pettini, S. 152
Pettit, Z. 285–286
Pfanstiehl, C. 116
Pfanstiehl, M. 116
phonetic synchrony 50–51
Phrase-based Statistical Machine Translation (PBSMT) 524, 526
Piano, The 285–286
Pinker, S. 245, 249
Pitt, B. 55
Piva, A. 289
planned conversation 192–193
Plastic Bertrand 424
pluricentric language areas 407
Pobol y Cym (De Vallei) 409
politeness 245–248
polyglot films 57
polysystem theory 429–430
Pool, L. 300
pop-up glosses 358, 371
Postman, L. 216
Practice of Everyday Life, The (de Certeau) 442
pragmatics 242–255
prefabricated orality 193
prefiguration 460–462
Prescott, M. 132
presence 219
primacy effect 233
Prison Break 440
Prix de beauté 19
production stages 508–509
ProFile project 139
prosody 55–56, 213–214
prosumers 31, 187, 419, 425, 427, 437, 442–443
Psy 427
psycho-cognitive issues 40
psycholinguistics 209–220
pull-protocols 88–89

Pulp Fiction 226, 227, 228, 229–230, 232–235, 237–238
Pulver, A. 164
Pym, A. 161, 470

Quaglio, P. 193
Quargnolo, M. 17
Queen, R. 290–291
Queer as Folk 303
queer theory 299–300
'queer translation' 302–303

Radiohead 420
Rajendran, D. J. 104, 353, 357
Ramos, M. 213, 217
Ranma Project 440
Ranzato, I. 51, 302, 303
Raw, L. 161
Rayner, K. 352
reaction 40, 368
readability of subtitles 35, 90
reading index for dynamic texts (RIDT) 361–362
reading practices 179–180, 181
real-time captioning services 524
recency effect 233
reception studies 367–379
redubbing 24
redundancy effect theory 485
Reel Voice system 56
Reeves, K. 55
Reference Corpus of Contemporary written Dutch (SoNaR) 410
register 283
register-specificity 324–326
Rehm, G. 75
Reiser, E. M. 218
Reisistance on Tour 507
Relevance Theory 248–252, 253
Remael, A. 1, 33, 37, 57, 72, 102, 193, 194, 228, 232, 233, 238, 247–248, 248, 470, 491
remediation 456
renarration 430
Renoir, J. 54, 164
repercussions 40, 368, 377
Reservoir Dogs 230
resource integration principle 260
respeaking 96–108, 141, 142, 519, 520, 525
Respeaking – Process, Competences, Quality 103
response 40, 368
resubtitling 24
revoicing 66
rhythm 261, 268
rhythmo-band 22, 53
Rica Peromingo, J. P. 322
Ricento, T. 403

Rickard, N. S. 213
Riggins, S. 405
Ring, The 164, 166–167
Ringu, Ring 161, 165, 169
Ring Virus, The 161, 166–167
rise of the volunteer 187
Rittmayer, A. 286–287
Rizk, P. 457, 461
Roaring Girl Productions 506–507
Roberson, D. 214–215
Rodríguez, K. T. 445
Rodríguez-Arancón, P. 489
Rodríguez Martín, M. E. 193
Romaine, S. 408
Romance 286–287
Romero-Fresco, P. 57, 58, 86, 89, 102, 324–325, 356, 372, 375, 470, 504, 508
ROM hacking 146, 437, 445
Rossi, F. 325
Rouch, J. 500
Rough Sea at Dover 182
Royce, T. 261, 268, 278
Rozema, P. 300
rule-based machine translation (RBMT) 519, 527
Rundle, C. 490–491
Russell, B. 214
Russian Formalism 226
Ryan, M. L. 225–226, 229, 230

saccades 351–352, 359, 360, 361–362
Sailor Moon 440, 445
Saint, The 74
Sala Robert, E. 88
Saldanha, G. 403
Salt, B. 16
Salway, A. 120, 236, 319, 321, 326
Sánchez, D. 524
Sánchez Mompeán, S. 55–56, 59
Sandford, J. 90
San qiang pai an jing qi/A Woman, A Gun and A Noodle Shop 166
Santamaria, L. 469
Santos, J. 420
Sanz Ortega, E. 50, 53, 57
Sapir-Whorf hypothesis 214
Satoshi, K. 303, 305
SAVAS 105–106, 525
Sawaf, H. 528
Sayles, J. 506
scanlation 437
Schacter, S. 213
schemas 212
Schiffrin, D. 203
Schmidt, T. 341
Schmitt, N. 199
Schules, D. 443

Scott, J. 298
Scott, J. W. 298
scripting 100
Seas Beneath 18
'second screen' phenomenon 521
Secret City 506
segmentation 341–342
self-censorship 148, 152–153, 154
self-mediation 456
Selim, S. 455
semasiological approach 323
Sepielak, K. 68, 71–72, 74–75
Şerban, A. 248, 502
setting, tracking 271–272
Sex, Lies et les Franco-Manitobains (Prescott) 132
Sex and the City 300–301
Sexton, J. 185
Sherlock 40, 502–503
Shogun Assassin 422
Sifianou, M. 247
signal delay 99
Silence est d'or, Le 17
silent period 15–17, 49, 162, 499
Silverman, K. 297, 299, 306
simplification 327
Simpsons, The 55, 292
simultaneous shipment (sim-ship) 148, 150
Singer, J. 213
Sinha, A. 58
skopos theory 161, 429
slang 72–73, 283, 290, 327–328
Sliding Doors 198–199
Slingshot Hip Hop 421
Slumdog Millionaire 58, 460
smart subtitles 493
Smith, I. R. 166
Smith, T. 218, 505
Smoke 285–286
Snyder, J. 210, 217, 476
social dimension of reception 377
sociolect 283, 290–291
sociolinguistics 281–293
socio-narrative theory 430
software 56–57, 138–139, 141, 473, 490–492, 517–518, 522, 525; *see also* machine translation (MT) applications; speech recognition
Software Publishers Association (SPA) 147
Soleil, S. 426
Somwe Mubenga, K. 245
Sotelo Dios, P. 329, 342
sound, transition to 17–18
Sousa, S. C. M. 528
Spade, D. 297
spatial factors, for subtitling 33–34
Spears, B. 428–429

Specker, E. A. 360
speech acts 243–245
speech recognition 96–108, 138, 141, 336–337, 519, 525–526; *see also* automatic speech recognition
speech synthesis 529–530
Speed Racer 438
'speed subbing' 441
Sperber, D. 251, 254, 255
Spicks and Specks 424
spoken discourse 192–205
Spolsky, B. 281, 282, 283
Sponholz, C. 469
spontaneous conversation 192–193
Spring Breakers 428
StageTEXT 131, 138, 139, 141
standardization 282, 288–289, 327–328
Star Trek 71
Statistical Machine Translation systems 410
stenotypists 97–98
Sternberg, M. 226, 227, 288
Steyn, F. 353, 361, 370
Stiller, B. 72–73
Streamline Productions 440
Strella 303, 304
subjectivity 121–122
subtitling: abusive 460–462, 502; activism and 454, 456–462; assessment of 477–478; beginnings of 18; compared to literary translation 163; conversational features in 193–201; creative 502; for deaf and hard of hearing audiences 82–92, 101, 209, 262, 373–375, 425–426, 472–473, 498, 499; description and discussion of 31–42; dubbing versus 375, 504; early process for 516; eye-tracking and 351, 353, 354–355, 362, 369–372, 411, 503–504; filmmaking process and 500–501; in games 151; language learning and 375–377, 406, 483–487; of linguistic variation 285–293; multimodality and 263, 275–277; narratology and 232–234; part-subtitling 58, 502; presentation rate for 356; reception studies and 368, 373–375; reversed 485, 487; rules for 356–357; smart 493; of song lyrics 419–420, 422; in sound period 20–21; through speech recognition 96–108; training for 468–478
SUMAT 410, 527–528
Suojanen, T. 153
Supernatural 440
surtitling 130–142, 372
Susam-Sarajeva, S. 418, 426
suspense 227–228
Svelch, J. 441, 443
Swan Song of the Valkyries 440
Swinton, T. 54
Sydorenko, T. 376

Symphogear 440
synchronization 50–52, 66, 68–69, 71–72, 134–135, 342, 478, 486, 503
'synchronized' films 17
syntactic adaptations 37
Szarkowska, A. 69, 70, 124, 353, 356, 374, 529

taboo expressions 287–288
Talaván, N. 484, 487, 488–489
Tapping the Power of Foreign Language Films: Audiovisual Translation as Cross-cultural Mediation 254
Tarantino, Q. 38, 58, 226, 230, 422, 506, 510
Tarkan 426
Taylor, C. 55, 263, 491
Taylor, C. J. 376
Taylor, J. 56
technological determinism 180–181
technologization 56–57, 516–530
television 179, 184, 423–424
template workflow 518
temporal factors, for subtitling 34
Tetsuan Atom 438
text pairs 24–25
text reduction 37
text-to-speech AD 123, 529
Textual Poachers (Jenkins) 442
theatre 114–115, 116, 130–142
Theory of Second Language Acquisition 487
Thibault, P. 491
Thibault, P. J. 260, 263
Thieves 23
Thomas, J. 242
Thompson, J. 183, 184
Threepenny Opera, The 162–163
Timberlake, J. 428
Tirkkonen-Condit, S. 203, 325–326
TIWO (Television in Words) Audio Description Corpus 318, 319, 321, 326, 410
Tlaxcala 458, 461
Todorov, T. 225
Toffler, A. 442
Top of the Pops 423
Totò che visse due volte 289
Toury, G. 315, 401, 402
Tracce Corpus 410
training 468–478, 505
Trainspotting 408
TRAMA research group 472
TraMOOC 527
transcreation 152
transcription 317
transitioning minority languages 405
transitivity system 278
Translate for Justice 455
translating dissolve 16
translation hacking 437

551

translation management systems 520–521
translation memories (TMs) 334–335, 518, 528
translation quality assessment (TQA) 153
translation theory 401
Translectures project 102, 105–106
transmedia tactics 442
Tremblay, G. 179, 180
True Blood 440
Trueswell, J. C. 140
Trump, D. 455
Truth Conditional Semantics (TCS) 244
Tseng, C. 261–262, 263, 268, 272, 277–278
Tuchman, G. 296
Tuning Educational Structures in Europe Project 471
Tuominen, T. 377
Turist Ömer Uzay Yolunda/Tourist Ömer in Star Trek 166
Twain, M. 290–291
Twelve Monkeys 167
2001: A Space Odyssey 177
Tymczyńska, M. 477
Tymoczko, M. 2, 453, 454, 455, 456, 457

Udo, J.-P. 501–502
UFO Robot Grandizer 438
UK Communications Act 131
Umwelt 212, 213
UN Convention on the Rights of Persons with Disabilities 84, 92
Understanding Media (McLuhan) 179
Unique Item Hypothesis 203, 326, 327
Universal Declaration of Human Rights 130
Universal Declaration on Cultural Diversity 92
universal design 501–502
universals 327
Usai, P. C. 25
user-centered translation (UCT) 153–154
User Generated Content 521
Uszkoreit, H. 75

Valdeón, R. A. 201
Vandaele, J. 236
Van Dam, D. 505
van de Poel, M. 376
Vanderplank, R. 406, 484, 485–486
van der Veer, B. 102
Van Dijck, J. 442
Vanilla Sky 164
van Leeuwen, T. 260–261, 263, 268, 278
van Rensbergen, J. 369
Van Waes, L. 103
Vasey, R. 16
Vellar, A. 443
Velotype 97
Venuti, L. 161, 180, 287, 441, 455
verbal-visual prelude 276

verbatim subtitles 89–90
Verbatim Test 105
Vercauteren, G. 228
Verevis, C. 167, 168
Vermeer, H. J. 209, 211
Vermeulen, A. 490
Vernallis, C. 421
Vertov, D. 164
ViaVoice 518
Vicky the Viking 438
video games 145–156, 473, 523
Video Rewrite 56
viewing speed 356
Viki Global TV 437, 444–446, 524
Vilaró, A. 236, 358, 359
Vimeo 463–464
Vincendeau, G. 19, 162, 164
Virkkunen, R. 139
virtual reality (VR) 156
VISP (VIdeos for SPeaking) 490
visual perception 216
Vlance, H. 426
VocalEyes 141
voice: dubbing and 54–55, 56, 59; gender studies and 306
voice-over translation 24, 64–77, 151, 472
Volk, M. 528
von Bolváry, G. 21
von Flotow, L. 298, 407
von Helmholtz, H. 215–216
von Trier, L. 423
VTB4All Project 377

Waddington, C. 478
Wahl, C. 25
Walsh, J. 401–402
Walther, J. B. 386
Wang, W. 285
Wang, Y. 161
Ward, P. 90
Wardhaugh, R. 282
Watson, E. 54
Web 2.0 186–188, 437
Webb, H. 97
webpages, translation of 336
Weinberg, H. 21
Westfront 1918 18
Westwell, G. 65
Wheatley, C. 21
Where are my Children 16
Whitman-Linsen, C. 50, 55
Wildgruber, D. 213
Williams, N. 484
Williams, R. 180–181
Willse, C. 297
Wilson, C. 427
Wilson, D. 251, 254

Wilson, G. M. 229, 231
Winke, P. 353, 355, 361
Winner, M. 161
Winterbottom, M. 292
Wittgenstein, L. 236
Wong, D. 165, 169
Wooding, D. S. 140
Words of Women from the Egyptian Revolution 456, 458, 460–461, 462, 463
World According to Hollywood 1918–1939, The (Vasey) 16
Wozniak, M. 71
Wright, N. S. 166

Yau, W. P. 292–293
YouTube 419–420, 424, 458, 463–464, 521, 528
Y-Tritty 427
Yuan, X. 248

Zabalbeascoa, P. 403
Zanettin, F. 316
Zanotti, S. 327
Zick, R. G. 105
Zoolander 72–73
Zuzume, R 420
Zwei Herzen im 3/4 Takt 21

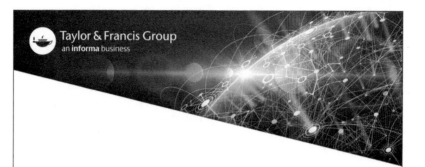